CHOICE Reviews in Women's Studies 1990-96

edited by

Helen MacLam
CHOICE **Magazine**

Association of College and Research Libraries
A division of the American Library Association
Chicago 1997

The paper used in this publication meets the minimum requirements of American National Standard for Information Sciences-Permanence of Paper for Printed Library Material, ANSI Z39.48-1992.

Library of Congress Cataloging-in-Publication Data
Choice reviews in women's studies, 1990-96 / edited by Helen MacLam.
        p. cm.
        Includes bibliographical references and indexes.
        ISBN 0-8389-7881-9 (alk. paper)
        1. Women's studies-Book reviews.   2. Women-Social conditions
-Book reviews. I. MacLam, Helen.   II. Association of College and
Research Libraries.   III. Choice (Chicago, Ill.)
HQ1180.C56 1996   96-52113
305.4'07--dc21

Printed in the United States of America.

01 00 99 98 97   5 4 3 2 1

SOCIAL & BEHAVIORAL SCIENCES
227

INDEXES
405

PREFACE

C*hoice Reviews in Women's Studies: 1990–96* is the latest addition to the *Choice* bibliography series. As a result of the growth of interest in ethnic studies and women's studies over the past two decades and the concomitant development of academic programs in these fields, *Choice* received many requests from collection development librarians and faculty for a source that would identify works needed to build basic collections in these areas. We responded by publishing compilations of reviews in subject areas of expressed interest: *African and African American Studies*; *Asian and Asian American Studies*; *Latino Studies*; *Native American Studies*; and now *Women's Studies*.

When *Choice* first considered issuing a separate compilation of women's studies reviews, the volume of material to be winnowed was substantial. The volume has now become enormous as publication in women's studies has moved ahead in all directions. This gathering of reviews, well over 2,000, has been drawn from the last six *Choice* volume years. The number of titles falling under the rubric of women's studies has grown from 239 in volume 28 (1990-91) to 496 in volume 33 (1995-96).

These reviews demonstrate movement and change in women's studies scholarship in recent years, not only in the published material itself, but also in the perspective of those reviewing—some are feminist, some are not; some view this body of knowledge through a postmodern lens, others bring an empirical approach to their assessments. What is undeniably clear is that women and their concerns are now represented in every life arena as well as every academic discipline.

Such richness of representation, however, has created a corresponding problem in organizing the material in this compilation. The essential question was how to maintain some degree of logical consistency in internal arrangement while also taking into account considerations of space, numbers, and aesthetics. In general, reviews have been divided into the major sections used in the magazine itself, and subdivided into smaller units of related works. Works that are general, comparative, or interdisciplinary have been grouped together at the beginning of each section. In some cases, e.g., Language and Literature, and History, Geography, and Area Studies, larger subdivisions have been further broken down by region and period. An attempt was also made to place figures or events that span chronological divisions according to the period in which they flourished or with which they are most closely identified. In other instances, e.g., Psychology and Sociology, sections have been divided not only by specialties within disciplines but also topically, reflecting new or significant bodies of literature. Placement decisions in some cases are admittedly arbitrary; failing any other applicable rationale, titles have been placed according to Library of Congress classification number.

It is important to note one other feature. As in the magazine itself, works relevant to specific groups of women, e.g., African American, lesbian, may be located by using the Topical Index, which appears along with the name and title indexes. No attempt has been made to determine the in-print status of titles in this volume.

ABOUT *CHOICE*

Choice:*Current Reviews for Academic Libraries* is a publication of the Association of College and Research Libraries, a division of the American Library Association. Directed toward academic librarians and faculty, *Choice* publishes concise, informed evaluations of significant recent scholarly publications—both print and electronic— in more than 40 disciplines spanning the humanities, science and technology, and social and behavioral sciences.

Choice has reviewed more than 200,000 titles since its founding in 1964, with an emphasis on works suitable for undergraduate collections, and has become the most widely used selection tool for academic library materials. Each of the 11 issues published annually contains approximately 600 reviews. Because most titles are reviewed within six months of publication, *Choice* usually provides the first professional, postpublication commentary on a scholarly work.

Choice reviews are brief—averaging 190 words—but critical. Grouped by discipline, reviews usually compare works with standard literature of the field. Reviewers are primarily teaching faculty from institutions across the United States and Canada, individuals chosen for their subject expertise, their active involvement with undergraduate students and curricula, their diverse viewpoints and backgrounds, and their sensitivity to scholarly trends. Reference publications are reviewed by practicing academic librarians, many of whom are subject specialists with advanced degrees.

Titles for review are selected by *Choice* subject editors, most of whom have experience as college or university librarians with responsibilities for collection development. They examine more than 22,000 scholarly and trade books annually and monitor publishers' catalogs and professional journals for materials of potential value to undergraduate collections. Assignment for review is based on numerous criteria, fully articulated in *Choice*'s Selection Policy, published in the September 1993 issue of the magazine. Chief among these criteria are relevance to undergraduate curricula and academic library collections, originality of scholarship, comprehensiveness of coverage, expertise of authors, and quality of scholarly apparatus, e.g., bibliographies, appendixes, and indexes. Revised editions, edited collections, and conference proceedings are reviewed more selectively, and textbooks and reprinted materials are generally not reviewed. It should also be noted that *Choice* considers only English-language publications and only finished copies; galleys or uncorrected proofs are not assigned. Each fall, *Choice* editors identify the most distinguished titles reviewed during the previous year for the Outstanding Academic Books feature, which appears annually in the January issue. This feature recognizes approximately 600 works and is highly regarded by publishers and by collection development librarians as a checklist for necessary acquisitions.

Other Products

Choice Reviews-on-Cards, also published 11 ties a year, supplements the full magazine. Further, *Choice* CD-ROM and online tools enable users to search the more than 50,000 reviews published since 1988. In addition to the bibliographic series described earlier, *Choice* has directed the compilation of three editions of *Books for College Libraries* (3rd ed., 1988) and the 11th edition of the *Guide to Reference Books* (1996), both published by the American Library Association. *Vocational and Technical Resources for Community College Libraries* (1995), published by the Association of College and Research Libraries, was also produced by *Choice* staff.

Choice Bibliographic Format

Choice's bibliographic entry format is derived from the Library of Congress (LC) cataloging when available and includes pagination, presence of bibliography and indexes, and ISBN and LC classification number when available. The designation "afp" indicates that the book has been printed on acid-free paper—a conservation concern for librarians. Each review carries a unique record number, and indexes reference reviews by these numbers. Publisher information is in its briefest form; the words "university" and "press" are omitted unless they are needed to distinguish presses with the same name. Only numbered series are identified in an entry. Price information for both cloth and paper editions reflects prices provided by publishers at time of publication.

WOMEN'S STUDIES

The Emergence of Feminist Scholarship

omen's Studies as an academic field is both a unique and a significant outcome of what has been variously designated as the feminist movement, the women's rights movement, or the women's liberation movement. By definition a *movement* assumes activity rather than contemplation or academic direction. Under what conditions, then, does activism result in intellectual inquiry and scholarly analysis?

The feminism of a century ago was not part of an important scholarship concerning "women's place" analogous to the hundreds of summaries of such work contained in this collection. A hundred years ago, women were scarcely an influential presence in public life generally, or in academe specifically. Professorial women existed, but they were few and marginalized within the academy. They were powerless to counter widely or effectively the prevailing view that (white) male supremacy was an inevitable, even desirable, concomitant of superior male intellectual capacities and stamina for competition and achievement. More important, 19th-century feminism did not encourage women to rethink their own assigned roles. Rather, women focused their attention on their right to be heard and to exert influence on the basis of those very roles. Thus, the first feminists were largely preoccupied with gaining access to the ballot box and with using the vote on behalf of family support and preservation.

Women of the time were generally committed to the ideal of "true womanhood" and its dominant credo that women were both weaker and more virtuous than men. The very delicacy of sense and sensibility that ill-suited them for participation in the public world was also considered the source of women's special strengths in the private world of family and domesticity. Women built their case for the right to vote on the accepted *feminine* ideology of the day. As wives and mothers, caretakers and nurturers, women had a special moral and civilizing voice to bring to the ballot box. If women's separate sphere of nurture, domesticity, and virtue was as essential to the social order as both men and women had been led to believe, then the vote was necessary to legitimate the status of women and to provide a channel of expression for their distinctive concerns. Women, especially middle-class women, campaigned for the vote not to unseat "family values" but to underscore them, not to transform the feminine (nor, by implication, the masculine) but to expand its domain through selfless reform, including temperance, to better the lot of those less fortunate. And finally, there is the unattractive truth that many white women of high social standing were offended, if not outraged, that the vote was withheld from them at a time when "even" immigrant men and men of color could vote.

The passage of the Nineteenth Amendment to the U.S. Constitution, following decades of organized leadership and the vocal support of thousands of women and men, must be recognized as a monumental accomplishment. But it was not founded on a broad-based critique of the social structure and context of male-female relationships or of the ongoing differential by sex of power and rights. Even the expansion of educational opportunities for women that began in the latter half of the 19th century did not imply a scholarship *of* women. Rather it entailed a scholarship *for* women, one that self-consciously accommodated the ideology of separate spheres. For postslavery black women, the separate sphere consisted of both race and sex. On behalf of their race, black women received instruction—with a heavy overlay of Christian missionary fervor—in curriculum that would allow them to serve their community in the respectable feminized occupations of nursing, teaching, librarianship, and social work. The school environment of middle-class African American girls also assured the development of their skills in the domestic arts, and carefully cultivated their manners and appearance.

Although a liberal arts education had become more accessible to white women, it was tailored to the expectations of a white, male-dominant society. Even the elite "seven sister" colleges, purported to be the female educational equivalent of the prestigious male "ivy league" colleges, were careful *not* to educate women to aspire to or compete with men for the high reaches of professional life. Overall, women's colleges were male-defined by their presidents, their boards, their donors, and/or their faculties. The curriculum was less demanding (and typically included home economics in some guise) and the faculty generally less accomplished than at men's colleges. A great emphasis was placed on physical education to ensure that female students' intellectual labor did not rob them of potential reproductive energy—a fear commonly expressed by male physicians of the day. The residential environment was styled to resemble the domestic life from which students had come, and to which they would return as adult wives and mothers. In these settings they dined family style, were subject to strict dress codes and curfews, and accountable to the housemother, who supervised in loco parentis the propriety of student conduct. The early women's college graduates were not intended to question the conventions of femininity. Rather, their education was meant to result in a schooled femininity that would manifest itself in educated motherhood and genteel wifehood—the class-appropriate complement to prominent and successful husbands. A career—most often in teaching, sometimes in settlement work—was considered acceptable for white women who did not marry.

Nonetheless, the "separate spheres" ideology gradually lost its force as highly educated women created innovative, vital, and highly respectable public roles for themselves as pioneer activist educators and reformers. By example they encouraged younger women to do the same. Further, the effect of both world wars was to blur the boundaries of a once highly differentiated social world. Women entered new occupational arenas and perforce the rigid class and sex-role conventions of earlier decades began to crumble. Educational opportunities for women expanded steadily throughout the first half of the 20th century to the point where the college-educated woman became commonplace. As early as the 1930s, women accounted for fully 40 percent of all college graduates; this percentage (representing, of course, an increase in actual numbers) remained steady into the 1960s. In these same decades, women earned ten to 15 percent of all doctorates, though their actual representation in academe declined precipitously from 1930 to 1960. However, the scope of women's public engagements—including military service—left no doubt of their energy, vigor, and capacity for independence.

In other words, a stable femininity no longer served as the implicit standard for the measure of masculinity. Thus the years following World War II were ones in which the message of the media and the purpose of social policy was to set the social order back on track generally and, specifically, to restore men to their rightful roles. The result was a glorification of marriage and family life. Politically, the nation once again focused on internal concerns. Personally, families turned inward, protective of their own emotional and material well-being. For many in the middle class this meant an escape to the burgeoning suburbs, a commuter husband in avid pursuit of career success married to a capable, educated wife who channeled her time and talents into high-level housekeeping and childrearing.

It was among such women that Betty Friedan in 1963 discovered and named the "problem that has no name." She called it "the feminine mystique," the ideal of "the suburban housewife ... the dream image of the young American women and the envy ... of women all over the world. She was healthy, beautiful, educated, concerned only about her children, her home. She had found true feminine fulfillment." In talking to Friedan, however, these privileged women spoke not of fulfillment, but its opposite—loneliness, isolation, despair, emptiness. The creation of a woman's autonomous selfhood was proposed as the logical solution to the problems created by the "mystique." What this meant specifically to Friedan and to the educated women she represented was that women should and could pursue and enjoy careers of their own, in parity with men.

In calling for liberation from their domestic cocoons, middle-class women turned their personal frustrations into a political movement. In 1966 the National Organization for Women was established to take action against any "conditions which now prevent women from enjoying the equality of opportunity and freedom of choice which is their right as individual Americans and as human beings." Compared to the single-issue focus on the vote of the old feminism, the new feminism called for nothing less than the full participation—and the elimination of all barriers to such participation—of women in all sectors of society. The demand then was for women's self-actualization, a diffuse goal requiring change and challenge in all arenas of social life.

When self-actualization is the issue, reflection is soon to follow. The field of women's studies took root in the earliest challenges to the social and psychological analysts, above all Freud, who were charged with deriving their assumptions about woman's nature from the nature of her socially prescribed roles. Questions about sex differences in cognitive and perceptual abilities loomed large in the early years of feminism, because sexual stereotypes were a barrier to women's occupational participation, especially in the elite male professions of law, medicine, university teaching, the clergy, and top-level business management.

Feminism has meant many things to many people since its resurgence nearly 35 years ago. Although it encompasses a wide spectrum of issues, one single issue continues to stand out: the insistence of women on breaking through the bastions of male occupational privilege and claiming some of that territory for themselves. Perhaps this goal is elitist, but it is also inevitable when there exists a critical mass of educated women who are excluded, because of sex, from the professions that seem to offer the very self-actualization—in the form of intellectual challenge, command of knowledge, power, status, and rewards—that is already open to their own husbands, brothers, and fathers.

It became incumbent on women to demonstrate through scholarship and research a favorable comparison of male and female intellectual abilities and personality traits, and to clarify the powerful role of socialization in shaping the domains of masculinity and femininity. Similarly, feminist scholars launched an assault on assumptions pertaining to the nuclear family as natural, evolved, and functional. They traced the theologies, ideologies, material conditions, and economic interests that underpinned the idealization of the nuclear family as a social form.

Such work by women already positioned in the academy offered essential support to those seeking entry to graduate and professional schools. Although not abundant, there were by the 1960s enough women established in relatively senior positions across a variety of academic disciplines to welcome feminism into the academy. And there was no shortage of women students eager to follow their lead. By the late 1960s, individual women's studies courses began to appear, especially in the humanities and social sciences.

Within their professional disciplinary associations, women scholars organized around feminist concerns. From the outset academic feminism embraced both activism and analysis, and emphasized the connection between the two by pressing for university reform. In this regard feminist scholars in the 1970s and 1980s made major contributions to the redefinition of women's roles and to new concepts of women's rights. At the same time, they documented the patterns and mechanisms of discrimination against women in their private and public lives. Within academic institutions they questioned male standards of productivity, male-defined structures of work; they took stands against sexual harassment and assault, and for affirmative action, comparable worth, and salary equity.

As academics, women also questioned the very form and content of their own individual disciplines and found them to be less the product of value-free, objective inquiry than of male interests, bias, values, and priorities. Scholarship, they asserted, both as career and subject matter, was socially constructed by men, tailored to the roles of men, and dominated by stereotypical male norms in directing what is worth studying, what is not, and how. Indeed, the hallmark of women's studies has been its ongoing challenge to the perspectives and paradigms established and taken for granted by centuries of male scholarship and intellectual dominance.

Women's studies continues as it began about 25 years ago—a combination of confrontation and dialogue with male hegemony in the academy. North American campuses are now home to more than 600 undergraduate and many dozens of graduate programs in women's studies, representing scores of disciplinary concentrations and orientations. National and international journals in all areas of women's studies now—in 1996—number well over 200. There is considerable and continual debate on what the place—interdisciplinary, mainstream, separatist, multidisciplinary, oppositional—and impact of women's studies should be in the structure of the academic world. What is most important, though, is that women's studies *does* unquestionably have a place in that world.

As the contents of this volume clearly show, women's studies is not a single academic field but many, and its scholarship, to judge from its productivity in the last five years alone, is alive and well. Whether women's studies will eventually evolve as a substantively and conceptually singular and distinct discipline remains to be seen. What matters in the present moment is what women's studies scholars have already achieved. They have reclaimed the lives of women and restored them to their social, cultural, literary, historical, and scientific places in the world. In bringing women back in, feminist scholarship has stimulated the reconfiguration, and thereby the reinterpretation, of potentially all of human experience and accomplishment. Perhaps most valuable, as is evident from the reviews published here, are the genuine efforts of feminist scholarship to critique and correct for its own early elitism, and to fashion a knowledge base that is inclusive of the lives and experiences of women in all classes and cultures.

Martha R. Fowlkes
Professor of Educational Leadership
University of Connecticut, Storrs, CT
November 1996

◆ REFERENCE

WS-0001 Orig
The 1995 information please women's sourcebook, ed. by Lisa DiMona and Constance Herndon. Houghton Mifflin, 1994. 591p indexes ISBN 0-395-70067-1 pbk, $13.95

A compendium of statistics, resources, guidelines, and advice for women concerning education, work, child care, health, well-being, fertility, sexuality and relationships, divorce and custody, retirement, politics, violence, and activism, this makes a handy desk reference. The statistics alone justify the price. Short essays and articles scattered throughout are an added bonus and make this more than just a dull gathering of statistics. Appendixes list important judicial and legislative decisions; documents, newsletters, and publications; and book and periodical resources. The organization and subject indexes provide additional access. Highly recommended for college, university, and public libraries as well as any organization that serves women or families.—*J. E. Peelle, Kenyon College*

WS-0002 E176 95-45052 CIP
American first ladies: their lives and their legacy, ed. by Lewis L. Gould. Garland, 1996. 686p index afp ISBN 0-8153-1479-5, $95.00

Gould's book covers 38 wives of presidents, from Martha Washington to Hillary Rodham Clinton. Excluded are ex-wives, wives married after the presidency, and other female relations who may have performed hostess duties. The biographical essays provide fascinating summaries, with each entry indicating the location of primary resources, relevant biographies, and suggestions for further research. Due to the broad nature of the work, the essays are of greatest use to undergraduates and the general public, but advanced researchers will find the work helpful. Although other anthologies have attempted to provide information on the role of the wife of the president, *American First Ladies* represents the most comprehensive, up-to-date resource available. Highly recommended for any reference or women's studies' collection.—*D. Lee, Mississippi State University*

WS-0003 E98 91-2961 CIP
American Indian women: a guide to research, by Gretchen M. Bataille and Kathleen M. Sands. Garland, 1991. 423p (Women's history and culture, 4) index afp ISBN 0-8240-4799-0, $57.00

Bataille and Sands, authors of *American Indian Women: Telling Their Lives* (CH, Oct'84), continue their significant contributions to scholarship on Native American women with this annotated bibliography covering "scholarly and literary work by and about Indian women in the US and Canada." With 1,573 entries, it is the most comprehensive bibliography to date on this topic. The entries are divided among eight topical sections: bibliographies and reference works; ethnography, cultural history, and social roles; policies and law; health, education, and employment; visual and performing arts; literature and criticism; autobiography, biography, and interviews; and film and video. The introduction carefully spells out exclusions (e.g., materials not in the English language; dissertations and theses; juvenile works) and refers readers to other important reference tools, such as Rayna Green's *Native American Women: A Contextual Bibliography* (CH, Jan'84). There is a good index by time period, tribe, name, and subject. Recommended for academic and larger public libraries with Native American collections.—*C. E. Carter, California State University, Fresno*

WS-0004 PQ509 95-39490 CIP
Beach, Cecilia, comp. **French women playwrights of the twentieth century: a checklist.** Greenwood, 1996. 515p (Bibliographies and indexes in women's studies, 24) bibl index afp ISBN 0-313-29175-6, $79.50

Beach has combed library catalogs, reference works, checklists of performances, theatrical periodicals, and literary studies to produce a list of thousands of plays by French women writers, some well known but most quite obscure, to complement her admirable earlier volume, *French Women Playwrights before the Twentieth Century: A Checklist* (CH, Apr'95). The checklist is limited to plays written by French women and/or performed between 1900 and 1990. In addition to the major genres, Beach includes one-woman shows and other cafe-theatre

shows, but not the puppet theater, musical hall, and cabaret. Very basic biographical information is given for each author. Each play entry gives the title of the play and variant, genre, number of acts, and whether in prose or verse; coauthor(s) or composer(s) when appropriate; place and date of publication and of at least the first performance and performing company; and coded references and sometimes full call numbers of holding Parisian libraries or archives. A title list and several bibliographies complete the volume. Though it may seem churlish to ask for more, a chronological list of the plays and a listing by genres would also have been useful. Academic collections.—*E. Sartori, University of Nebraska—Lincoln*

WS-0005 Orig
Brennan, Shawn. **Resourceful woman,** by Shawn Brennan and Julie Winklepleck. Visible Ink, 1994. 833p index ISBN 0-8103-8594-5 pbk, $17.95

Intended as both a reference and browsing book, this unique directory/anthology has a great store of useful information. Entries for reference works, publishers, periodicals, institutes, government agencies, academic programs, libraries, videos, online services, awards, etc., are interfiled in one alphabet under 15 broad topics. Entries sometimes include minimal information, but there is always a name, address, and phone number; most briefly describe the content or purpose of the source. On almost every page are well-chosen poems, photographs, and excerpts that illuminate the topic. Some topics are treated at length (for example, education, kinship, and violence against women); aging, sexuality, and youth are very brief and seem like afterthoughts. Although there are sources for lesbian materials throughout the book, the reader has to hunt for them because there is no separate section and no subject index. There is an author/title index and a selected list of feminist booksellers. Librarians will not like the book's organization; it is not a quick lookup. However, a patron browsing in this book will find a wealth of information and leads. Recommended for all libraries.—*B. K. Lacks, California State University, Fresno*

WS-0006 Orig
Brownmiller, Sara. **An index to women's studies anthologies: research across the disciplines, 1980-1984,** by Sara Brownmiller and Ruth Dickstein. G.K. Hall, 1994. 494p indexes afp ISBN 0-8161-0589-8, $150.00

A continuation of Susan Cardinale's *Anthologies By and About Women* (CH, Sep'82), this excellent index is a much-needed service to anyone interested in research on women. It provides enhanced author and subject access to material about women that has been published in "edited works of essays, proceedings, and primary research across all subject disciplines, whose primary focus is on women or feminist issues." Well-organized and easy to use, the book includes citations for nearly 500 anthologies (with tables of contents) and subject, author, and keyword indexes. Selection of titles for inclusion was based on searches of the online catalogs at the University of Oregon and in the University of California system and on the publication *New Books on Women and Feminism* (1979-) from the University of Wisconsin. A useful system of cross-references based on a set of 13 broad umbrella terms (e.g., "Discriminate" and "Law") further increases the value of this work. A second volume, covering works published between 1985 and 1989, is being compiled currently and should be as welcome an addition to libraries as this title. Highly recommended for all libraries. All levels.—*B. Stafford, University of Illinois at Urbana-Champaign*

WS-0007 HQ1206 89-39974 CIP
Carter, Sarah. **Women's studies: a guide to information sources,** by Sarah Carter and Maureen Ritchie. McFarland/Mansell, 1990. 278p index ISBN 0-89950-534-1, $39.95

Women's studies faculty, librarians, and students owe a vote of thanks to Carter and Ritchie (University of Kent, UK) for their comprehensive, beautifully crafted bibliography—a true guide to the literature. International in scope, this work complements and extends the coverage in Joan Ariel's *Building Women's Studies Collections* (1987) and Susan E. Searing's *Introduction to Library Research in Women's Studies* (CH, Oct'85), with 1,076 annotated entries, primarily from the period 1978-88. The guide is arranged in three sections: general reference material; areas of the world; and special topics (arts and media, education, etc.)

Under each geographic area or special topic are lists of reference sources, periodicals, libraries or archives, and organizations. That cross-references (consisting of full author, title, subtitle, and reference number) are used liberally adds greatly to the usefulness of the work. For example, Patricia Addis's "Through a Woman's I", which first appears in the general section under "Bibliographies of Personal Writings," is also cited under "American History—Diaries" and "American Literature—Bibliographies." An author/title index completes the work. Everything about this guide is well done: the selection of titles, the good annotations, the excellent organization, and even the typography. It is a very readable, very useful book. A must purchase for every academic library.—*B. K. Lacks, California State University, Fresno*

WS-0008 HQ1410 96-4308 CIP
Cullen-DuPont, Kathryn. **The encyclopedia of women's history in America.** Facts on File, 1996. 339p bibl index afp ISBN 0-8160-2625-4, $45.00

With 500 entries averaging less than half a page each, this is not the ideal encyclopedia of US women. Nevertheless, the book has strengths. Entries, selected for inclusion by Cullen-Dupont, are well written and cover an appropriately wide range of topics: individuals, events, writings, firsts, policies, and laws. References in the entries point to the 18-page bibliography. An appendix of 34 documents adds depth. One might argue that the Arthur and Elizabeth Schlesinger Library on the History of Women in America (Harvard) deserves a separate entry or that *Herstory* merits mention. These quibbles do not detract from the book's value; it offers solid information in concise form. Recommended for academic, public, and school libraries.—*P. Palmer, University of Memphis*

WS-0009 PS147 95-31815 CIP
Davis, Cynthia J. **Women writers in the United States: a timeline of literary, cultural, and social history,** by Cynthia J. Davis and Kathryn West. Oxford, 1996. 488p bibl index afp ISBN 0-19-509053-5, $45.00

Originally intended to be an addendum to *The Oxford Companion to Women's Writing in the United States*, ed. by Cathy N. Davidson (CH, May'95) this title became a book in its own right. The term "writing" is broadly interpreted, encompassing nonfiction, fiction (including mysteries), award-winning children's authors, editors, songwriters, etc. The women included were born in the US or thought of as American; Canada and Mexico are excluded. The book is in chronological order and within each year is divided into "Texts" and "Contexts" on the same page. "Texts" lists the writers in alphabetical order with the type of writing; "Contexts" lists historical and other significant events, especialy those pertaining to women. There is a list of works consulted and an index, which unfortunately does not index "Texts." Useful as a companion to the major work or alone, this title is recommended for colleges and university women's studies programs, but for major public libraries it is not a necessary purchase. The juxtaposition is the important factor, because the information on the writers is minimal. *The Companion* does include a very abbreviated time line of women's writing.—*T. M. Racz, Eastern Michigan University*

WS-0010 HQ1883 93-13702 MARC
Encyclopedia of women's associations worldwide: a guide to over 3,400 national and multinational nonprofit women's and women-related organizations, ed. by Jacqueline K. Barrett; Jane A. Malonis, associate editor. Gale, 1993. 471p indexes afp ISBN 1-873477-25-2, $80.00

The editors of *EWAW*, which lists emerging and established women's organizations worldwide, intend that their book be used to promote communication and networking. For example, this new affordable directory includes 95 women's groups in the Russian section, all founded since 1989. The recent formation of such groups and the sketchiness of other entries, illustrate the fragility of these budding societies and their need for support and representation. The plurality of groups are from the US (1,027 out of 3,435) while some countries have only a single entry (Lithuania, Algeria, Bhutan) and others none at all (particularly countries of the Commonwealth of Independent States). Those interested in women's issues will be able to locate regional contacts or associations involved in particular activities. The directory arrangement is geographic, with alphabetic and "activ-

ities" indexes (e.g., arts, politics, peace, health, economics, sports). Entries compiled from *Encyclopedia of Associations, Encyclopedia of Associations: International Organizations* and from questionnaires, contain, when available, address, phone, fax, year founded, description, and publications. Highly recommended.—*P. Keeran, University of Denver*

WS-0011 HQ1236 93-17515 CIP
Franck, Irene. **The women's desk reference,** by Irene Franck and David Brownstone. Viking, 1993. 840p ISBN 0-670-84513-2, $27.50

By the authors of the highly regarded *Parent's Desk Reference*, this sourcebook focuses on social, political, and health issues pertaining to women. Alphabetically arranged entries include key people, organizations, programs, and conferences. For major topics like abortion, breast cancer, health equity, and the women's rights movement, the authors provide a guide that lists organizations, readings, and other resources for more information. Tables, statistics, and checklists supplement the text of many other entries. The authors provide an overview of the topic, note controversies, and explain their importance to women. Entries range from a few sentences to several pages in length, and most include liberal cross-references and boldface terms indicating related topics. An appendix includes texts of key documents, statistics and tables, and a timeline of women's rights. The book includes some historical and international entries but emphasizes contemporary American women's experiences. Combining Lisa Tuttle's *Encyclopedia of Feminism* (CH, Apr'87) and Christine Ammer's *New A-to-Z of Women's Health* (1991), this sourcebook succeeds as a basic reference source and is recommended for subject collections, and undergraduate and large public libraries.—*L. Krikos, Ohio State University*

WS-0012 HQ1410 94-9355 CIP
Frost-Knappman, Elizabeth. **The ABC-CLIO companion to women's progress in America,** by Elizabeth Frost-Knappman with Sarah Kurian. ABC-Clio, 1994. 389p bibl index afp ISBN 0-87436-667-4, $55.00

While researching her book *Women's Suffrage in America*, written under the name Elizabeth Frost (CH, Feb'93), which focused on the 19th century, Frost-Knappman became curious about "women's public achievements since the founding of the colonies." This book, covering the years 1619-1993, is the result. The bulk of the book is devoted to an alphabetical listing of topics, organizations, individuals, laws, and court cases that illuminate women's progress. The text is accompanied by contemporary illustrations. Articles are succinct and authoritative, and written with admirable clarity. It is unfortunate that two worthwhile reference books on American women's history have come out at the same time. Dorothy Weatherford's *American Women's History* (1994) is similar in content and format, covers many more topics, but lacks an index. Weatherford's articles tend to emphasize different aspects of the same topics, so that the two books complement one another. Academic libraries should have both titles, but if a choice has to be made, this reviewer recommends the Frost-Knappman because of its unique chronology, excellent bibliography, and detailed subject matter.—*B. K. Lacks, California State University, Fresno*

WS-0013 CT3203 91-41182 CIP
Golemba, Beverly E. **Lesser-known women: a biographical dictionary.** L. Rienner, 1992. 380p bibl indexes afp ISBN 1-55587-301-4, $65.00

Listing more than 750 women, this dictionary is international in coverage and spans the years 1600 to the present. Arranged chronologically, entries provide name, dates, country of origin and accomplishment, race or ethnicity (for US women), a five- to ten-sentence summary of achievements, and codes to the 783 sources listed in the back of the book. The women are indexed by name, country, and profession. Golemba intends to highlight unrecognized accomplishments, yet many of the women are very well known (e.g., Aphra Behn, Dorothea Lange, Emma Goldman, Kathe Kollwitz, Beryl Markham, and Elisabeth Vigee-Lebrun). Most of the sources are readily available: *Continuum Dictionary of Women's Biography*, ed. by Jennifer Uglow, (CH, Dec'89), Joan and Kenneth Macksey's *Book of Women's Achievements* (1976), *Liberty's Women*, ed. by Robert McHenry (CH, Nov'80), and many other standard titles. The volume's highest value may be its coverage of African, Asian, South American, and Eastern European women. This rather expensive title is recommended for comprehensive collections.—*L. Krikos, Ohio State University*

WS-0014   HQ1121   94-41762 CIP
Greenspan, Karen. **The timetables of women's history: a chronology of the most important people and events in women's history.** Simon & Schuster, 1995 (c1994). 459p index ISBN 0-671-67150-2, $35.00

Similar in format to Bernard Grun's *Timetables of History* (CH, Mar'76), this volume highlights the major events and chief participants in women's history. Covering a broad time period, 4000 BCE to 1992, and with no geographical limits, this chronology cannot be comprehensive, but it offers an array of quick facts that demonstrate the magnitude of women's historical influence and achievement through the ages. Entries are arranged by year in ten topical columns: general, daily life, humanities, occupations, education, performing arts/entertainment/sports, religion/philosophy, science, statecraft/military, and reform. Famous women are listed along with the obscure. There are some problems with indexing and format, but overall the volume is easy to read and use. A subject index lists items by year and category. More than 60 brief essays focus on key individuals and events (e.g., Christine de Pizan) or give an overview of issues and trends (women in medicine). Some 100 photographs and line drawings help make the book attractive. Useful on reference shelves, high school through research libraries.—*M. J. Finnegan, Salem Public Library*

WS-0015   BS680   95-35831 CIP
Gruber, Mayer I. **Women in the biblical world: a study guide. [v.1:] Women in the world of Hebrew scripture.** American Theological/Scarecrow, 1995. 271p (ATLA bibliography series, 38) indexes afp ISBN 0-8108-3069-8, $39.50

Gruber's bibliography is divided into 18 sections ranging from "Women in Hebrew Scriptures" to "Women and Womanhood at Ugarit" and contains works dating from 1779 to 1993, with a concentration on post-1970 literature, as if to prove the author's claim that secondary scholarship on women in the Bible was generally neglected until then. A search in *Religion Indexes* of the American Theological Library Association (ATLA), however, finds numerous sources from 1949 to the present not cited in this list of 2,964 works. Gruber includes books, articles (both scholarly and semipopular), collections, and unpublished theses. He claims his bibliography differs from others on the topic by including works in modern Hebrew and Arabic. He lists such references in English translation (his?) with the original language noted in parentheses, a method that may make locating the original difficult. There are author and subject indexes, as well as an index of biblical references. Gruber's work might be recommended to a specialist in the field as a handy reference for bibliographic citation and for some of the rarer items, but its cumbersome format makes it less appealing (and less useful) to most users than ATLA's *Indexes*.—*V. R. Hotchkiss, Southern Methodist University*

WS-0016 have 1st ed.   HQ1115   94-48253 CIP
Humm, Maggie. **The dictionary of feminist theory.** 2nd ed. Ohio State, 1995. 354p bibl ISBN 0-8142-0666-2, $59.50; ISBN 0-8142-0667-0 pbk, $20.00

After flourishing in the eighties, the publication of feminist dictionaries has come almost to a standstill. This second edition continues the excellence while expanding the scope of the first edition (CH, Sep'90). The average length of entries is two paragraphs, although some (e.g., abortion, essentialism, language, marriage, postcolonialism, sexuality, womanculture) are given a full page. Humm assumes common beliefs among feminists but does not attempt to homogenize them. She gives general overviews of concepts and explains differences and distinctions within feminism. This edition's 354 pages compares with the first edition's 278. Terms added include "Autobiography," "Backlash," "Binary," "Rey Chow," and "Citizenship." Some entries have been expanded (e.g., "Helen Cixous"), others shortened (e.g., "Consciousness-raising"). In the preface to the first edition, Humm explained that she excluded terms in critical theory such as "Deconstruction" and "Postmodernism" because she believed they received enough attention elsewhere. Without retracting that statement, she has added both "Deconstruction" and "Postmodernism," as well as theorists Ann Kaplan, Sandra Gilbert and Susan Gubar, and Trinh Minh-ha (look under Minh-ha). Cross-referencing is uneven: Gilbert and Gubar share a single entry, but there is no reference from one to the other. Catherine MacKinnon lacks her own entry, although she is referred to many times throughout the book. Birth and death dates are not included in personal name entries. Books or articles from which theories are derived are iden-

tified by publication date to enable readers to refer to those works in the bibliography. This is sometimes confusing: none of Melanie Klein's works are referenced in her entry, so readers do not know the time period in which she lived and worked. Small criticisms aside, this book is probably the best scholarly source for defining French and Anglo-American theory.—*P. N. Arnold, Central Michigan University*

WS-0017 have   HQ1115   89-16237 MARC
Humm, Maggie. **The dictionary of feminist theory.** Ohio State, 1990. 278p bibl ISBN 0-8142-0506-2, $39.95; ISBN 0-8142-0507-0, $14.95

Making accessible "some of the commonest terms and issues in current English-speaking feminism" (pref.) is Humm's primary objective. Especially for students approaching feminist theory for the first time, this volume offers succinct, scholarly definitions within such diverse fields as sociology, psychology, history, literature, and the arts. Feminist theoretical intersections with Marxist, liberal, deconstructionist, and postconstructionist theories are made; entries on issues as diverse as race, gender, sexuality, work, family, ecofeminism, pacifism, and antipornography introduce the reader to "the argument. . .that feminism. . .has an indigenously produced theoretical tradition of some sophistication" (pref.). Humm explicates those conceptual tools required for the understanding of sexual, political, and economic discrimination and delineates those analyses useful for feminist politics. Without a doubt, readers will be led to those texts in which the dictionary's ideas first appear. Entries from "Abolitionist feminism" to "Zetkin, Clara" (writer about "the woman question from a socialist perspective") are followed by an extraordinarily comprehensive bibliography. This is an absolutely essential reference book for all public and academic libraries and information centers.—*N. S. Osborne, SUNY College at Oswego*

WS-0018   Orig
The International who's who of women. Europa Publications Ltd., 1992. (Dist. by UNIPUB) 553p index ISBN 0-946653-85-2, $350.00

Biographical details of "5,000 women of importance," many of them national or international household words, are presented in this first edition. Entries treat established figures as well as those rising in prominence, and emphasize geographic, employment, and cultural diversity. Names were recommended by an international panel of specialists and personnel from embassies and national and international organizations. Biographical entries, compiled from replies to questionnaires, include title; academic degrees; address; telephone, telex, and fax numbers; date and place of birth; nationality; family details; education; career; honors; publications, films, plays, recordings; and leisure interests. Exceptionally useful are the indexes (by career, name, nationality, and profession) and appendixes (an abbreviations list and an International Telephone Code table with instructions for its use). By themselves, the latter constitute excellent national and international sources. Populist researchers may hope for additional volumes that treat women who are less "eminent and distinguished." Valuable and unique, this work promises to be useful to academic, public, and business libraries, and to corporations, the media, and organizations and associations.—*N. S. Osborne, SUNY College at Oswego*

WS-0019   HQ1418   91-22206 CIP
Mehaffey, Karen Rae. **Victorian American women, 1840-1880: an annotated bibliography.** Garland, 1992. 180p (Garland reference library of the humanities, 1181) afp ISBN 0-8240-7142-5, $25.00

Mehaffey has provided a useful though somewhat limited bibliography on the average Anglo-American woman living in the Northeast or northern Midwest during the middle of the 19th century. She specifically excludes the famous, wishing instead to provide information about the lives of more ordinary women from this era and area, noting that modern historians have often ignored these women until recently (pref., p. xi). Sources listed are both primary—diaries, advice and etiquette books, cookbooks, consolation literature—and secondary, mostly books, with some articles and nonbook material noted. The bibliography is divided into seven chapters: "The Victorian Woman," "The Fashion Plate," "The Genteel State," "Social Gaiety," "A Wife and Mother," "The Cult of Domesticity," and "Faith and Mourning." Each chapter has an introductory essay providing insight into the role of the title topic in Victorian women's lives; materials are then listed alphabetically, with each entry giving full bibliographic information,

OCLC record number, and a descriptive annotation. Among numerous bibliographies on women in American history, a few cover Victorian women, e.g., Virginia R. Terris, *Woman in America* (1980) and Jill K. Conway, *The Female Experience in Eighteenth and Nineteenth Century America* (CH, Apr'83). However, even though the curent bibliography is limited to published books found through the OCLC database, it does pull together many more sources than any other bibliography on the Victorian American woman. Lack of an index makes this source less useful than it could be. Recommended for university libraries supporting women's studies programs or departments.—*C. S. Faries, Pennsylvania State University, University Park Campus*

WS-0020 HQ1180 91-3792 CIP
Miller, Connie. **Feminist research methods: an annotated bibliography,** by Connie Miller with Corinna Treitel. Greenwood, 1991. 279p indexes afp ISBN 0-313-26029-X, $45.00

Has feminism changed the content and character of research? Do feminist researchers behave differently? This pioneering bibliography cites more than 400 English-language sources published between the 1920s and 1990 that explore these questions in relation to research tasks, techniques, and approaches. The articles, books, and reports identified here represent work by feminists across a broad range of disciplines from anthropology to science to urban planning (literary criticism, philosophy, education, nursing, and medicine are the noted omissions). While acknowledging feminist resistance to segmented knowledge and compartmentalization, Miller and Treitel nevertheless organize their work by subject-oriented chapters, reasonably assuming that most users will approach the material in this manner. Annotations are informative and readable, their usefulness enhanced by the introductions to each chapter which provide an overview of the annotated sources and "outline the consequences of the feminist critique." Subject and author indexes offer additional access. Together with Wendy Frost's *Feminist Literary Criticism* (CH, Oct'88), this bibliography begins to map critical terrain in research and scholarship extending far beyond the boundaries of women's studies. An essential addition to all upper-division undergraduate and research collections; also recommended for large public libraries.—*J. Ariel, University of California, Irvine*

WS-0021 E98 92-19990 CIP
Native American women: a biographical dictionary, ed. by Gretchen M. Bataille. Garland, 1993. 333p (Biographical dictionaries of minority women, 1) index afp ISBN 0-8240-5267-6, $40.00

This first in a new series of volumes of biographical sketches of minority women includes brief descriptions of 240 Native American women past and present, ably edited by Bataille (Arizona State Univ.), a specialist in this field, who with Kathleen M. Sands also produced the recent *American Indian Women: A Guide to Research* (CH, Nov'91). A good introductory overview is followed by a selected bibliography of other works on Native American women. The entries, arranged alphabetically, vary in length because they were written by 62 contributors. Each entry concludes with a list of references on the woman described. Several indexes follow the entries: one by broad and somewhat arbitrary "areas of specialization" (e.g., "activism," "cultural interpretation"); one by decades of birth; one by state/province of birth; one by tribal affiliation; and finally, a general index of subjects and names. The indexes will help facilitate comparative research. Recommended for all Native American and women's studies collections and all larger academic reference collections.—*C. E. Carter, California State University, Fresno*

WS-0022 E185 91-35074 CIP
Notable Black American women, ed. by Jessie Carney Smith. Gale, 1992. 1,334p index afp ISBN 0-8103-4749-0, $75.00

With this volume, Smith adds to her list of credits (e.g., *Images of Blacks in American Culture*, CH, Dec'88) another fine reference source on African Americans. It contains 500 signed biographies of historical and contemporary women from all walks of life. The scope of the book makes omission inevitable, but the entries include the essential few and expand on that number with important figures often hard to locate elsewhere. The well-written entries by qualified contributors include bibliographies, and many give the location of pertinent archival collections. Judicious use of quotations, personal interviews, and pho-

tographs adds dimension to various entries. Unfortunately, the indexes are flawed. The entries are arranged by each woman's best-known surname, hyphenated or not; but since the subject index does not cross-reference among married, maiden, and professional names, some confusion is likely. In the list of contents by area of endeavor, overlapping categories such as "writer" and "author" do not include the same names, and no cross-referencing between such areas exists. Despite these minor flaws, the volume is recommended for all libraries, and is essential for collections in African American or women's studies.—*M. F. Jones, Muskingum College*

WS-0023 G200 89-39701 CIP
Robinson, Jane. **Wayward women: a guide to women travellers.** Oxford, 1990. 344p bibl indexes ISBN 0-19-212261-4, $29.95

Robinson, a former London antiquarian bookseller specializing in works of travel and exploration, compiled Wayward Women as a reference guide to what seemed an important but little-documented body of literature. She applies the delightful double entendre "wayward" to some 400 women writers, mostly of British extraction, who traveled to other countries. Listings of their firsthand travel accounts published in book form are preceded by brief details of these accounts and biographical sketches. Authors are grouped in chapters with intriguing titles and short, illuminating introductions. Sample titles: "An Up-to-Anything Free-Legged Air" and "Quite Safe Here with Jesus." The volume concludes with four appendixes: maps, a list of useful reference books (mostly British), and geographical and author indexes. Robinson's excellent effort should be compared with Marion Tinling's *Women into the Unknown: A Sourcebook on Women Explorers and Travelers* (CH, Jun'89), which has biographical sketches and bibliographies of 42 women, also primarily British. Together the two books suggest possibilities for the creation of a variety of reference sources about women travelers of different countries, perhaps by mode of travel. Wayward Women is recommended enthusiastically for all libraries and for readers ranging from armchair explorers to technical rock climbers.—*N. S. Osborne, SUNY College at Oswego*

WS-0024 HQ1662 92-4516 CIP
Ruthchild, Rochelle Goldberg. **Women in Russia and the Soviet Union: an annotated bibliography.** G.K. Hall, 1994 (c1993). 203p indexes afp ISBN 0-8161-8989-7, $40.00

An inclusive bibliography of 875 numbered, annotated entries, each giving complete bibliographical information including pagination, and citing indexes and bibliographies. The work is divided into nine sections beginning with reference works and bibliographies, and general works. Succeeding chapters follow historic periods. "Folk and Peasant Culture" includes fairy tales and songs; "The Ancient and Medieval Periods to 1682" continues with more tales, epics, history and laws; three following chapters cover the period of the monarchs, with a separate chapter for Catherine the Great, 1762-96. The work concludes with two largest sections: "Reform, Reaction, and Revolutions, 1855-1917," and "The Soviet Period, 1918-1991." Within each period, entries are alphabetical by author. All are in English, although numerous translations are included, and most are books, but there are also periodical articles, chapters of books, and doctoral dissertations. There are author, title, and subject indexes and cross-references throughout the bibliography and the indexes. Ruthchild (Norwich Univ.) is a specialist in Russian/Soviet studies and founder and first president of the Association for Women in Slavic Studies. A specialized reference tool for students, teachers, and researchers in Russian/Soviet women's studies, history, and folklore.—*R. P. Sasscer, Catholic University of America*

WS-0025 U21 91-40430 CIP
Seeley, Charlotte Palmer, comp. **American women and the U.S. armed forces: a guide to the records of military agencies in the National Archives relating to American women,** rev. by Virginia C. Purdy and Robert Gruber. National Archives and Records Administration, 1992. 355p index ISBN 0-911333-90-8, $25.00

Seeley provides access to holdings in the National Archives the records of federal military agencies that discuss women as wives and mothers of servicemen, as suppliers of military goods and services, and as participants in and victims of war. Arrangement is by agency, then by record group. Records are described in some detail and more than 50 pages of index entries under personal names and subjects further enhance access. This supplementary guide to a subset of archival records is similar to guides to Native American and black history records which have been published in the past decade. It will fill a need in comprehensive women's history collections. Although well-prepared, easy to use, and reasonably priced, this guide's use will be limited to serious researchers who plan to use the Archives.—*K. F. Jones, California State University, Sacramento*

WS-0026 HQ1420 96-1521 MARC
Statistical handbook on women in America, comp. and ed. by Cynthia M. Taeuber. 2nd ed. Oryx, 1996. 354p bibl index afp ISBN 1-57356-005-7, $54.50

Compiled from data collected by such government sources as the Bureau of Labor Statistics, this statistical handbook presents a portrait of women—birth, education, family life, health, economic and social circumstances, and death. The work is arranged alphabetically by title within five sections in tabular format. The tables (more than 260) and charts (more than 80) are assigned letters and numbers, which are used to access them from the table of contents or by subject from the index. Each section is introduced by a four- to five-page essay describing the significant aspects of the information. Coverage is broad, including topics from birth expectation and child care to occupations and living arrangements. The publication furnishes substantial information about young women. Most of the material compares data over decades and varies in currency, with the most recent covering early 1995. Tables offer a variety of reliable, interesting, and useful statistics that respond to questions relating, e.g., to the need for married women to work or preparation for professional and managerial careers. Although the data may be found scattered in standard government sources, they are conveniently located here in one volume. Recommended for collections on women's issues.—*M. Rosenthal, Nassau Community College*

WS-0027 HQ1150 91-4175 CIP
Statistical record of women worldwide, comp. and ed. by Linda Schmittroth. Gale, 1991. 763p index afp ISBN 0-81038349-7, $89.50

As statistical compendiums go, this seems to be a reasonable compilation, conveniently presenting a broad spectrum of data—about 50% focused on US women and 50% on women "worldwide." "Worldwide" can mean focus on an individual city or country, five countries, or many countries. The annotated "List of Sources Consulted" gives a description of the original source as well as bibliographic information. Source notes appearing with each table may give information concerning the definition of terms, other information appearing in the original source, warnings about the data, or even sources of further discussion on a topic. The "Subject and Geographic" index gives additional access to the tables, though the subject terms are not always immediately recognizable in the terminology of the tables themselves, e.g., the table listed under the subject term "Welfare Recipients" uses the term "Government Transfers." The table just above it, which is not listed under "Welfare," has a column heading "Welfare Dependence." Another minor irritation is that US statistics are not always labeled as such. Printed on ANSI standard permanent paper, sewn and cased in serviceable, paper covered boards. Recommended for both academic and public libraries.—*J. E. Peelle, Kenyon College*

WS-0028 CT3320 93-13325 CIP
Sweeney, Patricia E. **Biographies of British women: an annotated bibliography.** ABC-Clio, 1993. 410p index afp ISBN 0-87436-628-3, $75.00

A welcome companion to the author's *Biographies of American Women: An Annotated Bibliography* (1990), this volume treats more than 2,000 British women, 1600-1992. Arranged alphabetically by name, each entry contains vital dates, followed by alphabetical listings of biographical accounts, memoirs or recollections by friends and families, and critical analyses of the person's works and contributions. Many listings are annotated with brief synopses. Extensive cross-references provide both *see* and *see also* links to other relevant entries. An appendix lists all entries by profession or field of interest, and an author/title index is provided. This work focuses primarily on women who were born in the UK or the British Empire and resided most of their lives in the UK, although a few famous emigrants such as Mother Mary Jones are also included. Biogra-

phies had to be at least 50 pages long to be included. Coverage is by no means even, with particular weakness in the fields of politics, government, and social reform movements. While in some instances this volume adds recent resources, it succeeds best as a supplement to more comprehensive resources such as the *Europa Biographical Dictionary of British Women* (CH, Jul'89) and the *International Dictionary of Women's Biography* (CH, May'83).—*E. Patterson, Emory University*

WS-0029 HQ1122 93-41513 CIP
Trager, James. **The women's chronology: a year-by-year record from prehistory to the present.** H. Holt, 1994. 787p index afp ISBN 0-8050-2975-3, $40.00

"Aimed in some small way at correcting historical oversights," this reference tool is apologetically brought to us by the author of *The People's Chronology* (CH, Jan'80). The more than 13,000 entries are flagged with icons that represent 30 themes (political events, human rights, population, crime, science, health and medicine, religion, education, literature, art, sports, economics and everyday life, etc.). The use of these graphic symbols seems to be unnecessary because the indexing is extensive. Three-fourths of the entries chronicle the activities of 18th-, 19th-, and 20th-century women. Very few of the events assigned to the dates between three million BCE and 1700 are attributed to women. Instead, they are historical events that affected women. Trager has included black-and-white photographs and a short bibliography. Recommended for general and undergraduate academic libraries as a complement to Kirstin Olsen's *Chronology of Women's History* (CH, Dec'94).—*R. L. Ruben, Western Illinois University*

WS-0030 HQ1904 94-38500 CIP
U.S. women's interest groups: institutional profiles, ed. by Sarah Slavin. Greenwood, 1995. 645p index afp ISBN 0-313-25073-1, $99.50

This informative source book describes some of the prominent women's organizations in the US. Since the editor did not attempt to identify every women's organization, her book is not meant to be as inclusive as *Encyclopedia of Women's Associations Worldwide*, ed. by J.K. Barrett (CH, Feb'94), which lists 3,400 groups, or the National Council for Research on Women's *NWO: A Directory of National Women's Organizations* (1992-), which lists 477. The information here is mainly based on responses to a questionnaire. Nearly 200 women's organizations, from AIDS Coalition to Zonta International, are included. Special efforts were made to list every major organization of color, except sororities. Many religious groups representing various denominations are included. To be listed organizations had to meet one or more of five criteria: (1) there is some connection to women; (2) membership is confined to women; (3) they serve specific women's interests; (4) they represent a traditional women's role; and (5) they take positions on issues of concern to women. Each organizational profile gives origin and development, organization and funding, policy concerns and tactics, and further information (the latter lists the organization's publications and a bibliography). The information about policy and tactics can be useful to those interested in an organization's previous activities and future directions. The book describes legislative issues on which some of these organizations took stands and what their future tactics will be. It also cites interorganizational relationships and activities. Cross-references include former names of organizations and names of merged groups. Although organizations included are somewhat random—those that returned the questionnaire—this sourcebook represents diversity in both organizations and emphases. Useful both to identify women's issues groups and as an overview of the women's movement. Highly recommended for libraries supporting women's studies and related programs.—*E. L. Yang, University of Colorado at Denver*

WS-0031 Orig
Von Salis, Susan J., comp. **Revealing documents: a guide to African American manuscript sources in the Schlesinger Library and the Radcliffe College archives.** G.K. Hall, 1993. 174p index ISBN 0-8161-0613-4, $50.00

This finder's tool will give researchers interested in African American life as portrayed in primary sources an introduction to the Schlesinger/Radcliffe collections. Schlesinger Library is known for its resources in women's studies and history. Begun in 1943, the library focuses on the suffrage movement, women's rights and legal status, women in politics, and many other areas relating to women. However, during its first 30 years, any material having to do with black America was acquired by happenstance. In 1955 the first papers of an African American woman, Roberta Church, were received. Since that time, the papers of about 30 women, including Pauli Murray, Edith Sampson, Dorothy West, June Jordon, and Florence Kennedy have been added. Although these materials constitute a minuscule part of the Schlesinger/Radcliffe collections, this text describes in a thoughtful and deliberate manner the African American women's papers and portions of other papers in the library/archive that mention African Americans or related topics. The book has four parts: "The Papers of Black Women"; "Collections in Schlesinger Containing Materials of or About African Americans"; "Papers of African Americans in the Radcliffe College Archives"; and "Radcliffe College Archives Containing Materials of or About African Americans." Research collections.—*C. Snelling, Chicago State University*

WS-0032   E185   93-33079 CIP
Williams, Ora. **American black women in the arts and social sciences.** 3rd ed., rev. and enlarged. Scarecrow, 1994. 387p index afp ISBN 0-8108-2671-2, $57.50

Expanding as well as updating previous editions (CH, Feb'74; May'79), this bibliographic survey provides an invaluable resource for the study of African American women. It provides checklists of materials in reference, the literary arts, audiovisuals, and performing arts (including culinary arts). Bibliographies of the works of West Coast women replace earlier editions' individual bibliographic essays (only librarian Dorothy Porter Wesley and choral director Eva Jessye are featured in this volume). A general chronology and one concentrating on the West Coast trace significant dates in African American women's history. Resource lists, expanded and better organized than those in the previous edition, include music directors and conductors; college presidents; African American periodicals, newspapers, collections, and resource centers; and selected ideas and achievements. Libraries that own the earlier editions should retain them for the biobibliographic profiles, photographs, and lists of unpublished materials. Although not entirely comprehensive, this book, in conjunction with earlier editions, provides a valuable search tool and points out gaps in African American studies scholarship. Recommended for all libraries and a necessary purchase for African American and women's studies collections.—*M. F. Jones, Muskingum College*

WS-0033   HQ1438   91-24898 CIP
Women in the West: a guide to manuscript sources, ed. by Susan Armitage et al. Garland, 1991. 422p (Women's history and culture, 5) ISBN 0-8240-4298-0, $59.00

This extensive bibliography identifies the manuscript sources, oral histories, and photographic collections available in 20 states of the trans-Mississippi West for multicultural research in Western women's history. More than 1,500 repositories, ranging from archives and museums to religious orders and tribal councils, completed questionnaires on their general holdings on women, with special emphasis on women of color. The entries are arranged alphabetically by state, city, and repository name, and include address, contact person, phone number, hours, and available services, such as photocopying or microform readers. The size of the repository is identified as small (under 10 items or collections), medium (11 to 50), large (50 to 100) or extensive (more than 100). Entries include general descriptions of the holdings, separate paragraphs describing multicultural materials, and mentions of items or collections "of special note." Scholars interested in the history of women, the West, and diverse cultures will find this bibliography invaluable.—*K. F. Jones, California State University, Sacramento*

WS-0034   Orig
Women's information directory: a guide to organizations, agencies, institutions, programs, publications, services, and other resources concerned with women in the United States, ed. by Shawn Brennan. Gale, 1993. 795p index afp ISBN 0-8103-8422-1, $75.00

A handy guide to a wide variety of resources for women in the US, *WID* includes more than 10,000 entries divided into 26 chapters accessible through a "Master Name and Subject Index." The users guide describes the scope, what is included in each entry, arrangement, sources of information, and how the entries are indexed for each of the chapters. Entries normally include contact information. The majority of the information was culled from other Gale publications, some from government or private organization publications, and some from original research. One chapter gives more than 400 video titles and another has 30-plus electronic resources including electronic bulletin boards and their e-mail addresses. Though there is much overlap, *WID* does not totally replace *DWM: A Directory of Women's Media* (16th ed., 1992, from the National Council for Research on Women) which includes radio, TV, music, theater, dance, speakers, and other performance groups not covered in *WID*. Perhaps the two publications should get together and pool their resources. Its convenience will make *WID* worthwhile to both academic and public libraries. It is printed on recycled, permanent paper.—*J. E. Peelle, Kenyon College*

WS-0035   CIP
The Women's information exchange national directory, comp. by Deborah Brecher and Jill Lippitt. Avon Books, 1994. 338p index ISBN 0-380-77570-0 pbk, $10.00

This directory seeks to provide a comprehensive, though not exhaustive, listing of women's groups, networks, and services—with attention to a broad range of social, political, ethnic, and age concerns—to facilitate resource sharing and communication among women. The organizations and programs listed were selected from the National Women's Mailing List, which includes more than 12,000 women's groups. The directory is arranged by subjects, including arts, booksellers, education, foundations, health, legal services, lesbian and gay organizations, women of color, political groups, publishers, religious groups, sports, science, special interests, violence, history, rights, work, and others. This is a convenient, affordable resource recommended for academic and public libraries and women's centers and services.—*J. E. Peelle, Kenyon College*

WS-0036   KF478   95-46893 CIP
Women's legal guide, ed. by Barbara R. Hauser with Julie A. Tigges. Fulcrum, 1996. 526p bibl index ISBN 1-55591-913-8, $39.95; ISBN 1-55591-303-2 pbk, $22.95

A handy, well-organized, comprehensive compendium, *Women's Legal Guide* aims to help women make informed decisions by providing information and guidance in negotiating both straightforward and complex legal questions. Beginning with a chapter on selecting and working with a lawyer, this handbook is arranged in five broad sections: personal/body issues, family law, women's rights at school and in the workplace, business law, and life planning. Twenty-nine female attorneys contribute chapters focusing on a wide range of expected legal issues of particular concern to women including health care, marriage and divorce, spousal and family violence, sexual harassment, and retirement and estate planning. Of particular note, however, are chapters dealing with timely and relevant issues such as child care planning for seriously ill mothers, sports, legal rights of lesbian women, disabilities, and legal issues for refugee women. Chapters are enhanced by bibliographies and organizational resources for further information and assistance. A glossary and comprehensive index round out the volume. Priced reasonably enough for personal collections, and essential for academic and public libraries.—*J. Ariel, University of California, Irvine*

WS-0037   HQ1115   88-32806 CIP
Women's studies encyclopedia: v.1: Views from the sciences, ed. by Helen Tierney. Greenwood, 1989. 417p bibl index afp ISBN 0-313-26725-1, $59.95

More a collection of position statements than an encyclopedia, as that term is generally understood. The editor's introduction identifies some of the major problems: "partial and incomplete. . ., overconcentration of articles in some areas and gapping omissions in others. . . .The bibliographic apparatus is therefore very limited. . . .Most articles are limited just to the United States. . . .The lack of a uniform feminist perspective. . .the lack of uniformity of organization. . . Cross-references have been reduced to a minimum." When one adds to that litany considerable evidence of poor editorial control and quixotic indexing, it is difficult to welcome this volume, let alone its two planned companions. Their areas of coverage are not stated. This volume, subtitled "A View from the Sciences," ranges sporadically through "fields that can be considered, in some, sense, as science': natural, behavioral, and social sciences, health and medicine, economics, linguistics, political and legal sciences" (introd.). The 247 articles, which range from one sentence to four pages in length, are written for an educated user who is not a specialist on the topic of the article. Articles are signed, unless written by the editor; 121 contributors, virtually all US academics, are listed. The overall aim was "a reference tool that includes the results of feminist research on women from various academic perspectives"; yet in a view from the sciences there is no article headed "Biology" and no reference this reviewer could find to the important collection Women Look at Biology Looking at Women (CH, Mar'80). Nor are there articles on women in the sciences, but there are articles on teaching and librarianship. The two-sentence article "Feminism" ends with references to seven specialized feminisms, but omits the article "Radical Feminism." From "Divorce" there is a reference to "No-Fault Divorce," but the articles give different dates for the California law and different numbers of states to adopt the idea. "Sexually Transmitted Diseases" cites a master's thesis on chlamydia trachomatis, but the article on that condition has no references at all. There are no entries under personal names, but some personal names appear in the index. Frances Perkins is indexed (p. 259) as the first woman cabinet member, but the first congress-woman, woman senator, and Supreme Court Justice are not indexed from the same article, p. 258. Many entries are useful summaries of research, as promised: the economics articles are the most consistently factual and "encyclopedia-like." Too many articles end with platitudes or pious hopes: "Most men and women continue to depend on their friends, relatives, and lovers. . ." (Dependency); "However, most women whose children have left home find they are happier than they have been in years" (Empty Nest Syndrome); ". . .as more high school girls realize that mathematics is vital to their futures, the gap in test scores should gradually close" (Math Anxiety). Ideally, this volume should be recalled and the whole encyclopedia rethought, reedited, and really indexed. Realistically, it will be bought, shelved, cited in student papers, and forgotten, perhaps to be rediscovered by future scholars as a period miscellany of some received wisdom on its scattering of topics.—*V. Clark, Choice*

WS-0038 HQ1115 88-32806 CIP
Women's studies encyclopedia: v.2: Literature, arts, and learning, ed. by Helen Tierney. Greenwood, 1990. 381p bibl index afp ISBN 0-313-27357-X, $59.95

The second volume of the Women's Studies Encyclopedia focuses on a narrower range of disciplines and is therefore more cohesive than the first volume (CH, Feb'90). It also includes more articles about other countries and cultures. With few exceptions the quality of the signed articles is very good. Within each two- to three-page essay, the material is presented chronologically with references for further reading (a format also followed in the shorter articles, which are primarily definitions). Problems noted with cross-references and indexing in the first volume continue here. For example: there is a cross-reference from "Poets U.S." to "African-American, Chicana, and Native American," but in the index there is no reference to "Chicana"; there are no cross-references between "New Woman in Victorian Literature" and "Stereotypical Heroine in Victorian Literature;" and the index does not list "New Woman" under "Victorian." There are some puzzling omissions: an essay "Italian Artists (Fifteenth Through Eighteenth Centuries)," but nothing on a later period; "Magazines, Women's (Nineteenth-Century)," but nothing about the great flowering of feminist periodicals in the 1970s. Despite these flaws, both volumes of this set contain a wealth of useful information. Recommended.—*B. K. Lacks, California State University, Fresno*

WS-0039 HQ1115 88-32806 CIP
Women's studies encyclopedia: v.3: History, philosophy, and religion, ed. by Helen Tierney. Greenwood, 1991. 531p bibl index afp ISBN 0-313-27358-8, $65.00

Names of consultants and contributors occupy eight pages of the *Women's Studies Encyclopedia* which, as its subtitle indicates, contains articles on selected topics in women's history, religion and philosophy. Articles average 1,000 to 1,500 words; most include a short, representative bibliography. Philosophy articles include statements of classic philosophers. Articles on the history of women are organized under nation or area for women outside the US and Europe; under the name of the nation or people concerned for Europe (except Britain and France since the Reformation); and under subject headings for post-Reformation British, French, and US women's history. In the index, page numbers set in italics indicate the location of a main entry. This volume could be useful to undergraduate students in need of basic definitions and information; recommended for libraries

that own the other two volumes (CH, Feb'90, Jun'91), to complete their collection.—*N. S. Osborne, SUNY College at Oswego*

WS-0040 Orig
Women's studies index, 1989. G.K. Hall, 1990 (c1991). 502p ISBN 0-8161-0510-3, $125.00

This new annual is a welcome, needed addition to the women's studies field. The advisory board consists of four well-known women's studies librarians and scholars and their experience is evident in both coverage and arrangement. Access is provided to 78 important American and international journals and magazines—feminist and mainstream women's periodicals plus titles in related fields. Both popular and scholarly titles are represented. Coverage incudes current news, the arts, education, work, politics, health, spirituality, and much more. Titles by and about women of color, lesbians, and Third World women are represented. This source indexes titles more completely than Women Studies Abstracts (1972-) or Studies on Women Abstracts (1983-) and is much easier to use. Authors, subjects, and cross-references are in a single alphabet. Each citation of an item provides all the standard information, with the helpful addition of the full journal title. There are subject headings for creative works as well as for book, film, play, and video reviews. The volume is physically durable; future editions should increase the number of journals covered. Highly recommended for all academic reference collections.—*L. Krikos, The Ohio State University*

WS-0041 Orig
The World's women, 1995: trends and statistics. United Nations, 1995. 188p (Social statistics and indicators, series K, 12) bibl ISBN 92-1-161372-8 pbk, $15.95

Representing an initial compilation of data on women worldwide, the first edition of this work appeared in 1991. This latest edition was produced in preparation for the Fourth World Conference on Women and was intended to enable governments to take action for gender equality. The 1991 edition dealt with education, population, public life, health, childbearing, and work. In the second edition, coverage of media, violence against women, poverty, the environment, refugees and displaced persons, and 50 years of women in the UN and in peacekeeping have been added. The purpose of the volume is to present statistics on how women fare in different parts of the world. Information is presented globally and regionally, broken down into Latin America and the Caribbean, sub-Saharan Africa, Northern Africa and Western Asia, Southern Asia, Eastern and Southeastern Asia, and developed regions. Key conclusions are highlighted in the margins, e.g., "too many women lack access to reproductive health services." Material is extremely well organized and information is displayed in an attractive manner. A resource book for research, teaching, or policy making. Undergraduates and above.—*S. Reinharz, Brandeis University*

◆ Education

WS-0042 LC1757 95-106 CIP
Dobkin, Rachel. **The college woman's handbook,** by Rachel Dobkin and Shana Sippy. Workman Publishing, 1995. 640p bibl index ISBN 1-56305-559-7 pbk, $14.95

Near the end of this volume, Dobkin and Sippy ask for "feedback, please": What issues are important to college women today? What information or resources would have been helpful as you started college? What services would have been important to you as an undergraduate student? What campus events are occurring that others should know about? These questions indicate the goals of this resource-ful, "peer-to-peer guide." Major sections include "Aspects of Academic Life"; "Money and Home"; "Mental and Physical Health"; "Sexual and Reproductive Matters"; "Fighting Back" (harassment, violence against women, and home and travel safety); and "Defining Yourself" (community service, activism, and organizational leadership). Humorous and suitable illustrations, and the user-friendly language of traditional undergraduate women, help readers get the most out of their education. Librarians who are asked survival questions, parents sending their children to college, college counseling centers, and those seeing friends off to college, would do well to use this lively, provocative, and honest handbook. Extensive resource guides, sidebars packed with information, "lively lexicons," and direct quotes from undergraduate women make these 24 chapters a good investment, worthwhile and appropriate for high school and undergraduate reference collections, with perhaps a second copy for circulation.—*N. S. Osborne, SUNY College at Oswego*

WS-0043   LC212   90-19600 MARC
Grambs, Jean Dresden. **Sex differences and learning: an annotated bibliography of educational research, 1979-1989,** by Jean Dresden Grambs and John C. Carr. Garland, 1991. 280p (Garland bibliographies in contemporary education, 11) indexes afp ISBN 0-8240-6641-3, $35.00

Research studies appearing in journals and covering sex differences in learning in grades K-12 are the focus of this bibliography. Studies included have American subjects, appeared 1979-1989, and are selected only from journals likely to be available in large libraries. The 795 entries are arranged in 23 categories with author and subject indexes for the entire bibliography. Annotations provide brief information on methodology and findings, with cross-references to related entries. Grambs (who died in 1989) and Carr have published frequently, both separately and together, on topics in education and diversity. Their knowledge is apparent in the work's design and annotations. The key to a purchase decision is whether a library needs a bibliography on this topic. Recommended for large education collections with focus on K-12. Useful to graduate students and faculty, as well as to those doing research on related topics, and to educational administrators.—*P. Palmer, Memphis State University*

WS-0044   LC212   93-24315 CIP
Stitt, Beverly A. **Gender equity in education: an annotated bibliography.** Southern Illinois, 1994. 168p index afp ISBN 0-8093-1937-3, $24.95

Begun in 1985 and completed in early 1993, this bibliography was created for sex equity staff, administrators, teachers, and counselors "in their attempts to overcome gender role stereotyping and sex bias in schools." A majority of the resources included were published over a decade ago, reflecting the intense interest in vocational education, nontraditional careers, and sex equity on the parts of national and state agencies, school boards, and organizations of that era. Most of these titles are still available for purchase. Citations are grouped under 23 alphabetically arranged categories that range from "Agriculture and Industry" to "Women's Studies." Stitt (information systems and women's studies, Southern Illinois Univ. at Carbondale) chose to include what campus curriculum committees would call "classics." This is a particularly useful resource for libraries that never had (or have discarded) the Women's Equity Action League's *WEAL Washington Report* and *TABS Aids for Equal Education* resources. For sex equity research—particularly for materials on cultural diversity—this bibliography must be supplemented by more current resources, but it is a fine volume leading to timeless materials. All levels.—*N. S. Osborne, SUNY College at Oswego*

WS-0045   LC1756   90-20408 CIP
Touchton, Judith G. **Fact book on women in higher education,** comp. by Judith G. Touchton and Lynne Davis. American Council on Education/Macmillan, 1991. 289p bibl index ISBN 0-02-900951-0, $39.95

Compiled by the highly respected Office of Women in Higher Education, this fact book is the newest of a series copublished by the American Council on Education and Macmillan. It is designed to provide comprehensive information relating to the status of women of all races and ethnic groups in US higher education. Priority was given to primary sources from government, private, and professional organizations. More than 85 charts, tables, and graphs are provided for 7 broad areas: demographic and economic data pertinent to education; high school and the transition to higher education; enrollment; earned degrees; faculty; administrators, trustees, and staff; and student aid. Each area notes highlights and trends and supplements graphics with narrative comments. The fact book is completed by a guide to the sources, a bibliography, and reproduction of the source tables. Though statistical data on women in education are provided in several other sources, most recently in *Statistical Handbook on Women in America,* ed. by Cynthia Taeuber (1991), those volumes do not match the thoroughness of this title. Highly recommended.—*L. Krikos, Ohio State University*

WS-0046   LA2311   93-28033 CIP
Women educators in the United States, 1820-1993: a bio-bibliographical sourcebook, ed. by Maxine Schwartz Seller. Greenwood, 1994. 603p bibl index afp ISBN 0-313-27937-3, $99.50

This fine assemblage of biographies introduces readers to 66 women educators whose professional lives mirror "common themes." The excellent introduction and overview organizes the historical context, grouping entries under "The Pioneers, 1820-1870," "Expanders and Reformers, 1870-1920," "Losses and Gains, 1920-1960" (suffrage, feminism, gender equity), and "Pursuing Equality and Excellence, 1960-1993." The editor acknowledges that the women included are "representative of many others who have made similar and often equally important contributions." Entries are arranged alphabetically by last names; each entry concludes with notes and "works by" and "works about" the subject. Scholar contributors with "special expertise on the particular educator" wrote the bio-bibliographies, including discussion on the impact of gender on their subjects' lives. Some living educators are listed; refreshingly, bibliographies differ in length and style of writing. Indicating that disabilities, race, tribal identities, and restrictive environments were as important as gender issues in many women educators' lives, the editor made a genuine effort toward inclusion and diversity; however, lesbians are not mentioned in her overview, nor is the term to be found in the index. An appendix that lists educators chronologically by the historical periods mentioned above makes this source especially accessible to scholars of women's history and the history of education. The selected bibliography is brief but germane. This useful source is recommended without reservation to all libraries, academic and public.—*N. S. Osborne, SUNY College at Oswego*

◆ Fine Arts

WS-0047   Orig
Germaine, Max. **A Dictionary of women artists of Australia.** Craftsman House, 1992 (c1991). (Dist. by Scientific and Technical Book Service, Ltd., Bush Terminal, 32 Thirty-Third St., Brooklyn, NY 11232) 486p ISBN 976-8097-13-2, $55.00

The artists listed in this dictionary are living professionals, nine tenths of whom were born in Australia. Information was provided by the artists themselves or by their agents. Painters, sculptors, printmakers, ceramists, and performance artists are listed in a straight dictionary arrangement with no indexes. A fair selection of aboriginal artists is included, but there is no way of separating them out. (Most of them appear to be in the N's, however, and are members of about eight families.) Entries include brief biographical and professional information, publications, and places where paintings are represented. Longer entries have a brief bibliography. There is rather less information on the aboriginal artists. A selection of 27 good-quality color illustrations in the center shows a sample of these artists' work. Germaine has previously compiled three editions of *Artists and Galleries of Australia* for Craftsman House, the latest in 1990. This dictionary is a unique and up-to-date publication and is recommended for libraries collecting in art, Australia, or women's studies.—*P. Brauch, Brooklyn College, CUNY*

WS-0048   N72   93-822 MARC
Langer, Cassandra. **Feminist art criticism: an annotated bibliography.** G.K. Hall, 1994 (c1993). 291p indexes afp ISBN 0-8161-8948-X, $55.00

Langer, a commentator on feminist art criticism issues, has compiled a valuable bibliography of 1,100 selected works, written over the last century, about women and art. The majority are in English and were published in the 1970s and '80s. The author arranged the volume in chapters covering reference tools, books, exhibition catalogs, and articles. Within each section, numbered entries are in alphabetical order by author or by title and are made accessible through author and subject indexes. Future editions should include a title index. Included are all the standard names and texts associated with scholarship about women and art, plus interesting, lesser-known references (e.g., "The Girl Art Student in Paris," 1883). The descriptive, paragraph-long annotations discuss the work's place and influence within the literature and, sometimes, refer to other relevant citations for those new to the field. The result is a valuable overview of feminist criticism. Each entry works individually, and all are tied together by Langer's grasp of the literature and insightful comments. For all academic libraries and public research libraries with art or women's studies collections.—*P. Keeran, University of Denver*

WS-0049 N6503 94-49710 CIP
North American women artists of the twentieth century: a biographical dictionary, ed. by Jules Heller and Nancy G. Heller. Garland, 1995. 612p (Garland reference library of the humanities, 1219) bibl index afp ISBN 0-8240-6049-0, $125.00

The Hellers have compiled an extensive biographical dictionary of 20th-century women artists born prior to 1960 who worked primarily in the US, Canada, and Mexico. Their book does much to remedy the paucity of basic biographical information about women artists. More than 100 contributors, including academics, curators, and artists, wrote the 1,500 entries; no major omissions were detected. Artists were selected if they demonstrated a serious commitment to the visual arts by participating in specific types of exhibitions, and by paper trails of reviews, articles, or monographs. Accounts of individual artists, averaging 330 words, describe general artistic characterizations, media of choice, biographical and professional backgrounds, representative exhibitions and awards (including dates), and include brief bibliographies. This information will satisfy basic information needs as well as provide avenues for further research about Canadian, Mexican, and American women artists. Although color photographs would have been preferable, some 100 glossy black-and-white photographs are of high quality and illustrate the varied styles and media used by these artists. This valuable reference book should be in every art, academic, and large public library collection.—*P. Keeran, University of Denver*

WS-0050 N8354 93-27248 CIP
Piland, Sherry. **Women artists: an historical, contemporary and feminist bibliography.** 2nd ed. Scarecrow, 1994. 454p bibl afp ISBN 0-8108-2559-7, $59.50

Piland, coauthor of the lst edition (CH, Sep'79), adds 29 artists in this edition and makes corrections to the first edition. The first section of the bibliography is a list of general works, divided into three categories: (1) books, including microfilm collections, slide sets, and dissertations; (2) periodicals, plus papers delivered before societies; and (3) catalogs. The second section, the main part of the work, consists of individual artists grouped by century, beginning with the 15th century and earlier, and continuing into the 20th century with a cutoff birth date of 1930. Artists in each century are arranged alphabetically, as are the citations about them. There is a biography of each artist. The work concludes with a short selected bibliography on needlework that includes books and periodicals. Works listed in each section are annotated, many at length. This work continues to be an extremely valuable reference source, especially for women artists prior to the 20th century. Bibliographies for 20th-century artists are not comprehensive, and because of the 1930 cutoff date, some will not be listed. There are still no indexes or cross-references. Academic and general collections.—*R. P. Sasscer, Catholic University of America*

WS-0051 TT835 92-13726 CIP
Quilt groups today: who they are, where they meet, what they do, and how to contact them. American Quilter's Society, P.O. Box 3290, Paducah, KY 42002, 1992. 336p ISBN 0-89145-999-5 pbk, $14.95

This interesting, well-produced directory is the first in a projected series and was compiled from survey forms completed by individual quilt groups. Entries are arranged by US states and 16 foreign countries. Each entry offers address, area served, group size and expertise, and meeting frequency and location. Descriptions of the groups were taken from the survey forms, along with notes of annual events and donations; they often offer lively reading and a feel for the nature of the group. A number of the entries also include photographs. The guide does not claim to be comprehensive, but the number of groups included in this first edition is very impressive, with 69 in California alone and 28 from New Zealand. A survey form is included for groups who would like to be included in the next edition. The publication of this directory reflects a growing interest in both the history and art of quilting. The 1991 *Encyclopedia of Associations* lists a membership of 70,000 in the American Quilters Society, and the recent publication of quilt literature demonstrates increasing academic interest in the field. *Quilts*

in America, by Patsy and Myron Orlofsky, a major and standard history of the field first published in 1974, has been reprinted (1992), as has Marie Webster's 1915 *Quilts: Their Story and How to Make Them* (1992), alas with its color plates reproduced in black and white. *Abstract Design in American Quilts: A Biography of an Exhibition*, by Jonathan Holstein (1991), demonstrates "awareness of American quilts as an art form and social document." Two beautiful studies of regional quilting were also published last year: *Nebraska Quilts & Quiltmakers*, edited by Patricia Cox Crews and Ronald C. Naugle (1991) and *Quilts in Community: Ohio's Traditions*, by Ricky Clark, George W. Knepper, and Ellice Ronsheim (1991). Both of these volumes offer state history, art history, biography of quilters, and quilting analysis, amid lovely reproductions. The heritage and current creation of quilts is of interest to social historians, art historians, women's historians, artists, collectors and, of course quilters. Especially considering its very reasonable price, this directory is highly recommended to most public and academic libraries, both for reference and for browsing, together with other works as local interests and curricula dictate.—*N. Taylor, Earlham College*

◆ Health Sciences

WS-0052 RT34 87-29076 CIP
American nursing: a biographical dictionary, v.2, ed. by Vern L. Bullough, Lilli Sentz, and Alice P. Stein. Garland, 1992. 389p (Garland reference library of the social sciences, 684) indexes afp ISBN 0-8240-7201-4, $95.00

The review of Volume 1 (CH, Oct'88) noted that "since nursing has been one of the few professions available to women as a career. . .[this dictionary] provides an interesting perspective on the evolution of women's education and work roles over the last 150 years." In Volume 2 an effort has been made to include more nonwhite women who may or may not have received formal training as nurses, but whose curative powers give reason to acknowledge their work. This inclusion not only makes the work a useful reference for multicultural studies but highlights the essence of all medical professions, which is both to heal and to alleviate the pain of dying. This volume covers 215 persons; and as in Volume 1, individual articles are followed by lists of publications by the subjects and by bibliographies of sources of information about them. The text is followed by four indexes: "Decades of Birth," "First Nursing School Attended," "Area of Special Interest or Accomplishment," and "States & Countries of Birth." In the introduction the editors ask readers to suggest further names for inclusion in Volume 3, which is scheduled for publication in 1997 or 1998. Highly recommended for academic libraries serving either nursing programs or women's studies programs.—*K. Bradley, Bellevue Community College*

WS-0053 RG525 92-14975 CIP
Encyclopedia of childbearing: critical perspectives, ed. by Barbara Katz Rothman. Oryx, 1993. 446p index afp ISBN 0-89774-648-1, $74.50

Birth studies as a scholarly discipline is new compared to the ancient practice of midwifery or the well-developed specialty of obstetrics. This fine encyclopedia examines childbearing from nontechnical perspectives: social, political, literary, psychological, artistic, etc. Some 250 signed entries, alphabetically arranged, average more than a page in length. Each is followed by a bibliography of related, mostly current resources. Topics are decidedly eclectic and sometimes surprising ("Childbearing in Science Fiction," "Diapers, Environmental Concerns"). Most examine historic aspects as well as current trends in such areas as "Posture for Labor and Birth," "Formula Marketing," and "Naming Practices." A "Guide to Related Topics" groups entry titles by category—e.g., "Adoption," "Cross-Cultural Perspectives," "New Procreative Technologies." A useful directory of organizations and resources and an excellent index conclude the volume. Rothman, a respected sociologist and author of several important books on pregnancy and motherhood, rejoices in the diversity of the material while acknowledging its limitations (e.g., childbearing practices of only a few non-American cultures are treated). The more than 200 contributors are specialists with backgrounds in sociology, nursing, midwifery, medical anthropology, and a variety of other fields. A prefect starting point for undergraduates and general readers, the book is handsomely printed on permanent paper, with a few black-and-white photographs and drawings. Highly recommended.—*L. N. Pander, Bowdoin College*

WS-0054   HQ111   91-3211 CIP

Kantha, Sachi Sri, comp. **Prostitutes in medical literature: an annotated bibliography.** Greenwood, 1991. 245p (Bibliographies and indexes in medical studies, 6) indexes afp ISBN 0-313-27491-6, $49.95

Large medical or research libraries where there is interest in human sexuality will find this book useful. Although a researcher could find similar information by searching relevant databases and using *A Bibliography of Prostitution,* ed. by V.L. Bullough et al. (1977), Kantha gathers the material in one place and includes citations from the years 1890 to 1989, thereby saving a scholar a lot of footwork. The bibliography is divided into ten chapters and has an author and subject index. It includes material from scientific journals, government documents, books, dissertations, and a few research reports. No popular material is covered, which is too bad, since this excludes Sydney Barrows's *Mayflower Madam* (1986), which contains a good description of the psychology of modern prostitutes and madams. Recommended if there is a need for this information.—*N. Kupferberg, Montana State University*

WS-0055   RG133   92-56679 CIP

Partridge-Brown, Mary. **In vitro fertilization clinics: a North American directory of programs and services.** McFarland, 1993. 234p index afp ISBN 0-89950-817-0 pbk, $28.50

The first of its kind, this directory provides a general listing of clinics in North America offering in vitro fertilization (IVF), gamete intrafallopian transfer (GIFT), and/or zygote intrafallopian (ZIFT) services. For the approximately ten million men and women in North America suffering from some type of fertility problem, this resource gives valuable data on assisted reproduction programs. It allows readers to compare specific programs and make an educated decision. The directory lists 250 programs, giving for each: name, address, telephone number, procedures offered, drugs used, anesthesia options, egg retrieval method, cost breakdown, program starting date, rate of success, requirements or restrictions, and names of supervising physicians. Written from the point of view of a fertility patient, this book covers diagnostic testing and conventional infertility solutions, describes each of the assisted reproductive technologies (ARTs), explains how they differ, and offers an alphabetic program profile. The directory should help prospective patients make more informed decisions about infertility choices. Recommended for reference collections of academic and health science center libraries.—*J. M. Coggan, University of Florida*

WS-0056   RC607.A26   90-7732 CIP

Watstein, Sarah Barbara. **AIDS and women: a sourcebook,** by Sarah Barbara Watstein and Robert Anthony Laurich. Oryx, 1990 (c1991). 159p bibl indexes afp ISBN 0-89774-577-9, $36.50

Similar in format, content, and indexing to David A. Tyckoson's annual *AIDS* (2nd ed., CH, May'87). Each section begins with a one or two page overview followed by an annotated bibliography of sources commonly held by academic libraries—e.g., Morbidity & Mortality Weekly Report or New England Journal of Medicine. Related statistical tables carry headings ranging from "Pediatric AIDS Totals—New York City" to "Cases by Race." The appendix includes lists of audiovisual resources, hotlines, and organizations, plus a glossary and list of sources for continuing research. There are author, subject, and title indexes with references to page numbers. For selectors the decision to buy or not will be based heavily on convenience: sources such as Academic Index (on Infotrac), Social Sciences Index, and Tyckoson's AIDS do not give easy subject access to the broad topic of women and AIDS. One must search under broad headings like "Women-Health & Hygiene," or "Women-AIDS-Social Aspects," etc., to pull together sources. Libraries that have experienced heavy use of Tyckoson's *AIDS* or *AIDS Information Sourcebook,* ed. by H. Robert Malinowsky (CH, Jul'88) will want this title.—*T. C. Trawick, Troy State University*

◆ History, Geography & Area Studies

WS-0057   [CD-ROM]

American journey: history in your hands: women in America. Research Publications International, 12 Lunar Dr., Woodbridge, CT 06525, 1994. ISBN 0-89235-158-6, $179.00. 1 disc; user guide; teacher's guide. System requirements: IBM-PC 386 or higher; 510K free RAM; color display; 5 MB free hard drive space; DOS 5.0 or higher.

American Journey is designed to complement the high school history curriculum by providing easy access to more than 200 documents and 500 pictures on women's history. Document types include letters, diaries, treaties, and legislation. The images of paintings, photographs, and drawings are sharp and clear on a good monitor; a disc with maps is available, but must be specifically requested. Audio clips are also built in for computers with sound cards. Although any printer may be used for text files, a laser printer is required for copying pictures. The system is very easy to install. Use of a mouse is recommended, but keyboard commands allow for good maneuverability.

The opening screen has five selections: Search Options, Picture Album, Historical Overview, Key Topics, and About This Disc. Users may search via full text, chronologically, or by selecting from listings of index terms, documents, and pictures. The best place to begin using the system is Key Topics. This segment will quickly orient users by showing them eight screens containing brief descriptions of historical segments such as "Earliest Americans: Native Americans," "Colonial women through the eyes of the law," "Role of women in building a new nation," and so forth. Each subject area has a lengthy overview, with certain names and terms highlighted in blue. Immediate access to a picture or portion of text may be gained by selecting a highlighted term. Full text searching should be used primarily when looking for a specific person or historic event. A full text search for "Anita Hill," for example, resulted in two hits: one in key topics (New Women's Movement) and another in documents (her congressional testimony regarding Clarence Thomas's Supreme Court nomination). Although a topic such as temperance can also be searched full text, words that are too common will stall the system and require a reboot. All search screens allow users to view related items, see source citations, begin a new search, or go back to the main menu. Printed helps include a 32-page user guide and a 95-page teacher guide outlining the disc contents. Although geared to the high school curriculum, this could well serve as a supplementary source for undergraduate courses in women's history. Recommended for high school, public, and academic libraries.—*G. D. Barber, SUNY College at Fredonia*

WS-0058   HQ1593   CIP

Banks, Olive. **The biographical dictionary of British feminists: v.2: A supplement, 1900-1945.** New York University, 1990. 241p indexes ISBN 0-8147-1146-4, $75.00

Articles ranging up to 2,000 words sketch a select company of 68 women and 7 men and extend to 1945 the coverage of Volume 1 (CH, Nov'85). The 1900-1930 overlap signals the addition of a few women who would have been eligible for the earlier volume. In contrast to Volume 1, nearly two thirds of whose subjects also appeared in such standard references as the *Europa Biographical Dictionary of British Women* (CH, Jul'84), Volume 2 treats women who have received less attention elsewhere: only 26 in the Europa; only 14 of the women-but 6 of the 7 men-in DNB. In part, this seeming indifference reflects the lack of a single focus for feminist activity after the extension of the franchise to women under 30 in 1928. The activities of these women are less easy to characterize and several of the articles "reach" for a feminist theme in their subjects' lives. Articles cite published sources, including the DNB and the *Dictionary of Labour Biography,* but references are not exhaustive: for example, those on A. Susan Lawrence do not include the long obituary in the *Fabian Quarterly.* The subject index, with more than 300 specific topics and institutional names, is a great improvement over the limited analysis under 22 broad subject terms used in Volume 1. A valuable addition to collections in 20th-century British history or women's history.—*V. Clark, Choice*

WS-0059   E185 *have*   92-39947 CIP

Black women in America: an historical encyclopedia, ed. by Darlene Clark Hine. Carlson, 1993. 2v. 1,530p bibl index afp ISBN 0-926019-61-9, $195.00

The unique viewpoint of the African-American woman's experience permeates every aspect of the 804 essays in this encyclopedia, from the topics of the entries to the strength of language in each description. The signed essays range in length from two paragraphs to 25 pages, and accompanying bibliographies indicate that many are based on rare or unpublished sources of information. Although Jesse Carney Smith's *Notable Black American Women* (CH, Jun '92) contained material on a number of the 641 figures included, many are not covered in any standard reference source. In addition, this encyclopedia contains 163 topical articles, including general discussions of slavery and free black women during the Civil War, historical accounts of black women's organizations, and articles on stereotypes such as Aunt Jemima and Mammy. Some 450 black-and-white photos scattered through the text are striking; while sources such as *The Negro Almanac* (5th ed., 1989) include similar photographs, this is the first to exhibit so many archival photos of black women. The entries are followed by a chronology of black women in the US, beginning with the first three women put ashore at Jamestown in 1619, then tracing famous firsts and important events through 1992. Following the chronology is an excellent annotated bibliography of basic resources in the field. The index is detailed and accurate, with fine cross-references, and the list of biographical entries by profession is useful and clearly defined. Hine, editor of *Black Women in United States History: From Colonial Times to the Present* (16v., 1990) and author of books on African-American history (e.g., *Black Women in White: Racial Conflict and Cooperation in the Nursing Profession*, CH, Mar '90), has produced a sound work that will be a standard reference source for years to come. Highly recommended for all libraries.—*M. F. Jones, Muskingum College*

WS-0060   G1201   94-29084 CIP

Fast, Timothy H. **The women's atlas of the United States,** by Timothy H. Fast and Cathy Carroll Fast. rev ed. Facts on File, 1995. 246p bibl index afp ISBN 0-8160-2970-9, $75.00

Based on the 1990 census and other data up through 1993, this edition updates the first, which drew on the 1980 census and other data prior to 1990. Text and maps have been added to illuminate 1990s issues such as homelessness and AIDS, and computer graphics have made the maps more attractive and easy to read. The organization of the first edition has been retained, beginning with a general section on demographics followed by six topical sections. Sections on politics, education, and health have been expanded, but maps showing particular occupations have been dropped. New to this edition are multiracial data and maps in some topical sections. The introduction and text for each section have been rewritten, and the index expanded and made easier to use. The "Bibliography for Maps" gives the data sources. Timothy Fast, geographer and coauthor of the first edition, and Cathy Carroll Fast, AutoCAD specialist, present a wealth of information in a very accessible format. This is an important reference work. Highly recommended for undergraduates and general readers.—*B. K. Lacks, California State University, Fresno*

WS-0061   HQ1410   89-17120 CIP

Handbook of American women's history, ed. by Angela Howard Zophy. Garland, 1990. 763p (Garland reference library of the humanities, 696) index afp ISBN 0-8240-8744-5, $95.00

Designed to aid students, teachers, and librarians new to the field of American women's history, this one-volume handbook succeeds admirably in its goal to provide fundamental introductory information. History is broadly defined, with entries discussing the sex-gender system and soap operas included along with more "traditional" or familiar topics such as protective legislation or the Settlement House movement. Controversial issues are handled sensitively and respectfully, with no important topic off-limits. The Handbook's greatest strength, however, lies in its explicit recognition of the racial, ethnic, sexual, and class diversity that is becoming the hallmark of reflective and accurate American women's history. The entries, arranged alphabetically, are clear and concise, covering critical moments in women's history as well as highlighting some less well known people, places, and events. "See also" references are provided to help make connections among important concepts as well as to elaborate on an idea. Entries

include brief lists of references, giving the more curious or adventuresome readers access to additional sources of information. An excellent index leads to major entries as well as to topics covered within entries. Attention to detail, concern for the subject, and ease of access to the information make this a worthwhile addition to any academic collection.—*E. Broidy, University of California, Irvine*

WS-0062   HQ1593   95-1038 CIP

Hannam, June. **British women's history: a bibliographical guide,** comp. by June Hannam, Ann Hughes, and Pauline Stafford. Manchester, 1996. (Dist. by St. Martin's) 150p index ISBN 0-7190-4652-1, $79.95

Part of the "History and Related Disciplines Select Bibliographies" series, this guide presents a critical selection of more than 3,400 English-language monographic and periodical works. Numbered items are grouped in four broad sections covering general works and methodology, and medieval, early modern, and modern periods. In each section a listing of general works is followed by a detailed subject arrangement that carries from section to section. Most entries are annotated; most works were published before 1993 in Great Britain. Cross-references are provided, and author and abbreviation indexes are included. The enormous growth of the literature in this field has led to such selectivity and specialization that sometimes it is possible to lose sight of the big picture. Excellent guides like those in this series, which present a thoughtful balance between the breadth and depth of research in the field, are a welcome resource for students and instructors in need of scholarly but selective introductions to the literature. Although they did not attempt the comprehensiveness of a work such as Barbara Kanner's *Women in English Social History, 1800-1914* (CH, Oct '90), the compilers have managed to pack a tremendous number of valuable resources into a slim but extremely well organized and usable volume. Academic collections.—*E. Patterson, Emory University*

WS-0063   D107   89-28282 CIP

Jackson, Guida M. **Women who ruled.** ABC-Clio, 1990. 190p bibl afp ISBN 0-87436-560-0, $39.00

Jackson's encyclopedic work encompasses women rulers, living or deceased, since the beginning of recorded history. Much care is evident in the preparation of this book, as each ruler's entry is complete with dates, names, and occasionally an illustration. An excellent chronology precedes the entries, and the introduction surveys the regions of the world where women have ruled as monarchs, chiefs, and presidents, thus giving a good understanding of the particular backgrounds from which these women came. The author admits that some rulers have a hazy history and may, in fact, have been fictional persons. However, each ruler, whether real or fictional, has a complete biographical sketch which should help the reader more fully comprehend the role women rulers have played in world history. The notes and bibliography at the end of the book encourage the reader to delve more fully into this topic. Recommended for both undergraduate and graduate libraries.—*D. Seaman, Baylor University*

WS-0064   E159   93-28701 CIP

Sherr, Lynn. **Susan B. Anthony slept here: a guide to American women's landmarks,** by Lynn Sherr and Jurate Kazickas. Times Books/Random House, 1994. 579p bibl index ISBN 0-8129-2223-9 pbk, $18.00

The whimsical title of this book sparks an interest in the inveterate traveler to follow in the footsteps of the great women of this country. Sherr and Kazickas have updated and expanded their earlier feminist travel guide, *The American Woman's Gazetteer* (CH, Dec '76). The new volume includes many of the landmarks mentioned in the *Gazetteer* and covers an additional 500 sites. Women new to the travel guide include Golda Meir, Bess Truman, and Mother Clara M. Hale. As the authors point out in the introduction, this guide is only a sampling of those honored for their contributions. It is arranged alphabetically by state and city and includes addresses and some photographs. Sites not open to the public are identified. Hours of operation and costs are not included. A similar travel guide is Marion Tinling's *Women Remembered: A Guide to Landmarks of Women's History in the United States* (1986). The two titles cover many of the same sites, but each includes landmarks not mentioned by the other. This guide makes great reading for travelers and armchair travelers alike. A useful addition to any travel collection.—*D. A. Forro, Michigan State University Libraries*

◆ Language & Literature

WS-0065 Z286.F45 86-4714 MARC

Clardy, Andrea Fleck. **Words to the wise: a writer's guide to feminist and lesbian periodicals & publishers.** Rev. and updated. Firebrand Books, 1990 (c1986). 54p ISBN 0-932379-16-8, $4.95

Libraries serving the intended clienteles of these two works—publishing scholars in the case of Clardy and library and information professionals in the case of Gough and Greenblatt—will find both books absolute gems. Both works also offer bibliographic and directory information that will make them useful in reference collections serving undergraduates, although the format of the Gough and Greenblatt volume (essays followed by appendixes) diminishes its overall usefulness. Indeed, it may be relegated to the stacks, where it will be underused. Its valuable appendixes provide, among other things, a core list of nonfiction books, a filmography, a discography, a bibliography of AIDS-related materials, and other helpful lists, including one of publishers and mail-order houses. This material might more usefully have been presented as a reference volume in its own right. Clardy's guide, more limited in scope, lends itself more readily to reference collections. There is, of course, overlap in the publishers list; but in addition to addresses, phone numbers, and contact names, Clardy provides brief statements about each publisher that give a fair idea of which might be most receptive to particular topics or themes. In addition, Clardy furnishes charts, both for book publishers and for periodicals, that give quick answers to such important questions as to whether a press accepts unsolicited material and whether publication guidelines are available. The need for revision and updating of this sort of list is mentioned; unfortunately the format here does not lend itself to updating, just to a new edition. Both these books are well worth acquiring. In the case of the Gough and Greenblatt volume, however, librarians will need to draw attention to the reference dimensions of this valuable resource.—*E. Broidy, University of California, Irvine*

WS-0066 Can. CIP

Davis, Gwenn. **Drama by women to 1900: a bibliography of American and British writers,** comp. by Gwenn Davis and Beverly A. Joyce. Toronto, 1992. 189p (Bibliographies of writings by American and British women to 1900, 3) indexes ISBN 0-8020-2797-0, $100.00

Based on major library catalogs (NUC pre-1956, British Library) and the OCLC database) as well as on basic drama dictionaries and bibliographies, this work is part of a series that aims to "reestablish the range and variety of printed books published by women from 1475-1900." Arranged alphabetically by author, the listing contains extensive cross-references to pseudonyms and variant spellings. Each entry names an author, with life dates, play title, and citation, including dates of publication or performance and publisher; some entries contain a descriptive statement such as "monologue" or "imaginary conversation on anarchism." The informative and readable opening essay is a good introduction to drama by women. The first of two appendixes groups dramatists chronologically into periods; the second lists actresses—with no reference to performances or periods. The "subject" index is primarily of genre ("comedy," "verse"), plus a few specific topics ("Easter," "U.S. Revolution"). An "Index of Adaptations and Translations" is largely unhelpful; arranged by original author, it lists adaptor, but does not include a corresponding entry number in the bibliography section. The camera-ready, two-column format is difficult to read and unattractive. This book will be useful primarily for scholars and researchers already familiar with drama by women and needing verification of publication or performance information.—*J. M. Parker, St. Olaf College*

WS-0067 PN849 95-7479 CIP

Fister, Barbara. **Third World women's literatures: a dictionary and guide to materials in English.** Greenwood, 1995. 390p bibl index afp ISBN 0-313-28988-3, $75.00

Fister's concise addition to the reference literature on women writers focuses specifically on the "Third World," which the compiler limits to "the countries of the Caribbean, Central and Latin America, Africa, the Middle East, South Asia and Asia," the latter excluding Japan, Australia, and New Zealand. Three types of entries are provided: biographical entries on individual writers (some of whom, such as the Palestinian poet Fadwa Tuqan and Punyakante Wijenaike of Sri

Lanka, may be new to Western audiences), entries on individual works of literature, and 15 short thematic essays on issues and ideas. Each is followed by a bibliography of selected works and criticism published through 1994. Appendixes list authors by region and country, birth year (beginning in 1648 with Juana Ines de la Cruz), further resources on Third World women and their literatures (including a useful list of publishers), anthologies of their work, and criticism arranged by geographic region. Indexing is provided by author, subject, and title. Most useful for libraries that have not previously purchased more detailed reference sources in this field (e.g., *Caribbean Women Novelists*, CH, Sep'93). Graduate; faculty.—*R. B. M. Ridinger, Northern Illinois University*

WS-0068 PR830.W6 90-39517 CIP

Fuderer, Laura Sue. **The female bildungsroman in English: an annotated bibliography of criticism.** Modern Language Association of America, 1990. 47p index ISBN 0-87352-962-6, $12.50

This "initial effort" to list criticism of female bildungsromane written in English by women authors fills a useful niche, slight as the book is. With the rise of feminist criticism in the 1970s came increased interest in the female protagonist of the bildungsroman, traditionally a male-oriented genre. By gleaning criticism on women's novels of adolescence and self-discovery and their heroines, Fuderer facilitates and promotes research in this developing area. Though selective, the 133 entries—books, chapters, articles, and dissertations published primarily from 1972 to 1987—seem quite inclusive. The brief annotations, an informative introduction, and a list of more than 275 bildungsromane cited in the criticism covered, and an index of authors—both as subjects and critics—are all helpful. The surprising absence of a bildungsroman like Nadine Gordimer's *The Lying Days* (1953) means that critics have paid scant or no attention to its genre. Definitely a good purchase for any library serving students of literature; but CIP subject cataloging needs amplification: the headings "Heroines in Literature" and "Bildungsroman" should be added.—*M. H. Loe, SUNY College at Oswego*

WS-0069 PN56 94-24137 CIP

The Gay and lesbian literary heritage: a reader's companion to the writers and their works, from antiquity to the present, ed. by Claude J. Summers. H. Holt, 1995. 786p bibl index afp ISBN 0-8050-2716-5, $45.00

Literature by and about lesbians and gay men plays a vital role in representing personal lives and identities and in the construction of social realities. The 350 essays compiled in this volume document this rich and varied cultural heritage, meeting the needs of researchers and the interests of browsers. Summers covers a broader historical range and a greater number of writers than comparable titles, notably *Gay & Lesbian Literature*, ed. by Sharon Malinowski (CH, Sep'94), and *The Gay and Lesbian Literary Companion*, by Sharon Malinowski and Christa Brelin (1995). The particular strength of this work lies in its substantive overviews of national and ethnic literatures and its topical essays on significant literary movements or genres, including AIDS, children's literature, coming out stories, cross-dressing, mystery, travel, and war. Author entries range from brief accounts to in-depth critical analyses of major figures, although the definition of "major" is not clear and is sometimes perplexing. Certain highly influential contemporary writers (e.g., Tony Kushner, Kate Millet) appear only in topical essays. The index to entries and writers points to information on all authors, even those embedded in the essays, but biographical entries for each writer would be preferable. Liberal cross-references to related topics and brief bibliographies follow each entry. Recommended for academic and public libraries.—*J. Ariel, University of California, Irvine*

WS-0070 PN56 93-47362 MARC

Gay & lesbian literature, ed. by Sharon Malinowski. St. James Press, 1994. 488p indexes afp ISBN 1-55862-174-1, $85.00

The vitality and increasing recognition of the field of gay and lesbian literature finds another reflection in this impressive compilation of biographical, bibliographical, and critical information tracing the accomplishments of prominent writers since 1900. This work covers more than 200 novelists, poets, short story writers, dramatists, journalists, editors, and writers of nonfiction whose work has contributed significantly to the lesbian and gay literary, social, and political landscape. Two introductory essays on gay male literature and lesbian literature precede and frame the alphabetical entries. International in scope and featuring authors selected for the lesbian or gay thematic content of their work rather than their sexual identity, this volume serves as a useful companion to the recent bio-bibliographical sourcebooks *Contemporary Lesbian Writers of the United States*, ed. by Sandra Pollack and Denise Knight (CH, Mar'94) and *Contemporary Gay American Novelists*, ed. by Emmanuel S. Nelson (CH, Jul'93). Informative and well-organized, each entry provides biographical information and lists of writings by and about the author, followed by a signed critical essay focusing on the importance of the author's work "to his/her own literary canon specifically and to the gay and lesbian literary or historical world generally." In addition to a general index to the featured entries, indexes provide multiple access by nationality, gender, subject, genre, and recipients of gay and lesbian literary awards. Lists of additional authors of gay and lesbian literature and of important published anthologies round out the volume and serve as useful guides for further investigation. Highly recommended for both academic and public libraries.—*J. Ariel, University of California, Irvine*

WS-0071 PR830 94-16123 CIP
Great women mystery writers: classic to contemporary, ed. by Kathleen Gregory Klein. Greenwood, 1994. 432p bibl indexes afp ISBN 0-313-28770-8, $49.95

Spanning the range of styles and sleuths, this work features 117 writers from 19th-century pioneers to the currently prominent. Readers might legitimately quibble over omissions, but this book is impressive—a must wherever mysteries are popular. Two-page essays venture beyond the bland with insight into structure, major themes, and detectives, as well as brief author biographies. Compiled by "scholar-critics," entries also include bibliographies of the writers' publications and critical sources. Advice on whether a writer's corpus should be read in sequence and on similar authors increases usefulness. A lively account of trends and major players, the introduction details the history of women in the genre. Seven appendixes cover award winners, mystery-related activities, the advocacy group Sisters in Crime, categories, an e-mail discussion group, and booksellers. Pseudonyms, authors, and titles are indexed. This work holds the answers to many questions, and it is solid entertainment, a treat for mystery lovers. All collections.—*P. Palmer, University of Memphis*

WS-0072 PN471 93-47648 CIP
Great women writers: the lives and works of 135 of the world's most important women writers, from antiquity to the present, ed. by Frank N. Magill. H. Holt, 1994. 611p index afp ISBN 0-8050-2932-X, $40.00

This guide combines biographical, bibliographic, and critical analysis for 135 selected authors of poetry, drama, and fiction. Primary focus is on Western writers, more than 80 percent of them 20th century. The alphabetically arranged entries include principal works, other literary forms, achievements, a biographical sketch, an unsigned critical essay, and a brief selected bibliography. Contributing reviewers are listed; an index of writers and individual and collected works completes the guide. Information on these authors is available elsewhere, e.g., in concise form in *The Bloomsbury Guide to Women's Literature*, ed. by Claire Buck (CH, Mar'93), or Virginia Blain's *The Feminist Companion to Literature in English: Women Writers from the Middle Ages to the Present* (1990). More extensive coverage for many of the represented writers can be found in *Dictionary of Literary Biography* volumes. Recommended for libraries seeking a single, reasonably priced compilation of biobibliography and criticism for well-known authors from a range of genres and geographic, historical, and ethnic backgrounds. Other libraries may find this guide limited and redundant compared with other sources. Public and undergraduate libraries.—*N. Knipe, Colorado College*

WS-0073 PR508 92-35190 CIP
Jackson, J.R. de J. **Romantic poetry by women: a bibliography, 1770-1835.** Oxford, 1993. 484p indexes afp ISBN 0-19-811239-4, $75.00

As the title indicates, this is a record of verse published by women between 1770 and 1835. The bibliography is actually based on the author's *Annals of English Verse, 1770-1835* (1985). Most of the volumes are works written in or translated into English by known individual authors; however, there are entries for multiple authors, anonymous authors, collections, and others. Besides using

names from *Annals*, Jackson undertook a very thorough search for additional women authors of the period. He traveled to libraries worldwide, consulting various catalogs, individual books, collections, and unpublished sources. More than 2,584 volumes were ultimately recorded and arranged by poet, with each entry given all available publication information. Of additional interest and benefit are the biographical headnotes, which provide background information on unfamiliar authors. Several detailed indexes provide easy access. This reliable and thorough bibliography complements other reference sources on historic women poets. Recommended for larger academic libraries.—*S. R. Moore, University of Southwestern Louisiana*

WS-0074 PL725 94-617 CIP
Japanese women writers: a bio-critical sourcebook, ed. by Chieko I. Mulhern. Greenwood, 1994. 524p bibl index afp ISBN 0-313-25486-9, $95.00

This reference work is a welcome addition to the rapidly expanding interest within Japanese studies, as well as more generally, in women writers. It contains substantial essays (six to nine pages long including short bibliographies) on 58 writers from the ninth century to the present. Generally characterized as a male-dominated society, Japan has had a healthy representation of prominent women writers throughout its history except during the Edo period (1603-1867), when a repressive government and commercially based literature essentially excluded women's participation in literary endeavors. Women treated in the volume are correctly designated as "mainstream writers," not falling into a subgenre of "women's literature." Though they provide historical context and biographical data, these biocritical essays focus primarily on literary achievement. The subjects of the essays have all received previous treatment in English in the form of translations and critical study. The book endeavors to kindle more general interest in Japanese women writers by listing all these sources and providing stimulating introductions to the authors. The Japan specialist and the novice alike can enjoy these essays. Mulhern's editing maintains consistency while not stifling the individuality of each of the 19 scholarly contributors. Upper-division undergraduate and above.—*R. G. Sewell, Rutgers, The State University of New Jersey, New Brunswick*

WS-0075 PE1460 91-13819 CIP
Maggio, Rosalie. **The dictionary of bias-free usage: a guide to nondiscriminatory language.** Oryx, 1991. 293p afp ISBN 0-89774-653-8 pbk, $25.00

A reorganization, revision, and extension of Maggio's *The Nonsexist Word Finder* (CH, Jan'88). Reorganization consists in some rewriting of the original "Appendix A: Writing Guidelines" and its repositioning before the dictionary proper. Appendix B, a 17-page section of readings, and the four-page bibliography have been omitted. Within the 5,000 term dictionary (to judge from a 4 percent sample), about 24 percent of entry words are new; about half that many have been deleted; discussions of 27.5 percent have been very slightly revised; 38 percent remain the same; 10 percent have undergone major rewording/revision. Some added or revised entries are mini-encyclopedic essays on a topic rather than definitions. Scope is extended, as the title indicates, to forms of bias beyond sexism, notably racism/ethnicity and handicap/disability. Slightly more than half the apposite quotations that head letter divisions of the word list are new; some have been moved for no obvious reason. A worthy enterprise, occasionally seeming over-earnest even to one who routinely edits out biased language. In at least one case a definition is mistaken both in its etymology and its implied connotation. Useful in any library, but the 1988 edition should be retained for its bibliography.—*V. Clark, Choice*

WS-0076 PL782.E1 89-1319 CIP
Mamola, Claire Zebroski. **Japanese women writers in English translation: an annotated bibliography.** Garland, 1989. 469p (Garland reference library of the humanities, 877) index afp ISBN 0-8240-3048-6, $52.00

This annotated bibliography is an outcome of the author's interest in Japanese women writers, which was acquired while teaching a course on the history of modern Japan for Appalachian State University. The bibliography is in three parts: Heian period (794-1185) writings (13 titles); fiction from the 19th century through

1987 (209 titles); and nonfiction for the same period (361 titles). In each part, works are arranged alphabetically by the last name of the author and then by original Japanese title when known, or by the translated title. The scope of the bibliography, as stated in the preface, includes works originally written either in English or in other languages. It also includes works in collections and periodical articles. In the introduction the author lists the themes of Japanese women's writings. Annotations are descriptive and include comments on the lives of the authors. Annotations are short, but long enough to indicate subject. The bibliography covers a long period and varied authors. Index and listings of specialized works by Japanese women. Recommended for students at any level interested in reading works by Japanese women.—*H. Ikehara, emeritus, Eastern Michigan University*

WS-0077   89-1319 CIP
Mamola, Claire Zebroski. **Japanese women writers in English translation: v.2: An annotated bibliography.** Garland, 1992. 452p (Garland reference library of the humanities, 1317) index afp ISBN 0-8240-7077-1, $72.00

The author attempted to locate, read, and annotate everything written by native Japanese women that has been translated into or was originally written in English. The structure of the present volume differs from that of Volume 1 (CH, Jan'90). It is in four parts: fiction (87 titles), nonfiction (413 titles), specialized works (837 titles, not annotated), and dissertations (48 titles, not annotated). Works in collections and articles in periodicals are included as well as monographs. The works cited treat various subjects—e.g., education, family relationships, political concerns, Hiroshima/Nagasaki A-bomb experiences, aspects of the culture. Poetry and books for very young children are excluded. Annotations are descriptive. Works of different periods covering various topics are listed in one alphabet by the author's name with index at the end. Not for research, but recommended for general readers and students at any level interested in sampling Japanese women's writings.—*H. Ikehara, emeritus, Eastern Michigan University*

WS-0078   PN471   94-25180 CIP
Masterplots II. Women's literature series, ed. by Frank N. Magill. Salem Press, 1995. 6v. 2,629p indexes afp ISBN 0-89356-898-8, $500.00

In this set, the compilers meet well the challenge to cover women's writing from the ancients to contemporary times. Although one might quibble over exclusions or inclusions, finding fault with the four-to-five-page essays proves more difficult. Each of the 536 signed entries covers a literary work. They are not limited to fiction but include social criticism, diaries, memoirs, history, etc. The clear authoritative essays focus on context, content, analysis, and related sources. Character lists, first production date and location for plays, time period, and setting are given. The geographic index lists authors from 27 countries, while other indexes provide access by author, title, and type of work. The latter is subdivided into categories; for example, "Novel and Novella" has 23 subdivisions including domestic realism (36 entries), science fiction (6 entries), and social realism (37 entries). Recommended for libraries that find other Masterplots sets useful.—*P. Palmer, University of Memphis*

WS-0079   PR9369   93-37446 CIP
Nadine Gordimer: a bibliography of primary and secondary sources, 1937-1992, comp. by Dorothy Driver et al. H. Zell, 1994 (c1993). 341p (Bibliographical research in African literatures, 4) indexes afp ISBN 1-873836-26-0, $75.00

Nadine Gordimer is the third African to have won the Nobel Prize for Literature (in 1991, following Wole Soyinka in 1986 and Naguib Mahfuz in 1988). She has written not only novels and short stories, but a considerable body of social and literary commentary. This bibliography is a gold mine of information for research on this distinguished writer, and the fitting tribute to her its compilers intend it to be. The introduction provides insights into Gordimer's work and its South African context. The body of the bibliography is comprehensive: a chronology of Gordimer's life and work; a chronological list of her writings, arranged by genre, including reviews by her and interviews of her; and chronological lists of critical writings and reviews, the latter grouped by the work reviewed. Included are reviews of works of criticism by Gordimer. There is a list of these on Gordimer, a list of films based on her writing, and a list of biographical works. This mass

of information is handily arranged and made more accessible by comprehensive indexes of names and titles. Impressive research sources are listed. The authors used the extensive collection of the National English Literary Museum in South Africa, as well as other South African libraries, and a full range of databases. Gordimer also allowed the compilers to consult her private collection. This is a thorough and professional piece of work, invaluable for research on an author whose message and insights have relevance worldwide. Highly recommended; upper-division undergraduates and above.—*G. Walsh, Boston University*

WS-0080   PN849   92-37915 MARC
Paravisini-Gebert, Lizabeth. **Caribbean women novelists: an annotated critical bibliography,** comp. by Lizabeth Paravisini-Gebert and Olga Torres-Seda. Greenwood, 1993. 427p (Bibliographies and indexes in world literature, 36) indexes afp ISBN 0-313-28342-7, $69.95

The compilers focus not so much on novels and novelists, as indicated by the title, but on all genres by and about Caribbean women writers who have published at least one novel since 1950. The writers range from the well known, like poet Audre Lorde, to the obscure, such as Dinorah Castillo. Embracing the Caribbean islands' linguistic groups, this far-ranging compilation covers primary sources with special thoroughness and testifies to the research skills and scholarship of its compilers, as well as the valuable cooperation of other experts and research centers. Brenda F. Berrian and Aart Broek's *Bibliography of Women Writers from the Caribbean, 1831-1986* (1989) includes many more writers, but this new work is easier to use with its annotations, author arrangement, and various indexes. Entries give brief biographical information and list primary sources (novels, excerpts, short fiction, poetry, plays, essays, children's literature, translations, autobiography, criticism, and other media) and secondary works (reviews, criticism, interviews, and bibliographies/biographical sources). Some readily available critical sources are inexplicably omitted in this otherwise well-executed work. Still, a welcome addition for libraries that support upper-division and graduate programs.—*M. H. Loe, SUNY College at Oswego*

WS-0081   PE1460   94-29281 CIP
Schwartz, Marilyn. **Guidelines for bias-free writing,** by Marilyn Schwartz and the Task Force on Bias-Free Language of the Association of American University Presses. Indiana, 1995. 100p bibl index afp ISBN 0-253-35102-2, $15.00; ISBN 0-253-20941-2 pbk, $5.95

Schwartz's small volume contains a wealth of information for writers and editors seeking guidelines on bias-free language. Each chapter follows a standard format: traditional usage is discussed, alternative terms suggested, and examples provided. The beginning chapter on gender, the most lengthy, distinguishes between gender-neutral and nonsexist language. It includes the more frequent problems writers face (e.g., generic "he" and feminine suffixes "ess"), plus the less common areas of acknowledgments, bibliographic citations, and indexes. The strength of the remaining four chapters—race, ethnicity, citizenship and nationality, and religion; disabilities and medical conditions; sexual orientation; and age—is the section that defines specific terms. The volume concludes with a brief bibliography and index. The manual is the result of work by the AAUP Task Force on Bias-Free Language to address the presence of sexist language in scholarly publications. Since there seem to be few style manuals on bias-free language, this volume is recommended for purchase, especially for academic libraries.—*J. P. Burton, West Chester University of Pennsylvania*

WS-0082   Orig
Swanson, Jean. **By a woman's hand: a guide to mystery fiction by women,** by Jean Swanson and Dean James. Berkley Books, 1994. 254p indexes ISBN 0-425-14143-8 pbk, $10.00

This guide is intended to be a "voyage of discovery" for mystery lovers. The authors, who clearly love their subject, have sought to fill a gap in the critical literature on women mystery writers. The result is an engaging source covering more than 200 English-language writers, with emphasis on American, Canadian, and English writers. Coverage begins in 1977 when Marcia Muller introduced her series featuring Sharon McCone, considered to be the first modern fictional female private eye. Also included are authors whose careers began before 1977 who consistently published after that date. Arranged alphabetically by author, entries range from a half page to over a page and include a surprising amount of detail. Included are biographical details as they relate to the authors' writing, analysis of their style and character development, and insights on what appeals to readers. Bibliographic information is provided for series and for other notable works of the more prolific writers. Awards and award nominations are also noted. Each entry ends with a referral to authors of similar novels. This unique feature will be invaluable to casual readers and students alike. The entries are indexed by type of detective, regional setting, series character, and author. This reasonably priced book belongs in all public and undergraduate academic libraries.— *L. O. Rein, George Mason University*

◆ British & European

WS-0083   PR115   90-21780 CIP
Alston, R.C. **A checklist of women writers, 1801-1900: fiction, verse, drama.** G.K. Hall, 1991 (c1990). 517p ISBN 0-8161-7295-1, $65.00

In essence, a circumscribed index, whose limitations are candidly set forth, to the British Library's 19th-century holdings in three genres of creative writing by women. Alston, an eminent bibliographer, formerly on the BL staff, has identified 14,730 works of fiction, 2,079 of verse, and 298 dramas by scanning the library's pressmarks for those genres as assigned in classification schemes used up to about 1918. The scope is stated as "works written by women published in English in the British Isles and British dependent territories [not including] works written in insular vernaculars. . .[or] Latin." Works meant for "pre-pubertal" children are excluded. Alston acknowledges the probabilities of missed pseudonymous and anonymous works and the weakness of BL holdings of Canadian writers (a supplementary name list is appended), while saluting BL holdings for Australian and New Zealand women. A second appendix—set run-on!—lists about 50 works not in the BL but held in other UK libraries. Entries are spare: name only, no dates; titles; place and date of first (or earliest held) edition; pressmark. Name cross-references are made to the form used in the BL *General Catalogue*. Running heads for authors' names are helpful, but the typographic differentiation of names from titles on the closely set three-column pages is not so distinct as it might be. An index to places of publication outside London and Edinburgh, naming both authors and works, will be valuable to scholars of regional literatures. Alston's list overlaps by nine years J. Grimes and D. Daims's somewhat similar attempt, *Novels in English by Women, 1891-1920* (CH, Sep'81). Also seen by its compilers as a preliminary checklist, this work includes both US and UK authors, author dates, very brief annotations, and citations to reviews of about 15,000 titles. Both volumes will be wanted in large collections used by scholars.—*V. Clark, Choice*

WS-0084   Z2174   94-28703 CIP
Beach, Cecilia, comp. **French women playwrights before the twentieth century: a checklist.** Greenwood, 1994. 251p (Bibliographies and indexes in women's studies, 22) bibl index afp ISBN 0-313-29174-8, $65.00

Beach's checklist of published and manuscript plays by French women playwrights will be extremely valuable to scholars in women's studies. Women playwrights in the era covered are generally unknown. To produce a play, one needed connections in the theater world and money, and women often had neither. This checklist, which covers the 16th through the 19th centuries, will rescue many playwrights from oblivion or obscurity and bring forward dramatic works by writers known for their work in other genres. The book is intelligently conceived. Playwrights are grouped alphabetically by name in each century. Under each name entry, dramatic works are listed chronologically. Beach provides variations in name and spelling and/or pseudonym, with cross-references, dates of publication and/or performance of the dramatic work, date of birth and death when known, other professional activities, and other genres practiced by the author. Extremely valuable is the identification of a holding library for each title. Beach's work will make readers long for more information about these playwrights, many of them prolific and famous in their time, and for an explanation of why they are largely absent from literary history. Her compilation makes it easier for others to reclaim these writers. Recommended for upper-division undergraduates and above.—*E. Sartori, University of Nebraska-Lincoln*

WS-0085   PR113   89-26844 CIP
Bell, Maureen. **A biographical dictionary of English women writers, 1580-1720,** by Maureen Bell, George Parfitt, and Simon Shepherd. G.K. Hall, 1990. 298p ISBN 0-8161-1806-X, $32.50

Editors Bell (Open Univ.), Parfitt, and Shepherd (both at Univ. of Nottingham) have framed standard biographical data with an introduction and critical appendixes that provide historical and cultural background for the period. Based on much of the same source material as Hilda L. Smith's, *Women and the Literature of the Seventeenth Century* (CH, Oct'90), this work overlaps, to some degree, both Smith and *A Dictionary of British and American Women Writers, 1600-1800*, ed. by Janet Todd (CH, Jun'85). Entries include patronym, places of birth and residence, occupation, religion, husband's name and occupation, and references to works written. Sources are not cited as they are in Smith; coverage starts and ends earlier than Todd's, and duplicate entries are not so extensive. This compilation on more than 550 English women writers is useful for locating information on those women not included elsewhere and for the unique addition of critical essays on prophetic writing, Quaker women, petitions, letters, the role of men as "gatekeepers," and women and publishing. Recommended for academic libraries with comprehensive women's studies reference collections.—*N. Knipe, Colorado College*

WS-0086   PN471   92-10415 CIP
The Bloomsbury guide to women's literature, ed. by Claire Buck. Prentice Hall General Reference, 1992. 1,171p ISBN 0-13-689621-9, $40.00; ISBN 0-13-089665-9 pbk, $20.00

A companion to *Bloomsbury Guide to English Literature* (1989), this work provides more than 5,000 biographical, bibliographical, and critical entries for women authors and fiction by women, from all time periods and nationalities. Thirty-six brief but fascinating essays, organized by countries or regions, treat the historical and cultural contexts for authors, and the differences and similarities in women's literature. An extensive brief-entry section, arranged alphabetically, contains name, work, and thematic entries, and includes brief bibliographies and synopses of works. Frequent cross-references strengthen the sense of commonality and connectivity in women's writing. Prose, poetry, and a range of popular fiction genres are included, but nonfiction is excluded. Lesser-known figures and non-Western writers are emphasized. An important criterion for inclusion is the availability of works in English translation, but some authors for whom few or no translations are available are included to represent all nationalities and periods. Closely resembling *Feminist Companion to Literature in English* by Virginia Blain et al. (CH, Feb'91), *Bloomsbury's* narrower focus on fiction eliminates some well-known writers, Although other sources provide considerably more detail (e.g., *Modern American Women Writers*, ed. by Elaine Showalter, 1991, or *Biographical Dictionary of English Women Writers*, ed. by Maureen Bell, George Parfitt, and Simon Shepherd, CH, Jan'91), *Bloomsbury* stands out both for its emphasis on lesser-known writers and works and its illumination of the contextual links of women writers across boundaries of history, region, and culture. It is gratifying that extensive resources now exist to support research on women writers (particularly Western writers) and that works like *Bloomsbury* venture beyond the mainstream to introduce, however briefly, many new faces. Advanced undergraduate; graduate; faculty.—*E. Patterson, Emory University*

WS-0087   PC3904   94-27639 CIP
Double minorities of Spain: a bio-bibliographic guide to women writers of the Catalan, Galician, and Basque countries, ed. by Kathleen McNerney and Cristina Enríquez de Salamanca. Modern Language Association of America, 1995 (c1994). 421p bibl ISBN 0-87352-397-0, $50.00

Covering women authors who have written in Spain's minority languages—Catalan, Galician, and Basque—this guide reveals pluralistic dimensions of the Iberian peninsula culture, which has centralized its discourse and literature in the Spanish of Castile. To encourage rethinking the traditional canon and recognition of languages, literatures, and women writers that have been overlooked or ignored for political reasons, the editors and their network of 40 contributors have gathered and organized biographical, bibliographical, and critical information for nearly all the 472 writers identified. The chronological coverage begins with anonymous medieval poems, but most material is from the 19th and 20th centuries, including recent decades when these languages achieved legal status. The editors have embraced all creative writing, from the traditional genres to memoirs and children's stories, disregarding quantity of publishing as a criterion for inclusion. The list of available Spanish translations of the Catalan, Galician, and Basque texts is important; including this kind of material in college curricula can be revitalizing. Thorough and unique, this guide is essential for research collections; other libraries supporting the Spanish major will find it beneficial, although some needs will be met by an earlier guide for which McNerney edited the non-Castilian entries, *Women Writers of Spain* (CH, Oct'86). [Advice and specific language for this review contributed by Georgina J. Whittingham, Dept. of Modern Languages, SUNY College at Oswego.]—*M. H. Loe, SUNY College at Oswego*

WS-0088   PN481   91-6930 CIP
An Encyclopedia of Continental women writers, ed. by Katharina M. Wilson. Garland, 1991. 2v. 1,389p (Garland reference library of the humanities, 698) afp ISBN 0-8240-8547-7, $175.00

Several reference books on British and American women writers have appeared in the last few years, but Wilson's is the first on Continental women writers. It is a remarkable work, notable for the quality of the writing as well as for its range and depth. The signed entries are written with sympathy and verve, generally emphasizing the writers' experiences as women. Each provides biographical data and an overview of the writer's work, followed by brief citations of primary and secondary sources. One of the chief virtues of this work is its comprehensiveness. It includes women writers from antiquity to the present who lived anywhere in Europe from the Atlantic to the Urals and wrote in any of the languages spoken and written on the Continent, among them Hungarian, Albanian, Greek, Romanian, Polish, and even Hebrew, in addition to French, German, Spanish, and Russian. The term "writer" has been interpreted liberally to encompass women who wrote pamphlets, memoirs, and scientific works or produced translations, as well as those who wrote novels, poetry, essays, and dramas. A work of this scope cannot avoid omissions (for instance Rahel Levin Varnhagen, Marie von Ebner-Eschenbach, Santa Teresa de Avila, Julia Kristeva, and Monique Wittig) nor errors (Mme de Tencin was neither unfrocked nor a canoness). The quality of the bibliographies varies. A preface outlining the bases for selection and an appendix listing the writers by country would have been helpful. However, these criticisms pale before the achievements of this generative (in this context one hesitates to use "seminal") work, which belongs in all libraries.—*E. Sartori, University of Nebraska-Lincoln*

WS-0089   PR6063   93-50597 CIP
Fletcher, John. **Iris Murdoch: a descriptive primary and annotated secondary bibliography,** by John Fletcher and Cheryl Bove. Garland, 1994. 915p (Garland reference library of the humanities, 506) indexes afp ISBN 0-8240-8910-3, $130.00

Fletcher and Bove have compiled a detailed bibliography of the Irish-born novelist and philosopher. Though three other full-length bibliographies exist, (Laraine Civin, *Iris Murdoch*, 1968; Thomas Tominaga and Wilma Schneidermeyer, *Irish Murdoch and Muriel Spark*, 1976; and Kate Begnal, *Iris Murdoch*, CH, May '88), these lack the comprehensive coverage of the volume at hand. The compilers' ambitious goal, one they carry out in style, is to record Murdoch's vast output of known works, both in English and in translation—novels, essays, poems, editorials, radio broadcasts, and reviews—and to list all published criticism of her work by others. In the case of English and American first editions of the full-length works, the compilers supply abundant detail: pagination, collation, and a full description of title pages and bindings. In citations of reprints and foreign editions, the compilers include the basic details—publisher, place, date, and number of pages. The bulk of the volume, some 600 pages, is given over to an annotated listing of books, articles, theses, interviews, and reviews that evaluate Murdoch's writing. The volume closes with an appendix, in which the compilers locate and describe manuscript and correspondence collections. This impressive and carefully compiled bibliography will be essential for any future serious study of Murdoch's life and work. Upper-division undergraduate and above.—*D. C. Dickinson, University of Arizona*

WS-0090   PQ149   91-2519 CIP
French women writers: a bio-bibliographical source book, ed. by Eva Martin Sartori and Dorothy Wynne Zimmerman. Greenwood, 1991. 632p indexes afp ISBN 0-313-26548-8, $85.00

Well-edited and well-written this biographical dictionary provides excellent introductory information on the 52 French women writers selected for inclusion—some well-known, some, as the editors admit, "unknown even to the specialist." The major criterion for inclusion was a substantial body of published work. Readers may question whether this was consistently applied (Elsa Triolet, for example, was not included), but most names one would expect to find are there. Editorial principles are clearly stated in a brief preface, and an introduction surveys the position of women in French literary life from the 12th century to the current period. The signed articles are each approximately ten pages long, and all follow the same format: a biography, a discussion of major themes, a survey of criticism, and a bibliography of primary works, English translations, and selected critical studies. An effort has been made to provide more extensive bibliographical information for the lesser-known authors. Since the articles appear in alphabetical order by biographee, the chronology and list of authors by date of birth at the end of the volume are helpful. Title and subject indexes are also included. Although many of these authors will be discussed in volumes of the ongoing "Dictionary of Literary Biography" series, there is nothing else like this compilation currently available. Highly recommended at all academic levels.—*V. W. Hill, University of Wisconsin-Madison*

WS-0091   PR6045   91-12218 CIP
Haule, James M. **A concordance to the novels of Virginia Woolf,** by James M. Haule and Philip H. Smith. Garland, 1991. 3v. 3,806p (Garland reference library of the humanities, 1005) afp ISBN 0-8240-6339-2, $450.00

It is "the unique role of language in the work of Virginia Woolf that has encouraged the compilation of this union concordance to her nine novels," proclaim the compilers (preface). Based on the first American editions of the novels (published by Harcourt Brace), the concordance combines into one sequence the separate listings for each novel of the compilers' earlier publication in microfiche, *Concordances to the Novels of Virginia Woolf* (v.1-7, 1981-86; repr. 1988 with v. 8-9, 1988). In an alphabetical sequence, each headword notes the frequency of occurrence. Beneath each headword, each occurrence of the word appears in context with several preceding and following words, citing the location by title, chapter, page, and line. Articles, prepositions, individual letters, and assorted frequently used words omitted from the concordance appear in a separate list which gives the frequencies of each. The headwords from the main concordance appear in two appended listings, the first arranged alphabetically, the second by frequency. The functional design and the attractive typefaces employed for the camera-ready text make this concordance a model of its kind. Upper-division undergraduate and graduate collections.—*W. S. Brockman, University of Illinois at Urbana-Champaign*

WS-0092   PR2965   91-27900 CIP
Kolin, Philip C. **Shakespeare and feminist criticism: an annotated bibliography and commentary.** Garland, 1991. 420p (Garland reference library of the humanities, 1345) indexes afp ISBN 0-8240-7386-X, $55.00

Kolin identifies and annotates relevant scholarship on feminist views of Shakespeare's plays and poems, including books, essay collections, articles, and dissertations published between 1975 and 1988, 1975 being the publication date of Juliet Dusinberre's *Shakespeare and the Nature of Women* (CH, May'76). Kolin's is the first annotated bibliography on feminist criticism. *The Woman's Part: Feminist Criticism of Shakespeare*, ed. by C.R.S. Leuz et al. (CH, Mar'81) is unannotated and outdated. Kolin's extensive introduction deals with various aspects of his subject. The 439 bibliographic items are arranged by year of publication and then alphabetically by author within each year. Annotations are extensive, informative, and nonevaluative. For books they are followed by reviews and their sources. Articles are entered under the original publication year. Dissertations are not annotated but references are given to entries in *DAI*. A variety of studies are included that shed light on Shakespeare's views on and representation of women, sex, and gender, for example, studies of Elizabethan and Jacobean culture and theater conventions of role-playing, language, desire; psychoanalytical studies that address feminist concerns; and responses that challenge feminist criticism such as items 220, 290, 421, and 430. Various indexes—author, play/poem, subject. This work is highly recommended for public, college, and university libraries.—*P. Kujoory, University of the District of Columbia*

WS-0093　　　　PG2997　　　　92-9246 MARC
Nemec Ignashev, Diane M. **Women and writing in Russia and the USSR: a bibliography of English-language sources,** by Diane M. Nemec Ignashev and Sarah Krive. Garland, 1992. 328p (Garland reference library of the humanities, 1280) index afp ISBN 0-8240-3647-6, $51.00

While the focus of this much-needed bibliography, compiled by students and two professors at Carleton University, is on women writers it also lists writings about Russian/Soviet women in general. The work is divided into four major sections: primary sources, biographical and critical sources, supplementary sources, and bibliographies. Although the first and most of the second section—about two-thirds of the whole volume—form an unambiguous and logical arrangement, some of the subsections are less well defined; thus a number of citations appear several times in various places. Brief biographical paragraphs (like those in Margery Resnick and Isabella de Courtivron's *Women Writers in Translation: An Annotated Bibliography 1945-1982*, CH, Jun'84) would have considerably added to this work's appeal to a less initiated reader. The introduction does not spell out precisely enough the parameters of the work, i.e., the period covered and types of publications included. Also, from the introduction: "OCLC" is not an abbreviation of the On-Line Catalog of the Library of Congress and "regular serial periodicals" is a redundant expression. These are, however, minor points and do not detract from this work's usefulness to researchers and students, undergraduate up.—*L. Siegelbaum, Michigan State University*

WS-0094　　　　PR6045　　　　91-11183 CIP
Packer, Joan Garrett. **Rebecca West: an annotated bibliography.** Garland, 1991. 136p (Garland reference library of the humanities, 1158) index afp ISBN 0-8240-5692-2, $20.00

Packer has updated G.E. Hutchinson's 740-item primary bibliography, *A Preliminary List of the Writings of Rebecca West, 1912—1951* (1957), with 193 items published through 1989, plus 173 secondary sources. Her solid annotations will facilitate research on West, whose eclectic, sometimes brilliant, writing spanned most of this century and included political journalism, literary reviews and criticism, travel writing, fiction and history. The arrangement functions (works by RW: books, stories and essays, reviews; works about RW: books/dissertations, articles, reviews); but additional subdivisions like nonfiction, fiction, addresses, and interviews would aid research. Except for a few inexplicable omissions, the introduction provides a survey of RW's work and its reception. The index lists writers and titles, but not subjects. As an update, this bibliography must be used with Hutchinson's work, which is not widely available. One wishes Packer had provided at least a complete list of RW's books. Still, this is a good start on West. Recommended for women's studies, history, and literature collections.—*M. H. Loe, SUNY College at Oswego*

WS-0095　　　　PQ6055　　　　92-42432 CIP
Spanish women writers: a bio-bibliographical source book, ed. by Linda Gould Levine, Ellen Engelson Marson, and Gloria Feiman Waldman. Greenwood, 1993. 596p bibl indexes afp ISBN 0-313-26823-1, $95.00

This collective biography looks both at the relatively narrow topic of Spanish female writers and the broader one of feminist literature. Combining biography and bibliography permits the editors to go beyond a mere listing of titles and provide brief critical biographies for each author. The choice of 50 authors was imposed on the editors, and their explanation of their selection is convoluted, but all the authors are established and relatively well known in the English-speaking world. The contributors are all scholars in Hispanic studies, as the depth and perceptiveness of the biographies attest. To facilitate use by students or other readers, entries are in standard format, each having a succinct biography, "Major Themes," "Survey of Criticism," and a brief bibliography. There are title and subject indexes and useful appendixes (e.g., "Works Available in English Translation"). Although the book will interest many academic and public libraries, the price for a useful but nonessential work will limit purchase to research libraries.—*D. R. Brown, DePaul University*

◆ North American

WS-0096　　　　PS147　　　　78-20945 CIP
American women writers: a critical reference guide from Colonial times to the present. v.5: Supplement, ed. by Carol Hurd Green and Mary Grimley Mason. Continuum, 1994. 522p index ISBN 0-8264-0603-3, $95.00

Volume 5 of this well-established reference guide expands coverage with 145 new entries, including African American, Asian American, Native American, lesbian, Chicana, and Latina writers such as Rita Dove, Michelle Cliff, Jamaica Kincaid, Sandra Cisneros, and Cherríe Moraga, among others. Updated entries for 90 writers included in the preceeding four volumes (CH, Jan'80, Nov'80, Sep'81, Jul'82) provide additional critical references. As in the earlier volumes, the range of writers covers both lesser- and well-known writers of poetry, fiction, and drama and a few journalists, essayists, and authors of children's literature. Written by a number of contributors in a consistent style, brief entries are both biographical and critical, providing an overview of a writer's work. References to works not mentioned in the critical essay and a critical bibliography complete each entry. This supplement addresses earlier gaps in coverage of minority writers and is recommended for all libraries.—*N. Knipe, Colorado College*

WS-0097　　　　PS3525　　　　91-47702 CIP
Bennett, Joy. **Mary McCarthy: an annotated bibliography,** by Joy Bennett and Gabriella Hochmann. Garland, 1992. 442p (Garland reference library of the humanities, 1251) indexes afp ISBN 0-8240-7028-3, $70.00

Bennett and Hochmann have applied the same enthusiasm and energy to Mary McCarthy as they did to *Simone de Beauvoir* (CH, Jul'89). The result is an exhaustive bibliography of more than 1,760 items on a writer once described by Norman Mailer as "our First Lady of Letters." The bibliography covers the years 1935 to 1991 and is divided into two sections, works by McCarthy and works about her. Works by McCarthy include books, essays, short stories, book reviews, theater and film reviews, translations, letters to the editor, and interviews. Original publication dates are provided with notes on additional publication information. All editions of books are listed, including foreign editions. Works on McCarthy include general criticism, book reviews, North American theses, biographies, and obituaries. All entries are arranged chronologically within the sections. Descriptive annotations, explanatory notes, and cross-references are provided for many of the entries. Author and named person/title indexes. A few idiosyncrasies should be noted. Explanatory notes are lacking in the entries for book reviews and theater/film reviews by McCarthy, and one often has no immediate way of knowing who or what is being reviewed. Since both titles and authors of reviewed items are listed in the index, could they not have been included in the entry texts? Similarly, the named person/title index excludes McCarthy's short stories, again for no obvious reason. Finally, in a work of this magnitude, some minor errors are inevitable. This is the first full-length bibliography on McCarthy since Sherli Evans's *Mary McCarthy* (1968), and it will be an important acquisition for academic and large public library collections.—*L. O. Rein, George Mason University*

WS-0098　　　　PS153　　　　93-6561 CIP
A bibliographical guide to African-American women writers, comp. by Casper LeRoy Jordan. Greenwood, 1993. 387p (Bibliographies and indexes in Afro-American and African studies, 31) index afp ISBN 0-313-27633-1, $65.00

Arguably, no other publication is "nearly as comprehensive in covering the vast panorama of the attainments of black women in the creative literature field." The compiler (Clark Atlanta Univ. School of Library and Information Science) documents bibliographically the contributions of black women writers from Lucy Terry (1730-1821), the first African-born female writer-poet in North America, to more familiar writers of the 1990s (e.g., Terry McMillan, Alice Walker, Gloria Naylor). Genres represented include poetry, memoirs, biographies, short fiction, diaries, etc. Although book reviews and works in science and social science are omitted, privately published works and products of small literary presses, both outlets for many women writers, are not overlooked. Writers are listed alphabetically and each is assigned a discrete number; for each writer, primary and secondary works are listed separately and are assigned separate numbering sequences within the author's number. This scheme will permit easy updating for future additions and revisions. The only work that covers so vast an array of African American women writers; highly recommended for all libraries.— *G. T. Johnson, Central State University (OH)*

WS-0099   PS228.V5   89-11963 CIP
Butler, Deborah A. **American women writers on Vietnam: unheard voices: a selected annotated bibliography.** Garland, 1990. 312p (Garland reference library of the humanities, 1278) indexes afp ISBN 0-8240-3528-3, $41.00

Although Butler makes no claims for comprehensiveness, this bibliography is the best single source on American women writing on the Vietnam War. The compiler includes factual, personal, and fictional books, articles, book chapters, and dissertations covering the period from 1954 to 1987. There are 781 English-language works represented in succinct annotations that are designed to be descriptive. This lack of critical evaluation could be a weakness for some purposes, but there are some exceptions to this rule in a very few entries. One wishes, however, that a controversial work like Lynda Van Devanter's *Home Before Morning* (1983) had been given the evaluative one-liner at the expense of a solid classic like Frances Fitzgerald's *Fire in the Lake* (CH, Jan'73). Also, given the broad topical organization, a subject index would have been a helpful alternative to skimming all entries under a given theme. These comments in no way negate the overall value of this bibliography. The annotations are obviously the result of actual examination of each item, and the title and author indexes work well. There is no comparable work. The standard bibliographies on the war just do not cover women writers, compilers, and editors in any depth. A much needed tool that is a worthy addition to general and women's studies reference shelves. Recommended for undergraduate, graduate, and large public library collections.—*C. L. Sugnet, University of Arizona*

WS-0100   PS374   93-10822 CIP
Carter, Susanne, comp. **Mothers and daughters in American short fiction: an annotated bibliography of twentieth-century women's literature.** Greenwood, 1993. 132p (Bibliographies and indexes in women's studies, 19) indexes afp ISBN 0-313-28511-X, $49.95

Twentieth-century short fiction by American women forms the basis of this slender bibliography in which nearly 250 stories are annotated. The arrangement is by seven categories of mother-daughter interaction: Abuse and Neglect, Aging, Alienation, Death, Expectations, Nurturance, and Portraits. The thematic arrangement allows for well-written chapter introductions but does not allow for listing in more than one category. Annotations are useful, being fairly lengthy and incorporating both summaries and criticism. The publisher's use of page numbers identical in size and typeface to entry numbers leads to needless confusion when both are justified to the right margin. Recommended for libraries with substantial literature or women's studies collections but other libraries may want to consider balance between price and scope.—*P. Palmer, Memphis State University*

WS-0101   PS374   91-33399 CIP
Carter, Susanne. **War and peace through women's eyes: a selective bibliography of twentieth-century American women's fiction.** Greenwood, 1992. 293p (Bibliographies and indexes in women's studies, 14) indexes afp ISBN 0-313-27771-0, $55.00

Carter (Southwest Missouri State Univ. Library) has compiled an interesting and useful selected bibliography of 374 works of fiction that reflect attitudes of women writers toward war and peace from WW I through the Vietnam War and nuclear war. Each chapter covers the literature of a separate war and includes an introduction, sections on novels and short fiction, and a bibliography of literary criticism and sources. Each entry includes an evaluative synopsis of the cited novel or short story. Author, title, and subject indexes complete the volume. The unique focus of women's fictional perspectives on war and peace sets this bibliography apart from other works such as Lucy Dougall's *War and Peace in Literature: Prose, Drama, and Poetry Which Illuminate the Problem of War* (1982). Carter's selective bibliography will provide access to material useful to students of social activism, women, peace, and nonviolence. Highly recommended for public and academic libraries at all levels.—*N. Knipe, Colorado College*

WS-0102   PS153   92-39468 CIP
Contemporary lesbian writers of the United States: a bio-bibliographical critical sourcebook, ed. by Sandra Pollack and Denise D. Knight. Greenwood, 1993. 640p bibl index afp ISBN 0-313-28215-3, $99.50

Greenwood's biobibliographical sourcebooks are useful to map work in new and important fields of scholarship. This volume joins *Contemporary Gay American Novelists* (CH, Jul'93) to provide an invaluable foundation for the study of contemporary lesbian and gay literature in the US. Knowledgable contributors provide highly readable essays covering 100 authors, both prominent and newly emerging, "who, at some point during the 1970-1992 period, had written as self-identified lesbians." In a five-part format, each essay provides biographical information; a discussion of major works and themes; an overview of critical reception of the writer's work; and a two-part bibliography of works by and studies about the author. Since the work of many of these writers has not yet received scholarly attention, the contributors' efforts to document reviews and critical reception in more ephemeral publications is nothing short of remarkable. The diversity of lesbian voices in fiction, poetry, and drama find wide representation in the many essays on Asian, Black, Chicana, Latina, and Native writers; but the otherwise well-constructed index lacks references by ethnicity. A list of publishers of lesbian writers, selective periodicals and journals of interest, and an extensive bibliography of selected nonfiction on lesbian issues cap the volume, further enhancing its reference value. Highly recommended for academic libaries at all levels and for medium and large public libraries.—*J. Ariel, University of California, Irvine*

WS-0103   PS374   93-30644 CIP
DellaCava, Frances A. **Female detectives in American novels: a bibliography and analysis of serialized female sleuths,** by Frances A. DellaCava and Madeline H. Engel. Garland, 1993. 157p (Garland reference library of the humanities, 1685) indexes ISBN 0-8153-1264-4, $26.00

An analytical essay with which this book opens discusses trends in the development and role of the female detective in American novels over the past 100 years, and is followed by bibliographic entries for individual sleuths. Entries discuss the character, identify the author, and list the books in which the character has appeared (detectives who have appeared only in short stories are not included). The book is indexed by author, by character, and by book title. An observation rather than a criticism: the subtitle might better be "census" than "analysis" of serialized female sleuths, since the authors almost always focus on enumeration of characters' demographic traits (age, occupation, marital status, sexual orientation, etc.). Within this context, however, this is a worthwhile addition to reference works in the field, particularly since a significant number of contemporary mystery writers feature women sleuths. Complementing such previous works as Kathleen Gregory Klein's *The Woman Detective: Gender & Genre* (CH, Mar'89) and Patricia Craig's and Mary Cadogan's *The Lady Investigates: Women Detectives and Spies in Fiction* (1981), *Female Detectives in American Novels* is recommended for purchase by any library with an interest in detective and mystery fiction.—*D. Highsmith, California State University, Fullerton*

WS-0104   PS3545.H16   89-25034 CIP
Garrison, Stephen. **Edith Wharton, a descriptive bibliography.** Pittsburgh, 1990. 514p index ISBN 0-8229-3641-0, $100.00

As a companion to Kristin Lauer and Margaret Murray's *Edith Wharton: An Annotated Secondary Bibliography* (CH, Oct'90), Garrison's comprehensive primary bibliography of Wharton's writings rounds out the research apparatus for this major American novelist. Full and detailed descriptive information on contents and physical properties is provided for Wharton's books, pamphlets, and collections of her writings. The compiler also includes complete bibliographic and publishing information through 1986 for titles in which any material by Wharton first appears (including poetry and letters), and for first publication of Wharton writings in newspapers and magazines. The lengthy entries for Wharton's books, pamphlets, and collections also include serialization, a facsimile of title and copyright pages, later printings in English, and even library locations of copies of each printing. The volume is most useful in identifying lesser-known writings by Wharton and providing locations for these materials, such as her general report "War Charities in France," and her contribution to the compilation Breaking Into Print (1937), a collection of essays by authors describing the difficulties of publishing. The bibliographic scholarship reflected in this volume is most impeccable and complete. The index is especially useful; one valuable feature being the inclusion of entries for publishers, thus allowing quick identification of all Wharton publications produced by a particular firm. This primary bibliography is recommended for most academic libraries because of its subject's stature in American literature.—*J. A. Adams, SUNY at Buffalo*

WS-0105   PS338   92-42768 CIP
Gavin, Christy. **American women playwrights, 1964-1989: a research guide and annotated bibliography.** Garland, 1993. 493p (Garland reference library of the humanities, 879) index afp ISBN 0-8240-3046-X, $75.00

Gavin presents information on approximately 150 modern American women playwrights, listing for each selected plays, playscripts, profiles, interviews, press reviews, preview articles, and critical studies. Other features include a bibliographic essay and a 110-entry annotated bibliography of general works. The topic is timely and the contents useful, but format and indexing are awkward. Entries for individual playwrights are arranged alphabetically and often cover several pages. Since there are no running heads for playwrights' names, finding a desired section is tiresome. Nor are playwrights indexed or listed individually in the table of contents. The only index covers some authors of critical writings about plays and playwrights, but it is selective and occasionally inaccurate (some index entries refer to nonexistent entry numbers). Authors of critical works are indexed only if they wrote entries the compiler annotated (e.g., of 19 reviews of JoAnne Akalaitis's *Dead End Kids*, 7 are annotated and thus indexed, while 12 are not annotated, hence not indexed). Despite these frustrating production flaws, the work contains valuable information not readily available in other sources. Recommended for libraries with large theater collections.—*P. Palmer, Memphis State University*

WS-0106   PR9188   92-35184 CIP
Gerry, Thomas M.F. **Contemporary Canadian and U.S. women of letters: an annotated bibliography.** Garland, 1993. 287p (Garland bibliographies of modern critics and critical schools, 21) bibl index afp ISBN 0-8240-6989-7, $45.00

Using as criteria that these writers have written both poetry and/or fiction and literary criticism and/or theory, Gerry has compiled a bibliography of 16 Canadian and US women authors (slight emphasis on Canadian) for whom annotated bibliographies are not available, e.g., Nicole Brossard, Jane Rule. Each chapter is devoted to one author with her works arranged in chronological order, categorized, and numbered. The annotations are substantive except for fiction and poetry which have none. In the last chapter "Related Bibliographies" Gerry lists 18 additional women authors and at least one major bibliography that has been published about each. Although a few of the first group of 16 have one or more entries in Wendy Frost's *Feminist Literary Criticism: A Bibliography of Journal Articles, 1975-1981* (CH, Oct'88), Gerry's coverage is much more extensive. Many of the authors also appear in one or more of the Gale series on authors and literary biography, but this work fills a niche in feminist literary criticism. Gerry need not have apologized for being a man but writing about women. Recommended for women's studies collections in colleges and universities.—*T. M. Racz, Eastern Michigan University*

WS-0107   PS3531.O752   90-43628 CIP
Hilt, Kathryn. **Katherine Anne Porter: an annotated bibliography,** by Kathryn Hilt and Ruth M. Alvarez. Garland, 1990. 354p (Garland reference library of the humanities, 507) indexes afp ISBN 0-8240-8912-X, $58.00

This bibliography covers materials published through 1988 with several 1989 and 1990 entries. Part 1, works by Porter, includes books; translations of books; stories published in books and periodicals; essays, letters, and poems; journalism, including pieces not listed in other bibliographies; and book reviews. Entries are listed chronologically. Part 2, works about Porter, lists bibliographies; biographies and interviews, many never before listed; general criticism; criticism of individual works; book reviews; and dissertations. Here entries are listed alphabetically by author or title of work. All entries give full bibliographic information

when known plus short annotations. Indexes of authors, of editors or translators, and of Porter titles allow for easy identification of citations. Because of its currency and inclusion of newly discovered works. Hilt and Alvarez's bibliography replaces Louise Waldrip's *A Bibliography of the Works of Katherine Anne Porter* (1969) and Robert F. Kiernan's *Katherine Anne Porter and Carson McCullers: A Reference Guide* (CH, Dec'76). This bibliography will be useful to both Porter scholars and graduate literature students. Recommended for university-level libraries.—*C. S. Faries, Pennsylvania State University, University Park Campus*

WS-0108   PS153   93-40618 CIP
Jewish American women writers: a bio-bibliographical and critical sourcebook, ed. by Ann R. Shapiro et al. Greenwood, 1994. 557p bibl index afp ISBN 0-313-28437-7, $89.50

This reference work presents 57 authors, each of whom receives an alphabetically arranged entry that includes a one-page biography, an essay on the author's major themes, survey of criticism, and bibliographies of works by and about the author. The 56 contributors represent an impressive array of institutions. The writers chosen range from the well known to the forgotten and obscure. Some of the authors have voluminous trails of criticism; others are too young or too off the beaten track to have much written about them at this point. The book also includes an interpretive essay on autobiographical writings and a useful glossary of Hebrew, Yiddish, and Aramaic terms. The index would have been more useful had it included themes and topics in addition to names and titles. The operative principle of the sourcebook is inclusiveness; not all writers deal with Jewish themes, but they all have some connection to Judaism, if only having been born into a Jewish household. This is a useful first step for anyone looking for a single place to find basic information. The editors do not claim that this work presents the canon of Jewish American women's literature, but rather offer the work as a starting point. Highly recommended for all academic libraries.—*B. Adler, Valdosta State University*

WS-0109   PS3503.O195   90-47804 CIP
Knox, Claire E. **Louise Bogan: a reference source.** Scarecrow, 1990. 315p (Scarecrow author bibliographies, 86) indexes afp ISBN 0-8108-2379-9, $39.50

Drawing on files of *The New Yorker* (where Bogan was poetry editor 1931-1969), collected materials at Harvard and Amherst, the Berg Collection at the New York Public Library, and the Library of Congress (where Bogan was consultant in poetry), Knox has compiled an exhaustive, annotated bibliography on Bogan. Knox (Northeastern University) extends the work of Jane Couchman's 1976 bibliography published in *The Bulletin of Bibliography* and a Library of Congress bibliography published with William Jay Smith's memorial lecture *Louise Bogan: A Woman's Words* (1972). Part 1 covers works by Bogan and includes sections on her poetry, criticism, translations, and short stories as well as less accessible journals, poems on records and tapes, lectures, and letters. Part 2 is based on works about Bogan and includes general criticism and dissertations, bibliographies, awards, and memorial speeches. Annotations in Part 1 draw heavily on Bogan's own language and point of view; all the annotations are evaluative. Author and title indexes of both Knox's sources and Bogan's work complete the volume. Similar to other "Scarecrow Author Bibliographies," this reference source is only the eighth out of 87 titles published in that series to focus on a woman. Recommended for all academic libraries.—*N. Knipe, Colorado College*

WS-0110   PR9199   91-11385 CIP
McCombs, Judith. **Margaret Atwood: a reference guide,** by Judith McCombs and Carole L. Palmer. G.K. Hall, 1991. 735p indexes afp ISBN 0-8161-8940-4, $60.00

In an annotated bibliography of 2,000 items, McCombs (Canadian poet, Atwood scholar) and Palmer (academic librarian) have admirably accomplished their stated purpose, "to create a text that serves to document accurately the critical reputation of Margaret Atwood." International in scope, the completeness of the bibliography owes much to Atwood's making her private archive available to the authors. Citations to journal and newspaper articles, interviews, book reviews, and dissertations cover the years from 1962 through 1987, with some reference to significant anthologies published in 1988 and 1989. Author and subject indexes are provided. It would have been helpful to readers had Atwood's works been identified by genre (e.g., novel, poetry.) Because of the number of works cited (286 in the year 1986), it would also have been helpful if citations, which are arranged chronologically and by author within each year, had first been subdivided by title of work. The book greatly expands and updates Alan J. Horne's two-volume *Margaret Atwood, an Annotated Bibliography* (1979-80). For further citations readers are referred to Palmer's "Current Atwood Checklist," published annually since 1986 in *Newsletter of the Margaret Atwood Society*. This excellent work is highly recommended.—*B. K. Lacks, California State University, Fresno*

WS-0111 PS3505 93-10381 CIP
Meyering, Sheryl L. **A readers guide to the short stories of Willa Cather.** G.K. Hall, 1994. 286p indexes afp ISBN 0-8161-1834-5, $60.00

WS-0111a PS3505 92-42434 CIP
March, John. **A readers companion to the fiction of Willa Cather,** ed. by Marilyn Arnold with Debra Lynn Thornton. Greenwood, 1993. 846p afp ISBN 0-313-28767-8, $99.50

Willa Cather wrote more than 60 short stories. More than a listing of critical books and articles on Cather's stories, Meyering's *Guide* provides information on the publication history of the stories and biographical and external influences. Arranged in simple alphabetical order by story title, the guide will be of great help to undergraduates, providing a discussion of the thematic relationship of each story to other Cather works and a comparison of critical perspectives, followed by a list of books and articles referred to in the comparison. An earlier annotated bibliography, *Willa Cather, a Reference Guide* by Marilyn Arnold (1986), remains a valuable resource because it covers all Cather's writings, includes some foreign criticism, and contains items of criticism dating back to the time of Cather's writing. Arnold arranges critcism by year of publication rather than by the title of the novel or story, making it less appealing to undergraduates than Meyering. Although one might expect Arnold to include everything in Meyering and more, this is not the case; for Cather's short stories, Meyering has more listings than Arnold, most dated after 1970. Recommended for all undergraduate collections and also useful to more advanced researchers.

March's *Reader's Companion* was also edited by Arnold. Throughout his life, March carried on an enormous correspondence devoted to tracing motifs, proper names, and allusions in Cather's poems, stories, novels, and essays. Each entry identifies a person, motif, or literary or artistic work, followed by a description of its use by Cather and a coded reference to its location in her works. In the introduction, Arnold indicates that March's selection of items as somewhat idiosyncratic, including some, like "cocktail," which readers scarcely need look up, but making some surprising omissions, such as the Rock in *Death Comes for the Archbishop*. Arnold added sources that were omitted for some quotations, expanded March's identification of many people by last name only, added cross-references, changed March's listings for women characters under their married names, and corrected his tendency to describe women in relation to their husbands or fathers. The *Companion* is impressive both for the knowledge of literature, art, and music Cather possessed, apparent in her many allusions, and for the detail of March's effort. The *Companion* makes one want to reread Cather's works more closely, or read those not yet read. Recommended for upper-division undergraduates, graduate students, and researchers.—*A. Maio, University of Hartford*

WS-0112 PS151 90-52917 CIP
Modern American women writers, ed. by Lea Baechler and A. Walton Litz. Scribner, 1991. 583p index ISBN 0-684-19057-5, $85.00

This work includes essays on 41 American women writers who have published since the 1870s. The women span a wide range of regions, racial/ethnic groups, and genres, including poets such as Emily Dickinson or Sylvia Plath, playwrights like Susan Glaspell, short-story writers such as Flannery O'Connor, novelists like Toni Morrison or Anne Tyler, and intellectuals such as Charlotte Perkins Gilman or Susan Sontag. Both academics and practicing writers contributed the essays, which provide detailed accounts of the writers' lives, thorough critical analysis of their works, and bibliographies listing important primary and secondary works. The introduction by Elaine Showalter does a fine job of outlining the historical and cultural contexts of women's writing in America, and a useful chronology supplements this introduction. One index lists writers, titles, and subjects. Other reference works do cover American women writers, the most

detailed being the four-volume *American Women Writers: A Critical Reference Guide from Colonial Times to the Present*, ed. by Lina Mainiero (CH, Jan, Nov'80; Sep'81; Jul'82). Mainiero's work spans a greater time period but has shorter essays that list only a few primary and secondary works. Because of its currency and more detailed essays, *Modern American Women Writers* would be a useful addition to college and university library reference collections.—*C. S. Faries, Pennsylvania State University, University Park Campus*

WS-0113 PS374 93-8642 CIP
Modern women writers, ed. by Matthew J. Bruccoli and Judith S. Baughman. Facts on File, 1994. 100p index afp ISBN 0-8160-3000-6, $18.95

Adapted from *Facts on File Bibliography of American Fiction, 1866-1918* (CH, May '93) and *Facts on File Bibliography of American Fiction, 1919-1988* (CH, Feb'92), this concise bibliography includes information through the end of 1992, complete listings of primary works, and selected secondary references. Authors include: Willa Cather, Kate Chopin, Carson McCullers, Joyce Carol Oates, Flannery O'Conner, Katherine Anne Porter, Gertrude Stein, Anne Tyler, Eudora Welty, and Edith Wharton. Entries are divided into bibliographies, primary works, location of existing manuscripts and archives, biographies, critical studies, collections of essays, special issues of journals, chapters in books, and critical articles. The "Checklist for Students of American Fiction" includes 68 historical, literary, and reference works and five journals to aid in research, with an indication of computerized sources. Designed for high schools, community colleges, and general libraries, the volumes in the "Essential Bibliography of American Fiction" series provide concise references for a limited number of representative writers. African American authors, e.g., Toni Morrison, are covered in another series volume, *Modern African American Writers* (CH, Jul'94), requiring multiple purchases for more comprehensive coverage. Recommended for general, undergraduate, and community college libraries.—*N. Knipe, Colorado College*

WS-0114 PS147 94-26359 CIP
The Oxford companion to women's writing in the United States, ed. by Cathy N. Davidson and Linda Wagner-Martin et al. Oxford, 1995. 1,021p bibl index afp ISBN 0-19-506608-1, $49.95

The 771 signed, alphabetically arranged entries in this one-volume source include short biographies and extensive essays; coverage is thematic, chronological, geographic, multicultural, theoretical, and practical. Essays on women's bookstores, presses, and lesbian publishing are incorporated in a range that includes Colonial to contemporary writers and treats issues such as race and racism, health, essentialism, feminist film theory, ecofeminism, friendship, gossip, and eating disorders. Davidson (Duke) and Wagner-Martin (Univ. of North Carolina at Chapel Hill) have compiled an impressive and diverse portrait of women and women's writing in the US. Short bibliographies conclude each entry; an extensive bibliography and name/topic index, as well as timelines of social history and women's writing, complete the dictionary. Some authors—e.g., poet Mary Oliver, novelists Gail Godwin and Barbara Kingsolver, and theorist bell hooks—are missing or included in survey essays rather than given individual entries. Despite occasional gaps, this survey is a celebratory addition to women's writing in the US and provides concise topical information not easily found elsewhere in a single source. Recommended for all libraries.—*N. Knipe, Colorado College*

WS-0115 PS3513 92-42696 CIP
Papke, Mary E. **Susan Glaspell: a research and production sourcebook.** Greenwood, 1993. 299p (Modern dramatists research and production sourcebooks, 4) indexes afp ISBN 0-313-27383-9, $69.50

Although Glaspell's fame rests primarily on her one-acter *Trifles* (1916), University of Tennessee-Knoxville feminist critic Papke (*Verging on the Abyss*, 1990) makes a strong argument throughout this exhaustive guide for a reexamination of Glaspell's significance in the American canon, both as dramatist and minor novelist. The 314 annotated citations and 195 reviews are supplemented by a bibliography of Glaspell's primary works, lengthy detailed plot summaries of all staged works, production histories, summary reviews for first and subsequent major productions, and an excellent brief biocritical study. Papke sometimes underplays Glaspell's literary shortcomings, but her detailed summations and inclusion of obscure sources should provoke further investigation. As the only research guide available on Glaspell, this volume is essential, along with V.A. Makowsky's *Susan Glaspell's Century of American Women* (CH, Sep'93), for all collections focusing on American theater history or feminist literature. Highly recommended for all academic libraries.—*A. J. Adam, Prairie View Agricultural and Mechanical University*

WS-0116   PS151   94-10993 CIP
Sakelliou-Schultz, Liana. **Feminist criticism of American women poets: an annotated bibliography, 1975-1993.** Garland, 1994. 332p (Garland bibliographies of modern critics and critical schools, 17) indexes afp ISBN 0-8240-7084-4, $50.00

Sakelliou-Schultz lists articles, books, and dissertations written by feminist literary critics in English in this bibliography. The 32-page introduction provides a useful overview of issues that have animated this school of criticism since 1975 and summarizes a range of opinions regarding the goals of feminist scholarship, the possibilities of a distinctive feminist theory of literature, the ability of male critics to assess female writers fairly, and more. Points of view are accompanied by references to specific works in the bibliography. Sakelliou-Schultz distinguishes "feminist practice," or the analysis of poems, from works that deal mainly with feminist theory. Accordingly, every item is categorized as one or the other. Annotations will be useful to serious students and scholars. Others, unfamiliar with the terminology of literature, deconstruction theory, or feminism, may be lost. Some references lack annotations, and some dissertation entries simply cite *Dissertation Abstracts International.* Although name/subject and author indexes are supplied, an index to journal and monograph titles would have been useful. This work updates, in part, an earlier Garland bibliography, Wendy Frost and Michele Valiquette's *Feminist Literary Criticism: A Bibliography of Journal Articles, 1975-1981* (CH, Nov'88). Recommended for undergraduate, graduate, and research collections.—*M. P. Shapiro, American University*

WS-0117   PS243   93-47349 CIP
Slocum, Robert B. **New England in fiction, 1787-1990: an annotated bibliography.** Locust Hill, 1994. 2v. 980p indexes afp ISBN 0-933951-54-X, $100.00

Slocum's specialized bibliography lists 4,975 English-language novels and short fictional works with a New England setting or themes. Sentimental, picaresque, historical, realistic, detective, and gothic fiction are included, but juvenile titles (for those under age ten) are omitted. Arranged alphabetically by author, entries include full citations with pagination. Cross-references lead from given names to pseudonyms under which particular titles were published. Full indexes by title, subject, and place make the work easy to use; a chronological index covers the years 1787-1865. Annotations are descriptive rather than critical; most are plot summaries, and many include quotes from contemporary reviews. Slocum's introduction includes a superficial overview of New England literary history, emphasizing regional themes and the prominence of women authors. In view of the bibliography's narrow focus and high price, it is recommended only for research collections with major interests in New England literary history, regionalism, or minor American fiction writers. Smaller collections can continue to rely on Perry Westbrook's more scholarly *Literary History of New England* (CH, Apr'89).—*E. J. Carpenter, Oberlin College*

WS-0118   PN4879   91-12151 CIP
Zuckerman, Mary Ellen, comp. **Sources on the history of women's magazines, 1792-1960: an annotated bibliography.** Greenwood, 1991. 297p (Bibliographies and indexes in women's studies, 12) indexes afp ISBN 0-313-26378-7, $49.95

Popular women's magazines are the focus of this bibliography. Although her work is more extensive than Nancy K. Humphreys's *American Women's Magazines: An Annotated Historical Guide* (CH, May'90), Zuckerman does not include information on the underground sources that Humphreys does. Instead, she concentrates on the popular women's magazine industry and the historical context of that industry. The bibliography includes unpublished manuscripts and dissertations which, along with the book and periodical resources, were gathered for the author's dissertation in journalism history. A few sources are included for questionable reasons (for example, Erica Jong's *Fear of Flying*), but the bulk of the sources are excellent and the annotations are clearly and con-

cisely written. In addition to general sources on the history and criticism of the magazines, Zuckerman includes useful material on images of women in other media, sources on advertising and market research, and biographical resources on the magazines' publishers. Highly recommended for colleges and universities with collections in women's studies, advertising, or journalism history.—*M. F. Jones, Muskingum College*

◆ Performing Arts, Communication & Media

WS-0119   PN1998   90-43743 CIP
Acker, Ally. **Reel women: pioneers of the cinema, 1896 to the present.** Continuum, 1991. 374p index ISBN 0-8264-0499-5, $34.95

Scholarship on women in the cinema is currently a hot topic, so this new reference source comes at an opportune time. Acker, a writer and filmmaker, states that her book is "about the manipulation of history" (xvii), and her insightful introduction, telling why this is so, is followed by a selective yet well-organized work giving brief sketches of "pioneer" women in the film industry. Acker has focused on women in mainstream cinema who have worked on feature films; two exceptions are inclusion of women in the early days of cinema, when "feature" was not clearly defined, and women of color who work primarily on short films or documentaries. *Reel Women* includes portraits of women directors, producers, writers, and editors; actresses turned director or producer; even animators and stunt women from the earliest days of filmmaking to the present. Under most categories, an introduction precedes the biographical sketches organized under silent and sound eras. Shorter miscellaneous bios are also included under "short takes." Each woman's career profile is followed by a list of her films. More than 100 photographs, many never seen before, enhance this source, along with a select bibliography. Other sources on women in film—including Louise Heck-Rabi's *Women Filmmakers: A Critical Reception* (CH, Feb'85), Anthony Slide's *Early Women Directors* (CH, Dec'77), and Sharon Smith's *Women Who Make Movies* (CH, Sep'75)—cover only a handful of women who have shaped American film. Because of its ease of use, currency, and coverage, Acker's work is recommended for reference collections in research libraries.—*C. S. Faries, Pennsylvania State University, University Park Campus*

WS-0120   PN2287   91-25094 CIP
Barranger, Milly S. **Jessica Tandy: a bio-bibliography.** Greenwood, 1991. 150p (Bio-bibliographies in the performing arts, 22) bibl index afp ISBN 0-313-27716-8, $39.95

WS-0120a   PN2287   91-24008 CIP
Carrier, Jeffrey L. **Tallulah Bankhead: a bio-bibliography.** Greenwood, 1991. 267p (Bio-bibliographies in the performing arts, 21) index afp ISBN 0-313-27452-5, $42.95

WS-0120b   ML134   91-16233 CIP
Rivadue, Barry. **Mary Martin: a bio-bibliography.** Greenwood, 1991. 234p (Bio-bibliographies in the performing arts, 18) indexes afp ISBN 0-313-27345-6, $39.95

WS-0120c   PN2287   91-21528 CIP
Schultz, Margie. **Irene Dunne: a bio-bibliography.** Greenwood, 1991. 312p (Bio-bibliographies in the performing arts, 19) disc index afp ISBN 0-313-27399-5, $45.00

These four titles constitute the latest additions to a series that has previously included celebrities Jean Arthur, Cary Grant, Julie Andrews, and Milos Forman, to name a few. Each volume provides a brief biographical sketch of the individual along with a thorough listing of credits in all the arenas in which the subject worked. A bibliography of secondary sources finishes each volume. The biobibliography on Mary Martin is no exception. Rivadue documents Martin's career from 1938 to 1990. A short biographical sketch gives the basic outline of Martin's life, but for information in more depth readers should be referred to either Shirley P. Newman's *Mary Martin on Stage* (1969) or, better, Martin's own autobiography *My Heart Belongs* (CH, Jul'76). The strength of Rivadue's title is the detailed listing of Martin's work. Martin's stage performances fill the longest section, listing all of her plays in chronological order. This section also states when and where a show opened and how long it ran; gives all major credits including set and costume design, music and lyrics, dance direction, etc.; lists casts; cites critical reviews; and includes comments by the author. The second section, a discography, lists Martin's recordings alphabetically and then those available on 78s. The broadcasting section gives all of Martin's performances and appearances on radio and television in chronological order. The filmography lists Martin's films in chronological order, noting cast, director, producer, and songs performed. Rivadue also cites reviews and provides a synopsis of each film along with his own comments. Finally, the bibliography lists books and magazine and newspaper articles about Martin, 1938-1990. Most of the alphabetically arranged entries are annotated. Appendixes include a chronology of Martin's life, awards won, endorsements she has made, and locations of her archives. General index and song index. Several black-and-white photographs show Martin at various stages of her career. The other three new volumes are similar in format and scope, with some unique aspects tailored to each performer. For example, the work on Irene Dunne has an appendix listing the magazine covers that featured the actress, and Tallulah Bankhead's biobibliography has an appendix "The Use of Her Name in Books and Films." However, all three volumes provide thorough listings of the performer's work, a good bibliography, and illustrations. This admirable series should provide quick access to information on performers for many researchers. Recommended for reference collections in university libraries with large film or theater departments.—*C. S. Faries, Pennsylvania State University, University Park Campus*

WS-0121   PN2287   93-37191 CIP
Barranger, Milly S. **Margaret Webster: a bio-bibliography.** Greenwood, 1994. 230p (Bio-bibliographies in the performing arts, 47) bibl index afp ISBN 0-313-28439-3, $65.00

Webster was of that company of British giants who completed, in the middle third of the 20th century, the transition from 19th-century modes and methods of Shakespeare production to the "modern" mode associated with such theaters as Stratford, Ontario's. Offering a biography and chronology and annotated lists of productions, recordings, awards and honors, archival collections, and works about and by Webster, Barranger's bio-bibliography abounds in documentary evidence but leaves the researcher with sound-bite accolades—Webster as the first women to do this or that—rather than a clear idea of the context in which she worked or of what her productions were like. The text would be more helpful if it listed reviews with the entry for each production rather than in a separate section, and the commentary on those productions would be more useful if, instead of summarizing plots, it discussed Webster's views on the plays. Quick checks of standard sources reveal items omitted from the bibliography. The writing is serviceable but fails to create interest, and the volume's design is doggedly utilitarian. For research collections in women's studies and theater history.—*R. H. Kieft, Haverford College*

WS-0122   PN2287.J59   89-25834 CIP
Carrier, Jeffrey L. **Jennifer Jones: a bio-bibliography.** Greenwood, 1990. 140p (Bio-bibliographies in the performing arts, 11) index afp ISBN 0-313-26651-4, $35.00

This work has seven sections: a biography; a chronology of highlights of Jones's life; a filmography with selected reviews; a listing of radio, theater, and television appearances; a list of awards and nominations; an annotated bibliography of references in books, magazines (many in movie/fan magazines), and newspapers; and an index of names and film titles. There are a dozen illustrations; appendixes include New York Times obituaries for Jones's husbands, Robert Walker and David O. Selznick. Other works on Jones are *The Films of Jennifer Jones* by W. Franklyn Moshier (1978), which has some biographical information as well as film details, with many illustrations, and *Star-Crossed: The Story of Robert Walker and Jennifer Jones*, by movie publicist Beverly Linet (1986). Carrier's book is part of the series "Bio-bibliographies in the Performing Arts," which offers four other 1990 volumes on women performers: *Ann Sothern*, by Margie Schultz; *Alice Fay*, by Barry Rivadue; *Maureen O'Sullivan*, by Connie J. Billips; and *Ava Gardner*, by Karin J. Fowler. Volumes in the series have similar formats— biography, filmography, chronology, etc., and, when appropriate, discographies

and song sheets, as well as references to archival material. These volumes are generally recommended for film collections, depending on interest in their subjects, though the tendency to make assumptions or to repeat gossip is occasionally irresistible to some of the authors. Acknowledging that something is gossip may not mean it can then be used with impunity.—*M. McCormick, University of California, Los Angeles*

WS-0123   ML128   94-45222 CIP
Ericson, Margaret D. **Women and music: a selective annotated bibliography on women and gender issues in music, 1987-1992.** G.K. Hall, NY/Prentice Hall International, 1996. 400p indexes afp ISBN 0-8161-0580-4, $95.00

Devoted to publications relating to gender issues in music, all published within a few years, this volume is a testament to the growth of women's studies in this discipline. Developed from a series of annual bibliographies designed to fill a need expressed by members of the Music Library Association, this bibliography's 1,836 expertly annotated citations include "a diverse range of topics, perspectives, and viewpoints" and sections listing scores, sound recordings, and media. Since the volume is oriented toward issues, biographical references are excluded. Arranged by topic, each section covers a broad subject (e.g., "Feminist Musical Aesthetics," "Women in Jazz and Popular Music"); many sections are divided into subtopics. There are name and subject indexes. Although most of the works cited are in English, this volume is international in scope. Recommended for large or inclusive music libraries and academic libraries supporting women's studies.—*J. L. Patterson, University of Wisconsin—Eau Claire*

WS-0124   PN1998   95-7395 CIP
Foster, Gwendolyn Audrey. **Women film directors: an international bio-critical dictionary.** Greenwood, 1995. 443p bibl indexes afp ISBN 0-313-28972-7, $79.50

Foster describes this excellent reference book as "the first of its kind, not a study of one aspect of women as filmmakers, but a dictionary of women filmmakers, working in film to create new feminist visions of beauty and transcendent power." She also points out that feminist criticism must "allow for violently opposing viewpoints." The alphabetically arranged entries include women from 37 countries, from 1896 to 1910 (Gene Gauntier and Alice Guy) to the present. For each director Foster provides a brief biography, discussion of important films, brief critical comments, and a selected filmography and bibliography. The clearly written, intelligent comments lean toward feminist interpretations of many of the films. Her introduction cites a number of relevant books. This should be an indispensable volume for film and feminist studies collections. Appendixes list the directors by nationality and by decade.—*J. Overmyer, emerita, Ohio State University*

WS-0125   PS153   93-17078 CIP
Furtado, Ken. **Gay and lesbian American plays: an annotated bibliography,** by Ken Furtado and Nancy Hellner. Scarecrow, 1993. 217p afp ISBN 0-8108-2689-5, $27.50

If recent publishing trends are any measure, lesbian and gay studies clearly represent a hot new cultural and academic frontier. Furtado and Hellner provide a welcome addition to the increasing number of reference sources for this rapidly growing literature, at the same time effectively combating continued invisibility in mainstream sources (evidenced, for instance, by the absence of a category in Samuel French for gay, lesbian, or transgendered plays). This bibliography updates and expands Terry Helbing's *Gay Theatre Alliance Directory of Gay Plays* (CH, Oct'81), most notably in the addition of lesbian material, reflecting the richness of gay and lesbian theater and culture today. Arranged alphabetically by author, the nearly 700 plays represent "works containing major characters whose gay or lesbian sexuality is integral to the play's message, and plays whose primary themes are gay or lesbian." A coding system identifying plays by category (gay, lesbian, musical, AIDS, coming out, historical, etc.), in addition to a title index, lists of agents, playwrights, and theaters, and an extremely selective bibliography, all enhance use. While not comprehensive, this catalog still provides the most extensive listing yet available. Recommended for college, university, and large public libraries.—*J. Ariel, University of California, Irvine*

WS-0126　　　　ML106　　　　92-32211 CIP
Grattan, Virginia L. **American women songwriters: a biographical dictionary.** Greenwood, 1993. 279p bibl indexes afp ISBN 0-313-28510-1, $39.95

More casual than scholarly, this volume by a former teacher of English uses mostly other biographical dictionaries and newspaper articles as its main sources. Many important sources are left out, for example, Judith Tick's *American Women Composers Before 1870* (CH, Sep'83) and Hazel Carby's famous article "'It Jus Be's Dat Way Sometime'" (in *Unequal Sisters*, ed. by Ellen C. DuBois and Vicki L. Ruiz, 1990). In addition, the latest editions of sources are not always used. For example, the first edition of Aaron Cohen's *International Encyclopedia of Women Composers* (CH, Mar'82) is cited instead of the second (CH, Sep'88). "Songwriters" to the author means lyricists as well as composers; however, only American-born artists are included. Thus, important early composers such as Augusta Brown and Faustina Hodges are excluded. This dictionary has fewer than 200 entries and is arranged into 10 sections according to genre. At the beginning of each section, there is a brief history of the genre. Each entry includes dates, a short biography, and sources; the most significant song is also featured. Despite its shortcomings, this dictionary is still useful for a public or school library.—*J. Tsou, University of California, Berkeley*

WS-0127　　　　ML134　　　　91-26745 CIP
Hartig, Linda. **Violet Archer: a bio-bibliography.** Greenwood, 1991. 153p (Bio-bibliographies in music, 41) index afp ISBN 0-313-26408-2, $39.95

A brief but complete biography precedes the heart of this book—the bibliographies of works, recordings, and writings by and about contemporary Canadian composer Violet Balestreri Archer, born in Montreal in 1913 and still teaching and working on new commissions. Works are listed by genre; there is also an alphabetical index and a chronology by Hartig, music librarian at the University of Wisconsin-Milwaukee. Because Archer is a talented and prolific composer and educator and is not well known in the US, this volume will be of use to many performers and conductors, especially to those specifically seeking choral and instrumental compositions by women.—*J. P. Ambrose, University of Vermont*

WS-0128　　　　ML128　　　　91-3210 CIP
Heinrich, Adel, comp. **Organ and harpsichord music by women composers: an annotated catalog.** Greenwood, 1991. 373p afp ISBN 0-313-26802-9, $55.00

In addition to a main, worldwide list identifying about 750 composers (from the 17th century to women born in the 1960s) and naming their works for organ and harpsichord, Heinrich's book contains several other features: an instrumentation index, a title index, a list of publishers and libraries, very brief biographical sketches (5 to 10 lines) and a chronological listing of composers by country that includes names from the main list and from two speculative appendixes: a list of about 250 women known to have composed for organ or harpsichord but for whom compositions have not been identified and a list of about 75 women composers who played organ or harpsichord and may have written works for those instruments. A final four-page section is headed "Sources/Further Reading." The title and instrumentation indexes would be more convenient to use if they included page number in addition to composer references. Overall, this is a useful tool that pulls together information from more than 50 sources; however, an overwhelming majority of these women can be found in Aaron I. Cohen's *International Encyclopedia of Women Composers* (2nd ed., CH, Oct'88). For tight acquisitions budgets, Cohen is the wiser purchase. Heinrich's work is recommended only for academic libraries wishing comprehensive holdings.—*K. A. Abromeit, Wright State University*

WS-0129　　　　P94.5.W65　　　　90-23780 CIP
Lent, John A., comp. **Women and mass communications: an international annotated bibliography.** Greenwood, 1991. 481p (Bibliographies and indexes in women's studies, 11) indexes afp ISBN 0-313-26579-8, $75.00

According to Lent (Temple University), women and feminism were virtually ignored in the media literature until the 1970s. Lent's 27 years of international communications experience have helped uncover a goldmine of historical and current resources on women and media worldwide. Following the first chapter on

global and comparative studies, each chapter is devoted to a different geographical area, featuring historical studies, media images of women, women as audience, women practitioners (journalists, filmmakers, directors, broadcasters), and women's media. An excellent introduction briefly summarizes the literature and provides lists of journals selectively or thoroughly surveyed. Included are fugitive materials, conference and seminar papers, non-UMI dissertations, and a list of relevant organizations and periodicals. Two other brief bibliographies on this topic (curiously absent here), Marjan Flick's *Bibliography for Women in Media Research* (Bergen, Norway, 1977) and Marcia Pulyk's *A Bibliography of Selected Materials on Women in the Mass Media* (Ottawa, 1978), do not compare with this work, the only large-scale bibliography of its kind. Strongly recommended for college and university.—*S. G. Williamson, Annenberg School of Communications, University of Pennsylvania*

WS-0130　　　　PN2285　　　　91-52639 CIP
Rainey, Buck. **Sweethearts of the sage: biographies and filmographies of 258 actresses appearing in western movies.** McFarland, 1992. 632p bibl index ISBN 0-89950-565-1, $95.00

These are affectionate biographies of "B" Western heroines (and some major stars), women struggling to succeed in a male-dominated film genre. To be included, an actress must have made at least eight films. Other criteria include personal charisma, popularity in her own day, contribution to the medium, and the importance of the films themselves. The four sections trace the changing role of women in Westerns through the decades: Part 1, the pre-1920 era; Part 2, the '20s; Part 3, the '30s and '40s; and Part 4, from the '40s to the present day. Within each section, biographies are arranged alphabetically. Each entry begins with a one-line italicized tag summarizing the actress's contribution (e.g., for Fritzie Ridgeway, *the Mona Lisa of the Range*) followed by details of her career and personal life, and synopses of selected films. Detailed filmographies are provided, including full cast information, and there is a generous selection of black-and-white photographs. A general bibliography and title index are included. The book serves an important reference function in providing access to difficult-to-locate information, and succeeds in evoking "the innocent pleasures of by-gone days." Delightful for browsing. Highly recommended for serious film collections, women's studies collections, and wherever there is strong interest in Western or silent/early sound films.—*L. E. Jorbin, Cleveland State University*

WS-0131　　　　PN1590　　　　91-16333 CIP
Steadman, Susan M. **Dramatic re-visions: an annotated bibliography of feminism and theatre, 1972-1988.** American Library Association, 1991. 367p indexes ISBN 0-8389-0577-3, $45.00

Steadman has organized this extensive bibliography into eight chapters which cover theory, feminist theaters and theater groups, pioneering women playwrights, 20th-century women playwrights, feminist reassessment of men's playwriting, performers/performance issues/performance art, selected play collections, and conferences, festivals, and organizations. Each chapter is further divided into book and monograph sources, periodical citations, serials, and annuals. All references are to works in English. A section of 30 selected works published after 1988 expands the coverage to 1990. A lengthy introduction provides theoretical and historical background, a discussion of feminist theater and performance issues, and a list of 120 references cited. Indexes are included to names, titles, categories (country, time period, specialization or ethnic group), and subjects. Although critical works on feminist theater have begun to appear in the last several years, e.g., Helene Keyssar, *Feminist Theatre* (1984); *Performing Feminisms: Feminist Critical Theory and Theatre*, ed. by Sue-Ellen Case (1990), this useful bibliography draws together a wide range of material from many sources. Highly recommended for all library collections.—*N. Knipe, Colorado College*

WS-0132　　　　ML128　　　　91-38146 CIP
Walker-Hill, Helen. **Piano music by Black women composers: a catalog of solo and ensemble works.** Greenwood, 1992. 143p (Music reference collection, 35) bibl disc index afp ISBN 0-313-28141-6, $42.95

Walker-Hill, a pianist and musicologist, has produced a long-needed catalog of the piano works of 55 black women composers. As the author points out in the preface, compositions by white women are now gaining prominence, but those by minority women are still being ignored. As partial compensation, a short but informative sociohistorical essay on black women composers is included in the introduction, and a short biography begins each composer's entry. Lists of works include both solo and ensemble pieces, and some works are annotated. The annotations and the appendix "Easy and Moderate Pieces for Teaching" should be especially useful for piano teachers. The appendix "Ensemble Instrumentation" should be useful for performers. The other appendixes are a "Chronology of Surviving Piano Works Before 1920" (presumably for historians but not that helpful), and a useful list headed "Available Published Piano Music." (Curiously, publisher information is not always included in individual work list entries.) A very short bibliography, a discography, and an index round out the volume. Although brief, the catalog is still a useful source for piano teachers, performers, and to a lesser extent, scholars.—*J. Tsou, University of California, Berkeley*

◆ Physical & Biological Sciences, Technology

WS-0133   T36   92-34400 CIP
Bindocci, Cynthia Gay. **Women and technology: an annotated bibliography.** Garland, 1993. 229p (Women's history and culture, 7) indexes afp ISBN 0-8240-5789-9, $39.00

This select bibliography of 570 entries focuses on secondary works (articles, books, published conference proceedings, and dissertations, all in English) published 1979-91, most before 1990. The bibliographer intends to summarize briefly the scholarly research on women and technology. The first 40 pages offer general resources—bibliographies, review essays, guides, indexes, biographies, and collected essays. The remainder of the book is arranged in 16 categories: Agriculture/Food Technology, Architecture, Clerical, Communications, Energy/Ecology, Engineers/Inventors, Health, Home Work, Household Technology, Industrial Work, Labor Organization, Military/War, Reproductive Technology, Transportation, Women in Development, and Work. Technology is defined so broadly that only a sampling can be provided in each category (e.g., under Health there are only 11 entries). A more appropriate title might be "Women and Work." Subject and author indexes are provided. Online and CD-ROM databases are omitted. Unfortunately, the typeface is unattractive. Nevertheless, one hopes works like this will inspire research in this topic.—*M. J. Finnegan, Salem Public Library*

WS-0134   Orig
The History of women and science, health, and technology: a bibliographic guide to the professions and the disciplines, ed. by Phyllis Holman Weisbard and Rima D. Apple. 2nd ed. University of Wisconsin System Women's Studies Librarian, 430 Memorial Library, 728 State St., Madison, WI 53706, 1993. 100p index Free on request.

The first edition (1988) focused on developing new college courses about the history of women in science and related fields, supporting integration of new feminist scholarship into existing survey courses, and providing guidance for professionals to explore the history of women in these disciplines. This updated and expanded edition contains a section of biographical and historical works for older children. This basic bibliography will be of considerable interest to feminist scholars and to those interested in shrinking the gender gap in science. It is organized in six parts: overviews, women in the scientific professions, health and biology, home economics/domestic science, technology, and children and young adult literature. The author index provides easy access. Invaluable for those designing new gender-centered courses, those wanting to make the history of women in these professions more accessible, and those seeking core lists of readings in these specialized areas. Recommended for academic, science, and health center library collections.—*J. M. Coggan, University of Florida*

WS-0135   QD21   92-40224 CIP
Women in chemistry and physics: a biobibliographic sourcebook, ed. by Louise S. Grinstein, Rose K. Rose, and Miriam H. Rafailovich. Greenwood, 1993. 721p index afp ISBN 0-313-27382-0, $99.50

The incompatibility of women and science is a persistent belief. As stated in Margaret Rossiter's *Women Scientists in America* (CH, Apr'83), women are linked

to emotional, delicate, and noncompetitive behavior while science is viewed as rational, tough, competitive, and masculine. To help dispel this myth, one need only refer to *Women in Chemistry and Physics* to find compelling stories of women who have worked either with or around a male-dominated field, making substantial contributions in research, education, and scholarly publications. The editors have compiled a representative collection of biobibliographies of women in the physical sciences spanning some three centuries. Entries are arranged alphabetically and follow a three-section format: Biography, telling the individual's life story; Work, detailing the significant contributions made to her discipline; and Bibliography, listing works by and about each woman. Several appendixes include biographical, discipline, and chronological information. An index is provided as well as short biographies of contributors, all accomplished in their own right. Of interest to general readers and handy for science and women's studies collections. Highly recommended for public and academic libraries.—*N. Chipman-Shlaes, Governors State University*

◆ Religion, Philosophy, Classical Studies

WS-0136   B72   92-227406 MARC
Barth, Else M. **Women philosophers: a bibliography of books through 1990.** Philosophy Documentation Center, 1992. 236p index ISBN 0-912632-91-7, $39.00

One of a growing number of works that focus attention on philosophical writings about and/or by women, this bibliography lists, without description or evaluation, nearly 2,000 books and dissertations from Western European and English-speaking countries. Every title was either listed somewhere as a philosophical writing, written by a person holding a university position in a philosophy department, or satisfied "one or more of the several current definitions of 'philosophy.'" Many books by feminists are included, but only a few of the topical headings—e.g., "Sexual/Gender Oppression and Politics"—are nontraditional. An index of names, a separate section on major philosophers arranged in alphabetical order, numerous cross-references, and a five-page analytic table of contents listing nearly 200 major and minor areas or schools of philosophy all facilitate access to topics and writers. The failure to put page numbers in the table of contents and topic section numbers on each page results in much awkward page-thumbing. Strongly recommended for all academic libraries.—*L. Kincaid, Boise State University*

WS-0137   BL715   91-26649 CIP
Bell, Robert E. **Women of classical mythology: a biographical dictionary.** ABC-Clio, 1991. 462p index afp ISBN 0-87436-581-3, $49.00

With the current focus on women in the field of classical studies this biographical dictionary is a timely piece of work. Bell's dictionary follows a simple alphabetic arrangement that makes it much easier to consult than his *Dictionary of Classical Mythology* (CH, Dec'82), which was arranged by subject. The new dictionary contains the names of both notable and not so notable women of classical myth who are not easily found in other convenient sources on myth such as Pierre Grimal's *The Dictionary of Classical Mythology* (1986) or *The New Century Handbook of Greek Mythology and Legend* (CH, Oct'72) Bell's dictionary is not for the scholar but for the interested student who needs a ready reference source. The biographical entries, ranging from a single sentence to three pages in length, are easily understood and provide sufficient information for further study. An additional and original feature of this dictionary is selective citation, following each entry, of classical authors by whom each of these female figures have been mentioned. The dictionary also contains an alphabetical list of masculine names titled "The Men in Their Lives." Recommended for most public and undergraduate libraries.—*J. C. Jurgens, Northeastern Illinois University*

WS-0138   BL458   91-47603 CIP
Carson, Anne. **Goddesses & wise women: the literature of feminist spirituality, 1980-1992: an annotated bibliography.** Crossing, 1992. 248p index ISBN 0-89594-536-3, $39.95

Carson's first bibliography, *Feminist Spirituality and Images of Divine Femi-*

nine (CH, Oct'86), covered materials from 1833 to 1985. This new work includes books, articles, periodicals, AV materials, and theses from 1980 to early 1992. Almost all entries have annotations, commendably unbiased; arrangement is either by broad topic or by form. A new twist is the inclusion of some materials critical of or hostile to feminist spirituality. The greatest drawback to the work, as with its predecessor, is its dearth of access points, all the more frustrating with such a complex topic. There is no author index, and the subject index is frustratingly brief and often misleading: only one entry under the concept of the four directions, when many works include it; interviewees are not always indexed; to find European wicca one must review all "Wicca" entries. The work is nonetheless an indispensable delight, even if one must read item by item to find its riches. The diversity of the field is well demonstrated by entries on ritual, art work, liturgy, anthropology, health, psychology, ecology, sexuality, astrology, archaeology, and even comedy (*Pagans-poof*, a parody of pagan periodicals, includes an article "Occult Use of French Fries," p. 132), as well as spirituality. The weakest section, on re-visioning Christianity and Judaism (Carson acknowledges other, better sources on this topic) is more than balanced by the sections on periodicals, AV materials, and especially children's literature, a boon for those looking for alternatives to traditional tales of wicked witches and patriarchal gods. Essential for collections in women's studies, spirituality, and popular culture.—*M. R. Pukkila, Colby College*

WS-0139   Z7963x   Can. CIP
Finson, Shelley Davis, comp. **Women and religion: a bibliographic guide to Christian feminist liberation theology.** Toronto, 1991. 207p index afp ISBN 0-8020-5881-7, $70.00

Finson's bibliography offers a catalog of resources for faculty and students wishing to explore the issues of women in Christian churches or their contribution to church leadership. Its entries include books, articles, dissertations, reports, and other material published between 1975 and 1988. The topics range through the Bible, the history of the Christian church, Judaism, inclusive language, sexism, Mariology, the Christian ministry, pastoral care, spirituality, worship, and other related topics. The focus throughout is on Christian feminist resources. Since the arrangement is topical, an author index is provided. The material cited in this volume goes beyond what is contained in standard religion indexes. Recommended for libraries building collections in Christian theology or women's studies.— *E. Peterson, Montana State University*

WS-0140   BR117   94-30157 CIP
Kadel, Andrew. **Matrology: a bibliography of writings by Christian women from the first to the fifteenth centuries.** Continuum, 1995. 191p bibl indexes afp ISBN 0-8264-0676-9, $24.95

Kadel has produced an accessible and thorough basic bibliography of works by and about early women religious writers. One might quibble with the term "matrology" since very few of these authors commented on the Bible in the tradition of the patristic writers, and even fewer have been recognized as authoritative voices of the church; but the term should be understood to cover the writings of Christian women from the 1st to the 15th centuries, an impressive breadth of coverage. The work is arranged chronologically with brief descriptions of almost 250 women writers and lists of primary and some secondary works. English-language translations and studies are always included, because, as Kadel notes, his work is intended for "undergraduates and general readers as well as scholars in a number of different disciplines." Medievalists will find the work useful for ready reference and basic bibliography. Kadel may need to revise this bibliography on a regular basis as scholarship, translations, and editions continue to appear. One could not ask for a more conscientious bibliographer of this popular area of research. General; academic.—*V. R. Hotchkiss, Southern Methodist University*

WS-0141   BS491   91-44831 CIP
The Women's Bible commentary, ed. by Carol A. Newsom and Sharon H. Ringe. Westminster-J. Knox, 1992. 399p afp ISBN 0-664-21922-5, $19.95

In this volume, 41 outstanding women biblical scholars provide commentary from a feminist perspective for each book of the Old and New Testaments. Most chapters begin with a general introduction to the Biblical book and, as relevant, include such topics as major themes, authorship, date, literary form, or structure. However, rather than writing a complete commentary, the authors have spent the majority of each article addressing those issues and portions of scripture judged

to be of particular interest to women. With no index, this commentary will seldom be used for reference, but will give those studying the Bible, both women and men, an excellent introduction to critical feminist biblical interpretation. Recommended for public libraries and all college and university libraries.—*J. E. Sheets, Baylor University*

◆ Social & Behavioral Sciences

◆ Business, Economics

WS-0142   HD6223   93-38803 MARC
Ghorayshi, Parvin, comp. **Women and work in developing countries: an annotated bibliography.** Greenwood, 1994. 223p indexes afp ISBN 0-313-28834-8, $59.95

This is a welcome contribution to the growing literature on women in the Third World. The introduction covers general works, organizing them into such categories as "The Developing World and the Global Economy," "Theoretical Considerations," and "Gender and Work." The main body of the bibliography is organized by geographical region—Africa, Asia, Latin American and the Caribbean, and the Middle East—and subdivided into sections, e.g., "Social Construction of Gender" and "Women's Experience of Wage-Work." A final chapter lists audiovisual resources. The numbered entries, covering books, articles, reports, and dissertations, are two to three sentences long and contain cross-references by entry number. A preface draws the material together conceptually and outlines the overall organization of the bibliography. The work also contains an appendix of women's organizations and research centers and indexes by author, country and region, and subject. Well conceived and well written, this bibliography should prove useful to those interested in women's issues and international development. There is no current comparable resource. Recommended for upper-division undergraduate and graduate collections.—*G. M. Herrmann, SUNY College at Cortland*

WS-0143   HD6073   95-41230 CIP
Maman, Marie. **Women in agriculture: a guide to research,** by Marie Maman and Thelma H. Tate. Garland, 1996. 298p (Women's history and culture, 11) indexes afp ISBN 0-8153-1354-3, $46.00

Well organized and extensively annotated, Maman and Tate's research guide is unique and valuable in incorporating and synthesizing cross-cultural information concerning women and their roles in agricultural history, education, and economic development. Multidisciplinary in nature, information in this field is widely scattered, and publications, especially those derived from overseas conferences and symposia, are often difficult or impossible to acquire. Knowing this, one better appreciates the usefulness of this bibliography, which includes information reasonably accessible in US academic libraries or through interlibrary loan, and primarily in the English language. In addition, it is a welcome and practical source for use by teachers, researchers, and students in other disciplines ranging from women's studies to anthropology. Additional sections include citations to related and earlier bibliographies on women in agricultural sciences, an overview of relevant electronic resources and indexes, a section noting journals publishing frequently in this area, citations to dissertations and theses, and author and subject indexes. This comprehensive research guide is recommended for college and university libraries.—*M. A. Miasek, Corvallis-Benton County Public Library*

WS-0144   HD6095   93-23533 CIP
Schneider, Dorothy. **The ABC-CLIO companion to women in the workplace,** by Dorothy Schneider and Carl J. Schneider. ABC-Clio, 1993. 371p bibl index afp ISBN 0-87436-694-1, $55.00

A useful guide to the history of women and work in the US. Arranged alphabetically, entries treat issues, strikes, court cases, biographies, occupations, organizations, and events. They range in length from a brief definition of "sandwich generation" to a two-page entry on "protective legislation." Biographies average about 175 words. Entries include a *see also* section of cross-references and abbreviated bibliographic references. Complete citations are found in the lengthy bibliography at the end of the book. Well-written and well-organized, this guide also contains an introduction providing a historical overview, a chronology of events, and a subject index. As a glance at the approximately 50 black-and-white illustrations reveals, this work includes material on US minorities, such as Althea Gibson and Jesse De la Cruz. Entries cover historical material (e.g., "Triangle Shirtwaist Fire") and contemporary struggles (e.g., "Guerrilla Girls"). Although much of the information is available in other reference works, *Women in the Workplace* affords a handy guide to this important topic. Recommended for all levels.—*G. M. Herrmann, SUNY College at Cortland*

WS-0145   Orig

The women's business resource guide: a national directory of over 600 programs, resources and organizations to help women start or expand a business, by Barbara Littman and Michael Ray. Resource Group, P.O. Box 25505, Eugene, OR 97402, 1994. 131p index ISBN 1-884565-01-8 pbk, $21.95

Women currently own 30 percent of businesses and are opening new ones in significant number. This guide is designed to assist women in starting and expanding a business. Information about more than 600 organizations, programs, government agencies, publications, information sources, training workshops and seminars, and counseling services is organized into five chapters: "Training, Technical Assistance and Counseling"; "Information Sources"; "Selling to the Government"; "Membership Organizations"; and "Program and Resource Listings." The authors recommend skimming the first four chapters to identify areas of interest before seeking addresses in chapter 5. A "Quick Find Guide" directs readers to listings of such important resources as Small Business Administration regional offices, Office of Women's Business Ownership representatives, and state women's business advocates. The guide also includes a prefatory explanation of federal agencies. A complement to Claudia Jessup and Genie Chipps's *The Woman's Guide to Starting a Business* (3rd ed., 1991), which is more of a how-to manual for establishing businesses, this well-researched and clearly organized guide is a must for libraries supporting business programs and useful for all others.—*G. M. Herrmann, SUNY College at Cortland*

◆ Political Science, Law

WS-0146   K644   91-0731 CIP

DeCoste, F.C. **Feminist legal literature: a selective annotated bibliography,** comp. by F.C. DeCoste, K.M. Munro, and Lillian MacPherson. Garland, 1991. 499p (Garland reference library of social science, 671) indexes afp ISBN 0-8240-7117-4, $65.00

DeCoste's annotated bibliography is designed to provide access to pertinent English-language journal articles concerning women's issues upon which the law has an influence. Also included are articles written in French and published in French Canadian periodicals. The time frame is generally the decade of the 1980s (approximately January 1980 to November 30, 1990). The citations are arranged in the following 14 categories: abortion and reproduction, constitutional law, criminal law, family law, feminist theory, judges and courts, first nations and race, labor and employment, legal education, legal history, legal practice, lesbianism and sexual orientation, pornography, and prostitution. Each category constitutes a chapter. When it is appropriate to categorize an article in more than one chapter, the overlap is indicated by including the cite but not repeating the annotation. In addition to legal periodicals, other sources are included, namely social science journals, humanities journals and alternative press periodicals. Chapter 15 lists relevant bibliographies; Chapter 16 contains annotations of book reviews; symposia are noted in Chapter 17. Three indexes (author, topic, and journal) enhance the reference value of this compilation. It is recommended for academic libraries supporting women's studies programs.—*H. Q. Schroyer, Purdue University*

WS-0147   KFR4758   93-8805 CIP

Eisaguirre, Lynne. **Sexual harassment: a reference handbook.** ABC/Clio, 1993. 217p index afp ISBN 0-87436-723-9, $39.50

This entry in the "Contemporary World Issues" series provides easy access to quick information about sexual harassment. A limited chronology notes the most significant legislation, court decisions, trends, and political events. A brief biographical chapter lists important figures who have been involved in the debate about sexual harassment (e.g., Phyllis Schlafly, Catharine MacKinnon, Anita Hill). Following a listing of laws and legislation are a resource directory of organizations and a short bibliography of books, articles, and films basic to the field. M.D. McCaghy's *Sexual Harassment: A Guide to Resources* (CH, Jul'85) is a more comprehensive bibliography with substantive annotations, and much of the rest of the information in Eisaguirre's volume, such as biographies and laws, can be found in other sources. While *Sexual Harassment* is thus necessarily limited in scope, it will prove useful for undergraduates.—*E. Winter, California State University, Bakersfield*

WS-0148   JC599   92-56649 CIP

Hardy, Gayle J. **American women civil rights activists: biobibliographies of 68 leaders, 1825-1992.** McFarland, 1993. 479p index afp ISBN 0-89950-773-5, $45.00

Hardy's book will provide inspiration for many research projects, from high school term papers to doctoral dissertations. Each entry focuses on one individual and includes three major sections: a chronological biography; background information; and bibliographical information (e.g., books and shorter works by and about each person, primary source materials, biographical sketches, media materials [i.e., films, slides, sound recordings], and other works such as plays). Hardy skillfully pulls together information not otherwise available in one source, and her expertise as a reference librarian shapes the form of the book. The crisp and factual style maintains brevity without sacrificing depth. In comparison with *Women Champions of Human Rights; Eleven U.S. Leaders of the Twentieth Century*, by Moira Davison Reynolds (1991), Hardy's work treats more people, has more extensive bibliographies, and includes ten excellent appendixes. Unfortunately, there are no photographs. College students and faculty are most likely to use this book, but it has great value at the secondary level. Recommended for all academic and public libraries.—*M. Caterson, American University*

WS-0149   HQ1237   95-21267 CIP

Hartel, Lynda Jones. **Sexual harassment: a selected, annotated bibliography,** by Lynda Jones Hartel and Helena M. VonVille. Greenwood, 1995. 158p (Bibliographies and indexes in women's studies, 23) indexes afp ISBN 0-313-29055-5, $59.95

The pervasive and increasingly complex nature of sexual harassment has sparked public debate on a wide range of issues. Until fairly recently, sexual harassment was considered a private issue, but the explosive media coverage of the Packwood, Tailhook, and Shannon Faulkner controversies has brought this issue to the public's attention. Hartel and VonVille have compiled an exhaustive and well-organized bibliography, selecting works that have made a scholarly, original, or creative contribution to the literature. Purposefully omitted are editorial comments, generic works, or popular press publications (including Packwood, Tailhook, or Faulkner). The 534 entries are organized into four main parts and 18 chapters. Part 1 examines the history, theories, and consequences of sexual harassment, part 2 addresses the issue of various workplace settings, part 3 discusses sexual harassment in academic, social, and living environments, and part 4 explores the legal ramifications and negotiation process. A brief chronology of significant sexual harassment legislation and publication is appended, with thorough subject and author indexes following the appendix. Academic collections.—*A. E. Bonnette, University of Southwestern Louisiana*

WS-0150   HQ1410   92-38990 CIP

Huls, Mary Ellen. **United States government documents on women, 1800-1990: a comprehensive bibliography. v.1: Social issues; v.2: Labor.** Greenwood, 1993. 2v. 502, 481p (Bibliographies and indexes in women's studies, 17; 18) indexes afp ISBN 0-313-26712-X, v.1; ISBN 0-313-28157-2, v.2; $79.50 ea.

Yearly, US government agencies publish works about every possible subject, including women, who make up half the US population. Huls (College of St. Catherine Library), using US government sources and commercial indexes, especially those of the Congressional Information Service, lists in two volumes some 7,000 government publications on women, both those that are factual and those that present government policies and perceptions. Executive and congressional publications predominate; technical reports, ERIC studies, article reprints, and federal court cases are excluded. Volume 1 treats social issues in 21 chapters, volume 2 treats labor in 20; some publications on labor appear in volume 1 as well. Topics range from general issues to politics, education, health, and family. Chapters vary in length: while Women Offenders has 135 entries and Violence Against Women, 139, the chapter on women entrepreneurs is more than twice as long as that on clerical workers, and lists more recent publications. Each chapter begins with a brief historical essay defining the issue and highlighting significant publications. The entries themselves, in chronological order in each chapter, include a complete citation (including corporate or personal author, Superintendent of Documents number or Serial Set number) and a terse abstract. Each volume has indexes for personal authors (many are themselves women) and subjects and a list of abbreviations. Especially useful in libraries with large collections in government publications or women's studies, but valuable for any collection.—*E. F. Konerding, Wesleyan University*

WS-0151   KF9325   92-45133 CIP
Leonard, Arthur S. **Sexuality and the law: an encyclopedia of major legal cases.** Garland, 1993. 709p (American law and society, 3) index afp ISBN 0-8240-3421-X, $95.00

In assembling major legal cases concerning sexuality and the law in the US, Leonard describes more than 100 decisions handed down primarily between 1970 and Jan 1, 1992. Some earlier decisions on eugenic sterilization, sexual privacy, speech, and association are also included, where appropriate, in a range of subjects covering the law and sexuality as related to reproduction, sexual conduct, the family, free speech and free association, and discrimination (both civilian and military and in the federal government and educational institutions). Also treated are cases concerning immigration and naturalization and estates and trusts. Leonard, (New York Law School) intends the encyclopedia as an overview for the professional, but he discusses each case in its social context and in such clear English, that the work also provides a wealth of information for general readers. Each section contains a bibliography; case references are documented, and both a table of cases and a good subject index are included. Recommended for law libraries, social science and health science collections, and public libraries.—*N. L. Powell, Catholic University of America*

WS-0152   JF1525   93-36559 CIP
Mahoney, M.H. **Women in espionage: a biographical dictionary.** ABC-Clio, 1993. 253p bibl index afp ISBN 0-87436-743-3, $65.00

The role of women in espionage has long been a topic that fascinates novelists and spy buffs. Mahoney, a retired CIA officer, seeks with this biographical dictionary to help those looking for quick background information on notable female agents. The time frame is comprehensive (there are entries for the biblical figures Jezebel and Delilah) but the author emphasizes the 19th and 20th centuries. The organization is straightforward. The main body is an alphabetical listing by name, and there is a bibliography, a list of acronyms and abbreviations for the names of intelligence organizations, and a name-subject index. Each entry has its own list of sources, usually no more than four or five general or popular books. Entries vary in length according to the importance or notoriety of the subject. As one might expect, Mata Hari has the longest entry with four pages. Judith Coplon and Ethel Rosenberg, both celebrated as spies for the Soviet Union in the US, get three pages each. There are numerous *see* and *see also* references. This source is well organized and easy to use, but there are some defects: cross-references between spies and the governments for which they worked would have been helpful; several dates are inaccurate. A very general source with little new for intelligence scholars or specialists, but general readers will find it useful. Recommended for undergraduate and public libraries.—*W. F. Bell, University of North Texas*

WS-0153   DA591   92-38071 CIP
Mikdadi, Faysal. **Margaret Thatcher: a bibliography.** Greenwood, 1993. 269p (Bibliographies of British statesmen, 18) indexes afp ISBN 0-313-28288-9, $85.00

She would approve being classed with British states*men*, for central to Thatcher's career stands the belief that hard work and independence are the keys to success. No Old Boy network or affirmative action for her; she delighted in outclassing the Establishment at its own game. In her ten years as prime minister, Thatcher transformed the political and social face of Britain. Although a dizzying array of books and articles have analyzed her political philosophies, this is the first attempt to draw together the writings on Thatcher and Thatcherism. This series' first foray into the 20th century follows the pattern of earlier volumes, providing a lengthy and valuable introductory essay on Thatcher's personal and political life, a chronology, and writings by and about Thatcher arranged in 16 topical sections. Only nonfiction journal and newspaper articles, books, theses, and reviews are listed; manuscripts and Cabinet papers are excluded. Many entries have abstracts and some have cross-references. Works the compiler found most useful are starred, but not all those warrant an abstract. There are author and brief subject indexes. Although nearly all the sources listed can be found using indexes available in most large libraries, it is convenient to have them gathered in one volume. The arrangement is not always consistent: the general periodical section lists some articles separately by title and date, whereas other sections are alphabetical by main entry. Nevertheless, a helpful introduction for students of the "Iron Lady."—*E. Patterson, Emory University*

WS-0154   LC212   90-24364 CIP
Paludi, Michele A. **Academic and workplace sexual harassment: a resource manual,** by Michele A. Paludi and Richard B. Barickman. State University of New York, 1991. 215p index ISBN 0-7914-0829-9, $39.50; ISBN 0-7914-0830-2 pbk, $12.95

Aptly titled, this volume is a resource manual rather than a monograph. As such, it provides a variety of materials in a convenient single source: legal definitions, sample university and college sexual harrassment policy statements, a bibliography of research literature, classroom exercises, sample questionnaires, source directories for audiovisual material. It is thus likely to be useful to a variety of audiences concerned with sexual harassment on campus, from students and instructors to members of campus committees charged with developing guidelines or investigating complaints. Although it should be widely available in college and university libraries, this compendium would have benefited from some simple improvements: the layout and typography should have set off special "boxed" material more clearly from the text proper; the redundancies could easily have been eliminated, e.g., by establishing a common bibliography for all chapters; annotations on the content of the audiovisual materials and the most frequently cited research literature would have made them more accessible.—*M. M. Ferree, University of Connecticut*

WS-0155   JK721   93-19100 CIP
Ross, Lynn C. **Career advancement for women in the federal service: an annotated bibliography and resource book.** Garland, 1993. 251p (Public affairs and administration, 28) index afp ISBN 0-8153-1058-7, $40.00

Intended for a wide audience—human resource managers, researchers, career-seekers and employees concerned with career planning—this selective bibliography, which also furnishes background and theory, treats a broad range of issues important to women's participation in the federal bureaucracy. These include structural and organizational discrimination, family responsibility, inequitable pay, negative stereotyping, mentoring, and networking. The 479 numbered entries cite English-language books, articles in important popular and scholarly legal and management journals, government documents, reports, and congressional hearings, and are arranged in 11 chapters. The work provides descriptive, nonevaluative annotations, one to four sentences in length, and lists current sources 1986-91 with some older references, the latter to provide historical perspective or because of classic importance. Most chapters conclude with a list of other resources: pertinent laws and regulations, executive orders, administrative directives, organizations, and publications. Author index. A valuable addition to the literature, this well-written source, unique in scope and content, touches on high-profile material and will be of special interest to career, management, and women's studies collections.—*M. Rosenthal, Nassau Community College Library*

WS-0156 HN55 92-38161 CIP
Walls, David. **The activist's almanac: the concerned citizen's guide to the leading advocacy organizations in America.** Simon & Schuster, 1993. 431p index ISBN 0-671-74634-0 pbk, $18.00

A timely almanac that clearly fills a need by gathering a wealth of information on more than 100 advocacy organizations in the US. A search by subject in OCLC's WorldCat ("social action," "citizens associations," "social reformers," etc.) turned up a few out-of-date guides on activism, but not nearly so many as are found in this directory of multi-issue organizations (progressive or conservative) or those concerned with environment, peace and foreign policy, or human rights. To be included, organizations had to be "national in scope," have a "membership structure that promotes individual involvement," be open to the general public, be nonprofit, and be oriented "toward changing public policy." The almanac lists for each group: purpose, background, current priorities, structure, resources, and publications and services. There is also a section of bibliographic notes. From the background sections emerge the personalities that shape the organizations: Saul Alinsky as super organizer, Faye Wattleton as super advocate, Phyllis Schlafly as superwoman (who "wrote nine books while raising six children"). The author, responding to what he sees as a new wave of social activism like those of the 1930s and 1960s, provides accounts that explain new ways of "attacking political, social, economic, and ecological injustice." General and academic readers, all levels.—*R. E. South, University of Oregon*

WS-0157 HQ1236 91-32804 CIP
Who's who of women in world politics. Bowker-Saur, 1991. 311p index afp ISBN 0-86291-627-5, $95.00

This volume compiles biographical information on approximately 1,500 politically active women from more than 115 countries. Entries, listed alphabetically, focus on the main aspects of each woman's personal, professional, and political lives and include contact addresses. Information is current as of July 1991 (not recent enough to reflect the dissolution of the Soviet Union). Statistical tables on the number of female heads of state and the female share of cabinet and national legislative posts broken down by broad regions (Africa, Asia, and the Pacific) and by specific countries supplement the biographies. An index lists the name and political position of each entrant by country. A political directory that provides each country's government structure, similar to the one in *Who's Who in European Politics* (CH, Jun'91), would have been quite helpful. Together with *Women's Movements of the World: An International Directory and Reference*, ed. by Sally Shreir (1988), this source greatly enhances women's networking possibilities worldwide. Regularly updated editions are promised by the publisher. Recommended for most academic libraries, lower-division undergraduate and up, and particularly for women's studies collections.—*L. Krikos, Ohio State University*

WS-0158 JX1293.U6 89-48298 CIP
Women in International Security (Project). **Internships in foreign and defense policy: a complete guide for women (& men),** prep. by Women in International Security. Seven Locks, 1990. 103p afp ISBN 0-932020-75-5, $10.95

Women in International Security, a national, nonpartisan organization, seeks to promote the career prospects and professional development of women working in the traditionally male-dominated fields of international relations and foreign and defense policy. This first of several directories planned to advance this effort identifies internships that can provide invaluable opportunities to gain experience and informal career counseling, and to develop networks and credentials. This well-organized, informative directory names approximately 80 organizations "concerned with military or defense matters, foreign policy, and national policy and budget issues" that offer summer or academic-year internships. Arranged alphabetically by organization name, entries describe the organization and the representation of women, internships available with dates and duration, qualifications and application procedures, funding, and academic credit provided. Brief but informative prefatory chapters address the value of doing an internship and strategies to find the right one. The volume concludes with an annotated bibliography of other directories covering broader subject areas, as well as a sample resume and letters. Three indexes list organizations by name, issue orientation, and type. Recommended for all academic libraries; essential for those supporting international relations, peace studies, or women's studies.—*J. Ariel, University of California, Irvine*

◆ Psychology, Sociology

WS-0159 BF692 90-32466 CIP
Beere, Carole A. **Sex and gender issues: a handbook of tests and measures.** Greenwood, 1990. 604p indexes afp ISBN 0-313-27462-2, $85.00

Beere (psychology, Central Michigan Univ.) has written another useful reference book. This latest is actually a continuation of *Gender Roles: A Handbook of Tests and Measures* (CH, Jul'90). In her attempt to update her first book, *Women and Women's Issues: A Handbook of Tests and Measures* (CH, Apr'80), she identified too many measures for one volume. So she split the tests into two categories: gender issues and gender roles. Those dealing with issues are included in this current volume; 211 tests related to roles are identified in the previous volume, Gender Roles. The book under review identifies 197 tests on many different topics including sexuality, pregnancy and childbirth, contraception and abortion, and eating disorders. Many of the test entries contain the following information: title, author, variable measured, instrument type, description, sample items, administration, reliability, validity, and test availability. The tone of the entries is descriptive in nature rather than critical or evaluative. Beere has been extremely thorough in gathering information and has taken great care with accuracy. She has even attempted to view each instrument before including it in this book. Students and faculty will find Sex and Gender Issues worthwhile and easy to use. Highly recommended for four-year college and university libraries.—*K. Condic, Oakland University*

WS-0160 HQ767 91-15231 CIP
Costa, Marie. **Abortion: a reference handbook.** ABC-Clio, 1991. 258p index afp ISBN 0-87436-602-X, $39.50

Costa, a freelance writer and researcher, has contributed this volume to ABC-CLIO's "Contemporary World Issues" series. Following the general format of its series predecessors, the work is intended to be a basic, one-stop resource, and also to serve as a guide for further research. The first three chapters cover the historical context of abortion from Greek times through July of 1991 and supply biographical sketches of key figures in the current abortion debate and facts and statistics, including information on laws, mortality rates, abortion techniques, incidents of harassment of abortion providers, and public opinion polls. The last three chapters are brief, annotated lists of abortion-related organizations, print and nonprint resources. A glossary of abortion terminology and comprehensive index are included. Within its space limitations, a very useful and needed compendium for general readers and college students from first year through graduate level who are beginning work on abortion issues or who need quick references.—*E. Winter, California State University, Bakersfield*

WS-0161 HQ759 90-24981 CIP
Dixon, Penelope. **Mothers and mothering: an annotated feminist bibliography.** Garland, 1991. 219p (Women's history and culture, 3) index afp ISBN 0-8240-5949-2, $26.00

Dixon's annotated bibliography contains 351 listings of journal articles and books based on research studies written by professionals and published from 1970 through 1990. The majority of the materials were published in the US; however, some works of British authors are also included. Articles from popular magazines such as *Ms.* are not cited. The bibliography is divided into the following topical chapters: mothers and mothering, mothers and daughters, mothers and sons, single mothers, lesbian and black mothers, mothering in the family, children, feminism, psychoanalysis, and reproductive issues as they relate to mothering. Each chapter starts with general information about the topic, and is followed by a bibliography. Citations, with full bibliographic data except price, are arranged by author. The book is concluded with an author index. This publication is essential for college, university, and large public libraries that support students in professional programs in family and women's studies, sociology, and psychology.—*S. D. Gyeszly, Texas A&M University*

WS-0162 RC451 91-4562 CIP
Female psychology: an annotated psychoanalytic bibliography, ed. by Eleanor Schuker and Nadine A. Levinson. Analytic, 1991. 678p bibl indexes ISBN 0-88163-087-X, $59.95

This comprehensive annotated bibliography of the psychoanalytic literature on female psychology was edited by two academic psychoanalysts to fill a recognized need. Schuker (Columbia Univ.) and Levinson (Univ. of California, Irvine) cover more than 2,000 articles, essays, and books from the psychoanalytic literature and related disciplines. Both theoretical and clinical material is included, from Freud to the present. Selections are primarily from contemporary American literature, extending to 1991. The 28 chapters are organized into 5 sections: historical perspectives from the early psychoanalysts to contemporary views; developmental stages and issues from infancy to old age; adult female sexuality, character, and psychopathology; clinical issues related to patient-analyst relationships; and suggested reading lists for various academic levels. Each chapter has an introduction with an overview and insight into the controversial issues covered. Within each chapter, entries are listed chronologically rather than alphabetically. Annotations are primarily descriptive summaries relating the conclusion of each author to other works. Author and subject indexes are thorough. Although it emphasizes psychoanalytic research, this bibliography is recommended for both upper-division undergraduate and research libraries concerned with the psychology of women.—*E. Tonn, Vermont College of Norwich University*

WS-0163 BF175 92-6812 CIP
Feminism and psychoanalysis: a critical dictionary, ed. by Elizabeth Wright. B. Blackwell Reference, 1992. 485p index ISBN 0-631-17312-9, $59.95

Wright and her associates have attempted to combine psychotherapy and feminism in a dictionary format. The result is a critical appraisal of approximately 130 psychoanalytic terms, including themes, theorists, disciplines, and applications, in feminist thought. Sample entries include "Object-relations theory," "Nancy Julia Chodorow," "Science," and "Pornography." Items are not defined objectively but are "explored, historized [*sic*], and politicized." An attempt has been made to present opposing sides of controversial issues,—e.g., differing views of Freudian and Lacanian theories are represented. The editors solicited articles from scholars throughout the world in either feminist studies or psychoanalysis, but the dictionary is written mainly by feminists. As a critical dictionary, its format is exemplary. The subject index is thorough, and numerous bibliographic citations conclude each entry, but its content deserves caution. All entries are written with a feminist mindframe, a philosophical outlook that may offend some readers. Some prior knowledge of psychoanalysis is required to comprehend this work fully. A unique dictionary that will find a home only in feminist collections.—*K. Condic, Oakland University*

WS-0164 HQ767 91-12625 CIP
Fitzsimmons, Richard. **Pro-choice/pro-life: an annotated, selected bibliography (1972-1989),** comp. by Richard Fitzsimmons and Joan P. Diana. Greenwood, 1991. 251p index afp ISBN 0-313-27579-3, $45.00

This useful bibliographic guide is unique in covering both sides of the abortion controversy, drawing from monographic and periodical literature, minus newspaper articles. Very brief, objective annotations are provided. Entries are listed alphabetically by author or title. This would have been a far more valuable tool had it used a more detailed subject index; Library of Congress subject headings do not adequately describe the complexity of the abortion issue. Such topics as "post-abortion trauma" and "decision-making" are lost among the numerous numerical entries under "Abortion—Psychological Aspects," or other such general headings. The compilers would also have been more accurate to use the term "anti-abortion" instead of "pro-life" in light of the number of entries exhorting those who call themselves "pro-life" to be consistent and to take a stance against war, capital punishment, mercy killing, the bombing of abortion clinics and the like, exhortations that attest the anti-abortion focus of the movement. Eugenia Winter rejects both "pro-life" and "pro-choice" terminology in her more narrowly focused, but more academically oriented bibliography—*Psychological and Medical Aspects of Induced Abortion* (CH, Dec'88). Although it is especially good for public libraries since much coverage is devoted to popular periodicals, *Pro-Choice/Pro-Life* can also be used in all levels of academic libraries.—*G. M. Herrmann, SUNY College at Cortland*

WS-0165 HQ75 92-21941 CIP
Garber, Linda. **Lesbian sources: a bibliography of periodical articles, 1970-1990.** Garland, 1993. 680p (Garland gay and lesbian studies, 9) afp ISBN 0-8153-0782-9, $75.00

Intended as a starting place for research, this admirable bibliography lists articles by or about lesbians published in 64 lesbian and feminist journals. A concise preface explains the scope, methodology, and vocabulary choices. The liberally cross-referenced table of contents doubles as a subject index. More than 120 broad subjects include standard topics (e.g., sociology, economics, psychology) as well as more specifically lesbian topics (butch/femme, coming out, music festivals). Most subjects are further subdivided by personal name or geographic region. Complete citations, listed alphabetically by author within each category, repeat under all pertinent subjects. Lists of archives, special journal issues, and journal issues included complete the source. It includes most important journals and the range of topics, including racial, ethnic, and international coverage, is both useful and gratifying. There is no name index. Complements Clare Potter's *Lesbian Periodicals Index* (1986) and Delores Maggiore's *Lesbianism: An Annotated Bibliography and Guide to the Literature, 1976-1991* (1992; 1st ed., CH, Jul'88). Highly recommended for academic collections.—*L. Krikos, Ohio State University*

WS-0166 HQ1075 92-45080 CIP
International handbook on gender roles, ed. by Leonore Loeb Adler. Greenwood, 1993. 525p bibl index afp ISBN 0-313-28336-2, $95.00

Adler's handbook generally focuses on gender roles as perceived in 31 countries, primarily on the Asian, Latin American, and African continents. Arranged aphabetically by country, each chapter follows a standard organization: an introduction and overview section is followed by a brief exposition on male and female life cycles (including infancy, early childhood, youth, adolescence, adulthood, and old age), a summary and concluding section, and a list of references. The references are collected in a select bibliography at the end, together with a general author, subject, and title index. A brief biographical note is provided for each contributor. The scope of this work is commendable, but the sum is less than its parts. The criteria for selection are unclear and the level of research and writing varies widely from chapter to chapter. The general organization of chapters is intended to provide a useful cross-cultural review of developmental periods, but in practice this approach gives the user an uneven and often only cursory introduction to themes. Beginning students may find the bibliographies useful, since they provide a more multinational view of selected themes extensively and effectively covered in other works such as Susan Basow's *Gender: Stereotypes and Roles* (3rd ed., 1992). Advanced students will be better served conducting their own direct research in the extensive literature in psychology, anthropology, sociology, women's studies, and related areas.—*E. Patterson, Emory University*

WS-0167 HQ809 95-44080 CIP
McCue, Margi Laird. **Domestic violence: a reference handbook.** ABC-Clio, 1995. 273p index afp ISBN 0-87436-762-X, $39.50

Although violence against women and the desire to end it is not a new concern, the modern battered women's movement began in 1971 in England and quickly spread to the US by way of the feminist movement. This relatively inexpensive volume is a cornucopia of information on this "hot topic" and complements other books in the "Contemporary World Issues" series, although the emphasis here lies clearly on the US. The volume includes definitions of domestic violence, the types and causes of such abuse, a chronology showing the dilemma is not new and the path toward domestic tranquillity has not been straight, short biographical sketches of post-Revolutionary War persons involved in the struggle for and against equal gender rights, a lengthy section of facts, statistics and legal issues involved in domestic violence, an annotated list of national and state organizations, and a long list of books, articles, newsletters, professional publications, and nonprint resources. Information is factual and concise, but there are a few errors in dates; e.g., Susan B. Anthony is said to have attended the 1948 Women's Rights Convention. Community college, public, and college and university libraries will want this book because it provides a quick source of current, concise data; the bibliographies lead to more specific aspects of the subject.—*S. R. Johnson, Meridian Community College*

WS-0168   HQ185   94-331 CIP

Nash, Stanley D. **Prostitution in Great Britain, 1485-1901: an annotated bibliography.** Scarecrow, 1994. 226p index afp ISBN 0-8108-2734-4, $32.50

Nash has pulled together all important British secondary and primary source literature on the subject of prostitution from 1485 to 1901. Descriptive, evaluative annotations are arranged in three time periods—Tudor-Stuart Britain (1485-1700), 18th century, and 19th century—and subdivided by primary and secondary source formats. Extensive cross-references link individual works. The lengthy index accesses subjects, names, and titles of works included within entries; authors and title main entries are not indexed. Most works were personally examined by the author. The 28-page introduction discusses not only the evolution of the literature of prostitution but also the major events and key issues that have affected its history. Although only British sources are cited, most should be readily available in the US. This bibliography is very specialized, but reasonably priced and well executed. It should be included in comprehensive British history and women's studies collections. Upper-division undergraduates and above.—*K. F. Jones, California State University, Sacramento*

WS-0169   HQ111   92-5112 CIP

Prostitution: a guide to sources, 1960-1990, ed. by Vern L. Bullough and Lilli Sentz. Garland, 1992. 369p (Garland reference library of social science, 670) indexes afp ISBN 0-8240-7101-8, $56.00

A useful compilation of nearly 2,000 books and periodical articles, mostly in English, this work has problems in scope, indexing, and coverage. The subtitle implies the sources included will fall between 1960 and 1990, but many older reprints are included. The index of personal names is really an author index and should be identified as such. Persistent searchers can find Jane Addams, Josephine Butler, and others under the subject heading, "reformers and activists," but name entries would have been helpful. Some entries under "biographies and autobiographies" could be included under "biographies, individual" where they receive name identification; entry 314, a biography of Josephine Butler, is an example. Government documents are not included but should be. Important associations, such as the International Abolitionist Federation, the Josephine Butler Society, and the Third World Movement Against the Exploitation of Women are omitted from the short list of associations. Despite these flaws, this collection is unique since it pulls together the largest number of citations of any recent work on the subject.—*K. F. Jones, California State University, Sacramento*

WS-0170   HM19   90-43376 CIP

Women in sociology: a bio-bibliographical sourcebook, ed. by Mary Jo Deegan. Greenwood, 1991. 468p indexes afp ISBN 0-313-26085-0, $75.00

Feminist scholar Deegan (*Jane Addams and the Men of the Chicago School,* CH, Feb'89) has edited one of the first reference sources to document the contributions of women to the field of sociology. The 51 women included were all born before 1927 and represent all sociological eras from the 1840s to the present. Efforts were made to include women worldwide and to reflect ethnic, political, and ideological diversity. A lengthy introduction explains methodology, defines terms, lists criteria for inclusion, provides overviews of the eras, and briefly discusses epistemology. Arranged alphabetically, the entries, seven to ten pages each, contain succinct summaries of achievements, short biographies, explanations of major themes, sources for critiques of the subject's works, and selective bibliographies of the most important primary and secondary materials. Name and subject indexes are helpful but could have been more comprehensive. Similar in format and physical appearance to other Greenwood titles, Ethel Kersey's *Women Philosophers* (CH, Feb'90) and *Women in Psychology,* ed. by Agnes O'Connell and Nancy Russo (CH, Feb'91), this source fills a gap and is recommended for most academic libraries.—*L. Krikos, Ohio State University*

◆ Sports & Physical Education

WS-0171   Orig

Abromowitz, Jennifer. **Women outdoors: the best 1900 books, programs & periodicals.** Jennifer Abromowitz, RD 1 345C, Williamsburg, MA 01096, 1990. 179p index $28.00

Abromowitz, a former teacher of and about adventuresome women in the wilderness, suffered an "overload of pesticides and chemicals which damaged her immune system. . . , derailing her outdoor activities for the long term. . . ." Her bibliography, a 15-year labor of love, salutes such women and outdoor activity. The main selection of books is arranged by about 60 topics, a complete list of which constitutes the table of contents. Examples are canoeing, dogsledding, and foraging. A section of approximately 200 children's books offers a valuable "outdoor child" bibliography for educators, librarians, or parents. A bookstore and catalog resources section, a short but accurate periodicals listing, and information on outdoor programs especially for women (addresses, directors' names, brief annotations) complete this unique and necessary reference volume. Abromowitz acknowledges the certain existence of many other adventure writings "hidden in libraries, attics and. . .archives" or preserved only "in our genes, in spirit, and on the wind." Her book is a fine start in compiling a wealth of specific literature about women travelers, adventurers, and explorers. One caveat, however: the index requires a magnifying glass to read; the next printing/edition must make the print in the index larger. Both public and academic libraries at any level.—*N. S. Osborne, SUNY College at Oswego*

WS-0172   GV697   91-50946 CIP

Davis, Michael D. **Black American women in Olympic track and field: a complete illustrated reference.** McFarland, 1992. 170p index afp ISBN 0-89950-692-5, $24.95

Davis presents this book in attempt to pay tribute to the African American women who have participated in and contributed to the Olympic events of track and field. A section titled "Olympic Checklist" is a chronological list of female African American athletes who have competed in the Olympics, their events, placements, and time or distance. The main body of the book is the biographical profiles. The entries range in length from a minimum of the name, event or position, and year(s) of involvement to, at the maximum, a detailed profile. The randomness in variations of length presents an inconsistent picture of the women listed, thus failing to capture the qualities that set these women apart. The introduction glosses over some of the issues of African American women in track and field. There is no discussion of improvement, changes, or development for these women and track and field events, and this lack of historical context is disappointing. The appendix is more a commentary on the issue of sex testing in track and field. A list of related biographical works would have contributed to the value of this resource. There are few sources on this topic and none are complete in coverage. In this regard, Davis's book complements *Black Women in Sport,* by Tina S. Green et al. (1981) and James A. Page's *Black Olympian Medalists* (CH, Jul'91). General readership.—*M. C. Su, Pennsylvania State University, Altoona Campus*

WS-0173   GV1834   92-42635 CIP

LeCompte, Mary Lou. **Cowgirls of the rodeo: pioneer professional athletes.** Illinois, 1993. 252p index afp ISBN 0-252-02029-4, $22.50

This welcome source offers a fresh look at the history of women's professional rodeo. LeCompte relies on primary sources from archives of various institutions and organizations that collect in the history of the West and rodeo to document the history and heritage of this fascinating profession, 1896-1992. She combines biographical information about many of the important women who contributed to women's rodeo with the history of women's participation in this sport. Interspersed throughout is the author's commentary on coinciding and related developments in women's sport history as a contrast to rodeo. As interesting and informative as these digressions are, they detract at times from the rodeo focus. The book includes photographs, extensive footnotes, a very good index, appendixes of tables of women who participated in rodeo until 1955, and a bibliography of primary and secondary sources used in compilation. LeCompte succeeds in presenting the history of this professional women's sport in a very different perspective from that of Joyce G. Roach's *The Cowgirls* (1977; 2nd ed., 1990) and Teresa Jordon's *Cowgirls* (1982). This book is essential for libraries that collect in women's studies, the history of the West, or sports.—*M. C. Su, Pennsylvania State University, Altoona Campus*

WS-0174 GV709 90-20557 CIP
Remley, Mary L. **Women in sport: an annotated bibliography and resource guide, 1900-1990.** G.K. Hall, 1991. 210p indexes afp ISBN 0-8161-8977-3, $35.00

In this work Remley offers a chronological insight into monograph publications in the area of women in sport. The entries are grouped into four time frames: 1900-1930, 1931-1960, 1961-1975, and 1976-1990s. Each time frame is introduced with an essay commenting on the period. Because of the nature of this format, this volume is not simply an updated edition of Remley's *Women in Sport: A Guide to Resources* (1980). The number of references is expanded considerably and subjects such as body-building, football, and the Iditarod (Alaskan dogsled) race are now included. The majority of resources are American with a few exceptions from Canada and Britain. All entries for books cited have annotations which range from short to lengthy. Chapters within books are also cited as well as works with biographical information. Chapter 5 identifies other sources from which to obtain information: periodicals, national sports organizations,

and halls of fame. Author, title, and subject indexes are included. Recommended for all academic institutions, especially those with sport and or women's studies programs.—*M. C. Su, Pennsylvania State University, Altoona Campus*

WS-0175 GV697 92-199 CIP
Woolum, Janet. **Outstanding women athletes: who they are and how they influenced sports in America.** Oryx, 1992. 279p index afp ISBN 0-89774-713-5, $39.95

Besides listing awards and winners of various sporting events, Woolum in a timely resource on a topic of growing interest provides historical, biographical, and bibliographical information. The historical portion is an excellent overview that summarizes the development of participation by women in American sport. An Olympic section covers inclusion of women and comments on American women in the Olympics. A biographical chapter has essays with bibliographies on 60 individuals chosen by Wollum (including such non-Americans as Olga Korbut) who have influenced or contributed to the growing presence of American women in sport. A bibliographic chapter annotates a variety of books ranging from specific sports to general sources. R. J. Condon's *Great Women Athletes of the 20th Century* (CH, Mar'92) contains similar biographical information but is more popular in tone. Unfortunately, bibliographies by M. L. Remley (CH, Jun'91) and Michele Shoebridge (1987), both called *Women in Sport*, are omitted from this otherwise useful listing. Appendixes include lists of Olympic medalists, awards, and championships, and a list of athletes by sport. Good index. Recommended for all public and academic libraries.—*M. C. Su, Pennsylvania State University, Altoona Campus*

◆ HUMANITIES

WS-0176 PN56 93-46282 CIP
Adams, Alice E. **Reproducing the womb: images of childbirth in science, feminist theory, and literature.** Cornell, 1994. 267p bibl index afp ISBN 0-8014-2945-5, $34.95; ISBN 0-8014-8161-9 pbk, $14.95

Interdisciplinary scholars interested in the newly burgeoning area of gender and science will welcome the timely publication of this book. Adams trains post-structuralist methods of analysis on a wide variety of literary, medical, and psychoanalytic texts. The fictions of Ernest Hemingway, Aldous Huxley, Joanna Russ, Marge Piercy, and a host of other authors are juxtaposed to scientific articles on reproductive technology and with eye-opening effect to Lennart Nilsson's lush fetal photographs. Obstetric and literary writings that represent the mother as fragmentary environment to a seemingly autonomous fetus contrast vividly with writings from mothers' perspectives, including the author's own. Adams situates herself among other feminist theorists who both critique psychoanalysis and use it as an analytic frame. *Reproducing the Womb* covers some well-trod ground in its readings of Lacan, Kristeva, and Irigaray, but also brings fresh insights to them. In fact, the clarity with which Adams presents these theorists makes her book valuable to nonhumanists who find their style forbidding. Now that feminist scholars in humanities and sciences are increasingly joining together for faculty seminars and team-taught courses, this book provides a fine meeting ground. Upper-division undergraduate and up.—*L. W. Rabine, University of California, Irvine*

WS-0177 PN1995 94-25317 CIP
Bobo, Jacqueline. **Black women as cultural readers.** Columbia, 1995. 248p bibl index afp ISBN 0-231-08394-7, $49.50; ISBN 0-231-08395-5 pbk, $16.50

Bobo's work is a pathbreaking study of African American women's responses to literature and film. Making judicious use of theoretical approaches developed in John Fiske's *Understanding Popular Culture* (CH, Jul'90), Bobo (Univ. of North Carolina at Chapel Hill) focuses on a small group of middle-class African American women as they process contemporary literature (by Terry McMillan, Alice Walker) and film (the work of Julie Dash, *The Color Purple*) that addresses their own experiences. Although scholars recognize "call and response" as crucial to African American culture, this is the first convincing study of a contemporary black community's application of the process. Emphasizing the tradition of black women's culture as resistance, the author reveals how the interpretive community of her study is able to apply cultural texts to their own lives in a way that effectively edits out distorting elements introduced by the mass market. Bobo's readings of her core texts are solid, but her most important contribution lies in the fascinating and incisive interviews. This work should command the attention of all scholars of American popular culture. All academic collections.—*C. Werner, University of Wisconsin—Madison*

WS-0178 PS366 95-10288 CIP
De Grave, Kathleen. **Swindler, spy, rebel: the confidence woman in nineteenth-century America.** Missouri, 1995. 270p bibl index afp ISBN 0-8262-1005-8, $37.50

This is a treasure trove of information on actual and fictional 19th-century American women who were able to trick society as swindlers, soldiers, spies, and gold diggers. They used deception not simply to delude but to survive, as in the case of Ellen Craft, who successfully disguised herself as a white man to escape slavery. From the many accounts she examines—memoirs, novels, newspaper stories, biographies—De Grave (Pittsburg State Univ., Kansas) deduces that the 19th century was "an unusually fertile time for American women to manipulate their environment by deceit." She discusses conditions leading to these activities and explains why less attention has been paid to confidence women than to their male counterparts. In recounting the stories of these adventuresses, crooks, impersonators, subversive wives, and subversive writers, the author speaks with admiration—not of the women's criminal activities, but of their "assertive attitude toward life and strong confidence in their own skill." A rich bibliography of primary and secondary sources ranges from Belle Boyd's account of being a Confederate spy (*Belle Boyd, in Camp and Prison*, 1865) to Elaine Abelson's 1989

study of shoplifting in Victorian department stores (*When Ladies Go a-Thieving*, CH, Sep'90). All collections.—*J. S. Gabin, University of North Carolina at Chapel Hill*

WS-0179 NX180 93-50585 CIP
Feminist subjects, multi-media, ed. by Penny Florence and Dee Reynolds. Manchester, 1995.(Dist. by St. Martin's) 218p bibl index ISBN 0-7190-4179-1, $59.95; ISBN 0-7190-4180-5 pbk, $12.95

The contributors to this collection seek to traverse disciplines and to fuse critical approaches with creative and autobiographical ones. The book's multimedia scope accommodates writing about painting (Manet, Cassatt, Kahlo, Morisot), surrealist poetry, family photography, *Thelma and Louise, Carmen*, television natural history programs, and feminist approaches to war, reading, memory, and the body. The contributors, most of whom work in Britain, range from practicing artists to established academics working in a variety of media and disciplines. Especially noteworthy are Griselda Pollock's beautiful epistolary piece on Manet's *A Bar at the Folies-Berg*D`ere*—which opens the painting's historical context to the 19th-century women's movement while developing a provocative interpretation of the barmaid's ungloved hands—and Annette Kuhn's moving and adept analysis of family photographs of herself, which become a charged site of power struggle between mother and daughter. Though the quality of the pieces is uneven, the collection as a whole is engaging and would provide an effective introduction to cultural methodologies in women's studies for an upper-division undergraduate, a beginning graduate student, a feminist artist, or a general reader. A number of the selections make valuable contributions that would be of interest to advanced researchers as well.—*S. Duhig, Southern Illinois University at Carbondale*

WS-0180 DD256 95-10296 CIP
Gättens, Marie-Luise. **Women writers and fascism: reconstructing history.** University Press of Florida, 1995. 185p bibl index afp ISBN 0-8130-1401-8, $39.95

Gättens (Southern Methodist Univ.) discusses four principal texts: Christa Wolf's novel *Patterns of Childhood* (1980); Virginia Woolf's *Three Guineas* (1938), an analytical essay about what role the "daughters of educated men" can play in British society; Ruth Rehmann's autobiographical search for a pastor's life, *Der Mann auf der Kanzel* (1979); and Helga Schubert's *Judasfrauen* (1990), which retells ten "case histories" as stories of female denunciation in the Third Reich. The common theme of the four works is how repression of women contributed to the establishment of dictatorships and to the practice of war. Different reactions to "fascist" domination by men and the different compulsions under which these narratives are constructed define the book's critical focus. Proceeding with interpretive caution and substantiated by flexible recourse to primarily "feminist" theory (and its jargon), Gätten's study presents perceptive readings of "postmodern" inventions and interventions that reassemble gendered history. Her attention follows the argumentative momentum inherent in the texts more than their narrative structuring as works of the literary imagination. General readers; upper-division undergraduates; graduates.—*M. Winkler, Rice University*

WS-0181 E185 94-32738 CIP
Holloway, Karla F.C. **Codes of conduct: race, ethics, and the color of our character.** Rutgers, 1995. 225p index ISBN 0-8135-2155-6, $24.95

Holloway combines literary analysis, political commentary, and autobiographical meditations in a manner that makes a major contribution to the understanding of the cultural significance of race and gender. Drawing on her experience as a black woman teaching at a prestigious mainstream university, Holloway (Duke Univ.) addresses issues with public policy implications much more directly than she has done in the writing that established her reputation in African American literary studies (e.g., *The Character of the Word*, CH, Sep'87; *New Dimensions of Spirituality*, CH, Feb'88). Her central thesis is deceptively clear: the reality of racism in the US makes it impossible to separate ethical conduct from ethnic identity. *Codes of Conduct* makes its real contribution, however, in presenting case studies of African American women, language, and children. Holloway's chapter on how black women's bodies determine political dynamics contains an excellent comparison of the experiences of Anita Hill, Phyllis Wheatley, and Zora Neale Hurston. The one problem with this frequently lyrical book is Holloway's occasional lapses into an arcane academic vocabulary that adds little to her analysis and may alienate some potential readers. Nonetheless, this title adds an important voice to the ongoing discussions of the importance of race and gender in American cultural life. Upper-division undergraduates and above.— *C. Werner, University of Wisconsin—Madison*

WS-0182 PN2594 93-3664 CIP
Kaplan, Joel H. **Theatre and fashion: Oscar Wilde to the suffragettes,** by Joel H. Kaplan and Sheila Stowell. Cambridge, 1994. 220p bibl index ISBN 0-521-41510-1, $49.95

In this well-illustrated, entertaining, and scholarly study—"the first book to explore the complex relationship between theatre, fashion, and society in the late Victorian and early modern era"—Kaplan and Stowell focus on the intimate relationship between fashion and stage production in the works of many playwrights, including Oscar Wilde, Henry Arthur Jones, Arthur Pinero, and Bernard Shaw. The society drama of the time provided fashionable audiences with reflections of their own class and with a standard for appropriate public attire. Moreover, actresses were "living mannequins" for the fashionable dressmakers of the day. Modes of dress on stage also undermined the traditional condemnation of the "fallen woman" by dressing her in beautiful, elegant gowns—an ironic contrast, since her dress was expected to befit her fallen state. By the early 20th century, suffragette plays presented heroines who were "assured without being masculine, committed without being hysterical, well dressed without being seductive" as "models for feminist action." In their illuminating account, Kaplan and Stowell include much on theatrical history and personalities that should have a wide appeal. Highly recommended for all academic libraries. Upper-division undergraduate and up.—*K. Beckson, Brooklyn College, CUNY*

WS-0183 PR478 95-4350 CIP
Koritz, Amy. **Gendering bodies/performing art: dance and literature in early twentieth-century British culture.** Michigan, 1995. 218p bibl index afp ISBN 0-472-10616-3, $37.50

Approaching literature figures in the context of dance, Koritz (Tulane Univ.) reveals significant connections between literature and dance; she positions dance as central in shaping aesthetics and ideology in British culture between 1890 and the 1920s. She traces dance of the music hall, Maud Allan, Isadora Duncan, and Ballets Russes de Diaghilev (as experienced by Oscar Wilde, W.B. Yeats, George Bernard Shaw, T.S. Eliot, Edward Gordon Craig, and Arthur Symons) as catalysts in the development of aesthetic theory—a theory that in turn shaped critical evaluations of dance and exerted powerful influences on it. The author is knowledgeable about interdisciplinary content and methodology; her well-researched and stimulating discussion embraces dance history and gender and cultural studies. Her themes include the devaluation of the dancer, which occurred simultaneously with the increased acceptance of women on the British stage, and the separation of the work of art from the creative artist (which denied the dancer status as artist, and reserved that elite designation for composers, directors, and choreographers). This thematic ideology characterized aestheticism, symbolism, and modernism and affected dance artists at the time. The author argues that although the definition of dance as an elite art required the separation between dancer and creative artist (as exemplified by Ballets Russes de Diaghilev), it stymied the careers of early female modern dancers such as Maud Allan and Isadora Duncan. Upper-division undergraduate and above.—*C. T. Bond, Goucher College*

WS-0184 NX650 95-16143 MARC
Lewis, Reina. **Gendering Orientalism: race, femininity and representation.** Routledge, 1996. 267p bibl index ISBN 0-415-12489-1, $59.95; ISBN 0-415-12490-5 pbk, $18.95

Lewis examines how gender, Orientalism, and imperialism affected the production and responses to art in the late 1800s. Using the disciplines of art and literary criticism, the sociology of knowledge, and feminist analysis, Lewis contends that gender, ethnicity, social class, and political forces such as nationalism and "respectability" led to multiple contending perspectives. In two cases studies readers see how painter Henrietta Browne and writer George Eliot approached their works and how various audiences responded. Browne painted harem scenes less sexual and more personalized than her male counterparts, and Eliot's *Daniel Deronda* (a 19th-century "Guess Who's Coming to Dinner?") created a sympa-

thetic portrayal of an "acceptable" Jew. These artists violated some norms, but not others. The book's strengths include its visual art and examples of multiple influences. It has serious problems, however. Lewis makes unnecessary use of jargon, e.g., "positionalities," "deconstructing," and "discourses." She also needs to better link various disciplines and provide a fuller explanation of women's roles in colonialism. Graduate, faculty.—*S. D. Borchert, Lake Erie College*

WS-0185 P301 95-3298 CIP
Reclaiming rhetorica: women in the rhetorical tradition, ed. by Andrea A. Lunsford. Pittsburgh, 1995. 354p bibl index afp ISBN 0-8229-3872-3, $59.95; ISBN 0-8229-5553-9 pbk, $22.95

In the mid 1960s, Edward P.J. Corbett and others reidentified rhetoric as a discipline and as a tradition. Since then this reviewer has wished for this revisiting of the field in search of its excluded women. As James J. Murphy purports in his foreword, this text is but an enthymeme in the discourse to follow, not a beginning only but a solid foundation for future work. Women rhetoricians are identified as part of the rhetorical tradition in historical order: Aspasia, Diotima, Margery Kempe, Christine de Pisan, Mary Astell, Mary Wollstonecraft, Margaret Fuller, Ida B. Wells, Sojourner Truth, Laura (Riding) Jackson, Susanne K. Langer, Louise Rosenblatt, and Julia Kristeva. Lunsford (Ohio State Univ.) includes also a chapter on the formal study of rhetoric in women's colleges in the 19th century, particularly the Seven Sisters colleges, and a chapter on the history of rhetoric with respect to the suffrage movement at those same colleges. Demonstrating that in the centuries of women's silenced tongues there were always some women who raised their wise and eloquent voices, this text presents a lesson in history as well as in rhetorical theory and women's studies. The contributors write with scholarly passion and interdisciplinary expertise. Recommended for libraries that serve undergraduate and graduate students in many fields: education, English composition and literature, history, philosophy, and women's studies.—*T. B. Dykeman, Fairfield University*

WS-0186 AE5 92-9857 CIP
Thomas, Gillian. **A position to command respect: women and the eleventh *Britannica*.** Scarecrow, 1992. 212p bibl index afp ISBN 0-8108-2567-8, $25.00

Thomas's delightful little work presents an interesting insight into the cultural and historical climate that helped give rise to one of the most fascinating and enduring publications of its era, the famed 11th edition of the *Encyclopaedia Britannica*. Providing a captivating (if brief) publication history of the *Britannica*, this work focuses primarily on the efforts of its women contributors and how their work reflected the era that Virginia Woolf later identified as a historical moment "when human character changed." Short biographical entries are provided for all 35 contributors, some of them not widely covered in other general biographical or women's studies resources. Where appropriate, additional readings on the individuals are listed. The main section of this work addresses the struggles these women had in achieving not just an appointment to the *Britannica* staff but, in the words of one contributor, Francis Strong (later Lady Emilia Francis Dilke), a "position to command respect" in their own society. Through their stories, and in broader chapters which range from issues such as women's education, women in publishing and journalism, women's clubs and support groups, to women's real and ideal place in the family, this book is a marvelous encapsulation of a turning point in society and scholarship. Well-written and engaging from start to finish, this work would be a fine addition to already strong women's studies collections.—*E. Patterson, Emory University*

WS-0187 HM101 94-29007 CIP
Walters, Suzanna Danuta. **Material girls: making sense of feminist cultural theory.** California, 1995. 221p bibl index afp ISBN 0-520-08977-4, $40.00; ISBN 0-520-08978-2 pbk, $14.00

Walters has written an excellent monograph explaining and summarizing the scholarly literature in the field of feminist cultural studies, no mean task. Her accomplishment is even greater in that she writes in an accessible style that makes her ideas understandable to an audience larger than the academy. Indeed, she notes that a major problem of cultural, literary, and film criticism in the last two decades is that it has been laden with the jargon of semiotics and psychoanalysis. Walters offers a readable analysis of the liberal feminist literature on images of women in film as well as on the later scholarship, which has largely ignored this material and has explored the subject within a Marxist, Freudian, or Lacanian perspective. She also looks at communications research and then offers her own intertexual, contextual framework, which devotes a great deal of attention to spectators, the audience who absorbs, responds to, and integrates the visual, aural, and oral messages sent. Highly recommended for all levels.—*J. Sochen, Northeastern Illinois University*

WS-0188   Z232   91-41505 CIP
Willis, J.H.. **Leonard and Virginia Woolf as publishers: the Hogarth Press, 1917-41.** University Press of Virginia, 1992. 451p bibl index ISBN 0-8139-1361-6, $29.95

Drawing on a wide range of published sources as well as a cache of 32 rediscovered archival files, this very engaging history of the Hogarth Press covers the period from its inception in 1917 to Virginia Woolf's suicide in 1941. The Woolfs published a total of 474 titles during this period, among them works by Maynard Keynes, T.S. Eliot, Gertrude Stein, Christopher Isherwood, and Vita Sackville-West. Their most famous rejected manuscript was Joyce's *Ulysses*. As Freud's English publishers, they played a critical role in the dissemination of psychoanalytic thought, and as a vehicle for Leonard Woolf's political concerns, the Hogarth Press published a large number of works on imperialism, disarmament, pacifism, and feminism. Most significantly, the Press gave Virginia Woolf the creative freedom she needed in her own work (although she also had to waste many hours reading unsolicited manuscripts). This story of two intellectuals successfully (if idiosyncratically) managing as complicated a business as publishing is endlessly fascinating. The best parts, as always, are the quotations from Virginia Woolf's diaries and letters. Highly recommended for larger collections of English literary and intellectual history.—*S. Lehmann, University of Pennsylvania*

 Art

WS-0189   NB237   95-205689 MARC
Bernadac, Marie-Laure. **Louise Bourgeois.** Flammarion, 1996. (Dist. by Abbeville) 191p bibl filmography ISBN 2-08013-600-3, $35.00

Bourgeois's distinctive, organically abstract sculpture has received much attention in the era of postmodernism because of the themes of sexuality, the body, and autobiography that they address. Organized chronologically, this newest addition to the growing body of monographic texts on this venerable artist presents the development of her art decade by decade, with chapters organized into sections that focus on particular themes or series of works. What sets Bernadac's book apart from others is the degree to which the biography and psychic life of the artist guide the author's interpretive analyses, in terms of both content and style. Indeed, for Bernadac, a curator at the Musée National d'Art Moderne in Paris, each of Bourgeois's works is the resolution of personal trauma. The consistency of this approach, although conveying an interesting and meaningful aspect of this sculpture, does so, at times, at the cost of oversimplification. The exclusion of other interpretive possibilities and historical connections allows for only a particular understanding of the artist's work, and in this sense the usefulness of the book is limited. The book does, however, function as an interesting supplement to more broadly based texts on the artist. Undergraduate through faculty; general.—*S. L. Jenkins, University of Southern California*

WS-0190   N8354   95-47948 Orig
Inside the visible: an elliptical traverse of 20th century art in, of, and from the feminine, curated and ed. by M. Catherine de Zegher. MIT, 1996. 495p index ISBN 0-262-54081-9 pbk, $35.00

Culminating an ambitious cross-cultural project, this catalog marks the revamping of the exhibition *Inside the Visible* (subtitled *Begin the Beguine in Flanders*), initiated at the Béguinage of Saint-Elizabeth, Kortrijk (Flanders, Belgium) and organized by the Kanaal Art Foundation from April 16, 1994, to May 28, 1995. In fact it documents th exhibition with a full complement of 37 artists and more than 125 works as "further elaborated and organized by the Institute of Contemporary Art, Boston" shown from January 30 to May 1996, then downscaled for a venue at the National Museum of Women in the Arts in Washington, DC, from June 15 through Sept. 15, 1996, with another scheduling in Britain

to follow. De Zegher is an art historian and a cofounder of the Kanaal Art Foundation. Her goal was "to develop an exhibition concept that bypasses the artificiality of 'oppositional thinking' while acknowledging the work of deconstructionism, feminism, and poststructuralism, which has been instrumental in revealing the operations that tend to marginalize certain kinds of artistic production while centralizing others." Unfortunately, jargon hinders the reader from realizing this show's demanding significance. Works range from the 1930s to the 1990s; artists are most often European or Latin American, many of them little known in the US. (Short but helpful biographical sketches are given at the back of the volume.) With some exceptions, the pieces are generally abstract, minimalist, conceptual in nature, video and/or performance art, participatory, environmental, site-specific, and often multimedia. Arcane and almost technical in its definition of art; nevertheless, recommended for highly specialized collections on the 20th century and feminism. Graduate; faculty.—*M. Hamel-Schwulst, Towson State University*

WS-0191   ND548   94-42772 CIP
Perry, Gill. **Women artists and the Parisian avant-garde: modernism and 'feminine' art, 1900 to the late 1920s.** Manchester, 1996 (c1995). (Dist. by St. Martin's) 186p bibl index ISBN 0-7190-4164-3, $79.95; ISBN 0-7190-4165-1 pbk, $24.95

Perhaps the strongest criticism of this book should be for its brevity. Perry (art history, Open University) organizes the text around little-known Emilie Charmy, whose career coincides with Fauvism and Cubism. But the work of Charmy (and Maria Blanchard, Jacqueline Marval, Alice Halicka, Marevna) exists in a "fragile space" outside of what are now considered "major" art movements. The space was fragile, says Perry, because these artists did not fit into art critics' accepted interpretation of "feminine" art. The works of better-known artists Marie Laurencin and Suzanne Valadon are discussed in counterpoint: their non-threatening approach explains their inclusion in art historical survey texts. The role of Berthe Weill, an art dealer whose writings provide persuasive documentation of Perry's ideas, is examined for her promotion of now-marginalized artists and for her "navigation" of a masculine terrain. The text would be stronger if other artists were given as rich treatment as Charmy receives, although the arguments are convincing and ideas of feminist art historical predecessors (i.e., Griselda Pollack) are tempered with considerable reason. General; upper-division undergraduate; graduate; faculty.—*E. K. Menon, Mankato State University*

WS-0192   TR654   94-46914 CIP
Reframings: new American feminist photographies, ed. by Diane Neumaier. Temple University, 1996 (c1995). 319p afp ISBN 1-56639-331-0, $49.95

This is an ambitious, exceptional book in its scope, breadth, and inclusiveness. Edited by Diane Neumaier, with all women contributors, it is a collection of contemporary, photo-based artworks and critical essays that examines feminist perspectives on the politics of visual representation and its impact on women's lives. Neumaier does not shy away from the difficult questions that conflicting interpretations present. Instead she embraces a diversity of opinion and, at times, conflicting points of view to explore a wide range of American feminist issues and experiences. The threads that unite the book are the recurring themes—frequently visualized through self-representation—of gender, ethnicity, sexual orientation, class, and age. The book is divided into eight dense chapters that combine artworks and essays by known and unknown artists. Neumaier purposefully utilizes artworks by feminist women artists in an attempt to remedy a lack of exposure to their work, and she thus provides opportunities for a more developed feminist critique. Excellent color and black-and-white reproductions; brief notations about photographic images, artists, and critics. A welcome addition that richly intersects art, photography by women, and feminist theory. Most highly recommended. General; undergraduate through professional.—*J. Natal, Nazareth College of Rochester*

WS-0193   ND1329   95-16654 CIP
Sheriff, Mary D. **The exceptional woman: Elisabeth Vigée-Lebrun and the cultural politics of art.** Chicago, 1996. 353p bibl index afp ISBN 0-226-75275-5, $40.00

A court painter to Marie Antoinette, Vigée-Lebrun is a part of the feminist hidden heritage rediscovered in the 1970s. Although she has inspired exhibition catalogs and book chapters since, this is the only recent English-language book devoted to the artist. But it is not a traditional biography. Beginning with the notion of professional exceptionality—i.e., the idea that something elevated this artist to a status above her peers—Sheriff (art history, Univ. of North Carolina, Chapel Hill) reviews specific incidents, other art and literature of the period, and Vigée-Lebrun's portraits. The author uses a variety of analytical methods: feminist, psychoanalytical, literary, formalist, and even medical-anatomical. Although most previous publications on Vigée-Lebrun emphasize the French court, Sheriff also examines the artist's postrevolutionary relationships with Madame de Stael and Emma Hamilton. This book is best described as a series of essays about the publicly political nature of the Royal Academy and royal portraiture, and the more subtle political undercurrents of family and self-portraiture. Vigée-Lebrun is a recurring character, but the real focus is on the role of ordinary (and extraordinary) women in French society and within the artistic community. Extensive notes and bibliography. Recommended. Upper-division undergraduate; graduate; faculty.—*M. M. Doherty, University of South Florida*

◆ History, Theory & Criticism

WS-0194　　　93-87805　　　Orig
Bad girls. New Museum of Contemporary Art, New York/MIT, 1994. 144p bibl ISBN 0-262-70053-0 pbk, $19.95

This exhibition catalog, which includes trenchant essays by museum director Marcia Tucker and others, documents a current genre of artwork that functions outside of mainstream art practices in order ultimately to effect change in the status of women by disrupting stereotypes of conventional femininity in favor of alternative and multiple points of view. If, as Tucker suggests, artistic practice expresses a society's ordering of its power relationships, then the "bad girls" in this exhibition—who use videos, cartoons, music, comics, fiction, and also traditional artistic media—seem intent on undermining these relationships through a reliance on a variety of strategies, including parody, appropriation, use of the grotesque, and role reversal. Although both the artworks and the essays can be characterized as transgressive and funny, the essays also provide art historical and social precedents, as well as theoretical interpretations, for the objects in the exhibition. The inclusion of this stimulating publication, with its "bad girls" exhibition compendium and bibliography, is a must for any library with an interest in feminist or contemporary art. Lower-division undergraduate through graduate; faculty.—*S. L. Jenkins, University of Southern California*

WS-0195　　　ND237　　　92-46895 CIP
Bearor, Karen A. **Irene Rice Pereira: her paintings and philosophy.** Texas, 1993. 324p bibl index afp ISBN 0-292-73858-7, $34.95;

Bearor's fine book will appeal to a wide range of readers interested in American intellectual history of the first half of the 20th century. Pereira is a little-known woman painter whose interests can be related to the Abstract Expressionist movement of the 1940s. This is the first complete study of Pereira, and it contributes significantly to the rediscovery of female achievement characteristic of much recent scholarship. Although the author admirably reviews Pereira's options and limitations as an artist and a female, the book does not make its greatest contributions around the discussion of Pereira. It is a thorough analysis of the variety of issues that were so much a part of American intellectual foment between the wars. Thus, the book presents some of the first discussions of Spengler, Jung, Freud, Einstein, Dewey, et al., in the context of their impact on Pereira's general circle—that is, the politicized, intellectual, and/or creative urban American milieu. The author never convinces the reader that Pereira is a truly important artist, and does not seem to have intended to. This is a solid and exceptional "fabric" study, presenting an even weave of the context around artistic achievement in America and in the first half of the 20th century. Undergraduate; graduate; faculty; general.—*D. J. Johnson, Providence College*

WS-0196　　　N7638　　　94-31440 CIP
Bergman-Carton, Janis. **The woman of ideas in French art, 1830-1848.** Yale, 1995. 261p bibl index afp ISBN 0-300-05380-0, $30.00

The evaluation of images of women is the subject of this valuable but uneven book. The author examines images from popular culture and fine art to isolate and interpret what is dubbed the "woman of ideas"—an intellectual or politically "dangerous" female construct studied less frequently than prostitutes or fashion plates. A product of 18th-century literary salons and the influence of St. Simonist philosophy, this "woman" was first fully developed in Daumier's prints and then evolved in Salon paintings as representations of women reading (including Mary Magdalene) or under the guise of "the muse" or "the Sphinx". George Sand (a real "woman of ideas") was reinvented in the satirical press. Documentation supporting some of Bergman-Carton's themes remains tenuous; although original primary research has been conducted, the author heavily relies on secondary sources to examine crucial issues linked to both political history and the feminist movement. In general she provides a stimulating reading of artworks, although occasionally the interpretations move beyond what is provable or even reasonable. Nevertheless, this lucidly written book will provide scholars of the July Monarchy (and of women's studies in general) much to think about. Graduate; faculty.—*E. K. Menon, St. Olaf College*

WS-0197　　　ND237　　　95-30528 CIP
Bloemink, Barbara J. **The life and art of Florine Stettheimer.** Yale, 1995. 303p index afp ISBN 0-300-06340-7, $45.00

WS-0197a　　　Orig
Sussman, Elisabeth. **Florine Stettheimer: Manhattan fantastica,** by Elisabeth Sussman with Barbara J. Bloemink. Whitney Museum of American Art, New York, 1995. (Dist. by Abrams) 143p bibl afp ISBN 0-8109-6815-0 pbk, $39.95

Sophisticated yet naive, public but highly personal, developed in the center of the modern art world but removed from the mainstream, painter-poet-set designer Stettheimer approached each discipline on her own terms, creating worldly yet folksy apparitions in each medium of her work. Her unique family life, which she shared with her sisters Carrie and Ettie, is fully documented in her art, as is the social milieu in which the sisters thrived. In time, her circle included Duchamp, Stieglitz, O'Keeffe, Lachaise, Nadelman, and many others. Sussman, creator and author of an earlier exhibition at the Institute of Contemporary Art, Boston (1980), serves as guest co-curator, with Barbara Bloemink, for the Whitney Museum exhibition, *Manhattan Fantastica*. Bloemink provides an essay for the Whitney catalog, as does noted art historian Linda Nochlin. The catalog is superbly documented with numerous illustrations and photographs of the artist and her world, chronology, bibliography, and notes. Bloemink's own book does not duplicate but supplements the exhibition catalog by providing a continuous narrative of the artist's career. It contains photos of the artist's living spaces; friends; her more obscure paintings; reproductions of her painted screens; costumes and sets; and excerpts from her published collection of poems, *Crystal Flowers* (1949). Bloemink's monograph presents Stettheimer not as a lyrical or eccentric artist but rather a satiric chronicler of the cultural scenes of her day, a perceptive conscience of the modernist era. Graduate; faculty; general.—*L. Doumato, National Gallery of Art*

WS-0198　　　NB237　　　93-28375 CIP
Bourgeois, Louise. **Louise Bourgeois: the locus of memory, works, 1982-1993,** by Charlotta Kotik, Terrie Sultan, and Christian Leigh. Brooklyn Museum/Abrams, 1994. 144p bibl index ISBN 0-8109-3127-3, $45.00

This catalog of an expanded version of Bourgeois's 1993 Venice Biennale exhibition focuses on the artist's production of the last decade as the culmination of a stylistically independent creative pursuit of more than 40 years. Although general information is provided regarding background, training, and use of various methods and materials, each of the essays also provides both didactic and interpretive information about specific sculptures and installations, with great attention paid to recurrent themes of anxiety, alienation, fear, pain, identity, sex, and death. Bourgeois's deeply autobiographical content, use of organic forms, allusions to the human body, subversive impulse, and exploration of the marginal are seen as foreshadowing the premises of feminist art in the early 1970s. Her work is also discussed in terms of its relation to contemporary issues regarding gender, sexuality, and the right to individuality; she is considered a significant influence on many of today's important artists, particularly those who deal with the human body from a psychological point of view. For these reasons, this

book would be an important inclusion in any library that serves students of art.—
S. L. Jenkins, University of Southern California

WS-0199   N6853   94-30122 CIP
Callen, Anthea. **The spectacular body: science, method and meaning in the work of Degas.** Yale, 1995. 244p bibl index ISBN 0-300-05443-2, $50.00

In a generally contentious tone, Callen explores the life conditions and status of women in the late 19th century, using contemporary art—especially that of Degas—for a measure and mirror. But despite the book's wealth of information—socioeconomic, political, legal—the role of art seems contrived and incomprehensibly reversed. The historical facts are important in another context, but the very questionable cause-and-effect linkage with art here presented may easily damage the ideals and aims it is intended to serve. If anything, the artists of the time most often sought out the individuality, spirit, charm, grace, and dignity natural to women then and now. Notwithstanding a somewhat acerbic social demeanor, Degas was inherently generous, a positive influence for *all* artists of his time, and a major force in the revolutionary freedoms born of Impressionism. Degas's inspired blend of subtle, rich color and shadow, of supple line and form is his splendid defense. To see it as destructive in intent, narrow, or biased is incompatible with aesthetic reality and the judgment of generations. Awkward reasoning pervades this book—e.g., the severely critical evaluation of Degas's elegant and gracefully personable studies of Mary Cassatt. Yet the book has attractions. The artist's extraordinary virtuosity is beautifully represented. Art libraries with already existing full collections of Impressionist (and, particularly, of Degas's) work may consider this book an interesting variant for research purposes and controversial opinions. Notes; selected bibliography. Faculty.—*C. Pascoe, College of Mount Saint Vincent*

WS-0200   GT2073   Orig
Carter, Alison. **Underwear, the fashion history.** Drama Book, 1992. 161p index ISBN 0-89676-120-7, $29.95

Thoroughly modern Carter traces the development of the undergarment industry as she melds fashion, social, and industrial history, focusing primarily on women's undergarment fashions from 1490 to 1990. Her chronicle is straightforward with only a soupçon of the inevitable erotic and male fetish overtones. She highlights trends in fashionable silhouettes as undergarments moved in lock step with outer garments, providing their structure. Cycles of concealing and revealing show that the current revival of innerwear as outerwear is not so new as it may seem at first blush. Carter classifies undergarments as second skin, fulfilling functions of modesty, warmth, and hygiene; and as second skeleton, architectural contraptions, distorting natural contours by constricting or enlarging. She traces 360-degree sea changes from the obligatory fig leaf to early body coverings through tight lacing, returning to nonrestrictive, minimalist yet highly inventive lingerie of the 20th century. Indentifying manufacturers and designers she describes garments (and their mutations) ranging from chemises, camisoles, petticoats, and knickers to stays, S-bend corsets, hoops, bustles, and both men's and women's padded garments. Surviving garments and 107 illustrations (32 in color) from paintings, catalogs, advertisements, cartoons, and photographs authentically document her study. She includes details of fabrics, cut, construction, colors, ornamentation, health concerns, dress reform movements, and technological innovations. Also included are a glossary, bibliography, and list of companies and trade names. Recommended for academic costume and fashion history collections.—*M. F. Morris, East Carolina University*

WS-0201   89-50634 Orig
Chadwick, Whitney. **Women, art, and society.** Thames & Hudson, 1990. 384p bibl index ISBN 0-500-18194-2, $24.95; ISBN 0-500-20241-9, $14.95

For approximately two decades, feminists have been attempting to create and maintain a place for women artists in mainstream art historical literature; Whitney Chadwick succeeds in this endeavor through a modified approach. She integrates women's roles in society with art history because, philosophically, there is no progressive history of women artists. As Chadwick unequivocally states, "the historical and critical evaluation of women's art has proved to be inseparable from ideologies which define her sic place in Western culture generally." The

volume uses as an outline the standard art historical time periods as chapters; these are documented through the works of women painters, sculptors, architects, decorative artists, and performance artists, and with works depicting significant individual females. Since it seeks to summarize the existing literature presented from a cultural standpoint, this book emerges as an ideal source for students and scholars alike. Numerous illustrations and an extensive bibliography supplement the text.—*L. Doumato, National Gallery of Art*

WS-0202   N6847   90-25889 CIP
Clayson, Hollis. **Painted love: prostitution in French art of the Impressionist era.** Yale, 1992. 202p bibl index afp ISBN 0-300-04730-4, $45.00

Clayson deals with an important and fascinating topic—the image of the prostitute in late 19th-century French painting. Societal conditions produced by the industrial revolution forced many poor working-class women of the 19th-century to turn to prostitution for their economic survival. This rise in prostitution was frequently interpreted as a threat to the moral structure of the bourgeois family and thus became a political issue. The author, a student of T.J. Clark (*The Painting of Modern Life: Paris in the Art of Manet and his Followers*, CH, Jun'85), delves further into some of the topics so tantalizingly presented by her mentor. While focusing on such major figures as Degas and Renoir, she discusses their paintings in the context of works by lesser-known artists such as Eva Gonzales and Henri Gervex. Her examination of these artists is built on a feminist-Marxist foundation and is polemic in tone. The text is amply illustrated with 93 illustrations, most in black and white, which are well chosen and present some interesting and little-known works by well-known artists including Manet and Cezanne, as well as works by artists popular in the 19th century but unfamiliar today. There is a useful bibliography and helpful index. Both undergraduate and graduate students in the humanities could benefit from this book.—*E. Kosmer, Worcester State College*

WS-0203   Orig
Curtis, Penelope. **Barbara Hepworth: a retrospective,** by Penelope Curtis and Alan G. Wilkinson. Tate Gallery, 1995 (c1994). (Dist. by Washington) 168p bibl ISBN 1-85437-141-X pbk, $40.00

The four essays in this retrospective catalog offer a straightforward, chronological account of Hepworth's stylistic development from earlier figurative work, inspired by an interest in non-Western art and a truth-to-materials attitude, through geometric and organic abstraction, to the abstracted figural and multipart sculptures that became her stylistic hallmark. Much of the discussion addresses Hepworth's achievements in relation to the work of her husband, modernist painter Ben Nicholson, and Henry Moore, one of the foremost British sculptors. Indeed, the final chapter of the catalog is an interesting comparison of the critical reception and government support received by both Hepworth and Moore, who were once art school colleagues. Together, the essays are a clear attempt to rectify a seeming lack of recognition of the artist's accomplishments. To this end, the catalog also includes a chronology of public commissions, a rather extensive biography, and a reading list. Though perhaps not the definitive publication on this much-honored but relatively lesser known artist, this is among the more recent books on Hepworth that should become part of a basic collection of 20th-century art literature.—*S. L. Jenkins, University of Southern California*

WS-0204   ND249x   Can. CIP
Davis, Ann. **Somewhere waiting: the life and art of Christiane Pflug.** Oxford, 1991. 303p index ISBN 0-19-540857-8, $39.95

As curator of a one-woman exhibition of the work of Christiane Pflug, Ann Davis chose to write the first biography of this woman artist through the extensive use of primary materials: unpublished manuscripts and letters; interviews with the artist's mother, husband, and children; and most importantly, through the works of art themselves. Pflug, painting in a realist style, documents the banal scenes and fixtures of her daily existence as mother and housewife in suburban Toronto; the paintings include such titles as "Over the Kitchen Sink," "Cottingham School in Winter," and "McDermott's Truck." Pflug's life was a most unhappy one; she escaped Nazi Germany to Paris, left Paris for Morocco, and finally came to Toronto, where the adjustment to North America (and the constricting duties as wife, mother, and daughter) plunged her into a deep depression that ultimately led to her suicide. Davis's straightforward text, the color and black-and-white illustrations, and useful notes make this an important biography on an artist whose brief career made a significant contribution to the history of Canadian painting. Recommended for all readers, from the most scholarly to the novice.—*L. Doumato, National Gallery of Art*

WS-0205   ND553   91-30544 CIP
Dealing with Degas: representations of women and the politics of vision, ed. by Richard Kendall and Griselda Pollock. Universe, 1992. 224p index ISBN 0-87663-628-8 pbk, $16.95

Since the 1870s, Degas and his art have been popular subjects for journalists, scholars, and critics. Several recent publications show Degas as a rich territory for specialized studies and alternative interpretations. Beginning with Eunice Lipton's *Looking Into Degas: Uneasy Images of Women and Modern Life* (CH, May'87) Degas's life, times, and art have been subjected to even greater sociocultural exploration. *Dealing with Degas* is an overtly feminist investigation of class and gender politics relative to the interpretation of Degas. The text features nine papers from a 1988 Tate Gallery symposium plus three essays added to expand the scope of the investigation. Editors Kendall, who curated a companion exhibition, "Degas: Images and Women," and Pollock, a noted feminist art historian, contribute excellent introductory essays that place the volume in clear context. The remaining 7 contributors, all accomplished authors, provide well-conceived and intelligent essays offering new perspectives on Degas's respresentation of women. Taken as a whole, this is a well-written book that achieves a meaningful encounter between feminism and art history. There are 8 color plates of fair quality, 51 useful black-and-white illustrations, and excellent notes of use to scholars. This book must be viewed within the context of more standard literature on the artist such as *Degas* by Jean Sutherland Boggs, et al. (CH, Feb'89) and Carol Armstrong's *Odd Man Out: Readings of the Work and Reputation of Edgar Degas* (1991). Should be acquired by libraries with an interest in modern art and is a must for institutions committed to women's studies.—*J. A. Day, University of South Dakota*

WS-0206   NE2043.25   89-70715 CIP
Etched in memory: the building and survival of artistic reputation, by Gladys Engel Lang and Kurt Lang. North Carolina, 1990. 437p bibl index afp ISBN 0-8078-1908-5, $45.00

The Langs (sociology, University of Washington) apply social science methods to a sample of 286 American and British etcher/printmakers active from 1880 to 1940. Scholarly monographs on etchers are a rarity, and this one also serves as a model for sociological art history, a history of popular taste, and a contribution to the literature of women artists (half the sample.) The authors set the stage by tracing the popularity of etching from 16th-century Holland through its "revival" in 20th-century America and Britain. Narrowing the focus, they seek out factors (social, economic, gender-related, educational) that influenced the etchers' career paths. These comparisons lead the Langs to downplay aesthetic considerations and to conclude that the survival of an artist's reputation hings on the ability to produce a sizeable and accessible oeuvre, to keep extensive records, and to associate with famous artists. This controversial but well-written work belongs in university, college, and large public library collections. Recommended.—*M. M. Doherty, University of South Florida*

WS-0207   ND1040   90-11001 CIP
Flowering in the shadows: women in the history of Chinese and Japanese painting, ed. by Marsha Weidner. Hawaii, 1991 (c1990). 315p index afp ISBN 0-8248-1149-6, $35.00

In the introduction editor Weidner is especially perceptive in disentangling many of the misconceptions of women that Westerners have persisted in taking in regard to the East Asian role of women. The ten essays in this volume make it abundantly clear that while the Confucianist and Buddhist religious traditions common both to China and Japan discourage the positive role of women as artists, patrons, and collectors, some considerable obscurity is due to the fact that the Western artistic tradition itself has given women a subordinate role. Two of the essays are extremely welcome translations of accounts of women of the Japanese Heian period and the Chinese Mongol or Yuan period, and are quite moving. Two of the essays extensively discuss the didactic Confucianist literature such as the *Ladies*

Classic of Filial Piety and the Buddhist handscrolls titled *Tales of Gishōand Gangyō*to articulate the complex social position of women. Two further essays by Patricia Fister on the cultural background and training of Japanese women artists are excellent. The extensive notes that follow all the essays are as fascinating as the individual portraits they describe. This volume represents both careful and extremely readable scholarship, which would make it first-priority acquisition for any collection of East Asian materials.—*R. W. Hostetler, Heidelberg College*

WS-0208   ND1452   92-23436 CIP
Franits, Wayne E. **Paragons of virtue: women and domesticity in seventeenth-century Dutch art.** Cambridge, 1993. 271p bibl index ISBN 0-521-43129-8, $60.00

Jacob Cats's most popular manual of domestic behavior, *Houwelijck* (1625), provides the organization for this well-considered, lucid monographic study of the depiction of states of a woman's life. By prescribing proper accomplishments for a woman's roles from cradle to grave, Cats presents a positive model for a woman in Dutch culture; this nurturing and spiritually sustaining model proclaims, maintains, and reinforces the patriarchal nature of that society. The author correlates Cats's book with Dutch imagery, and deepens the meaning and influence of that text by surveying other 17th-century publications, especially emblem books. He takes a temperate course through the thicket of symbolic and allegorical interpretation. The extent to which Cats's prescriptions were followed is hard to measure; similarly elusive is an estimate of the mix of ideal and real behavior presented in *Houwelijck* and Dutch imagery. This study belongs to the purviews of several major disciplines: art history; the field of word/image relations; women's studies; and the history of the family. Highly recommended for academic and public libraries. Advanced undergraduate; graduate; faculty; general.—*A. Golahny, Lycoming College*

WS-0209   N72   93-43147 CIP
Garb, Tamar. **Sisters of the brush: women's artistic culture in late nineteenth-century Paris.** Yale, 1994. 207p bibl index ISBN 0-300-05903-5, $45.00

In this updated dissertation, Garb (University College, London) concerns herself with French social attitudes and artistic politics rather than art works. She chronicles and expands on the major milestones: the founding of the Union of Women Painters and Sculptors, the creation of a Salon des Femmes, and the admission of women to the Ecole des Beaux Arts. Well-known painters (e.g., Cassatt, Morisot) here rate only a mention. Instead, Garb focuses on the most eloquent and politically active "sisters," Virginie Demont-Breton and Mme Leon Bertaux, using their words, paintings, and sculptures to recreate their world. On a more philosophical level, Garb looks at how 19th-century Parisians of both genders fretted over the question of a distinctly feminine art. In forums ranging from scholarly publications to cartoons, they debated quality, "appropriate" subject matter, and the potential for a reversal of sex roles. Superbly documented and well written, this book will be immensely valuable to both undergraduates and faculty. It examines in depth what has before been given only chapter-length treatment. Highly recommended.—*M. M. Doherty, University of South Florida*

WS-0210   ND3380.4.R65   90-34551 CIP
Hamburger, Jeffrey F. **The Rothschild Canticles: art and mysticism in Flanders and the Rhineland circa 1300.** Yale, 1991 (c1990). 336p (Yale publications in the history of art) bibl indexes afp ISBN 0-300-04308-2, $50.00

The Rothschild Canticles is a fascinating compendium of mystical images interspersed with short meditations drawn from liturgical, biblical, and theological sources—an instrument, as the author illustrates, for initiating the reader into "transcendent mysteries". Made c. 1300 in French Flanders or the Rhineland for an encloistered nun (most likely connected with Dominican circles), the manuscript proves an ideal vehicle for exploring the role of images in female spirituality and the interrelationship of art and text in late medieval mysticism. The study proceeds thematically, grouping miniatures of related theme together and progressing as does mystical contemplation from imitation of and identification with the Bride of the Song of Songs and the Virgin Mary to mystical union with God and the ultimate goal of mysticism, the vision of God himself, expressed in the Trinitarian images. Copiously illustrated with 225 black-and-white and 12 color plates, the volume also includes physical analysis of the manuscript and an edition of the text in appendixes. This is an interdisciplinary synthesis of art history and literature on spirituality and mysticism that demonstrates an impressive command of both subjects, presenting its recondite subject in clearly comprehensible and gracefully written prose. Will be of major importance to scholars in many fields.—*J. Oliver, Colgate University*

WS-0211　　　　NB163　　　　94-39539 CIP
Havelock, Christine Mitchell. **The Aphrodite of Knidos and her successors: a historical review of the female nude in Greek art.** Michigan, 1995. 158p; 39 plates bibl index afp ISBN 0-472-10585-X, $47.50

Havelock is to be tributed, as a much respected female professor emeritus of classical studies at Vassar, for disrobing Praxiteles' Aphrodite of Knidos of her 19-century guilty ambience. During an astute survey of current and old, German and English scholarship, Havelock dismisses the issues of what the original could have been like, and who the model might have been. The result is a great boost for femininity: if, for Greeks, beautiful nudity is a sincere representation of the godliness of male sexuality, the same is said by this lovely female nude and her successors. Current adulation of the semiotic Venus of Willendorf sounds humorous in contrast to this frank acceptance of the many picturesque spin-offs of the fourth-century religious piece. Even seeing the more direct appeal to the prurient of later Greco-Roman variations of the goddess, Havelock focuses on the still-intended sacredness. She believes that this reverent attitude, fostered by Praxiteles' ground-breaking monumental nude holy image, brought—to later courtesans and wives alike—self-respect and financial independence. All students of the classical and womanhood in general will enjoy this book—if they can take a little titillation. General; undergraduate through professional.—*E. L. Anderson, Lansing Community College*

WS-0212　　　　N6797　　　　95-47541 CIP
Helland, Janice. **The studios of Frances and Margaret Macdonald.** Manchester, 1996. (Dist. by St. Martin's) 207p index ISBN 0-7190-4783-8, $79.95

Admirers of the great Art Nouveau architect and designer Charles Rennie Mackintosh probably know of the art of two women who also made their mark in turn-of-the-century Glasgow, his sister-in-law Frances Macdonald and his wife Margaret Macdonald. Both worked in design, watercolor, and areas that united the fine arts with craft. Their efforts contributed to that explosion of creativity that marked Scotland as an artistic center of consequence, a fact recognized by their celebrated participation at the famous Vienna Secession of 1900. Much has already been written about the influence, especially Margaret's, on Mackintosh (see Timothy Neat, *Part Seen, Part Imagined*, Edinburgh, 1994). Helland (Concordia Univ.) avoids extravagant claims to concentrate on a judicious evaluation of the work of these two talented women. Although a professional art historian, Helland is also interested in the role played by class, gender, marriage, and collaboration in the art profession. Originally a doctoral dissertation, Helland's thoroughly researched book is agreeably free of jargon and pedantry; thus it is a good choice for general readers as well as for art and social historians and women's studies students. One wishes that the 62 good black-and-white illustrations had been supplemented by color plates. Undergraduate; graduate; faculty; general.—*W. S. Rodner, Tidewater Community College*

WS-0213　　　　N8354　　　　87-904 CIP
Heller, Nancy G. **Women artists: an illustrated history.** Rev. ed. Abbeville, 1991. 255p bibl index ISBN 1-55859-211-3 pbk, $29.95

On its initial publication *Women Artists* in 1987 (CH, Jan'88) was lauded as a readable narrative for scholar and novice alike, as a usable text for classes in art history and women's studies departments, and as a major source for color reproductions of paintings and sculpture by women. This new revised edition contains a seventh chapter, entitled, "New Currents," that documents the significant achievements of women artists from 1980 to the present. Organized in a similar manner to the earlier chapters, this contemporary study presents the works of painters, sculptors, and performance artists and provides extensive notes and bibliographic citations as well as color reproductions of works and portraits of the artists. *Women Artists* remains the most informative text in the field.—*L. Doumato, National Gallery of Art*

WS-0214　　　　ND212　　　　90-53708 CIP
Henkes, Robert. **American women painters of the 1930s and 1940s: the lives and work of ten artists.** McFarland, 1991. 236p index afp ISBN 0-89950-474-4, $29.95

The period of the 1930s and '40s were at best difficult times for all Americans, and most especially for women. Although the ten artists discussed in this volume lived through the Depression and WW II, their art reflects none of the tragedy or hardships endured. Henkes acknowledges that the selection of artists was based on personal favoritism and on the fact that all were great in their time but are now largely forgotten. MacIver, probably the most distinguished, shares with the other nine artists highly specialized subject matter presented in a witty and humorous way. The book is written as ten separate essays detailing the life of each artist while providing critical assessment of her individual artistic achievement. Texts are supplemented with black-and-white illustrations, notes, and a bibliography. Highly useful for undergraduate and general readers.—*L. Doumato, National Gallery of Art*

WS-0215　　　　ND553　　　　91-29966 CIP
Higonnet, Anne. **Berthe Morisot's images of women.** Harvard, 1992. 311p index afp ISBN 0-674-06798-3, $45.00

Higonnet, Morisot expert and biographer, attempts to take the traditional methods of the biographer and critic into the area of social history. By analyzing Morisot in context, particularly as a woman artist, the author allows readers to understand her limitations, Morisot's leadership, and her real place in history. This emphasis on historical context and on the artist's status as a woman is important and topical. Unfortunately, the questions Higonnet raises are somewhat more provocative than her answers, especially as they relate to Morisot's overwhelmingly female imagery: What do Morisot's paintings of the important women in her family—daughter, mother, and sisters—tell us about her life as well as the lives of many 19th-century women? How do her images of women and their relationships differ from those of her male colleagues? What is her relation to popular imagery, especially of the female? While these issues still await satisfying discussion, this is their first central appearance in the scholarly literature. Meanwhile, Higonnet's original biography still provides the clearest sense of Morisot as a painter, a woman, and an individual. All libraries.—*D. J. Johnson, Providence College*

WS-0216　　　　ND237　　　　93-4141 Orig
Hobbs, Robert. **Lee Krasner.** Abbeville, 1993. 127p bibl index ISBN 1-55859-651-8, $32.95; ISBN 1-55859-283-0 pbk, $22.95

In this fine addition to Abbeville's "Modern Masters" series, Hobbs (art history, Virginia Commonwealth) emphasizes the intellectual and personal qualities of Krasner's paintings and collages. This is only the second widely circulated monograph devoted solely to Krasner. The first, Barbara Rose's *Lee Krasner* (1983), takes a more formalist and less biographical approach. Ten years after Krasner's death, Hobbs is far freer to comment on her relationships with Jackson Pollock and other art world figures. Fortunately, Hobbs had interviewed Krasner extensively in connection with a group exhibition in the 1980s, and the text conveys an intimacy and insight inspired by those conversations. The book is well, if not lavishly, illustrated (50 color plates and numerous photographs). It concludes with a mini-chapter on technique, an excellent bibliography, a chronology, and lists exhibitions and public collections owning Krasner's work. Highly recommended to public and academic libraries as an affordable source on an important American Abstract Expressionist who has never received her due in terms of books and exhibitions.—*M. M. Doherty, University of South Florida*

WS-0217　　　　ND225　　　　95-17367 CIP
Independent spirits: women painters of the American West, 1890-1945, ed. by Patricia Trenton; with essays by Sandra D'Emilio et al. Autry Museum of Western Heritage/California, 1995. 304p index afp ISBN 0-520-20202-3, $60.00; ISBN 0-520-20203-1 pbk, $29.95

Published in conjunction with an exhibition by the same title and organized by the Autry Museum of Western Heritage in Los Angeles, CA, this book is committed to introducing the contributions of western women artists into the mainstream of American art. Concentrating on information rather than theory, it surveys the history of women artists between the closing of the "frontier" in 1890 and the end of WW II in the area west of the 98th meridian to the Pacific Coast. A primary thesis of the book is that during this period of dynamic western growth, women in the western US found themselves less restricted by tradition and social circumstances than women in the East and that a large number of independent, dedicated, and successful women artists there deserve to be recognized as a cultural force in America. Wisely recognizing that the West is not a monolithic culture, the book is divided into five distinct regions: California, the Northwest, the Southwest, the Rocky Mountain region, and the Great Plains. Following the introduction, nine essays focus on women artists by region. Editor Trenton, who curated the exhibition, is, like all the contributors, an established curator and scholar committed to social history. The book is well integrated, readable, authoritative, informative, and thought-provoking. Its 277 high-quality illustrations include 100 color plates, many published for the first time. A valuable resource for all libraries with a commitment to American art, western history, and women's studies. Undergraduate; graduate; faculty.—*J. A. Day, University of South Dakota*

WS-0218   ND259   94-45994 MARC
Kahlo, Frida. **The diary of Frida Kahlo: an intimate self-portrait,** introd. by Carlos Fuentes; essay by Sarah M. Lowe. Abrams, 1995. 295p bibl index ISBN 0-8109-3221-0, $39.95

Carlos Fuentes says it all in his splendid introduction: "How much more than [suffering and death] was in Kahlo...her *Diary* now shows us: her joy, her fun, her fantastic imagination." Added to Fuentes's colorful and poetic view of the prominent Mexican artist are an essay and insightful commentary and annotations by art historian Sarah M. Lowe, well-executed English translations of the entire diary, a chronology of the artist, and a selected bibliography. It is the faithful and handsome reproduction of the *Diary*, however, that deserves the most praise. The pages painstakingly simulate the original, flaws, inkspots, and all, giving the reader an immediate entry into the complex mind of an artist whose words and doodles reveal her character with poignancy and force. For the Kahlo aficionado, this work rounds out the stream of biographies, critical works, and documentaries on the artist which has been steadily flowing since the early 1980s. For the general public, it provides a live introduction to a suffering and stoic, yet humorous and optimistic, woman. The extraordinary production values give the *Dairy* a quality not often achieved in a printed text: a perfect marriage of form and content, of textual and visual elements. Undergraduate; graduate; faculty; general.—*S. T. Clark, California State University, San Marcos*

WS-0219   ND653   93-12478 CIP
Leyster, Judith. **Judith Leyster: a Dutch master and her world,** project directors, James A. Welu and Pieter Biesboer. Worcester Art Museum, 1993. (Dist. by Yale) 391p bibl index ISBN 0-300-05564-1, $60.00

This book contains eight introductory essays and a well-researched catalog section of 42 entries, 16 of which are devoted to Leyster and the remaining 26 to Peter de Grebber, Maria de Grebber, Frans and Dirck Hals, Jan Molenaer, and Hendrik Pot. Based on the pioneering work of Frima Fox Hofrichter, the essays present the results of the authors' thorough interdisciplinary investigations. There is new and important information about the artist and her environment; her biography and that of her spouse, Jan Miense Molenaer; the socioeconomic context; issues of gender, including the social factors affecting the position of professional women in the 17th century. Equally interesting are the results of new technical investigations of her work by the same team that conducted earlier research of Frans Hals's paintings. The catalog entries are traditional and focus predominantly on iconography. They present nevertheless a good overview with many well-chosen illustrations of the artistic career of this important master and some of her closest contemporaries. This appealing book on Leyster also contains a register and a methodically organized bibliography in the back. Appropriate for academic library patrons, all levels.—*H. J. Van Miegroet, Duke University*

WS-0220   N7429   93-29218 CIP
Lucie-Smith, Edward. **Race, sex, and gender in contemporary art.** Abrams, 1994. 224p bibl index ISBN 0-8109-3767-0, $39.95

This is an overview of artists whose sex, race, or sexual orientation is the central theme of their work. Lucie-Smith explores the impact these new voices have had on the contemporary art world in the US and in Britain, and he discusses recent

work in several non-Western countries. He devotes a chapter to each of the various groups, e.g., African American art, Chicano and Cuban art, racially based art in Britain, minority sexuality in art, feminist art, Aboriginal and Maori art, and the art of modern Africa and Asia. The author attempts to historicize works by citing art with similar themes in the recent and distant past. Although not the definitive work on "outsider" art, it is nonetheless a good basic source for the various movements and artists who have come in recent years to make up the avant garde. There are numerous good color plates of work by artists that are not often reproduced. A fine general bibliography accompanies each chapter. General; lower-division undergraduate through graduate.—*R. J. Merrill, University of Southern California*

WS-0221   ND237x   90-61820 Orig
Martindale, Meredith. **Lilla Cabot Perry: an American Impressionist.** National Museum of Women in the Arts, 1991. (Dist. by Northeastern) 164p bibl ISBN 0-94079-14-4 pbk, $32.95

This catalog was published to accompany the 1990 retrospective exhibition of Lilla Cabot Perry's work organized by the National Museum of Women in the Arts. Perry's art, produced between 1885 and her death in 1933, was critically acclaimed in her life but has been largely overshadowed since then by her role as an American advocate for Impressionism and as a friend of Claude Monet. The catalog documents the first major Perry exhibition since 1969 and provides a balanced view of the contributions of this noted American woman artist. Martindale, who curated the retrospective, offers a substantial, readable, and well-researched bio-critical essay charting Perry's artistic development. Perry emerges as a gifted and committed artist, who while limited by academic convention nonetheless incorporates the lessons of Impressionism into a personal style that earns her a reputable place in American art history. N.M. Mathews (Williams College Museum of Art) provides an effective and authoritative essay on social conditions facing aspiring women artists at the turn of the century. The text also features a reprint of Perry's reminiscences of Claude Monet, a section containing family reflections about the artist, and selections from Perry's memoirs and correspondence. Some 80 illustrations (54 high-quality color plates) clearly document Perry's artistic development. Offering the only comprehensive study of Perry's art and life currently available, this book should be acquired by libraries with an interest in 19th-century American art and will be especially valuable to women studies collections.—*J. A. Day, University of South Dakota*

WS-0222   ND237.H3434   90-80947 CIP
Mattison, Robert Saltonstall. **Grace Hartigan: a painter's world.** Hudson Hills, 1990. 156p bibl index afp ISBN 1-555-95041-8, $50.00

Mattison has had a longtime involvement with Hartigan exhibition catalogs. This first monograph on Grace Hartigan vividly pictures and sensitively analyzes her art and life from the 1950s through the 1980s. His careful observations and thoughtful interpretations here are mostly focused on those works that are reproduced in the 100-plus illustrations (64 in color). A list of plates, chronology, selected bibliography, list of exhibitions, notes, and index are useful additions to the essay and the illustrations. This book should serve as a model for the kind of art-historical study that Mattison recommends be made of those other older contemporary artists (like Louise Bourgeois and Marisol) whose work has been eclipsed, as Hartigan's had, by the shifting tastes in art styles. Highly recommended to college and university students of American art, modern art, and women's art.—*G. Eager, Bucknell University*

WS-0223   N72   91-16632 CIP
McCarthy, Kathleen D. **Women's culture: American philanthropy and art, 1830-1930.** Chicago, 1991. 324p bibl index afp ISBN 0-226-55583-6, $29.95

McCarthy's study documents the vital role of women as promoters of the visual and decorative arts; unlike their male counterparts, women volunteer more time than money to reinforce the efforts of cultural organizations. Museums play a very important part of the story with such celebrated women as Isabella Stewart Gardner, Gertrude Vanderbilt Whitney, and Abbey Aldrich Rockefeller. The essays in this volume focus not only on philanthropists but also on curators and artists; dynamic and resourceful women art professionals like Juliana Force and art movement creators such as Candace Wheeler are noted for their contributions and for the influence they brought to these fields of endeavor. Beginning with the period of the Civil War, McCarthy delineates the steady development of professionalization and gender in philanthrophic institutions and implements this methodology through to the present. Black-and-white reproductions, notes, and a bibliography supplement the well-written text. For college and university libraries.—*L. Doumato, National Gallery of Art*

WS-0224   Brit. CIP
New feminist art criticism: critical strategies, ed. by Katy Deepwell. Manchester, 1995. (Dist. by St. Martin's) 210p index ISBN 0-7190-4257-7, $69.95; ISBN 0-7190-4258-5 pbk, $19.95

The essays in this anthology collectively address the difficulties faced by feminist artists and art critics in the 1990s as they work to find a negotiable space between artistic practice and critical theory. Much recent feminist writing has relied heavily on the employment of such poststructuralist theories as deconstruction, psychoanalysis, and semiotics. Indeed, many of the 22 essays in this book discuss the shortcomings inherent in this shift away from the practical and the political. Written by British critics, curators, academics, and artists, they emphasize a broad framework of concerns and are organized into sections focusing on issues that impact feminist art-making, including censorship, the role of art institutions, and the production of marginalized media such as textiles and other "crafts." The importance of this book lies precisely in the timeliness of these discussions of issues that are crucial to the future direction of feminism. Despite certain drawbacks to this book, such as the unevenness of the texts and a singular emphasis on a British feminist point of view, its overall direction merits attention and inclusion in collections of writing on feminist art.—*S. L. Jenkins, University of Southern California*

WS-0225   N6537   91-560 CIP
Peters, Sarah Whitaker. **Becoming O'Keeffe: the early years.** Abbeville, 1991. 397p bibl index ISBN 0-89659-907-8, $39.95

Although Georgia O'Keeffe remains a popular artist and virtual folk hero, critics increasingly question the significance of her work within the larger context of modern American art. O'Keeffe's well known passion for secrecy creates a sense of mystery about her life which has generated many books but has retarded serious scholarship leading to mature evaluation of an artist's contributions. Recently, there has been an encouraging breakthrough in O'Keeffe scholarship with books such as this which eschew the "show and tell" approach in favor of a solid bio-critical perspective. Peters limits her study to the period between 1915 and 1930, when O'Keeffe defined her essential artistic beliefs and style. The book offers a full, authoritative analysis not only of O'Keeffe's development but also of the artistic influence she, in turn, exerted upon Steiglitz and his circle. Intellectually conceived and meticulously researched, the book does an excellent job of placing O'Keeffe within her larger artistic context. Peters is particularly convincing in her expositions of O'Keeffe's artistic influences; less so when speculating about the artist's personal motivations and feelings. This well-written, well-researched book (with thorough notes and an extensive bibliography) is supported with 162 excellent illustrations (46 in color). Other recent publications on O'Keeffe, including Anita Pollitzer, *A Woman on Paper* (CH, Dec'88); Roxana Robinson, *Georgia O'Keeffe* (CH, Mar'90); and Barbara Lynes, *O'Keeffe, Steiglitz and the Critics* (CH, May'90) have an important place in the literature on the artist; however, Peters's book helps to set a new standard for O'Keeffe scholarship. For all libraries with a commitment to modern American art.—*J. A. Day, University of South Dakota*

WS-0226   ND1290   90-1860 MARC
Pointon, Marcia. **Naked authority: the body in western painting, 1830-1908.** Cambridge, 1990. 160p bibl index ISBN 0-521-38528-8, $49.50; ISBN 0-521-40999-3, $18.95

Pointon's six essays that make up this slender volume offer a critical assessment both of the nudes in famous 19th-century paintings (e.g., Manet's *Dejeuner sur l'herbe*, Delacroix's Liberty on the Barricades, and Eakins's *The Agnew Clinic*) and of their well-known, late 20th-century interpreters (e.g., K. Clark, J. Berger, M. Fried, and T. J. Clark). The rise of gender studies has brought new possibilities to study of the body, ever an object of intense interest. In art history the traditional aestheticized nude, male and female, has happily been super-

seded by the policitized, psychologized, and deconstructed body. Pointon brings to bear on her readings of the naked figure not only a thorough knowledge of 19th-century history and art, but also a familiarity with a broad range of theoretical work, resulting in a number of original insights. Theory has not displaced the canonical images, which are well reproduced within the text. The language of theory in which the book is written will, however, make it difficult to read for those who have not been initated into its mysteries.—*A. J. Wharton, Duke University*

WS-0227   N72   94-1543 CIP
The Power of feminist art: the American movement of the 1970s, history and impact, ed. by Norma Broude and Mary D. Garrard. Abrams, 1994. 318p bibl index ISBN 0-8109-3732-8, $49.50

Since its advent in the early 1970s, the feminist art movement in the US has proved to be a multifaceted and revolutionary value system as well as an early expression of postmodernist change. This book, which aims to document and define the originating phase of the movement, comprises a substantial introduction plus 16 essays grouped into four sections, which document (1) the feminist art education programs of the early '70s; (2) the development of the movement via influential publications, organizations, and exhibitions; (3) feminist art's challenge to modernism through the return to serious political and personal content based on a postmodernist aesthetic; and (4) the status and impact of feminist art in the 1980s and 1990s. Coeditors Broude and Garrard (American Univ.) enjoy substantial reputations as commentators on feminist art. Their expertise is readily apparent in the judicious selection of the 18 contributing scholars, artists, and critics. The book as a whole is authoritative, well written, meticulously documented, and unusually cohesive for a work with so many contributors. It is much enhanced by its 270 high quality illustrations, of which 118 are in full color, and by a good bibliography, excellent notes, and an illustrated time line. The book lives up to its billing as the first history and analysis of the origins of the feminist art movement; it will become a standard in the study of the subject. Recommended for all libraries with a commitment to contemporary art. General; undergraduate through professional.—*J. A. Day, University of South Dakota*

WS-0228   N6999.P67   89-242 CIP
Sarab'ianov, Dmitrii V. **Popova,** by Dmitri V. Sarabianov and Natalia L. Adaskina; tr. by Marian Schwartz. Abrams, 1990. 396p index ISBN 0-8109-3701-8, $85.00

Liubov Popova was a major figure in the emergence of modern art in Russia between 1914 and 1932. Although popular in Russia and comparatively well known in the West, Popova has not received the critical attention accorded to a number of her associates, most notably Vladimir Tatlin and Aleksander Rodchenko. This first comprehensive work on Popova published in English offers a detailed chronological study of her artistic development between 1912 and her death in 1922. The authors, both respected Soviet art historians with substantial expertise on Popova, provide two lengthy and significant essays that contribute considerable depth to the understanding of Popova's personal artistic development and her role in the short-lived effort to apply modern art to social ends in pre-Stalinist Russia. The text is ably translated from the original French but is, nonetheless, a bit laborious in style. This large-format, well-bound volume includes 433 excellent illustrations, of which 133 are full-color plates. The usefulness of the text is further enhanced by extensive notes, a good chronology, and a solid index. This work has the makings of a standard on the work of Popova and is recommended for all libraries with a commitment to the study of modern art and especially of 20th-century Russian art.—*J. A. Day, University of South Dakota*

WS-0229   NB237   91-15632 CIP
Sherwood, Dolly. **Harriet Hosmer, American sculptor, 1830-1908.** Missouri, 1991. 378p index afp ISBN 0-8262-0766-9, $29.95

Biography is the hardest form of history to write, for it requires the analysis of the historian and the literary gifts of the novelist. Sherwood partially succeeds. Her research has been thorough, and she has consulted contemporary letters and literary works as well as recent feminist histories and histories of 19th-century culture. Nonetheless, her book is narrative and anecdotal. It lacks much analysis because of its strictly chronological organization, which is similar to the earlier *Harriet Hosmer Letters and Memories*, ed. by Cornelia Carr (1912). Perhaps the book would have been enhanced through divisions in subject—such as Hosmer's work, friendships, travels—or through a fuller picture of cultural history in the 19th century. Sherwood's description of Hosmer's relationships to women and of her associations with the circle of Charlotte Cushman is reasoned, intelligent, and sensitive. This reader wished for more photographs of Hosmer's work, or of other people important to the text. Nonetheless, a biography of Hosmer is long overdue, and Sherwood's book makes that contribution at last.—*J. A. Barter, Amherst College*

WS-0230   ND237   91-8278 CIP
Simon, Joan. **Susan Rothenberg.** Abrams, 1991. 205p bibl index
ISBN 0-8109-3753-0, $75.00

In this first comprehensive monograph to be published about the life and work of Susan Rothenberg, Simon characterizes this much-exhibited artist, who initially gained recognition in the 1970s for reductivist paintings of horses, as a link between minimalism and neoexpressionism. The book's scope is broad and its tone promotional, with an emphasis on Rothenberg's aesthetic intentions and contextual development. Joan Simon, an established writer and curator who specializes in contemporary art and a former managing editor of *Art in America*, has known the artist since the early '70s, and this association contributes a congenial biographical dimension to the fluid and confident text. The large format effectively supports the 161 illustrations, of which 87 are in full color; they are of uniform high quality and were intelligently selected to complement the thrust of the text. The book includes a good chronology, exhibition history, and bibliography. The overall result is a handsome, well-researched monograph on an established contemporary artist who may or may not achieve the prominence predicted by Simon. There is no doubt, however, that this will be the standard work on Susan Rothenberg for some time to come and should be acquired by libraries with a commitment to contemporary American art.—*J. A. Day, University of South Dakota*

WS-0231   NE1321   95-16908 CIP
Swinton, Elizabeth de Sabato. **The women of the pleasure quarter: Japanese paintings and prints of the floating world.** Hudson Hills/Worcester Art Museum, 1996 (c1995). 195p bibl index afp ISBN 1-55595-115-5, $65.00

Swinton's valuable study of the popular culture of premodern Japan was produced in conjunction with an exhibition organized by the Worcester (Mass.) Art Museum and examines the life-experience of the women—courtesan, Geisha, and prostitute—who formed the iconic core of a public, alternative culture in the urban centers of Tokugawa Japan. Simply put, in separate persuasive essays the authors explore the real lives of set-apart women who dominated, from their positions at center and pinnacle, a distinct urban entity whose values, ideals, aspirations, and significances they shaped and personified. They were treasured, living works of art, and their proper realm (the Pleasure Quarter) was an artful reconstitution of the fabled universe of an Imperial past, tailored to the sensibilities of a prosperous working class. Self-identified patterns of language, movement, and social behavior/expectation sustained and defined a complex social experience that was both distinct from, and resonant with, that of the world at large. The arts, represented in effective illustrations—many in full color—give flesh and substance to the ideas proposed in the essays. An individual commentary is paired with each picture, and there are, as well, minibiographies of each artist, a glossary, and a bibliographical list. Highly recommended for all readers. General; undergraduate through professional.—*D. K. Dohanian, University of Rochester*

WS-0232   TR647   Canadian CIP
Thomas, Ann. **Lisette Model.** National Gallery of Canada, 1990. (Dist. by Chicago) 362p bibl index ISBN 0-88884-605-3, $39.95

Under the guise of an exhibition catalog, Thomas has written a fascinating, informative, and richly illustrated biography on the life and times of photographer Lisette Model. Meant to long outlive the retrospective exhibition that the book accompanied, the work draws heavily from the unpublished contents of the Model archive at the National Gallery of Canada (consisting of photographic prints, negatives, teaching notebooks, and correspondance) to place Model's work within a biographical and art-historical context. Such attention is long overdue given Model's powerful influence both as an artist and teacher. Thomas fol-

lows Model through her formative years in Vienna in the early 1900s, on to her immigration to the US during the 30s and traces her development as a freelance photographer and legendary teacher for 33 years. Included is a unique chapter about Model's most famous student, Diane Arbus, and their friendship. With more than 300 illustrations and reproductions of Model's work, a chronology, and an extensive bibliography, this book is highly recommended—a must for every library. All levels.—*J. Natal, Alfred University*

WS-0233   ND237   94-16030 CIP
Udall, Sharyn R. **Inside looking out: the life and art of Gina Knee.** Texas Tech, 1994. 178p bibl index afp ISBN 0-89672-336-4, $29.00

An engaging, brief introduction to the little-known but meritorious American modernist painter Gina Knee, born Virginia Schnaufer (1898-1982). Udall is a feminist art historian who emphasizes Knee's real dilemma of being caught between the professional demands of her own art and the requirements of a domestic sphere as the wife of the active portraitist Alexander Brook. "Quietly, obsessively, she fought to keep her art alive and on track [though it was sometimes] driven underground by conflict at home." Knee's forte was watercolor with gouache, with a personal style forged from her experiences of life in the Southwest influenced by the art of John Marin and Paul Klee, where subjects were often landscapes and cityscapes, or glimpses of abstracted nature in general. Late in her career she turned more frequently to oils, sometimes practicing a style a bit comparable to that of her abstract expressionist neighbors on Long Island. She spent an episodic but evidently very private personal life, marrying three times, living in many different locations, including, finally, New York. Knee's paintings could not be described as unknown in her lifetime. She had a longtime New York dealer, Marian Willard, and participated in award-winning group and solo shows throughout the country. She is certainly worthy of wider recognition as an artist. Recommended for modernist art history and women's studies collections. Graduate; faculty.—*M. Hamel-Schwulst, Towson State University*

WS-0234   NX550   94-44722 CIP
Visions of the 'neue Frau': women and the visual arts in Weimar Germany, ed. by Marsha Meskimmon and Shearer West. Scolar, 1995. 187p bibl index ISBN 1-85928-157-5, $64.95

Renowned European scholars here contribute essays conveying the numerous roles women undertook during Germany's Weimar period. The essays explore the numerous contributions by women to the visual arts, ranging, e.g., from producers and patrons of art to subjects and objects in visual representations. The writers employ methodologies that include social-historical, psychological, political, feminist, and postmodernist theories and discuss a range of issues, from high to popular art and from fine arts to mass media, covering both familiar material (e.g., German expressionistic film and sculpture—though with fresh analysis) and rarely explored areas (e.g., women as collectors and dealers). Unifying many of the essays is the theme that the Weimar period was a remnant of 19th-century imperialism that helped create the milieu in which the Neue Frau emerged. The 34 images that are included are in black and white; often this is because the original object has long since been destroyed. These essays are important for not privileging the male experience and for highlighting the importance of women in the visual arts of the Weimar era. A worthy compilation that explores a fascinating aspect of German art and a worthwhile acquisition. Upper-division undergraduate; graduate; faculty; professional.—*K. A. Rusnock, University of Southern California*

WS-0235   Orig
Women in the Victorian art world, ed. by Clarissa Campbell Orr. Manchester, 1995. (Dist. by St. Martin's) 208p index ISBN 0-7190-4122-8, $69.95; ISBN 0-7190-4123-6 pbk, $19.95

A sturdy volume of no-nonsense essays growing out of the 1991 Cambridge symposium on women and historical change in the Victorian art world, held for the centenary retrospective of the artist/activist Barbara Leigh Smith Bodichon (1827-91). Strictly an academic study, this is the work of nine contributing professors, curators, and writers (among whom are several recognized experts in British feminist history with well-known books to their credit), who examine "the social and economic backgrounds of women artists, their opportunities for professional training, their reputations both as women and artists in art and fiction and the constraints imposed on them by the social mores of the period." Discussed are such topics as the Victorian feminist campaign to gain access to Royal Academy schools, and the activities of the Society of Female Artists is discussed. An interesting statistical study literally maps out the sphere of public and private spaces for women in West End London during the period—e.g., organizations where they could find lodging, etc. Another chapter identifies the importance of ceramic collector Lady Charlotte Schreiber. Yet Barbara Bodichon's fine works are analyzed and shown with only seven black-and-white illustrations. Copious endnotes usefully substitute for a bibliography. Recommended for specialized Victorian collections. Graduate; faculty.—*M. Hamel-Schwulst, Towson State University*

◆ Painting, Sculpture, Metal Work, Textiles

WS-0236 ND237.N43 90-38684 CIP
Belcher, Gerald L. **Collecting souls, gathering dust: the struggles of two American artists, Alice Neel and Rhoda Medary,** by Gerald L. Belcher and Margaret L. Belcher. Paragon House, 1991. 304p bibl index afp ISBN 1-55778-336-5, $22.95

A dual biography of two women who early in their lives shared the dream of becoming famous and successful artists. For Alice Neel, the dream became reality; for Rhoda Medary, it went unfulfilled. Neel's international reputation as a painter makes her a likely subject for a biography; not so Medary, who gave up her art for the sort of conventional family life that seldom commands serious public attention. Gerald Belcher is a professor who specializes in women's history and Margaret Belcher is an editor who has worked on the memoirs of Rhoda Medary. The authors largely eschew art history and criticism in favor of developing a story that finds meaning in the way two women artists faced the constraints society placed upon their lives and dreams. The story is told in an easy, lively voice with enough romanticism to be engaging without becoming too self-conscious. The book is well researched and offers much new information on Alice Neel that may be useful to other scholars. The 31 black-and-white photographs are useful only as references because of their small size and poor quality. Despite its rather happenstantial thesis, this is an intriguing and well-written book that will find appreciative general readers.—*J. A. Day, University of South Dakota*

WS-0237 NK9112 91-11425 CIP
Edmonds, Mary Jaene. **Samplers & samplemakers: an American schoolgirl art, 1700-1850.** Rizzoli, 1991. 168p bibl index ISBN 0-8478-1396-7, $40.00

This exhibit catalog builds on recent scholarship on the sampler as a form of material culture. Samplers are often misunderstood and Edmonds sets out to achieve three goals: (1) to portray samplers' embroidery as indisputable evidence of Colonial education for women in America; (2) to attempt to identify the often anonymous teacher and the location of her school room; and (3) to assist the reader in identifying specific patterns or design formats that will allow for the classification of more school-girl embroidery. Edmonds brings experience as a collector of samplers to her research. This volume is clearly object oriented, as it is a standard exhibition catalog in format—with detailed captions and handsome color illustrations. The captions draw on extensive genealogical searches and reveal insights into the lives of the makers of approximately 70 samplers. Edmonds succeeds in two of her three goals, providing a new understanding of the identity of the teachers and schoolrooms and the classification of specific patterns and design formats. While samplers can be considered as evidence of Colonial education, the educative process of the period and the cultural history of this age needs further development to achieve the author's third goal. However, this work is a fine addition to the scholarship in this area and is also a welcome addition to the study of women's material culture.—*C. K. Dewhurst, Michigan State University*

WS-0238 NK9112 90-70394 CIP
Fox, Sandi. Los Angeles County Museum of Art. **Wrapped in glory:** **figurative quilts and bedcovers, 1700-1900.** Thames and Hudson/Los Angeles County Museum of Art, 1990. 167p ISBN 0-500-01499-X, $35.00

Fox, curator at the Los Angeles County Museum, has chosen to focus on figurative quilts from 1700 to 1900. She examines this textile tradition through her selection of 36 representative examples. These remarkable pieces were also collected for an exhibition at the Los Angeles County Museum. The pictorial elements in the quilts display a wide array of themes: universal symbols, such as the Tree of Life and biblical stories; world events, such as the Crystal Palace exhibition; and more individual issues in the makers' lives, such as the suffrage movement and poignant personal accounts. At the time when European stylistic dominance was evolving into an independent American style of the middle class, the quilt-makers drew inspiration from pattern books, political cartoons, and fashion plates as well as from other popular publications, and their work reflected quite accurately contemporary fashions and life-styles. Fox gives detailed data on the techniques, materials, dimensions, date, and maker of each quilt. A comprehensive history gleaned from public and private records accompanies each entry. Extensive annotations expand on the background to these often exquisite, highly artistic textiles, in which the quilt-makers vividly express the world around them. This attractively designed volume includes a great number of high-quality color photographs of the quilts and their details, as well as pictures of contemporary publications and period photography. Highly recommended reading for those interested in textiles or women's studies.—*M. Tulokas, Rhode Island School of Design*

WS-0239 89-51744 Orig
Glanville, Philippa. **Women silversmiths, 1685-1845: works from the collection of The National Museum of Women in the Arts,** by Philippa Glanville and Jennifer Faulds Goldsborough. Thames & Hudson, 1990. 176p bibl index ISBN 0-500-23578-3, $45.00

Seldom has there been published a more informative and eye-filling book about silver, and never before one about women silversmiths. The primary concern is the collection of silver by women that is in the National Museum of Women in the Arts, but the book is also concerned with the history and usage of domestic silver. The two essays, well written by two museum curators, are superbly illustrated by 98 color plates of the silver pieces, with close-ups of their details, and of paintings of the period with close-ups of silver therein. The photographic reproduction is of outstanding quality. Also outstanding is a well-edited index; a short glossary; a biographical list of registered British and Irish women silversmiths, 1685-1845; a select short bibliography; and clear photographs of the collection's silvermarks. All art collections.—*L. C. Belden, The Henry Francis DuPont Winterthur Museum*

WS-0240 N6923.G73 89-43706 CIP
Grisi, Laura. **Laura Grisi: a selection of works with notes by the artist,** Essay-interview by Germano Celant. Rizzoli, 1990. 273p ISBN 0-8478-1222-7, $60.00

Laura Grisi, who emerged on the international art scene as a representative of young Italian modernists in the 1966 Venice Biennale, has since distinguished herself as a committed avant-garde artist who reflects the mercurial nature of the art world of the last two decades. Working sequentially in several major trends, including pop and conceptual art, Grisi's production is marked by an intensity of effort and contemporary sensibility. The book offers an overview of the artist's career to date largely via an "essay-interview" by Germano Celant (curator of contemporary art, the Solomon R. Guggenheim Museum). This textual device works fairly well, as it offers Celant the opportunity to provide Grisi's work with some critical context while allowing the artist to personalize her art. As one might imagine, this combination of criticism and autobiography results in an informal and loosely focused essay. The book contains more than 200 illustrations of Grisi's work (many excellent color reproductions), accompanied by brief notes by the artist, and a substantial selection of biographical photographs, an exhibition history, and a thorough bibliography. This is a beautifully produced publication on a noteworthy artist, but unfortunately its value is largely limited to a pictorial survey of Grisi's work. Recommended for libraries with a strong commitment to contemporary art and with money to spare.—*J. A. Day, University of South Dakota*

WS-0241 ND653 90-191032 Orig

Hofrichter, Frima Fox. **Judith Leyster: a woman painter in Holland's Golden Age.** DAVACO, Beukenlaan 3, 8085 RK Doornspijk, Netherlands, 1990 (c1989). 144p, 159 plates bibl indexes ISBN 90-70288-62-1, $160.00

Known primarily for her depictions of people engaged in seemingly everyday activities, Judith Leyster (1609-1660) also made portraits, one still-life, and botanical illustrations. Her imagery is distinguished from that of most 17th-century Dutch painters by its feminist nuances of meaning. At last, Hofrichter makes the artist's achievement available in a comprehensive and modern format, which is both eminently readable and thoroughly researched. Three chapters discuss Leyster's life and its documentation, her style, and critical fortune. The catalogue raisonné includes 46 authentic paintings, 7 problematic works, 12 lost works, 18 incorrectly attributed paintings, 1 etching, and extensive comparative material. A book that has its inception as the author's 1979 dissertation, it is complemented by her interpretive articles on single paintings (*The Proposition, Self-Portrait,* and *Tric-Trac Players*), which have appeared in journals or essay collections between 1975 and 1983. Hofrichter, to her credit, does not republish her earlier articles here but, rather, summarizes their findings. Also complementing this study is Hofrichter's 1983 exhibition catalog, *Haarlem, the Seventeenth Century,* which establishes Leyster's artistic milieu in its historical background. The works of Judith Leyster are now taught in standard undergraduate art surveys. Well worth its cost, this volume is essential for all academic libraries supporting programs in art and in women's studies.—*A. Golahny, Lycoming College*

WS-0242 NB1210.M3 89-77342 CIP

Kasson, Joy S. **Marble queens and captives: women in nineteenth-century American sculpture.** Yale, 1990. 293p bibl index afp ISBN 0-300-04596-4, $40.00

Between 1830 and 1880 a form of American neoclassic sculpture celebrated the Ideal via subjects derived from literature, history, and mythology. Kasson (American Studies, University of North Carolina, Chapel Hill) revisits this now largely obscure period and genre to examine the portrayal of women in the context of social history. She demonstrates how the period idealized women as fragile, vulnerable, and submissive, while expressing an ambivalence and anxiety about their evolving role in a society undergoing rapid economic and social change. The first two chapters do an excellent job of outlining the social context of Ideal sculpture in relation to the artists, patrons, and audiences involved. The rest of the book discusses major sculptures from the period, such as Hiram Powers's The Greek Slave, to illustrate the relationship of Ideal sculpture to its larger cultural context and to the reconstruction of gender. The well-written, thoroughly researched text provides a wealth of insights derived from a variety of sources, from personal correspondence to popular press and literature. These insights are strengthened by excellent citations, a solid bibliography, and 103 appropriate and instructive reproductions. For libraries serving upper-division undergraduate and graduate students interested in 19th-century American art and/or women's studies.—*J. A. Day, University of South Dakota*

WS-0243 Can. CIP

Lambton, Gunda. **Stealing the show: seven women artists in Canadian public art.** McGill-Queen's, 1994. 215p bibl index ISBN 0-7735-1188-1, $55.00; ISBN 0-7735-1189-X pbk, $24.95

This slim volume attempts to be both a survey of seven Canadian women artists who are leaders in the public art of that country and a polemical tract asserting connections between the work of women artists and art appropriate for the public domain. Each chapter is devoted to the work of one of the artists, Marcelle Ferron, Anne Kahane, Rita Letendre, Gathie Falk, Joyce Wieland, Jerry Grey, and Colette Whiten. These artists are not widely known outside of Canada, and despite the inclusion of exhibition and public commission lists, the lack of illustrations (only 21 in all) undermines this book's ability to introduce them to a wider audience. Although the author concludes that women's art, in its ability to "raise consciousness and transform culture," is most appropriate as public art, she admits that the public work of these artists has not engendered the kinds of debate or highlighted the primary issues familiar in today's public dialogue. General; researchers; professional.—*R. J. Onorato, University of Rhode Island*

WS-0244 ND553.M88 90-81567 CIP

Mount Holyoke College/Art Museum. **Perspectives on Morisot,** ed. by T.J. Edelstein. Hudson Hills/Mount Holyoke College Art Museum, 1990. 120p index afp ISBN 1-55595-049-3, $35.00

A welcome fulfillment of the promise held by the landmark 1986 Berthe Morisot exhibition organized by the Mount Holyoke College Art Museum in association with the National Gallery of Art. The catalog by Charles Stuckey and William Scott, *Berthe Morisot: Impressionist* (CH, Jan'88), invited additional critical and historical commentary to assist in the reevaluation of this important French artist. This volume, a compendium of lectures from a Mount Holyoke symposium in conjunction with the exhibition, includes essays on various aspects of Morisot's life and art by seven established women art historians with broad expertise in the arts and an interest in viewing Morisot from a female perspective. While diverse in subject, the essays are surprisingly consistent in their readable tone and fine scholarly quality. The text, well supported by 23 good-quality color plates of Morisot's paintings and 53 black-and-white illustrations, admirably achieves its goal of augmenting the meaningful scholarship available on Berthe Morisot and, as such, should be acquired by all libraries with a serious interest in modern art and the study of women artists. One caution: *Perspectives on Morisot* is a companion to, and not a substitute for, *Berthe Morisot: Impressionist*—still the best biocritical source available on the artist and notably superior in the number and quality of its color plates of Morisot's work to anything currently on the market.—*J. A. Day, University of South Dakota*

WS-0245 NB955 93-26843 CIP

Rose, Barbara. **Magdalena Abakanowicz.** Abrams, 1994. 224p bibl ISBN 0-8109-1947-8, $49.50

Rose's elegant and profusely illustrated monograph documents the life and work of the world-renowned Polish sculptor. Organized as a concatenation of 16 essays treating each major series of the artist's works in chronological order, the book provides a good introduction to Abakanowicz's life and work. The many large plates notably include the artist at work as well as installation views, complementing the text's attention to the artist's working process, and her technical and material innovations. Along with the standard biographical chronology, the chronologically arranged bibliography and exhibition history make this book useful to college-level researchers. Abakanowicz has been the subject of numerous exhibitions and articles; most important to American audiences was the large retrospective exhibition at the Chicago Museum of Contemporary Art in 1982. Although not as detailed as the Chicago catalog, this study by a well-known scholar is a solid piece of work that updates our view of this important artist. General; lower-division undergraduate through graduate.—*A. Pappas, University of Southern California*

WS-0246 NB236 89-26846 CIP

Rubinstein, Charlotte Streifer. **American women sculptors: a history of women working in three dimensions.** G.K. Hall, 1990. 638p index afp ISBN 0-8161-8732-0, $50.00

Although contemporary women sculptors are acknowledged, the historical achievements of women sculptors throughout the decades continue to pass unrecognized. Ceramics, textiles, and other design media are areas in which women have traditionally carried on creative work. By abolishing the hierarchical categories established to differentiate high from low art, the significance of women's role in low or decorative arts is accorded its just position. Rubinstein begins her survey with the baskets and ceramics of early Native Americans and documents each progressive phase of sculpture through to the three-dimensional works of the 1980s. The volume is handsomely produced but regretably limited to black-and-white illustrations; color often proves vital to sculpture as an art form and intensifies its aesthetic appeal. Despite this minor flaw, *American Women Sculptors* will assume a prominent position in every art reference collection next to Rubinstein's companion volume, *American Women Artists* (CH, Mar'83).—*L. Doumato, National Gallery of Art*

WS-0247 91-60404 Orig

Taylor, Ina. **The art of Kate Greenaway: a nostalgic portrait of childhood.** Pelican, 1991. 128p bibl index ISBN 0-88289-867-1, $34.95

This new biography of one of Britain's most revered illustrators has an abundance of illustrative matter: sketches, drawings, and full-color reproductions of paintings abound. In captions, Taylor does a good job of relating scenes or details in Greenaway's paintings to aspects of her life; however, photographs with which to compare these painted observations are not included (there are only six photos in the book pertaining to Greenaway's life). The text does an adequate job of telling Greenaway's story, but it does not do so in-depth nor with so much insight as Rodney Engen's *Kate Greenaway: A Biography* (1981). This latter book is filled with photos and drawings that help to enrich the very well written biography; but it is, unfortunately, meager in full color representations of Greenaway's work. The Taylor book may be recommended for its generous array of color plates, but for a substantial account of Greenaway's life, read Engen.—*C. Larry, Northern Illinois University*

WS-0248   NE539   92-20937 CIP
Winnan, Audur H. **Wanda Gág: a catalogue raisonné of the prints.** Smithsonian Institution Press, 1993. 315p bibl index afp ISBN 1-56098-221-7, $75.00

Remembered as an illustrator of children's books, Gág was also a technically sophisticated printmaker in New York of the 1920s and 1930s. Her landscapes and interior scenes are reminiscent of Van Gogh; occasional urban subjects resemble those of the American Scene group. Winnan (no art credentials given) provides a biographical essay based on interviews, exhibition catalogs, newspaper reviews, and Gág's writings. Included in the volume are lengthy excerpts from Gág's diaries and correspondence, a chronology, and glossary. The chronological catalogue raisonné of 122 lithographs, etchings, and woodcuts includes few book illustrations (those were mostly drawings.) Catalog entries describe states and editions, and identify preparatory drawings. (Many are illustrated alongside the print.) Also included are eight color illustrations of Gág's paintings. This volume is most valuable as the first major catalog of Gág prints; it is most interesting as an ironic tale of a Minnesotan from an immigrant family who became a sexually and politically liberated urban woman but whose popular image remains that of a minor rustic sketcher of cats and rabbits. Recommended to college and university collections.—*M. M. Doherty, University of South Florida*

◆ Architecture, Photography

WS-0249   TR647   95-889 CIP
Lowe, Sarah M. **Tina Modotti: photographs.** Abrams/Philadelphia Museum of Art, 1995. 160p bibl index ISBN 0-8109-4280-1, $45.00

Lowe, an art historian who specializes in photography and Latin American art, describes Modotti as the "best-known unknown photographer of the twentieth century"—an assessment based on Modotti's notoriety, earned through an eventful and complex life. Italian-born Modotti was a model, movie star, and revolutionary communist as well as a photographer. The brevity of her seven-year career as a photographer, her political activism, and her relationship with Edward Weston each in its own way contributed to suppressing awareness of Modotti's artistic accomplishments. In the past 15 years, there has been a resurgence of interest in her photography, and more critical attention has been paid to her rich cultural context, especially the period 1923-30 spent in postrevolutionary Mexico as a member of an international modernist community. This catalog for a touring exhibition by the same title, curated by Lowe and organized by the Alfred Stieglitz Center of the Philadelphia Museum of Art, is the first in-depth, art-historical study of the artist's work. Lowe demonstrates an acute aesthetic sensitivity to Modotti's photographs and a zeal for reconstructing the artist's cultural biography. Her substantial biocritical essay on Modotti is clearly organized, readable, and precisely researched. The text is supported by 140 excellent duotone illustrations, which present the full range of Modotti's photographic vision. A significant contribution to the history of photography; recommended to all libraries with a commitment to modern art and women's studies. Undergraduate; graduate; faculty; general.—*J. A. Day, University of South Dakota*

WS-0250   TR140   91-22451 CIP
Michaels, Barbara L. **Gertrude Käsebier: the photographer and her photographs.** Abrams, 1992. 192p bibl index ISBN 0-8109-3505-8, $45.00

Although not as well known as Stieglitz, Kasebier was nonetheless one of the foremost Pictorialists of the New York school at the turn of the century. Her influence extended beyond her highly acclaimed photographs to a wide range of photographic friends and acquaintances who were influenced by her technique and philosophy. This book builds on William I. Homer's *A Pictorial Heritage: The Photographs of Gertrude Kasebier* (1979), and goes beyond it. The material is presented chronologically with particular topics analyzed in depth and detail. For example, Michaels identifies several of Kasebier's American Indian portrait subjects, discusses their personalities and relation to mainstream culture, and compares Kasebier's photographs to others of the same type. She discusses Kasebier's portrait subjects and studies of women and children within the context of current ideology and addresses the question of Kasebier's feminism. Michaels also explores Kasebier's relationships with other Pictorialists and demonstrates the strengths and weaknesses of this personal and professional network. The book is well documented, carefully thought out, and well written. Highly recommended for college, university, and public libraries.—*S. Spencer, North Carolina State University*

WS-0251   NA7461   94-43109 CIP
Prussin, Labelle. **African nomadic architecture: space, place, and gender,** by Labelle Prussin with Amina Adan et al. Smithsonian Institution Press/National Museum of African Art, 1995. 245p bibl index afp ISBN 1-56098-358-2, $55.00

The first comprehensive survey of African nomadic architecture, this richly illustrated volume also turns out to be a study of art produced by women, since it is they who are primarily responsible for making the structures, setting them up, and collapsing them. With a ritual-inspired aesthetic so unlike that of Western architecture, these moveable buildings and their furnishings are models of functional elegance previously little appreciated in the art history of Africa. The leading author, whose previous works on the mud mosques of the Western Sudan are definitive, and the five contributors have assembled more than 200 drawings, photographs (two dozen in color), and maps that help the reader appreciate for the first time the effort, skills, beauty, and meaning of these buildings and the textiles, leatherwork, basketry, and other crafts that adorn them. The fresh perspective, authoritative scholarship, and astonishing brilliance of the "huts" may make this book, in the words of Robert Farris Thompson in the foreword, "one of the classics of twentieth-century architectural history."—*D. J. Crowley, University of California, Davis*

WS-0252   TR139   94-6713 CIP
Rosenblum, Naomi. **A history of women photographers.** Abbeville, 1994. 356p bibl index ISBN 1-55859-761-1, $60.00

Given the proliferation of books on the history of photography, a work surveying the contributions of women to this art form was perhaps inevitable. One is encouraged that the author is Naomi Rosenblum, a well-respected scholar whose *A World History of Photography* (CH, Apr'85) is a standard text. Beginning with the proposition that women's role in the development of photography is understudied and undervalued, Rosenblum produces a broad-ranging survey of the contributions of 233 women photographers between 1835 and 1950. The book's nine chapters are organized chronologically and culminate with the chapter "The Feminist Vision." The author effectively relates women photographers to the dominant social values of the time, and she writes clearly and concisely, using specific examples to elucidate broad general trends and features of the time. With 263 illustrations, including 35 color plates, the book offers an excellent visual survey of its subject. The section of biographies of the artists considered in the text is valuable; for, although succinct and formal, they include new information on a number of previously obscure women photographers. Other publications explore women's contributions to photography, most notably *Women Photographers*, edited by Constance Sullivan (CH, Dec'90), but Rosenblum is the first to do it so extensively and comprehensively. This will be a standard work in its area, and it provides a firm foundation for additional scholarship on the role of women in photography. A "must" acquisition for all libraries committed to photography and art history. General; undergraduate; graduate; faculty.—*J. A. Day, University of South Dakota*

WS-0253   NA2543   91-16024 CIP
Weisman, Leslie Kanes. **Discrimination by design: a feminist critique of the man-made environment.** Illinois, 1992. 190p index afp ISBN 0-252-01849-4, $24.95

Using skyscrapers, department stores, shopping malls, maternity hospitals and public housing, Leslie Weisman presents the feminist approach to spatial perspective and documents the privileges and penalties in gender, race, and class. The question of building communities that foster relationships of equality and environmental wholeness is the emphatic theme of this volume. Practical advice is offered to planners, architects, politicians, and social activists, making this book a useful and unique tool on many levels. *Discrimination by Design* is a pioneering work that will pave new territory not only for feminists but for all those who are prepared to rethink environmental and societal issues.—*L. Doumato, National Gallery of Art*

WS-0254   TR650   90-30722 CIP
Women photographers, ed. by Constance Sullivan. Abrams, 1990. 263p ISBN 0-8109-3950-9, $65.00

An important, ambitious collection of photographs that examines women's contributions to photography from the mid-19th century to the present. The title Women Photographers does not adequately reveal the questions that editor Sullivan and Eugenia Parry Janis (author of the essay) ask about the relationship between the feminine and photography in their attempt to write a history of photography that includes the presence of the feminine spirit. Sullivan's selection of photographs, culled from public and private collections worldwide, lies at the heart of the book. Of the 73 photographers included in the collection, there are a number of emerging artists as well as many known artists, represented here by previously unpublished work. The 200 photographs are beautifully reproduced; a detailed list of plates is included. This is an important addition to any library.—*J. Natal, Alfred University*

◆ Communication

WS-0255   PN4888   92-41011 MARC
Beasley, Maurine H. **Taking their place: a documentary history of women and journalism,** by Maurine H. Beasley and Sheila J. Gibbons. American University, in cooperation with Women's Institute for Freedom of the Press, 1993. 359p bibl index afp ISBN 1-879383-09-8, $51.00; ISBN 1-879383-01-1 pbk, $14.95

A first-of-its-kind presentation of material on the historical development of women in journalism, from 1790 to the present. Extensive original documents, all written by women journalists, make an outstanding contribution to a field that so far has had only three book-length overviews of American women journalists: Ishbel Ross, *Ladies of the Press* (1936), Marion Marzolf, *Up from the Footnote*, (CH, Mar'78), and Kay Mills, *A Place in the News* (1988). The materials included by Beasley and Gibbons, not generally available, give fascinating insight into the American experience of women journalists: a 1790 petition to the US Senate; editorials by early women editors; autobiographical data; letters to newspapers; magazine articles; Civil War writings; columns; early work of African American women; work of war correspondents, journalists, and sob sisters; and articles by present-day, ground-breaking women journalists in print and in broadcasting. Extensive bibliographies supporting each historical era further enhance the usefulness of this work, as does a valuable overview of the women's movement and parallel developments of women's participation in journalism. Highly recommended for undergraduate and graduate collections supporting courses on women and mass communication, journalism history, and the women's movement.—*M. R. Grant, Wheaton Graduate School (IL)*

WS-0256   HQ1237   93-37025 CIP
Conceptualizing sexual harassment as discursive practice, ed. by Shereen G. Bingham. Praeger, 1994. 206p bibl index afp ISBN 0-275-94593-6, $55.00

These ten original essays by feminist communication scholars make a major

contribution to the literature on sexual harassment and at the same time model the discursive, conversational approach thcy tout: authors refer to one another's essays throughout, and concluding essays provide critical reflections on the work as a whole. Although the title of the book and indeed the titles of most of the essays seem almost a parody of turgid academic discourse, the essays themselves are exceptionally well argued, scrupulously researched, and provocative. Each essay subscribes to the general premises that discourse is fundamentally ideological and that it creates our social realities. Discourse examined ranges from the Anita Hill/Clarence Thomas hearings to working women's storytelling strategies in response to sexual harassment. Each essay provides clear, concise explication of the often complex theoretical frameworks employed, thereby ensuring access for the uninitiated without penalizing the more advanced reader. The bibliography is outstandingly comprehensive and current. Highly recommended for researchers in gender communication issues, graduate and advanced undergraduate collections.—*T. Gleeson, Neumann College*

WS-0257   PN1992   93-32536 CIP
D'Acci, Julie. **Defining women: television and the case of Cagney and Lacey.** North Carolina, 1994. 344p index afp ISBN 0-8078-2132-2, $45.00; ISBN 0-8078-4441-1 pbk, $16.95

D'Acci analyzes gender construction in American television from feminist, postmodern, and poststructuralist viewpoints, using *Cagney and Lacey* (*C&L*) as a case study. Her main point is that meanings of gender are multiple, shifting, socially constructed, and constantly negotiated and contested. The players in *C&L*'s gender construction struggle were the network, the *C&L* TV team, the advertisers, the press, the women's movement, and the audience. D'Acci examines their roles in the review of *C&L*'s stormy history. She draws on personal research (including interviews), in-house files (including executive memos and fan mail), press coverage, and academic literature to make her points. Scholars who inform her analysis include Judith Butler, Teresa De Lauretis, John Fiske, Christine Gledhill, Stuart Hall, and Annette Kuhn. The result? A masterful synthesis and summary of relevant research (especially in the endnotes, which should have been footnotes) that only occasionally catches fire theoretically. The study is marred by an excessively pedantic, repetitious prose style and by the lack of a bibliography. For scholarly audiences only, graduate level and above.—*C. Hendershott, New School for Social Research*

WS-0258   HX84   95-37607 CIP
Dearborn, Mary V. **Queen of Bohemia: the life of Louise Bryant.** Houghton Mifflin, 1996. 365p bibl index ISBN 0-395-68396-3, $24.95

Portrayed as Sophie Macdonald in Somerset Maugham's novel *The Razor's Edge* (1944), Louise Bryant lived life on the edge of communism and lesbianism and in the center of bohemianism. Married to both radical John Reed and diplomat William Bullitt, Bryant inhabited the distant worlds of Russia's Bolshevik Revolution and Paris's 1920s. In between were Provincetown and Greenwich Village. For six years the only Western reporter in what was then known as the Near East, she secured interviews with Lenin and Trotsky; in Italy she gained an exclusive with Mussolini. Although Bryant's career lasted for only a short period, she nevertheless made her mark with mature, objective reporting. In her pivotal chapter about Bryant as journalist, "Toward Another Life," Dearborn demonstrates her competency as a biographer; an alcoholic by the mid-1920s, Bryant was diagnosed with Dercum's disease, a painful condition affecting the nerves for which there was no cure or treatment, and Dearborn tells the last ten years of her sad and tortured life with reasonable dispassion. With 16 pages of photos and extensive notes, this book is a worthwhile addition to all libraries. It is far more comprehensive than Virginia Gardner's *"Friend and Lover": The Life of Louise Bryant* (CH, Mar'83).—*S. W. Whyte, Montgomery County Community College*

WS-0259   P94   94-490 CIP
Douglas, Susan J. **Where the girls are: growing up female with the mass media.** Times Books/Random House, 1994. 340p index ISBN 0-8129-2206-9, $23.00

This well-written and extensively documented work offers a fresh, significant analysis of the confusing and contradictory media images of the girls and women of America's postwar era. Douglas reclaims a span of cultural history frequently ignored: from the girl group music of the mid-1950s and '60s, to the sitcom heroines of television shows like *Bewitched* and *The Flying Nun*, to network news departments' trivialization of the ERA, to the narcissistic advertisements of the Reagan era. In a witty and often humorous style, Douglas shows how the very ambiguity of the media messages flooding the increasingly important female teen and young-adult market accelerated the media-denigrated feminist movement. This book convincingly argues that in order to understand these ironic dynamics, scholars and students must move beyond the standard feminist political histories and explore the cultural histories of the millions of women consuming popular culture who become feminists. Even the young feminists of the 1990s who, for reasons explained in the book, preface their remarks with "I'm not a feminist, but—" are included. For feminist, media, and popular culture studies, sociology, and psychology. All levels.— *M. R. Grant, Wheaton Graduate School (IL)*

WS-0260　　　　　P120　　　　　93-43408 CIP
Fay, Elizabeth A. **Eminent rhetoric: language, gender, and cultural tropes.** Bergin & Garvey, 1994. 156p bibl index afp ISBN 0-89789-309-3, $49.95

Fay's important update of the discipline of rhetoric distinguishes and analyzes six new tropes in current discourse. In five short chapters this book argues that rhetoric as purposeful manipulation of language to gain political ends is being used as an unacknowledged weapon targeting women. The author focuses on discourse that knowingly does not "disclose its designs" and uses tropes that contribute to the dissembling of "the rhetor's actual goal." The purpose is "to point out recognizable patterns in word usage so that paying attention can be easier" for those attempting to read closely. In the arenas of pedagogy, media, literature, and intellectual debate about feminism the author examines the rhetoric of La Baron Russell Briggs, Jane Austen, Toni Morrison, Chef Jeff Smith, McNeil/Lehrer, Francis Fukuyama, Catherine MacKinnon, Susan Faludi, and Camille Paglia to demonstrate when rhetoric does and does not utilize these tropes. To question the "transmission of ideology" in devious rhetoric, this text suggests reading with scrutiny in order to produce meaning rather than merely to perceive meaning. Recommended for classes in communication, advanced composition, journalism, and advanced women's studies at both the undergraduate and graduate levels.— *T. B. Dykeman, Fairfield University*

WS-0261　　　　　P94　　　　　95-8204 CIP
Feminism, multiculturalism, and the media: global diversities, ed. by Angharad N. Valdivia. Sage Publications, CA, 1995. 332p indexes afp ISBN 0-8039-5774-2, $44.00; ISBN 0-8039-775-0 pbk, $19.95

This groundbreaking collection explores the intersecting variables of groups marginalized by the media. Contributors examine gender, race, class, sexual orientation, geography, and ethnicity in relation to feminist multicultural issues. This work supplements *Cultural Studies*, ed. by Lawrence Grossberg, Cary Nelson, and Paula Treichler (1992), which addresses cultural and societal commonalities among groups marginalized by the media. Part 1 of the present title examines personal, institutional, and organizational interventions. Part 2 focuses on the need to consider texts in their sociocultural context. Part 3 discusses the challenges of this distinctive research approach: i.e., scholars must be conversant with many literatures and methodologies and in touch with current popular culture and socio-historical context. The editor provides useful examples of media mismanagement of complex multicultural events and chapters on Jewish, lesbian, and African American media "absence." Highly recommended for students of feminism, multiculturalism, cultural studies, communication theory, and media analysis. Upper-division undergraduate and above.— *M. R. Grant, Wheaton College (IL)*

WS-0262　　　　　PS374　　　　　95-9467 CIP
Garvey, Ellen Gruber. **The adman in the parlor: magazines and the gendering of consumer culture, 1880s to 1910s.** Oxford, 1996. 230p index afp ISBN 0-19-509296-1, $45.00; ISBN 0-19-510822-1 pbk, $17.95

This book traces the ways in which advertising interacted with fiction and became an integral part of the American magazine while conditioning the readers, especially females, to become consumers. Garvey (Jersey City State College) studies trade cards (collected into scrapbooks by adolescents) and the influence of those cards in integrating the commercial, social, educational, and religious

worlds, then considers the contests advertisers promoted to get readers into the ads at the back of the magazine. One of the more interesting topics is the development of the consumers' practice of using brand names for products as a cultural short-hand, but even more fascinating is the account of the debate in the 1890s over the effect of women riding bicycles, as the progressives argued that riding would strengthen the female body for motherhood while the conservatives insisted that this exercise would masculinize women and endanger their sexual health by promoting masturbation. Generously supplied with illustrations, this carefully documented book gives fresh insights into turn-of-the-century America. Upper-division undergraduate through faculty.— *J. D. Vann, University of North Texas*

WS-0263　　　　　　　　　　Brit. CIP
Geraghty, Christine. **Women and soap opera: a study of prime time soaps.** Polity/B. Blackwell, 1991. 211p index ISBN 0-7456-0489-7, $52.95; ISBN 0-7456-0568-0 pbk, $15.95

A feminist analysis of nighttime soap operas from the US, Britain, and Australia, this book forms part of a feminist academic tradition of revalidating cultural forms that give women pleasure, forms that have often been reviled. The book's strongest emphasis, therefore, is placed on the role of women in soap opera, as well as the pleasure and values offered to them as the implied audience. The opening section analyzes how soaps organize their narratives and how they tend to mix various genres; the middle section of the book examines the appeal soaps make to women; and the final few chapters explore how the format has expanded, addressing issues of race, class, and gender in a more dramatic way, so as to engage new audiences. The book is well written and researched, summarizing much of the previous feminist work in the field. A knowledge of the programs discussed would assist in comprehension of the analysis, but the book remains suitable for the general, as well as the academic, reader.— *A. Goldson, Brown University*

WS-0264　　　　　PN1992　　　　　94-41723 CIP
Heide, Margaret J. **Television culture and women's lives: Thirtysomething and the contradictions of gender.** Pennsylvania, 1995. 173p bibl index afp ISBN 0-8122-3253-4, $28.95; ISBN 0-8122-1534-6 pbk, $12.95

Since the publication of Tania Modleski's crucial *Loving with a Vengeance: Mass-Produced Fantasies for Women* (CH, Feb'83), feminist scholars of television have continued to produce critical insights about the most influential medium of American life. Heide's new book, which focuses on the dramatic series *Thirtysomething*, adds to the body of analysis an important discussion of the interrelationships between the television text and the experiences and sensibilities of women viewers. The author's treatment employs cultural and literary theory, feminist scholarship, and sociological methodology to gauge the ways female spectators construe the gender issues embedded in the show's storylines. Examining both the narrative strategies of the text and the complex response patterns of the audience, she demonstrates how women simultaneously identify with and distance themselves from the story characters, using popular television inventively as an instrument to sort out the sex role conflicts of their own lives. Heide's discussion is cogent and intelligent, though her reliance on viewer interviews sometimes preempts analysis of the text itself; she eschews postmodern approaches to the material when such a critical framework would have deepened her analysis. Undergraduate through faculty.— *L. Babener, Montana State University*

WS-0265　　　　　P94　　　　　88-12696 MARC
Howell, Sharon. **Reflections of ourselves: the mass media and the women's movement, 1963 to the present.** P. Lang, 1990. 194p (American university studies. Series XXVII, Feminist studies, 1) bibl ISBN 0-8204-0523-X, $46.95

The past decade has witnessed an explosion of books on the rise of the women's movement and the second wave of feminism. Using gender, race, and class as categories of analysis, scholars have examined the rich tapestry of women's evolving political, social, and cultural worlds. Regrettably, Howell's book does not make much of a contribution to this burgeoning field. Unevenly written, it leaves the reader wondering about context, let alone historical precedent. Problems begin right on the title page. Although subtitled "The Mass Media and the Women's Movement, 1963 to the Present," for all intents and purposes the book stops at 1980. A misleading subtitle may be the least of the book's shortcomings, but given the keen interest in the field, libraries might be tempted to purchase it solely on the basis of the title, although one hopes the hefty price tag will serve as a deterrent.—*E. Broidy, University of California, Irvine*

WS-0266   Orig
Macdonald, Myra. **Representing women: myths of femininity in the popular media.** E. Arnold, 1995. (Dist. by St. Martin's) 250p bibl index ISBN 0-340-63221-6, $59.95; ISBN 0-340-58016-X pbk, $16.95

Macdonald uses Roland Barthes's definition of "myth" to look at popular media (primarily film, magazines, advertisement, and television) representing femininity and to consider why women "collude" with these media myths of femininity. She does not, in fact, answer that question adequately. Still, this is an extremely useful synthesis of examinations of media images, including an unexpected but invaluable chapter analyzing disciplinary approaches to the issue (including sociology, psychology, psychoanalysis, historical analysis, and cultural studies) and a glossary of terms. American readers will find much to learn here, even when the author is relying on British popular media. Not surprisingly, given the nature of her textual evidence, Macdonald's treatment is almost exclusively devoted to representations of white femininity. She mentions aging women, albeit superficially, but her work is relatively uninformed by gerontology. Macdonald is often more descriptive than analytical, but her discussions of film are especially strong. The bibliography is very brief if helpful. A welcome addition to such classics as Kathryn Weibel's *Mirror, Mirror* (CH, Feb'78), Marjorie Rosen's *Popcorn Venus* (CH, Apr'74), and Susan Douglas's *Where the Girls Are* (CH, Mar'95). All levels.—*J. de Luce, Miami University*

WS-0267   HQ1236   93-31206 CIP
McDermott, Patrice. **Politics and scholarship: feminist academic journals and the production of knowledge.** Illinois, 1995 (c1994). 197p index afp ISBN 0-252-02078-2, $36.95; ISBN 0-252-06369-4 pbk, $13.95

McDermott's book offers more than its title suggests. By focusing on the emergence of some key feminist journals, the author takes the reader through a journey that covers the origins and conflicts among women's studies scholars in the establishment of feminist academic journals. The journey ends with a cogent analysis of the relationship between political agenda and the production of knowledge in general. The balance between achieving academic legitimacy as a scholarly journal and adhering to an explicit feminist politics is at the heart of this accessible and compelling analysis. Even the thorny question of what qualifies as feminist scholarship finds its way into this brief but important book. McDermott makes clear that the tension between maintaining scholarly forms and conventions while manifestly retaining the explicit feminist contribution of the publication remains a constant challenge for the editors and writers involved in the production of feminist journals. Upper-division undergraduate and above.—*D. Kaufman, Northeastern University*

WS-0268   PN1992   91-46255 CIP
Mellencamp, Patricia. **High anxiety: castastrophe, scandal, age, and comedy.** Indiana, 1992. 414p index afp ISBN 0-253-33744-5, $39.95; ISBN 0-253-20735-5 pbk, $18.95

A collection of essays that look at the state of culture premised on women's everyday life and logic. The works span a decade of Mellencamp's writing, ranging through a variety of topics analyzed from a feminist perspective, including aging, gossip, sex, money, comedy, and catastrophe. Although not exclusively focused on media, the book does largely discuss issues of ideology and representation, concentrating on film, television, and women's magazines. In addition, the book includes several essays on contemporary independent video. Despite the range of subject matters, Mellencamp (art history, Univ. of Wisconsin-Milwaukee) makes an argument and a movement through the collection, which follows the changes in her own intellectual focus, for instance, from youth to age, from sex to money, from film studies to television studies, from theory to the everyday, and from academia to journalism. Despite this progression, however, each chapter can also stand alone. Undergraduates and general readers.—*A. Goldson, Brown University*

WS-0269   PN4874   93-41331 CIP
More than a muckraker: Ida Tarbell's lifetime in journalism, ed. with introd. by Robert C. Kochersberger. Tennessee, 1994. (bibl index afp) 242p ISBN 0-87049-829-0, $36.95

A book on Ida Tarbell is published approximately every ten years. Kochersberger's follows Mary E. Tomkins's *Ida M. Tarbell* (CH, Feb'75) and Kathleen Brady's 1984 *Ida Tarbell: Portrait of a Muckraker* (CH, Jan'85). Why so much interest in an increasingly obscure early 20th century writer? This book shows through Tarbell's own writings that she helped to invent modern journalism and was a practitioner of investigative business reporting as well as of muckraking. The essays, speeches, articles, and book excerpts by Tarbell show her development as a journalist. Best known for writing about business, she established her reputation with "The Rise of the Standard Oil Company" in *McClure's Magazine* (1902), included here. In *The Business of Being a Woman* (1912), contradictions appear as the career journalist writes about women in the home and on the job. Kochersberger has chosen the selections well, providing timely introductory material. Though some of Tarbell's prose is confusing, much of her writing rings with the clarity resulting from concrete illustrations. Recommended for all general and academic libraries with journalism collections/interests.—*S. W. Whyte, Montgomery County Community College*

WS-0270   PN1992   94-44239 CIP
Mumford, Laura Stempel. **Love and ideology in the afternoon: soap opera, women, and television genre.** Indiana, 1995. 165p index afp ISBN 0-253-32879-9, $27.95; ISBN 0-253-20965-X pbk, $12.95

This volume joins a number of salient feminist readings of soap opera, including Tania Modleski's all-important *Loving with a Vengeance: Mass-Produced Fantasies for Women* (CH, Feb'83); *Female Spectators: Looking at Film and Television*, ed. by Deidre Pribram (CH, Jul'89); *Television and Women's Culture: The Politics of the Popular*, ed. by Mary Ellen Brown (CH, Jun'91); and Martha Nochimson's *No End to Her: Soap Opera and the Female Subject* (CH, Oct'93). Mumford emphasizes her double perspective as both academic critic and long-time soap-opera viewer in order to erase the gap between audience and analyst that has characterized some earlier work on the genre. The author revisits and revises standard definitions of soap opera and probes its paramount conceptual issues: the relationship between public and private worlds in the soap-opera universe; the structural matrix that intertwines nonlinear development with patterns of closure; and, most important, the strategies of the genre to provide spectator gratification while conveying the ideology of patriarchal capitalism. The discussion is articulate and well-grounded in previous scholarship, though it lacks the incisiveness of the work of thinkers like Modleski and Brown, whose feminist reclamation of soap opera seems more compelling than Mumford's thoughtful critique. Despite useful footnotes, a works cited list is wanting. Upper-division undergraduates and up.—*L. Babener, Montana State University*

WS-0271   PN4882   95-30628 CIP
Outsiders in 19th-century press history: multicultural perspectives, ed. by Frankie Hutton and Barbara Straus Reed. Bowling Green State University Popular Press, 1995. 251p index ISBN 0-87972-687-3, $37.95; ISBN 0-87972-688-1 pbk, $19.95

This is a collection of articles, not a cohesive book. The selections are unified only in that all the "minority presses" treated represented groups that were ignored or discounted by the American "mainstream." The individual articles are interesting; they cover newspapers arising from ethnic groups (Jews, African Americans, Spanish speakers, Chinese Americans, Native Americans), women, and peace groups. The articles are well documented, well edited, and easy to read, so that they are easily accessible to readers on all levels. The volume would have benefited from a longer introduction that made more of the common elements in the separate stories and commented on the treatment in the mainstream press that made these minority presses necessary. This book might make interesting supplemental reading for courses dealing with American minority cultures or the history of the 20th-century press. Undergraduate collections.—*M. Cherno, University of Virginia*

WS-0272 PN1992 90-21274 CIP
Press, Andrea L. **Women watching television: gender, class, and generation in the American television experience.** Pennsylvania, 1991. 238p bibl index afp ISBN 0-8122-8169-1, $38.95; ISBN 0-8122-1286-X pbk, $16.95

Press examines how television shapes the gender identity of women in the US. Using "feminist methodology," blending traditional theories of identification, Marxist theory, and social scientific studies of the mass media audiences, the author asks how women's self-conceptions correspond to television images, whether women identify with the female characters they see on television, and whether women use television images in forming their own self-images. Press begins by reviewing current literature about television's effects and then examines a history of how women have been depicted on television. In the central section, the book focuses on the response of women of different classes and different generations to television programs. In a departure from much of the existing work on women and television, the author emphasizes class as a major factor in determining women's level of identification. The book is well researched and, although structured around interviews, provides a good summary of current theory in the field. Appropriate for public libraries and all levels of academic libraries.—*A. Goldson, Brown University*

WS-0273 HQ76 93-30242 CIP
Queer words, queer images: communication and the construction of homosexuality, ed. by R. Jeffrey Ringer. New York University, 1994. 348p indexes afp ISBN 0-8147-7440-7, $50.00; ISBN 0-8147-7441-5 pbk, $17.95

An interesting, readable, wide-ranging collection designed for an audience that believes "in the value of examining the language, nonverbal acts, and symbols of gay men and lesbians." Ringer provides a fine balance of personal reflections, statistical analyses, and scholarly studies. Included are strong essays on portrayals of gay men and lesbians on television (where narrative strategies often deny the validity of the very gay lives they present), on gay male political campaigns (in which approaches grounded in folly—e.g., Harvey Milk's campaign—help manage the transition between two worlds), and on the ontological shifts necessary to the process of coming out in the classroom. This political collection addresses the sense of isolation that gay men and lesbians experience when their rightful place in public discourse is denied. Several essays concern the rhetorical strategies and absences within the private discourse of gay and lesbian couples. This is fascinating reading for anyone wishing to know more about how culture both creates and distorts gay selves. Useful for courses in language theory and principles of human communication, the collection is an excellent addition to *Lesbian Texts and Contexts*, ed. by Karla Jay and Joanne Glasgow (1990), *Sexual Practice, Textual Theory*, ed. by Susan J. Wolfe and Julia Penelope (CH, Oct'93), and *Lesbian Teachers* by Madiha Didi Khayatt (1992). Advanced undergraduate; graduate; faculty.—*L. Winters, College of Saint Elizabeth*

WS-0274 PN4784 95-42313 CIP
Rivers, Caryl. **Slick spins and fractured facts: how cultural myths distort the news.** Columbia, 1996. 250p index afp ISBN 0-231-10152-X, $24.95

Rivers (Boston Univ.) provides a chatty, well-written, and timely dissection of the cultural myths and ideologies that frame media accounts. As a semiautobiographical observation by a media insider (Rivers both practices and teaches what she preaches), this book is entertaining and thought provoking. However, as a contribution to media studies, it lacks conviction. Although the book is filled to the brim with references, and although Rivers's deconstructions of cultural myths are interesting, her assertions would have had more depth and impact had she used a method such as content analysis or frame analysis. In addition, nonfeminists will probably not last much beyond the first few chapters, alienated by the cheerful pro-woman stance. Despite these weaknesses, Rivers's book presents a less alarmist, more wryly scolding viewpoint of media machinations than Susan Faludi's *Backlash* (1991). As such, it should be part of any undergraduate library collection focusing on women's studies, journalism, and/or sociology.—*P. D. Schultz, Alfred University*

WS-0275 NC1425 93-10570 CIP
Sheppard, Alice. **Cartooning for suffrage.** New Mexico, 1994. 276p bibl index ISBN 0-8263-1458-9, $37.50

Thanks to Sheppard (SUNY, Fredonia), students of history will be able to integrate new and fascinating information on women cartoonists into their understanding of the women's suffrage movement. "Lou" Rogers, Blanche Ames, and Rose O'Neill are three of the women cartoonists readers meet in this book. These women were not only pioneers in a male field, they also defied general expectations by acting as political cartoonists, artists who satirized the accepted truths about women's place in society and their exclusion from the political realm. The women cartoonists tried, through arguments of justice as well as expediency, to convince the American public that women deserved the vote and were perfectly capable of using the franchise wisely. Recognizing the importance of visual presentations in reaching a large audience, the cartoonists tried to publish their work in the mainstream press as well as in the publications of the organized women's suffrage movement. Well illustrated with many examples of the cartoons discussed, the book gives readers a good sense of the quality and the angle of vision of the cartoonists. General and academic readers, upper-division undergraduate and above.—*J. Sochen, Northeastern Illinois University*

WS-0276 PN1992 93-18121 CIP
Simpson, Amelia. **Xuxa: the mega-marketing of gender, race, and modernity.** Temple University, 1993. 238p index afp ISBN 1-56639-101-6, $34.95; ISBN 1-56639-107-5 pbk, $14.95

Xuxa (pron. Shoo-sha) is an enormously popular blond, female Brazilian performer who assumes the disparate roles of sex symbol and children's idol. Simpson (Romance languages and literatures, Univ. of Florida) deconstructs the images and "media texts" of the Xuxa phenomenon and finds in them a coldly cynical manipulation of Brazil's cultural contradictions (the myth of racial democracy and the white ideal of beauty; the expectation that a woman be both vamp and virgin; the First World aspirations in the midst of Third World poverty). Although Simpson fails to articulate a coherent theory of media effects, she does provide an incisive semiotic reading of Xuxa. The research is meticulous, the writing very good, the illustrations helpful, and the insights often brilliant. For sheer clarity and wit, Mark Crispin Miller's *Boxed in: The Culture of TV* (1988), admiringly cited by Simpson, remains the exemplar of this semiotic/Marxist approach to media criticism. But *Xuxa* is an important contribution to the field, and as Xuxa begins to export her show and image throughout the Americas, a book-length, English-language work is certainly timely. Highly recommended for undergraduate and general collections.—*T. Gleeson, Neumann College*

WS-0277 E185 94-9087 CIP
Wells-Barnett, Ida B. **The Memphis diary of Ida B. Wells,** ed. by Miriam DeCosta-Willis. Beacon Press, 1995. 214p bibl index ISBN 0-8070-7064-5, $24.00

This volume gives intimate glimpses into the private life of Ida B. Wells-Barnett once known as "the princess of the press." Wells-Barnett was a black journalist and civil rights activist who was perhaps best known for her antilynching efforts. The diary concentrates on her early life in Memphis during the 1880s, when she broke many bounds commonly surrounding young women. A school teacher, she chafed at teaching. A journalist, she was rarely paid for her work. Though always lacking money, she invariably dressed with taste and elegance. For a long time disdaining marriage, she enjoyed male company. The diary demonstrates her strong religious faith, her self-criticisms, and her powerful, candid opinions about her friends, acquaintances, and colleagues. She did not suffer fools gladly. This book gives scant information about her life as a public figure, although an extensive introduction and notes introducing each section help. Readers should see Wells-Barnett's autobiography *Crusade for Justice* (1970), an important companion volume. The editor translates and clarifies terms, initials, and acronyms. The exhaustive bibliography is very useful; photos are less so. Appropriate for upper-division undergraduate and above.—*R. Halverson, Arizona State University*

WS-0278 PN1992 92-945 CIP
Williams, Carol Traynor. **It's time for my story: soap opera sources, structure, and response.** Praeger, 1992. 253p bibl index afp ISBN 0-275-94297-X, $47.95

The premises underlying this very useful book are that soap opera's powerful appeal is based on archetypes both Oedipal and Proppian (from folklorist Vladimir Propp); that it is psychologically credible; that the pleasures of telling the story are polysemous for writers, producers, and audiences. Williams's introduction is both a valuable overview and critique of current feminist and post-modern scholarship. She provides a sound introduction on the radio roots of soaps as well as on their affinity with and difference from melodrama. She detects parallel dramatic effects in Jacobean tragicomedies. Using detailed examples from 11 soaps viewed over several years, she provides new insights into the overall content, particularly the strengths and weaknesses of the "issue stories." Using interviews with writers and producers plus commentary in *Soap Opera Digest*, she demonstrates how characters drive the stories. Diagrams take the reader through the intricacies of "blocking and weaving" the plots. In her final section Williams (Roosevelt Univ.) demonstrates why "fans" are active viewers and are "more trustworthy," when interviewed in depth over a period of time, than the students who are the usual sources of empirical studies. Her conclusion that the soaps have "resonance, complexity and spacious vision" is persuasive. Undergraduate; graduate; faculty.—*M. J. Miller, Brock University*

WS-0279   CIP
Women in mass communication, ed. by Pamela J. Creedon. 2nd ed. Sage Publications, CA, 1993. 398p index ISBN 0-8039-5386-0, $50.00; ISBN 0-8039-5387-9 pbk, $25.00

Although saddled with an overly earnest sense of political correctness, this is a provocative overview of issues related to women in mass communication, both in the workforce and in the classroom. Because more than two thirds of students currently enrolled in journalism and mass-communication education are women, the field is ripe for ferment in its values and hierarchy of power. Yet gender has wrought little change in the field. This book attempts to address this disparity by offering a "re-visioned" approach to transforming gender values in mass-communication education and practice. The results are occasionally muddled, but overall worthwhile. The book is organized into three sections: theoretical perspectives, women in mass-communication industries, and the mass-communication classroom. Revisions from the first edition are substantial and include the addition of an index and new and updated chapters. Upper-level undergraduates and above; community college students; professionals.—*P. D. Schultz, Alfred University*

WS-0280   PN5124.W58   89-77034 CIP
Young, Alison. **Femininity in dissent.** Routledge, 1991 (c1990). 190p bibl index ISBN 0-415-04788-9, $55.00

Young's intention in this stimulating and provocative book is to analyze the discourses produced by the news media in their coverage of the antinuclear protests at Greenham Common in England. Drawing on the theories of post-structuralists such as Michel Foucault and Jacques Derrida and of feminists such as Luce Irigaray, Catherine Clement, and Helene Cixous, Young considers the issue of the power of the media. She examines how sexual difference is represented, and, in the process of representation, how it is constructed. Because the Greenham Common protesters were women, the media could fashion a mythology that articulated various themes of womanhood in their stories. Focusing their debates on concepts of femininity, maternity, the family, violence, and the nature of the liberal state, the media helped to create categories of normalcy and deviance based on sexual difference. By demonstrating how a woman's peace protest can be represented as a criminal activity, as a witches' coven, as a threat to the state, the family, and the liberal order, Young shows how definitions of criminality and deviance are brought into existence and imbued with meaning. Must reading. All levels.—*S. K. Kent, University of Florida*

WS-0281   Brit. CIP
Zoonen, Liesbet van. **Feminist media studies.** Sage Publications, CA, 1994. 173p bibl index ISBN 0-8039-8553-3, $65.00; ISBN 0-8039-8554-1 pbk, $21.95

Although, as Van Zoonen notes, the media have played a central role in feminist critique, questions of gender are scarce in the mass communication literature and feminist media studies remain marginalized. Here is a strong effort to remedy the situation, an overview that initiates the newcomer and offers topics and methods for the previously initiated. Van Zoonen takes the position that audiences are active producers of meaning, and rather than fearing the "turn," welcomes post-structuralist contributions to feminist media politics. Her summary of ethnographic method leaves much to be desired (particularly the thin sketch of ethnomethod-

ology). The absence of pivotal work on language, media, and gender (e.g., by Dale Spender, Cheris Kramarac, Casey Miller, Kate Swift) is offset, however, by the inclusion of international and cross-cultural material and perspectives. All levels.—*V. Alia, University of Western Ontario*

◆ Language & Literature

WS-0282   PS374   90-47290 CIP
Ammons, Elizabeth. **Conflicting stories: American women writers at the turn into the twentieth century.** Oxford, 1991. 234p index afp ISBN 0-19-506030-X, $32.50

Ammons (Tufts University) presents a useful and at times pioneering analysis of turn-of-the-century American women writers. Arguing that their fiction forms "a diverse yet unified body of work," Ammons depicts these "Progressive Era women writers" as "clearly breaking with the past, and the major break. . .consisted in their avowed ambition, with few exceptions, to be artists" rather than professional writers, as their 19th-century predecessors had viewed themselves. The 17 writers discussed are diverse in terms of ethnicity, race, and class. Ammons acknowledges this diversity in various ways, some of which represent a significant departure from earlier studies of these writers. For example, she attends to the racism—by commission and omission—in the work of white feminists such as Chopin, Gilman, Stein, and Cather. Additionally, she reads texts by African American, Chinese American, and Native American women to reveal their critique of the racism of white feminists. Her analysis, achieved in part by her juxtaposition within chapters of artists from different traditions, is persuasive and goes a long way to achieve her stated goal for this project: "the need to understand the relationship between the literary past of women of color and that of white women. . .that race in combination with gender be recognized and analyzed." Strongly recommended for undergraduate and graduate collections.—*E. R. Baer, Washington College*

WS-0283   PS366   91-32766 CIP
Autobiography and questions of gender, ed. by Shirley Neuman. F. Cass, 1992 (c1991). (Dist. by International Specialized Book Services) 214p ISBN 0-7146-3422-0, $29.50

Heretofore, the consideration of gender has not seemed important in what has come to be regarded as the traditional approach to the study of autobiography. This form, generally written by men, can be said to be characterized by a sense of stability, coherence, and unity, with measured attention to levels of generality. However, with the proliferation of "Women's Studies," political and sociological attention to gender has emerged, becoming often a dominant factor in the depiction of "self" and life experience. Some contributors to this volume therefore distinguish a "feminine style" in life writing. Editor Neuman is also a contributor with her essay on "Autobiography, Bodies, Manhood" and with her introduction, which goes the circle in placing each essay in the total context. The other contributors are all scholars already established in what we have come to call "Women's Studies." Although reading through the essays in the order printed has its merits, it is possible to center in on individual contributions, a choice that might be made by the undergraduate student, whose interests might be limited or who do not care for a particular emphasis or particular style. What is important is that women too have their stories to tell, as well as men, in racially or financially oppressive life situations.—*D. Kolker, Cleveland State University*

WS-0284   PN3401   91-9513 CIP
Bammer, Angelika. **Partial visions: feminism and utopianism in the 1970s.** Routledge, 1992 (c1991). 198p bibl index ISBN 0-415-01518-9, $55.00; ISBN 0-415-01519-7 pbk, $16.95

A significant proportion of utopian writing in recent years has taken the form of feminist reinterpretations of classic texts or "discoveries" of feminist novels, both historical and present-day. Bammer correctly identifies the 1970s as the golden period of this writing and constructs a meaningful discussion of its underlying patterns. The central argument, in oversimplified form, is that utopian writing is best when the utopia is only partially formulated. A fully formed ideal society would by definition be unchangeable and therefore conservative. For this reason, Bammer focuses on utopia as process, and contends that the feminist utopian novels and writings of the 1970s were largely responsible for realigning ideas of utopia. The author discusses an impressive number of utopian texts and takes the critique of utopia beyond the definitional debate. The content is thus important beyond the feminist viewpoint, and helps to synthesize various strands of the utopian dialectic. Also, Bammer has translated and evaluated several utopian works available only in German. Upper-division undergraduates and above.— *E. J. Green, Prince George's Community College*

WS-0285   PQ3939   92-7520 CIP
Barney, Natalie Clifford. **Adventures of the mind,** tr. with annotations by John Spalding Gatton. New York University, 1992. 290p bibl index afp ISBN 0-8147-1177-4, $40.00; ISBN 0-8147-1178-2 pbk, $13.95

Barney (1876-1972) was one of the most colorful and truly international writers and hostesses. She went from Dayton, Ohio, to Paris at the turn of the century, where at 20, rue Jacob she presided over a great salon for 60 years. In the US we have seen biographies, but few translations of her work (all written in French). This is the first complete and richly annotated English translation of the first volume of her memoirs (published in 1929 in Paris), which many critics consider her finest work. (Unfortunately, the title does not identify this as the "memoirs of. . . .") Barney's entries—memories, letters, poetry—on Oscar Wilde, Anatole France, Remy de Gourmont (who called her his Amazon), Gertrude Stein, Djuna Barnes, Max Jacob, and a dozen others, make it a rich association indeed. The bibliography lists full information on Barney's sources, for she quoted at length. The valuable annotations, which take 68 of the 267 pages, help to make this an indispensable volume for 20th-century literary studies. Undergraduate; graduate; faculty.—*N. R. Fitch, University of Southern California*

WS-0286   PR830   93-30645 CIP
Barreca, Regina. **Untamed and unabashed: essays on women and humor in British literature.** Wayne State, 1994. 191p bibl index afp ISBN 0-8143-2136-4, $29.95

After an introduction in which she finds that "most books on comedy in literature ignore writings by women authors ..." Barr examines works of Jane Austen, Charlotte Brönte, George Eliot, Elizabeth Bowen, Muriel Spark, and Fay Weldon. She believes that women's humor "is about our reclamation of certain forms of control over our lives," and she supports this thesis with a careful analysis of such examples as Charlotte Lennox's *The Female Quixote* (1970), Austen's *Northanger Abbey,* Brönte's *Jane Eyre* and *Villete,* and Eliot's *The Mill on the Floss* and *Middlemarch.* She finds that Bowen's female characters break down established patterns, and that Spark "does not accept convention." Barreca concludes: "We will read women writers best when we allow for their humor, their laughter, and their appetite for dislocation." Her detailed analysis, witty insight, and the wide range of writers she examines make her book an important discussion for anyone interested in women, fiction, and humor or, indeed, anyone interested in literature. General and academic audiences.—*A. Jenkins, Georgia Institute of Technology*

WS-0287   PR468   91-28965 CIP
Basham, Diana. **The trial of woman: feminism and the occult sciences in Victorian literature and society.** New York University, 1992. 253p bibl index ISBN 0-8147-1174-X, $37.50

Victorian occultism with its experiments in mesmerism, spiritualism, and seances was a movement parallel with that of emerging feminism. It gave support both to feminist discourse and to conventional patriarchal language. Seeking the validation of science, occultism emphasized its relationship with animal magnetism, electrical energy, and other fields under scientific study. Pairing the biographies of real women taken up by occultism with representations of feminine occult powers in literary works such as Florence Nightingale's *Cassandra,* Charlotte Bronte's *Shirley,* Lucie Duff Gordon's *The Amber Witch,* and Elizabeth Barrett's *Aurora Leigh,* Basham demonstates the linkage of such powers with the search for greater autonomy. The study has useful insights for Victorian feminist scholars. Some will find its linkage of female hysteria, menstruation, and mesmeric fluids persuasive, but the sporadic injection of semiotic and psychoanalytic (Lacanian) critique to provide an ideological framework impedes

rather than enhances this study. Bibliography of primary and secondary sources. Recommended for scholars, faculty, and graduate students.—*R. E. Wiehe, University of Lowell*

WS-0288   PR9205.A515   90-80896 CIP
Caribbean women writers: essays from the first international conference, ed. by Selwyn R. Cudjoe. Calaloux Publications, 1990. 382p bibl afp ISBN 0-87023-731-4, $37.50; ISBN 0-87023-732-2, $14.95

Cudjoe's landmark volume analyzes Caribbean feminist traditions, giving space to writers' own statements. The section "In Their Own Voices," which constitutes the bulk of the text, presents Lorna Goodison, Erna Brodber, Beryl Gilroy, Marlene Philip, Rosa Guy, Valerie Belgrave, and others, on their art, their roles in processes of social change. The volume is framed by an opening historical "context" provided by Lucille Mair and Rhoda Reddock, among others, and by a closing "overview" of Spanish-, French-, and Dutch-speaking writers. Writers were requested, notes Cudjoe in his introduction, to address how their work represents the development of a Caribbean literary tradition and "to what degree" their work "has been influenced by feminist concerns." Cudjoe traces the historical development of a Caribbean women writers' tradition from Mary Prince's slave narrative (1831), into this century with writers like Una Marson, Louise Bennett, and Jean Rhys. Reddock's essay usefully locates an indigenous feminist tradition that challenges the notion that feminism was "a 1960s import into the Caribbean." Her definition of feminism sets the tone for most of the writers' statements. This book is particularly useful for the writers' statements, remarkable examples of theorizing the politics of identities, language uses, and colonial education systems through autobiography and the personal voice. One wishes that in compiling this volume, entirely in standard English, an attempt had been made to recreate the writers' own lived patois forms of English to counter the notion that thought processes that entail theorizing need to be conducted in standard English.—*K.H. Katrak, University of Massachusetts at Amherst*

WS-0289   PE1404   94-28621 CIP
Composing social identity in written language, ed. by Donald L. Rubin. L. Erlbaum, 1995. 252p bibl indexes afp ISBN 0-8058-1383-7, $59.95

The ten scholarly articles in this volume explore the ways that individual choice interacts with cultural norms to construct a writer's identity, as it is "jointly erected by writer and reader." In an informative 30-page introduction, Rubin (Univ. of Georgia) defines the three kinds of social identity examined in the articles: ethnic, gender, and role-relational (adaptation to the audience or potential readers). The articles deal with controversial topics of current political and social importance: e.g., the functions of dialect in the speech and writing of African Americans, differences in male and female language usage, and strategies of persuasion. Each article sets theoretical background, evaluates earlier studies, and analyzes the methods and results of the author's research. Conclusions are based on empirical evidence—interviews, students' writings, teachers' evaluations. Most of the authors are widely published linguists or rhetoricians with academic affiliations. Extensive bibliographies, tables of statistics, and analyses of numerous examples of student writing enhance the value of the articles to specialists and advanced students in sociolinguistics and ethnic and gender studies. Upper-division undergraduates and above.—*E. Nettels, College of William and Mary*

WS-0290   PR868   94-10269 CIP
Copeland, Edward. **Women writing about money: women's fiction in England, 1790-1820.** Cambridge, 1995. 291p bibl index ISBN 0-521-45461-1, $49.95

Meticulously researched and solidly written, this study makes a valuable contribution to the understanding of women's literature. Copeland (Pomona College) takes as his subject "the consumer agenda of women's fiction, 1790-1820." The author provides discussions of fiction of the 1790s (including gothic), in which women were usually depicted as victims of imposed impoverishment; fiction after 1800, which recognizes the empowerment of women through their control of domestic economy; and Jane Austen's use of money and rank "to convey social meaning and power." He also offers a provocative analysis of 19 illustrations from *The Lady's Magazine* and readings of several novels dealing with women's employment, including the profession of writing. Copeland's strength is close textual analysis, informed by the perspectives of economic history and cultural studies. He makes nodding references to Bakhtin, Derrida, Jameson, Poovey, and others. He provides one particularly useful tool: a scale that enables readers to calculate costs, competencies, and worth (e.g., if a character is described as having an annual income of a thousand pounds, what does that mean in terms of rank and consumer power?). The exhaustive and useful bibliography includes both primary sources (many of them obscure) and secondary sources. Highly recommended for upper-division undergraduates and above.—*E. R. Baer, Gustavus Adolphus College*

WS-0291   PR116   CIP
Cosslet, Tess. **Women writing childbirth: modern discourses of motherhood.** Manchester, 1994. (Dist. by St. Martin's) 184p bibl index ISBN 0-7190-4323-9, $59.95; ISBN 0-7190-4324-7 pbk, $17.95

By making childbirth more visible as a "life-changing event for women," Cosslet (Lancaster Univ., UK) contributes to the "recovery of maternal subjectivity," her aim in this book. She undertakes a fairly comprehensive study of the literature of 20th-century women in four regions: Africa (e.g., Buchi Emecheta and Doris Lessing), the US (e.g., Toni Morrison, Doris Betts, Nikki Giovanni, Erica Jong, Sylvia Plath, Adrienne Rich, and Alice Walker), Canada (Margaret Atwood), and Great Britain (e.g., Enid Bagnold, Vera Brittain, A.S. Byatt, Margaret Drabble, and Fay Weldon). She also ranges widely in her use of theorists, moving easily from Susan Griffin to Julia Kristeva, from Jane Tompkins to Marianne Hirsch, from Barbara Ehrenreich to Hélène Cixous. She concludes her study with an autobiographical epilogue, which also includes information about interviews with contemporary women who have had difficult childbirth experiences. Cosslet has read the medical literature on childbirth and moves deftly between those texts and fiction and poetry. Her critique of "natural childbirth" as a largely male construct which both valorizes and stereotypes "primitive women" will be of special interest to feminist critics. A valuable study for women's literature as well as for medical, premedical, and nursing students. Recommended for such specialized collections. Academic and general audiences.—*E. R. Baer, Gustavus Adolphus College*

WS-0292   PE1404   94-21538 CIP
Dooley, Deborah Anne. **Plain and ordinary things: reading women in the writing classroom.** State University of New York, 1995. 273p bibl index afp ISBN 0-7914-2319-0, $44.50

Seldom do freshman composition teachers get the opportunity to think about their work as much more than academic drudgery. Dooley's book managed to shake this reviewer out of that ennui. Dooley (Nazareth College) examines the teaching of writing in a meditation that ranges from English Romantic poets to contemporary African American women writers. Her theory of orality is based on her study of Australian Aboriginal women's songs, and her theories of women's writing are largely dependent on French feminist theorists. The body of the text, however, shows how she uses women's writing, in particular that of Virginia Woolf, Joanna Field, and Adrienne Rich, to access a particular approach to writing— that is, writing as a means to connecting not just with the world around us but, more importantly, with ourselves. She invites teachers to create narratives with students about how they construct relationships to knowledge and how approaches to knowledge may be different but valuable. Ultimately, however, she invites readers to think about the teaching of composition as profound, exciting, and having everything to do with the literature we prefer to teach. Graduate students; faculty; professionals.—*J. Tharp, University of Wisconsin—Marshfield-Wood County*

WS-0293   CT25   95-46088 CIP
Evasdaughter, Elizabeth N. **Catholic girlhood narratives: the Church and self-denial.** Northeastern University, 1996. 271p bibl index afp ISBN 1-55553-269-1, $28.95

"A Catholic woman writing an autobiography is already a subversive," declares Evasdaughter in this study of 33 memoirs, spanning lifetimes from 1836 to the present in the US, France, Spain, Ireland, Guatemala, and Canada. Her intent in studying Catholic women's autobiographies is to demonstrate that, as a group, they have "suffered a repression of their human possibilities by their Church in the name of 'the Catholic woman' and have repudiated this training both as girls and as autobiographers." The resulting book, the first study of its kind, is persuasive. Much of that persuasion is based on the author's explication of Catholic theological doctrine about women in documents ranging from the Baltimore catechism to Augustine, Aquinas, and papal texts, and her convincing connection between what she

calls "Catholic gender formation" and self-images, submissions, frustrations, and resistances delineated in these autobiographies. Though raised as a Protestant, Evasdaughter converted to Catholicism and as a former Dominican nun is well versed in this doctrine. Some of the texts—by Sarah Bernhardt, Mary McCarthy, Simone de Beauvoir, Colette, Rigoberta Menchu—will be familiar to readers of women's literature; for the many less familiar texts, Evasdaughter provides helpful summaries. While demonstrating awareness of recent theory on women's autobiography, Evasdaughter develops her own typology of personal narratives available as options to Catholic women. Strongly recommended for all academic and public collections.—*E. R. Baer, Gustavus Adolphus College*

WS-0294   Z1039   93-18195 MARC
Flint, Kate. **The woman reader, 1837-1914.** Oxford, 1993. 366p index ISBN 0-19-811719-1, $38.00

Flint (Oxford), author of a well-received *Dickens* (CH, Dec'86) and editor of *The Victorian Novelist: Social Problems and Social Change* (1987), turns her attention to women readers of Victorian and Edwardian literature and to the many critics and advisers who were ready to see women's reading as a social problem. The first four of the book's five parts are, in effect, an extensive bibliographic essay. In Part 1, Flint includes a mixture of 19th-century commentators and moderns (e.g., Richard Altick) and more recent secondary work embodying feminist scholarship (e.g., Elizabeth Flynn, Suzanne Hull, Caroline Lucas, Patrocinio Schweickart). Part 2 surveys 19th-century studies and advice in several categories of publications: medical, physiological, and psychoanalytic; practical advice and instruction manuals; the literature of girls' education; and reviews and criticism in the periodical press, including journals of the developing women's movement. Readers themselves speak through journals, letters, and autobiography, addressing reading practices in general (Part 3) and the reading of fiction—with special chapters on so-called "sensation" fiction and "new woman" fiction in Part 4. In and among the rich tapestry of references Flint weaves her own text, framed with an opening chapter on theory and a conclusion that admits, almost with relief, recognition of the "heterogeneity of the woman reader." The seemingly exhaustive bibliography fails to cite Amy Cruse's *The Victorians and Their Books* (1935), mentioned in the text. Staff in all libraries; advanced undergraduate and graduate students; faculty.—*V. Clark, Choice*

WS-0295   94-61440 Orig
Foster, Shirley. **What Katy read: feminist re-readings of 'classic' stories for girls,** by Shirley Foster and Judy Simons. Iowa, 1995. 223p bibl index ISBN 0-87745-493-0, $19.95

Those who remember Jo March, Anne Shirley, and Mary Lennox from their childhood reading will find Foster and Simons's book thought-provoking. But even readers who do not remember these popular girl heroines will be interested in the author's articulate discussion of girls' reading habits and how such reading can be both socializing and subversive. Through close readings of such classic North American and British girls' novels as *The Secret Garden*, *The Daisy Chain*, *Little Women*, *Anne of Green Gables*, and *The Wide, Wide World*, Foster and Simons focus on this often disregarded area of literature. The authors point out that scholars should study girls' literature with greater care, since such books help to form a "collective cultural inheritance" for many girls. Taking a feminist approach to the texts they examine, the writers create lucid, persuasive argument for the importance of *all* girls' books, not only the ones studied here. For scholars of children's literature, this book is a must read. But, even more broadly, any person interested in how gender influences reading will appreciate this study. All academic collections.—*S. A. Inness, Miami University*

WS-0296   PS2719   93-23813 CIP
Gates, Joanne E. **Elizabeth Robins, 1862-1952: actress, novelist, feminist.** Alabama, 1994. 297p bibl index afp ISBN 0-8173-0664-1, $39.95

Gates's critical biography uses previously unavailable primary material and recent feminist perspectives to retrieve the life and art of Elizabeth Robins. Balancing a passion for acting with prolific writing, Robins left America to become a leading interpreter of Ibsen's heroines on the English stage and to produce 21 published novels, plays, and collections of stories, 37 works of nonfiction, and 62 unpublished plays, fictions, and nonfictions. While Robins's achievements as an actress stem from her dedication to the moral purpose of a truly artistic theater, her strength as a writer comes from her readiness to transform personal experience into meaningful investigations of the differences between men and women's natures, the significance of women's silences, and contemporary feminist issues. Discovering the artistic power in speaking with two voices, Robins found privacy, as well as greater self-expression, in her shifting personae: widow, actress, pseudonymous author, independent theater manager, sister, expatriate, invalid, adventurous Alaskan traveler, mother substitute, militant suffragette. Gates's own strengths are careful research and a multifaceted style and subject. All academic levels.—*S. N. Mayberry, Alfred University*

WS-0297 PJ5013 92-33134 CIP
Gender and text in modern Hebrew and Yiddish literature, ed. by Naomi B. Sokoloff, Anne Lapidus Lerner, and Anita Norich. The Jewish Theological Seminary of America, 1993 (c1992). (Dist. by Harvard) 274p bibl index ISBN 0-674-34198-8, $35.00

Most of the essays in this important pioneering collection originated as presentations at a conference held at the Jewish Theological Seminary, having the theme "Feminist Criticism and Modern Jewish Literature." The avowed aim of this volume is to further explore the implications of feminist readings in the modern literature of the Jewish languages, Hebrew and Yiddish. The result is an exceptionally stimulating and insightful discussion. The first section, "On Women in Literature," ranges from the study of individual writers (Esther Raab, Yocheved Bat Miriam, Bialik, Appelfeld, and Yehoshua) to general analyses of the cultural condition of the woman writer in Jewish society. This is followed by a shorter section, "By Women in Literature," devoted to three revealing personal essays (by Chava Rosenfarb, Ruth Almog, and Amalia Kahana-Carmon), in which the circumstance of the female writer is powerfully rendered. The volume concludes with valuable selected annotated bibliographies on gender studies in Yiddish and modern Hebrew literatures, thus prolonging the vital discourse so ably initiated in this collection. The editors' intentions are fully realized: gender studies of Yiddish and Hebrew texts have resulted in new forms of knowledge and understanding. Undergraduate and up.—*M. Butovsky, Concordia University*

WS-0298 P120 95-16959 CIP
Gender articulated: language and the socially constructed self, ed. by Kira Hall and Mary Bucholtz. Routledge, 1995. 512p bibl ISBN 0-415-91398-5, $22.95

This rich and diverse collection, bringing together 19 essays representing what the editors call "the state of the art in language and gender research," commemorates the 20th anniversary of Robin Lakoff's groundbreaking *Language and Women's Place* (1975). The editors survey responses to feminist linguistics and map the current field. The essays are in three sections representing contemporary "analytic stances": "how cultural paradigms of gender relations are perpetuated through language"; "women's innovative use of language to subvert this dominant belief system"; and "how women construct social identities and communities that are not determined in advance by gender ideologies." Topics include female police officers' appropriation of masculine language, discourse analysis of the Anita Hill hearings, "butch speech" in lesbian authors' novels, and "code switching" among African American teachers and among Chicanas in New Mexico. Among the contributors are such senior scholars as Jenny Cook-Gumperz, Penelope Eckert, Michele Foster, Susan Gal, Lakoff, Sally McConnell-Ginet, and Elinor Ochs. Accessible and well informed, this is a crucial acquisition for all academic libraries.—*R. R. Warhol, University of Vermont*

WS-0299 PN849 91-4788 CIP
Green cane and juicy flotsam: short stories by Caribbean women, ed. by Carmen C. Esteves and Lizabeth Paravisini-Gebert. Rutgers, 1991. 273p bibl ISBN 0-8135-1737-0, $34.00; ISBN 0-8135-1738-9 pbk, $11.95

This wide-ranging collection of short stories, with one written by each of 27 women, is drawn from 11 Caribbean societies: Antigua, Cuba, Dominica, the Dominican Republic, Guadeloupe, Haiti, Jamaica, Martinique, Puerto Rico, Surinam, and Trinidad. The stories, which are of good quality and representative of the themes and styles of the region, are presented, for no apparent reason, in the alphabetical order of their authors' names. Some authors, like Jean Rhys and Jamaica Kincaid, are well known to English-speaking readers. Many stories depict gender, racial, and colonial exploitation. Two of the longer sto-

ries are especially moving: Olga Nolla's "No Dust is Allowed in this House," which reveals the tensions in an upper-class Puerto Rican household, and Olive Senior's "Bright Thursdays," about a young girl fostered by her father's parents in Jamaica. The translations from French, Dutch, and Spanish appear fluent. An introduction and selected bibliography are useful, but the map calls Belize "British Honduras" and omits Barbados altogether. For college, university, and public libraries, along with *Her True-True Name*, ed. by Pamela Mordecai and Betty Wilson (1989).—*O. N. Bolland, Colgate University*

WS-0300 PN494 92-53860 CIP
Harlow, Barbara. **Barred: women, writing, and political detention.** Wesleyan/University Press of New England, 1993 (c1992). 292p bibl index ISBN 0-8195-5249-6, $40.00; ISBN 0-8195-6258-0 pbk, $17.95

The literature of revolution and incarceration has come a long way—especially for women—and this book attempts to chronicle its most recent and most feminist manifestation in the world's "hot spots." The argument is that the growing number of women involved in revolutionary activities has generated a new kind of educational literature in and about the "university of the prison." We are told that this is "forcing a radical rethinking of the mobilizational tactics and structures of contestation that historically have been articulated on masculinist grounds by protest movements and resistance organizations." Harlow has allocated chapters in six areas where she feels such rethinking is exemplified and thus merits closer scrutiny: Northern Ireland, Israel/Lebanon, Egypt, South Africa, El Salvador, and the US. In all areas what is needed is the recognition of the political status of prisoners and "by both state and the resistance movement, of the political status of women." At times judgmental and inflammatory, the narrative nevertheless constitutes an in-depth study of social agendas and political struggles, which are pieced together from stories, narratives, novels, diaries, autobiographies, and even film. This depth is both the book's strength and its weakness. The bibliography is important, unique, and up-to-date. But perhaps because of the political focus, the style is often jargon-ridden and very abstract as it tries to discover a descriptive flow that will encompass and direct without polarizing. The attempt is not always successful. Advanced undergraduate; graduate; faculty.—*E. J. Zimmermann, Canisius College*

WS-0301 PR9205 92-33056 CIP
The Hart sisters: early African Caribbean writers, evangelicals, and radicals, ed. with introd. by Moira Ferguson. Nebraska, 1993. 214p index afp ISBN 0-8032-1984-9, $40.00

Long-forgotten works by early authors of the African Caribbean are reappearing today and undergoing scholarly analyses. In a lengthy introduction to the spiritual writings of the "free colored" sisters Anne Hart Gilbert and Elizabeth Hart Thwaites of Antigua, Ferguson contributes to the fund of knowledge and appreciation that present-day students require for a fuller understanding of African Caribbean literature. Ferguson discusses the implications in the prose works of the Hart sisters, who defied the mainstream island society as they labored to assist all persons of color, especially those men and women still in slavery. Each woman wrote a history of Methodist activities detailing personal accounts of spiritual conversions, courageous attempts to evoke sympathy for the slaves' plight, and strong criticisms of those in control of the island society's institutions of power. This book is an interesting addition to the growing body of black autobiographical prose works. Recommended for all Caribbean, black studies, and religious history collections. Undergraduate; graduate; faculty.—*A. Costanzo, Shippensburg University of Pennsylvania*

WS-0302 PS409 95-31825 CIP
Inscribing the daily: critical essays on women's diaries, ed. by Suzanne L. Bunkers and Cynthia A. Huff. Massachusetts, 1996. 296p bibl index afp ISBN 1-55849-010-8, $55.00; ISBN 1-55849-011-6 pbk, $18.95

Students, scholars, amd diarists will enjoy and benefit from reading this volume in part or whole. The editors quote generously from diaries, and the bibliography suggests further reading in every direction. After the editors' informative survey of the seminal and the exploratory work in the field, 15 accessible, jargon-free essays expand the "discussion of the diary itself" and contribute to "the ongoing assessment of its place within autobiography, writing by women, and the audience and cultural communities." A second section, "Women's Diaries and the Cultural Matrix," discusses a great variety of diaries, from those of 19th-century French *jeune filles* to those of contemporary diarists. Almost regardless of race, time, place, or person, the diaries presented are asylums of freedom. In keeping, sharing, rereading, and sometimes rewriting diaries, women find comfort, courage, knowledge, companionship, joy, healing, and self in the freedom from patriarchal control by family, husband, church, and society. Several essayists demonstrate how some diarists successfully control reality with the choices involved in diary writing. The variety of situations, uses of diaries, and new ideas about women's diaries in this collection is enormous. All levels.—*P. A. McHaney, formerly, Georgia State University*

WS-0303   PR830   94-40947 CIP
Lewes, Darby. **Dream revisionaries: gender and genre in women's utopian fiction, 1870-1920.** Alabama, 1995. 199p bibl index afp ISBN 0-8173-0795-8, $36.95

Lewes (Lycoming College) says this study is both "narrower in scope and broader in detail" than Nan Bowman Albinski's similarly titled *Women's Utopias in British and American Fiction* (CH, Feb'89). Lewes focuses on the "new kind of utopian narrative" that emerged in the late 19th century as a result of middle-class women's "experiences with contemporary politics, fashion, health, education, and employment." The "apparent failure of the suffrage movement" in the late 1860s and the success of Edward Bellamy's *Looking Backward: 2000-1887* (1888) were important factors in the large-scale production of women's utopias between 1870 and 1920. Lewes contrasts the urban, futuristic settings and "public heroines" of most British women's utopian studies with the frontier landscapes and domestic protagonists of American works. She also demonstrates that many literary utopias—such as that in Charlotte Perkins Gilman's *Moving the Mountain* (1911)—helped to bridge the "schism" between evangelical and rationalist forces in the women's movement by shaping "disparate dreams into a unified pattern of reconciliation." A valuable appendix describes about 150 women's utopian works between 1621 and 1920. Strongly recommended for all academic libraries, upper-division undergraduate and above.—*J. W. Hall, University of Mississippi*

WS-0304   PN6068   94-31075 CIP
Moving beyond boundaries: v.1: International dimensions of black women's writing; v.2: Black women's diasporas, ed. by Carole Boyce Davies (v.1 & 2) and 'Molara Ogundipe-Leslie (v.1). New York University, 1995. 2v. 252, 333p bibl indexes ISBN 0-8147-1237-1, v.1; ISBN 0-8147-1239-8, v.2; $50.00 ea.; ISBN 0-8147-1238-X pbk, v.1; ISBN 0-8147-1240-1 pbk, v.2: $18.95 ea.

Davies's eclectic two-volume collection of creative and critical writing by black women from various countries does not claim to be comprehensive, but it represents numerous voices in a variety of genres, including poetry, autobiographical and critical essays, and fiction. Authors of these pieces range from newly discovered Brazilian poets to well-known feminist critic bell hooks and poet Sonia Sanchez. Introductions by the editors define their "trans-national project" as crossing genre and national boundaries with "short pieces from writers from a number of cultural sites, speaking reflectively and creatively on their existences." Davies articulates the political agenda of the collection as one that recognizes and seeks to overcome historically imposed silence or retaliation by publishing black women's voices that, in passionate writing, "express resistance" to oppression. Volume 1 centers on poetry in addition to some prose pieces; volume 2 includes interviews, literary criticism, and substantial bibliography. Upper-division undergraduates upward.—*B. Braendlin, Florida State University*

WS-0305   PN56   90-27053 CIP
Narrating mothers: theorizing maternal subjectivities, ed. by Brenda O. Daly and Maureen T. Reddy. Tennessee, 1991. 297p bibl index afp ISBN 0-87049-705-7, $42.50; ISBN 0-87049-706-5 pbk, $19.50

This collection of 15 essays by various feminist scholars centers on the construction of the concept of motherhood in narratives written by 20th-century English and North American women. Central to these novels and autobiographies, as the introduction notes, is a focus on "maternal subjectivity," an identity informed by the decision not only to have children, but to care for them. Narrators and characters are thus seen as practicing motherhood not just in a personal, individual way but in a relational way that extends caretaking to all children and that expresses a "concern for the future of the human race." Informing the critiques of specific texts are psychoanalytic and cultural theories of subjectivity, language, and social practices currently in vogue among feminist critics. The central issue of female desire is explored in several essays, particularly those on lesbianism and feminist teaching. Political importance emerges in discussions of surrogate motherhood, adoption, and societal regulation of the female body. The collection includes an extensive bibliography. Graduate and upper-division undergradate levels.—*B. Braendlin, Florida State University*

WS-0306   PR878   95-52470 CIP
The New nineteenth century: feminist readings of underread Victorian fiction, ed. by Barbara Leah Harman and Susan Meyer. Garland, 1996. 286p (Wellesley studies in critical theory, literary history and culture, 10) bibl index afp ISBN 0-8153-1292-X, $50.00

Consider this statistic from John Sutherland's very helpful foreword to this book: approximately 50,000 novels were published during the Victorian period, from the pens of an estimated 3,500 novelists. The most ardent scholar has read or analyzed less than 10 percent. This book is about the task of rethinking that granite-etched reading list of 19th-century novels, a list used in the classroom for five generations. These 15 essays on "underread" Victorian fiction treat the work of novelists normally considered "second tier"—Anne Brontë, Wilkie Collins, Charles Reade, Walter Besant, George Moore, George Gissing—and those so minor as to appear hardly ever on any syllabus anywhere—Sarah Grand, George Egerton, Flora Annie Steel, and Geraldine Jewsbury. Again and again the essayists make the point that many fine novels are unread and therefore unappreciated; that many "minor" novels give unique insights into such historical events as the Beecher trial and the Bengal Mutiny; and that a fuller knowledge of these unfamiliar novels would bring a deeper appreciation of the Victorian female novelist, since most of the lesser-known novels in the Victorian period were written by women. This intelligent and reasonable argument for a rethinking of the English fictional canon will be a good addition to both undergraduate and graduate libraries.—*P. W. Stine, Gordon College*

WS-0307   88-70199 Orig
Out of the Kumbla: Caribbean women and literature, ed. by Carole Boyce Davies and Elaine Savory Fido. Africa World, 1990. 399p bibl ISBN 0-86543-042-X, $49.95; ISBN 0-86543-043-8, $15.95

Aime Cesaire's *Cahier d'un retour au pays natal* (Paris, 1947) focused critical attention on the literary achievements of writers from the French-, English-, and Spanish-speaking Caribbean nations. With few exceptions, however the writers to whom the literary establishment turned its attention were men. In the present seminal collection of essays Caribbean women writers receive the kind of critical attention their male counterparts have enjoyed in the years since Cesaire's *Cahier*. Alice Walker's notion of "womanism" provides the primary theoretical framework for these essays. But as Sylvia Wynter observes in her brilliant "After/Word," this "womanist/feminist" theoretical approach has underscored the tensions and contradictions between the two terms in interesting ways. For example, although the Cuban poet Nancy Morejon dismisses certain feminist movements as products of a consumer society, she seems only cautiously optimistic about the relevance of "womanism" for "underdeveloped countries." Yet Morejon's poetry is very "woman-centered." However, as she explains in an interview with Elaine Savory Fido, her "woman-centeredness" must be seen in relation to the very rich and complex "mixed" Cuban culture. Similarly, most of the other writers who have contributed to this collection seem much more concerned with how the female presence in Caribbean literature enhances and intensifies its richness and complexity than with establishing bipolar (male/female) oppositions. Consequently, for readers with little or no knowledge of the Caribbean environment, *Out of the Kumbla* provides a comprehensive overview of its cultural context(s) as well as a commentary on how this literature developed. Essential for anyone interested in Caribbean, Third World, or world literature.—*S. Adell, University of Wisconsin—Madison*

WS-0308   PS153   93-2991 CIP
Outwrite: Lesbianism and popular culture, ed. by Gabriele Griffin. Pluto, 1994 (c1993). 204p bibl index ISBN 0-7453-0687-X, $49.95; ISBN 0-7453-0688-8 pbk, $17.95

Drawing variously on sociological research on the subject of audience responses as well as on deconstructive, psychoanalytic, and reader-response theory, the eight essays and brief introduction composing *Outwrite* generally emphasize that lesbians are active rather than passive consumers of popular culture. In addition to entries on lesbian cinema, lesbian music, and visual representations of lesbian sex, there are five essays focusing on literature, including lesbian romance and science fiction. Most of the contributors are affiliated with British universities, but the authorial stance vacillates, even in some cases within a single essay, between the scholarly and the personal. Attempting to fill a perceived gap in lesbian cultural studies, the collection tends to present somewhat idiosyncratic overviews rather than detailed readings or fully developed theories. None of the essays has been previously published, but Pauline Palmer's entry on lesbian thrillers overlaps slightly with her contribution to *What Lesbians Do in Books* (ed. by Elaine Hobby and Chris White (1991). Recommended for comprehensive lesbian, gay studies, and popular culture studies collections. Undergraduates and up.—*F. Michel, Willamette University*

WS-0309   PS153   93-2467 CIP
Palmer, Paulina. **Contemporary lesbian writing: dreams, desire, difference.** Open University, 1993. (Dist. by Taylor & Francis) 141p bibl index ISBN 0-335-09039-7, $79.00; ISBN 0-335-09038-9 pbk, $27.50

Palmer examines the intersections of personal, cultural, and literary politics in writing by and about lesbians in the last 25 years. She discusses the freedoms afforded by the lesbian feminist movement, the increasing power of feminist presses, and the influence of lesbian and gay studies programs as well as the queer politics movement on the theory and practice of lesbian fiction. Palmer questions the distance between the obscurity and elitism of some poststructuralist lesbian theory and the simple pleasure in reading lesbian texts. For US readers, this study's Anglo-American focus is particularly valuable, as Palmer describes and analyzes the reimaginings for late 20th century lesbian readers of popular genres such as the thriller, the science fiction story, and the gothic tale. Especially perceptive are her discussions of the politics of S-M and Butch-Femme identification, the role of the freak and the master in lesbian comic novels, and the final chapter on fantasy, narrativity, and sex in the works of J. Winterson, J. DeLynn, and S. Schulman. A balanced and interesting study. Upper-division undergraduate and up.—*L. Winters, College of Saint Elizabeth*

WS-0310   PN3426.W65   90-49120 CIP
Redefining autobiography in twentieth-century women's fiction: an essay collection, ed. by Janice Morgan and Colette T. Hall. Garland, 1991. 305p (bibl afp ISBN 0-8240-7392-4, $43.00

These 17 essays by new scholars in the field of literary and feminist criticism discuss 20th-century woman-authored autobiographical fiction in the contexts of contemporary narrative and gender theories and of the historical production of texts. Placing each author in her historical time and country, the essayists discuss the play of fiction and facticity in writings by a wide variety of American and European authors, including among others Colette, Doris Lessing, Marie Cardinal, Marguerite Duras, H.D., Isabel Allende, Clarice Lispector, Maxine Hong Kingston, and Christa Wolf. The essays offer provocative insights into issues of female autobiography, presenting sociopolitical as well as aesthetic reasons (e.g., censorship) to explain why women inscribe their lives in fictionalized formats. The collection underscores the necessity of defining gender contextually and of recognizing autobiographical and narrative differences among women of various nationalities. Accessible to students, the essays will be valuable especially to teachers who want to broaden their range of texts in women's studies and world literature courses.—*B. Braendlin, Florida State University*

WS-0311   PR868   95-33313 CIP
Small, Helen. **Love's madness: medicine, the novel, and female insanity, 1800-1865.** Oxford, 1996. 260p bibl index afp ISBN 0-19-812273-X, $65.00

Beginning with a penetrating analysis of an inscription on Sarah Fletcher's 1799 gravestone in Dorchester Abbey—which reads in part "She sunk and died a Martyr to Excessive Sensibility"—this investigation into the treatment of "love's madness" ranges through the fiction and theory of women and madness in the 18th and 19th centuries. Small (Univ. of Bristol, UK) cogently and lucidly argues that the very notion of madness brought on by love and its disappointments represents contested ground. Focusing on texts both widely known and obscure,

but bringing to all the same discriminating and lively intelligence, the author succeeds in doing exactly what she ascribes to such authors as Jane Austen: she breathes new meaning and life into old and constricted conventions. She demonstrates that both doctors of the times and scholars of our own time have failed to read such texts in their historical contexts or to observe the degree to which women's madness was (and is) a "convention" among other literary conventions. Chastising and correcting past readings by scholars as renowned as Elaine Showalter (e.g., *The Female Malady: Women, Madness, and English Culture, 1830-1980*, CH, May'86) with wit and patience, Small embeds every reading in both literary and medieval history. The result is a fascinating and rewarding contribution to the reader's understanding of every text she considers. Academic and general collections.—*R. Nadelhaft, University of Maine*

WS-0312   PR610   95-40616 CIP
Sword, Helen. **Engendering inspiration: visionary strategies in Rilke, Lawrence, and H.D.** Michigan, 1995. 266p bibl index afp ISBN 0-472-10594-9, $44.50

Sword (Indiana Univ.) analyzes the gendered nature of inspiration for the poets Rilke, Lawrence, and H.D., exploring how inspiration has been constituted in different fashions by these writers. The author understands inspiration as being intricately linked to modernism, with the three poets representative of a much larger literary circle of modernist writers who wrote about the nature of the muse. She wishes "to recognize inspiration and gender not merely as compelling thematic issues but also as the formative elements of a modernist poetics." She builds a persuasive argument for the centrality of inspiration as it figures in the works of the poets. In each of the individual chapters on the three writers Sword shows herself to be a notable scholar who is able to integrate a vast range of literary knowledge. Only the closing chapter, focusing on Yeats and "Leda and the Swan," falls a trifle short of its fellows, but it still provides a thoughtful reflection on Leda as "a compelling yet highly problematic symbol for the visionary poet." Any literary scholar interested in the nature of poetic inspiration will find this book intriguing. Upper-division undergraduate and above.—*S. A. Inness, Miami University*

WS-0313   CT22   93-42403 CIP
Wagner-Martin, Linda. **Telling women's lives: the new biography.** Rutgers, 1994. 201p bibl index ISBN 0-8135-2092-4, $22.95

Wagner-Martin's intelligent analysis of women's biographies is insightful, fascinating, and much needed. The author says that the attacks on her *Sylvia Plath: A Biography* (CH, Feb'88) prompted her to realize that "telling women's lives has become so dangerous that writers must think twice ...." She feels that while biographies of men tell "the personal success story," those of women "demand different kinds of information," with one focus on the person's "interior life and another on the external values and conflicts." In crisp, clear style Wagner-Martin discusses such issues as the trap of the stereotype and overcoming it (George Eliot in the 19th-century view "fell short"); viewing women as wives, mothers, and relatives of the famous (the daughters of Margaret Mead and Marie Curie); and the problem of biography as being partly fiction (Kitty Kelley's biography of Elizabeth Taylor). She also considers the difference in the ways men and women biographers treat the wives of famous men, e.g., as Nora Barnacle, James Joyce's wife. Anyone will read women's biographies with a fresh eye after this. Indispensable for women's studies and English libraries. All levels.—*J. Overmyer, Ohio State University*

WS-0314   PS153   91-27069 CIP
Wilentz, Gay. **Binding cultures: Black women writers in Africa and the Diaspora.** Indiana, 1992. 141p bibl index afp ISBN 0-253-36585-6, $29.95; ISBN 0-253-20714-2 pbk, $10.95

This is the third book-length comparative study of black women's literature in Africa and the African diaspora to appear in the last three years. Similar to F. Lionnet's *Autobiographical Voices* (CH, Jan'90) and K. Holloway's *Moorings and Metaphors* (CH, Jun'92), this study argues that African cultural values continue to inform the artistic expressions and mother/daughter relationships of black women living in the diaspora. Using a cultural methodology consisting of Marxist, feminist, and Afrocentric criticism, Wilentz draws from historical, anthropological, sociological, and folkloric studies of black women in West Africa and the US. Common to West African and African American women novelists and playwrights, Wilentz argues, is their success in retaining the "orality of the spoken word and the active presentation of the oral tradition" within the confines of Western genres. Hence she suggests the term "oraliterature" in reference to the African novels *Efuru* by Flora Nwapa and *Foriwa* by Efua Sutherland, and the play *The Dilemmas of a Ghost* by Ama Ata Aidoo. The African American novels discussed in the second section as continuing the oraliterary tradition of the Africans are Alice Walker's *The Color Purple*, Toni Morrison's *Song of Solomon*, and Paule Marshall's *Praise-song for the Widow*. Wilentz's jargon-free, intelligent discussion of these six titles will appeal to students in African, African American, and women's literature courses, as well as general readers interested in the emerging field. The bibliography will be useful for teachers and scholars.—*A. Deck, University of Illinois at Urbana—Champaign*

WS-0315 PS152 91-32103 CIP
Winter, Kari J. **Subjects of slavery, agents of change: women and power in Gothic novels and slave narratives, 1790-1865.** Georgia, 1992. 172p bibl index afp ISBN 0-8203-1420-X, $30.00

A study that yokes Gothic novels and slave narratives seems at first improbable. Winter (Univ. of Vermont) has, however, illuminated both genres by this comparative study. Starting with Aristotle's views of slavery as informing the foundation of the Western social order, Winter asserts that "the oppression of women and male slaves can be understood fully only when the ideology of male domination is examined in conjunction with the ideology of slavery." She is careful, though, not to equate the status of slave and female. Reading "both genres as sites of ideological struggle," Winter states that her primary concern is "to examine how female Gothic novels and slave narratives engaged the dominant classist, racist, patriarchal discourse and created possibilities for new, feminist ways of thinking." Her sweep is sometimes dizzying, as she moves between Ann Radcliffe and Toni Morrison, Frederick Douglass and Charlotte Bronte. In addition, the book's organizational structure is rather idiosyncratic, being based on the movement of an Emily Dickinson poem which first represents the horrors of patriarchy, traces attempts at resistance and escape, and ends with images of enclosure again. Nonetheless, those readers already familiar with texts in both genres will find Winter's analysis often startlingly innovative and persuasive. Her prose is fluid and deft, informed but not burdened by theory. Strongly recommended for undergraduate and graduate collections.—*E. R. Baer, Gustavus Adolphus College*

WS-0316 PN842 94-12697 CIP
Women of the world: Jewish women and Jewish writing, ed. by Judith R. Baskin. Wayne State, 1994. 382p index afp ISBN 0-8143-2422-3, $39.95; ISBN 0-8143-2423-1 pbk, $18.95

Feminist criticism describes the condition of women writers in a male-dominated culture and charts the ways in which they fashioned literary identities out of their often narrow and confined situations. This ambitious and excellent collection of 17 essays focuses on the historic situation of Jewish women writers, tracing the problematics of being Jewish and a writer from the Middle Ages to the present and as conveyed in the Jewish languages of Hebrew and Yiddish, as well as in English and Spanish. The essays range from broad contextual surveys on women in Medieval Hebrew literature or radical women writers in America, to studies of individual talents including Dvora Baron, Esther Raab, Anzia Yezierska, and Cynthia Ozick. In particular, the essays that deal with the social, political, and cultural circumstances that confronted Jewish women writers in America—many were recent immigrants from East-European societies—are impressive in their informative coverage and historical insights. They comprise a self-contained area of concentration that covers the disruptive transition from the traditional to the modern. A helpful index is appended, as are biographical notes on the contributors. This volume makes a valuable contribution to studies in Jewish literature, feminist theory and aesthetics, and comparative literature. General; undergraduate and up.—*M. Butovsky, Concordia University*

WS-0317 PN56 94-24666 CIP
Wu, Qingyun. **Female rule in Chinese and English literary utopias.** Syracuse, 1995. 225p bibl index afp ISBN 0-8156-2623-1, $34.95

Wu's cross-cultural study seeks "to transcend Eurocentrism in feminist utopian study" by engaging both Western and Eastern literary traditions. By "feminist," Wu does not necessarily mean something written by a woman: four of the eight texts considered are by men who situate strong female figures in utopian idylls (in two cases, with a "pre-feminist" slant). The texts best known to Western readers—Spenser's *The Faerie Queene*, Charlotte Perkins Gilman's *Herland* (1979), Ursula Le Guin's *The Dispossessed* (1974)—are thoughtfully discussed. However, it is their pairing with comparable Chinese utopias that provides a fresh reading of each. Of the four Chinese utopias considered, only one has an adequate recent English translation—Bai Hua's *Remote Country of Women* (1988; cotranslated by Wu and Thomas O. Beebee, CH, Jan'95)—and two have no English translation. However, Wu's jargon-free discussion makes all the books accessible to the attentive reader. A return to the matrilineal prehistory of Chinese culture recovers the goddess myths that led to figures like the woman warrior, countering the stereotype that China has always and only oppressed its women with customs like foot binding. Wu's demonstration that feminist utopias dramatize the liberation of both genders from hierarchies of domination is a provocative contribution to gender studies. Recommended at the upper-division undergraduate level and above.—*M. J. Emery, Cottey College*

◆ Criticism

WS-0318 PR3065 91-29716 CIP
Adelman, Janet. **Suffocating mothers: fantasies of maternal origin in Shakespeare's plays,** *Hamlet* **to** *The tempest.* Routledge, 1992. 379p indexes ISBN 0-415-90038-7, $49.50; ISBN 0-415-90039-5 pbk, $15.95

"Selfhood grounded in paternal absence and in the fantasy of overwhelming contamination at the site of origin...." Thus Adelman states her thesis in examining Shakespeare's tragedies from *Hamlet* through *Antony and Cleopatra*, where she finds a pattern of struggle by tragic heroes to define their masculinity apart from the smothering influence of maternal engendering and love. The helpless infant, a fairly common Shakespearean image, becomes the focal image for the struggle of the heroes to assert their gender identity—separation from the maternal body, helplessness in the face of the world's demands, rejection of the female world of nurturance, all are documented in one after another male protagonist or supporting character. Adelman traces "a psychologized version of the Fall" (publisher's term) in Shakespeare's attempt to dramatize infantile helplessness and male attempts to liberate themselves from maternal power, from mothers both present and absent. The argument is persuasive, thoroughly grounded in both the plays' texts and myriad psychological studies copiously noted in the abundant notes that make up a good third of the volume. Adelman's readings of the tragedies contain provocative insights and radical reinterpretations of familiar Shakespearean scenes. Yet readers will be rewarded for adding this "unsettling" (publisher's term) view to their Shakespearean canon. Three indexes, full bibliographical notes. Recommended for upper-division undergraduate and graduate students, and faculty.—*M. H. Smith, College of St. Catherine*

WS-0319 PR888 94-45726 CIP
Allan, Tuzyline Jita. **Womanist and feminist aesthetics: a comparative review.** Ohio University, 1995. 152p bibl index afp ISBN 0-8214-1109-8, $34.95

Allan (Baruch College) distinguishes feminist and womanist aesthetics—à la Alice Walker's definition of "womanist" as expressing audaciousness, woman centeredness, and "whole(some)ness")—then uses these definitions to explore four modern novels: Virginia Woolf's *Mrs. Dalloway*, Margaret Drabble's *The Middle Ground*, Alice Walker's *The Color Purple*, and Buchi Emecheta's *The Joys of Motherhood*. With all but Woolf, Allan examines several earlier works by each author to create an aesthetic context for studying the major work; in Woolf's case, however, she barely mentions earlier work before reading *Mrs. Dalloway*, which she perceives as filled with Woolf's ambivalences about class, race, imperialism, and female sexuality. On the whole, Allan agrees with Walker's judgment that white feminism is unable to affirm woman, especially when woman is of color, of lower classes, of culture other than European or American. But Walker's womanism, too, is narrow and racist since it includes only women of color—and not even all of them. After an unpromising introduction (dominated, like so much literary criticism of the past 25 years, with murky, jargon-ridden verbosity), Allan settles down to write in a sensible, humane, clear, direct voice revealing important strengths (Walker) and weaknesses (Drabble, Emecheta) in these novelists' aesthetics concerning femaleness. Undergraduate collections.—*S. B. Darrell, University of Southern Indiana*

WS-0320 PR878.F45 90-35039 CIP
Ardis, Ann L. **New women, new novels: feminism and early modernism.** Rutger, 1990. 217p bibl index ISBN 0-8135-1581-5, $35.00; ISBN 0-8135-1582-3, $14.00

"Modernism" continues to be reexamined in recent feminist criticism, especially since Sandra Gilbert and Susan Gubar's *No Man's Land* (CH, Apr'88). Ardis focuses on the place of the "New Woman" novel, 1880-90, in British modernism and makes a valuable contribution to the study of early modern fiction. Why was the unattached late-Victorian woman labeled "odd," "wild," "superfluous," and "new"? This literary character demystified the ideology of "womanliness," the inevitability of the marriage plot, and the mimetic standards of didactic realism. Yet modernist critics have long relegated the "New Woman" to derogatory footnote status. This interesting study describes the rise and fall of the New Woman, her marginalization and exclusion from the cannon. Among the topics examined are matters of aesthetic deficiency, ideological self-consciousness, intertextuality, and the distinction between popular culture and high art. It explains her dismissal as a reflection of unease with the angry aesthetic of political engagement, a topic that today continues to decenter the modernist aesthetic. Includes extensive notes, a bibliography of New Woman authors, and helpful index. Recommended for all collections on the history of the novel.—*S. A. Parker, Hiram College*

WS-0321 PR457 93-23001 CIP
At the limits of Romanticism: essays in cultural, feminist, and materialist criticism, ed. by Mary A. Favret and Nicola J. Watson. Indiana, 1994. 291p index afp ISBN 0-253-32156-5, $39.95; ISBN 0-253-20853-X pbk, $14.95

While the term "classicism" implies restrictive formalities, "romanticism" generally suggests an individuality of thought and expression—a liberality in literature. A closer examination of historic romanticism, however, discloses an undervaluation of the efforts of women writers, narrative verse and prose, most of its journalism and decorative arts. Issues of gender and genre from roughly the period between the French Revolution of 1789 and the Reform Act of 1832 have been largely ignored. The 13 essays written by leading authorities on individual romantic subjects that make up this volume explore some uncharted terrain. A long introduction brings the objectives of this study into focus; but, then, at times it would seem these erudite explorations were written essentially for advanced students of romanticism, those quite familiar with the works of Bialostosky, de Man, Foucault, Rieder, among a dozen or so other such theoreticians. As for the essays themselves, "Wordsworth and Romanticism in the Academy," "Transfiguring Byronic Identity," and "Butchering James Hogg" are especially provocative and rewarding. A few are highly informative and worthwhile. Others are at best somewhat tendentious and a bit ponderous. Graduate; faculty.—*G. A. Cevasco, St. John's University (NY)*

WS-0322 PN56 93-13830 CIP
Castle, Terry. **The apparitional lesbian: female homosexuality and modern culture.** Columbia, 1993. 307p bibl index afp ISBN 0-231-07652-5, $29.95

Castle aims to fill a gap that she perceives in gay literary criticism: the lack of an adequate theory about lesbians in literature. Her theory is informed by an interest in ghosts as a literary subject and her perception that prominent critics like Eve Kosovsky Sedgwick have concentrated on males in their theoretical work. Castle argues against the notion that lesbian sexuality appears only with the introduction of the term "lesbian" in the late 19th century. Also, she observes that many instances of social interaction between two women employ spectral imagery when approaching the potential for such sexual interaction. From these two points, she argues that lesbian sexuality seems to pose an even greater threat to heterosexual hegemony than male homosexuaity does. In developing her own model for lesbian fiction, she reverses Sedgwick's concept that male homosexual relations are plotted as a triangle with a female as the mediating figure; for lesbians, Castle postulates a "counterplot," a triangle that uses two women with a male as the mediating figure. Castle develops her argument in nine chapters that move from personal experience through theoretical groundwork to considerations of specific lesbian figures for exemplary details. The writing is clear; the support is witty and graceful, with relevant portraits for helpful illustration. Substantial list of works cited. Recommended for undergraduate and graduate libraries.—*J. J. Marchesani, Pennsylvania State University, Mckeesport Campus*

WS-0323 PN98 92-12699 MARC
Changing subjects: the making of feminist literary criticism, ed. by Gayle Greene and Coppélia Kahn. Routledge, 1993. 283p index ISBN 0-415-08685-X, $49.95

The essays in this collection are autobiographical recollections by several prominent American feminist literary scholars of how they were introduced to feminist theory and criticism over the past three decades. Scholar-teachers like Nancy K. Miller, Rachel Blau DuPlessis, Bonnie Zimmerman, Barbara Christian, and Shirley Geok-lin Lim, among others, who came of age personally and professionally in the 1960s and 1970s, describe the real-life and reading experiences that inform their feminist criticism. As they weave narratives of family obligations, relationships with male and female partners, employers, colleagues, and students with their readings of literary and theoretical texts, they inscribe themselves as lovers, wives, mothers, professors, scholars, and politically involved citizens. Thus the collection is both a record of academic women's personal/professional experiences and one version of the history of second-wave feminism. It vividly illustrates the combination of personal and political that has been the basis of feminist thought and practice during this era. The references to each article together provide an extensive bibliography of feminist literary criticism. Advanced undergraduate; graduate; faculty.—*B. Braendlin, Florida State University*

WS-0324 PR878.F45 90-8166 CIP
Crosby, Christina. **The ends of history: Victorians and "the woman question."** Routledge, 1991. 186p index ISBN 0-415-00935-9, $49.95

Crosby's provocative and well-written volume sets out to illustrate the twin Victorian passions for history and for women and to explore the logic of their relations to one another. Crosby builds her book around the interesting idea that history, as defined by the Victorians, represented a generic history of "man" or "mankind," which in turn excluded other categories of humankind, such as "woman," "savages and primitive men," and "the poor" from the charmed circle. On the other hand, Victorians made a substantial effort to understand the nature of woman. To illustrate her theory the book's four chapters discuss: Daniel Deronda and F. Hegel's *Philosophy of History*; Henry Esmond and T. B. Macaulay's *History of England*; *Little Dorrit*, W. Collins's *Frozen Deep* , and H. Mayhew's *London Labour and the London Poor*; and *Villette*, Patrick Fairbairn's *Typology of Scripture*, and J. Ruskin's *Modern Painters*. There is a concluding chapter of summary. In each chapter Crosby discusses "the strange familiarity of history' and the troubling but necessary difference of women'." George Eliot, Crosby says, is a "woman writer who is deeply identified with the idea of Man, i.e. history whose writing displays the consequences of that incongruity." Although the scholarly notes are well documented, there is no formal bibliography, a regrettable omission. The book presents advanced and responsible feminist critical theory and will surely stimulate debate about the redefinition of history by feminist critics. Levels: graduate and upper-division undergraduates.—*R. T. Van Arsdel, emerita, University of Puget Sound*

WS-0325 PR830.P3 90-23907 MARC
David, Gail. **Female heroism in the pastoral.** Garland, 1991. 258p (Gender & genre in literature, 2) bibl index afp ISBN 0-8240-7107-7, $37.00

Much more focused than its title may indicate, this study offers a stimulating argument. David brings to light fundamental cycles in the journey of the hero: in the pastoral from the Renaissance through the 19th century, the male achieves acclaim or success by moving from urban to pastoral to urban setting, whereas the female achieves maturity and intimacy by moving from pastoral to urban to pastoral setting. In a methodical analysis, the author focuses on the progress of Montemayor's Felismena, Sidney's Pamela, Burney's Evelina, Radcliffe's Emily, Austen's Elinor and Marianne, Brontë's Catherine and Cathy, Gaskell's Ruth, and George Eliot's Maggie, depending heavily on nominal, geographical, and seasonal archetypes, but filtering these through feminist rereadings (especially Chodorow, Heilbrun, Moers). The limited number of female heroes treated here makes one wonder about those who participate in narratives with more complex issues of regendering (Hardy's Bathsheba?), but the pattern David outlines seems to work effectively as a basis that will further feminist criticism. The footnotes, bibliography, and index are excellent. Recommended for libraries wishing to enhance collections in women's studies.—*W. C. Snyder, St. Vincent College & Seminary*

WS-0326   PR6035.H96   90-31402 CIP

Emery, Mary Lou. **Jean Rhys at "World's End": novels of colonial and sexual exile.** Texas, 1990. 219p bibl index afp ISBN 0-292-71126-3, $24.95

This title suggests another psychosexual angle into which to corner the critically elusive works of Jean Rhys. Emery's discerning, sympathetic study overcomes the disadvantages of agendas by making Rhys's marginality—with respect to Caribbean, modernist, and feminist literatures—the departure for pluralistic readings of the novels. She rejects "the conflation of author and character," which has been the standard critical stance, by placing first the discussion of Rhys's last, best-known novel, *The Wide Sargasso Sea*, and by suggesting cultural, social, and political contexts. The readings are prefaced by a two-part critical exploration of the trope of "masking." Although the second part is less pointed, this section raises theoretical questions resulting from considering the intersection of marginalities and asserting a creative vision for Rhys, questions that have importance for feminist readers and other contemporary critics. Expository endnotes and a bibliography showing diverse and thorough research complement a study highly recommended as a critical resource that will be useful to graduate students and upper-division undergraduates.—*S. Landon, formerly Middlebury College*

WS-0327   PS152   89-78222 CIP

Engendering men: the question of male feminist criticism, ed. by Joseph A. Boone and Michael Cadden. Routledge, 1991 (c1990). 333p bibl index ISBN 0-415-90254-1, $49.95

A collection of essays concerning feminist criticism as practiced by men. A number of powerful and interesting articles offer new insights into both methodology and particular texts. The perspectives of gay male critics are addressed as well. Throughout, the authors and editors assert that matters of gender are legitimately and necessarily central to the stance of the literary critic; the editors acknowledge their indebtedness to women feminist critics who encouraged them both to attempt and to claim inclusion within the expanding ranks of feminist analyses. Though jargon sometimes clutters these essays, the best essays are full of vital insights and ideas that will allow readers new access to some key works of literature, from Hawthorne to Oscar Wilde. Of particular value are the essays in Section 3, "Cleaning Out the Closet(s)"; Michael Warner's "Homo-Narcissism; or, Heterosexuality" is a thoughtful and intense analysis of the heterosexist bias of psychoanalytical language as it equates narcissism with homosexuality and then contributes to critical assumptions unthinkingly perpetuating a specific historical equation. There is much to welcome in this collection. Appropriate for students at graduate and upper-division undergraduate levels.—*R. Nadelhaft, University of Maine at Orono*

WS-0328   PR888   91-6849 CIP

Greene, Gayle. **Changing the story: feminist fiction and the tradition.** Indiana, 1991. 302p bibl index afp ISBN 0-253-32606-0, $45.00; ISBN 0-253-20672-3 pbk, $17.50

Greene (Scripps College), coeditor of two anthologies, *The Woman's Part: Feminist Criticism of Shakespeare* (CH, Mar'81), and *Making a Difference: Feminist Literary Criticism* (CH, Apr'86), turns her attention in this book to the 1970s fiction of Doris Lessing, Margaret Drabble, Margaret Laurence, and Margaret Atwood. Her focus is on what she terms "feminist metafiction": books about "protagonists who turn to reading for validation of self and escape from circumstances." Greene sets her analysis within the framework of debate between Anglo and French feminist critics and, by her own admission, uses eclectic approaches: Marxist and deconstructive for *The Golden Notebook*, French feminist for *The Waterfall*, intertextual for *The Diviners*, and psychoanalytic for *Lady Oracle*. Greene's study is exhaustively researched (more than 70 pages are devoted to notes and bibliography), densely and tightly written, and yet eminently readable. Her introduction is a tour de force, which is followed by three chapters tracing themes, especially that of the mad housewife, in women's literature prior to feminist metafictions; then four chapters are devoted to that main topic. The concluding chapter, "Whatever Happened to Feminist Fiction?", a kind of literary counterpart to Susan Faludi's *Backlash* (1991), presents a bleak assessment of recent work by Atwood, Lessing, and Drabble. Greene asserts that such novels as *The Handmaid's Tale* and *The Radiant Way* "express unqualified disillusionment" in that the protagonists are no longer able to revise their worlds by the acts of writing and reading. Strongly recommended for all academic libraries.—*E. R. Baer, Washington College*

WS-0329   PR888   90-49252 CIP

Hanley, Lynne. **Writing war: fiction, gender, and memory.** Massachusetts, 1991. 151p afp ISBN 0-87023-738-1, $24.95; ISBN 0-87023-748-9 pbk, $12.95

Unusual as it is powerful, this study consists of linked essays interspersed by short stories, all based on the general theme of women and war. Hanley (Hampshire College) begins by taking issue with Paul Fussell's important work, *The Great War and Modern Memory* (1975), calling it a narrow analysis of war literature, based exclusively on the writings of white English and American men. The author sees Fussell's study deliberately suppressing war texts written by women, especially pernicious in this period of canon formation. As remedy, Haley critically examines the writings of women who make the matter of war a central part of their evolving thought: Virginia Woolf, Joan Didion, and Doris Lessing, in particular. She isolates bellicosity as a dominant structure of consciousness leading to war, proclaiming this more a male way of thinking than female, a point also made by Susan Jeffords's *The Remasculinization of America: Gender and the Vietnam War* (CH, Feb'90). Hanley's short stories, her war literature, cover the impact and aftermath of war. The stories movingly express fear, dislocation, monstrousness. Both essays and stories are accessible, a clear explication of an important feminist critical stance. Highly recommended for advanced undergraduate and graduate libraries.—*B. Adler, Marian College*

WS-0330   PN57   93-37016 CIP

Images of Persephone: feminist readings in Western literature, ed. by Elizabeth T. Hayes. University Press of Florida, 1994. 212p index afp ISBN 0-8130-1262-7, $29.95

Hayes's collection of essays would be useful in a graduate or undergraduate seminar in women's studies, cultural studies, or literature with a focus on mythic criticism or feminist criticism. Aside from Hayes's opening essay, "The Persephone Myth in Western Literature," which presents a coherent summary of the Greek sources of the Demeter/Persephone/Hecate myth, the ten remaining essays discuss how the myth evolves and is perpetuated in specific works of American, English, and French literature. The essays are arranged chronologically by primary author: Chaucer; Shakespeare; Quinault and Lully; Hawthorne; Atherton; D.H. Lawrence; Beckett; Atwood; Cixous; and Morrison, Hurston, and Walker. All of the essays provide a detailed, close reading of a work by one of these authors, an overview of the scholarship of that work, and a 20 to 50 item bibliography. They also explore aspects of the Demeter/Persephone myth that can be used to understand how Western society has upheld patriarchal values and condoned aggressive male sexuality at the cost of female autonomy. Four versions of the myth appear in the appendixes.—*B. M. McNeal, Slippery Rock University*

WS-0331   PR658   91-25081 CIP

Jankowski, Theodora A. **Women in power in the early modern drama.** Illinois, 1992. 237p bibl index afp ISBN 0-252-01882-6, $34.95; ISBN 0-252-06238-8 pbk, $14.95

Jankowski's study illustrates how radically common assumptions about women in the Renaissance have shifted. This shift was fueled by groundbreaking books and studies such as *Rewriting the Renaissance*, ed. by M.W. Ferguson et al. (CH, Feb'87). Jankowski knows and refers to almost all such recent criticism; her problem, in fact, is that although her specific topic promises a new and fascinating focus, she primarily catches onto and rides the tail of this critical tiger. After a jargon-ridden introduction on "theorizing and politicizing," she does offer her readers an excellent chapter on women in early modern England. Even here Jankowski's strength lies in the efficiency and brevity with which she summarizes what by now has become revisionist orthodoxy about women's positions in early Renaissance England. Her own analysis is less cogent. She appropriates M. Axton's idea in *The Queen's Two Bodies* (London, 1977), which was itself adapted from E. Kantorowicz's exhaustive examination, in *The King's Two Bodies* (1957), of the medieval and Renaissance theory that the king has "two bodies," one mortal and potentially dying (the body natural) and the other immortalized in the continuity of the crown (the body politic). Jankowski accurately reviews and then skews this doctrine, pulling it in odd directions to fit the pattern of her own analysis of power in Lyly, Marlowe, Shakespeare, and Webster. Although containing moments of genuine insight, this book on the whole hits one or two steady, repetitive drumbeats. Extensive notes; thorough bibliography. Recommended only for those libraries that can afford a complete collection of Shakespearean criticism.—*M. C. Riggio, Trinity College (CT)*

WS-0332   PR858   94-28979 CIP
Johnson, Claudia L. **Equivocal beings: politics, gender, and sentimentality in the 1790s: Wollstonecraft, Radcliffe, Burney, Austen.** Chicago, 1995. 239p index afp ISBN 0-226-40183-9, $34.95; ISBN 0-226-40184-7 pbk, $14.95

Johnson (Princeton Univ.) argues that the 1790s idealization of "sentimental man" profoundly unsettled notions of gender. Men appropriated traits traditionally assigned to women (tenderness, sensitivity), effectively displacing women, who became hyperfeminine or took on traditional male traits only to be condemned as unsexed, "equivocal beings." Sentimentality subverted old roles and offered women neither empowerment nor equality. Johnson studies how Mary Wollstonecraft, Ann Radcliffe, and Fanny Burney responded, in their novels, to the gender roles imposed by sentimentality. In *Maria or, The Wrongs of Woman* Wollstonecraft begins to imagine a life for women outside the straitjacket of sentimental heterosexuality. Burney and Radcliffe are ambivalent and do not ultimately challenge the underlying social and political structures—rendering their fiction aesthetically flawed and ideologically incoherent. Johnson's overview of the political and ideological issues of the period is convincing; her reading of the novels is less so. She uses much more critical jargon than she did in her excellent first book, *Jane Austen: Women, Politics, and the Novel* (CH, Jan'89), which explored similar themes more effectively. Even in this study, her brief epilogue on Austen is the strongest section. Graduate and research collections.—*K. P. Mulcahy, Rutgers, The State University of New Jersey, New Brunswick*

WS-0333   PR830.W6   90-55116 MARC
Langbauer, Laurie. **Women and romance: the consolations of gender in the English novel.** Cornell, 1990. 271p bibl index afp ISBN 0-8014-2421-6, $35.00; ISBN 0-8014-9692-6, $10.95

Post-Foucault post-structuralism informs this study of the structural linkages between gender and the "genre" of romance. Arguing that romance cannot be defined by contrast to the formal realism of the novel or as wish fulfillment, Langbauer examines the marginality of romance. She critiques Ian Watt's *Rise of the Novel* (1957) and Fredric Jameson's *The Political Unconscious* (CH, Jun'81). The novel's phallocentric order is challenged as the dominant discourse, and another discourse is posited, one that takes gender battles into account in fiction. This leads to an examination of Charlotte Lennox's *The Female Quixote* and the writings of Mary Wollstonecraft, George Eliot, and Charles Dickens. An index and thorough list of works cited are included. This feminist study is of limited use to a general reader because of its reliance on esoteric critical idioms. Suitable only for advanced students of critical theory.—*S. A. Parker, Hiram College*

WS-0334   PR778   90-42210 CIP
Levy, Anita. **Other women: the writing of class, race, and gender, 1832-1898.** Princeton, 1991. 174p bibl index afp ISBN 0-691-06865-8, $35.00; ISBN 0-691-01493-0 pbk, $9.95

The "writing" of the subtitle is early treatises in sociology, anthropology, and psychology, as well as *Wuthering Heights*, an example of domestic fiction. Like many other recent commentators, Levy asserts that although seeming only to describe, these writings simultaneously privileged certain forms of behavior while marginalizing others. Her particular focus in this revisionist account is the behavior, including sexual behavior, of the Victorian wife and mother, the middle-class angel in the house against whom are measured (and found wanting) women of other classes, races, and sexual behaviors. Although her thesis is ingenious, her analyses are less impressive. At times, she misrepresents the materials she describes and makes rather sweeping generalizations based on very slight evidence. Moreover, she analyzes her writings out of context and seems to relegate all concern for "real" social problems to mere rhetorical strategy. In spite of its shortcomings, however, this is a thought-provoking study. Extensive notes and bibliography.—*J. L. Culross, Eastern Kentucky University*

WS-0335   PN98   91-7404 CIP
Miller, Nancy K. **Getting personal: feminist occasions and other autobiographical acts.** Routledge, 1991. 164p bibl index ISBN 0-415-90323-8, $39.95; ISBN 0-415-90324-6 pbk, $13.95

Miller's collection of essays reprises several talks and lectures she presented at various occasions during the 1980s. She discusses subjects ranging from autobiography to pedagogy, exploring issues raised by feminism. Miller compares the conflicts expressed by those who represent themselves as "feminist" to the challenges offered by literary theory, especially in the new emphasis on autobiographical or personal criticism. Viewing the current move to personal expression in critical writing as "at least the sign of a turning point in the history of critical practices," Miller constructs in this collection a mini-autobiography of a critic who writes the personal into her critical theory, a technique she calls "narrative criticism." By reviving the occasion in which each essay was written, Miller provides a context for the feminist issues she explores and demonstrates how critics and teachers speak from positions defined by particular times, places, and ideologies. The collection will interest scholars and teachers of autobiography, as well as feminist theorists and critics.—*B. Braendlin, Florida State University*

WS-0336   PR878   93-43751 CIP
Mitchell, Judith. **The stone and the scorpion: the female subject of desire in the novels of Charlotte Brontë, George Eliot, and Thomas Hardy.** Greenwood, 1994. 228p (Contributions in women's studies, 142) bibl index afp ISBN 0-313-29043-1, $49.95

In this analysis of 12 novels using gender relations theory Mitchell (Univ. of Victoria, Canada) wishes to know "the extent to which these authors permit their heroines to look, speak, feel and act on their desire within the (heterosexual) erotic encounter." After a strong opening chapter outlining feminist theory, Mitchell provides succinct and perceptive readings of the three novelists; she concludes that Brontë is the most disruptive of Victorian sexual paradigms, Hardy the least so. A recommended purchase for all libraries that serve readers of Victorian novels, and especially valuable for institutions with interest in feminist criticism, since the opening chapter will stimulate debate about feminist assumptions even where these novelists' work is not an issue. Equally important, the book is written in a jargon-free style, so that any postsecondary students with an interest in the subject should be able to grapple successfully with the author's arguments. Undergraduate and up.—*M. Minor, Morehead State University*

WS-0337   91-13126 CIP
Modleski, Tania. **Feminism without women: culture and criticism in a "postfeminist" age.** Routledge, 1991. 188p indexes ISBN 0-415-90416-1, $39.95; ISBN 0-415-90417-X pbk, $13.95

Modleski argues that contemporary feminist criticism ("postfeminism") not only fails to serve the interests of women but also threatens to undermine the threat that feminism originally posed to patriarchy. Interest by "gynocritics" (Elaine Showalter) has shifted from an exploration of female culture to gender studies, an area that concerns itself with the social construction of male and other sexualities. This shift has redirected attention away from exclusively female literature back to male literature and theories. The advent of "male feminists" has transformed the feminist movement from a struggle against patriarchy into a struggle *within* it, in which men appropriate feminism and find empowerment as feminists but do so only at the expense of women, whose voice they have usurped. Debates over essentialism have similarly excluded notions of women *as women* from feminism. Certain films show how female roles have been taken over by men (*Three Men and a Baby*), men have retreated into a phantasmatic youth (*Big*, Pee-Wee Herman films), women and "the feminine" have become targeted as the enemy (*Top Gun, Full Metal Jacket, Heartbreak Ridge*), and homosexual panic informs male melodramas (*Dead Poets Society*) and action films (*Lethal Weapon*). Films of the feminist age thus reveal a feminism without women.—*J. Belton, Rutgers, The State University of New Jersey, New Brunswick*

WS-0338   RC685   91-46465 CIP
Morey, Ann-Janine. **Religion and sexuality in American literature.** Cambridge, 1992. 276p (Cambridge studies in American literature and culture, 57) bibl index ISBN 0-521-41676-0, $44.95

An advanced work aimed toward graduate students and faculty specialists in literary criticism. Nevertheless, it can be a useful reference for advanced undergraduates in such interdisciplinary areas as American studies, women's studies, semiotics, and communication studies. The book deals with the relationship between religion and sexuality in American fiction, a topic which has received little attention in other sources. Morey's analysis of how male and female writers differ in their treatment of the connection between religion and sexuality is a particularly valuable contribution. Drawing on both 19th-century and contemporary fiction, Morey examines how cultural ideas about male and female identity are shaped through the use of language. She also demonstrates how the narrative form reflects issues of control, authority, and resistance. Recommended for academic libraries.—*H. L. Minton, University of Windsor*

WS-0339 PR9340 91-30118 CIP
Motherlands: Black women's writing from Africa, the Caribbean and South Asia, ed. by Susheila Nasta. Rutgers, 1992 (c1991). 366p bibl index ISBN 0-8135-1781-8, $36.00; ISBN 0-8135-1782-6 pbk, $12.95

Divided into three sections, "Breaking the Silence: New Stories of Women and Mothers," "Mothers/Daughters/Sisters?" and "Absent and Adopted Mother(land)s," this collection of essays demonstrates the links in women's creative works from different global areas, specifically as demonstrated in their attempts to discover new forms and languages to express women's experiences in patriarchal societies and to subvert continuing traditional, colonial, and neo-colonial gender stereotypes. Canonical figures—Bessie Head, Ama Ata Aidoo, Buchi Emecheta, among others, appear, in addition to many less well known writers, including Lorna Goodison, Rebeka Njau, and Anita Desai. Uniting many of these essays are their authors' examinations of the themes of history and contemporary culture; particularly useful are their political interpretations of the concept, "mother," especially as manifested in ideas of "motherhood," "mother tongue," "mother land," as well as their analysis of the writers' examinations of mother/daughter relationships and the (re)creation of the self. Because of its inclusive nature, *Motherlands* adds to the essential comparative dimension present but not prominent in the handful of available critical collections focusing upon black women writers.—*A. A. Elder, University of Cincinnati*

WS-0340 PS153 92-4927 CIP
New lesbian criticism: literary and cultural readings, ed. by Sally Munt. Columbia, 1992. 207p ISBN 0-231-08018-2, $40.00; ISBN 0-231-08019-0 pbk, $15.00

This volume extends the series of lesbian and gay studies under the general editorship of Lillian Faderman and Larry Gross. Earlier volumes in the series have considered lesbian life in America and lesbian sexuality. This one considers literary theory and its cultural context. The introduction by its editor, Sally Munt, identifies key questions in positioning lesbian literary criticism amid literary criticism generally and in relation to gay male criticism more particularly. Since all but three of the contributors are based in Britain, the volume provides a trans-Atlantic perspective. Its ten essays range from more theoretical studies by Bonnie Zimmerman, Reina Lewis, and Munt herself to more applied studies by Anna Wilson, Gillian Spraggs, and Lisa Henderson. Among the topics addressed are lesbian bars, Greyhound Bus stations, and lesbian pornography. A bibliography for further reading lists more than 200 titles. Undergraduate; graduate.—*J. J. Marchesani, Pennsylvania State University, McKeesport Campus*

WS-0341 PR120.M45 90-35674 CIP
Out of bounds: male writers and gender(ed) criticism, ed. by Laura Claridge and Elizabeth Langland. Massachusetts, 1991 (c1990). 344p afp ISBN 0-87023-734-9, $42.50; ISBN 0-87023-735-7, $16.95

A much-needed collection of feminist essays on male writers as diverse as Milton, Sterne, Blake, Keats, Shelley, Browning, Whitman, Hardy, Forster, Frost, Faulkner, and Durrell. The essays particularly concern canonical male writers who wish to escape or redefine patriarchal language. The editors' emphasis upon resistance to what Jane Marcus has elsewhere called "the languages of patriarchy" leads to valuable close textual reading of Browning's dramatic monologues, Shelley's use of silence, and Durrell's "homoerotic negotiations in the colonial narrative." The editors wisely include essays on writers that many feminist critics choose to ignore. This would be an important addition to any course on contemporary feminist thought. Particularly good are V.C. Knoepflmacher on Browning, Elizabeth Langland on E.M. Forster, and Frank Lentricchia on Robert Frost.—*L. Winters, College of Saint Elizabeth*

WS-0342 PN56 90-19351 CIP
Rape and representation, ed. by Lynn A. Higgins and Brenda R. Silver. Columbia, 1991. 326p afp ISBN 0-231-07266-X, $35.00

Higgins and Silver's thought-provoking, theoretically sophisticated collection of essays is essential reading not only for any literary critic but also for any reader concerned with culture's recurrent representation of, if not acquiescence to, the brutal victimization of women through sexual violence. This collection of 14 brilliant, lucid essays preceded by a concise but far-ranging introduction contends with a wide variety of pervasive myths (e.g., Philomela); framing institutions (e.g., medieval rape laws, US lynching practices); well-known works from a variety of genres (e.g., Hardy's *Tess*, Keats's "Ode on a Grecian Urn," Resnais's *Last Year at Marienbad*); lesser-known works (e.g., Clarice Lispector's *The Hour of the Star*, Sony Labou Tansi's *La Vie et Demie*). While all the authors might be in sympathy with one another's projects, the essays are far from programmatic and serve to add meaning to one another, thus contributing to a richly textured whole that will provide countless avenues for further questioning of our literary heritage for its potential challenge to, or complicity in, the cultural construction of violence against women. Appropriate for upper-division undergraduates, graduate students, faculty, and general readers.—*E. Robertson, University of Colorado at Boulder*

WS-0343 PS152 94-40053 CIP
Ratcliffe, Krista. **Anglo-American feminist challenges to the rhetorical traditions: Virginia Woolf, Mary Daly, Adrienne Rich.** Southern Illinois, 1996. 227p bibl index afp ISBN 0-8093-1934-9, $29.95

Ratcliffe's thesis is Bathsheba's lament in Hardy's *Far from the Madding Crowd*: "'I have the feelings of a woman, but I have only the language of me.'" The first chapter presents a dense and complex overview of that language's dimensions, focusing on Roland Barthes's "The Old Rhetoric." Then Ratcliffe (Marquette Univ.) spends a chapter on each author, "extrapolating" their Anglo-American feminist theories of rhetoric "from their feminist texts about women, language, and culture." The final chapter focuses on feminist pedagogy. Although the first chapter is informative, much of the book does not apply directly to the three writers, whose rhetorical views are very different. In addition, it is filled with current critical jargon (e.g., "problematize," "valorize," "foreground" as a verb). And despite the presentation of 13 suggestions in chapter 5, practical application seems elusive. However, the superb 20-page bibliography makes this book useful for upper-division undergraduates and above.—*J. E. Steiner, Drew University*

WS-0344 PN98 94-14784 CIP
Rereading modernism: new directions in feminist criticism, ed. with an introd. by Lisa Rado. Garland, 1994. 395p (Wellesley studies in critical theory, literary history, and culture, 4) afp ISBN 0-8153-1189-3, $60.00

This collection of 17 essays (three of which are reprints) focuses upon a number of female modernist writers, including H.D. (Hilda Doolittle), Marianne Moore, Djuna Barnes, Gertrude Stein, Rebecca West, Dorothy Richardson, and Virginia Woolf, who are often ignored by students of modernism. Whether these "lost" women writers of the modernist period will prove to be true counterparts of the central male writers such as Joyce, Lawrence, Pound, Eliot, Hemingway, Faulkner, Lewis, Proust, and Kafka, they are currently undergoing a resuscitation from semioblivion. In treating these women writers as both feminists and modernists, this volume takes its place alongside other works of the new era in modernist scholarship marked by the publication of Shari Benstock's *Women of the Left Bank* (CH, Apr'87), Sandra Gilbert and Susan Gubar's *No Man's Land* (CH, Apr'88), and Bonnie K. Scott's *The Gender of Modernism* (1990). The essays in this volume raise questions about the definition of modernism and the shape of feminist theory. Upper-division undergraduate.—*S. M. Nuernberg, University of Wisconsin-Oshkosh*

WS-0345 PR457 94-39710 CIP
Romantic women writers: voices and countervoices, ed. by Paula R. Feldman and Theresa M. Kelley. University Press of New England, 1995. 326p index afp ISBN 0-87451-711-7, $49.95; ISBN 0-87451-724-9 pbk, $19.95

The 13 essays in this book, which focuses particularly on the imaginative literary output of women Romantic writers, are divided into four sections—"Reimagining Romantic Canons"; "Textual Strategies"; "Nationalism, Patriotism, and Authorship"; and "Performance and the Marketplace." Because this is a relatively unexplored area, the close documentation is helpful, as is Feldman and Kelley's cogent introductory essay detailing the direction and parameters of the various literary contributions. If a major revisiting of the Romantic period is in order once female contributions are properly assessed, then similar assessments need to be even more closely scrutinized, e.g., *Romanticism and Feminism*, ed. by Anne Mellor (CH, Sep'88), Marlon Ross's *The Contours of Masculine Desire* (1989), *Women Romantic Poets*, ed. by Jennifer Breen (1992), *The Authority of Experience*, ed. by Arlyn Diamond and Lee Edwards (CH, Sep'77), Ellen Moers's *Literary Woman* (CH, Dec'76), Elaine Showalter's *A Literature of Their Own* (CH, Nov'77), and *The Norton Anthology of Literature by Women*, compiled by Sandra Gilbert and Susan Gubar (1985). And, finally, interested scholars should see *The Johns Hopkins Guide to Literary Theory & Criticism*, ed. by Michael Groden and Martin Kreiswirth (CH, Jul'94), under the entry "Feminist Theory and Criticism," for a well-annotated discussion. Recommended for general and academic audiences.—*R. E. Carlile, Darton College*

WS-0346 PN56 91-14705 CIP
Roof, Judith. **A lure of knowledge: lesbian sexuality and theory.** Columbia, 1991. 285p bibl index afp ISBN 0-231-07486-7, $40.00

In this complex and richly textured work Roof seeks to uncover and analyze representations of lesbians and lesbian sexuality in literature, cinema, psychoanalysis, and literary criticism. Through examinations of such divergent texts as soft-core pornographic films, "lesbian" feature films, the psychoanalytical theorizing of Nancy Chodorow, and the recent work of a number of well-known (and frequently cited) feminist literary critics, Roof reveals the heterosexual assumptions at the core of most depictions of lesbian existence. Although the plot summaries of popular cinema appear at first glance to provide some orientation for the reader, grounding in far more arcane matters makes or breaks one's understanding of the text. Without a firm grasp of the language of critical theory, the reader must turn frequently to the dictionary for definitions of terms such as scopophilia while wondering where to look for a concise explanation of the Lacanian "mirror stage." Although obviously intended for a theoretically sophisticated audience, parts of the work are remarkably accessible, even to the uninitiated. Strongly recommended for libraries supporting critical studies programs.—*E. Broidy, University of California, Irvine*

WS-0347 PR6045 94-25607 CIP
Rosenman, Ellen Bayuk. **A room of one's own: women writers and the politics of creativity.** Twayne, 1995. 133p (Twayne's masterwork studies, 151) bibl index afp ISBN 0-8057-8374-1, $22.95; ISBN 0-8057-8594-9 pbk, $12.95

This superb study of one of the basic texts of feminist criticism begins with a section on literary and historical context, including discussion of Woolf's background, of the importance of a *A Room of One's Own*, and of its critical reception both in 1929 and 50 years later. The focus, however, is a close "reading" of the text. First, Rosenman emphasizes the centrality of Woolf's conceptions of patriarchy and feminism in understanding her purpose in *Room* and her insistence on the effects of the material conditions of a writer's life on her art. Rosenman then turns to Woolf's construction of "a new literary history" based solely on women's writing, her invention of Judith Shakespeare to illustrate problems women writers face, and her elucidation of women's distinctive concerns as writers. The penultimate chapter analyzes the nonlinear, indirect form of *Room*, as well as its use of a number of fictional techniques, and of irony and allusion. In the last chapter, Rosenman provocatively explores contradictions in Woolf's thinking. Two of these are her "insistence on a gender-specific tradition" and her formulation of the concept of androgyny, each of which "runs counter to much of Woolf's argument" in *Room*. This thoughtful, thorough book is essential to all college and university libraries.—*J. E. Steiner, Drew University*

WS-0348 PN691 95-42861 CIP
Sigal, Gale. **Erotic dawn-songs of the Middle Ages: voicing the lyric lady.** University Press of Florida, 1996. 241p bibl index afp ISBN 0-8130-1381-X, $49.95

In this provocative study, Sigal (Wake Forest Univ.) reassesses the role of the "female" voice in medieval lyrics. Focusing specifically on the alba—a 12th-century French genre characterized by the plaints of adulterous lovers parting at dawn—Sigal considers the female contribution to these reciprocal expressions of romantic love and finds that the "lyric ladies" of the albas provide a balance to the more idealized representations of silent and repressed women in the more familiar and conventional courtly lyrics. Sigal wants to "correct [the] misreadings" of earlier studies of romance lyrics, in particular those of Maureen Fries and Doris Earnshaw. Five chapters of analysis situate the texts in relation to various troubadour traditions using a comparative methodology; the author provides examples from Old Provencal, Old French, Middle High German, and Middle English, all presumably written by men but with a "ventriloquism," Sigal argues, that is "empathic" in its identification with female passion. Though somewhat overstated in its aims, this is an intriguing demonstration of the various critical perspectives that can be productively applied to this often-neglected genre. Upper-division undergraduate level and up.—*C. S. Cox, University of Pittsburgh*

WS-0349 PS147 90-10835 CIP
Tradition and the talents of women, ed. by Florence Howe. Illinois, 1991. 379p index afp ISBN 0-252-01685-8, $44.95; ISBN 0-252-06106-3 pbk, $17.50

Essays in honor of Mary Anne Ferguson, whose early feminist scholarship was instrumental in implanting women's studies in the academy. With Ferguson's exemplary work in mind, editor Howe sought out essays that address the complex relationship between gendered literary practice and original female expressiveness, celebrating the richness and complexity of women's creative traditions. The 15 essays—ranging in subject from Virginia Woolf, Charlotte Brontë, and Jane Austen to Djuna Barnes, Gloria Anzaldua, and Anne Moody—are meant to probe the ways women use imaginative expression to build, communicate, and inscribe a female subculture within patriarchy. Although individual essays are incisive and theoretically informed, the rationale behind the inclusion and grouping of essays needs to be more sharply articulated. Nonetheless, the collection is a welcome complement to the now manifold body of feminist literary scholarship from the last two decades, reconsidering established writers, evaluating anew the contributions of less laureled writers, and reconceptualizing the shaping power of "tradition" in women's writing. For all academic libraries.—*L. Babener, Montana State University*

WS-0350 PS374 94-16130 CIP
Tucker, Lindsey. **Textual escap(e)ades: mobility, maternity, and textuality in contemporary fiction by women.** Greenwood, 1994. 149p (Contributions in women's studies, 146) bibl index afp ISBN 0-313-29156-X, $49.95

Tucker (English, Univ. of Miami) provides another interesting addition to the growing body of feminist critiques of modern fiction. Drawing heavily on psychoanalytic theory and recent critics such as Irigaray and Cixous, she teases out images of mobility and maternity from works by Sylvia Plath, Margaret Atwood, Toni Morrison, E.M. Broner, Monique Wittig, and others. She argues that women writers, in the mode of members of marginal groups, are more confrontational than men, more subversive, and more playful. Thus, the "escap(e)ades" or wild pranks serve as means of counterwriting, revitalization, and transformation as they allow the author (and her characters) to develop strategies for escape—from containment, entrapment, and objectification. Her thoughtful study explores these playful journeys that contemporary feminist writers construct, building the intellectual, cultural context for these devices. Her attention to both obvious and hidden meanings, to patterns of escape and maternal imagery, to extensive psychoanalytic scholarship, and her imaginative interpretations make this an extremely useful new title in the "Contributions in Women's Studies" series. Graduate; faculty.—*N. Tischler, Pennsylvania State University, University Park Campus*

WS-0351 PS152 94-30723 CIP
Walker, Nancy A. **The disobedient writer: women and narrative tradition.** Texas, 1995. 205p bibl index afp ISBN 0-292-79095-3, $30.00; ISBN 0-292-79096-1 pbk, $13.95

Walker (Vanderbilt Univ.) is interested in what she calls "disobedient" writers: women who revise classic texts in order to highlight classist, racist, or antifeminist messages. Addressing a wide range of texts—including biblical stories, fairy tales, frontier stories, sentimental novels, and autobiographies—this study shows how women have revised and rescripted older narratives, in the process creating entirely new ones that challenge the status quo. In order to develop a persuasive argument, the author is careful to examine a variety of canonical and noncanonical writers, including Caroline Kirkland, Fanny Fern, Margaret Halsey, Margaret Atwood, and Anne Sexton, to name only a few. What emerges is a fascinating analysis of the way in which revisionary tendencies have been "an integral part of writing as a woman in the Anglo-American tradition." Particularly notable is the book's chapter on fairy tales, which explores how such authors as Edith Nesbit, Fay Weldon, and Angela Carter have revised the fairy tale formula to reveal how traditional fairy tales have perpetuated feminine gender stereotypes. This thought-provoking book will interest any feminist scholar, whether undergraduate, graduate student, or professor.—*S. A. Inness, Miami University*

WS-0352   PS2127x   Can. CIP
Walton, Priscilla L. **The disruption of the feminine in Henry James.** Toronto, 1992. 179p bibl index afp ISBN 0-8020-5987-2, $40.00

Drawing heavily on recent critical theory (Derrida, Naomi Schor, Luce Irigaray, Helene Cixous) Walton argues that James's texts "subvert their explicitly Realist nineteenth century ideology" through their "self-reflexive attempts to bind women." This "masculinism" is evinced, for example, in *The Portrait of A Lady* where Walton finds that "the novel suggests that Isabel is free to choose, but that because she is female and hence somewhat irrational and unstable she will choose erroneously. The text, therefore, works to justify patriarchal authority, for the circumscription of women is presented as a kindness, a means of helping them to help themselves." Such readings will surely be disputed. A corrective may be found in the subtle commentaries of Millicent Bell's recent *Meaning in Henry James*, (CH, Feb'92). Of interest to specialists.—*J. J. Benardete, Hunter College, CUNY*

WS-0353   PR830   90-8200 MARC
Where no man has gone before: women and science fiction, ed. by Lucie Armitt. Routledge, 1991. 234p bibl index ISBN 0-415-04447-2, $59.95

Written predominantly by women scholars and science fiction authors in England, these demonstrate the increasing academic interest in women's SF, and it explores the complexity and scope of contemporary fictional visions as presented by major women SF writers. Building on the critical base established by such recent studies as Sarah Lefanu's *Feminism and Science Fiction* (CH, Jan'90; UK title, *In the Chinks of the World Machine*), and Nan B. Albinski's *Women's Utopias in British and American Fiction* (CH, Feb'89), this compilation aims to focus additional critical analyses of the female voices of major writers C.L. Moore, Ursula LeGuin, and Doris Lessing, among others, then turns to explorations of specific themes evident in SF written by women: (pro)creativity, the alien, machines as a psychological replacement for women, the significance of language. The final part examines problems inherent in the SF genre specifically, creating positive female characters; the blurring of boundaries between SF and horror, fantasy, and romance; and marketing strategies which, by labeling genres, tend to limit readership. As a whole, the essays and the fiction they discuss transmit a resigned recognition of the "otherness" of women, that women's fictional quest is still the search for an alternative reality in which the social and cultural centrality of women is possible. Included are essays by SF writers Josephine Saxton, Gwyneth Jones, and Lisa Tuttle, as well as scholars Sara Lefanu, Moira Monteith, and Susan Bassnett. These essays add to the growing body of scholarship addressing SF written by women as well as feminist literary concerns, but, being broad-surface examinations, they do not contribute to the depth of such scholarship. Recommended for academic libraries with strong collections in science fiction or feminist literary criticism.—*J. A. Adams, SUNY at Buffalo*

WS-0354   PN99   94-40962 CIP
Women critics, 1660-1820: an anthology, ed. by the Folger Collective on Early Women Critics. Indiana, 1995. 410p bibl index afp ISBN 0-253-32872-1, $39.95; ISBN 0-253-20963-3 pbk, $19.95

This anthology of writings by European and American women adds a salient body of work to the canon of literary criticism. The compilation features theoretical and applied commentary from a range of female critics, most of whom are known primarily for their imaginative writings—e.g., Aphra Behn, Mary Wollstonecraft, Phillis Wheatley, Ann Radcliffe, and Jane Austen. The editors have culled critical discourse from essays, letters, prefaces, fictional excerpts, and other sources to demonstrate the richness and intellectual sophistication of the female critical tradition, which has reposed in relative obscurity. A meticulous set of biographical sketches, notes, and bibliographical references amplifies the usefulness of the collection. However, the editors' disclaimer that "our purpose is not to forge from this diverse group of writers a distinctly female critical tradition" leaves this reviewer puzzled about the reasons for the anthology if not to address overtly the ways in which gender has shaped the conventions of criticism. A more sharply argued feminist rationale would have enhanced the collection as a scholarly pedagogical tool, but it is nonetheless a valuable new resource for academic collections.—*L. Babener, Montana State University*

WS-0355   PN98   91-426 CIP
Writing the woman artist: essays on poetics, politics, and portraiture, ed. by Suzanne W. Jones. Pennsylvania, 1991. 453p bibl index afp ISBN 0-8122-3089-2, $44.95; ISBN 0-8122-1343-2 pbk, $17.95

The scope of this critical volume is narrow. All the essayists featured are women; all the poets and novelists they discuss are women; and all the fictional artists of the texts in question are women as well. The collection is a hall of mirrors where we can easily see the Grail pursued by those involved: a feminine voice that repudiates the highly sentimentalized convention of early women writers, one free of paternalistic conventions and that negates, for example, a literary world where "men write poems and women inhabit them." Among the more esoteric pieces here is Josephine Donovan's "The Pattern of Birds and Beasts: Willa Cather and Women's Art." Donovan notes that although Cather rejected the sentimentalist emotionalism prevalent in the women writers of her time, affected a masculine appearance, and often chose a masculine narrator, she often connected herself through her characters to mother-figures whose domestic talents were artisanal in nature. Cather thus moves away from both masculine and feminine forms and toward a new androgynous mode. The narrowness of the text is balanced by a great range of writers: Bishop, Rich, H.D., Brookner, and Woolf, and is especially valuable for research on the woman artist: painter, sculptor, writer, or performer. Graduate level.—*J. A. Dompkowski, Canisius College*

◆ Theory

WS-0356   PS374   93-12466 CIP
Barr, Marleen S. **Lost in space: probing feminist science fiction and beyond.** North Carolina, 1993. 231p index afp ISBN 0-8078-2108-X, $39.95; ISBN 0-8078-4421-7 pbk, $14.95

Barr's intention, reiterated in a number of these essays, is to prevent the further marginalization or even the disappearance of feminist science fiction. To this end, Barr reads LeGuin and other feminist writers of science fiction in the context of postmodern fiction, contemporary experimental fiction, and any other category that promises serious and mainstream consideration. Her redesignation of the works of such writers as LeGuin, Charnas, and Tiptree does not guarantee their survival, but it does suggest at least one tactic intended to deghettoize the works of challenging and thoughtful feminists who use science fiction and fable to deconstruct the condition of women in patriarchy. In these readings, Barr insists on making connections to contemporary politics, from the recent presidential elections to the Holocaust. Reviewing Sally Gearhart's *The Wanderground: Stories of the Hill Women* (1978), which uses the Holocaust as a historical reference point, Barr connects the hunting down and killing of women with her own immediate condition ("I am a Jew who is writing this piece in the University of Dusseldorf's humanities building [with Dachau] within excursion distance by train.") Barr's essays are provocative and immediate, her perspective often apocalyptic. This is a valuable book. Advanced undergraduate; graduate; faculty; general.—*R. Nadelhaft, University of Maine at Orono*

WS-0357 PN56 94-32674 CIP
Bartkowski, Frances. **Travelers, immigrants, inmates: essays in estrangement.** Minnesota, 1995. 183p bibl index afp ISBN 0-8166-2362-7 pbk, $17.95

"Informed by feminist psychoanalytic theory," this book addresses the discovery of self in bodies that have been "gendered or sexed (or) raced." Bartkowski (Rutgers Univ.) hopes to "create a mosaic of discoveries" wherein the reader will "see mirrored certain structural repetitions in the construction of identities." This mosaic is that of the traveler, appropriate in that the journey motif must be the oldest and most profound of all of metaphors for the human condition. The modern traveler must confront and recount cultural, racial, gender, and political dislocations ("essays in estrangement") that manifest the construction of a self. The traveler in search of the exotic, the immigrant who (to the self at least) feels compelled to experience the "other," and the inmate in the context of the Holocaust: each is a wayfarer experiencing wonder, shame, and sometimes horror in the unfolding of the self. Bartkowski's methodology involves detailed introductions and running commentaries on chosen texts. The immigrants section, for example, includes writings of black (Hurston), Chicana (Cisnero), and Jewish (Hoffman) women who experience both wonder and shame "immigrating" to different America. These writers, like those discussed in the other sections, "provide a textual unfolding of the relation between wonder and shame." A difficult but interesting postmodern approach to an (emerging) psychogenre of travel writing. Upper-division undergraduates and above.—*E. J. Zimmermann, Canisius College*

WS-0358 PR778 95-43861 CIP
Bohls, Elizabeth A. **Women travel writers and the language of aesthetics, 1716-1818.** Cambridge, 1995. 309p (Cambridge studies in Romanticism, 13) bibl index ISBN 0-521-47458-2, $49.95

Without new historicist readings of travel literature, scholars might wrongly assume that privileged British women of the 18th and early 19th centuries were restricted to the narrow province of a polite and amateurish appreciation of aesthetic experience. Bohls (Univ. of Illinois at Urbana-Champagne) presents women writers who "broke out of masculine tutelage" and made significant contributions to modern aesthetic theory during its formative period. Bohls's introduction charts essential developments in aesthetic theory and practice in the 18th century. Bohls analyzes Lady Mary Wortley Montagu's difficulty in taking up the role of power spectator in her famous accounts of Turkish harems and Janet Shaw's account of colonial slaves in the West Indies in the 1770s. The author describes the gathering momentum of scenic tourism and landscape gardening and explains the dominant theories of Burke, Kant, William Kent, William Gilpin, and others. She reads Dorothy Wordsworth's journals as examples of making an aesthetic of the commonplace and works by Mary Wollstonecraft and Ann Radcliffe as creative redefinitions of the picturesque and the beautiful. A final chapter on Mary Shelley's *Frankenstein* is stunning in its judgments on the profound meaning of the aesthetic experience of the creature. Essential for collections on aesthetic theory and the history of romanticism. Upper-division undergraduate and up.—*S. Pathak, Johns Hopkins University*

WS-0359 PN3401 90-8117 MARC
Breen, Jennifer. **In her own write: twentieth-century women's fiction.** St. Martin's, 1990. 146p bibl index ISBN 0-312-04240-X, $35.00; ISBN 0-312-04241-8 pbk, $12.95;

Breen (Polytechnic of North London) has a curiously pragmatic view of the purpose of fiction, a view resulting perhaps from her dual training (social science and 20th-century literature, according to the dust jacket). She states in her "Conclusion" chapter: "Women, who now live politically under a late decadent patriarchy in which a fortunate minority of women have been co-opted as honorary men, must adopt a reading strategy whereby we examine to what extent each work of fiction supports the structure of unequal power relationships between men and women or to what extent the fiction subverts this unequal structure." Her goal in writing this brief book is to "discover subversive meanings in underrated women's novels" and indeed, she touches on literally dozens of books by British, Australian, Indian, West Indian, African, and American women writers. Those novels that are subversive, that show work rather than sexual relationships at the center of a woman's life, are singled out for praise. Indeed, Breen badgers women writers for too great an emphasis on sexual relationships: "Where is

our late twentieth-century female Conrad?" she cries. Finally, it is Breen's unremitting insistence that fiction must be a tool for social change (to her, the only appropriate measure for fiction's success) that renders her analysis too simplistic and predictable. Nonetheless, the book has its usefulness. Divided into chapters according to topics—sexuality, work, mothering, alternatives to marriage, politics and war; and racial stereotypes—the book provides helpful introductions to women's fiction about these topics. The bibliography has the virtue of including several lesser-known writers. Recommended only for large undergraduate collections.—*E. R. Baer, Washington College*

WS-0360 PN61 94-17926 CIP
Bridging the gap: literary theory in the classroom, ed. by J.M.Q. Davies. Locust Hill, 1994. 373p (Locust Hill literary studies, 17) bibl index afp ISBN 0-933951-60-4, $38.00

J.M.Q. Davies (Northern Territory Univ./Australia) has edited an excellent collection of essays exploring how literary theory influences pedagogy; it will appeal to both the novice and the adept in theory. The 20 essays address, among other topics, postcolonial theory, theology, politics, narratology, deconstruction, psychoanalytic theory, reader-response theory, and black women's autobiography. Gerald Graff's essay urging a "dialogical curriculum" extends his familiar work in teaching cultural conflict. Simon Barker's "Literary Theory in the Study of Shakespeare" and Davies's essay "*Paradise Lost* and the Theory Survey" usefully examine the ways in which newer critical approaches enlighten older texts. Most provocative is psychologist Colin Martindale's essay ("Shouldn't These Theories Be Tested?"), which argues for a way of quantitatively justifying critical judgments based on evaluation of measurable responses: if the "proper subject matter of literary studies is not objective texts" but "texts as perceived and understood," then literary studies must be a "a sub-discipline of the behavioral sciences." Recommended for undergraduate and graduate libraries; select bibliography and index.—*C. Baker, Armstrong State College*

WS-0361 PR6019 95-6475 CIP
Brivic, Sheldon. **Joyce's waking women: an introduction to *Finnegans wake.*** Wisconsin, 1995. 162p bibl index ISBN 0-299-14800-9, $45.00; ISBN 0-299-14804-1 pbk, $17.95

WS-0361a PR6019 95-6622 CIP
Ingersoll, Earl G. **Engendered trope in Joyce's Dubliners.** Southern Illinois, 1996. 193p bibl index afp ISBN 0-8093-2016-9, $29.95

The poststructuralist theories of Derrida, Lacan, and their followers structure both these books. Ingersoll's "engendered tropes" means (masculine) metaphor and (feminine) metonymy, concerned primarily with empowerment rather than sex. Characters may shift "gender" in fields of masculine mobility and freedom versus feminine confinement and vulnerability. After reviewing Lacanian readings of Joyce, Ingersoll (SUNY College at Brockport) rearranges *The Dubliners*, principally around travel. The first three stories focus on the desires of "rambling boys." Next come the confined females of "Eveline," "The Boarding House," and "Clay," with Eveline a paradigm of feminine domestic confinement; the "feminized," confined, and vulnerable men of "A Little Cloud," "A Painful Case," and "Ivy Day"; and the exploited women of "A Mother." Male empowerment is explained as "the joking male" in "Two Gallants," "After the Race," "Counterparts," and "Grace." The climactic "The Dead" is analyzed by the "gender" of travel, with Gabriel desiring travel but experiencing metaphoric perception of his place. The analysis of "Clay" is outstanding

In *Joyce's Waking Women*, Brivic (Temple Univ.) bases his discussion on traditional assumptions about *Finnegans Wake*—permeable characters and dream structure, deconstructive theories built on dissociated words or fragments of text, and avoidance of narrative and of Victorian acts. He justifies Joyce's female creations from the viewpoint of the male feminist. Joyce aims at understanding the mind of woman; he addresses his works to women and practices both seduction and rejection in presenting masculine conflicts with feminine resolutions. Brivic's gender analysis will be better appreciated by those familiar with his *The Veil of Signs: Joyce, Lacan, and Perception* (1991), which discusses language that creates reality, gender delineations, and the unknown and mystical Other. Woman's fluidity and shiftiness opposes man's fixity and stability, a position not technically sexist because of woman's creativity and the male feminist's attack on patriarchal authority and structures in language and politics. The complex *wak-*

ing of women is a process of discovery and development. Imposition of theory on the text causes tenuous and frequently almost invisible linkages that promote endless speculation and conjecture. Both books are highly recommended for upper-division undergraduates and graduates—*G. Eckley, emeritus, Drake University*

WS-0362 PS374.D57 90-11143 CIP
Brown, Gillian. **Domestic individualism: imaging self in nineteenth-century America.** California, 1991 (c1990). 266p (The new historicism: studies in cultural poetics, 14) index afp ISBN 0-520-06785-1, $24.95

Gillian Brown's seminal contribution in this study is to extend understanding of how the rise of 19th-century domesticity was a development within the history of possessive individualism, rather than—as many feminist critics have previously argued—apart from and counter to it. Domesticity is neither a totalizing nor a monolithic force; rather, Brown claims, it is a "working machinery, one that has served and continues to serve many purposes." Thus in some cases (e.g., abolition) it inspires reformist politics; in other instances (e.g., suffrage) it appears reactionary. Nor is domesticity uniquely tied to the female. Instead, it is central to the American male's sense of self as well, flavoring it with the values of interiority and privacy. Brown centers her argument on readings of Stowe, Hawthorne, and Melville, but she extends these readings by linking texts to a provocative series of cultural subjects: abolitionism, mesmerism, consumerism, architecture, interior design, agoraphobia, hysteria. Her method is, as she puts it, "generally deconstructionist" and informed by current feminist theory and new historicism. Dense, stimulating, and important, this book is mainly for graduate students and faculty.—*L. W. MacFarlane, University of New Hampshire*

WS-0363 PR868 91-14574 CIP
Cohen, Paula Marantz. **The daughter's dilemma: family process and the nineteenth-century domestic novel.** Michigan, 1991. 226p index afp ISBN 0-472-10234-6, $27.50

Cohen's highly original and readable book introduces "family systems theory" into literary-critical analysis of the British novel. Cohen summarizes the history of the systems-theory movement in psychology, applies it to interpretations of canonical novels (and, in some cases, their authors' lives), and uses it to reveal ideological assumptions about gender, domesticity, and closure in fiction. The introductory chapter, "The Family and the Novel," aptly sets up the frame for readings of family-system configurations in *Clarissa, Mansfield Park, Wuthering Heights, The Mill on the Floss,* and *The Awkward Age.* Taking a previously unexplored feminist stance, Cohen identifies "a potential for female empowerment emerging in nineteenth-century culture," which structural analysis from a systems perspective brings into view. Careful definition of terms and explanation of assumptions should make this book accessible to literary scholars at the undergraduate level; its insights into a new literary application of psychological methodology will make it valuable to their professors, as well.—*R. R. Warhol, University of Vermont*

WS-0364 PR888 91-3571 CIP
DeKoven, Marianne. **Rich and strange: gender, history, modernism.** Princeton, 1991. 248p index afp ISBN 0-691-06869-0, $39.50; ISBN 0-691-01496-5 pbk, $12.95

This comprehensive and closely reasoned study by a leading critic of feminist theory and modernist literature offers brilliant readings of narratives and poetry by British and American writers of the late 19th and early 20th centuries. In chapters pairing works by male and female writers (e.g., *Lord Jim* and *The Awakening,* "Melanctha" and *The Nigger of the "Narcissus"*), DeKoven develops her thesis that modernism is neither reactionary nor subversive but is expressive of "unresolved contradiction or unsynthesized dialectic," revealed through analysis of the multiple perspectives, modulations in tone, disruptions of linear time, and the function of water imagery as a locus of meaning in each text. Establishing gender as the primary category, she shows how modernist works simultaneously assert and subvert conventional polarities of masculine and feminine and established hierarchies of class and race. The study summarizes earlier definitions of modernism, explores connections between feminist criticism and modernism, demonstrates the importance of female writers in the development of modernism, and illuminates even such exhaustively studied works as *The Heart of Darkness*

and *The Turn of the Screw.* Extensive notes with references to dozens of secondary works enhance the value of the book. Highly recommended to all specialists and students of modern literature and feminist theory.—*E. Nettels, College of William and Mary*

WS-0365 HQ1587 90-38351 CIP
Determined women: studies in the construction of the female subject, 1900-90, ed. and introd. by Jennifer Birkett and Elizabeth Harvey. Barnes & Noble Books, 1991. 213p index ISBN 0-389-20950-3, $46.75

Determined Women is a disparate collection of feminist literary criticism and social commentary that contains articles on German, French, Canadian, and American women writers. Because the contributors treat different cultures as well as different genres (both fictional and nonfictional), the essays vary greatly in their value to the reader. An analysis of three Canadian short stories cannot be given the same weight as oral interviews with contemporary German women or an analysis of French car advertising. Though the editors believe that all of the essays illustrate the effects of patriarchy and the efforts made by women to transcend cultural bonds, this reviewer is less sure of the meaning and importance of each contribution. Only for libraries with extensive women's studies collections.—*J. Sochen, Northeastern Illinois University*

WS-0366 PS2127 95-11137 CIP
Ender, Evelyne. **Sexing the mind: nineteenth-century fictions of hysteria.** Cornell, 1995. 307p bibl index afp ISBN 0-8014-2826-2, $42.00

Ender's book is a subtle, difficult, and very European. Some readers will be put off by its dense poststructural collaboration of literature, feminism, and psychoanalysis and by its relentless, intense, close engagement with texts. To others it will seem like the only way to read. Ender has a deep historical grasp of the making of gender ideology in the 19th century, and she pursues a kind of literary typology of hysteria, tracking it as a profoundly ambivalent psychocultural response to an ideology that in different hands exhibits varying degrees of surrender and resistance. She analyzes "what might be some of [the] consequences, for a history of the subject and for a history of the relations between men and women" of the enforced "law of gender" or "grammar of the sexes"; she wants to understand the *writing* of the hysteric as "an effigy of the mind haunted by a question of gender." She weaves together astonishingly fresh, absorbing takes on Henry James, George Eliot, Freud, and particularly George Sand. Ender's idiomatic ease in English, French, and German gives the reader confidence in her critical authority and steeps her argument in a rich multilingual compost of primary and secondary sources. Language crossover, however (the book was originally composed in French), may also account for the outrageous number of typos throughout the text. There is an ample, learned bibliography and user-friendly footnotes and index. Graduates; researchers.—*F. Alaya, Ramapo College of New Jersey*

WS-0367 PR888 95-13834 CIP
Felber, Lynette. **Gender and genre in novels without end: the British *Roman-Fleuve*.** University Press of Florida, 1995. 205p bibl index afp ISBN 0-8130-1402-6, $39.95

In four chapters and a short epilogue analyzing Anthony Trollope's Palliser series, Dorothy Richardson's *Pilgrimage,* and Anthony Powell's *A Dance to the Music of Time,* Felber tentatively traces the evolution of the British roman-fleuve, arguing that "feminine" narrative techniques (such as oblique, sprawling, contrapuntal exposition and diffused, unclimactic closure) are essential components of the genre. This study compels readers to reconsider both their previous conclusions about multivolume works and their presuppositions about narrative techniques. Although Felber's clear definitions and copious examples make prior knowledge unnecessary, those already familiar with recent debates about *écriture féminine* will find this work somewhat more accessible initially. In a few places Felber seems to forget that the sexual meanings of terms such as "climax," "fecundity," and "ejaculatory" are metaphors when applied to literary works; they cannot be taken literally or pushed too far. For the most part, however, she makes it clear that "feminine" and "masculine" writing techniques are not the exclusive property, respectively, of women and men. This study contains an excellent bibliography and a good but incomplete index. Despite several repetitious passages and a few minor errors, the copy editing is far better than average. Upper-division undergraduates and above.—*D. R. Eastwood, United States Merchant Marine Academy*

WS-0368　　　　HQ1190　　　　91-5556 CIP
Finke, Laurie A. **Feminist theory, women's writing.** Cornell, 1992. 216p bibl index afp ISBN 0-8014-2547-6, $33.95; ISBN 0-8014-9784-1 pbk, $11.95

　　Relying heavily on such theorists as Foucault and, especially, Bakhtin, Finke argues in this book for a critical "complexity" that explores the "cultural and historical specificity of oppression, resistance, co-optation, and subversion which marks writing by and about women." To explore the tensions between female writing and cultural representations of "woman," Finke examines the ways the love lyrics of female troubadours and the narratives of female mystics (usually recorded by men) enable women to claim power, however unconsciously, in a feudal, patriarchal, and largely homosocial culture. In another chapter she analyzes the style of *A Vindication of the Rights of Woman* (1792) to demonstrate the difficulty with which Mary Wollstonecraft must negotiate the tensions between the public and private spheres assigned to men and women in 18th-century notions of bourgeois individualism. A final chapter argues for a dialogic, historically and politically based theory of aesthetic value. With its extensive bibliography, Finke's work is an important contribution to ongoing theoretical discussions, appropriate for upper-division undergraduates, graduate students, and faculty.— *M. A. Dalbey, Eastern Michigan University*

WS-0369　　　　PR830　　　　92-26024 CIP
Fraiman, Susan. **Unbecoming women: British women writers and the novel of development.** Columbia, 1993. 189p bibl index afp ISBN 0-231-08000-X, $35.00

　　Fraiman addresses debates about the content and structure of the female bildungsroman and proposes a socioeconomic, rather than a psychoanalytical, approach to the genre. She examines the novel of female development as produced by popular Georgian and Victorian novelists like Burney, Austen, Charlotte Brontë, and Eliot, as well as conduct books that once arbitrated feminine norms; in so doing, she points out the obstacles and diversity of paths women have faced as they apprenticed to adulthood. Each novel is approached as containing a dissenting story ("counternarrative") that breaks up the course of female development. These obstructions, humiliations, and diversions "deform" the women characters and challenge the myth of courtship as education. Fraiman in Chapters 1 and 4 self-consciously composes a poetics of women's writing, gynocriticism that is indebted to the post-1980s "gorgeous explosion" of feminist theories and critical interpretations. Her focus is a feminist historicism that addresses "gender" by making clear specific meanings in women's lives. A poststructuralist viewpoint is argued: identity is provisional and adult selves are always fluid and emergent. Consequently, this study does not substitute a female path to adulthood for a male one, but offers examples of many incoherent and class-specific notions that create a larger, cacophonous discourse about female formation. Accessible but critically sophisticated, this interesting study builds on work by such scholars as Gilbert, Gubar, Modleski, Radway, and Hirsch. Advanced undergraduate; graduate.—*S. A. Parker, Hiram College*

WS-0370　　　　PS374　　　　94-27508 CIP
Freeman, Barbara Claire. **The feminine sublime: gender and excess in women's fiction.** California, 1995. 202p index afp ISBN 0-520-08863-8, $35.00

　　Freeman (Harvard Univ.) defines the "feminine sublime" as "a domain of experience ... in which the subject enters into a relation with an otherness ... that is excessive and unrepresentable." It emphasizes the primacy of the individual. This otherness, seen as opposed to a misogynist view of what is typically thought of as feminine, is represented in various ways, depending on the author. Toni Morrison sees African American literature in the American canon as an example of an "unspeakable thing unspoken." Kate Chopin in *The Awakening* sees the ocean as the central character: "words at their most sublime have the force and feel of water." Freeman sees examples of the misogynist view of the sublime in the works of Kant, Mary Shelley, and Jean Rhys. She discusses the theoretical writings

on this subject in the works of Edmund Burke and Longinus, for whom the sublime is "a kind of ... excellence of discourse." Freeman's intricate arguments will be seen by some as challenging, by others as esoteric. This work will interest graduate students and researchers in women's studies and English literature.— *J. Overmyer, emerita, Ohio State University*

WS-0371　　　　PR5368　　　　91-31421 CIP
Gainor, J. Ellen. **Shaw's daughters: dramatic and narrative constructions of gender.** Michigan, 1992. 282p bibl index ISBN 0-472-10219-2, $32.50

　　Students of Shaw and of women's studies will want to read this new study that brings a feminist perspective to bear on the Shavian corpus. We think of Shaw as a champion of women's rights, and in many ways he was. But Gainor tries to show that, for all his advanced thinking, Shaw remained a child of his age— and that age, like most in recorded history, was decidedly patriarchal. What emerges from the prose and dramatic works, Gainor says, is a pattern that marks the male as the paradigm "emancipated" women emulate. In Shaw, men retain their privileged status as makers of culture and educators of daughters, while women generally stay locked in their gender-defined roles as wives and mothers, only to be marginalized as they grow old. Even in so enlightened a reformer as Shaw, who believed that men and women are equals except for anatomical differences that hardly matter, the male bias is said to endure. Sure to generate interest and discussion, *Shaw's Daughters* is recommended for all academic libraries.— *H. I. Einsohn, Middlesex Community College*

WS-0372　　　　PN98　　　　91-24137 CIP
Gallop, Jane. **Around 1981: academic feminist literary theory.** Routledge, 1992. 276p index ISBN 0-415-90189-8, $42.50; ISBN 0-415-90190-1 pbk, $13.95

　　Jane Gallop—known for her work on Lacan and literary criticism—has written an impressively comprehensive account of recent feminist literary theory. *Around 1981* is not a book for beginners, but rather a carefully nuanced critique of 12 influential feminist anthologies published between 1972 and 1987. Rather than following chronology, Gallop begins "around 1981," at a point where she herself "entered into contact with the mainstream of academic literary feminism in the United States," backs up to the first feminist critical anthology, then considers where feminist criticism has gone since. By performing "symptomatic readings" attending as much to the "differences within" any given anthology as to the "differences between" collections, Gallop carefully avoids oversimplifying the books she summarizes. She also avoids the schematic categorization of feminist criticism and theory into "schools" (e.g., "French feminism" versus "Anglo-American feminism") common in earlier accounts of feminist theory (such as Toril Moi's *Textual/Sexual Politics* (1985) and Janet Todd's *Feminist Literary History* (CH, May'89). Gallop's attention to differences in writers' race, class, nationality, age, and literary positioning make this an important book: required reading for specialists in the field.—*R. R. Warhol, University of Vermont*

WS-0373　　　　PN771　　　　92-54152 CIP
Gerhart, Mary. **Genre choices, gender questions.** Oklahoma, 1992. 261p (Oklahoma project for discourse & theory, 9) bibl index afp ISBN 0-8061-2450-4, $27.95

　　An overview of the relations of gender and genre to the interpretation of literature. A specialist in hermeneutics and religion, Gerhart argues that both genre and gender are historical, not essential or eternal, categories. Although this is not a new observation, Gerhart elaborates upon it by systematically analyzing the intersections of gender and genre in literary history and theory, and focusing on their respective impact upon readers' understanding of texts. Gerhart's range of reference stretches from the Bible to postmodern "new novels." Proposing "genre and gender testing" as a means of evaluating interpretations, Gerhart concludes that "having a theoretical basis for differences in interpretations makes it more likely that readers will be prepared to make use of those differences in public discourse." The book is clearly written; it does not engage directly in contemporary feminist-theoretical debates, but alludes to them. Accessible to advanced undergraduates, useful for graduate students or scholars seeking a broad perspective on gender and genre.—*R. R. Warhol, University of Vermont*

WS-0374 PN98 93-5982 CIP
Gilmore, Leigh. **Autobiographics: a feminist theory of women's self-representation.** Cornell, 1994. 255p bibl index afp ISBN 0-8014-2778-9, $37.50; ISBN 0-8014-8061-2 pbk, $14.95

In *Autobiographics*, Gilmore (Cambridge-Portland) inscribes her "feminist theory of women's self-representation" as a "technology of resistance," allying her "genealogy" of women's autobiography with the work of recent feminist theorists (notably, Judith Butler and Teresa de Lauretis), which resists reifying critiques of subjectivity, exploring instead relational matrices for writing/reading/analyzing the "truthscape" of agency. *Autobiographics* highlights the strategic "estrangement from dominant codes of meaning" pursued by an experientially rich range of autobiographers, including Margaret Cavendish, Sandra Cisneros, Julian of Norwich, Mary McCarthy, Hannah Tillich, Monique Wittig, and Ida Bauer (Freud's *Dora*), each of whom "engages" and "restructure[s] the space the writing subject occupies." Against an insightful interrogation of the regulatory, (de)authorizing links between gender and genre, Gilmore counterposes "autobiographics" to revise the "critical histories of [autobiographical] reception" as well. Readings of lesbian writers Gertrude Stein, Cherríe Moraga, and Audre Lorde most cogently illustrate autobiographics; within these texts, identity, like autobiography, remains "irreducible to a single answer," serving instead as "occasions for experimentation." Graduate; faculty.—*S. Bryant, Alfred University*

WS-0375 PR858.C69 90-41569 MARC
Green, Katherine Sobba. **The courtship novel, 1740-1820: a feminized genre.** University Press of Kentucky, 1991. 184p index afp ISBN 0-8131-1736-4, $23.00

The best thing about this study is the desire it produces to read or reread the women novelists it examines. Noncanonical "discoveries" like Mary Collyer, Jane West, and Mary Brunton are read alongside Frances Burney, Charlotte Lennox, Eliza Haywood, and the long-canonical Jane Austen. The readings, which tend toward plot summary with commentary, are sometimes fresh and interesting. Readers will want to look at the texts themselves to test Green's hypotheses about the development of what she terms a "feminized genre," a genre primarily written for women and frequently written by them, the "courtship novel." Theoretically speaking, Green's model of textual analysis is rather disappointing. Readers may be unpersuaded by her efforts to construct novels about courtship and marriage as a separate genre. And her reliance upon Lawrence Stone's theory of the rise of affective individualism is suspect, though she claims to distance herself from it in the introduction. Similarly, she seems to wish to embrace poststructuralist theories of subjectivity and gender, but keeps falling back on essentialist conceptions of what it means to be a man or a woman, to be masculine or feminine. Yet her study is very approachable, and her evenhanded treatment of interesting and neglected women writers alongside their more famous counterparts is timely and useful.—*D. Landry, Wayne State University*

WS-0376 PN810 93-14673 CIP
Griffin, Gabriele. **Heavenly love?: lesbian images in twentieth-century women's writing.** Manchester, 1994 (c1993). (Dist. by St. Martin's) 202p bibl index ISBN 0-7190-2880-9, $69.95; ISBN 0-7190-2881-7 pbk, $19.95

A balanced and interesting treatment of writing by and about women. Griffin includes both canonical lesbian fiction (H.D. and Radclyffe Hall) and recent work by writers less frequently studied. Her broad historical scope helps put into context contemporary lesbian science fiction and narratives of female friendship. This close reading helps undercut the traditional division between "popular" and "high" culture, even as it charts the series of shifts in the representation of lesbians from "deviant" to "defiant." Through her treatment of writing by older lesbians on the subjects of illness, caretaking, and community building, Griffin suggests how culturally encoded images of lesbians have changed in the course of the 20th century. She makes a convincing case for the argument that lesbian culture is now thriving as a result of women's liberation and the advent of the gay and civil rights movements. These cultural shifts resulted in cause-oriented female-bonding fictions unthinkable in the first half of this century. Griffin provides a superb theoretical structure against which to weigh lesbian fiction of sexuality/eroticism as well as narratives of romantic love. A solid addition to *The Safe Sea of Women* by Bonnie Zimmerman (1990) and *Surpassing the Love of Men* by Lillian Faderman (1981). Advanced undergraduate; graduate; faculty.—*L. Winters, College of Saint Elizabeth*

WS-0377 PR4038.P6 90-10866 CIP
Handler, Richard. **Jane Austen and the fiction of culture: an essay on the narration of social realities,** by Richard Handler and Daniel Segal. Arizona, 1990. 175p (The Anthropology of form and meaning) bibl index afp ISBN 0-8165-1171-3, $22.95

This study of Jane Austen's novels by two anthropologists who regard Austen as social theorist and ethnographer is original and might seem extreme, but as applied social analysis it is a useful bridge between disciplines: it focuses on cultural and social issues in Austen's novels that students like to examine. Handler and Segal's approach makes more sense than that of much contemporary self-referential literary criticism, especially since it tends to avoid the jargon often associated with the social sciences. Based on clearly defined principles of courtship and marriage, the study occasionally lapses into puzzling tangents: a chapter on dialogue with an extended analogy that is much longer than any point about Austen's novels or the belabored concerns with incest that seem to go beyond the need of the ethnographic strategy to defamiliarize. Its serious treatment and tone contrast with Austen's own dry ironies; a more relaxed and exploratory style would be more engaging. The list of references is sound, but the index is far too brief. Recommended for upper-division undergraduate and graduate students.—*T. Loe, SUNY College at Oswego*

WS-0378 PR830 95-25088 CIP
Haroian-Guerin, Gil. **The fatal hero: Diana, deity of the moon, as an archetype of the modern hero in English literature.** P. Lang, 1996. 261p (Writing about women, 21) bibl index afp ISBN 0-8204-3025-0, $53.95

Haroian-Guerin (Syracuse Univ.) examines the ways that writers such as George Eliot, Nathaniel Hawthorne, James Joyce, and Edith Wharton reshaped the goddess Diana. In particular, she argues that Diana became a model for the modern heroine in these authors' works. As the author writes, Diana was "one of the most free-spirited and independent females," which helps to explain her appeal as a cultural icon in a period when views of women's socially acceptable roles were changing dramatically. The author provides close analysis of such fictional women as Jane Eyre, Hester Prynne, Molly Bloom, and Lily Bart, showing the ways that these women embody Diana. Although Haroian-Guerin's argument is intelligent and unique, this reviewer wishes that she had expanded her thesis to include some less well known authors, which would have made her book even more intriguing. Also, she could have given even greater thought to the culture surrounding the novels and how it reenvisioned Diana. But perhaps these are topics for a longer study. This book would be a suitable addition to any academic library's collection in gender studies.—*S. A. Inness, Miami University*

WS-0379 PR878 94-31064 CIP
Harsh, Constance D. **Subversive heroines: feminist resolutions of social crisis in the condition-of-England novel.** Michigan, 1994. 203p bibl index afp ISBN 0-472-10566-3, $37.50

Following the lead of such scholars as Catherine Gallagher (*The Industrial Reformation of English Fiction*, CH, Jan'86) and Nina Auerbach (*Woman and the Demon*, CH, Feb'83), Harsh examines seven novels published from 1839 to 1854 to show how their "covert feminism" brought about the "resolution" to the social crises brought on by the industrial revolution (Carlyle's condition-of-England question, discussed in such works as *Past and Present*, 1843, and *Chartism*, 1839). Harsh (Colgate Univ.) goes on to show how novels published after 1854 were unable to continue the "genre's feminist analysis or make use of its imaginative power." Her analyses of major "texts"—from Frances Trollope's *The Life and Adventures of Michael Armstrong* (1840) to Dickens's *Hard Times* (1854)—are most persuasive when she does not resort to generalizations but examines specific scenes and characters. For instance, her discussion of the women in *Hard Times*, in her chapter titled "Victimized Women," looks at the "plight" of these "victims" and the various ways Dickens used their victimization as a subversive commentary on the social ills of the time. Her especially useful discussion of Louisa demonstrates the "forceful" role a victimized woman could play and provides a nice extension of the angel-demon thesis expounded by Auerbach. Upper-division undergraduate; graduate; researchers; faculty.—*M. Timko, Queens College, CUNY*

WS-0380   PR585   89-71135 MARC
Hoeveler, Diane Long. **Romantic androgyny: the women within.** Pennsylvania State, 1991 (c1990). 274p index afp ISBN 0-271-00704-4, $29.95

Hoeveler (Marquette University) argues convincingly that the English Romantic poets' fascination with androgyny reflects their need to absorb the "symbolic feminine." She demonstrates that each of the six canonical male poets felt his creativity insured when his mental being was made whole, transformed, or idealized by an androgynous absorption of the female essence—seen as Mother, Sister, Beloved, Femme Fatale, or Muse. Hoeveler's chapters correspond to these figures, an organization that yields useful comparisons between works such as *Jerusalem* and *Prometheus Unbound*, or *Christabel* and *Lamia*. The book is appropriate for faculty, graduate students, and upper-division undergraduates; Hoeveler's practice of augmenting her psychoanalytic methodology with reference to a variety of contemporary feminist critics will expose students to the possibilities of theoretical dialogue. In the ongoing investigation of English Romanticism's insistent male-centeredness, Hoeveler's book complements studies such as the collection edited by Anne K. Mellor, *Romanticism and Feminism* (CH, Sep'88) and Marlon B. Ross's *The Contours of Masculine Desire* (1989) by offering a convincing reminder of why this literary period has been so resistant to feminization.—*W. L. Hotchkiss, California State University at Long Beach*

WS-0381   PR878   95-18035 CIP
Kahane, Claire. **Passions of the voice: hysteria, narrative, and the figure of the speaking woman, 1850-1915.** Johns Hopkins, 1995. 196p bibl index afp ISBN 0-8018-5161-0, $45.00; ISBN 0-8018-5162-9 pbk, $14.95

Using Freud's Dora case, Alice James's diary, Florence Nightingale's *Cassandra*, Charlotte Brontë's *Shirley* and *Villette*, James's *The Bostonians*, Conrad's *The Heart of Darkness*, and Ford's *The Good Soldier*, Kahane seeks to show that hysteria as represented both by narrative incidents and style is "a subversive mode of discourse that articulates a dis-ease with the cultural ordering of desire." The pun typifies the author's close but sometimes overclever attention to diction, as she examines her chosen texts for signs of suppressed rage manifested in visual, auditory, respiratory, and vocal disturbances characteristic of ego conflict displaced onto the body or represented within the narrative discourse. Kahane claims that hysteria arose in the late 19th century as a response to the militant "loud-mouthed woman." This subtle study suffers from a stream of psychoanalytic jargon, and it never articulates clearly which of several conflicting theories—Freud's, Lacan's, Klein's, or Kristeva's—it adheres to. The author's specific examples indicate that rage is a personal ego conflict (Conrad's fear of women as devouring horror)—but also culturally engendered by bad psychoanalytic theories (Freud allows "little place for the integration of rage in women's liberation")—or a fixed human condition of patriarchal language. Recommended for graduate students or faculty with a good knowledge of psychoanalytic theories.—*R. E. Wiehe, University of Massachusetts at Lowell*

WS-0382   PS228   91-45539 CIP
Kaplan, E. Ann. **Motherhood and representation: the mother in popular culture and melodrama.** Routledge, 1992. 250p bibl indexes ISBN 0-415-01126-4, $52.50; ISBN 0-415-01127-2 pbk, $16.95

Kaplan makes an important contribution to current feminist theorizing about motherhood as an institution and about representations of the mother in popular culture. Arguing that dominant cultural products—especially mainstream film melodramas—are seldom interested in a mother's subjectivity, Kaplan shows that just when attention begins to focus on that subjectivity, it is displaced by concern with the fetus. The book's first section focuses on history and on psychoanalytic discourse. The second, much longer section looks at representations of (white, mostly middle-class) motherhood in 19th-century women's writings, including *East Lynne, Herland*, and *Uncle Tom's Cabin*; in films from 1930 to 1960, including *Stella Dallas* and *Imitation of Life*; and in films, advertisements, and social science texts from the 1980s. This is an ambitious, fascinating book that helps us to understand not only the particular materials Kaplan analyzes, but also why the 1990s are sure to be a transition period in developing mother-discourses.—*M. T. Reddy, Rhode Island College*

WS-0383   PR858   90-45534 CIP
Kowaleski-Wallace, Elizabeth. **Their fathers' daughters: Hannah More, Maria Edgeworth, and patriarchal complicity.** Oxford, 1991. 235p index afp ISBN 0-19-506853-X, $29.95

Kowaleski-Wallace views her work as "a study of patterns of complicity—or the motivations behind women's identifications with their fathers, of the forms their complicity can take, and of the consequences of that identification." She examines Hannah More and Marie Edgeworth as daughters who "define themselves in opposition to a representation of nature that is consistently 'other'." More's *Strictures on the Modern System of Female Education* (London, 1799) and her work with William Wilberforce and Evangelicalism are analyzed in terms of feminist theory. The discussion of *Female Education* centers around More's attitude to Milton and his daughters, and to his characterization of "mother" Eve. More's "relationship to the Evangelical movement was paradoxical even though it has been widely praised." For Maria Edgeworth there is a chapter on "Domestic Ideology in *Belinda*" and another on "The Politics of Anglo-Irish Ascendancy." Kowaleski-Wallace cites Lawrence Stone's *The Family, Sex and Marriage in England, 1500-1800* (CH, May'78), Marilyn Butler's *Romantics, Rebels, and Reactionaries* (CH, Jul'82), as well as Kristina Straub's *Divided Status: Fanny Burney and Feminine Strategy* (CH, Jul'88). In each case she develops her own theme of "patriarchal complicity." The whole argument of this study is cast in feminist theory; there is no documented background of fact and no placing of More and Edgeworth in the larger context of the development of the novel or religious discourse. As such the book is a valuable addition to women's studies collections. Upper-division undergraduates and above.—*A. Jenkins, Georgia Institute of Technology*

WS-0384   PS153   93-6235 CIP
The Lesbian postmodern, ed. by Laura Doan. Columbia, 1994. 267p index afp ISBN 0-231-08410-2, $49.50; ISBN 0-231-08411-0 pbk, $16.50

The politically correct will recognize the fundamental problems raised by a male reviewer's evaluation of a book titled *The Lesbian Postmodern*. Others will avoid the problem, taking shelter under the Roman notion that "nothing that is human is foreign to me." So far as they are valid, these observations are directed at both parties. *The Lesbian Postmodern* is a collection of 13 essays on topics as seemingly dissimilar as Judith Raiskin's "Inverts and Hybrids: A Lesbian Rewriting of Sexual and Racial Identities" and Erica Rand's "We Girls Can Do Anything, Right Barbie? Lesbian Consumption in Postmodern Circulation." In her introduction, editor Laura Doan notes that the book "promises to unsettle, rather than settle, a complex array of questions" arising from the "highly contested terms" used in the title. "Feminist resistance to postmodernism is well documented," Doan points out, as "some feminists are concerned about the perceived loss or collapse of political agency" inherent in this cultural trend. The individual contributions to the volume vary in style but all remain above the level of mere polemic or diatribe. As a contribution to women's studies, lesbian and gay studies, gender theory and cultural trends, *The Lesbian Postmodern* is often insightful, provocative, and deeply critical of those patriarchal and heterosexual assumptions that marginalize lesbians. General and academic audiences.—*D. A. Barton, California State University, Long Beach*

WS-0385   PS1541   90-48721 CIP
Loeffelholz, Mary. **Dickinson and the boundaries of feminist theory.** Illinois, 1991. 179p index afp ISBN 0-252-01789-7, $32.50; ISBN 0-252-06175-6 pbk, $13.95

A rich synthesis of some of the more fruitful lines of inquiry in recent Dickinson criticism: deconstructionist, feminist, historicist, Lacanian. The book ranges widely and cogently over the entire modern corpus of Dickinson studies, acknowledging a debt to M. Homans (*Women Writers and Poetic Identity*, CH, Apr'81), Joanne Feit Diehl (*Emily Dickinson*, CH,Feb '87) and J. Arac (*Critical Genealogies*, CH, Jan'88) and arguing the value of a Lacanian, rather than object relations, approach to psychological readings of the poet. Slow reading and necessarily dense in the best sense of the term, this book yields finally both deeper insight into the ambiguities of Dickinson's work and rewarding readings of a number of poems as disparate as "I Never Told the Buried Gold," "Proud of My Broken Heart, Since Thou Didst Break it," and "Of All the Sounds Despatched Abroad." A final chapter applies Loeffelholz's approach to Emily Brontë and to Adrienne Rich, both placing Dickinson on a historical continuum and demonstrating the validity of this approach to other women poets. Excellent notes. Highly recommended for graduate students and beyond.—S. R. Graham, Nazareth College of Rochester

WS-0386 PR116 92-5265 CIP
Loeffelholz, Mary. **Experimental lives: women and literature, 1900-1945.** Twayne, 1992. 256p bibl index afp ISBN 0-8057-8976-6, $22.95; ISBN 0-8057-8977-4 pbk, $13.95

The introductory chapters of this volume are outstanding. Loeffelholz's goal of combining new critical theories with modernism is aptly suited to the subject of women and modernism. The discussion of imagism is very thorough, and the author's grasp of the development of the novel through the work of Virginia Woolf, Richardson, and Wharton is exceptional. Loeffelholz is so thorough that there is a risk of seeing this fine work used as a trot by harried undergraduates who are looking for quick analysis of course readings. For everyone else, the short reviews of the literature will trigger fond memories of the great accomplishments of women writers. General; beginning undergraduate.—H. Susskind, Monroe Community College

WS-0387 DA16 94-7593 CIP
McClintock, Anne. **Imperial leather: race, gender and sexuality in the colonial contest.** Routledge, 1995. 449p index afp ISBN 0-415-90889-2, $55.00; ISBN 0-415-90890-6 pbk, $18.95

McClintock's magisterial study—"a sustained quarrel with the project of imperialism, the cult of domesticity, and the invention of industrial progress"—is a daring articulation of the race-class-gender triad. The axis of British Victorian metropolis/(South) African colony provides her spatial and temporal organizing principles. Within these constraints McClintock (Columbia Univ.) shows that "the cult of domesticity," usually seen as a cultural production of industrial capitalism at "home," involved an erasure of women's labor everywhere—which made domesticity "an indispensable element both of the industrial market and the imperial enterprise." A bold redefinition of "fetishism" challenges and enlarges Freudian and Marxist paradigms, and allows the author to move freely across the elaborate text of empire (including an astonishing range of visual images) from Olive Schreiner to H. Rider Haggard's *King Solomon's Mines* to the photo archive and diaries of Arthur Munby and, more importantly, the diaries of his wife-servant (*The Diaries of Hannah Cullwick, Victorian Maidservant*, CH, Jun'85). Such encyclopedism is impelled by a moral urgency to uncover both how power uses culture to control and how the disempowered use culture to resist. At the end McClintock asks that (male) postcolonial criticism mind both "the gendered dynamics of the subject" and the need for alternative historical narratives that resist the power of the "progress" myth. Rich, learned notes with full citations; well-integrated and indexed illustrations and text. Upper-division undergraduates; graduates; researchers.—F. Alaya, Ramapo College of New Jersey

WS-0388 PR830 91-24921 CIP
McCormick, Marjorie. **Mothers in the English novel: from stereotype to archetype.** Garland, 1991. 205p (Gender & genre in literature, 1) bibl index afp ISBN 0-8240-7131-X, $30.00

Behind this discussion of the fictional depiction of mothers lies archetypal scholarship about the Great Mother goddess; it also draws on stereotypes that have appeared in such genres as the fairy tale and Shakespearean drama. McCormick concentrates on how novelists, both men and women, have regarded motherhood, a transformative experience where individuality is subsumed under a powerful role identity. Mothers have been depicted as monstrously self-involved or as selflessly resembling Madonnas; they have been revered, feared and laughed at. This literary study is especially interesting when it explains the evolution of such paradigms at the end of the Victorian era. It then focuses on E.M. Forster's Mrs. Moore, Virginia Woolf's Mrs. Ramsay, and Doris Lessing's Kate Brown. An informative and provocative analysis, this work is indebted to such related studies as Estella Lauter's *Feminist Archetypal Theory* (1985) and Marianne Hirsch's *The Mother/Daughter Plot* (CH, Apr'90). McCormick's thematic analysis is recommended for upper-division college collections on the history of fiction and women's studies.—S. A. Parker, Hiram College

WS-0389 PN171 93-43224 CIP
Men writing the feminine: literature, theory, and the question of genders, ed. by Thaïs E. Morgan. State University of New York, 1994. 207p index ISBN 0-7914-1993-2, $49.50

This excellent collection continues "the conversation between women and men about theories of sexual difference, feminism, and gender identity which arose during the 1980s." The first four essays investigate what happens when male authors "write the feminine," or create female characters' consciousness, in fiction and poetry; four more essays consider the role the "gaze" plays in structuring gender in literary texts; and the last four consider the role(s) of men in feminist theory and criticism. The essays analyze texts by British, American, and French authors from the 1600s to the present, including George Herbert, William Wordsworth, D.H. Lawrence (in relation to Emily Brontë), John Hawkes, Denis Diderot, Paul Verlaine, Randall Jarrell, John Berryman, and William Faulkner—the latter being considered (provocatively enough) as a "lesbian author." The book draws on psychoanalytic, deconstructionist, and poststructuralist theories of gender. It will be a valuable resource for specialists in gender studies and feminist theory, and would be suitable for graduate students and sophisticated upper-division undergraduates.—R. R. Warhol, University of Vermont

WS-0390 PR788 91-15720 CIP
Mills, Sara. **Discourses of difference: an analysis of women's travel writing and colonialism.** Routledge, 1992 (c1991). 232p bibl index ISBN 0-415-04629-7, $55.00

Mills constructs a new theoretical framework for the analysis of women's travel writing. In the first section she investigates the limits of traditional approaches—both the conventionally biographical and the more theoretical work of Edward Said. The second section analyzes the discussion of gender within the study of colonial discourse, arguing persuasively that theories of colonial discourse cannot simply add gender and stir, but "themselves need to be reconsidered in the light of feminist analyses." Michel Foucault's work influences the discussion of the numerous constraints upon the production and reception of women's travel writing. In the last section Mills explores three case studies: *My Journey to Lhasa* (1927) by Alexandra David-Neel, *Travels in West Africa* (1897) by Mary Kingsley, and *The Indian Alps and How We Crossed Them* (1876) by Nina Mazuchelli. Some of the painstaking negotiation of Foucault seems poignantly destined for a short shelf life. Too, in avoiding "more cohesive but partial readings," the study offers readings that are, as Mills acknowledges, unwieldy and constantly modified. But this often illuminating work resists easy generalizations and outlines significant areas for research. Appropriate for graduate students and faculty.—B. Kalikoff, University of Puget Sound

WS-0391 PR830 94-31366 CIP
Nichols, Nina daVinci. **Ariadne's lives.** Fairleigh Dickinson, 1995. (Dist. by Associated University Presses) 221p bibl indexes afp ISBN 0-8386-3582-2, $36.50

Nichols describes this book as a work in progress "on establishing an archetype," for use as a literary tool. Establishing a basic Ariadne pattern, Nichols applies her Ariadne archetype—which blends aspects of lost preheroic, Cretan myth with the heroic Greek mythic tradition—to several 19th- and 20th-century works (e.g., *Jane Eyre*, *The Scarlet Letter*, *The Awakening*, and *The Mill on the Floss*). She sees Ariadne as the mythic pattern behind the heroine's rebellion: "For no matter her story or its genre, as an avatar of Ariadne she transgresses against some taboo or cultural norm, placing herself in a conflict leading to death." Nichols's readings are speculative and sometimes illuminating. This reviewer often had difficulty seeing the relationship between Ariadne and the fictional character suggested by Nichols, and the strategies for drawing the connections sometimes seemed strained and complex to the point of impenetrability. This is a hard book to work through, though it is meticulously researched and reveals a subtle, intelligent mind. It has copious notes and a good bibliography and index. Recommended for graduate level and above, especially for those interested in myth and literature.—S. F. Klepetar, St. Cloud State University

WS-0392 PR830 93-4158 CIP
Novy, Marianne. **Engaging with Shakespeare: responses of George Eliot and other women novelists.** Georgia, 1994. 271p bibl index afp ISBN 0-8203-1596-6, $50.00

The juggling act hinted at in this book's title tosses up the women's novel tradition, Shakespeare's reception-history, and George Eliot's relationship to the male canon and manages to hold all three in the air in one amazing arc. Novy explores the tradition of women "shaping and responding to Shakespeare's cultural presence" from Aphra Behn to Angela Carter, with emphasis on Austen, Brontë, and (centrally) Eliot, the "female Shakespeare." Novy is "engaged" both with the texts and in an extended dialogue with other critics, particularly (but not exclusively) feminists, on the issue of whether women writers have been typically hostile or receptive to the male canon. She convincingly traces a thread of "appropriative creativity" in their "writing back" at Shakespeare, changing his plots, embracing and repudiating his "sympathy," and developing an "increasing self-consciousness about the gender-crossing involved in appropriating him." At Eliot's hands, she argues, these tangled choices become a dense web, and then a "bridge" to the ways of women with Shakespeare in this century from Cather, Woolf, Murdoch, and Atwood to the "cultural hybridity" of such writers as Gordimer, Carter, Naylor, Smiley, and Drabble. Both text and notes are dense; Novy's style, deliberate at best, needs a stronger editorial hand. Rich bibliography and detailed subject index. Upper-division undergraduate and up.—*F. Alaya, Ramapo College of New Jersey*

WS-0393 PR830 90-19979 CIP
Parkin-Gounelas, Ruth. **Fictions of the female self: Charlotte Brontë, Olive Schreiner, Katherine Mansfield.** St. Martin's, 1991. 203p bibl index ISBN 0-312-05709-1, $39.95

Ruth Parkin-Gounelas (University of Thessaloniki, Greece) states her intent in the introduction: "This study treats the work of three generations of post-Romantic women writers of fiction as precursors (and in some sense initiators) of the contemporary, neo-feminist preoccupation with female selfhood." Specifically, the text focuses on Charlotte Brontë, Olive Schreiner, and Katherine Mansfield; two chapters are devoted to each of the three writers, the first presenting the author's view of the task of a writer (drawing on journals and correspondence), and the second analyzing her fiction. Parkin-Gounelas is conversant with a wide array of contemporary literary theory—feminist, psychoanalytic, semiotic, deconstructionist—and brings it to bear in a deft way on her topic. Citing the "uncomfortable paradox" that, although all women's texts have been viewed (read: demeaned) as autobiographical, women are not included in standard histories of autobiography, Parkin-Gounelas argues that, until recently, women have been inhibited in their efforts at self-inscription. Her argument is strengthened by her acknowledgment of Barthes's assertion of the "death of the author" and by her discussion of the usefulness of that concept for women writers, their fiction, and their traditions. Recommended for graduate and undergraduate collections.—*E. R. Baer, Washington College*

WS-0394 PE1074.75 89-48169 CIP
Penelope, Julia. **Speaking freely: unlearning the lies of the fathers' tongues.** Pergamon, 1990. 281p bibl index afp ISBN 0-08-036556-6, $37.50; ISBN 0-08-036555-8, $16.95

Penelope has blended scholarly reflection and immoderate polemics into a work that is alternately thought-provoking and exasperating. She surveys and analyzes numerous topic areas of linguistics (such as the history of English, the growth of prescriptivism, sex differentiation in languages of the world, and current English syntax) from an overtly feminist perspective. Her examples are abundant, clear, current, and appropriate, and her analyses often provide fresh insights into the subject matter; however, the polemic aspects may be extremely obtrusive or even offensive to most readers, especially in the 37-page introduction. The reader is also frequently distracted by Penelope's overabundant use of boldface and underlining and by her unconventional, politically motivated use or rejection of capital letters (e.g., u.s., Lesbian) and of x for Christ (e.g., xtianity). This book is recommended for libraries with strong feminist collections. Appropriate for faculty and for upper-level undergraduate and graduate students who have some acquaintance with linguistics and are able to separate legitimate scholarship from political rhetoric. Very informative endnotes and glossary.—*L. Bebout, University of Windsor*

WS-0395 PN56 91-52597 CIP
Powers, Meredith A. **The heroine in Western literature: the archetype and her reemergence in modern prose.** McFarland, 1991. 234p bibl index afp ISBN 0-89950-615-1, $32.50

Joseph's Campbell's well-known *Hero with a Thousand Faces*, which clarifies the archetypal voyage of the hero and offers role models to fire the imagination of young males, is all too clearly a masculine guide. Powers, like others who have recognized the lack of female models for self-affirmation in the Western cultural heritage, has gone in search of the archetypal heroine. Unable to find her in the Hebrew and Greek myths, except in the distortions wrought by patriarchal cultures who reduce her to secondary status, ostracize her, or omit her entirely, Powers goes back to prehistoric times to find the early tribal autonomous goddesses. She then finds these goddesses' correlatives in characters in contemporary fiction, thus revalidating the unseen goddess's presence and revealing her again as a model for female autonomy. This study is a necessary rereading and rethinking of archetypal images and valuable for all students of literature and myth. Excellent bib., notes, and index.—*N. B. Palmer, Western Maryland College*

WS-0396 PS169.P36 89-6118 MARC
Refiguring the father: new feminist readings of patriarchy, ed. by Patricia Yaeger and Beth Kowaleski-Wallace. Southern Illinois, 1989. 319p afp ISBN 0-8093-1529-7, $32.50

Given the current preoccupation of women's studies with the deconstructive/psychoanalytic approach, particularly in regard to incest and patriarchy, as well as the long-established concern with sounding out a feminist philosophy, *Refiguring the Father* is an excellent addition to a rapidly expanding body of research. Because it is a collection of essays, most written by established scholars in the field although some are by less experienced but competent writers, the whole work is consistent in themes but not in development. Mainly, the essays revalue, rethink standard literary works, from the obligatory Greek myths to Faulkner and Henry James. Wise inclusions are the popular but influential work of Alcott and the Elsie Dinsmore series. The volume, a part of the fine "Ad Feminam" series, is typical of writing in women's studies in being thoroughly and precisely documented. The essays assume substantial knowledge of a wide range of literature and literary history, as well as considerable psychological and philosophical sophistication. Although each of the 15 essays is clearly written and well thought out, the collection is a demanding one, aimed at scholars and not beginners.—*T. S. Kobler, Texas Woman's University*

WS-0397 PS374 92-25385 CIP
Roberts, Robin. **A new species: gender and science in science fiction.** Illinois, 1993. 170p bibl index afp ISBN 0-252-01983-0, $29.95; ISBN 0-252-06284-1 pbk, $12.95

Roberts's useful survey of science fiction takes its point of departure from Mary Shelley's *Frankenstein* and uses that text along with key myths, such as that of Demeter, to trace the development of feminist values in 19th- and 20th-century science fiction. Despite the title, which suggests that this book will examine closely the uses of science in science fiction, the primary emphasis is rather on gender issues. In particular, the author discusses "proto-feminist" works as a way of illustrating the developmental nature of science fiction as it reflects the growth of feminist thought in the 19th and 20th centuries. The examination of texts is not exhaustive, and the author would have done well to include some discussion of pre-Hellenic versions of the myths she relies on; but the book is a valuable compilation of readings of some of the most significant science fiction by key authors of our time. Gender issues are central to science fiction, reflecting as it does the culture out of which it comes; this book helps readers to trace the meaning of gender as it has evolved in feminist thought and fiction. Undergraduate; general.—*R. Nadelhaft, University of Maine at Orono*

WS-0398 PR888 90-10249 CIP
Robinson, Sally. **Engendering the subject: gender and self-representation in contemporary women's fiction.** State University of New York, 1991. 248p bibl index ISBN 0-7914-0727-6, $44.50; ISBN 0-7914-0728-4 pbk, $14.95

This study reads fiction by Doris Lessing, Angela Carter, and Gayl Jones in light of contemporary gender theory. Robinson argues that feminist theory must dismantle the essentialist notion of Woman that has emerged from the texts of Western humanism, while articulating ways in which women authors create new, historically contingent identities. In order to theorize how women become subjects in contemporary culture, it is necessary to hold in tensive suspension both

"Woman" and "women," the general and the specific, and to engage simultaneously in a negative critique of master narratives that define women monovocally and in affirmative politics that insist on female-constructed polyvocal self-definitions. Robinson follows this method as she demonstrates in her readings of contemporary fiction how women negotiate the cultural texts that seek to define them and how they position themselves in the discourses in ways that allow resistance and transgression of control. The book includes extensive notes and bibliography.—*B. Braendlin, Florida State University*

WS-0399   PR6045   95-32134 CIP
Schroeder, Steven. **Virginia Woolf's subject and the subject of ethics: notes toward a poetics of persons.** E. Mellen, 1996. 248p bibl index ISBN 0-7734-8923-1, $89.95

Schroeder bases his exploration of ethics on the notion that the fundamental question of ethics centers on the same relationships as those in social science: structure/society and individual/society. He defines a discipline of ethics in dialogue with social theory and uses this framework to discuss Augustine's *Confessions* and Woolf's *A Sketch of the Past*. The author defines Augustine's concepts of time and memory and his autobiographical account as a prototype for the way narrative structures have reproduced social structures in the West and he contrasts Augustine with Woolf's autobiographical acts in *Sketch* and in other writings (including *A Room of One's Own* and *Three Guineas*). Woolf undermines the structure established by Augustine and develops a poetics of persons that remakes the world and redefines autobiographical practice. Recommended for graduate students, researchers, and faculty.—*N. Allen, Beaver College*

WS-0400   PR830   92-45112 CIP
Sharpe, Jenny. **Allegories of empire: the figure of woman in the colonial text.** Minnesota, 1993. 190p index afp ISBN 0-8166-2059-8, $39.95; ISBN 0-8166-2060-1 pbk, $14.95

In a lengthy and heavily annotated introduction, Sharpe charts themes to be developed in the book. These include the psychology of colonialism; the importance of the 1857 Indian Mutiny; political power that permitted both domination and subordination. She stresses that the raping of white women by Indian men "was not a part of the colonial landscape in India prior to the 1857 uprisings," and that it signaled a crisis in British authority, which regarded the "violated bodies of English women as a sign of the violation of colonialism." References to E.M. Forster's *A Passage to India* (1924) and Paul Scott's *The Raj Quartet* (1966-75) appear repeatedly throughout, the latter being central to the sixth and final chapter. Successive chapters (2-5) deal with the rise of women in an age of progress, journalistic reports and popular histories of the Indian Mutiny, the rise of memsahibs in an age of empire, and Flora Annie Steel's *On the Face of Waters* (1896). Sharpe writes out of her own Anglo-Indian experiences, and one of her strengths may well be her extensive knowledge of unusual research materials. She defines her terms, distinguishing between colonialism and imperialism; sepoys are Indian soldiers in the British army; the terms Hindoo, Indian, and native are interchangeable; and Anglo-Indians are "British residents in India" or a "community in exile." The notes are rich with archival references, and a brief appendix lists selected published and unpublished sources. Faculty.—*R. T. Van Arsdel, emerita, University of Puget Sound*

WS-0401   PN471   93-27252 CIP
Skoller, Eleanor Honig. **The in-between of writing: experience and experiment in Drabble, Duras, and Arendt.** Michigan, 1993. 161p bibl index ISBN 0-472-10260-5, $39.50

Taking the authority of experience within recent Euroamerican feminist thought as a premise, Skoller's readings of Drabble, Duras, and Arendt are developed in order to ask the further question: Why is it that so few women prose writers have appeared in the canonical rosters of contemporary experimental authors? The introductory chapter of this short study argues that the relation between "women's experience and literary experiment" must be centrally posed in coming to terms with such a question. The approaches to the three writers chosen to exemplify the complexities of this relation are variously linguistic, semiotic, psychoanalytic, and deconstructive, precisely to demonstrate their respective connections to language and world history. From Drabble's *The Needle's Eye* (CH, Nov'72), to Duras's *Hiroshima Mon Amour*, to Arendt's *Rahel Varnhagen*,

Skoller locates the work of these authors within the several contending fields of literary criticism and feminist theory. Recommended for college libraries.—*B. Harlow, University of Texas at Austin*

WS-0402   PR878   94-1597 CIP
Stockton, Kathryn Bond. **God between their lips: desire between women in Irigaray, Brontë, and Eliot.** Stanford, 1994. 273p bibl index afp ISBN 0-8047-2312-5, $39.50; ISBN 0-8047-2344-3 pbk, $13.95

Designed to explore desire between women as a form of "spiritualism," Stockton examines Charlotte Brontë's *Villette* and George Eliot's *Middlemarch* from the viewpoint of French feminist Luce Irigaray, who transforms psychoanalyst Jacques Lacan's identification of women's "lack" into her theory of "elegant absence." Underlying this discussion is Karl Marx's explanation of work as masculine "capitalist exchange," which excludes women, and its consequences, such as women's mirrored relations and their self-pleasure in desiring. Carlyle embodies Victorians' spiritual materialism, and poststructuralists are new Victorians who replace "God" with the "body." Biography is also scrutinized to reveal the novelists' spiritual heritage and its reflection in their work. Brontë's Paul Emanuel is described as a Christ figure who represents hetero-erotic relations modeled on feminine fractures and serves as a telescopic end point for desire between women. Eliot's oddly masculine narrator glances at women, often paired women, as potential objects of desire. Both novels reveal that spirituality nurtures sexual desire and class leveling. Built upon a repudiation of Ian Watt's influential *The Rise of the Novel* (1957), which emphasizes masculine bourgeois individuality, this challenging and stimulating application of recent feminist and poststructuralist theory offers immersion in close reading of two major texts and a useful rethinking of Victorian theorists. Upper-division undergraduate and up.—*S. A. Parker, Hiram College*

WS-0403   PS374.S54   89-29777 MARC
Stout, Janis P. **Strategies of reticence: silence and meaning in the works of Jane Austen, Willa Cather, Katherine Anne Porter, and Joan Didion.** University Press of Virginia, 1990. 228p bibl index ISBN 0-8139-1262-8, $27.50

In a monograph as tautly written as the work of the authors she discusses, Stout proves out her thesis that women writers have used reticence instead of statement to put forward feminist points of view. Beginning with Jane Austen and working through Willa Cather and Katherine Ann Porter to Joan Didion, the book describes the deliberate, probably socially induced, omissions of the four writers. Undoubtedly well chosen for their laconism and reticence, all four writers offer tightly composed works of fiction that provide silence instead of polemics, both because of the constraints on women's lives and, obviously, because the nature was, or is, to write so. Using wit, compression, and suggestion, all four—from the great Austen to the contemporary Didion—have expressed more than they have stated. Stout's thesis is an appealing one, well reinforced by her thorough examinations of the prose. Whether these writers were consciously setting out feminist ideas by conscious omissions is not so important as the fact that their works have achieved that effect. Some knowledge of the work of Austen, Cather, Porter, and Didion is required for the best use of this book, which serves as valuable literary and stylistic as well as feminist analysis. Like most good work in women's studies, it is thorough in documentation. Recommended for graduate and upper-division undergraduate students.—*T. S. Kobler, Texas Woman's University*

WS-0404   Brit. CIP
Traub, Valerie. **Desire and anxiety: circulations of sexuality in Shakespearean drama.** Routledge, 1992. 182p index ISBN 0-415-05526-1, $57.00; ISBN 0-415-05527-X pbk, $15.95

A volume in the series "Gender, Culture, Difference," edited by Catherine Belsey, which is dedicated to the construction of a feminist cultural history. Traub is working in the domain (though with a difference) established by theorists of the history of sexuality from Foucault to Thomas Laqueur and Natalie Zemon Davis, and particularly, as the word "circulations" in her title suggests, by Stephen Greenblatt. Her particular contribution is to offer readings that not only are feminist but also insist on the separation of gender and sexuality as issues for consideration. Traub views Shakespeare's texts as sites for the playing out of the erotic possibilities of early modern England. After an occasionally jargon-laden introduction, individual texts are discussed as sites for the containment or marginalization of the feminine by an anxious phallocentric culture. Just as Laertes advises Ophelia to keep her "chaste treature locked," or contained, so the sequestering of Hermione as statue in *The Winter's Tale* is seen as a strategy to contain and disarm her "unmanageable" sexuality. Cressida's troublesome sexuality is viewed as a metaphor for the invasion of venereal disease into early modern society. In a particularly bold reading, Traub equates Falstaff ("False-staff") with the female "grotesque body," which Hal must eventually repudiate. The latter part of the book deals with the circulation of homoerotic energy (both male and female) in Shakespeare's "transvestite" comedies. Useful endnotes.— *T. K. Lerud, Elmhurst College*

WS-0405 PN471 94-38181 CIP
Violence, silence, and anger: women's writing as transgression, ed. by Deirdre Lashgari. University Press of Virginia, 1995. 351p bibl index ISBN 0-8139-1492-2, $55.00; ISBN 0-8139-1493-0 pbk, $19.95

Lashgari (California State Polytechnic Univ.) has put together a useful collection of 21 essays that apply contemporary theory to establish a point of view toward writings by women who are not extremely well known in the US. The editor's announced intention is to bring together "ideas about silence and anger and the need to speak out against violence." A very good introduction forcefully establishes the theoretical stance. The essays that follow are more useful academic criticism than the title suggests. Although Virginia Woolf and Adrienne Rich are included, the text brings theory to bear on writers not usually part of academic discourse—e.g., Janice Mirikitani, Etel Adnan, Sherley Anne Williams, Nawal el Saadawi, Mary Gordon, Sylvia Molloy, and Elsa Joubert. Recommended for university libraries, upper-division undergraduate upward.— *Q. Grigg, Hamline University*

WS-0406 PS374.F45 89-25701 MARC
Waxman, Barbara Frey. **From the hearth to the open road: a feminist study of aging in contemporary literature.** Greenwood, 1990. 205p (Contributions in women's studies, 113) bibl index afp ISBN 0-313-26650-6, $38.00

Waxman (University of North Carolina, Wilmington) traces the changing image of aging women in popular magazines and fiction. She asserts that a new genre is emerging, which she dubs the *Reifungsroman*, or "novel of ripening." She compares this to the more familiar term bildungsroman, as each kind of fiction portrays a character's growth, but at a different stage of life. The characteristics of this new genre, according to Waxman, include a confessional tone, a rambling narrative, exploration of sexual passion, a journey/quest motif, the desire to name, and dreams/flashbacks that allow the character to come to terms with her past. The establishment of this new genre and the creation of a bibliography are the most valuable aspects of the book. Waxman's analysis of individual works of fiction is competent but lacklustre, offering few new insights. She includes the following writers: Doris Lessing, Alice Adams, Elizabeth Taylor, Barbara Pym, Paule Marshall, Margaret Laurence, and May Sarton; she devotes her opening chapter to the depiction of old age in periodical literature of 1890-1920 and of 1950-1980s, establishing a backdrop for her discussion of contemporary fiction. The overall impact of Waxman's book is to point out a rather dramatic move away from ageism in recent fiction by and about women. Recommended only for large collections.—*E. R. Baer, Washington College*

WS-0407 93-60971 Orig
Wolmark, Jenny. **Aliens and others: science fiction, feminism and postmodernism.** Iowa, 1994. 167p bibl index ISBN 0-87745-446-9, $29.95; ISBN 0-87745-447-7 pbk, $14.95

Although slim, Wolmark's volume tackles substantive questions regarding the "intersections" of science fiction with feminism and postmodernism. As she develops her concept of these intersections in her opening chapter, she focuses on the destabilization of boundaries between binary oppositions such as male and female, and the challenge to the inequalities of power that result in dominant and subservient roles. Subsequent chapters examine how a variety of writers from Octavia Butler to Marge Piercy have achieved this destabilization and mounted this challenge by adapting or subverting features of science fiction such as aliens,

cyborgs, cyberspace, and the genre's own conventions for narrative. Along the way, Wolmark is able to suggest how the shifting fortunes of feminism over the past 25 years are reflected in an increasingly problematic view of gender and identity. Closely focused and deftly argued, Wolmark's concise volume should stimulate further study of these issues. For interested scholars, the volume includes nine pages of notes, 16 pages of bibliography, and an index. Recommended for libraries serving upper-level undergraduates as well as graduate students.— *J. J. Marchesani, Pennsylvania State University, Mckeesport Campus*

WS-0408 PR830 91-42254 CIP
Wolstenholme, Susan. **Gothic (re)visions: writing women as readers.** State University of New York, 1993. 201p bibl index ISBN 0-7914-1219-9, $44.50; ISBN 0-7914-1220-2 pbk, $14.95

This is a fine, if difficult, theory-driven book. It demands either a current interest in feminist writer/reader theory on the issue of a "female Gothic" tradition, or an ability to negotiate the intersection of feminism and narratology. Expressly employing the decoding logic of Lacanian psychoanalysis "through the medium of film theory," Wolstenholme adds to a mounting critical literature on the gothic a number of fresh insights into the dynamics of female creativity over the swift course of the 100 years that divide Radcliffe's *Italian* and Shelley's *Frankenstein* from Wharton's *House of Mirth*. Or, better, that unite them: she argues that it is the sign of "Gothic-marked texts" to acknowledge the "monstrosity" of the woman-artist and pay homage to the devious storytelling "arts" of their foremothers, who grasped the anarchy of a narrative in which woman is both "icon" and author—object and subject. Using a pictorial aesthetic of "visions" or "scenes," or employing several narrators, gothic fiction resists the masculine narrative poetics of sequence and action and generates post-gothic "re-visions" that "threaten the very power relations they accommodate." Chapters on Brontë and Eliot explore romance and realism as narrative politics; the chapter on *Uncle Tom's Cabin* breaks new ground, explicating Stowe's subversions of sexism *and* racism. Well researched, with illustrations brilliantly interpolated, and illuminating endnotes and bibliography. Advanced undergraduate; graduate; faculty.—*F. Alaya, Ramapo College of New Jersey*

WS-0409 PR830.W6 90-12010 CIP
Wyatt, Jean. **Reconstructing desire: the role of the unconscious in women's reading and writing.** North Carolina, 1990. 271p bibl index afp ISBN 0-8078-1915-8, $32.50; ISBN 0-8078-4285-0, $12.95

In this study of several 19th- and 20th-century British and American novels by women, including the artist novel, Wyatt explores possibilities for personal and sociopolitical changes by readers attuned to unconscious fantasies of female desire in fiction. Using theories of the unconscious derived from Freud, Jacques Lacan, Julia Kristeva, and Nancy Chodorow, Wyatt identifies a latent energy source in the human personality, which may resist and even transform debilitating social constructions of female identity and restrictive economic opportunities for women. When preoedipal fantasies, reflecting that energy source, are expressed in women's fiction, they challenge traditional patriarchal fantasies—especially those involving father-daughter relationships—that entrap women in the ideology of romantic love, which denies them autonomy. Wyatt hopes for the eventual attainment of a new equality for women that might emerge when readers who recognize female desire in fantasy begin to mobilize it in their own lives. African American women's novels are especially helpful in encouraging change because they embody a respect for maternal love and values and a concept of extended family that counters the traditional "gender-bound" patriarchal nuclear family. Appropriate for graduate and upper-division undergraduate students —*B. Braendlin, Florida State University*

WS-0410 PR149 95-53949 CIP
Wynne-Davies, Marion. **Women and Arthurian literature: seizing the sword.** Macmillan, UK/St. Martin's, 1996. 237p bibl index ISBN 0-312-16047-X, $45.00

In this ambitious, diffuse, and theory-laden book, Wynne-Davies (Univ. of Dundee) combines a primarily materialist-feminist critical stance with Bakhtinian dialogic and chronotopic (intersecting time/space) concerns to examine Arthurian works and/or their authors from the 14th to the 20th centuries. The author's theoretical and textual choices are sometimes an uneasy fit: discussions of Spenser's (only marginally Arthurian) *Faerie Queene* and a single bizarre story by the contemporary fantasist Jane Yolen seems quixotic when placed next to Chaucer's "The Wife of Bath's Tale," *Sir Gawain and the Green Knight*, and Malory's *Le Morte D'Arthur*. More productive is the conjoining of Lady Charlotte Guest's translation of *The Mabinogion*, Tennyson's *Idylls of the King*, and Julia Margaret Cameron's photographic illustrations to the latter text, a discussion made more interesting by the fact that these Victorians knew each other and discussed Arthurian subjects. A concluding chapter considers the emergence of 20th-century women writers Mary Stewart (the Merlin trilogy and "the Mordred book," *The Wicked Day*) and Marion Zimmer Bradley (*The Mists of Avalon*) in addition to Yolen's short story "Evian Steel." An awkward style suffers further from jargony diction—both "aporia" and "scopophilia" appear with annoying frequency. But the book is worth reading, if only as a pioneering look at an unjustly neglected topic. Upper-division undergraduates through faculty.—*M. Fries, SUNY College at Fredonia*

◆ African & Middle Eastern

WS-0411   PQ3980   94-26083 CIP
Almeida, Irène Assiba d'. **Francophone African women writers: destroying the emptiness of silence.** University Press of Florida, 1994. 222p bibl index afp ISBN 0-8130-1302-X, $34.95

D'Almeida takes the point of view that, prior to 1969, the original date of publication of Thérèse Kuoh-Moukoury's *Rencontres essentielles* (Adamawa, 1981), there was a silence in print by French-speaking African women, one that women felt the need and the duty to break. This silence was due to the dominance of patriarchies in African society. D'Almeida's book examines novels and autobiographies by nine writers who have published since 1975, all of whom use writing to critique the patriarchal order, to champion the cause of women and the community, and to preserve positive aspects of tradition. She approaches these writers through an artificial hierarchy of social categories, beginning with a representation of the self, moving to women's position within the family, and finally concluding with the writers' concerns for society as a whole. She concludes that "writing had allowed women to speak the unspeakable, to utter words, ideas, concepts that are forbidden to them within the conventions laid out by patriarchal society." She feels that it would be premature to say that this emptiness of silence has been destroyed. Yet, "if the story is told, the silence, and its emptiness, may be destroyed." Excellent notes. Undergraduate and up.—*S. R. Schulman, Central Connecticut State University*

WS-0412   PJ8005   94-9898 CIP
Arebi, Saddeka. **Women and words in Saudi Arabia: the politics of literary discourse.** Columbia, 1994. 357p bibl index afp ISBN 0-231-08420-X, $49.50; ISBN 0-231-08421-8 pbk, $17.50

This is a thorough ethnographic study of the writings of nine Saudi women. Most of the poets, essayists, and fiction writers, among the earliest women in Saudi Arabia to receive public education, became active in the 1980s, the decade of greatest change. These women are uncompromising in their challenge to male discursive power and to oppressive social norms; they refuse marginalization but force attention to the injustice of segregation. Arebi argues that they use literature as a political tool to go public, to reinterpret religion, tradition, and history, and to effect social transformation while remaining invisible. They often use densely symbolic language to bypass the censor. Aerbi has conducted interviews with each woman and translated lengthy examples from her work; she then added textual analyses highlighting themes. This format has entailed repetition and a didactic quality perhaps better suited to a high school textbook. Nevertheless, this is an important contribution to the growing scholarship on Arab women intellectuals and an unusual insight into the creative world of women thought to be immobilized by living in one of the world's most severe patriarchies. Undergraduate.—*M. Cooke, Duke University*

WS-0413   PK6561   91-40933 CIP
Daneshvar, Simin. **A Persian requiem: a novel,** tr. by Roxane Zand. G. Braziller, 1992 (c1991). 279p ISBN 0-8076-1273-1, $22.50; ISBN 0-8076-1274-X pbk, $12.50

The 1980s saw a massive increase in the number of Middle Eastern novels translated into European languages and especially into English. Unprecedented attention has been paid to women's writings so that finally the Western reader has access to some household names in Iran and the Arab world. *A Persian Requiem* is a translation of a 1969 work by Simin Daneshvar, Iran's leading woman writer, the first novel by a woman to be published in Iran. Its popularity continues until today. Entering into the heart of an aristocratic southern family at the end of WW II, it tells the story of women's charitable works, of local intrigue, of tribal resistance and revolts, of collusions with the enemy, of the struggle to survive and the wages of trying to help others less fortunate to survive the British occupation. This family saga, which traces through a period of social and political transformation, weaves an absorbing tale sensitively and elegantly translated by Roxane Zand.—*M. Cooke, Duke University*

WS-0414   PS3554   96-3143 CIP
Drew, Eileen. **The ivory crocodile: a novel.** Coffee House, 1996. 289p ISBN 1-56689-042-X, $21.95

Moroccan-born Drew has in this first novel written of Caucasian Nicole Spark, who goes to the fictitious African country of Tambala to teach English. Nicole is sponsored by AfricEd, not a government agency, as she carefully points out. Nevertheless, she is drawn into the political situation of the country and into the personal lives of her students, fellow Americans in Africa, and such friends as Mpovi, the wife of the *préfet* of her school. Nicoli, as she is called, wants desperately to belong, even allowing Mpovi to dress her in the pagne, the Africaqn women's dress, and to braid her hair in order to attend a wedding. But she can never fit in. Drew limns the problems of an outsider trying, however sincerely, to understand and become part of a foreign culture. Symbol-lovers will have a field day with this novel, especially with the crocodile of the title. It is literally a hollow ivory knickknack, but it represents Nicole herself: "endowed with white luck, I was sacred as an idol, precious as a god carved from tusk." But she sees herself finally as a fraud: "I'd wanted to see ivory and crocodiles for what they were. And yet ... it's an emblem, I see now, of our expatriate idyll, of ivory as dinner table art, of crocodiles as cute." Drew has written with affection and understanding of believable, mostly likable, definitely sympathetic characters. Very highly recommended for all collections.—*J. Overmyer, emerita, Ohio State University*

WS-0415   PR9369   Orig
Head, Bessie. **A gesture of belonging: letters from Bessie Head, 1965-1979,** ed. by Randolph Vigne. Heinemann/SA Writers, 1991. 229p index ISBN 0-435-08059-8 pbk, $12.50

This collection of letters joins three other recent publications—*Tales of Tenderness and Power* (1989), *The Tragic Life*, ed. by C. Abrahams (1990), and *A Woman Alone* (CH, Jul'91)—that provide rich contexts for the work of Bessie Head, the late Southern African writer. The 107 letters initiated by Head's exile in Botswana were written from October 1965 to July 1977 and addressed to compiler Vigne, former editor of *Africa Today* and Head's colleague in both political activism and journalism in Cape Town. Many of the recurring themes in her fiction appear here: Head's alienation from the Botswanas; her general emotional and intellectual isolation; sexual brutality, but especially against women; her increasing sense of an impending mental breakdown; her search for roots; the destruction of black life by tribalism and colonialism; and African as well as white racism. Of significant literary interest is the light the letters shed on the composition and reception of her works. Present also, however, is a disquieting strain of paranoia and contradictory responses. In view of these elements, of particular helpfulness are Vigne's brief summaries following the letters from a particular locale, explaining what was actually happening to Head at the time and clarifying her references. Appropriate for public libraries and all levels of academic libraries.—*A. A. Elder, University of Cincinnati*

WS-0416   PR9369   94-39707 CIP
Horton, Susan R. **Difficult women, artful lives: Olive Schreiner and Isak Dinesen, in and out of Africa.** Johns Hopkins, 1995. 312p bibl index afp ISBN 0-8018-5037-1, $45.00; ISBN 0-8018-5038-X pbk, $15.95

In this maddening and delicious book Horton's aim is to save confounding contradictions (e.g., woman/not woman, past/future, self/other, real/imagined,

African/European, black/white) from incoherence without denying their contrariety and the psychic cost of the effort—in her subjects or in the reader—to separate, resolve, or "oscillate" between them. Her idiosyncratic treatment of these two very different writers who happen to have African common ground gains credibility with each chapter; the reader sees them as part of a historical continuuim of "self-formation" planted squarely in time yet bearing witness to the present. Both subjects benefit: Schreiner comes together in all her self-ravaging complexity, making no apology for her unfinished literary business; Dinesen perversely disintegrates into brilliant *personae*. Horton's decisions on what to read, and how to read it, revitalize every text she chooses, from photos to fetishes, including life acts and choices besides the usual letters, essays, and fictions. She negotiates a minefield of race, class, and gender issues (surcharged here with the powerful nationalist and ethnic ordinance of her African material) with an open, adroit deployment of theory and historiography. Attentive to the public and political uses of criticism, she never quite sidelines the need for "play" that brings readers to literary "*langscapes*" in the first place. Upper-division undergraduates and above.—*F. Alaya, Ramapo College of New Jersey*

WS-0417   PK6413   91-28640 CIP
Milani, Farzaneh. **Veils and words: the emerging voices of Iranian women writers.** Syracuse, 1992. 295p bibl index afp ISBN 0-8156-2557-X, $34.95; ISBN 0-8156-0266-9 pbk, $16.95

Farzaneh Milani introduces this first full-length study in English of Iranian women's writings by situating herself: an Iranian living in America yet succeeding from this place of exile in balancing worlds of opposing values. Like its author, *Veils and Words* maintains throughout an almost impossible cultural, literary, and theoretical equilibrium. Debts to Western and Middle Eastern scholars of literary and feminist criticism are openly acknowledged; writers' jugglings of the modern and the traditional, the conventional and the revolutionary are analyzed to find that space in which they may fruitfully co-exist. She persuasively links women's publications with their unveiling as with their enforced veiling in the post-Iranian Revolution era. She describes her agenda as being less a survey than an attempt to highlight those women whose works have "marked important new beginnings concerning notions of veiling/unveiling." Although Milani pays most attention to poets, including Qorrotol'Ayn, Farrokhzad, Saffarzadeh, and Behbahani, she does devote a section to fiction and autobiography. This work powerfully and sensitively analyzes writings of which students of literature everywhere should be aware.—*M. Cooke, Duke University*

WS-0418   PR9369   91-9431 CIP
Monsman, Gerald. **Olive Schreiner's fiction: landscape and power.** Rutgers, 1991. 201p index ISBN 0-8135-1724-9, $45.00

This well-written study of Olive Schreiner's works is a fine addition to Ruth First and Ann Scott's 1980 biography (*Olive Schreiner*, CH, Feb'81) and Joyce Berkman's 1989 study (*The Healing Imagination of Olive Schreiner*, CH, Mar'90). Monsman discusses most of Schreiner's works, concentrating on her three novels—the autobiographical novel, *The Story of an African Farm* (1883); the fundamentally political novel, *Trooper Peter Halket of Mashonaland* (1897); and the posthumous *From Man to Man* (1927). Her juvenile novel *Undine* as well as several short stories are also included. One third of the book is devoted to *The Story of an African Farm*. Schreiner's works present rich insights into the marginal world of women in late 19th-century South Africa, as well as an alternative voice to the dominant, technologically driven colonialism of her age. As the child of missionary parents she became deeply aware of the inconsistencies between Christian teachings and colonial realities. Monsman presents a thorough analysis of Schreiner's profoundly feminist voice, clearly describing her double alienation from both European patriarchal and African societies, and suggesting parallels between racial imperialism and sexual exploitation. Footnotes are adequate, as is the index, but a bibliography is lacking. A reading of at least one of Schreiner's works is strongly recommended before reading this book. Levels: graduate and upper-division undergraduate.—*C. Pike, University of Minnesota*

WS-0419   PJ7731   91-10102 CIP
Naddaff, Sandra. **Arabesque: narrative structure and the aesthetics of repetition in the *1001 nights*.** Northwestern University, 1991. 156p bibl index afp ISBN 0-8101-0976-X, $26.95; ISBN 0-8101-0990-5 pbk, $14.95

Structuralism, poststructuralism, narratology, and classical Arabic rhetorical theory methodologically inform Naddaff's examination of "narrative structure and the aesthetics of repetition" in the *1001 Nights*. The study takes its title from the patterns designed in the *Nights* and in their cultural context. Unlike Ferial Ghazoul's innovative *The Arabian Nights: A Structural Analysis* (Cairo, 1980) and its similar theoretical approach, however, Naddaff's analysis focuses on one specific story cycle from the larger work: "The Story of the Porter and the Three Ladies." This exemplary cycle exhibits, according to the critic, the connections between narrative and gender, the textual and the sexual, that distinguish the *Nights* as a whole. Beginning with the role of figural language, especially metaphor, in the stories, as constitutive of an "écriture feminine," Naddaff goes on to examine in particular the functions of repetition in the stories told by the ladies, the porter, and the three dervishes as these affect and are affected by desire, difference, and time. The three ladies, like Sheherazade herself, threaten patriarchy by their autonomy and self-determination, and must, it is argued, eventually be contained by the conservative imperatives of a narrative strategy of repetition. *Arabesque* combines comparative literary theory with a contemporary gender-studies emphasis to produce a compelling reading of this important story cycle from a world classic, one that will be useful to students and teachers alike. Recommended for graduate and undergraduate libraries.—*B. Harlow, University of Texas at Austin*

WS-0420   PR9369.3.N4   90-26832 CIP
Ngcobo, Lauretta. **And they didn't die: a novel.** G. Braziller, 1991 (c1990). 245p ISBN 0-8076-1263-4, $19.95

The great success of this novel is its compelling portrayal of ordinary rural women in South Africa—their experience of penury, drought, labor, child rearing, and separation from husbands and sons. The plot demonstrates that the courage, ingenuity, determination, and heroism of the protagonist are typical of the women in her circumstance. The constraints and supports of the communal values and organizations, including the Christian church, are explored, especially the obedience due from a wife to her mother-in-law, the chastity due to her absent husband, the difficulty of maintaining conjugal love despite a spouse's separation or unemployment, the consequences of defying or submitting to the pass laws, and the political oppression itself. The reasoning, motives, and emotions of the characters are reported more than revealed, unconvincingly for prison guards and collaborators, inadequately for children and male white oppressors. The heavy reliance on authorial explication is relieved by striking, unromanticized events, engaging suspense, and historical allusions. Verisimilitude and structure are sacrificed in the final pages, which rush through a decade in order to create an optimistic—if not happy—ending.—*D. F. Dorsey, Clark Atlanta University*

WS-0421   PR9379   93-35009 CIP
Odamtten, Vincent O. **The art of Ama Ata Aidoo: polylectics and reading against neocolonialism.** University Press of Florida, 1994. 202p bibl index afp ISBN 0-8130-1276-7, $32.95; ISBN 0-8130-1277-5 pbk, $16.95

This study examines the evolution of one of Ghana's most important writers over the past 30 years, Ama Ata Aidoo. It is also, indirectly, a sociopolitical study of Ghana during this period. It attempts to address what the author sees as an important shortcoming in contemporary African letters—the disparity between the exciting, innovative imaginative literature of Africa and the weakness and dependency of its literary criticism. This study aims at a "polylectic" reading of Aidoo's works. Its eye is on the importance of the underlying oral literature from which Aidoo has drawn so much inspiration. It also aims to follow the African writer's lead by critically reading against neocolonialism. In both respects this book is a modest success. Ama Ata Aidoo has been giving a strong voice to African women since 1964. Her works draw from a variety of sources and defy easy labeling—hence Odamtten's use of the term polylectic. A reader must be familiar with at least some of Aidoo's works to gain from this study (which includes two plays, a collection of short stories, two innovative novels, and a collection of poetry). The strongest sections are the discussions of Aidoo's well-known plays, *The Dilemma of a Ghost* (1965) and *Anowa* (1970). In Aidoo's collective works, the reader will come to understand, among other things, important tensions between long-held Ghanaian views about the importance of economic independence for women and colonial and neocolonial ideals. This is a study, in short, of one of Africa's leading feminists from a country with a rich tradition for many aspects of contemporary feminism. Important reading for anyone interested in Ama Ata Aidoo. Upper-division undergraduate and up.—*C. Pike, University of Minnesota*

WS-0422 PR9387 95-37391 CIP
Ogunyemi, Chikwenye Okonjo. **Africa wo/man palava: the Nigerian novel by women.** Chicago, 1996. 353p bibl index afp ISBN 0-226-62084-0, $29.95; ISBN 0-226-62085-9 pbk, $15.95

For all its political and economic problems, Nigeria has been the most prolific literary nation in sub-Saharan Africa. To name only a few of its worthies—Chinua Achebe, Wole Soyinka, Christopher Okigbo, Amos Tutuola, Lenrie Peters, J.P. Clark—is to note that the best-known and most widely read Nigerian writers are men. Ogunyemi intends to redress that imbalance by concentrating on the contributions of eight Nigerian women novelists, including Flora Nwapa, the first African woman to publish an English novel in England. Ogunyemi indicates by her title that African women have much to say and deserve a place in the conversation and growing body of African literature. After two chapters in which she discusses women's new role in the language of the marketplace, mythological sources, the place (or lack of place) in Nigerian creative circles for women, and how best to engender the discourse of African literature, Ogunyemi turns to a detailed discussion of the lives and works of her female tale-tellers. She devotes separate chapters to the first generation (Nwapa, Adaora Ulasi, and Buchi Emecheta) and a last chapter to five younger women (Funmilayo Fakunle, Zaynab Alkali, Eno Obong, Ifeoma Okoye, and Simi Bedford), who deserve to be better known. This book skillfully combines literary criticism, content analysis, and African "womanist" ideology. It should be in any library that seeks geographical and gender breadth and will be very valuable to any undergraduate or graduate school where African literature is in the curriculum.—*P. W. Stine, Gordon College*

WS-0423 PN6519 91-14605 CIP
Schipper, Mineke. **Source of all evil: African proverbs and sayings on women.** I.R. Dee, 1991. 97p bibl ISBN 0-929587-73-1, $15.95

"Woman is the source of all evil; only our souls save us from the harm she does," according to a Fon proverb in Benin, hence the title of Schipper's collection of African proverbs, drawn from South Africa, Ethiopia, Kenya, and other African countries. There can be little doubt that her intent is to demonstrate a negative view of African men toward women. Other examples: "A woman is like the Merino sheep: her beauty is judged by her backside"; "If you really love your wife you have to beat her." As with any collection of proverbs there are some whose metaphorical sense is lost and must be interpreted; hence, "Women have only crooked words", i.e., women keep no secrets and seldom tell the truth. Negative proverbs such as these form a large part of the collection but do not account for its entirety; others celebrate a woman's affection, wisdom, or courage: "The man may be the head of the home; the wife is the heart"; "If you want peace, give ear to your wife's proposal"; "The mother grabs the sharp end of the knife." Schipper organizes her collection by theme. Her introduction is thoughtful and considers the many problems of dealing with proverbs. One of these is that they are best analyzed as they are used in conversation—something she cannot do when she is taking materials from published sources (which she properly cites). This is a good acquisition for any college library.—*D. Westley, Boston University*

WS-0424 PR9369 90-5906 CIP
Schreiner, Olive. **"My other self": the letters of Olive Schreiner and Havelock Ellis, 1884-1920,** ed. by Yaffa Claire Draznin. P. Lang, 1993 (c1992). 583p index afp ISBN 0-8204-1360-7, $79.95

No previously published collections of Olive Schreiner's letters have focused exclusively on her correspondence with Havelock Ellis. Yet, what an amazing slice it is, capturing in many ways the entire multilayered sexual consciousness of the late 19th century. More than half of the 607 notes and letters included here are Schreiner's (367). Nevertheless we see—intensely in the rapidly exchanged early correspondence, more discontinuously later on—two brilliant, vanguard writers, both vigorous feminists, bold political activists, and pioneers in the rearticulation of the psychological and social implications of sexuality, writing themselves into, and nearly out of, sexual existence over the course of 36 years. They explored their own emotions, psychosomatically, relentlessly, vividly, sighting

a new horizon of freedom, but too burdened with history and pain, and in some sense too shackled to science, ever to experience it. Editor Draznin has done a service to specialists and nonspecialists alike because there exist no other collected Ellis letters. This work supplements, rather than supplants, two earlier Schreiner collections, but it also defines a higher standard of editorial rigor, printing from holographs exclusively. Comprehensive introduction (a primer in editing), good notes, extensive index. All levels.—*F. Alaya, Ramapo College of New Jersey*

WS-0425 PQ3988 92-46725 CIP
Woodhull, Winifred. **Transfigurations of the Maghreb: feminism, decolonization, and literatures.** Minnesota, 1993. 233p index afp ISBN 0-8166-2054-7, $44.95; ISBN 0-8166-2055-5 pbk, $16.95

More than a survey of recent Maghrebian literatures written in French, Woodhull's readings here of the issues of feminism and decolonization in those literatures offer a critique of contemporary poststructuralist theories and the politics of postcolonialism and immigration. Disputing the current attempts, in France especially but with analogues in Euro-American thought more generally, to separate poetry from politics, Woodhull argues for the persistence of conflicts, from the era of colonialism and anti-colonial struggle to the present, between feminism and nationalism. Her own analyses proceed historically, beginning with Kateb Yacine's 1954 novel, *Nedjma*, and concluding with French novels of the 1980s and their representations of the former colonies. That history is not a singular one, however, and Woodhull's argument is one that traverses and recrosses the Mediterranean in its examination of immigrant writing in France, including the "beur" culture, and its reconstructions of women as historical agents. The novels of Assia Djebar and Leila Sebbar function importantly in this critical examination. Woodhull proposes a crucial realignment of literary history, feminist debates, poststructuralist theory, and colonial and postcolonial studies, as well as close rereadings of important works of the Maghrebian narrative. Recommended for graduate and undergraduate libraries.—*B. Harlow, University of Texas at Austin*

WS-0426 PJ7525 94-1007 CIP
Zeidan, Joseph T. **Arab women novelists: the formative years and beyond.** State University of New York, 1995. 363p bibl index afp ISBN 0-7914-2171-6, $74.50

This invaluable book presents for the first time, in any language, the variety and energy of Arab women novelists. Zeidan (Ohio State Univ.) builds on his Arabic-language bibliography (1986) of almost 500 Arab women writers who have published during the 20th century. Though touching on the writings of dozens of novelists, the author has summarized and analyzed at length the work of 11 novelists. He divides progress in the development of Arab women's literary interests into three stages: members of the Pioneering Generation, active until the late 1940s, whose "apologetic and hesitant" novels dealt with historical themes or described social problems outside their cultures; the "Quest for Personal Identity" stage (the 1950s and 1960s) encompasses women who wrote about their frustrated searches for self-fulfillment in a harsh society; and, last, novelists in search of national identity. Zeidan highlights the Palestinian question and the Lebanese civil war. The book ends with a chronological listing of Arab women's journals. Despite some misgivings about the totalizing framework, this reviewer applauds the scope of Zeidan's book and his clear commitment. A must for all libraries with Middle Eastern, women's studies, and non-Western literature collections.—*M. Cooke, Duke University*

◆ Asian & Oceanian

WS-0427 PL2895 94-9956 CIP
Bai, Hua. **The remote country of women,** by Bai Hua; tr. by Qingyun Wu and Thomas O. Beebee. Hawaii, 1994. 376p afp ISBN 0-8248-1591-2, $38.00; ISBN 0-8248-1611-0 pbk, $14.95

The Remote Country of Women tells the stories of Sunamei, a girl becoming a woman in the ancient matriarchal ways of the Mosuo people of Sichuan and Yunnan, and of Liang Rui, an intellectual caught in the sweeping conflicts of the nation. In the two intertwined plots, which are largely set in the violent days of suffering and brutality during the Cultural Revolution, the reader not only shares a great range of experiences, some familiar, some strange, but also gains information about Mosuo traditions that will tempt the curious anthropologist in all of us. Though the translation loses the feel of English idiom at times, this historical novel deserves wide readership as a piece of inventive fiction and as a dramatic picture of the many faces of China. It is part of the new series "Fiction from Modern China" published by the University of Hawaii Press under the general editorship of Howard Goldblatt. Recommended for lower-division undergraduate through faculty readership.—*J. G. Holland, Davidson College*

WS-0428 PL2840 90-21300 CIP
Ch'en, Hsüeh-chao. **Surviving the storm: a memoir,** by Chen Xuezhao, ed. by Jeffrey C. Kinkley; tr. by Ti Hua and Caroline Greene. M.E. Sharpe, 1991 (c1990). 147p index afp ISBN 0-87332-601-6, $29.95

The second of a two-volume set and the only volume now available in English, this is the memoir of Chen Xuezhao (1906-), a writer whose life intersects many of China's revolutionary upheavals this century. During the May 4th era (late 1910s to 1920s), young Chen Xuezhao became acquainted with leading intellectuals such as Lu Xun, Mao Dun, and others as a fledgling writer, and for a few years following, she lived in Paris. After returning to China she became attracted to the Chinese communist movement, eventually moving, in the early 1940s, to Yan'an, the communist capital, where she was befriended by many of China's top communist leaders, including Zhou Enlai and his wife Deng Yingchao. Chen joined the party in 1945. This book details her difficulties as a party member and writer after 1949. Her outspokenness and unusual background complicated her relations with local party officials. Chen encountered serious problems in the anti-Rightist campaign of the late 1950s and the Cultural Revolution (1966-76), when she became a victim of personal animosities and shifting tides of politics and ideology. Only in the late 1970s was Chen allowed to write freely. Her two-volume memoir was an outgrowth of the new policy toward writers and intellectuals. *Surviving the Storm* is the second title in M.E. Sharpe's new series of autobiographies and memoirs by women from the Third World. Recommended for libraries with collections of East Asian literature and history.—*C. N. Canning, College of William and Mary*

WS-0429 Orig
Choy, Elsie. **Leaves of prayer: the life and poetry of He Shuangqing, a farmwife in eighteenth-century China: selected translations from Shi Zhenlin's *West green random notes*.** Chinese University Press, 1993. (Dist. by Chinese American Educational and Cultural Center of Michigan, 325 E. Eisenhower Parkway, Ann Arbor, MI 48108) 243p ISBN 962-201-489-5, $32.00

He Shuangqing was a talented young woman who was married at age 18 to an illiterate farmer. She lived in the early 18th century in East China in the region between Shanghai and Nanjing. Her combination of intelligence, beauty, and ability to compose good poetry drew the attention of a local scholar, Shi Zhenlin and his circle of friends, many of whom address poems to He Shuangqing and received poems from her in return. The book consists of a biographical study based upon several enticing, anecdotal glimpses into the unhappy domestic life of He Shuangqing through translations from Shi Zhenlin's random notes, and English translations of He's 48 extant poems. She is not to be considered a major Chinese poet, but she is a good poet, and a tragically good example of a "virtuous wife" who remained true to her brutish husband, even while receiving the expressions of admiration and interest from other men of much greater means. He Shuangqing died at age 22, while the young men who admired her poetry were traveling north to take the imperial civil service examinations. Choy's translations are accurate, readable, and often moving. Chinese texts are included with all translations. Undergraduate; general.—*J. W. Walls, Simon Fraser University*

WS-0430 Orig
Chughtai, Ismat. **The crooked line: Terhi lakir,** tr. by Tahira Naqvi. Heinemann, 1995. 335p ISBN 0-435-95089-4 pbk, $11.95

In this fine novel translated from the Urdu, the author writes of her young heroine, "Girls generally nurse a desire to get married, but of late Shamman had been experiencing a desire to hit people." Why this should happen in an Indian Muslim family of the 1920s is explained by Chughtai with a polish and sensibility reminiscent of Jane Austen and the late Victorians. Written in 1944, the

work revolves around Shamman, an unwanted female child whose rebellious nature grows in proportion to the sexual, cultural, and political oppression she experiences growing up in a traditional middle-class family. Chughtai details the innermost dimensions of feminine consciousness, describing Shamman's evolving sense of self as she comes of age during a period of unprecedented upheaval in India. Sexual identity in particular is incisively redefined in terms of self-awareness, empowerment, even political identity. Set against the Indian nationalist currents of the times, this richly textured and sobering feast of a book, in apparently seamless translation, merits widespread attention.—*T. Carolan, Kingston College*

WS-0431 PL840 91-48130 MARC
Copeland, Rebecca L. **The sound of the wind: the life and works of Uno Chiyo.** Hawaii, 1992. 255p bibl index afp ISBN 0-8248-1409-6, $28.00

Uno Chiyo, born in 1897, has been a teacher, femme fatale, award-winning novelist and autobiographer, kimono designer, and advice columnist. This volume, a biography together with translations of three of her stories, originated in Copeland's Columbia PhD dissertation. The biography, pleasingly and intelligently written, also sheds light on the situation of Japanese women writers generally. Copeland judges Uno a minor writer as compared to the great 20th-century Japanese male authors, but readers who know her ironic *Confessions of Love* (CH, Oct'89) in Phyllis Birnbaum's exquisitely simple translation may well disagree. Copeland's own translations do not fare well: attempts like hers to render dialect in one language into dialect in another draw too much attention to themselves and away from their material, seeing as how (a favorite expression!) they tend to sound and look unnatural even when the translator has a better ear. Goodness! (Another favorite expression.) The two stories subjected to this treatment survive, but just barely. Good illustrations; misleading bibliography, which may leave novices thinking that works of other authors are by Uno. Recommended for women's studies and Asian collections.—*M. Ury, University of California, Davis*

WS-0432 GR305 94-1706 CIP
DasGupta, Sayantani. **The demon slayers and other stories: Bengali folk tales,** collected and written by Sayantani DasGupta and Shamita Das Dasgupta. Interlink Books, 1995. 167p bibl ISBN 1-56656-164-7, $24.95; ISBN 1-56656-156-6 pbk, $12.95

The 20 tales and nine poems in this anthology are collected under five headings: marriage and adventure, family unity, cunning, greed and piety, and the supernatural. Clearly this arrangement is rather arbitrary; another editor might well have seen a connection between marriage and family, piety and the supernatural, and greed and cunning. Yet the tales themselves are interesting, admonitory, and illustrative of generations-old mores and roles—especially women's roles. However, the long and interesting introduction is markedly partial to Hindu interests (and those clearly Brahman) and not relevant to the tales themselves. We are told, for example, that the Raj "brought Bengali society to its nadir," and that "during this time child marriage, hypergamy, sati ... the cult of Thagi (ritualistic highway robbery and murder) and human sacrifice proliferated." Clearly this interpretation of history is at odds with the facts, as is the assertion that Bengali Hindus were responsible for all the social reforms in India and even for "securing Indian freedom in 1947." Even other Indians would question the statement that in Bengal there is noteworthy veneration for the mother—both mortal and divine. General audiences.—*A. L. McLeod, Rider University*

WS-0433 PL4758 92-14647 MARC
Ilaṅkōvaṭikaḷ. **The Cilappatikāram of IlaṅkōvAṭikaḷ an epic of South India,** tr. by R. Parthasarathy. Columbia, 1995 (c1993). 426p bibl index afp ISBN 0-231-07848-X, $17.50

This book is the first poetic translation of the *Cilappatikāram* ("The Narrative of the Anklet," 5th century CE), the earliest long poem in Tamil, a south Indian language with a rich classical literature going back to the 1st century CE. Ilaṅkō Atikal, said to have been a prince who became a Jain monk, tells the epic tale of the heroine Kannaki's avenging of the unjust death of her husband, the merchant Kōvalan, and of her apotheosis as the chaste-wife goddess Pattini. With a woman for its central character, the *Cilappatikāram* is unique among world epics.

Its rich description of the three ancient Tamil kingdoms make it the Tamil national epic. Its literary excellence places it among the world's great long poems, and the Kannaki narrative's focus on women and the sacred invites comparison with Greek tragedy. A poet in English as well as a Tamil scholar, Parthasarathy (Skidmore College) has given us a vibrant, lively, accurate version of the *Cilappatikāram* He has also provided stimulating comparative perspectives from which to approach the text. Undergraduate and graduate students, general audiences; comparative literature, Indian literature and culture.—*I. V. Peterson, Mount Holyoke College*

WS-0434 PL2443 94-22076 CIP
Lu, Tonglin. **Misogyny, cultural nihilism, & oppositional politics: contemporary Chinese experimental fiction,** by Lu Tonglin. Stanford, 1995. 235p bibl index afp ISBN 0-8047-2463-6, $39.50; ISBN 0-8047-2464-4 pbk, $14.95

Lu Tonglin (Univ. of Iowa) surveys and studies the experimental fiction of the late 1980s in contemporary China, using the works of Mo Yan, Can Xue, Zhaxi Dawa, Su Tong, and Yu Hua. This experimental fiction is of particular interest in China because it radically subverts socialist realism. This in-depth study holds that in this literature "misogyny serves as both a basis for and a limit on its subversive function vis-à-vis communism." In trying to break away from the past, be it Confucianist or Communist, these writers exhibit a cultural nihilism that ironically ties them again to the past because of their misogynist discourse. In the same way, this generation's oppositional politics of rejecting the existing social order serves to link it to the patriarchal past, which again only leads to failure. The author concludes that only when Chinese women are treated equally can China be democratic. With its feminist perspective, this study throws new light on the way both experimental fiction and contemporary China can be explained. The book also contains extensive notes and a Chinese character list. Recommended for upper-division undergraduates and above.—*Y. L. Walls, Simon Fraser University*

WS-0435 PL832 92-33630 CIP
Tansman, Alan M. **The writings of Kōda Aya, a Japanese literary daughter.** Yale, 1993. 214p index afp ISBN 0-300-05724-5, $27.50

A fascinating account of a literary woman (1904-90) whose identity and existence were totally subsumed by her father, the Meiji literary giant Koda Rohan (1867-1947), who taught this sensitive daughter how to properly sweep and scrub the floor, cut tofu, apply makeup, manage the house—everything except how to write. Tansman's portrayal of Aya reveals a woman brought up by a stern Confucian gentleman-scholar who meant no harm but who had absolute power over her, went into unprovoked rages, belittled her, took for granted everything she did for him. In an abysmal, obsessive father-daughter relationship (modern psychoanalysts would call this co-dependency), Aya internalized her pain and anger, rationalized her plight, failed in marriage, and engaged herself in the only "rebellion" she instinctively knew how to carry out: writing. Her autobiographical works never strike at the root of her misery, partriarchy, but instead turn her own internalized anger against herself and other women. Popular among conservative Japanese male critics, her literature poses no threat to men. Tansman does not follow through with his claim that Aya's writings have a subversive intent. If this claim is true, it has nothing to do with what she wrote but rather with the act of writing itself. And although Tansman tries to ignore gender as if it were irrelevant, gender was very much on Aya's mind. Four of her short stories appear at the end of this book. Tansman's translations of them and of the many extensive passages from other works incorporated into his discussion are excellent. Highly recommended for women's studies, Japanese literature, and psychology courses.—*M. N. Wilson, University of Virginia*

WS-0436 PL782 91-24354 CIP
Unmapped territories: new women's fiction from Japan, ed. by Yukiko Tanaka. Women in Translation, 1991. 163p ISBN 1-879679-00-0 pbk, $10.95

The choice of seven stories for this collection is brilliant, the translations superb: the confidence, feminist energy, and sense of humor displayed by these Japanese women are in perfect accord with the subjects treated. Why men should never take wives for granted ("The Rain at Rokudo Crossroad" by Kazuko Saegusa); the invisible, magical, omnipresent power of feminine imagination ("Candle Fish" by

Minako Ohba); a female office worker confronts a ladder-climbing male chauvinist ("Sinking Ground" by Mizuko Masuda); the outrageous, and therefore female, odyssey of an amorous heroine ("Straw Dogs" by Taeko Tomioka); a woman trying to find the source of her own feminine mystique ("The Marsh" by Yuko Tsushima). These feminist writers offer no apology for their uninhibited sexuality and assertiveness. Nor do they seek approval for their endeavors from any patriarchy. Their voice is unmuffled, their perspective unfiltered. This collection, Tanaka's third to date, firmly establishes a new female literary tradition: "being ambiguously women" (to paraphrase Deborah Cameron's words), they no longer allow the patriarchal authority to determine their identity. The publication of this book is timely because what these feminist writers are exploring is a perfect metaphor for a Japan now desperately seeking self-assertion among "white" nations. Enthusiastically recommended for college courses in women's studies, Japanese/world/comparative literature, anthropology, and history.—*M. N. Wilson, University of Virginia*

WS-0437 PK2098 94-26786 CIP
Varma, Maha Devi. **Sketches from my past: encounters with India's oppressed, a translation of Mahadevi Varma's** *Ateet Ke Chalchitra* **by Neera Kuckreja Sohoni.** Northeastern University, 1994. 142p afp ISBN 1-55553-198-9, $21.95

Varma, who wrote in Hindi, paints in *Chalchitra* poignant real-life portraits of oppressed women and men in preindependent India. In her stories of oppressed women we see victims of society, but most of her women defy their condition in small, subtle ways and discover some strength in themselves. The author herself appears in her work as the questioning, ironic prober, pointing out the realities and injustices of patriarchal Indian society. True to her feminism, she inquires into alternatives for women within the societally imposed roles of mother and wife. Sohoni's translation of Varma augments the growing collection of feminist literary works made known in the English-speaking world and to feminist criticism. Although the translation on the whole captures the strength of Varma's writing, this reviewer questions the lack of scrupulousness in using the idioms of American English to translate Hindi, which sometimes creates a discordant note when reading Varma Devi in her Indian context. General; graduate; faculty.—*P. Venkateswaran, Nassau Community College*

WS-0438 PN56 95-13353 CIP
Wu, Yenna. **The Chinese virago: a literary theme.** Council on East Asian Studies, Harvard University, 1995. (Dist. by Harvard) 313p (Harvard-Yenching Institute monograph series, 40) bibl index ISBN 0-674-12572-X, $39.00

Wu (Univ. of California, Riverside) carefully examines the literary representations of the Chinese virago—the jealous, shrewish, fierce wife—and her counterpart, the husband who fears her. Although sporadic studies have been done on jealous wives and henpecked husbands, this is the first study devoted solely to the historical and topical study of this theme up to the Qing Dynasty (ended 1911). Wu draws her material from many sources: fiction, drama, history, and anecdote. Few of the works she examines are written by women, because very few traditional Chinese writers were women. Through these works, one sees that a typical Chinese virago—most of the time forced to be one because of her social situation—abuses her husband, his concubine(s), and even his family. In five chapters, the author deals with sociopsychological foundations, archetypes and antecedents, condemnation, caution and reform, and comedy. The introduction is well written, but the book does not offer any conclusions and lacks in-depth critical analysis. Wu's major contribution is the many images of viragos and henpecked husbands she presents. Nearly one-third of the book is devoted to notes, selected bibliography, glossary and index. Academic collections.—*Y. L. Walls, Simon Fraser University*

WS-0439 Orig
Wu, Yenna. **The lioness roars: shrew stories from late Imperial China.** Cornell University, East Asia Program, 1996 (c1995). 156p (Cornell East Asia series, 81) bibl ISBN 1-885445-71-7, $20.00; ISBN 1-885445-81-4 pbk, $12.00

This volume contains translations of eight Chinese tales of various lengths from the 17th and 18th centuries. Wu (Univ. of California, Riverside) is also the author of a comprehensive study of the Chinese shrew theme, *The Chinese Virago: A Literary Theme* (CH, Apr'96). The stories translated here are about fierce wives and their henpecked husbands, and some are tales of the taming of the shrew. Of the eight stories, one is written by Li Yu (1610-80), one by Aina Jushi (c. 17th century), five by Pu Songling (1640-1715), and one by Yuan Mei (1716-97). The translations read well and provide interesting, unusual, and sometimes hilarious stories from the Qing Dynasty. One can read them as stories alone or study them as social texts revealing or parodying some aspects of family life of the time or as political parables of the Qing Dynasty whose Han Chinese writers often felt and resented the "oppressive" rule by the Manchus. The Chinese character list is less than adequate, but the selected bibliography of primary source material in Chinese and secondary source material in Chinese, Japanese, and English is useful for readers who wish to pursue further studies of the shrew theme in Chinese literature. All collections.—*Y. L. Walls, Simon Fraser University*

◆ British

Medieval - 18th Century

WS-0440   PR858   91-43583 CIP
Ballaster, Ros. **Seductive forms: women's amatory fiction from 1684 to 1740.** Oxford, 1992. 232p bibl index ISBN 0-19-811244-0, $49.95

Ballaster examines three women Tory novelists (Aphra Behn, Delarivier Manley, and Elizabeth Haywood) and their novels, to point out that use of the seduction plot enabled them to engage the reader's interest through fiction and to support their political views—to suggest to their readers that the theme of "love" could be a powerful means of personal and political statements. Ballaster provides a careful and precise background, considering 17th-century novels and such studies as J.J. Richetti's *Popular Fiction Before Richardson* (1992), J. Spencer's *The Rise of the Woman Novelist* (CH, May'87), and M. McKeon's *The Origins of the English Novel, 1600-1740* (CH, Sep'87) to explain her own views. She finds Behn's fictions "challenge the amatory forms traditionally associated with the woman writer"; that Manley's fiction "stands on the borders. . .of discrete discursive territories"; that "all undergo a series of inversions and rearticulations"; and that Haywood's romances of the 1720s "locate a form of feminine resistance. . .her narrative strategies subverting the rigid gender oppositions" of her plots. Ballaster argues cogently for the view that Behn, Manley, and Haywood were professional women who challenged "masculine" power both in fiction and in party politics. In a style that is never dull, never full of jargon, Ballaster engages the reader in an exciting examination of early women's fiction. An important book. Advanced undergraduates, graduate students, faculty, and general readers.—*A. Jenkins, Georgia Institute of Technology*

WS-0441   PR4057   92-39712 CIP
Barbauld, Anna Letitia. **The poems of Anna Letitia Barbauld,** ed. by William McCarthy and Elizabeth Kraft. Georgia, 1994. 399p bibl indexes afp ISBN 0-8203-1528-1, $65.00

Editors McCarthy (*Hester Thrale Piozzi*, 1985) and Kraft (*Character & Consciousness in Eighteenth-Century Comic Fiction*, CH, Jun'92) have produced a thorough edition of all the known verse of a poet who was widely admired by her contemporaries and whose skills were occasionally envied by the likes of Wordsworth. The gracefully written introduction provides a brief critical survey of Barbauld's work, emphasizing its heterogeneous content (e.g., religion, political and historical events, domestic matters, progress, and innovation) and varied tone (ranging from reverent to serious to whimsical and satiric.) There is also a history of the poems (Barbauld's disappearance from literature for 150 years is blamed largely and rather facilely on the animus of the major romantics, especially Coleridge) and a detailed discussion of the editors' textual and other editorial procedures. The edition prints 161 authentic and ten conjectural poems, arranged by date of composition (though this sometimes must mean by date of first printing), plus descriptions/discussions of lost poems and doubtful and spurious attributions. The notes to the poems, comprising a quarter of the volume, are detailed and informative with-

out being pedantic, and include variant readings. The edition concludes with a bibliography and two indexes. An admirable example of meticulous scholarship and good editorial sense. Recommended for all college and university libraries.— *C. B. Dodson, University of North Carolina at Wilmington*

WS-0442   PR275   94-39910 CIP
Bartlett, Anne Clark. **Male authors, female readers: representation and subjectivity in Middle English devotional literature.** Cornell, 1995. 212p bibl index afp ISBN 0-8014-3038-0, $32.50

In the Middle Ages male authors wrote devotional literature for nuns and for lay women that was often misogynic. In fact, these writers made patriarchal values the norm. Evidence of resistance on the part of women is scarce, which seems to suggest passivity and mute acceptance. Bartlett (DePaul Univ.) shows otherwise by looking at the context of this literature. A medieval codex with devotional literature might contain misogynic material; nevertheless, other types of writing with different perspectives were usually included, as Bartlett's appendix—a list of books owned by Medieval English nuns and convents—shows. Also, because meaning is accepted in the reader's, not the writer's context, a particular social context can challenge and undermine antifeminism with different values. For example, the image of the nun as the spouse of Christ, who is pursued like a heroine in a medieval romance by a knightly suitor, recognizes and strengthens feminine identity. The methodology of this study is convincing since the material is studied in its context without one narrow perspective. As a result, enlightened, cultural discourses that respect feminine identity and subjectivity are uncovered. Any study of devotional literature for women in the Middle Ages can profit from this approach. Upper-division undergraduate and up.—*J. F. O'Malley, Slippery Rock University of Pennsylvania*

WS-0443   PR3317   95-5205 Orig
Behn, Aphra. **The rover; The feigned courtesans; The lucky chance; The emperor of the moon,** ed. by Jane Spencer et al. Oxford, 1996 (c1995). 400p afp ISBN 0-19-812154-7, $74.00

This collection of four comedies by Aphra Behn is a welcome addition to the growing number of available works by 17th-century women authors. *The Rover*, Behn's best-known play, was first attributed to a male author. *The Feigned Courtesans* is a surprisingly pro-Catholic play; *The Lucky Chance* explores courtship and marriage from a woman's perspective; and *The Emperor of the Moon* is a farce filled with spectacle and unusual stagecraft. Spencer provides annotations; a glossary; select bibliography; an introduction to Behn's life, her place in Restoration drama, and performance aspects of her plays; and comments on the four comedies in this edition. Recommended for upper-division undergraduates and above.—*J. P. Baumgaertner, Wheaton College (IL)*

WS-0444   PR858   93-33407 CIP
Benedict, Barbara M. **Framing feeling: sentiment and style in English prose fiction, 1745-1800.** AMS Press, 1995 (c1994). 261p (AMS studies in the eighteenth century, 26) bibl index ISBN 0-404-63526-1, $45.00

Abandoning the language of an older critical approach to the study of novels, which examines the author's "point of view" or "angle of narration," Benedict (Trinity College) here applies an analytic method to the spate of sentimental English literary fictions that dominated the last half of the 18th century—works ranging from Oliver Goldsmith's *The Vicar of Wakefield* and Lawrence Sterne's *Tristram Shandy* to Jane Austen's *Sense and Sensibility*. She stresses the way authors frame their stories and characters' feelings to reveal their significance and, very often, the feminist implications of the sensibility, sensitivity, and sentiment that characterize their subject matter. Benedict's new approach and thorough examination of this group of less frequently studied fictions is a significant contribution to advanced study of the English novel, British publishing history, and social relationships between the Age of Reason and the Romantic period. Upper-division undergraduates and above.—*A. E. Jones Jr., emeritus, Drew University*

WS-0445   PR858   90-47980 CIP
Brophy, Elizabeth Bergen. **Women's lives and the 18th-century English novel.** South Florida, 1991. (Dist. by University Presses of Florida) 291p bibl index afp ISBN 0-8130-1036-5, $29.95

A successful attempt to focus on how 18th-century novels present a rather accurate picture of ordinary women in their struggle to fulfill certain expectations demanded of them by society. This study clearly reinforces the major thesis that these novels, particularly the ones dealt with here, helped to improve considerably the self-image of 18th-century women themselves. Brophy (College of New Rochelle) proves her major thesis in various ways. She extensively quotes from letters, diaries, and journals as well as conduct books of the period; and she clearly connects these extracts to her lucid discussion of works that appeared between 1744 and 1799 by seven novelists (Samuel Richardson and Henry Fielding, plus Sarah Fielding, Charlotte Lennox, Sarah Scott, Clara Reeve, and Fanny Burney). Her discussions are guided primarily by the stages of a woman's experience—daughter (mainly the matter of courtship), wife, widow, or spinster. Illustrations, notes, and an adequate index. Highly recommended to anyone interested in women's studies, cultural and social history, and the 18th-century novel at undergraduate or graduate levels.—*R. G. Brown, Ball State University*

WS-0446 PR3316.A4 Can. CIP
Burney, Fanny. **The Early journals and letters of Fanny Burney: v.2: 1774-1777,** ed. by Lars E. Troide. McGill-Queen's, 1991 (c1990). (Dist. by Toronto) 311p index ISBN 0-7735-0539-3, $65.00

This second installment in the sumptuously produced edition of Frances Burney's early journals and letters will be welcomed by readers of the first (CH, Feb'89); the same high standards of editing and production are evident. And the plot of the journals themselves thickens as Burney matures into the novelist who wrote *Evelina*. Reading these entries, one gets an increased sense of Burney's socially observant eye, her phenomenal memory for gesture and conversation, and her small stature and susceptibility to illness. Among the great events of everyday life in Queen Street are the appearance of Omai, a Tahitian more polite than certain spoiled English gentlemen; James Bruce, the explorer just returned from Abyssinia; and the singer Lucrezia Agujari, who "neither Eats, Drinks, sleeps or Talks, without considering in what manner she may perform those vulgar duties of Life so as to be most beneficial to her Voice." Such public obsession with the perfecting of one's art was a luxury that Burney herself could scarcely credit at this period. An instructive and pleasurable read.—*D. Landry, Wayne State University*

WS-0447 PR3458 94-33011 CIP
Campbell, Jill. **Natural masques: gender and identity in Fielding's plays and novels.** Stanford, 1995. 324p bibl index afp ISBN 0-8047-2391-5, $45.00; ISBN 0-8047-2520-9 pbk, $16.95

This excellent study of Fielding's works takes as its central metaphor the masque (or mask), which, Campbell (Yale) convincingly argues, Fielding used throughout his career to explore the often complicated relationships among biological sex, gender, sexuality, and identity. The author is impressive both in her scope (she surveys all the major works—especially the plays, *Joseph Andrews*, *Tom Jones*, and *Amelia*—and traces Fielding's changing opinions over time) and in her incisiveness, for she reads closely and has something important to say in nearly every sentence. She deftly relates Fielding's concerns about gender and identity to such larger questions as the development of the early novel, Milton's Eve, 18th-century theories of motherhood, the role of gender and sexuality in contemporary politics, and the relationship between gender and genre (novel, epic, satire, etc.). Deeply learned but never obscure, thoroughly up-to-date but never merely trendy, this is a major work: essential reading not only for Fielding scholars but also for upper-division undergraduate and graduate students.—*J. T. Lynch, University of Pennsylvania*

WS-0448 PR2499 92-36294 MARC
Cary, Elizabeth. **The tragedy of Mariam, the fair queen of Jewry, by Elizabeth Cary, Lady Falkland; with** *The Lady Falkland: Her Life,* **by one of her daughters**; ed. by Barry Weller and Margaret W. Ferguson. California, 1994. 328p bibl afp ISBN 0-520-07967-1, $45.00; ISBN 0-520-07969-8 pbk, $16.00

Elizabeth Cary (Lady Henry Falkland), c. 1585-1639, wrote the first original play by a woman published in England, *The Tragedy of Mariam, The Fair Queen of Jewry* (1613). She was also the first English woman writer to be the subject of a biography, *The Lady Falkland: Her Life* (written 1643-49, first published in 1861). Weller and Ferguson have edited these two works (in one volume)

with such exquisite care and enthusiastic appreciation that they should become definitive editions. *The Life* seems more interesting than *The Tragedy of Mariam*, a bewildering closet drama about Herod the Great's second wife, based on the *Antiquities* of Josephus and written in turgid rhyme. Though it may illuminate concerns of 17th-century women, Lady Falkland's own life is far more dramatic. Fascinating anecdotes about her reveal a lovable, exasperating, strong, pious, and learned woman. ("She had read very exceeding much.") With an excellent introduction, full textual and content notes, and several bibliographies usefully arranged by subject, this work is a fine example of the many recent publications which recover the lives of relatively unknown women and their literary contributions. All levels.—*J. M. Green, Kent State University*

WS-0449 PR437 94-19823 CIP
Chernaik, Warren. **Sexual freedom in restoration literature.** Cambridge, 1995. 268p index ISBN 0-521-46497-8, $54.95

In theory, libertinism—"a dream of human freedom" and the self-gratifying pursuit of (mainly sexual) pleasure—has obvious antifeminist implications. In practice, however, it is self-contradictory: its pleasures lead to pain and its freedom turns into enslavement; moreover, as this serious study illustrates, male libertinism entails female libertinism. Chernaik (Univ. of London) investigates these paradoxes in Restoration literature, primarily in the writings of Rochester and Aphra Behn, though also in the works of other dramatists of the period and less renowned women writers (e.g., Sarah Fyge). The pairing of Rochester and Behn is not an antifeminist backlash; if libertine freedom was "deeply problematical" for both, Chernaik shows that the woman was better able to handle it—to embrace it "wholeheartedly as a fact of nature"—than the man was. Though the book is relevant to modern debates on sexual politics, Chernaik's thesis is primarily literary: libertine freedom was a "necessary illusion" for both Rochester and Behn, "nurturing the imagination by its very unattainability." A valuable supplement to Dale Underwood's *Etherege and the Seventeenth-Century Comedy of Manners* (1957). Upper-division undergraduates and up.—*G. R. Wasserman, Russell Sage College*

WS-0450 PR5841 93-33718 CIP
Conger, Syndy McMillen. **Mary Wollstonecraft and the language of sensibility.** Fairleigh Dickinson, 1994. (Dist. by Associated University Presses) 214p bibl index afp ISBN 0-8386-3553-9, $39.50

Seeking a better way to explain some of the problems and paradoxes of Wollstonecraft's life and works, Conger suggests that her study will consider "the language of sensibility and its fictions;" she points out the fictions as well as the theory of sensibility. In the Preface there are such topics as "The Power of Metaphors," "Women and Language," and "Women Language, and Madness." Conger analyzes Wollstonecraft's private correspondence; *Mary, A Fiction: A Vindication of the Rights of Men; A Vindication of the Rights of Woman*; "Cave of Fancy"; *French Revolution*; and *Letters in Sweden*, concluding with the unfinished *Maria*. Conger finds many parallels between Wollstonecraft and the "darker Werther-like fictions of sensibility." Wollstonecraft and Werther "embrace ... the notion of sensibility .... they do not simply entertain its ideas; they live them ..." Conger reveals a wide knowledge of Wollstonecraft and of sensibility in her text, the footnotes, and the bibliography. She demonstrates her thesis in pertinent details, citing appropriate passages from the works. She writes clearly and explains the work in the context of her subject. Conger's book is a very important addition to the study of Wollstonecraft and "the language of sensibility." General; undergraduate and up.—*A. Jenkins, Georgia Institute of Technology*

WS-0451 PR1286 94-33366 MARC
Counterfeit ladies: *The life and death of Mal Cutpurse—The case of Mary Carleton,* ed. with introd. by Janet Todd and Elizabeth Spearing. New York University, 1995 (c1994). 165p ISBN 0-8147-8214-0, $50.00

Counterfeit Ladies presents two 17th-century autobiographical pamphlets (*Mal Cutpurse*, 1662, and *Mary Carleton*, 1663) that chronicle the lives of two notorious female rogues, Mary Frith (Moll Cutpurse) and Mary Carleton, known to the Restoration as "The German Princess." Frith's pamphlet narrates her lengthy career in fencing stolen goods and procuring. Despite her sobriquet, she kept a discreet distance from actual theft and seldom ran afoul of the law. The less fortunate Carleton reveals details of her past but centers the narrative on her recent trial and acquittal on a charge of bigamy. The works make lively reading, each offering information about the 17th-century underworld. Together, they also serve to document the plight of women who chose not to marry. As literature, they are precursors to the novel as well as early examples of criminal autobiography. In a lengthy introduction, the editors explore questions related to authorship, genre, and social relevance. Numerous explanatory notes serve to clarify ambiguities and obscure passages in the two pamphlets. Graduate and research collections.—*S. Archer, Texas A&M University*

WS-0452   PR858   92-30851 CIP
Craft-Fairchild, Catherine. **Masquerade and gender: disguise and female identity in eighteenth-century fictions by women.** Pennsylvania State, 1993. 190p bibl index afp ISBN 0-271-00918-7, $30.00; ISBN 0-271-00919-5 pbk, $14.95

Craft-Fairchild sets out "to analyze the relationship of masquerade to the construction of femininity in eighteenth-century fiction by women" (introduction); her analysis of the novels discussed is clear and to the point. In five novels from the late Restoration and early 18th century—Aphra Behn's *The Dumb Virgin*, Mary Davys's *The Accomplished Rake*, and Eliza Haywood's *The Masqueraders*, *Fantomina*, and *The City Jilt*—she finds "the female protagonists ... effect role reversals ... that leave the fundamental terms of representation intact." In two novels of a later period—Elizabeth Inchbald's *A Simple Story* and Frances Burney's *The Wanderer*—she finds "the dissolving of gender difference between lovers is coupled with an increased emphasis on the savagery of rivals and, more important, on the patriarchal tyranny of fathers." *A Simple Story* is "subversive" in that "it probes the psychological underpinnings of patriarchal authority"; in *The Wanderer* both female characters "fail to escape the masquerade of femininity." Illustrations supporting Craft-Fairchild's thesis are carefully chosen; her arguments are persuasive. She cites a wide range of scholars who have written about masquerade—e.g., Terry Castle (*Masquerade and Civilization*, CH, Feb'87), Jane Spencer (*The Rise of the Woman Novelist*, CH, May'87), Mary Anne Scholfield (*Masking and Unmasking the Female Mind*, CH, Dec'90). An important contribution. Advanced undergraduate; graduate; faculty.—*A. Jenkins, Georgia Institute of Technology*

WS-0453   PR3316   91-22254 CIP
Cutting-Gray, Joanne. **Woman as "nobody" and the novels of Fanny Burney.** University Press of Florida, 1992. 169p bibl index afp ISBN 0-8130-1106-X, $24.95

Cutting-Gray provides a self-professedly postmodern reading of Burney's novels and her earliest diary (1768-78), in which she addresses herself to "Nobody." From this rhetorical gambit, the author fashions a whole argument about the problematical relation between women and the discourses of reason and rank in civil society. Themes derived mainly form Lacan, Derrida, and Luce Irigaray animate this book: purloined letters, the symbolics of patronyms and patriarchy, women's relative namelessness, their status as counters to be exchanged between men, and the construction of a gendered cultural system in which man embodies reason and woman becomes a name for the irrational and unknowable. Burney was certainly preoccupied by questions of name, rank, and signification, and her narratives often seem to be interrupted or disturbed by the unwritable at crucial moments that decide her heroines' fates. Yet this book's particular take on poststructuralist theory and Burney's oeuvre may strike readers as rather thin. When Cutting-Gray interprets Willoughby's purloining of Evelina's letter to Orville, we are more likely to remember her invocation of Lacan's "Seminar on 'The Purloined Letter,'" with her reminder that "*Pur-loigner* in the French means to put aside or put amiss, to suffer, a letter in sufferance trapped in a discourse it does not initiate, a letter effectively silenced," than anything substantial about Burney or 18th-century discourse.—*D. Landry, Wayne State University*

WS-0454   PR111   92-9227 CIP
Ezell, Margaret J.M. **Writing women's literary history.** Johns Hopkins, 1993. 205p bibl index afp ISBN 0-8018-4432-0, $32.95

Ezell (Texas A&M) investigates why feminist literary history has lost so many pre-1700 women writers. Using a feminist historicist approach, she examines critical studies published between 1660 and 1990 to uncover the critical assumptions behind the presentation of women's writing, especially the methods by which women's writings were categorized and organized in literary histories. Working from the 20th century back to the 17th, Ezell shows how Virginia Woolf's construction of Judith Shakespeare (in *A Room of One's Own*) was contigent on 18th- and 19th-century biographical and encyclopedic works that silenced or negated some women writers by memorializing (canonizing) others. Ezell shows how Woolf's incomplete version of women's literary history is manifest in recent works, particularly anthologies, on women writers. Writings by Quaker women, which in their diversity and style defied categorization, and works by the coterie writers of the 17th and 18th centuries, serve as examples of the types of writings that have been lost. This vital and theoretically sound study is certainly among the most important of recent contributions to women's literary history. Highly recommended. Advanced undergraduate; graduate; faculty.—*S. Pathak, Johns Hopkins University*

WS-0455   PR4148   92-56604 CIP
Freed, Eugenie R. **"A portion of his life": William Blake's Miltonic vision of woman.** Bucknell, 1995 (c1994). (Dist. by Associated University Presses) 159p bibl index afp ISBN 0-8387-5265-9, $60.00

This is a beautiful, large-format book with many illustrations, some full page, some in color. Freed's scholarship is far ranging, but the many notes remind the reader that this ground has been gone over before: there has been much recent feminist interest in Blake's representations of women, and the Blake/Milton connection has been discussed from the first. The emphasis here is on the concept of "femaleness" in Blake, and on its relation to Blake's modifications of such archetypal female figures in Milton as Eve and Sin in *Paradise Lost* and the chaste Lady of *Comus*. Freed's argument is well knit and amply illustrated, but the writing style is dense—lucid enough for those who already know Blake and Milton and take it slowly, but unsuitable for beginning Blakeans. Perhaps the most original discussion concerns Ololon, of Blake's *Milton*, with its intriguing argument as to the derivation of the name from *lo*, the Hebrew word of negation in the Decalogue. The study's conclusion hopes to mitigate feminist accusations of misogyny, arguing that Blake ultimately transcends the images and biases of his patriarchal sources. For graduate students and faculty.—*J. D. McGowan, Illinois Wesleyan University*

WS-0456   PR113   94-9208 CIP
Gallagher, Catherine. **Nobody's story: the vanishing acts of women writers in the marketplace, 1670-1820.** California, 1994. 339p (The new historicism, 31) index afp ISBN 0-520-08510-8, $38.00

One would hope that this confusing title, which aims to set the stage for Gallagher's new historicist arguments about the "disembodiment" of female authorship in the Restoration and 18th century, will not lead prospective readers to think that she is dealing with minor or insignificant writers. Gallagher's nobodies are none other than Aphra Behn, Mary Delarivier Manley, Charlotte Lennox, Frances Burney, and Maria Edgeworth; each in her way created herself as an abstraction of an authorial persona thereby lending new cultural power to plays, fictions, and other writings of the period. In the peculiar literary marketplace that sustained the image of the playwright as prostitute, Gallagher situates Behn as the most ingenious Restoration playwright for her stagy and explicit sexuality. Tensions between fiction, femininity, and politics are analyzed in the satires and in the slanderous (but immensely popular) tales of Manley, Lennox, and Burney, which are more wholesome; they wrote as "genuine proper purveyors of original tales." Edgeworth's writings are grounded in clear and distinct general principles and a peculiar blend of late 18th century patriarchalism and productivism. In sum, Gallagher analyzes each writer's career in the context of the literary marketplace that sustained it and in the powerful revisionist terms of property, gender, and possession. Graduate; faculty.—*S. Pathak, Johns Hopkins University*

WS-0457   PR698   94-7584 CIP
Gill, Pat. **Interpreting ladies: women, wit, and morality in the Restoration comedy of manners.** Georgia, 1995 (c1994). 209p index afp ISBN 0-8203-1664-4, $35.00

Moral issues are perhaps too often discussed in studies on the Restoration comedy of manners. Yet despite a surfeit of such criticism, links between morality, rhetoric, and gender have been superficially treated, as if the plays themselves could not yield anything deeper or more insightful. Gill (Western Michigan Univ.) posits that female protagonists and female spectators have been misread because the playwrights were uneasy about female knowledge in matters of sexual duplicity, hypocrisy, and sexual desire. The author analyzes the comedies of Etherege, Wycherley, and Congreve, showing that they were so imbued with aristocratic, conservative "English masculinity" that satiric practices obscure the plays' moral indeterminacy and slippage. Discussing major comedies by each playwright, Gill uses Freud's theory of obscene wit to analyze the reassuring testimonies of male privilege harbored in Etherege's *She Would If She Could* (1668) and *The Man of Mode* (1676), Wycherley's *The Country Wife* (1675) and *The Plain-Dealer* (1677), and Congreve's *The Way of the World* (1700). A final chapter offers the counterexample of Aphra Behn, whose female protagonists are less naive and moral but more knowledgeable and discursively honest than those of her male contemporaries. Recommended for all serious drama collections.—*S. Pathak, Johns Hopkins University*

WS-0458   PR428   95-36592 CIP
Hall, Kim F. **Things of darkness: economies of race and gender in early modern England.** Cornell, 1995. 319p bibl index afp ISBN 0-8014-3117-4, $45.00

Not until very recently has research into race and racial consciousness in early-modern English literature been recognized as a subject. In the late 1980s and the 1990s scattered studies began appearing, but Hall's eagerly awaited volume is the first book-length study of the subject. Hall examines race in a wide range of materials and issues: travel literature; sonnets as a subtext for English colonialism; drama and its cultural anxieties over England's imperial expansion; the writings of women, principally Lady Mary Wroth and Elizabeth Carey; and the visual arts, especially portraiture and cameos. The author does not claim that the book is comprehensive, but this genuinely and remarkably trailblazing work covers more territory than any study before it. The book has its problems; it is too quick to generalize and like other new historicist studies too confidently locates the general in a few particulars. But the limits of the book pale beside its signal accomplishment, which is to undo the erasure of race from early-modern literary study. A major study recommended for all academic collections at the upper-division undergraduate level and above.—*P. Cullen, CUNY Graduate Center and College of Staten Island*

WS-0459   PR1928   92-30016 CIP
Hallissy, Margaret. **Clean maids, true wives, steadfast widows: Chaucer's women and medieval codes of conduct.** Greenwood, 1993. 224p (Contributions in women's studies, 130) bibl index afp ISBN 0-313-27467-3, $47.95

Focusing on ideologies surrounding women's speech, movement, and dress, Hallissy surveys the ways medieval law and custom ordained and defined the estates of secular women (virgins, wives, and widows) and attempts to show how Chaucer's secular heroines directly or indirectly subvert prevailing authority. As one might expect, she gives most attention (and a separate chapter) to the Wife of Bath, though Grisilde, Criseyde, May, Dorigen, Custance, and others receive considerable attention. (Oddly, Hallissy does not mention Alison of the "Miller's Tale," who should provide strong support for her thesis.) There is little that is new here. Though the subject is thoroughly researched (the text of fewer than 200 pages has nearly 700 footnotes, mostly in secondary sources), the results are not so much original understandings of Chaucer's attitudes toward women as they are a compendium of contemporary scholarly thought. The more provocative ideas reside in Hallissy's sources. Thus, the book is more suitable for nonspecialists than for advanced students or scholars of medieval literature. Undergraduate; general.—*M. A. Dalbey, Eastern Michigan University*

WS-0460   PR658   92-39168 CIP
Hansen, Carol. **Woman as individual in English Renaissance drama: a defiance of the masculine code.** P. Lang, 1993. 217p (American university studies. Series IV, English language and literature, 156) bibl index afp ISBN 0-8204-2009-3 pbk, $27.95

This intriguing study begins with the idea that the negative biblical view of Eve results in an "image of woman as weak and guilty" that is "the central one in the English Renaissance." A woman facing the authority of father or hus-band must accept, circumvent, or actively defy it. But, Hansen argues, such dramatists as Shakespeare, Middleton, and Webster "time and again appear to question this tradition, and ultimately to reverse it." Her purpose in the book is "to trace the growing emergence of strong women characters in selected plays" from the period. The author shows the questioning of paternal authority in such characters as Egeus, Capulet, and Lear. The authority of the husband is explored in *Othello*, *Much Ado*, and *Hamlet*, where Shakespeare's sympathies are seen as complex rather than conventional. Several plays, including Webster's *The Duchess of Malfi*, are used "to show how a kind of verbal violence appears as a corollary to the masculine code" of authority. The defiant woman appears, for example, as Paulina in *The Winter's Tale*, as Webster's Duchess, and as Beatrice-Joanna in Middleton's *The Changeling*. The ultimate illustration is Cleopatra, who attains authority equal to men. Useful bibliography. Advanced undergraduate; graduate; faculty; general.—*R. E. Burkhart, Eastern Kentucky University*

WS-0461   PR1928   91-13025 CIP
Hansen, Elaine Tuttle. **Chaucer and the fictions of gender.** California, 1992. 301p index afp ISBN 0-520-07133-6, $42.50

Certain to spark controversy while setting the stage for future revisionist studies, Hansen (Haverford College), author of *The Solomon Complex: Reading Wisdom in Old English Poetry* (1988), here presents a feminist reading of several Chaucerian texts while debunking the traditional "myths"—Chaucer as father of English poetry and "friend to woman." Rejecting the notions of a "universally human" Chaucer and a "literary father figure," Hansen argues that in Chaucer's writings "women characters and the feminine are deployed as the battleground over which authority, selfhood, and unity can be established." Finding Chaucer's texts to reflect problems of gender identity the poet himself experienced, Hansen observes that two kinds of men were feminized by 14th-century courtly conventions—the lovers and the poets. Particular texts she examines include "The Wife of Bath," *Book of the Duchess*, *House of Fame*, *Parliament of Fowls*, *Troilus and Criseyda*, "The Clerk's Tale," "The Merchant's Tale," and "The Franklin's Tale." Although some may fear feminist criticism of Chaucer as destructive, Hansen concludes that it protects against "slipping from a critique of objectivity into apolitical relativism" and "may also offer a way in which to make masterworks more available and interesting" to those for whom "they were not written."—*D. D. Evans, Bemidji State University*

WS-0462   PR418   93-28752 CIP
Hutson, Lorna. **The usurer's daughter: male friendship and fictions of women in sixteenth-century England.** Routledge, 1994. 295p bibl index ISBN 0-415-05049-9, $69.95

This original study explores the relationship between 16th-century English culture and its literary representations of women. Hutson (Univ. of London) focuses on economic dependency and affective bonds; her main argument is that women are portrayed in 16th-century literature as signs of credit that serve to forge alliances and friendship between men. Such portrayals not only restricted these women, but also legitimated authorship as a distinctly masculine activity. Her introduction situates the analyses in relation to historical transition and literary production. Six chapters—under the headings "Mental Husbandry," "Anxieties of Textual Access," and "The Theatre of Clandestine Marriage"—develop such topics as the moral parameters of economic behaviors, friendship as capital investment, legal rhetoric and credit relations, and the legal discourses of Renaissance humanism. In connection with these topics Hutson considers a range of continental and English texts, including Erasmus's correspondence, the prose fictions of William Painter and George Pettie, the "Elizabethan prodigal" dramas of George Gascoigne and Isabella Whitney, and Shakespearean comedy. Upper-division and graduate students, as well as teachers, of early modern literature, 16th-century culture, and gender studies will find much of interest in this challenging and accomplished book.—*C. S. Cox, University of Pittsburgh—Johnstown*

WS-0463   PR555.W6   89-25216 CIP
Landry, Donna. **The muses of resistance: laboring-class women's poetry in Britain, 1739-1796.** Cambridge, 1991 (c1990). 325p index ISBN 0-521-37412-X, $39.50

Although it is safe to assume that relatively few students of 18th-century English poetry have heard of Mary Collier, Mary Leapor, or Ann Yearsley, Landry

(Wayne State University) argues that the obscurity of these poets does not reflect a lack of aesthetic merit. Instead, their neglect stems from the class and gender bias of the dominant literary culture, for these writers were doubly disadvantaged as women and members of the working class. Landry's work exemplifies the new brand of politically engaged scholarship in which the critic's ideology is very much to the fore. In addition, she exhibits an unfortunate stylistic debt to feminist theory, Marxist historical writing, and the fashionable theories of Derrida, Foucault, Lacan, etc. At times the worthy attempt to gain new scholarly attention for unjustly neglected authors bogs down in a morass of impenetrable critical jargon; Landry misses few buzzwords. To her credit, she expresses an awareness of the danger of naively imposing late 20th century attitudes onto earlier writers, but nonetheless she too often falls into that very trap—crediting her subjects with nuances of political thought scarcely available to those not conversant with radical feminist theory, Marx, Derrida, Foucault, Lacan, et al. Of value primarily for comprehensive graduate level collections in women's studies and literary history.—*K. P. Mulcahy, Rutgers, The State University of New Jersey, New Brunswick*

WS-0464　　　　PR658　　　　93-27476 CIP
Levine, Laura. **Men in women's clothing: anti-theatricality and effeminization, 1579-1642.** Cambridge, 1995 (c1994). 185p (Cambridge studies in Renaissance literature and culture, 5) bibl index ISBN 0-521-45507-3, $59.95; ISBN 0-521-46627-X pbk, $16.95

The subject of this book is not cross-dressing as a theatrical practice but rather the ways in which antitheatrical tracts and plays of the Elizabethan/Jacobean period reflect cultural anxieties about masculinity and the notion of a stable self. Levine (Wellesley College) sheds new light on subjects previously explored by Jonas Barish (*The Antitheatrical Prejudice*, CH, Oct'81) and Stephen Greenblatt (*Renaissance Self-Fashioning*, CH, May'81). Her brilliantly argued introductory chapter examines the work of antitheatrical writers, whose attacks on cross-dressing indicate a pervasive fear that femininity is a "default position" and that masculinity must be performed in order to exist. Subsequent chapters analyze Shakespeare's *Troilus and Cressida* and *Antony and Cleopatra* and Jonsons's *Epicoene* and *Bartholomew Fair*, showing how the two playwrights acknowledged the anxieties of the antitheatricalists and defended theatrical practice. The last two chapters examine the theatricality of two nondramatic works: James I's *Daemonologie* and the anonymous *Newes from Scotland*, a tract on witchcraft. The reader will appreciate Levine's clear, jargon-free writing style and the endnotes, which provide a valuable survey of recent scholarship. A must for all library collections in English Renaissance literature. Upper-division undergraduate and up.—*J. W. Lafler, Institute for Historical Study*

WS-0465　　　　PR113　　　　92-9506 CIP
Lewalski, Barbara Kiefer. **Writing women in Jacobean England.** Harvard, 1993. 431p index afp ISBN 0-674-96242-7, $45.00

Lewalski (Harvard) tells the story of the "breakthrough to female authorship" in the early 17th century. Her command of primary (including archival) and secondary material enables Lewalski to explain with admirable clarity how "in their lives and works these Jacobean women collectively challenged patriarchal ideology, resisting the construct of women as chaste, silent, obedient, and subordinate; and they rewrote the major discourses of their era in strikingly oppositional terms." Lewalski's careful accounts of the gender polemicist Rachel Speght, the poet and historian Elizabeth Cary, the poet Aemilia Lanyer, and the author of romance fiction Mary Wroth provide handy summaries and judicious readings of works still insufficiently known. This study will be most welcome to teachers who wish to bring female authors into their courses in 17th-century literature. Illustrated with portraits of the authors (some really patrons rather than pen wielders); very richly annotated. A must for academic collections.—*E. D. Hill, Mount Holyoke College*

WS-0466　　　　PR2007　　　　91-26069 CIP
Lochrie, Karma. **Margery Kempe and translations of the flesh.** Pennsylvania, 1992 (c1991). 253p bibl index afp ISBN 0-8122-3107-4, $24.95

Lochrie presents both a reevaluation of Margery Kempe's work in the light of current feminist literary theory and a call for a reassessment of the ways in which scholars have constructed the medieval mystical tradition. Reading Kempe's mys-

tical utterances in the context of medieval gender ideology, particularly the association of woman with the flesh (in Augustinian theology that disruptive principle which pulls against the spirit), Lochrie argues that her mystical practices, including her "excessive" laughter and weeping, both challenge masculine ideology about the separation of body and spirit and establish an authorizing locus for feminine access to the divine. Lochrie further argues that Kempe's marginalization by modern scholars results in part from the relatively recent discovery of the full manuscript of her book and in part from our own cultural associations of masculinity with spirituality and authority and of femininity with physicality and mundane experience. With its extensive notes and excellent bibliography of both primary and secondary materials, Lochrie's work is a valuable contribution both to feminist theory and to medieval studies.—*M. A. Dalbey, Eastern Michigan University*

WS-0467　　　　DA501　　　　92-41757 CIP
Lowenthal, Cynthia. **Lady Mary Wortley Montagu and the eighteenth-century familiar letter.** Georgia, 1994. 261p index afp ISBN 0-8203-1545-1, $40.00

Feminist formalism finds new life in this study, which is almost entirely preoccupied with Lady Montagu's correspondence as a textual phenomenon. Aside from a few paragraphs on the vagaries of the late 17th and early 18th century postal service in Britain, Lowenthal shows little interest in material culture or current debates within early-modern social history, prefering to theorize about letters. Her Lady Mary is primarily compelling as a figure of aristocratic womanhood, whose gender and class status are often at odds with her literary ambitions, and whose notions of social life owe more to the codes of theatrical representation as performance than to those of novelistic representation of inner being. As a meditation on 18th-century epistolary discourse, this book offers some useful insights. As a study of Montagu, it relies heavily on Halsband's and I. Grundy's biographical and bibliographical research. No new evidence from manuscripts or private papers is forthcoming. In the Turkish embassy letters, Lowenthal's treatment of Montagu's orientalism is less illuminating than L. Lowe's analysis in *Critical Terrains: French and British Orientalisms* (CH, Jul'92). This is a readable book. However, hungry for more of Montagu's wit and richly detailed observation, readers will revert to Halsband's biography and finally to the correspondence itself. Upper-division undergraduates and up.—*D. Landry, Wayne State University*

WS-0468　　　　PR1928　　　　90-48826 CIP
Mann, Jill. **Geoffrey Chaucer.** Humanities, 1991. 222p bibl index ISBN 0-391-03707-2, $39.95; ISBN 0-391-03708-0 pbk, $12.50

Mann (Girton College, University of Cambridge) attempts successfully to break new ground in feminist studies in Chaucer's writing. She accomplished this not by following any set "school" of feminine criticism, but by showing how woman was to be represented for herself, not from a male standpoint, either positive or negative. Thus, in Mann's view, Chaucer presented woman "at the centre instead of at the periphery, where she becomes the norm against which all human behavior is to be measured." In supporting this claim, Mann ranges widely through Chaucer's works with chapter titles such as "The Surrender of Maistrye," "Suffering Woman, Suffering God," and "The Feminised Hero," and concludes with a discussion of the "Nun's Priest's Tale." Although the book reads easily, the reader will find much intellectual stimulation with which to exercise the critical imagination. Finally, it is refreshing to find a book whose feminist approach avoids special pleading. Appropriate for graduate students and faculty.—*L. L. Bronson, Central Michigan University*

WS-0469　　　　　　　　90-70034 Orig
Martin, Priscilla. **Chaucer's women: nuns, wives, and amazons.** Iowa, 1990. 254p index ISBN 0-87745-293-8, $29.95

Martin bases this reading of Chaucer's work on the assumption that "Chaucer recognizes. . .the implications of traditional restriction of written discourse to a male clerical class," and that he explores those implications as he addresses his major subject, the problematic relationships between the sexes. One would wish that her study (one of a very few book-length analyses of Chaucer's women) brought more forcefully original insights to his poetry. But although Martin offers some interesting observations on gendered discourse in Chaucer's works—and on equally gendered silence—most of her perceptions strike an experienced reader of Chaucer with a sense of deja vu. Her readings are thoughtful, sensible, and often sensitive, but not particularly original. For more stimulating theoretical arguments, one might better go to Carolyn Dinshaw's *Chaucer's Sexual Poetics* (CH, Oct'90). Nevertheless, though Martin's book, lamentably, lacks a bibliography, it would be a useful critical study for undergraduate libraries.—*M. A. Dalbey, Eastern Michigan University*

WS-0470   Orig
Miles, Robert. **Ann Radcliffe: the great enchantress.** Manchester, 1995. (Dist. by St. Martin's) 201p bibl index ISBN 0-7190-3828-6, $49.95; ISBN 0-7190-3829-4 pbk, $19.95

Miles (Sheffield Hallam University, UK) proclaims that his purpose is to "help scotch the view of Radcliffe as a literary primitive." More specifically, he seeks to "draw out the context" in which Radcliffe wrote, and this he does in chapters devoted to the aesthetic and historical contexts, intending to "argue against the preconception of Radcliffe as a 'conservative' writer" and to demonstrate how Radcliffe "'re-invent[s]' the Gothic romance." Although these latter two goals have been accomplished already by the many recent studies of the female Gothic, especially those written by feminist literary critics, Miles dismisses these approaches as "read[ing] against the grain of Radcliffe's apparent intentions." His own theoretical approach shifts in an almost dizzying way, from biographical to new historical to psychoanalytic to structuralist. This is regrettable, particularly since he states in his introduction that he intends the book for a "student audience primarily." Miles provides somewhat helpful suggestions for further reading in his annotated bibliography. The text suffers from a number of typos. Comprehensive undergraduate collections only.—*E. R. Baer, Gustavus Adolphus College*

WS-0471   PR2399   95-26151 CIP
Miller, Naomi J. **Changing the subject: Mary Wroth and figurations of gender in early modern England.** University Press of Kentucky, 1996. 279p index afp ISBN 0-8131-1964-2, $34.95

Wroth (1587-1653) was the author of the first published sonnet sequence in English by a woman, the first novel published by a women, and one of the first plays published by a woman. Up to now she has been considered primarily in relation to canonical male authors—in particular, Sir Philip Sidney, her uncle. In her time she was excoriated for her choice of subject matter and her gender, called by one male writer a "hermaphrodite in show, in deed a monster"; to this day she continues to be read, Miller (Univ. of Arizona) contends, as "not-Shakespeare," marginalized by contemporary critics. Miller uses a combination of new historicist, materialist feminist, and French feminist theory "to interrogate the multiple conjunctions and disjunctions that emerge when 'dominant' and 'marginal' texts are juxtaposed." Attempting to demonstrate that women's voices were not always weakened by domestic relations to men, Miller considers the figuration of maternity in mothers' advice books, in literary works by Wroth's male "fathers," and in works by female authors. She shows how Wroth refigures Shakespeare's families of absent mothers into families that emphasize mothers' relationships and maternal authority. Miller also shows how Wroth uses the figuration of political authority provided by Queen Elizabeth and the court of Queen Anne. In spite of its ponderous style and irritating use of clichéd parlance, this book presents an important new viewpoint that will probably influence the study of Renaissance texts by women. Upper-division undergraduate and up.—*J. P. Baumgaertner, Wheaton College (IL)*

WS-0472   PR769   93-46260 CIP
Moore, Judith. **The appearance of truth: the story of Elizabeth Canning and eighteenth-century narrative.** Delaware, 1994. (Dist. by Associated University Presses) 278p bibl index afp ISBN 0-87413-494-3, $42.50

After Elizabeth Canning's month-long disappearance from her London home in 1753, two women were convicted of imprisoning her in an attic for four weeks. But before the sentence was carried out an alibi turned the defense into prosecution, and Canning was tried for perjury, convicted, and deported. Moore scrutinizes not only the celebrated case itself (which drew the attention even of Fielding) but also the dozens of conflicting accounts, fictional and nonfictional, circulating from the 18th through the 20th century. Her unnamed guiding spirit is Pirandello, for the real subject of *The Appearance of Truth* is the impossibil-

ity of finding the truth in a field of competing narratives. Class, gender, and sexuality, recurring topics in the pamphlet wars over Canning, are central in contemporary novels such as *Pamela*, and Moore analyzes the complex relation between tract and novel, fact and fiction. Though the writing is clear and lively, the pace is uneven: slow in the documentation (more than her case requires), rushed in the analytical chapters. But the case makes for fascinating reading, and *The Appearance of Truth* is recommended for academic collections.—*J. T. Lynch, University of Pennsylvania*

WS-0473   PR2323   93-27167 CIP
Moulsworth, Martha. **"My name was Martha": a Renaissance woman's autobiographical poem,** ed. by Robert C. Evans and Barbara Wiedemann. Locust Hill, 1993. 117p bibl afp ISBN 0-933951-53-1, $22.50

Martha Moulsworth's 1632 poem, "Memorandum," recently discovered in a commonplace book in Yale University's Beinecke Library, is printed here for the first time. Written by a 55-year-old woman who chronicles her life in 55 couplets, it is one of the earliest examples of autobiographical poetry. The poet also makes a remarkably progressive claim for equal rights to education for women ("two Vniversities we haue of men/ o thatt we had but one of women then"). The thrice-widowed Moulsworth creates a self-portrait that reveals her indebtedness to her clergyman father, who saw to it she was educated, and her enjoyment of all three husbands, especially the third with whom she "led an easie darlings life," exercising her "will in house, in purse in Store ...." The editors, both of whom teach at Auburn University, provide a close reading of the poem, pointing out its complex mixture of tones, and place the poem in its historical context, considering its identity as autobiography and as feminist discourse. An important discovery for Renaissance scholars, the book is also accessible to general readers. Highly recommended. Undergraduate; graduate; faculty.—*J. P. Baumgaertner, Wheaton College (IL)*

WS-0474   PR3613   95-10377 CIP
Munns, Jessica. **Restoration politics and drama: the plays of Thomas Otway, 1675-1683.** Delaware, 1995. (Dist. by Associated University Presses) 269p bibl index afp ISBN 0-87413-548-6, $42.50

Munns (Univ. of New Orleans) has published essays about Otway in *Restoration, English Literary History*, and other journals. Here, she provides a detailed account of Otway's plays, arranging them by genre and, so far as possible, presenting them in chronological order. The book emphasizes the women in the plays, who are viewed not as "types of antiwoman" but as women whose love for their mates leads them to challenge male assumptions of primacy. Otway's most famous play, *Venice Preserv'd* (1682), is discussed in a chapter that argues for the inseparability of the play's sexual and political content and also responds to male critics' hostility to Belvedere's sensuality. (Since, however, these critics include Leigh Hunt, Byron, and three others cited from 1958, 1959, and 1969, perhaps the matter is not urgent news.) Not much has been published on Otway of late—the most recent book is Kerstin Warner's *Thomas Otway* (CH, Jan'83)—so the value of Munns's book lies in its currency. Recommended for graduate students and research libraries.—*J. Wilkinson, Youngstown State University*

WS-0475   PR2323   95-22413 CIP
"The muses females are": Martha Moulsworth and other women writers of the English Renaissance, ed. by Robert C. Evans and Anne C. Little. Locust Hill, 1995. 315p (Locust Hill literary studies, 20) indexes afp ISBN 0-933951-63-9, $32.00

This collection of short essays offers valuable explorations of Martha Moulsworth's recently discovered poem "Memorandum" (appearing for the first time in Moulsworth's *"My Name Was Martha": A Renaissance Woman's Autobiographical Poem*, CH, Mar'94), including newly uncovered details about the author's life that sometimes provocatively contradict the persona she created. The authors—Germaine Greer, Anthony Low, John Shawcross, and Frances Teague, among others—take diverse approaches to the poem, investigating, for example, its biblical resonance, its viability as an early poetic expression of mutual love in marriage, its punning marginalia, and its place in the genre of 17th-century autobiographical works by women. The appendix includes an edited text of the poem, photographic reproductions of the handwritten text discovered in the Beinecke, transcripts of the wills of Moulsworth and her three husbands, the funeral sermon for Moulsworth, and a helpful chronology of women writers of the English Renaissance. This engaging, meticulously reconstructed biography results from historical detective work and careful attention to, analysis of, and contextualization of a hitherto unexplored poem by a newly discovered author. Highly recommended for all collections.—*J. P. Baumgaertner, Wheaton College (IL)*

WS-0476 PR448.W65 90-30542 CIP

Myers, Sylvia Harcstark. **The Bluestocking circle: women, friendship, and the life of the mind in eighteenth-century England.** Oxford, 1990. 342p bibl index ISBN 0-19-811767-1, $64.00

Myers (California State, Hayward, before her death in 1988) combed the primary sources in both print and manuscript to produce a new account and assessment of the famous Bluestocking circle of mid- and later-18th-century English literary life. Her new study supersedes such old standards as Myra Reynolds's *The Learned Lady in England, 1650-1760* (1920). Its combining of biographical chapters on such women as Elizabeth Montague, Catherine Talbot, Elizabeth Carter, and Hester Thrale with accounts of the social and literary events contributes to a reader's understanding of the intellectual climate of the times and, most particularly, the way in which the position of women in that period explains the phenomenon of the Bluestocking circle. For students of 18th-century English literature, social history, and the contributory currents of modern feminism, this will be a pleasantly informative and scholarly source. It offers occasional glimpses of such major literary figures as Pope, Samuel Richardson, Samuel Johnson, Walter Scott, and others from a new perspective; above all, it demonstrates fairly conclusively, without arguing the case, that it was the effort to achieve intellectual development and mutual respect, rather than lesbian attraction, as some have hinted, that best explains the nature of the Bluestocking phenomenon. For collections of considerable depth in related areas.—*A. E. Jones Jr., emeritus, Drew University*

WS-0477 PR858 94-47663 CIP

Nelson, T.G.A. **Children, parents, and the rise of the novel.** Delaware, 1995. (Dist. by Associated University Presses) 252p bibl index afp ISBN 0-87413-558-3, $37.50

Nelson's interesting, readable volume challenges the notion that the marginal role of children in early English novels is a carryover of the Restoration libertine view of parenthood as a comic misfortune or, more seriously, a curtailment of the life force. Nelson (Univ. of New England) calls attention to a sympathetic turn away from the begettor and toward the child in Augustan comedy (beginning in the 1690s); he also focuses (in novels written before 1750) on the use of the language of sentiment in representing children as figures of hope and new life and the reserving of comic treatment for their rejectors. The book extends studies like Leah Marcus's *Childhood and Cultural Despair* (CH, May'79) and, to some extent, qualifies modern criticisms of patriarchy in these works, without, however, idealizing the fictional family by ignoring the retention of older cultural attitudes. Since the early novel does not yet portray children subjectively, Nelson examines their depiction as part of a structural relationship with mothers and fathers. He is enlightening on even the most familiar fictional families and most rewarding on lesser-known examples, e.g., those of Sara Fielding's *The Governess* and Bernard Mandeville's *The Virgin Unmask'd*. Highly recommended for general and academic readers.—*G. R. Wasserman, Russell Sage College*

WS-0478 PR658 90-23374 CIP

Newman, Karen. **Fashioning femininity and English Renaissance drama.** Chicago, 1991. 182p index afp ISBN 0-226-57708-2, $32.00; ISBN 0-226-57709-0 pbk, $11.95

A slim but suggestive exploration of the construction of gender in an assortment of Renaissance texts: medical illustrations, marriage treatises, play texts, consumer goods, and dress. Newman calls for a "different kind of textual intercourse, a promiscuous conversation of many texts," and that is exactly what she delivers. She combines New Historicist, Marxist, and feminist approaches with psychoanalysis and the theories of Derrida and Bakhtin. Newman begins with the fragmentation of the female body, particularly into reproductive organs. She shows how the marriage tracts' repeated desire for ordered family life reflected acute anxiety about the future of the commonwealth. In *The Taming of the Shrew* she sees the theatrical realization of the *skimmington*, the public shaming and subjection of the shrewish wife. *Macbeth*'s witches represent the inversion of cultural codes of femininity, including maternal relations, while *Othello*'s Iago hyperbolizes contemporary views of race and gender. Newman concludes with a brilliant discussion of the relation of women to the growing consumerism of the early Jacobean age as represented in Jonson's *Epicoene*. A must for scholars and graduate students and appropriate for upper-division undergraduates.—*V. M. Vaughan, Clark University*

WS-0479 PR756 95-11801 CIP

Nussbaum, Felicity A. **Torrid zones: maternity, sexuality, and empire in eighteenth-century English narratives.** Johns Hopkins, 1995. 264p index afp ISBN 0-8018-5074-6, $45.00; ISBN 0-8018-5075-4 pbk, $14.95

Nussbaum looks at Johnson's *Life of Mr. Richard Savage* and *Rasselas*, Richardson's *Pamela* and *Pamela II*, Defoe's *Roxana*, and Opie's *Adeline Mowbray*. In *Roxana* the author finds "women are alienated from each other's sexual, maternal, and wage labor, an alienation exacerbated by the demands of empire." Roxana's feminism is "an economic and sexual independence purchased at the cost of her daughter's life." Scholars of the emergent empire in the 18th century should see sexuality in terms of feminism's internal struggles and its "Othering." Nussbaum discusses polygamy in African narratives and in England, examining Mary Wollstonecraft's work, Anna Falconbridge's narrative of her voyages to Sierra Leone, and Lady Mary Wortley Montagu's description of her time in Turkey. She also looks at prostitution, romance, sati, and a variety of other subjects found in travel literature, thereby providing a view of both the Englishwomen and the Other woman. A discussion of deformity leads her to *The Spectator*'s "Ugly Club" and Sarah Scott's *Millennium Hall*. Nussbaum succeeds in making the "ideological working of empire and Englishwomen's complicity within it more legible." Complete notes provide many citations to other work. Upper-division undergraduates and above.—*A. Jenkins, Georgia Institute of Technology*

WS-0480 PR457 94-27188 CIP

Re-visioning romanticism: British women writers, 1776-1837, ed. by Carol Shiner Wilson and Joel Haefner. Pennsylvania, 1994. 329p bibl index afp ISBN 0-8122-3231-3, $39.95; ISBN 0-8122-1421-8 pbk, $16.95

Aptly titled and enterprising, this collection of 14 essays mixes commentary by established Romantic critics with that of newer voices in the field. The volume maintains a sense of coherence even though it does not privilege any singular critical mode and ranges from autobiography, dissent, and domesticity to religion and gender in Welsh writers, botanical themes in poetry, "literary anti-history," and theater theory. Writers Felicia Hemans, Mary Robinson, Charlotte Smith, and Anna Laetitia Barbauld are given voice in a number of the articles, whereas writers such as Hannah More, Joanna Baillie, Maria Edgeworth, Mary Lamb, and Jane Taylor are placed in more limited critical contexts. Every article is focused, well directed, crisply written, threaded with grace or humor or passion. The scholars reveal themselves as long-standing investigators of a topic about which they care and which they want readers to discover, respect, or understand. Interesting points of view, important contributions by all critics, superb job by the editors. Bibliography separates primary and secondary works, is careful and current with a fast-moving field. Exemplary scholarship. Upper-division undergraduate and up.—*W. C. Snyder, St Vincent College & Seminary*

WS-0481 PR2399 91-390 CIP

Reading Mary Wroth: representing alternatives in early modern England, ed. by Naomi J. Miller and Gary Waller. Tennessee, 1991. 240p bibl index afp ISBN 0-87049-709-X, $39.50; ISBN 0-87049-710-3 pbk, $18.95

Seldom does one find an anthology of critical perspectives in which the essays are uniformly intelligent and well written. *Reading Mary Wroth* offers a wide range of viewpoints and theoretical stances, yet each essay reveals some crucial facet of the most accomplished woman writer in Stuart England. The initial biographical section, for example, pairs Margaret Hannay's traditional account of Mary Wroth's relationship to her aunt, the Countess of Pembroke, with Gary Waller's feminist, psychoanalytic reading of her attraction to her cousin, William Herbert, Third Earl of Pembroke. The second section is New Historicist in focus, situating Wroth's poems (the sonnet cycle *Pamphilia to Amphilanthus*), play (*Love's Victory*), and prose romance (*The Countess of Montgomery's Urania*) in the context of Jacobean court politics and culture. The third section is comparative, placing Wroth's work in relationship to the poems of the Venetian courtesan Veronica Franco and the plays of William Shakespeare. A final section examines the construction of the female subject within Wroth's writings and those of her contemporaries. This collection is indispensable for anyone seriously interested in Lady Mary Wroth's work and its meaning for English Renaissance culture. Appropriate for students at or beyond upper-division undergraduate level.—*V. M. Vaughan, Clark University*

WS-0482   PR3317   93-12243 CIP
Rereading Aphra Behn: history, theory, and criticism, ed. by Heidi Hutner. University Press of Virginia, 1993. 336p index ISBN 0-8139-1442-6, $45.00; ISBN 0-8139-1443-4 pbk, $17.95

By a familiar paradox, the contributors to this collection repeatedly claim that Aphra Behn has been omitted from the "canon" of English letters—meanwhile citing those from Alexander Pope and Leigh Hunt to Edmund Gosse and Virginia Woolf, who have been fascinated by her work. In fact Behn is one of many writers (often, but far from exclusively, women) who faded from anthologies and literary histories during the great contraction known as New Criticism and is now being "rediscovered." The 13 essays presented here treat most of the genres in which Behn worked (plays, poems, fiction, dedications, with most emphasis on well-known works such as *Oroonoko* and *The Rover*). The authors foreground their theoretical stances (Marxist, feminist, deconstructive, new historicist) in order to demonstrate Behn's importance in furthering the political ends of those stances (in destabilizing Restoration constructions of gender, capitalism, or race). The result is a series of intelligent but partial readings, and a volume that will nourish current rethinking of Restoration literary studies, though perhaps for less time than its authors might have hoped. Graduate; faculty.—*D. L. Patey, Smith College*

WS-0483   PR2343   93-20209 CIP
Roberts, Katherine J. **Fair ladies: Sir Philip Sidney's female characters.** P. Lang, 1993. 130p (Renaissance and baroque studies and texts, 9) bibl afp ISBN 0-8204-2145-6, $42.95

This slim and expensive book argues that Sir Philip Sidney's fictional portrayal of female characters moves steadily away from stereotypically "negative theories about women" towards a degendered appreciation of their "individuality." Roberts's first chapter outlines the virtues and vices expected of women as they are typically portrayed (1) in a handful of influential courtesy books of the age, and (2) in selected works of "popular literature" and literary antecedents for Sidney's *Arcadias*. The middle three chapters consider: (1) the *Old Arcadia*, focusing on Gynecia as a female character who, untypically, is permitted to "step out of the passive role of the virtuous Renaissance woman to think, feel, and act like a man"; (2) the figure of Stella in Sidney's sonnet cycle; and (3) the *New Arcadia*, focusing on Sidney's revision of Pamela and Philoclea into "intelligent creatures capable of rational thought and moral responsibility" who possess "many of the virtues often reserved for heroes." In a brief concluding chapter, Roberts speculates about what influences might have encouraged Sidney to break out of cultural stereotypes of women. Roberts's unpretentious clarity of style and argument makes the book accessible to undergraduates, but her lack of sophistication in exploring the cultural, literary, social, and theological contexts limits its usefulness for advanced students. Undergraduate.—*J. E. Skillen, Gordon College*

WS-0484   PR275.R4   89-24836 MARC
Robertson, Elizabeth. **Early English devotional prose and the female audience.** Tennessee, 1990. 227p bibl index afp ISBN 0-87049-641-7, $29.95

In this thoughtful study of the six 13th-century works of devotional prose making up the so-called "AB texts," Robertson posits that their focus on the female body, their use of quotidian imagery, and their affective style—all of which constitute what is frequently regarded as a female style of writing—derive rather from male clerics' beliefs about the nature of women, who were seen as trapped in their bodies, and, indeed, the nature of all uneducated audiences (which included women), all of whom were bound in the corporal world. Introductory chapters provide valuable overviews of the condition of the female religious in England and of medieval views of female spirituality. These are followed by individual studies of the *Ancrene Wisse*; *Hali Meidenhad*; the lives of saints Katherine, Mar-

garet, and Juliana; and the homily "Sawles Warde." Concluding chapters suggest the debt of these works to the Anglo-Saxon vernacular tradition and to the affective piety of Anselm and the Victorines. The book, which contains an excellent bibliography, is well suited for a range of academic readers.—*M. A. Dalbey, Eastern Michigan University*

WS-0485   PR2983   95-21677 CIP
Shakespearean tragedy and gender, ed. by Shirley Nelson Garner and Madelon Sprengnether. Indiana, 1996. 326p bibl index afp ISBN 0-253-32964-7, $39.95; ISBN 0-253-21027-5 pbk, $17.50

This useful collection takes stock of 20 years of gender studies of Shakespeare's tragedies. (Eight of the dozen essays have been published in some previous form). Five essays demonstrate Shakespeare's consistent displacement of dangerous female energy from the center to the periphery of the action. The richness of male tragic subjectivity is thus seen as developed at the expense of depth in depicting female tragic subjects. Three essays analyze a tragic wife (Desdemona): the flaws in Othello's domestic polity, Desdemona's Venetianness, and her differences from Emilia and from the Duchess of Malfi (the latter essay is worth the price of the volume). The final four essays are the most miscellaneous, wrestling with whether Shakespeare is truly contemporary and concluding, reluctantly, that he is not. Whatever the reader's politics, this compendium demonstrates the substance of gender studies. It also shows that such studies are part of a "movement": the essays retain their original bibliographies, which illustrate the centrality of writers like Janet Adelman, Linda Bamber, Jonathan Dollimore, Diane Dreher, Peter Erickson, Jean Howard, Lisa Jardine, Carol Thomas Neely, Marianne Novy, Mary Beth Rose, and Valerie Traub. Highly recommended for large collections of Shakespeare studies.—*D. O. Dickerson, Judson College*

WS-0486   PR3698   93-49538 CIP
Spector, Robert D. **Smollett's women: a study in an eighteenth-century masculine sensibility.** Greenwood, 1994. 196p (Contributors to the study of world literature, 56) bibl index afp ISBN 0-313-28790-2, $55.00

In this superbly argued study, Spector, the undisputed expert on Smollett and his works, has emphasized the thesis that Smollett's fiction essentially represents the "male-dominated world of 18th-century England" and therefore primarily appeals to the masculine mind. Spector concentrates on suggesting some of the shaping forces behind the development of Smollett's special masculine approach such as his marital relationship with Anne, his insistence on heroic, manly conduct, and his disdain of homosexual behavior. Spector applies this analysis in great detail to Smollett's heroines, who represent the best that 18th-century society could produce and whose duty it was to uphold the highest ideals of womanhood despite the fact that they were essentially asexual. His Hogarthian view of the often harmful effect of a woman's vanity and his typical 18th-century notions of a woman's sexuality can be seen in Smollett's treatment of fallen women and women as victims. The last chapter is devoted to the matter of Smollett's comic and grotesque female characters, who served his satiric and humorous purposes exceedingly well, given his tendency to create memorable caricatures and stereotypes; indeed, Smollett's choice of the epistolary technique provided him with the opportunity to create a convincing structure and to develop a remarkable variety of female characters, some of whom go beyond the limitation of stereotype and caricature. Highly recommended. Upper-division undergraduate and up.—*R. G. Brown, Ball State University*

WS-0487   PR3637   92-42647 CIP
Thomas, Claudia N. **Alexander Pope and his eighteenth-century women readers.** Southern Illinois, 1994. 309p bibl index afp ISBN 0-8093-1886-5, $39.95

Thomas's book is the latest feminist take on canonical 18th-century male writers. Thomas's reception study considers Pope's attitude toward women in an 18th-century context, arguing that Pope is not quite the misogynist wasp tradition has made him out to be, and that women reacted to his vision of an ideal domesticity sometimes favorably, sometimes contentiously. Women participated in Augustan literary culture by reading, responding to, and imitating nearly all of Pope's corpus; Thomas does a service by assembling these readings of and reactions to such works by Pope as the *Essay on Man*, his translation of the *Iliad*, "Eloisa to Abelard," and the Horatian satires. However, weak organization buries even her best insights in a mass of paraphrase that passes for close reading. Her attention to specifics instead of generalities goes too far, and her reticence to explore the implications of her material results in too many missed opportunities for a focused feminist or historical critique. Useful for more inclusive collections. Graduate; faculty.—*J. T. Lynch, University of Pennsylvania*

WS-0488   Can. CIP
Ty, Eleanor. **Unsex'd revolutionaries: five women novelists of the 1790s.** Toronto, 1993. 189p index afp ISBN 0-8020-2949-3, $40.00; ISBN 0-8020-7774-9 pbk, $18.95

This study, like Ruth Salvaggio's *Enlightened Absence* (CH, Oct'89), is an example of what Gayatri Spivak might call "essentialist, humanist, deconstructivist feminism." Working back and forth between French feminist theory and studies of women's psycho-sexual development by Nancy Chodorow and Carol Gilligan, Ty discovers many correspondences between these recent feminist findings of women's linguistic and psychic differences from men and the probing fictions of 1790s British women writers. This decade is rich in female novelistic experiments, and an investigation, like the present one of novels by Mary Wollstonecraft, Mary Hays, Helen Maria Williams, Elizabeth Inchbald, and Charlotte Smith, is certainly needed. Readers will have to decide for themselves whether they find Ty's rather heavy-handed interpretive apparatus illuminating or obfuscatory. The best chapter analyzes Inchbald's *A Simple Story*, a novel that might have been designed to illustrate Ty's argument about the Law of the Father. One can regret that the book as a whole reads more like a series of commentaries on selected novels than a well-integrated study of women's literary production in the period, and that the individual readings in general bring so little news. Advanced undergraduate; graduate; faculty.—*D. Landry, Wayne State University*

WS-0489   PR2399   92-42532 CIP
Waller, Gary. **The Sidney family romance: Mary Wroth, William Herbert, and the early modern construction of gender.** Wayne State, 1993. 328p bibl index afp ISBN 0-8143-2436-3, $39.95

Waller (Univ. of Hartford), author of *English Poetry of the Sixteenth Century* (CH, Feb'87) and coeditor of *Sir Philip Sidney and the Interpretations of Renaissance Culture* (1984), assembles here a vast array of interdisciplinary supports, especially psychoanalysis and feminist theory, for his speculations about William Herbert, (who was Earl of Pembroke, Lord Chamberlain, and Shakespeare's patron) and Mary Sidney Wroth, lady-in-waiting, who were for a time lovers and apparently produced two illegitimate children. Both Wroth and Herbert were formed by the "family romance" of the famous, powerful Sidney family—he a nephew, and she a niece of Sir Philip Sidney—although their lives were very differently "gendered." Waller emphasizes Wroth, whose serious, powerful works were almost unknown until recently: a collection of Petrarchan love poetry, *Pamphilia to Amphilanthus*; a long prose romance, *The Countesse of Mountgomeries Urania*; and an unperformed pastoral drama, *Love's Victory*. In her writing, the courageous and fascinating Mary Wroth sought the autonomy granted to Sidney family men but denied their women. Waller describes these works in useful detail, concluding that Wroth is the most important woman writer of the early modern period. Her poetry, liberally quoted, is moving still. Waller analyzes less convincingly the cousins' inner lives, "in the (obvious) absence of direct evidence and a paucity of documentation." His compassion and enthusiastic research do not entirely validate all his conclusions with equal authority, but his flashes of insight illuminate the lives of these two cousins and of our own. Graduate; faculty.—*J. M. Green, Kent State University*

WS-0490   PR113   89-36296 MARC
Williamson, Marilyn L. **Raising their voices: British women writers, 1650-1750.** Wayne State, 1990. 339p index ISBN 0-8143-2209-3, $39.95

A feminist survey of English women writers from 1650 to 1750, beginning with Margaret Cavendish, the first Englishwoman to write for publication. Her successors are divided into two schools headed by Katherine Philips (1631-64) and Aphra Behn (1640-89). Philips (also known as the "Matchless Orinda") used the classical *beatus vir* convention to praise the retired life. Away from the masculine ethos of politics and commercialism, women could assert their private virtues, especially their idealized friendships with other women. Thus Philips never challenged traditional gender roles, but hoped to reform the woman's role

within patriarchal marriage. Behn, in sharp contrast, offered a radical critique of marriage ideology, asserting woman's sexuality as a natural force. Her cavalier comedies exposed marriage as oppressive to both men and women. Behn also competed with men, writing plays for performance and fiction for sale. Williamson shows the literary daughters of Philips and Behn as constituting a natural transition to the female novelists of the 18th century, particularly in their emphasis on free choice in marriage partners. The survey approach with its brief snippets of text necessarily frustrates, but it does expose the reader to many unfamiliar women writers. Useful for graduate students, upper-division undergraduates, and general readers.—*V. M. Vaughan, Clark University*

WS-0491   PR2399   95-2654 CIP
Wroth, Mary, Lady. **The first part of *The Countess of Montgomery's Urania*,** ed. by Josephine A. Roberts. MRTS (Medieval & Renaissance Texts & Studies), 1995. 821p (Medieval & Renaissance Texts & Studies, 140) indexes afp ISBN 0-86698-176-4, $60.00

Wroth's *Urania* is the earliest known prose fiction by an Englishwoman. The editor (Louisiana State Univ.), who also edited *The Poems of Lady Mary Wroth* (CH, Jan'84), here provides a critical edition of the text published in 1621, collated from 29 extant copies, including one with Wroth's handwritten notes and changes. Roberts provides lengthy critical and textual introductions, which include literary, political, social, and personal contexts that help explain this "highly complex fiction." These introductions include references to the forthcoming second volume, which will include part 2 of *Urania*, extant only in a holograph manuscript, and a comprehensive subject index to both parts. Following the text in the present volume are extensive textual apparatus; commentary; genealogical tables; and indexes of characters, places, and first lines of poems in part 1. The bibliography is in the footnotes and commentary. Older reference works ignore or scant Wroth's achievement, and undergraduates without encouragement will overlook this work. It will nevertheless become essential and standard in any complete collection of English Renaissance or feminist literature for decades to come. Upper-division undergraduates and above.—*D. C. Homan, emeritus, Bethany College (KS)*

◆ British 19th Century

WS-0492   PR4838   92-23190 MARC
Alwes, Karla. **Imagination transformed: the evolution of the female character in Keats's poetry.** Southern Illinois, 1993. 210p bibl index afp ISBN 0-8093-1835-0, $29.95

Alwes examines Keats's portrayal of mortal and immortal maidens appearing primarily in the poetry of 1817-1819. She contends that, "more than comprise a symbol of the female as a romantic lover," these portrayals reflect Keats's attempts to "search for identity." Readers of Keats are well aware of his struggle to move among "uncertainties, mysteries, doubts," striving for that degree of comfort that characterizes the person who has achieved a high degree of tolerence for ambiguity. Alwes's discussions of the female character in Keats, the association with one mode of creativity—that is, the feminine—are well grounded, interesting, and informative. Readings of individual poems sometimes seem idiosyncratic or strained as she attempts to support her thesis. For example, her reading of "La Belle Dame Sans Merci" takes little notice of the medieval/Renaissance tradition of courtly love. On the other hand, her attempt to bring a feminist critical perspective to her theme challenges and stimulates the reader to consider her approach seriously. Beginning students of Keats will benefit more from the traditional scholarship of Walter Jackson Bate, Jack Stillinger, and David Perkins, but advanced students and scholars will find this study arresting. Alwes's conclusion—that Keats reconciles his two passions, women and poetry, in "To Autumn"—is well supported and taken. Endnotes and bibliography are excellent, but a feminist critic might wonder at the omission of Amy Lowell, herself a passionate student of Keats. Graduate; faculty.—*V. L. Radley, Russell Sage College*

WS-0493   PR468   93-17254 CIP
Anderson, Amanda. **Tainted souls and painted faces: the rhetoric of fallenness in Victorian culture.** Cornell, 1993. 250p bibl index afp ISBN 0-8014-2781-9, $35.00; ISBN 0-8014-8148-1 pbk, $14.95

As the subtitle suggests, Anderson's subject is not so much the prostitute in Victorian literature as it is the rhetoric the Victorians used to construct "fallenness." This condition, Anderson argues, is defined less by sexual transgression than by the inability to take deliberative moral action. The fallen woman is determined; she is doomed and powerless to avert her fate. Thus, she becomes a kind of cultural scapegoat, the outcast who allowed the (unfallen) Victorians to reassure themselves that they retained autonomy, the ability to act, reason, and control their destinies. Using this notion, Anderson analyzes novels by Dickens and Gaskell, as well as Rossetti's "Jenny" and Elizabeth Barrett Browning's *Aurora Leigh*. She handles the poems reasonably well, but the novels are perhaps so large that they elude her efforts to contain and describe them. Following her analyses, she appends a lengthy discussion of issues involving the determined and autonomous character types in the contemporary politics of poststructuralism. The entire work is fully documented with extensive notes and a lengthy bibliography. Graduate; faculty.—*J. L. Culross, Eastern Kentucky University*

WS-0494   PR4897.L2   90-13473 MARC
Bennett, Betty T. **Mary Diana Dods, a gentleman and a scholar.** W. Morrow, 1991. 303p index afp ISBN 0-688-08717-5, $22.95

While producing her invaluable edition of Mary Shelley's collected letters, Bennett encountered the scholarly riddle at the heart of this book. In Shelley's circle were three characters, two men and a woman, whom Bennett at first was unable to identify with much precision. A meticulous and vigorous investigation led her to the remarkable conclusion that the three individuals were all one, a woman, Mary Diana Dods. The illegitimate daughter of a Scottish earl, Dods first wrote for *Blackwood's* as David Lyndsay and then later, with the aid of Shelley, passed herself off as Walter Sholto Douglas, the "husband" of Shelley's friend Isabel Douglas. This charade was conducted in Paris for more than two years and ended with Douglas's death in debtors' prison around 1830. Bennett presents her hypothesis persuasively, despite its inherent incredibility. But the characters involved are unimportant even to Shelley scholars, and the facts presented have to be overinterpreted to shed any light on psychological or gender issues. However, as a narrative about complex detective work by an extremely talented 20th-century literary scholar, the book may well interest others engaged in similar enterprises.—*M. M. Garland, Ohio State University*

WS-0495   PR4681   94-10513 CIP
Bodenheimer, Rosemarie. **The real life of Mary Ann Evans: George Eliot, her letters and fiction.** Cornell, 1994. 295p index afp ISBN 0-8014-2988-9, $33.95

We should all write letters to Bodenheimer and thank her for this book. Here we have the first full-scale study of George Eliot's correspondence (as collected in nine volumes by Gordon Height, Yale Univ. Press, 1954-74), helpfully organized by topic, and connected thematically to both life and fiction. Every paragraph is filled with information and insight, as issues both familiar (public and private) and not so familiar (Eliots's stepsons) are treated with immense and quiet sophistication. Unlike so much contemporary criticism, which spends half its time ostentatiously arm wrestling with theory or theorists, Bodenheimer shows clear awareness of contemporary accounts of biographical or epistolary subject construction (and there are substantial bibliographical guides in these areas), yet for the most part allows Eliot and her contemporaries to provide their own best contexts. Both the fictive nature of letters and the autobiographical "reality" of fiction are well discussed in this very welcome book. General and academic audiences.—*S. C. Dillon, Bates College*

WS-0496   PR4711   92-292 CIP
Bonaparte, Felicia. **The gypsy-bachelor of Manchester: the life of Mrs. Gaskell's demon.** University Press of Virginia, 1992. 310p bibl index ISBN 0-8139-1390-X, $37.50

Basing her study on the thesis that Elizabeth Gaskell was not, as most critics have insisted, an angel in the house, Bonaparte skillfully and at times convincingly demonstrates that there was, in fact, an "inner demon," a creature born to be a "gypsy-bachelor" existing within the author of *Mary Barton, Cranford, North and South*, and *Wives and Daughters*—novels we have been asked to read as products of "the very incarnation of a Victorian dissenting minister's wife" rather than the secret documents of a tormented secret self. In this mixture of biography and criticism, Bonaparte, ignoring chronology, traces images, diction, characters, letters, and plots to find the "subversive" text that enables one to see how Gaskell did, indeed, find and "write" her secret self. Whether or not one is persuaded by Bonaparte's approach—at times one senses a bit of strain in the readings—one has to admire the thoroughness of method and the depth of conviction. The result, as controversial as the author's procedure may be, is a positive one. It helps to emphasize the direction of Catherine Gallagher's *The Industrial Reformation of English Fiction 1832-1867* (CH, Jan'86), thus furthering understanding of this neglected author and the significance of her novels, especially in the context of the time in which she wrote.—*M. Timko, Queens College, CUNY*

WS-0497   PR4688   91-28717 CIP
Brady, Kristin. **George Eliot.** St. Martin's, 1992. 209p bibl index ISBN 0-312-06059-9, $24.95

After a definition of Eliot as icon, Brady begins with a brief biography to "consider Eliot's life. . .in terms of her overdetermined position as a feminine gendered subject within partriarchy." Brady's repetitive insistence on Eliot's "status of commodity in an economic exchange among men," however, leads at times to a narrative almost as reductive of complex human motivation as those by biographers (from Bray to Haight) who construct her life within the (less explicit) ideologies of patriarchy, and who see her, in particular, as a woman who must find a man to lean on. More willing to tolerate ambiguity in Eliot's own texts, Brady gives full attention to the ways in which, in each of the fictions (including the short stories and *The Spanish Gypsy*), "the apparent resolutions. . .finally expose the privileging by patriarchy of the masculine and its negation of woman's desire." If the terms of Brady's analysis tend to be predictable, her sensitivity to the varieties of exposure that the plots present gives the four chapters of readings a vitality and sense of discovery that redeems them from cliché. As at the end of Eliot's last novel, one leaves Brady's short book with some skepticism about its answers but great respect for its questions.—*W. W. Heath, Amherst College*

WS-0498   PR468   93-35955 MARC
Brown, Penny. **The captured world: the child and childhood in nineteenth-century women's writing in England.** St. Martin's, 1994 (c1993). 222p bibl index ISBN 0-312-12058-3, $39.95

In the 19th century, the child received unprecedented attention as a popular literary topic. Traced by Phillipe Ariès in *Centuries of Childhood* (1962) and placed in British context by social historians such as James Walvin in *A Child's World* (1982), the movement toward Locke's and Rousseau's idealization of children invented a view of them as primally innocent and individually important. Going beyond the limiting male emphases of writers such as Pattison and Grylls, this valuable study examines many significant women writers' prose stories about children that were written for an adult audience. It explains how they interpreted childhood in light of their preconceived spiritual, philosophical, and literary ideologies, which mirror the child figures' subordination as a reflection of their own desire to rebel against the gendered status quo. Symbols of children range between didactic, sentimental innocence, and Calvinist emphasis upon discipline and obedience. The treatment of innovative, realistic foregrounding of children as life-like characters is most engaging. Including notes and bibliography, this highly readable and interesting study is recommended for all undergraduate and graduate collections of Victorian literature.—*S. A. Parker, Hiram College*

WS-0499   PR5642   94-36979 CIP
Clarke, Micael M. **Thackeray and women.** Northern Illinois, 1995. 235p bibl index afp ISBN 0-87580-197-8, $30.00

As George Eliot and Charlotte Brontë noted, Thackeray wrote about significant patterns of his era's gender ideology. Because of his wife's madness, he educated his daughters and followed contemporary gender issues with special diligence; for example, he derived plot material for his novels from Caroline Norton's test case, which provided insights into divorce, child custody, and married women's property rights. Thackeray critiqued gender inequities but, despite his liberal views, has been unevenly understood by critics, who have debated the meaning of "feminism," failed to appreciate his irony, and miscalculated the historical meaning of socially constructed plots. Clarke (Loyola Univ. of Chicago) surveys Thackeray's formative years and canon, revealing the novelist's brilliant, conscious partisanship of the Victorian women's movement. Modern scholars like Dorothy Van Ghent, Gordon Ray, and Eve Kosofsky Sedgwick have studied Thackeray's treatment of patriarchs. Nina Auerbach's *Woman and the Demon* (CH, Feb'83) and Richard Barickman, Susan MacDonald, and Myra Stark's *Corrupt Relations* (CH, May'83) approached his gender analysis. Wide-ranging discussions of Victorian gender are provided in *Victorian Women*, ed. by Erna Olafson Hellerstein et al. (CH, Jul'81), and Mary Poovey's *Uneven Development* (CH, Apr'89). However, Clarke's unique study offers the first in-depth analysis of Thackeray's treatment of birth, madness, and motherhood among Victorian women. Recommended for all college and academic libraries.—*S. A. Parker, Hiram College*

WS-0500   PR115   89-24205 CIP
Clarke, Norma. **Ambitious heights: writing, friendship, love: the Jewsbury sisters, Felicia Hemans, and Jane Welsh Carlyle.** Routledge, 1990. 245p bibl index ISBN 0-415-00051-3, $55.00; ISBN 0-415-00052-1, $16.50

Jane Carlyle spent decades in the center of London literary and intellectual life. After her sudden death in 1866, her husband, Thomas, studied and edited her letters, which began a controversy that has existed to this day: Was Jane Carlyle a self-abnegating martyr or a shrew? This question remains both relevant and interesting, rather than voyeuristic, because Jane Carlyle's thwarted literary ambitions can be seen as a paradigm of troubled Victorian womanhood. Before marriage an ambitious writer, after marriage an ardent letter writer, Jane Carlyle receives fascinating treatment in this studious examination of frustrated aspirations. Clarke considers Jane Carlyle's life, friendships, and work. For 25 years, she was friends with Geraldine Jewsbury, whose life offers a counterpoint and comparison. Virginia Woolf in 1935 discussed Jane and Geraldine, initiating interest in the forces of permission and prohibition that shaped Victorian women's selfhood. Light is also shed on the interesting, but largely ignored figures of the Jewsbury sisters and Felicia Hemans. Helpful notes and bibliography complete this provocative study which carefully traces the complex friendships and interactive dynamics of these currently neglected Victorian figures. Reliant upon modern feminist scholarship, Clarke's significant contribution draws on the collected letters of the Carlyles and on unpublished papers, and she corrects the narrow judgments of such commentators as J.A. Froude (*Life of Carlyle*, 1883), Waldo Dunn (*Froude and Carlyle*, 1930), and John Clubbe (*Froude's Life of Carlyle*, 1979). Strongly recommended for students of Victorian culture and women's studies.—*S. A. Parker, Hiram College*

WS-0501   PR788   91-17499 CIP
Corbett, Mary Jean. **Representing feminity: middle-class subjectivity in Victorian and Edwardian women's autobiographies.** Oxford, 1992. 240p bibl index afp ISBN 0-19-506858-0, $36.00

So many subjects, or "subjectivities," crowd this absorbing narrative that it may be hard to conceive how tightly and even suspensefully built it is. Corbett's subject is really subjectivity itself, and her historiography of the (gendered) self, also explicitly controlled for other ideological factors such as middle-class, white, and English, makes a vital contribution to the history of consciousness. Arguing that "concepts of the self. . .are historically and culturally variable," she boldly positions her study within the major social paradigm shifts of late 18th-century Romanticism and WW I, and then traces the subtle, richly grained manifold of the public/private self from Wordsworth and Carlyle (as exemplary public male subjects) through a host of women's self-representations, literary and not-so-literary, known and obscure, from Mary Howitt to Sylvia Pankhurst. Corbett resolutely de(con)structs the hegemony of the "normative" or "unitary" self theorists, who have dominated autobiography studies in the past. But, more important, she both challenges and reconciles feminist revisionists lately torn between "sexual" essentialism and "gender" artificialism. Difference, she affirms, is still difference, even when it is located within the subjective "experience of gender," rather than biology. "It is 'consciousness of gender' and class and race that makes possible and necessary exploration of the social subject." Dense, well-written endnotes, comprehensive bibliography, and proper-name index, plus wonderful blank end-papers for note-taking. Levels: graduate and upper-division undergraduate.—*F. Alaya, Ramapo College of New Jersey*

WS-0502   PR5908   92-37636 CIP
Cullingford, Elizabeth Butler. **Gender and history in Yeats's love poetry.** Cambridge, 1993. 334p bibl index ISBN 0-521-43148-4, $54.95

Cullingford examines dozens of Yeats's lyric poems by reading them in the context of the following: Irish myth and history; gender definitions and relations in 19th- and 20th-century Ireland and England; Yeats's female friends and loves, particularly these women's activities in the suffragist and Republican movements; his interest in the occult; the influence of pre-Raphaelite writers and painters on Yeats; his work as a Protestant, a senator, and an artist opposing the patriarchy and sexual politics of Ireland's Catholic Church and of the de Valera government—as well as much recent Yeats scholarship and Cullingford's own feminist approach to these love poems and their contexts. This study offers new, important readings of Yeats and his development as thinker and poet, focusing on Yeats's ambivalent and changing attitudes toward women and Woman and Mother Ireland. Of special note are her readings of "Leda and the Swan," "Among School Children," the Crazy Jane poems, "A Woman Young and Old," and "The Wild Old Wicked Man." Some readers will find much to quarrel with here, but clearly Cullingford has raised the level of interpretive quarrels through her careful research and argument. Good notes, exceptional bibliography. Highly recommended for undergraduate and graduate libraries and for scholars of modern poetry, Irish history, and women's studies.—*S. B. Darrell, University of Southern Indiana*

WS-0503   PR468   95-32733 CIP
David, Deirdre. **Rule Britannia: women, empire, and Victorian writing.** Cornell, 1995. 234p bibl index afp ISBN 0-8014-3170-0, $29.50

"Women, empire, and Victorian writing," David declares, "form a rich ideological cluster and a compelling subject for cultural analysis." Her objective is to find in Victorian writing the dominating attitudes toward empire, with particular emphasis on women writers, on women as represented in the texts, and on women as objects of sacrifice in the imperial world. For source material the author turns to "significant cultural documents" such as political essays, parliamentary reports and speeches, missionary literature, and travel writing, in addition to traditional fiction. The six chapters consider Wilkie Collins's *The Moonstone*, Thomas Macaulay's parliamentary speeches, and letters written home from India by Emily Eden; Charles Dickens's *The Old Curiosity Shop* and *Dombey and Son*; Charlotte Bronte's *Jane Eyre* combined with travel writing about Jamaica and literature about the Indian practice of suttee; education of the native Indian population and a legal case in Calcutta in the mid-1880s in which a female missionary was accused of loose behavior; assertive women in the imperial metropolis, the new imperialism, adventure fiction of H. Rider Haggard, and Tennyson's empire poetry; and Emilia Gould in Conrad's *Nostromo* and gender differences in constructing empire. This is a relatively new area of scholarly investigation, begun only as recently as 25 years ago, but David's excellent, detailed bibliography indicates that much progress has been made. This highly original and provocative book is recommended for upper-division undergraduates and above and for the general reader.—*R. T. Van Arsdel, emerita, University of Puget Sound*

WS-0504   PR4036   90-47976 CIP
Fergus, Jan. **Jane Austen: a literary life.** St. Martin's, 1991. 201p index ISBN 0-312-05712-1, $35.00

Fergus provides precisely what her subtitle promises, "a literary life," even though, as she is quick to point out, material for any biography of Austen is "scanty." Her knowledge of the period in which Austen wrote and her authoritative treatment of what is known about Austen's professional life—especially through letters and other primary sources—serve to make a virtue out of any paucity of detail. The study synthesizes its own useful critical analyses and informed conjectures together with a range of information about the conditions of authorship for women during Austen's life and selected references to current critical commentary on Austen's works. There is a generous amount of hard data—the circumstances governing the writing, who the publishers were, how many copies were sold, how much money was paid—but the handling of more abstract topics, such as Austen's tone, her sense of style, and her predilections in choosing topics and themes is especially adroit, with an astuteness and clarity well suited to its subject. Researchers will appreciate the extensive notes and ample index. Highly recommended for undergraduate and graduate libraries.—*T. Loe, SUNY College at Oswego*

WS-0505 PR4392 92-7873 CIP
Franklin, Caroline. **Byron's heroines.** Oxford, 1992. 280p bibl index ISBN 0-19-811230-0, $59.00

In this highly original book, Franklin examines Byron's heroines as cultural constructs emanating from the role of women in Regency Britain. In contrast to the well-known Byronic hero, who remains a fairly consistent character, Franklin explores the various manifestations of Byron's female characters. She shows Byron's ongoing concern with the issue of sexual role differentiation, both as an aristocratic critic of bourgeois society and as a Romantic writer who projects the feminine as the repressed lost self of an idealized masculinity. *Don Juan* is examined as a response to the contemporary debate on the role of women in society, and each of the women in the work is analyzed as a representative of this issue. Franklin's discussion of Manfred is especially interesting. In her discussion of Astarte, she moves beyond the well-known incest issue to consider Manfred's quest for Astarte as a desire to transcend the polarized sexual roles of dominance and submission. Although this is a fairly technical study, advanced readers interested in Byron's representations of women in the early 19th-century will find this book a worthy endeavor.—*M. S. Johnston, Mankato State University*

WS-0506 PR778 92-55127 CIP
Frawley, Maria H. **A wider range: travel writing by women in Victorian England.** Fairleigh Dickinson, 1994. (Dist. by Associated University Presses) 237p bibl index afp ISBN 0-8386-3544-X, $38.50

Victorian women travel writers were an intrepid group, and a comprehensive study of their exploits is certainly welcome. This author, however, also develops an ancillary modern cultural theme: that women used their travel writing to prepare themselves for further professional development and writing in other areas. It is a fresh approach and one that suggests many new interpretations of travel writing. Frawley succeeds in demonstrating the ways in which women's minds were opened during and after their travel. She also analyzes the work not only of the well-known names, but also the myriad of less well-known women who traveled to the four corners of the earth. The book is well written, meticulously researched, rich with evocative material, and valuable for its definitive bibliography. Academic and general audiences.—*R. T. Van Arsdel, emerita, University of Puget Sound*

WS-0507 Orig
Gordon, Lyndall. **Charlotte Brontë: a passionate life.** W.W. Norton, 1995 (c1994). 418p bibl index ISBN 0-393-03722-3, $27.50

Gordon (St. Hilda's College, Oxford) infers Brontë's states of mind from the Brontë sisters' writings more than from the autobiographical events they contain. Readers without close knowledge of the novels and poems will often find the allusiveness obscure and will be uncertain about the chronology of many sequences of actual events. Gordon brilliantly explains the bearing that Charlotte's relationship with her publisher George Smith had upon the character of Graham Bretton and upon the plot of *Villette* (1853), although it is not clear whether the cooling owed more to Smith's business responsibilities and the opposition of his mother or to Charlotte's great need that Smith show his interest by writing letters. Gordon's overall theory that Charlotte's basic need is for words—for example, in their aspect of preserving desire for future fulfillment—is also drawn on to explain the passionate correspondence with M. Heger as a deeply needed alternative to his person. Gordon emphasizes Charlotte's sense of her independent self and the self-sufficiency of her heroines, not her or their rebelliousness or sexuality; she says that Bertha Mason Rochester is *not* infused with "feminist sentiment." Illustrations. General and academic audiences.—*D. Kramer, University of Illinois at Urbana-Champaign*

WS-0508 PR115 92-5277 CIP
Gorsky, Susan Rubinow. **Femininity to feminism: women and literature in the nineteenth century.** Twayne, 1992. 213p bibl index afp ISBN 0-8057-8975-8, $22.95; ISBN 0-8057-8978-2 pbk, $13.95

Gorsky seeks to illuminate the nature of women's experience and the literature that both shaped and reflected that experience by considering women's "real" lives and their depiction in literature. To discuss women's political, social, and economic lives, Gorsky relies on a variety of secondary sources, presenting a general view of women's experience under many headings, from "Schools for Girls" to "Medicine." Gorsky then illustrates the treatment of each issue by references to literature of the times. The result is a curious mixture of social history and brief considerations of a very varied mix of fictional texts. There is no discussion of literary material in terms of its formal or affective design; events or characters in literature serve as examples of whatever theme brings them into the section. Texts used range widely from the popular and ephemeral to those that continue to represent some of the most searching examinations of women's experiences. The resulting flattening of literature diminishes the significance of the major texts and suggests a difficulty in Gorsky's approach. The author claims that literature both reflects and affects "reality," but since she does not indicate what about literature makes it a powerful agent for imaginative understanding—and even change—the book eventually becomes a repetitive catalog of subject headings and titles of published fiction.—*R. Nadelhaft, University of Maine at Orono*

WS-0509 PR4984 93-22864 CIP
Harriet Martineau in the London *Daily News*: **selected contributions, 1852-1866,** ed. by Elisabeth Sanders Arbuckle. Garland, 1994. 451p (Garland reference library of the humanities, 1600) index afp ISBN 0-8153-0835-3, $70.00

This anthology of articles, written by Martineau between 1852 and 1866 for the *Daily News*, will save scholars many trips to newspaper repositories. The editor, whose *Harriet Martineau's Letters to Fanny Wedgwood* appeared in 1983, sketches the history of the paper and Martineau's life. When she began her 14-year stint on the *Daily News* at age 50, Martineau was already a well-known reforming journalist, travel writer, novelist, and historian with philosophic interests. Isolated psychologically by deafness and geographically by residing in the Lake District, she often relied on *The Times*, sent by train from London, for her topics. Years of thinking about political and social issues, and her well-honed literary skills, enabled her to grasp and organize facts, and produce informed and imaginative responses to persons and events in the news. The 40 contributions collected here fall into five categories: concerns of women; social and economic issues, such as cholera, temperance, and railways; the Crimean War; British politics and foreign affairs; and American developments, including the anti-slavery movement. An appendix listing some 1,500 of her *Daily News* articles by date, subject, and first words is based on the work of R.K. Webb, whose biography of Martineau in 1960 came early in the revival of scholarly interest in her remarkable life. An index enriches this useful (if costly) compilation. Graduate; faculty.—*M. S. Vogeler, emeritus, California State University, Fullerton*

WS-0510 PR5398 94-18535 CIP
Hill-Miller, Katherine C. **"My hideous progeny": Mary Shelley, William Godwin, and the father-daughter relationship.** Delaware, 1995. (Dist. by Associated University Presses) 249p bibl index afp ISBN 0-87413-535-4, $38.50

In her introduction Hill-Miller notes that Mary Shelley's relationship with her husband, Percy Bysshe Shelley, has received more attention than her relationship with her father, William Godwin. She also says that "while commentators had analyzed Shelley's *Frankenstein* from almost every conceivable viewpoint, little was written about Shelley's lesser-known novels, in which father-daughter relationships play a key role." Hill-Miller's scholarly account demonstrates the importance of Shelley's relationship with her father in those "lesser-known novels." The author uses "incest" to refer "not to a physically intimate act but instead to the sexual, and therefore taboo, emotions that naturally and universally exist between fathers and daughters." Such emotions are central to *Mathilda*, *Lodore*, and *Falkner*. Hill-Miller is especially good on the allusions to *Oedipus* in *Mathilda* and to Shelley's use of Godwin's novels. For instance, *Falkner* is read as a revision of Godwin's *Deloraine* and as "the literary culmination" of the father-daughter relationship. Hill-Miller's work is informed by both the pertinent criticism on Shelley and "contemporary feminist revisions of psychoanalysis." Recommended for upper-division undergraduates and up.—*T. Ware, Queen's University at Kingston*

WS-0511   Can. CIP

Ingham, Patricia. **Dickens, women and language.** Toronto, 1992. 152p bibl index ISBN 0-8020-2891-8, $50.00; ISBN 0-8020-7760-9 pbk, $19.95

Many previous studies have focused on Dickens's female characters and his use of imagination, notably M. Slater's *Dickens and Women* (CH, Jul'83), but this is the first to make use of the modern critical approaches of linguistic and feminist analysis. Noting that Dickens's characters have been subjected more persistently to biographical comparison than those of other Victorian novelists, the author rejects the notion of relating them to Dickens's mother, wife, sisters-in-law, daughters, and mistress. Instead she "relocates such figures where they belong: in the text, and not in some specious hinterland behind it." To do this, she uses the first chapter to define her methodology of linguistic analysis and to "characterize the individual reworking by Dickens of images of women." Chapters that follow address: "nubile girls," (marriageable virgins with no knowledge of their attractiveness); "fallen girls," (fallen from nubile girlhood); "excessive females, "(wives and companions for their husbands); "passionate women," (adulteresses); and "true mothers," (nurturing and cherishing). A postscript ably analyzes Dickens's correspondence, showing the way in which he shifted his expressed views of various female members of his family until he developed entirely fictional "literary exemplars." A provocative study, well and clearly written, with a sensibly limited bibliography.—*R. Van Arsdel, emerita, University of Puget Sound*

WS-0512   PR4038   95-22180 CIP

Jane Austen and discourses on feminism, ed. by Devoney Looser. St. Martin's, 1995. 197p bibl index afp ISBN 0-312-12367-1, $39.95

Looser (Indiana State Univ.) has collected ten original essays on Jane Austen and feminism, some by established Austen scholars—e.g., Jocelyn Harris (author of *Jane Austen's Art of Memory*, CH, Jun'90), Glenda Hudson (*Sibling Love and Incest in Jane Austen's Fiction*, CH, May'92), and Laura Mooneyham (*Romance, Language, and Education in Jane Austen's Novels*, CH, Jul'88)—and some by newcomers. The collection does not seek to answer the troublesome question "Was Jane Austen a feminist?" but it addresses the historical and theoretical issues that form the contexts for that question. Part 1 considers Austen in historical and social context; part 2 "reassesses some of the central arguments (feminist and otherwise) in Austen criticism today"; and part 3 offers two feminist readings each for the "less-often-theorized novels" *Northanger Abbey* and *Mansfield Park*. The essays in the second part are especially interesting, including Laura Mooneyham White's analysis of the persistence of the marriage plot in Austen's novels, Jocelyn Harris's critique of Sandra Gilbert and Susan Gubar on Austen, and Glenda Hudson's assessment of "masculine and feminine values" in Austen's fiction. A welcome, though brief, addition to Jane Austen criticism. Upper-division undergraduate and above.—*R. R. Warhol, University of Vermont*

WS-0513   PR5114   94-3528 MARC

Jay, Elisabeth. **Mrs Oliphant, 'a fiction to herself': a literary life.** Oxford, 1995. 355p bibl index afp ISBN 0-19-812875-4, $39.95

WS-0513a   PR114   94-19751 CIP

Margaret Oliphant: critical essays on a gentle subversive, ed. by D.J. Trela. Susquehanna University, 1995. (Dist. by Associated University Presses) 190p index afp ISBN 0-945636-72-5, $33.50

These two titles treat a 19th-century writer whose elephantine corpus includes some 98 novels, 50 short stories, 25 works of nonfiction, more than 300 essays and reviews, and an autobiography (written between 1849 and 1899). Jay's life and critical commentary describes a woman who was a major presence in the 19th-century world of publishing, where she had to fight constantly against male domination. The relentless pace of her output, which supported children, nieces, a nephew, and her brothers, made her fiction uneven in quality. Writing several serialized novels simultaneously while also reviewing for *Blackwood's Magazine*, she compromised strong characterization, most notably of weak men (whom she observed firsthand in her own family), with slack plotting and melodramatic stereotyping. While conservatively upholding marriage and family life as women's destiny to satisfy the commercial market, she adeptly showed masculine misunderstanding, exploitation, and denial of women's sacrifices. As Jay (Roosevelt Univ.) makes evident, Oliphant's realism details the erosion of women's lives by a masculine-dominated society. Oliphant's reputation declined in the early 20th century, and Jay's patient recovery of Oliphant's ideas, analysis of the author's contemporary reputation, and somewhat daunting reference to literally dozens of novels puts Victorian scholars in her debt. The chapters "A Woman

of Letters"—showing tensions within Oliphant's work—and "The Women and Her Art"—appraising her style and voice—are particularly useful. Jay's non-linear approach seems appropriate for a career that circled and regrouped rather than progressed. The bibliography, chronology, and ample citations (including unpublished materials) provide solid ground for this needed major study of an author whose work is largely inaccessible now. Upper-division undergraduates and above.

Supplementing Jay's study is Trela's essay collection, which will be a helpful adjunct for graduate students and specialists. The subtitle, a *a Gentle Subversive*, suits this trenchant ironist who undercut sentimentality about marriage and domestic life. This collection of scholarly short studies written by respected feminist Victorian scholars includes Linda Peterson's account of Oliphant's recasting of the female bildungsroman and Esther Schor's discussion of Oliphant's supernatural fiction (she did *that* too). Thanks to these two volumes, Oliphant is now not merely a reference but a real presence who, but for her own busyness in supporting her dependents, might have been a major writer like George Eliot.—*R. E. Wiehe, University of Massachusetts at Lowell*

WS-0514   PR878   94-20113 CIP

Jenkins, Ruth Y. **Reclaiming myths of power: women writers and the Victorian spiritual crisis.** Bucknell, 1995. (Dist. by Associated University Presses) 200p bibl index afp ISBN 0-8387-5278-0, $35.00

Jenkins's meticulously researched volume seeks to evaluate the role of organized religion, particularly among the middle and upper classes, in reducing women to a subservient role in society. Jenkins (California State Univ., Fresno) tells us that "the Church marginalized women from spiritual power" and "women lived in a culture that revered an active life of good works and industry, but defined and evaluated the female by a passive model." The author examines the spiritual crises that this formula effected in the lives and careers of four Victorian women: Florence Nightingale, Charlotte Brontë, Elizabeth Gaskell, and George Eliot. Nightingale and Brontë claimed the individual's right to belief free from authority, but Gaskell and Eliot designed an alternative ethical vision based on the individual's benevolent relation to her community through charitable acts. These views are traced through critical analysis of the works of the three novelists and of Nightingale's writings on revisionist theology. The afterword examines the qualities of hymns written by 19th-century women. This original and thought-provoking study draws on both modern feminist criticism and such Victorian commentators as Sarah Stickney Ellis. The book could serve as a useful seminar text and is recommended for academic collections at the upper-division undergraduate level and above.—*R. T. Van Arsdel, emerita, University of Puget Sound*

WS-0515   PR4036   91-41186 CIP

Kaplan, Deborah. **Jane Austen among women.** Johns Hopkins, 1992. 245p index afp ISBN 0-8018-4360-X, $29.95

To be at once "feminist yet historically informed," Kaplan mines little-read letters and diaries by Austen's friends and neighbors as well as conduct books to elaborate two conflicting "cultures" in which women around 1800 participated: a larger, patriarchal "gentry culture" and a narrower, homosocial, potentially subversive "women's culture," sustained in families, and by letters and visits. Kaplan proceeds to find these two cultures at play first in Austen's life and then in her works, in readings of the juvenilia, the "middle" pieces *Lady Susan* and *The Watsons*, and finally *Pride and Prejudice*. She is most persuasive in showing how fully, in both spheres, Austen accepted "gentry ideology"; evidence for the voice of subversion is thin. Kaplan speculates that Austen eschewed marriage precisely to follow her vocation as novelist, and finds her middle works, written for family and friends, most ideologically innovative; the great novels, intended for a wider public, abandon this early promise, though occasionally—as in the sprightly voice of Elizabeth Bennet, a displacement of the voice of "women's culture" into the public sphere—Austen does hint a feminist critique. Graduate and advanced undergraduate.—*D. L. Patey, Smith College*

WS-0516   PR4681   94-37436 CIP

Karl, Frederick R. **George Eliot, voice of a century: a biography.** W.W. Norton, 1995. 708p index ISBN 0-393-03785-1, $30.00

Toward the end of this biography, Karl notes that "we have little sense of [Eliot's] internal world." This is a serious problem for a biography of a powerfully intellectual and creative person; Karl's compensatory strategy is to interweave great amounts of day-to-day details with quick summaries of the intellectual concerns and historical and social events of the 19th century. Karl implicitly contends that little in Eliot's writing is not either a direct or a transmuted reflection of her life events and contemporary pressures; he demonstrates that the attributes of such as Adam, Maggie, Dorothea, and Gwendolen can be compassed without special psychological pleading. Since Gordon Haight's biography *George Eliot* (CH, Dec'69), several useful revaluations have appeared—Ruby Redinger's *George Eliot: The Emergent Self* (CH, Dec'75), Ina Taylor's *A Woman of Contradictions: The Life of George Eliot* (CH, Jun'90), Rosemarie Bodenheimer's *The Real Life of Mary Ann Evans* (CH, Apr'95), and others. Karl's account supersedes all previous studies in its range of coverage and in its mature common sense and lucid insights, even if these suffer in comparison with Eliot's own—lacking her warm dispassionate empathy and brilliance and her surgical phrasing. Also, Karl's emphases are curious: he gives a more careful sustained analysis of John Cross's leap into the Grand Canal than of the reasons Eliot began to write fiction. Though overlong (and in small print!), this astute book warrants attention from the general as well as the scholarly reader.—*D. Kramer, University of Illinois at Urbana-Champaign*

WS-0517   PR878   94-29336 CIP
Kranidis, Rita S. **Subversive discourse: the cultural production of late Victorian feminist novels.** St. Martin's, 1995. 143p bibl index ISBN 0-312-10739-0, $39.95

This slender volume analyzes fiction by women in the last two decades of the 19th century and protests that though novels by women "could be seen to have some cultural value, feminist novels were not seen to possess it as 'fine literature.'" Kranidis discusses the impact of social and political change in late Victorian culture and deals with such subjects as "high and low culture" and "new journalism." One chapter assesses publishing and women in the literary marketplace and another looks at the feminist writers' "mission" (to "assail and dismantle the privileged [male] authorial and cultural perspective and the ensuing categorization concerning literary value"). Kranidis also discusses unconventional female characters created by such male writers as George Gissing, George Moore, George Meredith, and Henry James. Though this book is intelligently researched and the bibliography up-to-date with modern feminist scholarship, this reviewer wonders how a book that refers often to the "new journalism" fails to mention Joel Wiener's authoritative *Papers for the Millions: The New Journalism in Britain, 1850s to 1914* (1988). Nor does the author appear to have consulted Karl Beckson's *London in the 1890s* (CH, Oct'93) or *The 1890s: An Encyclopedia of British Literature, Art, and Culture*, ed. by G.A. Cevasco (CH, Dec'93). This book will no doubt promote discussion, both agreement and challenge, among the graduate students it targets.—*R. T. Van Arsdel, emerita, University of Puget Sound*

WS-0518   Orig
Lane, Maggie. **Jane Austen and food.** Hambledon, 1995. 184p bibl index afp ISBN 1-85285-124-4, $35.00

Every so often, an author publishes a book simple in concept yet fresh, witty, and insightful. The reader marvels at the ingenuity and ponders why no one thought of this before. Such is the case with Lane's study of Austen's attitudes toward eating, food preparation, housekeeping, hospitality, social class, and gender. Admitting the topic of food is "merely background," Lane delivers substantive analysis of characters and describes how Austen's evaluation of their moral worth is based on how they eat, keep house, and entertain. Austen's own feelings about food appear ambiguous because most of her protagonists (with the exception of Emma) disregard it; however, in her letters, Austen thoroughly enjoyed writing about food. Author of *Jane Austen's Family* (1984) and *Jane Austen's England* (CH, Mar'87), Lane uses a sociological approach in bringing together letters, novels, family papers, 18th-century cookbooks, and histories. Most interesting is the chapter "Gender and Greed," in which Lane employs a feminist approach to food and writes that "Austen is quite clear that both sexes must be allowed the full play of their moral autonomy and that a healthy society values equally the contributions each can make." Recommended for general readers and scholars.—*J. L. Thorndike, Lakeland College*

WS-0519   92-60971 Orig
Leighton, Angela. **Victorian women poets: writing against the heart.** University Press of Virginia, 1992. 321p bibl index ISBN 0-8139-1426-4, $45.00; ISBN 0-8139-1427-2 pbk, $14.95

Although studies of Victorian women writers have preceded this one—e.g., K. Hickok's *Representations of Women* (CH, Dec'84), E. Moers's *Literary Women* (1963), E. Showalter's *A Literature of Their Own* (CH, Nov'77), and S. Gilbert and S. Gubar's *The Madwoman in the Attic* (CH, Jan'80)—few have concentrated on little-known or forgotten Victorian women poets. Notable exceptions are, of course, Elizabeth Barrett Browning and Christina Rossetti, well-known poets whom Leighton features in this book. Leighton also examines Felicia Hemans, Letitia Elizabeth Landon (L.E.L.), Augusta Webster, Michael Field, Alice Meynell, and Charlotte Mew. Perhaps most striking is Leighton's chapter on Michael Field, a writer who in fact was two writers, Katherine Bradley and her niece, Edith Cooper. These remarkable women, relatives, loving friends, and collaborative poets, produced poetry for more than 40 years. They counted among their acquaintances many major male figures of their day. Yet today "Michael Field" is a name almost no one knows. Augusta Webster dropped quickly into oblivion although known and admired by many contemporaries. And Charlotte Mew, who died as recently as 1928, is presented as "a love poet who, at some level, has ceased to believe in love," once again stimulating the reader's interest. Well researched and carefully documented, highly readable and informative, Leighton's contribution is an important source for feminist critics as well as for anyone interested in discovering more about once-significant Victorian women poets—who might well become so once again.—*V. L. Radley, SUNY College at Oswego*

WS-0520   PR4886   92-41443 CIP
Levy, Amy. **The complete novels and selected writings of Amy Levy, 1861-1889,** ed. by Melvyn New. University Press of Florida, 1993. 566p afp ISBN 0-8130-1199-X, $49.95; ISBN 0-8130-1200-7 pbk, $24.95

Levy, from a cultured, Orthodox Jewish family, matriculated at Newnham College, Cambridge. At 28, she died by her own hand, leaving a considerable literary legacy for one so young. This volume reprints her three novels: *The Romance of a Shop* (1888); *Reuben Sachs: a Sketch* (1889); and *Miss Meredith* (1889). *Reuben Sachs* may be of most interest because of the accusation, on its publication, that it was antisemitic. Levy published widely in periodicals of the 1880s, including *Temple Bar, Cambridge Review, Gentleman's Magazine*, the *Jewish Chronicle*, and Oscar Wilde's *Woman's World*. Wilde thought highly of her opinions, which were of a feminist cast, and her talent, which he described as marked by "sincerity, directness, and melancholy." In an able and insightful introduction, the editor asserts that Levy's work deserves a modern audience, pointing out the breadth of her learning across various disciplines and the sharpness of her perception of human nature. He concludes that *Reuben Sachs*, rare and out of print today, is suitable as a text for a course examining Jewish fiction of the late 19th century, because "it raised numerous questions about the despair of an educated Jewish woman in late Victorian England." Advanced undergraduate; graduate; faculty.—*R. T. Van Arsdel, emerita, University of Puget Sound*

WS-0521   PR4891   94-12992 CIP
Loudon, Jane (Webb). **The mummy!: a tale of the twenty-second century,** introd. and abridgment by Alan Rauch. Michigan, 1994. 299p afp ISBN 0-472-09574-9, $42.50; ISBN 0-472-06574-2 pbk, $16.95

The Mummy is Loudon's only novel; she was then a 23-year-old British author who went on to write nonfiction, mainly about gardening. Its date, 1827, puts it in the Romantic Period. Rauch, in his introduction, suggests it should be seen as an optimistic version of Mary Shelley's *The Last Man*, published the previous year. The novel itself is a combination of ingredients: (1) the Gothic novel, with an Egyptian emphasis; (2) futuristic science fiction—robot doctors, lawyers, and judges, a tunnel for walking beneath the Irish Sea, transportation by balloons; (3) a complicated love story, with three happy and two unhappy endings; and (4) various political and military matters, including an elective queenship in England and an Irish conquest of Spain. The revival of the pharaoh Cheops seems to be by electric shock near the beginning of the novel but is said to have been supernatural at the end. There is much moralizing by the author and the characters. Rauch's shortening of the book is not indicated in a scholarly manner, but his preface suggests he cut about one-ninth; at one point, two persons are promoted/demoted for actions omitted from a previous battle. The full text is necessary for advanced research, but this should do for undergraduate work on science fiction, women's studies (stereotypical roles despite the queendom), and 19th-century studies. For large or specialized collections.—*J. R. Christopher, Tarleton State University*

WS-0522 PR5238 95-16345 Orig
Marsh, Jan. **Christina Rossetti: a writer's life.** Viking, 1995 (c1994).
634p bibl index afp ISBN 0-670-83517-X, $29.95

As she does in her earlier studies of Pre-Raphaelites, e.g., *Pre-Raphaelite Women* (CH, May'88), Marsh here builds on strong foundations of pertinent primary and secondary documents, which she assimilates with authoritative control and considerable verve. The all-too-familiar solemn, reclusive, exceedingly religious Christina (who earlier scholars have revealed as harboring intense, repressed passions for several men) appears here as a wholly human (and humane), temperamental, humorous woman in daily life (especially in her early years) and a dedicated author of considerable artistic accomplishment. Here, too, the reader finds a female poet who is given just dues in terms of a tradition of Victorian poetry by women, from E.B. Browning onward. Brother William Rosetti's long-honored reticences in his many chronicles of his family and friends, which kept Christina's true stature from emerging, are here replaced with considered views of individuals' personal lives and artistic endeavors. Some readers will not like the psychoanalytic approach to Christina's writings, but it is illuminating. All collections.—*B. F. Fisher IV, University of Mississippi*

WS-0523 PR4681 91-13710 CIP
McSweeney, Kerry. **George Eliot (Marian Evans): a literary life.** St. Martin's, 1991. 156p bibl index ISBN 0-312-06574-4, $35.00

This is a notable addition to the St. Martin's series "Literary Lives." Aiming at the general reader, as well as at undergraduate and graduate students, McSweeney traces Eliot's development as an artist, enlacing his account of each novel with the biographical events and social context which it transmutes, an account he enhances with aptly chosen quotations from other critics. Moreover he deftly introduces Eliot's own theories of fiction at appropriate points, and with unobtrusive skill reveals how her philosophical ideas, scientific lore, and historical knowledge are embodied in her poetry and fiction. He summarizes, judges, and suggests; his guide to further reading sends the student to (with hardly an exception) the best scholarship and criticism of Eliot's life and works available. Full of admiration for Eliot's best work (as in *Middlemarch*), he is firmly specific about what he judges to be her failures (as in parts of *Daniel Deronda*) and the reasons therefor. He writes a lucid, readable style, mercifully free of current critical jargon, and has produced an admirable introduction to the work of this great, insurgent, Victorian novelist. Adequately indexed.—*J. W. Bicknell, emeritus, Drew University*

WS-0524 PR468 92-22902 CIP
Mellor, Anne K. **Romanticism and gender.** Routledge, 1993. 275p bibl index ISBN 0-415-90111-1, $49.95; ISBN 0-415-90664-4 pbk, $14.95

Mellor argues lucidly and compellingly that "our current descriptions of Romanticism are unwittingly gender-biased"; that "the highly selective group of texts, almost all poems, almost all written by men" we designate as British Romantic literature largely excludes not only the works of the many women writers of the era but also female values and concerns. Drawing upon the writings of Wollstonecraft, Austen, Radcliffe, and Dorothy Wordsworth, among others (including Keats and Emily Brontë as "ideological cross-dressers"), Mellor shows how such writers offer implicit and explicit critiques of the portrayal of gender in canonical Romantic texts. She describes this alternative vision as "feminine Romanticism," an ideology celebrating rationality and responsibility over passion, the family as a political model over the patriarchy, and a relational, subjective notion of the self over the egotistical sublime. This important book challenges, qualifies, and expands our understanding of British romanticism. Highly recommended for undergraduate and graduate collections.—*C. Walker, Carleton College*

WS-0525 PR115 92-45186 CIP
Mermin, Dorothy. **Godiva's ride: women of letters in England, 1830-1880.** Indiana, 1993. 181p bibl index afp ISBN 0-253-33749-6, $35.00; ISBN 0-253-20824-6 pbk, $12.95

This book begins by comparing 19th-century British women authors with the legendary figure of Lady Godiva, whose "powerlessness is her power, her nakedness her shield." The book explores the now-familiar paradoxes raised by women's having published their work in a Victorain world where they were

supposed to restrict their activities to the private realm. In a highly condensed, clear, and readable form, Mermin outlines the history of Victorian women's writing, drawing on biographical details from the lives of the Brontës, E.B. Browning, George Eliot, Elizabeth Gaskell and others. In addition to sketching out women's contributions to Victorian fiction and poetry, the book surveys the impact of religion and science—among other cultural influences—upon female authors. Acknowledging the constraints that social and cultural conditions placed upon Victorian women, Mermin argues that those same conditions also "gave impetus, energy and significant form to women's writing." This brief study should be enormously helpful to students seeking an introduction to feminist approaches to Victorian writers. Undergraduate; graduate; general.—*R. R. Warhol, University of Vermont*

WS-0526 PR878.W6 90-32879 CIP
Morris, Virginia B. **Double jeopardy: women who kill in Victorian fiction.** University Press of Kentucky, 1990. 182p index afp ISBN 0-8131-1751-8, $20.00

Morris argues that women's homicidal violence in Victorian fiction emerges from "the abuse they suffered at the hands of the men they killed." Women killers thus "do not subvert masculine control; they assault it." After quick but helpful chapters on earlier fictions and Victorian legal theory and practice, the study offers individual thematic readings of works by Dickens, Eliot, Braddon, Collins, and Conan Doyle. Morris's methodology combines interdisciplinary and new critical approaches. *Double Jeopardy* is informed by relevant scholarship—Boyle and Hughes, Auerbach and Showalter. Some insights are useful: Morris contextualizes Hardy's Tess as a victim of domestic violence who fights back. But others are timid and familiar, as if to review for those seated after intermission: "Mothering was highly valued in Victorian England as a woman's most critical contribution to the family and to the society at large." These simple observations seem to flatten out the prose. The study is straightforward and fast-moving, and therefore recommended for public, community college, and undergraduate libraries.—*B. Kalikoff, University of Puget Sound*

WS-0527 PR4037 90-48428 CIP
Mukherjee, Meenakshi. **Jane Austen.** St. Martin's, 1991. 167p bibl index ISBN 0-312-05794-6, $24.95

Though her novels have consistently received critical attention, Jane Austen's contributions have never been "assessed according to her sex" asserts this brief, highly focused study-an imbalance it seeks to correct. Part of the problem of employing such a critical approach is that Austen's ironic narrative stances and parodic structures often render her own perspectives elusive and, since she has been a canonical figure so long, it is difficult to see her now as more than a crypto-feminist. Such questions are clearly raised and addressed, however, along with issues such as Austen's handling of marriage, narrative closure, class, and her connections with other female writers. More specific attributes especially rewarded by a feminist reading, like the desirability of physical strength, the sense of space and enclosure, or modes of secrecy and concealment, are examined as well. The tone is balanced and scholarly, and the assertions substantiated by frequent reference to novels and a range of criticism. Missing elements and irregularities in the bibliography will cause researchers problems; the index is too sparse. Recommended for undergraduate and graduate libraries.—*T. Loe, SUNY College at Oswego*

WS-0528 PR878 95-10932 CIP
Nord, Deborah Epstein. **Walking the Victorian streets: women, representation, and the city.** Cornell, 1995. 270p bibl index afp ISBN 0-8014-3196-4, $39.95

Nord (Princeton) poses the question: "If the rambler [in the 19th century] was a man, and if one of the primary tropes of his urban description was the woman of the streets, could there have been a *female* spectator or a vision of the urban panorama crafted by a female imagination?" Her study provides not only an affirmative answer to this question but also a lively picture of the denizens of the Victorian streets that is more inclusive, chronologically and thematically, than related studies by such recent social historians as Judith Walkowitz (*City of Dreadful Delight*, 1992) and Martha Vicinus (*Independent Women*, CH, Dec'85). Furthermore, Nord argues that the "particular urban vision of the female observer, novelist, or investigator derives from her consciousness of transgression and trespassing ...." Discussions of "urban observers" include such writers as De Quincey, Lamb, Elizabeth Gaskell, Dickens, and Beatrice Webb (who, like other female writers, assumed a "disguise" to observe women "at work"). Nord's readable, illuminating study sheds light on the Victorian woman in the street as "tainted" by her gender, whether prostitute or respectable middle-class woman. Recommended on all academic levels.—*K. Beckson, Brooklyn College, CUNY*

WS-0529 PR878 93-30912 CIP
Nunokawa, Jeff. **The afterlife of property: domestic security and the Victorian novel.** Princeton, 1994. 152p bibl index afp ISBN 0-691-03320-X, $24.95

Nunokawa's highly focused study has only 124 pages of text and treats only four representative Victorian novels (*Little Dorrit*, *Dombey and Son*, *Daniel Deronda*, and *Silas Marner*), but nonetheless fully articulates an issue that should be crucial to studies of 19th-century fiction—the idea of women as commodity. It is a deft and creative analysis that makes an informed use of a variety of different historical, political, socioeconomic, and gender-oriented critical sources. Nunokawa's concern is to elaborate upon the diverse refractions that the capitalist consciousness takes in these narratives regarding women, not only in terms of "the market and marketable property," but also in other "forms of capital ... beyond the cash nexus," especially in the notion of women as "safe property." Such sophisticated cultural concepts can be elusive or difficult to define, but this study is thoughtfully written and well organized—making a thoroughly convincing exegesis and argument. Readers with some familiarity with contemporary literary and cultural theory will benefit the most: for upper-division undergraduates and above. Skimpy index, useful notes and list of works cited.— *T. Loe, SUNY College at Oswego*

WS-0530 PR5398 92-14568 CIP
The Other Mary Shelley: beyond *Frankenstein*, ed. by Audrey A. Fisch, Anne K. Mellor, and Esther H. Schor. Oxford, 1993. 300p index afp ISBN 0-19-507740-7, $49.95

These 14 essays (all but one written for this volume) exemplify the changing critical fortunes of Mary Shelley, once neglected or treated as a writer who had almost accidentally produced a single odd masterpiece, but now taken seriously as a major author, with increasing attention being accorded her other works. This critical rediscovery stems in large part from the work of feminist scholars who see Shelley as a trenchant critic of her culture and, in particular, of the excesses of Romantic individualism. Both established scholars and younger critics are represented in these essays, and the overall quality is high. S. Wolfson demonstrates the important role Mary played as editor of Percy Shelley's works, arguing persuasively that it was she who defined her husband and his canon for subsequent readers. P. Cantor illuminatingly reads Shelley's tale "Transformation" as a response to Byron's unfinished *The Deformed Transformed* and a critique of the darker side of Romanticism. M. Paley and Fisch offer contrasting readings of Shelley's apocalyptic novel *The Last Man*—Paley seeing an ironic rebuke to Romantic optimism, and Fisch viewing Shelley's novel of a devastating plague in terms of our contemporary plague, AIDS. One caveat: several essays are marred by excessive indulgence in critical jargon, thus effectively limiting their audience to a tiny academic elite. Recommended for graduate-level collections in Romanticism and women's studies.—*K. P. Mulcahy, Rutgers, The State University of New Jersey, New Brunswick*

WS-0531 PR4687.3 89-20474 CIP
Perkin, J. Russell. **A reception-history of George Eliot's fiction.** UMI, 1990. 197p bibl index afp ISBN 0-8357-2011-X, $39.95

Perkin's intelligent, well-written study of critical reactions to George Eliot's fiction fills a gap in George Eliot studies. Perkin's aim is to place Eliot criticism in the context of reception theory as formulated by the contemporary German critic Hans Robert Jauss. A lucid introduction explains Jauss's theories, which are then applied to the reception of George Eliot's fiction. Chapter 2, "George Eliot in the 1850s," concentrates on Adam Bede and Scenes of Clerical Life, Chapter 3, "The Reception of Daniel Deronda," is largely confined to British reviews. Henry James and Virginia Woolf are the focus of Chapter 4, F.R. Leavis and Barbara Hardy, the focus of Chapter 5. Chapter 6 surveys "Marxists Reading George

Eliot," i.e., Felix Holt. Feminist and deconstructive approaches to Middlemarch preoccupy the final chapter. In addition to detailed notes, and a selective unannotated bibliography, there is an index. In spite of omissions (*Romola* and *Silas Marner* receive short-shrift), a concentration on British criticism, and some misprints, Perkin's study is strongly recommended for graduate students, faculty, and upper-division undergraduate students.—*W. Baker, Northern Illinois University*

WS-0532 PR1286 95-24400 CIP
Prose by Victorian women: an anthology, ed. by Andrea Broomfield and Sally Mitchell. Garland, 1996. 729p (Garland reference library of the humanities, 1893) afp ISBN 0-8153-1970-3, $75.00; ISBN 0-8153-1967-3 pbk, $24.95

This book includes 35 essays (first published 1824-98) by 16 authors. Edited mostly by Mitchell's graduate students at Temple Univ., the essays include introductions, bibliographies, and notes. Like *Victorian Women Poets*, ed. by Angela Leighton and Margaret Reynolds (1995), and the three-volume *The Woman Question*, by Elizabeth Helsinger, Robin Sheets, and William Veeder (CH, Feb'84), this book makes available writings that are valuable for 19th-century studies. It includes some familiar works (by Harriet Martineau and George Eliot), but its special contribution is its representation of work by less familiar writers, including Lady Elizabeth Eastlake and Vernon Lee. Some of the essays (including Mary Russell Mitford's) are important chiefly for literary reasons, but others are interesting in connection with social issues, including race, economics, and "the woman question" (e.g., Sarah Grand's "The New Woman and the Old," Alison Caird's "The Morality of Marriage," and Frances Power Cobbe's "Wife-Torture in England"). Like *Victorian Britain: An Encyclopedia*, also edited by Mitchell (CH, May'89), this book is an important resource for upper-division undergraduates and specialists alike. Strongly recommended for all academic libraries.—*T. Hoagwood, Texas A&M University*

WS-0533 PR878.C513 90-10758 MARC
Reynolds, Kimberley. **Girls only?: gender and popular children's fiction in Britain, 1880-1910.** Temple, 1990. 182p bibl index ISBN 0-87722-737-3, $24.95

The author traces the development of a subgenre, girls' fiction, and its readership. For contrast, boys' fiction is also analyzed. Both subgenres are related to societal expectations for passive femininity and dominant masculinity during Victorian and Edwardian times. Although the conclusion strikes at the idea that historical children's literature affects our understanding of today's fiction for young people and their development of sexual identity, this concept lacks development. The author is a lecturer at Ealing College of Higher Education. She evaluates authors for girls such as L.T. Meade and E.E. Green, and discusses G.A. Henty and R.B. Reed as writers perpetuating male standards. However, the best contribution is the analysis of periodicals: *The Boy's Own Paper* and *The Girl's Own Paper*. For academic libraries with historical, British literature collections. Notes and bibliography are thorough.—*H. F. Stein, Spoon River College*

WS-0534 FR878 93-27468 CIP
Reynolds, Kimberley. **Victorian heroines: representations of femininity in nineteenth-century literature and art,** by Kimberley Reynolds and Nicola Humble. New York University, 1994 (c1993). 195p bibl index ISBN 0-8147-7361-3, $40.00; ISBN 0-8147-7362-1 pbk, $16.95

In this provocative feminist interpretation of the Victorian heroine, Reynolds and Humble postulate a traditional dichotomy between the "angel in the house" and the sexually aware—and therefore depraved—woman, only to offer a revisionist reading: that women with explicitly erotic sensibilities were protagonists in the fiction of Charlotte Brontë, Braddon, Eliot, and Collins, and subjects in paintings by Alma-Tadema, Leighton, and Albert Moore, among others. So lightweight a "straw woman" is easy to knock down; yet there is merit in their reading, which compels readers to feel the impact of Victorian feminine sensuality. The authors are equally tendentious in reading masculine autobiography as bildungsroman but feminine autobiography as less egocentric and linear. No short work can encompass the Victorian, of course, but this book disregards both recent scholarship—e.g., Richard Jenkyns's *Dignity and Decadence* (CH, Nov'92)—as to neoclassicism and femininity, and major primary sources (e.g., Thackeray, Trollope, Christina Rossetti, and periodical literature). The reader must also cope with misspellings, a miscounting of Collins's children, and a reversed cover illustration. Advanced undergraduate; graduate; faculty.—*D. Rutenberg, University of South Florida*

WS-0535 PR4711 91-42287 CIP
Schor, Hilary M. **Scheherezade in the marketplace: Elizabeth Gaskell and the Victorian novel.** Oxford, 1992. 236p index afp ISBN 0-19-507388-6, $29.95

Previous studies have depicted Gaskell as an amateur, writing to assuage her grief at losing a son, and as a nonprofessional observer outraged at social injustice. Schor argues that Gaskell consciously wrote for publication and coveted the opportunity to be a "public voice." Gaskell is shown to be very much a woman of her time, influenced by Wordsworth, Darwin, and Pre-Raphaelite aesthetics, and capable of standing up to Charles Dickens in publication matters. Schor seeks to separate Gaskell from so-called "domestic" fiction (safe, easy, and comfortable) and to show her as familiar with the problems of industrialization and able to tackle controversial subjects such as prostitution and working-class politics. The first of the book's three sections analyzes *Mary Barton* (1848) and *Ruth* (1853) in terms of variations on the conventions of narrative and literary apprenticeship; the second discusses *Cranford* (1883) and *North and South* (1855) to assess conditions of publication; and the third turns to *Sylvia's Lovers* (1863) and *Wives and Daughters* (1866) to study authorial questions confronting Gaskell. Schor freely acknowledges her debt to Marxist and feminist critics. A provocative study, marred only by the lack of a bibliography and excessive use of the first-person pronoun. This is certainly a different picture from that painted by Winifred Gérin in her definitive *Elizabeth Gaskell* (CH, Dec'76).—*R. Van Arsdel, emerita, University of Puget Sound*

WS-0536 PR4692 93-13641 CIP
Semmel, Bernard. **George Eliot and the politics of national inheritance.** Oxford, 1994. 168p index afp ISBN 0-19-508567-1, $39.95; ISBN 0-19-508657-0 pbk, $16.95

Semmel, an outstanding historian at City University of New York, here enters the field of literary criticism with considerable success. The George Eliot he presents emerges as less a liberal than we are used to—not a Positivist so much as a Burkean conservative whose primary concern in her mature fiction was preserving the English identity by celebrating its cultural and social heritage in the face of the bewildering changes which were transforming 19th-century English life. Where Suzanne Graver had argued in *George Eliot and Community* (CH, Oct'84) that Eliot sought to create a new community through her readers, Semmel's point is more that, for Eliot, this community already existed. Good notes and index. Recommended for academic collections, lower-division undergraduate through faculty.—*M. Minor, Morehead State University*

WS-0537 PR4757 92-716 CIP
The sense of sex: feminist perspectives on Hardy, ed. by Margaret R. Higonnet. Illinois, 1993. 270p index afp ISBN 0-252-01940-7, $42.50; ISBN 0-252-06260-4 pbk, $15.95

This collection of 13 essays by well-established Victorian/Edwardian authorities such as Knoepflmacher and Kincaid, is also cosmopolitan in nature, drawing on the work of scholars from Australia, eastern and western Canada, and Germany, in addition to those from the US. The book seeks to analyze the novels of Thomas Hardy, applying the theories of modern feminist criticism, with its strong emphasis on gender studies; and attempts to assess the multiple meanings readers attach to and construct through sex. The collection builds on three basic premises: (1) that feminist criticism offers "formidable tools for the study of texts by men"; (2) that "gender study is not a domain of or about women"; and (3) that one must examine the codes of both masculinity and feminity because "the grammar of gender regulates the construction of texts." Hardy's work is particularly suited to this type of examination because he wrote when there was much debate about the myth of the so-called New Woman, toward which his attitude was ambivalent. A number of critical tools are employed in this study: gender analysis, new historicism, psychoanalysis and film studies, theories of ideology and discourse. Analysis tends to center on *Tess of the d'Urbervilles* and *Jude the Obscure,* but eight additional Hardy novels are considered. Those committed

to the theories of feminist criticism might well find this stimulating; traditionalists may find it less satisfactory.—*R. T. Van Arsdel, emerita, University of Puget Sound*

WS-0538 PR5238 95-40019 CIP
Smulders, Sharon. **Christina Rossetti revisited.** Twayne/Prentice Hall International, 1996. 183p (TEAS, 517) bibl index afp ISBN 0-8057-7050-X, $22.95

Interest in Victorian author Christina Rossetti has grown steadily in recent years, as evidenced by such studies as Anthony Harrison's *Christina Rossetti in Context* (CH, Jun'88), Kathleen Jones's *Learning Not to Be First: The Life of Christina Rossetti* (1992), Jan Marsh's *Christina Rossetti: A Literary Biography* (1994), and Dolores Rosenblum's *Christina Rossetti: The Poetry of Endurance* (CH, Sep'87). Smulders's book continues this critical inquiry, serving as a fine introduction to the elusive writer's life and work. The author gives a good reading of Rossetti's most famous poem, "Goblin Market," placing it in the context of the group of writers and artists known as the Pre-Raphaelite Brotherhood. But more important, she stresses how Rossetti is an author who should be known for more than just one poem. She gives a thorough analysis of many other Rossetti poems and fictional works (the latter a category almost entirely neglected by most critics). Recommended for collections of poetry and fiction criticism at the upper-division undergraduate level and above.—*L. J. Parascandola, Long Island University—Brooklyn Campus*

WS-0539 PR4757 94-46928 CIP
Stave, Shirley A. **The decline of the goddess: nature, culture, and women in Thomas Hardy's fiction.** Greenwood, 1995. 165p (Contributions to the study of world literature, 63) bibl index afp ISBN 0-313-29566-2, $49.95

Tracing archetypal patterns in Hardy's Wessex novels, Stave focuses on *Far from the Madding Crowd, The Return of the Native, The Woodlanders, Tess of the D'Urbervilles,* and *Jude the Obscure.* The author examines Hardy's two world views and his adaptation of the dualistic tension between agrarian and industrial life, pagan and Christian principles. She illustrates how the earth goddess is gradually defeated in the novels by messianic biblical narratives, which generate such features as frightening ecclesiastical figures, rustics with agency, gender revisionism, and the eventual destruction of the pagan goddess via the triumph of Victorian sexual and social ethics. This detailed, densely written, and challenging work picks up on such earlier scholarship as Merryn Williams's *Thomas Hardy and Rural England* (CH, Jan'73), Marlene Springer's *Hardy's Use of Allusion* (CH, Feb'84), and Rosemarie Morgan's *Women and Sexuality in the Novels of Thomas Hardy* (CH, Nov'88). It is a forceful discussion built on contemporary critical precepts and is recommended to advanced readers of Hardy, the Victorian novel, and women's or gender studies scholars. Helpful chapter notes. All academic collections.—*S. A. Parker, Hiram College*

WS-0540 PR4038 92-39954 CIP
Stewart, Maaja A. **Domestic realities and imperial fictions: Jane Austen's novels in eighteenth-century contexts.** Georgia, 1993. 209p bibl index afp ISBN 0-8203-1540-0, $35.00

Writing from the perspective of "post-structural feminist and colonial theories," Stewart reads Austen's novels for the responses of women to the disruption of paternalistic conventions during the expansion of the British Empire. She identifies her entry to her subject as "the narrative in her [Austen's] novels that depicts the struggles for mastery between the older son and the younger sons ... who return after a circuit in international trade ... to contest the supremacy of their hitherto privileged brother." During the male struggle for supremacy, Austen's women respond by making the traditional country home a maternal domestic space that masks colonial aggression with new models of female virtue and subjectivity. Stewart's reading of Austen's novels reveals a context of aggressive male behavior and female response that adds historical and literary dimension to them and to their author. The book includes an introduction and a bibliography of works cited. Recommended for scholars of Jane Austen, collections of women's studies, and graduate libraries. Advanced undergraduate; graduate; faculty.—*W. W. Waring, emeritus, Kalamazoo College*

WS-0541   PR4194   94-14198 CIP
Stone, Marjorie. **Elizabeth Barrett Browning.** St. Martin's, 1995. 254p bibl index ISBN 0-312-12210-1, $24.95

Convincing, well-written, Stone's book details Elizabeth Barrett Browning's daring poetic experiments, which challenged the status quo of a male-centered ideology, frequently with subversive discourse. Stone (Dalhousie Univ.) relates EBB to Romanticism and to contemporary women writers such as Gaskell; examines neglected manuscripts; discusses EBB's poetic development; and critiques individual works. For example, her *A Drama of Exile* (1845) shifts from the dominant male to the female perspective and draws on Prometheus, the fire thief of Aeschylus; Milton's destructive Satan; and Byron's Cain. Because of the heroism and tragedy of the form, the ballads circumvent the Victorian stereotype of the pure, self-sacrificing heroine as the strong, angry protagonist rejects the role men have designed for her. *Aurora Leigh* (1857) presents the heroine as a poet-prophet, like those drawn by Victorian male poets. Stone's final and most interesting chapter details the development of the myth that EBB's only significance is her influence on Robert Browning. The author redefines EBB's place in Victorian literature and counters the male-oriented view that relegates the poet to minor status. Upper-division undergraduate; graduate; researcher.— *M. S. Stephenson, University of Texas at Brownsville*

WS-0542   PR5716   90-38878 CIP
Sutherland, John. **Mrs Humphry Ward: eminent Victorian, pre-eminent Edwardian.** Oxford, 1990. 432p bibl index ISBN 0-19-818587-1, $29.95

This absorbing and beautifully written biography charts the life of Mrs. Humphry Ward (nee Mary Arnold, 1851-1920), from her marriage to an obscure Oxford tutor to international acclaim as a novelist, commanding great wealth and social position. Sutherland makes two important points: first, being an Arnold (she was granddaughter of Dr. Thomas Arnold and niece of Matthew Arnold) was "the most important single fact" of her life; second, she was both "eminent Victorian" and "pre-eminent Edwardian," whose career peaked during the Edwardian era. Mary Arnold endured a wretched childhood: isolated, lonely, and emotionally deprived. But the effects of these early experiences were offset by her years at Oxford, where she was introduced to influential people in the world of ideas, such as Walter Pater, Mark Pattison, and Benjamin Jowett. She had a part in the founding of Somerville College for women at Oxford, one of a number of ways in which she worked for social betterment (though she was opposed to female suffrage). In 1888 her *Robert Elsmere*, which dealt with questions of faith and doubt, was published and became a runaway best-seller, establishing her career. Throughout the Edwardian era she published a series of novels, which, though increasingly dated, were successful. For these, Sutherland has provided excellent critical commentary. This is a rich, full book, not easily summarized; it is notable for meticulous and distinguished scholarship and many perceptive insights into character. The author of *Victorian Novelists and Publishers* (CH, Mar'77), Sutherland gives a good picture of Ward's often complicated negotiations with Smith, Elder. Sensitive and dramatic, this is the definitive biography of Ward.—*R. T. Van Arsdel, emerita, University of Puget Sound*

WS-0543   PN4888   90-23922 CIP
A voice of their own: the woman suffrage press, 1840-1910, ed. by Martha M. Solomon. Alabama, 1991. 233p bibl index afp ISBN 0-8173-0526-2, $32.95

A collection of essays dealing with the role of early women's periodicals in the movement that culminated in the adoption of the suffrage amendment in 1920. Its early chapters are an overview of the genre; later chapters are devoted to individual periodicals and are written by a talented group of historians. Contributing authors are faculty members in communications, journalism, and speech communications. The periodicals described include *Lily, Una, Revolution, Woman's Journal, Woman's Tribune, Woman's Column, Farmer's Wife,* and *Woman's Exponent.* The book is especially valuable in that it traces changes in the women's movement from an emphasis on a new self-image for women to suffrage. It contains too few examples of the content of these papers, but those it does include are elucidating. Writing is straightforward and clear, but not sprightly. Documentation is superb. Endnotes are helpful guides to seminal works in women's journalism. The index is useful, and the bibliography is excellent. A useful acquisition for upper-division undergraduates.—*R. Halverson, Arizona State University*

WS-0544   Can. CIP
Walton, Priscilla L. **Patriarchal desire and Victorian discourse: a Lacanian reading of Anthony Trollope's Palliser novels.** Toronto, 1995. 180p bibl index afp ISBN 0-8020-0655-8, $45.00

This psychoanalytic reading of Trollope's six late Victorian political novels (1864-80) is intended as a contribution to feminist criticism, and it should be judged as such rather than in traditional terms. As a determinant of the standing of the Palliser fiction in the Trollopian oeuvre, the book has no value, since it ignores all of Trollope's voluminous writings, even his letters, with the exception of the *Autobiography* (1875-76) and the subject novels. However, as a rigorous, almost unrelenting application of the Lacanian theory of a centric subject and its peripheral other, it is a tour de force. It takes as its premise a structure of phallocentric patriarchy and marginalized individuals, mainly women, necessary to the function of a system that Walton (Carleton Univ.) regards as emanating from humanistic logic. As cultural studies grow more important in graduate English departments, books like Walton's may become mandatory for serious students of Victorian fiction. There is an alternative to this book, however. Walton has encapsulated her critique of the Palliser series in a contribution to the *Reference Guide to English Literature,* ed. by D.L. Kirpatrick (CH, Feb'92), and scholars interested in a briefer and non-Lacanian feminist approach to the series might consult it instead. Nonetheless, this book deserves consideration.—*D. Rutenberg, emeritus, University of South Florida*

WS-0545   PR468   93-15979 CIP
Winnifrith, Tom. **Fallen women in the nineteenth-century novel.** Macmillan, UK/ST. Martin's, 1994. 178p bibl index ISBN 0-312-10173-2, $49.95

Treating three female and three male Victorian novelists, Winnifrith's somewhat misnamed study considers the link between these authors' lives and their treatment of Victorian sexual codes. Such an old-fashioned biographical approach makes easy reading, but no new ground is broken here. The book concentrates on known texts and questions of artistic sincerity regarding Victorian sexual conventions and conduct. Authors are evaluated in terms of their endorsement or condemnation of extant mores. Social contexts, not surprisingly, render Austen as conventional, while Charlotte Brontë and George Eliot convey a more individualized view of morality. Thackeray is both a rake and a prude, while Dickens and Hardy receive credit for their more complex attempts to deal generously with the complex female dynamics of whoredom. The study's final chapter provides an overview of minor novelists who inadequately grapple with such issues as shame and the double standard. The text's notes are interesting. Covers the same ground as Nancy Armstrong's more theoretical study *Desire and Domestic Fiction* (CH, Nov'87). A pleasant but light read for afficionados of Victorian fiction. Undergraduate; general.—*S. A. Parker, Hiram College*

◆ British 20th Century

WS-0546   Orig
Berry, Paul. **Vera Brittain: a life,** by Paul Berry and Mark Bostridge. Chatto & Windus, 1995. 581p bibl index ISBN 0-7011-2679-5, $35.00

Berry and Bostridge have written the first biography of Vera Brittain, one of Britain's best known 20th-century female authors. The book quotes extensively from a large mass of manuscript material not previously used and draws on the personal knowledge of Berry, Brittain's friend for more than two decades and her literary executor. The authors have produced a very full account that alters in important respects the self-portrait Brittain presented in her volumes of autobiography. Although Berry and Bostridge had the cooperation of Brittain's daughter, Shirley Williams, their study is surprisingly candid. It is especially valuable for its discussion of Brittain's semidetached marriage (often portrayed as a model of feminist marriage), her close relationship with the writer Winifred Holtby, and her struggle to become a successful author. Given the importance of feminism in Brittain's life, it is unfortunate that the authors are unsuccessful in conveying the nature of her feminism or her role in the British feminist movement. Recommended for readers at all levels.—*H. L. Smith, University of Houston—Victoria*

WS-0547   PR6003   93-24543 CIP
Birch, Sarah. **Christine Brooke-Rose and contemporary fiction.**
Oxford, 1994. 253p bibl index afp ISBN 0-19-812375-2, $45.00

Why is Christine Brooke-Rose (b. 1923) so little known? Author of the novels *Out*, *Such*, and *Thru* (no, these aren't the titles of aborted Henry Green fictions), she grew up trilingually. She wrote her Ph.D thesis at the University of London on medieval studies. Though she lives in France, she continues to write in English. But the main influences on her work—Bakhtin, Robbe-Grillet, and the *Tel Quel* Group—are foreign. Augmenting her status as an outsider is the truth that, as a fictional innovator who even challenges the authority of the subject-object dualism, she flies in the face of the social realism usually associated with English prose narrative. Perhaps modern English-language fiction boasts no freer spirit than this feminist, who includes in her work elements of fantasy, science fiction, and linguistic analysis. Birch shows that, in shying away from Brooke-Rose, the critical establishment has missed a big chance both to refresh and expand its agenda. Covering a great deal of ground, Birch explores important issues raised by her subject, including the conflation of linguistic and sexual terminology in order to unearth ties between language and reality. Birch's own language flows rhythmically most of the way, and it usually sidesteps the jargon undermining so much of today's criticism. She deserves a bouquet for the wit and invention with which she conveys the artistry of her profound, polyphonic subject.—*P. Wolfe, University of Missouri—St. Louis*

WS-0548   PR6052   94-32195 CIP
Boland, Eavan. **Object lessons: the life of the woman and the poet in our time.** W.W. Norton, 1995. 254p ISBN 0-393-03716-9, $23.00

Published poet, essayist, recipient of many awards, and college teacher, Boland offers a splendid, disquieting, piercingly sharp, and intellectually and emotionally moving account of the life of a woman poet today. Here, as the title suggests, she reveals a woman learning lessons about herself, her country (Ireland), the overwhelming exclusive maleness of the poetic tradition—and most of all, the powerfulness of language once she began to discover her powerlessness. Boland's sharing of the defining moment that characterizes and sets a poet—for her, reading of Aeneas's journey in Virgil's *Aeneid*—not only vindicates the value of reading great literature but also demonstrates how its very historical limitations create courage, insight, and direction in the young. Boland's book recounts the celebrations and disappointments that marked her life. She has walked directly into the male poetic tradition and has triumphed over its courtings and its restricted paths. Boland has not been seduced by those feminists who call for a separatist vocation for the poet. Although this is not a book of confession, Boland writes so directly about her life and poetry that she casts light for all—and offers powerful hope for our language and lives. All levels.—*C. B. Darrell, Kentucky Wesleyan College*

WS-0549   PR9639   94-4107 CIP
Burgan, Mary. **Illness, gender, and writing: the case of Katherine Mansfield.** Johns Hopkins, 1994. 217p bibl index afp ISBN 0-8018-4873-3, $29.95

One of the most persuasively reasoned psychobiographies of a creative writer, this work aims, as its title indicates, to examine the relation between illness and gender in the genesis of Mansfield's short stories. (Mansfield died of tuberculosis in 1922, but had experienced other illnesses earlier.) The interrelatedness of illness and gender is too complex an issue to be dealt with thoroughly in a first examination like this, however, and Burgan (Indiana Univ.) is more successful with the part played by illness than with that played by gender. Although she looks at gender throughout, it is the aspect of illness that she keeps in steady, clear focus. When she discusses individual stories such as "The Pear Tree" in relation to the circumstances of Mansfield's life, she is often brilliantly insightful and writes with admirable clarity; but when she discusses psychiatric theory she writes so abstractly that much of what she says goes over the reader's head, from the sheer effort required to concentrate. As the most thoroughly considered analysis of psychological conflicts underlying some of Mansfield's stories, the book constitutes essential Mansfield reading. Graduate; faculty.—*J. B. Beston, Nazareth College of Rochester*

WS-0550   PR888   92-8868 CIP
Contemporary British women writers: narrative strategies, ed. by Robert E. Hosmer. St. Martin's, 1993. 214p index ISBN 0-312-07480-8, $39.95

This collection of essays is the first of three proposed volumes intended to introduce and promote the fiction of contemporary British women writers to an American audience. The ten authors discussed range from the well-known Muriel Spark, Fay Weldon, and Angela Carter to the lesser-known Anita Brookner, Sybille Bedford, A.S. Byatt, Isabel Colegate, Penelope Fitzgerald, Susan Hill, and Molly Keane. Written in readable styles and including plot summaries where necessary, the essays cover salient themes, literary devices, and to some extent social issues of the female-authored fiction. Although most of the essays pay some attention to political feminism in relation to contemporary female authorship, they eschew feminist theory. One notable exception is Walter Kendrick's essay on Angela Carter, which discusses issues of sexual (or gender) politics in her work. Each essay includes a brief biographical sketch of the author, a bibliography of writings by her, and a bibliography of writings about her work. These components provide scholars, teachers, and students with valuable research tools that encourage critical assessment of these newcomers to the literary canon.—*B. Braendlin, Florida State University*

WS-0551   Orig
Daring to dissent: lesbian culture from margin to mainstream, ed. by Liz Gibbs. Cassell, 1994. 237p index ISBN 0-304-32794-8, $55.00; ISBN 0-304-32796-4 pbk, $15.95

Gibbs's volume of essays about lesbians and contemporary culture, chiefly in England, makes a notable contribution to the burgeoning field of queer studies. Essays by writers such as Mary Wings, Nina Rapi, Liz Yorke, and Barbara Wilson examine a variety of issues; they would be excellent reading material for anyone interested in an introduction to lesbian studies or upper-division undergraduates. The strength of many of the essays in this collection is their coverage of a broad range of materials. Readers are given an overview of lesbians in mainstream and alternative theater, as well as in television, radio, and queer cinema. Particularly thorough is Veronica Groocock's study of lesbian depictions in journalism, both mainstream and alternative, from the 1960s to 1990s. A few pieces in the anthology are more limited in scope, such as Mary Wings's essay on the lesbian subtext of du Maurier's *Rebecca*. But all the essays demonstrate the validity of the editor's claim: "Lesbians are ... at the cutting edge of the creative process, developing and designing an ever more colorful culture, one which has the potential to inform and alter wider society." Academic and general audiences.—*S. A. Inness, Miami University*

WS-0552   PR6037.P29   90-40537 CIP
Edgecombe, Rodney Stenning. **Vocation and identity in the fiction of Muriel Spark.** Missouri, 1990. 165p bibl index afp ISBN 0-8262-0750-2, $22.50

Edgecombe, focusing on "vocation" in five of Spark's 18 novels and on her conversion to Roman Catholicism, attempts—on the whole, successfully—to view her novels as "extended epigrams" and her Catholicism as "ballast and weight" for her sometimes flat and trivial technique. *The Bachelors* (1960) recalls 18th-century poems and Ivy Compton-Burnett's novels. The formulaic beginning of *The Girls of Slender Means* (1963), set off against the end of WW II, enables Spark to contrast evil and good. The "epiphanic" *The Mandelbaum Gate* (1965) focuses on one woman's "polarities" (Catholicism and divorce, Judaism and her Gentile heritage). *The Abbess of Crewe* (CH Mar'75), a "masterly jeu d'esprit," is characterized by "efficiency" and "elegant heartlessness." *The Takeover* (1976), seen as "vocation misconceived," centers on the con-artist leader of a "pagan cult." Spark may indeed emphasize "vocation" in these five radically different novels as she moves from "rigorous conformity" in doctrine toward a sense of "self-determination" and a diminution of a "sense of the transcendant other," but one questions whether "atheistic presumptions prevail" in most contemporary fiction. This closely reasoned, generally persuasive study is good but far from the last word on this talented, perplexing writer. Recommended for large collections of modern British fiction and criticism.—*P. Schlueter, Warren County Community College*

WS-0553   PR6073   94-20493 CIP
Fay Weldon's wicked fictions, ed. by Regina Barreca. University Press of New England, 1994. 234p index ISBN 0-87451-642-0, $29.95

Weldon, the British novelist, playwright, and critic best known for her satirical *The Life and Loves of a She-Devil* (1983), has authored more than 50 scripts for the BBC and English commercial television networks, including two episodes of *Upstairs, Downstairs* and a five-part dramatization of Jane Austen's *Pride and Prejudice.* Her 19 novels have won critical praise on both sides of the Atlantic, and her outrageously witty and candid treatment of the universal predicaments of women has already been dubbed "Weldonesque." Weldon is a major literary figure whose art deserves serious critical attention, but this collection of 13 essays, put together by Barreca (Univ. of Connecticut), is uneven and woefully lacking in scholarly apparatus. Shortcomings of this volume include its lack of a bibliography of works by and about Weldon, its inadequate citations to the five short, nonfiction pieces by Weldon that are included, and its failure to indicate which of the contributed essays are original and which are reprints. Weldon fans will appreciate this book, but scholars will find it only partially satisfying. General readers only.—*S. M. Nuernberg, University of Wisconsin-Oshkosh*

WS-0554   PR129   92-39302 CIP
Ferguson, Moira. **Colonialism and gender relations from Mary Wollstonecraft to Jamaica Kincaid: East Caribbean connections.** Columbia, 1993. 175p bibl index afp ISBN 0-231-08222-3, $29.50

As pointed out in the conclusion to this book, Ferguson examines a series of "authors' conversations about colonial and gender relations." Drawing on contemporary approaches to issues of patriarchy and slavery, class and sexuality, race and gender, the five central chapters of the book investigate both the historico-political contexts and the textual constructions of these strained relations and their contributions to the struggles for women's emancipation and the abolition of slavery. Mary Wollstonecraft is presented as a "political pioneer" for the ways, limited as they may be, in which she uses "colonial slavery as a reference point for female subjugation." From England to Antigua, then, the work of the lesser known Hart sisters, African Caribbean women, is read for its contribution to establishing black women's historical role in determining new cross-Atlantic formulations on the question of gender and race. Continuing that exchange, Ferguson reads Jane Austen's *Mansfield Park* for the parallels it establishes between gender relations at home and power relationships between colonizer and colonized. The final two chapters, on Jean Rhys's *Wide Sargasso Sea* and on Jamaica Kincaid's *Annie John* and *A Small Place*, bring that conversation into the 20th century and the contemporary challenge to a historical process consistently recalcitrant in the face of socio-political change. Recommended for graduate and undergraduate libraries.—*B. Harlow, University of Texas at Austin*

WS-0555   PR6045.O72   89-10957 CIP
Ferrer, Daniel. **Virginia Woolf and the madness of language,** tr. by Geoffrey Bennington and Rachel Bowlby. Routledge, 1990. 169p ISBN 0-415-03194-X, $37.50

Using semi-Freudian, semi-semiotic methods, this French thesis aims to demonstrate how Woolf's "madness" becomes part of the substance and especially the discourse, or formal fiber, of four of her novels. But though dealing with the causes and effects of this "madness" (a term the author admittedly uses only because Woolf did) Ferrer does not touch upon the current dispute about the real nature of the illness; and when he concludes by demonstrating similar effects in that sanest of all writers, Daniel Defoe, he may seem to compromise his own case. On *Mrs. Dalloway* he is rather dull, partly because he is humorless, or seems to be; and on *Between the Acts* he is a disappointment in every way. However, on *To the Lighthouse* and *The Waves* he is fascinating; he will be called everything from inspired to farfetched, but he should absorb the attention of all Woolf enthusiasts for his dash and daring. His analysis of one sentence in *To the Lighthouse* will provide matter for many a lively argument. Recommended for all graduate libraries.—*J. Hafley, St. John's University (NY)*

WS-0556   PS3511   94-42094 CIP
Frederics, Diana. **Diana: a strange autobiography.** New York University, 1995. 242p afp ISBN 0-8147-2632-1, $35.00; ISBN 0-8147-2635-6 pbk, $15.95

Reissued in the series "The Cutting Edge: Lesbian Life and Literature," this minor classic of Lesbian literature (first published in 1939) is again in print. Julie Abraham's introduction successfully locates the interests it offers to research in the historical construction of discourses of lesbian life and sexuality. She also probes the problematic of genre: autobiographies that borrow narrative patterns from lesbian novels, and vice versa. The identity of Diana Frederics has never been established, thus these questions are particularly provocative in the case of her "autobiography." What neither Jay nor Abraham asks is why this text has remained popular; in print in one form or another for almost 50 years, the book has a remarkable longevity. This reviewer suggests that *Diana* offers one of the more fruitful sites for exploring polyvalent levels of lesbian identity formation and affirmation; thus many kinds of readers can find self-affirmation within the text. *Diana*'s return to print should interest at least three readerships: lesbian readers who use the book as a tool for self-understanding; general readers who wish a historical insight into older formations of lesbian life; and lesbian/gay scholars developing analyses of lesbian textuality, in particular genre blurring, liminality, and polyvalency.—*D. N. Mager, Johnson C. Smith University*

WS-0557   PR478   94-24561 CIP
Goldman, Dorothy. **Women writers and the great war,** by Dorothy Goldman with Jane Gledhill and Judith Hattaway. Twayne/Prentice Hall International, 1995. 156p (TLS, 7) bibl index afp ISBN 0-8057-8858-1, $26.95

Goldman argues that the experience and impact of WW I were not confined to frontline combatants. In their roles as nurses, ambulance drivers, munitions workers, lovers and mothers, women experienced the war with an intensity equal in many ways to that of men, and they produced an important literature of that experience. Integrating other scholarship on this subject—Paul Fussell's *The Great War and Modern Memory* (1975), Claire Tylee's *The Great War and Women's Consciousness* (1990), Modris Eksteins's *Rites of Spring* (CH, Oct'89), and the work of Susan Gilbert—Goldman considers "widely respected" prose writers such as Wharton and Woolf as well as the "inferior but interesting." There are good chapters on the search for an adequate form: romance (with its quest motif) and modernist fragmentation are extensively treated. The argument is clear and generally persuasive, balancing attitudes and topics that women writers shared with their male counterparts with domestic and gender concerns that were largely or uniquely women's. Very good bibliography. All academic collections.—*G. Grieve-Carlson, Lebanon Valley College*

WS-0558   PR6023   94-33418 CIP
Greene, Gayle. **Doris Lessing: the poetics of change.** Michigan, 1994. 285p bibl index afp ISBN 0-472-10568-X, $39.50

Most recent books on Lessing have been novel-by-novel primers expounding familiar themes and concepts. Greene's astute, well-informed book is a welcome exception, at once both analytical and personal. The "change" in the title applies to Lessing's evolution as a writer, to her reluctance to be identified too closely with causes such as feminism, and to her profound consciousness-raising influence in her readers' lives. Especially important are Greene's fresh look at *The Four-Gated City* (1969); her discussion of *The Memoirs of a Survivor* (1975); her balanced treatment of Lessing's mysticism; her sensitive discussion of *The Good Terrorist* (1985); and her consideration of Lessing's "reluctance" to create endings that might lead her to write series of books even though "few writers are so fixated on the End" as Lessing. Greene (Scripps College) does not discuss all of Lessing's writings, just those "where Lessing uses the writing as a 'growing point' and a probe, as an 'instrument of change.'" Hence, in addition to the novels cited above, Greene treats only two each of the "Children of Violence" and "Canopus" sequences, *The Golden Notebook* (1962), *The Summer Before the Dark* (1973), and *Diaries of Jane Somers* (1984). This highly recommended book, which is certain to have a major impact on Lessing studies, should be owned by all academic libraries.—*P. Schlueter, Warren County Community College*

WS-0559   PR808   95-4572 CIP
Harris, Janice Hubbard. **Edwardian stories of divorce.** Rutgers, 1996. 214p bibl index afp ISBN 0-8135-2246-3, $42.00; ISBN 0-8135-2247-1 pbk, $18.00

Readers may be misled by the title of this book. It is not an anthology of Edwardian short fiction but a stylishly written and amply documented discussion of the issues raised during the Edwardian campaign for divorce reform. Harris means her book to complement existing studies (e.g., Roderick Phillips's *Putting Assunder*, CH, Jun'80, and Lawrence Stone's *Broken Lives*, CH, Mar'94, among others). She distinguishes between the "stock story," embodying conservative attitudes—which was heard in the divorce courts and reported with commentary in the tabloid press—and the "counterstory," which was offered by advocates of divorce reform and individuals seeking relief from troubled marriages. Many such challenges to the status quo were heard by the Royal Commission on Divorce and Matrimonial Causes. That commission's 1912 report is the subject of an especially informative chapter. Harris discusses Edwardian divorce novels, which she calls a neglected subgenre of the period's fiction. She cogently argues that such novels presented ambiguities and complexities of marital discord not found in court testimony, newspapers, or the evidence presented to the Royal Commission. Harris concludes with a summary of the commission's recommendations and their fate, and a discussion of Edwardian surveys on women's attitudes toward divorce. Upper-division undergraduate, graduate, and research collections; general readers.—*M. S. Vogeler, emeritus, California State University, Fullerton*

WS-0560   PR6019.O9   89-10075 CIP
Henke, Suzette A. **James Joyce and the politics of desire.** Routledge, 1990. 288p bibl index ISBN 0-415-01056-X, $47.50; ISBN 0-415-01057-8, $15.95

Henke's study draws heavily from Freud, Lacan, and Kristeva to explore the part that sexual stereotypes and gender roles play in the fiction and drama of James Joyce. In reaction to some recent negative appraisals of Joyce from several feminist critics, Henke, a feminist herself, asserts that Joyce's language is actually an attempt to undermine the authority of a patriarchal culture. Henke traces the emergence of what she calls the salvatory female in Joyce's writing, from Gretta Conroy and Bertha Rowan to Molly Bloom and Anna Livia Plurabelle. These female characters speak a language different from that of their male counterparts, and such *écriture feminine* introduces the element of play into discourse in a carnivalesque way that subverts the male desire for certainty and closure. Joyce's women are the true poets of the imagination, since, though trapped in the limited roles in which male society has imprisoned them, yet they sing of a linguistic freedom that cannot be denied. Though Henke may occasionally get bogged down in her own language, she provides many solid insights as she moves through the texts, and her book will prove of interest and profit to those with an interest both in James Joyce and contemporary critical theory, especially at the graduate level.—*M. H. Begnal, Pennsylvania State University, University Park Campus*

WS-0561   PR6003   93-49675 CIP
Hoogland, Renée C. **Elizabeth Bowen: a reputation in writing.** New York University, 1994. 369p bibl index afp ISBN 0-8147-3501-0, $50.00; ISBN 0-8147-3511-8 pbk, $17.95

This volume clearly states its purpose: to remedy Bowen's reputation as a writer because "it has not kept up with the times, nor has her work received the serious critical attention it deserves." The remedy: to "recognize Bowen for what she also is, a truly radical, innovative, and critically practicing feminist." This remedy will be accomplished by removing Bowen from a "primarily patriarchal tradition," placing her in "a lesbian feminist perspective," and applying to her works an "understanding shaped by feminist theory." After these explanations, matters become increasingly difficult because of (1) two terminologies, her own and one borrowed from a list of critics who have helped shape (de) and (re) constructionist thought, and (2) a syntax which at crucial moments will tax the patience of even the most disciplined of grammarians. This reviewer recommends the volume only to those who (a) have a reasonable grasp of literary critical-theoretical tradition; (b) understand at least the rudiments of "feminist" reconstructionist theory; and (c) combine an openness to new theory with a patience for terminology which identifies feminism with lesbianism, among other strained relationships. A preface, introduction, and notes may help. Faculty; professionals/practitioners.—*F. L. Ryan, Stonehill College*

WS-0562   PR6037   94-18997 CIP
Huse, Nancy. **Noel Streatfeild.** Twayne, 1994. 163p (TEAS, 510) bibl index afp ISBN 0-8057-4515-7, $22.95

Noel Streatfeild was a significant children's writer. Born in 1895, her first

vocation was the stage. She was a prolific writer, publishing adult books and romance serials (under the name Susan Scarlett). It was not until 1936, with the Christmas reviews of *Ballet Shoes*, that she became famous. Children's books followed, all of them being retitled in America to end with the word *Shoes*. Streatfeild's main contribution was to use the family as a site for the career development of young women. Her themes were contemporary—the role of women, class system, and family structure. She was credited with giving "girls' books" a new respectability. Huse (professor of English and director of Women's studies at Augusta College, Illinois) is currently president of the Children's Literature Association. The main sources of information about Streatfeild are Angela Bull's *Noel Streatfeild: A Biography* (London: Collins, 1984) and Barbara Wilson's *Noel Streatfeild* (1964; Bodley Head, 1961). This work is designed for undergraduate students but should please those of us reared on her books.—*G. B. Cross, Eastern Michigan University*

WS-0563   PR8752   93-24067 MARC
Innes, C.L. **Woman and nation in Irish literature and society, 1880-1935.** Georgia, 1994 (c1993). 208p bibl index ISBN 0-8203-1597-4, $35.00; ISBN 0-8203-1598-2 pbk, $18.00

In this short, meaty book, Innes endeavors to explore the role played by women in the creation of the conscience (not just the consciousness) of the people of Ireland in the period 1880-1935. The first half goes over the already well-known literary representations of Ireland as maiden or mother and then focuses largely on the treatment of women in selected writings of Joyce and Yeats. Some Joyce characters (e.g., Molly Bloom) are seen to accurately reflect their surrounding social and economic system, while others (Gerty McDowell) are not able to question it. Yeats, alas, appears to have an unfortunate habit in his poems of obscuring subversive female protest. In the second half, Innes points out the way in which Irish women, rendered powerless as individuals, effectively formed collective political and cultural organizations. In forceful and original appreciations, Innes traces the emergence of formidable women in politics (Maud Gonne, Constance Markievicz) and literature (Lady Gregory, Elizabeth Bowen). He concludes that the process of the recognition of women in Ireland is a version of the larger postcolonial ideology. His study dips and darts abruptly from major to incidental matters, but its vision and learning qualify it as a sound introduction to its area of consideration. Upper-division undergraduate and up.—*R. J. Thompson, Canisius College*

WS-0564   Orig
Jamie, Kathleen. **The Queen of Sheba.** Bloodaxe Books, 1995 (c1994). (Dist. by Dufour Editions) 64p ISBN 1-85224-284-1 pbk, $14.95

This is Scottish poet Kathleen Jamie's third collection of poems. The imaginative world she creates is filled with strong voices and an appealing oddness. Rather than opt for the tonal flatness so prevalent in much contemporary verse, Jamie combines her originality of perception with strange new angles on ordinary experience and a propensity for making the cadences of English enriched with Scotch dialect seem completely natural, even to those unfamiliar with some of the vocabulary. The voices and experiences of women are particularly strong in these poems. One woman photographs her baby in the shadow of tenements, unaware that she has the power to choose a more appealing backdrop just across the street. "School Reunion" is a haunting pastiche of memories of the past and images from the present, with projections of future reunions and the inevitable slide into a time when the women will mirror the images of their own mothers. These poems force readers into the position of voyeur with the relentless reminder that these are privileged glimpses of private moments. They also reveal a hunger for myth in a culture trapped in the plastic of shopping malls. For all collections with an interest in contemporary poetry. Jamie promises to be a major voice.—*J. P. Baumgaertner, Wheaton College (IL)*

WS-0565   PR808   94-34792 MARC
Joannou, Maroula. **'Ladies, please don't smash these windows': women's writing, feminist consciousness and social change, 1918-38.** Berg, 1995. 236p bibl index ISBN 1-85973-022-1 pbk, $19.95

This is an important feminist survey of English women novelists between the two World Wars. Joannou is evenhanded in her treatment of the writers, from the less known, like Leonora Eyles, to the well known, like Virginia Woolf.

She also touches on a wide variety of topics—e.g., spinsterhood, the history of feminism, patriarchialism, and factionalism within the feminist cause itself. Lesbianism, which is only narrowly dealt with by the writers she surveys, is seen simply as one issue among many. Since Joannou writes from what she calls a "socialist-feminism" viewpoint, she insists on a close relationship between feminism and political ideology. There is no similar work of American origin. A British study, Nicola Beaumann's *A Very Great Profession: The Woman's Novel 1914-39* (1983), deals with many of the same authors and ideas but without the political overtones and Joannou's advanced feminist perspective. A valuable addition to feminist literary criticism, recommended for upper-division and graduate levels.—*J. J. Patton, Atlantic Community College*

WS-0566   PR9639.3.M258   90-45880 CIP
Kaplan, Sydney Janet. **Katherine Mansfield and the origins of modernist fiction.** Cornell, 1991. 233p bibl index afp ISBN 0-8014-2328-7, $29.95; ISBN 0-8014-9915-5 pbk, $12.95

Katherine Mansfield's editors and critics have, until recently, been mainly men, but the rise of feminist literary criticism has attracted skillful women critics, of whom Sydney Janet Kaplan is one. She sees Virginia Woolf and Oscar Wilde as the main influences on Mansfield (though acknowledging the role of George Eliot), but she demonstrates Mansfield as having greater "innovativeness" than Woolf and identifies "At the Bay" and "Prelude" as the most significant stories, in terms both of modernist technique and of feminist theory. Although Kaplan is not entirely convincing in her treatment of "encoded sexuality" and the role of city life in Mansfield's writing, she convinces in her depreciation of the influence of Chekhov and in her view that Mansfield's early letters (especially those of 1908)—which she quotes and analyzes in detail and with skill—reveal signs of her every later innovation: interior monologues, extended metaphors, impressionistic descriptions, tropes, patterns, and phrases even. Persuasive in its well-informed scholarship, Kaplan's study of Mansfield's changing sexuality, her relationship with D.H. Lawrence, her struggle with genre and technical issues, is truly commendable and enlightening and deserving of widespread attention. Recommended for all libraries.—*A. L. McLeod, Rider College*

WS-0567   PR9639   93-25541 CIP
Katherine Mansfield—in from the margin, ed. by Roger Robinson. Louisiana State, 1994. 209p index afp ISBN 0-8071-1865-6, $27.50

The subtitle of this book indicates its main concern: to bring Katherine Mansfield in from a marginal status and place her in a central position within modernism. In her own time and for years after her death, Mansfield was indeed a marginal figure, especially as a colonial living in England. One hundred years after her birth, her reputation is secure; Robinson precisely specifies the nature of her original achievement: the ways in which she predated Joyce and Woolf. Her achievement is analyzed by a number of different scholars at two different conferences, one in New Zealand and one in the US, on the centenary of her birth (1988); this collection of 12 studies has been compiled from their papers. On the whole, the best essays are those by established Mansfield critics such as Cherry Hankin and Gillian Boddy, but there is also a forceful study by Perry Meisel of two very disparate stories, "*Je ne parle pas français*" and "Bliss," in which the reader is drawn into rejecting both the cynicism of the one and the naïveté of the other. Meisel demonstrates Mansfield's skill in making the reader supplement what is lacking in both texts and shows how each story needs the other for coherence. Editor Robinson's introduction admirably brings the collection together, drawing attention to its organization and overall unity. All levels.—*J. B. Beston, Nazareth College of Rochester*

WS-0568   PR6053   90-26185 CIP
Kritzer, Amelia Howe. **The plays of Caryl Churchill: theatre of empowerment.** St. Martin's, 1992 (c1991). 217p index ISBN 0-312-06091-2, $39.95

Kritzer's comprehensive study of Caryl Churchill's plays, though the first to appear, will surely remain a standard. In chapter after chapter, from the radio plays of the 1960s to the television plays of the 1970s to the most recent stage plays, Kritzer sustains a level of analysis that is both admirable and revealing. Her portrait of Churchill, a materialist-feminist acutely alert to the potential of drama, is gleaned almost exclusively from the plays, which collectively offer a social analysis of oppression and a political agenda of empowerment. Kritzer's readings of the little-known plays, often the first, are intelligent and perceptive. But it is her readings of the familiar plays—*Cloud Nine*, *Top Girls*, *Serious Money*—that are bound to attract attention. For here she focuses on the materials of oppression—on sex and gender, for example, and on labor and capital—with startling acuity. Her concluding chapter offers an excellent overview of Churchill's work, rehearsing the issues, techniques, and challenges her plays engage. One wishes only that Kritzer had not reviewed the theoretical positions of others in her introduction, which yields to a vocabulary she herself does not employ. This is a feminist analysis of the first rank, a book that opens up the possibility for a broader understanding of Britains foremost female playwright. Undergraduate; graduate; faculty.—*J. Schlueter, Lafayette College*

WS-0569   PR6003   91-2202 CIP
Lassner, Phyllis. **Elizabeth Bowen: a study of the short fiction.** Twayne, 1991. 192p bibl index afp ISBN 0-8057-8336-9, $24.95

Lassner's overview of Bowen's work is new and often insightful: "Beginning her career in the twenties, a time marked by all sorts of liberation for women, Bowen infused her short stories with an energizing spirit that stands in marked contrast to the loss and despair expressed by her male colleagues of this period." However, when it comes to critical analysis of individual stories Lassner, although good on the private themes, tends to exclude the rest. "Summer Night" is Bowen's most ambitious WW II story—it is almost a novella. In it, as in her wartime novel *The Heat of the Day*, Bowen tries to explain (as did Greene, Waugh, and others) how her generation "muffed the catch." The theme is too ambitious for the story and Bowen is forced into using a rhetorical figure in the person of Aunt Fran. There are well-chosen selections from Bowen's own reviews and thoughts on the short story; a useful overview of Bowen's critical reception includes essays by William Trevor and Eudora Welty. Good primary and secondary bibliography. Undergraduate collections at any level.—*S. Donovan, St. Thomas University*

WS-0570   PR6023   93-7829 CIP
Lewiecki-Wilson, Cynthia. **Writing against the family: gender in Lawrence and Joyce.** Southern Illinois, 1994. 301p bibl index afp ISBN 0-8093-1881-4, $34.95

This provocative study leads to a rethinking of Lawrence and Joyce in ways that are significant but will not be congenial to all readers since it is heavily psychoanalytic. Focusing on the depiction of family relationships and gender roles by these two authors, Lewiecki-Wilson devotes her lengthy first chapter to providing background, initially on Freudian theory, especially that related to the Oedipus complex, and then on relevant theories of Bakhtin, Lacan, various feminist theorists, and object-relations psychologists, to the end of building a case that the texts of both novelists "implicitly challenge our thinking on feminist issues such as family form, female sexuality, and gender." This chapter, despite its focus, is remarkably free from jargon. Chapter 2 discusses Lawrence's *Sons and Lovers*, *The Rainbow*, and *Women in Love*; chapter 3, Joyce's *Portrait of the Artist as a Young Man* and *Ulysses*. Chapter 5 relates Lawrence's *The Man Who Died* and Joyce's *Finnegans Wake* to Egyptian myth, in which Freud had a strong interest. While most readings are intelligent, Freudian constructs and jargon become increasingly prominent. Finally, in a basically well written book, the number of grammatical errors is unsettling. Graduate; faculty.—*J. E. Steiner, Drew University*

WS-0571   PR6062.I895   90-42348 CIP
Livia, Anna. **Incidents involving mirth: short stories.** Eighth Mountain Press, 1990. 190p afp ISBN 0-933377-14-2, $22.95; ISBN 0-933377-13-4, $9.95

Livia's collection of short fiction, focused on the passions and perils of lesbian love, is saved from tedium by several first-rate stories in which the writer's imagination, wit, compassion, (reserved for women) as well as the vitality of her language create memorable tales. Women's love in the best stories offers a fresh perspective on a wide variety of social and political concerns: the nature of freedom, the cruelties of prejudices, the terrors of failed communication, the saving grace of all loves. Despite the verbal wit and comic hyperbole that distinguish almost all the stories, the tone falters when the author follows Jeanette Winterson and Angela Carter to write her own feminist fairy tales or Doris Lessing to write her own science fiction parables. In these (and elsewhere in the collection), the characters are too predictable, and the doctrine too shrill for the making of wholly successful fiction.—*J. Sudrann, emerita, Mount Holyoke College*

WS-0572 PR6025 93-29203 CIP
Love from Nancy: the letters of Nancy Mitford, ed. by Charlotte Mosley. Houghton Mifflin, 1993. 538p index ISBN 0-395-57041-7, $35.00

Out of approximately 8,000 surviving letters of Nancy Mitford (1904-73), Charlotte Mosley, wife of Nancy's nephew, has published approximately 500. Nancy "clearly realized that ... [her letters] would one day be published," so fortunately for the reader, she wrote with not only the recipient but the outsider plainly in mind. She intended the letters to contribute to her memoir; when the brother of a correspondent said he had burnt all her letters, someone said, "In that case you've burnt a fortune." Mosley adds lengthy and fascinating footnotes, not only to identify people, places, and events, but to quote sections of books or comments referred to. She also provides informative introductions to each section. Nancy's correspondents included not only her parents, sisters (Jessica Mitford among them), husband, and lover, but such notables as Evelyn Waugh, Harold Acton, and Cyril Connelly. These letters, in fact, give a picture of a class and an era. She discusses such matters as her writing (novels, newspaper columns, and histories), her clothes, WW II hardships, her preference for Paris over England, her reading, and, toward the end, her cancer. Very much herself on paper, Nancy is ebullient (at times even babbling), knowledgeable, irreverent, humorous. Photos, chronology, family tree, biographical notes, and facsimile pages. Highly recommended for history, literary, and women's studies collections. Undergraduate through professional.—*J. Overmyer, Ohio State University*

WS-0573 PR6045 92-22238 CIP
Mepham, John. **Virginia Woolf.** St. Martin's, 1992. 135p bibl index ISBN 0-312-08603-2, $29.95

Mepham, author of criticism on both Virginia Woolf and Modernist texts, has here arranged and ordered criticism of Woolf's life and works as part of the "Criticism in Focus" series. This volume is exceedingly useful, as much for the even-handed discussion as for Mepham's own readily confessed biases and analyses. The seven chapters divide Woolf criticism in a reasonable fashion; Mepham identifies some works as deserving of commentary in more than one of his categories, and he is not rigid in his system. The variety of biographical approaches receives thorough treatment, and readers at several levels will benefit from the concise but careful way in which Mepham identifies the various strains of interest in aspects of Woolf's life, from the familial to the feminist. Though Mepham confesses occasionally to some skepticism, he is never snide, and his approach to a rich and complex critical outpouring is welcome. Advanced undergraduate; graduate; general.—*R. Nadelhaft, University of Maine at Orono*

WS-0574 PR6045 91-9081 CIP
Mepham, John. **Virginia Woolf: a literary life.** St. Martin's, 1991. 222p index ISBN 0-312-06204-4, $24.95

A solid recounting of Virginia Woolf's writing life. Mepham chooses to focus on Woolf's series of experiments with prose style. He suggests that with each work she willfully varied both her style and her subject matter. He emphasizes the lesser-studied early and late novels and nonfiction, suggesting that Woolf "did not even write the same *kind* of book twice." The greatest strength of this work is Mepham's objectivity. Unlike many of Woolf's biographers, Mepham seems not to have a personal stake in Woolf's madness, hardships, or her family of origin. A balancing addition to Quentin Bell's biography of his aunt (*Virginia Woolf: A Biography*, CH, Feb'73) and to Phyllis Rose's excellent *Woman of Letters* (CH, Dec'78). For upper-division undergraduates, graduate students, and faculty.— *L. Winters, College of Saint Elizabeth*

WS-0575 PR6063 94-42084 CIP
Morrissy, Mary. **Mother of pearl: a novel.** Scribner, 1995. 281p ISBN 0-684-19667-0, $22.00

Morrissy's prose has a punch that takes the reader beyond the facade and into the psyche. This very interesting first novel plunges the reader into the off-center consciousness of Irene Godwin and the seemingly dead-end, working-class

life of Rita Spain. At the center is the mystery of the loss and recovery and loss again of Pearl or Hazel Mary or Jewel, the daughter of two mothers, a female Moses in the bulrushes. Morrissy traces her characters' dark, emotional struggle for an understanding of motherhood and daughterhood in a world informed by violence and insensitivity. Ireland's tormented history is reflected in these anguished women's attempts to come to terms with their own realities. It would not do to give away the solution to a mystery, but suffice it to say that *Mother of Pearl* is a gripping narrative that places the reader in the hands of a compelling and accomplished storyteller. Highly recommended for all collections.— *M. H. Begnal, Pennsylvania State University, University Park Campus*

WS-0576 DA684 95-45742 CIP
Paterson, John. **Edwardians: London life and letters, 1901-1914.** I.R. Dee, 1996. 330p index afp ISBN 1-56663-101-7, $27.50

The author of this dense but very sprightly study seems to have read everything and forgotten nothing that the major Edwardian writers said about each other and their books, publishers, agents, critics, and nonliterary friends. Patterson (Univ. of California at Berkeley) deploys his riches of anecdotes and excerpts from letters, memoirs, and biographies in three sections. "London Denied," the shortest, focuses on the lure of the countryside for the urban dweller. "London Deliver'd," by far the longest section, details the metropolis's myriad attractions—politics, publishing, leisure, art, and the rich variety of Edwardian challenges to conventional views of sex, marriage, and social class. "London Declined" locates evidence of disillusionment with the period's initial enthusiasms, such as liberal reforms, Fabianism, the Court Theatre, and Impressionism. Famous names appear, but few minor ones; the research is primarily in printed sources. Textual references to literature are limited to titles or brief summaries. There is some vagueness about dates, and at times the light tone slides into flippancy. Overall, however, 40 pages of endnotes authenticate the enterprise. Like Karl Beckson's analogous *London in the 1890s* (CH, Oct'93), the book will reward upper-division undergraduate and graduate students and their teachers.—*M. S. Vogeler, emeritus, California State University, Fullerton*

WS-0577 PR6045 93-43714 CIP
Phillips, Kathy J. **Virginia Woolf against empire.** Tennessee, 1994. 267p bibl index afp ISBN 0-87049-833-9, $24.95

This study of Woolf's fiction focuses on Woolf as a cultural critic who satirizes social institutions and suggests that seemingly diverse institutions such as imperialism, the military, and marriage reinforce each other. Phillips establishes a synergistic relationship between Leonard Woolf's anti-imperialist writings and Virginia Woolf's critique of social systems in her novels. With insightful departure from a narrow definition of modernism that defines Woolf as championing the personal above social action, Phillips presents Woolf's satiric characters as products of dangerous ideologies. Reading female characters as coconspirators in the patriarchal structure, she refutes readings that suggest that Woolf's indirect manner results from societal demands that women suppress feelings toward men and readings that suggest that characters represent Woolf's unconscious repression of anger. Judicious use of diaries, essays, and, in particular, *Three Guineas* as a gloss on the fiction reinforces the centrality of Woolf's social commentary. Thoughtful readings of *Jacob's Room*, *To the Lighthouse*, and *Orlando* are invaluable. Accessible to upper-division undergraduates and graduate students; a must read for scholars who teach Virginia Woolf's fiction.— *N. Allen, Beaver College*

WS-0578 PR478 92-46074 CIP
Rediscovering forgotten radicals: British women writers, 1889-1939, ed. by Angela Ingram and Daphne Patai. North Carolina, 1993. 319p index afp ISBN 0-8078-2087-3, $45.00; ISBN 0-8078-4414-4 pbk, $17.95

The focus of these 13 essays is on radical women writers whose work during a 50-year period dealt with social issues such as marriage, socialism, votes for women, their reproductive rights, eugenics, war, and the rise of the Nazis. The subject of one essay, Marie Stopes, has never dropped from sight since her groundbreaking marriage manual *Married Love* appeared in 1918, but Lesley A. Hall usefully complicates our perception of Stopes by discussing ambiguities in her neglected novel. Several essays show women novelists expanding socialist discourse to include feminist goals, some by utilizing the romance genre, others the utopia genre. Why have these thoughtful women been neglected? This volume blames gender bias, canonical aesthetic standards, and high modernism's indifference to the fiction writer's social values. Also relevant might be the frustrations of historical research, nicely illustrated here by the co-editors' engaging account of discovering that "Irene Clyde," who published a ground-breaking gender-free utopian novel in 1909, was actually Thomas Baty, who from 1916 until his death in 1954 lived in Japan and acted as legal advisor to its foreign office! A well-conceived and amply documented book. Recommended. Advanced undergraduate; graduate; faculty.—*M. S. Vogeler, emeritus, California State University, Fullerton*

WS-0579   PR6035   94-4170 CIP
Richardson, Dorothy. **Windows on modernism: selected letters of Dorothy Richardson,** ed. by Gloria G. Fromm. Georgia, 1995. 712p index afp ISBN 0-8203-1659-8, $65.00

Compiling this volume was surely a labor of love, for Fromm (Univ. of Illinois at Chicago) spent years reading Richardson's 1,800 extant letters to make her selection. The introductory materials and scholarly apparatus are superb. Alas, the quality and interest of the letters vary greatly. The early ones, starting in 1901, are by far the least interesting. Fromm's splendid biography *Dorothy Richardson* (CH, Jul'78) had already used copiously the most important information in them. They deal mainly with daily concerns: Richardson's domestic routine; doings of her husband, artist Alan Odle; the progress of her writing; problems with publishers, money, health, housing; gossip about friends; and reactions to her fellow authors and to her regular reading, which was wide-ranging. Ideas of any sort are virtually absent. Then, starting around 1933 and continuing until her last letters in 1952—as her "inspiration" for the ongoing "chapters" of her four-volume *Pilgrimage* (1915-1967) and energy to write them gradually dry up— Richardson's letters begin to include some ideas, largely related to politics (German and English), religion, literature, and differences between men and women. By this time, however, many of the letters are repetitious. A more judicious pruning throughout would have been welcome. Upper-division undergraduate collections and above.—*J. E. Steiner, Drew University*

WS-0580   PR6023   94-16871 CIP
Rowe, Margaret Moan. **Doris Lessing.** St. Martin's, 1994. 137p bibl index ISBN 0-312-12192-X, $24.95

The 11th title in the feminist series "Women's Writers" this text treats Lessing's fiction in eight concise chapters. The most attractive formulation is Chapter 5, "Parables of Inner Space," which discusses *Briefing for a Descent into Hell* (1971) along with two novels. The phrasing of other headings accurately outlines the author's approach to Lessing's development. Rowe takes a certain time to establish tone and methodology; thus, some readers will prefer another treatment of Lessing's early life and first fiction. Comparisons with Schreiner, George Eliot, and others are more helpful later in the text, where they are briefer than at the outset. A strong feature is the measured use of quotations from Lessing herself. There is interesting analysis of major texts, clearly marking Rowe's stance toward selected critics, as illustrated in the discussion of *The Fifth Child* (1988). The book ends rather sharply with a defense of the role of academic criticism in evaluating Lessing's oeuvre. Includes a select bibliography but lacks a chronology. This short study presents an evolutionary definition of Doris Lessing as an author continuously experimenting with original means of literary expression. General; undergraduate.—*E. Glass, Rosemont College*

WS-0581   PR888   95-3579 MARC
Scott, Bonnie Kime. **Refiguring modernism: v.1: The women of 1928: v.2: Postmodern feminist readings of Woolf, West, and Barnes.** Indiana, 1996 (c1995). 2v. 318, 217p bibl index afp ISBN 0-253-32936-1, v.1, $39.95; ISBN 0-253-32937-X, v.2, $34.95; ISBN 0-253-20995-1 pbk, v.1, $18.95; ISBN 0-253-21002-X pbk, v.2, $15.95

This ambitious work aims to revise the history of modernism, defined here as the period from about 1910 to mid-20th century, by including women writers hitherto neglected. Scott's basic critical metaphor is the web, which she applies as a means of examining the interconnections between women writers—principally Virginia Woolf, Rebecca West, and Djuna Barnes—and the major male figures of the movement—Pound, Lewis, Eliot, Joyce, Lawrence, and Forster. The first

volume traces these relationships through historical and biographical continuities. Family ties, professional and social acquaintances, and marriage and love relationships are interwoven in the cross-fertilization of ideas, experimentation, and artistic production characterized as "modernism." The second volume focuses on close readings of the works of Woolf, West, and Barnes. It purports to apply the theories developed in the first volume but is less imaginative and at times somewhat plodding. Although correlated in approach and theory, the two volumes are independent; neither is necessary for comprehension of the other, and critical and documentation apparatus is complete in each. Recommended for undergraduate and graduate collections.—*H. Jaskoski, California State University, Fullerton*

WS-0582   PR6005   90-24121 CIP
Shaw, Marion. **Reflecting on Miss Marple,** by Marion Shaw and Sabine Vanacker. Routledge, 1991. 111p bibl ISBN 0-415-01794-7 pbk, $14.95

As the authors of this new study of Agatha Christie's Miss Marple novels demonstrate, that writer's importance to modern letters cannot be overestimated. In a century that has produced tens of thousands of mystery fictions avidly consumed by a manifestly diverse readership, Christie's work remains at the fulcrum of the canon; her 17 novels featuring spinster detective Miss Marple continue to win admirers and invite critical attention. In their incisive and deftly written study, Shaw and Vanacker document the ways in which Christie's protagonist must be understood as a feminist heroine whose genius is her crafty ability to utilize the misogynist and ageist prejudices of her culture to her advantage as a sleuth. Exploiting her marginal status in cunning ways and discerning, through her uniquely female perspective, salient insights into the disturbed domesticity that constitutes Christie's criminal domain, Miss Marple turns detection into the vindication of the feminine. Readers of this volume might wish that its authors had expanded their succinct discussions of individual novels; a study as perceptive and articulate as this one merits expansion. Complementing Kathleen Klein's *The Woman Detective* (CH, Mar'89), it is a major contribution to popular culture and feminist scholarship. For all libraries.—*L. Babener, Montana State University*

WS-0583   PR6037   92-4795 CIP
Sproxton, Judy. **The women of Muriel Spark.** St. Martin's, 1992. 158p index ISBN 0-312-08116-2, $35.00

Generalities abound, beginning with the assertion that Spark's "achievement in constructing female character is unrivalled in the twentieth-century Catholic novel." Sproxton (University of Birmingham) reminds us that Spark is no feminist; she neither asserts women's rights nor criticizes "a society which might seek to repress women." Rather, Spark's female characters often are searching for a dignity and possession of mind that will vindicate their spiritual integrity. The first of four chapters, "Mature Women," treats characters portrayed confronting "essential problems" in *The Comforters, Robinson, The Mandelbaum Gate, Loitering with Intent*, and *A Far Cry from Kensington*. Next Sproxton turns to "Women of Power," characters who are strong yet have no apparent catalyst: Jean Brodie (*The Prime of Miss Jean Brodie*), Selina Redwood (*The Girls of Slender Means*), Alexandra (*The Abbess of Crewe*), Maggie Radcliffe (*The Takeover*), and Margaret Murchie (*Symposium*). Spark's most bizarre women are grouped in a chapter titled "Women as Victims" which discusses *Momento Mori, The Bachelors, The Public Image* and *The Driver's Seat*. A final chapter, "Narrative and Faith," rounds up Spark's Catholic characters, male and female, for a final glance. Sproxton's combination of plot summary and superficial character analysis does little to delineate the internal dynamics of Spark's female characters or explain Spark's achievement in creating them. The book is further compromised by flat, uninspiring writing, too few quotes from the novels, and no references to other scholarship on Spark. David Lodge's *The Novelist at the Crossroads* (CH, May'72) is briefly quoted in Sproxton's introduction.—*S. Pathak, Johns Hopkins University*

WS-0584   PR6045   91-10235 CIP
Virginia Woolf and war: fiction, reality, and myth, ed. by Mark Hussey. Syracuse, 1991. 273p bibl index ISBN 0-8156-2537-5, $29.95

These 13 essays by 15 academics were begun as a 1989 discussion topic about how Woolf reflects and uses the two world wars and Spanish civil war her lifetime included. The essays are very uneven in quality, but William J. Handley's on *Jacob's Room*, is splendid, by far the best thing here and arguably the best thing ever done about that novel. (Handley, a UCLA graduate student, bears watching.) This crucial passage in Handley's essay ought to have been assigned reading for all the other critics: "In exposing the conventions of realism and focusing on her own textuality, on the thing itself that the text forms and is, Woolf challenges the hierarchical relationships that treat a thing as a means and not as an end in itself. An active reading of a Woolfian text does not give the reader a directive or program to follow but is still political if it effectively confuses the rigidity of conventional, purposive relationships." Disregard of this leads to the strident, axe-grinding hysteria that characterizes too many of the other essays, although there are several decidedly rewarding performances, especially those by Karen L. Levenback, Josephine O'Brien Schaefer (on Woolf and Cather), and Patricia Laurence.—*J. Hafley, St. John's University (NY)*

WS-0585 PR888 94-15015 CIP
Woolf and Lessing: breaking the mold, ed. by Ruth Saxton and Jean Tobin. St. Martin's, 1994. 208p bibl index ISBN 0-312-12051-6, $39.95

Though scholars have long noted similarities in the writings of Virginia Woolf and Doris Lessing, this first extended comparison of influence and "affinities" is exemplary in detailing specific parallels. The eight essays, mostly by well-known Lessing scholars, approach their subjects variously: in terms of Woolf's demonstrable influence on the fragmented persona in Lessing's *The Golden Notebook* (1962) (Claire Sprague, Christine W. Sizemore, Jean Tobin); as approaches to postmodernism (Roberta Rubenstein on consciousness and "nostalgia," Magali Cornier Michael on "Subjectivity"); as manifestations of the Demeter myth (Lisa Tyler), in their "fascination with mental life as an important root/route of literature" (Linda E. Chown); and, in an important essay by Ruth Saxton, in their sense of the centrality of woman's body to a sense of identity. The volume is particularly a major contribution to Lessing scholarship in that it delves into assumed but unexamined territory, thus setting it apart from previous thematic or whole-career analyses. Highly recommended for all libraries.—*P. Schlueter, Warren County Community College*

◆ Canadian

WS-0586 PR9499 93-18145 MARC
Bharati Mukherjee: critical perspectives, [ed.] by Emmanuel S. Nelson. Garland, 1993. 236p (Garland reference library of the humanities, 1663) bibl index afp ISBN 0-8153-1173-7, $38.00

Mukherjee has attracted considerable critical attention from postcolonial, feminist, and deconstructionist academics. The present book is a collection of a dozen studies that grew out of a recent academic conference. Most are by young, new critics and suggest that in Mukherjee they have found a subject worthy of their analysis and evaluation, though too often they find it necessary, apparently, to write in the jargon of the critical theories that they espouse. This is especially to be noted in one essay that considers "Sociopolitical Critique as Indices and Narrative Codes ... in *Wife* and *Jasmine*" and which concludes that the odd turns of plot in these novels create "a new sort of postcolonial narrative logic." The case is not persuasively put. Likewise, one essay on narrative voice and gender roles is (as the editor suggests) an "intriguing interpretation," but it is far from convincing. Yet other essays (clearly written and well thought out) do present a clear case for regarding Mukherjee as a major voice of postcolonial, expatriate, feminist, and immigrant writing, one in whose works violence plays a central role. In fact, perhaps the most engaging essay is "Creating, Preserving, Destroying: Violence in Bharati Mukherjee's *Jasmine*." Gender, race, power, ethnicity, and Americanness are all addressed in these essays, which invite rather than preempt further studies. Undergraduate; graduate; faculty.—*A. L. McLeod, Rider College*

WS-0587 PR9188 90-38417 CIP
Fraser, Wayne. **The dominion of women: the personal and the political in Canadian women's literature.** Greenwood, 1991. 190p (Contributions in women's studies, 116) bibl index afp ISBN 0-313-26749-9, $42.95

Fraser (Ridley College, Ontario) argues compellingly the tight connection between the personal and the political in Canadian women's fiction. Defining the

"essence of femininity" as a sense of "relatedness," Fraser chronologically traces the parallel progress and mutual encouragement of feminism, women's fiction, and Canadian nationalism, meticulously identifying seven stages, from colonial dependence (via Brooke, Traill, Jameson, Moodie) through imperialism to an ambivalent emancipation in the 1920s and 1930s (Duncan, McClung, Ostenso), 1940s and 1950s isolationism (Ethel Wilson), 1960s nationalism (Laurence) and anti-Americanism (Atwood), and a final maturity and (measure of) autonomy in the 1970s and 1980s (again Laurence, Atwood). In firm command of the 17 texts (entirely fiction, not the larger "literature" the title promises) by 10 authors that he has chosen to illustrate his thesis, Fraser uses massive textual, critical and historical reference in a generally graceful and unforced manner. A useful bibliography and index bring to a close a study which convinces us that women's writing is one of the best places to see what is happening in Canada. Unpretentious and accessible to the literate generalist, the book will be of particular interest and value to upper-level undergraduate students of Canada, of Canadian literature, and of women's writing.—*L. B. Thompson, University of Vermont*

WS-0588 PS8089x Can. CIP
Hodkinson, Yvonne. **Female parts: the art and politics of women playwrights.** Black Rose Books, 1992. (Dist. by Paul & Company) 163p bibl ISBN 0-895431-07-7, $34.95; ISBN 0-895431-06-9 pbk, $15.95

Canadian female playwrights are almost unknown in the US and little known in Canada, so this book is a welcome addition to recent books about women writers. In the introduction Hodkinson states that "in Canada, the pursuit of a female vision is unique in that it examines the notion of gender and female identity through the lens of cultural mythology." The first chapter presents a survey of female playwrights, from the 19th-century "expounding a feminist vision" to contemporary playwrights. The following chapters examine in detail plays by five Canadian women. These plays explore, in a variety of styles, the problems women face in Canada—immigration, existence within the constraints imposed by a patriarchal society, the impact of the wilderness on women, etc. The author sums up her beliefs in an afterword, noting that the playwrights in the study are trying to enlarge female consciousness by presenting challenges to the conditions that have "alienated women from the mainstream of Canadian life." The author's style is clear and interesting, and the plays are appropriate to her discussion. For graduate and upper-division undergraduate students.—*Y. Shafer, University of Colorado at Boulder*

WS-0589 PR9199 95-24442 CIP
Howells, Coral Ann. **Margaret Atwood.** St. Martin's, 1996. 185p bibl index ISBN 0-312-12891-6, $35.00

Howells (Univ. of Reading, UK), author and editor of books on Gothic fiction, Canadian women novelists, and Jean Rhys, presents here an excellent introduction to the work of the Canadian novelist and poet. Published in the "Modern Novelists" series, which closely examines texts as introductions to 19th- and 20th-century writers, this study focuses on Atwood's eight novels, a book of short stories, and her analysis of Canadian literature, *Survival* (1972). Indeed, Howells claims that " ... 'survival' in a context of environmental change which is both ecological and ideological" is a key term for understanding Atwood's work. Grouping Atwood's fiction by topics—wilderness, feminism, power politics, the Gothic—Howells adroitly demonstrates Atwood's experimentation with genres, her use of Adrienne Rich's concept of "re-vision," and her intertextual relations with other authors. Howell's prose is crisp and clear; she capably traces the evolution of Atwood's themes and ideology; she makes judicious use of her comprehensive knowledge of both existing Atwood criticism and of Atwood's manuscripts. Her chapter on Atwood's most popular novel, *The Handmaid's Tale* (1985), is perhaps the most innovative, reading the novel in light of the work of Helene Cixous. This book can be profitably used by student and scholar alike.—*E. R. Baer, Gustavus Adolphus College*

WS-0590 PR9199 93-6300 MARC
Margaret Atwood: writing and subjectivity: new critical essays, ed. by Colin Nicholson. Macmillan, UK/St. Martin's, 1994. 261p index ISBN 0-312-10644-0, $49.95

Of these 13 essays on the works of Margaret Atwood, three deal with her poetry, three with her short fiction, and the rest with her novels: *Surfacing*

(1972), *Lady Oracle* (CH, Feb.'77), *Life Before Man* (CH, May'80), *The Hand-maid's Tale* (CH, May'86), and *Cat's Eye* (1988). Nearly all emphasize the ways in which Atwood's Canadian heritage influences her writing. Several focus on her point-of-view characters and the ways in which they reflect Atwood herself and the feminist voice as well. Nearly all stress Atwood's complexities. Some essays are highly readable; some are couched in academic jargon. Some insights are forced, others valid. Among the latter: Judith McCombs's note that Atwood transforms into poetry some of T.S. Eliot's myths and symbols from "The Waste Land"; Sherrill Grace's point that one should not confuse the "I" of Atwood's novels with the author herself; David Ward's comment that *Surfacing* is deliberately indeterminate, dealing as it does with "internal frontiers." This collection will be of some interest for women's studies libraries. Contains a photograph, footnotes, notes on contributors. Upper-division undergraduates and up.—*J. Overmyer, Ohio State University*

WS-0591   Can. CIP
Miscegenation blues: voices of mixed race women, ed. by Carol Camper. Sister Vision: Black Women and Women of Colour Press, P.O. Box 217, Station E, Toronto, Ont. M6H 4E2, Canada, 1994. 389p ISBN 0-920813-95-X pbk, $16.95

The more than 50 contributors to this collection of autobiographical creative and critical texts display a gamut of emotions ranging from anger to ecstasy as they explore and express mixed-race identity. Camper's introduction transvalues the term "miscegenation" by returning it to its original meaning of "mixed marriage" and "mixed race," negating any racist connotation that would link "miscegenate" with "degenerate" and might forbid or decry the racial mixing that informs her own identity and life experience. Her anthology similarly intends to counter "popular culture's tiresome, racist images of racially mixed women" with a variety of texts that celebrate mixed-race identity. At the same time, many of the autobiographical poems and essays reveal insecurities, uncertainties, and unresolved tensions in the lives of woman living in a racist society. The collection enriches the canon of autobiography and the field of feminist theory as it raises provocative questions about gender, race, and class. Upper-division undergraduate and up.—*B. Braendlin, Florida State University*

WS-0592   PR9199   95-35711 CIP
New perspectives on Margaret Laurence: poetic narrative, multiculturalism, and feminism, ed. by Greta M.K. McCormick Coger. Greenwood, 1996. 232p (Contributions in women's studies, 154) bibl index afp ISBN 0-313-29042-3, $59.95

Valuable to students and Laurence scholars alike, the 18 essays in this collection of "predominantly American scholarship" are assembled under four headings: "Language, Theme, and Image," "Narrative Structure," "Multiculturalism," and "Feminist Perspectives." Coger contends that Laurence has been largely neglected by American critics despite the fact that she is anthologized and read. The editor provides an excellent summary of Laurence's life and literary achievement and a list of critical treatments of her works in the US. Michel Fabre's essay on metaphorical networks and structural opposition in Laurence's *The Stone Angel* is available for the first time in English in this collection. Readers especially interested in multiculturalism and feminist perspectives may also wish to consult the *New Oxford Book of Canadian Short Stories in English*, selected by Margaret Atwood and Robert Weaver (1995); Beverley Daurio and Luise von Flotow's anthology of Quebec women's fiction, *Ink and Strawberries* (1988); and Irène Assiba d'Almeida's *Francophone African Women Writers* (CH, Apr'95). All collections.—*S. R. Schulman, Central Connecticut State University*

WS-0593   PS8089x   Canadian CIP
Re(dis)covering our foremothers: nineteenth-century Canadian women writers, ed. by Lorraine McMullen. University of Ottawa Press, 603 Cumberland, Ottawa, Ontario K1N 6N5, 1990. 203p (Reappraisals, Canadian writers, 15) ISBN 0-7766-0197-0, $19.95

McMullen (University of Ottawa) here offers 17 essays that energetically promote the rediscovery and recovery of marginalized or erased 19th-century Canadian women writers in the first gender-focused volume in the University of Ottawa's annual "Reappraisals" series. The collection has five phases: manifesto; research guide; consideration for specific literary modes; resurrection of the van-

ished; and re-vision of the few survivors. First McMullen and three others make compelling introductory cases for a foremotherly tradition and the necessity of valuing both individuals and types of writing that have been unjustly dismissed. Then the problems, gaps, strategies, and practical solutions in past, present, and future research are addressed. Next four articles investigate particular genre/gender issues concerning autobiography, journalism, anthologies, and the literature of emigration. The final phase of the book offers new perspectives on a trio from the small group of canonized early Canadian women writers: Moodie, Trail, and Duncan. Each essay is accompanied by a list of works cited and short endnotes where needed. The book as a whole is a useful and persuasive addition to both Canadian literary and women's studies and would interest general readers of 19th-century literature.—*L. B. Thompson, University of Vermont*

WS-0594   PS3569   94-23647 CIP
Savageau, Cheryl. **Dirt road home: poems.** Curbstone, 1995. 92p afp ISBN 1-880684-30-6 pbk, $11.00

Libraries whose collections include Savageau's first volume, *Home Country* (CH, Jan'93), will want to carefully consider purchasing the current collection, since the first book's "poems make up the heart of this new volume." However, the poems in this collection, taken on their own, provide an intriguing look at the personal history of a woman with a French Canadian, Abenaki Indian background. Savageau has mastered the art of the storyteller as well as the skill of the poet. Her poems are accessible and often touching, as in the ending of the final poem, "All Night She Dreams": "Meanwhile there is walking in balance / there is clear thought / and song / rising from her lips / like smoke, like mist / like welcome clouds / like some green and beautiful plant." Much here makes this volume fit into a collection of oral history or women's studies as easily as into a traditional poetry collection. All levels.—*S. Raeschild, University of Cincinnati*

WS-0595   Can. CIP
Smart, Patricia. **Writing in the father's house: the emergence of the feminine in the Quebec literary tradition.** Toronto, 1991. 300p bibl index afp ISBN 0-8020-2732-6, $45.00; ISBN 0-8020-6771-9 pbk, $18.95

Smart (Carleton University, Ottawa) has done more than translate her excellent *Écrire dans la maison du père* (new ed., Montreal, 1990). The English version is an adaptation of the French, even to the redesigning of the diagrams, to make it accessible to a larger audience, less familiar with the literature of Quebec. The new edition adds a useful index and list of works cited. Winner, in its first edition, of the prestigious Governor General's award in 1988 for its reexamination of Quebec's literary canon, or the "Father's House of culture," the book documents the existence of a female literary tradition starting with Laure Conan in the 19th century. Smart provides a context for this tradition with a feminist analysis of male works, including those of Hubert Aquin about whom she has published an important book (*Hubert Aquin, agent double*, Montreal, 1973). She makes good use of many theoretical texts, both feminist and nonfeminist, by European, Canadian, and US scholars, as well as wide-ranging references to Quebec's literary production over the past century. Her feminist rereadings of Laure Conan and Gabrielle Roy are remarkable, and her analyses of Germaine Guèvremont, Anne Hébert, and France Théoret are also enriching. A beautifully written, perceptive study of some of the finest writers of our time, winners of major French literary prizes: women of French-speaking Canada. Uniquely important. A must for all academic library collections.—*A. M. Rea, Occidental College*

WS-0596   PS8587x   Can. CIP
Sweatman, Margaret. **Fox.** Turnstone Press, 607-100 Arthur St., Winnipeg, Man. R3B 1H3 Canada, 1991. 200p ISBN 0-88801-154-7 pbk, $11.95

In the general strike that swept Winnipeg in 1919, 30,000 workers participated, three ministers preached a new "social gospel," and one boy was shot to death by frightened police. Canada was changed forever, a social safety net emerged, pro-labor parties appeared, and three imprisoned strikers were elected to Manitoba's legislature. Sweatman's remarkable first novel examines the women of the period, from the poor to the wealthiest, from conservatives to "New" women whose sisters exist in Shaw, Dos Passos, and Hemingway. *Fox* traces women's roles in the struggle for justice after the war, when immigrants met xenophobes, wages fell, and babies starved. This is a panorama, as Sweatman puts it, of "the familiar brutal erotic" of history's "pentimento": here, the picture hidden beneath the familiar historical canvas reveals love undergoing metamorphosis, a new gender-consciousness growing, and religion and nationhood unexpectedly modulating. The brushstrokes include journal entries, news accounts, telegrams, stories, poetry, even missing photographs: ways of recording dreams and imaginings amid the facts of cultural perturbation. Recommended for undergraduate, graduate, and public library literature and history collections.—*R. H. Solomon, University of Alberta*

WS-0597   Can. CIP
Verduyn, Christl. **Lifelines: Marian Engel's writings.** McGill-Queen's, 1995. 278p bibl index afp ISBN 0-7735-1337-X, $44.95; ISBN 0-7735-1338-8 pbk, $19.95

This excellent study examines Engel's works chronologically, omitting only her two children's books and the nonfiction volume *The Islands of Canada*, coauthored with J.A. Kraulis (1981). Drawing heavily on feminist literary scholarship and her considerable knowledge of postmodern studies, Verduyn (Trent Univ.) analyzes Engel's writings as works "concerned with women's experience and women's expression of the world. [Engel] was interested in female identity and creativity, and the constraints to their development." What Verduyn correctly calls "the woman-focused outlook of Engel's writing" is most impressively demonstrated in her treatment of the difficulties "facing women committed to living and working in their own terms as artists and writers." No other scholar has made such extensive use of Engel's notebooks to illuminate her life and art, and no other commentator has offered such a solid critical overview of Engel's efforts. Moreover, Verduyn's readings of specific works—such as *The Bear* (CH, Jan'77), about which much has been written—invariably offer new and utterly persuasive insights. Lucid, thorough, and massively researched, this landmark study elevates Engel to her deserved place of prominence in Canadian letters. Upper-division undergraduates and above.—*C. G. Masinton, University of Kansas*

WS-0598   Can. CIP
Warne, Randi R. **Literature as pulpit: the Christian social activism of Nellie L. McClung.** W. Laurier, 1993. (Dist. by Humanities) 236p (Dissertations SR, 2) bibl afp ISBN 0-88920-235-4 pbk, $25.00

Warne analyzes the life and work of Nellie L. McClung (1873-1951), a prolific and influential Canadian writer who worked for religious and social reform, temperance, and suffrage. Warne writes that "McClung believed literature had a crucial role to play in the creation of a better Canada," and shows how this literature revealed McClung's agenda as well as Canadians' affinity for her writing. McClung wrote four novels, novellas, volumes of stories and essays, as well as articles for popular Canadian journals. Through the 1940s she published a syndicated newspaper column called "Nellie McClung Says," and was affectionately known in her homeland as "Our Nell." This book examines McClung's major works, discusses "the centrality of religion for her feminist social activism," and shows how she refuted the antifeminist arguments of her times, particularly as espoused by Stephen Leacock and Sir Almroth Wright. Warne's study might create renewed interest in McClung's writings, and certainly expanded attention outside Canada. But without the availability of primary sources this interest would be difficult to pursue; at this time only two novels—*In Times Like These* (1915, orig.; 1972) and *Purple Spring* (1921, orig.; 1992)—have been reissued, and all of her other work is out of print. Thorough documentation, bibliography, and supplementary primary materials, but no index. Best suited for specialized collections in Canadian history, religious history, and women's studies.—*J. S. Gabin, University of North Carolina at Chapel Hill*

WS-0599   Can. CIP
Zimmerman, Cynthia. **Playwriting women: female voices in English Canada.** Simon & Pierre, 2181 Queen St. E., Suite 301, Toronto, Ont. M4E 1E5, Canada, 1994. 235p (Canadian dramatist, 3) bibl index ISBN 0-88924-258-5 pbk, $22.00

The slimness of Zimmerman's book belies its richness. She focuses on six Canadian playwrights—Carol Bolt, Sharon Pollock, Margaret Hollingsworth, Erika Ritter, Anne Chislett, and Judith Thompson—offering a balanced mixture of fact and anecdote. The book is further valuable for its readability and conciseness. Zimmerman gracefully avoids the opaque jargon of most critical texts;

play summaries are just long enough to whet the reader's appetite. The book's title is misleading, since the volume is not simply a discussion of feminist topics. Those playwrights, Zimmerman points out, write not only about women's topics but also about women developing a voice to highlight crucial social issues of their time. The text is also an interesting general history of theater in Canada, including such aspects as collective workshops and alternative theater. In addition, Zimmerman gives the reader unfamiliar with Canadian literature a sense of what she calls the Canadian personality and the Canadian artistic personality. Unfortunately, the playwrights discussed are not well known in the US. They definitely should be. Upper-division undergraduate; graduate; faculty.—*J. A. Dompkowski, Canisius College*

◆ Classical

WS-0600   BS680   91-4272 CIP
"Women like this": new perspectives on Jewish women in the Greco-Roman world, ed. by Amy-Jill Levine. Scholars Press, GA, 1991. 260p (Early Judaism and its literature, 1) index afp ISBN 1-55540-462-6, $24.95; ISBN 1-55540-463-4 pbk, $15.95

This volume contains 11 essays on women in the canonical (biblical) and non-canonical (apocryphal) literature of the Hellenistic period, by scholars of religious studies and classics. The focus is on Jewish women, and the aim of the volume is twofold: to correct the bias against Judaism in feminist theology, and to apply the methodology of women's studies to the study of Jewish women in this era. The essays, arranged in chronological order, discuss principally Ben Sirah, Philo, Pseudo-Philo, II and IV Maccabees, Jubilees, Joseph and Aseneth, the Testament of Job, Tobit, the Gospels, and the Acts of Paul and Thecla. Feminist analysis has been a latecomer to biblical studies, and although these essays are an important and valuable first step, as a group they lack a certain degree of theoretical sophistication. This appears especially in a tendency to comb the texts for examples of women acting independently of men or taking initiative, and to interpret these as inspirational or reassuring. Nevertheless, the discussions are all scholarly and well researched, and none fails to raise questions and analyze issues that ought to interest and instruct students and scholars of all theoretical and methodological persuasions.—*M. A. Katz, Wesleyan University*

WS-0601   PA4167   94-6749 CIP
The Distaff side: representing the female in Homer's *Odyssey*, ed. by Beth Cohen. Oxford, 1995. 229p bibl index afp ISBN 0-19-508682-1, $45.00

This volume includes 11 essays originally presented at a 1992 conference on representations of female figures in Homer's *Odyssey*. Three well-argued and well-written introductory essays provide an excellent overview: Graham reviews the problems of dating the *Odyssey* and argues that a late 8th-century BCE date effectively reflects how the epic illuminates the role of Greek women in the colonization of the western Mediterranean; Schein describes the various types of female characters in the epic and evaluates their importance; Buitron-Oliver and Cohen present artifacts—vases, seals, painting, coins—representing female characters and scenes in the *Odyssey* (the Sirens, Scylla, Athene, Penelope, and so forth). Then follow four mainly literary and four mainly art-historical essays. Individual essays discuss, for instance, the importance of Athena in manipulating Odysseus' return to Ithaka (Murnaghan); Penelope's moral choices (Foley); the olive-tree-bed (Zeitlin); artistic renderings of the footwashing scene in *Odyssey* 19 (Havelock). This beautifully produced book includes 60 black-and-white photographs of artifacts (readers will wish for color, however). Full notes appear at the end of each essay, and the editor includes a substantial bibliography and index. Readers will not discover new or profound ideas here, but the essays reveal wide research, good thinking, and sound scholarship. Upper-division undergraduate upward.—*S. B. Darrell, University of Southern Indiana*

WS-0602   PA3074   91-40115 CIP
Holst-Warhaft, Gail. **Dangerous voices: women's laments and Greek literature.** Routledge, 1993 (c1992). 227p bibl index ISBN 0-41507249-2, $35.00

Why did the ancient Athenians set legal limits on women's mourning for the dead? In a clearly presented discussion, Holst-Warhaft attempts to answer this question from theoretical and comparative perspectives. From the themes of women's lamentations still sung in Mani she deduces that women do not eulogize the dead so much as call attention to their own fate, and that they emphasize values of family and individual over those of community, urging restitution or revenge whenever appropriate. As such, she argues, women's lamentations in Athens were thought to have posed a potential threat to the city, especially in times of war, as evidenced by the rhetoric of the state funeral oration for the war dead. Holst-Warhaft attempts to show that a similarly negative value was placed on women's lamentation in Athenian tragedy. Her argument is not always convincing, however; in order to prove her point she must interpret the action of the plays *ironically*. But why assume that the Athenians disapprove or portray as monstrous women's celebration of the traditional values of individual and family, if in plays such as Sophocles's *Electra* and Euripides's *Hecabe* (which Holst-Warhaft does not discuss) lamentation serves the same purposes as it does in modern Mani, to give women opportunity to demand just restitution of property and to plot revenge for murder? Advanced undergraduate through graduate.— *M. R. Lefkowitz, Wellesley College*

WS-0603   PA3978   93-17257 CIP
Rabinowitz, Nancy Sorkin. **Anxiety veiled: Euripides and the traffic in women.** Cornell, 1993. 246p bibl index afp ISBN 0-8014-2845-9, $37.50; ISBN 0-8014-8091-4 pbk, $14.95

Rabinowitz regards the dramas of Euripides as encoded documents that, when deciphered, provide a key to the understanding of fifth-century BCE Athenian sociology and psychology. As she reads them, the plays were designed to reinforce the values of Athenian society, specifically those that support male domination. In her view, women are praised only if their actions, heroic or otherwise, serve the purposes of men; and she discovers in the dramas an anxiety on the part of both the poet and his society about women who instead seek to act in their own best interests. The book warns modern readers not to accept this value system uncritically: "the modern reader must recognize the forces of control for what they are in order to capitalize on the resistance that is inscribed in the myth ...." Her Euripides is not a poet interested in portraying many sides of complex moral and religious issues so much as a moralist uneasily representing a social code. Such an analysis, however cogently argued, probably tells us more about the gender preoccupations of our own society than it does about those of Euripides or of ancient Athens. Advanced undergraduate; graduate; faculty.— *M. R. Lefkowitz, Wellesley College*

WS-0604   PA3622   90-48642 CIP
Sappho's lyre: archaic lyric and women poets of Ancient Greece, tr. with introd. and notes by Diane J. Rayor. California, 1991. 207p bibl afp ISBN 0-520-07335-5, $29.95; ISBN 0-520-07336-3 pbk, $10.95

Although Rayor's rhythmic unrhymed verse does not attempt to reproduce the elaborate metrical structures of the original lyrics, she has taken considerable care to represent accurately what the poets said without imposing her own interpretation or modern emphasis. The result is closer to the Greek originals, but less immediately accessible and racy than the translations of some of the same poems in *Games of Venus*, ed. by Peter Bing and Rip Cohen (1991). Rayor also includes a complete translation of the small corpus of women poets who saw themselves as Sappho's successors, though most of these lived centuries later and wrote in another style and for occasions different from those that inspired the earlier poets. As in Sappho's case, the distinctively female qualities of their verse (if any) might be better appreciated when compared with the work of their own male contemporaries. A helpful introduction concentrates on the poems themselves rather than the little that is known about their authors, and it provides a guide to recent scholarship. Appropriate for general readers.—*M. R. Lefkowitz, Wellesley College*

WS-0605   PA409   95-20124 CIP
Williamson, Margaret. **Sappho's immortal daughters.** Harvard, 1995. 196p index afp ISBN 0-674-78912-1, $24.95

Williamson's lucid and absorbing study successfully presents what can be known about the cultural context of Sappho's life and work. Using social, political, and literary materials that influenced and reflect Sappho's experience, the

author (Univ. of Surrey) reconstructs the atmosphere in which Sappho lived, breathed, and worked. References abound, providing readers with reproductions of relevant vase paintings, fragments of contemporary poetry, and a brief annotated bibliography for further research. It is of particular note that this interpretation of Sappho locates her within her culture in the broadest sense, not as an anachronism or a marginal figure but instead deriving much of the intensity of her lyrics from the tradition in which Williamson sees them embedded. The many strands of investigation come together, finally, in the analysis of the songs locating Sappho in the religion, society, and culture of the Homeric tradition. Aphrodite emerges as not simply Sappho's "patron goddess" but as the carrier of her sense of self: Sappho transforms the identity of Aphrodite as she transforms the conventions of the love relationship itself. This study insists on both reflective and integrative reading. Understanding Sappho in such a variety of contexts enriches both the fragmentary texts and their readers. General; upper-division undergraduate through faculty.—*R. Nadelhaft, University of Maine*

WS-0606   PA3016   95-2906 CIP
Zeitlin, Froma L. **Playing the other: gender and society in classical Greek literature.** Chicago, 1996. 474p bibl indexes afp ISBN 0-226-97921-0, $60.00; ISBN 0-226-97922-9 pbk, $19.95

Playing the Other brings together nine of Zeitlin's outstanding essays on ancient Greek literature. The work collected in this volume focuses on Athenian drama (seven of the nine chapters), especially Aeschylean and Euripidean tragedy, but the prestigious texts of the early Greek epic tradition, Homer's *Odyssey* and Hesiod's *Theogony* and *Works and Days*, also receive sophisticated critical scrutiny. Although all but one of the essays have been previously published, often more than once, and the recent essays have enjoyed wide circulation as orally delivered papers, their collection here constitutes a valuable resource for students of women's studies and Greek literature. Indeed, in many respects the collection can be read as a history of feminist criticism in the study of ancient Greek literature. Several of the essays have justly become classics in the field, especially the earliest pieces reprinted here ("The Dynamics of Misogyny: Myth and Mythmaking in Aeschylus' *Oresteia*" and "Travesties of Gender and Genre in Aristophanes' *Thesmophoriazousae*"). All are as fresh and exciting to read today as when they were first published. The volume should constitute an attractive addition to any library.—*A. M. Keith, University of Toronto*

◆ Germanic

WS-0607   PT2603.A147   90-4953 CIP
Bachmann, Ingeborg. **Malina: a novel,** tr. by Philip Boehm. Holmes & Meier, 1991 (c1990). 244p ISBN 0-8419-1192-4, $24.95

This is the first translation to appear in English of Bachmann's last completed novel, and it is an immensely sensitive handling of difficult material. Part of the "Modern Voices" series, it contains a translator's note and glossary, as well as an afterword by Mark Anderson, all extremely helpful to the reader, who can never hope to penetrate the layers of pain and obfuscation that purport to describe a Viennese woman writer, living with a mysterious man (alter ego) named Malina, in love with the Hungarian, Ivan, and tormented by unresolved attitudes toward her father. Stylistic elements are reminiscent of music—specifically, grand opera—and provide moments of macabre humor. Presently appearing in a movie version in Germany, this novel, with its famous last line "It was murder," its interest to feminist critics, and its dreamlike evocation of Viennese culture, is a necessary adjunct to collections of Bachmann's outstanding short stories, also recently translated—e.g., *The Thirteenth Year* (CH, Feb'88) and *Three Paths to the Lake* (CH, Jul'90). Recommended for all libraries.—*E. Glass, Rosemont College*

WS-0608   Orig
Contemporary Norwegian women's writing: an anthology, ed. by Janet Garton. Norvik, 1996 (c1995). (Dist. by Dufour Editions) 253p bibl ISBN 1-870041-29-1 pbk, $24.95

This title in the publisher's Scandinavian and Baltic series represents women's writings in Norway from 1973 (Bjørg Vik's essay "Is It True That Women Are Oppressed?" which appeared in the first issue of the journal *Siren*) to 1989 (an excerpt from Herbjørg Wassmo's novel translated into English as *Dina's Book*). As Garton says in her introductory material, the collection reflects a variety of genres and subjects; the 12 authors range from Bergljot Hobaek Haff, born in 1925, to Lisbet Hiide, born in 1956. The editor's "Notes on Authors" provides good historical and biographical information, and a helpful bibliography of publications in Norwegian and English translation concludes the volume. Anger, passion, and politics abound in these pages; but the brevity of the pieces in spite of competent translation precludes full engagement with the original. Recommended only for libraries collecting Scandinavian and Baltic literature and for those with extensive holdings in women's studies. Graduates; researchers; faculty.—*J. G. Holland, Davidson College*

WS-0609   PT8950   93-11754 CIP
Dunn, Margaret. **Paradigms and paradoxes in the life and letters of Sigrid Undset.** University Press of America, 1994. 104p index afp ISBN 0-8191-9280-5, $29.50

Dunn's opening assertion that "I envision Sigrid Undset as the major character in each of her novels" is obscured by her need to find paradigms and paradoxes in the texts. In brief chapters on *Kristin Lavransdatter* (1920), *The Master of Hestviken* (1925), *The Wild Orchid* (1931), *The Burning Bush* (1932), *Ida Elizabeth* (1932), and *Madame Dorothea* (1939) that are little more than outlines, she analyzes the novels in terms of paradigms drawn from such diverse sources as James Joyce, T.S. Eliot, Teilhard de Chardin, The Benedictine Rule, Thomas Berry, and John Bradshaw, this last choice enough to cast suspicion on the whole argument. There is little here about Undset's life beyond a few scattered and generally unconnected biographical details; the last chapter touches on Undset's exile in the United States during WW II, her friendship with a variety of American women (including Willa Cather), and her letters to her sister in Stockholm collected by Arne Skouen in *Sigrid Undset Skriver Hjem* (Sigrid Undset Writes Home,Oslo, 1982). Dunn clearly knows the texts well, and she seems to have detailed information about Undset's public and private selves gathered over what she characterizes as "my twenty-seven years of relationship with Sigrid Undset." Unfortunately, forcing the texts to align with the diverse paradigms weakens her use of this potentially rich material. Graduate; faculty.—*R. R. Kettler, Miami University (OH)*

WS-0610   PT1853   96-82 CIP
Ebner-Eschenbach, Marie von. **Their pavel,** tr. by Lynne Tatlock. Camden House, 1996. 151p afp ISBN 1-57113-078-0, $55.95

If the movies are any indication, classic novels by women writers (e.g., Austen, Wharton, Alcott, and the Brontës) are once again in vogue. Unlike scholars of English and American studies, however, scholars of German literature are hard pressed to find even a few significant women authors from periods prior to 1945. Is it any wonder then that several works have appeared recently about and by one of the more celebrated of this minuscule group, the Austrian Marie von Ebner-Eschenbach? Ferrel V. Rose provided an excellent treatise on Ebner-Eschenbach (*The Guises of Modesty*, CH, Nov'94); now Tatlock has published her translation of one of the author's better-remembered works, *Das Gemeindekind* (1887). Although this novella had already appeared in translation a century ago (titled *The Child of the Parish*), the scarcity and the stilted and somewhat archaic style of that edition make Tatlock's version welcome indeed. Ebner-Eschenbach's story of the slow and indefatigable rise of the orphaned son of an executed murderer, who is reared by his village only out of a sense of its legal obligation, is consistent with prevailing Victorian and Hapsburg era literary tastes. This highly readable rendition preserves both the spirit and the tenor of the original. Not a book for just students and scholars of literature, readers of all backgrounds and tastes should enjoy it.—*C. L. Dolmetsch, Marshall University*

WS-0611   PT2423   91-35930 CIP
The education of Fanny Lewald: an autobiography, ed. and tr. by Hanna Ballin Lewis. State University of New York, 1992. 341p bibl index ISBN 0-7914-1147-8, $57.50; ISBN 0-7914-1148-6 pbk, $18.95

Part of the series "Women Writers in Translation," this autobiography of the popular writer of more than 50 books recounts the early experiences of the eldest daughter of middle-class Jewish parents in Königsberg. It is a helpful source of information about the position of Jews, the 19th-century middle class, and a woman's education. Lewald (1811-89) is remarkable for her evolution from dutiful daughter to independent writer. She earned a comfortable living and used her freedom to advance the cause of emancipation for others. She also commented on many of the prominent figures of her day. The text is greatly abridged, containing "less than fifty percent of the original text." Omissions are summarized where they occur. Regrettably, there are several lapses in the editing of a generally good translation. Valuable as a document of social history, the book is not without its flaws. Lewald dwells on the obvious, exalts her role, harangues, and sentimentalizes. The translator provides essential notes to obscure references along with a good bibliography and index, making this an accessible resource for the interested student or general reader.—*E. Glass, Rosemont College*

WS-0612   PT2415   94-38323 CIP
Gustafson, Susan E. **Absent mothers and orphaned fathers: narcissism and abjection in Lessing's aesthetic and dramatic production.** Wayne State, 1995. 314p bibl index afp ISBN 0-8143-2503-3, $39.95

This innovative analysis views Gotthold Lessing's dramas (*Miss Sara Sampson*, *Emilia Galotti*, and *Nathan der Weise*) through the lens of Kristevan psychoanalysis, with secondary reference to Freud, Lacan, et al. Using *Laokoon*, but also other theoretical writings and correspondence, Gustafson provides a well-grounded, lengthy basis for interpretations that "underscore ... the centrality of the abject mother and the ideal father throughout Lessing's dramatic and aesthetic work." The author also incidentally illuminates the use of snake imagery (note the fearsome Gorgon illustration on the jacket) while shedding original light on several subordinate characters. Gustafson provides English translations of all German passages, makes outstanding use of her comprehensive bibliography and footnotes that contrast her arguments with those of recent critics, and sets forth her assertions in a persuasive way. The term "abjection" may seem unusual, but it proves to be necessarily descriptive of women throughout. There is a remarkable wealth of new insight into female characters and, more significantly, into the various categories of fathers foregrounded by Lessing. This excellent and intriguing book is recommended to student and critic alike.—*E. Glass, Rosemont College*

WS-0613   PT671   95-50130 CIP
Hart, Gail K. **Tragedy in paradise: family and gender politics in German bourgeois tragedy, 1750-1850.** Camden House, 1996. 136p bibl index afp ISBN 1-57113-037-3, $52.95

Analyzing German bourgeois tragedy, Hart (Univ. of California, Irvine) discovers something new: "the ritual removal of women." She locates the source for the genre's image of woman in an English play, George Lillo's "Image of Woe," in which the character Sarah Millwood's aggressive sexuality destroys the lives of the male characters. Gotthold Lessing consciously draws on Lillo's drama in the classic bourgeois tragedy *Miss Sarah Sampson* (1789), in which all women disappear, leaving two men to raise a family together. Proceeding to analyze Goethe, Klinger, Heinrich Leopole Wagner, Kleist, Schiller, and Hebel, Hart sees men constantly encroaching on turf traditionally assigned to women. For example, Lessing's man of sensibility rendered the feminine unnecessary for the family, while Kleist turns "grace," a conventionally feminine attribute, into an exclusively masculine affair. Hart's well-written analysis judiciously and deftly alludes to Eve Kosofsky Sedgwick's ideas on homosociality in British literature. Hart argues, however, that the German tradition is about the sheer expulsion of women, rather than the use of women as items of exchange. Her work makes a nice addition to a genre thought to be well known and performs the service of bringing German studies in contact with American gender studies. Upper-division undergraduate; graduate; faculty.—*R. D. Tobin, Whitman College*

WS-0614   PT289   90-46558 CIP
In the shadow of Olympus: German women writers around 1800, ed. by Katherine R. Goodman and Edith Waldstein. State University of New York, 1992. 264p bibl index ISBN 0-7914-0743-8, $49.50; ISBN 0-7914-0744-6 pbk, $16.95

The introduction to this book views women's writing in a comparative and historical context. In Germany, the public sphere where bourgeois authors found a voice and a readership emerged relatively late, coinciding with the French Revolution and the turn toward German classical and romantic aesthetics as an alternative to French terror. Women writers were not trained to meet these aesthetic norms and responded ambivalently to the roles ascribed them. The "shadow of

Olympus" refers to Goethe's preeminent position around 1800 and his continuing domination of literary history to the detriment of other voices, including Friederike Helene Unger, Sophie La Roche, Sophie Mereau, Rahel Varnhagen, Charlotte von Stein, Bettine von Arnim, Caroline Schlegel-Schelling, Therese Huber, Henriette Fröhlich, Sophie Albrecht, and Benedikte Naubert. These women wrote in dialogue with Goethe and other male authors, appropriating and being appropriated, creating alternative literary forms, plots, and visions. Jeannine Blackwell's study of the marriage plot in conjunction with family, church, and state control over women is particulary illuminating. The separate sections for texts, notes, and bibliographies are awkward. Clearly written, this first sustained gynocritical examination of this period in English is valuable for upper-division undergraduates as well as for graduate students and faculty.—*I. Di Maio, Louisiana State University*

WS-0615   PT2621   94-24281 CIP
Kaschnitz, Marie Luise. **Long shadows: stories,** tr. by Anni Whissen. Camden House, 1995. 149p bibl afp ISBN 1-57113-021-7, $39.95

Well known for her pre-WW II novels and her postwar books of essays, short prose, and poetry, Kaschnitz, following the death of her husband in 1958, turned to radio plays and short stories until her death in 1974. Here 21 short stories, ably translated by Anni Whissen, depict the loneliness and insecurity of individual human destiny. Frequent themes are loss and anxiety—from the pains of childhood to the indignities of old age—written always from a women's perspective. The author sets seven of these stories in Italy and often employs Greek and Roman mythology, using long inner monologues, diary, and journal methods (Rilke-style) sometimes called controlled improvisation. "Long Shadows" shows Rosie meeting a boy (Pan) naked on the beach. Ashamed (as she is), he vanishes under a setting sun that casts long shadows. Other stories with equally apt titles follow: "Black Lake," "Red Net," "Ghosts," "Everlasting Light," and more. The 25-entry bibliography provides additional access to an author whose star continues to rise in the English-speaking world. Partly through readings on college campuses and partly due to German-government-sponsored lectures during the 1960s and '70s, Kaschnitz enjoys a modest, popular following in America. Suitable for sophisticated general and scholarly audiences; upper-division undergraduate and above.—*L. J. Rippley, St. Olaf College*

WS-0616   PT735   93-42072 CIP
Kosta, Barbara. **Recasting autobiography: women's counterfictions in contemporary German literature and film.** Cornell, 1994. 219p bibl index afp ISBN 0-8014-2889-0, $35.00; ISBN 0-8014-8203-8 pbk, $13.95

Kosta delineates the post-1968 German student revolt and its awakening impact on feminist biography. Previously women wrote from a defensive or justificative posture; now they script the "autograph" of their history, reflecting the cultural engendering in which the woman self is defined by connection to others, the male self by isolation. German feminine autobiography presented here supplies a network of dialogues in which diversity links with self-reflection resulting in narrative discursivity. What began as feminist outlets for rage against, and indictments of, males has matured into paradigms of linguistic self-representation. The text becomes a working station, a fabric, a polyvalent network of voices that uses memory to interarch across time not with freeze-frame memory but in a simultaneity of events, a technique that improves by a dialogue of tenses on traditionally male/logical sequences. Because of Germany's Nazi past, German feminist writers inevitably confront the "father," the foregone nationalist Fatherland identity, which renders Kosta's study more relevant than if it treated any other culture. Post-Nazi Germany therefore has also produced the cinematic epistolary to expose the Reich's victimization/devaluation of the woman, and to reposition her in contemporary society. Thoroughly documented in footnotes with biblio/filmography and an index, this even-handed, unpolemical remapping of the autobiography belongs in all libraries whose clientele numbers serious readers. General and academic audiences.—*L. J. Rippley, St. Olaf College*

WS-0617   PT2512   93-12435 CIP
Powell, Hugh. **Louise von Gall: her world and work.** Camden House, 1993. 230p bibl index afp ISBN 1-879751-55-0, $59.00

More than half of this study is devoted to the "world" of Louise von Gall (1815-55). Powell's objective is to "illuminate her environment of humanitarian thinkers"

as well as to appraise Gall's achievement. Although characters in *Vormärz* prose fiction frequently did serve as mouthpieces for their authors, Powell's consistent conflation of characters' and authors' views on politics, society, technology, and economics, rendered through lengthy direct quotations, lacks analysis. He fails to critically address the notion that authors not only "mirror" the world, they construct fictional worlds. Nevertheless, one can appreciate the attention paid lesser-known authors' reflections on the enormous changes taking place in 19th-century German lands. The effect that the failed 1848 revolution had on the fictional form of liberal writers, particularly on the oft-cited works of Karl Gutzkow, however, requires elaboration. Powell's most valuable contribution is his examination of the liberal aristocrat Louise von Gall's life and work, especially her—ultimately fatal—struggle to gain an authorial voice while fulfilling duties as wife and mother; her literary treatment of the poet Annette von Droste-Hülshoff, who had had strong literary and emotional ties to Gall's husband, Levin Schücking; and her treatment of contemporary issues. Appendixes provide supplementary documentation. Undergraduate; graduate; faculty; general.—*I. Di Maio, Louisiana State University*

WS-0618   PT1853   94-5460 CIP
Rose, Ferrel V. **The guises of modesty: Marie von Ebner-Eschenbach's female artists.** Camden House, 1994. 213p bibl index afp ISBN 1-879751-69-0, $49.95

Although some writers justifiably fade into obscurity after their lifetimes, others deserve a better fate. Such is the case for the Austrian Marie von Ebner-Eschenbach (1830-1916). As Rose indicates in her introduction, Ebner-Eschenbach succeeded with her narratives despite both her lack of a substantial formal education and the prevailing attitude of her day to disregard even the most serious literary efforts of women. Starting as a dramatist, Ebner-Eschenbach soon moved more successfully to prose; both genres, however, provide examples used in this study. Rose convincingly explains that this author was not a simple conservative aristocrat as past scholars have claimed, but rather a more socially conscious and critically aware observer, albeit one laboring under the constraints of her time, especially her own high social standing and her intentional use of acceptable, noncontroversial authors such as Friedrich Schiller and Franz Grillparzer as role models. Although Rose's study focuses primarily on three specific texts, the reader is made aware of the larger body of Ebner-Eschenbach's writings. This study is extremely well documented and well written. The only fault, if any, may be said to be the rather curious title, which suggests a more limited scope for this work than it actually has. Indeed, this work should not only help to restore the reputation of Marie von Ebner-Eschenbach in the literary canon, it should also be regarded as a fine example in the study of otherwise neglected authors. Graduate; faculty.—*C. L. Dolmetsch, Marshall University*

WS-0619   PT8928   92-14129 CIP
Skram, Amalie. **Under observation,** tr. by Katherine Hanson and Judith Messick. Women in Translation, 1992. 369p bibl ISBN 1-879679-03-5 pbk, $15.95

In *Under Observation*, first published in 1895 as *Professor Hieronimus* and *Paa St. Jørgen*, the important Norwegian Danish naturalistic writer Amalie Skram tells her autobiographical story of the treatment of female psychiatric patients in her day. An introduction by Elaine Showalter and essays and notes by the translators supply a historical and biographical setting. Hanson and Messick should be given credit for closer local accuracy here and there, but it is in the English translation of this *Künstlerroman* by Alice Stronach and G. B. Jacobi (London, 1899) that the sensibility of the painter Else Kant more truly springs to life. The dulling of the edged verbal precision of this master of free indirect discourse may have contributed to the mistaken designation of Kant as narrator and arguably oversimplified reading in the introduction (pp.3 and xi). Beyond helpful background information this reviewer found little insight into Skram's artistic power in the analyses accompanying the text. Such worthy books published by Women in Translation in the future will benefit from more rigorous editorial scrutiny. Recommended with reservation.—*J. G. Holland, Davidson College*

WS-0620   PT1853   93-26091 CIP
Steiner, Carl. **Of reason and love: the life and works of Marie von Ebner-Eschenbach (1830-1916).** Ariadne, CA, 1994. 233p bibl index ISBN 0-929497-77-5, $29.50

Marie von Ebner-Eschenbach (1830-1916) gained recognition rather late in life; by 1890 she was considered the foremost woman author writing in German. To this day, she is appreciated more for her advocacy of kindness and compassion as the proper response to social inequities, than for her political astuteness in the portrayal of aristocratic abuses. A gentle didacticism rather than psychological subtlety, the variety of characters and themes depicted in her many stories and five novels rather than stylistic versatility, are thought to be her hallmark. Yet, it had been her first and abiding ambition to establish herself in an exclusively "male" genre: heroic tragedy in the classical mold of Schiller. However, after many frustrations with the theater, she looked to Turgenev as the model for her prose. Steiner's introductory study traces the evolution of this struggle in her life. Since only seven of Ebner's stories have been translated recently—the bibliography lists English versions from the 1890s and new interpretive work selectively—descriptive plot summaries, sometimes coupled with homey comments, predominate in a book that, in the end, is sustained more by the appeal of Ebner's "humanist message" than by its own momentum as scholarship. General and academic audiences.—*M. Winkler, Rice University*

WS-0621 PT5411 93-37518 CIP
Women writing in Dutch, ed. by Kristiaan Aercke. Garland, 1994. 713p (Women writers of the world, 1) afp ISBN 0-8153-0231-2, $95.00

As explained in the introduction, this title has been carefully chosen to represent fairly a number of writers who differ greatly from one another: across time, formal orientation, and geography. Hoping to construct an anthology free of polemical cant or canonical aspirations, editor Aercke has selected 16 women who wrote or are still writing in Dutch, whose work is presented in translation along with introductory essays by scholars almost as varied as the authors themselves. Given the range of talents among the writers and the translators, some of the authors will be more readily comprehended than others. The earliest authors, fascinating in description, are somewhat less enthralling to read. With Maria Petijt, however, a mystic who lived between 1623 and 1677, the anthology becomes startlingly direct; her "unmediated" mysticism has an immediacy that speaks across the centuries. Not until the final author, Maria Stahlie, born in 1955, does another writer speak with such an unmistakable voice, though several of the other contributors are memorable. The introductory essays are unfailingly helpful, often interesting in their own right. What remains unclear, given the lack of knowledge on this side of the Atlantic of the body of Dutch literature, is what this choice represents. The introductory remarks conclude with a long list of writers who "could, and probably should" have been included. Perhaps this volume will create a climate receptive to the translation and distribution of the work of other women writing in Dutch. General; upper-division undergraduate through faculty.—*R. Nadelhaft, University of Maine at Orono*

◆ Romance
French

WS-0622 PQ1963 94-48885 CIP
Allison, Jenene J. **Revealing difference: the fiction of Isabelle de Charrière.** Delaware, 1995. (Dist. by Associated University Presses) 171p bibl index afp ISBN 0-87413-566-4, $33.50

In her analysis of Isabelle de Charrière's feminocentric fiction Allison (Univ. of Texas at Austin) stresses the originality and inventiveness of this Dutch-born French writer. The author's analysis is greatly enhanced by her 20th-century, gender-related perspective. Allison shows how narrative form (in addition to plot) can perpetuate patriarchal structures, a point she illustrates with quotations from such works as *Le Noble* and *Letters trouvées dans des portefeuilles d'émigrés*. She contends that Charrière's literary techniques undermine traditional, repressed images of women. Charrière understands discourse to be gendered. Allison cites two novels illustrating two types of discourse: *Lettres écrites de Lausanne* represents the monophonic epistolary novel (a feminine genre); *Sir Walter Finch et son fils William* uses the philosophe's language (a masculine genre). Allison provides useful references to such Charrière specialists as Janet Whatley and Isabelle Vissière and to feminist scholars such as Elizabeth Goldsmith, Joan Landes,

and Carole Pateman. Recommended for students of women's or gender studies and 18th-century literary studies at the upper-division undergraduate level and above.—*L. A. Russell, Rosemont College*

WS-0623 PQ637 90-31075 CIP
Beasley, Faith E. **Revising memory: women's fiction and memoirs in seventeenth-century France.** Rutgers, 1991 (c1990). 288p bibl index ISBN 0-8135-1585-8, $42.00

In this rich, suggestive, and beautifully written work, Beasley focuses on the use and conception of history in memoirs and historical novels by three women authors of the opening years of the reign of Louis XIV, the Duchesse de Montpensier, Madame de Lafayette, and Madame de Villedieu. Acknowledged since the 17th century to be the originators of the historical novel and innovators in the writing of memoirs, these women have not, until recently, been studied as a group and as founders of a literary tradition. Beasley's goal is to determine what inspired them to develop the history-affiliated genres they worked with. Analyzing their texts with respect to the role the authors and other women played in public life and on the cultural scene, Beasley sees the works as questioning the accepted historical record of the time. She concludes that the authors' fundamental purpose was to offer "an alternative narrative of the past, a particular history designed to undermine the patriarchal, official history advanced by the Sun King, Louis XIV." Although Beasley owes much to the feminist literary criticism of Joan De Jean and Nancy K. Miller as well as to the work of feminist historians Natalie Zemon Davis, Joan Kelly, and Joan Scott, she goes well beyond them in the way she integrates literary and historiographical perspectives.—*R. A. Picken, Queens College, CUNY*

WS-0624 PQ2431 93-28437 CIP
Besser, Gretchen Rous. **Germaine de Staël revisited.** Twayne, 1994. 180p bibl index afp ISBN 0-8057-8286-9, $23.95

This title is but the latest in a series of works about the enduring legacy of one of the foremost intellectuals during the turbulent years of the French Revolution. Well-balanced in its presentation, it stands in sharp contrast to the vituperative attack made in Christopher Herold's biased *Mistress to an Age* (1958), Anthony West's unwarranted, violent diatribe, *Mortal Wounds* (1973), or Charlotte Hogsett's commendable *The Literary Existence of Germaine de Staël* (CH, Apr'88). Besser's objective is to introduce a new generation of readers to Madame de Staël's novelistic fiction, political thoughts, and iconoclastic demands for sexual equality. Sagaciously, she pays only scant attention to *Delphine* (1802) and *Corinne* (1807), two outdated novels. Instead, Besser chooses to emphasize de Staël's decisive role in the "literary and political orientation" of the nascent Romantic movement in western Europe. Although Besser gives de Staël due credit for her anticipation of sociology, she also points out her penchant for romantic love, ludicrous pride, and the vitriolic antisemitism present in her minor prose works. Besser's all-to-brief seminal introduction to Madame de Staël's life and works will undoubtedly strike a responsive chord in admirers and detractors alike. This cogent, clear, easily readable study is very highly recommended for public and university libraries.—*R. Merker, Grambling State University*

WS-0625 PQ155 92-38403 CIP
Burns, E. Jane. **Bodytalk: when women speak in Old French literature.** Pennsylvania, 1993. 277p bibl index afp ISBN 0-8122-3183-X, $36.95; ISBN 0-8122-1405-6 pbk, $14.95

Inspired by the feminist theories of Luce Irigaray and Teresa de Lauretis, Burns offers an original and often exciting interpretation of numerous Old French texts: several fabliaux, the *Jeu d'Adam*, *Philomena*, Chrétien de Troyes's *Erec et Enide* (the best chapter, in this reviewer's opinion), and Béroul's *Tristan*. Burns develops the intriguing thesis that, like prototypical Mae Wests, the heroines of these works exhibit a "doubled speech," a "bodytalk" that, although grounded in the dominant voice of the culture, nonetheless manages to call it into question and thereby gain for the heroines some status as speaking subjects. Although a poststructuralist approach predominates, with ingenious displays of word play ("con"/"conte"/"connoistre"/"conjointure"), the readings are modulated by unmistakable wit and buttressed by scholarly expositions of classical and medieval ideas as formulated by Plato, Aristotle, Galen, Augustine, and Aquinas. Regardless of one's critical persuasion, Burns's study raises basic questions regarding the interpretation of medieval texts and is sure to become—well, seminal. Graduate; faculty.—*C. M. Reno, Vassar College*

WS-0626   PQ1575   91-31266 CIP
Christine, de Pisan. **The book of the duke of true lovers,** by Christine de Pizan; tr. by Thelma S. Fenster and Nadia Margolis. Persea Books, 1992 (c1991). 162p bibl ISBN 0-89255-163-1, $24.95; ISBN 0-89255-166-6 pbk, $11.95

The epithet, the "Simone de Beauvoir of the Middle Ages," bestowed on Christine de Pisan in Robert Sabatier's *La poésie du Moyen Age* (Paris, 1975) is borne out in this new English translation (the only previous one in archaic English dating from 1908, with several subsequent reprintings). A champion of intelligent, articulate women and the first French woman to make a living from her writing, Pisan was anything but a "blue stocking." This new translation, in which the charm of her creation and the seriousness of her message are rendered in readable contemporary language, is significant in its fidelity to context and discourse, not only of the work itself, but to the newness of her "gentle" feminist thought in relation to the period in which she lived. The six illustrations are authentic reproductions directly from Harley manuscript 4431 and appear in the book at approximately the same place in which they occur in the manuscript. The introduction includes a useful discussion of the clothing worn by the subjects in the illustrations, providing the reader with insight into costume and ornament of mid 15th-century France. Also included are a brief guide to medieval lyric forms, excellent introductory notes, and informative endnotes. Level: Advanced undergraduate and above.—*M. R. Bonfini, Immaculata College*

WS-0627   PQ1575   92-41941 CIP
Christine, de Pisan. **The writings of Christine de Pizan,** sel. and ed. by Charity Cannon Willard. Persea Books, 1994. 384p bibl index afp ISBN 0-89255-180-1, $35.00; ISBN 0-89255-188-7 pbk, $13.50

In *The Writings of Christine de Pizan*, Willard provides the reader with a wide range of skillfully chosen excerpts of canon texts and of many hitherto untranslated texts. She organizes this book thematically into eight chapters, including "The Courtly Poet," "The Defense of Women," "The Biography of Charles V," "The Fate of France," and "The Life of the Spirit." These themes reflect Christine de Pisan's progression and her development as a writer as well as her versatility as a thinker. The editor focuses on Christine de Pisan as a witness of her society and invites the reader to discover the multifaceted author through primary texts. Each chapter begins with a concise and informative introductory essay. The bibliography section is complete and well documented. No prior knowledge of Christine de Pisan is needed to read this book, which is clearly written and well conceived. It can be used in an introductory course on medieval literature or on the French author herself. The wide selection of the texts and the quality of the translations also make it useful to advanced students and scholars. All levels.—*A. Caillaud, Grand Valley State University*

WS-0628   PQ2663   90-26785 CIP
Cixous, Hélène. **"Coming to writing" and other essays,** ed. by Deborah Jenson; tr. by Sarah Cornell et al. Harvard, 1991. 214p index afp ISBN 0-674-14436-8, $24.95

These six essays from Hélène Cixous, particularly the title essay, are almost unclassifiable by American expectations, but this volume with its informative/appreciative introduction and conclusion by Jenson and Susan Rubin Suleiman, goes far to extend a reader's recognitions. Cixous, important as she is as a feminist theorist and activist, is equally important as an accurate emotional sounding board for women everywhere. As such, her articulation of powerful, if delicate, perceptions in lucid prose/poetry compels the attention of European and American readers, even anti-feminists. For undergraduates, the essays will be either opaque or intensely revealing. Graduate students and faculties in women's studies or literature will welcome the literary, emotional but nonsentimental tone in a field often overanalytical or overimpersonal. Cixous can be unashamedly subjective because the power of her prose is philosophically sound and grounded in the most ancient traditions of European literature. The translation has been made with extreme care, care almost intrusive in its attempt to transmit the subtleties of style and thought in the elusive Cixous, an exactness which will be valued by scholars.—*T. S. Kobler, Texas Woman's University*

WS-0629   PQ2663.I9   90-41111 MARC
Cixous, Hélène. **The book of Promethea—Le livre de Promethea,** tr. by Betsy Wing. Nebraska, 1991. 211p afp ISBN 0-8032-1443-X, $29.95; ISBN 0-8032-6343-0 pbk, $10.95

To those who follow the French intellectual scene, Hélène Cixous is well known as a prolific writer, a perceptive critic, and an engaged feminist. For those less familiar with her, this impressive translation of a work originally published in 1983 can serve as a revealing introduction to all three facets of her career. This "autobiographical" tale of the passionate love between two women derives its evocative power from Cixous's practice of "writing from the body" in order to reveal the inextricable links between linguistic and social structures, and their relationships to the suppression of women's voice(s). As the title indicates, Cixous deploys a savvy decentering of Western mythologies and notions of the self to make a space for feminine experience. She uses wordplays and clichés in a strategy aimed at subverting the notion of "neutral language." The problem of translation of (feminine) experience into writing is at the heart of her project. Near the end of her text, the narrator senses success: "I wrote Promethea in our language. But she would not lose anything even in translation." Happily, Betsy Wing's remarkably faithful rendering of the book keeps that promise. Appropriate for upper-division undergraduates.—*G. Moskos, Swarthmore College*

WS-0630   PQ3949   92-8134 CIP
Condé, Maryse. **I, Tituba, black witch of Salem,** tr. by Richard Philcox. University Press of Virginia, 1992. 227p bibl ISBN 0-8139-1398-5, $19.95

Condé is one of the most prolific writers of the Caribbean and perhaps the most powerful woman's voice in contemporary literature of the Americas. Her interpretation of the Salem witch trials, recast from her own dreams, is a remarkable work of historical fiction that is a haunting and powerful reminder of the dangers of intolerance of differences. Tituba, the black witch of Salem about whom there is little factual information, tells her story in the first person narrative in the traditions of African oral history. The imaginative and provocative language takes the reader on a dark journey in the history of the Americas. Richard Philcox's translation is admirably done. The book contains a foreword by Angela Davis and an afterword by Armstrong Scarboro that includes an interview with Condé. Condé's historical note is helpful to the reader. The glossary of Creole words and phrases invented by the author is also included. Highly recommended for the general reader.—*A. J. Guillaume Jr., St. Louis University*

WS-0631   PQ1561   93-16139 Orig
The Danse macabre of women: ms. fr. 995 of the Bibliothèque Nationale, ed. by Ann Tukey Harrison. Kent State, 1994. 162p bibl index afp ISBN 0-87338-473-3, $24.00

The *Danse macabre des femmes* offers a rare and fascinating glimpse into the daily life of French women toward the end of the 15th century. The version of the work reproduced in this edition is an undated manuscript, Ms. fr. 995 of the Bibliothèque nationale. Harrison's edition includes a lengthy introduction, a chapter by Sandra Hindman (art history, Northwestern Univ.) commenting on the illuminations that accompany the text, and a facsimile of the entire manuscript (including several color plates). Each page of the manuscript is accompanied by a transcription, translation, and notes, all conveniently presented on the facing page. The format of the edition is remarkably well designed and attractively presented. Although not a literary masterpiece, the *Danse macabre des femmes* is a valuable source for those interested in medieval social history. The text and the images provide a striking representation of the late medieval fascination with death. It will be a valuable addition to undergraduate- and graduate-level collections.—*D. A. Fein, University of North Carolina at Greensboro*

WS-0632   PQ637   91-28239 CIP
DeJean, Joan. **Tender geographies: women and the origins of the novel in France.** Columbia, 1991. 297p bibl index afp ISBN 0-231-06230-3, $35.00

DeJean's interdisciplinary study situates the origins of the French novel in twin historical currents: the changing status of women, and the rise of absolutism after the failure of the Fronde. It brings fresh documentary support and fresh argument to bear on primary materials well known through older research; Henri

Coulet's *Le roman francais jusquá la Révolution* (1967) remains indispensable. Arguing a strong feminine continuity, and restricting her scope to novels written by women, as well as to the *roman d'analyse*, DeJean makes a convincing return to the theory of collective authorship, throwing new light on the *salons* and their political implications. Lafayette's *La Princesse de Clèves* is thus restored to its complex historical context, so frequently ignored in narrowly psychological readings. DeJean also contributes to current discussion of canon formation, blaming Boileau and government-sponsored classicism for the despised status of the novel. Her bibliography of women's writing from 1640 to 1715, in addition to the bibliography of works cited, will be a useful reference tool. The text and all long quotations are in English, and the work should be of interest to students of history as well as of literature and feminism. Graduate and upper-division undergraduate levels.—*J. Warwick, York University*

WS-0633 PQ2607 95-15342 CIP
Delarue-Mardrus, Lucie. **The angel and the perverts,** tr. by Anna Livia. New York University, 1995. 227p bibl afp ISBN 0-8147-5080-X, $45.00; ISBN 0-8147-5098-2 pbk, $14.95

This first English translation of *Ange et les pervers* (1930), by the prolific French writer prominent in the 1920s, is a notable addition to the works of lesbian literature in English. The translator's lengthy introduction describes Delarue-Mardrus and her life, discussing how she fell passionately in love with women throughout her life, although married for a number of years to Joseph-Charles Mardrus, the translator of the *Arabian Nights*. Livia refers to the narrative that follows as "a novel of social turbulence." Reminiscent of Djuna Barnes's *Nightwood*, Delarue-Mardrus's book is a roman à clef that includes portraits of such people as Natalie Clifford Barney and Renée Vivien. The narrator, a hermaphrodite named Mario/Marian, records his/her experiences in the sexual underworld of Paris. Being a hermaphrodite allows Mario/Marian the opportunity to explore the lives of both lesbians and gay men. What is more important, Mario/Marian serves as an often bitter commentator on social life and the blurring of boundaries between the genders. The combination of Livia's excellent introduction and an intriguing novel about gender bending makes this book an excellent choice for anyone interested in studying the construction of gender. All collections.—*S. A. Inness, Miami University*

WS-0634 PQ1925 91-13244 CIP
Farrell, Michèle Longino. **Performing motherhood: the Sévigné correspondence.** University Press of New England, 1991. 302p bibl index afp ISBN 0-87451-536-X, $45.00; ISBN 0-87451-537-8 pbk, $22.95

In this provocative volume, Farrell breaks new territory by reexamining from a feminist point of view the correspondence of Mme de Sévigné, one of the few major women authors of French literature not to have attracted concentrated attention from feminist scholars. Farrell's basic purpose is to try to understand why Sévigné's correspondence was so readily integrated into the normative canon of the 17th-century literature, a process that began during that author's lifetime. Her examination of the correspondence, particularly Sévigné's letters to her daughter, leads her to the conclusion that the correspondence is in fact a public performance of the maternal role. And by acting out the role that had already been scripted for her by a patriarchal society, Sévigné was able to enter the male domain of writing. Farrell suggests that her "superb talent as writer . . . was undisputed because she absorbed and represented the code governing appropriate generic behavior for women in her time." Farrell's well-written study is informed by a deep and comprehensive understanding of 17th-century French society and buttressed by scrupulous scholarship. It will have to be taken into account in all future work on Mme de Sévigné. The volume contains extensive notes and a useful bibliography.—*R. A. Picken, Queens College, CUNY*

WS-0635 PQ2603 94-20972 CIP
Feminist interpretations of Simone de Beauvoir, ed. by Margaret A. Simons. Pennsylvania State, 1995. 324p bibl index afp ISBN 0-271-01412-1, $45.00; ISBN 0-271-01413-X pbk, $15.50

Throughout much of her relationship with Sartre, Beauvoir insisted that she had little to do with the development of existentialism. Yet as these essays show, she may have been the one who initiated it. The essays reveal that theirs was not a relationship in which Sartre paved the philosophical path and Beauvoir simply followed. Many of the essays focus on *The Second Sex* (English translation, 1953), but their theoretical and stylistical approaches vary. For example,

Eleanor Holveck ("Can a Woman Be a Philosopher?") links Beauvoir with the blues singer Bessie Smith to make her point that the "Beauvoirian Housemaid" will find a way to philosophize, and Jeffner Allen's essay challenges Beauvoir's Sartrean "myth-making" in light of her posthumously published letters and diaries by weaving together personal narrative and critical discourse. Taken together, the essays all point to the complexity of Beauvoir's oeuvre and the impact it had on both Sartre and 20th-century philosophy. Readers with little or no knowledge of existentialism and Beauvoir's writing may lose their way in these scholarly essays. Others will find them provocative and never dull. Highly recommended for upper-division undergraduate, graduate, and research collections.—*S. Adell, University of Wisconsin—Madison*

WS-0636 PQ2431 90-42141 CIP
Germaine de Staël: crossing the borders, ed. by Madelyn Gutwirth, Avriel Goldberger, and Karyna Szmurlo. Rutgers, 1991. 248p index ISBN 0-8135-1636-6, $45.00

An excellent selection of 17 essays by contributors who are either 18th- or 19th-century French literature specialists or eminent Staël scholars who bring to this work their expertise in attempting to "cross the borders" of the feminine mentality of another era. There is admittedly a danger in the effort to reinterpret an author's work in the "light of current feminist thought"; however, the authors manage to avoid the usual pitfalls in examining De Staël's "own brand of feminism," which, they admit, "may not be ours." A broad range of topics is covered, including freedom, power, travel, new frontiers, Romanticism, and the French Revolution as they influence or are treated by Mme de Staël in her works. Many of the essays carry excellent explanatory endnotes; the index is ample; the bibliography covering works by Staël and by others is impressive, including recent (to 1988) critical studies on her writings. Although the style of the introduction is turgid, the preface is admirably succinct and invites the reader to explore the chapters that follow. This work performs well its "effort to get at the meaning of her [Germaine de Staël's] elusive works that do not fit genre categories." Recommended for upper-division undergraduates and graduate students.—*M. R. Bonfini, Immaculata College*

WS-0637 PQ2607 88-46147 CIP
Glassman, Deborah N. **Marguerite Duras: fascinating vision and narrative cure.** Fairleigh Dickinson, 1991. (Dist. by Associated University Presses) 151p bibl index afp ISBN 0-8386-3337-4, $31.50

Of the many books to appear recently on the contemporary French novelist and filmmaker Marguerite Duras, this study is one of the better, at once critically sophisticated and accessible. Glassman writes in effect an introduction to Duras's work by concentrating on three key areas: (1) an early transitional novel, *Moderato Cantabile*, and a thematically related film, her important *Hiroshima mon amour*; (2) the "India cycle," especially the novel *Lol V. Stein* and its fascination with madness as well as the related film *India Song*; and (3) the latest autobiographical phase in Duras's work, centering on the best-selling *L'Amant* as well as interviews that seem destined to become part of the Duras canon. This approach leaves out a great deal of work, but it allows Glassman to concentrate on the categories she discerns, especially on the psychosexual dynamics that underwrite Duras's semi-fictional creative universe. Perhaps the most important principle that Glassman finds is in the play of the visual fascination of fantasy that is set against the works' imposition of narrative order. This fascination underlies the "visual triangulation of desire" that is ubiquitous in Duras's work and seems to play some role in the fascination with madness therein. A good study for graduate students and advanced undergraduates, as well as collections of criticism dealing with women's issues.—*A. Thiher, University of Missouri—Columbia*

WS-0638 95-69365 Orig
Godwin-Jones, Robert. **Romantic vision: the novels of George Sand.** Summa Publications, AL, 1995. 322p bibl ISBN 1-883479-06-1, $43.95

Godwin-Jones (Virginia Commonwealth Univ.), a longtime Sand specialist, has produced a solid study—a careful analysis of a "representative cross-section of Sand's entire *oeuvre*." Tracing the evolution of Sand's narrative strategies, the author emphasizes the roles of the narrator and the reader. He shows that although Sand greatly admired the ideas of Félicité de Lamennais and Pierre

Leroux, similar notions were already in place in her early works; she did not suddenly transform her thinking after contact with the two reformers. Godwin-Jones also comments perceptively on Sand's treatment of religion. Although particularly useful for its inclusion of German sources, little known to most Sand scholars, the volume unfortunately relies on them for critical reactions in Sand's own time. Further, the book would have benefited from good editing, for example to eliminate sexist language and the tedious overdependence on the verb "to be." Though not groundbreaking like Isabelle Hoog Naginski's *George Sand: Writing for Her Life* (1991) or Naomi Schor's *George Sand and Idealism* (CH, Jan'94), this work has its place in an extensive collection on an author who has captured much scholarly attention over the past 20 years. Undergraduate collections.—*A. M. Rea, Occidental College*

WS-0639   PQ149   95-4889 CIP
Going public: women and publishing in early modern France, ed. by Elizabeth C. Goldsmith and Dena Goodman. Cornell, 1995. 249p index afp ISBN 0-8014-2951-X, $39.95

The role of women in both literary and historical movements has been unknown or overlooked for too long. Only recently has their role been recognized for its importance and relevance. This collection adds valuable insight into French women from the 17th and 18th centuries. The 14 essays treat "publishing" in its most literal meaning, i.e., putting something in print. Among the printed items discussed are, of course, literary works but also memoirs, guild tracts, legal briefs, letters, a manual on midwifery, and a "lewd novel." Because this volume can be considered both literature and history or cultural history, it could fall through the cracks and end up being ignored by both literary scholars and historians. This would be unfortunate, since both groups would profit from reading it. A worthwhile addition in feminist scholarship; upper-division undergraduate and above.—*C. E. Campbell, Cottey College*

WS-0640   PQ155   90-26337 CIP
Gravdal, Kathryn. **Ravishing maidens: writing rape in medieval French literature and law.** Pennsylvania, 1991. 192p bibl index afp ISBN 0-8122-8247-7, $29.95; ISBN 0-8122-1315-7, pbk $13.95

Feminist Gravdal's previous book dealt with transgressive parody in Old French literature, a theme that relates to the present thesis, namely, that medieval discourse most often legitimized rape. By focusing on the male characters' dilemmas and by drawing the audience's attention away from the female victim, most rape scenes in medieval French literature are romanticized, politicized, or aestheticized. Male violence against women intimates a frustrated expression of love, and female suffering, often depicted in tandem with male aggression, creates not sympathetic but erotically appealing situations. Gravdal exploits the ambivalence, ambiguity, and paradox of the issues, from "ravishing," i.e., overwhelmingly beautiful, to "ravishing" meaning rape and/or abduction. Her wide net reaches from Ovid's *Metamorphoses* to the 10th-century German author Hrotsvitha of Gandersheim; from 13th- and 14th-century legal precedents on rape cases to rather complex and sometimes frightening representations of sexual assault in 12th-century Arthurian romance; and then to an elaboration of the theme in the *Roman de Renart* and in the Provençal *pastourelle* lyric (all texts are translated). In this virtually exclusively male world, the author finds little empathy for the suffering female victims of forced coitus, as represented in medieval literature, but then, such a notion does smack of our late 20th century ethos. For upper-division undergraduate and graduate libraries.—*R. J. Cormier, Wilson College*

WS-0641   PN98.W64   89-31136 MARC
Herrmann, Claudine. **The tongue snatchers,** tr. with an introd. by Nancy Kline. Nebraska, 1991 (c1989). 145p bibl index afp ISBN 0-8032-2346-3 pbk, $9.95

Kline (Barnard College), herself a writer, knows well both the French language and Herrmann's work. These qualifications combine to make an excellent translation, faithful to the original yet gracefully expressed in English. Herrmann's 1976 assessment of the "colonization" of female culture and her encouragement of both men and women to learn each other's language remain appropriate today, but only ten pages have previously been available in English (*New French Feminisms*, ed. by Elaine Marks and Isabelle de Courtivron, CH, May'80). Kline's notes, kept to a minimum in this attractive volume, point out wordplays, give use-

ful cultural background, and include a 1988 update by Herrmann concerning the changes in France since the book's publication. With Hélène Cixous's "Le Rire de la Méduse" (*L'Arc*, 61, 1975), to which Kline links this volume in her first-rate introduction, *The Tongue Snatchers* is a founding text of French feminism. Eminently accessible, it well deserves inclusion in its entirety in undergraduate collections.—*A. M. Rea, Occidental College*

WS-0642   PQ629   89-29319 CIP
Hewitt, Leah D. **Autobiographical tightropes: Simone de Beauvoir, Nathalie Sarraute, Marguerite Duras, Monique Wittig, and Maryse Conde.** Nebraska, 1990. 259p bibl index afp ISBN 0-8032-2354-4, $25.00

Hewitt's treatment of the issue of gendered identity in autobiography is both informed and intelligent. Her choice of five authors (de Beauvoir, Sarraute, Duras, Wittig, and Conde) who are "at the margins of ecriture feminine's theories" precludes facile reductions of their writings. At the same time, Hewitt deftly situates each, in respect to one another and to the ongoing development of French feminism. Her book is staged as a fascinating and vital dialogue among these important writers, highlighting their many shared traits while preserving the diversity of their approaches. Abundant notes are helpful in placing these writers within the tradition of autobiography through and against which they write. The use of English translations, with French text in notes, makes the book easily accessible to the wide audience it deserves. Excellent bibliography.—*G. Moskos, Swarthmore College*

WS-0643   PQ149   95-50716 CIP
Holmes, Diana. **French women's writing, 1848-1994.** Athlone, 1996. 320p bibl index ISBN 0-485-91004-7, $85.00

The international "Women in Context" series brings a new and rich approach to women's studies. Covering the past 150 years, the series traces women writers of Norway, Sweden, Italy, Germany, and France from their quest for emancipation to their current social and professional status. The present volume offers a varied selection of writers, some internationally recognized, others less well known. Holmes (Univ. of Keele) provides in each of her three chronological sections a survey of selected writings in relation to literary theory and critical questions; she studies each writer and her works against the background of French society of that period. Holmes includes such writers as George Sand, Colette Yver, Renée Vivien (1848-1914); Colette, Simone de Beauvoir, Elsa Triolet (1914-1958); and Chantal Chawaf, Marguerite Duras, Christiane Rochefort, Annie Ernaux (1958-1994). She builds her text on the significant differences between male and female writers in relation to literary forms, "a difference which is not fixed and constant but historically specific and evolving." A useful bibliography covers women's writing and cultural theory, the history of French women and feminism, women writers in France, and individual writers. General; upper-division undergraduate through faculty.—*L. A. Russell, Rosemont College*

WS-0644   PQ2605   92-28589 CIP
Huffer, Lynne. **Another Colette: the question of gendered writing.** Michigan, 1992. 194p bibl index ISBN 0-472-10307-5, $37.50

Other recent volumes on Colette (at least ten over the past ten years) have covered some of the same topics: maternal and paternal models, sexuality, and the sewing trope. Nicole Ward Jouve, in her 1987 *Colette* (CH, Feb'88), used some of the same theoretical sources. No other study, however, compares in the prodigious scope of research on Colette, feminism, and poststructuralist theory. Huffer (Yale), like her subject, is "hyperbolically intertextual," as revealed by her notes and bibliography, which constitute more than one fifth of the text. The extensive notes allow Huffer to expand on her revisionary reading of Colette's "subjectivity as gendered textual form," to suggest future projects, and, at times, to disagree with prominent critical figures. The book also includes in its dense analysis of Colette's narrative strategies some sensitive explications of well-chosen passages. The metaphorical point of view adopted by Huffer proves Colette a far more conscious and complex artist than generally thought. Advanced undergraduates with a grounding in literary theory will discover in this book, which only rarely succumbs to jargon, a model of analysis and research, and a stellar example of dissertation revision, sharply focused, benefiting from the maturity brought by reading and reflection beyond the PhD. A must for Colette scholars. Highly recommended.—*A. M. Rea, Occidental College*

WS-0645   PQ637   94-9807 CIP
Jensen, Katharine Ann. **Writing love: letters, women, and the novel in France, 1605-1776.** Southern Illinois, 1995. 217p bibl index afp ISBN 0-8093-1849-0, $29.95

Once the reader has waded through the vaginalogocentric jargon of Sandra M. Gilbert's argument *ad feminam* in the introduction and the author's preface and prologue, this book becomes very interesting. Jensen (Louisiana State Univ.) posits the theory that there was a stereotypical "Epistolary Woman," "seduced, betrayed, and suffering," whose writings of love letters were automatically considered secondary literature at best. The author then presents five authors whose works do not fit the stereotype—Marie-Catherine Desjardins, Anne Ferrand, Françoise de Graffigny, Marie Jeanne Riccoboni, and Julie de Lespinasse. Each of these women proved that she could write self-consciously rather than emotionally, creating fiction rather than tortured love letters. Once this break with the Epistolary Woman occurred, the epistolary novel came to be valued, and women writers of the 17th and 18th centuries became empowered. It was only with the coming of the French Revolution that men became leery of this new-found power and worked to suppress it. Graduates; researchers, faculty.—*C. E. Campbell, Cottey College*

WS-0646   PQ155   92-36813 CIP
Krueger, Roberta L. **Women readers and the ideology of gender in old French verse romance.** Cambridge, 1994 (c1993). 338p (Cambridge studies in French, 43) bibl index ISBN 0-521-43267-7, $59.95

The author of this engaging study of the roles women have played as producer (especially Marie de France, Christine de Pisan) and product (among whom Briseida, Guenevere, La Pucele de Gaut Destroi, Queen Eufeme, La Belle Jehane) of the Old French romance epos provides her readership novel and highly cogent perspectives for the reevaluation of the Old French romance. Krueger is widely read in that body of the romance that illustrates what could be said to have been *la matiére de la cour*, which instructed, and cajoled, women to aspire to be part of the predominant, fashionable (read: acceptable) social class typologies for mother, daughter, loved-one. However, her analytical method might perhaps have been broadened by more reference to the world of the later hybrid romance, i.e., the poems of the *Cycle de la croisade* that echoed the extraordinary contacts being made with the cultured societies and women of the Middle East, contacts that occurred all throughout the period of the Crusades and during the expansion of the courtly ethic to non-European courts. In this way, the literary process of evolution/emancipation of women that Krueger's study chronicles would have been further enhanced by considerations of the pervasive influence of new empirical data about the roles eastern women played and were portrayed to have. Recommended to graduate students of comparative literature and culture as well as specialists of medieval mores.—*T. E. Vesce, Mercy College*

WS-0647   PQ1860   95-32324 CIP
Lalande, Roxanne Decker. **Intruders in the play world: the dynamics of gender in Molière's comedies.** Fairleigh Dickinson, 1996. (Dist. by Associated University Presses) 231p bibl index afp ISBN 0-8386-3592-X, $37.50

In this seminal study, Lalande (Lafayette College) promises to address a pressing need: an interpretation of Molière from a feminist perspective. Inspired by the work of Johan Huizinga, the author frames gender issues within a theory of comedy as ludic activity. Here comedy becomes the site of a "play world," a retreat from social and ethical reality. Lalande argues convincingly that this play world, like its empirical correlate, is patriarchal and based on the marginalization of threatening feminine Otherness. These observations ground the most impressive insights of the study. Lalande's discussion of the stakes and dynamics of gender persuasively establish models of feminine exclusion/empowerment and a typology of feminine Otherness in Molière's comedy. She draws from currents in contemporary feminist thought that have resulted from an interrogation and displacement of major concepts of psychoanalytic theory. Regrettably, many of these are not explicitly presented, contextualized, and problematized: for example, some discussion of the imaginary, the symbolic, and the real—concepts central to most of Lalande's work—would have helped situate and elucidate her argument. (Surprisingly, there is no bibliographic entry for Lacan.) But this is one minor flaw in a remarkable performance. Lalande's study will undoubtedly find its place among the important works on feminine alterity in Molière and in the comic sphere.—*E. R. Koch, Tulane University*

WS-0648   PQ653   93-38693 CIP
Lukacher, Maryline. **Maternal fictions: Stendhal, Sand, Rachilde, and Bataille.** Duke University, 1994. 219p index afp ISBN 0-8223-1432-0, $35.00; ISBN 0-8223-1436-3 pbk, $15.95

Lukacher considers the proliferation of pseudonyms in modern French literature in an attempt to understand what it tells us about the authors. Balzac, Stendhal, George Sand, Rachilde, and Bataille provide her with opportunities for detailed analysis influenced primarily by Freud and Luce Irigaray. The author notes that in every case these writers had problematic feelings about their mothers and, perhaps consequently, about their own sexuality. In several of the cases there was a difficult relationship with or absence of fathers as well, but for Lukacher's argument the maternal seems unquestionably the more important. Balzac learned of his mother's adultery at a key point in his career, whereas Stendhal suffered from a life-long, unfulfilled yearning for his mother. Stendhal was perhaps filled with guilt, given on the one hand his intense, erotic love for her and on the other her early death. George Sand never quite came to terms with her mother, and Rachilde detested hers. Finally, Bataille's pseudonymous, pornographic works reveal a guilt-laden, almost psychotic, maternal relationship. Lukacher concludes that the pseudonym keeps the father at a distance and allows each of the authors to confront the mother, although in none of these instances were they able to resolve the conflicts and tensions engendered by the relationship. Always a response to crisis, pseudonymity reveals the instability of identity. Specialists in psychological criticism and in the authors analyzed will find this an interesting study with numerous, shrewd insights along the way.—*A. H. Pasco, University of Kansas*

WS-0649   PQ1215   93-47317 CIP
The lunatic lover: and other plays by French women of the 17th and 18th centuries, ed. by Perry Gethner. Heinemann, 1994. 344p ISBN 0-435-08637-5 pbk, $17.95

It is surely a laudable project to anthologize for the English reader six plays illustrating major genres cultivated during the two centuries of French classicism: tragedy, tragicomedy, tearful comedy, comedy-ballet, and farce. (The major genre absent is comedy proper.) This undertaking assumes even greater importance when we consider that (1) the playwrights chosen all being women, the collection has relevance to feminist studies; (2) all the plays have been out of print since the early 19th century; and, (3) only one of them has ever before been rendered into English. Thus, we owe a great debt of gratitude to editor-translator Gethner (French, Oklahoma State Univ.), who provides in addition for each work ample, carefully weighed critical introductions as well as illuminating scholarly notes on less obvious references in the texts. He has also had the admirable courage to approximate the "*alexandrin*" meter of the originals in his modern, though sometimes flat, blank-verse iambic pentameters. Readers may, however, experience some disappointment if their expectations are too high, for none of the plays included is, by Gethner's own admission, "a forgotten masterpiece"; nor is specifically feminine sensibility much in evidence. The present volume will serve rather (no faint praise) as a sampling of the passing literary tastes, the "*mentalité*," of a great age in France—and, tangentially perhaps, as a reminder that our contemporary value systems are no more permanent. General and academic audiences.—*P. Koch, emeritus, University of Pittsburgh*

WS-0650   PQ145   95-9627 CIP
Marks, Elaine. **Marrano as metaphor: the Jewish presence in French writing.** Columbia, 1996. 187p bibl index afp ISBN 0-231-10308-5, $24.50

In this provocative and timely book, Marks (Univ. of Wisconsin) uses history, literary theory, and psychoanalysis to "take note of a Jewish presence without establishing a rigid Jewish difference." She examines a wide range of authors—from Garnier and Racine to Cohen and Derrida—to demonstrate the inevitability of intertexuality and assimilation in literary texts. Marks views this "contamination" as a positive condition, for it opens up the space of the "Marrano," the metaphor she has chosen to express the value of multiple identities. (Marrano is the name Christians gave to Jews in Medieval Spain who converted to Christianity in order to escape persecution, but who remained faithful to Judaism.) Commenting on "the acceptance of being Jewish and being assimilated, of being Jewish and ... being other(s) at the same time," she provides intelligent and meticulous readings that deftly illustrate the links between antisemitism, misogyny, homophobia, and the "death of God." At the same time, the book is a passionate and persuasive attempt to complicate simplistic notions of identity politics. For example, in a fascinating chapter on the critical reception of Renée Vivien, Marks shows how Charles Maurras's fear of lesbianism and Gayle Rubin's welcoming of it both betray an essentializing and exclusionary vision. The book is beautifully written and compelling. Marks's arguments will likely be controversial, but no one can deny their power to captivate and challenge the reader. Upper-division undergraduate and up.—*G. Moskos, Swarthmore College*

WS-0651   PQ288   93-34207 CIP
Massardier-Kenney, Françoise. **Translating slavery: gender and race in French women's writing, 1783-1823,** ed. by Doris Y. Kadish. Kent State, 1994. 346p (Translation studies, 2) bibl index afp ISBN 0-87338-498-9, $27.00

This monograph series proposes to study the myriad and varied approaches to translation and to bring together in a coherent and accessible form this variety of thought and tradition related to translation processes and procedures. Volume 1, *Translation as Text* (1992), discusses text-based translation and emphasizes the social and behavioral sciences, following and continuing the German language series, "Übersetzungswissenschaftliche Beiträge." The present volume offers a critical and humanistic definition evolving from the American school and integrating critical and ideological factors such as race and gender. In addition to the new translations of significant literary texts of the revolutionary period by such French women writers as Olympe de Gouges, Germaine de Staël, and Claire de Duras, voicing their opposition to oppression of slaves and women, the translators offer detailed commentaries on their translations. A transcript of a dialogue between two translators, "Black on White: Translation, Race, Class, and Power," illustrates clearly the complex issues involved in the process: the influence of the translators' background, their power over an author, the motivation for decisions. Appendixes provide the original French texts and notes. Upper-division undergraduate through professional.—*L. A. Russell, Rosemont College*

WS-0652   PQ653   93-13966 CIP
Matlock, Jann. **Scenes of seduction: prostitution, hysteria, and reading difference in nineteenth-century France.** Columbia, 1994. 422p bibl index afp ISBN 0-231-07206-6, $60.00; ISBN 0-231-07207-4 pbk, $18.00

Among the many strengths of this book is the wealth of different materials from 19th-century France therein collected. *Scenes of Seduction* treats the construction of feminine sexuality in works as far ranging as the novels of Balzac and Eugène Sue, the writings of pioneer sociologist Alexandre Parent-Duchâtelet and medical doctor Jean-Etienne-Dominique Esquirol, the prison memoirs of accused murderess Marie Cappelle-Lafarge, and the feminist newspapers *Tribune des femmes* and *L'Opinion des femmes,* among other works. They are all read as discourses, and as such, subjected to Foucaldian analysis. Foucault's work in turn is subjected to feminist critique. Through her exhaustive analysis, Matlock demonstrates the attempt to construct feminine sexuality across class lines. While prostitution was obsessively studied as the essence of proletarian sexuality, hysteria became the focus of debates around the "mystery" of middle-class women's sexuality. The popular novel itself came to be characterized within the terms of this aberrant feminine sexuality. Important reading for scholars of 19th-century French studies, and a sterling example of cultural studies on past historical periods. Upper-division undergraduate and up.—*L. W. Rabine, University of California, Irvine*

WS-0653   PQ2603   93-1101 CIP
Moi, Toril. **Simone de Beauvoir: the making of an intellectual woman.** Blackwell, 1994. 324p bibl index afp ISBN 0-631-14673-3, $54.95; ISBN 0-631-19181-X pbk, $21.95

The present study purports to analyze the life and work of Simone de Beauvoir from a feminist perspective. The book is not an autobiography in the traditional sense, for it does not seek to cover the subject's whole life in a balanced manner. Nor is it a critical analysis of de Beauvoir's writings, since it is especially concerned only with three texts: *L'invitée, Le deuxième sexe,* and *Mémoires d'une jeune fille rangée.* Thus, Moi coins the term "personal genealogy" to describe her book. Also, since Moi wants to dialogue with other feminists as well as respond

when appropriate to the various dreaded "patriarchs" who have commented on de Beauvoir, she needs special tools. To this end, she uses "reception studies, sociology of culture, philosophical analysis, psychoanalytic inquiry and feminist theory" to make her arguments. Although the present work surely reflects the concerns of an academic special interest group that is very much in fashion these days, it does not dull our wits with jargonized pleadings. In fact, it is written in a pleasant and engaging style that can be read with ease and profit by the noninitiated. Its brutal honesty about the private lives, political compromises, and literary achievements of both de Beauvoir and Sartre is, in fact, refreshing. This is a serious and important contribution to de Beauvoir studies. Upper-division undergraduate and up.—*D. O'Connell, Georgia State University*

WS-0654   PQ1240   94-30885 CIP
Plays by French and Francophone women: a critical anthology, ed. and tr. by Christiane P. Makward and Judith G. Miller. Michigan, 1995 (c1994). 345p afp ISBN 0-472-10263-X, $47.50

This is the latest of a number of works that fall within a narrow sector of literary activities known as "French Feminism," a term coined in France and popularized throughout the world in the early 1960s and 1970s (see, e.g., *A New History of French Literature,* ed. by Denis Hollier, CH, Mar'90). The current anthology benefits from an excellent introduction and ample footnotes that give readers a broad perspective of the type of plays and dramas written and performed before live audiences in the "post-1968 years when women were forced to come to terms with the fact that their concerns as women were neglected or dismissed by most of their male-counterparts." Though the seven plays included here represent a wide diversity of topics closely related to the unique experience of being female, each poses a "direct challenge of the male-dominated status quo." Indeed, all of the plays refuse to articulate "the correct model of a happy family." And almost all—be they Canadian, African, Martinican, or Antillean—have a common thread of music and dance. Among the works included are Michèle Foucher's humorous "The Table: Womenspeak," the delightful Martinican Ina Césaire's "Island Memories: Mama N and Mama F," and the more melodramatic "The Name of Oedipus," by French author and critic Hélène Cixous. Admittedly, not all of the works will appeal equally to all readers.—*R. Merker, Grambling State University*

WS-0655   89-142722 Orig
Plays by women: an international anthology, book two, [ed. by Françoise Kourilsky and Catherine Temerson]. Ubu Repertory Theater Publications, 1994. 267p ISBN 0-913745-42-1 pbk, $15.95

The title of this anthology is slightly misleading, since the five "international" women writers—Reine Barteve, Denise Bonal, Maryse Condé, Werewere Liking, and Abla Farhoud—not only all write originally in French but they all have a strong base in French or francophone theater, and most have had direct connections with Paris. Thus, these plays represent diverse aspects of one larger linguistic tradition, rather than a broadly international sampling of plays. This said, the collection itself superbly reflects the links as well as the distances between French Arabic, Creole, Canadian immigrant, and Parisian female drama. Each play is passionately driven by concerns that (though not ideologically limited) are in the best and broadest sense political, as well as personal. The texts are clean, clear, timely, and powerful. The volume as a whole reflects the Ubu Repertory Company at its best; plays which were produced or received staged readings in April and May 1994, are already available in a handsomely bound, paperback edition that contains production information with a minimum of critical apparatus. Since the earlier Ubu Rep. anthology *Plays by Women: An International Anthology* (1988) is now unavailable, this new anthology is a welcome addition. Abla Farhoud, whose *The Girls from the Five and Ten* (translated from *Les Filles du 5-10-15* cents) stood out in the previous volume, has once more a potential hint in her powerful *Game of Patience* (translated from *Jeux de patience* by Jill MacDougall). Other plays in translations by J.G. Miller, B.B. Lewis and C. Temerson, and R. Miller are equally strong. This volume is recommended for anyone wanting to sample francophone women's drama in its best English translations. All levels.—*M. C. Riggio, Trinity College (CT)*

WS-0656   PQ2635   92-12415 CIP
Ramsay, Raylene L. **Robbe-Grillet and modernity: science, sexuality, and subversion.** University Press of Florida, 1992. 301p

(University of Florida humanities monograph, 66) bibl index afp ISBN 0-8130-1145-0, $39.95

In this ambitious work the critic studies the dominant themes in the novels and films of Robbe-Grillet, the most important practitioner of the French New Novel. She organizes her themes in terms of the categories of science, myth, myths of women, sado-eroticism, eroticism and power, and, finally general considerations of Robbe-Grillet, postmodernism and his abusive fantasies about women. There is some repetition here, and much theoretical discussion that only obliquely relates to Robbe-Grillet. The critic, a feminist, seems to have trouble, understandably, about how to deal with Robbe-Grillet's constant portrayal of women as victims of rape or as vampires. She wants to conclude that these portrayals of domination and submission are enacted in new forms that work against the sexual politics they portray—and are ultimately feminist. Hence, much theoretical meandering. An interview with the writer concludes the book. Probably of interest only to libraries maintaining complete collections of criticism of modern French literature or advanced women's studies.—*A. Thiher, University of Missouri—Columbia*

WS-0657   PQ239   93-26577 CIP
Renaissance women writers: French texts/American contexts, ed. by Anne R. Larsen and Colette H. Winn. Wayne State, 1994. 242p bibl index afp ISBN 0-8143-2473-8, $39.95

This book is a compilation of 12 essays by the editors and ten other scholars of French Renaissance literature, both men and women. The topics are many and varied, ranging from "Women Addressing Women" to "Chastity and the Mother-Daughter Bond," but all relate to the formation of women's literary identity. The authors studied include Louise Labé, Catherine des Roches, Marguerite de Navarre, Pernette de Guillet, Marguerite de Valois, Hélisenne de Crenne, Jeanne Flore, and Marie de Gournay. The essays are grouped under three headings comprising revisionary practices, the female body, and the "politics of reception." Genres treated include sonnets, elegies, memoirs, novellas, translations, plays, dedicatory epistles, and novels. There is no one critical style that dominates these essays. Instead, each scholar has presented the topic under discussion from an interesting and unique perspective, as varied as typography and the theme of carpe diem. Upper-division undergraduate and up.—*C. E. Campbell, Cottey College*

WS-0658   PQ2011   94-45438 CIP
Schaub, Diana J. **Erotic liberalism: women and revolution in Montesquieu's *Persian letters*.** Rowman & Littlefield, 1995. 199p bibl index afp ISBN 0-8476-8039-8, $57.50; ISBN 0-8476-8040-1 pbk, $22.95

Schaub offers scholars a new reading of Montesquieu's *Persian Letters* under this somewhat misleading title. This epistolary novel is a study of domestic, political, and religious despotism. By regrouping the letters into various combinations, rather than following the order of the text, Schaub has been able to arrive at a new understanding of the work. Her interpretations are persuasively defended but should be compared with other points of view (e.g., that in Judith Shklar's *Montesquieu*, CH, Sep'88). Schaub argues that the key to all of Montesquieu's work is his concept of despotism and that all of his work is tied together, the *Persian Letters* being the beginning of the whole. The work is developed around a harem—as a means of tying together sexual, religious, and political despotism—and is written in epistolary form as a means of presenting varying points of view. Though Schaub relies on others for much of the translation from original texts, her own translations are excellent. There are copious and very helpful notes. Upper-division undergraduates and above.—*J. E. Parker Jr., Wake Forest University*

WS-0659   PQ2607   93-9411 CIP
Schuster, Marilyn R. **Marguerite Duras revisited.** Twayne, 1993. 185p (TWAS, 840. French literature) bibl index afp ISBN 0-8057-8298-2, $22.95

Schuster (Smith College), author of articles on women writers including Duras, surveys Duras's work to date, except her theater; nothing in English is as recent or complete. Schuster examines Duras's "creative impasse" of 1971 and her subsequent move to film. In her film analyses, Schuster demonstrates the "explicitly female subjectivity" of the separated voice and image tracks and the increas-

ingly controlling female authorial voice. She chronicles Duras's return to the written word and reflections on the process of reading and writing. Using a broad sampling of theory, expecially North American and French feminisms, Schuster shows how Duras "mirror[s] critical debates" and sometimes precedes them. Within a positive study, Schuster incorporates postcolonial and recent gay/lesbian theory to posit Duras's complicity with the dominant ideology in her portrayal of sexuality, race, and ethnicity. The heavily theoretical introduction should not discourage; the chapters are more accessible. The annotations of the bibliography and the sensitivity to problems of translation will also aid undergraduates. Supersedes Alfred Cismaru's *Marguerite Duras* (CH, Apr'72), which predated most of the films and much of the fiction. A "must" for any French literature collection. Advanced undergraduate; graduate.—*A. M. Rea, Occidental College*

WS-0660   Orig
Sellers, Susan. **Hélène Cixous: authorship, autobiography and love.** Polity, 1996. 191p bibl index afp ISBN 0-7456-1254-7, $49.95; ISBN 0-7456-1255-5 pbk, $19.95

Cixous (1937-) has published an abundance of works, including novels, plays, autobiography, and philosophical works. Her principal subject is feminine writing: she attempts to upset the rigid patriarchal status quo that has dominated society since the Greeks. According to Sellers, Cixous' prerequisite for writing is "the correlation between loss and self-definition"; she hopes to "challenge the present modes of perception and representation" and in so doing create a new concept of the relationship between the self and the Other. To accomplish this she must use language that she sees as life-inventing itself, since without words there is no life. Her painful reaction to the loss of her father is somewhat mitigated when she realizes what she has received from her mother. Cixous's ideas are forceful but her style makes for difficult reading. Expressions like "write the body" and "write the other" are irritating, and the endless succession of an/other, his/story, s/he m/other and (re)create, (re)birth, and (re)inscribe leave the reader with an uncomfortable impression of either/or and both/and. The endless puns are neither amusing nor informative. Nevertheless, Seller's introduction to Cixous should be read if one wants to understand the importance of the feminine writing movement in contemporary literature.—*F. C. St. Aubyn, emeritus, University of Pittsburgh*

WS-0661   PC3365   95-2961 CIP
Songs of the women troubadours, ed. and tr. by Matilda Tomaryn Bruckner, Laurie Shepard, and Sarah White. Garland, 1995. 194p (Garland library of medieval literature, 97A) index afp ISBN 0-8153-0817-5, $42.00

This anthology of lyrics assumed to be by *trobairitz*—female poets of Southern France—showcases these female voices from c. 1170 to c. 1260, when they unaccountably ceased. An excellent introduction—which provides literary, historical, cultural, and linguistic context—makes a good case for the problematic female authorship of the material. A useful bibliography provides information on dictionaries and grammars, anthologies and translations, and literary, historical, and textual studies. Substantial endnotes, about one quarter of the book, contain minibiographies of named poets and judicious textual, explanatory, and interpretive commentary, with cross-references to the most important previous scholarship (including especially Angelica Rieger's monumental critical study in German, *Trobairitz*, 1991). Wisely eschewing any attempt to render in rhyme-poor English the "virtuosic" rhyming of the originals with resultant "unacceptable losses and distortions" of the texts, the editors offer colloquial and often sprightly unrhymed English translations en face with the Occitan. The index would have benefited from brief definitions of the poetic terms. Highly recommended for upper-division undergraduate, graduate, and faculty audiences.—*M. Fries, SUNY College at Fredonia*

WS-0662   PQ2431   94-45742 CIP
Staël, Germaine de. **Delphine,** tr. with introd. by Avriel H. Goldberger. Northern Illinois, 1995. 469p bibl afp ISBN 0-87580-200-1, $50.00; ISBN 0-87580-567-1 pbk, $22.95

Staël's epistolary novel set in the first two years of the French Revolution has been, until very recently, almost completely disregarded by critics and readers alike. But Goldberger's new English translation may bring it new life. Goldberger, who follows in the steps of Staëlian scholars Madelyn Gutwirth (ed. of *Germaine de Staël: Crossing the Borders*, CH, Mar'92) and Gretchen Rous Besser (*Germaine de Staël Revisited* CH, Sep'94), has selected as her primary reference Simone Balayé and Lucia Omacini's French critical edition of the book (1987). She has eliminated sentences and expressions that would strike contemporary readers as archaic or confusing. Of particular interest is the detailed introduction, which focuses on the historical and political perspectives of the times and on the active role that Staël played during the last years of the 18th century and the first two decades of the 19th. Numerous explanatory notes and a chronology comparing the novel with historical events shed further light on a work of fiction whose protagonists championed divorce and the rights of women. Although *Delphine* will probably never be considered the first major French novel of the 19th century, this remarkable translation is highly recommended for general readers and students who wish to have a better understanding of the time.—*R. Merker, Grambling State University*

WS-0663　　　　PQ648　　　　92-33052 CIP
Stewart, Joan Hinde. **Gynographs: French novels by women of the late eighteenth century.** Nebraska, 1993. 251p bibl index afp ISBN 0-8032-4227-1, $35.00

Stewart opens a fascinating window onto 18th-century France by considering little-known but, in the day, successful novels by women: Le Prince de Beaumont, Elie de Beaumont, Riccoboni, Charrière, Montolieu, Souza, Cottin, and Genlis. Although Stewart's purpose is not literary, her exquisite analyses of such novels as Montolieu's *Caroline de Lichtfield* (1786)—here in the light of Le Prince de Beaumont's version of "Beauty and the Beast" (1758)—add pleasure to her description of the novels' portrayal of economic and sexual exploitation growing primarily from arranged marriages that turned women into chattel. If she were "virtuous"—the single most important female quality—a woman had few choices other than marriage, which was frequently abhorrent, and the convent. The best situation for most was to be a widow, and countless heroines refuse to give up that blissful state for another marriage. In short, Stewart shows us women trapped "by economic and affective systems in which pretense and opportunism are their only tactical weapons." A fine, readable book recommended for undergraduates, graduate students, and specialists.—*A. H. Pasco, University of Kansas*

WS-0664　　　　PQ2605　　　　94-36702 CIP
Strand, Dana. **Colette: a study of the short fiction.** Twayne/Prentice Hall International, 1995. 182p (Twayne's studies in short fiction, 59) bibl index afp ISBN 0-8057-4500-9, $23.95

Strand (Carleton College) situates Colette within feminist debates on "women's writing," positing in her short fiction blurred boundaries within which some female narrators are seen as ontologically and linguistically rebellious. Strand turns to such writers as Cixous, Kristeva, Chodorow, and Kahn to show how the mother-daughter relationship creates for Colette "a temporary haven from patriarchal space" and how Colette deprives "looking" of its pleasure in order to eroticize the experience itself. Colette's fiction appears polysemic and ambiguous to Strand in its shifting of moral grounds and in its unconventional treatment of such taboos as lesbianism and incest. She points repeatedly to Colette's representation of "woman's unchanging status in patriarchal society as a sexual object" while asserting that Colette replaces "the dominant system of beliefs with a matriarchal counterorder" and that in her work the woman's "self" is able to "achieve an accommodation with the world through the intervention of desire." Strand makes this novel analysis more interesting by including five representative samples of previous approaches to Colette. The reader, however, is not ultimately convinced of any female character's ability to liberate herself from "phallic rule" or "to reappropriate herself as a subject of a desire that *still* enjoys full expression, *even if* only in her own discourse" (emphasis added). All levels.—*Y. Jehenson, University of Hartford*

WS-0665　　　　PQ2607　　　　94-8745 CIP
Vircondelet, Alain. **Duras: a biography,** tr. by Thomas Buckley. Dalkey Archive Press, Illinois State University, Campus Box 4241, Normal, IL 61790-4241, 1994. 378p bibl index afp ISBN 1-56478-065-1, $24.95

This first full-length, worshipful biography of Marguerite Duras (1914-), French author of novels, plays, and film scripts (*Hiroshima mon amour*) attempts to imitate her "fluent writing." Intertwined are past, present, and future, fiction and reality, life and legend. Vircondelet, writing in the present tense with flash forwards, uses a style that is lush, poetic, vivid, elliptical, and repetitive. The atmospheric miasma which helps the reader experience life from Duras's perspective gives short shrift to her family members and friends and makes it difficult to winkle out facts: her birth as Marguerite Donnadieu in Indochina; her shocking teenage affair with a Chinese man; her marriage to and divorce from Robert Antelme; the birth of her son Jean Mascolo to her lover; her joining and leaving the Communist Party; her work for the French Underground in World War II; her living with Yann Andrea, a much younger homosexual. Despite alcoholism, emphysema, and a five-month coma, as well as decidedly mixed reviews for her work, Duras has become a cult figure. Vircondelet focuses on various of her thematic images: the beggar woman of Savannahket "with her bundle of crying flesh," whom Duras saw as a child; her identification with the Jews and all outcasts; her attraction to the sea and the nightship, "the dark ink of the written word." Some may view this book as a work of art; others as an attenuated frustration. Contains photos. Suitable for women's studies and romance language libraries. Academic and general audiences.—*J. Overmyer, Ohio State University*

WS-0666　　　　PQ653　　　　92-13863 CIP
Waller, Margaret. **The male malady: fictions of impotence in the French romantic novel.** Rutgers, 1993. 229p bibl index ISBN 0-8135-1908-X, $48.00

Political, social, and sexual impotence as a somewhat disguised source of power is the paradoxical theme underlying early 19th-century French novels from Chateaubriand to Sand. This feminist study of the famous *mal due siècle* convincingly demonstrates that such marginalized male outcasts as those represented by Chateaubriand, Constant, and Stendhal, unlike their 18th-century fictional predecessors, derive a new source of power over women from their silence, withdrawal, and refusal to exercise the usual male prerogatives (namely conjugal union); this allows them, whatever their failings, to confirm that "men are still on top." Recalling that most 18th-century libertine and sentimental novels had concealed their "androcentrism under an apparent feminocentrism," Waller notes the early Romantic novel's overt fixation on the male. In each of the chapters in this cogently organized and very readable study she rereads from a refreshingly new perspective not only *René*, *Adolphe*, and *Armance* but also two novels by women authors, de Staël's *Corinne* and Sand's *Lélia*. The latter "subverts and revises the meaning of the male malady by making it female," and through this reversing of gender roles shows just how much the famous *vague à l'âme* promoted in *René* is indeed a disguised form of power. Advanced undergraduate; graduate; faculty.—*W. L. McLendon, formerly, University of Houston*

◆ Romance
Hispanic

WS-0667　　　　PQ6605　　　　92-22741 CIP
Alayeto, Ofelia. **Sofía Casanova (1861-1958): Spanish poet, journalist and author.** Scripta Humanistica, 1992. 203p (Scripta Humanistica, 89) bibl index ISBN 0-916379-95-7, $54.50

For her time, Sofía Casanova (1861-1958) was a bold woman. As poet, novelist, and journalist, she became the main intellectual link between Spain and Poland, particularly during WW I and WW II. In this intellectual and literary biography, Alayeto documents the 830 articles Casanova wrote as foreign correspondent from Poland for ABC, also tracing Casanova's transformation from the young intellectual who entertained writers like Campoamor, Pardo Bazán, Pérez Galdós, and Benavente; through her marriage to Wincenty Lutoslawski, a Polish philosopher; to her involvement in the political affairs of Poland; and to being called Spain's intellectual ambassador to Eastern Europe by Francisco Franco. Focus is principally on Casanova's personal life, but the study also includes short commentaries on her 30 or so books that are just now beginning to be studied by feminist scholars. The biography is well organized, but frequent editorial remarks and awkward English constructions, especially in the introduction, interrupt the flow of the text. Of general interest to students of modern Spanish literature who are interested in uncovering ignored women writers.—*C. E. Klein, Beaver College*

WS-0668 PQ7539 93-25965 CIP
Alegría, Claribel. **Fugues,** tr. by D.J. Flakoll. Curbstone, 1993. 143p
English and Spanish. ISBN 1-880684-10-1 pbk, $10.95

The translator of this brilliant book of poems is Alegría's husband and frequent collaborator, Darwin J. Flakoll. Although the predominant theme of the collection is death, there are political poems, autobiographical poems, self-portraits, revisions of classical and Latin American myths, and verses dedicated to other Latin American women writers, such as Alejandra Pizarnik and Nancy Morejón. Of particular interest are the rewritings of classical myths from a feminist perspective. In "Carta a un desterrado," Penelope urges Odysseus not to return, while in "Galatea ante el espejo," Galatea repudiates Pygmalion's love with biting sarcasm. In similar fashion, Malinche in another text, denies having betrayed her homeland, asserting that it is her people who betrayed her. Like all of Alegría's poetry, these verses treat indistinctly the personal and the political with an incandescent lyrical expression enhanced, paradoxically, by the colloquial tone and precise physical description of events, objects, persons, and experiences. Unfortunately, the absence of any supplementary material, such as biographical or critical information, which could aid students to contextualize the poetry, makes this a difficult text for use in the classroom. Notwithstanding, this superbly translated collection will be of great interest to specialist and general readers.—*S. A. Cavallo, Loyola University of Chicago*

WS-0669 PQ9697 93-791 CIP
Alencar, José de. **Senhora: profile of a woman,** tr. by Catarina Feldmann Edinger. Texas, 1994. 198p ISBN 0-292-70449-6, $30.00; ISBN 0-292-70450-X pbk, $12.95

Set in Rio de Janeiro in the context of Brazil's 19th-century empire, Alencar's novel dramatizes the character and circumstances of a woman whose life was lived in conflict with controlling forces of her times and society: poverty, legitimacy, wealth, honor, and power. Aurélia's story unfolds as narrative, biography, and drama, fueled by her own fatal beauty, her perception of the hypocrisies of society and its values, and her ultimate struggle to use inherited wealth both to avenge years of helplessness and to shape reality by the sovereign exercise of feminine power. The suggestive theme of the novel lies in a conflict, seemingly irreconcilable in view of the dominant values of her society, between her role as an independent and powerful woman and inner ideals and desires. Through the dowry system, she purchased a husband, to whom she was passionately attracted but who had betrayed her in earlier circumstances because of her poverty. Alencar dramatizes the "unnatural" relationship of this master and her slave, in this case wife and husband, as permitted by law and wealth. The author's acute perception of the untenable position of women in Brazilian society is attenuated in the novel's conclusion when the male's authority and sexuality as husband are reestablished, and Aurélia's instruments of control—marriage contract and wealth—are neutralized. Edinger's introduction is limited and derivative; the translation captures Alencar's difficult, ornate vocabulary. Undergraduate; graduate programs in woman studies; general readers.—*K. D. Jackson, Yale University*

WS-0670 PQ6663 93-34853 CIP
Amell, Alma. **Rosa Montero's odyssey.** University Press of America, 1994. 107p bibl index afp ISBN 0-8191-9353-4, $34.50

This slim volume adds to the growing criticism on the contemporary Spanish journalist and novelist Rosa Montero. As the author states, her intent is not to study the formal structures of Montero's oeuvre, but to trace the development of her themes from her first novel, *Crónica del desamor* (1979), to her most recent work, *Bella y oscura* (1993). According to Amell, Montero's personal and novelistic odyssey is motivated by "the author's quest to understand the dialectics between the human being and the universe." Related themes are the conflict between the female protagonists' search for love and relatedness and their desire for autonomy in a male-dominated world; the disintegration of traditional values in a morally depraved and corrupt society; the essential loneliness of all people in an absurd universe where death is the only absolute reality. Montero's book will be useful to general readers and students of 20th-century Spanish narrative, and to feminist literary scholars. Unfortunately, such occasional errors in spelling and usage as "letargy" for "lethargy" and "despisefully" for "despicably" mar this otherwise useful study. General and academic audiences.—*S. A. Cavallo, Loyola University of Chicago*

WS-0671 PQ7297.C2596 89-20530 CIP
Another way to be: selected works of Rosario Castellanos, ed. and tr. by Myralyn F. Allgood. Georgia, 1990. 146p bibl afp ISBN 0-8203-1222-3, $25.00; ISBN 0-8203-1240-1, $12.95

Allgood (Samford University) has chosen some two dozen items from the prose and poetry of Mexico's premier woman writer. Some material was already accessible in translation elsewhere; some was unpublished and made available by friends or family of Castellanos. The poetry section is bilingual, so readers may appreciate the original versions and the choices a translator must make. Generally, Allgood's choices are satisfying, although at times she misses or avoids the expressive peculiarities of Spanish (e.g., "sentadito" as simply "sitting there"). Selections favor Castellanos's writings about indigenous Mexico, with fewer from her feminist work. There is a very selected bibliography. The introduction, which seems outdated, claims that few translations of Castellanos have been done, although, curiously, the bibliography does refer to three important English-language collections, all 1988: *Meditation on the Threshold,* tr. by J. Palley; *A Rosario Castellanos Reader,* tr. by M. Ahern; and *The Selected Poems. . .,* tr. by M. Bogin. With Allgood's volume added to those three, uninitiated readers have a good opportunity to enjoy this important writer, and Castellanos experts on occasion to evaluate the sometimes surprising differences among translations of the same work. The volume is recommended for academic and public libraries.—*K. F. Nigro, University of Cincinnati*

WS-0672 PQ7519 94-13983 CIP
Belli, Gioconda. **The inhabited woman,** tr. by Kathleen March. Curbstone, 1994. 412p ISBN 1-880684-17-9, $22.95

Gioconda Belli, the Nicaraguan writer, has gained an international reputation for her poetry, which is both personal and politically compromised. *La mujer habitada* (1988) is a narrative manifestation of these same concerns, presented in lyrical terms, but nonetheless realistic in its depiction of contemporary guerrilla warfare. Lavina, the upper-middle-class protagonist, is an architect who enters the political world of her lover Felipe, involved in the National Liberation Movement against the dictatorship of the "Great General" in the fictitious country of Faguas (Belli's own participation in the Sandinista struggle against Somoza in Nicaragua has been well documented.) Also, running parallel to the 1973 narrative strand is the story of the Nahuatl woman-warrior Itzá, her lover Yarince, and their courageous resistance to the Spanish invaders. The two worlds and epochs converge when the soul of the Indian woman inhabits (and strengthens) the body and mind of the modern protagonist. The inevitable tragic (yet hopeful) conclusion parallels the historical reality of the Conquest, and prefigures the success of the Sandinista Revolution. Belli's rendering of the twin stories is linguistically beautiful and thematically convincing. *The Inhabited Woman* is a searing document about a human rite of passage, and also a fine suspense novel. Unobtrusive translation. All levels.—*J. Walker, Queen's University*

WS-0673 PQ8097 94-27110 CIP
Bombal, María Luisa. *House of mist; and, The shrouded woman:* **two novels,** tr. by the author. Texas, 1995. 259p afp ISBN 0-292-70836-X, $40.00; ISBN 0-292-70830-0 pbk, $19.95

When these two novels, *La última niebla* (1935) and *La amortajada* (1938), were first published, the Chilean author was acclaimed as an outstanding example of avant garde in Latin America, her work an outspoken critique of the stifling lives of its upper-class women. *La amortajada* was awarded Santiago's "Premio Municipal de Novela" and translated into English by the author as *The Shrouded Woman* (1948). *La ultima niebla* became the basis of Bombal's longer English version, *House of Mist* (1947). In 1982, Richard and Lucía Cunningham translated the original 1935 Spanish version as "The Final Mist," and it was published, along with other short works by Bombal, in *New Islands and Other Stories* (CH, Feb'83). The present volume, which republishes Bombal's original translations, reveals the superiority of the original Spanish version of "The Final Mist" and of the Cunninghams' translation. Bombal's translation gives the reader a *House of Mist* in which the enigmatic, nameless protagonist of the original work is given a name and a biography and is encoded in a narrative that merges fairy tale, melodrama, and coincidence. In the 1935 and 1982 versions, on the other hand, there is no letting up of the despairing emptiness of a heroine who chooses to live in fantasy rather than to act. This edition provides an excellent foreword by Naomi Lindstrom and, along with the Cunningham collection, demonstrates the evolution of an author Carlos Fuentes once called "the mother of us all."—*Y. Jehenson, University of Hartford*

WS-0674   PN98   91-27789 CIP
Castillo, Debra A. **Talking back: toward a Latin American feminist literary criticism.** Cornell, 1992. 344p bibl index afp ISBN 0-8014-2608-1, $42.50; ISBN 0-8014-9912-7 pbk, $14.95

An important contribution to the study of Latin American women writers, re-valorizing and foregrounding images and narrative strategies that have usually been rendered as "feminine" (i.e., powerless) and instead rendering them as powerful. Beginning with the metaphor of the kitchen and ending with that of housekeeping the book defamiliarizes words, giving new meaning to conventional strategies and analyzing the women's writing from a new perspective. Castillo posits that "one of the springs of vitality in women's writing comes from its association with other marginalized groups," and she uses seven narrative categories to show how this is done. Her first chapter is an exploration of what a possible Latin American feminist literary practice would look like. In the rest of the book she analyzes American Latinas and Latin American women writers from the perspective of the narrative tactics outlined in the first chapter: Helena Maria Viramontes (silence); Luisa Valenzuela (appropriation); Rosario Ferré, Julieta Campos (cultivation of superficiality); Clarice Lispector (negation); Rosario Castellanos, Maria Luisa Puga (marginality); Denise Chávez, Maxine Hong Kingston ("In a Subjunctive Mood"). This is a very informative book, which blends text and critical theory in a nonassuming and insightful way. The chaper on Luisa Valenzuela is excellent. Recommended for college and university levels.—*Y. Jehenson, SUNY College at Oswego*

WS-0675   PQ6144   93-17102 CIP
Charnon-Deutsch, Lou. **Narratives of desire: nineteenth-century Spanish fiction by women.** Pennsylvania State, 1994. 223p bibl index afp ISBN 0-271-01007-X, $28.50

Noting the exclusion of women writers from the 19th-century Spanish canon, Charnon-Deutsch states her purpose "to explore what gender may have to do with writing practices that are commonly marginalized to the periphery of dominant realist discourses." Desire in the Spanish domestic novel relates either to a woman's wish for adventure and culture in the embodiment of another person (resulting in disappointment or self-destruction) or to her conforming to societal expectations of women ("social masochism"). Applying modern feminist theory, she looks at women's lives in 19th-century Spain and how the attitudes about sex and gender were manifested in their writing. Writers studied include Cecilia Böhl de Faber and María del Pilar Sinués de Marco to exemplify female subjectivity and domesticity; Rosalía de Castro and Emilia Pardo Bazán related to desire and knowledge; and several lesser-known turn-of-the-century novelists, such as Delors Monserdà i Vidal and Catalina Albert i Paradís. The illustrations from contemporary women's periodicals are appropriate additions to a book for students of literature and/or women's studies. Upper-division undergraduate and up.—*C. E. Klein, Beaver College*

WS-0676   PQ7125   91-15702 CIP
Cypess, Sandra Messinger. **La Malinche in Mexican literature from history to myth.** Texas, 1992 (c1991). 239p bibl index afp ISBN 0-292-75131-1, $25.00; ISBN 0-292-75134-6 pbk, $12.95

Cypess provides a thorough consideration of the character and impact of La Malinche, Hernán Cortés's collaborator, translator, and mistress. The introductory chapter, "La Malinche as Palimpsest," promises a complex analysis of this personage in Mexican history and mythology. Subsequent chapters, however, deliver an uneven experience for the reader, with shifts in emphasis and focus. A panorama of prehispanic society in Mexico and the Conquest addresses a general audience unfamiliar with Mexican history. Elaborate analyses of little-known works by similarly obscure Mexican authors (e.g., Ireneo Paz's *Amor y suplicio*) would interest primarily Mexican literature specialists. Thorough treatment of more important works (e.g., Elena Garro's *Los recuerdos del porvenir*) adds to the canon but detracts from the study's focus on La Malinche's key role in the Mexican psyche. The inclusion of US writers of Mexican background, given the book's emphasis on Mexican literature, appears unjustified.

Notwithstanding these problems, as well as a somewhat confusing theoretical framework, the study provides a readable, new perspective on a fascinating figure that persists in Mexican mythology, art, thought, and culture.—*S. T. Clark, California State University, San Marcos*

WS-0677   PQ7081   94-48679 CIP
A dream of light & shadow: portraits of Latin American women writers, ed. by Marjorie Agosín. New Mexico, 1995. 342p bibl ISBN 0-8263-1633-6, $32.50

Each of the 16 chapters in this book elaborates on the life and work of a woman who gained recognition through both her writings or artistic activities and her political activism. The women are all well-known figures in their own countries, but their backgrounds vary. Since each chapter was written by a different person, there are pronounced differences in approach and analysis. Some chapters stress biography; others focus on the subject's written work. The preface offers some theoretical discussion of the life and work of these women in the context of their societies; the book's main perspective, however, places these figures under a metaphor conceptualized by the image of the garden, an image that emphasizes their relative isolation and the odds against which they struggled. Unfortunately, Agosín (Wellesley College) gives no information on the individual contributors to the book, their positions, or what they have written before. Coverage is uneven: although the preface mentions the Argentinian playwright Griselda Gambaro, there is no entry for her. Only eight of the entries include bibliographical information. Some countries (e.g., Cuba and Venezuela) are not represented at all. General audience and upper-division undergraduates.—*O. B. González, Loyola University of Chicago*

WS-0678   PQ7081   90-23146 CIP
García Pinto, Magdalena. **Women writers of Latin America: intimate histories,** tr. by Trudy Balch and Magdalena García Pinto. Texas, 1991. 258p index afp ISBN 0-292-73862-5, $30.00; ISBN 0-292-73866-8 pbk, $13.95

Published originally as *Historias Intimas* (Ediciones del Norte, 1988) this volume reflects both the increasing critical attention paid to women Hispanic writers and the growing interest in Latin American literature. These are candid, intimate, wonderfully structured interviews, whose impressive impact reveals the interviewer's considerble skill, as well as her thorough knowledge of the writings of her subjects. In these engrossing and insightful interviews the subjects reveal the obstacles overcome, the motivation, the personal and social experiences, the strategies that resulted in their distinguished literary careers. The penetrating questions which probe the individual creative process are interspersed with judiciously selected quotations from the respective author's work. Although one might have preferred one or two other authors than those presented here, no one can dispute the caliber of those chosen. Ten women writers form four different countries and Puerto Rico speak openly of their lives, their art, and the reciprocal bearing of the one upon the other. Though of special interest to the Latin American specialist, these interviews hold interest for those concerned with women's literature as well as for the aspiring writer. Highly recommended for college, university, and public libraries.—*F. Colecchia, Duquesne University*

WS-0679   PQ6635   95-17404 MARC
Hartfield-Méndez, Vialla. **Woman and the infinite: epiphanic moments in Pedro Salinas's art.** Bucknell, 1996. (Dist. by Associated University Presses) 185p bibl index afp ISBN 0-8387-5295-0, $34.50

In contrast to other studies that treat Salinas' poetry exclusively or investigate the search for an ideal, Hartfield-Méndez's world focuses on the totality of Salinas' work as a basis for his paradigms of woman and the epiphanic moment. Citing prototypes like Joyce's epiphanies, Wordsworth's "spots of time," and other privileged moments in modern literature, the author (Emory Univ.) begins with literary influences on Salinas and proceeds to look at how he writes about the relationship of woman and man in that special moment. The work is thematically rather than chronologically organized. Using frequent textual references in Spanish with accompanying English translation, the author discusses Salinas' works in terms of memory and myths based on cultural archetypes, the perception of woman as elusive, the dual function of space and numbers, and the treatment of time and space. Hartfield-Méndez concludes by showing how the poet rejects a memory of a real woman in favor of forgetting and replacing her with an artistic creation that functions as the epiphanic moment. As a tightly documented study based on well-established critics, this work will be useful to graduate students and researchers.—*C. E. Klein, Beaver College*

WS-0680   PQ6555   93-8458 CIP
Jagoe, Catherine. **Ambiguous angels: gender in the novels of Galdós.** California, 1994. 236p bibl index afp ISBN 0-520-08356-3, $40.00

Jagoe's critical study is an outstanding example of feminist criticism and revises "commonly held views of" Benito Pérez Galdós's "feminism." The volume discusses the concept of the angel in the house, the ideological implications of Pérez Galdós's nonfictional writings on women, and the evolution of Pérez Galdós's ideology, especially in regard to gender. Among the novels examined are *Gloria*, *La familia de León Roch*, *La de Bringas*, *El amigo Manso*, *Fortunata y Jacinta*, *La loca de la casa*, *El abuelo*, and *Tristana*. It would have been interesting to have seen Jagoe's discussion of *Doña Perfecta*, whose chief protagonist is a woman. On the whole Jagoe communicates her views without forcing the reader to learn and understand a new critical vocabulary. Solidly basing her study on contemporary accounts of women's role in 19th-century Spanish society as well as on recent Galdósian criticism, Jagoe disagrees with much that male critics have written about gender in Pérez Galdós's novels. Her work will force a reevaluation of gender in the novels of the Spanish author. Graduate; faculty.—*H. C. Woodbridge, emeritus, Southern Illinois University-Carbondale*

WS-0681   PQ7082   94-33936 CIP
Jehenson, Myriam Yvonne. **Latin-American women writers: class, race, and gender.** State University of New York, 1995. 201p bibl index ISBN 0-7914-2559-2, $57.50

In this uneven overview, Jehenson (Univ. of Hartford) highlights the revolutionary nature of Latin American women writers. Grouping her essays around themes such as "building bridges," the power of words and newly heard voices, the author attempts to deliver both a panoramic and an incisive look at writers who run the gamut from the upper-class Argentinean Victoria Ocampo to Nobel Laureate Rigoberta Menchú, a writer of humble origins. Jehenson covers all genres and includes a bibliography of critical works on specific writers. A perusal of these reveals that there is still much work to be done to acknowledge the contributions of women writers vis-à-vis their male counterparts. The main problem with this study, however, is the lack of critical base and focus. There is a long chapter on Ocampo but one page on Menchú; a detailed analysis of works by Argentinean Griselda Gambaro but a superficial, two-page essay on the prolific Rosario Castellanos. The predominance of Southern Cone writers to the detriment of those of other regions; the omission of such important writers as Clarice Lispector, and of Latin American writers in the US; the frequent, superfluous references to world writers; the disembodied theoretical concepts; and the many errata diminish Jehenson's efforts. Although much remains to be done in the serious study of Latin American women and their accomplishments, this work contributes to the growing literature and will be useful to scholars at all levels.—*S. T. Clark, California State University, San Marcos*

WS-0682   PQ7297   93-37776 CIP
Jörgensen, Beth E. **The writing of Elena Poniatowska: engaging dialogues.** Texas, 1994. 172p bibl index afp ISBN 0-292-74032-8, $27.50; ISBN 0-292-74033-6 pbk, $12.95

The key question suggested here is whether the Mexican writer Elena Poniatowska has been able to overcome the barriers that exist between her privileged background and her subject matter. The European-born aristocrat, well respected in her adopted nation as a journalist and writer of "testimonial literature," remains an elusive figure. In her introduction, Jörgensen avows a feminist bias in her approach to the works, which start with a set of interviews with major artistic figures, *Palabras cruzadas* (1961), and end with *La "Flor de Lis"* (1988), a novel. Using a distracting first-person style, Jörgensen seeks to give validity to a writer who defies classification, by placing her as a challenge to the concept of hegemonic (or here defined as "monologic") discourse. This belabored and facile definition of the concept indicts a whole society and its establishment, to the detriment of some of its major figures. A detailed, well-documented chapter on the novel *Hasta no verte, Jesús mío* (1969) does little to enlighten readers on the work's real merits, instead focusing on the forced relationship between the outspoken peasant Jesusa Palancares and her educated and privileged interpreter. Jörgensen makes use of such critical theorists as Derrida in an attempt to provide a structure to Poniatowska's disjointed style, as we see in *La noche de Tlatelolco* (1971). What the author accomplishes, instead, is to demonstrate the reason why major writer status has eluded Poniatowska in her country and abroad. Upper-division undergraduate and up.—*S. T. Clark, California State University, San Marcos*

WS-0683   PN98   92-16023 CIP
Kaminsky, Amy K. **Reading the body politic: feminist criticism and Latin American women writers.** Minnesota, 1993 (c1992). 160p index ISBN 0-8166-1947-6, $39.95; ISBN 0-8166-1948-4 pbk, $13.95

Arguing on the one hand that Anglo-American and Continental feminism cannot be applied directly to Latin American women writers without a consideration of the latter's cultural and political context, and on the other hand, that feminist theory has more to reveal about these writers than many of them would acknowledge, Kaminsky offers insightful, often stunning readings of works by Alicia Partnoy, Elena Garro, Cristina Peri Rossi, Sylvia Molloy, and Gaby Brimmer (who worked in collaboration with Elena Poniatowska on her autobiography). The motif of the exile (because of politics, sexual orientation, physical handicap) is explored, with analogies made between the body as physical presence, on the one hand, and sexual and textual writing, on the other. In all instances, Kaminsky insists that feminist critical discourse must deal with the concrete and the wordly, that like feminist practice, it must concern itself with responsibility and the possibility for real (not just theoretical) transformation. These are some of the most intelligent and compelling essays written by a North American academic about the writing of Latin American women whose reality is anything but academic. Advanced undergraduate; graduate; faculty.—*K. F. Nigro, University of Cincinnati*

WS-0684   PQ7378   93-7644 CIP
Kutzinski, Vera M. **Sugar's secrets: race and the erotics of Cuban nationalism.** University Press of Virginia, 1993. 287p bibl index ISBN 0-8139-1466-3, $40.00;

Sugar's Secrets traces the development of Cuba's African cultural substratum, an ethnic component in the development of Cuban national identity. Racial dichotomies emerged as blacks confronted European-oriented mainstream cultures, with the result that blacks became a socially underprivileged group. Kutzinski observes this process especially in the mulatta, a "symbolic container for all the tricky questions about ... race, gender, and sexuality." Her interdisciplinary analysis includes the examination of printed representations of black people, such as the "marquillas," wrappers used by Cuban manufacturers to advertise their product. The marquillas show that social control is achieved through representation of race and gender (of mulattas in most cases). *Sugar's Secrets* is an impressive feminist analysis of Afro-Cuban literature. Rather than just enumerating sexist and thematic aggressions against black female characters, Jutzinski offers a newer approach to determining how these stereotypes arise and how they function in historical settings. Highly recommended to graduate students. General; upper-division undergraduate and up.—*R. Ocasio, Agnes Scott College*

WS-0685   PQ6498   94-19476 CIP
María de Zayas: the dynamics of discourse, ed. by Amy R. Williamsen and Judith A. Whitenack. Fairleigh Dickinson, 1995. (Dist. by Associated University Presses) 257p bibl index afp ISBN 0-8386-3572-5, $41.50

The work of this 17th-century Spanish author has in recent decades been the subject of numerous critical studies—as the bibliography of this collection attests—but this is the first book-length study of her in English. The 12 essays presented here are divided into sections titled "History/Literature: The Dynamics of Interdependent Discourses," "Competing/Completing Discourses: Sexual/Textual Dynamics," "The Dynamics of Desire," and "The Dynamics of Narrative." Notes and references appear at the end of each essay. The introduction notes that "the reader will hear several distinct voices approaching their inquiries with divergent interests and methods." All Spanish quotations are translated into English, which should make the volume more accessible to those who do not read Spanish. This volume should be useful to those interested in feminist critical theory and its application, and to scholars in the field of 17th-century Spanish novel and short story. Upper-division undergraduate and above.—*H. C. Woodbridge, emeritus, Southern Illinois University-Carbondale*

WS-0686 PQ7081 95-37411 CIP
Martínez, Elena M. **Lesbian voices from Latin America: breaking ground.** Garland, 1996. 223p (Latin American studies, 7) bibl index afp ISBN 0-8153-1349-7, $35.00

Martínez (Baruch College, CUNY) presents an overview of the works of five well-known Latin American women who are representatives of the emerging field of lesbian literature: Magaly Alabau, Sylvia Molloy, Rosa María Roffiel, Nancy Cárdenas, and Luz María Umpierre. A short introduction sets the theoretical background, emphasizing four thematic categories: the erotic, the autobiographical, the self-reflective, and the sociopolitical. In five independent chapters Martínez traces the themes and the literary techniques used by the five writers. The author's purpose is twofold: to define and categorize lesbian Latin American literature, and to provide a strong theoretical framework pertinent to the cultural and sexual realities that are the focus of the Latin American lesbian literary text. This captivating study, which sets up a series of issues for further analytical investigation, joins a strong, emerging critical movement initiated by David William Foster's *Latin American Writers on Gay and Lesbian Themes* (CH, Apr'95). Recommended for general readers and undergraduate and graduate students interested in an overview of Latin American lesbian literature.—*R. Ocasio, Agnes Scott College*

WS-0687 PQ7253 92-18246 CIP
Mouth to mouth: poems by twelve contemporary Mexican women, ed. by Forrest Gander; tr. by Zoe Anglesey et al. Milkweed Editions, 1993. 233p ISBN 0-915943-71-9 pbk, $14.95

A bilingual anthology that includes poems by women who came of age in the 1970s and 1980s. There are well-known authors (Carmen Boullosa, Kyra Galván) and lesser-known figures worthy of recognition: Elsa Cross, Myriam Moscona, etc. The introduction by Julio Ortega contextualizes writers and their role in the process of democratization that followed the Massacre of Tlateloco. The volume is divided into 12 sections; each begins with brief bio-bibliographical notes, followed by personal declarations of authors' poetics and selection of poems. Poems evidence a variety of themes and styles—e.g., erotic, experimental, autobiographical, and social or political. Translations are excellent and generally faithful to originals. Gander, the editor and translator of some texts, is a poet, as are all of the translators. This explains their deftness at rendering rhythm, tone, and diction of originals. The anthology advances scholarship in Hispanic letters, contemporary poetry and women's studies. Can be used at undergraduate and graduate levels, in classes in Spanish and English, and would be appropriate in a course on the poetry of women of color.—*S. A. Cavallo, Loyola University of Chicago*

WS-0688 PQ7297 95-3795 CIP
O'Connell, Joanna. **Prospero's daughter: the prose of Rosario Castellanos.** Texas, 1995. 263p bibl index afp ISBN 0-292-76041-8, $35.00; ISBN 0-292-76042-6 pbk, $17.95

As the years go by since Castellanos's tragic death in 1974, it becomes more and more apparent that Spanish American letters has lost one of its most gifted narrative, poetic, and journalistic voices; that voice is now being reclaimed by feminists on both sides of the Rio Grande. O'Connell's book is an important addition to the excellent work already done—*A Rosario Castellanos Reader*, ed. by Maureen Ahern (1988); Perla Schwartz's *Rosario Castellanos: mujer que supo latín* (1984); *Homenaje a Rosario Castellanos*, ed. by Ahern and Mary Seale Vasquez (1980); and Germaine Calderón's *El universo poético de Rosario Castellanos* (1979). In a highly lucid and accessible prose, O'Connell (Univ. of Minnesota) begins her study of the Mexican author by examining the evolution of the *Tempest* anthology traditionally used to symbolize the relations between colonizer and colonized. She analyzes the figure of Prospero's daughter Miranda as the embodiment of the difficult situation of many women intel-

lectuals: because of their social status and race, they are automatically identified with the power of the colonizer, but as women living in a male-dominated world, they are in fact condemned to a role of subordination. O'Connell's insightful reading convincingly demonstrates how Castellanos uses writing to subvert the limitations that society imposed on her as just another of Prospero's daughters. Upper-division undergraduate upward.—*J. J. Hassett, Swarthmore College*

WS-0689 PQ9677 91-22132 CIP
One hundred years after tomorrow: Brazilian women's fiction in the 20th century, tr. and ed. by Darlene J. Sadlier. Indiana, 1992. 241p afp ISBN 0-253-35045-X, $35.00; ISBN 0-253-20699-5 pbk, $12.95

A superb addition to the increasing number of anthologies dedicated to Brazilian literature. What is remarkable about this volume is the harmonious balance between established writers—e.g., Raquel de Queiroz, Clarice Lispector, and Lygia Fagundes Telles—with the writers who emerged in the 1970s and are writing today. Sadlier's interesting and well-documented introduction celebrates the accomplishment of Brazilian writers over a period of 100 years, and thus brings back forgotten writers into critical attention. Sadlier's translations are accurate and reflect the musicality and strength of the language. A good addition to academic and public library collections on Latin American women writers.—*M. Agosin, Wellesley College*

WS-0690 PQ6055 90-55690 CIP
Ordóñez, Elizabeth J. **Voices of their own: contemporary Spanish narrative by women.** Bucknell, 1991. (Dist. by Associated University Presses) 250p bibl index afp ISBN 0-8387-5203-9, $38.50

Hispanic women writers, whether from Spain or Latin America, have generally been ignored by critics, who dismiss them as borderline. More recent criticism, including the present volume, has dispelled this judgment. The author focuses on 11 women writers of the post-Spanish Civil War period. Divided into three sections—"Preludes," "In sotto voce," and "Gathering Choices"—the writers considered range from Laforet to Martin Gaite and Garcia Morales. Since much of prevailing criticism views women as a "subset of the male species; and their work, therefore, as marginal," Ordóñez has elected to examine each work included here "in terms of its relationship to the prevailing discourses of its time." This approach reveals a surprising heterogeneity among these writers. More significantly, the author suggests that a fair and objective evaluation of women writers requires viewing them from a female perspective, free of the norms imposed by a male-dominated cluture. It is the latter that has deprived not only these writers but women writers elsewhere of an unbiased assessment of their rich and varied contribution to human letters.—*F. Colecchia, Duquesne University*

WS-0691 PQ8549 93-17895 CIP
Parra, Teresa de la. **Iphigenia: (the diary of a young lady who wrote because she was bored),** tr. by Bertie Acker. Texas, 1994 (c1993). 354p afp ISBN 0-292-71570-6, $37.50; ISBN 0-292-71571-4 pbk, $17.95

Teresa de la Parra (1895-1936) is a novelist whose work has not been very well known, not even to Latin American readers. However, her writings constitute an important step in the elucidation of a feminine consciousness in Latin America. Originally published in 1922 as a serial in Spanish and French versions, *Iphigenia* appeared in book form in 1924, becoming an instant success in her native Venezuela. This is mostly an autobiographical narration that can best be described as a "novel of impressions." The protagonist, 18-year old María Eugenia Alonso, who as a motherless child had grown up in France, returns to Venezuela to a world that is largely foreign to her. She sets out to describe her passage into adulthood, which gradually becomes a search for a feminine identity in a patriarchal society that victimizes her. María Eugenia falls prey to a "Monster with seven heads that are called society, family, honor, religion, morality, duty, conventions, and principles." Clearly a first novel, the text suffers from overdrawn sections that detract from the overall quality, but that attest to its origins as a serial. Ably translated by Bertie Acker, useful if short introduction by Naomi Lindstrom. Recommended for general, undergraduate, and graduate readership.—*G. Gómez Ocampo, Wabash College*

WS-0692 CIP

Pedrero, Paloma. **Parting gestures: three plays,** tr. by Phyllis Zatlin. Estreno, 1994. 63p (Contemporary Spanish plays, 6) ISBN 0-9631212-5-1 pbk, $6.00

Many of the compelling virtues as well as the dispiriting lows of Pedrero's theater writing are revealed in these one-act plays. The poetic realism that characterizes her works may occasionally lose its fluid, colloquial freshness in Zatlin's dutifully correct translation, but the unifying theme of frustration born of defective human communication is a solid binding force in each piece. *The Color of August* (*El color de agosto*, 1989), which focuses on the intense relationship of a Madrid artist and her former model, is dramatically forceful. It convincingly conveys a conflict of contemporary women struggling with issues of passion, deceit, and latent lesbianism. It offers a harvest of symbolic and psychological meanings that warrant a section (sadly neglected in this publication) devoted to critical analysis. The least successful play is *The Voucher* (*Resguardo personal*, 1988), an insipid and untidy piece of tasteless trivialization. Bridging the sublime and ridiculous is *A Night Divided* (*La noche dividida*, 1989), which brings together an improbable pair of lonely, despairing people marred by dependency and alienation. All three plays will appeal to readers and actors interested in feminist studies: Pedrero's female protagonists are agonizingly alive and committed; their male counterparts are flat, boring, and revolting. Upper-division undergraduate and up.—*D. R. McKay, University of Colorado at Colorado Springs*

WS-0693 PQ6105 89-46402 CIP

The Perception of women in Spanish theater of the golden age, ed. by Anita K. Stoll and Dawn L. Smith. Bucknell, 1991. (Dist. by Associated University Presses) 276p index afp ISBN 0-8387-5189-X, $42.50

Literary texts can be appreciated in any number of ways, and this collection of essays by North American specialists in the Spanish *comedia* offers eloquent testimony to that assertion. Three parts follow an excellent introduction—(1) theoretical approaches, (2) taking the woman's part, and (3) rape, politics, and sexual inversion. All 14 essays center on the perception of women in Spanish drama of the 16th and 17th centuries, and the attempt throughout is to interrogate familiar materials by posing questions that seem pertinent to today's critical temper. B.W. Wardropper's insights into the *comedia* as comedy are borne out at every turn, especially the notion of woman as a subversive force in social structures. On the other hand, H.R. Hays's pioneering and fundamental *The Dangerous Sex: The Myth of Feminine Evil* (CH, Jan'65) is nowhere mentioned. Otherwise, contributions are of uniformly high quality and are eminently readable. While appropriate for all audiences, the primary readership will be specialists in the Spanish *comedia*, feminists, and others interested in women's studies.—*J. A. Parr, University of California, Riverside*

WS-0694 PQ6085 95-22660 CIP

Pérez, Janet. **Modern and contemporary Spanish women poets.** Twayne/Prentice Hall International, 1996. 198p (TWAS, 858. Spanish literature) bibl index afp ISBN 0-8057-4627-7, $24.95

This chronological study brings women poets writing in Spain's phallocentric, misogynist society out of a silence of centuries into the light of literary respectability and critical exegesis. Pérez's pioneering panorama is a timely attempt to establish a feminine canon that privileges domestic space, colloquial registers, and a high degree of orality. Denied access to formal education, Spain's women poets made a virtue of necessity, a ploy that has finally brought them overdue acclaim: autodidacticism led to the use of free verse and the prose poem, forms whose naturalness, simplicity, and freedom are nearer to modern taste. The time warp that reduced these women's participation in contemporary male "generations" allows readers to recenter them within a meaningful tradition for today's writers and readers. While affirming clearly identifiable antecedents, Pérez (Texas Tech Univ.) begins with Romanticism and ends her overview of the modern period with Franco's death in 1975. Significant women writing in Castilian, Catalan, Galician, and Basque—within and outside Spain—are reviewed; major figures are foregrounded (Carmen Conde, exceptionally, is allotted a whole chapter), but minor poets are also recognized, adding enormously to the value of this survey. Though it lacks textual analysis, Pérez's eclectic approach makes for enjoyable reading that will inform, stimulate, and excite both professionals and the merely curious. All collections.—*K. M. Sibbald, McGill University*

WS-0695 PQ9607 91-27454 CIP

Quinlan, Susan Canty. **The female voice in contemporary Brazilian narrative.** P. Lang, 1991. 205p (American university studies. Series XXII, Latin American studies, 7) bibl index ISBN 0-8204-1281-3, $40.95

During the last 15 years, Brazilian fiction as well as criticism has been granted the space so much deserved within the general framework of current Latin American studies. The book under review is a welcome addition to the studies dedicated to Brazilian literature. The study is particularly useful because of its scope and introductory nature. It clearly documents the development of Brazilian narrative from its beginnings to the present. Quinlan also adds important information on the relationship of Brazilian women's writing to the theory of feminist criticism. A much-needed study in this area particularly because the very writers chosen allow the reader to understand the rich tradition in Brazilian women's fiction. For graduate and undergraduate students.—*M. Agosin, Wellesley College*

WS-0696 PQ7082 94-17119 CIP

Reinterpreting the Spanish American essay: women writers of the 19th and 20th centuries, ed. by Doris Meyer. Texas, 1995. 246p bibl afp ISBN 0-292-75167-2, $25.00

This is a very important and wholeheartedly welcome contribution to the study of the essay in Latin America. The essay, a genre that "covers a literary terrain that is vast and remarkably varied," as Meyer (Connecticut College) puts it, has generally had a low status in most histories of Latin American literature. This regrettable situation is even more serious in the case of essays by women, which to a large extent have been absent from most other studies of the genre, e.g., Martin S. Stabb's *In Quest of Identity* (1967) and John Skirius's *El Ensayo hispano americano del siglo xx* (1981). Meyer's volume is a definite corrective to this situation: it looks at the Latin American essay in all its richness and diversity and reveals the contribution of women writers to the important traditions of the genre, restituting visibility to what she ironically calls the "literary disappeared." Individual chapters cover authors ranging from Flora Tristán (born 1803) to contemporary writers such as Carmen Naranjo and Margo Glantz. Recommended for all levels and academic and public libraries.—*G. Gómez Ocampo, Wabash College*

WS-0697 PQ7087 95-3564 CIP

Rereading the Spanish American essay: translations of 19th and 20th century women's essays, ed. by Doris Meyer. Texas, 1995. 324p afp ISBN 0-292-75179-6, $40.00; ISBN 0-292-75182-6 pbk, $19.95

This volume, companion to *Reinterpreting the Spanish American Essay: Women Writers of the 19th and 20th Centuries*, also ed. by Doris Meyer (CH, Jan'96), is essential to any Latin American collection. The editor has done a superb job of collecting some of the most important writings by women about women ever to come from that region. From works by relatively obscure writers (Eduarda Mansilla, Peru; Nellie Campobello, Mexico) to those by better known individuals such as Victoria Ocampo and Cristina Peri Rossi, every selection in this anthology is an eye-opener to the status of women in Latin American societies. A multiplicity of voices examine issues that run the gamut from the social to the personal and shed light on the constructs of power as they relate to gender, religion, morality, politics, and economics. It is surprising that many of these essays are hard to find in their Spanish-language originals, and it boggles the mind that most of them have never before been translated into English. Happily, these able translations now make them available to a much wider readership. The essays are preceded by short, useful introductions. This reviewer is pleased that footnotes are kept to a minimum, but an index of names and places would have been very useful. Recommended for all levels.—*G. Gómez Ocampo, Wabash College*

WS-0698 PN849 93-42502 CIP

Rodríguez, Ileana. **House/garden/nation: space, gender, and ethnicity in postcolonial Latin American literatures by women,** tr. by Robert Carr and Ileana Rodríguez. Duke University, 1994. 223p bibl index afp ISBN 0-8223-1450-9, $49.95; ISBN 0-8223-1465-7 pbk, $16.95

Twentieth-century Caribbean literature offers a rich selection of works by women witnessing the transition to modernity. This text examines that topic in two sections. Part 1 covers the masculine perspective with emphasis on economic development, property rights, the accumulation of capital, and the relationships between lineage and patriarchy, land and power, and literature and politics.

Examples are drawn from such noted authors as Gallegos, Rivera, and Güiraldes. Part 2 studies the feminine perspective through a careful analysis of works by five authors: Venezuelan Teresa de la Parra; Cuban Dulce María Loynaz; Jamaican Jean Rhys; Guadeloupan Simone Schwarz-Bart; and Nicaraguan Gioconda Belli. There is a logical, rational argument that is well developed through the chronological progression of the works. Although the influences of Spain, England, France, and Africa in the Caribbean are shown, such cultural differences as well as national identifications are seen to pale beside the overriding issue of greater participation by women and ethnic minorities in expanding political and economic spheres on a global level. Recommended for graduate students, researchers, and faculty.—*M. V. Ekstrom, St. John Fisher College*

WS-0699   PQ6055   94-21028 CIP
Scarlett, Elizabeth A. **Under construction: the body in Spanish novels.** University Press of Virginia, 1995 (c1994). 232p bibl index ISBN 0-8139-1532-5, $37.50

Looking at what she calls the intersections of textuality and physicality, Scarlett traces prominent women's and men's writing in Spain from the late 19th century through the 1980s. Beginning with the body as text in Emilio Pardo Bazán's *Insolación* (1892) and working through to Adelaida García Morales's *El silencio de las sirenas* (1985), Julio Llamazares's *Lund de lobos* (1985), Soledad Puértolas's *Queda la noche* (1989), and Antonio Muñoz Molina's *Beltenebros* (1989), she shows that over time, bodily flexibility between the genders increases as rapprochement in writing continues. Noteworthy discussions relate to Rosa Chacel, José Ortega y Gasset, and bodily discourse; disguises and codification of the female body in Mercè Rodoreda's novels; body politics in novels of Franco's Spain (Camilo José's *La familia de Pascual Duarte*, 1945); Carmen Martín Gaite's *Entre visillos* (1958); and Luis Martín-Santos's *Tiempo de silencio* (1962); and nomads and "schizos" as representative of postmodern trends in writing. Concluding that the body can never be constructed at total liberty from social norms, Scarlett sets new parameters for future investigations of other writings. A solid addition to gender studies in Spanish literature in upper-level undergraduate and graduate courses.—*C. E. Klein, Beaver College*

WS-0700   PQ7133   91-30584 CIP
Schaefer, Claudia. **Textured lives: women, art, and representation in modern Mexico.** Arizona, 1992. 163p bibl index afp ISBN 0-8165-1250-7, $29.95

Schaefer's feminist approach unites four 20th-century Mexican artistic figures, each the center of an essay. The lead—and lengthier—chapter examines the much-heralded artist Frida Kahlo. The other chapters treat three women writers. In Rosario Castellanos's case Schaefer chooses little-known essays instead of the poetic and fictional production. The chapter on Elena Poniatowska addresses biographic, epistolary works. The final essay analyzes the novel *Arréncame la vida* by the journalist Angeles Mastretta. Citing the Latin root of *text* in *texture* and *textile*, Schaefer justifies mixing genres to link "marginal" discourse to that which is dominant (female versus male). This approach works in the first two essays. Kahlo's in particular—despite the frustrating lack of illustrations—yields penetrating insights into the artist's successful translation of her art to visual form, as well as convincing parallels between Kahlo's world and Mexico's struggle in a modern era. The book's second half does not deliver, particularly the last essay, which cannot find its promised focus on the novel and Mexican popular music. Schaefer's insistence on translating *every* Spanish word into English, the footnote overuse, and the paucity of quoted text material make the reading laborious. Nevertheless, the brilliant Kahlo chapter alone makes this book worth acquiring for upper-division undergraduates, graduate students, and faculty.—*S. T. Clark, California State University, San Marcos*

WS-0701   PQ6670.U8   89-38371 CIP
Tusquets, Esther. **The same sea as every summer,** tr. by Margaret E.W. Jones. Nebraska, 1990. 196p afp ISBN 0-8032-4422-3, $22.95; ISBN 0-8032-9416-6, $9.95

A first-person, present-tense narrative of a woman, about age 50, who is a university professor of Italian literature. Though born into the bourgeoisie of her city (probably Barcelona), she has always been in conflict with the values and activities of her family and class. A man named Jorge, who came into her life when she was young and who has been everything her family and class were not, has inexplicably committed suicide, and the narrator/protagonist loses the will to continue the liberating path he set her upon. For 30 years hers is the loneliness of one whose mother, daughter, and successful husband neither care for nor understand her. After a crisis in her life, she seems to be on the verge of a new liberation but discovers that her will for trying was lost 30 years before. This novel begins well, but it bogs down tremendously—a rather common development in the Spanish feminist novel of the late '70s and early '80s. Regardless of its literary merits, however, it is an important cultural document. A volume in the "Nebraska European Women Series," it could be of interest to anyone reading in or studing contemporary feminism; and because it is by a major contemporary Spanish writer, it is recommended for purchase by academic and public libraries. Jones's translation from the Spanish serves well to bring Tusquets to the English-speaking general reader.—*S. Miller, Texas A & M University*

WS-0702   BX4700   95-4365 CIP
Velasco, Sherry M. **Demons, nausea, and resistance in the autobiography of Isabel de Jesús, 1611-1682.** New Mexico, 1996. 133p bibl index ISBN 0-8263-1664-6, $35.00

Isabel de Jesús published her diaries in 1685, a time when women religious were discouraged from writing, encouraged to report revelations and mystic experiences to their confessors, and required to obtain authorization before writing their experiences/revelations down. Although the work of some women mystics was recognized (e.g., Santa Teresa), most works were analyzed and often linked to considerations for sainthood or accusations of heresy. Velasco (Univ. of Kansas) ably captures the misogyny, demonology, anxiety of writing, particularly on religious matters, and opposition to suppression of writing by women like Isabel de Jesús. The author notes that Isabel uses the devil—whose attempts to prevent her from doing God's work, i.e. writing "religious doctrine," cause her nausea or other illnesses—as a device to express "her disgust toward misogynist ideology," to protect against reprisals of heresy, and to criticize the male clergy who tried to suppress women's writing. Isabel's rhetorical devices, the quotations written in the Spanish of the 17th century, and the sources and analyses on demonology and heresy (including illustrations) make this interesting and well-documented study valuable for researchers in rhetoric, linguistics, history, and literature. Upper-division undergraduate and above.—*M. Garza-Randeri, Texas Woman's University*

WS-0703   Orig
What is secret: stories by Chilean women, ed. by Marjorie Agosín. White Pine, NY, 1996 (c1995). 303p (Secret weavers series, 9) afp ISBN 1-877727-41-5 pbk, $17.00

This long-needed collection responds to a growing interest in Latin American women writers. Poet, critic, academic, Agosin (Wellesley College) divides the anthology into five sections that interweave the rich styles of the varied Chilean terrain with themes of myth, physical appearance, sensuality, motherhood, and confrontations between self and state. The 37 stories combine into one texture Chilean women, landscape, and history. Their style is forceful yet sensitive; their secret is no longer a silence but a creative urge to express conflict or harmony between the inner and public selves, that which is marginal yet artistically seeking justified recognition. Agosin provides useful biographical sketches of the authors, all of whose work dates from 1900. The writers are both well known and unknown—novelists, essayists, journalists, lawyers, professors, literary critics. Two stories were originally written in English. Accurate and admirable translations capture original styles in an attractive format. The book's flaws include some typos, disconcerting spelling variations of names, and the omission of any story by one of the author's profiled.—*A. Zimring, Roosevelt University*

WS-0704   PQ7488   91-26038 CIP
When new flowers bloomed: short stories by women writers from Costa Rica and Panama, ed. by Enrique Jaramillo Levi. Latin American Literary Review, 1991. 208p bibl ISBN 0-935480-47-1 pbk, $14.95

A welcome contribution of new voices, linked by culture, geography, and political history, but nevertheless demonstrating in vast differences of content and technique how misleading such labels as "women writers" or "Latin American" actually are. Most of these new and talented writers are virtually unknown. It is noteworthy that their stories do not deal with political strife, revolution, or group survival, and that their "conventional" themes are suffused with a genuine feminine consciousness. The stories run the gamut of conventional themes, with characters ranging from the lowly and humble to middle-class, including as narrators innocent children who do not understand the adult world. Traditional romantic themes are evident as are the experimental, like surrealism, metafiction, supernatural Gothic tales in contemporary garb, or even humorous, black comedy subversions of the conventional story of the suicidal woman. The selection is truly a joy to read and the stories are accessible to general readers. Therein lies the book's primary importance: to acquaint Anglophone readers with new and talented women writers.—*Y. Jehenson, SUNY College at Oswego*

WS-0705 PQ6490 93-33884 CIP
Yarbro-Bejarano, Yvonne. **Feminism and the honor plays of Lope de Vega.** Purdue, 1994. 324p (Purdue studies in Romance literatures, 4) bibl index afp ISBN 1-55753-044-0, $39.95

Critics are like cattle; they move in herds. Yarbro-Bejarano is one of a select group of younger critics who intone the neo-Marxist mantra in its refurbished, fin de siècle forms of "ideology" and "cultural studies." One expects an analysis of subject formation, along with some Foucauldian flourishes, to embellish the orthodox overtures to race, class, and gender. One is not disappointed. There is a stupefying sameness about the rhetoric of such studies, even when they are nuanced, as this one is. The readings tend to be as predictable as any advanced by the late (and often great) British School. This opus centers on gender and is modestly feminist. It endeavors to amplify and diversify the Lopean canon, while applying feminist theory. It corroborates what has often been demonstrated: feminist theory contributes to our understanding and appreciation of both text and context. Gender, sexuality, power, control, and subversion are concepts that intermingle and interpenetrate throughout the critic's discourse, along with several others, like desire, lack, and Spanishness. The study is readable, dutifully documented, and should be warmly embraced by feminists, cultural studies buffs, and the canon-shy. Graduate; faculty.—*J. A. Parr, University of California, Riverside*

◆ Romance
Italian

WS-0706 PQ4063x 91-67977 Orig
Amoia, Alba della Fazia. **Women on the Italian literary scene: a panorama.** Whitston, 1992. 151p bibl index ISBN 0-87875-428-8, $25.00

Amoia's survey of Italian women prose writers is useful in some ways and disappointing in others. Its utility resides in the introduction to and description of many 20th-century women writers, whose work is undoubtedly little known by English-language readers. The book is marred, however, by its tendency to make pronouncements on the value of these works, rather than to present deep analyses of them. The title of the study is itself misleading, for one might expect a diachronic study of women writers through the centuries, or an inclusion of women poets as well as prose writers of a given period. Instead, it is simply declared that no poets will be included, and the brief comments on women writers of earlier periods are superficial, adding little to an understanding of the historical context for the modern works under consideration. Although presumably written for non-Italian readers, the book does not provide titles of translated works in the slim bibliography, even though many are in fact available in English translation. If the book is intended for use by Italianists, it is too unscholarly; if general readers or nonspecialists are the targeted audience, it fails to make obvious the availability of materials in English that such a readership would need. There are some good insights, but overall the book is very uneven.—*R. West, University of Chicago*

WS-0707 90-39079 CIP
Bullock, Alan. **Natalia Ginzberg: human relationships in a changing world.** Berg, 1991. (Dist. by St. Martin's) 261p bibl index ISBN 0-85496-178-X, $26.00

A monograph for "Berg Women's Series," Bullock's study of Natalia Ginzburg is a carefully presented, well-documented introduction to her works. Although often read in intermediate and advanced language courses because of the simplicity of her style and although regularly translated into English, Ginzburg has not yet received extensive critical analysis, as Bullock's excellent bibliography demonstrates. This book remedies that void admirably by offering a valid thematic approach to the subject. Bullock's first chapter centers on Ginzburg's personal relationship to her vocation, carefully outlining the vicissitudes of the writer's involvement with her craft, including shifts in her style and subject matter. The following four chapters center on character analysis in her stories, novels, and plays. Three of the four focus on female protagonists in their struggles to endure and find meaning; the last chapter is dedicated to male characters, who are generally of secondary importance. Bullock proceeds in a chronological fashion but, given his thematic organization, rediscusses many of the primary sources from different angles. Elements of Ginzburg's life are integrated when deemed appropriate. All in all, this is a significant introductory study of a well-known contemporary writer.—*F. A. Bassanese, University of Massachusetts at Boston*

WS-0708 PQ4055.W6 89-28436 MARC
Contemporary women writers in Italy: a modern renaissance, ed. by Santo L. Arico. Massachusetts, 1990. 238p bibl ISBN 0-87023-710-1, $29.50

This excellent collection of essays on 12 Italian women writers sheds new light on a long-neglected element of Italian literature and culture. As Arico points out in his lucid introduction, writing by women has received scant critical attention in Italy and has also been overlooked by Italianists who address an English-speaking audience. Thus, this volume fills a gap and treats such major writers as Anna Banti, Camilla Cederna, Fausta Cialente, Oriana Fallaci, Natalia Ginzburg, Armanda Guiducci, Gina Lagorio, Gianna Manzini, Dacia Maraini, Elsa Morante, Lalla Romano, and Francesca Sanvitale. In addition to Arico, 12 other scholars of contemporary Italian literature have contributed essays, which are of a high quality and provide an accurate picture of current scholarship on this topic. Moreover, the plurality of critical viewpoints and the variety of authors discussed give the volume a panoramic quality. Although the individual essays serve as an in-depth introduction to the various authors, the volume as a whole provides an accurate overview and point of departure for further study. Handsomely published with an extensive bibliography, this volume provides an Italian perspective on an issue of great moment. Highly recommended for both the academic specialist and the general reader.—*J. Welle, University of Notre Dame*

WS-0709 PQ4572 91-44808 CIP
Finucci, Valeria. **The lady vanishes: subjectivity and representation in Castiglione and Ariosto.** Stanford, 1992. 329p bibl index afp ISBN 0-8047-2045-2, $39.50

While acknowledging that Castiglione and Ariosto showed some sympathy to women, Finucci argues that their fictional constructs have little historical verisimilitude. She holds that there is a great discrepancy between what the text says and what the subtext reveals. She then proceeds to give a thoroughgoing deconstruction of their male depiction of femininity. drawing on the resources of Freudian psychoanalysis with Lacanian refinements and a dash of Barthes and Althusser, with excursions into mythology and the fine arts. In the case of Castiglione the presence of women in the discourse is shown to be merely a matter of convenience, as a frame for the expression of male views about them. The chapters on Ariosto are more complicated, filled with ingenious deconstructions of the female characters: the mysterious Angelica as the narcissistic woman, "textual archetype of an obscure, inaccessible, longed for and yet seemingly easy to obtain Madonna"; Olimpia, in three stages, phallicized by being made a murderer, dephallicized, and finally fetishized; Isabella, projection of male desires; Bradamante, masquerading in men's armor but in the end a victim of her femininity. New insights may be gained from this reading, especially in the application of Freudian analysis, but the often contorted critical language poses an obstacle to intelligibility. The bibliography is admirable.—*C. Fantazzi, University of Windsor*

WS-0710 PQ4174 93-10867 CIP
Lazzaro-Weis, Carol. **From margins to mainstream: feminism and fictional modes in Italian women's writing, 1968-1990.** Pennsylvania, 1993. 223p bibl index afp ISBN 0-8122-3195-3, $34.95; ISBN 0-8122-1438-2 pbk, $16.95

Lazzaro-Weis's scholarly book offers a well-written, extensively researched, and theoretically propelled presentation of contemporary women's writing in Italy.

Chapter 1 proposes a personal reflection on recent American and French theories as the author believes they relate to feminism, cultural studies, psychoanalytical criticism, and genre, with some reference to their reception in Italy. Italian feminism is the focus of the chapter 2, as the author explores cultural and sociopolitical attitudes and their relationship to writing during the past few decades. The following sections deal specifically with female texts, broadly distributed according to genre: confession, romance, bildungsroman, historical novel, detective fiction. Writers treated include familiar names such as Anna Banti, Maria Bellonci, and Dacia Maraini; lesser-known figures like Francesca Duranti, Giuliana Ferri, and Rosetta Loy; and relatively unknown writers such as Fiora Cagnoni and Marisa Volpi. The author's intention is to clarify these writers' position vis-à-vis literary conventions by analyzing differences and similarities in female narratives as they confront traditional literary frameworks and expectations. Theory is utilized extensively not only to define Italian feminism and women's fiction but also to show displacements and accomodations women employ within genre categories and conventions. A complex, provocative, and demanding book. Graduate; faculty.—*F. A. Bassanese, University of Massachusetts at Boston*

WS-0711   PQ4055   95-38296 CIP
Wood, Sharon. **Italian women's writing, 1860-1994.** Athlone, 1995. 320p (Women in context series, 2) bibl index ISBN 0-485-91002-0, $85.00; ISBN 0-485-92002-6 pbk, $29.95

A rich panoramic view of a complex topic, this title explores the situation of women novelists from the Italian political unification to the present. Wood (Univ. of Strathclyde) introduces each of the book's three broad chronological divisions with a chapter covering the political situation, cultural environment, and socioartistic status of women. Individual chapters are dedicated to significant authors, from Neera to Dacia Maraini. In the section on contemporary women, the analysis of individual writers gives way to two thematic chapters devoted, respectively, to the reappraisal of motherhood and to three current novelists representing feminist and postmodernist views. Wood takes care to integrate critical theory in an accessible, nonjargony manner, with an emphasis on a feminist approach. Although she highlights some novelists—e.g., Sibilla Aleramo and Francesca Duranti—others (e.g., Annie Vivanti) receive only passing mention in the introductory chapters. Poetry and minor works are treated cursorily, and such poets as Vittoria Aganoor or Antonia Pozzi are not included. Nevertheless, this is an excellent volume for anyone curious about modern women writers, their lives, sociocultural backgrounds, and major fiction. All the essays are lucid and informative. Notes and a selected bibliography are provided, including a list of English-language translations.—*F. A. Bassanese, University of Massachusetts at Boston*

◆ Slavic

WS-0712   PG3476   91-29985 CIP
Amert, Susan. **In a shattered mirror: the later poetry of Anna Akhmatova.** Stanford, 1992. 274p bibl index ISBN 0-8047-1982-9, $37.50

More specialized than the standard works in English on Akhmatova (Sam Driver, *Anna Akhmatova*, CH, Jun'73; Amanda Haight, *Anna Akhmatova: A Poetic Pilgrimage*, CH, Feb'77), this rich study concentrates on the difficult post-1935 poetry and traces metapoetic themes, especially the poet's plight in Russian society after the 1920s. Amert (Univ. of Delaware) examines Akhmatova's essay on Pushkin and a number of poems to expose the "secrets of [her] craft." Instead of always analyzing entire poems or cycles, Amert investigates the "framing texts" of *Requiem* ("Instead of a Foreword," "Epilogue"); "Prehistory," a 58-line poem in blank verse; "Tails," the metapoetical second half of *Poem Without a Hero*; the lyric cycle *The Sweetbriar Blooms*; and the sixth of *The Northern Elegies*. She shows how, in spite of its surface fragmentariness, the imagery evolves to produce a coherent portrait of Akhmatova as poet. Akhmatova paradoxically reveals herself through the device of concealment, especially a complex web of literary allusions, which Amert deftly, often brilliantly, untangles. She also places Akhmatova in her literary tradition by investigating the poetry in light of her affinities with other poets, especially Pushkin. Citation of works in the original and in accurate English translations renders the book accessible to the non-

specialist. Excellent use of sources, informative footnotes, extensive bibliography, and sensitive readings of the texts make this book indispensable to students of Akhmatova, Russian poetry and poetics, and women's studies.—*C. A. Rydel, Grand Valley State University*

WS-0713   PG3015   92-33089 CIP
Andrew, Joe. **Narrative and desire in Russian literature, 1822-49: the feminine and the masculine.** St. Martin's, 1993. 257p bibl index ISBN 0-312-09123-0, $39.95

Andrew's study is recommended for two reasons: (1) it provides an interesting example of "gender study," which is a perspective many trained in the field of Slavic literatures have not been exposed to; (2) it provides valuable information on two writers, Elena Gan and Mariya Zhukova, who have, unfortunately, received little critical attention in the past. This book is not for the novice, for it assumes an intimate knowledge of Russian literature from Pushkin to Dostoevsky. Separate chapters are devoted to Pushkin, V. F. Odoevsky, Gan, Zhukova, Herzen and a short discussion of Dostoevky's *Netochka Nezvanova*. Although not every reader will agree with some of the basic theses or analyses, especially those concerning Pushkin's "southern poems," all readers will acknowledge this book's stimulating, thought-provoking content as viewed from a feminist perspective. Copious footnotes. Graduate; faculty.—*E. Yarwood, Eastern Washington University*

WS-0714   PG3213   93-26542 CIP
An Anthology of Russian women's writing, 1777-1992, ed. by Catriona Kelly; tr. by Catriona Kelly et al. Oxford, 1994. 535p index afp ISBN 0-19-871504-8, $60.00; ISBN 0-19-871505-6 pbk, $22.50

Conceived as a companion volume to her *A History of Russian Women's Writing, 1820-1992* (CH, Nov'94), Catriona Kelly's anthology stands on its own merit as the first historical anthology of Russian women's writing to appear in English or Russian. Selected from fiction, poetry, and drama, the works are presented in generally chronological order. Kelly has sought to display a diversity of genre, themes, and voices; to this end, she has alternated pieces of varying genres or thematic concern. In the interest of presenting texts and authors not commonly anthologized, such major writers as Gippius, Akhmatova, and Tsvetaeva are represented by fewer and in some cases less accessible works than are usually included in introductory collections. While Kelly's exhaustive notes afford invaluable guidance on background, subtext, and translation, a university course surveying Russian women's writing would necessarily supplement this anthology with more material from these authors' canons. The editor also acknowledges "a corrective bias toward the past" in her selections. While serving the aim of historical overview, the number and variety of 19th-century pieces allows the discovery of intriguing reverberations to more modern works. Readers seeking a more contemporary focus will consult other collections, such as Helena Goscilo's *Balancing Acts* (CH, Sep'89). In addition to the notes and an introductory discussion of historical and thematic perspectives, readers are aided by brief biographical notes and the Russian texts of the poems. General and academic audiences.—*N. Tittler, SUNY at Binghamton*

WS-0715   PG3476   94-1266 CIP
Burgin, Diana Lewis. **Sophia Parnok: the life and work of Russia's Sappho.** New York University, 1994. 355p bibl index afp ISBN 0-8147-1190-1, $50.00; ISBN 0-8147-1221-5 pbk, $17.95

Clearly a labor of love, this volume—disarmingly gutsy in the context of Russian culture—is the first book-length biographical anglophone study of Sophia Parnok (1885-1933), a Jewish lesbian poet of the Silver and early-Soviet Age (1893-1920s). Whereas Russian criticism has stubbornly ignored or denied Parnok's lesbianism, Burgin embraces it as the organizing principle of her monograph. Integrating generous extracts from Parnok's poems into the narrative of her lived experience, Burgin charts Parnok's life along an unwavering lesbian curve, projecting both life and verses against a deftly delineated cultural background. Although partisan in her treatment and occasionally too ready, perhaps, to translate Parnok's poetry in somewhat unmediated fashion into biographical probability, Burgin succeeds in vividly conveying a sense of Parnok's personality, values, and poetic allegiances. She rightly credits Parnok with introducing the lesbian voice into Russian poetry, concisely identifies the hallmarks of Parnok's poetic development and, with the aid of extensive archival sources, allows readers to sample (if only in translation) the range of Parnok's poetic creativity. However nonconformist in her sexual orientation, Parnok opted for a traditionalist poetics. In addition to lyrics, she wrote literary criticism and reviews, and a highly successful opera libretto as well as produced translations. Apart from a few minor stylistic gaffes, the book is written in an accessible and lively style and makes for absorbing and thought-provoking reading. General and academic audiences.—*H. Goscilo, University of Pittsburgh*

WS-0716   PG3456   94-6501 CIP
Chekhov, Anton Pavlovich. **Stories of women,** tr. by Paula P. Ross. Prometheus Books, 1994. 308p afp ISBN 0-87975-893-7, $28.95; ISBN 0-87975-901-1 pbk, $15.95

A collection of Chekhov's stories grouped thematically is a good idea and Ross provides a variety of stories about women from Chekhov's early, middle, and late periods, although she would have done better to present them chronologically rather than haphazardly. Included are known works: "Name Day Celebration," "Anna Around the Neck," "The Sweetie" (usually translated as "The Darling"), and "The Bride to Be" along with a host of lesser-known works. Notable for their absence are "The Grasshopper," "In the Cart," and "At Home." The translations are well done with a few exceptions. Ross states in the introduction that her translations may be too "literal," but translating *zaterebila oborochku*, for example, as "wanted to have a chance to protest" instead of Robert Payne's much more accurate "picked at the trimmings of her dress" (*The Image of Chekhov*, 1963) is hardly literal. Ross does not follow the standard transliteration systems, so her rendering of Russian names is disconcerting: Mihighlovna for Mikhailovna, Mihighel for Mikhail, Kizmich for Kuzmich, etc. Chekhov's genius as a short story writer, however, transcends these shortcomings. Recommended to general readers and undergraduates.—*E. Yarwood, Eastern Washington University*

WS-0717   PN98   93-8711 CIP
A dialogue of voices: feminist literary theory and Bakhtin, ed. by Karen Hohne and Helen Wussow. Minnesota, 1994. 207p index afp ISBN 0-8166-2295-7, $44.95; ISBN 0-8166-2296-5 pbk, $17.95

This collection of new essays brings together ten perspectives on Mikhail Bakhtin and feminist theory, placing them in dialogue with one another. The editors' introductory essay explains Bakhtin's central concerns (principally the concepts of dialogism, carnival, and chronotopes), and critiques previous feminist work that has incorporated Bakhtin. The editors strive to represent a diversity of voices, though their own position is forcefully argued in the introduction. The collection includes essays that argue both for and against Bakhtin's potential usefulness to feminism, as well as essays that assign precedence either to Bakhtinian theory or to feminism. The essays discuss a wide variety of genres, including "nature writing, 19th-century novels by British women, contemporary romances, Irish and French lyric poetry and contemporary Latin American prose" as well as Hollywood film. One unusual essay stands out: Virginia Purvis-Smith's autobiographical account of a church service, heavily annotated with scholarly, theoretical, personal, and critical reflections on the experience. The book is a valuable addition to collections geared to faculty and graduate students.—*R. R. Warhol, University of Vermont*

WS-0718   PG2981   93-8650 MARC
Dialogues/Dialogi: literary and cultural exchanges between (ex)Soviet and American women, by Susan Hardy Aiken et al. Duke University, 1994. 415p bibl index afp ISBN 0-8223-1375-8, $64.95; ISBN 0-8223-1390-1 pbk, $19.95

Unique in its effort to encompass not only modern Soviet/Russian and American women's writing (Grekova, Petrushevskaia, Makarova, Nergaki, Olsen, Bambara, Phillips, and Silko), but also discussions of these texts by an American feminist (Aiken), an American Slavist (Barker), and two "Soviet" Americanists (Koreneva and Stetsenko), this material-rich volume attempts a genuine exchange between two cultures on the issue of gender. The results are uneven and the dialogues could, and should, have been more extensive and "gloves off," but the collection has enough invaluable information, incisive commentary, and flashes of admirable insight to attract a broad readership. While few may read the entire volume, the diversity of the contents guarantees thought-provoking reading for

virtually anyone interested in women's prose and its cultural contexts. Of special note are the fine translations of the excellent Petrushevskaia and Makarova texts, as well as the new English version of the previously twice-translated Grekova story; the fine afterword and comprehensive bibliography; and the analyses of female creativity, motherhood, and the process of narration. Duke University Press deserves gratitude for making the paperback version available at a reasonable price. Recommended for general readers and for all academic levels.—*H. Goscilo, University of Pittsburgh*

WS-0719   PG3476   94-9243 CIP
Feiler, Lily. **Marina Tsvetaeva: the double beat of heaven and hell.** Duke University, 1994. 299p bibl index afp ISBN 0-8223-1482-7, $34.95

Independent scholar and translator Lily Feiler has written an excellent new biography of Marina Tsvetaeva. With its focus on the poet's psychological makeup, the book complements the already existing, traditional studies of Tsvetaeva's life and works (Simon Karlinsky, *Marina Cvetaeva: Her Life and Art*, CH, Feb'68; *Marina Tsvetaeva: The Woman, Her World and Her Poetry*, CH, Nov'86; Elaine Feinstein, *A Captive Lion: The Life of Marina Tsvetaeva*, CH, Dec'87) and offers new insights about the poet. Rather than conduct a literary exegesis on the poetry itself, Feiler treats the life as a literary study, tracing the psychological themes and images that made up the whole woman as well as laid as the basis of her complex, often contradictory, sometimes cruel relationships with people as child, mother, wife, lover, and friend. Tsvetaeva's all-consuming need for love as a woman and recognition as a poet first and foremost motivated her to sacrifice all—even people she loved—for the sake of her poetry. Feiler also studies the sexual and political forces that contributed to the formation of an essentially self-destructive personality. Well-written and nonjudgmental, this objective presentation of the truth offers much that is new and valuable, even to those scholars already acquainted with Tsvetaeva's life and poetry. It is also suitable as an introductory study of the poet. General and academic audiences.—*C. A. Rydel, Grand Valley State University*

WS-0720   PG3286   94-40988 Orig
Half a revolution: contemporary fiction by Russian women, ed. and tr. by Masha Gessen. Cleis, 1995. 269p ISBN 1-57344-006-X pbk, $12.95

This readable collection of contemporary Russian women's short fiction contains several stylistically and thematically rewarding selections that convey the range of current Russian women's prose. Especially notable are the imaginative folklore-steeped psychological minimasterpieces by Nina Sadur, a sample of Valeria Narbikova's postmodernist prose, and a chilling tale of alienation by Yelana Tarasova. The lesbian text by Natalia Shulga, though somewhat timid in conception and short on narrative momentum, impresses by its powers of nuanced description. All the entries have something to recommend them. Though the translations are accurate and read naturally, in a few cases they do not manage to capture the distinctive originality of the Russian text. Sadur and Narbikova in particular (the latter, admittedly, a nightmarishly difficult author to translate because of her ironic wordplay) sound neutralized in the English version. The absence of any other translation of Narbikova, however, makes this one particularly valuable. The overly brief preface and the introduction, like the commentary preceding each selection, are pitched at the general and undergraduate reader.—*H. Goscilo, University of Pittsburgh*

WS-0721   PG2997   92-46343 CIP
Holmgren, Beth. **Women's works in Stalin's time: on Lidiia Chukovskaia and Nadezhda Mandelstam.** Indiana, 1993. 225p bibl index afp ISBN 0-253-32865-9, $35.00; ISBN 0-253-20829-7 pbk, $14.95

Building on various sources, especially C.R. Proffer's *Widows of Russia*, Holmgren (Univ. of North Carolina) examines the role of women as unofficial memoirists of the Stalin era through sensitive analysis of the works of L. Chukovskaia (*To the Memory of Childhood*, CH, Mar'89; *Sof'ia Petrovna*, tr. as *The Deserted House*; *Spusk pod vodu*, *Going Under*; and *Notes on Anna Akhmatova*) and Nadezhda Mandelshtam ("Father," "Family," "Girls and a Boy," *Hope against Hope*, and *Hope Abandoned*). An introductory chapter looks at the political, social, and cultural aspects of Stalinism to explain how women became the custodians of culture in their not-altogether-private domestic spheres. Holmgren shows how Socialist Realism works, and "alternative" texts such as O. Mandelshtam's essays and poetry, Pasternak's *Doctor Zhivago*, and Bulgakov's *Master and Margarita* set literary models for real-life writers. On the other hand, Akhmatova's works gave women their own voice and helped to transform them from readers and preservers to authors. Holmgren sets out to show the path taken by each woman to evolve as a writer. She also looks at their legacy to Russian women. This fine book, with its copious, informative notes and good bibliography, will interest students of 20th-century literature and theorists of autobiography, feminist criticism, and gender studies. Upper-division undergraduate and up.—*C. A. Rydel, Grand Valley State University*

WS-0722   PG2997   93-26238 CIP
Kelly, Catriona. **A history of Russian women's writing, 1820-1992.** Oxford, 1994. 497p bibl indexes afp ISBN 0-19-815872-6, $39.95

Conceived as a companion to her equally mammoth *An Anthology of Russian Women's Writing, 1777-1992* (CH, Nov'94) this quirkily selective and opinionated survey of two centuries of women's prose, poetry, and drama covers an immense territory of gendered cultural activity. Divided chronologically into four sections (1820-80, 1881-1917, 1917-53, 1954-92), the study identifies each period's prevailing trends in female authorship, capping each overview with a chapter on three or four figures deemed representative of the pertinent era. Many specialists, this reviewer included, will contest Kelly's choices, emphases, and critical judgments, not the least of which concerns the inclusion of separate chapters on Akhmatova and Tsvetaeva (subjects of an already sizable scholarship). For a more complete and balanced picture of Russian women's writing, one would have to supplement this history with other sources. Kelly realizes as much, having consciously opted for the zealot's "inspiration," not the chronicler's exhaustiveness, as her authorial mode. The sheer wealth of information (Kelly excels at supplying a palpable social context) and the astuteness as well as the dubiousness of some of Kelly's challenging pronouncements make polemics with her worthwhile. Despite its frequently authoritative tone, Kelly's history provides a veritable feast for thought—the stimulus to debate and further inquiry that is Kelly's avowed goal, one that she indisputably achieves. A long but rewarding read! Undergraduate and up.—*H. Goscilo, University of Pittsburgh*

WS-0723   Orig
Lives in letters: Princess Zinaida Volkonskaya and her correspondence, [comp.] by Bayara Aroutunova. Slavica, 1994. 224p index ISBN 0-89357-251-9, $24.95

Princess Zinaida Volkonskaya is one of the more enigmatic personalities in Russian cultural history during the first half of the 19th century. Confidante of Tsar Alexander I, organizer of salons attended by luminaries in the arts (such as the poet Alexander Pushkin), a poet and novelist herself, and an operatic soprano, Volkonskaya defied conventional opinion on the proper behavior of a lady in high society. She was also prey to severe depression leading on occasion to nervous collapse. In the mid-1830s, she converted to Roman Catholicism, moved to Italy, and became deeply involved in religious charities. In her introduction to this collection of letters written primarily to Volkonskaya and held at Harvard University, Aroutunova provides a sketch of Volkonskaya's life and its historical context. The most significant letters are from Alexander I and from Cardinal Consalvi (Vatican Secretary of State), who regarded her highly. Most of the letters were written in French and have been reproduced in that language with no translation. Each letter is exhaustively annotated. Despite occasional stylistic and editorial lapses, the book is handsomely produced, with an index and a section of illustrations. Recommended for research libraries.—*W. C. Brumfield, Tulane University*

WS-0724   PG3213   93-22986 CIP
Lives in transit: a collection of recent Russian women's writing, ed. by Helena Goscilo. Ardis, 1995. 327p afp ISBN 0-87501-100-4, $39.95

Goscilo (Univ. of Pittsburg) here collects 23 short stories and roughly ten pages of lyric poetry by 20th-century Russian women writers, most of them still living. In both the lengthy introduction and in the choice of works itself, the editor emerges once again as the introducer and explicator of a new wave in women's writing in Russia. Though feminism per se remains an elusive term for political and artistic analysis alike, the more so in Russia, this collection testifies to a grow-

ing discomfort with and need for revision of previous or conventional views on women's writing. Although many of the stories are not at all politically oriented, Goscilo has masterfully selected writing that involves a feminine opinion—whether in the normative or social sense or as an experience evolving into the conflict in the story. The book may be read as a whole—producing a concentrated if kaleidoscopic view of women's artistic views; or, any single story can stand on its own merit, each one written with energy and translated effectively. This book should be read by everyone interested in Russia today. All collections.—*C. Tomei, Columbia University*

WS-0725   PG3365   93-5570 CIP
Mandelker, Amy. **Framing Anna Karenina: Tolstoy, the woman question, and the Victorian novel.** Ohio State, 1994 (c1993). 241p bibl index afp ISBN 0-8142-0613-1, $39.50

Rarely does a study of a literary masterpiece of the stature of *Anna Karenina* generate a perspective which breaks new ground to the extent that Amy Mandelker's does. Attacking the generally accepted notion of Tolstoy the misogynist, Mandelker provides convincing arguments for an opposite interpretation of *Anna Karenina*. Her contention that *Anna Karenina* is not a realistic novel is not as convincing, but she does provide a thought-provoking argument. In addition, her finely researched and well-documented analyses of Tolstoy's use of framing, his manipulation of imagery—especially his use of light and shadow—and his connection to the "woman question," among others, compel readers to reassess their traditionally accepted notions of the novel. Mandelker's ideas on Tolstoy and the Victorian novel provide an interesting beginning and should lead to further studies. Overall a stimulating, unique perspective on Tolstoy and the era in which he lived. Footnotes; bibliography; index. Highly recommended. General and academic audiences.—*E. Yarwood, Eastern Washington University*

WS-0726   PG3096   95-1989 CIP
A Plot of her own: the female protagonist in Russian literature, ed. by Sona Stephan Hoisington. Northwestern University, 1995. 164p afp ISBN 0-8101-1224-8, $49.95; ISBN 0-8101-1298-1 pbk, $16.95

Hoisington (Univ. of Illinois at Chicago) has edited an excellent, cohesive anthology of criticism, which in its "revisionist" stance offers fresh readings of 19th- and 20th-century classics. The contents include articles by C. Emerson on Pushkin, J. Costlow on Turgenev, A. Mendelker on Tolstoy, H. Murav on Dostoyevsky, G.S. Morson on Chekhov, E. Beaujour on Fedin and Bulgakov, Hoisington on Zamiatin, T. Durfee on Gladkov and N. Ostrovsky, and H. Goscilo on the only female author included, Petrushevskaya. Gary Rosenshield's insightful afterword discusses the "limitations of gynocriticism" and the "misguidedness of 'feminist critique'" and offers an interesting analysis of Dostoyevsky's "The Meek One." Though the critics do not all agree with each other, they do challenge some basic assumptions of feminist criticism, i.e., that male authors stereotype female characters and victimize them and that "gender or class ... defines one and determines one's critical approach." These critics focus on main women protagonists to show that they "are inextricably linked with the fundamental issues raised by the novels they inform" and that Russian writers "challenge and subvert gender assumptions." Highly recommended for students of Russian literature, world literature, and women's studies. Upper-division undergraduate and above.—*C. A. Rydel, Grand Valley State University*

WS-0727   96-3383   CIP
Present imperfect: stories by Russian women, ed. by Ayesha Kagal and Natasha Perova. Westview, 1996. 202p afp ISBN 0-8133-2675-3, $65.00; ISBN 0-8133-2676-1 pbk, $17.00

Kagal (*Times of India*) and Perova (*Glas*) have chosen stories and a novel excerpt that most typify the "new woman's prose" and cover in a wide range of styles such taboo topics in Russia as prostitution, illegitimacy, pragmatic marriages, promiscuity, lascivious enjoyment of sex, women's sensuality, mugging, and the handicapped. The authors, who generally exhibit a strong feminist bias and/or write in an easily identifiable woman's voice, include Ulitskaya, Vasilenko, Scherbakova, Polyanskaya, Klimova, Palei, and Nina Sadur. Only two authors make a man their hero, Yekaterina Sadur in a fantastic mien and Lydia Ginzburg in a traditional mode. Helena Goscilo (Univ. of Pittsburgh) provides an informative and competent introduction, which first surveys recent Russian women's writing and then defines the new trends. Half of these decent translations have appeared in other places (notably *Glas*). The editors give Russian sources for only four works but do offer brief sketches of the contributors. Though specialists will want to consult the originals, this collection will appeal to general readers, undergraduates, and those interested in Russian and/or women's studies.—*C. A. Rydel, Grand Valley State University*

WS-0728   PG2997   93-21143 CIP
Women writers in Russian literature, ed. by Toby W. Clyman and Diana Greene. Greenwood, 1994. 273p (Contributions to the study of world literature, 53) index afp ISBN 0-313-27521-1, $65.00

Faced with a tremendous undertaking both with respect to gender studies in Russia—which generally lag far behind the West—and evaluating Russian literature as a whole, Clyman and Greene achieve an unprecedented success in the conception and execution of their task. Each of the 14 essays, classified by period and genre, attempts to express the long-muted position of women in a literary milieu, spanning the time from the first writing in Russia about a millennium ago to the present and including literature written during glasnost and in emigration by Russian women authors. Each essay represents a new synthesis without involving the too-frequent bias of a contemporary cultural or feminist ideology. Thus feminists have the raw material to aid them in their understanding of Russian women writers, but the general reader with a different background will profit equally. For all readers interested in the fabric of women's literature and women in a literary society, this book represents the highest achievement to date in Russian studies. All levels.—*C. Tomei, American University*

◆ United States
Comparative, Historical & Critical Works

WS-0729   PS153   95-23531 CIP
Allen, Carolyn. **Following Djuna: women lovers and the erotics of loss.** Indiana, 1996. 142p bibl index afp ISBN 0-253-33023-8, $35.00; ISBN 0-253-21047-X pbk, $13.95

In this fascinating addition to the growing body of literary criticism on women's studies and lesbian fiction in particular, Allen (Univ. of Washington) discusses modern and contemporary women writers (Monique Wittig, Michèle Causse, Nicole Brossard, Mary Fallon, Jane Bowles, Jeanette Winterson, Rebecca Brown, Jane DeLynn) who have acknowledged Barnes as an influence on their thematic and stylistic preoccupations. The analysis focuses on fictions about "the erotics between women" in situations of obsession and inequalities of power, where "the threat of loss is always in the air." Allen divides women's writings into the erotics of nurture, the erotics of risk, and the erotics of excess. Especially insightful are the chapters on Jeanette Winterson's debt to Barnes and on the nonlinear story and interplay between frame-tale and affective narrative in Rebecca Brown's *The Terrible Girls* (1992). This fine volume joins Phillip Herring's *Djuna* (CH, Mar'96), *Nightwood: The Original Version and Related Drafts*, ed. by Cheryl J. Plumb (1995), and Eve Kosofsky Sedgwick's *Epistemology of the Closet* (1990). Upper-division undergraduate through faculty; professional.—*L. Winters, College of Saint Elizabeth*

WS-0730   PS430   93-21788 CIP
American women humorists: critical essays, ed. by Linda A. Morris. Garland, 1994. 441p (Garland studies in humor, 4) bibl index afp ISBN 0-8153-0622-9, $72.00

Treating various aspects of the humor of American women these 21 essays discuss traditional forms, including "Mother Wit" in African American autobiography and humor as "a weapon in the social arsenal." Ten essays on individual writers examine work by and about, for example, Kate Sanborn, whose anthology *The Wit of Women* (1885) countered the stereotype of women being devoid of humor, Frances Whitcher, author of *The Widow Bedott Papers* (1856), and Marietta Holley, also known as "Josiah Allen's Wife." Other essays discuss the characteristics of feminist humor, and the types and intents of women's literary

wit from the Colonial period to modern "domestic humorists." A generous sampling of primary material includes excerpts from poetry and fiction, as well as jokes and puns. One essay includes substantial discussion of works by non-American writers. If the author wanted to move beyond the written tradition, she should have presented a more inclusive view. However, this point is counteracted by the volume's general value as a fine tool providing solid material from which readers can move to more detailed studies. Introduction by Morris; chronology of significant publications; extensive bibliography; index. Will enhance collections in American studies and women's studies. Recommended for undergraduates, graduates, faculty.—*J. S. Gabin, formerly, Queens College, CUNY*

WS-0731   PS374   94-8739 CIP
American women short story writers: a collection of critical essays, ed. by Julie Brown. Garland, 1995. 367p (Wellesley studies in critical theory, literary history, and culture, 8) bibl index afp ISBN 0-8153-1338-1, $60.00

The 20 essays in this collection address gender and genre as they relate to short stories written by women in the US during the 19th and 20th centuries. Presented in a largely chronological order, the readings raise such issues as antislavery, women's suffrage, social reform, modernism, popular culture, ghost stories, magazine fiction, lesbianism, working women, Native Americans, African Americans, and Latinas. The work of writers such as Elizabeth Stoddard, Edith Wharton, Eudora Welty, Fannie Hurst, Leslie Silko, and Dorothy Parker (among many others) is dynamically presented. In her introduction, Brown emphasizes the importance of each of the titles in terms of literary study—since some have been neglected in scholarly writing—and their particular combination here. Concluding the volume are two substantial bibliographies of primary and secondary sources, making this anthology useful for students, teachers, and critics alike. Recommended for undergraduate and graduate libraries.—*B. Harlow, University of Texas at Austin*

WS-0732   PS374.W6   89-36066 CIP
Bardes, Barbara. **Declarations of independence: women and political power in nineteenth-century American fiction,** by Barbara Bardes and Suzanne Gossett. Rutgers, 1990. 231p index ISBN 0-8135-1500-9, $36.00; ISBN 0-8135-1501-7, $13.00

Bardes and Gossett's well-written and detailed study explores the ways in which 19th-century fiction reflected and influenced public attitudes toward women's independence. They argue that the novels they examine "both index the cultural debate about women and political power and take an activist role within that debate. Fiction impinges on history, just as history impinges on fiction." The study encompasses a wide variety of 19th-century texts, including a number of female authors' works that have been traditionally ignored, and covers a broad range of issues, from women's performance in the workplace to women's property rights. A welcome addition to women's literary and cultural studies, and highly recommended for academic libraries. Notes provided.—*P. L. Walton, University of Lethbridge*

WS-0733   PS374   94-11283 CIP
Baym, Nina. **American women writers and the work of history, 1790-1860.** Rutgers, 1995. 307p bibl index ISBN 0-8135-2142-4, $48.00; ISBN 0-8135-2143-2 pbk, $17.95

This is a comprehensive study of historical writing by American women before the Civil War; and as Baym (Univ. of Illinois at Urbana-Champagne) notes in her introduction, "there is so much more of it than one could have imagined." Her research led to more than 350 titles by more than 150 authors, in various genres. Textual illustrations are frequent, yet this volume is not an anthology but a scholarly study referring readers to extensive primary and secondary sources. Some writers' names will be familiar—Margaret Fuller, Catharine Beecher, the Grimké sisters—but scores will be new to readers of both traditional and feminist-oriented American studies. These authors used the public sphere of publishing to uphold and promulgate ideas within the private spheres of home libraries, reading circles, and schools, and most upheld the status quo. Though a few composed poems of protest, others supported popular prejudices. The literary genres and subjects these women chose may have been diverse, but their ideologies often were not, reflecting the prevailing Anglo-Protestant culture. But Baym's main picture is "a view of American women participating with gusto in the work of writing history"—participating in dynamic literary activity to such an extent that they exerted great control over popular reading habits and therefore over the way Americans perceived history. Upper-division undergraduate and above.—*J. S. Gabin, University of North Carolina at Chapel Hill*

WS-0734   PN841   91-24257 CIP
Black women's writing, ed. by Gina Wisker. St. Martin's, 1993. 189p index ISBN 0-312-06864-6, $35.00

Ten critical essays (one by a man) discuss the topic within the context of the British university system and provide useful perspectives from teachers and students. Wisker, who is senior lecturer in English at Anglia Polytechnic in Cambridge, explains the aims of the collection as introducing readers to "the range of writing by Black women" and bringing "into the open some of the tensions and difficulties of its publication, and, more centrally, of its reception in the largely white literary establishment. . . ." This recognition of inherent problems in the teaching of black women's writing without an understanding of cultural and historical context also provides helpful suggestions and critical insights not found in most books on black women's literature. Writers discussed include Alice Walker, Toni Morrison, Zora Neale Hurston, Buchi Emecheta, Ntozake Shange, Joan Riley, Grace Nichols, Ama Ata Aidoo, and Bessie Head. There are also notes on contributors, brief chapter endnotes, and a bibliography. The value of this collection is in its depth: we learn to be better readers and teachers from the insights shared. The black British woman's perspective addressed here is both unique and universal in asking for recognition. The writing is accessible and interesting, especially for teachers.—*D. S. Isaacs, Fordham University*

WS-0735   PS366   94-38417 CIP
Braham, Jeanne. **Crucial conversations: interpreting contemporary American literary autobiographies by women.** Teachers College Press (Columbia University), 1995. 159p bibl index afp ISBN 0-8077-6279-2, $38.00; ISBN 0-8077-6278-4 pbk, $17.95

Braham's new contribution to the study of women's autobiography joins an assemblage of important texts published in recent years, including *Women's Autobiography*, ed. by Estelle Jelinek (CH, Oct'80); Jelinek's *The Tradition of Women's Autobiography from Antiquity to the Present* (CH, Jan'87); Sidonie Smith's *A Poetics of Women's Autobiography* (CH, Jun'88); *The Female Autograph*, ed. by Donna Stanton (1987); *The Private Self*, ed. by Shari Benstock (CH, Apr'89); *Life/Lines*, ed. by Bella Brodzki and Celeste Schencke (CH, Jul'89); Carolyn Heilbrun's *Writing a Woman's Life* (1988); *American Women's Autobiography*, ed. by Margo Culley (CH, May'93); and *De/Colonizing the Subject*, ed. by Sidonie Smith and Julia Watson (1992). Braham (Clark Univ.) focuses on the personal narratives of contemporary American women writers, all of whom "see the sharing of their life stories as a crucial part of their literary mandate." She also addresses the structural properties of their work that reflect and underscore gender: fractured and pluralistic subjectivity; a contextual and communal rather than individualistic view of human experience; an appeal to the power of "felt truth"; a dynamic and fluid rather than fixed conception of memory; and an empathetic sensibility that sees the reader as a sharer. Though this book is not a theoretical advance, the writing is lucid and the application of other feminist theories of life writing to modern texts yields thoughtful, if somewhat abbreviated, commentary. All academic collections.—*L. Babener, Montana State University*

WS-0736   PS374   93-37419 CIP
Budick, Emily Miller. **Engendering romance: women writers and the Hawthorne tradition, 1850-1990.** Yale, 1994. 288p index afp ISBN 0-300-05557-9, $32.50

One need not agree with every point the author makes in this remarkable study to be mightily impressed with its scope, the aptness and lucidity of its argument, and the level of insight it brings to bear, both on the individual works discussed and on the overall development of the romance tradition in American letters. In only 245 pages of text, Budick manages at least to touch significantly upon a substantial number of salient texts in the tradition, and features close readings of *The Scarlet Letter*, *The Portrait of a Lady*, *The Sound and the Fury*, and *As I Lay Dying*. Of great value in and of themselves, these discussions prepare the way

for an in-depth look at four 20th-century women romancers: Carson McCullers, Flannery O'Connor, Toni Morrison, and Grace Paley. In what this reviewer would call a post-feminist synthesis, Budick brings together the richness of earlier feminist criticism, especially the psycholinguistic theories of Lacan, a deep understanding of Emerson and the contemporary philosophy of Stanley Cavell, and a profound grasp of the American literary tradition to develop a closely argued and convincing thesis concerning the historically persistent antipatriarchal bias of the American romance, its essentially skeptical stance, and its attacks, latent or overt, on sexism and racism. Well written and wonderfully humane, this book belongs in every collection of American literature. Strongly recommended for any serious student of American literary criticism. Upper-division undergraduate and up.—*S. R. Graham, emerita, Nazareth College of Rochester*

WS-0737   PS152   95-20049 CIP
Castiglia, Christopher. **Bound and determined: captivity, culture-crossing, and white womanhood from Mary Rowlandson to Patty Hearst.** Chicago, 1996. 254p bibl index afp ISBN 0-226-09652-1, $38.00; ISBN 0-226-09654-8 pbk, $13.96

Castiglia offers strong postmodern feminist readings of an emergent genre in American literature. Moving from Rowlandson's 1682 captivity narrative to Susanna Rowson's captivity romance *Reuben and Rachel* (1798), the author argues that the recurring "trope of captivity" offered white women writers a vehicle to challenge predominant constructions of race, gender, and nation. Castiglia brings his analysis to 1993, discussing how captivity figures as a revolutionary force in Barbara Deming's *Prisons That Could Not Hold* (1985), and as a reinscription of dominant power relations in Cassie Edwards's *Savage Sunrise* (1992). His insightful chapter on the representations of the Patty Hearst experience continues his exploration of the ways in which ministers, editors, and filmmakers limit the radical implications of this genre. Joining scholars to challenge earlier monolithic views of a women's domestic literary tradition, Castiglia notes female writers were not alone in desiring escape from the domestic; however, unlike men, women often found a community of women rather than isolation in these wilderness spaces. Full of information, astute analysis, and bibliographic and critical perspectives for graduate students, researchers, and faculty.—*S. Danielson, Portland State University*

WS-0738   PN1672   95-13373 CIP
Chaudhuri, Una. **Staging place: the geography of modern drama.** Michigan, 1995. 310p bibl index afp ISBN 0-472-09589-7, $34.50

Chaudhuri's sophisticated and well-written study for graduate students and their teachers explores modern drama's preoccupation with the seemingly irreconcilable discontinuities between the notions of home and homelessness, belonging and exile. These concepts manifest themselves in the pathological displacements that figure prominently in the disquieting image of America as a place resplendently awash in a wealth of social, political, and cultural conflicts. In charting the imaginative transformations the idea of place has undergone on the contemporary stage, Chaudhuri (New York Univ.) maintains that "dramatic structure reflects deeply ingrained convictions about the mutually constructive relations between people and place." In this evolving discourse, who one is and what one can be are inextricably tied to particular experiences of place. Traversing the terrain mapped by this nascent "geography of modern drama," the author takes us from naturalism to multiculturalism, by way of realism, expressionism, and environmentalism; the playwrights encountered along the way include the familiar, the perhaps unfamiliar, the white, the minority, and the multicultural. The readings of individual plays are fresh and invigorating and the scholarly apparatus—index, endnotes, and bibliography—helps keep the engaged traveler squarely on course. Highly recommended.—*H. I. Einsohn, Middlesex Community-Technical College*

WS-0739   PS153   92-46452 CIP
Cheung, King-Kok. **Articulate silences: Hisaye Yamamoto, Maxine Hong Kingston, Joy Kogawa.** Cornell, 1993. 198p bibl index afp ISBN 0-8014-2415-1, $33.95; ISBN 0-8014-8147-3 pbk, $14.95

This study interprets the role of silence in the work of three creative women writers. King-Kok Cheung, who is herself Chinese American, explains in the 26-page introduction that her aim "is to show that each of the three authors has developed her own unique bicultural idiom and that 'Western' suppositions must occasionally be suspended to catch its nuances." By both including and challenging feminist theory and theories of race and culture, Cheung articulates the nuances that bring added understanding of the work by these writers. The volume examines three kinds of silence. "Rhetorical Silence" discusses the work of Yamamoto, who uses double-telling to explore her Anglo-American and Japanese American literary tradition. "Provocative Silence" uncovers the Chinese American legacy in the works of Kingston. "Attentive Silence" discusses Kogawa's *Obasan*, a novel based on her experiences in British Columbia during WW II. Cheung's unraveling of text is illuminating and complicated because she challenges the critical theories and assumptions surrounding gender, race, and ethinicity. "We need two-way traffic in ethnic and feminist studies ..., " she states in the "Coda." The bibliography and terminology clarification add authenticity to this intellectually challenging discourse. Graduate; faculty.—*D. S. Isaacs, Fordham University*

WS-0740   PS3563   94-13045 CIP
Coiner, Constance. **Better red: the writing and resistance of Tillie Olsen and Meridel Le Sueur.** Oxford, 1995. 282p bibl index afp ISBN 0-19-505695-7, $45.00

This "first book-length study to explore Tillie Olsen's and Meridel Le Sueur's relationships to the American Communist Party" presents the complexity of those relationships, their agreements and disagreements. The literary Left was patriarchal, and the Communist Party leaned strongly toward expecting women to be housewives only. Coiner (SUNY at Binghamton) presents brief biographies of both women and discusses their writings: for Le Sueur three pieces of reportage, her novel *The Girl*, and three short stories; for Olsen *Yonnondio*, *Tell Me a Riddle* and three other stories, and *Silences*, her account of why some people do not write. Coiner foregrounds the "working-class" aspect of both authors as well as the "heteroglossia" ("a multiplicity of social voices"). Le Sueur's reportage is clipped prose with short declarative sentences; Olsen's style is more complex. Both wrote about "women's issues" from women's perspective, not common in the 1930s. Olsen in particular fused feminism to "other forms of radical analysis." Coiner concludes that the Left "failed to attract numbers ... partly because it has historically both feared and trivialized people's 'nonmaterial' needs," a position both Le Sueur and Olsen redressed. This thought-provoking analysis contains photos and will be of wide interest. Very highly recommended for women's studies and history libraries.—*J. Overmyer, emerita, Ohio State University*

WS-0741   PS153   93-14499 CIP
Connor, Kimberly Rae. **Conversions and visions in the writings of African-American women.** Tennessee, 1994. 317p bibl index afp ISBN 0-87049-818-5, $32.50

Connor traces a recurrent pattern of emphasis on and concern with identity formation in African American women's writings. Chapter 1, "Conversations," contains her main argument: rather than turning away from sin, conversion in these particular black women's writings refers to the various characters' efforts to move away from social stereotypes and toward stable, conscious levels of a spiritual identity. These dramas of conversion into selfhood, she contends, draw on available religious categories that may not be sanctioned by existing theological categories but are influenced by broader cultural categories which include religion. Chapter 2, "Voluntary Converts," discusses Harriet A. Jacobs's "*Incidents in the Life of a Slave Girl* (1861), Sojourner Truth's *Narrative of Sojourner Truth* (1850), and Rebecca Jackson's *Gifts of Power* (CH, Dec'81) as texts that are spiritual and literary antecedents to the novels she studies in chapter 4, "Involuntary Converts": Toni Morrison's *Sula* (1973), Paule Marshall's *Praisesong for the Widow* (1983), and Alice Walker's *The Color Purple* (1982). Chapter 3 "Called to Preach," focuses on Zora Neale Hurston's *Dust Tracks on a Road* (1942) and *Their Eyes Were Watching God* (1937) as transitional pieces between the two larger groups of texts. Ample notes to each chapter; useful bibliography. Recommended for academic and public libraries with large holdings in African American literary criticism.—*A. Deck, University of Illinois at Urbana—Champaign*

WS-0742   PS147   90-12006 CIP
Coultrap-McQuin, Susan. **Doing literary business: American women writers in the nineteenth century.** North Carolina, 1990. 253p bibl index afp ISBN 0-8078-1914-X, $29.95; ISBN 0-8078-4284-2, $10.95

Coultrap-McQuin presents case studies of five women writers of 19th-century America: E.D.E.N. Southworth, Harriet Beecher Stowe, Mary Abigail Dodge (Gail Hamilton), Helen Hunt Jackson, and Elizabeth Stuart Phelps (Ward). The opening chapter analyzes the ambiguities of a cultural context shaped by Victorian gender ideologies, a spectrum ranging from conservative "true womanhood" to liberal "new womanhood." The second, equally useful, chapter describes the subtly gendered continuum of role definitions for publishers: from antebellum gentleman publisher to Edwardian businessman publisher. The case studies that follow carefully place each writer at the intersection of these social prescriptions, which, Coultrap-McQuin argues, often supported female authorship while simultaneously devaluing female texts. Through her history of each woman's interaction with her publishers Coultrap-McQuin develops a beautifully detailed composite portrait of women's literary professionalism. The range of individual experience is striking, as is her finding that, although authorship had its difficulties for these women, anxiety over their right to write was not among them. The book builds on previous scholarship by historians such as Christopher Wilson and represents a valuable addition to our understanding of 19th-century literary production and its cultural context.—*S. W. Sherman, University of New Hampshire*

WS-0743   E85   92-42189 CIP
Derounian-Stodola, Kathryn Zabelle. **The Indian captivity narrative, 1550-1900,** by Kathryn Zabelle Derounian-Stodola and James Arthur Levernier. Twayne, 1993. 236p (TUSAS, 605) bibl index afp ISBN 0-8057-7533-1, $22.95

In this interdisciplinary cultural analysis of the Indian captivity narrative the authors argue critically that captivity victimized the captors far more than the captives. With a three-century scope, a comprehensive range of sources, and a heavy emphasis on the physical, psychological, and sometimes religious victimization of women, the authors show that innumerable and substantially fictitious images of torture, starvation, and murder created vicious but popular anti-Indian propaganda and intentionally served not only expansionist American politics but helped create cultural seeds for 19th-century wars of removal and genocide. Giving the American captivity narrative renewed life and innovative levels of discourse, the authors blend new historicism with contemporary feminism and offer a thoroughly fascinating historiographic and rhetorical analysis that travels beyond existing canonical works in the field. Highly recommended for advanced classroom use, this study adds fresh dimensions to a growing corpus of analytical and critical works on the Indian captivity narrative in its traditional and yet expanding media manifestations. Well suited for graduate students in women's studies, American literature, and folklore scholars, and for an advanced general readership.—*R. C. Doyle, Pennsylvania State University, University Park Campus*

WS-0744   PS374   92-33985 CIP
Devine, Maureen. **Woman and nature: literary reconceptualizations.** Scarecrow, 1992. 239p bibl index afp ISBN 0-8108-2612-7, $29.50

Devine considers the themes of nature, gender, and words or literarity in seven novels by women written in the 1970s and early 1980s. She applies the critical frames of ecofeminism and gynocriticism to the writing of Margaret Atwood (*Surfacing*), Margaret Laurence (*The Diviners*), Alice Walker (*The Color Purple*), Gloria Naylor (*The Women of Brewster Place*), Marilyn Robinson (*Housekeeping*), Marge Piercy (*Woman on the Edge of Time*), and Sally Miller Gearhart (*The Wanderground*). According to Devine, the novels share the common theme of the need to establish a female identity, and all treat in an interesting manner the relationship of woman to nature. Most successful is her explication of the particular novels in terms of the themes of nature and gender. Less successful and certainly unsystematic are her accounts of ecofeminism and gynocriticism, especially in her brief overview of the controversial concept of androgyny. Devine asserts but does not establish the perniciousness of dualistic thinking, the fundamental standard by which she evaluates the novels. Undergraduate.—*K. Begnal, Utah State University*

WS-0745   PS374   93-19916 CIP
DuCille, Ann. **The coupling convention: sex, text, and tradition in black women's fiction.** Oxford, 1993. 204p bibl index afp ISBN 0-19-507972-8, $39.95; ISBN 0-19-508509-4, $15.95

This engaging study examines the ways in which the marriage plot or "coupling convention" has been appropriated by black women novelists in order to explore and critique racial and sexual ideology and practices, and to "reclaim and resexualize the black female body." Spanning the period from 1853 to 1948, duCille's analysis includes works by Brown, Harper, Hopkins, Kelley, Faucet, Larsen, and Hurston. However, even as she surveys the tradition of black women's writing, duCille interrogates the very notion of tradition, arguing *against* a single black cultural source or a common black female experience and voice, and *for* a conceptualization of tradition that takes into account the multiplicity, fluidity, and complexity of cultural signifiers and constructs. Despite her, at times, overly generous readings of what she deems neglected texts, duCille has written an informative, perceptive book that illuminates the development of African American women's literature and extends the boundaries of critical theory and practice. Recommended for graduate and undergraduate collections.—*L. S. Burns, Tuskegee University*

WS-0746 PS261 92-9375 CIP
The female tradition in southern literature, ed. by Carol S. Manning. Illinois, 1993. 290p index afp ISBN 0-252-01951-2, $34.95

Manning (Mary Washington College), the author of a previous volume on Eudora Welty, (*With Ears Opening Like Morning Glories*, CH, Feb'86), sets out here to revise our pieties about the southern renaissance. She states her premise in her introduction: "We give attention to women writers and their motifs and themes that have been slighted by established theory. And we look at threads that connect some writers—threads that reveal a female tradition in Southern literature. . . . The implications of the volume are revisionist and feminist." Several of the authors of individual essays (some of which are new and some revisions of earlier publications) will be familiar to students or scholars of southern women's literature: Thadious Davis, Peggy Whitman Prenshaw, Louise Westling, Suzanne Jones, Anna Shannon Elfenbein, and novelist Doris Betts. Taken as a whole, the essays present a coherent and persuasive case for rethinking the role of women writers in the southern renaissance (a role heretofore largely neglected by critics), indeed for rethinking the boundaries, causes, and impact of the renaissance itself. Additionally, several of the essays offer fine new insights on authors such as Zora Neale Hurston, Flannery O'Connor, Alice Walker, Gail Godwin, Caroline Hentz, Caroline Gordon, Eudora Welty, and Katherine Ann Porter. But perhaps the collection's greatest contribution is the tracing of intertextual connections among southern women writers, both the well known and the little known. Strongly recommended for undergraduate and graduate collections.—*E. R. Baer, Gustavus Adolphus College*

WS-0747 PE1405 94-43034 CIP
Feminine principles and women's experience in American composition and rhetoric, ed. by Louise Wetherbee Phelps and Janet Emig. Pittsburgh, 1995. 433p bibl afp ISBN 0-8229-3863-4, $59.95; ISBN 0-8229-5544-X pbk, $22.95

The 20 essays in this book present the observations, thoughts, and studies of teachers, professors, and scholars concerned with the role and growth of feminism in rhetoric and composition. The editors, having experienced the problems of women involved in writing programs, "publish[ed] a call for papers intended to provoke and reveal the hidden thoughts and writing of women in composition and rhetoric about their experiences, their principles, the history of the field, its topics and issues—all reinterpreted from a feminist perspective." The 14 essays in part 1 deal with issues ranging from the role of teen mothers, to historical matters from the age of the Greeks to the present, to such specialized concerns as Vietnamese women in the literary process. The six essays in part 2, "Reconfigurations and Responses," address the issues raised in the first part as they fall into two broad classifications, "political or pedagogical" and "heteroglossic and multimodal," providing a thought-provoking and useful paradigm. The study is replete with a thick texture of scholarly and literary allusions and corollary information, and it contains detailed bibliographical information. Graduate and research collections.—*W. B. Warde Jr., University of North Texas*

WS-0748 PS648 91-50813 CIP
Follow my footprints: changing images of women in American Jewish fiction, ed. by Sylvia Barack Fishman. University of New England, 1992. 506p bibl ISBN 0-87451-544-0, $45.00; ISBN 0-87451-583-1 pbk, $24.95

A rich source of short stories and excerpts from novels, this anthology charts the changing portrayals of Jewish women by Jewish writers from the middle of the 19th century to the present. Strong and resourceful Jewish women (both traditionalists and those responsive to change) and Jewish women victimized by poverty, repression, and cultural norms are depicted by I.L. Peretz, Sholom Aleichem, and I.B. Singer. Sholem Asch, Chaim Grade, Abraham Cahan, Anzia Yezierska, and Henry Roth tell of the Jewish American immigrant experience with its frequent sacrifice of traditional religion for assimilation and acculturation. Philip Roth and Herman Wouk portray the overprotective, domineering "Jewish Mother" and the materialistic and sexually manipulative "Jewish American Princess" stereotypes. Contemporary women writers (Olsen, Gornick, Paley, Roiphe, Goldreich, Goldstein, and Ozick) chronicle women's conflict between American and Jewish values and address the implications of the Holocaust and the Israeli State for Jewish identity. Jewish feminist writers revive the solider women of Yiddish literature, respond to misogyny and patriarchal oppression, and delineate women coping with society's punitive attitude toward assertive, verbal Jewish women. Insightful introduction, brief but helpful biocritical descriptions of each author, glossary of Yiddish and Hebrew terms, supplementary reading list. Highly recommended for readers at all levels.—*S. L. Kremer, Kansas State University*

WS-0749 PS153 92-23916 CIP
Foster, Frances Smith. **Written by herself: literary production by African American women, 1746-1892.** Indiana, 1993. 206p index afp ISBN 0-253-32409-2, $35.00; ISBN 0-253-20786-X pbk, $12.95

Foster's study of early African American women writers brings together a fine collection of research and new ideas on works published up to 1892. Thus her book complements the critical treatment in Hazel Carby's *Reconstructing Womanhood* (CH, Jul'88), which focused on black women's writing in the latter part of the 19th and early 20th centuries. Starting with the poets Lucy Terry Prince and Phillis Wheatley, Foster then considers the writings of Jarena Lee, Harriet Jacobs, Elizabeth Keckley, Frances Ellen Watkins Harper, Octavia Victoria Rogers Albert, and Anna Julia Cooper. These and other authors are seen as coming out of a tradition of black women's oral and written works, most of which have been lost or forgotten. Many of the writers used existing literary modes, such as the slave narrative and women's fiction, but adapted them for their special purposes in order to convey startling ideas to distrustful audiences. Foster's incisive probes of the historical ramifications and literary contributions of black women in early America are forceful and exhaustive. She helps us to understand and appreciate the difficult and courageous work performed by the foremothers of 20th-century black women's literature. Well written and thoroughly researched. Highly recommended for all readers and students of American literature and African American, ethnic, and women's studies.—*A. Costanzo, Shippensburg University of Pennsylvania*

WS-0750 PS153 95-40678 CIP
Gardaphé, Fred L. **Italian signs, American streets: the evolution of Italian American narrative.** Duke University, 1996. 241p bibl index afp ISBN 0-8223-1730-3, $39.95; ISBN 0-8223-1739-7 pbk, $16.95

There is much gnashing of teeth among Italian American scholars about why their ethnic group has not produced a greater literature in the US. Over the past 80 years American writers of Italian descent have created significant literary texts that receive little, if any, critical attention. Inspired by W.E.B. Dubois's argument that critical activity is a certain indicator of a tradition's sophistication, Gardaphé (Columbia College, Chicago) sets out to demonstrate that there is an Italian American literature beyond Mafia stories. Mindful of the distinctive "signs" generated through codes specific to Italian American culture, he examines the works of 15 authors (including Helen Barolini, Mary Caponegro, Tina DeRosa, and Carole Maso), beginning with the strongest of the immigrant narratives (Marie Hall Ets's *Rosa, the Life of an Italian Immigrant*, which, though dating from 1918, was not published until 1970) and ending with the subtler ethnicism of Don DeLillo. Gardaphé omits such important writers as Robert Ferro, Rocco Fumento, Len Giovannitti, and Joe Papaleo but this, according to Gardaphé, is no oversight; his goal is not to catalog the writers of an entire ethnic group but to present a new perspective by which its literature can be read and interpreted generally. This is truly a pioneering effort, since the papers of some of the authors he assesses (John Fante, Pietro di Donato) remain in private collections, unprocessed and unavailable to scholars. All academic libraries serving upper-division undergraduates and up; also useful in feminist collections.—*J. Shreve, Allegany College of Maryland*

WS-0751   PS310   95-42906 CIP

Gendered modernisms: American women poets and their readers, ed. by Margaret Dickie and Thomas Travisano. Pennsylvania, 1996. 321p index afp ISBN 0-8122-3312-3, $44.95; ISBN 0-8122-1550-8 pbk, $18.95

The editors of this collection provide a way to use gender to redefine women poets and their place in modernism and postmodernism. Too often poets have been defined in relation to strong male influences, as in the case of H.D. and Laura Riding. Wisely, the contributors to this volume offer new ways of reading that contradict former perceptions. They consider why women poets do not assimilate or fit easily into fixed patterns and traditions. Gender does matter. Of particular interest is Dickie's reading of Gertrude Stein's eroticism and the poet's reasons for secrecy in terms of the period in which she worked. Lisa Steinman's reading of Marianne Moore exposes the contradictions of previous readings. She observes: "That Moore's work contains such recognitions has everything to do with her own, local circumstances as a woman." Travisano dissects the Bishop phenomenon by showing how and why her status changed from minor to major. Excellent, thought-provoking material for all readers.—*H. Susskind, emeritus, Monroe Community College*

WS-0752   PS374   92-39385 CIP

Greiner, Donald J. **Women without men: female bonding and the American novel of the 1980s.** South Carolina, 1993. 135p bibl index afp ISBN 0-87249-884-0, $24.95

Greiner's most important contribution is to consider the fiction of often-overlooked women writers such as Marilyn Robinson, Joan Chase, Mona Simpson, Joan Didion, and Gloria Naylor. His stated aim is to "investigate the complexities of female bonding" by considering female novelists who have "revised the canon by rewriting rather than repudiating" male writers' tales of the wilderness experience. Greiner questions whether the newly found bonds of women's friendships "are maintained with the fervor one expects of Natty-Chingachgook and Huck-Jim." In a work ostensibly concerned with women's experience, it is remarkable that Greiner uses the last chapter to consider the fiction of Frederick Busch, John Irving, Larry Woiwode, and Douglas Ungar. Although his aim seems to be to hear women writers' narratives, Greiner does not seem to understand women's friendships and the fragile but lasting qualities that hold them together against all odds. Recommended only to strong-minded readers who can recognize a political subtext when they see one. Greiner certainly resists political correctness (an admirable trait), but his work may be at the expense of women's freedom. An interesting companion to Leo Marx's *The Pilot and the Passenger* (1988), Rachel M. Brownstein's *Becoming a Heroine* (CH, Jan '83), and Carolyn Heilbrun's *Writing a Woman's Life* (1988). Advanced undergraduate; graduate; faculty.—*L. Winters, College of Saint Elizabeth*

WS-0753   PS338   92-35621 CIP

Hall, Ann C. **"A kind of Alaska": women in the plays of O'Neill, Pinter, and Shepard.** Southern Illinois, 1993. 146p bibl index afp ISBN 0-8093-1877-6, $34.95

A brief, tightly focused poststructuralist study of ten plays. Taking her title from a Harold Pinter play about people in frozen conditions, Hall seeks to demonstrate "the extremely affective political, social, and cultural power of drama and theatre." As she notes, "From a feminist perspective, approaching the works of male-authored dramas provides important insights into the nature of gender, women, and patriarchy." Her introduction crams a quick summary of key figures in feminist psychological literary criticism into a few pages. She then selects her particular approach, explains it, and attacks the texts, one author at a time. She studies the women in a few of the authors' plays, relates them to other women in the experience and creative histories of the authors, and then assesses the results. Hall does show that these male authors are sometimes more sympathetic to women than previously assumed. Providing no real summary of the plays or introduction to them, Hall zeroes in on her topic. She assumes a scholarly audience sympathetic to feminist theory, comfortable with the ideas of such critics as Lacan and Irigaray, and acquainted with the oeuvres of the modern playwrights. She has a practitioner's eye for stagecraft, physical appearance, tone, and audience. Her judgments are frequently political rather than aesthetic, dealing with male oppression, the fixing of women in stereotypical roles, and the heroine's violation of the patriarchy-imposed roles as victory. Advanced under-

graduate through professional.—*N. Tischler, Pennsylvania State University, University Park Campus*

WS-0754   PS374   94-40316 CIP

Hapke, Laura. **Daughters of the Great Depression: women, work, and fiction in the American 1930s.** Georgia, 1995. 286p index afp ISBN 0-8203-1718-7, $45.00

In a masterful integration of history and literature, Hapke (Pace Univ.) incisively analyzes the many ways that fiction in the 1930s reflected and reinforced the widespread hostility and exploitation suffered by women in the work force during the Depression. Notable for its comprehensiveness, the book draws material from letters, autobiographies, photographs, newspapers, government surveys, New Deal legislation and reports, and the careers of writers and other professional women such as Dorothy Thompson and Frances Perkins. Hapke thus creates a rich historical context for the study of scores of novels about female workers in a variety of settings, including factories, textile mills, offices, farms, labor unions, and domestic service. The author compares prominent mainstream male writers (e.g., Sherwood Anderson, Sinclair Lewis, John Steinbeck, and James Farrell) with influential black writers (e.g., Langston Hughes, Richard Wright) and with lesser-known "militant" women writers (e.g., Agnes Smedley, Muriel LeSueur) whose "female revisions of male ideology" undermined but failed to subvert the conventional view of woman's proper role as mother and helpmeet. Like the author's *Tales of the Working Girl: Wage-Earning Women in American Literature, 1890-1925* (CH, Jan'93), this is a groundbreaking work, outstanding for its clarity, scope, exemplary scholarship, and wealth of fact and insight. Highly recommended to all students of American literature and history and women's studies.—*E. Nettels, College of William and Mary*

WS-0755   PS374   92-10568 CIP

Hapke, Laura. **Tales of the working girl: wage-earning women in American literature, 1890-1925.** Twayne, 1992. 167p (Twayne's literature & society series, 2) bibl index afp ISBN 0-8057-8855-7, $26.95; ISBN 0-8057-8860-3 pbk, $13.95

The first comprehensive scholarly study to trace the changing representations of the working woman in American literature of the post-Civil War era. Drawing on the fiction and essays of more than 100 writers, Hapke defines the differing attitudes and goals of authors and their characters expressed in successive depictions of the female worker—as sexually exploited victim, as fallen woman, as aspirant to the middle class, and as militant protester. Muckraking journalism, autobiography, and stories and novels of women in factories, sweatshops, stores, and offices are all analyzed in relation to prevailing ideologies of gender and class and to the impact of such institutions as the settlement house, clubs for working girls, and women's trade unions. The integration of literary criticism and social history yields fresh insights into well-known works by Dreiser, Edith Wharton, and Stephen Crane, among others, as well as scores of novels and stories by writers who have received little if any critical attention. Clear and concise in style, enhanced by a wide-ranging annotated bibliography, this book is highly recommended to all specialists and to students, undergraduate onward, of American studies and women's history.—*E. Nettels, College of William and Mary*

WS-0756   PS261   90-28801 CIP

Harrison, Elizabeth Jane. **Female pastoral: women writers re-visioning the American South.** Tennessee, 1992 (c1991). 166p bibl index afp ISBN 0-87049-707-3, $22.50

Harrison (Berea College) makes a significant addition to the already burgeoning number of critical studies of Southern women's literature. This book consciously uses poet Adrienne Rich's notion of re-vision—"the act of looking back, of seeing with fresh eyes, of entering an old text from a new critical direction"—to provide innovative readings of the works of Ellen Glasgow, Margaret Mitchell, Willa Cather, Harriette Arnow, Alice Walker, and Sherley Williams. Specifically, Harrison suggests a new interpretation of the Southern women writers' relationship with the land. Her study can be usefully likened to Annette Kolodny's *The Land Before Her* (CH, May'84), which revolutionized understanding of the relationship of women writers to the West. Harrison posits that, whereas the Southern Agrarians, a conservative coterie of white male writers, indulged in a nostalgic return to the rural past as a way of dealing with the socio-political problems of the South, women writers spanning a century have undertaken a radical revisioning of community: "By dissociating the woman protagonist from her presentation *as* landscape, the female pastoral first allows her to develop autonomy." Thus, the quest, not the romance, is the plot of these fictions, which bring women characters into new relationships with other women as well as with men. Harrison's prose is lucid and persuasive; her bibiography of a dozen pages is a rich resource. Strongly recommended for undergraduate and graduate collections.— *E. R. Baer, Gustavus Adolphus College*

WS-0757　　　PS153　　　91-16803 CIP
Holloway, Karla F.C. **Moorings & metaphors: figures of culture and gender in Black women's literature.** Rutgers, 1992. 218p index ISBN 0-8135-1745-1, $36.00; ISBN 0-8135-1746-X pbk, $14.00

Holloway's book advances the study of black women's fiction in two different, but extremely important directions. This is one of a few sustained comparative studies of African and African American women's literature. Françoise Lionnet's *Autobiographical Voices* (CH, Jan'90), is the only other cross-cultural discussion to date. Moreover, Holloway bases her comparison on what she sees as the similar figures of language used by Ama Ata Aidoo, Octavia Butler, Buchi Emecheta, Gayl Jones, Toni Morrison, Flora Nwapa, Ntozake Shange, and Efua Sutherland to express their creative visions. The inversive, recursive, and subversive figures of language in black women's literature, she argues, can be assessed only when the cultural points of initiation (the "moorings") are acknowledged in each case. This enables a fuller understanding of the spirituality in black women's literature, namely the centrality of two related metaphors—the African goddess and the African American slave woman ancestor—that reflect the unity of soul and gender in these writers' imaginations. This book will spark debate, but it will also set a standard for a theoretical study of black women's literature that is overdue. Recommended for upper-division undergraduate and graduate courses on black women's literature.—*A. Deck, University of Illinois at Urbana—Champaign*

WS-0758　　　PS374　　　95-17736 CIP
Inness, Sherrie A. **Intimate communities: representation and social transformation in women's college fiction, 1895-1910.** Bowling Green State University Popular Press, 1995. 196p bibl index ISBN 0-87972-683-0, $29.95; ISBN 0-87972-684-9 pbk, $13.95

This study draws attention to the dozens of novels, short stories, plays, scholarly articles, and popular essays depicting life at women's colleges published during the American Progressive Era. A relatively new phenomenon at the time, the college woman was seen by many as a threat to the institution of marriage and to the dominant male power structure. In seven chapters Inness (Miami Univ.) discusses the role of commodities in college life; the character of women's "crushes" on each other; the significance of female athletics; the all-around girl; the scholarship girl; the function of the college maid; and how the "college literature" controlled the threat posed by educated women. This well-researched book offers an unusually thorough bibliography and covers much interesting and arcane material. The so-called Seven Sisters colleges—Barnard, Bryn Mawr, Mount Holyoke, Radcliffe, Smith, Vassar, and Wellesley—serve as representative institutions for the study. One caveat: although the book offers a very heavy sociological analysis of women's colleges, the discussion of college fiction is not as successful. All collections.—*R. T. Van Arsdel, emerita, University of Puget Sound*

WS-0759　　　PS151　　　92-42215 CIP
Jones, Margaret C. **Heretics & hellraisers: women contributors to *The Masses*, 1911-1917.** Texas, 1993. 227p bibl index afp ISBN 0-292-74026-3, $27.50; ISBN 0-292-74027-1 pbk, $12.95

The question raised by this book is: Why should *The Masses* be remembered as a radical magazine run by the Greenwich Village Socialists Max Eastman, Floyd Dell, and John Reed and not also as an important forum for socialist feminist ideas and ideals? Jones identifies more than 30 women, including Helen Hull, Mary Heaton Vorse, Cornelia Barnes, Elsie Clews Parsons, Dorothy Day, and Inez Irwin, whose contributions to *The Masses* helped to shape the nation's intellectual discourse on issues such as patriarchy, war, peace, suffrage, ethnicity, birth control education, and women's labor rights. This book reclaims an impor-

tant aspect of the history of feminism in America because it shows how women who were active in a variety of causes kept sight of those issues that affected the majority of women. Students of women's literature, class-conscious feminism, and radical journalism in pre-WW I America will find this book and its scholarly apparatus extremely useful. Undergraduate; graduate; faculty; general.— *S. M. Nuernberg, University of Wisconsin-Oshkosh*

WS-0760　　　PS153　　　93-21789 CIP
Kafka, Phillipa. **The great white way: African American women writers and American success mythologies.** Garland, 1993. 223p afp ISBN 0-8153-1160-5, $35.00

Using Henry Louis Gates Jr.'s definition of "signifying" in the African American social and literary tradition as a coded, complex language ritual that both praises and satirizes previous discourses, Kafka demonstrates how African American women writers signify on pervasive American male and female success myths. The male myth of socioeconomic success derives from Benjamin Franklin via Booker T. Washington, while the "Cinderella" myth of escape from the drudgery and confinement of the domestic sphere has been and continues to be disseminated by numerous discourses throughout American cultural history. Kafka illustrates the complex signifying processes at work on these myths in literature, ranging from Phillis Wheatley's poetry through Alice Walker's *The Color Purple*. Her study reinforces in a specific way a generally accepted view in contemporary literary criticism of African American literature as double-voiced discourse, written, as Kafka argues, "from an African American/European American *complex* of perspectives." Scholars and teachers interested in the "American Dream" motif in US literature will find Kafka's study particularly useful. Advanced undergraduate; graduate; faculty.—*B. Braendlin, Florida State University*

WS-0761　　　PS151　　　95-39871 CIP
Keating, AnaLouise. **Women reading, women writing: self-invention in Paula Gunn Allen, Gloria Anzaldúa, and Audre Lorde.** Temple University, 1996. 240p bibl index afp ISBN 1-56639-419-8, $49.95; ISBN 1-56639-420-1 pbk, $18.95

Despite its misleading, trendy title this is a thoroughly useful study. Keating (Eastern New Mexico Univ.) grounds her readings on feminist, queer studies, performative, and identity-politics frameworks, achieving the rare feat (these days) of using theory to make the authors urgent, available, and seductive (rather than using the texts to display theory). The author establishes her overarching theme in chapter 3, "Transformational Identity Politics." She follows with a chapter focused on each of the three authors, but at every point she also reads each against the other two. Thus, she offers readers several valid and useful ways to enter the three authors' works. Keating makes this particular grouping seem inevitable and necessary, never coincidental, while never losing sight of the autonomous integrity of each author. The final chapter somewhat belatedly attempts to make good on the book's title as Keating shares autobiographically her own "transformational" experience as a reader; this material is interesting, but in the nature of an afterword. Readers seeking more than a cursory reading of each or all of these important current writers will be well served by Keating's nuanced and probing study. All academic collections.—*D. N. Mager, Johnson C. Smith University*

WS-0762　　　PS374　　　91-35996 CIP
Levy, Helen Fiddyment. **Fiction of the home place: Jewett, Cather, Glasgow, Porter, Welty, and Naylor.** University Press of Mississippi, 1992. 265p bibl index afp ISBN 0-87805-554-1, $35.00

In much American women's fiction, the home place challenges "both the forest and the marketplace, arenas of male competition," says Levy (George Mason University). By connecting the house with domesticated nature, "and by the twin creativities of garden and sewing room," Levy's six authors link women's physical work to artistic creativity. They also display a "didactic, quasi-religious intent" in presenting "cooperative communal relationships" as an alternative to the "competitive individualism" that some of their own early female protagonists emulate. The ideal toward which these women's works evolve is the portrayal of "the female seer within a nurturing egalitarian homeland." Levy's concerns include the American cultural context, "female authorial language," the mother-daughter dynamic, and the female body. Her strongest chapters are those on Ellen Glasgow and Eudora Welty, and her inclusion of the contemporary African American author Gloria Naylor is noteworthy. This study complements, but is not superior to, Ann Romines's *The Home Plot: Women, Writing, and Domestic Ritual* (CH, Oct'92), which treats Jewett, Cather, Welty, Mary Wilkins Freeman, and Harriet Beecher Stowe. Bibliography and index. Recommended for general readers and for all academic libraries.—*J. W. Hall, University of Mississippi*

WS-0763   PS153   89-70968 CIP
Ling, Amy. **Between worlds: women writers of Chinese ancestry.** Pergamon, 1990. 212p bibl index afp ISBN 0-08-037464-6, $37.50; ISBN 0-08-037463-8 pbk, $16.95

Like the authors she studies, Ling is herself of Chinese ancestry, having come to the US at age six with her family. Her PhD is in comparative literature. The authors she studies include well-known and lesser-known writers: Edith Maud Eaton, Winnifred Eaton, Adet Lin, Lin Tai-yi, Helena Kuo, Mai-mai Sze, Han Suyin, Maria Yen, Yuan-tsung Chen, Nien Chang, Eileen Chang, Hazel Lin, Virginia Lee, Bette Bao Lord, Chuang Hua, Diana Chang, Jade Snow Wong, Maxine Hong Kingston, and Amy Tan. Although only five of them were born in the US, all have written prose works in English and all have published in the US. With the exception of one, all have been published in the 20th century. Ling provides biographical sketches and studies the themes, styles, and structures of their works interwoven with historical and social backgrounds. This is a well-managed and ambitious work which, one hopes, will inspire many more studies. Its bibliography of US-published women prose writers of Chinese ancestry is an important guide and an impressive result of thorough research. Recommended for all libraries, and particularly libraries of colleges and universities offering ethnic studies and women's studies.—*Y. L. Walls, Simon Fraser University*

WS-0764   PS374   94-41573 CIP
Marchalonis, Shirley. **College girls: a century in fiction.** Rutgers, 1995. 209p bibl index ISBN 0-8135-2175-0, $45.00; ISBN 0-8135-2176-9 pbk, $16.00

Marchalonis (Pennsylvania State Univ.) examines works written between the 1870s and the early 1930s that take as their subject an innovation in 19th-century American life: women's higher education, especially that pursued in institutions modeled on such pioneering colleges as Vassar, Smith, and Wellesley. She focuses less on the literary value of these unabashedly popular works and more on their revisions of and compromises with earlier models of womanhood. Indeed, the most interesting aspects of the study are the ambivalences resulting from the works' dual commitment to uphold "womanly" roles and create "green worlds" in which college life transforms self-definition and expands women's space. Though even the best of the works studied here exclude the possibility of legitimate female competition, sexual knowledge, or political activism, they are progressive when compared to later fiction that replaces same-sex friendship with obligatory heterosexual romance and reduces college experience to a backdrop for girls' adventure stories. The most problematic aspect of this study is that the works examined are rarely memorable (e.g., series novels such as Pauline Lester's *Majorie Dean, College Freshman*, 1922). Marchalonis's extensive use of plot summary and her decision not to relate the fiction more systematically with cultural context or with contemporary historical analyses of women's college experiences are limiting, particularly when she treats the fascinating and troubling exposés of college life in the 1930s. Recommended for undergraduate libraries with women's studies collections.—*M. L. Robertson, Sweet Briar College*

WS-0765   PS228   95-14890 CIP
Marek, Jayne E. **Women editing modernism: "little" magazines & literary history.** University Press of Kentucky, 1996 (c1995). 252p bibl index afp ISBN 0-8131-1937-5, $34.95; ISBN 0-8131-0854-3 pbk, $14.95

Marek (Franklin College) looks at several important Little Magazines and their women editors from a feminist perspective. *Poetry* (ed. Harriet Monroe), *The Little Review* (ed. Margaret Anderson), *The Egoist* (ed. Harriet Shaw Weaver), and *The Dial* (ed. Marianne Moore) and their female staffs are all discussed. Marek also explores Ezra Pound's relationship with each of the editors, de-emphasizing the importance of Pound's traditionally perceived influence on modern British and American literature in the first three decades of the 20th century. Pound is presented here as a man who "thought of women as subordinates who could offer money, hard work, and approbation in support of literary men." This is a radically different position from those that have emphasized the extensive influences Pound exerted (even to the extent of coining the phrase "The Pound Era"). Although scholarly resources are not lacking on either the persons or journals considered here (e.g., Ellen Williams's *Harriet Monroe and the Poetry Renaissance*, CH, Oct'77), Marek's focus is unique, and she includes a significant amount of previously unpublished material. Recommended to academic collections in publishing history, the history of Little Magazines, the history of modern literature, and women's studies. Upper-division undergraduate and up.—*A. R. Nourie, Illinois State University*

WS-0766   PS374   94-10663 CIP
McDowell, Deborah E. **"The changing same": black women's literature, criticism, and theory.** Indiana, 1995. 222p index afp ISBN 0-253-33629-5, $29.95; ISBN 0-253-20926-9 pbk, $12.95

Any scholar, beginning or seasoned, looking for an introduction to black feminist criticism and theory would be well advised to pick up McDowell's collection of essays. Written over the last 15 years, they document many of the central critical issues to emerge from black feminist criticism—literary tradition, identity politics, shifting literary conventions, reader/reception politics, the construction of historical knowledge, and black feminists' relationships to the age of theory. Rather than provide a linear, chronological record of her changing ideas, McDowell (Univ. of Virginia) groups her essays thematically, with contemporary commentary on many of her earlier works. The result is a delightful dialogue with both herself and a rich variety of African American writers, critics, and theorists—Hazel Carby, Hortense Spillers, bell hooks, and Henry Louis Gates Jr., to name several. Her examinations of major contemporary novelists Alice Walker and Toni Morrison and of Harlem Renaissance writers Jessie Fauset and Nella Larsen provide important insights. Written with wit and style, this book is the mature work of an impressive scholar.—*J. Tharp, University of Wisconsin—Marshfield-Wood County*

WS-0767   PS153   95-10351 CIP
Memory and cultural politics: new approaches to American ethnic literatures, ed. by Amritjit Singh, Joseph T. Skerrett, and Robert E. Hogan. Northeastern University, 1996. 357p bibl index afp ISBN 1-55553-234-9, $50.00; ISBN 1-55553-254-3 pbk, $20.00

This collection of 15 essays focuses on cultural identity and how it is generated and maintained. The authors employ a variety of theoretical and historical methods to examine what it means to be an "American" in an increasingly diverse society. A focus on postcolonial approaches to questions of immigration provides a contrast between "old" and "new" immigrants and how identity formation proceeds in different ways. Of particular interest are the views of women who must deal with ethnicity, national origin, and gender in their struggle to define themselves. These essays investigate the relationships between memory and writing of ethnic authors who use the past to illuminate their current definitions of self. Memory is often repressed (as in the case of the Japanese internment during WW II) and in conflict with printed history; it is frequently both collective and personal. Several essays focus on how understanding the past—reliving the memories—can inform the present and how writers use this strategy to expand cultural identity. This collection brings to the fore racial, ethnic, and gender issues previously unexamined in most studies of immigrant and ethnic experience, emphasizing the importance of writers and scholars of ethnic literature who see the creation of literary texts, social change, and cultural politics as interwoven and necessary in the creation of a shared American history. All academic collections.—*G. M. Bataille, University of California, Santa Barbara*

WS-0768   PS310.F45   89-70037 CIP
Merrin, Jeredith. **An enabling humility: Marianne Moore, Elizabeth Bishop, and the uses of tradition.** Rutgers, 1990. 185p bibl index ISBN 0-8135-1547-5, $35.00; ISBN 0-8135-16233-4, $17.00

Merrin's book appears one year after David Kalstone's distinguished *Becoming a Poet: Elizabeth Bishop with Marianne Moore and Robert Lowell* (1989). Despite the apparent overlap, these are very different books. Merrin's omission of Lowell is no accident. She attempts, persuasively, to provide a feminist reading of two female poets largely ignored or dismissed by feminist theorists, and, in the process, she offers a theory of literary influence that makes better sense of the way these poets appropriated from and slyly quarreled with the (mostly male) literary tradition than can such widely discussed theories as H. Bloom's or those of such feminist voices as S. Gilbert and S. Gubar, A. Rich, or A. Ostriker. Merrin argues that the work of Moore and Bishop involves "an appropriately non-appropriative extension of feminism." There are fine chapters on Moore's use of 17th-century prose models (especially Sir Thomas Browne) and Moore's revisionist response to romanticism, and on Bishop's appropriations from George Herbert and her revisionist response to Wordsworth. Many points in the Herbert discussion are anticipated in T.J. Travisano's *Elizabeth Bishop: Her Artistic Development* (CH, Nov'88), but Merrin's sensitive and generally persuasive feminist reading presents the Bishop-Herbert connection in a new and interesting light. The most compelling chapter, however, is the last, in which Merrin argues cogently for the strength of Moore's and Bishop's insistence on humility, balance, complexity, and alertness and for the validity of this approach from a feminist perspective. Refreshing and sound, this study is strongly recommended to libraries serving advanced undergraduates and graduate students.—*T. Travisano, Hartwick College*

WS-0769 PS153 94-17670 CIP
Peterson, Carla L. **"Doers of the world": African-American women speakers and writers in the North (1830-1880).** Oxford, 1995. 284p bibl index afp ISBN 0-19-508519-1, $35.00

Peterson (Univ. of Maryland College Park) argues convincingly that there is a problem at the heart of recent canonization of 19th-century African American literature because scholars have embraced slave narratives to the exclusion of most other writing. Examining African American women speakers and writers, the author begins to flesh out a different vision of this body of literature. In the "orature" of Sojourner Truth, the spiritual narratives of Maria Steward and Jarena Lee, the ethnographic writing of Nancy Prince and Mary Ann Shadd Cary, the speeches of Frances Ellen Watkins and Sarah Remond, the novelization of political issues in various women's writing, and the extensive diaries of Charlotte Forten, a new genre, style, and narrative purpose becomes apparent. African American women writers and speakers emerge as courageous and clever women who had to position themselves carefully in order to find a space from which to speak, a space in which others would hear them. Although this reviewer had hoped to glean more tangible information from this work, Peterson provides a sophisticated theoretical analysis of her subjects. Upper-division undergraduate collections and above.—*J. Tharp, University of Wisconsin—Marshfield-Wood County*

WS-0770 PS628 94-45115 CIP
Plays by early American women, 1775-1850, ed. by Amelia Howe Kritzer. Michigan, 1995. 444p bibl afp ISBN 0-472-09598-6, $39.50

The eight well-chosen plays in this impressive anthology dispel the impression, left by American theater histories and anthologies, that Mercy Otis Warren wrote *The Group* in 1775 and then Anna Cora Mowatt wrote *Fashion* in 1850. In fact 30 women published and produced plays during this period. Though frequently melodramatic, the eight selected here are fascinating. A thread of patriotism and a concern for women's rights run through them. Half the playwrights were born in the US, half abroad; their theater lives were in the US. Playwrights represented are Mercy Otis Warren, Susanna Rowson, Judith Murray, Sarah Pogson, Mary Carr, Frances Wright, Louisa Medina, and Charlotte Barnes. Missing from the introduction's bibliography are Alice Brown's biography *Mercy Warren* (1896) and *Modern American Drama: The Female Canon,* ed. by June Schlueter (1990). Little is missing from the 165-name bibliography of women dramatists in the US before 1900. However, since Alice Duer Miller's plays of the second and third decades of the 20th century are included, Angelina Weld Grimké's landmark play *Rachel* (1920) and Rachel Crothers's first play, *The Three of Us* (1916), should have been listed. The introduction and bibliographies provide hints for further studies. All academic collections.—*D. E. Abramson, emerita, University of Massachusetts at Amherst*

WS-0771 PS374 92-21433 CIP
Price Herndl, Diane. **Invalid women: figuring feminine illness in American fiction and culture, 1840-1940.** North Carolina, 1993. 270p bibl index afp ISBN 0-8078-2103-9, $32.50; ISBN 0-8078-4406-3 pbk, $13.95

This book traces cultural representations of female illness during the century that marked the professionalization of medicine, the rise of the woman novelist, the increasing complexity of the literary marketplace, and wide-ranging debate over "the woman question." Price Herndl seeks to reconcile arguments interpreting women's illness as manifesting, resisting, and subverting patriarchy; and she hopes to mediate between, on the one hand, poststructuralist theories that discursive structures create the self and, on the other hand, humanist theories that individuals resist, transgress, and transform discourse. Drawing lucidly on Bakhtin, deconstruction, and cultural studies, Price Herndl's compelling individual readings of works by major writers (Harriet Beecher Stowe, Hawthorne, Wharton, James, Fitzgerald) and minor ones complement her examination of germ theory, psychic and somatic cures, medicine's place in the rise of capitalism, and the cultural forms—from fiction to advertisements to film—in which men and women used the trope of female illness. Advanced undergraduate; graduate; faculty.—*L. W. MacFarlane, University of New Hampshire*

WS-0772 PS374 91-50259 CIP
Rabinowitz, Paula. **Labor & desire: women's revolutionary fiction in Depression America.** North Carolina, 1991. 222p bibl index afp ISBN 0-8078-1994-8, $29.95; ISBN 0-8078-4332-6 pbk, $12.95

In this study of US fiction of the Depression written by radical women, Rabinowitz has attempted to "articulate how gender was constructed within the rhetoric of the literary Left during the 1930s and what effects that (gendered) construction had on the fiction of radical women," or to focus on "the ways in which sexuality and maternity reconstruct the 'classic' proletarian novel to speak about both the working-class woman and the radical female intellectual" (Dust jacket). Rabinowitz quotes from numerous other critics, both in support and in opposition, and she is at her best when analyzing specific novels, such as Tillie Olsen's *Yonnondio* (1974), Josephine Herbst's *Rope of Gold* (1939; CH, Sep'85), and Lauren Gilfillan's *I Went to Pit College* (1934). Regrettably, a promising idea for a critical study is to a degree undermined by the academic jargon in which much of it is written: "In effect, gendered class and classed gender are the *non-dit* of the genre." This study will therefore probably lose much of its intended audience, nonscholars who are curious about a little-known aspect of literary history. May be of use in women's studies collections.—*J. Overmyer, Ohio State University*

WS-0773 PS3535 94-23646 CIP
Rand, Ayn. **Letters of Ayn Rand,** ed. by Michael S. Berliner. Dutton, 1995. (Dist. by Penguin) 681p index afp ISBN 0-525-93946-6, $34.95

This collection of the letters of Ayn Rand (1905-82) extends from 1926 to two months before her death. They were written to friends, fans, the famous (Barbara Stanwyck, Cecil B. DeMille), those with whom she agreed or disagreed. Included are series of letters to architect Frank Lloyd Wright, author and columnist Isabel Paterson, and philosopher John Hospers. Rand was generous with her time: her letters are long and enthusiastic, and they answer fans' questions seriously and at length. There is, intentionally, only essential footnoting. As Leonard Peikoff says in his introduction, the letters "let you watch her" live her life; her "value judgments ... were absolutes to her." Berliner describes her letters as "more like polished documents than casual conversations." Rand firmly defends and explains her points. She vigorously opposed Communism and collectivism and supported capitalism and individualism. When correspondents ask for her philosophy, she refers them to precise passages in her books and becomes irritated with those who miss what seem to her obvious points. Like any author, she was concerned about advertising and sales of her books, and about the movie based on *The Fountainhead.* Readers will note an intelligent, determined mind. Includes a chronology. Recommended for English literature collections and women's studies programs at all levels.—*J. Overmyer, emerita, Ohio State University*

WS-0774 PS674 94-4794 CIP
Raub, Patricia. **Yesterday's stories: popular women's novels of the twenties and thirties.** Greenwood, 1994. 131p (Contributions in American studies, 104) bibl index afp ISBN 0-313-29259-0, $49.95

Raub's compact study is the first book on women's best sellers of the interwar period, when "the nature of the middle-class woman was being contested." Raub discusses two English works, E.M. Hull's *The Sheik* and Daphne du Maurier's *Rebecca,* but otherwise her focus is American woman writers. These include Willa

Cather, Edith Wharton, and Dorothy Canfield Fisher, though most of Raub's subjects are such now-forgotten authors as Kathleen Norris, Temple Bailey, and Olive Higgins Prouty. Some novels are treated in more than one of the six short chapters: "The Flapper and Her Sisters," "Married Women," "Divorced Women," "Women at Work," "Farming and Pioneer Women," and "Sacrificial Heroines." Raub explains that Prouty's *Stella Dallas* (1923), Fannie Hurst's *Imitation of Life* (1933), Anita Loos's *Gentlemen Prefer Blondes* (1926), and several other women's novels had second and even third lives in Hollywood film versions. She confirms Erik Löfroth's conclusion in *A World Made Safe: Values in American Best Sellers, 1895-1920* (1983) that the cultural values reflected in popular fiction are basically conservative. Primary and secondary bibliographies are included. Recommended for all academic libraries. Upper-division undergraduate and up.—*J. W. Hall, University of Mississippi*

WS-0775 PS153 94-18740 CIP
Rebolledo, Tey Diana. **Women singing in the snow: a cultural analysis of Chicana literature.** Arizona, 1995. 250p bibl index afp ISBN 0-8165-1520-4, $35.00; ISBN 0-8165-1546-8 pbk, $16.95

Rebolledo provides a literary history of Chicana writers. Oral histories document the creative, imaginative world of the pioneer Chicana. The discussion of three New Mexican writers—Nina Otero-Warren, Cleofas Jaramillo, and Fabiola Cabeza de Baca—illustrates how these writers embedded in their texts the ideology of resistance. This work studies how Chicana writers choose, define, and integrate traditional myths and archetypes into their texts. The study of *Coatlicue*, *La Llorona*, and *La Virgen de Guadalupe*, archetypes entrenched in the psyche of Chicanas, are significant for the student of the Chicana. Rebolledo's inclusion of a variety of literary pieces provides insight into the revisionary process that the Chicana writer has embarked on. As the author states, "To become ourselves, in the fullest way possible, one must integrate the serpents, the 'negative,' and accept the power of self-knowledge and self-expression that comes with it." Finally, Rebolledo illustrates that as Chicanas remember their past and write their narratives, they construct and reconstruct their own identity and acquire an "understanding of their historical role in families and communities." An excellent companion to *Infinite Divisions: An Anthology of Chicana Literature* (CH, Jan'94), this book includes an extensive bibliography on Chicana literature and criticism. Strongly recommended for all collections, particularly those serving students of women's literature.—*J. Luna Lawhn, San Antonio College*

WS-0776 PS3511 93-9957 CIP
Roberts, Diane. **Faulkner and southern womanhood.** Georgia, 1994. 246p bibl index afp ISBN 0-8203-1567-2, $35.00

Illustrating from most of Faulkner's novels and several short stories, Roberts (Univ. of Alabama) shows how the writer both "subverts" and "reinforces" six stereotypes of Southern womanhood: the Confederate Woman, the Mammy, the Tragic Mulatta, the New Belle, the Night Sister (or spinster), and the Mother. She summarizes earlier appearances of each stereotype in popular culture and literature, and she presents "the context in which Faulkner reactivates the character in his fiction"—a context that includes Jim Crow laws, lynchings, and boycotts, as well as the 1950s Dior dresses evocative of antebellum fashions. Bakhtin's distinction between "classical" and "grotesque" bodies influences Roberts's discussion of the racial and cultural "binaries" that often "collapse" in Faulkner's works. She also detects "slippage" in gender categories, as when Drusilla Hawk and Laverne Shumann "cross-dress" and inhabit "bisexual spaces." Roberts concludes with *Requiem for a Nun*, where "the categories are bankrupt, the [Mammy's] kitchen and the pedestal [of the Dixie Madonna] both now empty." The index omits critics cited in the text, but the bibliography is extensive. Recommended for all academic libraries. Advanced undergraduate; graduate; faculty.—*J. W. Hall, University of Mississippi*

WS-0777 Orig
Roberts, Diane. **The myth of Aunt Jemima: representations of race and region.** Routledge, 1994. 228p bibl index ISBN 0-415-04918-0, $55.00; ISBN 0-415-04919-9 pbk, $15.95

Roberts's book interprets writing by 19th and early 20th century white women about American slavery, with special focus on representations of the body. The book cites the double positioning of white women authors, who were "at once part of the ruling elite" by virtue of race "and marginalized" for their gender. Beginning with Aphra Behne's *Oroonoko*, it proceeds through a lengthy reading of Harriet Beecher Stowe's *Uncle Tom's Cabin* and a survey of Southern responses to Stowe. Subsequent chapters include an examination of British women's writing about American slavery (Frances Wright, Frances Trollope, and Harriet Martineau); an essay about the career of abolitionist Fanny Kemble; a reading of the miscegenation theme in Lydia Maria Child's fiction; and a study of representations of African American characters in fiction by early 20th century white women. Aunt Jemima and Jezebel are invoked as the already very familiar literary and cultural stereotypes of black women. Although the book does not make a startling argument, it draws upon most of the significant scholarship in this field and would provide a good introduction to the issues at stake. Upper-division undergraduate and up.—*R. R. Warhol, University of Vermont*

WS-0778 PS374 91-34053 CIP
Romines, Ann. **The home plot: women, writing & domestic ritual.** Massachusetts, 1992. 319p bibl index ISBN 0-87023-783-7, $45.00; ISBN 0-87023-794-2 pbk, $15.95

Romines (George Washington University) has brought together her own experience and her favorite writers in a lovingly crafted piece of literary criticism focused on domestic rituals. Her thesis is that the apparently trivial activities of the home are handed down from one generation to another as a kind of female legacy, which is deeply satisfying to the participants. Referring to this as a "study of Hestia's tales and the poetics of domestic ritual," she uses Stowe, Jewett, Freeman, Cather, and Welty as her examples, selecting works that demonstrate and enrich her points, weaving a web of interconnected ideas and themes. She uses contemporary critics, recent feminist theory, essays, interviews, and a wide range of other materials to explore her ideas. The symbolic value of these scenes can derive from large, important household occasions, "such as a family reunion or a home wedding, or it can be an ordinary household task such as serving a meal or sewing a seam." In all cases, the ultimate goal is the preservation of the shelter. The result is a fresh reading of some American classics by a lively and thoughtful reader, who enriches our awareness of the sources and resonances of these delightful works. Appropriate for upper-division undergraduates, graduate students, and faculty.—*N. Tischler, Pennsylvania State University, University Park Campus*

WS-0779 PS374 94-41242 CIP
Saunders, James Robert. **The wayward preacher in the literature of African American women.** McFarland, 1995. 169p bibl index afp ISBN 0-7864-0060-9, $27.50

Saunders book examines the figure of the black preacher as he is portrayed in literary works by black women, specifically, Nella Larsen's *Quicksand* (1928); Zora Neale Hurston's *Jonah's Gourd Vine* (1900); Paule Marshall's *Brown Girl, Brownstones* (1959); Gloria Naylor's *The Women of Brewster Place* (1982); and Terry McMillan's *Mama* (1987). Aware of the preeminence the African American preacher has traditionally enjoyed, Saunders analyzes the ways in which these novelists present some of the more troubling aspects of his character, for example, sexual promiscuity. He is careful to interpret the black preacher's character and actions, especially as they affect black women, in the context of a sexist society and culture, and he suggests that the dominance of the black male preacher is a reflection of patriarchal assumptions regarding male/female roles and aspirations. This work, with its useful insights into one of the most prominent figures in African American culture, is appropriate for general readers and undergraduates.—*L. S. Burns, Tuskegee University*

WS-0780 PS648 94-28678 CIP
Telling travels: selected writings by nineteenth-century American women abroad, ed. by Mary Suzanne Schriber. Northern Illinois, 1995. 304p bibl afp ISBN 0-87580-195-1, $35.00; ISBN 0-87580-561-2 pbk, $18.50

This anthology contains substantial excerpts from foreign travel books published by 16 American women between the 1830s and 1890s. Among the authors are the popular Harriet Beecher Stowe and Nellie Bly. Yet accounts by obscure women are the most interesting either because of their mode of travel, experiences, or point of view. The well-written introduction discusses travel writing in general and 19th-century women travelers in particular. The headnote for each excerpt provides biographical information about the author and critical comments about significant stylistic features of her travel account. Readers interested in American culture will find this anthology valuable because the writers frequently reflect on the political philosophy and customs of their American homeland, contrasting them to those of lands to which they journeyed. This is not an "adventure" book, and Schriber (Northern Illinois Univ.) acknowledges that many travelers—women and men—wrote "fairly tedious" accounts. Yet the selections excellently illustrate a range of ways in which women's issues were incorporated into popular travel books. The focus on women writers makes this anthology a valuable addition to the growing scholarship on travel literature. General readers; graduate students; researchers.—*D. C. Estes, Loyola University*

WS-0781 PS261 94-49536 CIP
Tracy, Susan J. **In the master's eye: representations of women, blacks, and poor whites in antebellum southern literature.** Massachusetts, 1995. 307p bibl index ISBN 0-87023-968-6, $42.50

Studies of antebellum southern plantation life and literature continue with this Marxist-feminist study of selected novels from the period. This is a well-cultivated subject, contributed to in recent years by Catherine Clinton, Eugene Genovese, Elizabeth Fox-Genovese, Mary Ann Wimsatt, Kathryn Lee Seidel, and Minrose Gwin, among others. Tracy (Hampshire College) looks at the novels of William Alexander Carothers, James Ewell Heath, John Pendleton Kennedy, William Gilmore Simms, George Tucker, and Nathaniel Beverley Tucker as documents of planter propaganda and reflections of idealizations and life experience in the early 19th century rather than as works of literary art. In fact, the author's introduction dismisses the artistic value of the novels with little comment, although the space and attention given to Simms suggests some aesthetic redemption for his efforts. This book does not supplant previous studies, but it extends the debate and discussion of the status and roles of planters, plantation mistresses, yeoman farmers, poor whites, and blacks. The strength of Tracy's effort lies in her linking the tradition of the southern novel to the English tradition represented by Richardson and in her considerations of whites who were not planters. Generalizations are balanced by very careful, full notes. All academic collections.—*T. Bonner Jr., Xavier University of Louisiana*

WS-0782 PS310 91-6294 CIP
Walker, Cheryl. **Masks outrageous and austere: culture, psyche, and persona in modern women poets.** Indiana, 1991. 221p index afp ISBN 0-253-36322-5, $39.95; ISBN 0-253-20666-9 pbk, $14.95

Following from Walker's book on 19th-century American women poets, *The Nightingale's Burden* (1982), this volume deals with six 20th-century women—Bogan, H.D., Lowell, Millay, Teasdale, and Wylie. Walker employs the traditional methods of literary history in relating social and cultural conditions to biography and thence Biography to the poetry. She successfully argues that the ambiguity or worse of women's position in a male-dominated society and the response of women poets to it pervade their work, whether for good or ill. Based on close reading and explication of the texts, Walker brings fresh insights to each poet. She deals even-handedly and sympathetically with writers who are not critically fashionable today. In method and outlook she is allied to such feminist critics as Alicia Ostriker (*Stealing the Language*, 1986) and Paula Bennett (*My Life a Loaded Gun*, CH, Apr'87). An important work of feminist-oriented criticism, recommended for all readers.—*J. J. Patton, Atlantic Community College*

WS-0783 PS3537 92-23098 CIP
Wallace Stevens and the feminine, ed by Melita Schaum. Alabama, 1993. 243p bibl index afp ISBN 0-8173-0666-8, $34.95

Three somewhat interrelated themes emerge from this absorbing essay collection on Stevens and the feminine principle in his writing and his life: (1) the "interior paramour" of his poems—the speaker's most intimate companion and confidant; (2) his disastrous longstanding marriage with Elsie Moll; (3) his deep attachment to his mother and, after her death, to her memory. Stevens's abstract yet romanticized treatment of the feminine is seen, in fact, as—among other things—the mother replacing the wife as his "interior paramour." Excessive psychoanalytical and postmodernist theorizing in a few of the essays becomes wearisome,

but that is offset by insightful critical and biographical interpretations by Roland Wagner on Stevens's "Concealed Self," Jacqueline Brogan on sexism *and* Stevens, Mary Arensberg on gender mythology, Rosamond Rosenmeier on Stevens's "rabbi" figures and wisdom acquisition (harking back to his Pennsylvania German ancestors), Daniel O'Hara and Lisa Steinman on Stevens's relation to Emerson, and Barbara Fisher on Stevens's "interior paramour": visualized as pythoness and other metaphorical figures, against the background of Solomon's epithalamium, "The Song of Songs." A very valuable addition to the burgeoning Stevens scholarship.—*S. I. Bellman, California State Polytechnic University, Pomona*

WS-0784 PS374 95-22338 CIP
Wood, Ruth Pirsig. **Lolita in Peyton Place: highbrow, middlebrow, and lowbrow novels of the 1950s.** Garland, 1995. 163p bibl index afp ISBN 0-8153-2061-2, $45.00

Wood (Univ. of Wisconsin—River Falls) has written a provocative book that joins Jane Tompkins's *Sensational Designs* (CH, Nov'85) in trying to revise the concept of canon. The author cites American novels from the 1950s, but not those candidates for the canon academics usually analyze. She is not writing theory in its usual manifestation, though she cites and elucidates many theoretical points. Rather, she takes the seemingly dated concept of highbrow-middlebrow-lowbrow and brings it to life with content analysis of the three types of novels. Her stated cause is to advocate the consumption of popular novels in schools, especially by women; her unstated thesis is to defend lowbrow novels as worthy of inclusion in the canon. Nabokov's *Lolita* is the takeoff point, a weak start since Wood considers it pornography rather than a cultural critique of a nation obsessed with teenage females. From *Lolita* she moves to firmer ground as she deals with many theoretical issues and novels. Although works from other decades (e.g., James Cain's *The Postman Always Rings Twice*) might have supported her point better than novels of the 1950s, the basic idea and the insights-in-passing are worthwhile. Many faculty and students will find this work useful.—*Q. Grigg, Hamline University*

WS-0785 PS374 94-32020 CIP
Yates, Norris. **Gender and genre: an introduction to women writers of formula Westerns, 1900-1950.** New Mexico, 1995. 181p bibl index ISBN 0-8263-1569-0, $35.00

This rich and useful study recovers the work of B.M. Bower, Caroline Lockhart, Vingie Roe, and more than a dozen other significant women writers of formula Westerns between 1900 and 1950. These women helped to shape the genre associated with the likes of Zane Grey and Louis L'Amour, but Yates (Iowa State Univ.) argues that they wrote "formula Westerns with a difference." One such difference is that the protagonists in their books were most often women. Yates points out that the depictions of these women protagonists evoke strongly the image of the ideal real women from the domestic novel of the 19th century. He demonstrates convincingly "how these writers not only participated in creating and sustaining the Western genre but in so doing created a subgenre of their own." Highly recommended for anyone interested in Western American literature and women's studies. Upper-division undergraduate and above.—*L. Evers, University of Arizona*

WS-0786 PS153 92-45119 CIP
Young, Mary E. **Mules and dragons: popular culture images in the selected writings of African-American and Chinese-American women writers.** Greenwood, 1993. 157p (Contributions in women's studies, 136) bibl index afp ISBN 0-313-28735-X, $45.00

An introduction and conclusion bracket four symmetrical chapters discussing stereotypes of African American and Chinese/Chinese American women, contrasted respectively with writing by African American and Chinese American women. The introduction traces development of race designations/attributes applied to African Americans and Chinese Americans in general, and women in both groups specifically. The middle chapters explore female stereotypes in writings of African American and Chinese American men as well as cultural products of the dominant culture. Although the title promises analysis of "popular culture images," only one nonliterary text, a cartoon series, receives extensive analysis; however, the introduction offers wide-ranging discussion based on law and journalism as well as fiction. The conclusion postulates that Chinese American women have not engaged the history of Chinese immigration and settlement as directly as African American counterparts. The book uncovers and offers brief analyses of many unstudied texts, relating them to development of race notions. Unfortunately, it suffers from poor writing, and caution is advised respecting uncritical use of secondary sources.—*H. Jaskoski, California State University, Fullerton*

WS-0787   PS153   94-33791 CIP
Zaborowska, Magdalena J. **How we found America: reading gender through East European immigrant narratives.** North Carolina, 1995. 359p bibl index afp ISBN 0-8078-2203-5, $45.00; ISBN 0-8078-4509-4 pbk, $18.95

Zaborowska celebrates immigrant and expatriate women writers who "have been left out of the so-called East European canon ... dominated by the celebrated male dissident avant-garde" (e.g., poets Czesław Miłosz and Joseph Brodsky). Zaborowska highlights Mary Antin, Elisabeth Stern, Anzia Yezierska, Maria Kuncewiczowa, and Eva Hoffman, and adds a final chapter on Nabokov for contrast. She thus offers valuable perspectives on a new genre heralded by her title. She notes dichotomies between female immigrant writers who see America as Eden and those who see it as a desert, the latter writing antistories, or antimyths to more romanticized tales. However, Zaborowska's defensive tone may cost her the following she hopes to enlist. The quote above is one example of this tone. At another point she claims that earlier "canonical approaches" to immigrant texts are simply "outdated," suggesting by her diction and its context that these approaches be swept into a literary dustbin. Such insistence, expressed in heavy feminist jargon, makes the first 40 pages of this book seem too long. Of Yezierska's happy endings Zaborowska later asserts, "[I do not] believe that we need a happy ending to her literary career to perceive her as equally good as, or even better than, the recognized male authors of a similar background, such as Henry Roth and Abraham Cahan, with whom she is always compared unfavorably." The richness of Zaborowska's topic has its own merits; she should therefore have resisted the urge to protest so much. Graduate and research collections.—*J. A. Dompkowski, Canisius College*

◆ United States
Colonial & 18th Century

WS-0788   PS149   94-48119 CIP
American women writers to 1800, ed. by Sharon M. Harris. Oxford, 1996. 452p bibl index afp ISBN 0-19-508453-5 pbk, $19.95

The many facets and forms of early American women's lives and literature are explored in this fascinating and welcome anthology, a significant contribution to the recovery and critical examination of women's texts. Bringing together canonical works (by Bradstreet, Rowlandson, Wheatley), lesser-known writings (by Murray, Rowson, Warren), and many works never before published or long out of print, Harris (Univ. of Nebraska) revitalizes the static portrait of American womanhood before 1800 by challenging not only longstanding assumptions about its (lack of) literary output but also its limited concern for matters outside the domestic sphere. Groups of readings of various forms—journal entries, letters, Native American oral tales, essays—explore women's education, business dealings, domestic responsibilities, political sentiments, and spirituality, among other matters. In a lengthy introduction, Harris offers a feminist framework through which the reader may situate the literary aesthetics of such prevalent forms of women's texts as letters and journals. Even without such theoretical apparatus, this anthology is valuable for its focus on a neglected period of women's literature and its diversity of writers and literary forms. All collections.—*J. K. Weinberger, Central Connecticut State University*

WS-0789   PR555   94-47993 CIP
Ferguson, Moira. **Eighteenth-century women poets: nation, class, and gender.** State University of New York, 1995. 164p bibl index afp ISBN 0-7914-2511-8, $44.50

Ferguson (Univ. of Nebraska, Lincoln) explores the neglected work of Mary Collier, Mary Scott, Ann Yearsley, and Janet Little. They are seen as constitut-

ing a tradition of working-class poets, expressing the concerns—and resentments—of the marginalized, and attempting to redefine patriotism in light of those concerns. Ferguson's detailed reading of the poems concentrates on the interplay of gender, class, and nationalism, and she illuminates how the poets grounded their appeal for justice in the emerging myths of ancient British liberties. This study considerably overlaps Donna Landry's *The Muses of Resistance* (CH, May'91). Landry covers three of Ferguson's quartet, plus another five poets, and her examination is longer, more comprehensive, and more theoretically informed. Ferguson's work, briefer and probably more accessible to undergraduates, is a good introduction to a set of writers only now being given due scholarly consideration; she is also among the first to examine Yearsley's unpublished poetic manuscripts. One major disappointment is the absence of any real consideration of poetic language or technique. Do these poets achieve a unique voice? Is there a tension between their often radical challenge to the ruling class and their adoption of the classical machinery of the pastoral tradition? Treatment of such questions would have expanded this study beyond its narrowly thematic scope. This is an optional purchase for collections that include the Landry volume.—*K. P. Mulcahy, Rutgers, The State University of New Jersey, New Brunswick*

WS-0790   Orig
Kenny, Maurice. **Tekonwatonti/Molly Brant (1735-1795): poems of war.** White Pine, 1992. 209p ISBN 1-877727-20-2 pbk, $12.00

Kenny has written a major poem on Tekonwatonti, a Mohawk woman who was the sister of Chief Joseph Brant and the common-law wife of Sir William Johnson. Johnson was a British military commander who led Native American armies in the French and Indian Wars, and after his death, Tekonwatonti and her brother led attacks on the Revolutionary armies. She died in exile in Canada. Her career places her at the heart of American history. Kenny begins with historical background, then tells Tekonwatonti's remarkable story. There is a considerable variety of genre in this book—dramatic monologues, narratives, quotations from documents, prayers, quoted oratory, lyrics. The style is flexible and often reaches great eloquence, though there are flat stretches and some unnecessary details. Kenny provides a glossary of characters and a chronology. He gives us insights into an extraordinary woman whose life reads like romance but conveys a tragic story full of relevance for today. A book for all collections.—*B. Almon, University of Alberta*

WS-0791   PS808   95-3580 CIP
Murray, Judith Sargent. **Selected writings of Judith Sargent Murray,** ed. by Sharon M. Harris. Oxford, 1995. 272p afp ISBN 0-19-507883-7, $39.95; ISBN 0-19-510038-7 pbk, $17.95

Union College Press's republication of Judith Sargent Murray's *The Gleaner* (CH, Oct'93; originally published in three volumes, 1798)—a compendium of essays, dramas, and fiction—confirmed Murray's position as a progressive thinker. Her feminism, republican principles, and educational and religious liberalism still have broad appeal, and she deserves to be better known as an early American author. The present volume, one in Oxford's "Women Writers in English 1350-1850" series, reprints four essays, a play (*The Traveller Returned*) and a novel (*Story of Margaretta*), about 30 percent of *The Gleaner*, and adds two early essays and 11 letters (or parts of letters) from the more than 2,000 preserved at the Mississippi Department of Archives and History. This is a convenient edition for undergraduates and nonacademic readers; Harris's introduction and (especially) annotations and her extraction of *Story of Margaretta* from the essays in which it was embedded make this volume an easier read than the original. On the other hand, much is lost from and relatively little is added to Murray's *Gleaner* here, which serious readers will still need.—*J. D. Wallace, Boston College*

WS-0792   PS847   95-7636 CIP
Only for the eye of a friend: the poems of Annis Boudinot Stockton, ed. by Carla Mulford. University Press of Virginia, 1995. 336p bibl index afp ISBN 0-8139-1613-5, $35.00

This painstaking, handsome volume will prove useful to scholars in a variety of disciplines. Stockton belonged to the Revolutionary War landed elite, and her poems reflect a sensitive yet energetic command of the modes, imagery, and subject matter of traditional 18th-century neoclassical poetry. Ready access to them provides valuable cultural insights into home-front history leading up to and including the Revolutionary War period, enhances the reader's understanding of the domestic and public status of well-to-do women of the time, and demonstrates the adaptation of English literary traditions to the emerging American scene. Especially interesting are poems that reveal household life, family relationships, and close bonds of friendship and those that applaud military occasions and the American heroes who emerged from them. Several poems in praise of George Washington and his accomplishments both on and off the battlefield show the very process of myth making as it occurs, and among the most interesting materials included in this meticulously annotated volume are Washington's gracious letters in response. Valuable to sophisticated readers in American studies and women's studies; a good addition to holdings in American poetry and 18th-century American literature, upper-division undergraduate and above.—*S. R. Graham, emerita, Nazareth College of Rochester*

◆ United States 19th Century

WS-0793   PS1017   95-6793 CIP
Alcott, Louisa May. **A long fatal love chase.** Random House, 1995. 242p afp ISBN 0-679-44510-2, $21.00

The discovery by Madeleine Stern and Leona Rostenberg of Louisa May Alcott's pseudonym (A.M. Barnard) led to the unearthing of numerous Alcott publications under this name. Often (and appropriately) characterized as "blood and thunder" tales, they were intended for adults, sport Gothic overtones, deal with such topics as hashish and feminism, and were penned by Alcott in a desperate effort to earn money. The present novel falls squarely in this category although it has not been previously published. The title aptly describes the plot. Purchased at an auction in manuscript form from Alcott's heirs and published in a handsome edition largely faithful to that original manuscript, this novel will be of interest more for its historical than for its literary value; for that reason, the lack of an introduction is regrettable. This is one of several books by or about Alcott scheduled for publication in this and the coming year (see, e.g., *Louisa May Alcott Unmasked: Collected Thrillers,*, edited by Stern, CH, Dec'95), several of which bring her "blood and thunder" tales back into print. Previous editions of these tales include *Behind a Mask: The Unknown Thrillers of Louisa May Alcott* (CH, Nov'75) and *Plots and Counterplots* (CH, Oct'76), both edited by Stern. Recommended for collections in American literature, women's literature, and Gothic literature.—*E. R. Baer, Gustavus Adolphus College*

WS-0794   PS1016   95-1501 CIP
Alcott, Louisa May. **Louisa May Alcott unmasked: collected thrillers,** ed. by Madeleine Stern. Northeastern University, 1995. 754p bibl afp ISBN 1-55553-225-X, $55.00; ISBN 1-55553-226-8 pbk, $24.95

Together at last! Alcott's readable thrillers (previously available in five separate anthologies) are united in one volume. Madeleine Stern's informative introduction outlines the discovery of Alcott's "sensation stories" (discoveries made by Stern, Leona Rostenberg, Victor Berch, and Daniel Shealy) and the stories' publication history, themes, and impact upon contemporary Alcott scholarship, especially that of feminist critics. This volume includes a chronological bibliography, prepared by Shealy, of all located Alcott thrillers (which demonstrates that four titles listed in the bibliography are unaccountably missing from this collection). Alcott's impressive energy, narrative skill, diligence, and professionalism are here once more demonstrated. All collections.—*J. J. Benardete, CUNY Hunter College*

WS-0795   PS1017   90-48069 CIP
Alcott, Louisa May. **Moods,** ed. with an introd. by Sarah Elbert. Rutgers, 1991. 284p ISBN 0-8135-1669-2, $35.00; ISBN 0-8135-1670-6 pbk, $13.00

Louisa May Alcott's first novel for adults has been unavailable in its first edition (1864) since the 19th century. Sarah Elbert (SUNY, Binghamton) brings it back into print in the Rutgers "American Women Writers" series, now 15 volumes strong, with reprints of "lost" works by such writers as Rose Terry Cook, Fanny Fern, Nella Larson, and E.D.E.N. Southworth. Elbert, whose earlier

work on Alcott includes a critical volume, *A Hunger for Home: Louisa May Alcott's Place in American Culture* (1987) and an introduction to another adult novel, *Work* (1974), has prepared an edition of *Moods* useful equally to the general reader and scholar. The text of the novel is pleasingly printed and not cluttered with footnotes. Enriching the novel is a 30-page introduction, which locates *Moods* in Alcott's body of work and focuses especially on the intertextual relationship of *Moods* to *Pilgrim's Progress* and *Jane Eyre*. Elbert has also included Henry James's 1865 review of the novel, originally published in *North American Review*, as well as the extensive revisions to the novel done by Alcott and published in 1882, and a bibliography. Highly recommended for general collections as well as for all appropriate special collections, such as American and women's literature.—*E. R. Baer, Washington College*

WS-0796   PS1541   90-70742 CIP
Bennett, Paula. **Emily Dickinson: woman poet.** Iowa, 1991 (1990). 223p index ISBN 0-87745-309-8, $27.50; ISBN 0-87745-310-1 pbk, $9.95

Bennett writes that her "first and chief aim is to make Dickinson accessible to teachers, students, and general readers" (introduction). Her second is "to show how—by placing her poetry within the context created by other American women poets—we can understand her for what she was—a nineteenth-century American 'woman poet' of a different kind: a poet who both drew from and critiqued the work of her peers." Bennett fulfills both aims beautifully. Gracefully situating each issue within the current critical discussion, she begins by looking at the "metaphysical basis for Dickinson's intellectual and linguistic experimentation," goes on to examine Dickinson's confrontation of traditional religious beliefs, then treats her construction of an alternative faith in nature, a faith both "woman-centered and materially-based." The final chapters explore Dickinson's psychological poems and her erotic imagery. Bennett concludes that "Dickinson's sexuality and her imagination were both homoerotic and autoerotic." Drawing on Luce Irigaray, among others, she argues that "this female-centered eroticism was one of the primary enabling factors in Dickinson's emergence as a strong woman poet." Here, as elsewhere, Bennett supports her point with finely textured, compelling readings of individual poems. This is a refreshing, persuasive study, well worth reading by seasoned Dickinson scholars as well as interested English majors.—*S. W. Sherman, University of New Hampshire*

WS-0797   PS2132   94-214 CIP
Church, Joseph. **Transcendent daughters in Jewett's *Country of the pointed firs*.** Fairleigh Dickinson, 1995 (c1994). (Dist. by Associated University Presses) 202p bibl index afp ISBN 0-8386-3560-1, $34.50

Church (Binghamton Univ.) bases this new study of Jewett's Dunnet sketches on the psychoanalytic theories of Melanie Klein. The "transcendent daughters" of his title refers to what Klein sees as a necessary stage in female development, when a daughter needs to "subsume" the internalized figure of the idealized father to which she has resorted to escape the figure of the negating mother. Church asserts that the narrator of *Country of the Pointed Firs* (1896) enacts the salutary process of "transcend[ing] a barren attachment to the father" and entering into beneficial relations with the mother, as seen by her relations with mature women such as the healer Mrs. Todd. Unfortunately, Church's use of psychoanalytic analysis reduces rather than illuminates the works. The palpable pleasures of *Country of the Pointed Firs* too often dissolve into a wearying and shadowy allegory in which characters lose their Maine solidity to become materializations of the figures of the narrator's internal drama. Church's totalizing use of Kleinian dynamics to explain so much action, character, and motive makes it too easy to dismiss the validity of these explanations, even when, as in the essay on "The Landscape Chamber," they seem provocative. Jewett awaits a deployment of psychoanalytic theory as convincing and contextualized as Sarah Way Sherman's more general treatment of the relation of mothers and daughters in *Sarah Orne Jewett, an American Persephone* (CH, Mar'90). Graduate; faculty.—*M. L. Robertson, Sweet Briar College*

WS-0798   PS1713   91-14275 CIP
Critical essays on Mary Wilkins Freeman, ed. by Shirley Marchalonis. G.K. Hall, 1991. 241p index afp ISBN 0-8161-7306-0, $40.00

Until her recent rediscovery through "feminist literary archaeology," Mary E. Wilkins Freeman, a best-selling New England writer at the turn of the century, had fallen into obscurity. But several of her most popular and deserving works—a novel, *Pembroke*, and a collection of short stories, including her famous story "The Revolt of Mother"—have been reprinted, and now Marchalonis (Pennsylvania State University, Berks Campus) offers a volume rich with resources for better understanding Freeman and her works. It is, according to James Nagel, general editor of this series, the first volume of essays ever published on Freeman, whom he terms "a neglected but important writer." The volume includes contemporaneous reviews (by William Dean Howells, Horace Scudder, and others); two essays by Freeman herself; 11 previously published critical essays (the most notable by F.O. Matthiessen, Susan Allen Toth, Marjorie Pryse, and Elizabeth Meese); and five new essays, commissioned for this collection. Marchalonis's introduction provides a useful overview of the writer's career and the trends in reviewers' response to her work. A chronology of major events and publications in Freeman's life and a section of notes on contributors would have improved this volume; nonetheless, it is the best resource available for both students and scholars of Freeman, and it is highly recommended for all collections.—*E. R. Baer, Washington College*

WS-0799　　　　PS217　　　　91-44238 CIP
The culture of sentiment: race, gender, and sentimentality in nineteenth-century America, ed. by Shirley Samuels. Oxford, 1992. 349p index afp ISBN 0-19-506354-6, $45.00

Interdisciplinary in scope, the essays provide an expansive treatment of the cult of sentimentality, ranging from art and popular culture to history and literature. While sentimentality is most often associated with the literature of the 19th century, Samuels points out that "the aesthetics of sentiment appear in advice books, statues, photographs, pamphlets, lyric poems, fashion advertisements, and novels." Samuels argues, "the sentimental complex also situates the reader or viewer: that is, the act of emotional response the work evokes also produces the sentimental subject who consumes the work." Redefining the boundaries of sentimentality, the essays provide the reader with "a more thoroughly situated and engaged sense of how sentimental texts produce effects and how social and cultural meanings are embodied." Notable are "Narratives of the Female Body: *The Greek Slave*," by Joy S. Sisson for its consideration of sentimentality in art and "Sentimental Figures: Reading *Godey's Lady's Book* in Antebellum America," in which Isabelle Lehuu "proposes that Godey's images of fashionably dressed women staged a potentially subversive culture." Graduate; faculty.—*R. McCaughey-Silvia, University of Rhode Island*

WS-0800　　　　PS1949　　　　95-8678 CIP
Curry, Jane. **Marietta Holley.** Twayne/Prentice Hall International, 1996. 114p (TUSAS, 658) bibl index afp ISBN 0-8057-4020-1, $22.95

Like 19th-century humorists Ann Stephens and Frances Whitcher, Marietta Holley (1836-1926), once as popular as her contemporary Mark Twain, has been "rediscovered." In this strong addition to the Twayne series, Curry extends and deepens the critical work of Nancy Walker and Linda Morris, mapping the contours of Holley's personal and literary life. The youngest of seven children, Holley suffered from chronic respiratory illnesses and chose to live with her mother and sister rather than to marry. She penned more than 40 volumes, often earning in excess of $100,000 for a creation. Holley's central vernacular character and pseudonym, Josiah Allen's wife Samantha, was born in 1869 in *Peterson's Magazine* and continued to explore "wimmens rites," temperance, racism, and spiritualism till her last book, published when Holley was 78. Her recurring literary strategies included Samantha's deadpan "housewife" humor and her use of husband Josiah and spinster Betsey Bobbe as literary foils. Curry also notes Holley's weaker social and literary elements: repetitions in later works and shortsightedness on issues of racial justice. An excellent and useful study of a "funny foremother" for all collections.—*S. Danielson, Portland State University*

WS-0801　　　　PS3363　　　　95-4332 CIP
Dean, Sharon L. **Constance Fenimore Woolson: homeward bound.** Tennessee, 1995. 236p bibl index afp ISBN 0-87049-898-3, $27.00

Dean (Rivier College) makes an avowed attempt to "recover" Woolson (most often mentioned in connection with Henry James) and her fiction in terms of 19th-century feminist issues as presented by 20th-century scholars. Accordingly, Dean

considers Woolson's work in terms of such issues as woman's search for a home, marriage, family, and the social position of spinsters and widows, as well as more familiar categories like regionalism and the contrast of European and American culture. She draws heavily on Woodson's life and family history to provide a "thick" context for her fiction, which, Dean argues, is "an invaluable source for understanding nineteenth-century issues" and deserves a more prominent place in the canon of American literature. Recommended for Americanists, feminists, and Jamesians at the upper-division undergraduate level and above.—*J. J. Benardete, CUNY Hunter College*

WS-0802　　　　PS1018　　　　89-42710 CIP
Delamar, Gloria T. **Louisa May Alcott and Little women: biography, critique, publications, poems, songs and contemporary relevance.** McFarland, 1990. 350p bibl index afp ISBN 0-89950-421-3, $29.95

The author states that this "work is the only reference which takes a triple approach to Alcott study. The biography section is a documentable telling of Alcott's life, incorporating numerous Alcott poems; a section on *Little Women* is a history and critical analysis of that book; and a third section discusses the Alcott legacy and contemporary relevance." Despite such comprehensive aims, there are significant omissions. Neither Martha Saxton's Louisa May (CH, Mar'78) nor Madelon Bedell's *The Alcotts* (CH, Mar'81) is discussed: the author notes only that after Aileen Fisher and Olive Rabe's We Alcotts (1968), a "few more biographies, laden with psychoanalytic interpretations, came in the last third of the 20th century as the entire field of literature began to be inundated with psycho-sociological critiques." Clearly feminist readings of Alcott are not engaged. The bibliography is nonetheless useful; the biography, though prosy, is informative; and some topics ("Alcott Sites as Literary Mecca") are helpful for the beginning researcher.—*J. J. Benardete, Hunter College, CUNY*

WS-0803　　　　PS2506　　　　92-33474 CIP
Dickenson, Donna. **Margaret Fuller: writing a woman's life.** St. Martin's, 1993. 247p index ISBN 0-312-09145-1, $35.00

Margaret Fuller (1810-50) is a complex and fascinating American writer, whose chief work is *Woman in the Nineteenth Century* (1845). A brilliant conversationalist and editor of the transcendentalist journal *The Dial*, she became a dramatic figure through her writings; her secret marriage in Italy to Giovanni Angelo Ossoli; her involvement in the Roman revolution (1848-49); and her tragic death in a shipwreck that also claimed her husband and son. Because she did not produce a work that has entered the canon of American literature as "major," interest in her has often focused on her relationships with other writers and the role of feminism in 19th-century America. This volume seeks to unravel how Fuller's reputation suffered at the hands of her male contemporaries, chiefly Emerson and Hawthorne, whose *The Blithedale Romance* (1852) is interpreted as containing a portrait of Fuller in the feminist Zenobia. The *Memoirs of Margaret Fuller Ossoli* (1852), published by Emerson and others, is here taken to be an exercise in denigration which helped to eclipse Fuller's true achievement. The only critic to escape the vitriol Dickenson liberally distributes here is Thomas Wentworth Higginson, who did not dismiss the full range of Fuller's talent. The book has telling points to make, but it is often a tedious polemic on St. Margaret and her enemies.—*H. J. Lindborg, Marian College of Fond Du Lac*

WS-0804　　　　PS303　　　　90-48495 MARC
Dickie, Margaret. **Lyric contingencies: Emily Dickinson and Wallace Stevens.** Pennsylvania, 1991. 196p indexes afp ISBN 0-8122-3077-9, $23.95

By focusing on the craft and the production of two great poets, Dickie (University of Georgia) illuminates the qualities of the lyric and its importance in American literature. For each poet in turn she analyzes the voice of the speaker in the poetry, the language characteristic of each author, and the audiences, real and imagined. Similarities and differences are illuminated through detailed analyses of many poems. By linking in this study a private woman of the 19th century with a public man of the 20th, Dickie presents a fairly comprehensive study of the relations between the lyric and American culture. In place of Emersonianism, which has usually been understood to unite these two poets, Dickie offers the philosophy of pragmatism as a better point of contact. Further, we come to see that the lyric is an overlooked genre in literary studies with historical preference going to the long poem. This is a useful book for scholars of poetry, the profession of literary studies, and women's studies.—*P. J. Ferlazzo, Northern Arizona University*

WS-0805   PS1541   95-11037 CIP
Doriani, Beth Maclay. **Emily Dickinson: daughter of prophecy.** Massachusetts, 1996. 230p indexes afp ISBN 0-87023-999-6, $35.00

As the tide of feminist readings of Dickinson ebbs, commentators focus more on placing her in the context of her times (Karl Keller, *The Only Kangaroo among the Beauty: Emily Dickinson and America*, CH, May'80, was one of the earliest of these) or addressing issues of form and style (e.g., Judy Jo Small's *Positive as Sound: Emily Dickinson's Rhyme*, CH, Apr'91, and Dorothy Oberhaus's *Emily Dickinson's Fascicles: Method & Meaning*, CH, Nov'95). The present title brings together both approaches, tracing the combined influence of the biblical books of prophecy and the rhetorical tradition of New England Puritan/Congregational preaching on both Dickinson's content and style. Doriani (Northwestern College) provides particularly useful commentary on Jonathan Edwards and Charles Wadsworth. Further, she places the poetry in the context of the kind of religious lyric being written by Dickinson's female contemporaries. In order to accomplish all this in a brief 200 pages, she was forced to scant her readings of the poems, often supplying readers instead with lists of relevant lyrics. Moreover, she tends to sacrifice the ambiguous, highly polysemous quality of much of Dickinson's poetry to establish the book's primary thesis. Still, this is a significant contribution to Dickinson scholarship and a corrective to some of the more extreme feminist readings of the poems. Recommended for collections in 19th-century American culture, as well as in Dickinson's life and work.—*S. R. Graham, emerita, Nazareth College of Rochester*

WS-0806   PS1294   93-4664 CIP
Dyer, Joyce. ***The awakening*: a novel of beginnings.** Twayne, 1993. 147p (Twayne's masterwork studies, 130) bibl index afp ISBN 0-8057-8382-2, $22.95; ISBN 0-8057-8383-0 pbk, $7.95

Kate Chopin's *The Awakening* (1899), after startling audiences upon publication, remained obscure until the last two decades. Now it is a staple of courses in American literature, women's literature, and southern literature. Dyer (Hiram College) has endeavored to present to readers a primer on the novel, introducing us, in concise and lucid prose, to its literary and historical contexts, its significance, and its critical reception. In this, she succeeds admirably. She also includes substantial readings of several key aspects of Chopin's novel: bird imagery, concepts of women's space, mythic scenes and references, depiction of the female artist, and various interpretations of Edna's suicide. Some of this interpretive material Dyer has previously published. All of it will be helpful to both teachers and students of the work. The volume is enriched by a careful chronology of Chopin's life, a substantial bibliography of Chopin's work and critical materials, and several photographs. Strongly recommended for all collections.—*E. R. Baer, Gustavus Adolphus College*

WS-0807   PS3332   91-44959 CIP
Evans, Augusta Jane. **Beulah,** ed. with an introd. by Elizabeth Fox-Genovese. Louisiana State, 1992. 420p afp ISBN 0-8071-1749-8, $45.00; ISBN 0-8071-1750-1 pbk, $16.95

The "Library of Southern Civilization" series brings the popular 1859 novel *Beulah* back into print with an excellent introduction by Elizabeth Fox-Genovese, author of *Within the Plantation Household* (CH, Sep'89). A model of domestic fiction, Evans's tale of an orphan's struggle to achieve independence as a teacher and writer frequently parallels Charlotte Brontë's *Jane Eyre*. More surprisingly, as Fox-Genovese explains, Evans also draws on Poe, Emerson, Coleridge, Carlyle, De Quincey, William Hamilton, and others who influence Beulah Benton's crisis of faith, the central concern of the book. Fox-Genovese provides biographical, historical, and cultural contexts for the story of Beulah's intellectual and emotional development from age 13 to 24, arguing that, to Evans's contemporaries, Beulah's eventual marriage to her guardian is a mark of Christian maturity, not a betrayal of her hard-won independence. The novel will be of great interest to students of women's literature, southern fiction, and the 19th-century novel, but the usefulness of this edition would be considerably enhanced by the addition of a bibliography and notes on the highly allusive text.—*J. W. Hall, University of Mississippi*

WS-0808   PS3332   91-30680 CIP
Evans, Augusta Jane. **Macaria, or, Altars of sacrifice,** ed. with an introd. by Drew Gilpin Faust. Louisiana State, 1992. 415p afp ISBN 0-8071-1661-0, $45.00; ISBN 0-8071-1662-9 pbk, $16.95

Like Evans's antebellum novel *Beulah* (also newly edited in 1992), *Macaria*—another tale of woman's self-realization, duty, and religious submission—is an important addition to the "Library of Southern Civilization" series. Faust, author of *The Creation of Confederate Nationalism* (1988), calls this 1864 best-seller the "quintessential war story for Confederate women," though the war dominates only the final fourth of the plot. As hospital volunteers for their "sacred cause," the amateur astronomer Irene Huntingdon and the artist Electra Grey resemble the lengendary Macaria, who saved Athens by sacrificing herself to the gods. Faust discusses the book as an uneasy "merger of the characteristic form of woman's fiction with that of the male war story." Evans wrote *Macaria* during a time of unprecedented challenge to "conventional gender roles" in "the very region where traditional notions of women's proper place had been most assiduously defended." Faust supplements her detailed introduction with "A Note on Augusta Jane Evans" and "A Note on Editions of *Macaria*," but there are no textual notes or bibliography. Recommended for general readers and for all academic libraries.—*J. W. Hall, University of Mississippi*

WS-0809   PS283   93-14023 CIP
Gallagher, Bernice E. **Illinois women novelists in the nineteenth century: an analysis and annotated bibliography.** Illinois, 1994. 206p afp ISBN 0-252-02065-0, $39.95

Gallagher's text provides an analysis and annotated bibliography of novels written by Illinois women and published between 1854 and 1893. Each work was selected for inclusion in the American section of the Woman's Building Library at the 1893 World's Columbian Exposition in Chicago. Gallagher has organized the book into two sections. The first describes the authors and their concerns; the second offers a synopsis of the 58 novels written by 36 authors. Gallagher argues that these novels are important because they provide "the first coherent collection assembled in America of works written, gathered, and cataloged by women." In addition, the work of these women writers "covered a broad range of human interest and proves a remarkable record of the social and intellectual history of the period." Gallagher's purpose is "to open this body of work to the scholarly investigation it deserves." She argues that such "neglected texts ... are valuable because they are particularly relevant to understanding the important religious beliefs, social practices, and economic and political environment that produced them." She sees these works as complex, rich, and more important than previously assumed, often providing "startling social critiques." The recovery of these texts by Illinois women novelists suggests perhaps that those novels submitted by other states to the exhibition might also prove valuable as scholars continue to evaluate and redefine the canon in American literature.—*R. McCaughey-Silvia, University of Rhode Island*

WS-0810   PS1018   93-17587 CIP
Keyser, Elizabeth Lennox. **Whispers in the dark: the fiction of Louisa May Alcott.** Tennessee, 1994 (c1993). 228p bibl index afp ISBN 0-87049-809-6, $32.95

Whispers in the Dark provides three remarkably useful services: it draws together and assesses the mass of Alcott criticism generated in the last 20 years; it provides well-contextualized readings of Alcott's corpus; and it bridges the prevailing critical gap between Alcott's "adult" fiction and her "juvenilia." Rather than seeing Alcott's adult fictions as subversive, radical and proto feminist, and her children's and domestic fiction as capitulations to those ideals, Keyser sees both as echoing similar themes in different registers. Their textual and rhetorical commonalities, and their conscious references to scenes in other Alcott pieces, highlight the critique of conventional values embodied even in the works most often considered conservative. To Keyser, this "stamp of intertextuality and self-referentiality" enables us to see Alcott's "imagination, if not always her conscious intent, with more ideological consistency and artistic control" than have often been ascribed to her. General and academic audiences.—*L. W. MacFarlane, University of New Hampshire*

WS-0811   PS1541.Z5   89-29460 CIP
Lease, Benjamin. **Emily Dickinson's readings of men and books: sacred soundings.** St. Martin's, 1990. 168p indexes ISBN 0-312-03650-7, $39.95

Lease (Northeastern Illinois) has used some of the biographical facts in Emily Dickinson's relationships to men, coordinated with the best information and scholarly conjectures about the circumstances of composition, to assist readers in understanding the significance of about 90 of Dickinson's poems on death, war, and immortality. The "readings" referred to in Lease's title are chiefly in the King James Bible; the 17th-century poets Vaughan, Traherne, and Herbert; Isaac Watts's hymns; and the periodical literature available in Dickenson's Amherst home. His book is a narrative series of illuminations and observations about the meaning of Dickinson's poems—not complete expositions, but useful clues to the metaphors that often startle or baffle even the experienced reader. The very full notes, the listing by first lines of the poems, and the excellent subject indexing are essential assets for students. Wherever Emily Dickinson's poetry is a subject of study, or even where she will be read attentively with appreciation, this book should be added to the shelves of good secondary criticism.—*A. E. Jones Jr., emeritus, Drew University*

WS-0812   PS153   91-47015 CIP
Lichtenstein, Diane. **Writing their nations: the tradition of nineteenth-century American Jewish women writers.** Indiana, 1992. 176p bibl index afp ISBN 0-253-33346-6, $24.95

Examining a body of work that has been almost entirely neglected—that produced by 19th-century Jewish American literary women, Lichtenstein makes a valuable contribution to Jewish studies and to women's studies. Rather than arguing for a canon that insists on meritocracy of texts, she describes a tradition based on ethnicity and gender. Many of the texts share common cultural values and myths and include Jewish, American, and female semiotic codes and similar themes, topics, and tropes. Central to Lichtenstein's analysis are the mythic ideals of "the Mother in Israel" and "the True Woman," myths about "the Jewish family functioning to preserve Judaism," and myths of "the specialness of Jews" which she contends provided the women a way to think and feel about themselves. Lichtenstein traces patterns of the writers' efforts to fuse both American and Jewish myths of womanhood as well as traditional and progressive gender expectations. Since marginality and ethnicity were essentially linked for the American Jewish woman writer, consciousness of dual loyalites appears as a recurrent theme of this literary tradition. More than 25 Sephardic and German Jewish writers are studied; most are rescued from obscurity, but some are of established reputation (e.g., Emma Lazarus and Edna Ferber). A significant record of the relationship of gender and Jewish ethnicity to American literary studies. Notes; comprehensive bibliography. Graduate students; researchers; faculty; general readers.—*S. L. Kremer, Kansas State University*

WS-0813   PS2502   94-18710 CIP
Margaret Fuller's New York journalism: a biographical essay and key writings, ed. by Catherine C. Mitchell. Tennessee, 1995. 228p bibl index afp ISBN 0-87049-870-3, $32.50

In this important study, Mitchell (Univ. of North Carolina at Ashville) adds yet another dimension to those offered in the recent explosion of books on Fuller's life by providing an intriguing look at her role in the history of American journalism. Mitchell's stated purpose in publishing this study is "to reclaim an often overlooked aspect" of Fuller's work, and at that she succeeds admirably. In a short but useful biographical essay, Mitchell cites criticisms of Fuller by *New York Tribune* editor Horace Greeley as the reason for the historical neglect, but she compellingly argues that, despite his complaints, Greeley actually valued Fuller's work and accorded her considerable latitude in overseeing the *Tribune*'s literary department. Mitchell also examines the history and political character of the *Tribune* and assesses Fuller's contributions. But the real value of this title lies in its retrieval of several of Fuller's articles on topics such as class struggles, prison and asylum reform, equal rights, abolitionism, and physical education. The only real deficiency in this otherwise fine volume is a surprisingly inadequate index that fails to provide a thorough listing of the subjects and figures referred to in the text. Recommended for undergraduates, graduates, and researchers.—*D. D. Knight, SUNY College at Cortland*

WS-0814   PS3174   91-40053 CIP
Morris, Linda A. **Women's humor in the age of gentility: the life and works of Frances Miriam Whitcher.** Syracuse, 1992. 253p bibl index afp ISBN 0-8156-2562-6, $32.50

Morris's book reclaims a historically neglected antebellum woman writer. Interweaving well-documented biography, close textual analysis of published columns, and social history, Morris recreates the context and analyzes the stylistic devices of this popular and influential female humorist. Whitcher satirizes the manners and mores of the emerging middle class in the young American republic through her finely crafted use of dialect. Her series of classic characters include the obsessive and self-absorbed Widow Priscilla Bedott, and her more subdued sister, Aunt Maguire. Episodes are often drawn from the author's life experiences as the wife of an Episcopalian minister in the provincial towns of upstate New York. Published frequently in *Godey's Ladies Book* and in Neal's *Saturday Gazette*, Whitcher's writings provided her a safe outlet for her insightful critiques and a modest income until her authorship was discovered. Morris's readership is broad, and she articulates connections between Whitcher and her well-known successor, Marietta Holley.—*S. Danielson, Portland State University*

WS-0815   PS1774   94-15269 CIP
Okker, Patricia. **Our sister editors: Sarah J. Hale and the tradition of nineteenth-century American women editors.** Georgia, 1995. 264p bibl index afp ISBN 0-8203-1686-5, $40.00

This is the first book-length study of Sarah J. Hale's career as editor of *Ladies Magazine* from 1828 to 1836 and then as literary editor of *Godey's Lady's Book* from 1837 to 1877. Okker (Univ. of Missouri—Columbia) attributes Hale's success in part to her belief in women's essential difference from men and in their separate spheres. But in addition to Hale's efforts to enhance women's status in their own domain—she coined the term "domestic science"—she sought to bring women into public life as members of professions and as reformers, though not into party politics. Okker discusses Hale's strategies to enhance authorship as a profession for women and her efforts to diversify their reading. Finally, a revisionist account of Hale's aesthetics of poetry and fiction argues persuasively that she favored neither sentimental nor moralistic verse, as often alleged, though her definition of realism in fiction was severely limited by her faith in the triumph of the good. A 53-page appendix identifies more than 600 19th-century American women editors and gives sources for information on them. Endnotes and an impressive bibliography attest to the high level of scholarship sustained throughout this important and well-written book.—*M. S. Vogeler, emeritus, California State University, Fullerton*

WS-0816   PS1711   91-48011 CIP
Reichardt, Mary R. **The uncollected stories of Mary Wilkins Freeman.** Mississippi, 1992. 332p afp ISBN 0-87805-564-9, $40.00

Twenty previously uncollected short stories by this turn-of-the-century writer are framed by Reichardt's useful introduction and impressive Freeman bibliography. Organized chronologically, stories like "Emmy" and "Friend of My Heart" repeat well-known Freeman themes of women's muted rebellion and internal strength. "Sweet-Flowering Perennial" suggests her skill with the popular mystery genre; at least five stories offer male protagonists. Several stories trace the ways in which women's artistic sensibility, as expressed through traditional "female" arts, provides a life-sustaining force for those often confined either by economic or family circumstance or by personal choice to a single life. Concluding this remarkable collection is Freeman's last published story, "The Jester." One of her undated and unfinished manuscripts, "The White Shawl," is offered with alternative endings. None of these stories offers a radical rereading of Freeman's work, but her wry, detached presentation of character and action allow the reader an uncomfortable nostalgia for a time before women had alternatives to domesticity and before technology had invaded every portal of their privacy.—*S. Danielson, Portland State University*

WS-0817   PS1713   91-32352 CIP
Reichardt, Mary R. **A web of relationship: women in the short stories of Mary Wilkins Freeman.** University Press of Mississippi, 1992. 186p bibl index afp ISBN 0-87805-555-X, $35.00

Freeman (1852-1930), a New England writer, has enjoyed a renaissance of interest in the past two decades. Her short stories had long been neglected until a Feminist Press edition with an afterword by Michele Clark (1974) and a selection edited by Marjorie Pryse (CH, Nov'83). In 1991 Shirley Marchalonis edited *Critical Essays on Mary Wilkins Freeman* (CH, Feb'92), the first such collection. Now Reichardt (Univ. of St. Thomas) has added another first to the growing Freeman bibliography: a full-length study of her short fiction. Signaling her focus with her title, Reichardt moves beyond other analyses, which concentrate on the rebellion of Freeman's women characters, to a study of the web of relationships in these character's lives. Specifically, Reichardt is interested in the moral struggle that results form the conflict between a desire for independence and "an equally strong desire to build and maintain relationships with others." Including chapters on biography and context, the volume introduces readers to heretofore unknown stories and provides fresh readings of old favorites, such as "The Revolt of Mother." Reichardt writes about the range of women's relationships in Freeman's stories: with parents, husbands, other women, and the Calvinist God. The appendix provides the first complete bibliography of Freeman's work. Undergraduate; graduate.—*E. R. Baer, Gustavus Adolphus College*

WS-0818   PS2133   90-20598 CIP
Roman, Margaret. **Sarah Orne Jewett: reconstructing gender.** Alabama, 1992. 246p bibl index afp ISBN 0-8173-0533-5, $28.95

This comprehensive study effectively demonstrates the many ways by which Jewett's fiction subverts conventional gender dichotomies dictating male and female roles in a patriarchal society. Analyzing a wide range of types in the novels and stories (e.g. the aristocratic woman, fairy godmother, independent single woman, paralyzed man, rebellious child), Roman progresses from adolescent characters' stagtegies of resistance, to the psychological destruction of characters trapped in conventional romantic relationships and "standard" marriages, to the fulfillment of both male and female characters who break free of rigid gender categories. Roman not only offers illuminating analyses of well-known works such as "The White Heron" and *The Country of the Pointed Firs*, but also shows the central importance of gender in scores of stories that have received little or no critical attention. Roman achieves a balanced view of Jewett which acknowledges the importance in the writer's life and in her fiction of opportunities both in communities of women and in male-dominated spheres. The argument is informed by concepts important in feminist criticism but is developed in nontechnical language that recommends the book to all students as well as to teachers of American literature and women's studies.—*E. Nettels, College of William and Mary*

WS-0819   PS2798   CIP
Sedgwick, Catharine Maria. **The power of her sympathy: the autobiography and journal of Catharine Maria Sedgwick,** ed. with introd. by Mary Kelley. Massachusetts Historical Society, 1993. 165p index ISBN 0-934909-35-0, $25.00; ISBN 0-934909-36-9 pbk, $8.95

Kelley (Dartmouth College) has performed an invaluable service to students of 19th-century American literature by editing and publishing the autobiography and journals of Catharine Maria Sedgwick, one of the country's first women fiction writers. The author of six novels and close to 100 tales published between 1822-1857, Sedgwick was a literary pioneer whose works and reputation helped open the field to other women writers in the 19th century. Some of her most important works have been reprinted in recent years, and now the publication of her autobiography and journals will make available in her own words Sedgwick's view on such topics as her childhood experiences, family relationships, educational background, and her ambivalence about her celebrated public career. Kelley's lucidly written and well-documented critical introduction is informative, and it places Sedgwick's writing in the social, political, and historical contexts of the years spanning the American Revolution and the Civil War. Moreover, Kelley traces the means by which Sedgwick negotiates the gender conventions of antebellum America in order to define a persona that was uniquely her own. An indispensable resource for any library.—*D. D. Knight, SUNY College at Cortland*

WS-0820   PS2133   92-24589 CIP
Silverthorne, Elizabeth. **Sarah Orne Jewett: a writer's life.** Overlook Press, 1993. 238p bibl index ISBN 0-87951-484-1, $22.95

A clear chronological account of Jewett's development as a Victorian woman and a writer, with useful attention to her early contribution to popular maga-

zines for "young people." Silverthorne treats Jewett's attachment to her father and her friendship with Theophilus Parsons, the Harvard professor of law who introduced her to Swedenborgianism and so resolved some youthful religious concerns. Jewett's relationship with Annie Adams Fields—often the subject of feminist speculation—is discussed, but nothing new appears. The documentary evidence of their years together was, of course, sorted and edited by Mrs. Fields, who survived Jewett and produced a volume of her letters. Those interested in evaluating the relationship will want to consider Fields's production of the epistolary legacy usefully summarized in Judith A. Roman's *Annie Adams Fields* (CH, Apr'91). Undergraduate (all levels); advanced undergraduate; graduate; general.—*J. J. Benardete, Hunter College, CUNY*

WS-0821   PS1332   94-19712 CIP
Skandera-Trombley, Laura E. **Mark Twain in the company of women.** Pennsylvania, 1994. 219p bibl index afp ISBN 0-8122-3218-6, $29.95

This study is of genuine interest to Twain specialists and American studies scholars. Skandera-Trombley (SUNY-Potsdam) successfully presents and supports her significant interpretation that Twain was highly influenced by the women in his life, principally Olivia Langdon and her family of Elmira, NY. The Langdons and their friends, along with many citizens of Elmira, were actively involved in reform movements such as women's suffrage and slave abolition. The author closely examines the long-accepted criticism of Van Wyck Brooks and Bernard DeVoto and convincingly modifies or refutes their conclusions on the social and cultural practices of the Langdon family, especially how they influenced Twain's personal and literary beliefs. Skandera-Trombley indisputably establishes Twain's acceptance of and reliance on the advanced thinking of his wife. Also, of unusual background interest are the two chapters on the city of Elmira (including Elmira College and Elmira Reformatory), abolition, feminism, and cultural advancements. Because it is trailblazing in its thesis, painstaking in its extensive research, and resolutely efficacious in its presentation, this monograph deserves full recognition and sincere accolades for its author. Bibliography and index are both superior in their thoroughness and reliability. Undergraduate and up.—*G. O. Carey, emeritus, Eastern Kentucky University*

WS-0822   PS1541.Z5   89-29073 CIP
Small, Judy Jo. **Positive as sound: Emily Dickinson's rhyme.** Georgia, 1990. 261p bibl indexes afp ISBN 0-8203-1227-4, $35.00

The last 20 years have seen an increasing flood of brilliant readers of Dickinson. But Small has the distinction of being the first to listen closely to the poet. As many have long suspected—and as the author convincingly demonstrates—Dickinson's ostensibly erratic, even bizarre, rhymes are purposeful and, in her best poems, not only enhance meaning, but direct it. Small has greatly advanced the next major task confronting Dickinson commentators: close attention to matters of technique. Only Cristanne Miller's recent study (*Emily Dickinson: A Poet's Grammar*, CH, Jul'87) has followed up two studies now more than 20 years old: Sirkka Heiskanen-Makela's *In Quest of Truth: Observations on the Development of Emily Dickinson's Poetic Dialectic* (Jyraskyla, Finland, 1970) and Brita Lindberg-Seyersted's seminal study, *The Voice of the Poet* (CH, May'69). Small's insightful and judicious study reminds us once again that great poetry is inseparable from great technique and that Dickinson's enduring appeal, far from a triumph of content over form, depends upon the remarkable fusion of the two. An excellent discussion of English rhyme generally is powerfully reinforced by specific application to Dickinson's poems, enlightening the reader about both. Highly recommended for upper-division undergraduate and graduate students and for would-be writers of poetry. Thorough notes.—*S. R. Graham, Nazareth College of Rochester*

WS-0823   PS1541   92-6368 CIP
Smith, Martha Nell. **Rowing in Eden: rereading Emily Dickinson.** Texas, 1993 (c1992). 286p bibl index afp ISBN 0-292-72084-X, $35.00; ISBN 0-292-77666-7 pbk, $13.95

Traditional Dickinson scholarship has interpreted the relationship between the poet and her sister-in-law, Sue Gilbert Dickinson, as close and usually friendly. They lived next door to each other and shared mutual family interests and problems, and suffered together through the occasional annoyances and jealousies that can surface between close family members. Further, the traditionalists have said, Emily appreciated Sue's interest in her poetry. Smith challenges the traditional point of view and argues that Emily was passionately in love with Sue, wrote poetry to and about Sue, and told the story of her hidden and painful love for Sue in many of her poems and letters. Smith asks serious and important questions about love and gender and poetic inspiration based upon the insights available through feminist and poststructuralist criticism. Further, she charges the literary establishment with creating layers of censorship upon the poetry, the letters, and the facts of Emily Dickinson's life in order to sustain a popular and acceptable myth about the poet. That myth portrayed her as a "New England nun" who withdrew from public life because of a love for an unnamed and unreachable man. Smith's book is a well-argued and insightful reinterpretation of the poet, which will be of interest to all readers of American literature and culture.— *P. J. Ferlazzo, Northern Arizona University*

WS-0824   PR9199   94-14202 CIP
Sui Sin Far. **Mrs. Spring Fragrance and other writings,** by Sui Sin Far; ed. by Amy Ling and Annette White-Parks. Illinois, 1995. 296p afp ISBN 0-252-02133-9, $39.95; ISBN 0-252-06419-4 pbk, $15.95

WS-0824a   PR9199   94-6448 CIP
White-Parks, Annette. **Sui Sin Far/Edith Maude Eaton: a literary biography.** Illinois, 1995. 268p bibl index afp ISBN 0-252-02113-4, $34.95

These companion books, a literary biography and a selected works, mark the rediscovery of turn-of-the-century writer Edith Maude Eaton (1865-1914). Popular in her time but forgotten until identified as the first Asian North American to publish English fiction, she wrote under the pen name Sui Sin Far. Eaton was raised in Canada by a Chinese-born mother educated in England and an unsuccessful English merchant father. Her most memorable fiction and journalism evoke her Chinese friends in Montreal, Seattle, San Francisco, and Boston. A self-doubting, malarial, rootless, unmarried intellectual woman of mixed race championing the Chinese, Eaton was the ultimate marginalized writer. White racism made her sympathize with the Chinese, with whom she chose to identify; her sister Winnifred, the first Asian North American *novelist*—originally more popular than Sui Sin Far—feigned the more prestigious Japanese identity and wrote as a Japanese under the name Onoto Watanna. Since Sui Sin Far was not culturally Chinese (and her mother was only partly so) the implications for the academic construction of anti-Orientalism as racism, and for ethnic authenticity as a literary touchstone, are mind boggling. Using race, gender, identity, and choice as the crux of her text, White-Parks (Univ. of Wisconsin, LaCrosse) has written a sympathetic and lucid life story that is factually definitive thanks to meticulous and imaginative historical use of literary sources. The collection of Sui Sin Far's writing likewise shows her to best advantage. The editors wisely placed her journalism about life in Chinatowns—demonstrating both her desire to ameliorate racism against "her people" and her status as cultural outsider—at the end of the volume. The fiction is better—historically important, richly ambiguous, and often surprising in its treatment of all manner of cultural and biological boundaries. Laypersons may like Sui Sin Far's stories not for their feminism and multiculturalism, but as Victorian comedies of manners sensitive to the downtrodden. Eaton's life invites further probing: her faith, use of language, conflict with her mother, and intriguing parallels to writer-journalist-activists in China.—*J. C. Kinkley, St. John's University (NY)*

WS-0825   PS374   91-46931 CIP
Tate, Claudia. **Domestic allegories of political desire: the black heroine's text at the turn of the century.** Oxford, 1993 (c1992). 302p bibl index afp ISBN 0-19-507389-4, $35.00

Tate's fascinating study of 11 post-Reconstruction domestic novels by African American women argues that what may read like idealized, bourgeois romances were in fact important contributions to emancipatory cultural discourse. Tate focuses here on novels that, with the exception of Harper's *Tola Leroy* (1892), were out of print for decades until the recent publication of the "Schomburg Library of Nineteenth-Century Black Women Writers" and are consequently still little known. Reconstructing the cultural conditions of these novels' production, Tate shows how the apparently apolitical "black Victorian love stories," in her phrase, provided an entry point into literature for their writers and also participated in the discourse of racial uplift fostered by black women's clubs during the 1890s. The first chapter, on maternal discourse as social protest, and the last, on Angelina

Weld Grimke's use of domestic tragedy as racial protest, which also takes the reader up to the present, are particularly strong. Highly recommended. Advanced undergraduate; graduate; faculty.—*M. T. Reddy, Rhode Island College*

WS-0826   PS1294.C63   90-37894 CIP
Toth, Emily. **Kate Chopin**. W. Morrow, 1990. 528p bibl index afp ISBN 0-688-09707-3, $27.95

This new biography of Kate Chopin has long been awaited by scholars aware of Toth's dissertation on Chopin, "That Outward Existence Which Conforms" (Johns Hopkins, 1975). Earlier biographies by Daniel Rankin (1932) and Per Seyersted (CH, Sep'70) do not reflect the insights of the past two decades of feminist literary criticism. Toth's biography is a big book, full of detail, replete with photographs, a chronology of Chopin's life, a bibliography of all her known writings, another of related works; and extensive documentation of sources. Some of the detail provided by Toth (Louisiana State University) is directly relevant to a better understanding of Chopin's work: for example, lists of childhood reading will be very helpful for intertextual study; some of the detail, however, is in the nature of human interest, even trivia. Toth has effectively used extensive quotations from Chopin's youthful commonplace book and other personal writing to illuminate her development as a writer; these materials, hitherto not easily available, will soon be forthcoming as *Kate Chopin's Private Papers*, edited by Toth and Seyersted. Toth also raises a provocative question about the fate of Chopin's best-known work, *The Awakening* (1899): it appears that it may not have been banned from libraries and its author from literary clubs as numerous scholars have previously claimed. Despite its occasionally grating tone, Toth's book is strongly recommended for all libraries. It will be the standard biography for some years to come.—*E. R. Baer, Washington College*

WS-0827   PS2506   94-18663 CIP
Von Mehren, Joan. **Minerva and the muse: a life of Margaret Fuller.** Massachusetts, 1995 (c1994). 398p index ISBN 0-87023-941-4, $40.00

Von Mehren's biography of the 19th-century journalist, educator, writer, and feminist thinker is a praiseworthy addition to the booming field of Fuller scholarship. With her meticulous research, Von Mehren has written a notable addition to previously published biographies, including Donna Dickenson's *Margaret Fuller: Writing a Woman's Life* (CH, Jan'94), Madeleine B. Stern's *The Life of Margaret Fuller* (rev. 2nd ed., 1991), and Charles Capper's monumental two-volume *Margaret Fuller: An American Romantic Life* (v.1, CH, Apr'93). Although Capper's work in particular achieves a broader historical and social scope, Von Mehren captures Fuller's individual character and the progress of her life. She portrays Fuller as divided between her Minerva side—the public intellectual—and the Muse side—the sensitive woman who sought intimacy. Von Mehren's exploration of these two sides of Fuller creates a lucid picture of what it must have been like to be a woman "determined on distinction," as Fuller once commented, in the early 19th century and pulled in different directions by societal forces. Because of its clarity and Von Mehren's careful research, this biography deserves a place in any large academic library and would be as suitable for upper-division undergraduates as for graduate students and professors.—*S. A. Inness, Miami University*

WS-0828   PS1541   91-10945 CIP
Walsh, John Evangelist. **This brief tragedy: unraveling the Todd-Dickinson affair.** Grove Weidenfeld, 1991. 230p bibl index afp ISBN 0-8021-1119-X, $19.95

A provocative reconsideration of several aspects of Emily Dickinson's biography that literary scholars had come to accept as indisputably settled. Richard Sewall (*The Life of Emily Dickinson*, CH, Jun'75), and Polly Longsworth (*Austin and Mabel*, 1984) had more or less established the definitive points of view regarding the love affair between Emily's brother, Austin, and Mabel Todd; the character and personality of Susan Dickinson; the nature of Mabel Todd's commitment to serving as the first editor of Emily's poetry; the situation surrounding Emily's death; and the land dispute between Lavinia Dickinson and Mabel Todd. Through a bold new interpretation of the record, Walsh presents an effective reinterpretation or modification of all of these items. Perhaps the most challenging of all has to do with the poet's death. The long-held belief was that her death was the result of physical deterioration relating to Bright's disease, a kidney ailment. Walsh proposes that Emily Dickinson, distraught over her brother's affair, the deaths of her favorite nephew, Gilbert, and of her beloved Judge Otis Lord, hastened her own death by refusing proper medical treatment and by ingesting a poison, such as strychnine. Such is the unsettling nature of this book, which seriously challenges scholarly complacency. Appropriate for graduate students and upper-division undergraduates.—*P. J. Ferlazzo, Northern Arizona University*

WS-0829   PS2523   91-20382 CIP
Warren, Joyce W. **Fanny Fern: an independent woman.** Rutgers, 1992. 374p index ISBN 0-8135-1763-X, $29.95

This superior biography brings a once-popular 19th-century writer, now unknown, to full, vivid life. Born Sarah Payson Willis (1811-72), this deacon's daughter, always a rebel, as an adult wrote and was known to all as Fanny Fern. Her "hostility and wit" in her essays, short stories, and novels revealed a writer of humor, realism, and energy. Her Boston newspaper columns made her the first woman newspaper columnist and the highest-paid newspaper writer. She scandalized critics by writing of such topics as venereal disease, prostitution, birth control, religious narrowness, and a questioning of male authority. Widowed, then divorced (her second husband spread lies about her), she enjoyed a successful third marriage. Warren chronicles Fern's friendships with Walt Whitman, Harriet Beecher Stowe, Horace Greeley, and Harriet Jacobs. Her *Ruth Hall* was praised by Nathaniel Hawthorne but criticized by other reviewers for its deviation from the role prescribed for women. This enthusiastic biography should revive an interest in Fanny Fern's writing. Contains photos and excellent notes. Very highly recommended for women's studies collections.—*J. Overmyer, Ohio State University*

◆ United States
20th Century (1900 - 1950)

WS-0830   PS3552   94-41552 CIP
Binstock, R.C. **Tree of heaven.** Soho Press, 1995. 212p ISBN 1-56947-038-3, $22.00

Winner of the Washington Prize, Binstock's second book (after the story collection *The Light of Home*, 1992) is a poetic miniature epic of 24 chapters narrated by two quixotic protagonists. One is a Japanese botanist, now an unhappy officer in occupied China who detests his soldiers' participation in "the rape of Nanking" and dislikes the Chinese, whom he neither understands nor respects; the other is a Chinese woman whom the reluctant captain saves from his men. The two engage in a dance of loving gestures, but the plot, which seems destined for a clichéd culmination of salvational love, curls instead toward lost hope and tragedy. The enemies approach their grail of love and rapport, but they carry the separate lands of their birth with them. Ancient habits color every action and thought, clinging like two native soils to young plants, nourishing but limiting movement. The title refers to the botanical "tree of heaven," the ailanthus plant, a weedy, stubborn growth as tough as the Chinese woman and her beaten nation, and as sun-seeking as the proud Japanese soldier-teacher. Like Amy Tan's *The Joy Luck Club* and the stories of Yukio Mishima, this novel tests and extends Western audiences. Highly recommended for all collections of American literature, women's studies, comparative literature, and Asian studies.—*R. H. Solomon, University of Alberta*

WS-0831   PS3505   94-17434 CIP
Brienzo, Gary. **Willa Cather's transforming vision: New France and the American northeast.** Susquehanna University, 1995 (c1994). (Dist. by Associated University Presses) 120p bibl index afp ISBN 0-945636-66-0, $28.50

The main concern of this book is to show how Cather's heightened awareness of domesticity permeates *Shadows on the Rock* (1931) and the fiction that followed it. Brienzo (Nebraska Wesleyan Univ.) concedes that the point is not new, acknowledging his debt to recent critics. Not having a new perspective to offer, Brienzo soon loses focus, and the book also becomes a study of Sarah Orne Jewett's influence on Cather and an account of Cather's use of her sources for

Shadows on the Rock. He becomes tentative, content to note or record rather than to interpret, other than in corroboration of a previous critic's observation. One misses a larger vision in the book. Brienzo does not see, for instance, how Cather throughout her career explores North American history in various aspects (she is far from being the regional novelist that she is commonly considered). And, although conscious of her strong interest in French culture, he never remarks how powerfully her exquisite style is influenced by her readings in French. The book is pleasant and interesting, but its material would have been more appropriately reorganized into an article or two. Recommended for all levels.—*J. B. Beston, Nazareth College of Rochester*

WS-0832   PS3523   95-13118 CIP
Burke, Carolyn. **Becoming modern: the life of Mina Loy.** Farrar, Straus & Giroux, 1996. 494p bibl index ISBN 0-374-10964-8, $35.00

Until now Loy has been the forgotten woman of modernism. Burke had access to family papers, so this assiduously researched and lushly detailed first biography is likely to be the definitive one. The narration is smooth with occasional gentle barbs. Loy, a cerebral/passionate vagabond, ranged across three continents before settling in New York and Aspen. Supported for decades by her father, Loy traveled, had servants, and pursued several arts. Once considered Marianne Moore's only rival, the poet was strikingly beautiful, sardonic, enigmatic, and "free." A friend of Gertrude Stein and Ezra Pound, she married Oscar Wilde's nephew; her friends, associates, and enemies constitute a who's who of modernism. The epitome of the "New Woman," she mixed a feminist personal style with a clinically detached view of romantic materials. Burke's perceptive work may not change the history of modernism, but it brings a fine, neglected poet to a new and wider audience. A comprehensive bibliography and generous samples of Loy's poems make it even more valuable for all collections of literary modernism and postmodernism. A jewel of the biographer's art. All collections.—*J. N. Igo Jr., San Antonio College*

WS-0833   PS3511   93-33642 CIP
Clarke, Deborah. **Robbing the mother: women in Faulkner.** University Press of Mississippi, 1994. 168p bibl index afp ISBN 0-87805-592-4, $30.00

Faulkner offers fertile territory for exploration of feminist issues. His comment that, "If a writer has to rob his mother, he will not hesitate; the 'Ode on a Grecian Urn' is worth any number of old ladies," serves as the springboard for a new study of his creativity as a figurative theft. Clarke (Pennsylvania State Univ.) demonstrates a genuine affection for Faulkner's work and a knowledge of the vast body of relevant literary criticism, as well as the rapidly growing gender criticism. Using several of Faulkner's major novels, Clarke locates and discusses the silences and omissions, the nonlinguistic communication—the modes of discourse associated with women. She also teases out examples of sexual and linguistic control associated with men, and demonstrates the potential in both genders for transgression of boundaries. Combining pairs of novels for discussion, she explores the evidence with considerable imagination and tenacity. Building carefully, Clarke convinces us that the intersection of the law of the father with the body of the mother, the physical and linguistic, is a source of Faulkner's amazing creativity. Upper-division undergraduate and up.—*N. Tischler, Pennsylvania State University, University Park Campus*

WS-0834   PS3523   93-32515 CIP
Davis, Thadious M. **Nella Larsen, novelist of the Harlem Renaissance: a woman's life unveiled.** Louisiana State, 1994. 492p index afp ISBN 0-8071-1866-4, $34.95

Meticulously researched and well-written this biography of Nella Larsen (1891-1964), Harlem Renaissance novelist, presents detailed and vivid accounts. Larsen was a "self-created persona," whose actual name, birth and death dates, parentage, and possible plagiarism of one short story are unclear. Davis does trace Larsen's schooling for and employment as a librarian and a nurse. She explores Larsen's marriage to and divorce from Elmer S. Imes, a noted scientist; her distancing from her "white" sister; her friendship with such notables as Carl Van Vechten and Walter White; and her alienation from the "upper classes of African Americans." Davis offers intelligent analyses of Larsen's two novels, *Passing* and *Quicksand*. This biography offers considerable insight into the fascinating people and circumstances of the Harlem Renaissance. Photographs, footnotes, an index, and a bibliography complete the volume. Highly recommended for Women's Studies, Black Studies, and English literature libraries.—*J. Overmyer, Ohio State University*

WS-0835   PS3507   94-13823 CIP
Edmunds, Susan. **Out of line: history, psychoanalysis, & montage in H.D.'s long poems.** Stanford, 1995 (c1994). 243p bibl index afp ISBN 0-8047-2370-2, $35.00

Edmund's psychoanalytic reading of H.D.'s three late long poems—*Trilogy, Helen in Egypt,* and *Hermetic Definition*—ingeniously mixes in a number of more social or "historicizing" orientations, including feminist and postcolonial perspectives, in an attempt to render the profound ambivalence (of all kinds, really, but especially between transporting psychic transcendence and painful social involvement) that the author (Syracuse Univ.) believes drives the poems' dynamics. Part of Edmunds's effort is, of course, for the purpose of elucidating the poems themselves, but a considerable part of it seems dedicated to the "rehabilitation" of the controversial psychoanalyst Melanie Klein, whose renegade (i.e., un-Freudian) concepts and theories, Edmunds argues, lie at the heart not only of H.D.'s meaning and rhetorical strategies but of work by such luminaries as Lacan and Kristeva. This extraliterary polemic sometimes grows tendentious, and Edmunds sometimes contrives readings simply to achieve accord with Kleinian ideas. Indeed, Edmunds herself acknowledges (in a poststructuralist "ambivalence" about her own interpretation) that there is no real evidence of H.D.'s deliberate application of Klein's thinking. These provocative, if sometimes arcane, readings offer insights into literary, mythic, and psychoanalytic concepts of the female principles at work in H.D.'s poetry. Graduate and research collections.—*R. J. Cirasa, Kean College of New Jersey*

WS-0836   PS3545   94-38996 CIP
Fedorko, Kathy A. **Gender and the gothic in the fiction of Edith Wharton.** Alabama, 1995. 198p bibl index afp ISBN 0-8173-0788-5, $34.95

Fedorko (Middlesex County College) traces and explores the psychic/sexual history of the characters in Wharton's works and of Wharton as well. Drawing on Jung and postmodern psychological and feminist critics such as Normand Holland, Leona Sherman, Jacques Lacan, and Julia Kristeva, the author establishes the idea that gothic literature "probed fears, spoke the unspeakable, meddled in the taboo ... especially incest." She shows how Wharton's works—from the less known short stories such as "Angel at the Grave," "The Eyes," and "Miss Mary Pask" to the major works including *Summer, The Age of Innocence,* and *The Gods Arrive*—are examples of what Joseph Wiesenfarth in *Gothic Manners and the Classic English Novel* (CH, Jul'89) refers to as the "new Gothic," which depicts "intense internal states rather than external terror." Divided into five chapters—one establishing the thesis and one for each of four epochs in Wharton's life, 1900-05, 1906-16, 1917-26, and 1927-37—this book provides the Wharton scholar with a new view of Wharton's inner life and the fictional characters reflecting that life. Upper-division undergraduate and above.—*B. M. McNeal, Slippery Rock University of Pennsylvania*

WS-0837   PS3545   94-34537 CIP
Ferrell, Nancy Warren. **Barrett Willoughby: Alaska's forgotten lady.** University of Alaska Press, 1994. 184p bibl index afp ISBN 0-912006-76-5 pbk, $14.95

Ferrell's *Barrett Willoughby* combines biographical narrative with supportive photographs and a comprehensive bibliography. Aimed at a general audience, Ferrell's work provides an overview of the life and works of a woman who captured the spirit of Alaskan life before the land became fully integrated into the United States. The daughter of immigrants, Florence Barrett was born in Wisconsin in 1886, not reaching her beloved Alaska til the late 1890s. After a series of Alaskan adventures and two divorces, Florence settled in San Francisco, where she became a secretary and pursued a writing career under the pen name Barrett Willoughby. For the next 35 years she made her living through her pen, frequently returning to Alaska to research her 11 works of fiction and nonfiction, and numerous articles. Each romantic adventure focuses on some aspect of outdoor life, from the salmon run to the fur trade. At least two, *Spawn of the North* (1932) and *Rocking Moon* (1925), became motion pictures. Ferrell's

focus on Willoughby's dedicated writing process and her thorough documentation of Willoughby's work make her biography an invaluable resource for future scholars. General; faculty.—*S. Danielson, Portland State University*

WS-0838   PS3545   93-35841 CIP
Fracasso, Evelyn E. **Edith Wharton's prisoners of consciousness: a study of theme and technique in the tales.** Greenwood, 1994. 138p (Contributions in women's studies, 140) bibl index afp ISBN 0-313-29155-1, $45.00

Although a few of Wharton's tales have been anthologized and singled out for commentary, her 11 volumes of 86 tales have been largely ignored by critics for a variety of reasons including her slight and pessimistic subject matter. Fracasso takes those stories of Wharton's considered most unworthy of attention and analyzes their thematic and technical achievement. The subject that dominates Wharton's short stories, in Fracasso's view, is the theme of imprisonment, of "prisoners of consciousness." The early techniques employed by Wharton to present her imprisonment theme include provocative openers, symbolic settings, dramatic irony and satire, eye imagery, revealing sign-posts, and an illuminating incident. In her later short fiction, she further develops irony and satire and uses new techniques such as explicit images of imprisonment, images of the heart, the frame, the flashback, and the interior monologue. Although not all of Wharton's tales concern imprisonment, some do, and Fracasso has brought them to light with a knowledgeable hand. Lower and upper-division undergraduates; pre-professional students.—*S. M. Nuernberg, University of Wisconsin-Oshkosh*

WS-0839   PS3507   90-33126 CIP
Friedman, Susan Stanford. **Penelope's web: gender, modernity, H.D.'s fiction.** Cambridge, 1991 (c1990). 451p index ISBN 0-521-25579-1, $39.50

This groundbreaking reading of Hilda Doolittle's innovative, often daring, prose refigures its and gender's contribution to modernism. Friedman (University of Wisconsin, Madison), author of *Psyche Reborn: The Emergence of H.D.* (1981), reads the discourses of H.D.'s impersonal, public poetry and her autobiographical, thus frequently suppressed, prose as oppositional, yet symbiotic. Within a "web" of current critical theories, some of which H.D.'s prose anticipates, Friedman sets up the "double weave" of H.D.'s narrative discourse through an analysis of the gynopoetic *Notes on Thought and Vision* (written in 1919 but published in 1982), and *Borderline* (1930), the anonymous cinema essay that infuses H.D.'s modernism with the marginalities of race, gender, and politics while simultaneously enacting that very marginality by concealing gender. Additional discussions include the prose's intertextuality and the "selves" which H.D. wove and rewove throughout her prose, including *Paint It Today, Bid Me To Live, Palimpsest, Tribute to Freud,* and *The Gift.* Collages inspired by H.D.'s photo album, an excellent "works cited" list, and a chronology of H.D's composition/publication complement this complex discussion. Recommended for upper-division undergraduates.—*J. C. Kohl, Dutchess Community College*

WS-0840   93-72625 Orig
Gilman, Charlotte Perkins. **Benigna Machiavelli.** Bandanna Books, 1993. 178p ISBN 0-942208-18-8 pbk, $7.95

Not a major literary accomplishment (like many of Gilman's fictional works, it is flawed), this newly published novel is important in the contribution it makes to the recovery of her lost works. The first-person protagonist-narrator devotes her life to the surreptitious performance of good deeds, often rationalizing her use of duplicity as a necessary means in achieving her objective. But the plot is thin and the denouement forced. Here, as in several of her works, Gilman uses the fictional backdrop to advance her social theories on such issues as child rearing, women's economic status, and effective household management. The publication of the novel is further weakened by the publisher's decision to "tone down" some of Gilman's melodramatic passages; yet no footnotes have been included to show how the original text has been altered. Moreover, the introduction offers little in terms of either historical contextualization or literary criticism, and it is riddled with inaccuracies—claiming, for example, that Gilman's monthly magazine, the *Forerunner,* began publication in 1906 (it actually began in 1909) and that the magnum opus of her long career, *Women and Economics,* was first published in 1898 by Putnam (it was, in fact, originally published in 1898 by Small, Maynard, & Co.). Overall, the novel's implausible story line, the absence of a comprehensive critical introduction, and the omission of footnotes render it of limited usefulness. Undergraduate (all levels); graduate; faculty; general.—*D. D. Knight, SUNY College at Cortland*

WS-0841 PS1744 94-4988 CIP
Gilman, Charlotte Perkins. **The diaries of Charlotte Perkins Gilman: v.1: 1879-87; v2: 1890-1935,** ed. by Denise D. Knight. University Press of Virginia, 1994. 2v. 943p bibl index ISBN 0-8139-1524-4, $89.50

Women's rights activist and author of the influential story "The Yellow Wall Paper" (1892) and other writings, Charlotte Perkins Gilman kept diaries from 1876 to 1887 and then again from 1890 to 1903. They cover the main events of her early life: her painful loss of her soul mate, Martha Luther, to marriage; her own disastrous marriage-on-the-rebound to the controlling Charles Walter Stetson (who forbade his wife the poems of Whitman, which he thought too racy); and her rapturous union with her first cousin George Houghton Gilman, who, until his sudden death from a massive cerebral hemorrhage, was her husband for 34 years. These diaries are essential to Gilman scholars and students of activism, though editor Knight (SUNY-Cortland) herself admits the diaries' "failure to conform to standards of literary excellence"; a typical entry records visits, meals, and the books Gilman read, and occasionally she seems to be trying to talk herself into believing that she is happier than she really is. Knight breaks the diaries into 34 chapters and provides helpful introductions that, invariably, are more engaging than the individual entries themselves. Graduates; faculty.—*D. Kirby, Florida State University*

WS-0842 PS1744 94-24905 CIP
Gilman, Charlotte Perkins. **A journey from within: the love letters of Charlotte Perkins Gilman, 1897-1900,** ed. and annot. by Mary A. Hill. Bucknell, 1995. (Dist. by Associated University Presses) 427p bibl index afp ISBN 0-8387-5293-4, $49.50

This collection of the letters of feminist Charlotte Perkins (1860-1935) to her cousin Houghton Gilman, before he became her second husband, represents less than half of the material in the 20-30 page letters she wrote almost daily. The letters reveal what Hill calls Perkins's "vivacious spontaneity," but, Hill notes, there are limitations: Houghton Gilman's letters are lacking; these letters reveal only a small part of Perkins's life; they are a private rather than a public journey; and they reflect a white, middle-class view. They are "alternately playful, coy, and deferential ... [and] intellectually assertive." Perkins alternates between rapt expressions of love ("I have you in my heart all the time"), concerns over the forthcoming marriage ("Please tell me ... that you particularly want me for yourself!"), and her solution to their relationship ("We must try to live like two friendly bachelors in apartments"). She tells Gilman of her relationship with Jane Addams of Hull House, the success or presumed failures of her lectures and her writings, her joy in being with her daughter (who was raised by her first husband), her sometimes ill health, her doubts and hopes. Hill's in-depth chapter introductions are lucid and useful. Highly recommended for women's studies.—*J. Overmyer, emerita, Ohio State University*

WS-0843 PS3545 89-40617 CIP
Goodman, Susan. **Edith Wharton's women: friends & rivals.** University Press of New England, 1990. 208p bibl index afp ISBN 0-87451-521-1, $27.50; ISBN 0-87451-524-6, $10.95

The seven chapters of this readable scholarly study effectively refute the long-standing claim that Wharton's life and fiction were marked by hostility to women. In extended analyses of ten novels and novellas, Goodman argues that Wharton's female characters achieve moral growth and a sense of identity primarily through their relationships with other women; that women, naturally each other's friends and guides, become enemies only when the exigencies of their society force them to become rivals. A chapter on A Backward Glance establishes the novelist's mother as the most important influence on Wharton's portrayal of competitive relationships between women. In Wharton's correspondence with Sara Norton, Goodman finds the model for the novelist's portrayal of women's friendships in the fiction. Through analysis of Wharton's fiction, letters, and autobiography, Goodman illuminates Wharton's relation to other women writers and her conception of her own art as a commingling of masculine and feminine qualities. Notable for its clarity, range of insight, and direct unequivocal statement, this critical-biographical study is a valuable addition to the growing body of Wharton criticism and gender studies, and it will be useful to graduate students and upper-division undergraduates.—*E. Nettels, College of William and Mary*

WS-0844 PS3505 93-44678 CIP
Harvey, Sally Peltier. **Redefining the American dream: the novels of Willa Cather.** Fairleigh Dickinson, 1995. (Dist. by Associated University Presses) 190p bibl index afp ISBN 0-8386-3557-1, $34.50

Harvey (Butte Community College) cites cultural histories, such as Christopher Lasch's *The True and Only Heaven: Progress and Its Critics* (1991), to develop contexts for the American Dream motif in Cather's 12 novels and four of her short stories. Even during the Depression years, Cather's "vision of America never ceased to recognize an imperfect but evolving dream of personal fulfillment," in "creative tension" with the individual's relationship to a larger community. According to Harvey, Cather opened up the American Dream to women and immigrants; in the "Old World values" of the latter, she found a "corrective" for Amerian materialism. Despite Cather's respect for the past and for the old culture of "character," Harvey argues that Cather is basically forward-looking, endorsing "the new culture of personality as a friendly climate in which an Amerian Dream of self-fulfillment can flourish." In contrast to most books about Cather, this one takes an American studies approach; Harvey quotes Lewis Mumford, George Santayana, and others among Cather's contemporaries, whose remarks on modern culture enhance a discussion of her fiction. The long bibliography and the index reflect Harvey's double interest in Cather as a literary artist and as a representative (and sometimes critic) of an era. Recommended for academic libraries, upper-division undergraduate and above.—*J. W. Hall, University of Mississippi*

WS-0845 PS3503 95-7630 CIP
Herring, Phillip. **Djuna: the life and work of Djuna Barnes.** Viking, 1995. 386p bibl index afp ISBN 0-670-84969-3, $27.95

This engaging, readable study details the painful life of Djuna Barnes, a master wit, a woman of beauty and style, and an elusive near genius. Barnes seemed to know everyone in the 1920s, but she never made it fully into the high modernist canon. Her personal and professional life was kept from full tragedy by the intervention of key figures, particularly T.S. Eliot, who championed the publication of her best work, the novel *Nightwood*. Herring unfolds a fascinating tale of painful sexual initiation, bisexuality, alcoholism, and debilitating illness. Particularly good is his analysis of the mixed motives and complex emotional ties in Barnes's most significant relationship, her intense love for Thelma Wood, who would betray her. This biography should encourage closer study of Barnes's work and will be enormously useful in women's studies and gay and lesbian studies classrooms, where it might be used with James Woodress's *Willa Cather: A Literary Life* (CH, Jun'88) and Gary Fountain and Peter Brazeau's *Remembering Elizabeth Bishop* (1994) to reveal the pressures on women artists who do not fit conventional categories. General; upper-division undergraduate and above.—*L. Winters, College of Saint Elizabeth*

WS-0846 PS3525 92-15343 CIP
Heuving, Jeanne. **Omissions are not accidents: gender in the art of Marianne Moore.** Wayne State, 1992. 195p bibl index afp ISBN 0-8143-2335-9, $32.95

Heuving undertakes a thorough examination of Moore's verse to show how a response to gender runs through it like a unifying thread, and so to refute unfair estimates of Moore, who was faulted (even by Pound and Jarrell) as sexless. From the early "understatements" to the final collage "overstatements," in which affirmation of her culture replaces the negativism of "adverse ideas" as discussed in the third chapter, Moore's work is shaped by efforts "to give expression to a universality and to herself as a woman." The chapter "An Artist in Refusing" reveals her conscious strategy in what she chose *not* to write—complaints about her second-class status in a masculine world—preferring lyrics as written *by* a woman to those written *about* women. As "superior" observers, Pound, Williams, and Eliot, in their three portraits of ladies, view their subjects as mirrors lighting up their own identities, against which Heuving contrasts Moore's "These Various Scalpels," in which their feminist peer addresses a beloved from her unique perspective, "the direct treatment of the thing." Although the density of Heuving's style limits appreciation of the poetry itself, this book comes at a welcoming moment in American social history.—*B. Quinn, formerly, College of Saint Teresa*

WS-0847   PS3545   90-19431 CIP
Holbrook, David. **Edith Wharton and the unsatisfactory man.** Vision Press/St. Martin's, 1991. 208p bibl index ISBN 0-312-03565-9, $39.95

In this study of a dozen novels and novellas by Edith Wharton, Holbrook explores the connection between the failure of characters to achieve fulfilling sexual relationships and their involvement in potentially incestuous attachments, especially those between middle-aged men and young women, as in *Summer, Twilight Sleep,* and *The Children.* Basing his interpretations on the assumption that Wharton as a child was strongly attracted to her father and may have been abused by him, Holbrook sees revealed in the plots of the fiction an "unconscious mythology" in which the mother is cast off in favor of the father and the incestuous relationship is vindicated. The book is clearly written and it illuminates important themes and narrative patterns in Wharton's fiction. Plot summaries occupy much of the space, however, and the book does not add substantially to recent studies such as R.W.B. Lewis's *Edith Wharton: A Biography* (CH, Jan'76) and C.G. Wolff's *A Feast of Words: The Triumph of Edith Wharton* (CH, Jul'77). Readers unfamiliar with other criticism of Wharton's fiction can learn a good deal from this book, but they should be warned that it contains some factual errors and many misspellings of characters' names.—*E. Nettels, College of William and Mary*

WS-0848   PS3507   91-10588 CIP
Hollenberg, Donna Krolik. **H.D.: the poetics of childbirth and creativity.** Northeastern University, 1991. 285p bibl index afp ISBN 1-55553-104-0, $25.00

This study of Hilda Doolittle by Hollenberg (University of Connecticut) is an interesting if narrow addition to the small corpus of H.D. criticism. As the subtitle suggests, the book focuses on one of H.D.'s recurring concerns—her own troubled experiences with pregnancy, childbirth, and motherhood—and uses that concern as a way of studying H.D.'s complete poetry and prose. Such a procedure is clearly a useful way of considering her work—and this book should be read by anyone interested in H.D.'s writing. Unfortunately, though, it also forces Hollenberg to overlook other, conflicting elements of H.D.'s complex poetics, most noticeably in the early work, which she suggests is limited (as a result of H.D.'s conflicted feelings about her procreative experiences) by a "poetic mode based on a strategy of self-effacement." Such suggestions are true, but only partly true. As is the case in its encounters with almost all of H.D.'s critics, the poetry is richer in its ambivalence and complexity than Hollenberg's readings allow.—*G. Burnett, Princeton University*

WS-0849   PS3531   93-46599 CIP
Kappes, Marcianne. **Track of the mystic: the spirituality of Jessica Powers.** Sheed & Ward, 1994. 182p bibl afp ISBN 1-55612-659-X pbk, $12.95

Kappes's book is an excellent introduction to the work of Jessica Powers (1905-1988), a poet whose audience has been limited by the inaccessibility of her books, several of which were privately printed by her Carmelite order. The poet works in the mystical tradition of Teresa of Avila, John of the Cross, and Theresa of Lisieux, but other spiritual voices also resound: Dickenson, Hopkins, Herbert, and Vaughan. At the heart of life in Carmel are contemplation, prayer, and manual labor, concerns reflected in the poems. Jessica Powers felt that poetry and contemplation were compatible so long as the poet does not give in to self-consciousness but always maintains humility before the work and before God. Of special interest to the poet are the feminine natures of God and the Holy Spirit, the transfer of attention from outer to inner geographies, and the strength of God's grace and mercy amidst inconsequential human actions. For those unfamiliar with Powers's poetry, the author quotes liberally from her work, often including entire poems. There is also a substantial and comprehensive bibliography, but no index. Of interest to collections emphasizing women's spirituality. General and academic audiences.—*J. P. Baumgaertner, Wheaton College (IL)*

WS-0850   PS3505   91-46127 CIP
Kaye, Frances W. **Isolation and masquerade: Willa Cather's women.** P. Lang, 1993. 204p (American university studies. Series XXIV, American literature, 30) index afp ISBN 0-8204-1764-5, $43.95

Kaye (Univ. of Nebraska) discusses Cather's novels and selected stories in the context of lesbian literature and American women's history. Sharon O'Brien's

Willa Cather: The Emerging Voice (CH, Nov'87) is an important influence on the discussion, though Kaye disagrees with O'Brien "in terms of Cather's development and her subsequent portrayals of women, disguised and undisguised, in her fiction." Unlike O'Brien and other critics who view Cather's depictions of strong women as "purely positive," Kaye believes that the heroines of *O Pioneers!* and *Song of the Lark*, for example, "are *exceptional* rather than *exemplary*" characters, created at "psychic costs" to Cather and producing "ambiguities" for the reader. Kaye emphasizes Cather's "distrust of women as a class" and her isolation from such reformist groups as the Women's Christian Temperance Union. Of special interest to Kaye are the works where a male character—like Jim Burden of *My Ántonia*—"masquerades" Cather's purported lesbianism in "an intense but unfulfilled relationship with the heroine." Notes. For literature, women's studies, and American studies collections. Advanced undergraduate; graduate; faculty.—*J. W. Hall, University of Mississippi*

WS-0851   PS1744   94-18591 CIP
Kessler, Carol Farley. **Charlotte Perkins Gilman: her progress toward utopia with selected writings.** Syracuse, 1995. 316p bibl index afp ISBN 0-8156-2644-4, $34.95; ISBN 0-8156-0304-5 pbk, $16.95

Kessler (Pennsylvania State Univ., Delaware County Campus) is the first scholar to devote an entire study to the utopian content of Gilman's fiction. In addition to providing a discussion that places utopianism in a cultural context, Kessler draws on several sources in situating her arguments, including Gilman's biography, personal correspondence, and nonfiction works. Unfortunately, the author overemphasizes biography—considering the wealth of information already available about Gilman's life—and her analysis of the fiction is comparatively slim and somewhat repetitive. Kessler's working definition of utopianism is broad, but she provides a service by reprinting ten of Gilman's difficult-to-locate utopian stories, written between 1908 and 1913. Less useful are chapter excerpts from four of Gilman's utopian novels. Most puzzling, however, is that Kessler virtually ignores the link between Gilman's introduction to Edward Bellamy's *Looking Backward*, her immersion in the nationalist movement, and her evolving utopian philosophy. Moreover, she does not discuss Gilman's experiences in communal living (most notably at Prestonia Mann's Summer Brook Farm in the late 1890s), which possibly influenced her utopian ideals. Kessler's endnotes, however, are well researched and informative. Despite several factual errors in Gilman's biography, the study is nonetheless an important starting point for further research into Gilman's utopian vision. Recommended for undergraduates, graduates, and researchers.—*D. D. Knight, SUNY College at Cortland*

WS-0852   PS1043   90-32410 CIP
Leider, Emily Wortis. **California's daughter: Gertrude Atherton and her times.** Stanford, 1991. 402p bibl index ISBN 0-8047-1820-2, $24.00

This splendid first biography of writer Gertrude Atherton (1857-1948) reveals a writer vastly popular in her day, who on the one hand had "courage, capacity for work, and independent spirit," and on the other "narcissism, competitiveness, worship of power, and lack of compassion." Leider brings to life this extraordinary woman who, widowed at 30 with one surviving daughter, was uninterested in home life, even in her own child, traveled about the world, and was friends with Ambrose Bierce and Gertrude Stein, among other notables. Leider also briefly discusses most of Atherton's more than 50 books, which include popular and historical novels, essays, short stories, histories (of California and San Francisco), and an autobiography. Leider, who spent ten years on this work, frankly discusses Atherton's racism, snobbism, ignoring of the common people both in life and her novels, and distaste for the carnal. Her novels, some shocking at the time but today unread, were too little edited and revised, asserts Leider, and are valuable mainly as social history, although the short extracts included read quite well. This biography has the narrative drive and revelation of personality of a novel itself. Includes acknowledgments, introduction, chronology, index, notes, bibliography, photos. Valuable for women's studies collections.—*J. Overmyer, The Ohio State University*

WS-0853   PS509   93-25552 CIP
Lesbian culture: an anthology, ed. by Julia Penelope and Susan J. Wolfe. Crossing, 1993. 561p ISBN 0-89594-591-6 pbk, $21.95

This rousing, optimistic, wide-ranging collection of essays, photos, memoirs, interviews, and poems of exhortation is about pride. Resembling an oral history on paper, this anthology seems primarily for a gay audience seeking to see its own reflection in works by canonical authors such as Andre Lorde, Radclyffe Hall, Judy Grahn, and Marilyn Frye as well as in new poetry and essays by lesser-known writers such as Crystos and Toni Armstrong, Jr. The editors make a serious attempt at cultural diversity. This work is likely to attract nonacademic readers who want a good laugh and a good time. Penelope and Wolfe present a battle cry and "a sign we are not alone." A solid and interesting contribution to the work of defining and creating a lesbian culture, it is a fine companion volume to *An Intimate Wilderness*, ed. by Judith Barrington (1991) and *Lesbians at Midlife*, ed. by Barbara Sang et al. (1991).—*L. Winters, College of Saint Elizabeth*

WS-0854 CT275 95-4345 CIP
Luhan, Mabel Dodge. **A history of having a great many times not continued to be friends: the correspondence between Mabel Dodge and Gertrude Stein, 1911-1934,** by Patricia R. Everett. New Mexico, 1996. 303p bibl index ISBN 0-8263-1640-9, $29.95

The awkward title of this work is Gertrude Stein's accurate assessment of her relationship with Mable Dodge. The two women knew everyone involved in the cultural life of the early 20th century, yet two more disparate personalities would be difficult to imagine. Stein's placid exterior hid a very active and creative mind that exerted a profound influence on the English language. Mable Dodge was a rich, spoiled socialite who flitted from Buffalo to New York to Paris to her villa in Italy. Dodge went through three husbands and finally settled with her fourth, a Native American, in Taos, New Mexico. She was instrumental in introducing Stein's writings to the American literary world in 1913, the year that the great Armory show in New York shook up the art world as nothing had before. Dodge played a part in the show's success, and of course Stein's revolutionary publications fit well into the spirit of the times. The Stein-Dodge correspondence continues to provide a view of a literary world still significant today. Upper-division undergraduate through faculty.—*F. C. St. Aubyn, emeritus, University of Pittsburgh*

WS-0855 PS3511 94-43835 CIP
McLendon, Jacquelyn Y. **The politics of color in the fiction of Jessie Fauset and Nella Larsen.** University Press of Virginia, 1995. 142p bibl index ISBN 0-8139-1553-8, $29.50

This analysis of the novels of two prominent Harlem Renaissance women sees their work as "revisionary and subversive." Both used their own lives and experiences to some degree; both used the "nineteenth-century stereotype of the mulatto as constructed by white writers" as a "political tool and an artistic device"; both attempted to present "more realistic mulattoes" as they "parodied, satirized, and altered" the self-loathing stereotype. Fauset blames white rather than black blood for the mulattoes' problems, portraying passing as wrong and black characters as anything but "hopeless and pitiable." Larsen's novels focus on alienation and the struggle toward selfhood, showing how women both resist and are limited by social constructs. Both Thadious Davis (*Nella Larsen, Novelist of the Harlem Renaissance*, CH, Jul'94) and Charles Larson (*Invisible Darkness: Jean Toomer & Nella Larsen*, CH, Apr'94) concur in the idea that Larsen's life heavily influenced her writing. Both authors see racism as only one of the issues of Larsen's work. McLendon's interesting study indicates a nonstereotypical view of the fictional mulatto and is recommended for all academic collections.—*J. Overmyer, emerita, Ohio State University*

WS-0856 PS3525 94-12823 CIP
Millay at 100: a critical reappraisal, ed. by Diane P. Freedman. Southern Illinois, 1995. 221p bibl index afp ISBN 0-8093-1973-X, $34.95

Coming not long after *Critical Essays on Edna St. Vincent Millay*, ed. by William Thesing (CH, Jul'93), this volume demonstrates that the revival of interest in Millay is not a seven-day wonder. It is a revival due largely to Millay critics of both sexes. Thesing's volume consists mainly of articles and reviews from a span of more than 70 years, a kind of history of Millay's critical reputation. The present 13 essays—11 by women—offer fresh approaches to the poet on a preponderantly feminist basis, e.g., Millay's use of the female body as "icon" and her role as a "female female impersonator." Readers unfamiliar with feminist critical rhetoric may feel somewhat distanced from the contents. In any case, Mil-

lay is here in the hands of sympathetic critics who offer a treatment that has eluded male critics who either cannot or will not practice gender-free criticism to determine her worth. Recommended to upper-division undergraduate and graduate students as an important addition to Millay studies and as a significant example of contemporary feminist criticism.—*J. J. Patton, Atlantic Community College*

WS-0857 PS3525 95-7167 CIP
Miller, Cristanne. **Marianne Moore: questions of authority.** Harvard, 1995. 303p index ISBN 0-674-54862-0, $35.00

By defining "authority" a number of ways, Miller (Pomona College) allows herself considerable latitude in applying the term to Moore. At times it apparently means a characteristic auctorial voice; at others an ideological position taken on, for example, politics or gender, a verse strategy, or simply an expression of self-assurance. Since Miller writes from an avowed "feminist poststructuralistic" perspective and focuses narrowly on Moore, she omits mention of most of Moore's immediate female contemporaries. In her final chapter she links certain later poets to Moore's "poetic," e.g., Gwendolyn Brooks, Adrienne Rich, and several less well known present-day women poets. Miller's subject receives little attention in other books on Moore. In *The Poetry of Marianne Moore* (CH, Sep'88), arguably the best study, Margaret Holley covers some of the same ground but in different terms: her use of the idea of "value" has a kinship with Miller's "authority." The development of Moore's distinctive poetic voice is clearly traced in Laurence Stapleton's *Marianne Moore: The Poet's Advance* (CH, Mar'79). Recommended particularly for specialists in Moore and, to a lesser extent, for those interested in recent American poetry in general. Academic libraries at the upper-division undergraduate level and above.—*J. J. Patton, Atlantic Community College*

WS-0858 PS3535 93-5786 CIP
A Muriel Rukeyser reader, ed. by Jan Heller Levi. W.W. Norton, 1994. 294p index ISBN 0-393-03566-2, $25.00

Levi's book is a treasure. Unlike other selections of Rukeyser's work, this reader includes large selections from her prose: part of her biography of the scientist Willard Gibbs (*Willard Gibbs*, 1942), her long essay "The Life of Poetry" (1949), and her lecture "The Education of a Poet" (1976). Levi's introductions to each publication, arranged chronologically, are written with tact and insight. Adrienne Rich's introduction adds to the understanding of this remarkable and inspired poet, who was a source of inspiration for Rich. Filled with moral and political passion, Rukeyser's engagement with public events from the two world wars to the Vietnam war informed her poetry. Ignored and despised as a "she-poet" in her early years, Rukeyser has become a beacon for many contemporary poets today. Her daring, her compassion, and her immense intelligence have always stood in contrast to timid academic fashion in poetry. This reviewer is one among the poets of her generation who fell in love with her poems from the early "Effort at Speech Between Two People" (*Theory of Flight*, 1935) to the affirmation of her last book, *The Gates* (1976). All levels.—*R. Whitman, Massachusetts Institute of Technology*

WS-0859 PS3527 93-20999 CIP
Nardi, Marcia. **The last word: letters between Marcia Nardi and William Carlos Williams,** ed. by Elizabeth Murrie O'Neil. Iowa, 1994. 242p bibl index afp ISBN 0-87745-445-0, $34.95; ISBN 0-87745-461-2 pbk, $16.95

O'Neil's careful scholarly research will fascinate a variety of readers: students and admirers of William Carlos Williams and his work, especially *Paterson*; feminist scholars, particularly those interested in the plight of the woman artist in mid-20th century; others interested in letters as a distinct literary genre; and finally those who are simply drawn to moving dilemmas. Intriguing from the purely human point of view, this exchange of letters between the poet and Marcia Nardi, the "Cress" of the letters in Books 1 and 2 of *Paterson*, along with a few related letters from others, not only sheds light on Williams's choices and intention for the poem, but also captures the poignant story of a female poet struggling mightily against lifelong social, economic, and personal handicaps. The person who emerges from these often stunning letters—and her increasingly problematic relationship with the usually patient, sometimes exasperated poet—not only justifies Williams's interest in her and her work, but the appropriateness of his choice of Nardi to underscore the vast differences between the male Paterson poet and the "woman." The letters bring to vivid life the most mysterious figure in the poem—the one whose remarkable voice always excites the curiosity of students. This slim volume is a significant contribution to Williams scholarship and provides valuable documentation on one woman poet's struggle to live and to work. Highly recommended for all levels.—*S. R. Graham, emerita, Nazareth College of Rochester*

WS-0860 PS3545 95-38196 CIP
Price, Alan. **The end of the age of innocence: Edith Wharton and the First World War.** St. Martin's, 1996. 238p bibl index ISBN 0-312-12938-6, $29.95

Price's absorbing, meticulously documented study chronicles Wharton's many activities, month by month, from 1914 to 1920, in aid of the Allied cause: she transported medical supplies to the front; she established refugee hostels in Paris, homes for displaced Belgian children, and hospitals for wounded soldiers; and she raised funds for these charities by direct solicitation, letters to the press, and concerts and auctions. More fully than earlier biographers, Price (Pennsylvania State Univ.) reveals Wharton's remarkable powers of organization and administration; her profound attachment to France and French civilization; and her fortitude as she suffered from exhaustion, recurrent illnesses, and grief in the loss of friends and relatives. A compelling picture of what one influential private citizen could accomplish, the book also conveys a vivid sense of daily life in wartime Paris, the controversial activities of the American Red Cross in France, and the devotion of Wharton's tireless coworkers, Mary Cadwalader Jones and Elisina Tyler. The book concludes with a brief but illuminating discussion of Wharton's fiction involving the war (e.g., *The Marne, A Son at the Front,* and *The Mother's Recompense*). Based on scores of newspaper articles, committee records, and unpublished letters, this book promises to be the definitive treatment of its subject, indispensable for a full appreciation of Wharton's character and art. Upper-division undergraduate; graduate; faculty.—*E. Nettels, College of William and Mary*

WS-0861 PS3525 90-20833 CIP
Pyron, Darden Asbury. **Southern daughter: the life of Margaret Mitchell.** Oxford, 1991. 533p index afp ISBN 0-19-505276-5, $26.00

Reading this massive, incredibly detailed biography of the author of *Gone with the Wind* is very much the same kind of experience as reading Mitchell's massive, incredibly detailed novel itself: no matter how strong one's initial impulse to disparage it, the story simply sweeps one away. Pyron (editor of the 1983 critical anthology *Recasting: Gone with the Wind in American Culture,* CH, Jan'84) says he first read *GWTW* in 1974 and discovered at the same time that "no one had 'done' either the novel or its author." *Southern Daughter,* no question about it, remedies that lack. The story of Margaret Mitchell's diverse family background, her childhood scribbling, her youthful amours as a "baby-faced vamp," her two marriages, her newspaper work, her "labor pains" in bringing forth her literary child, and all the turmoil that followed the worldwide success of her novel and its Hollywood film version have now been "done" to a degree that should satisfy not only every legitimate scholarly interest but even the nearly insatiable curiosity of Mitchell's most importunate fans. Those content with something less comprehensive should go not to the earlier lopsided biographies by Finis Farr and Anne Edwards, but to Elizabeth I. Hanson's concise but insightful *Margaret Mitchell* (CH, Jul'91).—*A. J. Griffith, Our Lady of the Lake University*

WS-0862 PS3537 94-46813 CIP
Quay, Joyce C. **Early promise, late reward: a biography of Helen Hooven Santmyer, author of "... And ladies of the club."** Knowledge, Ideas & Trends, 1131-0 Tolland Turnpike, Suite 175, Manchester, CT 06040, 1995. 134p bibl ISBN 1-879198-15-0 pbk, $14.95

Quay has written a brief, sympathetic, and accessible biography of Helen Hooven Santmyer who, at the age of 88, astounded the publishing world with her best seller, *...And Ladies of the Club* (1982). Using Santmyer's childhood journal, early novels, and personal letters, Quay dispels the view that Santmyer was a late bloomer. Although Xenia, Ohio, was the locus of Santmyer's inspiration, she was a graduate of Wellesley College and had traveled extensively in France and England, where she earned an advanced degree from Oxford. She published two novels in the 1920s, *Herbs and Apples* (1925) and *Fierce Dispute* (1929), now reissued along with a third, *Farewell Summer* (1988), previously unpublished. The Depression brought an end to her discretionary time and she supported her parents by teaching and as dean at Cedarville College and later as a librarian in Xenia. Retirement and encouragement from her partner, Mildred Sandoe, resulted in *...And Ladies of the Club.* Santmyer saw her work as an antidote to what she viewed as the socialism of the New Deal and to the cynicism of Sinclair Lewis's *Main Street* (1920). Quay's biography will have broad appeal to general readers and undergraduates.—*P. W. Kaufman, University of Massachusetts at Boston*

WS-0863 91-75024 Orig
Shaw, Patrick W. **Willa Cather and the art of conflict: re-visioning her creative imagination.** Whitston, 1992. 187p index ISBN 0-87875-423-7, $23.50

Shaw sees the 12 novels of Willa Cather (1876-1947) as expressing her own "homoerotic tensions" which were "the energy source for her creativity." All of her novels have motifs of a mysterious, fecund prairie which nevertheless "cannot nurture artistic sensibility." In them, a strong, intelligent female—who may be either a masculine or feminine persona—"struggles to prove her competence," and must finally separate herself from her milieu to "remain true to her psyche or art." Shaw also considers other tensions in Cather's fiction, always relating them to tensions within Cather's personal life. He sees some of her characters, such as Jim and Ántonia in *My Ántonia,* as representing divided parts of Cather's psyche; that these halves do not join indicates that "Cather did not reconcile the sexual tensions which marked her life." (Cather may have been a lesbian.) Although some scholars may object to the hyper-close relationship of this analysis to Cather's personal life, the end result is a challenging and intriguing addition to Cather scholarship. Undergraduate; graduate; faculty.—*J. Overmyer, Ohio State University*

WS-0864 PS3507 90-50088 CIP
Signets: reading H.D., ed. by Susan Stanford Friedman and Rachel Blau DuPlessis. Wisconsin, 1991. 489p bibl indexes ISBN 0-299-12680-3, $40.00; ISBN 0-299-12684-6 pbk, $16.50

These 18 previously published, some excerpted, essays are accompanied by a photobiography, selections from H.D.'s poem *Biography,* an updated chronology of H.D.'s writing, as well as highlights of H.D.'s life. The editors, Susan Stanford Friedman (University of Wisconsin-Madison), author of *Penelope's Web: Gender, Modernity, H.D.'s Fiction* (1990) and Rachel Blau DuPlessis (Temple University), author of *The Pink Guitar: Writing as Feminist Practice* (1990), both authorities on the life, works, and influences of Hilda Doolittle, have collected essays that span two decades of H.D. criticism by the most influential critics and that cover H.D.'s works currently being read or taught. Using a range of methodologies, the essays are organized in topical clusters with titles that evoke particular crystallized moments in H.D.'s career: "Lives"; "Images"; "Palimpsests, Prophecies; Rescriptings." An excellent bibliography, including dissertations. A required "handbook" for all readers of H.D.'s work. Recommended for graduate and undergraduate libraries.—*J. C. Kohl, Dutchess Community College*

WS-0865 PS3545 94-46344 CIP
Singley, Carol J. **Edith Wharton: matters of mind and spirit.** Cambridge, 1995. 261p (Cambridge studies in American literature and culture, 92) bibl index ISBN 0-521-47235-0, $49.95

Singley (Rutgers Univ., Camden) describes her book as "the first to explore the dimensions of Wharton's religious, spiritual, and intellectual search, and to place her life and writings in the context of American intellectual thought and religious history." This study of seven novels and several short stories challenges Percy Lubbock's "myopic observation" in his *Portrait of Edith Wharton* (1947) that Wharton was a novelist of manners who lacked any serious interest in "theoretic enquiry." From the "spiritual homelessness" portrayed in *The House of Mirth* and the "Calvinist tortures" of *Ethan Frome,* to the Platonic idealism of *The Age of Innocence* and Augustinian echoes in the late works *Hudson River Bracketed* and *The Gods Arrive,* Singley emphasizes the moral struggles of Wharton's characters during a period of doubt and disbelief. Nineteenth-century influences on the fiction include Darwinism, Emersonian transcendentalism, the aesthetics movement, and feminism. "Fragile Freedoms"—Singley's chapter on *The Reef* and *Summer*—suggests both the social and the metaphysical limitations of Wharton's characters, especially her women. Extensive bibliography and detailed index. Strongly recommended for upper-division undergraduates and above.—*J. W. Hall, University of Mississippi*

WS-0866   PS3505.A87   90-12486 CIP
Skaggs, Merrill Maguire. **After the world broke in two: the later novels of Willa Cather.** University Press of Virginia, 1990. 212p index ISBN 0-8139-1300-4, $25.00

While indebted to James Woodress (*Willa Cather: A Literary Life*, CH, Jun'88) and Sharon O'Brien (*Willa Cather: The Emerging Voice*, CH, Nov'87), Skaggs (author of *The Folk of Southern Fiction*, CH, Jul'73) offers "not a competing biography or psychobiography but rather an intellectual history, primarily derived from Cather's published work." Her inspiration is Cather's often cited remark that "the world broke in two in 1922 or thereabouts." Skaggs views the eight novels that Cather wrote after 1921 as an attempt to "find a way to weld her world whole again" after the personal traumas and public disappointments of the postwar years. In *One of Ours, A Lost Lady, The Professor's House, My Mortal Enemy, Death Comes for the Archbishop, Shadows on the Rock, Lucy Gayheart*, and *Sapphira and the Slave Girl*, Cather skillfully varies several recurring themes: desire, art and religion, cultural continuity, failure, strength, and miracle. Occasionally Freudian in her readings, Skaggs identifies the author with her characters, including the imperious Sapphira Colbert, in whom Cather finally "acknowledges the nature of her own blood, judges it coldly, and then accepts it." Index but no bibliography. Appropriate for all college-level Cather collections.—*J. W. Hall, University of Mississippi*

WS-0867   PS647   92-30446 CIP
The Sleeper wakes: Harlem Renaissance stories by women, ed. by Marcy Knopf. Rutgers, 1993. 277p bibl ISBN 0-8135-1944-6, $35.00; ISBN 0-8135-1945-4 pbk, $12.95

A crucial addition to the literature of the Harlem Renaissance, presenting a wealth of short stories by heretofore unpublished and/or underrepresented African American women writers of the 1920s and '30s. Nella Larsen, Jesse Redmon Fauset, Dorothy West, Marita Bonner, Alice Dunbar Nelson, Leila Amos Pendleton, and Eloise Bibb Thompson are, among others, included within the anthology; biographical notes are provided on all contributors. Knopf's careful research into back issues of *Crisis* and *Opportunity* magazines unearthed many of the works included here. Knopf, a graduate of the University of Cincinnati, provides within her substantial introduction a detailed literary and social history of the women writers of the Harlem Renaissance. In the foreword, noted African American studies scholar Nellie Y. McKay situates the state of research on the Harlem Renaissance, noting that the book " ... truly enhances efforts to bring the lives and experiences of black women writers into our lives and classrooms .... " A four-page bibliography offers further avenues of research. Recommended for public and academic libraries.—*J. Tharp, University of Wisconsin—Marshfield-Wood County*

WS-0868   PS3537   93-20225 CIP
Smith, Lillian Eugenia. **How am I to be heard?: letters of Lillian Smith,** ed. by Margaret Rose Gladney. North Carolina, 1993. 384p bibl index afp ISBN 0-8078-2095-4, $34.95

Scholars of the Civil Rights Movement, of southern women's literature, and of southern history owe Gladney (Univ. of Alabama) a considerable debt for creating such a meticulously edited and useful volume. Smith is perhaps best known for her novel *Strange Fruit* (1944) and for her prescient autobiographical work *Killers of the Dream* (1949), which pioneered analysis of the ineluctable connections between racism and sexism in the American South. Now, Smith's correspondence is available. Gladney's goal: "to construct a portrait of Lillian Smith that recognizes and challenges the attitudes toward gender and sexuality that have shaped and defined her life as a woman, her choices of self-definition, and her critical reception as a writer" (preface). Going far beyond the daunting task of selecting from among some 1,500 of Smith's letters (145 appear here in print), Gladney interweaves the letters with clear, concisely written explanatory paragraphs that at once provide insights about the contents of the letters and help to bind them together into a profile of Smith. Ample introductory material contains much new information about Smith's life, gleaned from the research into

25 different archives, including the effect of her intimate relationship with Paula Snelling on her beliefs. The collection begins with a letter dated 1917, written when Smith was almost 20, and ends with a letter dated August 1966, just a month before her death. The book's beautiful production makes it an extra pleasure to read. Strongly recommended for all collections.—*E. R. Baer, Gustavus Adolphus College*

WS-0869   PS3531   94-42285 CIP
Stout, Janis P. **Katherine Anne Porter: a sense of the times.** University Press of Virginia, 1995. 381p bibl index ISBN 0-8139-1568-6, $34.95

"Coherence is not the appropriate model for Porter's political and social views," says Stout (Texas A&M Univ.) in this highly recommended account of Porter's cultural context. Joan Givner accomplished much of the biographical groundwork in *Katherine Anne Porter: A Life* (CH, Apr'83, revised 1991), and Robert H. Brinkmeyer emphasized the changing focus of Porter's writing in *Katherine Anne Porter's Artistic Development: Primitivism, Traditionalism, and Totalitarianism* (CH, Nov'93), but Stout, more completely than her predecessors, places Porter against the shifting national and international backdrop of her times (1890-1980). Stout depicts the "noisy radicalism" of turn-of-the-century Texas, the socialist intellectual circles of Mexico and New York in the 1920s, the conservative agrarianism of the 1930s, the patriotism of the WW II years, and other movements that influenced Porter's life and work. She praises Porter's "consummate artistry," especially in the short stories, but does not ignore her "sexual adventurism" and racism. Porter's chronic restlessness, her writer's block, her hostility to feminists, and all her "troubled complexity" make more sense to the reader of Stout's well-documented, fascinating, essential study. Recommended for all academic and public libraries.—*J. W. Hall, University of Mississippi*

WS-0870   PS3537   94-23700 CIP
Wagner-Martin, Linda. **"Favored strangers": Gertrude Stein and her family.** Rutgers, 1995. 346p bibl index ISBN 0-8135-2169-6, $34.95

Historians of the modernist period in search of sustaining biographical fodder can pick the dry and familiar bones of the Bloomsbury group or turn to the meatier fare of American expatriot Gertrude Stein and her Parisian circle. Wagner-Martin (Univ. of North Carolina) offers a veritable banquet of anecdotes and details about Stein's exchanges on art, life, food, and literature with luminaries such as Hemingway, Matisse, Juan Gris, Picasso, Virgil Thompson, and many others. Incidents are retold with finesse and bolstered by plentiful and compelling primary sources. Emphasizing Stein's social genius, the author laces the book with a deep understanding of the style and substance of Stein's works and life. The most impressive aspect of Wagner-Martin's technique is her ability to connect Stein's work and her taking up, dropping, and revisiting of scores of friends and associates (including her brother, Leo) over the course of two world wars. This telling goes deeper and should prove more satisfying to connoisseurs of art and literary history than James Mellow's *Charmed Circle: Gertrude Stein & Company* (CH, Jun'74). Suitable for all academic collections.—*S. Pathak, Johns Hopkins University*

WS-0871   PS3545   90-41588 CIP
Waid, Candace. **Edith Wharton's letters from the underworld: fictions of women and writing.** North Carolina, 1991. 237p index afp ISBN 0-8078-1938-7, $29.95; ISBN 0-8078-4302-4 pbk, $10.95

Informed readers will want to take into account Candace Waid's readings of some of Edith Wharton's best works. Imperfect as the whole is (it is loosely structured around the myth of Persephone), chapters are very useful on *The House of Mirth, Ethan Frome, Summer, The Custom of the Country, The Touchstone*, and *Ghosts*. Waid (Yale) is an intelligent, perceptive, and authoritative reader with much to say about America's women and about Wharton's treatment of women writing and of women's texts. Waid's own text is critical and theoretically informed, but without any focus on theory, so that both academic and serious general readers will find it clear and often substantial. As the best full-length critical study of Wharton's work, this book should join R. W. B. Lewis's *Edith Wharton: A Biography* (CH, Jul'77) and Cynthia Griffin Wolff's *A Feast of Words* (CH, Jul'77) on all academic and many public library shelves. There is an introduction to Wharton and to her frequent reference to Persephone, and there are extensive and useful notes.—*Q. Grigg, Hamline University*

WS-0872 PS153 95-3132 CIP
Wall, Cheryl A. **Women of the Harlem Renaissance.** Indiana, 1995. 246p bibl index afp ISBN 0-253-32908-6, $29.95; ISBN 0-253-20980-3 pbk, $14.95

In critiquing the customary vision of the Harlem Renaissance, Wall (Rutgers Univ.) argues that Alain Locke's "new negro" paradigm "overstates the case for male writers" and "contradicts the experience of many woman." She contrasts optimistic male inventions of self with more claustrophobic biomythography in such women as Marita Bonner, Georgia Douglas Johnson, Anne Spencer, Bessie Smith, Gwendolyn Bennett, and others. Wall selects Jesse Redmon Fauset, Nella Larsen, and Zora Neale Hurston for this biographical and critical study. She surveys their works, places them in historical context, and evaluates their success. Readers see Fauset as influential for writers rather than a great writer; Larsen's "perilous" studies of the "intersections of race, class, and gender"; Hurston's elevation of the "cultural traditions of black people" in her folklore and fiction. In this essentially historical study with sound critical insight, Wall offers an effective alternate to the Harlem Renaissance of Locke/ Hughes/ McKay and the like. Suited to readers at all levels, the volume includes excellent photographs of key people and extensive notes.—*B. E. McCarthy, College of the Holy Cross*

WS-0873 PS3545 91-24547 CIP
White, Barbara A. **Edith Wharton: a study of the short fiction.** Twayne, 1991. 192p (Twayne's studies in short fiction, 30) bibl index afp ISBN 0-8057-8340-7, $26.95

White has written the most comprehensive study to date of Edith Wharton's short stories, giving thorough coverage to early, middle, and late groupings. The approach is story-by-story analysis, predominantly devoted to the narration and thematic content. There is, however, an emphasis on gender in dealing with character types and narrating speakers. Assessment is a major goal, and the volume sums up Wharton's accomplishments in the short story (some excellent and many lesser stories). White's book would be a useful guide in selecting stories to read. In spite of its competence, however, it will not be enlightening for experienced readers, though it has a useful bibliography, chronology, and index. The critic is knowledgeable and well read, but the approach is dated and unproductive. The body of the book is admirably compact (105p.) but is filled out by 151 lengthy notes and reprints of comments by Wharton on the short story and criticism by R.W.B. Lewis and Sandra M. Gilbert. Recommended for lower-level undergraduates.—*Q. Grigg, Hamline University*

WS-0874 PS2234 95-3005 CIP
Young, Bette Roth. **Emma Lazarus in her world: life and letters.** Jewish Publication Society, 1995. 298p bibl index ISBN 0-8276-0516-1, $34.95

Young sets out to debunk the myth of the Statue of Liberty poet as a literary recluse. Based on her discovery of 60 original letters, Young presents Lazarus as an engaged member in the society of prominent socialites and literati of America and England. The letters reveal an intelligent and respected writer who maintained correspondence and long-term friendships with Emerson, Hawthorne's daughter, Rose Lathrop, Thomas Ward, and Henry James; a writer received by Robert Browning and William Morris and praised by Turgenev; a social activist working on behalf of Jewish security. The bulk of the letters chronicle social life among genteel Victorians. A smaller portion convey the range of the writer's intellect, her literary projects, concerns about Russian antisemitic persecutions and her consequent support of Russian-Jewish immigrants, and her Zionist convictions. A strength of the volume is Young's critical introduction situating Lazarus among major 19th-century literary and intellectual leaders and repudiating earlier studies founded on her sister's characterization of Emma as a "tragic Jewish priestess." Young is especially critical of Allen Lesser and Heinrich Jacob, whom she judges to be factually incorrect, and Carole Kessner, whose hypotheses she claims are questionable. Recommended for all collections.—*S. L. Kremer, Kansas State University*

WS-0875 PS3515 92-45759 CIP
Zora Neale Hurston: critical perspectives past and present, ed. by Henry Louis Gates and K.A. Appiah. Amistad Press, 1993. 330p bibl index afp ISBN 1-56743-015-5, $24.95; ISBN 1-56743-028-7 pbk, $14.95

One of six volumes of the "Amistad Literary Series," this volume comprises 20 book reviews organized chronologically according to the publication dates of Hurston's seven major works; 14 essays by prominent literary critics (the major portion of the book), which Gates briefly summarizes in the lucid five-page preface, and he notes that Hurston "is the most widely taught black woman writer in the canon on American literature." This volume adds the context of the developing critical perspective to the study of Hurston's work and place in American literature. Included also are information on the essayists themselves, a chronology of Hurston's life, an updated bibliography, and an index for the volume itself. Notes follow each essay. The reviews were written between 1934 and 1948, but the essays were written between 1982 and 1992 and therefore document the prominence and complexity of Hurston's work recognized today. An invaluable resource both for the study of a single author and for the examination of literary criticism and attitudes toward a controversial author's work, this volume is readable, thought provoking, intelligent. Advanced undergraduate; graduate; faculty.—*D. S. Isaacs, Fordham University*

◆ United States
20th Century (1950 -   )

WS-0876 PS3566 91-50155 CIP
Alexander, Paul. **Rough magic: a biography of Sylvia Plath.** Viking, 1991. 402p index ISBN 0-670-81812-7, $24.95

This latest addition to the biographies of Sylvia Plath (1932-1962), prompted by a "strong admiration for Plath's work," places much of the blame for Plath's unhappiness and subsequent suicide on her husband, British poet Ted Hughes, whose affair with Assia Gutmann Wevill precipitated his and Plath's separation. Hughes is the villain here: Alexander states that he once choked Plath into near-unconsciousness and that Plath, after her marriage, sailed to America to abort her and Hughes's baby, fearing a loss of her Fulbright otherwise. Since the Plath estate (whose agent is Olwyn Hughes, Ted's sister, who once called Plath "pretty straight poison") often demanded changes in manuscript substance in exchange for quotation permission, Alexander did not consult with it. As a result there are few quotations from Plath; her individual, decisive, brilliant voice is missing. Alexander attempts no literary interpretations of her work, but he does, unlike Plath's other biographers, tell what happened after her death: to Hughes who remarried, to her grown children, and to *The Bell Jar* movie lawsuit. This account is readable, presents some new information, and is a worthy addition to the Plath oeuvre. It contains photos, notes, acknowledgments, but, oddly, no bibliography. Anne Stevenson, *Bitter Fame* (CH, Dec'89), presents Hughes as a near-victim; she discusses Plath's work, as does Edward Butscher, in *Sylvia Plath: Method and Madness* (CH, Jul'76).—*J. Overmyer, Ohio State University*

WS-0877 PS3551 94-34303 CIP
Anderson, Alice. **Human nature: poems.** New York University, 1995 (c1994). 87p afp ISBN 0-8147-0632-0, $25.00; ISBN 0-8147-0633-9 pbk, $12.95

Winner of the Elmer Holmes Bobst Award for Emerging Writers, *Human Nature* is courageous and often harrowing. Its 25 poems, notable for their candor, eroticism, and emotional trauma, are sometimes reminiscent of Sharon Olds, to whom they are dedicated, and of Sylvia Plath. Anderson exposes the psychologically complex world of a woman who has survived childhood incest. It is a world of violence, both physical and psychic, suffering, outrage, grief, horror. The adult narrator recalls herself as a small girl, when her father pulled her "back and forth across him like a washboard," when she heard her "house fill up with blood," when she concluded it was "Better to die than to be loved." The poems bear such titles as "What the Night Is Like," "The Suicide Year," "Little Girl Cadaver," and "Blue-Blackout." In "Defense," a fourth-grade girl slathers her small white body with a concoction of toothpaste, shampoo, jam, Windex, detergent, Turtle Wax, bleach, lip gloss, Vaseline, pine needles, dried worms, and urine, hoping vainly such reeking "sludge" will ward off advances of the father. Distressing poems indeed, but finally affirmative. "It's the human's nature to survive, welcome to the living," Anderson concludes. A strongly recommended collection.—*D. D. Kummings, University of Wisconsin-Parkside*

WS-0878　　PS3566　　92-5884 CIP
Arcana, Judith. **Grace Paley's life stories: a literary biography.**
Illinois, 1993. 269p bibl index afp ISBN 0-252-01945-8, $29.95

The life of Grace Goodside Paley (1922-), a doctor's daughter, and her work (three short story collections, one poetry collection) "resist separation," insists Arcana. Indeed, Paley's frequent protagonist, Faith Darwin Ashbury, is often taken to be Paley herself. Arcana sees Paley's "high level of integration in her life as a writer, teacher [at Sarah Lawrence College], mother [of two with one abortion], activist [many demonstrations and arrests for political activities], wife [two husbands], and friend" as the key to understanding both her comparatively low level of literary output and her life-related themes. Paley insists on the social responsibility of the artist; life comes first, literature second. Arcana also discusses Paley's language, which reflects Russian and Yiddish as well as English along with dialects of the Bronx and lower Manhattan. Paley emerges as a strong mother-figure and activist fiercely committed to every aspect of her life (except, perhaps, her writing), one who believes that "the world still has to be saved—every day." *Grace Paley: Illuminating the Dark Lives* by Jacqueline Taylor (CH, Feb'91) focuses solely on Paley's writing, particularly its colloquial "oral" language, which defies semantic and narrative conventions. Arcana's chattily written study is warm, appreciative, and wondrously insightful and should lead both new and old readers to Paley's writing. Includes photos and notes. Highly recommended for women's studies and literature collections. General; undergraduate and up.—*J. Overmyer, Ohio State University*

WS-0879　　PS3527　　94-28865 CIP
Bair, Deirdre. **Anaïs Nin, a biography.** G.P. Putnam, 1995. 654p index afp ISBN 0-399-13988-5, $39.95

Bair is the author of two previous biographies, *Samuel Beckett* (CH, Jan'79) and *Simone de Beauvoir* (1990). Here, her experience as a biographer reveals itself in both the quality and readability of the prose. This, along with her comprehensive coverage, makes this biography superior to Noel Riley Fitch's *Anaïs: The Erotic Life of Anaïs Nin* (1993), which has limitations indicated by its title. Nin is, of course, famous as one of the most prolific diarists of the 20th century, a habit begun at the age of 11 as her family embarked on a sea voyage to America after they were deserted by Nin's beloved father. Her diaries eventually numbered 69 volumes with another 30 or so notebooks of more random entries. She is also know for her long string of lovers and friends, who included June and Henry Miller, Otto Rank, Antonin Artaud, Edmund Wilson, Lawrence Durrell, and Gore Vidal. Bair terms Nin "a 'major' minor writer" and frequently points out the ways in which Nin anticipated many markers of the late 20th century, including exploration of sexuality, psychoanalysis, and women's autobiography. Bair availed herself of the Nin archives at UCLA and elsewhere and consulted with Rupert Pole, one of Nin's two (simultaneous) husbands. The result is a balanced and evenhanded book with more than 100 pages of tightly packed footnotes and many illustrations. Strongly recommended for all collections.—*E. R. Baer, Gustavus Adolphus College*

WS-0880　　PS3558　　93-42498 CIP
Bell, Betty Louise. **Faces in the moon: a novel.** Oklahoma, 1995 (c1994). 193p (American Indian literature and critical studies series, 9) afp ISBN 0-8061-2774-0 pbk, $10.95

In celebrating the voices of the Native American women of her childhood, Lucie, the central narrator of *Faces in the Moon*, implies that giving these women voice will be the novel's main action. Bell focuses on mixed-blood Cherokee women who eked out a hardscrabble living in Oklahoma cotton fields and whose accents owe more to their Georgia grandparents than to any knowledge of Cherokee. She provides a rich matrix for the creation and interplay of such voices: Lucie's mother, Gracie, and her aunt Rozella, who "chose mocassins over high heels," and Gracie's friend Lizzie Sixkiller, who looked "more like a Quaker than an Indian." However, Bell cannot fully depict poor white Cherokee life or enact the call and response of communal storytelling because it is more important for her to provide Lucie with an empowering relation with her now-dead mother, which causes Gracie's voice, her platinumed hair, and her 300-pound body to disappear from the narrative. Bell also has difficulty creating Oklahoma voices that are at once terse and resonant; Lizzie's speech is full of lines like "Thank you dear Lord for this here food we's 'bout to eat." Though Bell cannot yet match *Love Medicine* (1984), Louise Erdrich's interplay of poetic voices, or Linda Hogan's *Mean Spirit* (1990), an evocative portrayal of Osage oil boomers, this reviewer awaits

Bell's future efforts with interest. Recommended for large public and academic collections of Native American literature.—*M. L. Robertson, Sweet Briar College*

WS-0881　　PS3552.I7574　　90-19836 CIP
Birtha, Becky. **The forbidden poems.** Seal Press, 1991. 155p ISBN 1-878067-01-X, pbk $10.95

"I go by all my names/ third world/ black/ woman of color/ sister/hermana/ afroamericana la/ negra la/ lesbiana," says the speaker in one of Birtha's *The Forbidden Poems*. This strong first collection of verse (Birtha has two volumes of short stories, *For Nights Like This One*, 1983, and *Lover's Choice*, 1987) treats aspects of all these identities. Many of the poems deal with loss or absence, particularly of a lover or a child; others celebrate the strength derived from a women-centered community. Several, such as "Poem from a Clerk in the Law Library," display a biting humor. Despite a few overly sentimental lines, the majority of these poems have a stark, direct quality, which, as in "Doors" or "Plumstone," convey tremendous power. This power is reflected in the closing lines of "I Want More From You Than Words": "I've a river, rising/ coursing its current/ swift and strong/ through the core of me/ and I want—/ I want/ more from you/ than words." Recommended for collections with large holdings in poetry, African American, and/or women's literature.—*L. J. Parascandola, Long Island University—Brooklyn Campus*

WS-0882　　PS3525　　92-7180 CIP
Brightman, Carol. **Writing dangerously: Mary McCarthy and her world.** C. Potter, 1992. 714p index ISBN 0-517-56400-9, $30.00

This definitive biography of Mary McCarthy (1912-89), America's "First Lady of Letters," covers three areas—personal, political, and literary. Brightman details the upbringing of McCarthy and her brothers by relatives after their parents' deaths; her Jewish and Catholic ancestry and her Catholic schooling; her four marriages, the second of which to Edmund Wilson produced their only son, Reuel; and her large circle of friends, among them Hannah Arendt, Nicola Chiaromonte, Philip Rahv, Robert Lowell, Dwight Macdonald, and Elizabeth Hardwick. Among her enemies were Lillian Hellman and Simone de Beauvoir. Her leftist-leaning political life involved her in such issues as the Moscow trials, McCarthyism and the Cold War, the Waldorf Conference for World Peace, and Vietnam. Brightman discusses McCarthy's use of her life in such works as her novels *The Group* (1963), which was made into a movie; *The Company She Keeps* (1942), and *The Birds of America* (1971); and her nonfiction books such as *Memories of a Catholic Girlhood* (1957) and *Venice Observed* (1956). Brightman states that McCarthy's "respect for words and their mysteries. . .makes her literary example worth pondering." This complex, contradictory woman and writer lives again in this sympathetic, intelligent, coolly probing study. Essential for women's studies and literature collections.—*J. Overmyer, Ohio State University*

WS-0883　　PS3553　　92-34362 CIP
Castillo, Ana. **So far from God: a novel.** W.W. Norton, 1993. 251p index ISBN 0-393-03490-9, $19.95

Castillo has blended elements of surrealism, stream of consciousness, magic realism, flashbacks, internal monologue, the mundane and the miraculous, the ancient and the modern. She provides a wealth of information about customs, traditions, home remedies, folklore, and myth. A skillful mixture of Spanish and English adds to the realism of the rapidly moving, television-like, kaleidoscopic flow of events. The major characters in the novel's briskly unraveling plot are Sofia, the mother of four dysfunctional daughters: Esperanza, a television news reporter; Caridad, a drinking and promiscuous nurse; Fe, a bank employee in search of the good life; and la Loca, resurrected from death at the age of three. By the end of the narrative, all daughters are dead. The author's feminism is neither denigrating nor offensive. Her novel has reached a high degree of universality because of its frankness, sincerity, and avoidance of didactic invocations and stereotyping so abundant in the writings of militants of the Chicana narrative genre. With tact, taste, humor, and extraordinary literary prowess, she brilliantly exposes the socio-politico-economic concerns of a caring Mexican-American woman. It is an outstanding work of art by a first-rate novelist, writing in a genuine spirit of multiculturalism and not another piece of politicized literary resistance to "colonial oppression." Recommended for college courses as well as for college and public libraries.—*I. Molina, University of Cincinnati*

WS-0884   PS3553.H357   90-13332 CIP
Cherry, Kelly. **The exiled heart: a meditative autobiography.**
Louisiana State, 1991. 268p afp ISBN 0-8071-1620-3, $24.95

In this autobiography, Cherry chronicles her 25-year liaison with the Latvian composer Imant Kalnin as their attempts to marry are thwarted by the Soviet government. Her account is a memoir in the sense that the political background (the Cold War and détente) becomes as important as the personal story, yet it is written not by a statesman but by a poet-novelist and the story is not that of personal ambition but of frustrated love. Literary scholars and creative writers will appreciate the wide range of styles in this text, its mixture of vivid description and lyrical, poignant expressions of emotion that are only occasionally marred by turgid prose passages of philosophizing about personal existence and spirituality. The book will interest feminist theorists who study the role of ideology in the construction of subjectivity and critics who read it as context for analyzing Cherry's poetry. Appropriate for college and university libraries.—B. Braendlin, Florida State University

WS-0885   PS3515.E343   89-30985 MARC
Critical essays on Lillian Hellman, ed. by Mark W. Estrin. G.K. Hall, 1990 (c1989). 275p index afp ISBN 0-8161-8890-4, $38.00

This selection of essays on Lillian Hellman's work, life, and persona is an admirable addition to the "Critical Essays in American Literature" series. Editor Mark Estrin (English and film studies, Rhode Island College), a recognized authority on modern theater, has compiled and classified recent scholarly work on Hellman. His selections are balanced and exciting. He includes narrowly defined literary essays, feminist critiques, and wider-ranging commentaries—some of which were written especially for this collection. Because of the focus on recent scholarship, some of the lesser and earlier works receive short shrift. The most impressive sections are those that deal with Hellman's memoirs and her persona. Evenhanded and scholarly in his approach, the editor has included friends and enemies, all of whom are impassioned and eloquent. Sidney Hook, John Hersey, Martha Gellhorn, and Pauline Kael are among the most stimulating and contentious of the delightful cast of critics. Recent scholarship dealing with the genre of autobiographical writing and the uses of the persona, the nature and uses of lies, and the portraits of the aging writer are particularly fascinating. And through it all, this contentious, loyal, ferocious, dramatic woman appears in all her power. Recommended for academic and public libraries.—N. M. Tischler, Pennsylvania State University, University Park Campus

WS-0886   PS3554   93-39256 CIP
Danticat, Edwidge. **Breath, eyes, memory.** Soho Press, 1994. 234p ISBN 1-56947-005-7, $20.00

Danticat's first published novel moves back and forth between the author's two homes, Haiti and the US, touching on the characters' complex relationships to both places. The central protagonist must come to terms not only with her place in a long line of strong women, but also with the violence inflicted on them by strangers and by their own mothers. The "test," used by generations of Haitian mothers to ascertain their daughters' virginity, is revealed as a violation which cripples women's spirits and suppresses their sexuality. It also, inevitably, distorts mother/daughter relationships. The style of the novel is lyrical and often arresting, the narrative fast paced. The information it contains about Haiti, while incidental, is substantial. The characters are convincing and sympathetic. The sexual violation theme does, however, seem heavy-handed at times. The main character, Sophie, and her mother, for instance, have fewer dimensions than one might wish. In all, this is a very readable, moving story. General and academic audiences.—J. Tharp, University of Wisconsin—Marshfield-Wood County

WS-0887   PS647   95-19641 MARC
Daughters of the fifth sun: a collection of Latina fiction and poetry, ed. by Bryce Milligan, Mary Guerrero Milligan, and Angela de Hoyos. Riverhead Books, 1995. 283p afp ISBN 1-57322-009-4, $23.95

This worthy anthology marks the appearance of the first selection of Latina poetry and narrative to be presented by an important New York publishing house. Through their excellent introduction, the editors scrutinize a longstanding perception that most contemporary Mexican American writing has only recently transcended its oral tradition, a prejudice that overlooks the fact that this same writing, particularly in the Southwest, enjoys very deep literary roots that date back to the early 19th century. The editors use the term "Latina" in its most inclusive sense: readers will find texts by Dominican American, Cuban American, Puerto Rican American, Brazilian American, and Jewish Chilean American as well as Mexican American women. What these women have in common is their multicultural identity and their ability to survive on the borderlands of reality. Happily, this anthology provides an opportunity to read selections not only by the older and more established of these writers but also by a new generation of Latinas who, while recognizing their indebtedness to their elder sisters, are taking their writing in exciting and challenging directions. Recommended for all collections.—J. J. Hassett, Swarthmore College

WS-0888   PS3563   94-18767 CIP
Denniston, Dorothy Hamer. **The fiction of Paule Marshall: reconstructions of history, culture, and gender.** Tennessee, 1995. 187p bibl index afp ISBN 0-87049-838-X, $32.00; ISBN 0-87049-839-8 pbk, $15.00

Denniston's book joins the growing body of criticism on Marshall's oeuvre that examines the possibilities for spiritual wholeness among African diasporic peoples within "a racist, sexist, and materialistic society." She targets the "African cultural survivals" (oral narrative, the proverb tradition, ornate and highly performative language, nonlinear and nondualistic cosmologies) as they provide not only subject matter but "the essential framework for [Marshall's] artistry." Her chapter on *Brown Girl, Brownstones* (1959) best exemplifies the Barbadian cultural vernacular through which Marshall reveals her characters' mores and beliefs, via a wonderfully detailed reading of the sounds and figures of language of *Poets in the Kitchen* (1984). Denniston focuses as well on gender paradigms and interactions—notably, in her critical readings of "The Valley Between" (1954), Marshall's first published short story, and all of the novellas of *Soul Clap Hands and Sing* (1961). Lengthy citations and commentary and frequent emphasis on autobiographical connections substantiate Denniston's arguments, which, though wide-ranging conceptually and textually, cohere into an informative critique. All academic collections.—S. Bryant, Alfred University

WS-0889   PR9275   94-1309 CIP
Ferguson, Moira. **Jamaica Kincaid: where the land meets the body.** University Press of Virginia, 1994. 206p bibl index ISBN 0-8139-1519-8, $40.00; ISBN 0-8139-1520-1 pbk, $16.95

In this first complete and serious study of one of the most powerful female Anglophone writers in the Caribbean, Moira Ferguson paints a critically sensitive and poignantly accurate portrait. Through a highly stylized prose she expertly captures the tensions imprinted in Kincaid's novels and short stories between colonial degradation and the disillusionment of postcolonial realities. Each novel is carefully analyzed as an individual text and thoroughly examined as a chronicle of Antiguan life still unfolding. Ferguson offers detailed commentary and footnotes. The book is recommended for scholars of Caribbean literature and history and for those seeking a fuller comprehension of Kincaid's textual style and thematic development.—A. J. Guillaume Jr., Humboldt State University

WS-0890   PS3565   94-48867 CIP
Flannery O'Connor: new perspectives, ed. by Sura P. Rath and Mary Neff Shaw. Georgia, 1996. 225p bibl index afp ISBN 0-8203-1749-7, $35.00; ISBN 0-8203-1804-3 pbk, $18.00

These ten politically correct essays provide contemporary perspectives on Flannery O'Connor's work: its marketing and reception; gender, rhetorical, and stylistic issues; O'Connor's asceticism as a necessary corollary of her art; and her treatment of southern society. Essays by Marshall Bruce Gentry and Mary Neff Shaw on conflicts between O'Connor's narrators and her characters provide helpful close readings. Sarah Gordon's essay on "The Crop," an apprentice story depicting a would-be southern female writer's search for an appropriate subject, is especially instructive on the gender question. To find her own vision and voice, O'Connor had to reject the domestic role for women and society's demands that she "act pretty." Patricia Yaeger's startling essay on the grotesque indicts racist, sexist southern society as the source of deformity and sadism in O'Connor's fiction, the subject of which is not Catholicism but an absurd social system that makes insanity and cruelty the norm. Yaeger says O'Connor tortures both her characters and her readers in writing of precariously constructed values and contradictory codes in a society falling apart. These essays, all on the abuse of power, are cogently argued and well written with strong conclusions. All academic collections.—*M. S. Stephenson, University of Texas at Brownsville*

WS-0891   PS3557   92-16731 CIP
Fowler, Virginia C. **Nikki Giovanni.** Twayne, 1992. 192p (Twayne's United States authors series, 613) bibl index afp ISBN 0-8057-3983-1, $26.95

Fowler's literary biography of Nikki Giovanni, the poet who was among those at the center of the Black Arts Movement of the 1960s, fills a gap in available criticism on this important period in African American literature. Giovanni was one of the first black women poets at the time to read and record her poems with the accompaniment of African American music. The combination of her political views, her spiritual nature, and general tone of defiance appealed to a mass audience of African Americans during the 12 years between 1970 and 1982. In an effort to explain what she sees as a contradiction between Giovanni's continuing popularity as a speaker and her omission from critical studies of American poetry, Fowler provides a thoroughly researched book on the poet's life, the social and political context in which she writes, and the distinguishing features of each of Giovanni's published collections of poems. Particularly useful are the biographical introduction, the formal interview between Giovanni and Fowler included in the appendix, and the bibliography. This will prove useful to students of all levels and to the general reader. Recommended for all libraries with holdings in American poetry, African American literature, and American women's literature.—*A. Deck, University of Illinois at Urbana—Champaign*

WS-0892   PS3556   93-41001 CIP
Frye, Ellen. **Amazon story bones.** Spinsters Ink, 1994. 193p ISBN 1-883523-01-X, $21.95; ISBN 1-883523-00-1 pbk, $10.95

What would Greek mythology have been like if women had told the stories? In Frye's imaginative reconstruction, the tellers of the tales are Amazons. Their "myths" offer a clear sense of the limitations imposed on women's lives in the traditional accounts. The story bones of the title are animal bones kept in a pouch, shaken out, and "read" to the Gorgons by the Grey Ladies, the mysterious Graeae of Greek myth, but most of the tales are told by an old lady who returns after many years to find her granddaughter and her now aged and crippled Amazon partner. Before the patriarchal outsiders attacked their world, Amazon women would choose the men who would father their babies, and they raised only the female children; their partners in life were other women. Various characters from the Trojan war also figure in the story, described from a slave's rather than a master's point of view. These spare and elegant stories convey a sense of the mind-set of people in the bronze age, and the conditions in which they lived (with the exception of the tomatoes in the garden, which would not have appeared there until some three thousand years later). An attractive work of historical fiction. General readers.—*M. R. Lefkowitz, Wellesley College*

WS-0893   PS3565   94-49320 CIP
Frye, Joanne S. **Tillie Olsen: a study of the short fiction.** Twayne/Prentice Hall International, 1995. 232p (Twayne's studies in short fiction, 60) bibl index afp ISBN 0-8057-0863-4, $20.95

Frye's study offers a close analysis of Olsen's short stories, an invaluable interview with Olsen, and a short section of critical responses. Frey (College of Wooster) focuses on Olsen's commitment to writing about "life comprehensions," ordinary human experiences, especially those of women and working-class people. Olsen's intensely felt and expressed stories, told in "transformative" language, have caused many readers to empathize strongly with her characters. The interview with Olsen reveals the connections between the actual people and events of her life and her nonautobiographical stories. The critics' section discusses comments both apt and inapt. Invaluable for English department libraries, this work complements Constance Coiner's *Better Red: The Writing and Resistance of Tillie Olsen and Meridel Le Sueur* (CH, Oct'95), which focuses on the authors' relationship to the Communist Party; Mickey Pearlman and Abby Werlock's *Tillie Olsen* (CH, Dec'91), with its interview of Olsen and comments on her *Silences* and *Yonnondio*; Abigail Martin's briefer *Tillie Olsen* (CH, Jan'85); and Elaine Neil Orr's *Tillie Olsen and a Feminist Spiritual Vision* (CH, Dec'87), which gives a religious interpretation of Olsen's work. All collections.—*J. Overmyer, emerita, Ohio State University*

WS-0894   Orig
García Ramis, Magali. **Happy days, Uncle Sergio,** tr. by Carmen C. Esteves. White Pine, NY, 1995. 175p ISBN 1-877727-52-0 pbk, $12.00

This work by García Ramis (born 1946) is representative of a recent boom in Puerto Rican literature by women writers. A college professor, García Ramis is part of a current generation of women writers trained in literary theory and resolved to document women's issues in Puerto Rican society. *Happy Days, Uncle Sergio* (first published in Spanish in 1986), her first novel, traces Puerto Rican industrialization since the 1950s from the point of view of a girl narrator. The novel presents a series of vignettes illustrative of changes in Puerto Rican society, covering incidents that are important to children but that often are dismissed as trivial by adults. It is significant that many of those events treat differences in gender and consequent influence on the development of societal roles. A rich plot connects numerous characters (many of them adults) with the girl narrator, a sort of outsider in her family, since she constantly questions local traditions. This may be the novel's greatest innovation, because Puerto Rican literature has traditionally preferred to develop the social rebel in male characters, ignoring women and girls as prospective critics of their society. Recommended to all readers interested in contemporary Puerto Rican history and to feminist scholars.—*R. Ocasio, Agnes Scott College*

WS-0895   PS3557   95-9444 CIP
Glück, Tereze. **May you live in interesting times.** Iowa, 1995. 163p afp ISBN 0-87745-519-8, $22.95

In these elusive, subtle short stories Glück tempts the reader with surprises as she moves from the familiar to the exotic. On occasion Glück's wit sparkles like Grace Paley's. Her first-person narration resounds with moments of felt life. The women in her tales have lively interiors, despite their mundane situations. When Glück's women speak of emptiness, of impossible love, their tone is clipped, matter-of-fact. This device allows the pain to surface without sentimentality. Jean Rhys would recognize a kindred spirit in Glück's subjects. This is one collection of stories to be read slowly in order to savor its understated art. All levels.—*H. Susskind, Monroe Community College*

WS-0896   PS3503   91-21265 CIP
Goldensohn, Lorrie. **Elizabeth Bishop: the biography of a poetry.** Columbia, 1993 (c1992). 306p index afp ISBN 0-231-07662-2, $30.00; ISBN 0-231-07663-0 pbk, $15.95

Bishop, whose critical reputation has ascended rapidly since her death, was once widely regarded as an essentially passionless poet. Goldensohn decisively refutes this view. Basing her discussion on a comprehensive familiarity with Bishop's many unpublished poems, and particularly on a poem of lesbian eroticism, "It is marvelous to wake up together," which Goldensohn discovered in Brazil and arranged to have published in 1988, the author rereads Bishop's work in light of its pervasive but latent sexual charge. The book is skillfully written, with attention throughout to Bishop's subtly nuanced language. Its structure is unusual: it begins with Bishop's middle years in Brazil, then zig-zags tellingly throughout her career, early and late. Along the way Goldensohn provides illuminating readings of many of Bishop's poems. This remains a very important study of a poet whose significance seems to grow with each passing year. Those collections—graduate, undergraduate, and general—that have not yet acquired it should make haste to do so. Notes; 23 pages of photographs.—*T. Travisano, Hartwick College*

WS-0897   PS3545   94-12928 MARC
Gretlund, Jan Nordby. **Eudora Welty's aesthetics of place.** Delaware, 1994. (Dist. by Associated University Presses) 456p bibl index ISBN 0-87413-562-1, $47.50

Both scholars and ordinary readers of Eudora Welty will find much of interest in this hefty volume: a recent (1993) previously unpublished interview with the Mississippi writer, an expanded version of a previously published 1978 interview, an extensive analysis of an obscure early story ("Acrobats in a Park"), sensitive and stimulating discussions of all the novels and most of the stories, a keen appreciation of the cultural milieu reflected in Welty's work, and a valiant attempt to define an underlying "aesthetics of place." All these interesting elements, however, are here only to illustrate Gretlund's oft-repeated thesis that "Welty's fiction represents a cultural continuity of basic Agrarian ideas from their origin in their rural South to their presence in the urbanized South." The capital "A" in Agrarian is significant, for Gretlund insists on Welty's allegiance not just to some pastoral sentiment but to the principles of the Nashville Agrarians' 1930 ideological manifesto *I'll Take My Stand*—despite her own assertion in this 1993 interview that "I had no philosophy I was pursuing, and no aesthetics, I'm just writing as a tale-teller." Ultimately, the type of "literary Agrarian" Gretlund describes is vague enough to encompass half the Southern Renaissance. Academic and general audiences.—*A. J. Griffith, Our Lady of the Lake University*

WS-0898   PS3545   90-2732 CIP
Gygax, Franziska. **Serious daring from within: female narrative strategies in Eudora Welty's novels.** Greenwood, 1990. 160p (Contributions in women's studies, 114) bibl index afp ISBN 0-313-26865-7, $35.00

Believing with Virginia Woolf that language is gendered, Franziska Gygax, disregarding Welty's proclamation that she does not believe in all the issues of the women's movement and that as a writer she has never suffered any discrimination because of her sex, determines that one may gain insight into possible feminist views in Welty's works by exploring the language of her narrative strategies or those narrative devices that are indicative of female writing. She examines point of view in *Delta Wedding*; allusions and myths in *The Golden Apple*; dialogue in *Losing Battles*; and memory and concept of time in *The Optimist's Daughter*, all with the idea of determining what is essentially feminine. Although the subject is forced and the argument thin, Gygax adds to an already well-documented contention among feminists that most women writers by using men's language for expressing essentially feminine feelings give identity and emphasis to a dark, hidden area of women's makeup. This is not an important work. Unfortunately, it is representative of the slight treatment Welty's works are presently receiving and adds to a growing concern that Welty's works are not getting the serious consideration they deserve.—*R. L. Brooks, Baylor University*

WS-0899   PS3563   94-2195 CIP
Harding, Wendy. **A world of difference: an inter-cultural study of Toni Morrison's novels,** by Wendy Harding and Jacky Martin. Greenwood, 1994. 188p (Contributions in Afro-American and African studies, 171) bibl index afp ISBN 0-313-28980-8, $49.95

Offering "criticism at the interface," Harding and Martin use reading strategies that take into account the ways in which cultural determinants overlap in literary texts, the plurality of cultural referents that provide sites of dense complexity. Applied to the novels of Toni Morrison, this approach rejects any critical method based on binary oppositions in favor of more hybrid and dynamic principles of analysis and interpretation. More specifically, Harding and Martin are concerned with exploring the ways in which Morrison's novels straddle both Western and black literary and cultural traditions. By exploring such issues as representations of the self, gender, community, myth, ritual, and storytelling in Morrison's fiction, the authors seek to show how she works within and against Western traditions to create new narrative forms. An excellent selected bibliography is included. Although its sometimes dense prose and abstract critical vocabulary will not make this work easily accessible to general readers and many undergraduates, *A World of Difference* should attract the attention of sophisticated readers of Toni Morrison, graduate students, and literary critics.—*J. A. Miller, Trinity College (CT)*

WS-0900   PS3503   92-18960 CIP
Harrison, Victoria. **Elizabeth Bishop's poetics of intimacy.** Cambridge, 1993. 252p bibl index ISBN 0-521-43203-0, $59.95

In this meaty book, Harrison reads Elizabeth Bishop, who has lately won wide recognition as a great American poet, in the context of extensive quotations—typos carefully preserved—from Bishop's voluminous unpublished writing, including letters, workbooks, the many unfinished poems and stories, and drafts of published work. Harrison examines this material in the light of recent perspectives from gender and cultural studies. Harrison's promised discussion of Bishop as a pragmatist emerging from the tradition of William James and John Dewey is not as well sustained as her reading of the indirectly but insistently gendered character of Bishop's work. But this comparative neglect is consistent with

Harrison's obviously greater interest in Bishop as a self-censoring but intricately fascinating writer on sexuality and politics than in Bishop-as-philosophical-observer, as a poet whose skills make her an acknowledged master of the postmodern nature lyric. Hence, Harrison's reading of deft Bishop landscape poems like "Arrival at Santos" is disappointing. On the other hand, Harrison is strong, alert, and sometimes downright revelatory when engaged with poems and stories (especially unpublished writings) that deal with Bishop's inner-conflicts about sexuality, anger, politics, and culture. Not an introduction, this challenging contribution to Bishop studies is strongly recommended for advanced undergraduates, graduates, and faculty. Good bibliography and index.—*T. Travisano, Hartwick College*

WS-0901   PS3558   94-34999 CIP
Haynes, David. **Somebody else's mama.** Milkweed Editions, 1995. 340p afp ISBN 1-57131-003-7, $21.95

This impressive first novel illuminates the lives of a African American family in a small predominantly black midwestern town. Haynes explores a set of interconnected issues, including black class structure, politics, and gender relationships. Revoicing themes and motifs typically associated with African American women writers from Zora Neale Hurston—whose Eatonville is literary ancestor of Haynes's town—to Gloria Naylor and Ntozake Shange, Haynes is particularly astute in his treatment of male protagonist Al Johnson's emotional withdrawal. The center of the novel, however, is the relationship between Paula Johnson and Miss Xenobia Kezee, Al's mother, who moves in with the Johnsons when she can no longer live independently. One of the finest portraits of an aged woman in American literature, Miss Kezee links the historical experience of an older generation of black midwesterners with the relatively affluent present of some of their descendants. Forging a style that combines elements of literary and oral traditions, Haynes clearly establishes himself as a writer who should be read by anyone interested in the complexity of contemporary multicultural fiction. All collections.—*C. Werner, University of Wisconsin—Madison*

WS-0902   PS3569   91-36800 CIP
Hill, Dorothy Combs. **Lee Smith.** Twayne, 1992. 157p (TUSAS, 592) bibl index afp ISBN 0-8057-7640-0, $22.95

According to Hill (Georgetown University), Lee Smith writes for "self-repair," and her fiction describes the search "for that place—in art, in language, in self-assertion, in imagination, in passion—where wholeness lies." Beneath a "funny, fetching, come-hither" surface, Smith's short stories and novels deliver a radical message about "the sacralizing of the female and of female sexuality, seeing female flesh as sacred as male flesh." After the "watershed" novel *Black Mountain Breakdown* (1980), her "damaged" women characters began to realize possibilities for reconciliation and redemption in such popular books as *Oral History* (1983), *Family Linen* (1985), and *Fair and Tender Ladies* (1988). Her Appalachian settings have become known to critics as "Lee Smith country," and part of Smith's appeal is her discovery of a narrative voice for her mountain characters. Despite Hill's overemphasis on mythic elements—especially red-haired Aphrodite figures—this first book-length study of Lee Smith is valuable for its overview of her life, themes, and relationship to other Southern authors. Hill quotes from private conversations with Smith as well as from public lectures. Recommended for all libraries.—*J. W. Hall, University of Mississippi*

WS-0903   PS3558   93-7677 CIP
Hogan, Linda. **The book of medicines: poems.** Coffee House, 1993. 87p ISBN 1-56689-010-1 pbk, $11.95

This new volume of Hogan's poetry draws on the spiritual and ethical qualities of her American Indian heritage to explain why she needs (and, by extrapolation, we need) to be healed: she needs to recover her pre-rational roots as a metaphoric being commingling with the animals ("long-toothed partner/ in a sacrificial dance"), the elements ("there was no way back to the forest/ except to become a spring of clear water"), her dead ancestors ("This blood/ is a map of the road between us./ I am why they survived."), and the gender-laden origins of things ("Inside the dark human waters/ of our mothers/ ... we knew the drifts of continents/ and moving tides.") Those born into the Judeo-Christian tradition will have a harder time healing. Hogan's poetry is not, however, didactic, facile, or sentimental. She sees danger in her own traditions, as well as in the fact of being a woman. Her free verse is sharply focused, imagistic, and rhythmical. No point is belabored; rather the poet often uses the powerful device of a disconnected final image to carry the meaning of the poem. General; undergraduate and up.—*J. Nower, San Diego State University*

WS-0904 PS3558 95-24563 CIP
Hogan, Linda. **Solar storms: a novel.** Scribner, 1995. 351p ISBN 0-684-81227-4, $22.00

Solar Storms, the story of four contemporary Native American women who represent four generations of a Cree family, has three distinct parts. The first part—reminiscent of Leslie Silko's *Ceremony* (CH, Jul'77) and Louis Owens's *The Sharpest Sight* (CH, Jun'92)—deals with the female protagonist's search for her Cree roots after a lifetime in white foster homes. The second part describes the women's northbound journey to the ancestral Cree lands, a trip that permits the women to strengthen their bonds with nature and its powers. In the third part, which deals with the political situation surrounding hydroelectric projects, the protagonist realizes how her mother, physically and psychologically damaged by encounters with Euramerican greed, could have scarred her daughter's face and body as an infant. The protagonist becomes the symbol of the two cultures' encounters. *Solar Storms* is innovative in that it concentrates exclusively on the voices of Native women and their powers. The narrative is linear; there are occasional flashbacks of the older women, but none of the fragmented, complex narrative structure readers have come to expect from Native writers (see, for instance, Louise Erdrich's *Love Medicine*, 1986). All collections.—*B. Hans, University of North Dakota*

WS-0905 PS3558 94-22683 CIP
Huston, Paula. **Daughters of song.** Random House, 1995. 363p afp ISBN 0-679-41969-1, $23.00

This skillful first novel engages the reader from the beginning chapter. The coming of age story of a female pianist, it dramatizes the familiar issues of loyalty and love (typical of any novel with a 20-year-old protagonist) and brings into consideration the interesting additional complexities paramount in the lives of unusually talented creative artists in 20th-century America. The heroine, Sylvia, is studying piano far from home at a conservatory in Baltimore. The focus of her artistic struggle is a particularly difficult piece from Beethoven's late period, opus 111. The author does an admirable job of revealing Sylvia's development through her increasing understanding of this musical piece and the composer behind it. This charming work will find a ready audience within the college community because it deals with problems students themselves are confronting and, more importantly, because it offers realistic and yet optimistic possibilities for solutions to those problems. All levels.—*S. Raeschild, University of Cincinnati*

WS-0906 PS508 92-45101 MARC
Infinite divisions: an anthology of Chicana literature, [comp.] by Tey Diana Rebolledo and Eliana S. Rivero. Arizona, 1993. 393p bibl index afp ISBN 0-8165-1252-3, $40.00; ISBN 0-8165-1384-8 pbk, $19.95

This much-needed book is a compilation of writings by Chicanas. In addition to the contemporary Chicana writers such as Trambley, Cisneros, Castillo, Corpi, and Anzaldua, the editors have included samplings of works by early Chicanas such as Doña Eulalia Perez, Catalina Gurule, and Patricia Gallegos, as well as the works of familiar earlier Chicanas such as Nina Otero-Warren, Fabiola Cabeza de Baca Gilbert, and Cleofas M. Jaramillo. The editors' goal is to present a variety of writings that illustrate the complexity of the Chicana pyche; thus the use of the title, *Infinite Divisions*, an allusion to Bernice Zamora's poem, becomes a metaphor for the identity of the Chicana: "You insult me/ When you say I'm/ Schizophrenic./ My divisions are Infinite." In the end, the text becomes a historical recording of Chicana writings. Unlike the recent *Mirrors Beneath the Earth*, ed. by Ray González (CH, Oct'93) and *Pieces of the Heart*, ed. by Gary Soto (1993), the structure of *Infinite Divisions* makes the text a good tool for survey courses in ethnic literature or gender studies. Strongly recommended. General; graduate; undergraduate; faculty.—*J. Luna Lawhn, San Antonio College*

WS-0907 Orig
Jane's stories: an anthology of work by midwestern women, ed. by Glenda Bailey-Mershon et al. Wild Dove Studio and Press, Inc., 759 E. Stark Drive, P.O. Box 789, Palatine, IL 60078, 1994. 130p ISBN 0-9639894-0-5 pbk, $9.95

Not only short fiction but poetry, personal essays, "photo/vignettes," and other artwork are included in *Jane's Stories*. The title pays tribute to "the group of women called *Jane* who founded and operated an underground abortion providers' network in the days before Roe v. Wade." Biographical notes on the 30 authors and artists reveal a wide range of ethnic and professional backgrounds, but most contributors have ties to Chicago, rural Illinois and Indiana, or other midwestern settings, and many emphasize their feminist concerns. Sometimes this feminism is humorously displayed, as in Stephanie Harris's colorful poem, "Feminists Have the Best Earrings." In contrast, Marie Micheletti's futuristic story, "You Have the Right to Remain Silent," chillingly recalls Margaret Atwood's *The Handmaid's Tale* (1985). Many of the writers focus on relationships—with parents, children, lovers, students, and even (in Evelyn E. Shockley's poem "Connection") with a woman glimpsed on the street, "a Ghanaian princess, thinly disguised." Several titles evoke domestic scenes, but works like "Baking," "The Housewife's Autumn Hymn," and "There's No Place Like Home" are exposés rather than homages. For general readers with feminist interests.—*J. W. Hall, University of Mississippi*

WS-0908 PS3505 95-6127 CIP
Jennings, La Vinia Delois. **Alice Childress.** Twayne/Prentice Hall International, 1995. 157p (TUSAS, 652) bibl index afp ISBN 0-8057-3963-7, $22.95

Jennings (Univ. of Tennessee, Knoxville) calls Alice Childress's literary output a well-kept secret. An African American playwright, novelist, and young-adult-fiction writer, Childress (1916-94) is best known for her adolescent novel *A Hero Ain't Nothin' but a Sandwich* (1973). Long before it was popular to do so, Childress explored social and psychological themes from black women's perspectives. Furthermore, she disregarded the accepted taboos of teen novel writing and dwelt on the stark realities of drugs, racism, AIDS, homosexuality, divorce, and crime. An important aim of Childress's work was to destroy the myth of the black woman's emasculation of the black man. As a dramatist, Childress demonstrated how the African cultural heritage that has survived in America is an essential ingredient in the African American experience. Jennings provides a thorough and detailed study of the major characters in most of Childress's plays and novels. She concentrates on thematic issues of racial intolerance, sexual stereotyping, and class tension affecting black men and women. This careful, in-depth study is an excellent work of dedicated scholarship. Highly recommended for all literature, theater, and black studies collections.—*A. Costanzo, Shippensburg University of Pennsylvania*

WS-0909 PS3513 93-30366 CIP
Jonza, Nancylee Novell. **The underground stream: the life and art of Caroline Gordon.** Georgia, 1995. 464p index afp ISBN 0-8203-1628-8, $34.95

Known as the conservative southern lady married to poet Allen Tate, Gordon cultivated the myth that Tate was her mentor. Her self-mythologizing contrived this persona, but her interest in prose and aesthetics actually preceded her marriage. This detailed biography—which draws on letters, unpublished works, and manuscript drafts—presents a complex and unhappy woman and adds much to other biographical studies (including Frederick McDowell's biography *Caroline Gordon*, 1966; Ann Waldron's *Close Connections: Caroline Gordon and the Southern Renaissance*, CH, Feb'88; and Veronica Makowsky's *Caroline Gordon: A Biography*, CH, Oct'89). Jonza's new material emphasizes Gordon's matriarchal tradition, early journalism career, Catholicism, and alcoholism. Focusing on the would-be southern belle before and after her marriage, Jonza's view of this interesting life focuses on Gordon's self-destructive confusion: should she frankly celebrate human creativity or honor conventional gender roles? Jonza demonstrates that Gordon's decision to embrace a dishonest gender identity enervated her creatively and left a sad "unsexed" life. Useful for advanced students of 20th-century American letters. Upper-division undergraduate; graduate; faculty.—*S. A. Parker, Hiram College*

WS-0910 PS3569 95-911 CIP
Kennedy, Liam. **Susan Sontag: mind as passion.** Manchester, 1995. (Dist. by St. Martin's) 146p index ISBN 0-7190-3785-9, $35.00

Sontag has been an icon for more than three decades. Kennedy (Univ. of Birmingham) gives the pop celebrity, avant-garde, enfant terrible maverick her first extended critical examination. In this chronological treatment, the author presents Sontag as a cloistered cleric of letters, indebted to European intellectual culture and her New York City context. He identifies her key themes as isolation, self-sufficiency, transcendence of passions, and melancholy modernism. Eschewing the biographical subtext of her work, Kennedy discusses Sontag's metaphorical treatment of such subjects as "camp," photography, and illness; he emphasizes her commitment to the generalist's freedom to pursue personal taste (which explains Sontag's eclectic and pluralistic role as a social critic of mass culture). Her self-proclaimed occupation of the sphere of public liberalism is evident in Sontag's fiction, from her early novels *The Benefactor* (1963) and *Death Kit* (CH, Jan'68) to *The Volcano Lover* (1992). In recent years Sontag's literary work has turned toward theater and questions of the failure of intellectual community. With its useful notes, this interesting examination of an evolving figure is recommended for students of modern intellectual history.—*S. A. Parker, Hiram College*

WS-0911   PS3569   94-36113 CIP
Lester, Neal A. **Ntozake Shange: a critical study of the plays.**
Garland, 1995. 321p (Garland reference library of the humanities, 1441) bibl index afp ISBN 0-8153-0314-9, $49.00

Begun as a dissertation, this is the first full-length study of this significant American author. Lester begins by discussing Shange's major theatrical contribution, the choreopoem, which is "a theatrical expression that combines poetry, prose, song, dance, and music." He examines in depth Shange's unique use of language, her glorification of the heritage of all people of color, and the unflinching condemnation of racism and patriarchy in five of her works (*For Colored Girls Who Have Considered Suicide, When the Rainbow Is Enuf; Spell #7; A Photograph: Lovers in Motion; Boogie Woogie Landscapes*, one of three plays in *Three Pieces*; and *From Okra to Greens*). In the book's foreword, Shange expresses "excitement" about this book. Those interested in African American literature, women's literature and/or American theater will share this feeling. Lester has given a probing, scholarly analysis of an often misunderstood and underappreciated talent. Upper-division undergraduates and above.—*L. J. Parascandola, Long Island University—Brooklyn Campus*

WS-0912   E185   93-22731 MARC
Life notes: personal writings by contemporary black women,
[ed.] by Patricia Bell-Scott. W.W. Norton, 1994. 429p ISBN 0-393-03593-X, $25.00

This brilliant, exciting collecton of selections from the journals, diaries, and personal notebooks of contemporary African American women—some published but most unpublished—was, Bell-Scott says, compiled with four objectives: to honor the "nameless women and girls" who have recorded their lives; to share their rich experiences; to show "self-defining women" speaking for themselves; and to encourage others to write. The youngest correspondent is eight years old, the eldest 64. The eight divisions into which the writings are placed cover such topics as reflecting girlhood, violation and betrayal, and claiming a new self. All the writings are moving; they are also honest, at times painfully so, revealing heartbreak and joyous depths. One reads the anger of Jamaica Kincaid at the British conquerors of her island, Antigua, and the bravery of Audre Lorde, who is dying of cancer. There is, in short, as much diversity as one might find in any group of women, but these women, many having suffered for their skin color and place in the world, bring a special poignancy to their insights. Very highly recommended for African American studies and women's studies collections. Undergraduate (all levels); graduate; faculty; general.—*J. Overmyer, Ohio State University*

WS-0913   PS3562   92-40859 CIP
Lorde, Audre. **The marvelous arithmetics of distance: poems, 1987-1992.** W.W. Norton, 1993. 60p ISBN 0-393-03513-1, $18.95

In this, the author's final book of poems before her death, the greatness of Lorde's talent is evident. In "Legacy—Hers," the poet who is "Learning how to die" struggles to come to terms, not only with her own death but with the death of her lover. "Constructing my own/ book of your last hours/ how we tried to connect, . . . one bright Black woman/ to another bred for endurance/ for battle." Lorde explores the relationships between herself and her mother, friends,

lovers, and sisters, and in the passionately moving poem "Inheritance—His," she comes to terms with her father. "Who were you outside the 23rd Psalm?/ Knowing so little/ how did I become so much/ like you?" The poet's themes are a woven pattern made of grief, loss, rage. Looking back on Lorde's earlier books, one sees in this volume a poet who has grown in wisdom and whose poetry is finely honed, lyrical, and fearless. Like Alice Walker, Toni Morrison, Sonia Sanchez, and Lucille Clifton, she writes with clarity and courage. Highly recommended for academic and public libraries.—*M. Gillan, Passaic County Community College*

WS-0914   PS3566   90-49425 CIP
Macpherson, Pat. **Reflecting on *The Bell Jar**. Routledge, 1991. 101p bibl ISBN 0-415-04393-X pbk, $11.95

Macpherson's slim book draws heavily upon Sylvia Plath's psychological struggle, Foucault's theories, Cold War political dynamics, and feminist politics to interpret *The Bell Jar*. Fundamental to her thesis, but unconvincing, are the connections she asserts between national security as dramatized in the Rosenberg espionage trial and execution and the psychiatric regimen of electrotherapy that Plath and her heroine experienced. More convincingly sustained is Macpherson's analogy of the coercive effects of J. Edgar Hoover-era Cold War paranoia (with its insistence on political conformity and restricted modes of female identity) during the early stages of Plath's and her heroine's writing careers. Bolstering her arguments with the opinions of Michel Foucault, Raymond Williams, Doris Lessing, Adrienne Rich, and Marilyn Monroe, Macpherson reads Plath and Esther Greenwood as psychological victims of American political and sexist oppression, as representatives of societal betrayal of educated women forced to diminish their worth to gain public approval. Feminist interpretation based on matrophobia and self-hatred that were at the center of 1950s femininity is more cogently argued than is the writer's Marxist thesis.—*S. L. Kremer, Kansas State University*

WS-0915   PS3563   91-7248 CIP
Maddux, Rachel. **Communication, the autobiography of Rachel Maddux, and her novella, *Turnip's blood**, ed. with introd. by Nancy A. Walker. Tennessee, 1991. 209p afp ISBN 0-87049-699-9, $24.95

The publication of these writings of Rachel Maddux (1913-81) brings to fresh light the work of a little-known but fascinating author. Maddux published three novels, one work of nonfiction, and several short stories; she is best known for *A Walk in the Spring Rain*, which was made into a movie starring Ingrid Bergman and Anthony Quinn. Her autobiography, *Communication*, written when she was 28 and hitherto unpublished both conceals and reveals. Far from writing the standard and-then-I-did-this-and-said-that tale, she presents impressions rather than straight narration. Her revelations are honest, sometimes cruelly so, and the prose sings. The novella, *Turnip's Blood*, tells of a childlike woman who marries a much older man, to whom she brings happiness. But at the end she weeps knowing that she is emotionally growing up. Both works reveal a careful thinker writing in spare style, with considerable honest inner knowledge and no pretense. The interesting foreword by Susan Ford Wiltshire and the invaluable introduction by Nancy A. Walker, which traces Maddux's life and works up to her death, are both indispensable. Contains illustrations, preface, and bibliography. Recommended for women's studies and literature collections.—*J. Overmyer, Ohio State University*

WS-0916   PS3563   93-31513 CIP
Mairs, Nancy. **Voice lessons: on becoming a (woman) writer.**
Beacon Press, 1994. 166p bibl ISBN 0-8070-6006-2, $15.00

Mairs writes with a flair for the personal that often makes her personal essays wonderfully intimate. Her first collection, *Plaintext* (1986), was refreshing and original. In this work, she continues the exploration of her own life as the representative locale of experience by American women today. Her essay titles give some indication of both her quirkiness and her range, for example, "Reading Houses, Writing, Lives: The French Connection"; "The Literature of Personal Disaster"; and "Body at Work." Here, however, in her latest volume, she provides a much more extended feminist literary theory than previously as the surrounding membrane within which to understand her ideas. To some extent, this has a disorienting effect, creating within the reader an almost double vision as Mairs slides back and forth sometimes uncomfortably between the academic (which she eschews) and the quotidian with all its messy reality.

Nonetheless, this essay collection provides many lustrous moments. It would be a good addition and an effective balance in a library collection already full of more traditional essay selections or in any library with a solid feminist section. General and academic audiences.—*S. Raeschild, University of New Mexico*

WS-0917   PS3563   95-14834 CIP
Major, Devorah. **An open weave.** Seal, 1995. 182p ISBN 1-878067-66-4, $20.95

Major uses poetic prose to create a story about the town of Buttonhole, California, which was settled by African American cowboys who worked their way west and then established families. The novel focuses on three generations of women in one of those families: Ernestine, the blind grandmother who weaves the cloth and patterns that fill the walls of the house; Iree, the visionary and seer, whose epilepsy enhances her ability to see; and Imani, the strong-willed and proud teenage daughter. Major concentrates on the way the women give birth to and nurture one another. Central to these themes are Ernestine's blindness and her daughter's ability to see into the future and the past. Time is an open weave, a cloth of connection stretching back to everyone in the family, living and dead. Imani asks her grandmother, "Gramma? How come you never really finish your cloth? Just weave and weave. We got cloth all over the walls, but ain't none of it finished ...." "Nuthin' to finish Imani. Nuthin' never finished. Only things stop sometimes, and then start up again." So it is with the lives of these women, who know that "the one thing none of them ever let go of all the way was family." All collections.—*M. Gillan, Passaic County Community College*

WS-0918   PS3566   93-33848 CIP
Malcolm, Janet. **The Silent woman: Sylvia Plath & Ted Hughes.** Knopf, 1994 (c1993). 208p ISBN 0-679-43158-6, $23.00

Journalist Janet Malcolm's fascinating book is not a biography of Sylvia Plath and Ted Hughes, but a biography of several other biographies, concentrating on Anne Stevenson's writing of *Bitter Fame* (CH, Dec'89). She was edited and manipulated throughout by Ted Hughes' sister, Olwyn, who acted as her brother's protector, "the Cerberus of the Plath estate." As Malcolm remarks, "relatives are the biographer's hostile enemies." Like Stevenson and Malcolm herself, this reviewer, too, identified with Plath, as did so many other creative women struggling to find their roles in the 1950s and '60s. But despite this sense of identification and sympathy, the reader is left with new compassion for Ted Hughes, whose life has been so cruelly invaded by journalists and biographers. Although Malcolm claims she is exploring "the fundamental moral problem of journalism and biography that involve living people," and although she has interviewed every person who contributed material to the Plath myth, she comes off as much less objective than one would expect. As she herself concludes, "I have looked at my revisionist narrative and found it wanting. I have found every other narrative wanting." General; undergraduate.—*R. Whitman, Radcliffe College*

WS-0919   PS3547   94-7330 CIP
Marguerite Young, our darling: tributes and essays, ed. by Miriam Fuchs. Dalkey Archive, 1994. 143p afp ISBN 1-56478-055-4, $24.95

Can a collection that combines personal encounters, tributes, interviews, and nostalgia along with some serious critiques create sufficient interest to resurrect a novelist's major opus? *Miss MacIntosh, My Darling* (CH, Dec'65), a text of enormous heft comprising some 1,198 pages, has been compared to Proust's *Remembrance of Things Past*. Young's admirers also compare her writing to Joyce, Nabokov, and Virginia Woolf. Others cite the influence of William James. According to one of her former students at Iowa, Peter Marchant, Young encouraged her class to strive for inclusive writing, and to amplify emotions constantly. Young herself worked in a singular style of recovering life through memory and imagination. Joyce Petrolle, one of the critic-contributors, thus sums up the quality of Young's writings: "They fuse past, present, future, dream, wakefulness, fact and fiction in densely allusive, self-reflexive streams of consciousness that highlight the composite, textlike nature of consciousness." After a decade of minimalist fiction, Young might find a new readership for her work with this collection serving as enticement. General and academic audiences.—*H. Susskind, Monroe Community College*

WS-0920   PS3545   93-29518 CIP
Mark, Rebecca. **The dragon's blood: feminist intertextuality in Eudora Welty's *The Golden Apples*.** University Press of Mississippi, 1994. 304p bibl index afp ISBN 0-87805-661-0, $35.00

Welty's poetic prose is so lucid that it requires minimal criticism; it is so rich in allusions and so full of layered meanings that it invites analysis. *The Golden Apples* (1949) resonates with rich references to myth, literature, and culture. Mark picks this book apart like an intricately stitched tapestry, in which she spots multi-colored threads, interwoven and partially concealed. Using an acknowledged feminist, humanist, Marxist viewpoint, she seeks to prove that the work is a "detailed rewriting of the triumphant conqueror in early Greek and Celtic myth; as saviour in Christian theology; as defeated, lost, or cynical hero in early modernism." Story-by-story, she moves through the collection to make her case, pressing hard on her discussions of Faulkner, Frazier, and Joyce in particular. Although Mark's argument is very thorough and quite convincing, the reader is struck by Welty's own refusal to accept the label of "feminist," and her rejection of intertextualist criticism. Although an interesting analysis for teachers and critics who enjoy such "German thoroughness," the laborious dissection does of necessity ignore much of the poetic power of the language and the sheer delight of its imaging of reality. Mark's complex tapestry is far richer than its individual threads. Graduate; faculty.—*N. Tischler, Pennsylvania State University, University Park Campus*

WS-0921   PS3563   92-35600 CIP
Maso, Carole. **Ava: a novel.** Dalkey Archive, 1993. 274p bibl afp ISBN 1-56478-029-5, $19.95

A mysterious and richly allusive novel about the erotics of the liminal space between wakefulness and sleep as well as life and death, this novel is an interesting experiment in stream of consciousness. Using the narrator's reveries on the last day of her life, Maso is able to convey the bittersweet quality of memory and powerful longings for lost geographies of love and connection. Out of the fragments of Ava Klein's story, the reader pieces together a life of "passionate and promiscuous reading" and loving. In this dream-like prose poem, the narrator muses, "Almost everything is yet to be written by women about their infinite and complex sexuality, their eroticism." In her description of the evocative details of physical life, Maso contributes new insights into women's inner life. At moments in the narrative the innovative form seems a method the writer uses to avoid making necessary connections, yet the reader is also drawn into the inviting and provocative first-person narration. A novel worth reading for all interested in women's experience.—*L. Winters, College of Saint Elizabeth*

WS-0922   PS3563   95-125 CIP
McBreen, Joan. **A walled garden in Moylough: poems.** Story Line, 1995. 52p ISBN 1-885266-07-3 pbk, $10.95

These are intimate, subtle, controlled poems—more controlled than the reader would expect from the garish cover of the book. McBreen cultivates in the "walled garden" of poetic memory the affective presences of her mother and grandmother, but her reining in of gesture and language is so severe that seldom do these poems lift off the page into the reader's imagination. Too often they calculate a final effect, a frisson of closure, that seems Calvinistically predetermined. Many of McBreen's choices of poetic matter have already been licensed by Eavan Boland; in McBreen's lines one finds domesticity unstained by the externalizing politics of the past two decades. This work bears an odd resemblance to the second collection by another Irish poet—John Montague's *A Chosen Light* (1967). Recommended chiefly for library collections pertinent either to Women's studies or to Irish studies.—*T. D. Redshaw, University of St. Thomas*

WS-0923   PS3503   93-30390 CIP
McCabe, Susan. **Elizabeth Bishop: her poetics of loss.** Pennsylvania State, 1994. 273p bibl index afp ISBN 0-271-01047-9, $45.00; ISBN 0-271-01048-7 pbk, $16.95

McCabe's study of Elizabeth Bishop is an intelligent and sensitive treatment of an inadequately understood poet's descriptions of the strange, familiar-foreign objects in her lonely world. (The "man-moth" is a striking example.) A clear-thinking appreciator rather than an apologist for her subject, McCabe concedes (as did Bishop herself) that Bishop "is a poet of the small, the humble, the unmonumental." In order properly to present Bishop from an "eclectically untraditional" standpoint, the helpful introductory chapter is grounded in the literary movements of modernism and postmodernism. For the literary specialists it may be difficult to reconcile the author's equivocal "placement" of Bishop: that is, to accept McCabe's resistance to the available labels of "feminist, socialist, lesbian, poet," her "implicitly post-modern bias," and her belief that Bishop cannot be relegated to any one literary movement on the one hand, and her opinion that "the modern and the feminist permeate her work" on the other. Bishop's pervasive sense of loss—somewhat difficult to explain satisfactorily—informs this entire study. Other significant considerations include Bishop's "artifices of independence," her search for love, imagined and remembered places, and "questions of history." Highly recommended.—*S. I. Bellman, California State Polytechnic University, Pomona*

WS-0924 93-73475 Orig
Miller, Leslie Adrienne. **Ungodliness: poems.** Carnegie Mellon, 1994. 58p ISBN 0-88748-172-8, $16.95; ISBN 0-88748-173-6 pbk, $10.95

For her second book of poetry, Miller has chosen the title *Ungodliness*, its negation matching the sad photograph of the author on the back cover, face cupped in hands, eyes looking down. There is little to smile about in the contents: recollections of a Catholic girlhood, failed relationships, more-than-casual sexual encounters. Section titles ("Temples," "Idols," "Relics") indicate facets of belief outgrown but apparently not replaced. This poet has an exceptionally fine gift for recalling how a child feels, as in the kindergarten story about the lunch milk machine. She will never be accused of what she blames in "The Romantics," namely "To be too tender is to give ground"; however, when on vacation from college she judges her parents harshly, she has enough self-knowledge to agree with her mother that her behavior is hateful. Several selections call for development into short stories; perhaps the longer form would lessen the bleakness and brittle skepticism here. The author of this "collage of lovelessness" has much by way of technique (narrative and otherwise) to teach her creative writing students at the University of St. Thomas in St. Paul. Realism, however, makes readers eager for a sequel to "Ungodliness," which might include celebration of the affirmations the world contains. All levels.—*B. Quinn, formerly, College of Saint Teresa*

WS-0925 HQ1413 95-1727 CIP
Millett, Kate. **A.D., a memoir.** W.W. Norton, 1995. 325p ISBN 0-393-03524-7, $25.00

A.D. is a memoir in the inward turning, circular storytelling style of feminist biography. This is an account of imperfect martinis, paths taken and not taken, and hope in the form of an African violet. Nothing is straightforward in this compunctious tale of Millett's life. The surfaces of her experience are sliced thin, from many angles. Though some characters in the book are familiar to Millet readers, this work is an investigation of family. The axial relationship is Aunt Dorothy (A.D.), Millett's kin and object of lifelong yearning. Aunt Dorothy is an unrelenting (mostly indifferent) presence for Millett. A lamented lie Millett made to her aunt, whose endowment paid for Millett's study at Oxford, is polished and held to light. The lie and the loss of the nearly mythic aunt remain as distant as the aunt's beloved Han horse. There is no redemption for Millett; no atonement is permitted. Both the lie and the aunt are remote but brilliantly faceted in their telling. Millett and her books are rejected or disregarded by her Aunt Dorothy, and reunions imagined in New York reverie do not happen in the cold and distant St. Paul landscapes. A.D. is about class, ambivalence, art, money, and aristocracy, and all the ways in which they intersect in a particular Irish-American family. All levels.—*L. De Danaan, Evergreen State College*

WS-0926 PS628 93-11831 CIP
Moon marked and touched by sun: plays by African-American women, ed. by Sydné Mahone. Theatre Communications Group, 1994. 406p ISBN 1-55936-065-8 pbk, $14.95

Mahone's collection of eleven excerpts entitled *Moon Marked and Touched by Sun* adds a unique, important perspective to the literature about contemporary theater, women playwrights, and African American women writers. Mahone combines her experience as dramaturge at Crossroads Theater Company with her Afro-matricentric perspective and knowledge of today's theater. As she states, the playwrights included in this volume represent the "most compelling, thought-

provoking and stylistically fresh" voices in the vanguard of American theater. Playwrights included are Laurie Carlos, Kia Corthron, Thulani Davis, Judith Jackson, Adrienne Kennedy, Robbie McCauley, Suzan-Lori Parks, Aishah Rahman, Ntozake Shange, Anna Deavere Smith (recently nominated for a Tony award), and Danitra Vance. Each excerpt is preceded by an interview that includes discussion of vision and heroism, notes about the author and her work, a list of characters in the play, and an author's note. Mahone's readable introduction provides a useful context for this study of African American women's cutting-edge contribution to American theater. This collection introduces readers to innovative writing, African American women's work (excluded from most texts), and the dynamics of African American theater. Upper-division undergraduate; professional.—*D. S. Isaacs, Fordham University*

WS-0927 PS3545 93-41117 CIP
Mortimer, Gail L. **Daughters of the swan: love and knowledge in Eudora Welty's fiction.** Georgia, 1994. 213p bibl index afp ISBN 0-8203-1633-4, $40.00

Using the psychoanalytic theories of Carol Gilligan and Nancy Chodorow, Mortimer explores the complex relations between love and knowing in Eudora Welty's fiction. Mortimer examines the images of circle and labyrinth in Welty's stories and novels and suggests that these images evoke both the inside and outside status of the lover and the knower. Mortimer relies on Welty's own childhood quest for love and knowledge in readings of the failure of protective love in *The Optimist's Daughter* (CH, Sep'72). Through her often brilliant readings of Welty's works, Mortimer places the novelist in the tradition of Shelley, Keats, Coleridge, and Yeats—from whose poem "Among School Children" the book's title is drawn—because of their exploration of evocative images (circle, dome, labyrinth) that reflect the solitary aspects of human consciousness seeking knowledge. Mortimer's book ranges far and wide to explore the mythic elements of Welty's rich oeuvre. This welcome addition to the growing number of studies on Welty is recommended to academic and general audiences.—*H. L. Carrigan, Jr., Otterbein College*

WS-0928 PS3563 94-17412 CIP
Mosby, Katherine. **Private altars.** Random House, 1995. 322p afp ISBN 0-679-42896-8, $21.00

A stunning accomplishment, this first novel astonishes, delights, challenges, and satisfies the reader. The language is richly poetic, nuanced, and powerful. Mosby's beautifully wrought work has all a reader could want: romantic love, lost children, midnight adventures, accidents, fires, and startling discoveries. The outrageous adventures excite laughter, pity, anguish, longing, and understanding. The passionate and eccentric heroine, Vienna Daniels, marries a stolid Southerner and moves from her wealthy urban home to Winsville, a small Southern town, where she is as peculiar as a unicorn among mules. Educated in the classics, in love with nature, and comically out of touch with proper Southern behavior, she obliviously manages to enrage most of the town, alienate the women, and drive away her puzzled husband. Abandoned and impoverished at the beginning of the Depression with two small children to raise, she makes their lives a masterpiece of imagination and excitement. Mosby—a teacher at both Columbia and NYU—has an ear for conversation, an eye for detail, and a delight in "dappled" things. She is a bright new heir of the modern Southern renaissance. Academic and general audiences.—*N. Tischler, Pennsylvania State University, University Park Campus*

WS-0929 94-78069 Orig
Nye, Naomi Shihab. **Red suitcase: poems.** BOA Editions, 1994. 109p (American poets continuum series, 29) ISBN 1-880238-14-4, $20.00; ISBN 1-880238-15-2 pbk, $12.50

Naomi Shihab Nye's poems are tenuous, inoffensive, and bland. She writes about family, living in the contemporary urban world, a little on the Middle East. Passion is absent, as is wit. The writing is prosy, often banal, characterized by temporizing expressions: somewhat, some, seemed, perhaps, so, not exactly, and other locutions indicating the writer is unsure of the subject. A short poem on gingko trees is successful, and a poem for a little girl killed by the violence in the Middle East is touching. Recommended for institutions aiming at comprehensive collections of women's writing or poetry.—*H. Jaskoski, California State University, Fullerton*

WS-0930   Orig

Parson-Nesbitt, Julie. **Finders: poems.** West End Press, 1996. 60p ISBN 0-931122-83-X pbk, $8.95

Parson-Nesbitt's first collection of poems is laden with images drawn from the streets of the poet's native Chicago, her Jewish heritage, and her experience as a late-20th-century woman. Her use of catalogs is sometimes reminiscent of the original poet of the American streets, Walt Whitman, and of his literary heirs, the Beats. Incremental repetition is a recurrent prosodic strategy in *Finders*, and the poems seem written primarily for oral presentation in public readings, since little attention is given to considerations like compression of language, line breaks, and standardized punctuation. Although this reviewer can imagine that Parson-Nesbitt's work is dramatically effective before a live audience, a general prosaic flatness afflicts it on the page, making the reader wish a cassette accompanied the volume. Still, there is energy and conviction here, and Parson-Nesbitt is a poet to hope for. Recommended for larger poetry and women's studies collections.—*B. Galvin, Central Connecticut State University*

WS-0931   PS3565   91-8623 CIP

Pearlman, Mickey. **Tillie Olsen,** by Mickey Pearlman and Abby H.P. Werlock. Twayne, 1991. 159p (TUSAS, 581) bibl index afp ISBN 0-8057-7632-X, $19.95

The few but powerful works of the incomparable Tillie Olsen (b. 1912 or 1913) are here given a careful, reasoned analysis that makes connections between them and her life and that both refers to and attacks other interpretations. She was born Tillie Lerner in Wahoo, Omaha, or Mead, Nebraska, of Russian immigrant parents; left high school; was self-educated in public libraries; held a number of ill-paying jobs; was briefly a member of the Communist party; married union leader Jack Olsen; bore four daughters. Pearlman interviewed her, coming away with a feeling of "hopefulness and continuity" in her work. The author's analysis of Olsen's one incomplete novel, *Yonnondio*, and her five short stories ties them together "by their portrayal of the aching hardship of poverty and the themes of exile and exclusion," their characters belonging to the "wrong (working) class or wrong (nonwhite) race." Also present are "illness and disease, 'lost' children, nightmares, guilty or harrowing memories, and prolonged individual silences," with which the latter dealt specifically in Olsen's nonfiction book, *Silences.* An intelligent, thought-provoking study that contains Olsen interview, biography, introduction, chronology, notes, and selected bibliography. Essential for all literature and women's studies collections. *Tillie Olsen* by A. Martin (CH, Jan'85) covers essentially the same ground more briefly, with varying interpretations and review excerpts. *Tillie Olsen and a Feminist Spiritual Vision* by E. N. Orr (CH, Dec'87) gives a "religious interpretation" to Olsen's work, with some biographical details.—*J. Overmyer, Ohio State University*

WS-0932   PS151   95-8529 CIP

Perreault, Jeanne. **Writing selves: contemporary feminist autography.** Minnesota, 1995. 153p bibl index afp ISBN 0-8166-2655-3 pbk, $17.95

Perreault's provocative study of self writing extends the boundaries of autobiography beyond the narration of life events into "autography," the textual creation of a self-in-process, as "she who says I" engages with social institutions and discourses to construct and assert feminist agency. Perreault's readings of complex texts by four authors—Audre Lorde's *The Cancer Journals* (1980), Adrienne Rich's prose and poetry, Kate Millet's *The Basement* (1979), and Patricia Williams's *The Alchemy of Race and Rights* (1991)—demonstrate the courage exhibited by these authors in confronting disease, sexual and racial exploitation, and ethnocentrism. But the textual feminist selves-in-process in Perreault's analysis may be even more courageous in revealing "parts of one's self that one has had reason to keep silent," a voicing that "is frightening, painful, and even dangerous" to both writers and readers. Perreault's readings uncover the disturbing dark underbelly of feminist issues like writing on the body and sisterhood, issues rarely recognized in gender or genre theories. Of interest to graduate scholars and researchers of autobiography and feminist criticism. Extensive bibliography.—*B. Braendlin, Florida State University*

WS-0933   PS3570.Y45   90-12534 MARC

Petry, Alice Hall. **Understanding Anne Tyler.** South Carolina, 1990. 267p bibl index ISBN 0-87249-716-X, $24.95; ISBN 0-87249-742-9, $12.95

The five-page bibliography that concludes this first full-length study of Anne Tyler reveals the sparse attention previously paid to this important contemporary American author, and Petry (Rhode Island School of Design) has with this work fulfilled a need and perhaps provided an inspiration for students to continue to search for the patterns reappearing throughout Tyler's 11 novels. In establishing this emphasis, Petry explains that in the past, Tyler has been classified as a woman's writer, a Southern writer influenced by Faulkner, and even a Dickensian, all of which labels are disproved. Instead, this book suggests the strong influence of Hawthorne, Emerson, Thoreau, and 19th-century Russian playwrights, especially Chekhov. Although Tyler does not care for the strident feminist work of the early 1970s, she does admit to a preference for the fiction of Eudora Welty and Carson McCullers, Southern authors whose works also transcend categorization. Her humanistic purpose, "remaining functional" in the face of oppressive circumstances, reflects these influences. Petry proves a qualified guide for this subject. A separate chapter deals with each novel, and Petry's notes are conveniently arranged at the end of each. For graduate, undergraduate, and public libraries.—*A. Hirsh, Central Connecticut State University*

WS-0934   PS3563   94-48916 CIP

Pettis, Joyce. **Toward wholeness in Paule Marshall's fiction.** University Press of Virginia, 1995. 173p bibl index ISBN 0-8139-1614-3, $29.50

Pettis (North Carolina State Univ.) situates Marshall's work preeminently in the growing body of African American literature and criticism that privileges the quests and possibilities for spiritual wholeness. She reads Marshall's canon (four novels, one collection of novellas, and one of short stories) within a matrix of black feminist critical theory (Patricia Hill Collins, Paula Giddings, Deborah McDowell, Barbara Christian) and Afrocentric psychological perspectives (Joseph A. Baldwin, Linda James Myers). Chapter 1, "Generative Spaces," argues intriguingly, though insufficiently, for the uniqueness of Marshall's literary vision of "resolution" to cultural, historical "psychic fracturing" for all peoples of the African diaspora. (Sustained comparative readings of Marshall's contemporaries—e.g., Toni Morrison, Gloria Naylor, Alice Walker—would complicate and substantiate Pettis's theory.) Organized topically rather than chronologically, chapters examine the importance of literal and psychological communities to diasporic quests and the "pernicious" dynamics of race, class, and gender: *Praisesong for the Widow* (1983) represents "satisfactory closure" to Marshall's quest for "psychic equilibrium"; *Daughters* (1991) depicts a viable, postquest community of spiritually whole, self-enabled women. This excellent introduction and critical analysis is recommended for upper-division undergraduates and above.—*S. Bryant, Alfred University*

WS-0935   PS3568   95-4151 CIP

Redel, Victoria. **Already the world: poems.** Kent State, 1995. 56p afp ISBN 0-87338-530-6, $17.00; ISBN 0-87338-531-4 pbk, $9.50

WS-0935a   PS3568   94-42899 CIP

Redel, Victoria. **Where the road bottoms out: a collection of stories.** Knopf, 1995. 171p ISBN 0-679-42071-1, $20.00

These two new titles demonstrate the abilities of this compelling newcomer. *Already the World*, a fine contribution to the "Wick Poetry First Book Series," is a collection of narrative poetry focusing on a range of topics including sexuality, pregnancy, parenting, family, and grief. Redel divides the poems into three loosely thematic sections: the first set of poems revolves around issues of sexuality, gender, and identity; the second recounts familial roots and loss; and the third set explores motherhood. Interestingly, the poems in the third set are far shorter than those in the other two, which may reflect Redel's discovery that for new mothers time for writing is scarce and interrupted. Though Redel's poetry is never predictable, she tends to excel at two types of poems: the longer narrative piece that draws in the often extraneous details of life (exemplified in the lovely poems "Everyday" and "Behold") and short pithy poems that draw quickly to a point (as in "On the Table" and "Maybe There Is Nothing Special Going On").

This exciting new volume of poetry is joined by Redel's first collection of short stories, *Where the Road Bottoms Out*, an oddly fascinating addition to contemporary literature that is reminiscent of Grace Paley's short fiction. Two features in particular are striking: the style and the characters. Reading this book is like eavesdropping on strangers' conversations and getting only telegraphic or suggestive information. Readers must make their own connections and explanations or simply ponder the echoes and suggestions of a particular image or phrase. The lyrical, poetic effect of the stories is delightful if baffling—they confound any traditional sense of meaning. Furthermore, Redel shifts style entirely in each story, displaying an amazing range of ability. In part the fragmentary style of the stories seems tied to Redel's focus on children's perspectives and on parents' relationships with their children. She seems compelled to find fresh angles from which to view these connections, exploring the terrain of her story until the angle and frame provide that moment of surprise. Both titles are recommended for all academic and general collections.—*J. Tharp, University of Wisconsin—Marshfield-Wood County*

WS-0936   PS3537   93-26078 CIP
Roberts, Terry. **Self and community in the fiction of Elizabeth Spencer.** Louisiana State, 1994. 141p bibl index afp ISBN 0-8071-1879-6, $29.95

Terry Roberts (UNC/Chapel Hill) brings into focus the entire oeuvre of Elizabeth Spencer, a Southern novelist whose popularity has waxed and waned since the publication of her first novel *Fire in the Morning* (1948). The volume is organized chronologically with each chapter treating one or two books. Roberts sets about to demonstrate the evolution in her fiction of the theme of "the relationship of the individual to the community." He draws heavily on Peggy Prenshaw's study, *Elizabeth Spencer* (1985), rarely contradicting Prenshaw's findings but rather expanding on them. He also draws on his personal correspondence with Spencer, as well as several interviews he has conducted; these quotations add considerable original insight to his analysis. The only disappointment in Roberts's analysis is that he does not raise the question of gender as it relates to community. He would have done well to consult recent works on the distinctiveness of women's fictional tradition in the South. Not to acknowledge this growing trend in feminist literary criticism, to either build on it or disagree with it, is a serious omission when writing a book on a contemporary Southern woman writer. Useful bibliography. Recommended for large collections of Southern and women's literary criticism.—*E. R. Baer, Gustavus Adolphus College*

WS-0937   PS3566   91-26313 CIP
Rose, Jacqueline. **The haunting of Sylvia Plath.** Harvard, 1992. 288p bibl index afp ISBN 0-674-38225-0, $24.95

After nearly 30 years of critical controversy, Rose offers a view of Plath and Plath's writing that in a sense embraces and demolishes all sides. There have been those who read the poetry as expressions of pathology, of a frighteningly unhealthy death wish. Others hear an early call to feminist arms, a rebellion against patriarchal cruelty and control. Still others have argued rigidly to read the poems as literary objects in themselves, disregarding the life from which they sprang. Yet others have struggled to separate Plath's "original" texts from those edited by the Hughes family, her literary heirs. Rose, however, sees Plath as more than any one of these: she sees in the very controversy—in our own inability (or unwillingness) to grasp what Plath is all about—even more about ourselves and our culture than about Plath. Thus arises Rose's position that Plath "haunts" us, forcing us to grapple with issues that disturb us. Life/death, love/hate, sexuality/aggression, personal/political, fantasy/reality—in Plath's work we face the dichotomies, and it has been our fear of them (or our own twisted ways of dealing with them) that has distorted our critical assessment of the poetry. This book offers extraordinary insight, not only into the poetry of Sylvia Plath, but into the culture of our time and the biases of our own minds. May it find readers ready to abandon their own resistance. Recommended.—*A. Geffner, Taylor Business Insitute*

WS-0938   PS3569   91-8264 CIP
Rosenberg, Brian. **Mary Lee Settle's Beulah quintet: the price of freedom.** Louisiana State, 1991. 174p bibl index afp ISBN 0-8071-1674-2, $25.00

The Beulah quintet, according to Brian Rosenberg, is simply too valuable to be overlooked. He notes that serious historical fiction has been making a comeback recently, and asserts that Mary Lee Settle's massive quintet should be celebrated as a significant forerunner of this resurgence. He places the series in cultural and creative context, demonstrates Settle's particular value as a rare exam-

ple of an American woman's writing historical fiction in a sustained manner, and explores each of the novels in the series in some detail. Among the most valuable sections of the study is an interview with Mary Lee Settle, in which she outlines her own ideas and describes her mode of composition. The study, which includes a lengthy summary of critical responses, is designed more for critics and teachers than for the general reader. Rosenberg (Allegheny College, PA) presents a scholarly, but not ponderously documented explanation of Settle's modest reputation and her failure to attract big audiences to her extended exploration of a region of West Virginia. By placing the novels in their proper order and indicating the grand design, he has performed a valuable service to readers of historical fiction.—*N. Tischler, Pennsylvania State University, University Park Campus*

WS-0939   PS3569   95-18208 CIP
Schumacher, Julie. **The body is water.** Soho Press, 1995. 262p afp ISBN 1-56947-042-1 pbk, $21.00

This first novel revolves around the lives of Jane Haus, her eccentric father, and a strange, brilliant sister. These three are drawn together in the months of Jane's return to the family home. She has quit her teaching job. She is 28, single, and newly pregnant. As a study of a dysfunctional family, the novel rings tragically true. The reader learns of the family through flashbacks to Jane's childhood along the New Jersey shore in a place called Safe Haven. The mother is remote and sickly and takes years to die. Jane's pregnancy, the result of a casual affair, is tied up with her own emotions of being unwanted. Her baby is something she wants to care about, although her erratic upbringing does not persuade the reader of her ability to function rationally. Schumacher succeeds in creating an environment in which indeterminacy flourishes. Her writing is spare and haunting, at times reminiscent of Marilynne Robinson's *Housekeeping* (1980). Like flowing water, the novel moves. Just where is left uncertain. General and academic collections.—*H. Susskind, Monroe Community College*

WS-0940   PS310   91-6577 CIP
Schweik, Susan. **A gulf so deeply cut: American women poets and the Second World War.** Wisconsin, 1992 (c1991). 385p index ISBN 0-299-13040-1, $39.50; ISBN 0-299-13044-4 pbk, $14.50

A fascinating and wise study of the dynamics of gender in the politics of war and of war poetry. Schweik explores the experience of war as an ideological construct, traces its conceptual links to masculinity, and discusses poets whose work is concerned with the influence of war on civilians. Through her powerful analysis of poetry by H. D., Gwendolyn Brooks, Marianne Moore, Muriel Rukeyser, and Elizabeth Bishop, among others, Schweik explains the presence of women as subjects in the action and discourse of WW II. She gives center stage to women poets who consciously talk back to a male model of ironic distance—clearly present in the war poetry of Wilfred Owen and Robert Graves—and to male critics who allow no female participation in war except bereavement. This work will be particularly helpful in courses on modernist and/or contemporary poetry. An excellent companion work to Paul Fussell's *The Great War and Modern Memory* (1975) and *War Time* (CH, Jan'90) and Jon Stallworthy's *Oxford Book of War Poetry* (1984).—*L. Winters, College of Saint Elizabeth*

WS-0941   PS3503.A614   89-26358 CIP
Silence and power: a reevaluation of Djuna Barnes, ed. by Mary Lynn Broe. Southern Illinois, 1991. 424p bibl index afp ISBN 0-8093-1250-6, $29.95; ISBN 0-8093-1255-7 pbk, $13.95

The first full collection of contemporary criticism of the work of Djuna Barnes (1892-1982), whose cultlike celebrity and stylistic obscurity have probably kept her from broader attention. Several critical essays are devoted to each of the following: early journalism, poetry, and illustrations; one-act plays and short fiction; *Ryder*; *Ladies Almanac*; *Nightwood*; and *Antiphon*. The essays are written by scholars such as Catharine Stimpson, Jane Marcus, Mary Lynn Broe, Louise DeSalvo, and 15 other authorities on Barnes. Included also are seven reminiscences by Barnes's friends and biographers, a handsome section of photographs and illustration, and an excellent bibliography that updates Douglas Messerli's *Djuna Barnes: A Bibliography* (CH, Sep'76). Though limited largely to feminist criticism, this is a primary source for any study of Barnes, and essential for all university libraries.—*N. R. Fitch, University of Southern California*

WS-0942   PR9275   94-25608 CIP
Simmons, Diane. **Jamaica Kincaid.** Twayne, 1994. 155p (TUSAS, 646) bibl index afp ISBN 0-8057-3994-7, $23.95

Jamaica Kincaid's important literary career is examined by Simmons in this study of the US-Caribbean writer from her birth as Elaine Potter Richardson in Antigua in 1949 to her most recent essays in the *New Yorker.* Simmons's critical focus is on Kincaid's theme of loss and betrayal in two related registers, that of mother-daughter relationships and that of colonial domination. Pointing out that Kincaid has herself eschewed description as either a "black" writer or a "feminist" author, Simmons nonetheless traces the relevance of Kincaid's own autobiography and education in the Caribbean and the United States to her writing, both fictional and nonfictional. One chapter on style identifies the incantatory, ritual aspects of Kincaid's use of rhythmic repetition in her sentences and paragraphs. Another on literary influence emphasizes the importance of Milton's *Paradise Lost* and Bronte's *Jane Eyre* to Kincaid's oeuvre. The last four chapters concentrate on Kincaid's four published books: the collection of stories, *At the Bottom of the River* (1983), the two novels, *Annie John* (1985) and *Lucy* (1990), and finally the extended essay, *A Small Place* (1988), on "postcolonial Antigua." Recommended for university and college libraries.—*B. Harlow, University of Texas at Austin*

WS-0943   PS3569   93-634 CIP
Sornberger, Judith Mickel. **Open heart.** CALYX Books, 1993. 98p afp ISBN 0-934971-32-3, $19.95; ISBN 0-934971-31-5 pbk, $9.95

Sornberger's volume of poetry has the failings of it virtues. It speaks in a homely tongue of homely issues. It delves into women's lives for its themes and its metaphors. There is throughout the sense of personal history, or oral history. Sometimes all of this comes together in a poetry full of delight and discovery; more often, though, it delivers a poetry that is not quite resolved, sometimes forced, and sometimes corny. As an example of all this, the good as well as the bad, one could consider the opening to the "Pioneer Child's Doll": "Here, child, is what we mean by love:/ a block head doll of coarse-grained wood,/ eyes two knife-pricks, mouth a crooked stab." A library collection particularly strong in women's poetry and able to afford the luxury of another volume without requiring it to be the strongest example of women's writing today should add this book. Otherwise, it might be better to pass on it.—*S. Raeschild, University of New Mexico*

WS-0944   PS3569   94-36114 CIP
Sprecher, Lorrie. **Sister safety pin: a novel.** Firebrand Books, 1994. 253p afp ISBN 1-56341-051-6, $20.95; ISBN 1-56341-050-8 pbk, $9.95

This readable, funny, and engaging coming-of-age novel works best as a sociological review of the 1980s punk world that now seems quaint and distant and safe. These characters remind us that a carefully-developed BAD attitude most often masks engaging innocence and profound vulnerability. This sentimental novel of lesbian awakening, with its convincing love triangle, suggests that love is often found in the least likely places, unless we really think about it and realize that the choices we make eventually come to seem inevitable. Sprecher, who possesses a wonderful talent for the evocative detail, would benefit from trusting her reader enough to avoid editorializing on events. There is a genuine power of observation here, but it is diminished by a tendency to tell us how to respond. General; undergraduate.—*L. Winters, College of Saint Elizabeth*

WS-0945   PS3560   94-23529 CIP
Templin, Charlotte. **Feminism and the politics of literary reputation: the example of Erica Jong.** University Press of Kansas, 1995. 233p bibl index afp ISBN 0-7006-0708-0, $29.95

Through personal interviews and painstaking research, Templin (Univ. of Indianapolis) has produced the definitive account of Erica Jong and her writing. This thoughtful study explores Jong's oeuvre and includes chapters on her most famous books, including *Fear of Flying* (1976) and *Fanny* (1980). In particular, Templin is interested in Jong's literary reputation and questions why the author has never achieved wide critical acclaim. Templin explores how Jong's gender and the popularity of her fiction have influenced the critical reception of her books. Although Templin's study is insightful, her ideas also have broad critical implication and raise many questions. What role do reviews play in a book's success? In what way does the personal reception of an author influence her literary reputation? How does popularity influence a book's critical reception? Can a writer be a popular as well as a literary success? The book insightfully explores these issues and others, making it a must read for anyone interested in how popularity and financial success affect an author's literary reputation. Because of its clarity, this book would be suitable reading for a broad audience, including undergraduates, graduates, and professors.—*S. A. Inness, Miami University*

WS-0946   PS3572   94-40889 CIP
Verdelle, A.J. **The good Negress.** Algonquin Books, 1995. 299p ISBN 1-56512-085-X, $19.95

This work both meets and expands our expectations of the American female novel of development. Denise Palms, the 12-year-old narrator, lived with her maternal grandmother in Virginia before she rejoined her family in Detroit. Her journey from the rural south to the urban north parallels those made by thousands of American blacks during the years between the wars. The description of her growth from a naive, black dialect-speaking ingenue into an urban schoolgirl charged with the enormous tasks of running her mother's house shows just how difficult it was for many girls her age to make the transition. The family quickly takes Denise's passion for domestic orderliness for granted, so much so that no one remembers her 14th birthday. She gleans most of the lessons she learns about human relationships by observing her mother, stepfather, and two brothers. She mediates arguments and troubles with the law and determines to learn to speak "the king's English" in the manner of her pompous, black bourgeois schoolteacher. Yet Denise conveys most of her narrative in the rich and colorful African American dialect: she commands the folk language and understands the world through folk vernacular and beliefs. Denise arrives at the threshold of adulthood once she is able to speak the two versions of English, and to understand when to make that shift. Verdelle's truly fine debut novel belongs in the ranks of other classics in African American folk vernacular, e.g., Charles Chesnutt's *The Conjure Woman* (1899); Zora Neale Hurston's *Their Eyes Were Watching God* (1900); Toni Morrison's *The Bluest Eye* (1970); and Alice Walker's *The Color Purple* (1982).—*A. Deck, University of Illinois at Urbana—Champaign*

WS-0947   Orig
Vest, Hilda. **Sorrow's end: poems.** Broadside Press, 1993. 72p ISBN 0-940713-08-X pbk, $8.00

In her effort to convey the complexity known as the black experience in America, Vest successfully synthesizes the distinct themes of race, class, and gender in this collection of poems. One feels the intensity of the older female personae in "Australian Granddaughter," "A Woman's Prayer," "On Turning Fifty," and "Second Chance." There is finality to the overall collection as though the various speakers are nearing or have reached an end to mental suffering, or physical pain. Many of the poems convey Vest's admiration of black men, especially her husband of 25 years ("Twenty-Fifth Wedding Anniversary"), and her sensitivity to their plight in America ("Title for Doctoral Dissertation"); but a few poems vent her wrath against those men who cower under the weight ("Internment"), and fail to appreciate African American culture ("Excuses Excuses Excuses"). Broader topics sensitively portrayed include black political leadership, senseless child murders, drug addiction, and white American Civil Rights martyrs. Deft in her use of African American dialect in some poems, Vest clearly respects the black experience in all its dimensions. Recommended for all college and public libraries with holdings in African American and American women's literature.—*A. Deck, University of Illinois at Urbana—Champaign*

WS-0948   PS3572   93-29735 CIP
Villanueva, Alma Luz. **Weeping woman: La Llorona and other stories.** Bilingual Press/Editorial Bilingue, 1994. 161p ISBN 0-927534-38-X pbk, $13.00

In this collection of intense stories by Chicana poet and novelist Alma Luz Villanueva, the characters—usually poor Indian and Chicana women and children—are often in situations of crisis, facing violence, grief, and fear. Such crises seem to arise from the social and economic powerlessness of those characters, but they act with strength, determination, and dignity. They are depicted convincingly as conscious, moral agents who realize the consequences of their actions. Included are some vivid stories of sexuality, but the eroticism seems to take on dark undertones. The individual stories are linked together by the luminous motif of the seashell and by references to La Llorona, a figure of inspiration who in one story at least is the grandmother. The four stories of *el alma*, the soul, depict four possible lives of Luna, the young character in the first story. Several characters seem to be close to nature and to a mythic tradition, elements that give resonance to lives in such poor material circumstances, but rich nonetheless. Readers would have a hard time patronizing such characters. The volume is recommended to general readers, upper-division undergraduate students, faculty, and researchers.—*K. Begnal, Utah State University*

WS-0949   PS3552   92-26821 CIP
Ward, Carol M. **Rita Mae Brown.** Twayne, 1993. 191p bibl index afp
ISBN 0-8057-4000-7, $22.95

Ward's study recognizes the importance in contemporary literature of Rita Mae Brown not only as a lesbian author but also as a southern woman writer, a designation Brown indicates in interviews she prefers. Ward's analyses of Brown's novels demonstrate how Brown's "liberal ideology" and "traditional Southern values" combine to appeal to a wide range of readers interested in values and mores generated by the women's and gay liberation movements, as well as the cultural history of the South. Ward interprets Brown's fiction in light of her early political essays (1969 to 1975), which explore topics that inform her novels: relationships between the personal and the political, the interaction of social classes, the role of art in society, and lesbian sexuality. Although Ward's close readings of the novels may be problematical to some scholars because they eschew contemporary gender theory, they do provide a wealth of detail about the fiction. Ward also presents copious informative material about Brown's personal and professional life and numerous references to book reviews and interviews in her selected bibliography. Undergraduate and up.—*B. Braendlin, Florida State University*

WS-0950   PS3565   92-39467 CIP
Wesley, Marilyn C. **Refusal and transgression in Joyce Carol Oates' fiction.** Greenwood, 1993. 171p (Contributions in women's studies, 135) bibl index afp ISBN 0-313-28462-8, $45.00

At first glance, the title of this new study of some (not all; how could it?) of Oates's stories, novellas, and novels might appear awkward. In fact, it is inevitable, given the author's definition of "refusal" and "transgression" as strategies by which daughters and sons in Oates's work seek to escape the confines of the familial structures that have been imposed on them. Thus, this is also by necessity a charting of the routes for Oates's characters from relative entrapment to empowerment and liberation. Ultimately, Wesley argues that Oates is in fact a strong feminist, something evident to anyone who knows her but a fact sometimes lost on her critics, especially those of the earlier works in which supposedly "helpless" females appear. Though Wesley introduces a few diagrams to elucidate her thesis, she wears her extensive background in literary theory lightly; her prose is supple and lucid, and it is difficult to find fault more significant than her apparent failure to understand just what a race riot is. One assumes that this volume represents a slight updating of the author's doctoral dissertation at Syracuse, also Oates's alma mater. There is also a bibliography specific to this topic, which has now been covered with admirable thoroughness but also economy. Effective also is Wesley's use of Oates's unusually forthcoming commentary on her own narrational devices. A valuable addition to Greenwood's series on women's studies that also manages to transcend any ostensible limitations attached to that focus. Recommended. Undergraduate and up.—*J. M. Ditsky, University of Windsor*

WS-0951   PS3545   94-6067 CIP
Weston, Ruth D. **Gothic traditions and narrative techniques in the fiction of Eudora Welty.** Louisiana State, 1994. 202p bibl index afp
ISBN 0-8071-1897-4, $25.00

Welty's writing has sometimes suffered under the confines of the Gothic label, but Weston (Oral Roberts Univ.) explains how Welty transforms the Gothic traditions employed by the Grimm brothers, Austen, Cooper, Irving, Poe, Hawthorne, Faulkner, O'Connor, and McCullers. Drawing extensively and usefully from contemporary theory of the short story, narratology, dialogism, feminism, existentialism, structuralism, and folk and fine art, from a full range of criticism of Welty and the aforementioned writers and theories, from archival manuscripts,

letters, and interviews, and from the full Welty canon, Weston presents a new, clear, persuasive argument that Welty has reconfigured the Gothic in writing about human experience. Without repetition, Weston moves easily from Welty's early stories, where Gothic tradition is most evident, to the mature short fiction and novels in which Gothic spaces and techniques are rewritten in modernist and realistic style. Weston shows that the Gothic labyrinth (of space, time, and psyche), made realistic on the Natchez Trace, in houses, in the wilderness or the community, traps Welty's female heroes. They escape, though chaos results. Understanding and regard for Welty's genius are enlarged by Weston's scholarship. Undergraduate and up.—*P. A. McHaney, formerly, Georgia State University*

WS-0952   PS3573   92-18038 CIP
Wilner, Eleanor. **Otherwise.** Chicago, 1993. 129p afp ISBN 0-226-90029-0, $27.50; ISBN 0-226-90030-4 pbk, $11.95

The welcome proliferation of good poetry by women specifically addressing women's concerns adds a difficulty to the reviewer's task of sorting. The poet whose work sings to us without reference to any special sympathies, though, is singular in any group. That is the sort of poet one finds in this volume, a poet who deserves attention because of the strength of her poetry. Although Wilner's themes fit easily enough under the feminist rubric, they stand equally well with no label. Her far-ranging references—from classical antiquity and Bible stories to current politics and contemporary movies—add a breadth and depth to the volume's significance. The book is well balanced, a few very long poems alternating with a number of shorter lyrics. Images are fresh and yet unstrained, as in this from "The Bird in the Laurel's Song": ". . .and the sun,/ stretched out on its back, moved/ in a shiver of gold." Wilner's technical skill matches her thematic intensity, making this volume a rare treat which would be a valuable addition for a general poetry collection or one focused on women's writings. Undergraduate and beyond.—*S. Raeschild, University of New Mexico*

WS-0953   PS3569   95-23493 CIP
Wilson, Mary Ann. **Jean Stafford: a study of the short fiction.** Twayne/Prentice Hall International, 1996. 176p (Twayne's studies in short fiction, 62) bibl index afp ISBN 0-8057-7807-1, $23.95

This first in-depth study of Jean Stafford's more than 40 short stories reveals that she treated her subject—the lives of girls and women "from childhood to old age"—in terms of "female self-definition, powerlessness, and marginality." Wilson (Univ. of Southwest Louisiana) analyzes some of the major stories, dividing them into four categories: "The Innocents Abroad"; "The Bostonians and Other Manifestations of the American Scene"; "Cowboys and Indians, and Magic Mountains"; and "Manhattan Island." She also includes comments by 12 critics and reminiscences by two friends, Dorothea Straus and Peter Taylor (Taylor: "In life, Jean was, in a sense, always playing a role.... Her literary personality remains her best kept secret.") Wilson's readable, sane essays examine her stories in part as they relate to Stafford herself: "Stafford kept rewriting her own life in these stories." The essays also consider her style, her "ear for the telling phrase, the offbeat metaphor, the colorful analogy." With its notes and chronology, this valuable addition to the Twayne library should enlighten both those familiar and those unfamiliar with Stafford's work. Highly recommended.—*J. Overmyer, emerita, Ohio State University*

WS-0954   PS3573   91-45309 CIP
Winchell, Donna Haisty. **Alice Walker.** Twayne, 1992. 152p bibl index afp ISBN 0-8057-7642-7, $21.95

Winchell's literary biography of Alice Walker, one of the leading black women writers in the US today, is extremely valuable as both an introduction to the study of Walker and as a handy annotated reference to the most useful critical studies of Walker's fiction. Writing in a clear and lively style, Winchell carefully traces the parallels between each significant stage in Walker's life (her background as the daughter of Georgia sharecroppers, her education at two women's colleges, her involvement in the Civil Rights Movement in Mississippi, and her discovery of the writer Zora Neale Hurston), and Walker's particular interpretation of black life, especially black women's lives, in the US. Winchell relies on Walker's own autobiographical essays, contained in *In Search of Our Mother's Gardens* (CH, May'84) and *Living By the Word* (1988), to extract meaning from, rather than to impose interpretations on, Walker's four novels, two collections of short stories, and four volumes of poetry. This allows us to see Walker's preoccupation in all of her writings with her own and black people's struggle to regain the spiritual wholeness that racism, sexism, and poverty destroy. The first book-length discussion of a major contemporary black woman writer, it should be required reading for anyone interested in American, African American, and women's literature.—*A. Deck, University of Illinois at Urbana—Champaign*

WS-0955   PS628   93-11557 CIP
Women on the verge: 7 avant-garde American plays, ed. by Rosette C. Lamont. Applause, 1993. 369p ISBN 1-55783-148-3 pbk, $14.95

These seven plays illustrate the talent, diversity, "boldness, innovation, and poetry" of American women playwrights—the latter three, asserts Lamont, because "female artists have nothing to lose." The most conventional, in form at least, are Rosalyn Drexler's *The Hunger Artist,* an adaptation and expansion of Franz Kafka's short story, and Tina Howe's *Birth and After Birth,* a parody of a "normal" family that questions conventional views of both civilized and primitive ways of child-rearing. *Us* by Karen Malpede consists of 11 discrete scenes concerning male-female relationships and politics. *What of the Night?* by Maria Irene Fornes is made up of four short plays dealing with barrenness, both physical and emotional. *The Death of the Last Black Man in the Whole Entire World* by Suzan-Lori Parks considers, through an account of a lynching, the place of blacks in the world; its exaggerated African American language and characters mock white attitudes toward blacks. Joan M. Schenkar's *The Universal Wolf* amusingly and frighteningly deconstructs the idea of deconstruction in relation to Little Red Riding Hood. The most moving play is Elizabeth Wong's *Letters to a Student Revolutionary,* which deals with both the personal and political through two women, one Chinese American and one Chinese. In all these plays, in the absence of conventional characters and plots, language—both spare and lush—is hyper-important. This book should be of strong interest to drama departments. Undergraduate (all levels); graduate; general.—*J. Overmyer, Ohio State University*

WS-0956   PS3557   94-30115 CIP
Xie, Lihong. **The evolving self in the novels of Gail Godwin.** Louisiana State, 1995. 242p bibl index afp ISBN 0-8071-1924-5, $30.00

Applying feminist criticism and Bakhtinian analysis to the evolution of the understanding and writing of feminine bildungsroman, Xie examines Godwin's eight novels written between 1970 and 1991. The study shows Godwin's self-evolution in the personae of her fictional characters. Her heroines—southern women: daughters, wives, mothers, writers—decenter themselves to become self-actualized and self-authenticating. As Godwin matures, so do her characters; they encounter new middle-aged problems and seek solutions in contemporary processes of growth. The trapped, circumscribed women use "memory as the locus of growth" in ways similar to Godwin using the writing process, journal keeping, interviews, and hindsight/reflection. As the heroines proceed and change, so does Godwin's narrative style. Xie makes good use of all the extratextual commentary and published statements, but not of Godwin's manuscripts and working papers. Godwin and Xie aptly employ a variety of styles and analyses (multiple points of view, gender studies, narratology, heteroglossia, and the dialogic), and this book illustrates that Godwin is a successful writer of popular novels because her characters are contemporary and realistic. All academic collections.—*P. A. McHaney, formerly, Georgia State University*

◆ Performing Arts

◆ Dance

WS-0957   GV1799   92-17279 CIP
Adair, Christy. **Women and dance: sylphs and sirens.** New York University, 1992. 283p bibl index ISBN 0-8147-0621-5, $40.00; ISBN 0-8147-0622-3 pbk, $15.00

Combining dance studies and feminist thought, *Women and Dance* is an overview of women's participation in and contributions to the history of Western theatrical dance. It is a valuable book for anyone interested in situating dance within feminist studies, as well as for the dancer who is beginning to think about gender issues within the profession. Unfortunately, Adair's approach leads her to string together one quote after another in a seemingly endless series of general declarative sentences which rarely probe specific dances with any discursive depth. For instance, in a chapter headed "Cultured Bodies—the social construction of the body," Adair never extends the implications of her title by talking about how certain genres of dance construct different body types. This unwillingness to probe the contradictions that inevitably arise when one analyzes real bodies and specific dances allows her to suggest that it "has not, until recently, been deemed necessary to control our sexual activity because of women's lack of status and power in Western society"—certainly a peculiar pronouncement for a book whose subtitle is "Sylphs and Sirens." Undergraduate; pre-professional.—*A. Cooper Albright, Oberlin College*

WS-0958   GV1600   94-14738 CIP
Bodies of the text: dance as theory, literature as dance, ed. by Ellen W. Goellner and Jacqueline Shea Murphy. Rutgers, 1995. 263p index ISBN 0-8135-2126-2, $48.00; ISBN 0-8135-2127-0 pbk, $20.00

This challenging interdisciplinary work brings together essays by 12 internationally diverse scholars, an energetic forum for exploring the possibility of applying literary-critical skills to thinking about dance and the potential for direct consideration of dance in literary studies. These explorations result in provocative new perspectives on dance, literature, gender, power, identity, ethnicity, and sexual orientation. Shea Murphy effectively brings all of these together in her essay "Unrest and Uncle Tom ...," which is an excellent complement for the currently relevant video *Bill T. Jones: Dancing to the Promised Land* (1994). This essay is supported by interesting historical illustrations of posters advertising early performances of *Uncle Tom's Cabin* and current photographs of Jones's work. Goellner provides animated commentary on the function of gossip and its dance parallels in Faulkner's *Light in August.* Although most of the essays share their concepts with vigor through text alone, the powerful androgynous images that accompany the essay on French Canadian choreographer Marie Chouinard's work add important visual credence to that text. Every essay is generously footnoted, providing a rich bibliographic resource for serious scholars, graduate level and above, and professionals.—*C. W. Sherman, College of William and Mary*

WS-0959   GR550   93-27277 CIP
Canton, Katia. **The fairy tale revisited: a survey of the evolution of the tales, from classical literary interpretations to innovative contemporary dance-theater productions.** P. Lang, 1994. 186p (New connections, 9) bibl afp ISBN 0-8204-2309-2 pbk, $36.95

Canton views fairy tales through a new critical lens: postmodern dance. She analyzes Perrault and Grimm (using the writings of Zipes, Barchilon and Flinders, and John Ellis), describing the sociocultural milieu of those authors in order to "demythicize" the classic tales and highlight their purposes as conveyors of morals, values, and gender roles. She then traces the growth of dance from classical ballet through modern dance to postmodern, showing how each form is a reflection of the agendas of its time. She finishes with a detailed analysis of three postmodern dance pieces based on classic tales (Marin's *Cinderella,* Bausch's *Bluebeard,* and Kinematic's *Girl Without Hands*), showing how the choreographer's lives meshed with their cultures to subvert the "mythicized" stories. She uses folklorist Vladimir Propp's system to analyze the narratives of both stories and dances, and concludes that all three pieces remove the tales from the realm of timeless or neutral "truths" by revealing the values they support: affirmation of male power and female passivity, and legitimation of white male European supremacy. Though slightly marred by a repetitive style, a few typos, and an occasional awkward phrase, this is an unusual and useful study. Undergraduate; graduate.—*M. R. Pukkila, Colby College*

WS-0960 GV1588 92-27878 CIP
Dance, gender and culture, ed. by Helen Thomas. St. Martin's, 1993. 219p index ISBN 0-312-08881-7, $39.95

This collection, edited by sociologist Helen Thomas, explores various ways dance can be seen as a vehicle for investigating gender and culture. It extends some of the concerns evident in two other recent works, *Dance, Sex and Gender*, by American anthropologist/dance scholar Judith Lynne Hanna (CH, Oct'88) and *Women and Dance: Sylphs and Sirens*, by British dance writer Christy Adair (CH, May'93). Thomas's volume includes the work of writers from various disciplines in an effort to suggest ways that dance can serve as a productive site for inter- and intradisciplinary cultural study. Thomas's stated intentions are to explore ways that dance and gender intersect within particular cultural contexts; to demonstrate that dance can provide a rich resource for other disciplines and that it can, as well, gain from analytic and investigative techniques developed by those disciplines; and, finally, to affirm that nondancers can contribute to substantive discourse regarding dance. Most of the contributors write from a British perpective; three are American. Many of the 13 articles call upon feminist discourse previously developed in the arts, humanities, and social sciences. One of the strengths of the book is the dialogue that emerges when these articles are read in tandem. Extensive footnotes and bibliographies contribute to the book's use as an aid to further discussion and additional research. Recommended for advanced undergraduates, pre-professionals, and up.—*S. E. Friedler, Swarthmore College*

WS-0961 GV1785 87-36964 CIP
De Mille, Agnes. **Martha, the life and work of Martha Graham.** Random House, 1991. 509p bibl index ISBN 0-394-55643-7, $30.00

Agnes De Mille is an important American choreographer in both ballet (works such as *Rodeo* and *Fall River Legend*) and on the Broadway stage (*Oklahoma* and *Brigadoon*), and is the author of 12 previous books on dance. In this work she presents a private view of her friend and sometime heroine Martha Graham, one of the pioneers of American modern dance. Written in a conversational style and supported by quotes from Graham company members, dance critics, patrons of Graham's work, and by De Mille's own recollections, this work reflects De Mille's considerable experience as both a creator and an observer of concert dance. It is an intimate portrait, one which places greatest emphasis on Graham's early years as an independent artist and on exploring how her relationships with lovers, advisers, and patrons shaped her mature choreogaphy. De Mille is clear in acknowledging both her regard for Graham as a genius and her biases concerning various individuals and dance works. The book was written over a period of 25 years and joins earlier works by Merle Armitage (1937) and Don McDonagh (1973) and Graham's own posthumously published autobiography, *Blood Memory* (1991), as a guide to understanding this significant American choreographer and her career. There are some 50 well-chosen black-and-white photos, a chronicle of Graham's works, brief biographies of others who figure prominently in the book, notes, and a selected bibliography. Useful to scholars and students in the field, this work is also suitable for the general reader.—*S. E. Friedler, Swarthmore College*

WS-0962 PN1949 92-20825 CIP
Futterman, Marilyn Suriani. **Dancing naked in the material world.** Prometheus Books, 1992. 137p afp ISBN 0-87975-737-X, $26.95

In the tradition of Susan Meiselas's *Carnival Strippers* (1976) and a worthy complement to its photographs and firsthand commentary, Futterman's collection similarly looks, with camera and words, at marginalized exotic dancers in contrasting venues to traditional and now virtually nonexistent burlesque theaters. *Dancing Naked*'s subjects, along with at least one husband and patrons, photographed in Atlanta, Georgia, strip clubs over a period from 1979 to 1992, furnish the commentary. A less than satisfactory essay by an academic on the current world of exotic dancing and its sociological implications completes the book. The motivations of the dancers and their exploitation (largely by male owners and patrons) affect on the participating individual performers; a sense of envi-

ronment and of the character of the dancers is captured very effectively through Futterman's honest, yet artistic, black-and-white photographs and the words of the dramatis personae. This handsome volume is relevant to study in popular culture, feminist and gender exploration (especially on the body), and the ongoing investigation of the striptease phenomenon, quite anomalous in this day of blatant and easily accessible pornography.—*D. B. Wilmeth, Brown University*

WS-0963 GV1785 93-1737 CIP
Life into art: Isadora Duncan and her world, ed. by Dorée Duncan, Carol Pratt, and Cynthia Splatt; text by Cynthia Splatt. W.W. Norton, 1993. 199p index ISBN 0-393-03507-7, $40.00

A welcome addition to the ever-growing library of material about Duncan. The editors of this volume (one of them Duncan's great niece) use a wealth of previously unpublished family photographs and drawings that tend to make the oft-repeated details of Duncan's life come alive. The text draws from memories of families and friends, as well as from the dancer's own letters and personal archives. What emerges is a fascinating story of a woman interesting for more than leading an eccentric life: Duncan's art influenced future generations, and her technique is still practiced today. Evocative of the turbulent years preceding and immediately following WW I, this lavishly illustrated work puts the dancer's life in a rich cultural context. Undergraduates; faculty; professionals.—*J. L. Cohen, formerly, Los Angeles County Museum of Art*

WS-0964 GV1785 92-32232 CIP
Manning, Susan A. **Ecstasy and the demon: feminism and nationalism in the dances of Mary Wigman.** California, 1993. 353p bibl index afp ISBN 0-520-08193-5, $30.00

Manning's very important new book is the only source in English, aside from the two translations by Walter Sorell of Mary Wigman's own writings—*The Language of Dance* (1966) and *The Mary Wigman Book* (CH, Sep'75)—that provides a view of the German choreographer's significant place in the development of 20th-century dance. Manning (dance and cultural history, Northwestern Univ.) has created a challenging, engaging, demanding, and intensely informative new perspective on Wigman's work within a stimulating context, not only of feminism and nationalism, but also of modernism in the visual arts. Pointing out that the early modern dancers challenged the male gaze essential in 19th-century ballet, the author moves on to show how Wigman and other innovative choreographers moved toward, or away from, possibilities for female self-authorship and female spectatorship. In addition to an excellent overview of Wigman's life and whole career, the reader is provided a compelling new view of how the choreographer accommodated her work to the Third Reich and the National Socialist Cultural Ministry headed by Goebbels. Sixty-five clearly reproduced illustrations, many from the Mary Wigman Archive in Leipzig, support the text. The meticulously organized bibliography provides a rich resource of background information. The work of such dance historians as John Martin, Lincoln Kirstein, and Elizabeth Kendall and dance critic Deborah Jowitt is generously attributed throughout the text and serves to put this work in the context of world-class dance scholarship. Very highly recommended. Advanced undergraduate; graduate; pre-professional; professional.—*C. W. Sherman, College of William and Mary*

WS-0965 GV1623 94-12157 CIP
Martin, Carol. **Dance marathons: performing American culture of the 1920s and 1930s.** University Press of Mississippi, 1994. 182p bibl index afp ISBN 0-87805-673-4, $37.50; ISBN 0-87805-701-3 pbk, $16.95

Martin (New York Univ.) carefully documents dance marathons as complicated, controversial, and contradictory popular entertainments in America between the two world wars. The origins, developmental stages, demise, and derivatives of marathons are penetratingly analyzed and interpreted as a cultural construct of social dance, popular music, contests, vaudeville, exhibition, social Darwinism, and the working-class struggle for survival during the Great Depression. The work is organized according to three shifting paradigms—hourly endurance contests, theatricalized athletic competition, and extended theatrical spectacles—and discusses such recurring themes as realism; puritanism; patriotism; commercialization of leisure; differences of gender, generation, class; and the uncertain role of women and their physical, moral, and economic powers. Rhetorical questions, richly detailed descriptions, and a revisionist approach that situates the subject within discourses of feminism, popular entertainment, performance theory, and American history make this a useful interdisciplinary source. This is an excellent companion work to Frank Calabria's *The Dance Sleepwalkers* (CH, Sep'93), which approaches marathons from a perspective of psychoanalytic, mythic, and existential literary criticism. The two titles contribute to the field with initial digs into virgin territory. Upper-division undergraduate and above.— *C. T. Bond, Goucher College*

WS-0966   Can. CIP
Vigier, Rachel. **Gestures of genius: women, dance, and the body.**
Mercury Press, 1994. 238p afp ISBN 1-55128-012-4 pbk, $16.95

A Canadian with a background in philosophy and women's studies, Vigier focuses here on ways that dance has been used by women to construct social and spiritual meaning. Women in dance provide most of the material for this investigation. The book comprises three sections: the first is a brief and selective look at ways women have danced and been viewed throughout history; the second section records Vigier's impression of the impact of dance on three female artists (writers Zelda Fitzgerald and H.D. and painter Leonora Carrington); the final portion is a compilation of interviews with 12 female choreographer/dancers on the subject of the female body in dance. A very brief black-and-white photo essay (23 pictures) is also included. Vigier writes in a very colloquial style and is clear about the important role dance can play in the lives of women who, like herself, are not professionals as well as of those who pursue a career in dance. Unfortunately, the book's lack of complete reference citations and a bibliography severely restricts its use for students and scholars. Recommended for the general reader.—*S. E. Friedler, Swarthmore College*

◆ Film

WS-0967   PN2658   92-23507 CIP
Bach, Steven. **Marlene Dietrich: life and legend.** W. Morrow, 1992. 626p bibl disc index afp ISBN 0-688-07119-8, $25.00

Although Bach "spoke intermittently but at length" with Dietrich, this is not an official biography. He has written both the story of her life and a detailed discussion of the legend of this international star. The book is what a star-biography should be but rarely is. Dietrich, like Jay Gatsby, created herself. Bach, a student of Josef von Sternberg, believes that "he did not invent Marlene Dietrich, or even 'discover' her: he revealed her." There is a detailed discussion of the making of the seven Dietrich films Von Sternberg directed, beginning with *Der Blaue Engel* (1930) and ending with *The Devil Is a Women* (1935). Dietrich's other films are also discussed, including the 17 German films in which she appeared prior to *Der Blaue Engel*, which made her an international star. The book is very long, filled with facts; and in its factual accuracy and extensive research, it is superior to any other Dietrich biography. It is all here—the films, the romance, the sex, the glamour, the unconventional marriage, the Nazi sister, the friendship with Hemingway, the wartime work for the Allies, the tragedy, the pathos, the grandmother, the legs, the truth, and the legend. Bibliography, notes on sources, theater chronology, filmography, discography, and an outstanding collection of more than 100 photographs and stills. Recommended for all film collections.—*W. K. Huck, emeritus, Idaho State University*

WS-0968   PN1995   95-31390 CIP
Berenstein, Rhona J. **Attack of the leading ladies: gender, sexuality, and spectatorship in classic horror cinema.** Columbia, 1996. 274p bibl index afp ISBN 0-231-08462-5, $42.50; ISBN 0-231-08463-3 pbk, $15.50

Berenstein's lucid and well-crafted book offers yet another descent into the ideological maelstrom of "gender, sexuality, and spectatorship" in classic horror cinema film. The author (Univ. of California, Irvine) is agreeably conversant with traditional interpretations of the genre and with emerging theoretical constructs, especially those of Nöel Carroll, and she provides a superb and even-handed explication of those arguments with which she differs. Her insights into the performance aspects of such films as *Mad Love* (1935), *Dracula* (1931),

and *King Kong* (1933) flow from a vast pool of related cultural materials—contemporary reviews, marketing campaigns, fan mail, letters to the editors, and meaningful film stills. She reads classic horror films through a gender-bent lens, questioning basic critical assumptions of prevailing analyses of the genre, and challenges the dominant notions that horror films appeal to a sadistic male spectator and that their terrorizing narratives center on "heterosexual, albeit monstrous, desire." For those not yet weary of gay and lesbian studies of the media, Berenstein has initiated a lively attack on leading theories of horror films and gender. Of particular interest is her underlying apologetic for the open negotiation of homosexual relations. She has constructed a fascinating though not fully compelling perspective on the shifting roles of the screaming "women." Graduate students, faculty.—*T. Lindvall, Regent University*

WS-0969   PN2287   95-15671 CIP
Britton, Andrew. **Katharine Hepburn: star as feminist.** Continuum, 1995. 256p bibl filmography index ISBN 0-8264-0801-X, $24.95

The late Andrew Britton's *Katharine Hepburn: The Thirties and After* (1984) has been reissued here with a new subtitle (presumably considered more apt for the 1990s); some slight restructuring; an updated bibliography and filmography (and the addition of stage credits, though Hepburn's theater career is barely mentioned in the text); and, most significantly, the addition of more than 100 stills from Hepburn's films. Britton's analysis of Hepburn's screen persona in its various manifestations (with useful comparisons to other stars such as Greta Garbo and Bette Davis) is undeniably one of the more sophisticated star studies to date. His thought-provoking, insightful look at Hepburn on screen raises problems about class, female sexuality, film genre, camp, spinsterhood, and women's oppression within the context of conventional cinema (Britton notes that "Hepburn's presence is always more radical than her films"). Even the obligatory chapter on Hepburn and Spencer Tracy has some unorthodox conclusions. Because the first edition of this work is scarce, this new illustrated one will be a welcome addition to film collections and probably should be added to those holding the earlier edition as well. Upper-division undergraduates and above.—*D. B. Wilmeth, Brown University*

WS-0970   PN1995   90-46738 CIP
Byars, Jackie. **All that Hollywood allows: re-reading gender in 1950s melodrama.** North Carolina, 1991. 326p bibl index afp ISBN 0-8078-1953-0, $39.95; ISBN 0-8078-4312-1 pbk, $14.95

During the 1950s, a resurgence in the production of melodrama films paralleled the contradictory forces of the era's pro-family, patriarchal conservatism and the increased emergence of women seeking a place within the traditionally male-dominated workplace. While the melodramas of the 1950s were not necessarily overt social critiques (though the films of Douglas Sirk reveled in political ironies), they did provide a forum through which the question of gender roles and the social structure could be critically examined. Not surprisingly, this period of the genre has come under intense feminist scrutiny and in this book Jackie Byars is as concerned with previous critical writings on the films as she is with the films themselves. Armed with all the tools of contemporary film theory, Byars attempts to expand her study beyond the phallic-centered domain of Freud and Lacan as she pursues questions pertaining to class position and race and their interrelationship to gender roles within society. She successfully avoids the relativistic, ahistorical venue that has become increasingly predominant in film criticism, but the broad nature of her concerns remains sketchy, and her discussions of the actual films are interesting but all too brief. Though this is an important addition to the critical study of 1950s melodrama, it works better as an introduction to the gender/social concerns of the genre than as a comprehensive text in itself.— *D. Toth, Columbus Museum of Art*

WS-0971   PC1995   91-28571 CIP
Clover, Carol J. **Men, women, and chain saws: gender in the modern horror film.** Princeton, 1992. 260p bibl index afp ISBN 0-691-04802-9, $19.95

Clover's provocatively titled book is one of the most remarkably readable pieces of scholarship on the study of gender and horror films. She examines three species of the popular low culture genre of horror: slasher films, occult and satanic possession films, and rape/revenge films. In her psychoanalytic reading of these marginal films, based upon Laguer's "one-sex model" of gender construction, she argues that male spectators can and do identify with female victim/heroes. This thorough, well-informed, and intelligent work avoids the obtuse specialized jargon of much contemporary cultural theory and raises stimulating questions for feminist, genre, and audience studies. The bibliography is splendidly comprehensive for so focused a study. Finely tuned to stir debate, disagreement, and insight, it is highly recommended for academic libraries.—*T. Lindvall, Regent University*

WS-0972   PN1998   95-2325 CIP
Cohen, Paula Marantz. **Alfred Hitchcock: the legacy of Victorianism.** University Press of Kentucky, 1995. 198p index afp ISBN 0-8131-1930-8, $34.95; ISBN 0-8131-0850-0 pbk, $14.95

Building on her previous study of Victorian novels (*The Daughter's Dilemma: Family Process and the Nineteenth-Century Domestic Novel*, CH, Feb'92), Cohen (Drexel Univ.) here extends and expands that study into 20th-century films, and in so doing makes a valuable contribution to Hitchcock studies. Her thesis is that Hitchcock took film, which in its classic phase catered to the male gaze, and fused it with the feminine subjectivity of the late Victorian novel. She charts the course of this process, arguing that Hitchcock's transformation from action-suspense to psychological-suspense director was influenced both by Selznick and—more importantly—by what she calls the "daughter effect"—Hitchcock's relationship with his daughter Patricia. Although necessarily thin on any direct evidence about the actual nature of Hitchcock's relationship with his daughter and marred by occasional mistakes and misquotations, the book goes a long way toward fusing a psychoanalytic auteur approach to Hitchcock with the feminist approach of writers like Modleski and Wood. It also helps explain why Hitchcock has been both condemned as a misogynist and hailed as a protofeminist. He was both, though in the end, this reviewer believes, "his story" won out over "her story." Anyone seriously interested in Hitchcock should read this book. Upper-division undergraduates and above.—*W. A. Vincent, Michigan State University*

WS-0973   Orig
Francke, Lizzie. **Script girls: women screenwriters in Hollywood.** British Film Institute, 1994. 172p bibl index ISBN 0-85170-477-8, $45.00; ISBN 0-85170-478-6 pbk, $18.95

Francke starts off with a bang: her acknowledgments provide a comprehensive list of film and (to a lesser extent) television archives and resources, a thumbnail sketch of the terrain for the interested scholar. The extensive notes following each chapter illustrate two points: Francke has done her homework and, even though the film medium has completed its first century, its bibliography is still in its infancy. Some of the women featured were available for interviews; sadly, some of the pioneers had passed on before research for this volume began. Despite the occasional paucity of the record, Francke has pieced together a history that is itself a miniseries: talent, ambition, drama, betrayal, comedy, suspense, and even an occasional triumph are all here. The filmography includes 201 women and refreshingly brackets the male writing partners *after* the female. The comprehensive index has only one small shortcoming: given the interest in film genres and their many mentions in the text, inclusion of genre terms in the index terminology would have been nice. This history reads as engagingly as a novel, a must purchase for any library with women's history or a film history collection.—*D. A. Schmitt, St. Louis Community College at Meramec*

WS-0974   PN1995   93-7755 CIP
Fregoso, Rosa Linda. **The bronze screen: Chicana and Chicano film culture.** Minnesota, 1993. 166p index afp ISBN 0-8166-2135-7, $39.95; ISBN 0-8166-2136-5 pbk, $15.95

This well-researched and footnoted study combines film theory, close textual analysis, and social history to examine the emergence of a film culture by, for, and about Chicanas and Chicanos. Fregoso draws on a cultural-studies framework and feminism's critical discourse on film to explore the problematics of cultural identity, the "border" as transcultural experience, the subversive potential of humor, and gender and subjectivity in narrative discourse in such important Chicano and Chicana films as *Born in East L.A.*, *La Bamba*, *Break of Dawn*, *Después del terremoto*, and *La ofrenda*. No bibliography is included; the academic jargon may discourage undergraduate readers. This major study builds on and surpasses the work of editors Gary D. Keller (*Chicano Cinema: Research, Reviews, and Resources*, 1985) and Chon A. Noriega (*Chicano and Film: Essays on Chi-*

cano Representation and Resistance, CH, Jun'92). Recommended for libraries building substantial Chicano studies and film studies collections at the graduate level and above.—*D. West, University of Idaho*

WS-0975   PN1993   92-25618 CIP
Gender and German cinema: feminist interventions, ed. by Sandra Frieden et al. Berg, 1993. 2v. 332, 361p bibl index ISBN 0-85496-947-0, v.1 [*Gender and Representation in New German Cinema*]; ISBN 0-85496-323-5, v.2 [*German Film History/German History on Film.*]; $64.00 ea; ISBN 0-85496-243-3 pbk, v.1; ISBN 0-85496-324-3 pbk, v.2; $19.95 ea.

Much has been written about the male practitioners of the *Neue Kino*, but too little has been available about the equally important women filmmakers in the German "new cinema" movement, such as von Trotta, Sander, Ottinger, Export, and Stöckl. Discussions of their works, along with representative interviews, are the most valuable contribution of this collection which also includes treatments from a feminist perspective of works by Fassbinder, Wenders, and Straub/Huillet. Volume 2 deals, often excitingly, with German film history and the treatment of history in German film. Overall, *Gender and German Cinema* lacks a clear focus and individual pieces are of varying quality and interest; but at its best, as in B. Ruby Rich's essays on Sander's films and on Sagan's *Girls in Uniform*, or in Roswitha Mueller's piece on films by Stöckl and von Trotta, it attains a very high level. What is best—and saddest—about this collection is that it makes us realize how much the German women directors have been neglected and how hard it still is to see their works. Useful, however, are listings of rental sources.—*W. A. Vincent, Michigan State University*

WS-0976   PN2287   96-11764 CIP
Genini, Ronald. **Theda Bara: a biography of the silent screen vamp, with a filmography.** McFarland, 1996. 158p bibl index afp ISBN 0-7864-0202-4, $29.95

In this carefully researched study, Genini excavates the exotic career and life of the first and greatest silent film femme fatale. While providing a full biography of the nice Jewish girl born Theodosia Goodman (whose film name became known as an anagram for "Arab Death"), he unravels the fascinating trajectory of this cinematic vamp. The scope of Genini's research in contemporaneous newspaper, magazine, and journal articles is impressive; his marshaling of primary materials makes for an insightful and compelling narrative of the invention, exploitation, and erasure of the silver screen's first sex goddess. The work marches through Bara's film career, noting anecdotal and critical reviews, fan mail, publicity campaigns, including her sale of Liberty War Bonds. The human side of the cosmetically decorated and veiled actress who ushered the female vampire into American culture is affectionately woven into the story of her film and stage career. Photographs illustrate and chronicle the stages of her life. A useful volume on silent American film. All levels.—*T. Lindvall, Regent University*

WS-0977   PN2287   91-2951 CIP
Golden, Eve. **Platinum girl: the life and legends of Jean Harlow.** Abbeville, 1991. 248p bibl index ISBN 1-55859-214-8, $27.50

Eve Golden, a journalist and film buff, has written a readable biography of Harlow for both fans and students of American films. Her attention is focused on the life, the legends, and the films. The brief life of Harlow, who was dead of kidney failure at the age of 26, is told in detail. Golden presents her as a serious and hard working actress who was and still is a glamorous and legendary figure. The titles of two of Harlow's films refer to these legendary elements: *Platinum Blonde* and *Blonde Bombshell*. Golden is more concerned with the "platinum" than the "bombshell" elements in Harlow's life. She attacks and refutes Irving Shulman, author of *Harlow, an Intimate Biography* (1964), who presented Harlow as a sex goddess whose life was filled with many sensational scandals. Shulman's book is both inaccurate and sleazy. Golden's grasp of film history is at times weak: Columbia was not a major studio in the 1930's; *Scarface* was released by United Artists not Warner Bros.; *I Am A Fugitive From A Chain Gang* was released by Warner Bros., not RKO. Her critical opinions are sometimes off the mark: "Joan Crawford was an accomplished singer and dancer." The book contains a list of sources that does not include Shulman's book, although it is quoted and mentioned frequently in the text. There is a filmography and a lavish collection of stills, photographs, and posters. For undergraduate and public library collections.—*W. K. Huck, emeritus, Idaho State University*

WS-0978   PN1995   90-50647 CIP

Jacobs, Lea. **The wages of sin: censorship and the fallen woman film, 1928-1942.** Wisconsin, 1991. 202p bibl index ISBN 0-229-12880-6, $37.50; ISBN 0-229-12884-9 pbk, $15.00

In suggesting a very limited scope of a few movies about women punished or rewarded for lapsing into sin, the title of this book is modest, even misleading. Here is a work of unexpected scope and thoughtfulness. True, few specific movies are analyzed—*Anna Karenina, Stella Dallas, Back Street, Blonde Venus, Camille, I'm No Angel, Susan Lenox: Her Fall and Rise*—but hints, insights, and alert scholarship provide a large context: stage melodrama, opera, novels (Hardy, Trollope, Collins, Eliot, Zola, Flaubert), Victorian concepts of womanhood, social mobility, and, of course, popular ideas of morality. There are a fine bibliography, footnotes, and filmography. Whether the sexually transgressing woman is punished or rewarded, "such films helped to define the limits of what was permissible." Once the machine of censorship got rolling, the rules of censorship dictated particular "structures of narrative" (endings and motives, especially). Will the man have a key to an unmarried woman's apartment? Will the secretary have a mink coat? This is a book about the specifics of censorship during a 14-year period in the US. Better yet, this is a book about the principles of censorship. The tone is calm, the approach historical, the ideas—without exception—worth serious consideration in these current censorial times. College and university libraries.—*P. H. Stacy, University of Hartford*

WS-0979   PN1997   92-29569 CIP

Jean-Luc Godard's *Hail Mary*: women and the sacred in film, ed. by Maryel Locke and Charles Warren. Southern Illinois, 1993. 235p index afp ISBN 0-8093-1824-5, $29.95; ISBN 0-8093-1891-1 pbk, $14.95

This volume collects the papers presented at a 1987 conference (at Harvard University's Carpenter Center for the Visual Arts) on Godard's most controversial movie. Also provided are both English and French shot breakdowns for the two short films, which were released and shown together, Godard's *Hail Mary* and *The Book of Mary*, by his collaborator Anne-Marie Miéville. There are also two short 1985 Godard interviews. Editor Locke leads off the essays with a survey of the controversy. Coeditor Warren considers the theological implications of the Godard film's whimsy. Sandra Laugier approaches *Hail Mary* as pedagogy, especially related to psychoanalyst Francoise Dolto. Godard's iconography of women is examined by Laura Mulvey and in a jointly authored piece by Geraldine Bard and conference organizer Vlada Petric. David Sterritt defines connections between the Godard and Miéville films. Inez Hedges finds Godard making a film about filmmaking. Ellen Draper contrasts the "successfully feminine" film by Miéville with the "ineffectively masculine" film by Godard. Robert Kiely's Catholic response is informed and sensible. Gayatri Chatterjee provides a pertinent Eastern perspective. For theologian Harvey Cox, Godard critiques the "increasingly implausible 'religious' system—modernity." John Gianvito extols Godard's visceral positivism. A vital defense of and guide to an intriguing set of films. Advanced undergraduate and above.—*M. Yacowar, Emily Carr College of Art and Design*

WS-0980   PN1993   92-6408 MARC

Knight, Julia. **Women and the new German cinema.** Verso, 1992. (Dist. by Routledge, Chapman & Hall) 221p bibl index ISBN 0-86091-352-X, $54.95; ISBN 0-86091-568-9 pbk, $17.95

Critical accounts in English of New German Cinema have always focused on its founding fathers (Fassbinder, Wenders, Kluge, et al.), with only occasional asides in specialist journals to important women directors such as Von Trotta or Helke Sander. Though its dry prose betrays its origins as an academic dissertation, Knight's monograph therefore begins to fill an embarrassingly large gap in our understanding of this still vital movement. Building on pioneering studies in German, Knight provides brief accounts of the work of nearly 50 female directors who have worked in television and film, including the still too little known Helma Sanders-Brahms, Birgit Hein, Ulrike Ottinger, and Valie Export. Knight patiently outlines how the rise of the women's movement and the struggle to define a feminist aesthetic inflected an impressive variety of films. Unfortunately, she primarily offers only brief plot descriptions coupled with paraphrases of remarks by the filmmakers or their critics; she avoids any significant critical evaluation of individual films. The extensive bibliography and useful filmographies at the end, however, will become a crucial resource for further, necessarily more search-

ing assessments. Advanced undergraduate; graduate.—*S. Liebman, Queens College, CUNY*

WS-0981   PN1995   90-25290 CIP

Lant, Antonia. **Blackout: reinventing women for wartime British cinema.** Princeton, 1991. 262p bibl index afp ISBN 0-691-05540-8, $49.50; ISBN 0-691-00828-0 pbk, $15.95

Lant (cinema studies, NYU) has added to the canon of books about the impact of WW II on the lives of women, in this case British women as seen through the prism of popular film. For Lant a key metaphor of wartime movie culture is the "blackout" (the dimming of lights as a defense against aerial bombardment) during which encounters take place that in prewar days would have been both unlikely and unseemly. The resulting cinema "was no longer characterized by conventional gender distinctions." Moreover, she argues, such breaks with the past allowed British audiences to see the Hollywood movies that had dominated their prewar screens as "specific and national rather than universal and natural." And the resulting social changes for British women (at least for the term of the war) provided a theme of value "particularly for feminism." Lant's book is enhanced by a solid bibliography, forays into the Public Records Office and other repositories of primary sources, and uncommonly good graphics drawn not only from films but from propaganda posters and popular magazines. The generally well-crafted book is only occasionally clouded by the jargon that recent scholars, at the expense of clarity, have borrowed from the disciplines of psychoanalysis, linguistics, and Marxist social theory.—*T. Cripps, Harvard University*

WS-0982   PN1995   90-50903 CIP

Lawrence, Amy. **Echo and Narcissus: women's voices in classical Hollywood cinema.** California, 1991. 212p bibl index afp ISBN 0-520-07071-2, $37.50; ISBN 0-520-07082-8 pbk, $15.95

Amy Lawrence's research into certain ideological implications of early sound technology underpins her critical exploration of cinema's "image/sound hierarchy." As with patriarchal myth, woman, like sound, plays "Echo" to classical cinema's spectacle-driven, "vain and self-absorbed Narcissus." Rooted in silent film's conventions, classical Hollywood narratives tend to efface woman's voice, denying her the male subject's control, authorial presence, and right to discourse. Lawrence traces the historical problem of the "speaking woman" and yokes it to films with "crisis" structures (*The Spiral Staircase*) that "explicitly confront a woman's struggle to speak." Her fruitful readings of films enlarge the critical examination of woman/sound constructions and subversions. Sometimes the writing sparkles with lucidity and flair (*Sorry, Wrong Number*), unravelling complex codifications of Hollywood's compliant female. Regrettably, Lawrence's anthology of published essays and recent writing lacks a formal conclusion. For college and university libraries.—*J. Nicks, Brock University*

WS-0983   PN2287   94-46303 CIP

Leaming, Barbara. **Katharine Hepburn.** Crown, 1995. 549p index ISBN 0-517-59284-3, $27.50

Leaming's biography of Hepburn is more complete on her early life than other sources, including Hepburn's autobiography *Me* (1991) and Anne Edwards's *A Remarkable Woman* (1985). Fully half of the book focuses on the often dark, complex episodes of Hepburn's ancestors and the tragedies during her childhood (blighted by a series of family suicides). In addition, Leaming offers detailed accounts of Hepburn's romantic relationships with Spencer Tracy and John Ford, particularly the latter. Although she is a good biographer (*Orson Welles*, 1989), Leaming has written a biography that reads more like a fictional account (the unflattering portraits of Ford and Tracy seem exaggerated), in itself not an indictment, for this is gripping reading. But despite the fact that her note on sources suggests copious and lengthy research, there are no specific citations within the text (general notes are provided) and thus no direct way to corroborate statements. In an attempt to tell a good story some truths may have been embellished. And for those who wish insights into Hepburn the actress/artist, Leaming's account will prove unsatisfying. Yet there is much to admire in this effort, especially in Leaming's explication of the effect of the past and of personal relationships on the development of Hepburn the woman. General and undergraduate collections.—*D. B. Wilmeth, Brown University*

WS-0984   PN1998   94-30602 CIP
Loshitzky, Yosefa. **The radical faces of Godard and Bertolucci.**
Wayne State, 1995. 286p bibl filmography index afp ISBN 0-8143-2446-
0, $44.95; ISBN 0-8143-2447-9 pbk, $18.95

Brilliantly blending theory and explication, Loshitzky (Hebrew Univ. of
Jerusalem) provides the best discussion yet of the reciprocal influence of Jean-
Luc Godard and Bernardo Bertolucci. The author traces Godard's radicaliza-
tion in his 1968-78 films, especially the influence of Jarry's *Ubu*, autocriticism,
and self-reflexivity in *Tout va bien* (1971). The 1968 upheavals that led Godard
to repudiate his prepolitical films led Bertolucci to discover personal liberation in political revolution. In *The Spider's Strategem* (1970), *The Conformist*
(1970), and *Last Tango in Paris* (1972), Bertolucci explores "the tension between
private and public memory." The thematic and formal organization in *Tragedy
of a Ridiculous Man* (1981) completed Bertolucci's Oedipal exorcism of Godard,
suggesting his flight from the spiraling negativity of modern Europe. Godard
sought spiritual rejuvenation in his "triology of the sublime" (*Passion*, 1982;
Carmen, 1981; *Hail Mary*, 1983), in which recurring sky images show preoccupation with the impossibility of representing the sublime. Loshitzky also provides a dense multidisciplinary context for Bertolucci's quest for the Other in
The Last Emperor (1987) and *The Sheltering Sky* (1990). She offers feminist
reinterpretations of Godard's work "from his early libertine misogynism" to the
"meta-heresy of the sacralizing images of feminine flesh in his quasi-religious, cosmic period," and of Bertolucci's "poetics and politics of sexual indeterminacy." She concludes with a critique of *Last Tango* and of his general failure "to transgress patriarchal binarism." Whereas Godard's image of woman
is in constant flux, revealing his steadily increasing sensitivity, Bertolucci's
female characters never transcend the sexual domain. "Godard's seemingly
bizarre nouvelle religion and Bertolucci's search for uncontaminated civilizations [are] cultural and political symptoms [that reflect] ... the accumulative reactions to the political 1960s and 1970s, the apolitical 1980s, and to the even more
confusing 1990s with their celebratory rhetorics of a new world order,
perhaps masking a new world disorder." The notes are exemplary. Upper-
division undergraduate and above.—*M. Yacowar, University of Calgary*

WS-0985   PN1995   92-25407 CIP
Male trouble, ed. by Constance Penley and Sharon Willis. Minnesota,
1993. 316p index ISBN 0-8166-2171-3, $39.95; ISBN 0-8166-2172-1 pbk,
$16.95

Based on the 1988 special issue of *Camera Obscura: A Journal of Feminism and Film Theory*, this volume reprints seven contributions from that source
and adds six new essays. The editors note that in content and context and in
tone and approach the book version represents a significant advancement in the
examination of masculinity "from an explicitly feminist theoretical and historical
perspective." That advancement involves consideration of masculinity and
patriarchy neither as monolithic nor as a victimizing force but as "split and contradictory" and as "uneven and sometimes unsuccessful in its effects." These wide-
ranging and resourceful essays focus on "straight masculinity" (usually white)
"caught between fear of women and fear of homosexuality." Thus, concepts
historically and traditionally applied to women and gays can be used to explain
a troubled and troublesome masculinity that exhibits male hysteria, subjectivity,
gender uncertainty, masochism, and narcissism. After four essays that introduce recurring theoretical concerns, the volume focuses on the figurations and representations of masculinity in photography, television, and film. Four essays deal
with the themes, subtexts, gender role implications, and responses to the 1988 TV
program *Pee-Wee's Playhouse.* Four present resourceful and detailed close
readings of films ranging from early silents to *Picnic* (1956), *Strangers on A Train*
(1951), and *To Live and Die in L.A.* (1985). The concluding essay deals with
the television series *Thirty Something* as male domestic melodrama and "self-
ironic postmodern text." These readings reveal the historically and socially
shifting meanings and representations of masculinity (and its relations to women,
minorities, and sexual groups) as well as the "crisis-ridden" qualities that cause
male anxiety and resulting efforts to shore up or defend masculinity. Graduate
students and faculty interested in understanding the new directions and dimensions of feminist theory will find this a valuable, instructive book yielding cultural
information of substantial value and application.—*D. A. Noverr, Michigan State
University*

WS-0986   PN1995   95-42165 CIP
Maxfield, James F. **The fatal woman: sources of male anxiety in
American *film noir*, 1941-1991.** Fairleigh Dickinson, 1996. (Dist. by
Associated University Presses) 194p index afp ISBN 0-8386-3662-4, $32.50

Maxfield (Whitman College) uses 14 classic films noir to demonstrate the male
anxiety that emotional vulnerability cedes control to woman. The figure of the
dangerous, seductive woman embodies the male fear of loss of control, will,
and identity. The author rounds up the usual suspects. In *The Maltese Falcon*
(1941) Sam Spade is pragmatic, defensive, and determined to dominate everyone he meets. Stunted psychological development characterizes the heroes of *Double Idemnity* (1944) and *Murder My Sweet* (1944). The incoherent ending of
Howard Hawks's *The Big Sleep* (1946) maintains the effect of an inscrutable world,
with death the only certainty. Freudian forms of the Greek tragic hero are defined
in *Out of the Past* (1947) and *White Heat* (1949). In Hitchcock's *Vertigo* (1958),
John Boorman's *Point Blank* (1967), and David Lynch's *Blue Velvet* (1986) the
betrayal and vengeance narratives suggest the dream state. The modern spiritual void is played out with black humor in *Mean Streets* (1973), *Chinatown* (1974),
and *Prizzi's Honor* (1985). The *Grifters* (1990) is bleaker still, because its most
selfish murderer is the nurturer, the mother. *In Thelma and Louise* (1991) the massive legal assault shows the intensity of the patriarchy's fear of female denial of
its authority. Each chapter is clear, perceptive, and persuasive. However, the
analysis is so literary (versus cinematic) that the directors of *The Grifters* (Stephen
Frears) and *Thelma and Louise* (Ridley Scott) are nowhere named. All collections.—*M. Yacowar, University of Calgary*

WS-0987   PN1998   93-51496 CIP
Mayne, Judith. **Directed by Dorothy Arzner.** Indiana, 1995 (c1994).
209p filmography index afp ISBN 0-253-33716-X, $29.95; ISBN 0-253-
20896-3 pbk, $15.95

Between 1919 and 1943 Arzner moved from typist to script clerk to screen-
writer to editor to director of 16 credited films. The story of Arzner's success
as the only woman director in Hollywood is an interesting and compelling one;
she gained a reputation as a star maker for notable actresses like Clara Bow, brought
new dimensions to the "women's film" by focusing on women's communities and
relationships as shaped and complicated by social class, and survived three commercial failures. But the further range of Mayne's study involves an investigation
into Arzner's lesbian identity and the ways her lesbianism informed her films.
Mayne shows through resourceful readings of the film texts how Arzner drew complicated and complex portraits of women's lives; highlighted women's points of
view; showed the dynamics of female bonding or separation; and dramatized
encounters between women, suggesting the possibilities of other kinds of attractions and desires. The book is an excellent guide to lesbian feminist response theory. Mayne also provides substantial information on Arzner's directing philosophy and how the rise of powerful studio procedures proved disastrous to her
career. Only two areas of the book fail to satisfy. There is no discussion of
how Hollywood publicity photographs (heavily used in the book to investigate
Arzner's gendered persona) were used and no information on financial issues.
A fascinating and rewarding book; upper-division undergraduate and above.—
D. A. Noverr, Michigan State University

WS-0988   NX180   90-47160 CIP
McCormick, Richard W. **Politics of the self: feminism and the postmodern in West German literature and film.** Princeton, 1991. 262p
bibl index afp ISBN 0-691-06851-8, $45.00; ISBN 0-691-01483-3 pbk, $14.95

McCormick takes his definition of the term "postmodern" primarily from Linda
Hutcheon's *A Poetics of Postmodernism* (CH, Oct'88). He interprets six West
German literary or cinematic works from the period between 1968 and 1980 to
illustrate the cultural turn from the "rigid theoretical orthodoxy" (p.71) charac-
teristic of the Student Movement of the mid-60s to a renewed affirmation of
subjectivity. For McCormick, three trends shape the postmodern panorama of
these years: New Subjectivity (Peter Schneider's *Lenz* and Karin Struck's *Class
Love* are examples); a pessimistic interiority (*Devotion* by Botho Strauss and *Wrong
Move* by Peter Handke and Wim Wenders); and a "return to history" (the films
Germany, Pale Mother, directed by Helma Sanders-Brahms, and *The Subjective
Factor*, directed by Helke Sander). Through the representative nature of these
choices and the broad scope informing his interpretations, McCormick does
succeed in capturing the period. His book is plainly written, with vestiges of the

dissertation in occasional awkwardness and redundancy, and has copious notes and an exhaustive bibliography. Two stills as illustrations. Suitable for upper-division undergraduates or graduate students.—*M. Faber, Swarthmore College*

WS-0989 PN1995 95-7088 CIP
Me Jane: masculinity, movies and women, ed. by Pat Kirkham and Janet Thumim. St. Martin's, 1995. 296p indexes ISBN 0-312-12767-7, $39.95; ISBN 0-312-12768-5 pbk, $16.95

In *You Tarzan: Masculinity, Movies and Men* (CH, Dec'93), their collection of essays by male writers on the subject of cinematic masculinity, Kirkham (De Montfort Univ.—Leicester) and Thumim (Univ. of Bristol) assembled an often interesting but highly uneven group of articles. This well-edited companion volume of (almost all original) essays by female writers on such varied topics as star personae, personalized audience response, and transgendered characters offers a higher percentage of clear and valuable articles and a more "unified" perspective. Some problems remain: copy editing is still weak; several articles are labored; photographs are woefully few (two, to be exact—an especially odd and unfortunate shortcoming in a collection that refers frequently to mise-en-scènes and the physical attributes of actors). But the writing is generally good, and most of the essays provide close semiotic readings through clear description and cogent analysis; especially admirable are Margaret O'Brien on Oliver Stone's Vietnam films, Charlene Regester on Oscar Micheaux, and Kathleen Rowe on melodrama. Recommended for undergraduate and graduate collections in film studies, popular culture, and gender studies.—*T. Gleeson, Neumann College*

WS-0990 NX548 94-6589 CIP
Mueller, Roswitha. **Valie Export: fragments of the imagination.** Indiana, 1995 (c1994). 246p filmography index afp ISBN 0-253-33906-5, $49.95; ISBN 0-253-20925-0 pbk, $24.95

Mueller's sumptuously illustrated volume is the first in English devoted to this important Austrian avant-gardist. Mueller (German and comparative literature, Univ. of Wisconsin—Milwaukee) provides a comprehensive overview of the various modes—performance art, photography, film, expanded cinema, and video—in which Export's feminist and social concerns have been expressed since she began her career as a participant in the Fluxus art scene in Vienna during the early 1960s. Despite the author's occasional lapses into turgidity, most of the major works are concisely described and interpreted in the light of Export's theoretical agendas. The body, especially the female body as it intersects with and inflects technology, quickly emerged as Export's central focus. Mueller patiently charts the evolution of Export's work in the context of other contemporary artistic and political initiatives—action painting, happenings, the Wiener Group, and the rise of the feminist movement, among others. A thought-provoking interview between author and subject concludes the book. Though a useful filmography/videography is included, a bibliography of the artist's writings and of texts about her oeuvre is unfortunately omitted. Recommended for more advanced students (including undergraduates) and faculty.—*S. Liebman, CUNY Graduate School and University Center*

WS-0991 PN1995 93-13743 CIP
Multiple voices in feminist film criticism, ed. by Diane Carson, Linda Dittmar, and Janice R. Welsch. Minnesota, 1994. 547p index ISBN 0-8166-2272-8, $49.95

This will be an invaluable resource for anyone who studies and/or teaches feminist film criticism and may actually be the best available anthology on the subject. Containing essays by many of the leading feminist film scholars, the book is divided into three sections. Section 1, "Perspectives," provides overviews of feminist film theory and its use of such other important theoretical discourses as Marxism and psychoanalysis. Section 2, "Practice," looks at key texts, often exploring the intersections of gender and/or race, ethnicity, and sexual orientation. Section 3, "Course Files," should prove especially valuable for pedagogical purposes, providing outlines for six potential courses in the field, each with a theoretical framework and a suggested list of readings and screenings. There is even a "Partial List of Distributors and Resources." The editors have put together an admirable collection that goes far beyond the white, middle-class, heterosexual perspective that has characterized much of feminist film criticism. General readers; undergraduate and graduate students; faculty.—*R. E. Pearson, University of Pennsylvania*

WS-0992 PN1998 94-9603 CIP
Poague, Leland. **Another Frank Capra.** Cambridge, 1995 (c1994). 286p bibl filmography index ISBN 0-521-38066-9, $54.95

Poague believes that film criticism is a kind of "cultural conversation of critics with each other and the films they study." Each chapter of his revisionist study of Capra's films is a series of such conversations. He begins with short but meaningful autobiographical comments on his personal discovery of Capra's films. He sees Capra as a serious, modernist artist who is a "proto-feminist." Readers are given close readings of Capra's *Forbidden* (1931), *Mr. Deeds Goes to Town* (1936), *Lost Horizon* (1937), *Mr. Smith Goes to Washington* (1939), *It's a Wonderful Life* (1946), *Meet John Doe* (1941), and *You Can't Take It with You* (1938), a film often neglected by Capra's "populist" critics. Grounded in genre and gender theories and feminist psychology, this study is supplemented by notes and some frame enlargements (though Columbia Pictures, for whom Capra directed many of his films, chose not to give permission for extensive use of frame enlargements). Recommended for upper-division undergraduates, graduate students, researchers, and faculty.—*W. K. Huck, emeritus, Idaho State University*

WS-0993 PN1995.9.E96 90-10897 CIP
Rabinovitz, Lauren. **Points of resistance: women, power & politics in the New York avant-garde cinema, 1943-71.** Illinois, 1991. 250p bibl index afp ISBN 0-252-01744-7, $34.95; ISBN 0-252-06139-X pbk, $14.95

Three of the most important women in North American film history are sympathetically and thoroughly dealt with in this book: Maya Deren, Shirley Clarke, and Joyce Wieland. These filmmakers, says Rabinovitz, "are less interesting as simple auteur studies than as subjects of significant cultural formations in cinema and the art." Her readings of the central films of these women are thorough, although not spectacular. However, her strength is to locate each of them in the context of avant-garde filmmaking and art practice, and at the same time to modulate the concept of the avant-garde itself in order to draw out the feminist specificity of the works. The book thus ranges easily from history, to theory, to interpretation, and to biography. While it is useful on all those levels, it has the additional merit of focusing on what Rabinovitz calls the "reception practices" surrounding these films. That is, she charts the fate of the films in terms of their distribution, their critical and journalistic reception, and their place within feminist discourse and politics. This focus is what sets the book above the ranks of most film histories or auteur studies. Its illustrations are adequate and it offers full filmographies and bibliographies.—*P. Smith, Carnegie-Mellon University*

WS-0994 PN1995 94-39466 MARC
Rabinowitz, Paula. **They must be represented: the politics of documentary.** Verso, 1994. 264p index ISBN 1-85984-025-6 pbk, $19.95

In this abstract albeit personal collection of essays, Rabinowitz explores problems that politicized documentaries have posed for American bourgeois intellectuals. The text begins with a rereading of James Agee's *Let Us Now Praise Famous Men* (1941), contrasted with a shorter critique of Margaret Bourke-White and a survey of mass media representations of 1930s poverty. A second section, on the 1960s, encompasses both gender and Vietnam reportage (primarily nonvisual) and the family motif in docudrama and cinema verité. The final section reviews the challenges posed to the documentary by contemporary female filmmakers such as Chris Strand, Yvonne Rainer, Jill Godmilow, and Trinh T. Minh-Ha, and closes with comments on Rodney King. The book demands considerable grounding in both Marxist and feminist theories, which dominate discussion, and knowledge of the documentary works themselves, which are often introduced only briefly in the text. This "crisis of the representer" may also beg questions of alternative approaches/voices from those who represent themselves, within the US as well as outside of it, reflecting on documentaries as problematic forms. Nonetheless, a provocative interrogation. Upper-division undergraduates and above.—*G. W. McDonogh, Bryn Mawr College*

WS-0995 PN1992 92-3187 CIP
Rapping, Elayne. **The movie of the week: private stories/public events.** Minnesota, 1992. 162p (American culture, 5) bibl index afp ISBN 0-8166-2017-2, $39.95; ISBN 0-8166-2018-0 pbk, $14.95

Rapping (Adelphi Univ.), an increasingly prolific writer about television, here addresses fans and intellectuals alike. If not entirely successful, she has nonetheless attained much of her goal, particularly in an introductory essay that is worth the price of the book. She wished to inquire into a mass medium from the angle of feminism and thus chose the made-for-TV movie for its capacity for "the domestication of social issues." She aptly calls herself a "public intellectual," bent upon taking seriously the medium but using an accessible language free of scholarly cant. Rapping likes the genre of made-for-TV movies for its taking up "serious issues" in a form that genuinely affects its target audience, perhaps even moving it to action—"affective empowerment," she calls it. As examples she notes both the morning-after actions of viewers reported in the press and testimony such as that of a girl who felt suddenly confident in her sports skills after watching *Cagney and Lacey*. In this way TV movies become "women's movies" in that otherwise "unrealized political ideals" are set afoot in the minds of viewers as "cognitive mappings" (quoting Frederic Jameson). A small book, it glosses historical antecedents, empirical data, and other scholarly conventions, but engages the reader through anecdotes drawn from responses of the author's students. Useful index and very current bibliography. Both general and academic readers at all levels.—*T. Cripps, Morgan State University*

WS-0996   PN1995   90-20695 CIP
Rodowick, D.N. **The difficulty of difference: psychoanalysis, sexual difference, and film theory.** Routledge, 1991. 162p index ISBN 0-415-90331-9, $37.50

A fascinating and complex work best used by readers extremely familiar with the psychoanalytic theories of Sigmund Freud and Jacques Lacan. Rodowick attempts to recover and reexplain the power of Freud's theories on gender and sexual difference. This is not a work for those who wish extended and specific discussions of particular films. At its best, this is an interesting work in dialogue with feminist film theorists who speak for the power of the female gaze both within films themselves and among audience members. Should be read in conjunction with Laura Mulvey's *Visual and Other Pleasures* (1989) and Nancy Chodorov's *The Reproduction of Mothering* (CH, Nov'78).—*L. Winters, College of Saint Elizabeth*

WS-0997   PN1995   93-10970 CIP
Stacey, Jackie. **Star gazing: Hollywood cinema and female spectatorship.** Routledge, 1994. 282p bibl index afp ISBN 0-415-09178-0, $59.95; ISBN 0-415-09179-9 pbk, $16.95

The author (sociology, Lancaster Univ.) uses film study and women's film theory for the more immediate concern of women's studies. She follows the tradition of such male gaze academic gender theorists as Laura Mulvey, Mary Ann Doane, and Teresa de Lauretis and utilizes French psychoanalyst Jacques Lacan's mirror gratification study. Stacey, in furthering the work of these others, addresses the relationship of women spectators to their Hollywood ideals on screen by investigating the subjective reaction of British women in the 1940s and '50s to films in which the star was an object created by male directors and cinematographers. The spectator realizes that her relationship is not one of emulation but of desire, the recognition of the gap between herself and idealized image. As a result, Stacey studies the diversity of the forms of identification, her goal to arrive at "forms of intimacies between feminities." The data for this study draw on letters from and questionnaires sent to British women who would approximate the ages of the stars 40 to 50 years ago. This work, with its extensive notes, bibliography, appendixes, and stills (mostly studio publicity poses) is recommended for film and women's studies collections, upper-division undergraduate and above.—*A. Hirsh, Central Connecticut State University*

WS-0998   PN1995   94-46539 CIP
Staiger, Janet. **Bad women: regulating sexuality in early American cinema.** Minnesota, 1995. 226p bibl filmography index afp ISBN 0-8166-2624-3, $49.95

Staiger (Univ. of Texas at Austin) examines public discourse surrounding female sexuality in turn-of-the-century fiction and films, ranging from kinetoscope peep shows in the 1890s to *Traffic in Souls* (1913), *A Fool There Was* (1914), and *The Cheat* (1915). During this period Victorian reticence about sexuality gave way to a discussion about the changing status of women brought about by urbanization and industrialization and by the entry of women into the public sphere. Rather than repressing discussion of sexuality, the middle class became fascinated

with prostitution, white slavery, venereal disease, and the figures of the flapper and the new woman. Staiger's study focuses on the representation of "bad" or "troublesome" women and on the moral lessons such narratives provided middle-class women. She provides a survey of reform movements such as populism and progressivism, and she documents the history of censorship up to 1915. This excellent film scholarship represents a major contribution to the study of the reception of films and other works. It is written in an accessible style and should interest feminists, Americanists, and general readers.—*J. Belton, Rutgers, The State University of New Jersey, New Brunswick*

WS-0999   PN1998   91-42876 CIP
Trinh, T. Minh-Ha. **Framer framed.** Routledge, 1992. 276p index ISBN 0-415-90561-3, $59.95

Presents the scripts of three of Trinh T. Minh-Ha's unclassifiable films (poetic? documentary? fiction? political manifesto?): *Naked Spaces—Living Is Round*, *Surname Viet Given Name Nam*, and *Reassemblage*. Copious stills illustrate these works. In addition, nine interviews with Minh-Ha highlight her aesthetic, anthropological, and political theories, while she eloquently resists "boundaries and closure." As a Vietnamese woman discussing her films on West African cultures, she exemplifies in herself a sense of possibility, an openness to all human experience, which cannot be contained in theories: she repudiates "the comfort of categorization," although she propounds recognizable "schools" of contemporary criticism—radical feminist, postcolonial, postmodern, deconstructionist views. This unusual book is recommended, even for those who have had no opportunity to view Minh-Ha's films. She is a critic and theorist whose ideas emerge in her art: the best proof of their viability. Advanced undergraduate; graduate.—*R. D. Sears, Berea College*

WS-1000   PN1993   92-36398 CIP
Wexman, Virginia Wright. **Creating the couple: love, marriage, and Hollywood performance.** Princeton, 1993. 288p bibl index afp ISBN 0-691-06969-7, $49.50; ISBN 0-691-01535-X pbk, $16.95

Basing her discussion on the underlying assumption that life imitates film, Wexman (Univ. of Illinois at Chicago) analyzes the cinema's rituals of romantic love, courtship, and marriage, contending that Hollywood's ideology of romance and sexual fulfillment has significantly contributed to popular taste. Examination of the evolution of the couple as represented in film reveals that cinema called attention to the destabilization of the male and the empowering of the female, restructuring the expectations of a permanent marriage and happy, nuclear family. The first movies exerted their influence when actresses like Lilian Gish portrayed passive helplessness as ideal femininity. As women acquired economic and political power, they realized that men were not absolutely necessary for financial security or personal fulfillment. Films such as *The Big Sleep*, starring Humphrey Bogart and Lauren Bacall, and *Adam's Rib*, with Spencer Tracy and Katharine Hepburn, introduced the egalitarian couple, in which the woman aggressively refused to submit to male domination. Cinema's current emphasis on gender destabilization has sparked interest in promiscuity, homosexuality, and other alternative forms of sexual expression. Recommended for general readers with some background in film, undergraduates, and graduate students.—*E. Watson, Davenport College of Business*

◆ Music

WS-1001   Orig
American women composers: piano music from 1865-1915, by May Aufderheide et al.; ed. by Sylvia Glickman. Hildegard Publishing Company, Box 332, Bryn Mawr, PA 19010, 1990. 75p [score] pbk, $33.00

The 15 American women composers whose piano works are included in this collection, along with brief biographical notes, are for the most part unknown. Only three, Amy Beach, Helen Hopekirk, and Carrie Jacobs Bond are familiar, and the last, Bond, is best known for two songs, "I Love You Truly" and "A Perfect Day." Like those songs, most of the selections in this volume can be classified as "old-fashioned," that is, typical of much of the music composed by both men and women between 1865 and 1915: romantic, flowery, and of no great substance. There are two noteworthy exceptions: Philadelphia-born Celeste Heckscher, and Clara Gottschalk, sister of Louis Moreau Gottschalk. Their compositions in the collection are charming, and are of considerable musical interest. Regrettably the bulk of the works collected here seem to be rather pale imitations of what more well-known men were writing in these years. Studies continue to be done, analyzing why women did not, perhaps could not, write more artistically, more creatively. The Hildegard Publishing Company has contributed to sources for such studies by producing this collection, representative of published compositions by women. It should have a place in upper-division undergraduate or graduate libraries supporting programs in music and women's studies.—*J. E. Tucker, Northland College*

WS-1002　　　　MT820　　　　92-44414 CIP
Ashley, Douglas. **Music beyond sound: Maria Curcio, a teacher of great pianists.** P. Lang, 1993. 112p (American university studies. Series XX, fine arts, 19) index afp ISBN 0-8204-2101-4, $48.95

Curcio has been an important inspiration to many performing pianists on the world scene. Through her coaching and teaching she has influenced and nurtured these artists and made an international reputation for herself even after her own performing days had tragically ended. Ashley has compiled a paean to her. In Chapter 1 he provides a brief, skeletal biography and then uses the rest of the book to present her pedagogical and artistic ideas through a series of short chapters drawn from discussions with her, from master class comments, and from interviews with two of her most famous pupils. Some personal reminiscences by the author and a few photographs round out the work. The information presented is interesting and important to pianists, but not enough is given for a truly complete picture. Curcio's philosophies, while thought provoking, are described in such superficial manner that the reader does not gain an overall understanding of how she works with students, what the regimen of study is like with her. Numerous typographical, spelling, and grammatical errors also detract from the text. Nevertheless, because Curcio is one of the premiere teachers in the world of pianism, this book is recommended for larger libraries that support piano performance and instruction programs at advanced undergraduate and graduate level.—*D. L. Patterson, University of Wisconsin-Eau Claire*

WS-1003　　　　ML290　　　　CIP
Baldauf-Berdes, Jane L. **Women musicians of Venice: musical foundations 1525-1855.** Oxford, 1993. 305p bibl index afp ISBN 0-19-816236-7, $55.00

Far from being the quasi-orphanages described in writings about Vivaldi's violin concertos, the Venetian *ospedali grandi* were for over 350 years musical institutions of wealth and grandeur where patrons supported more than 300 external masters to teach more than 850 women the skills required of virtuosity. The works written for the *cori* or musicians of the *ospedali*, still uncataloged, number more than 4,000. The ecclesiastical independence of Venice from Rome allowed these grand charitable enterprises to permit females to become church musicians, and students ranging from orphans to such famous performers as Faustina Bordoni took advantage of the opportunity to receive the best training from European musicians of several countries. Although Venice itself has long been considered a center for the other arts, knowledge of music has been centered at San Marco. Baldauf-Berdes has opened a whole new and exciting area for research. Her extensive bibliography should provide the incentive for revelations about the history of women in Italian music and for the publication of "new" Venetian music. A major contribution to women's studies and to the history of music.—*J. P. Ambrose, University of Vermont*

WS-1004　　　　ML82　　　　93-18463 CIP
Cecilia reclaimed: feminist perspectives on gender and music, ed. by Susan C. Cook and Judy S. Tsou. Illinois, 1994. 241p index afp ISBN 0-252-02036-7, $34.95; ISBN 0-252-06341-4 pbk, $12.95

This work sets itself a fascinating task, which it accomplishes with distinction and interest. Ten essays—ranging from a discussion of the philosophy of feminist music criticism and musicology (Marcia J. Citron), through the psychology of rearing a child prodigy (Adrienne Fried Block on Amy Beach) and how the politics of representation influenced musical activities throughout history, to a tale of

gender and power in American balladry (Susan C. Cook)—revisit some familiar musical paths with new maps. Cook and Tsou promise in their introduction to "add untold dimensions to our previous understanding of music history and musical activity" and they do. They present the reader with "an attempt to right the inequities of male-female relations by rewriting aspects of our musical past ... ask[ing] new questions ... examin[ing] neglected source materials...." This collection traverses the tale of women in music from the English Renaissance, 17th-century France, 18th-century Italy, 19th-century American magazine (popular) music, arriving at a discussion of female images in current rap music. The distinguished essayists are joined in the common cause of rethinking and reviewing the history of music, a cause that will be taken all the more seriously because of the excellence of their contributions. This volume is a must for any music history shelf in any library serving undergraduates, graduates, and the general musical public. It will also be a valuable addition to the literature of women's studies, sociology, and ethnomusicology. The excellent bibliographic references attached to each article will serve future scholars as a springboard for research for years to come.—*S. Glickman, formerly, Franklin and Marshall College*

WS-1005　　　　ML3890　　　　92-2468 CIP
Citron, Marcia J. **Gender and the musical canon.** Cambridge, 1993. 307p bibl index ISBN 0-521-39292-6, $64.95; ISBN 0-521-44974-X pbk, $14.95

Citron (Rice Univ.) has written a dense, carefully thought out, and amazingly thorough treatment of the ways in which the concept of a musical canon intersects with considerations of gender. Far from acquiring position on the basis of abstract principles of quality, the so-called canonic repertoire has reached its preeminence by means of a complex process that also involves social values, commercial factors, and critical reception. Until very recently this process worked to the virtual elimination from the canon of music by women, hence to a devaluation of the products of women's creativity. This process also tends to be self-perpetuating, as the music most often performed, recorded, and taught is drawn from the very canon whose values it then reinforces. The book's only weakness is its analysis of the Cécile Chaminade sonata, which seems force-fit onto a model not suited to its unique qualities. Citron's reasoned voice speaks both originally and in images creatively drawn from a carefully documented wealth of interdisciplinary sources. Nor is Citron content merely to analyze the problem; she also suggests ways in which music by women can coexist with a canon that shows no signs of going away. Though not an easy literary pill to swallow, this is an important book that should prove enlightening especially to those who program and teach music. Advanced undergraduate and up.—*K. Pendle, University of Cincinnati*

WS-1006　　　　ML390　　　　92-40558 CIP
Citron, Stephen. **Noel and Cole: the sophisticates.** Oxford, 1993 (c1992). 360p bibl index afp ISBN 0-19-508385-7, $25.00

Citron, an author skilled both in music (*Songwriting*, 1985) and the musical theater (*The Musical from the Inside Out*, CH, Jul'92), calls on both talents for this well-written dual biography. In alternating chapters he recounts the lives of Noel Coward and Cole Porter, noting similarities and differences. Coward was "a total man of the theatre" whereas Porter concentrated solely on the music. Together they mirrored the first half of the 20th century, "chronicling it in their uniquely personal, urbane style." Even though they seem already well represented in the literature (recent works include Clive Fisher's *Noël Coward*, London, 1992, and Charles Schwartz's *Cole Porter: A Biography*, CH, Jan'78), Citron's work is welcome because of his own insights and new information. Most important, he furnishes numerous examples and analyses of selected songs, both lyrics and music. Good photographs enhance the text, and Citron adds a useful dual chronology of both lives, noting too what was happening in the US and British theater and in the world. Index and bibliography, but a poor job of documenting sources throughout the text and some editing slips. Even so this volume merits a place in all performing arts collections and larger academic and public libraries.—*R. D. Johnson, SUNY College at Oneonta*

WS-1007　　　　ML420　　　　92-39331 CIP
Cone, John Frederick. **Adelina Patti: queen of hearts.** Amadeus Press, 1993. (Dist. by Timber) 400p (Opera biography series, 4) bibl disc index ISBN 0-931340-60-8, $39.95

Perhaps she *was* the greatest singer in the world! "For she is an artist by nature, so perfect that perhaps there has never been her equal ... a marvelous voice, a very pure style of singing, a stupendous artist with a charm and a naturalness which no one else has ...," wrote Verdi after hearing her in his *La Traviata* in 1877. Cone's biography, the first in English since Hermann Klein's *The Reign of Patti* (1920), reads like a novel; and the diva (1843-1919) emerges as "stupendous" heroine, with her lovers, marriages, conquests, tours, incredible amounts of money, great acclaim, and diamonds! The author faces the truth that the recordings Patti made in 1905, when she was in her sixties, give little idea of the beauty her voice quite clearly must have created. Important information about the Patti career finds its place in the "Baptismal Record," pages and pages of notes and references, a discography, chronologies of her concert and opera performances, her operatic repertoire, and a useful index. There are about 150 color and black-and-white paintings and priceless photographs covering the star's entire career. Recommended for all interested in Patti and her career, and more important, in the milieu and financial possibilities of 19th-century performance practice. Both general and academic readers at all levels.—*J. Rayburn, Mercy College*

WS-1008 ML410 90-44831 MARC
DiMedio, Annette Maria. **Frances McCollin: her life and music.** Scarecrow, 1990. 168p (Composers of North America, 7) bibl indexes afp ISBN 0-8108-2289-X, $37.50

Pianist and teacher Annette Maria DiMedio has written a very brief, devoted, and careful account of the life and work of a remarkable woman composer. Blind from the age of five, McCollin was taught and encouraged by a musically literate family, developing her talents to the point where she won many awards, some under pen names because of her concern that she might win because of pity rather than her talent. She was a religious woman, and a pacifist; both interests determined many of her choices of texts for her choral music. McCollin received many performances of her music by groups ranging from the Philadelphia Mendelssohn Club to the Philadelphia Orchestra and the Curtis String Quartet. Much of it was published during her lifetime, enabling future generations to "rediscover" it. DiMedio writes that McCollin was "fortunate. . .[that she lived]. . .at a time when women composers were coming into their own." She also quotes Fanny Morris Smith in an *Etude* magazine article of 1901 who states that "the woman composer. . .has come to stay." Unfortunately, the woman composer has had to "reinvent" her history many times in the decades since then. The series in which this book is published, in which four of the eight volumes completed to date are about women, adds to the rediscovery process. DiMedio devotes 131 pages of the volume to a complete catalog of McCollin's music; lists of her awards, memberships and performances; and a recitation of her memorabilia left to the Free Library of Philadelphia. More discussion of her music vis-à-vis the work of other composers of the period would be welcome.—*S. Glickman, Franklin and Marshall College*

WS-1009 ML2100 95-19594 CIP
En travesti: women, gender subversion, opera, ed. by Corinne E. Blackmer and Patricia Juliana Smith. Columbia, 1995. 381p bibl index afp ISBN 0-231-10269-0 pbk, $17.50

This wide-ranging collection of essays by musicologists and literary critics addresses not only literal trouser roles ("*en travesti*") but also "women in opera—whether characters, performers, librettists, or composers—who figuratively 'put on the trousers': women who challenge and transgress the limits that normally define female identity on the lyric stage." Audience is a decisive element; several authors discuss reception history and take an autobiographical position. Beginning with her infatuation with Brigitte Fassbaender, Terry Castle charts an alluring history of Sapphic diva worship in the 19th and 20th centuries. Judith Peraino blends performance history, reception, listening experience, traditional harmonic analysis, and an examination of Purcell scholarship to form a wonderful queer reading of Purcell's *Dido and Aeneas* (1689). Focusing on Monteverdi's *Orfeo* (1607), Wendy Bashant unites music and literature to produce a new understanding of opera's complex display of gender and cross-dressing. Elizabeth Wood's articulate discussion of Ethel Smyth's operas locates her masquerading within the music and its encoded discourse. In a fascinating examination of literary sources, editor Smith demonstrates the evolving construction of Turandot as a lesbian character. This good companion to Wayne Koestenbaum's gay male perspective of opera (*The Queen's Throat*,

CH, Jun.'93), and it builds beyond the work of Catherine Clément (*Opera, or the Undoing of Women*, tr. by Betsy Wing, CH, Jun'89) to produce more nuanced readings. Highly recommended for all collections.—*J. M. Edwards, Macalester College*

WS-1010 ML410 91-8661 CIP
Ford, Charles. **Così: sexual politics in Mozart's operas.** Manchester, 1991. (Dist. by St. Martin's) 262p bibl index ISBN 0-7190-3487-6, $39.95

This is an unsettling book in more ways than one. The opening chapters discuss Enlightenment philosophy in the manner and jargon of a text in philosophy. Readers unaccustomed to this sort of writing may find much of this section nearly incomprehensible, while others may be disturbed that Ford appears not to have read any primary source in its original language. Indeed, he is often satisfied to quote excerpts of excerpts from secondary sources, also in English. After Chapter 4, Ford turns to the more familiar methods of history, but this area also has its problems. Too many of Ford's generalizations about opera before Mozart are uninformed by firsthand knowledge of the subject, gleaned from primary sources. Hence they tend toward overstatement, oversimplification, or plain error. Chapter 5 begins Ford's consideration of the music of Mozart's mature operas, in which he concentrates on *Così fan tutte* but includes much about *Don Giovanni* and *Figaro* as well. Alongside relatively straightforward and often insightful musical analyses, the author provides his own gender-sensitive interpretations of his findings that are sure to be controversial. Though some of his views on what Mozart accomplished are undercut by his lack of accurate historical perspective, and though one may disagree with his conclusions, one cannot doubt the integrity and thoroughness of his commentary.—*K. Pendle, University of Cincinnati*

WS-1011 ML394 CIP
Gaar, Gillian G. **She's a rebel: the history of women in rock & roll.** Seal Press, 1992. 467p bibl indexes ISBN 1-878067-08-7 pbk, $16.95

By placing women at the center of her examination of rock and roll, by asking new questions regarding women's experiences in this male-dominated industry, by giving value to the words women rockers use to articulate their own stories, and by confronting the sexual and racial stereotypes that have made women's lives and contributions invisible, Gaar reframes the history of rock and roll. *She's A Rebel* is not a book that merely fits women outsiders inside the male-defined rock and roll tradition; it is a book that subverts the assumptions of value that have long determined the story of that tradition. Within a basically chronological context, Gaar combines her astute reassessment of rock and roll trends with scholarly details on a myriad of women rockers (not just performers and composers, but managers, producers, etc.) and punctuates all with the words of the women themselves. What emerges is a rich and lively tapestry documenting the full range of women's involvement in rock and roll. Readers will lament the lack of source notes. General and academic readers at all levels.—*L. Whitesitt, Queens College, North Carolina*

WS-1012 ML3557 93-23221 CIP
Giglio, Virginia. **Southern Cheyenne women's songs.** Oklahoma, 1994. 243p bibl index afp ISBN 0-8061-2605-1, $29.95

Giglio's sympathetic and straightforward monograph is in the ethnomusicological mainstream of Native American studies. All her examples are placed in their cultural context relative to Frances Densmore's classic *Cheyenne and Arapaho Music* (1936) and Bruno Nettl's description of the southern Plains musical style (*North American Indian Musical Styles*, 1954). She follows David McAllester's widely accepted song translation paradigm (articulated in his 1949 *Peyote Music*); McAllester also contributed the foreword. The author's research is firmly grounded in cultural specifics derived from an extended and personally committed period of fieldwork. After introductory remarks concerning her relationship with the singers and their communities, her study consists of an overview of Cheyenne culture and history followed by chapters devoted to the principal women's genres: lullabies and children's songs, hand-game songs, war songs, social songs, spiritual songs, and "everyday songs." Two appendixes present comparative material from an Arapaho singer and list musical examples on a cassette tape (unfortunately without mention of its availability); maps, photographs, extensive musical examples and analyses, and a Cheyenne glossary are also included. Recommended for all academic and public libraries.—*M. Forry, University of California, Santa Cruz*

WS-1013   ML2829   92-37138 CIP
Gorrell, Lorraine. **The nineteenth-century German Lied.** Amadeus Press, 1993. (Dist. by Timber) 398p bibl indexes ISBN 0-931340-59-4, $39.95

Gorrell (Winthrop Univ.) has written a book of considerable importance to those who teach the history and literature of song. We have needed a work such as this, one that deals clearly and generously with the literary, cultural, and political environment that contributed to the development of the Lied and to the development of the piano, and also deals more than superficially with individual composers and their works. These accomplishments alone would be enough for Gorrell's book to be considered as a possible resource for undergraduate song literature classes. But Gorrell has done more: without calling particular attention to it and without slighting the commonly acknowledged master composers, she has included an introduction to the major women composers of the century, a well-proportioned look at their compositions, a description of the societally assigned roles they played, and an evaluation of the part they played in the rise of song as an important genre. This is a first in the field. Until now, the work of women Lied composers has been treated only in journal articles, biographies, or biobibliographic books. Indeed, a few of Gorrell's chapters began as periodical articles. This is an important new tool for undergraduate teaching. Appendixes (chronology, performance editions, and program planning), endnotes, bibliography, song indexes listing titles and composers. Both general and academic readers at all levels.—*M. S. Roy, Pennsylvania State University, University Park Campus*

WS-1014   ML82   93-40360 CIP
Gourse, Leslie. **Madame Jazz: contemporary women instrumentalists.** Oxford, 1995. 273p bibl index afp ISBN 0-19-508696-1, $27.50

Gourse describes the serious fight to gain instrumental equality for women in jazz in excruciating detail. She focuses on the contemporary scene—which makes her book a good follow up to the historical work done by Sally Placksin (*American Women in Jazz*, CH, Apr'83) and Linda Dahl (*Stormy Weather*, CH, Sep'84)—contending there have been major advances in the past ten years. Advances notwithstanding, the obstacles facing jazzwomen are monumental. This book will encourage young women considering careers as instrumentalists, but it also provides a realistic idea of the price they may have to pay to survive. Gourse includes numerous interviews and descriptions of women who have experienced a wide range of successes and failures. An appendix lists dozens of jazzwomen but the information is sketchy, inconsistent, and haphazard. Although recordings are mentioned throughout the book, there is no discography. As Gourse makes clear, this is hardly a definitive work; there are a number of areas worthy of further exploration and this reviewer expects to hear more from her. It would be fascinating to read about the equally serious plight of women in classical and popular music. All collections.—*C. M. Weisenberg, University of California, Los Angeles*

WS-1015   NL420   92-22001 CIP
Gourse, Leslie. **Sassy: the life of Sarah Vaughan.** Scribner, 1993. 302p index ISBN 0-684-19317-5, $25.00

In 1984 Gourse published a collection of profiles of jazz singers under the title *Louis' Children* (CH, Jul'84) in acknowledgement of Louis Armstrong's seminal role in the creation of a vocal approach to jazz music. Armstrong went far beyond the mere singing of the blues in a jazz manner to using his voice as imaginatively and creatively as anyone could use an instrument. The art of using the voice in an instrumental fashion reached its height with Sarah Vaughan. Gourse came to the Vaughan biography after successfully completing books on singers Nat Cole (*Unforgettable*, 1991) and Joe Williams (*Every Day*, CH, Oct'85), making her the premier biographer of jazz singers. Vaughan's career was launched when she won an amateur contest at the Apollo Theater while still a teenager. She came out of the big band era to become the most important modern jazz vocalist. When she died in 1990 at 66, Vaughan was recognized in and out of jazz circles as one of the most distinguished singers of the century and the last major jazz vocal inno-

vator. Gourse tells the story of her artistic accomplishments along with the personality traits of a woman who remained shy and insecure, had three failed marriages yet an unquenchable zest for living that shaped her life. Excellent though not definitive discography.—*C. M. Weisenberg, University of California, Los Angeles*

WS-1016   ML410   94-21509 CIP
Jenkins, Walter S. **The remarkable Mrs. Beach, American composer: a biographical account based on her diaries, letters, newspaper clippings, and personal reminiscences,** ed. by John H. Baron. Harmonie Park, 1994. 226p (Detroit monographs in musicology. Studies in music, 13) bibl disc index ISBN 0-89990-069-0, $35.00

Jenkins (Tulane Univ.) met Amy Cheney Beach, the preeminent American woman composer of the early 20th century, in 1935 and became her biographer after her death in 1944. Jenkins's study is enriched by Beach's private papers and published source material, including extensive concert reviews of her major works; it substantiates the established view of Beach as a gifted Boston pianist-composer, a prodigy during the 1880s, and the single woman composer to attain more or less equal status with the other so-called Boston Classicists in the 1890s. Jenkins chronicles her emergence as a national and even international figure in the early 20th century. Beach's music has suffered the benign neglect of the entire New England school throughout most of this century, but recent interest in feminist music has catapulted her back into prominence. Completed largely in the 1960s, this biography does not wrestle with issues that occupy current Beach scholars, e.g., a woman succeeding in a man's profession or restrictions on female education and opportunity; it nevertheless offers valuable information about Beach and how she was viewed by her contemporaries. Appendixes include publications about Beach, editions of her music, and a discography. Recommended for academic libraries, upper-division undergraduate and above, and large public collections.—*W. K. Kearns, University of Colorado at Boulder*

WS-1017   ML420   93-1757 CIP
Kesting, Jürgen. **Maria Callas,** tr. by John Hunt. Northeastern University, 1993. 416p bibl disc index afp ISBN 1-55553-179-2, $29.95

Readers with an interest in the superstar syndrome will welcome this translation of Kesting's biography of Maria Callas, first published in Germany in 1990. (Kesting is also author of the three-volume *Die grosse Sänger*, Düsseldorf, 1986, and a brief monograph on Luciano Pavarotti, 1991, neither available in English.) In this study of Callas he details the steps that led to a triumphant career as well as the events that contributed to career decline. In so doing, he offers critical analysis of live performances and recordings that brought about the unique Callas success, and he interprets the burning controversy her singing generated. He compares her with singers of the past through assessment of her vocal quality and her acting and stage demeanor, and through an examination of her personality and the events of her private life. Detailed descriptions of the chief performances, her approach to the roles she sang, attitudes of other singers toward her, impressions expressed by impresarios and conductors—all are fused into a narrative account that reaches 364 pages. Subjective judgments abound. The author's personal views on what constitutes good performance are evident throughout. John Hunt's translation from the German is serviceable and clear. There are 22 pages of illustrations, including a photographic record of the May 28, 1955, La Scala performance of *La Traviata*. Addition of discography, notes, and index produces a sizable volume. Chiefly of interest to those who enjoy delving into the lives of the famous, to Callas fans, and to lovers of the world of opera.—*R. Miller, Oberlin College*

WS-1018   ML400   92-6653 CIP
Matheopoulos, Helena. **Diva: great sopranos and mezzos discuss their art.** Northeastern University, 1992 (c1991). 333p index ISBN 1-55553-132-6, $29.95

Interviews with sopranos and mezzo-sopranos who have been prominent on international opera house stages serve as the basis from which Matheopoulos (*Divo*, 1986, and *Maestro*, CH, Sep'83) infers the present state of being an opera singer. The particular pitfalls that emerge are the dearth of fine teachers, shortened periods of technical study, the necessity for some of learning parts rapidly, chronic fatigue from travel, and conductors uninterested or untrained in working with singers. On the other hand, many of the singers point to wise training, careful pacing, extraordinary help, rich family lives, and a lot of good luck. Each discusses her most successful roles and the vocal problems inherent in them. Both a loving and a dignified introduction to favorite singers of the author, *Diva* will be of interest to all opera lovers and will encourage the sale of recordings and compact discs. Brief citations, most from popular opera journals, appear in the body of the text. Valuable for undergraduate and public libraries; of interest to graduate students and faculty. Pictures.—*M. S. Roy, Pennsylvania State University, University Park Campus*

WS-1019   ML417   95-10196 CIP
McCarthy, Margaret William. **Amy Fay: America's notable woman of music.** Harmonie Park, 1995. 196p (Detroit monographs in musicology/Studies in music, 17) bibl index ISBN 0-89990-074-7, $35.00

Fay has loomed large in the history of American music, not because she was a great pianist (though she was certainly a capable one), but because her activities represent important trends and stages in the careers of classical music performers in this country. As a young pianist Fay was among the first Americans to seek advanced training in Germany, and her account of her years there, *Music-Study in Germany* (1881), has enjoyed numerous reprintings, most recently in 1979. At a time when female music teachers seldom won the prestige accorded to their male counterparts, Fay turned out at least four noteworthy professionals. She also popularized classical music via her "Piano Conversations," lecture-recitals begun in Chicago in the 1880s, and her founding of music clubs for women in both Chicago and New York. In addition, her work dovetails well with the growing feminist movement of her day. McCarthy, a recognized authority on Fay, here provides a clearly written, meticulously researched account of the woman and the musician. Calling on a wealth of primary sources, McCarthy presents a detailed account of Fay's life, locating her within the historical and cultural context in which she lived, studied, and worked. This fine contribution to the history of music in America can be enjoyed by interested readers at all levels.—*K. Pendle, University of Cincinnati*

WS-1020   ML82   90-11169 CIP
McClary, Susan. **Feminine endings: music, gender, and sexuality.** Minnesota, 1991. 220p index ISBN 0-8166-1898-4, $39.95; ISBN 0-8166-1899-2, $14.95

This collection of feminist essays applies feminist discursive theory to a repertory ranging from Monteverdi to Madonna. McClary correctly takes the position that there has been little critical (as opposed to theoretical) discussion of music and posits a methodology that examines the construction of gender and sexuality in pieces like Tristan and Madonna and Prince's duet "This Is Not a Love Song"; gendered theory such as strong and weak cadences ("feminine endings") and beats, gender, and sex in musical themes; and the "effeminate" nature of music devotees from antiquity to Ives. Her division is tripartite: works in the canon, music by women who "problematize their sexual identity," and popular musicians like Laurie Anderson and Madonna, "who flaunts her own feminine ending." Tchaikovsky, sonata form, madwomen in opera, and Janika Vandervelde's "Jack and the Beanstalk" are all used in McClary's intriguing challenges to the "classic schema of Western masculine subjectivity." No one will read these essays without thinking about and hearing music in new and interesting ways. Exciting reading for adventurous students and staid professionals.—*J. P. Ambrose, University of Vermont*

WS-1021   Orig
Music, gender, and culture, International Council for Traditional Music, ICTM Study Group on Music and Gender; ed. by Marcia Herndon and Susanne Ziegler. Florian Noetzel Verlag, 1990. (Dist. by C.F. Peters, 373 Park Ave. S., New York, NY 10016) 307p (Intercultural music studies, 1) bibl index ISBN 3-7959-0593-1, $65.00

Because the recital is not the usual context for music by women, it is important that ethnomusicologists contribute to the discussion of relationships between music and gender. These contributions are meant to encourage the understanding of gender roles, identify lacunae, and disseminate research. All are based on extensive fieldwork in both developed and underdeveloped countries. Several common themes emerge. For example, there are public and private repertories, pre- and postmarriage music, and gender-specific ceremonial and ritual musics in most cul-

tures. Genres such as lullabies, laments, love songs, and fertility or agricultural rite songs are also gender specific. Gender identification is associated with instruments. Two biographical studies are included—one of Queen Salote, the most famous composer of 20th-century Tonga, and one of blues virtuoso Bessie Smith. Excellent black-and-white photos; extensive musical examples and notes. The bibliography should lead advanced students to more obscure studies. Only *Women and Music in Cross-Cultural Perspective*, ed. by Ellen Koskoff (CH, Apr'88), covers the same subject area. Both volumes are essential to the serious study of women in music, undergraduate level and up.—*J. P. Ambrose, University of Vermont*

WS-1022   ML3838   92-16317 CIP
Musicology and difference: gender and sexuality in music scholarship, ed. by Ruth A. Solie. California, 1993. 355p index afp ISBN 0-520-07927-2, $35.00

This important contribution to the field of music contains 15 original essays by prominent musicologists and ethnomusicologists, elegantly edited and with an introduction by Solie (Smith College). The book expands, with often brilliant insights, on issues presented in Susan McClary's *Feminine Endings* (CH, Jun'91). The essays encourage musical scholars to move beyond a formalistic or absolutist approach to music and to consider how works may reflect individual or cultural concerns with gender and sexual orientation. (There is very little on racial difference.) Much of the attention is on the works of the common practice period, but there are also essays on Britten, Ives, Ethel Smyth, and Francesca Caccini, on chant, and on popular and non-Western traditions. There is a philosophical bent to many of the essays; some warn against "essentialism" in criticism, for example, whereas others warn that charges of "essentialism" can be used to silence divergent views. The book shows the influence of multiple disciplines and should be of interest to scholars both within and outside the field of music. Several essays would be tough going for lower-level undergraduates.—*R. Lorraine, University of Tennessee at Chattanooga*

WS-1023   ML420   93-6387 CIP
Newman, Katharine D. **Never without a song: the years and songs of Jennie Devlin, 1865-1952.** Illinois, 1995. 291p bibl index afp ISBN 0-252-02081-2, $39.95; ISBN 0-252-06371-6 pbk, $16.95

Newman (formerly West Chester Univ., PA, and founder of MELUS, Society for the Study of the Multi-Ethnic Literature of the United States) has preserved a bit of American popular culture in this work on Devlin, orphan, wife, mother, singer, and inadvertent collector of a rich body of folk songs. The author met "Grandma Deb" (as Devlin was known) in 1936 and slowly unearthed her story: an extraordinarily hard and lonely youth passed from family to family, a capacity for hard work seldom encountered even then, a marriage troubled by her husband's drinking, and the surprising joys of her later years. Through all of this, Devlin maintained a love of singing and of songs, which she learned aurally because she could neither read nor write. Newman tells Grandma Deb's tale with an affection and respect that this reviewer has not encountered even in books about international opera divas. What gives this book its scholarly value is that Newman preserved the words and had the tunes notated by a musician. Eighty-five songs, most of them with their music, are included. Each song is documented by Devlin's own words and Newman's careful research into the history of the texts. In 1938, Newman also arranged for folklorist Alan Lomax to interview Devlin in her home and record her singing for the Library of Congress. This book will interest Americanists in music, literature, popular culture, and women's studies and the folk-song-loving general public. All collections.—*M. S. Roy, Pennsylvania State University, University Park Campus*

WS-1024   ML420   95-16155 CIP
Nicholson, Stuart. **Billie Holiday.** Northeastern University, 1995. 311p disc index ISBN 1-55553-248-9, $29.95

Any biography of Billie Holiday will be problematic. Nicholson's study is first-rate, more clearly organized, and less tendentious (if somewhat less informative) than Donald Clarke's *Wishing on the Moon* (1994). Nicholson lays out the tangled lines of Holiday's parentage and her bleak early life in two concise chapters; thereafter he follows her story in short periods (one to five years), including in each chapter descriptions of her touring, stage and club performances, and recording sessions as well as her nonperforming life. Nicholson is concerned with the relationship of Holiday the woman to Holiday the singer (or, as he calls her, the "song stylist"). He sees her career in part as the construction of an artistic persona (the loser in love and singer of sad songs) and in part as the conflation of this persona with her extramusical "victimhood" through racism, treatment at the hands of her male lovers and managers, and drugs. He concludes that Holiday's image "has rendered her a victim at the expense of her music, the one thing that made her unique." This well-researched book includes a 30-page annotated discography by Phil Schaap; an odd "tempo analysis" by Malcolm Nicholson that classifies 1933-43 recordings as "slow," "medium," or "fast" according to metronome marking but ignores everything else that affects the sense of tempo (including Holiday's phrasing and rhythm, which made even her fast numbers sound slow and relaxed); and an equally undigested list of titles and dates by Malcolm Nicholson entitled an "Analysis of the Live Recordings by Billie Holiday 1948-59." General and undergraduate collections.—*J. McCalla, Bowdoin College*

WS-1025   ML3160   94-1697 CIP
Patterson, Beverly Bush. **The sound of the dove: singing in Appalachian Primitive Baptist churches.** Illinois, 1995. 238p bibl index afp audiocassette ISBN 0-252-02123-1, $37.50

Music in Primitive Baptist churches consists solely of congregational singing of unaccompanied vocal music; the singing styles are based largely on oral tradition, but also on shape-note notation and modern hymnbooks. Patterson's detailed ethnomusicalogical study traces the history of the denomination, its strict reliance on the New Testament, and its emphasis on male dominance in things spiritual. Though women in the Primitive Baptist world are subservient, their informal role in the church is extremely important and influential. Patterson includes a fascinating chapter, "Woman as Singer and Symbol," on this topic. Though secondary literature was significant in the author's research, more fascinating and important is the audio record—oral comments gathered from members of these churches, coupled with recording of singing and commentary by Primitive Baptists. The accompanying audio cassette fleshes out the written notes and transcriptions. The bibliographic essay, excellent bibliography, and a valuable "note on the recording" provide a rounded and detailed view of music in the church. Highly recommended for anyone interested in the interdisciplinary investigation that ethnomusicology, practiced well, as in this instance, can bring to the study of a culture. All academic and public collections.—*C. W. Henderson, Saint Mary's College (IN)*

WS-1026   British CIP
Piaf, Edith. **My life,** tr. and ed. by Margaret Crosland. P. Owen, 1991 (c1990). (Dist. by Dufour) 120p ISBN 0-7206-0797-3, $30.00

Shortly before her death in 1963, Edith Piaf dictated her recollections, quasi-confessions, to journalist Jean Noli, who published them under the title *Ma vie* (Paris, 1964). Now they have been translated, by Margaret Crosland, author of a recent biography of the chanteuse (*Piaf,* 1985). The litany of love affairs, addictions, losses, and sufferings, while predictably painful and even pitiful, remains simultaneously stirring and heroic. The little sparrow shows herself as both selfish and selfless, abused and abusive, vulnerable yet indomitable. Her greatest love and loss would seem to have been the champion boxer Marcel Cerdan, who taught her kindness, and whose death in a plane crash in 1949 left her ever more dependent upon drink, drugs, and spiritualism. (The narrative, even if not accurate or wholly true, has the veracity of being Piaf's sense of herself, and, if not coherent or sequential, has a good fiction's design, circling back for a last, lingering look at the girl Edith and her first teenage lover, P'tit Louis, the first of many whom she left, and their baby daughter Marcelle, first of many to die.) One cannot really regret the absence of anything about Piaf's art and artistry, for, as she says, "My songs are myself, my flesh, my blood, my head, my heart, my soul," and thankfully we have her songs. A poignant glimpse at a troubled genius; a book for general readers and those who care about the price paid by entertainers for our entertainment.—*J. Ellis, Mount Holyoke College*

WS-1027   ML82   93-28495 CIP
Rediscovering the Muses: women's musical traditions, ed. by Kimberly Marshall. Northeastern University, 1993. 304p index afp ISBN 1-55553-173-3, $35.00

The title of this excellent collection references the active role of women

involved as musical creators rather than as muses. The 11 essays are unified by a focus on activities for which we have little notated music, e.g., composition for personal use, performance in oral traditions, and sponsorship. The cross-cultural content reminds readers of the importance of culture-specific interpretation but demonstrates that gender is a major determinant as artists choose between "public renown and ... private satisfaction." Carol Meyers clarifies a common misconception about female drummers in biblical Israel and uses this information to formulate ideas on the overall status of women in society. Nancy Sultan presents an insightful analysis of women's laments in Greek poetry and tragedy. Kimberly Marshall challenges the traditional assumption that "medieval depictions of music show real men and allegorical women." Both Paula Higgins and Suzanne G. Cusick consider larger, conceptual issues important to scholarship about women. This extensively documented and illustrated book gives musicians access to a body of scholarship that goes beyond the borders of the discipline. Highly recommended for all academic and public libraries.—*J. M. Edwards, Macalester College*

WS-1028   ML420   92-17103 CIP
Scott, Michael. **Maria Meneghini Callas.** Northeastern University, 1992 (c1991). 312p bibl index afp ISBN 1-55553-146-6, $29.95

Scott is well equipped to write on the career of the ultimate diva, Maria Callas. Not only does he have at his fingertips exact information on what Callas sang when and where, but he has listened to all recordings, read all reviews, articles, and books on his subject, and attended many of her performances. Thus he is in a position not only to offer facts and figures, but to evaluate what he has seen and heard. Though he is biased in the singer's favor, Scott's critiques are neither rose-colored nor unrealistic. He is at his best when evaluating the artistic and musical dimensions of Callas's work, though he is obsessed by high notes and is not well qualified to deal with the technical side of singing. He is also a clumsy, often inept writer, a fault for which editors on both sides of the Atlantic (the book was published first in England) ought to be heartily ashamed. Also, one may well become annoyed by his harping on Callas's weight, as well as by his assertions that when she decided to "become" what she clearly was already, a "woman" (i.e., to lose weight and dress stylishly), her voice had to suffer. Given Scott's meticulous record of her demanding career, it would have been surprising had her voice not shown some ill effects. In short, another Callas book, more detailed and fact-filled than most, but undeserving of unqualified endorsement.—*K. Pendle, University of Cincinnati*

WS-1029   ML82   91-8413 CIP
Women and music: a history, ed. by Karin Pendle. Indiana, 1991. 358p bibl disc index afp ISBN 0-253-34321-6, $27.50

Like other inclusive edited collections, this volume suffers from unevenness. Its first half does less well what Jane Bowers and Judith Tick accomplished in the collection they edited, *Women Making Music* (CH, Jul'86) where the scholarship was, partly because of its newness, more interesting and coverage more detailed—the Western art tradition only, 1150-1950. The second half is spotty in its ethnomusicological coverage—Europe and the British Empire, and a general "non-Western" chapter. Particularly useful in the American section is a chapter on North America since 1920 by J. Michele Edwards and Leslie Lassetter: it is comprehensive and so little else exists outside of monographs. The "Blues and Jazz" chapter considers only African American women and relegates the important area of ragtime to a footnote. The one chapter on feminist aesthetics is too general to be of much use. Readers should familiarize themselves with Susan McClary's *Feminine Endings* (CH, Jun'91) for this perspective. The bibliographies are adequate. The general list of recordings is limited to the set prepared to accompany *Historical Anthology of Music by Women,* ed. by James R. Briscoe (1987). Both public and academic libraries at all levels.—*J. P. Ambrose, University of Vermont*

◆ Theater

WS-1030   PN1590   93-16280 CIP
Acting out: feminist performances, ed. by Lynda Hart and Peggy Phelan. Michigan, 1993. 406p afp ISBN 0-472-09479-3, $49.50

In several ways, this anthology is a double volume. Each coeditor provides an introduction and contributes an essay. The 19 articles (six of them reprinted from periodicals) fall generally in two categories: documented accounts of solo female performers or performance groups and theoretical essays on the feminist politics of performance. Those in the latter category will be dense to those not initiated into the subtleties of performance theory, but they offer an important spectrum of alternative views. The reprinting of landmark essays by Jill Dolan and Elin Diamond (both have updated and revised their remarks) adds continuity, for Lynda Hart and Hilary Harris confront some of the earlier premises of feminist and lesbian/feminist performance theory. If the theoretical language is abstract and semantically refined, clarity dominates the performance accounts. Individual essays delineate the history and style of such groups as Monstrous Regiment and Siren Theatre Company in Britain and Split Britches and Spiderwoman Theater in the US. The confrontational tactics of Karen Finley and the transformative theater pieces of Robbie McCauley, Anna Deavere Smith, and Holly Hunter confirm diversity in the agendas of feminist performance styles. Perhaps lesbian theater and theory dominates, but analyses of Madonna's self-promotion, the staging of Zora Neale Hurston's life and works, and the antiabortion protests of Operation Rescue expand the scope of the collection. Advanced undergraduate and up.—*J. E. Gates, Jacksonville State University*

WS-1031   PN1590   94-12202 CIP
Aston, Elaine. **An introduction to feminism and theatre.** Routledge, 1995. 166p bibl index ISBN 0-415-08769-4 pbk, $14.95

Since the publication of Sue-Ellen Case's *Feminism and Theatre* (CH, Dec'88), there has been much important new work in feminist critical theory and theatrical practice. Aston's study, intended as a guide to theater students and practitioners, provides a new general overview, not without some omissions and flaws. Aston does an admirable job of relating critical theory to theatrical practice in chapters entitled "Staging Feminism(s)," "Black Women," and "Performing Gender: A Materialist Practice," and in the case studies in part 2. The 12-page bibliography is impressive, although Aston omits the pioneering *Women in American Theatre*, edited by Helen Krich Chinoy and Linda Walsh Jenkins (rev. ed., CH, Apr'88)—one of several instances of the author's Anglo-centrism. Aston's bias against realism and bourgeois feminism seems misplaced in an introductory study and often results in straw women to knock down. Her insistence that the medieval playwright Hrotsvit has been excluded from "the canon" betrays the narrowness of her focus; Hrotsvit's work appears in *Medieval and Tudor Drama*, edited by John Gassner (1963, 1987), a major anthology continuously used—in the US—since its original publication. A major disappointment is Aston's attenuated discussion of feminist critical theory, which consists chiefly of paraphrase and quotations. Designed primarily for British academic programs, the book cannot be recommended strongly for US libraries. However, it may serve as a useful adjunct to upper-division undergraduate collections in feminist theater.— *J. W. Lafler, Institute for Historical Study*

WS-1032   PR698   92-40746 CIP
Backscheider, Paula R. **Spectacular politics: theatrical power and mass culture in early modern England.** Johns Hopkins, 1993. 335p bibl index afp ISBN 0-8018-4568-8, $39.95

The jacket design, with its arresting but little-known engraving of actress Sarah Siddons, perfectly represents this study, which offers fresh, often challenging insights into familiar—and not-so-familiar—material from the Restoration and 18th century. Examining theatrical endeavors in relation to complex cultural processes, Backscheider (Auburn Univ.) draws on an impressive array of primary sources, both pictorial and written, and secondary materials, from traditional literary studies to political and cultural theory. In the first section, the author discusses new and stock pieces in the theatrical repertory of the early 1660s, along with the street pageants staged during the early reign of Charles II, in relation to the process of monarchic legitimation, popular resistance, and the molding of public opinion. The section that begins with plays by women includes a compelling

discussion of the non-dramatic works of Aphra Behn. In the final section, the author finds telling differences between gothic novels and gothic drama and offers new insights into the impact of Sarah Siddons on late 18th-century audiences. A few quibbles: The theoretical apparatus sometimes seems intrusive; the discussion of theatrical practice in the third section is thin and contains some errors. Highly recommended for upper-division undergraduates and above.— *J. W. Lafler, Institute for Historical Study*

WS-1033   PN2887   92-1720 CIP
Berliner, Louise. **Texas Guinan: queen of the nightclubs.** Texas, 1993. 221p bibl index afp ISBN 0-292-78111-3, $24.95

Few personalities so dominated the nightclub era of the 1920s as did larger-than-life Texas Guinan (1884-1933), club hostess, stage actress, and silent film performer. She nonetheless remains something of a peripheral figure in American culture, although her catch phrase "Hello, Suckers!" is well known. Acquainted with dozens of the more fascinating figures of the time (Rudolph Valentino, Walter Winchell, Mae West, Aimee Semple McPherson, etc.), Guinan led a life that left all too few tracks. This frustrating elusiveness, complicated by Guinan's proclivity to invent facts and events in her life, dominates much of this modest biography by Louise Berliner, grandaughter of the lawyer who defended Guinan at her notorious public nuisance trial in 1929. Still, the author does an admirable job in clearly capturing the essence of Guinan's character, the world in which she operated (primarily New York, but also Chicago and Los Angeles), and the after-hours life and atmosphere of the nightclub and speakeasy. Wonderful illustrations. Of special interest to popular culture collections. General; undergraduate; graduate; faculty.—*D. B. Wilmeth, Brown University*

WS-1034   PR739   92-29695 CIP
British and Irish women dramatists since 1958: a critical handbook, ed. by Trevor R. Griffiths and Margaret Llewellyn-Jones. Open University, 1993. (Dist. by Taylor & Francis) 193p bibl indexes ISBN 0-335-09603-4, $90.00; ISBN 0-335-09602-6 pbk, $32.50

A wonderfully coherent collection of nine essays addressing and illuminating a grossly neglected area of theater history, dramatic literature, and women's studies. Eight contributors with impressive credits address problems that women dramatists have faced during the last three decades in both fringe and mainstream theater in Britain and Ireland. The first half of the book surveys the achievements and challenges facing British and Irish women in theater writing and production. The second half devotes separate chapters to more specific issues related to black, Afro-Caribbean, and Asian playwrights, to lesbian theater, and to dramatists in Ireland, Wales, and Scotland. Spotlighted are Caryl Churchill, Sarah Daniels, Timberlake Wertenbaker, Ann Jellicoe, Pam Gems, Shelagh Delaney, Mary O'Malley, Margaretta D'Arcy, Charabanc, Michelene Wandor, Lisella Kayla, Liz Lochhead, Enid Bagnold, and Agatha Christie, among others. Contributors align playwrights with one of three approaches to form and ideology in women's theater writing: feminine/reflectionist (largely naturalistic), feminist/revolutionary (gender issue-based), or female/ritualistic (using a more physical, visual, poetic performance language—a theatrical Cixous-like "Ecriture Feminine"). This is an indispensable reference book with an impressive bibliography which may inspire further research. Advanced undergraduate; graduate; faculty.—*E. Kearney, formerly, Pomona College*

WS-1035   PS338   91-23952 CIP
Brown, Janet. **Taking center stage: feminism in contemporary U.S. drama.** Scarecrow, 1991. 171p bibl index afp ISBN 0-8108-2448-5, $22.50

Brown's new book is based, in part, on her *Feminist Drama: Definition and Critical Analysis* (CH, May'80) and is impressive in readability and clarity, and in a thoroughness that belies its small size. Brown has chosen a tidy Aristotelian structure for this work: it has, quite literally, a beginning, a middle, and an end. The introduction lays the foundation for feminist theater, tracing its late appearance to the humanitarian need to give voice to forgotten women. The broad center of the text is a rich discussion of 11 plays by both male and female playwrights (Norman, Shange, Rabe, and Wagner, among others) which have been commercially successful. Here the plot summaries, which can be too expansive, do not act as mere fillers. Rather, they serve as introduction to the plays for a theatrical neophyte, and as guides to their subtleties for a more experienced reader/theatergoer. Brown includes reviews from sources like *The New*

York Times, as well as comments from feminist critics with whom she appears well acquainted. The "Summary and Conclusion" reinforces the themes of the drama in question and stresses the role of emergent feminist theater as "observant of society." Among her closing notes Brown anticipates that the next step for commercially successful pieces she has spotlighted will be film. This slim text is itself worthy of taking center stage.—*J. A. Dompkowski, Canisius College*

WS-1036   PN2638   92-25987 CIP
Brownstein, Rachel M. **Tragic muse: Rachel of the Comédie-Française.** Knopf, 1993. 318p index ISBN 0-394-57451-6, $30.00

An analysis of the perception of the 19th-century French actress Rachel in her time and in "afterlives" as an inspiration to various writers. In contrast with earlier biographers, Brownstein (*Becoming a Heroine*, CH, Jan'83) is "interested, above all, in [examining] how Rachel and her life were embedded in legends." Moving from the romantic legend regarding Rachel's unrecorded birth as the child of Jewish itinerant peddlers, through her early success and her career at the Comédie-Française, her love affairs and family life, and her early death from consumption, the book shows a woman praised by many as the queen of tragedy, but criticized by others as a greedy, vulgar, ugly woman. In her analysis of the creation of Rachel the star (by herself and others), Brownstein reveals the opportunities, pressures, jealousies, and difficulties that contributed to the controversy regarding the actress during her lifetime and afterwards. In her depiction of the complexities of stardom, the author relates Rachel to the entire phenomenon of stardom, in the 19th century and later, and to other stars such as Sarah Bernhardt, Eleanora Duse, and Marilyn Monroe. In presenting the life of Rachel, the writer explores the question of the ultimate reality of the life of a star for herself and her audience. The relationship between the life of the theater and political and social changes informs the story of the actress. Excellent illustrations include paintings, sculptures, etchings, and caricatures. Both academic and general readers.—*Y. Shafer, University of Colorado at Boulder*

WS-1037   PN3307   94-935 CIP
Broyles-González, Yolanda. **El Teatro Campesino: theater in the Chicano movement.** Texas, 1994. 286p bibl index afp ISBN 0-292-72082-3, $37.50; ISBN 0-292-70801-7 pbk, $17.95

This text emphasizes the role of oral tradition as a forerunner of the Chicana/o theater movement. Through an examination of cultural identity and cultural survival, Broyles-González (Chicano studies, Univ. of California, Santa Barbara) places the secular Mexican performance tradition along with spiritual traditions in a long continuum of oral cultural practice. The chapter on the roles of women in El Teatro Campesino has been published elsewhere; the most in-depth segment of this study deals with an attempt to analyze the formulation of an alternative and native Chicana/o performance theory and practice of this leading American theater company. The function of social practices and educational processes in counterculture and resistance to the dominant society provide insight into indigenous performance in the context of Chicana/o culture. This welcome addition in critical theory about the Chicana/o theater movement is recommended for those researchers interested in theater practice and performance, women's studies, and cultural studies. The author includes several photographs and a helpful bibliography.—*E. C. Ramirez, University of Oregon*

WS-1038   PN2270   95-12132 MARC
Canning, Charlotte. **Feminist theaters in the U.S.A: staging women's experience.** Routledge, 1996. 271p bibl index ISBN 0-415-09804-1, $55.00; ISBN 0-415-09805-X pbk, $16.95

Another valuable addition to Routledge's growing list of publications in theater and performance, this volume offers a challenging new history of grassroots feminist theater in the US and effectively places feminist theater within the broader context of theater as a historical movement. The work is informed by interviews, which Canning (Univ. of Texas at Austin) effectively uses as a means for presenting a "complex picture of women's personal articulations of their artistic, political, and social positions." Between 1969 and 1989, the US witnessed an explosion of feminist theatrical activity, and the collective impact on theater that the author chronicles was profound. Canning's topics include feminism and radical politics, collectivity and collaboration, "representing community" through analyzing plays about mothers and daughters, and "representing the patri-

archy" through plays about violence against women. Valuable additions include an extensive bibliography and appendixes that list interviews, interview questions, and feminist theaters and producing organizations. Recommended for upper-division undergraduates and researchers interested in feminist and cultural studies, theater history, and performance.—*E. C. Ramirez, University of Oregon*

WS-1039   PN1590   93-17910 CIP
Cima, Gay Gibson. **Performing women: female characters, male playwrights, and the modern stage.** Cornell, 1993. 233p index afp ISBN 0-8014-2874-2, $28.95

Each substantial chapter of this book proposes a theory for understanding the performance style of the playwrights who, over a century, have revolutionized the modern stage: Ibsen, Strindberg, Brecht, Pinter, Shepard, Beckett. Cima (English, Georgetown Univ.) rejects the term "actress" as too diminutive, but her insistence on the term "female actor" seems cumbersome. By reexamining a playwright's impact on the culture through the lenses of specific female roles and performers, the author explores the dimensions of patriarchy and its subversions. In some cases, Cima uses historical documents to prove the multilayered significance of an original production; in others she takes hints from performers who give her the potential for a feminist re-vision of the text, or she offers clarification by refutation. Each playwright is matched to a specific term that demarcates his style: for Beckett, the No theater; for Pinter, the cinematic stage; for Shepard, the improvisational theater movement; for Ibsen, the critical actor who must have a command of what Cima terms the "autistic gesture." Hardly reductive, these equations add up to a clarification of the playwrights' differences and to Cima's encouragement to feminist directors and performers to explore subtext and reinvigorate modern performance style. Upper-level undergraduates and above.—*J. E. Gates, Jacksonville State University*

WS-1040   PS627   95-7465 CIP
Contemporary plays by women of color: an anthology, ed. by Kathy A. Perkins and Roberta Uno. Routledge, 1996. 323p ISBN 0-415-11377-6, $59.95; ISBN 0-415-11378-4 pbk, $18.95

This anthology of 16 full-length and excerpts of two plays resists the silencing specter of cultural "invisibility" by increasing awareness of and access to this substantial and rapidly growing body of literature. Notable writers and performers—including Glenda Dickerson and Breena Clarke, Pearl Cleage, Bina Sharif, Anna Deveare Smith, Cherrie Moraga, and the storytellers of Spiderwoman Theater—engage personal/political issues ranging from urban myths, racism and heterosexism, ancestral roots and revisionist histories, economic poverty and cultural richness to evoke "the poignancy of life" through unique yet resonant dramatic experiences of double consciousness. Perkins (Univ. of Illinois) and Uno (Univ. of Massachusetts) set the tone with their call-and-response introduction, juxtaposing personal, familial, and cultural memories and autobiographies against conventional American dramatic histories. Privileging the textures of orality and immediacy of performance, each playwright combats stereotypes by portraying multifaceted, multicultural "women who are human beings." Particularly insightful are the richly personalized "artistic statements" that, along with brief biographies and production histories, precede each selection. Photographs of contributors and an extensive bibliography of published plays by American women of color complete this aesthetically satisfying and politically provocative volume. All collections.—*S. Bryant, Alfred University*

WS-1041   PN2291   93-44133 CIP
Curry, Jane Kathleen. **Nineteenth-century American theatre managers.** Greenwood, 1994. 157p (Contributions in women's studies, 143) bibl index ISBN 0-313-29141-1, $49.95

This survey of over 50 known women theater managers, most of whom have been overlooked by recent scholars, provides a brief glimpse into their managerial activities. Curry includes women working in California during the gold rush, in New York City, in Philadelphia, and in some US cities outside traditional theatrical centers. The greatest attention is given to Laura Keene and Mrs. John Drew, two women who exemplify the highest achievement in theater management. The author includes information about the legal limitations and social restrictions these women faced, chronicling their ambitions, obstacles, and successes throughout the century. The title is misleading because it implies that all American women will be included: in fact, only "white women" are discussed. The author does not clarify why she deals exclusively with white women and only with those who have worked in the professional English-language theater, thus raising the question about whether nonwhites also made contributions in this area. The bibliography is valuable. Recommended for advanced undergraduates, graduates, and anyone interested in women in theater history and in nontraditional roles.—*E. C. Ramirez, University of Oregon*

WS-1042   PN2594   90-47664 CIP
Davis, Tracy C. **Actresses as working women: their social identity in Victorian culture.** Routledge, 1991. 200p bibl index ISBN 0-415-05652-7, $49.95; ISBN 0-415-06353-1 pbk, $16.95

Davis's important study, grounded in Marxist and feminist theory and the "New History" methodology of Lawrence Stone, discounts many of the findings of the only other recent books on the subject—Michael Baker's *The Rise of the Victorian Actor* (CH, Jan'79) and Michael Sanderson's *From Irving to Olivier: A Social History of the Acting Profession in England 1880-1983* (CH, Jun'85)—for being too narrowly limited to successful West End performers and casually assembled data. Davis (Harvard) includes suburban and provincial theater and music hall performers, and explodes many a myth about actresses with substantial evidence, ranging from census reports to court records. The chapters cover actual working conditions and wages, the equivocal social position of females in the profession ("Victorian actress" is almost oxymoronic), and the implicit and explicit erotic and pornographic implications of costume, gesture, and the playhouse environment. The 14 plates relate mostly to this last, semiotically treated, topic. Crucial reading for the serious theater historian, this book will also interest those concerned more generally with feminist and Victorian subjects.—*J. Ellis, formerly, Mount Holyoke College*

WS-1043   PN1590   93-40780 CIP
Dudden, Faye E. **Women in the American theatre: actresses & audiences, 1790-1870.** Yale, 1994. 260p bibl index afp ISBN 0-300-05636-2, $27.50

Well-known 19th-century female actresses Fanny Kemble and Charlotte Cushman are the centerpiece of this study. Dudden (history, Union College) documents their successes as a backdrop against which she portrays a theater environment unfavorable to a multitude of other talented actresses. Thomas Hamblin's cultivation of mass audiences at his Bowery Theatre in New York depended on his exploitation of women's talent—playwrights and performers who were either his mistresses or whose contracts provided only living expenses. English-born Laura Keene, managing her own companies, wavered between her goals of making the theater more respectable and cashing in on the demand for spectacle. Commercial interests tended to sensationalize the physical appearance of increasingly bare-legged and cross-dressed women. That Kemble refashioned her girlhood romantic image after enduring a bitter divorce trial and that Cushman defied many standards of a female star's image seem exceptions to the ways in which the American stage objectified women. Dudden's impressive historical documentation reinforces her uses of feminist performance theory. She provides new and personal ways to expose the questionable star status of women performers in these decades. The book provides ample scholarly annotations; high quality reproductions allow Dudden to comment on the way in which popularity was promoted through engravings, photographs, and illustrative souvenirs. Upper-division undergraduate and above.—*J. E. Gates, Jacksonville State University*

WS-1044   PN1590   92-11968 CIP
Gender in performance: the presentation of difference in the performing arts, ed. by Laurence Senelick. Tufts/University Press of New England, 1992. 348p index afp ISBN 0-87451-545-9, $49.50; ISBN 0-87451-604-8 pbk, $19.95

Senelick has assembled a collection of essays by notable contemporary writers who examine, from a variety of viewpoints, the question of gender on the stage. However, as he notes in his introduction, "The focus here is not so much on drama, the literary artifact, as on live performance, from Islamic passion plays to Wild West shows." The writers include theater historians, anthropologists, directors, and actors. The essays are international in scope, including studies of the Japanese Takarazuka Revue, the 17th-century emancipated women in the

Comedie Italienne, the German dance pioneer Mary Wigman, and Balinese performance. There is also a wide range in periods, with considerable analysis of past cross-dressing, as in the ancient Greek theater, as well as several analyses of modern elements such as drag performances at the turn of the century, and the work of the Omaha Magic Theatre. The book will be useful in theater, dance, and women's studies courses as well as in courses directly addressing gender and society. It definitely supports Senelick's introductory remark that, "Performance once again allows for the trying on and trying out of gender variations not always at one's disposal in narrower walks of life."—*Y. Shafer, University of Colorado at Boulder*

WS-1045   PR2822   92-14074 CIP
Gilbert, Miriam. **Love's labour's lost.** Manchester, 1993. (Dist. by St. Martin's) 137p bibl index ISBN 0-7190-2749-7, $59.95

Like the 11 previously released studies in Manchester University Press's useful series "Shakespeare in Performance," this compact volume examines how critical issues of interpreting a Shakespearean script have been dealt with in a representative range of significant productions. Gilbert (Univ. of Iowa) launches her study with a discussion of performance values that an Elizabethan audience might have most appreciated—e.g., pyrotechnics of language and delight in topical allusions. She follows this with a comparative analysis of the diverse qualities of the script that were "rediscovered" by modern scholars, directors, actors, and audiences (notably in terms of gender politics). Using detailed accounts of one 19th-century staging, four contrasting theater productions since WW II, and the 1984 BBC video version, Gilbert engagingly assesses the play's complex interpretive possibilities including the impact of casting, treatment of design, and the playing of key moments. The author's commentary interperses references to varied scholarly views and to noteworthy features of other stage productions. The lucid text sustains a focused enthusiasm. Upper-level undergraduates; graduate students; researchers, faculty, and practitioners.—*P. D. Nelsen, Marlboro College*

WS-1046   PN2287.B69   90-39331 CIP
Grossman, Barbara W. **Funny woman: the life and times of Fanny Brice.** Indiana, 1991. 287p bibl index afp ISBN 0-253-32653-2, $35.00

Grossman's work is superior in virtually every respect to the 1953 biography of the brilliant clown Fanny Brice (1891-1951) by Norman Katkov, *The Fabulous Fanny*, despite the candor and objectivity of that effort. Grossman's new scholarly biographical study offers not only a detailed chronology of Brice's four-decade career in the context of the times but perceptively analyzes her material and methods, providing vivid reconstructions of some of her more successful routines. Especially effective are discussions of her appearances in nine Ziegfeld Follies and, though she was not fundamentally a Jewish comic, her use of Yiddish dialect in much of her stage work. Grossman (theater, Tufts Univ.) builds effectively to the conclusion: "She could be irreverent and outrageous, but her name meant laughter, hilarious antics, and great fun." Brice, never successful in films, is remembered today principally for her radio career as Baby Snooks (1937-1951) and by the largely romanticized characterization of Brice by Barbra Streisand in *Funny Girl* and *Funny Lady*. Grossman's portrait and the facts of Brice's life emerge as far more complex (and fascinating) than the Streisand image and vehicles. Illustrated and thoroughly documented. Recommended for both public and academic libraries.—*D. B Wilmeth, Brown University*

WS-1047   90-81816 Orig
Henneke, Ben Graf. **Laura Keene: a biography.** Council Oak Books, 1990. 317p bibl index ISBN 0-933031-31-9, $19.95

Given the importance of Laura Keene not only as one of the first actress-managers in the US, but also as a theatrical innovator, it is surprising that she has been the object of relatively little scholarly study. This biography, the first to be published since John Creahan's *Life of Laura Keene* (1897), has been extensively researched. Henneke adds significantly to the information available in the biographical sketches in C.D. Johnson's *American Actress: Perspective on the Nineteenth Century* (CH, Jun'85) and *Notable Women in the American Theatre*, ed. by A.M. Robinson, et al. (CH, May'90), and he corrects numerous errors. How unfortunate, then, that such important work has been presented in a way that is off-putting to serious scholars. The gossipy style is a constant irritant, as are the manufacture of entire scenes and the endless speculation about what "Laura must have felt." The endnotes are awkward to use, and for far too much of the narrative no sources are given. But the inclusion of references to extensive unpublished material makes the bibliography a valuable tool for future research, and the book can therefore be recommended for theater collections in academic as well as public libraries.—*J. W. Lafler, Institute for Historical Study*

WS-1048   PN2592   91-27698 CIP
Howe, Elizabeth. **The first English actresses: women and drama, 1660-1700.** Cambridge, 1992. 226p bibl index ISBN 0-521-38444-3, $59.95; ISBN 0-521-42210-8 pbk, $17.95

There is much to be grateful for in this first full-length study of Restoration actresses since John Harold Wilson's *All the King's Ladies* (1958), not least the attention paid to the influence of actresses on the repertory. The brilliant and versatile Elizabeth Barry is given her due, especially her roles in comedy, which until now have not received adequate attention. Major figures (Gwyn, Mountfort, Bracegirdle) are discussed, but Howe also brings to light the contributions of many lesser-known but significant performers. The appendix listing the roles of 14 actresses, chronologically and by type, is a valuable tool for researchers. A feminist, Howe has chosen to focus upon issues of sexuality and gender; her bibliography includes recent works in this field. It is unfortunate that a more careful job was not done. There are some trivial errors; others are surprising and distressing in a work that appears to have originated as a dissertation. The assertion that playwright Katherine Philips "shunned exposure in the commercial theatre" is simply untrue; Nathan Field, not John Ford, is the coauthor of *The Fatal Dowry*; the date of 1698 for John Verbruggen's petition repeats the error of Allardyce Nicoll, long since corrected by Judith Milhous; the "obscure actress Mrs. Novice" is a misreading of "Norice" (a variant of "Norris"), a character actress whose career is far from obscure; the statement that pathetic heroines were superseded in the 1720s and 1730s by the heroes of bourgeois tragedies is one of several vast, unsupported, annoying generalizations. These and other flaws notwithstanding, the book will be a useful addition to theater collections in academic libraries.—*J. W. Lafler, Institute for Historical Study*

WS-1049   PN2638   92-32954 CIP
Kiernander, Adrian. **Ariane Mnouchkine and the Théâtre du Soleil.** Cambridge, 1993. 172p bibl index ISBN 0-521-36139-7, $54.95

Kiernander (Univ. of Queensland) writes with style and clarity from a perspective of personal experience with the Théâtre du Soleil and its director, Ariane Mnouchkine. The author presents an engrossing picture of Mnouchkine's approach to theater (enhanced by a 1988 interview, which follows the text) and of the history of Théâtre du Soleil's formation, its world-famous productions, and the critical response to its work. Kiernander worked with the company during the 1985 production of *Norodom Sihanouk* and focuses on that production to exemplify the unusual, often contradictory, elements in the company's rehearsals and performances. She also describes the productions of such important works as *The Kitchen, A Midsummer Night's Dream, L'Age d'or,* and *The House of Atreus.* The discussions present vivid descriptions of the use of the space in the the Cartoucherie, the visual effect of the settings and costumes, and memorable moments of exciting theatricality within the plays. Excellent photographs complement the descriptions. The chronology of productions indicates the range of countries and types of theaters in which the company has successfully performed. This is the first full-length study of an important director who has made significant contributions to contemporary theater practice. All levels.—*Y. Shafer, University of Colorado at Boulder*

WS-1050   PN1861   92-36504 CIP
Kintz, Linda. **The subject's tragedy: political poetics, feminist theory, and drama.** Michigan, 1992. 329p bibl index ISBN 0-472-10385-7, $37.50

Kintz's work is far-ranging reexamination of the nature of performance theory. Kintz first analyzes the masculine strategies of two of Sophocles' tragedies, *Oedipus Rex* and *The Women of Trachis,* showing how they endorse patriarchal values. In a transitional chapter, "Relearning Language," Kintz redefines Julia Kristeva's feminist contributions to Freudian criticism and moves further into the politics of subjectification by drawing upon the theories of Henry Louis Gates Jr., Sue-Ellen Case, and bell hooks. A chapter each is devoted to a critique of Mar-

sha Norman's controversial *'Night, Mother,* to a broader social and autobiographical reading of Adrienne Kennedy's plays, and to examination of the suppression of Mexican women in Rosario Castellanos's parodic and self-reflective play *The Eternal Feminine.* Throughout the study—broadly theoretical yet accessible and relevant—poststructuralist fascinations with fragmentation (and their feminist and political implications) provoke revisions in the traditional notions of a cohesive family and in myths of the idealized mother and daughter. Although in her introduction Kintz promises a relevant analysis of Virginia Woolf's *Between the Acts,* her afterword merely touches on that aspect of subjective experience in the novel that stresses the oxymoronic quality of a catharsis that can be simultaneously collective and individual.—*J. E. Gates, Jacksonville State University*

WS-1051   PS3505   94-41267 CIP
Lindroth, Colette. **Rachel Crothers: a research and production sourcebook,** by Colette Lindroth and James Lindroth. Greenwood, 1995. 141p (Modern dramatists research and production sourcebooks, 8) bibl indexes afp ISBN 0-313-27815-6, $59.95

Crothers (1878-1958) was, as one modern critic aptly labeled her, the Neil Simon of her day, with a string of Broadway successes from her first hit, *The Three of Us* (1906), to her last play, *Susan and God* (1937). To some extent her very strengths as a playwright—witty dialogue, deft comic plotting, a focus on timely (not necessarily timeless) issues confronting women—may have proved too narrow a range of talent to guarantee survival. The one previous book on Crothers, Lois Gottlieb's *Rachel Crothers* (CH, Feb'80), in "Twayne's United States Authors Series," consists primarily of play-by-play summaries and analyses, amplified with contemporary critical estimates. Colette Lindroth and James Lindroth are even more modest in intent, offering detailed plot summaries of Crothers's 24 full-length plays plus annotated primary and secondary bibliographies. Perhaps now, with such spade work done, some thoughtful, sympathetic, literate study of Crothers will flourish. This stylish, dedicated author-director, who also led war relief during both world wars, deserves a big biography with lots of illustrations. Although useful for serious students of the American theater and of women in the arts, this expensive book is a borderline purchase for most academic libraries.—*J. Ellis, formerly, Mount Holyoke College*

WS-1052   PN2205   91-19225 CIP
Nash, Elizabeth. **The luminous ones: a history of the great actresses.** P. Lang, 1991. 224p bibl index afp ISBN 0-8204-1577-4, $43.95

Nash presents information regarding actresses she regards as "luminous," beginning with Theodora in 523 and concluding with Eleanora Duse. A very brief chapter moves from antiquity to the Italian Renaissance; three chapters survey the actresses in France, England, and America from 1550 to 1876. The final four chapters focus on Rachel, Ristori, Bernhardt, and Duse. The book, which does not pretend to be an in-depth study, is largely based on secondary sources; and much of the material will be familiar to those who have studied theater history or read the existing biographies of many of the actresses included in the study. As an overview of the opportunities on the stage for women and an anecdotal picture of four major actresses, however, it will be useful. There are no photographs or illustrations to enhance the text. The selected bibliography (three and a half pages long) directs the reader to further research on the actresses discussed. Of interest to undergraduates and general readers rather than specialists, this book reflects the enthusiasm the author feels for the actresses throughout history who have thrilled and excited audiences.—*Y. Shafer, University of Colorado at Boulder*

WS-1053   PN2582   91-41480 CIP
The New woman and her sisters: feminism and theatre, 1850-1914, ed. by Vivien Gardner and Susan Rutherford. Michigan, 1992. 238p ISBN 0-472-10265-6, $37.50; ISBN 0-472-08168-3 pbk, $14.95

These dozen papers from a Manchester University conference circle the complex figure of the New Woman of the English 1890s more than define or describe her, extending to Yvette Guilbert in the tradition of the French chanson, to fictional depictions of opera prima donnas, and to an unconvincing argument for Lotta Crabtree as the inspiration for Belasco's *The Girl of the Golden West.* Edwardian drama fares best: in Jill Davis's shrewd reading of Shaw's sexual anxieties in his stereotyped women, Sheila Stowell's appreciative assessment of Cicely Hamilton's undeservedly neglected *Diana of Dobson's*, and Linda Fitzsimmons's examination of Elizabeth Baker's *Chains*. More superficial, but nonetheless richly informative, are papers on cross-dressing by music hall artistes, female daredevil aerialists, and Annie Horniman's management of the Gaiety Theatre, Manchester. Detailed chronological tables and a historical introduction by coeditor Gardner constitute the most generally useful portions of this stimulating collection. A welcome addition to feminist studies in the performing arts.—*J. Ellis, formerly, Mount Holyoke College*

WS-1054   PR6066.A33   Orig
Page, Louise. **Plays one: Tissue, Salonika, Real estate, Golden girls.** Methuen Drama, 1991 (c1990). (Dist. by Heinemann) 324p ISBN 0-413-64500-2 pbk, $14.95

Although Louise Page (b. 1955) is not well known in the US, either as produced playwright or subject for criticism, her dozen or so feminist plays have had successful runs and receptions in the UK. This first collection includes her four best-known works. *Golden Girls* (1985), long and choppy with abrupt, short scenes, is concerned with the members of a women's track team and the effects of competition, testing for drugs, and speculations about ethical behavior, and though well-intentioned seems too diffuse to make a coherent statement. *Real Estate* (1985), by contrast, is perceptive though contrived: a pregnant 38-year-old returns to her parents' home after avoiding all contact for 20 years and gradually takes over her mother's real estate office, leading the mother to leave home as suddenly as the daughter had and leaving unresolved mother-daughter conflicts, a frequent topic for Page. *Tissue* (1982) deals sensitively with breast cancer as well as women's varying reactions, from early adolescence to old age, to their breasts. And in the more experimental *Salonika* (1983), a WW I widow travels with her daughter to the Greek shore where her husband died and where he returns to speak to each of the women about death and their present relationships. The certainty that Page's reputation will rise as she becomes better known in the US makes this relatively inexpensive collection a worthwhile purchase for most libraries.—*J. Schlueter, Lafayette College*

WS-1055   90-62764 Orig
Paris, Yvette. **Queen of burlesque: the autobiography of Yvette Paris.** Prometheus Books, 1990. 188p afp ISBN 0-87975-639-X, $19.95

Paris (in private life Mrs. Barbara Ann Baker March) is a loving wife, a dedicated mother, and an inductee into the Stripper Hall of Fame. Her autobiography is a further entry in the publisher's series of socially stigmatized lives. The writing is totally honest if somewhat pedestrian; often Paris is so familiar with what she is describing that she forgets to be detailed. She was born into a working-class family and her account of growing up and her initiation into sex is matter of fact and quite appalling; however, her intelligence and her strong sense of self gave her the courage to make a good life and a successful career. Her decision to begin her career in burlesque grew out of a very real need for a second income for her family; her story of the creation of her act and her rise to success is classic. She is quite aware of her surroundings, and the section relating her experiences as a go-go dancer are truly horrifying; she also is able to indicate the closeness among performers in burlesque. Paris respects a professional, resents being prejudged, and seems almost untouched by the tawdry qualities of her workplace. As indicated, this is not a literary document; but it is a valuable perspective on a unique life from the point of view of a wholly admirable woman. Useful in libraries supporting women's studies, sociology, psychology, and popular culture.—*R. S. Bravard, Lock Haven University*

WS-1056   GV1157   94-10260 CIP
Riley, Glenda. **The life and legacy of Annie Oakley.** Oklahoma, 1994. 252p (Oklahoma western biographies, 7) bibl index afp ISBN 0-8061-2656-6, $24.95

Riley's study of the legendary Western icon Annie Oakley (1860-1926), actually born in Ohio and infrequently in the West during her lifetime, explores her life as "entertainer, sport shooter, lady, and western woman." This somewhat interpretative assessment focuses more on the latter three "dimensions" of Oakley's career than most biographies, while at the same time providing a solid, generally reliable account of Oakley's associations with "the Show Business," especially Buffalo Bill Cody's Wild West exhibition. Riley has corrected numer-

ous misconceptions regarding Oakley and her times, providing one of the more trustworthy, balanced studies to date (comparable to Shirl Kasper's *Annie Oakley*, 1992). Not found in other biographies is an analysis of distortions of the Oakley legend since her death, and a discussion of how sensibilities in various periods have colored depictions of the famous sharpshooter. There is a useful annotated essay on sources, though, in keeping with the series, there are no source citations in the text. Clearly well researched and stylistically straightforward (though somewhat spiritless), Riley's book is the best basic introduction to Oakley available. All public and academic collections.—*D. B. Wilmeth, Brown University*

WS-1057   PN2287   92-4414 CIP
Schanke, Robert A. **Shattered applause: the lives of Eva Le Gallienne.** Southern Illinois, 1992. 319p index afp ISBN 0-8093-1820-2, $39.95

This is a handsome book, with 40 pages of striking photographs and drawings of Eva Le Gallienne, with lists of her writings in one appendix and of her productions in another. May Sarton's brief foreword contains interesting observations about Le Gallienne's acting. The text itself is a disappointment. This is a biography hobbled by its thesis. The author seems determined to show that Le Gallienne, woman and actress, suffered from being a lesbian, "a man trapped in a woman's body." Lesbianism is evoked pathologically throughout the book. Le Gallienne's triumphs in the theater, though reported, are somehow belittled by Schanke's constant need to remind readers of her suffering and shame at being a lesbian. The psychologizing is so amateur and outmoded as to be embarrassing, and gossip poses as scholarly report. Le Gallienne, who died at age 92 in 1991, was an important actress-manager and director; she deserves a better biography. Until there is one, Schanke's may interest a general readership and intrigue theater scholars as well as psychologists.—*D. E. Abramson, emerita, University of Massachusetts at Amherst*

WS-1058   PR3095   94-34462 CIP
Shapiro, Michael. **Gender in play on the Shakespearean stage: boy heroines and female pages.** Michigan, 1995 (c1994). 282p index afp ISBN 0-472-10567-1, $37.50

Numerous scholarly publications examine issues of gender identity and sexual disguise in the plays of Shakespeare and his contemporaries—Laura Levine's *Men in Woman's Clothing* (1994), *Erotic Politics*, edited by Susan Zimmerman (1992), Lisa Jardine's *Still Harping on Daughters* (CH, Dec'83), to name only a few. Shapiro's engaging study is distinguished by the scope of interrelated topics it draws together and the balance of critical perspectives it brings to bear upon them. Shapiro (Univ. of Illinois) "traces cross-dressing as a dramaturgical motif, a theatrical practice, and a social phenomenon in early modern England." He contextualizes within the English theatrical heritage the custom of casting boy actors, called "play-boys," as female characters, notes the literary tradition of using cross-gender disguise as a plot device, and examines the multifaceted messages—from metatheatrical irony to psychological anxiety—that develop from sexual masquerade. In the chapter "A Brief Social History of Female Cross-Dressing," Shapiro integrates commentary on how dissembled gender identity was practiced beyond the formal arena of playhouse make-believe, and how the image of a female page on stage may have generated erotic resonance with audiences of the time. Useful appendixes and notes complement the core text. Recommended for all college and university collections.—*P. D. Nelsen, Marlboro College*

WS-1059   PT668   94-19407 CIP
Sieg, Katrin. **Exiles, eccentrics, activists: women in contemporary German theater.** Michigan, 1994. 239p bibl index afp ISBN 0-472-10491-8, $37.50

This feminist study deserves the attention of all interested in European theater. Though women have been title figures in nearly as many German plays as men, the work of women as playwrights, directors, and dramaturges has been completely ignored. Sieg (Univ. of California, San Diego) sets out to rectify the deficit in a two-part study of the 20th-century German stage. The first analyzes the work of Marieluise Fleisser, Erika Mann, and Else Lasker-Schüler, three women active in theater in pre-Hitler Germany; the second concentrates on the differing theatrical traditions of Gerlind Reinshagen, Elfriede Jelinek, and Ginka Steinwachs, all from the postwar era. Sieg's study initiates a critical debate about German theater history. Her writing is best in the clear synopses of the playwrights' works, in her fighting misconceptions, and in her detailed biographical sketches. Her theoretical chapters are tougher going as they bog down a bit in tried but dated clichés from German academic Marxism, literary deconstructionism, and militant feminist scholarship. Nevertheless, Sieg's work rightly challenges all, including those who reject said ideologies but approach her study with an open mind. Undergraduate and up.—*G. M. O'Brien, University of Minnesota—Duluth*

WS-1060 PR739 91-42072 MARC
Stowell, Sheila. **A stage of their own: feminist playwrights of the suffrage era.** Michigan, 1992. 170p bibl index ISBN 0-472-10334-2, $34.50

This tidy, interesting book, in combination with *Feminine Focus*, ed. by Enoch Brater (CH, Feb'90), and Janet Brown's *Taking Center Stage* (1991), forms a valuable package both of theatrical history and of the history of women in the arts. At first glance it appears that Stowell's topic, the feminist playwrights of the suffrage era, is too esoteric. Yet the author is quick to explain that she does not offer a study of plays limited to those concerned with the right to vote. Rather, she defines how the suffrage issue became the vehicle by which women writing in Edwardian England voiced their concerns about a system based on patriarchal oppression. Stowell continues with interesting information about the nature of these early performances, revealing the plays to be short, often monologues, duologues, pageants, and one-act comedies designed as part of an extensive afternoon or evening program. Ultimately the author must turn to the debate about whether this drama is propaganda or art. Stowell cautiously suggests that "art and propaganda do not exist as separate and unconnected areas of endeavor," and that "the art/propaganda divide is itself a kind of propaganda for art." In keeping with the historical flavor of the book, she notes how the women's theater of the 1960s, also political and didactic, was unaware of its Edwardian ancestry and thought itself to be the first feminist theater: an ironic note in a highly informative book. Undergraduate; graduate.—*J. A. Dompkowski, Canisius College*

WS-1061 PN2286 92-18349 CIP
Tanner, Jo A. **Dusky maidens: the odyssey of the early black dramatic actress.** Greenwood, 1992. 171p (Contributions in Afro-American and African studies, 156) bibl index afp ISBN 0-313-27717-6, $45.00

An excellent introduction to early African American female performers, their route from minstrel shows and vaudeville to musical comedies and drama. Until Tanner's study they have not received such specific and deserved attention. As singers and dancers these women were prized for their light skins, but as actresses they were often forced to blacken up to play servant/mammy roles. The richest chapters are those about three outstanding singers and dancers—Dora Dean, Sissieretta Jones ("Black Patti"), and Ida Forsyne—and those about early dramatic actresses Inez Clough, Lottie Grady, Anita Bush, Laura Bowman, and Abbie Mitchell. Most of them had careers abroad as well as in the US, e.g., Ida Forsyne, who was too dark for the Harlem clubs of the 1920s, spent ten years in Russia. Bush, Bowman, and Mitchell all organized acting troupes and founded acting schools. Tanner makes good use of a variety of sources. One could wish for more photographs, but the ten included are excellent. The bibliography is adequate. This is a much needed reference source for academic readers, beginning undergraduates and up, and it should appeal to general readers as well.—*D. E. Abramson, emerita, University of Massachusetts at Amherst*

WS-1062 PN1590 94-20057 CIP
Theatre and feminist aesthetics, ed. by Karen Laughlin and Catherine Schuler. Fairleigh Dickinson, 1995. (Dist. by Associated University Presses) 331p index afp ISBN 0-8386-3549-0, $45.00

Though this is a helpfully annotated volume of essays, its attempts to be nonprescriptive forfeit true dialogue about aesthetic theory and feminist theater. Specific studies of plays, playwrights, and theater artists range across cultures (Australia, Quebec, Russia, French Caribbean, England), yet they rarely build interest in a full exploration of the inherent oxymoron of an aesthetic theory of political theater. Most who approach the issue either favor pluralism or suggest alternatives. "Aesthetics of Marginality" defines Joan Littlewood and Buzz Goodbody's directorial innovations; very little inquiry is devoted to a tradition of aesthetics. In Patti Gillespie's informative essay, Aristotle is reduced to a

proscriber of form; Brecht and a feminist extension of Marxist criticism seem the only valid touchstones to mainstream theatrical tradition. Recent feminist performance theory has become spectator focused, but no contributor explores catharsis as political conversion. These case studies of underexamined playwrights may perpetuate the assumption that feminist theorists write only for themselves. The publishers grant reproduction rights of individual essays for a fee. No doubt those most in demand will be the essays on Marsha Norman's and Caryl Churchill's plays and on Hansberry's *A Raisin in the Sun*—because author Sheri Parks connects black feminist aesthetics to the availability of the play's videotape and thus makes accessibility to a wider audience an important feature of her analysis. Upper-division undergraduates and above.—*J. E. Gates, Jacksonville State University*

WS-1063 PN2598 94-28056 CIP
Tomalin, Claire. **Mrs Jordan's profession: the actress and the prince.** Knopf, 1995 (c1994). 414p bibl index ISBN 0-679-41071-6, $27.50

Dorothy Jordan (1761-1816) was arguably the greatest British comic actress/singer of her day. The facts of her life and especially her professional career are succinctly recorded in volume 8 of Philip Highfill, Kalman Burnim, and Edward Langhan's *A Biographical Dictionary of Actors, Actresses, Musicians, Dancers, Managers & Other Stage Personnel in London, 1660-1800* (1973, 1993). But Dora (her preference) was also a witty woman offstage—courageous, generous, and surprisingly unselfish. Her personal life—from triumphs to pathetic failure and personal tragedy—is nowhere better told than in Tomalin's book. Most sensitive and captivating is the author's recounting of Jordan's independent, sure handling of her professional career while living as the mistress of the Duke of Clarence, later King William IV, and giving him ten children (she had already had four children). After she had spent almost 20 years with Prince William, Dora's professional star waned in 1815. She was expelled from her home and almost cut off from her children. She died, in poverty and virtually alone, in France. Tomalin—author of *The Invisible Woman* (1990), a similar study of Dickens and his mistress, the actress Nelly Ternan, and other biographical works—recovers this fascinating and important theatrical figure in a biography that ranks with the best—well researched (including hundreds of letters) and illustrated. Recommended for all levels.—*D. B. Wilmeth, Brown University*

WS-1064 PS628 93-21858 CIP
Unbroken thread: an anthology of plays by Asian American women, ed. by Roberta Uno. Massachusetts, 1993. 328p afp ISBN 0-87023-855-8, $45.00; ISBN 0-87023-856-6 pbk, $18.95

A valuable addition to the repertory of Asian American plays, this outstanding collection of six plays by Genny Lim, Wakakoo Yamauchi, Momoko Iko, Velina Hasu Houston, Jeannie Barroga, and Elizabeth Wong provides some of the most significant work to date from women in this group. The range of experiences includes those of Chinese Americans, Japanese Americans, Amerasians, and Filipino Americans, covering such themes as immigration, isolation, captivity, reconnection, and liberty in a changing world. Uno (Univ. of Massachusetts) arranges the play texts in order of the historical era covered, an arrangement that reveals the silencing of Asians in the US—through laws, social practice, and the media—and the emerging voice of this once-marginalized group. A brief introduction provides an important history of significant Asian American contributions to the American stage, including names of notable actors and playwrights who have emerged from their silenced roles through the recent development of Asian American dramatic literature. Each play is accompanied by a profile of the playwright. An appendix of plays by 69 Asian American women lists almost 200 works, including production histories. Recommended for everyone interested in American, multicultural, and diverse theater history.—*E. C. Ramirez, University of Oregon*

WS-1065 PN2770 92-38338 CIP
Upstaging Big Daddy: directing theater as if gender and race matter, ed. by Ellen Donkin and Susan Clement. Michigan, 1993. 329p afp ISBN 0-472-09503-X, $42.50; ISBN 0-472-06503-3 pbk, $16.95

This collection of essays documents the achievements of feminist directors. Although the book is designed as a handbook for theater practitioners, the suggestions and guideposts, drawn from the personal experience of primarily university directors, may appear too self-celebratory and radically experimental to persuade those working in a popular theater environment. The book is well organized in the way it groups the essays: Esther Beth Sullivan's historical and theoretical overview serves as sourcebook for the several articles each on the different stages of a production, "Interpreting the Text," "Subverting the Text," "Constructing the Text," and "Rehearsing the Text." Admittedly, the experiences documented demonstrate also that feminist directing is difficult to compartmentalize and that a committed feminist director is also a playwright, dramaturge, designer, politicized teacher, and advocate to the public. There is little analysis of how innovative productions have affected mainstream theater nor very much documentation of how feminists have reinterpreted the classics. Rather, the powerfully moving personal accounts speak with a clarity that in itself seems to question one of the book's paradoxes, that feminist productions best confront the dominant ideologies of the patriarchy because their feminisms maintain their status at the margins of culture. Advanced undergraduate; graduate; faculty.— *J. E. Gates, Jacksonville State University*

WS-1066 PR6003.E282 89-5126 MARC
Women in Beckett: performance and critical perspectives, ed. by Linda Ben-Zvi. Illinois, 1990. 260p index afp ISBN 0-252-01658-0, $37.50

Essays in this collection represent gender criticism of Samuel Beckett. The 35 actresses, interviewers, directors, and critics who contribute to the book are limited in their discussion by focus on a selection from Beckett's canon. The playwright's treatment of women is primarily through the male characters (Molloy, Murphy, Krapp) affected by them, and for the most part reproduces negative, even misogynist stereotypes; only Winnie in *Happy Days* and Mouth in *Not I* receive consistent attention. Nevertheless, this volume yields some significant material. Elin Diamond, Shari Benstock, and others display the promise and problematics of feminist criticism. A dozen actresses, many having worked directly with Beckett, comment on performing the role of Winnie (perhaps the epitome of absurdism in the modern theater), the woman who contemplates survival in an uncaring universe from her position of being stuck, first to her waist, then to her neck, in a mound. Ben-Zvi herself has done a creditable task of collecting the material (only a tiny portion previously published, some of it originating at a recent MLA session). Her concluding essay points out the variant viewpoints from which others have analyzed *Not I*: for the influential French feminist Julia Kristeva, the play exists as a literary text by which she can disagree with Lacan; for Peter Gidal it is a stage piece in which femininity has both power and ungendered status. But, because Beckett allowed *Not I* to be filmed, Ben-Zvi argues for a potentially pornographic meaning, the mouth on video a "gigantic apperture," suggestive of the terror of the vaginal opening. With photographs, and a short excerpt from Beckett's unpublished "Dream of Fair to Middling Women."— *J. E. Gates, Jacksonville State University*

◆ Philosophy

WS-1067 B850 93-9573 CIP
American women philosophers, 1650-1930: six exemplary thinkers, ed. by Therese Boos Dykeman. E. Mellen, 1993. 389p bibl index ISBN 0-7734-9266-6, $89.95

Though the lack of female presence has been noted throughout the history of philosophy, the profession still is not making students aware of this dearth. Dykeman recognizes that many woman have performed the task of philosopher but have not been recognized for it or have been seen instead as historians, poets, idealists, or mystics. Dykeman unearths the representative works of six women from the 17th to the 20th century, displaying the power and breadth of their philosophical perspicuity by setting them within the larger context of the contemporary philosophical scene. The goal is to incorporate the women in the philosophical dialogue. Each woman's writings are accompanied by an introduction with criticisms, reviews, and pertinent comments; a chronology; a bibliography of primary and secondary sources; and a defense of the term "philospher" where appropriate. This book follows in the tradition of Nancy J. Holland's *Is Women's*

Philosophy Possible? (CH, Sep'91), Ethel M. Kersey's *Women Philosphers: A Bio-critical Source Book* (CH, Feb'90), Mary Ellen Waithe's three-volume *History of Women Philosophers* (1987-), and such journals as *Resources in Feminist Research* and *Hypatia*. It makes a significant contribution toward raising consciousness and invites students, teachers, and researchers to reflect on the long history of gender prejudice in philosophy. Recommended for all college and university libraries.—*J. M. Boyle, Dowling College*

WS-1068 BJ1533 95-45757 CIP
Babbitt, Susan E. **Impossible dreams: rationality, integrity, and moral imagination.** Westview, 1996. 242p bibl index afp ISBN 0-8133-2639-7, $65.00; ISBN 0-8133-2640-0 pbk, $19.95

Babbitt (Queen's Univ., Ont.) makes a radical feminist contribution to ethics and political theory. Her thesis is that in certain circumstances, especially for members of oppressed groups, people are unable to know their own interests and act autonomously without first undergoing a "transformational experience." Such an experience may be brought about by reading imaginative literature, adopting revolutionary values, and/or taking some unprecedented action. Her rationale is the Marxist idea that members of oppressed groups have almost always internalized false values or an attenuated sense of self, both of which make determination of one's true interests and autonomous action problematic. What makes Babbitt's argument interesting is that she defends a nonrelativistic position on transformational values. Not all are equally good or defensible in her view. The bulk of the book makes this case and, in the course of making it, provides excellent dissections of several influential conceptions of individual integrity, rationality, autonomy, essentialism, the erotic, naturalized epistemology, inductive inference, and much else. Some readers may be put off by the book's radical feminist premise that women in the US today constitute a deeply oppressed group. That would be a mistake. If one only grants that there are any deeply oppressed groups in the world, Babbitt's argument deserves a careful hearing. Undergraduate; graduate; faculty; general.—*R. B. Scott Jr., William Woods College*

WS-1069 BH301.C84 89-46346 MARC
Battersby, Christine. **Gender and genius: towards a feminist aesthetics.** Indiana, 1990. 192p bibl index afp ISBN 0-253-31126-8, $25.00; ISBN 0-253-20578-6, $9.95

An accessible and fascinating account of the history of the concept of genius in Western culture. Battersby's main concern is to show that the exclusion of women from the category of genius in the 19th century was neither a new phenomenon nor an unexpected one. Indeed, the very meaning of the word is linked to the Latin word for a male fertility spirit. Interestingly, although a woman could not be considered a genius, the qualities associated with the romantic genius were all feminine. Accordingly, Battersby concludes that it is not femininity that is devalued in Western culture but femaleness itself. A successful feminist aesthetic must focus on including women, not femininity. There is an adequate bibliography for those beginning to pursue these questions. The book is perfect for an undergraduate audience. More advanced scholars will find this a welcome addition to the growing field of feminist aesthetics.—*J. Genova, The Colorado College*

WS-1070 BJ1395 93-2697 CIP
Bell, Linda A. **Rethinking ethics in the midst of violence: a feminist approach to freedom.** Rowman & Littlefield, 1993. 296p bibl index afp ISBN 0-8476-7844-X, $64.00; ISBN 0-8476-7845-8 pbk, $22.95

Bell's excellent book (with a terrible title) reviews the ethical dilemmas faced by contemporary feminist philosophers. It does more than that, however; it is also a very good review of many of the dilemmas of contemporary ethics. Bell's thesis is that the feminist ethic of caring—first discussed by Carol Gilligan (*In a Different Voice*, CH, Oct'82) and advocated by Nell Noddings (*Caring*, CH, Nov'84) and others—is inadequate in a world of violence and oppression. Feminist ethics, Bell argues, must include a political consciousness that will enable feminists to avoid affirming the dominant political structures and may, at times, require the use of violence to fight violence. Her model for feminists is Sartre (and de Beauvoir), an ethics of authenticity and ambiguity. In developing her thesis Bell exposes the failure of traditional ethical theories, such as utilitarianism and Kantian ethics, to give satisfactory answers to those who are oppressed. Although ostensibly for feminists, her arguments are applicable to ethical debate generally and shed light on such difficult issues as the relationship between ends and means and the conflict between ethical ideals and violence. Bell's conclusion is somewhat disheartening or disappointing, but it is at least honest and should not detract from the depth and scope of her discussion. This book is a must for feminists and almost a must for ethics generally. Both general and academic readers at all levels.—*S. C. Schwarze, Cabrini College*

WS-1071   BD311   92-20270 CIP
Bigwood, Carol. **Earth muse: feminism, nature, and art.** Temple University, 1993. 375p bibl index afp ISBN 0-87722-986-4, $44.95; ISBN 0-87722-987-2 pbk, $16.95

Bigwood categorizes her work as a "cautious, ecofeminist, postmodern art/philosophy." She investigates Western philosophy's concern with the phallocentrism of Western Being, confronting woman's problem at an ontological level, and tracing the male-biased Western metaphysics all the way back to the Greeks, in "Heideggerian/feminist fashion." She stresses Aristotle's difficult reasoning to show that woman, being the receiver of the "form" from man, can only generate from herself a female as an "abnormal way of nature." Nietzsche had the same problem trying to build a metaphysics of woman. The author claims that a philosophy of woman has to be reworked, by renaturalizing the body (postmodernism/deconstruction), drawing from the phenomenology of Merleau-Ponty, to show that body is not purely cultural, yet is historical and certainly not fixed. She aims at showing that the relation of woman's body to the earth is positive: ground of her experience, her subjectivity, her personhood, ecologically replacing domination by caretaking. She envisions a meeting of ecology and economics center in the home; at the international level, a meeting of cultures, races, genders, even humans and nonhumans. The artistic work included represents feminine sexual/reproductive experience.—*M. -R. Barral, Gannon University*

WS-1072   HQ75   94-12527 CIP
Card, Claudia. **Lesbian choices.** Columbia, 1995. 310p bibl index afp ISBN 0-231-08008-5 pbk, $29.95

Card has written a work that is, alternately, extremely academic and highly personal. Relying both on her academic training as a philosopher and her position in the academy (and the community) as an out lesbian, Card tackles topics ranging from the ban on gays and lesbians in the military (focusing on the Clinton Administration's problematic "don't ask, don't tell" policy) to questions of battering, female on female incest, and sadomasochism in the lesbian community. She organizes the work into three parts. Part 1, though interesting, is not particularly controversial. Parts 2 and 3, however, challenge both conventional lesbian notions of their own "community" (a concept subject to challenge in and of itself) and, arguably, exposes members of the "community" to most unwelcome scrutiny. Although she is quick to point out that the alleged perpetrators of female-on-female incest often do not identify themselves as lesbian, Card's discussion creates the possibility of interpreting as "lesbian" (in a most negative sense) a wide variety of parental practices, ranging from spankings to enemas, and raises issues not fully addressed here of the debate over "recovered memory." On a structural level, her frequent references to and obvious reliance upon Sarah Hoagland's *Lesbian Ethics: Toward New Value* (1988) makes her book rough going for anyone unfamiliar with Hoagland's work. Nevertheless, this book should be in any collection supporting women's studies and/or lesbian and gay studies. Upper-division undergraduates and above.—*E. Broidy, University of California, Irvine*

WS-1073   HQ1190   90-55755 MARC
Code, Lorraine. **What can she know?: feminist theory and the construction of knowledge.** Cornell, 1991. 349p bibl index afp ISBN 0-8014-2476-3, $42.50; ISBN 0-8014-9720-5 pbk, $14.95

Feminist critiques of traditional disciplines invariably reach the same conclusion: the supposedly neutral and objective assumptions of mainstream ("malestream") traditions actually reflect the values, experiences, and interests of privileged white men. Carrying this critique to Anglo-American epistemology, Code eloquently demonstrates that instead of an objective standard whereby any knower can be determined to have any kind of knowledge, epistemology offers a subjectivist definition of knowing in which knowers are pre-

sumptively male, knowledge is paradigmatically the knowledge of physical objects, and the power relations that produce or suppress knowledge are putatively irrelevant. Code nonetheless hesitates to offer a "feminist epistemology." Because the received tradition is so inimical to feminist concerns, she contends, "feminist epistemology" is an impossibility. Instead, she proposes a feminist approach to epistemological questions that would be honestly subjective and relativist, acknowledging the knower's position, using knowledge of persons as paradigmatic, and having social and political accountability. Written for philosophers, this work is remarkably lucid and readable, and is accessible to students and faculty in women's studies and philosophy.—*L. Vance, Vermont College*

WS-1074   HX273   90-21458 CIP
Dunayevskaya, Raya. **Rosa Luxemburg, women's liberation, and Marx's philosophy of revolution.** 2nd ed. Illinois, 1991. 240p bibl index afp ISBN 0-252-01838-9, $32.50; ISBN 0-252-06189-6 pbk, $12.95

A reissue of a book that first appeared in 1982. The work has moved to an academic press, the price has increased substantially, and it has been enhanced by Adrienne Rich's foreword and some later commentary and proposed revisions by the author (who died in 1987). The body of the work is three separate essays— on Rosa Luxemburg, on the women's liberation movement, and on Marx himself. Dunayevskaya was articulating a Marxist humanism that searched for a doctrine of liberation in the Marxist tradition. She found that only Marx himself offered one, and that he had been, in Rich's phrase, "diminished, distorted, and betrayed by post-Marx Marxists and the emerging 'Communist' states." In dense, jargon-laden prose, these essays attempt to formulate a Marxist doctrine of revolutionary liberation, one that includes the movements of blacks, women, and the Third World as fundamental factors in the revolutionary process. Of interest primarily to those who share the author's point of view.—*J. Zimmerman, University of Pittsburgh at Greensburg*

WS-1075   HQ1190   90-46615 CIP
Duran, Jane. **Toward a feminist epistemology.** Rowman & Littlefield, 1991. 275p bibl index afp ISBN 0-8476-7635-8, $42.00

Are there ways of knowing that draw on and reflect the situation and experience of women? Answering affirmatively, Duran outlines a feminist epistemology (the gynocentric model) that emphasizes contextualization and communication reflecting the special situatedness of women. In carrying out this project she draws from contemporary analytic philosophy, establishing a connection through naturalized epistemology, which suggests that all epistemic justification depends on context. In addition to commenting on contemporary analytic epistemology, Duran provides helpful discussions of work by other feminist theorists, both American (Harding, Bordo, Hartsock, Keller, and Flax, among others) and Continental (Cixous, Irigaray, Kristeva). She also treats feminist work in nonphilosophical areas, particularly the sociology of knowledge. Duran is sensitive to the philosophical difficulties involved in her project—especially to the problem of using existing philosophical theory while avoiding its androcentric bias. The result is an important advance in feminist philosophy. Upper-division undergraduates and above.—*J. W. Meiland, University of Michigan*

WS-1076   B667   94-24499 CIP
Dzielska, Maria. **Hypatia of Alexandria,** tr. by F. Lyra. Harvard, 1995. 157p (Revealing antiquity, 8) index afp ISBN 0-674-43775-6, $29.95

Dzielska, described on the jacket as "an internationally recognized authority on the cultural life of the Roman empire," provides here an exemplary "retrieval" of the life and achievements of Hypatia of Alexandria (c.335-415). Dzielska traces in detail the modern literary legend of Hypatia—from the Enlightenment authors who claimed her as the last of the great pagan neoplatonists, through Victorian novelist Charles Kingsley, to today's feminists (as in *Hypatia: Journal of the Society for Women in Philosophy*). The author portrays the close circle of her students and provides the context for her public lectures; she concludes with 35 sober pages on the "life and death of Hypatia," interpreting her death as a kind of witch-burning in the transition from pagan Empire to Christian state. Dzielska is meticulous in her pursuit of facts from the widely scattered sources, and she provides a concise 10-page essay on the sources, thorough notes, and index of names. The translation is clear and readable; the book as a whole is a model of feminist scholarship in its sorting out of legend from facts. Given Hypatia's importance for the history of neoplatonic philosophy and for her work in mathematics and astronomy, every strong collection in women's studies needs this book. Upper-division undergraduate through professional.—*H. J. John, Trinity College (DC)*

WS-1077   B395   92-36046 CIP
Engendering origins: critical feminist readings in Plato and Aristotle, ed. by Bat-Ami Bar On. State University of New York, 1994. 247p bibl index afp ISBN 0-7914-1643-7, $44.50

This engaging collection of 11 articles by well-known feminist philosophers is the companion volume to *Modern Engendering* (CH, Jun'94). Elizabeth V. Spelman and Eve Browning Cole analyze class and gender in *Republic* and *Politics*; Judith Genova and Cynthia Hampton examine Plato's dualism; Christine Pierce suggests that Plato's epistemology privileges homoerotic women as well as men; Susan Hawthorne claims Diotima as "thinking through the body"; Cynthia Freeland argues for a sense in which Aristotelianism may be viewed as "gender-free" science. In contrast, Nancy Tuana, Deborah K. W. Modrak, and Christine M. Senack see Aristotle's insistence on male superiority as the root of his failures in logic and observation. As its editor notes, the book lacks a clear focus for its methodological assumptions. More sustained studies—such as Spelman's *Inessential Woman* (CH, Jun'89), Martha Nussbaum's *The Fragility of Goodness* (CH, Apr'87), Prudence Allen's *The Concept of Woman* (CH, Feb'86)—will be more helpful for limited libraries. Good references, notes on contributors, suggested readings, and index. Academic libraries at all levels.—*H. J. John, Trinity College (DC)*

WS-1078   HQ1221   91-21235 CIP
Explorations in feminist ethics: theory and practice, ed. by Eve Browning Cole and Susan Coultrap-McQuin. Indiana, 1992. 203p bibl index afp ISBN 0-253-31384-8, $35.00; ISBN 0-253-20697-9 pbk, $12.95

In an attempt to critique as well as explicate the initial agenda set by psychologist Carol Gilligan (*In a Different Voice*, CH, Oct'82) and philosopher of education Nel Noddings (*Caring: A Feminine Approach to Ethics and Moral Education*, CH, Nov'84), whose views challenge those of Kant, Rawls, and Kohlberg, this anthology presents selected papers from a conference that focused on the emerging area of feminist ethics. Thus it is grounded in a perspective that challenges the imbalance of dominant Western moral theories, especially those rooted in notions of rights and justice. These essays advance a reinterpretation of pivotal categories such as self-knowing, moral agency, and altruism. They analyze and defend an ethics of care, though they raise appropriate cautions about it as well. The authors advocate new directions in ethical theory including greater attention to interdisciplinary inquiry, greater sensitivity to human diversity, and a deeper regard for the context of commitment and intersubjectivity in moral decision-making. One of this work's most valuable contributions to the field of ethics as a whole is the long overdue recognition that historical distortions attributed to the predominantly masculinist tradition, still current in ethical theory, call for the corrective of a feminine perspective (gender-linked rather than sex-linked). Such a perspective could strike a needed balance by establishing values of empathy, nurturance, and contextual thinking as core elements in the project of moral thinking. A must for all students and researchers/faculty engaged in the study of ethics.—*J. M. Boyle, Dowling College*

WS-1079   PN98   90-47263 CIP
Feminism, Bakhtin, and the dialogic, ed. by Dale M. Bauer and Susan Jaret McKinstry. State University of New York, 1992 (c1991). 259p index ISBN 0-7914-0769-1, $49.50; ISBN 0-7914-0770-5 pbk, $16.95

Exploring the interface between the work of the sociolinguist Mikhael Bakhtin and contemporary feminist literary criticism, these essays are uniformly good—illuminating and insightful in what they do say and suggestive in terms of further thinking and application. They are unified thematically by an attempt to apply Bakhtin's theory of the dialogic, as developed in conjunction with his theory of the novel, to a broad range of contemporary issues in language and gender and feminist literary interpretation. The scope of the essays is far-ranging and interesting, from theoretical considerations of narrative, feminist dialogics, and the cultural criticism of Luce Irigaray to discussions of specific works by authors such as Alice Walker, Nadine Gordimer, and Joyce Carol Oates. All use the notion of dialogic to show how gender, class, and race are socially constituted. By drawing attention to the multiple discourses inherent in these definitions, the essays go far in showing how the dialogic can be expanded into an interpretive schema which recovers previously marginalized narratives and voices. The only serious criticism is that the introduction lacks a more detailed presentation of Bahktin's views that would have been useful for those interested in issues of language and gender but not closely acquainted with Bakhtin. The book fills a niche in bringing together feminist criticism and Bakhtin's theory. Recommended for libraries that serve graduate programs in literary theory, feminism and feminist criticism, and linguistics.—*M. Feder-Marcus, SUNY College at Old Westbury*

WS-1080   BD450   91-7653 CIP
Feminist ethics, ed. by Claudia Card. Kansas, 1991. 300p bibl index afp ISBN 0-7006-0482-0, $29.95; ISBN 0-7006-0483-9 pbk, $14.95

These 15 articles (grouped under the headings "Contexts, Histories, Methods," "Character and Moral Agency," and "Women's Voices and Care") offer a wide-angle view of developments in feminist ethics, illustrating as well as arguing the ethical significance of diversity, relationships, and moral communities. The practical interplay of ethical theory with personal relations and political life is spelled out in substantial articles on ethics and human survival (Ruth Ginzberg) and in "The Social Self and the Partiality Debates" (Marilyn Friedman). The ethical importance of feminist self-criticism pervades articles by Maria C. Lugones, Victoria M. Davion, and Elizabeth V. Spelman. Alison M. Jaggar provides an overview, "Projects, Problems, Prospects." The articles are readable, and the book is very well edited, with an extensive bibliography, notes on the contributors, and a thorough index (rare in such anthologies!) which facilitates the tracing of specific themes through the various essays. This updates the state of the questions since *Women and Moral Theory*, ed. by Eve Feder Kittay and Diana T. Meyers (1987). Recommended to entice beginning students into further study, and to clarify the cross-pollination of themes and issues for teachers and graduate students.—*H. J. John, Trinity College (DC)*

WS-1081   B831   95-8841 CIP
Finn, Geraldine. **Why Althusser killed his wife: essays on discourse and violence.** Humanities, 1996. 203p bibl index ISBN 0-391-03907-5, $49.95; ISBN 0-391-03908-3 pbk, $17.50

This volume of 13 short essays promotes the project of slipping between categories, of resisting the attraction of violence—namely the oppressive force of categories and the totalizing tendencies of political reason and science. Finn sees both theoretical rationality and science, in her own totalizing vision, as inherently oppressive—or, indeed, as she stipulates, as "violence." In the volume's title essay, Finn links the theoretical work of the famous Marxist scholar Althusser with his murder of his wife. Althusser's own confessional writing, "L'Avenir dure longtemps," is discounted as "too late," though it makes the same points. The essays—all as useful for advanced students in feminist theory as for students of postmodernism—raise an "uncompromising, critical voice" that attacks both modernism and postmodernism. Finn recommends inhabiting the "space between" representation and reality, a new "ethical" praxis that promotes particularity without rules, codes, principles, or guarantees. Upper-division undergraduate; graduate; faculty; general —*S. S. Merrill, Purdue University—Calumet*

WS-1082   BJ1533   93-25812 CIP
Friedman, Marilyn. **What are friends for?: feminist perspectives on personal relationships and moral theory.** Cornell, 1994 (c1993). 276p bibl index afp ISBN 0-8014-2721-5, $34.50; ISBN 0-8014-8004-3 pbk, $13.95

Friedman's analysis of personal relationships is a major contribution to the growing literature about the role of friendships in moral theory. In Part 1, Friedman argues that impartiality is an impractical ideal for humans to attain. Instead, we can identify and eliminate bias by closely examining the social practice of partiality. Part 2 explores a feminist ethics of care. Departing from Carol Gilligan's research on moral development, Friedman claims that care and justice do not define different moral perspectives. The modified concept of "enlightened care" described in Chapter 6 does not require women (or men) to sacrifice their own needs to be nurtured and cared for. Part 3 details the nature and value of friendships. In practice, friendships allow us to test moral guidelines because our commitments to particular persons reveal a different moral perspective. Clearly written and accompanied by an extensive bibliography, this work will be useful to scholars, and it is accessible to upper-division undergraduates in philosophy or women's studies.—*B. A. Dixon, SUNY College at Plattsburgh*

WS-1083　　　　RA564x　　　　91-72182 Orig
Gatens, Moira. **Feminism and philosophy: perspectives on difference and equality.** Indiana, 1991. 162p index ISBN 0-253-32551-X, $39.95; ISBN 0-253-28190-3 pbk, $14.95

Gatens points out that feminists, in constructing feminist theories, have made use of existing theories such as Marxism and psychoanalysis. However, these theories may embody sexual biases and may therefore lead feminists to conclusions "that are prejudicial to women." Gatens ferrets out these sexual biases, not only in earlier thinkers like Rousseau and John Locke, but also in recent thinkers such as Simone de Beauvoir, Carol McMillan, Mary Daly, and several prominent French feminists. The author's ultimate aim is to find an appropriate feminist stance toward philosophy that treats philosophy neither as neutral nor as obsolescent but as a resource for transformation. This useful book gives a subtle discussion of the complex matters of stance, perspective, and framework. Adding to its value for students is its lucid presentation, brevity, and lack of pretension. Recommended for advanced undergraduates and graduate students in philosophy and in women's studies.—*J. W. Meiland, University of Michigan*

WS-1084　　　　HQ1190　　　　93-17451 CIP
Grant, Judith. **Fundamental feminism: contesting the core concepts of feminist theory.** Routledge, 1993. 226p index ISBN 0-415-90825-6, $52.50; ISBN 0-415-90826-4 pbk, $16.95

Feminist theory has, Grant argues, been examined only in terms of the canons of the history of Western thought. She offers instead an analysis of feminist theory "as it has developed out of feminism itself." Grant takes issue with the work of a wide range of feminist political theorists, especially radical feminists who provided the theoretical bases for second wave feminism. She asserts that the core concepts of feminist theory found in these works—the category of woman, experientialism, and personal politics—are inherently contradictory and confusing. She analyzes theoretical strategies feminists have used to handle the problems with the core concepts and explores their implications in epistemology and in postmodernism. In her final chapter, Grant proposes four hypotheses that she believes will clarify feminist theory and provide a sound basis for feminist practice. The ideas are interesting and challenging. Libraries with collections in women's studies, gender studies, political science, and philosophy, especially those supporting graduate programs, will want to include this book. Upper-division undergraduates and above.—*J. A. Brown, Connecticut State University*

WS-1085　　　　HQ1190　　　　94-24016 CIP
Green, Karen. **The woman of reason: feminism, humanism and political thought.** Continuum, 1995. 211p bibl index ISBN 0-8264-0821-4, $24.95

Green's rather short work is essentially an essay and an argument. The author's expressed aim is to reconnect feminism to the Western humanist tradition. Her task is twofold: on the one hand, she argues against those feminists for whom rationalism is a male construct and male ideal, the function of which is to exclude woman from full participation in civic life. On the other, she also takes issue with rationalism itself, attempting to enrich the concept by including the nurturing, care-giving qualities traditionally (and in much contemporary feminism) associated with women. Green draws particularly on Christine de Pisan, Hobbes, Rousseau, and Mary Wollstonecraft in this endeavor. In addition, she uses evidence from Freud and later psychologists. Her attempt to combine rationalism and essentialism is sure to raise hackles. So will her use of thinkers generally considered misogynist, especially Rousseau and Freud, to promote feminism, and of the authoritarian Christine de Pisan and Hobbes to promote democratic humanism. For the most part, Green avoids jargon and writes in a comprehensible prose. The work will serve as an excellent starting point for debate for relatively mature students.—*J. Zimmerman, University of Pittsburgh*

WS-1086　　　　HQ1190　　　　95-9130 MARC
Griffiths, Morwenna. **Feminisms and the self: the web of identity.** Routledge, 1996 (c1995). 220p bibl index ISBN 0-415-09820-3, $49.95; ISBN 0-415-09821-1 pbk, $16.95

Griffiths argues that experience—if treated critically, with attention to politically situated perspectives—can provide a sound basis for epistemology. Thus, she employs this methodology by weaving autobiographical writings into her theoretical account of the formation of the self. In contrast to the traditional philosophical conception of the subject, she posits the metaphor of a "web" and claims that individuals exist in and through the various communities of which they are members. Arguing that the role of emotion has been neglected in mainstream theories of the self, Griffiths develops a theory of self-identity that focuses on both emotion and reason, specifically in human relationships of love and resistance, acceptance and rejection. In the final section of the book, Griffiths broadens her scope to explore language, communication, agency, and authenticity, which she considers in light of questions about political change. Drawing on diverse aspects of the philosophical tradition, she touches on many philosophical problems in a clear and readable style. Feminists interested in issues of identity and subjectivity will find this book an interesting read. Undergraduates.—*L. Schwartzman, SUNY at Stony Brook*

WS-1087　　　　HQ1190　　　　93-28611 CIP
Grosz, Elizabeth. **Volatile bodies: toward a corporeal feminism.** Indiana, 1994. 250p bibl index afp ISBN 0-253-32686-9, $35.00; ISBN 0-253-20862-9 pbk, $14.95

In this work Grosz (Monash Univ., Australia) reconfigures notions of the body from a feminist perspective. She bases her theorizing on an examination of the failures of the mind/body polarization dominating Western philosophy, including its valorization of the mind over the body and its linking of the feminine to the corporeal and the masculine to knowledge. First building on the writings of Freud and Lacan, Grosz discusses theories of psychical functioning, focusing specifically on the patterns through which these experiences provide meaning for physical existences. That is, she points out the ways subjects' inner lives serve as necessary sources of a unified and cohesive body image as well as an operative and dynamic body. Next she turns to the work of Nietzsche, Foucault, Deleuze, and Lingis to replace the primacy of consciousness with an emphasis on the body as a sociocultural artifact, a historically specific object to be created and marked by institutions and social structures. She then moves beyond these works to theorize sexual difference by way of a discussion of the characteristics of sexed bodies. Grosz argues that a recognition of distinct sexual entities provides space for the existence of difference, whereas a denial of separateness leads to an insistence by masculinist regimes on the existence of sameness. All university-level women's studies collections.—*D. Gimlin, SUNY at Stony Brook*

WS-1088　　　　HQ1206　　　　90-7091 CIP
Hekman, Susan J. **Gender and knowledge: elements of a postmodern feminism.** Northeastern University, 1990. 212p bibl index ISBN 1-55553-087-7, $25.00

Hekman's extremely timely and valuable work takes up, in a systematic way, the relationship between feminism and postmodernism. These two perspectives are usually seen as divergent: feminist philosophy, maintaining an ontological, epistemological, and ethical foundationalism, is rooted in the notion of an essential feminine nature or experience; postmodernism, by criticizing the notion of a privileged position for moral judgment and action, is seen as nihilistic in its tendencies. By focusing on the commonality of the critique both perspectives offer of Enlightenment rationality, Hekman argues that they can complement each other in very important ways. Postmodernism can show that the acceptance of any dichotomy (and Hekman here focuses on the rational versus the irrational, subject versus object, nature versus culture) will lead to a valorization of one at the expense of the other. Feminism, on the other hand, can extend Foucault's notion of discourse theory and offer an understanding of how gender is constituted by language. The book is an excellent resource for feminist theorists. Hekman's discussion includes virtually every major contributor to the philosophical foundations of feminism, and her bibliography is unusually extensive and complete, drawing from a wide range of fields. Highly recommended. Advanced undergraduates and up.—*M. Feder-Marcus, SUNY College at Old Westbury*

WS-1089   BF723   95-5634 MARC
Hekman, Susan J. **Moral voices, moral selves: Carol Gilligan and feminist moral theory.** Pennsylvania State, 1995. 188p bibl index afp ISBN 0-271-01483-0, $40.00; ISBN 0-271-01484-9 pbk, $16.95

Hekman sees in Carol Gilligan's work more than simply an alternative pattern of female moral development. She sees a paradigm shift to a relational, hermeneutical research method in psychology that is explicitly political and that challenges the epistemology behind traditional moral theory. This challenge results in the displacement of the Cartesian, autonomous, modernist subject in favor of a discursive subject constituted by the play of linguistic forces. Morality is not just another language game among many, but instead is constitutive of the discursive subject. Gilligan's model of the subject gives different moral voices equal standing, in contrast to the masculinist construction of morality as the disembodied application of abstract universal principles. This model thereby supports the feminist project. An imaginative, stimulating exploration of alternative ideas of subjectivity. Upper-division undergraduates and above.— *J. W. Meiland, University of Michigan*

WS-1090   HQ1196   90-9006 CIP
Holland, Nancy J. **Is women's philosophy possible?** Rowman & Littlefield, 1990. 194p bibl index afp ISBN 0-8476-7620-X, $33.50

"Women's philosophy" here is work "that arises from, explicitly refers to, and attempts to account for the experience of women." Holland (Hamline University) starts by using deconstructionist critique to show how Locke and Hume define experience so as to render women's philosophy impossible. She then turns to Continental resources for "feminist re-thinking of philosophy": Heidegger's being-with; Merleau-Ponty's phenomenology; the existentialisms of Sartre and Beauvoir; structuralism and semiotics (Barthes, Lacan, Foucault, and Derrida); and the "French Feminists"—Wittig, Kristeva, Cixous, and Irigaray. She ends with recommendations and examples (dealing with abortion and nuclear war) for a "deconstructive/phenomenological/hermeneutic approach to women's philosophy." Rich in allusions, dense in style, and difficult in content, the book brings together in intriguing and helpful ways very different approaches to feminist theory. (For easier starting points, see Alison M. Jaggar, *Feminist Politics and Human Nature*, 1983, and *New French Feminisms*, ed. by Elaine Marks and Isabelle de Courtivron, CH, May'80). Helpful bibliography and index; most useful for faculty and graduate students.—*H. J. John, Trinity College (DC)*

WS-1091   B3317   90-27059 CIP
Irigaray, Luce. **Marine lover of Friedrich Nietzsche,** tr. by Gillian C. Gill. Columbia, 1991. 190p afp ISBN 0-231-07082-9, $35.00

This text returns us to a premetaphysical, prepatriarchal and prelogical world both in its content and format. Irigaray powerfully inscribes the female voice within the masculine usurpation of it as untruth, the multiple, the other, disruption, rupture, threat, and death and also breaks free of this, mocks it, satirizes it from some other place. Her style is literary, poetic, descriptive, and programmatic as she responds to Nietzsche's, and to Greek and Christian portrayal of woman as ruse, deceit, and play. She weaves a web in the first section around and through the movement of the sea in all its tropes. The maternal womb, though unacknowledged, is portrayed as inhabiting all that Nietzsche, and with him the Western tradition, says of "woman as such." The dominant motif in male discourse of the connection between woman and death and the ensuing fear, flight, and attraction are explored by her to show how mysogyny is established. In the section marked "Veiled Lips," Irigaray details the Western male need for matricide and the consequent attempts to veil, repress, and "forget" this violence. Nonetheless, it surfaces as a "horror of nature," of the "wild," and as attempts to conquer, master, and subdue the other. Her third and final section, titled "When the Gods are Born," opens up the displacement of the goddesses and matriarchy as it is marked by the emergence of Zeus, Apollo, and Christ. Irigaray moves from the Greeks to the Christian subjugation of the mother, Mary, and rewrites this "virgin mother" as the eternal source of man. The fall of Mary, the figuration of Mary, is understood as paradigmatic and prophetic for the repression of women in the West. Despite her nonsystematic, nonlinear approach Irigaray puts forth a powerful argument in this text and offers an alternative vision for many of the seeming-archetypal assumptions of Western male patriarchal thought.—*I. E. Harvey, Pennsylvania State University, University Park Campus*

WS-1092   89-83247 Orig
James, Laurie. **Men, women, and Margaret Fuller: the truth that existed between Margaret Fuller and Ralph Waldo Emerson and their circle of transcendental friends.** Golden Heritage, 1990. 508p (The life and work of Margaret Fuller Ossoli (1810-1850), 3) bibl index ISBN 0-944382-02-9, $18.50

An exciting introduction to Fuller, Emerson, and their friends. James starts with the Fuller-Emerson relationship and then moves to the study of other relationships throughout their lives, but the book lacks a critical evaluation of Fuller's philosophy and of her most famous works. The surmises, the treatment of Fuller scholarship, and the vocabulary (e.g., "postpartum blues," "psyched") exclude it from professional academic acceptance under the canons of Carolyn G. Heilbrun and company; but it does fulfill their criterion of "feminine perspective." This is the third volume in a series written by James, the actress/writer of the one-woman dramas "O Excellent Friend!" and "Men, Women, and Margaret Fuller." The first volume, *The Wit and Wisdom of Margaret Fuller Ossoli* (1988), is a 90-page compilaton of snippets from Fuller's writings; the second, *Why Margaret Fuller Ossoli Is Forgotten* (1988), is a 62-page argument that Fuller deserves more, not less, attention than Emerson, claiming that prejudice has brought about the opposite. Good bibliography; good index. Recommended for every undergraduate interested in Margaret Fuller, US woman philosophers, and Transcendentalism.—*K. J. Dykeman, Fairfield University*

WS-1093   HQ1190   93-28965 CIP
Mann, Patricia S. **Micro-politics: agency in a postfeminist era.** Minnesota, 1994. 253p index afp ISBN 0-8166-2048-2, $44.95; ISBN 0-8166-2049-0 pbk, $17.95

Traditional gender roles and relationships have proved inadequate, in contemporary society, but reform and the creation of new roles has been difficult. Mann argues that standard beliefs, such as liberal notions of individual rights and Marxist conceptions of social justice, do not provide a sound basis for reconstruction. She suggests a new theory of persons as agents, centered around particular situations and issues—hence the term "micro-politics." Among specific issues to which this perspective is applied are the familial division of labor, the regulation of pornography, and the reconfiguration of parenting. In each case, Mann goes beyond current analyses, exposing deep complexities and multiple desires and needs to demonstrate that a different form of understanding is required. Another important contribution of this unusually constructive and thoughtful book is its focus on agency as interpersonal rather than atomic, as a fundamentally social rather than psychological phenomenon. Mann posits an individualism that responds to shifting identities by embedding individualism in the social fabric. Upper-division undergraduates and above.—*J. W. Meiland, University of Michigan*

WS-1094   BJ1031   91-44434 CIP
Manning, Rita C. **Speaking from the heart: a feminist perspective on ethics.** Rowman & Littlefield, 1992. 183p bibl index afp ISBN 0-8476-7733-8, $49.00; ISBN 0-8476-7734-6 pbk, $14.95

Manning (San Jose State Univ.) develops an ethics of caring, building on the work of Milton Mayeroff (*On Caring*, 1971), Carol Gilligan (*In a Different Voice*, CH, Oct'82), and Nel Noddings (*Caring*, CH, Nov'84, and *Women and Evil*, CH, Feb'90). She situates feminism in current ethical theory debates; lays out "desiderata for an adequate ethic"; and illustrates student responses to the caring/justice tension by reporting on a survey using the moles and porcupine fable. Then come detailed chapters titled "Just Caring," "Caring for Persons," and "Caring for Animals"; the work concludes with replies to feminist critiques of an ethics of caring. Manning's approach is well informed, fresh, and personal in her handling of the literature and in her use of her own experience of the complexities of caring in a wide range of relationships. This reader found unsettling the few lines on the duty of caring for starving children in Africa in contrast with a detailed and nuanced chapter on caring for animals; but Manning definitely takes issue with Noddings's claim that "universal caring" is impossible. She calls, in her conclusions, for an ethics of caring for each of the professions, and for a politics of caring. This reviewer hopes to see these realized. Undergraduate; researchers; faculty.—*H. J. John, Trinity College (DC)*

WS-1095   B791   92-36047 CIP
Modern engendering: critical feminist readings in modern Western philosophy, ed. by Bat-Ami Bar On. State University of New York, 1994. 280p index afp ISBN 0-7914-1641-0, $49.50

This comprehensive collection of feminist critiques of the Western canon includes essays on Descartes, Locke, Hume, Rousseau, Kant, Hegel, Marx, Nietzsche, and Dewey. Written in a variety of philosophical styles and from a variety of viewpoints, the essays provide a sourcebook of ideas for those beginning to question the so-called gender neutrality of Western philosophy. This reviewer knows of no other two volumes—the companion volume (*Engendering Origins*, CH, Jun'94) focuses on Plato and Aristotle—that bring such variegated and sophisticated critical scrutiny to bear on the thinkers of the Western tradition. Interestingly, the essays reveal a love/hate ambivalence with philosophy's founding figures. Though their sexism is apparent, so is the sexism, in many cases, of the very tools for undoing their narrow vision. Most rewarding, then, is that the details of the essays reveal a complex history and an even more complex response to that history from women philosophers writing today. A must purchase for all undergraduate and graduate libraries.—*J. Genova, Colorado College*

WS-1096   B3318   93-34551 MARC
Nietzsche and the feminine, ed. with introd. by Peter J. Burgard. University Press of Virginia, 1994. 349p bibl index ISBN 0-8139-1494-9, $49.50; ISBN 0-8139-1495-7 pbk, $16.95

Each essay in this fine collection focuses on some aspect of Nietzsche's comments regarding women. The arguments and positions of these essays are as diverse as Nietzsche's comments, a diversity that did not go unnoticed by the book's editor. Burgard (Harvard) has assembled an impressive group of writers and thinkers in this book. Of particular mention is Luce Irigaray's article, "Ecce Mulier? Fragments." Many of the other articles in this book, Burgard admits, *could* be seen as simply an introduction to her article, and indeed this is the case. Irigaray is one of the leading feminist thinkers in France today, and most of the other essays in this book either directly confront her work (e.g., David Farrell Krell), or they discuss other French theorists such as Derrida and Julia Kristeva, both of whom have much in common with Irigaray. In all cases, these articles seek to remove the stereotypical view of Nietzsche (a view handed down from Walter Kaufmann) as an undiluted misogynist and demonstrate instead that Nietzsche's position is far more problematic, complex, and ambiguous. This book is recommended for those interested in the role of the feminine in Nietzsche's philosophy; however, it does presuppose some prior familiarity with Nietzsche. Upper-division undergraduate; graduate; faculty.—*J. A. Bell, Southeastern Louisiana University*

WS-1097   HQ1190   95-13828 CIP
Nye, Andrea. **Philosophy & feminism: at the border.** Twayne/Prentice Hall International, 1995. 232p bibl index afp ISBN 0-8057-9763-7, $26.95; ISBN 0-8057-9778-5 pbk, $14.95

Nye has produced a synoptic review of feminist challenges and contributions to contemporary logic, ethics, epistemology, philosophy of language, and political theory. She reviews feminist challenges to models of individuality, language, discourse, power, and the notion of objectivity. Feminism contributes new methodologies, powerful critiques, and new visions of philosophical pedagogy. Such challenges do not require abandoning philosophy, as is sometimes suggested. The author argues that sustained, historicized reinterpretation of canonical works and contemporary scholarship can be directed toward normative and future-oriented philosophical discourse to move philosophy out of dogmatic doldrums. Specialists in Nye's topics might find her brevity frustrating. However, her succinctness is a valuable asset in this broad analysis of feminist attempts to make philosophy responsible for and reflective of diverse new constituencies, e.g., ethnic groups, women, gays and lesbians, and Third World peoples. For those interested in philosophy, women's studies, and general political and social theory, upper-division undergraduates and above.—*J. L. Croissant, University of Arizona*

WS-1098   BC57   89-28195 CIP
Nye, Andrea. **Words of power: a feminist reading of the history of logic.** Routledge, 1990. 190p index ISBN 0-415-90199-5, $45.00; ISBN 0-415-90200-2, $14.95

Words of Power is simultaneously provocative and illuminating. Nye approaches

major systems in the history of logic as systems of power, forms of thought embedded in history, which not only reflected the prevailing sociopolitical power arrangements but were definitive in forming a notion of rationality still used to perpetuate patterns of oppression. Beginning with Parmenides' logic as a flight from the uncertainty and ambiguity of the physical and, hence, feminine, world of birth and death, Nye goes on to consider the logics of Plato, Aristotle, the Stoics, the medievals, and Frege. Her discussion throughout aims at uncovering the concrete, existential ground from which these systems spring and to assess them critically by not only attending to what they include but by taking note of what is excluded as well. By doing this, Nye can point to the deeper structures of thought that have been discarded by male flight into the purity and certainty of abstract form. Nye's discussion of the various logics is both nuanced and precise. She offers criticisms of the systems in terms of their own internal categories and problematics as well as from a broader feminist perspective. An extremely important addition to the emerging canon of feminist philosophy. Highly recommended for college or university libraries.—*M. Feder-Marcus, SUNY College at Old Westbury*

WS-1099   Aust. CIP
Porter, Elisabeth J. **Women and moral identity.** Allen & Unwin, 1991. 223p bibl index ISBN 0-04-442332-2 pbk, $22.95

The thesis of Porter's clearly written and carefully argued book is that traditional categories of ethical philosophy inhibit the acceptance of women as full moral subjects. Offering analyses of the conceptions of moral dualism, nature, reason, and individualism that point to the masculinist bias implicit in these conceptions, Porter attempts to articulate a view of moral identity broad enough to encompass the moral experiences of both men and women. Although her treatment of the "gendered" nature of these philosophical categories is meticulous, Porter tends to rework ground already broken. Her criticism of these categories draws from work already done in feminist philosophy as the extensive referencing in the body of the text indicates. Porter does propose a new category, the notion of the rational, passionate self as a vehicle for overcoming gender bias and achieving a higher-order synthesis for moral identity, but again, it is not clear that she offers anything radically new here. Ultimately the great virtue of the book is the accessibility of its argument to the advanced undergraduate and its extensive citations of feminist thinkers and survey of the extant literature. It is not a book that fills a gap; rather, it is for those libraries with already extensive collections in feminist philosophy that need to keep up with current publications.—*M. Feder-Marcus, SUNY College at Old Westbury*

WS-1100   HQ1190   94-18086 CIP
Provoking agents: gender and agency in theory and practice, ed. by Judith Kegan Gardiner. Illinois, 1995. 342p index afp ISBN 0-252-02132-0, $44.95; ISBN 0-252-06418-6 pbk, $18.95

Feminism is about action, about individual and social change, not just about understanding the situation of women. Change requires action and effective agency. Essays in this volume address questions of what constitutes effective agency for feminists. Given postmodern critiques, can individuals act at all? How best should feminists organize to act effectively? Ellen Messer-Davidow argues that social-structural change requires building and acting through institutionalized practices. Sandra Lee Bartky engages postmodernism through interpretations of Foucault on power. Other writers deal with particular contexts of action, both historical and contemporary: AIDS activism, reproductive technologies, pornography, maternal agency. The result is a useful and stimulating collection combining theoretical elaboration and concrete analyses. Upper-division undergraduates and above.—*J. W. Meiland, University of Michigan*

WS-1101   HQ1190   90-46118 CIP
Ring, Jennifer. **Modern political theory and contemporary feminism: a dialectical analysis.** State University of New York, 1991. 229p index ISBN 0-7914-0753-5, $49.50; ISBN 0-7914-0754-3 pbk, $16.95

Are women and men fundamentally different, or are the differences really social constructs? What methods that do not beg the question can be used to find the answers? And what are the political implications, not only of possible answers, but also of the methods themselves? The view that difference is socially constructed—a popular feminist perspective—and that such constructs are inherent in dichotomous patriarchal thinking seems to imply that this way of thinking must be jettisoned. Ring points out that abandonment of dichotomous thinking eliminates the possibility that feminist thinking can make use of an already achieved understanding of the world. What is needed is a way of thinking that, unlike standard empiricism, will provide a value basis for political change and, unlike deconstruction, will accept enough of conventional epistemology to allow use of accumulated knowledge. Ring looks to dialectical thinking for a solution, first giving extended critiques of liberal empiricism (John Stuart Mill) and of other theories of dialectics (Hegel and Marx). Her own view—minimalist dialectics—emphasizes process and conflict and employs a notion of truth as momentary. This is a valuable and risk-taking exploration of basic epistemological questions, offering a new way out of real dilemmas. Graduate level.—*J. W. Meiland, University of Michigan*

WS-1102   HQ1075   94-9881 CIP
Ross, Stephen David. **Plenishment in the earth: an ethic of inclusion.** State University of New York, 1995. 430p bibl index afp ISBN 0-7914-2309-3, $74.50

There are currently three main theoretical models dominating environmental philosophy: deep ecology, social ecology, and ecofeminism. In the tradition of French feminist philosopher Luce Irigaray (*An Ethics of Sexual Difference*, 1993), this book is in the third genre. According to Irigaray, Ross, and other ecofeminists, "the question of our age" is "the question of sexual difference." The focus of the book, therefore, is to establish an ethic that is not based on hierarchy, domination, control, and distinction but one that is, in other words, an ethic of inclusion. The book richly details numerous key Western philosophers, especially Plato, Aristotle, Nietzsche, Foucault, Gilligan, and Heidegger. It is a scholarly, well-documented, highly creative work and, in this reviewer's opinion, a stimulating examination of the issues of power, gender, and diversity. However, those expecting environmental philosophy (as the cover of the text suggests) would prefer more discussion of the earth and the environment and would have greatly appreciated an introductory chapter situating Irigaray and ecofeminism in the larger debate with deep ecology and social ecology. Other philosophers may not care for the Foucauldian/Heideggerian literary style, which often incorporates dense and metaphorical language (e.g., the "alterity irreducible to myself"). Nevertheless, this book is surely an important contribution to philosophy of sexuality and gender. Graduate; faculty.—*R. F. White, College of Mount St. Joseph*

WS-1103   HQ767   95-47648 CIP
Rudy, Kathy. **Beyond pro-life and pro-choice: moral diversity in the abortion debate.** Beacon Press, 1996. 185p index afp ISBN 0-8070-0426-X, $23.00

Rudy's book is a provocative addition to the literature on abortion. It insightfully recounts the very "different" constructions of the issue of abortion by four competing communities of interpretation—the liberal, the Roman Catholic, the evangelical Christian, and the feminist—as well as conflicting views within Catholicism (double effect versus proportionalism) and in feminism (pro-life and reproductive rights). The thesis of this recounting is that the definition and description of abortion is intrinsically connected to its moral evaluation. Rudy also discusses the limitations of the debate as currently constructed, especially the emphasis on the legal notions of the "unified individual" and the "abstract right to abortion." She believes this wrongly frames the issues and leads to an either-or dilemma (pro-life or pro-choice). Instead, Rudy urges that account be taken of the real circumstances of the pregnant woman. In this light, she reviews the method of casuistry and Gillian's ethics of caring and argues that a combined methodology of these two views plus balance between justice and caring will refocus the abortion debate to caring for pregnant women and providing the conditions for real choice; accomplishment of this, however, requires government silence and repeal of the legal right to abortion. Even if one does not find all Rudy's arguments persuasive, this book will stimulate new and worthwhile discussion of the abortion issue. All levels.—*J. A. Kegley, California State University, Bakersfield*

WS-1104   HQ1190   91-142 CIP
Sawicki, Jana. **Disciplining Foucault: feminism, power, and the body.** Routledge, 1991. 130p index ISBN 0-415-90187-1, $42.50; ISBN 0-415-90188-X pbk, $13.95

Poststructuralist thought has often been seen as undermining feminism and other liberation movements by undermining the notions of rationality and truth on which their analyses depend. Sawicki aims to show that one facet of poststructuralist thought, namely Foucault's analysis of power in society, can instead serve to overcome present difficulties in feminism. For example, Foucault sees power as distributed throughout social practices and as an open system rather than as localized in key institutions. Consequently, effective resistance to power must take a different form from that prescribed by traditional revolutionary theories, a form that feminists might employ without creating a new and different oppression in the process. In discussing this and other topics, Sawicki throws light on central Foucauldian concepts and shows how Foucault's perspective is sympathetic to liberation. Her discussion is very sensitive to the complexities involved. This book is valuable both as a contribution to feminist theory and as a clarification of Foucault's approach. Upper-division undergraduates and above.—*J. W. Meiland, University of Michigan*

WS-1105   HQ1190   93-7337 CIP
Scheman, Naomi. **Engenderings: constructions of knowledge, authority, and privilege.** Routledge, 1993. 254p index afp ISBN 0-415-90739-X, $49.95; ISBN 0-415-90740-3 pbk, $15.95

The essays collected here (the earliest written in 1979) touch on a wide range of topics including art, competition, photography, and movies. But their main topic is Western philosophy, to which Scheman applies a feminist critique. An analytical philosopher by training (with a Wittgensteinian bent), her main quarrel with such philosophizing is that it treats the self as generic—a generic mind somehow related to a generic body. In true Wittgensteinian fashion, she finds that metaphysical and epistemological problems (as usually formulated) dissolve when readers understand that the subject is historically conditioned, that minds and bodies are differently constructed in different situations for different purposes. The essays constitute a serious challenge for analytic philosophy by making its notion of a problem itself problematic. Throughout the book, Scheman helps readers understand her journey to her present situated self. Recommended for upper-division undergraduates, graduate students, and faculty.—*J. W. Meiland, University of Michigan*

WS-1106   R724   91-14499 CIP
Sherwin, Susan. **No longer patient: feminist ethics and health care.** Temple University, 1992. 286p bibl index afp ISBN 0-87722-889-2, $39.95

Sherwin (philosophy and women's studies, Dalhousie University) presents a broad and solid account of the relevance of feminist ethics to health care ethics (or bioethics). Part 1 introduces "feminine" and "feminist" ethics and examines in depth the question of feminism's relation to moral relativism and to the meaning of human communities. Part 2 looks at "traditional problems": abortion, reproductive technologies, paternalism, and research; and Part 3 expands the "Bioethics Landscape" with treatments of "ascriptions of illness," "medical constructions of sexuality," and "gender, race, and class in the delivery of health care." Throughout, the emphasis is on the dominance relations that permeate the system of health care and constitute a major obstacle to fair and appropriate provision of care. There is a useful index. Although feminist treatments of special issues in bioethics abound (cf. Sherwin's 16 pages of references), this is the first comprehensive handling of feminist bioethics this reviewer has seen. (And I've been watching!) It should be in every library.—*H. J. John, Trinity College (DC)*

WS-1107   K642   91-46293 CIP
Steinbock, Bonnie. **Life before birth: the moral and legal status of embryos and fetuses.** Oxford, 1992. 256p index afp ISBN 0-19-505494-6, $29.95

Steinbock's book is valuable for all interested in the ethical/legal issues surrounding abortion, prenatal injury and liability, maternal-fetal conflict, and fetal/embryo research. The author provides an excellent historical overview of these issues, but she also addresses the issues from the stance of a particular theory of moral status, namely, interest theory. This gives coherence to her discussion as well as allowing testing of the viability of interest theory. Using the "ability to have interests" and "sentience" as the key concepts, Steinbock distinguishes moral status from moral worth, thus seeking to avoid the problems of granting personhood to prenatal beings while recognizing the respect that must be given to humanness and life and especially to late-gestation fetuses. She treats pro-life views fully and sympathetically while carefully distinguishing where her theory differs and disagrees. She argues for women's rights to privacy and bodily integrity while also disagreeing with some feminist positions on reproductive technology. Steinbock discusses many legal issues such as wrongful life/death and legal responsibility for the not-yet-born. She also gives the political/public policy context of the debates over fetal and embryo use. This very fine book does suffer from the lack of a summary chapter and a bibliography. All levels.—*J. A. Kegley, California State University, Bakersfield*

WS-1108 HQ1075 93-23909 CIP
Weiss, Penny A. **Gendered community: Rousseau, sex, and politics.** New York University, 1993. 189p bibl index afp ISBN 0-8147-9263-4, $40.00

Weiss (political science, Purdue) sets out, first, to shed light upon Rousseau's internal consistency and his interpretations of gender, justice, freedom, community, and equality; and second, to advance feminist theory through the study of Rousseau. Her book's main argument is "that Rousseau's defense of sexual differentiation is based on the contribution he perceives it can make to the establishment of community, and not on an appeal to some versions of 'natural' sex differences." Weiss examines Rousseau's program of sex differentiation and his educational plans for Emile and Sophie; rejects the biological determinist interpretation of his antifeminism; and argues instead that Rousseau's sex roles are designed as means to community. In her concluding chapters Weiss argues that Rousseau's sex-role strategy is self-defeating, and she compares the social agenda of feminists and communitarians from Plato to MacIntyre and from Sappho to Daly. Clear, rich, and coherent, the book succeeds splendidly in its intent to be "accessible and useful" to Rousseau scholars, feminists, and all those concerned with "gender equality, freedom and community." Essential for every library where these are live issues! Concisely written and well produced, with helpful notes, bibliography, and index. General and academic readers at all levels.—*H. J. John, Trinity College (DC)*

WS-1109 BJ1275 89-32986 CIP
Welch, Sharon D. **A feminist ethic of risk.** Fortress, 1990. 206p index afp ISBN 0-8006-2339-8, $9.95

Welch attempts to articulate a feminist theology of liberation vital enough to serve as the foundation for community of spirit that cuts across racial and class lines. Her analysis proceeds from two sources of ethical insight: the nuclear freeze movement and the literature of African-American women. American nuclear policy and the consequent peace movement provide Welch with the material for an analysis of the nature of power as it has traditionally functioned in Western ethics and allows her to suggest a new notion of power more genuinely in line with human community. Analogously, Welch's discussion of several major works by African-American women writers deepens her criticism of Western culture's conception of power and allows her to put forth new categories for forging a moral imagination that transcends social privilege. Welch's book is noteworthy for its attempt to bring together a number of critical traditions, including those of Foucault, Habermas, feminist theology, and liberation theology. She offers a cogent argument against the absolutist notion of power contained in traditional theology, and simultaneously presents a well thought out alternative—a notion of community based on the categories of limit, ambiguity, and risk. Welch's book is a very accessible presentation of major currents in contemporary feminist theology and her own vision is both provocative and deeply felt. An important contribution to the literature, recommended for all four-year college and university libraries serving departments of religion and women's studies.—*M. Feder-Marcus, SUNY College at Old Westbury*

WS-1110 HQ1190 90-40947 CIP
Whitford, Margaret. **Luce Irigaray: philosophy in the feminine.** Routledge, 1991. 241p bibl index ISBN 0-415-05968-2, $49.95

In a work quite remarkable in its scope, comprehensiveness, and precision of articulation, Whitford seeks to offer an overview of Irigaray's work to date and to provide a strong, sympathetic, and detailed account of the originality and power of Irigaray's vision. The text is divided between philosophy and psychoanalysis, fol-

lowing Irigaray's own double commitments, and is careful to show what is borrowed and what is rejected from both fields. Although closest to Lacan and Derrida, Irigaray parts company from them concerning her ultimately feminist commitments. Whitford details both the slippage used by Irigaray and fluid conceptuality, including "the female imaginary," as well as the exactitude of her position by showing how her critics have thus far misrepresented and misunderstood the vision at stake. "Philosophy in the feminine," Whitford argues following Irigaray, means to write, think, articulate, and describe experience *as* a woman, as women, not to think "like" a woman. To this end her rereadings of Plato's cavern, Hegel's Antigone, and Derridean deconstruction reveal that philosophy has always claimed the place of woman—man's version of her/it, as an object, a possession, his property and lost object at the same time. "Philosophy in the feminine," although still to be done, must speak as a female subject, from feminine subjectivity.—*I. E. Harvey, Pennsylvania State University, University Park Campus*

WS-1111 HQ1190 91-42974 CIP
Women and reason, ed. by Elizabeth D. Harvey and Kathleen Okruhlik. Michigan, 1992. 294p index ISBN 0-472-10220-6, $39.50

This cross-disciplinary collection of 13 essays includes considerations of "literature, art history, the history of medicine and science, and the theory of social science, political science and history." The essays are analyses of quite specific problems, weighted toward the 17th century. Agenda for the discussion is set by Genevieve Lloyd (*The Man of Reason*, CH, May'85); Carol Gilligan (*In a Different Voice*, CH, Oct'82); Sandra Harding (*The Science Question in Feminism*, CH, Dec'86); Carolyn Merchant (*The Death of Nature*, 1980); and Evelyn Fox Keller (*Reflections on Gender and Science*, CH, Jun'85). It is a wide-ranging and engaging collection, with introduction, notes on contributors, and a useful index—a rarity in such collections. Most helpful for feminist epistemology are essays by Alison Jaggar, Susan Bordo, and Lorraine Code. Recommended for extensive women's studies collections; advanced undergraduate, graduate, and faculty readership.—*H. J. John, Trinity College (DC)*

WS-1112 HQ1190 93-31618 CIP
Zerilli, Linda M.G. **Signifying woman: culture and chaos in Rousseau, Burke, and Mill.** Cornell, 1994. 214p index afp ISBN 0-8014-2958-7, $32.50; ISBN 0-8014-8177-5 pbk, $13.95

Although political theorists did not invent the concept of woman, Zerilli contends that some of them employ this concept symbolically to signify, among other things, class difference and political disorder. A standard feminist approach to political theory is to expose the defective ways in which major theorists represent and treat women. It is instructive to go beyond this approach to understand the deeper symbolic meanings of woman in these theories, i.e., woman as a sign rather than as an image. Zerilli's book illustrates this strategy through close reading of central texts by Rousseau, Burke, and Mill, all of whom, though very different from one another, make use of woman to set forth their political visions. Undergirding this analysis is a rejection of the referential model of language in favor of a post-Saussurean linguistics that emphasizes the instability of the sign and the generation of linguistic meaning through the play of differences. This book is a fascinating course in the reading of classic political texts using contemporary literary and linguistic approaches. Graduate; faculty.—*J. W. Meiland, University of Michigan*

◆ Religion

WS-1113 BQ6150 93-33586 CIP
Bartholomeusz, Tessa J. **Women under the Bōtree: Buddhist nuns in Sri Lanka.** Cambridge, 1994. 284p (Cambridge studies in religious traditions, 5) bibl index ISBN 0-521-46129-4, $59.95

This important book documents a significant episode in modern women's religious history. Using textual, historical, and anthropological methods, Bartholomeusz examines the revival and reinvention of monastic life for women in Sri Lanka in the 19th and 20th centuries as lay nuns, specifically the *upāsikārāmaya*, or lay nunnery. Although there is no officially sanctioned community of nuns in

Sri Lanka today, contemporary lay nuns, called *dasa sil mātā* (numbering about 5,000) follow lives of ordained nuns (the *bhikkhunī*) hoping to have a tradition of full ordination through a Mayana lineage recognized for them. The author focuses on several periods in Sri Lankan history, in which Buddhism has called women to world renunciation: (1) third century BCE, for which accounts in the *Mahāvaṃsa* and *Dīpavaṃsa* are crucial; (2) late 19th century, during which figures like Anagarika Dharmapala and "The Countess" were active in the lay nun movement, for which government and private archives are crucial; and (3) the contemporary period, during which the struggle vis-à-vis the male *saṅgha* and social stereotypes for women have been highlighted, for which the author's field studies in 1988-89 are crucial. Despite extended hardships, female Buddhist renunciants have been able to create semiautonomous communities (for the most part outside monks' control), finding fulfillment in their renunciation and making significant contributions to the resuscitation of Buddhism in Sri Lanka. This book provides a multidisciplinary analysis of the reemergence of Buddhist women renunciants. Extensive appendixes and notes; selected bibliographies. Undergraduate; graduate; faculty.—*E. Findly, Trinity College (CT)*

WS-1114   BV5095   92-15362 CIP
Beer, Frances. **Women and mystical experience in the Middle Ages.** Boydell, 1992. 174p bibl index ISBN 0-85115-302-X, $59.95

Beer has written a fascinating and detailed account of medieval spirituality from a feminine perspective. This includes a thorough analysis of the writings of three prominent women mystics (Hildegard of Bingen, Mechthild of Magdeburg, and Julian of Norwich) and of works written for the spiritual direction of women (*Nun's Rule* and the epistles of Richard Rolle). Additionally, her textual analyses center on such feminine concerns as empowerment, independence, view of body and creation, and attitude towards women. Each emerging theme is expertly placed in a historical and societal context, thus giving her analysis breadth as well as depth. For example, Mechthild's use of sexual imagery is placed in the wider context of bridal mysticism beginning with *Ezekiel* and *Hosea* and ending with the medieval writings of Bernard of Clairvaux and the societal influences of courtly love. The reader receives a thorough understanding of the times in which these ideas were generated along with their historical antecedents, and this is what makes the work different from other writings about medieval women— e.g., *Women Mystics in Medieval Europe*, ed. by E.Z. Brunn and G. Epiney-Burgard (CH, Mar'90). The clarity and liveliness of her writing make her scholarly analysis accessible and highly worthwhile to undergraduates as well as to graduate students interested in medieval and/or women's spirituality.— *A. McDowell, Ithaca College*

WS-1115   BX7800   93-13546 CIP
Bendroth, Margaret Lamberts. **Fundamentalism & gender, 1875 to the present.** Yale, 1994 (c1993). 179p bibl index afp ISBN 0-300-05593-5, $22.50

An important contribution to the study of gender in American Protestantism. The focus here is on fundamentalism. Bendroth does not contest the antifeminist image of fundamentalism, but she qualifies that perception. She notes that although fundamentalist leaders have sought to define the movement in masculine terms, women have always constituted the majority of fundamentalist adherents. This "numerical imbalance," she argues, has "created some potentially awkward contradictions between strict standards of female subordination and relatively permissive customs." As other scholars have documented before her, Bendroth confirms the fact that the sphere of approved feminine activities within fundamentalism became more restricted as the 20th century progressed. Only recently have fundamentalists been forced to reopen a discussion of gender roles. Bendroth unearths a helpful range of new material on the subject, but the argument of the book is weakened somewhat by her loose use of the label "fundamentalist." The historical development of themes could also be made clearer. Nonetheless, this is the most comprehensive study of the topic to date, and it deserves a place in advanced undergraduate and graduate library collections.—*D. Jacobsen, Messiah College*

WS-1116   BF109   90-55174 CIP
Bolen, Jean Shinoda. **Crossing to Avalon: a woman's midlife pilgrimage.** Harper San Francisco, 1994. 303p bibl index afp ISBN 0-06-250112-7, $22.00

Crossing to Avalon is an autobiographical account of a spiritual pilgrimage catalyzed by a physical pilgrimage to "sacred" sites in Europe. Bolen is a Jungian analyst, professor of psychiatry, and author of other books on women's spirituality. She describes her growing understanding of the "soul path" she is following and of the Goddess within. Bolen's prose is gentle, artful, and experiential. Though the book is labeled as a work of psychology, Jungian psychology is only implicitly used as a background for Bolen's musings. The book would have been better labeled a work of religious studies; the author herself connects her book with other works about "the Earth as Gaia, feminist theology, goddess archeology, women's spirituality, planetary consciousness, deep ecology" and other areas of contemporary reflection. Patriarchy, the cause of the suffering and spiritual oppression of women and men, can only be vanquished by the emergence of "goddess consciousness." An engagingly written autobiographical account of a now fairly common understanding of women's religious experiences. Suitable for acquisition by libraries collecting works on contemporary women's religious experience. General; upper-division undergraduate.—*S. L. Jones, Wheaton College*

WS-1117   BV2788   94-39195 CIP
A contest of faiths: missionary women and pluralism in the American Southwest, Yohn, Susan M. Cornell, 1995. 266p bibl index afp ISBN 0-8014-2964-1, $42.50; ISBN 0-8014-8273-9 pbk, $16.95

Although this book contains much worth commendation, its title and subtitle are somewhat misleading. The work does not focus on interactions between women missionaries and persons of differing religious faiths. "Contest of faiths" is, rather, a broadly applied metaphor used to organize the many conflicts that characterized the lives of Presbyterian women missionaries who worked among the Hispano-Catholic population in the Southwest in the late 19th and early 20th centuries. The book begins by tracing the struggle of the Presbyterian women who worked to organize a separate mission organization (Women's Board of Home Missions) in the later 19th century. Other chapters examine the internal conflicts faced by both the missionaries appointed by this board and their Hispano students. Attention is also given to the context of ideas that arose between the missionaries and their colleagues. Ultimately, the author explores the transition from voluntary evangelistic-based missions to government-supported social service and the part women missionaries and their leaders played in preparing the way for this change. Graduate; faculty.—*L. H. Hoyle, Georgetown College*

WS-1118   BX4496   93-23642 CIP
Costin, M. Georgia. **Priceless spirit: a history of the Sisters of the Holy Cross, 1841-1893.** Notre Dame, 1994. 268p bibl index afp ISBN 0-268-03804-X, $24.95

Helpful bibliographic works like Elizabeth Kolmer's *Religious Women in the United States* (1984) attest to the rapid proliferation of literature on American Catholic sisters (religious women/women religious) during the past three decades. Revisionist histories of individual orders and congregations of women in the US represent one important segment of this new literature. Sister M. Georgia Costin's book is a splendid example of what can happen in the new historiography of American women religious when it is informed by recent developments in social history and women's history. Grounded in a close reading of the congregation's chronicles and correspondence found in archival sources, this book takes a close look at the early history of the Sisters of the Holy Cross during the lifetime of their founder, Edward Sorin, and makes this history understandable to specialists in women's history who are not specialists in Catholic history. Undergraduate; graduate; general.—*D. Campbell, Colby College*

WS-1119   BV639.W7   90-35589 CIP
DeBerg, Betty A. **Ungodly women: gender and the first wave of American fundamentalism.** Fortress, 1990. 165p index afp ISBN 0-8006-2439-4, $9.95

A number of worthwhile treatments of American Protestant fundamentalism have been published in the last decade—e.g., G.M. Marsden's *Fundamentalism and American Culture* (1980), D.W. Frank's *Less than Conquerors* (CH, Jul'87), and J.D. Hunter's *American Evangelicalism* (CH, Sep'83). Some of these treatments focused on theological controversies between conservatives and "modernism," while others stressed the cultural and social changes in society to which fundamentalism was a moral reaction. DeBerg (theology, Valparaiso Univ.) points out that both of these approaches have ignored the important part played by changes in gender roles and family-centered issues. Although such changes were part of the processes of industrialization and urbanization of US society, they were defined by fundamentalists as moral changes with theological significance and biblical dimensions. By drawing on publications in the popular fundamentalist press from 1880 to 1930, DeBerg persuasively marshals evidence that fundamentalism appealed to many urban middle-class whites because of its religious defense of the diminishing Victorian gender ideology. Her book is both scholarly and of general interest. The documentation necessarily is profuse; there are 667 footnotes in 153 pages of text, and an annotated bibliography of primary sources. But DeBerg's writing is good and interested nonscholars will find it accessible. It is well organized and the argument is easy to follow.—*R. L. Herrick, Teikyo Westmar University*

WS-1120   BX137   94-18770 CIP
Doorn-Harder, Pieternella van. **Contemporary coptic nuns.** South Carolina, 1995. 253p bibl index ISBN 1-57003-034-0, $49.95

This study of contemporary female monasticism in the Coptic Christian community in Egypt is based on observations by a Protestant woman from the Netherlands with training in Islamic and religious studies. Rarely examined by social scientists, Coptic Christians—a religious minority in Muslim-dominated Egypt—are one of the largest communities of indigenous Christians in the Middle East. Focusing on the religious lives of Coptic nuns within broader ecumenical, spiritual, social, cultural, and historical contexts, Doorn-Harder examines the ways these women relate to the everyday world as well as to a transcendent reality. The author is particularly interested in how the revival of Coptic Christianity in Egypt since the middle of the 20th century affects the two major groups of nuns, contemplative and active. The book contains black-and-white photographs, notes, and a short glossary. It is a welcome addition to religious and women's studies in the Middle East. Upper-division undergraduates and above.—*L. Beck, Washington University*

WS-1121   BL625   93-3928 CIP
Eller, Cynthia. **Living in the lap of the goddess: the feminist spirituality movement in America.** Crossroad, NY, 1993. 276p index ISBN 0-8245-1245-6, $24.95

Drawing from many sources of modern feminist spirituality, including its literature, workshops, retreats, rituals, and personal interviews, Eller has produced a superb empirical and phenomenological rendering of this diverse and complex religious movement. She defines a spiritual feminist as an individual who seriously believes herself to be one and/or adheres to at least three of the five following characteristics: "valuing women's empowerment, practicing ritual and/or magic, revering nature, using the feminine or gender as a primary mode of religious analysis, and espousing the revisionist version of Western history favored by the movement." She analyzes feminist spirituality in terms of its organization and structure, demographics, conversion experiences of its adherents, origin, rituals, magic, understanding of the Goddess, and view of history. Additionally, she explicates the historical and modern movements that influenced it as well as the startling differences between it and feminist politics. This is an essential work for all libraries since no other book parallels this one in its scope, accuracy, vividness, and scholarship.—*A. McDowell, Ithaca College*

WS-1122   BX4667   90-39089 CIP
Finnegan, Mary Jeremy. **The women of Helfta: scholars and mystics.** Georgia, 1991. 171p bibl index afp ISBN 0-8203-1291-6, $30.00

At various times in the history of spirituality, there emerges a flowering of mystical activity, resulting from a clustering of mystics in a particular time and place. The Hasidim of 18th-century Poland are one famous example. Author Finnegan has written about another—holy women living in the Cistercian monastery of Helfta, during the 13th century, which was one of the most tumultuous periods of German history. Finnegan's book gives clear insight into the spiritual life of Helfta's leading women: the Beguine Mechtild of Madgeburg, who lived her later years at Helfta, the musical and lyrical Mechtild of Hackeborn, and the literary and devotional Gertrude the Great. The writings of these mystics, such as *The Flowing Light of the Godhead*, *The Book of Special Grace*, and *The Messenger*

of Loving Kindness, reveal a deep serenity, devotion, and spiritual insight that is a refreshing counterbalance to modern-day materialism. Their mystical experiences contain wonderfully vivid imagery, psychic awareness of other levels of reality, practical guidance both for themselves and their community, and intimate conversations with their Beloved (Christ). This work is for advanced undergraduates and up, who are interested in understanding the parameters of spiritual experience and/or life in medieval times.—*A. McDowell, Ithaca College*

WS-1123   BM729.W6   90-4389 CIP
Frankiel, Tamar. **The voice of Sarah: feminine spirituality and traditional Judaism.** Harper San Francisco, 1990. (Dist. by HarperCollins) 140p afp ISBN 0-06-063016-7, $18.95

This highly engaging work by a historian of religion, written from an Orthodox and feminist perspective, is an act of intellectual creativity and spiritual devotion. Under the form of interpretive narrative correlated with existential concerns, key feminine personages, mainly in ancient and modern Judaism (e.g., Sarah, Ruth, Esther, Judith, Shulamit, Channah, among others) offer the reader the opportunity to reappreciate them as practical models for contemplating a genuine femine spirituality. The key to this vision of a growing, reenlivening traditional Judaism is symbolized by the contrast between the "voice of Eve" (Chava) in Gen. 3 and "voice of Sarah" in Gen. 21:12. Feminists and nonfeminists will be potentially disarmed by the author's persuasive way of showing the multidimensional modes that being women can have in relation to "vital life force, body, sexuality, the inwardness of personal devotions, study, and meditation". Frankiel's thoughts on nature and the sacred are excellent. Through such archetypal women, however, the author envisions not the "destruction" but a revitalized experience of Jewish tradition—and the God it affirms. Candidly admitting this requires a "leap of faith," and an honest acceptance by women of their "own pain and difficulties as well as. .joys," Frankiel urges them to listen to such voices as they face a crisis-oriented modern world offering meagre "moral and spiritual guidance." Ultimately, Frankiel understands the perspective she offers to be "an adventure in spirituality," as much as a challenge to reenter the garden of Judaism with hope of a new and fuller revelation of the feminine.—*W. C. Beane, University of Wisconsin—Oshkosh*

WS-1124   BV5077   95-48804 CIP
Furlong, Monica. **Visions & longings: medieval women mystics.** Shambhala, 1996. 248p afp ISBN 1-57062-125-X, $20.00

Furlong, author of a biography of Thomas Merton (*Merton: A Biography*, 1980) has assembled an anthology of the works of six women, primarily mystics, of the European Middle Ages. Her book includes two letters of Héloise, who, although not a mystic, is included as a "counterpoint" to the celibate ardor of the other women. Furlong's introduction speaks to both the danger and the need to confront such strange voices from a distant time in an age such as ours. With brief biographies and excerpts from the writings of Hildegard of Bingen, Clare of Assisi, the Beguines, Catherine of Siena, Julian of Norwich, and others, Furlong's "Introduction" draws on studies such as Elizabeth Petroff's *Medieval Women's Visionary Literature* (CH, Nov'86) and *Body and Soul* (1994) and Peter Dronke's *Women Writers of the Middle Ages* (CH, May'85), adding some valuable insights of her own. While highlighting the misogyny of the ecclesial culture that stigmatized these women, Furlong also provides insight into the psychological impact of mystical experience on the personality of the mystic. With few notes and no bibliography, this compilation seems clearly designed for a more general readership and as an introduction to the mystics for undergraduate readers.—*M. Lichtmann, Valparaiso University*

WS-1125   BX5199.U53   89-77843 MARC
Greene, Dana. **Evelyn Underhill: artist of the infinite life.** Crossroad, 1990. 179p index ISBN 0-8245-1006-2, $18.95

Using new archival source material and her own knowledge of spiritual, psychological, and feminist theory, Greene has written a compelling and insightful biography of great 20th-century author of works on mysticism. Using Underhill's writings, Greene elicits her dynamic inner life and her struggles with such spiritual issues as pacifism in time of war, types of spiritual direction, the role of community or church in spirituality, mysticism in action, guiding retreats, and self-esteem. Underhill's gifts lie particularly in her eloquent, concise, and cogent descriptions of the spiritual life. The book is filled with these pithy, candid sayings that so accurately portray this process. Although similar to C.J.R. Armstrong's *Evelyn Underhill, 1875-1941: An Introduction to Her Life and Writings* (CH, Nov'76), Greene's book is more comprehensible, with less obtrusive commentary. The book is highly recommended for all those interested in spirituality and/or woman's studies.—*A. McDowell, Ithaca College*

WS-1126   BQ4570   92-9133 CIP
Gross, Rita M. **Buddhism after patriarchy: a feminist history, analysis, and reconstruction of Buddhism.** State University of New York, 1993. 365p bibl index ISBN 0-7914-1403-5, $44.50; ISBN 0-7914-1404-3 pbk, $14.95

Gross gives a feminist "revalorization" of Buddhism. Noting that the Buddhist treatment of women is problematic, but not irreparably so, the author provides what in many ways is a manual for rethinking Buddhism from a feminist perspective. Her concern is to work through a fourfold layering of androcentrism (creation of the canon, use of the canon, Western scholarship on the canon, and contemporary Buddhism itself) to find an "accurate and usable past." Gotama's reluctance to allow women to go forth, for example, must be placed within the context of the times, more serious consideration should be given to the *Therigatha*, the many Mahayana methods for dealing with liabilities against women (e.g., avoiding female rebirth, magical sex changes, gender-inclusive language) need to be rethought, and stories of Vajrayana *yoginis* like Yeshe Tsogyel need to be given due place. Moreover, because "the dharma is neither male nor female," key concepts in Buddhism that highlight its intersection with feminism (e.g., the ethics of nonviolence and the Bodhisattva path) need to be reemphasized. Gross then calls upon the modern Buddhist community to mandate and institutionalize gender equality through an androgynous vision that would take seriously, for example, issues of child care among laywomen and greater economic support for orders of nuns. A significant book deserving a prominent place in every collection of Buddhist hermeneutics.—*E. Findly, Trinity College (CT)*

WS-1127   BX1795   94-5008 CIP
Gudorf, Christine E. **Body, sex, and pleasure: reconstructing Christian sexual ethics.** Pilgrim Press, OH, 1994. 276p index afp ISBN 0-8298-1014-5, $19.95

Gudorf's book integrates the latest biological research into sexuality with reconsideration of scripture from the standpoint of a theology of incarnation. The author's goal is a foundational rethinking of Christian sexual ethics. She argues that scripture and traditional religious thought have been distorted by "procreationism"—a sexual ethic grounded on inaccurate views of the human body, the need to maximize reproduction, and the desire to maintain patriarchal control of woman. Moreover, the tradition's negation of the value of sexual pleasure is incompatible with the affirmation of embodiment in the incarnation and with the goodness of creation itself. As an alternative, Gudorf offers a new, but distinctively Christian, ethic of sexuality based on sexuality as a premoral good, mutual pleasure as a criterion of moral rightness, and the inalienable nature of what the author calls bodyright. Her book is full of practical information on sexuality, discussion of the relevance of recent scriptural interpretation to sexual ethics, and a constructive new appropriation of natural law. Some of the terminology is technical, but any educated Christian willing to think about the interrelationships of scripture, theology, and sexuality is likely to find this work fascinating and provocative. Undergraduate; graduate; faculty.—*L. L. Inglis, Buena Vista College*

WS-1128   BX2347   95-5122 CIP
Guider, Margaret Eletta. **Daughters of Rahab: prostitution and the church of liberation in Brazil.** Fortress, 1995. 235p (Harvard theological studies, 40) index afp ISBN 0-8006-7093-0 pbk, $16.00

Guider has made an important contribution to the documentation and analysis of current issues in the Catholic Church, particularly the portion of the Latin American church committed to Liberation Theology. Using outreach to prostitutes in Brazil as her case study, she marshals an array of materials and well-considered analysis to demonstrate not only a theological reflection on the issue but also social analysis of the changing role of the church. Her analysis of the church and changing times covers the period of official pastoral outreach to marginalized women (prostitutes) and shows an appreciation of broader historical developments. Thus, the reader is treated to a helpful synthesis of Brazilian church developments over the centuries and provided with the kind of contextual understanding necessary for a holistic approach to the church of liberation. Few other issues are so potent at revealing current conflicts and undercurrents within church debates and developments, and the author's work will therefore serve many audiences. The book contains an impressive and valuable documentation of the issue but is written in an approachable, scholarly tone. Suited for many levels of readers, from general and lower-division undergraduate to faculty and researchers. Recommended to all who seek to understand the Catholic Church in Latin America over the past two decades, particularly those interested in women's issues within the church—*B. T. Froehle, Georgetown University*

WS-1129   BX6447   92-19345 CIP
Higginbotham, Evelyn Brooks. **Righteous discontent: the women's movement in the Black Baptist Church, 1880-1920.** Harvard, 1993. 306p index afp ISBN 0-674-76977-5, $34.95

This landmark contribution to American religious history is the first full-scale study of the religious ideas and activities of a large cohort of African American women. Previous books on the religious activities of African Americans, such as *The Black Church in the African American Experience* by C. Eric Lincoln and Lawrence H. Mamiya (CH, Jul'91), tend to pay little attention to women. The few books that have studied the religious work of African American women, such as *Sisters of the Spirit*, ed. by William L. Andrews (CH, Oct'86), have focused on singular women prophets. Higginbotham's book is the first to study the religious work of a generation or more of African American Christian women. Higginbotham argues that women in African American Baptist churches between 1880 and 1920 worked against both racial and gender discrimination. Women figured importantly in the efforts of the National Baptist Convention to combat racism and to improve the conditions under which African Americans lived, while at the same time working toward greater equality and leadership as women within the Convention. This fine book is recommended for all libraries.—*A. Porterfield, Syracuse University*

WS-1130   BX4700   93-33715 CIP
Hildegard, Saint. **The letters of Hildegard of Bingen, v.1,** tr. by Joseph L. Baird and Radd K. Ehrman. Oxford, 1994. 227p bibl indexes afp ISBN 0-19-508937-5, $39.95

Abbess Hildegard of Bingen (1098-1179), 12th-century renaissance woman—visionary theologian, environmental mystic, medical writer, composer, poet, and dramatist—has been well described by Joan Ferrante as the Ann Landers of her day. The first of four projected volumes of her rich and abundant correspondence, this book is based on the authoritative critical text of Lieven Van Acker, in the impressive "Corpus Christianorum Continuato Medievalis" series. The translators graciously acknowledge the generous assistance of Barbara Newman, author of the splendid pioneer study *Sister of Wisdom* (CH, Mar'88). This first volume's 90 letters, clear and soberly close to the complex Latin originals, follow Van Acker's hierarchical ordering. They include correspondence from important crises in her eventful life—from her early visions, through her grief at the departure of her favorite young nun Richardis van Stade to be Abbess of Bassu, to the final conflict of her life, when Hildegard and her nuns were placed under interdict by the clergy of Mainz for burying in their cemetery a young man who allegedly died while excommunicated. Every library supporting a women's studies program should have this useful and seminal volume. The translation is a fine example of meticulous and exemplary editorial scholarship. The 26-page introduction is richly informative on the medieval letter genre. Good, short explanatory notes; concise bibliography; endnotes with excerpts from the original Latin; general index, especially helpful to researchers. General; undergraduate through professional.—*H. J. John, Trinity College (DC)*

WS-1131   Orig
Hogan, Linda. **From women's experience to feminist theology.** Sheffield Academic, 1995. (Dist. by CUP Services) 192p bibl indexes afp ISBN 1-85075-520-5 pbk, $19.95

Here is a splendid, succinct summary of the latest gleanings in feminist theology. Hogan has grouped together the three major strands—reformist, womanist, and post-Christian—in the context of women's experience and praxis.

The *reformist* utilizes the exemplary work of Elisabeth Schüssler Fiorenza and Rosemary Radford Ruether; the *womanist*, the work of an array of black women "who have not clearly identified their position"; and *post-Christian*, the work for those who have as their leading exponents Carol Christ and Christine Downing. The author coins the term "conceptual instability" to account for the wide diversities and constant reinterpretations churning through the dynamic, ongoing doctrinal, theological, and ethical stages of feminist hermeneutics. She focuses on the "growing unease with the assumed unitary nature of women's experience, which has undergirded much feminist theory." She rightly eschews all impulses to claim a universalist position in feminist theology, giving up "appeals to ontological reality for validation and appeal[s] instead to pragmatism." This book's exceptionally written survey adds a new and vital contribution to such admirable books as Margaret Daphne Hampson's *Theology and Feminism* (CH, Jan'91), Elizabeth Johnson's *She Who Is* (CH, Feb'93), and Francis Martin's *The Feminist Question* (CH, Jun'91). Undergraduate; graduate; faculty; general.—*D. W. Ferm, Colby College*

WS-1132   BR563   93-9220 MARC
Isasi-Díaz, Ada María. **En la Lucha = In the struggle: a Hispanic women's liberation theology.** Fortress, 1993. 226p bibl index afp ISBN 0-8006-2610-9 pbk, $13.00

In the 1970s, feminist theology emerged, with its focal point the liberation of women from all forms of human oppression. Elizabeth Johnson's *She Who* (CH, Feb'93) is the finest work yet written on this subject. In the 1980s womanist theology came on the scene, with a different focus on black women's experience and its tridimensional oppression: racism, sexism, and classism. Katie Cannon's *Black Womanist Ethics*, 1988, is the best model for black feminist theological discourse. And now we have "mujerista theology," featuring "a Hispanic woman who struggles to liberate herself not as an individual but as a member of a Hispanic community." Ada María Isaac-Díaz is the leading exponent, co-authoring her earlier *Hispanic Women: Prophetic Voice in the Church*, 1988. The liberation themes are all there—"the moral agency of Hispanic women," a preferential option for the poor and oppressed, base Christian and Hispanic communities, liberative praxis, conscientization, and the like—with some catchy phrases thrown in. This is a solid and well-written book. Advanced undergraduate; graduate; faculty.—*D. W. Ferm, Colby College*

WS-1133   BV5083   94-44562 CIP
Jantzen, Grace M. **Power, gender and Christian mysticism.** Cambridge, 1995. 384p (Cambridge studies in ideology and religion, 8) bibl index ISBN 0-521-47376-4, $64.95; ISBN 0-521-47926-6 pbk, $18.95

Both historically and philosophically, this compelling, massively documented study is a superlative contribution to medieval, religious, and feminist studies. It is fueled by Jantzen's discontent with the concept of mysticism set forth by William James and the many philosophers who have followed in his wake. In a twofold indictment, she faults James for (1) shoddy documentation and (2) the notion that the primary characteristic of mysticism is an intense, subjective, private, ineffable, psychological experience. To deal with the first, Jantzen undertakes close readings of major medieval writings (e.g., those of Dionysius, Eckhart, Hadewijk, Hildegard, et al.). To deal with the second, she offers as a corrective the view that Christian mysticism has important sociopolitical dimensions. Among the fruits of her overall analysis is the recognition that there have been distinguishable male and female traditions of Christian spirituality. Allowing for diversities within each, one notes the contrasts between them: the male tradition elevates the intellect, favors a body-soul dualism, and is misogynistic, whereas the female one exalts direct visionary experience, is holistic, and esteems womanhood and the feminine. Contained here are important lessons in regard to the just empowerment of women today. An essential acquisition. Upper-division undergraduate; graduate; faculty.—*C. MacCormick, emeritus, Wells College*

WS-1134   BT83   92-4178 CIP
Johnson, Elizabeth A. **She who is: the mystery of God in feminist theological discourse.** Crossroad, NY, 1992. 316p indexes ISBN 0-8245-1162-X, $24.95

"What is the right way to speak about God in the face of women's newly cherished human dignity and equality? This is the crucial theological question." John-

son's response is to range far and wide from the early church all the way to the present day to unearth God as the She Who Is, the "creative, relational power of being who enlivens, suffers with, sustains, and enfolds the universe." The author's rich rhetoric is replete with nifty phrases: "mothering the universe," "sheer exuberant relational aliveness," "sacramental anticipatory moments," "the dark radiance of love in solidarity," and so on. The crowning achievement of Johnson's remarkably effortless writing style is that she engages in a gentle, non-confrontational conversation with many of today's leading feminist theologians, among them Carol Christ and Judith Plaskow (*Weaving the Visions*, 1989), Anne E. Carr (*Transforming Grace*, 1988), Rebecca Chopp (*The Power to Speak*, CH, May'90), and Susan Brooks Thistlethwaite (*Sex, Race, and God*, 1989). Readers will find this incisive survey to be the finest yet written in the area of feminist theological discourse.—*D. W. Ferm, Colby College*

WS-1135   BX6239   94-191656 CIP
Juster, Susan. **Disorderly women: sexual politics & evangelicalism in revolutionary New England.** Cornell, 1994. 224p index afp ISBN 0-8014-2732-0, $32.95

Juster (history, Univ. of Michigan) builds on much recent work by women's historians on gender relations and the exercise of power. She focuses particularly on revolutionary and postrevolutionary Baptists in New England. Juster argues that the tenuous power afforded Colonial Baptist women by evangelical religion was significantly diminished during the revolutionary period as the Baptist churches sought legitimacy in the "quintessentially masculine" republican America. She further asserts that during this period, qualities viewed to be feminine (especially the quality of "disorder") came to define the very essence of sin. To further these arguments, Juster utilizes the official discourse of a wide range of Baptists, particularly in respect to church discipline, and analyzes conversion narratives from both the prewar and postwar periods. The result is a stimulating work, especially for those with a substantial background in women's history. Graduate; faculty.—*L. H. Hoyle, Georgetown College*

WS-1136   F73   93-32053 CIP
Kane, Paula M. **Separatism and subculture: Boston Catholicism, 1900-1920.** North Carolina, 1994. 415p index afp ISBN 0-8078-2128-4, $49.95

Kane revisits a small portion of the terrain covered by Robert E. Sullivan and James M. O'Toole in their edited volume *Catholic Boston: Studies in Religion and Community, 1870-1979* (1985). Kane provides a richly contextualized and very readable analysis of the different voices in which Boston Catholics spoke during the Progressive Era, encompassing fiction, poetry, essays, articles from the local Catholic press, apologetical works, and personal conversion narratives. She weaves a tapestry of early 20th century Boston Catholic life that illuminates its insularity and separatism, micro-managed by William O'Connell (archbishop 1907-44) through a complex web of militantly Catholic single-sex organizations, as well as the ways in which (resident and expatriated) Boston Catholic writers, artists, social reformers, and assorted professionals grappled with the forces of modernity in debates on economic, social, political, and explicitly gender-related issues. This lively study raises new and important questions for students and scholars in American social and religious history, as well as for specialists in women's studies and gender studies.—*D. Campbell, Colby College*

WS-1137   BX1407.W65   89-77880 MARC
Kenneally, James J. **The history of American Catholic women.** Crossroad, NY, 1990. 286p bibl index ISBN 0-8245-1009-7, $24.95

A groundbreaking work, the first comprehensive treatment of the experience of American Catholic women from the Colonial period through the 1950s. Kenneally's book and Mary Jo Weaver's *New Catholic Women* (1985), which covers the period from the 1960s onward, represent the only major works in an area that has been neglected by specialists in women's history and American Catholic history alike. Kenneally (history, Stonehill College) keeps the promise that he makes in his introduction—i.e., he demonstrates that "the thrust for equality in church and state by Catholic females from the 1960s to the present is merely a new phase of an enduring struggle." In so doing, he also illuminates the varieties of Catholic women's religious experience (social, political, economic, educational, and occupational) from the 17th century through the 1950s.

The History of American Catholic Women belongs in all libraries that have collections in women's history and American religious history.—*D. Campbell, Colby College*

WS-1138   BQ4570   94-7678 CIP
Klein, Anne Carolyn. **Meeting the Great Bliss Queen: Buddhists, feminists, and the art of the self.** Beacon Press, 1995. 307p bibl index ISBN 0-8070-7306-7, $25.00

Klein (Rice Univ.) has written extensively about Tibetan Buddhism, and her latest book focuses on Yeshey Tsogyel, wife of the Tibetan king Tri-song-day-tsen (c. 740-798). She is best known as the Great Bliss Queen, an enlightened being who manifests vast wisdom and compassion. She is identified also as the principal Sky Woman or *dakini*, and her festival is celebrated monthly. Klein describes the mandala, chants, meditation, and other cultic practices associated with her. Although her compassion extends to all living creatures, she has special relevance to women, and liturgy and iconography take notice of her womb and vulva as symbols of enlightenment. She is portrayed as "a passionately happy female deity" with whom ordinary Tibetan women might easily identify. Klein's book, however, is not limited to her role in Tibet. The author maintains that Buddhism and the Great Bliss Queen have much to offer to all woman—above all, as a way of resolving the "essentialist-postmodern debate" in contemporary feminism. Klein is well informed about feminist theory, and throughout her book she relates Buddhist insights to Western feminist thought. She may well be the first author to do so, and her book should interest students of Buddhism, feminists, and anyone concerned with cross-cultural conversation. Klein writes clearly, but she assumes some knowledge of Indo-Tibetan Buddhism and feminist theory. Endnotes, glossary. Recommended. Upper-division undergraduate; graduate; faculty.—*H. Peebles, Wabash College*

WS-1139   BL625   91-33777 CIP
Kraemer, Ross Shepard. **Her share of the blessings: women's religions among Pagans, Jews, and Christians in the Greco-Roman world.** Oxford, 1992. 275p bibl index afp ISBN 0-19-506686-3, $24.95

Kraemer attempts to reconstruct women's religious experience in the ancient world by applying a modified version of the anthropologist Mary Douglas's "group/grid" model to the scattered bits of information we possess. In 13 chapters treating Greek, Roman, Jewish, and Christian women in antiquity, and women as religious leaders in each culture, Kramer surveys a wealth of both primary and secondary source material. Her syntheses and reconstructions are necessarily speculative, but she provides good grounds for defending her major contentions—that women's religious experience in antiquity was a coherent and distinct social/psychological phenomenon, and that women's religious practices served both to reinforce traditional gender distinctions—and to offer alternative and even subversive opportunities for self-expression and self-definition. Kraemer applies the Douglas model creatively and judiciously, and brings to bear a prodigious amount of knowledge and scholarship in four separate fields. Hers is one of a very few books that discuss women and religion from a historical rather than a theological perspective, and the only such that treats women in the entire ancient Mediterranean world except for Egypt. This useful, informative, and enlightening compendium and analysis will be of interest to students and scholars alike, as well as to the general reader.—*M. A. Katz, Wesleyan University*

WS-1140   PR868   92-5418 CIP
Krueger, Christine L. **The reader's repentance: women preachers, women writers, and nineteenth-century social discourse.** Chicago, 1993 (c1992). 350p bibl index afp ISBN 0-226-45488-6, $29.95

This new feminist study of women's preaching and women's writing in 18th- and 19th-century British culture seeks to revise current assumptions about evangelicalism and female power. Krueger argues that women's social writing in the 19th century (particularly the "social problem novel" genre) had its roots in a hitherto unrecognized female preaching tradition. She contends that "evangelical hermeneutics briefly vitiated male domination of public speech, allowing women to use the authoritative language of scripture among men as they traditionally had with each other." Although women preachers achieved an enhanced social power they also "risked immasculation, appropriation, and

finally remarginalization." The first part of the book offers a history of British women's preaching; the second part contains in-depth studies of the early careers of Hannah More, Charlotte Tonna, Elizabeth Gaskell, and George Eliot, who saw their "social" writing as analogous to religious vocation. The approach is historical, biographical, and thematic, rather than rhetorical or stylistic. It would be of interest to specialists in 19th-century women's writing and/or in the history of evangelical preaching.—*R. R. Warhol, University of Vermont*

WS-1141   91-39580 CIP
Mack, Phyllis. **Visionary women: ecstatic prophecy in seventeenth-century England.** California, 1993 (c1992). 465p bibl index afp ISBN 0-520-07845-4, $40.00

Mack has produced a complex and subtly argued study of the importance and meaning of gender in shaping expressions of Quaker spirituality, from it origins to 1700. She has mined the voluminous writings and records of the early Quakers, including those of women of the laboring classes, to craft an exemplary study of the development of Quaker female spirituality. Conversant with the recent theoretical approaches of history, anthropology, post-Freudian psychology, and poststructuralism, Mack reveals their limits in understanding female religiosity and makes a case for reexamining religious expression in its social context and in terms of its goals and assumptions. She charts the Quaker movement's transition from sect—where women had authority as prophets, preachers, and mystics—to church—where their authority was confined to the women's meeting. For Mack, the change in the setting of women's spiritual creativity did not mark the death of female freedom but instead introduced a new political authority and the birth of modern feminism. Advanced undergraduate; graduate; faculty.—*J. Harrie, California State University, Bakersfield*

WS-1142   BT83   94-32318 CIP
Martin, Francis. **The feminist question: feminist theology in the light of Christian tradition.** Eerdmans, 1994. 461p bibl index ISBN 0-8028-0794-1 pbk, $29.99

From his vast reading of feminist theology in the light of Christian tradition, Martin (Dominican House of Studies, DC) has come to a twofold conclusion: that "feminism contained a profound and valid critique of our culture, and yet suffered from many of the deficiencies it sought to criticize." He understands feminism's potential harm to lie in the "uncritical way it has submitted to an understanding of God, the world and humankind that is at odds with the light of faith." Martin's masterful and majestic sweep of "the multifaceted reality that goes by the name of feminist theology" covers a "hermeneutical spiral" that ranges far and wide, from the early church through the Enlightenment, culminating in the "great waves" of feminism that extended from the latter half of the 19th century to the present day. Although this book does not include some major manifestations of contemporary feminist theology—e.g., womanist and *mujerista*—Martin's tour de force, which includes a superb bibliography, deserves its rightful place alongside Elizabeth Johnson's *She Who Is* (CH, Feb'93), with Kathleen Sands's *Escape from Paradise* (CH, Apr'95) a few lengths behind. Undergraduate; graduate; general.—*D. W. Ferm, Colby College*

WS-1143   BX4901   95-37249 CIP
McSheffrey, Shannon. **Gender and heresy: women and men in Lollard communities, 1420-1530.** Pennsylvania, 1995. 253p bibl index afp ISBN 0-8122-3310-7, $38.95; ISBN 0-8122-1549-4 pbk, $18.95

McSheffrey (history, Concordia Univ.) here offers a bold advance in the study of two arenas in the late medieval and early modern period of Christian history. She uses the Lollard communities in England (1420-1530) to challenge the prevailing assumption that women are attracted to heretical movements because these movements offer them more religious options. In fact, she concludes, "Lollardy was made by and, in a sense, for men." With deft moves, she deals with the gender issue in ways current scholarship will find unavoidable. Equally enlightening is the advancement of a picture of Lollardy as anticlerical, rationalistic, and scripturally fundamentalist. This description helps the reader understand Lollardy as transitional from late medieval Roman Catholicism to the reforming movements of 16th-century England. The book has the feel of a revised dissertation. (It is not so acknowledged, but McSheffrey's 1992 dissertation at the University of Toronto is similarly titled.) It offers a good summary of current literature, rich notation, and useful bibliography and index. Scholars and specialists in English history and this period will appreciate this fine contribution. Upper-division undergraduate; graduate; faculty.—*A. L. Kolp, Earlham College*

WS-1144 BX4705 93-23827 CIP
Merriman, Brigid O'Shea. **Searching for Christ: the spirituality of Dorothy Day.** Notre Dame, 1994. 333p bibl index afp ISBN 0-268-01750-6, $29.95

Writings on Dorothy Day have burgeoned in the two decades since William D. Miller's pioneering study, *A Harsh and Dreadful Love* (CH, Sep'73). The present work by Sister Merriman (Mt. Angel Seminary, Oregon) constitutes another addition to the massive corpus of works on Day. Merriman's revised thesis provides a concise outline of the ways in which Day's reading in scripture and in the works of Thomas à Kempis, Augustine, Dostoevsky, Tolstoy, Mounier, Maritain, and Furfey informed her spirituality. The author also addresses the relationship between Day and a handful of male monastics and clerics, including Thomas Merton, Virgil Michel, and Onesimus Lacouture, S.J. There are no surprises here for those who have kept up with Day scholarship, but many will be startled by what Merriman chose not to discuss. Why did she overlook James T. Fisher's revisionist treatment of Day in *The Catholic Counterculture in America* (CH, Apr'90)? Why is there no attempt to examine Day's spirituality in the light of growing literature on women's spirituality? What about issues of embodiment and female sexuality? Undergraduate; graduate.—*D. Campbell, Colby College*

WS-1145 BT704 89-42594 CIP
Miles, Margaret R. **Carnal knowing: female nakedness and religious meaning in the Christian west.** Beacon Press, 1989. (Dist. by Farrar, Straus & Giroux) 254p bibl index ISBN 0-8070-1306-4, $24.95

In *Image as Insight* (1985) Miles made a strong case for the importance of the visual to the understanding of historical existence. In the present work, Miles focuses on the artistic use of female nakedness in the Christian West, charging that it served as a "cipher for sin, sex, and death." She concludes that "the flesh" became marginalized in Christianity not—as is widely held—because of its self-identification with philosophy, but through representational practices that created the view that "knowledge at its best is free of the flesh." This view had the affect of "fatally undermining the Christian project of integrating the flesh," and is, at root, attributable to "the sexism of Christian societies." The only solution to this situation lies, Miles argues, in women's developing their own subjectivity and in this subjectivity becoming "valued in the public sphere, and reflected and cultivated in social practices and representations." Essential for religion, women's studies, and art history collections. Advanced undergraduates and above.—*S. H. Boyd, Regis College*

WS-1146 B765 92-31369 CIP
Milhaven, John Giles. **Hadewijch and her sisters: other ways of loving and knowing.** State University of New York, 1993. 171p bibl index afp ISBN 0-7914-1541-4, $39.50

Milhaven describes his book as a "call to discussion." He examines the very different way that the medieval mystic Hadewijch and several other medieval female mystics described the best way to know God. Unlike most thinkers in the Western tradition (most of whom, of course, have been male), who regarded only intellectual knowing as valuable, "Hadewijch and her sisters" asserted that bodily knowing was just as good a path to God. This bodily knowing used touch, rather than sight, as its basic metaphor, and challenged mainstream theology not only because it asserted the importance of the body in achieving a true knowledge of God, but also because it stressed that both God and the believer could gain by such knowledge and achieve what Milhaven terms "sufficiency in mutuality." The author, an expert in Catholic moral theology and ethics, brings to this consideration a broad knowledge of the Church fathers and medieval theologians, and links the ideas of these women with those of modern feminist thinkers who are also calling for incorporating the body into our basic paradigms of knowing in order to effect moral change. A thought-provoking essay, even for those not especially interested in medieval theology. General, advanced undergraduates, and above.—*M. E. Wiesner, University of Wisconsin—Milwaukee*

WS-1147 BX4705 90-15583 CIP
O'Connor, June. **The moral vision of Dorothy Day: a feminist perspective.** Crossroad, NY, 1991. 123p bibl index ISBN 0-8245-1080-1, $16.95

Throughout her life, Dorothy Day was advocate for a wide variety of causes, forcefully, thoughtfully, and consistently. O'Connor's study examines her as an ethicist and feminist. This sharper focus complements William D. Miller's *Dorothy Day: A Biography*. Day's religious worldview of personalism and pacifism undergirded her actions of feeding and housing the poor and opposing war in all of its manifestations. Her morality embodied care as well as justice, a hallmark of feminist morality, as Carol Gilligan has pointed out *In A Different Voice* (CH, Oct'82). Her concerns were broader than those of the middle-class origins of the 20th-century feminist movement and often left her at odds with the early feminist agenda. Feminism broadened its perspective to include women of color and issues of poverty just as Dorothy Day was retiring from public life. O'Connor, therefore, constructs a plausible, highly readable, stimulating dialogue. All undergraduate libraries should own this book, and it will be read with profit by students of religion, journalism, and feminist studies. There is also a first-rate bibliography.—*D. A. Brown, California State University, Fullerton*

WS-1148 BS575 91-40975 CIP
Pardes, Ilana. **Countertraditions in the Bible: a feminist approach.** Harvard, 1992. 194p bibl index afp ISBN 0-674-17542-5, $29.95

In a series of feminist, deconstructionist essays, Pardes explores "the tense dialogue between the dominant patriarchal discourses of the Bible and counter female voices which attempt to put forth other truths." Eve "performs the first independent act," gains wisdom (following Mieke Bal in a gnostic reading), and in naming Cain makes herself a creator; Miriam defies Moses' authority; Rachel, like Jacob a younger sibling, strives for power; Zipporah's story stems from that of Isis and Osiris; Ruth and Naomi, bonded together, retell the Rachel/Leah story; the Shulamite reveals female eroticism; Job's wife, also affected by the calamities, suspends trust. Making the most of fragmentary hints from a small unrepresentative sample, Pardes calls "into question the predominantly patriarchal base of monotheism." Interesting, faddish, at times deliberately obscure, the book makes no pretense of objectivity. Notes. For graduate libraries; to be read with its stated limitations in mind and not as a representative treatment of women in the Bible.—*M. S. Stephenson, The University of Texas at Brownsville*

WS-1149 BL1237 95-39811 CIP
Pearson, Anne Mackenzie. **"Because it gives me peace of mind": ritual fasts in the religious lives of Hindu women.** State University of New York, 1996. 315p bibl index afp ISBN 0-7914-3037-5, $68.50

This welcome new book examines a tradition of women's domestic rituals in South Asia known as *vratas*. Drawing on classical practices as described in the Sanskrit *Dharmasāstras*, Pearson details the relation of contemporary *vratas* or *vrats* to older expressions of the Hindu tradition, to the seasonal and festival life of the calendar, and to the life cycle stages of Hindu women as played out in communities of the north Indian city of Banaras. As rituals normally of and by women, *vratas* have as their beneficiaries all the members of the household, and the performance of these votive fasting rites are, in part, a way of meeting the obligations of women as wives, their *strīdharma*. As the author shows, however, knowledge of how to perform the rites is passed on by the women of each generation and their practice functions in important ways to bind women together as they pursue not only blessings for family members but also profound spiritual ends. The practice of *vratas* differ in each locality, but Pearson's discussion, based on extensive interviews, observations of domestic and public practice, and textual support from several periods highlights common thematic elements and shows that, indeed, the true beneficiaries are the women themselves. This contribution is a "must" for all undergraduates, graduates, and faculty.—*E. Findly, Trinity College (CT)*

WS-1150 BT83 91-28029 CIP
Pellauer, Mary D. **Toward a tradition of feminist theology: the religious social thought of Elizabeth Cady Stanton, Susan B. Anthony, and Anna Howard Shaw.** Carlson Publishing, 1991. 427p (Chicago studies in the history of American religion, 15) bibl index afp ISBN 0-926019-51-1, $60.00

Contending that "without a grasp of the religious aspects of the work of these women, it may be seriously questioned whether they have been adequately understood at all," Pellauer sets out to illuminate the reciprocal relationship between each woman's social analysis and her religious perspective. In all three cases, she finds that the "pivot point" between the social and religious dimensions is justice, centered on a particular social issue rather than on an analysis of the American social order in general. For each figure, Pellauer supplies a brief biography, notes on source documentation, discussion of the social issue in detail, description of the religious or theological position, and critical remarks. She provides a necessary corrective to the secularist bias of recent biographies of major figures such as Stanton and Anthony, but because of the book's price and the fact that it is a republication of her PhD thesis (University of Chicago, 1980) rather than a more accessible revision, it is recommended for upper-division undergraduates, graduate students, and faculty in women's studies and religion.—*S. H. Boyd, Regis University*

WS-1151   BX9354   91-8985 CIP
Porterfield, Amanda. **Female piety in Puritan New England: the emergence of religious humanism.** Oxford, 1992. 207p bibl index afp ISBN 0-19-506821-1, $29.95

Porterfield builds upon the scholarship of Caroline Walker Bynum, Ann Kibbey, E. Ann Matter, and many others in pursuing some of the questions she first raised in *Feminine Spirituality in America* (CH, Nov'80). She concentrates on six major figures in 17th-century Puritan New England: Thomas Hooker, Thomas Shepard, John Cotton, Ann Hutchinson, Ann Bradstreet, and Mary Rowlandson. Porterfield persuasively argues that despite significant differences in their spiritual perspectives, these six Puritans illuminate the grounding of Puritan spirituality in an "intensely religious form of humanism" bolstered by certain central images of female piety. Porterfield's analysis of the complex implications of female spirituality for male and female Puritans, and those living in different decades and socioeconomic milieus will be of interest to specialists in Puritanism, spirituality, and women's religious experience. Especially impressive is Porterfield's ability to treat 17th-century Puritan experience as part of a larger story—the evolution of Western Christian spirituality from the late medieval period through the Enlightenment. Upper-division undergraduates and graduate students.—*D. Campbell, Colby College*

WS-1152   BX4220   95-26813 MARC
Ranft, Patricia. **Women and the religious life in premodern Europe.** St. Martin's, 1996. 159p bibl index ISBN 0-312-12434-1, $39.95

Ranft seeks to present here "a selective history of Christian religious societies for Western women from their origin until the seventeenth century" in order to contribute to an evaluation of women's position in Western history. Drawing on the scholarship on women religious available only in the last generation, her study takes the form of a survey and taxonomy of major events, orders, and persons concerned with women's religious life. Beginning in the early centuries with the desert *ammas* (mothers), the book surveys women of both Eastern and Western monastic movements, new groups spawned by the *vita apostolica*, late medieval visionaries, and religious life for women of the Reformation era, as well as new religious orders in the early modern period. With its scant 131 pages of text covering such a lengthy time span, and with little "academic paraphernalia" (some major interpretive works are not listed in the selected bibliography), this study provides an introductory reference useful for a general readership and in lower-division undergraduate libraries.—*M. Lichtmann, Valparaiso University*

WS-1153   HQ1381   95-15090 CIP
Robb, Carol S. **Equal value: an ethical approach to economics and sex.** Beacon Press, 1996 (c1995). 198p index ISBN 0-8070-6504-8, $25.00

Robb (San Francisco Theological Seminary) has brought together theories used in Christian social ethics and reflections on practical applications to women's issues in the workplace. The text reflects the growing confidence of feminist theologians both to ground their deliberations in the biblical and ethical heritage and, at the same time, to criticize the injustices embedded in that heritage as the product of patriarchal institutions. Robb's practical conclusions reflect a growing feminist consensus on the direction and need for social change. Robb makes concrete policy proposals such as parental leave, overcoming harassment in the workplace by full integration, alternative models of marriage that prevent domestic violence, and direct challenges to the biblical "Holiness Codes" so often used to justify homophobia. The choice of issues is selective and not comprehensive, and one might wish that issues such as rape and the interaction of race and gender had also been included. Nonetheless, this author's contribution is her ability to make simple, straightforward links between the ethical theories with which she begins and the new claims of progressive sexual ethics. Particularly appropriate for seminary and religious libraries. Upper-division undergraduate through professional.—*L. L. Inglis, Buena Vista University*

WS-1154   BL1237   91-18883 CIP
Roles and rituals for Hindu women, ed. by Julia Leslie. Fairleigh Dickinson, 1991. (Dist. by Associated University Presses) 267p bibl index afp ISBN 0-8386-3475-3, $38.50

These essays on the variety of religious life among historical and modern Hindu women focus on centuries-old structures in a unique way. Rather than showing how women fall victims to ideologies that suppress and disenfranchise them, the authors of these essays rethink Hinduism as a tradition that provides women active ways to pursue satisfying and powerful religious lives. Covering women in public and domestic ritual and dance (both secular and sacred), as well as *satis*, *Śaiva bhaktas*, and ascetics, the authors move between myth and practice to show how religion shapes the details of daily life. Often invoking the methods of psychoanalysis, structuralism in ritual, textual exegesis, and oral history, for example, the essays are especially interesting for the way they highlight the depth of Hindu worship even among the most modern families. An excellent text for a course on Hinduism or on women in religion, with good notes, illustrations, and bibliography, this book is useful for both the educated general reader and the scholar and would make a good purchase for academic libraries, community college through graduate.—*E. Findly, Trinity College (CT)*

WS-1155   BV600   93-9306 CIP
Russell, Letty M. **Church in the round: feminist interpretation of the church.** Westminster, 1993. 253p bibl indexes afp ISBN 0-664-25070-X pbk, $14.99

Adding another volume to her feminist critiques of Christianity dating back to 1979 (i.e., *The Future of Partnership*, CH, Oct'79), Russell here focuses on the church as an institution. Moving beyond the feminist theological critique of the church by Rosemary Radford Ruether (*Women-Church*, 1985), Elisabeth Schüssler Fiorenza (*Bread Not Stone*, 1984), and her own *Household of Freedom* (1987), Russell seeks to create a new doctrine of the church. She starts with a spiral version of liberation theology's action/reflection model and then defines the nature of leadership necessary for replicating the model. Next she describes communities committed to solidarity with the oppressed, analyzing the ways in which they are changed by this advocacy stance. Finally, she outlines how ecclesiology must change in order to live out this vision, focusing on the doctrine of election, and showing how feminist spirituality enables the changes. Russell also provides helpful synthesis of a growing literature in the field. For all women's studies and religion collections.—*S. H. Boyd, Regis University*

WS-1156   BR195   CIP
Salisbury, Joyce E. **Church fathers, independent virgins.** Verso, 1991. (Dist. by Routledge, Chapman & Hall) 168p bibl index ISBN 0-86091-293-0, $34.95

Salisbury (Univ. of Wisconsin) is also the author of *Iberian Popular Religion, 600 BC to 700 BC* (1985) and *Medieval Sexuality: A Research Guide* (CH, Oct'90). That the literature narrating the alternative ascetic view of women was preserved for more than a millennium is warrant for the author's presentation here. In terms of its subject matter, the book may be divided as follows: (1) patristic views of sexuality and their rules for virgins; (2) exploration of ways seven women in the Escorial codex expressed their independence in violation of patristic prescriptions; (3) a theoretical base to establish the unifying principle of the ascetic view of women. Early church fathers viewed sex as reproduction, pollution, and marital intimacy (sometimes). Ascetic women with defiance and female strength were able to transcend gender requirements and finally gender itself. As a historian, Salisbury is less than objective, but the book is both history and fun. The author provides enough anecdotal humor to spice what might otherwise be a bland book, and she has enabled the Christian church to reclaim a part of its past that is an alternative to the Augustinian view of women and sexuality. Excellent notes and bibliography; adequate index. Appropriate for upper-division undergraduates, graduate students, and faculty.—*J. W. McCant, Point Loma Nazarene College*

WS-1157 BT83 94-9748 CIP
Sands, Kathleen M. **Escape from paradise: evil and tragedy in feminist theology.** Fortress, 1994. 212p index afp ISBN 0-8006-2636-2 pbk, $14.00

Sands's thesis, "the tragic consciousness as a heuristic foundation for theology," represents her attempt to come to terms with Christian theology and its feminist variants in the postmodern era. Engaging in lively conversation among her feminist peers in confronting the vexing problem of evil, Sands uses the fertile insights of Rosemary Ruether and Carol Christ as the bridge between the moral and intellectual advantages of rationalism and the mystical and aesthetic gains of feminist romantic dualism. According to the author, feminist theology and theology are "funny things," which emanate from "the imponderable sufferings of women, which flood the earth and accuse heaven," and which may, if unchecked, eventually lead to "the supposed death of feminism" and a "return to Paradise." This intriguing and thoughtful book is tough going. Unfortunately, its rambling rhetoric will captivate only the cadre of in-group "sisters in struggle," who too often enjoy saying "funny things" to each other. Far better to welcome and embrace is Elizabeth Johnson's eloquent *She Who Is* (CH, Feb'93). Undergraduate; graduate; faculty.—*D. W. Ferm, Colby College*

WS-1158 BV676 95-19950 CIP
Schmidt, Frederick W. **A still small voice: women, ordination, and the church.** Syracuse, 1996. 194p bibl index afp ISBN 0-8156-2683-5, $24.95

Although books on women and ordination have been published with some regularity in recent years, Schmidt offers a unique contribution to the discussion. He writes from the perspective of a sociologist, utilizing organization theory to explore the bureaucratic and cultural linkages within denominations that influence denominational responses to women in leadership. Although not always successful, Schmidt seeks to couch his findings in language that is comprehensible to a general audience. As the title might suggest, the author is also concerned with "enlarging" the voices of women in the church. He does this in a quite literal way by filling his book with extended quotations drawn from interviews and questionnaires completed by 40 ordained Protestant women and ten seminary-trained Catholic women. Schmidt gives particular attention to the stories and experiences of women in five denominations—Episcopal, United Methodist, Evangelical Lutheran, Southern Baptist, and Roman Catholic—dedicating a chapter to each one. In his conclusion, Schmidt offers his own observations regarding how denominational leaders can work toward the full involvement of women in the life and leadership of the church. Graduate; faculty; professional.—*L. H. Hoyle, Georgetown College*

WS-1159 BS2379 93-31336 CIP
Searching the scriptures: v.1: A feminist introduction, ed. by Elisabeth Schüssler Fiorenza with Shelly Matthews. Crossroad, NY, 1994 (c1993). 397p index ISBN 0-8245-1381-9, $29.95

These 24 essays by an international group of women scholars introduce a commentary project developed by the editor. Although future publications will directly engage the New Testament and contemporary texts, these studies consider the possibilities of feminist biblical interpretation using different sociohistorical perspectives (African, Asian, Asian American, Native American, *Mujerista*, and Womanist; ancient, medieval, 19th-century, modern; upper class and slave; pulpit and lectern) and critical methods (including excellent contributions on translation, literary criticism, and social, sociological, and anthropological approaches). Missing are lesbian perspectives and detailed considerations of heterosexism. Ostensibly ecumenical, the volume is overwhelmingly Christian in substance and tone; however, articles on Jewish women at the turn of the eras and on feminist antisemitism are welcome contributions. Familiar throughout are both condemnations of sexism, racism, ethnocentrism, and antsemitism in church and academy and appeals to the editor's hermeneutical strategies, but the varied perspectives of

the essays add new depth to such discussions. The collection's true test will be the commentaries themselves: the methodological and hermeneutical perspectives discussed here primarily in the abstract must now be applied to the texts. Recommended for all those engaged in biblical interpretation. Advanced undergraduate; graduate; faculty.—*A. -J. Levine, Swarthmore College*

WS-1160 BS2379 93-31336 CIP
Searching the Scriptures: v.2: A feminist commentary, ed. by Elisabeth Schüssler Fiorenza with Ann Brock and Shelly Matthews. Crossroad, NY, 1995 (c1994). 894p ISBN 0-8245-1424-6, $49.50

Like its companion, *A Feminist Introduction* (CH, Jun'94), the present volume grew out of discussions in the Women in the Biblical World section of the Society of Biblical Literature. Although it commemorates the centennial of the publication of Elizabeth Cady Stanton's *The Woman's Bible*, it takes a different theoretical and methodological approach. Rather than focusing on texts that concern women as did *The Woman's Bible*—and its direct successor, the *Women's Bible Commentary*, ed. by Carol Newsom and Sharon Ringe (CH, Apr'93)—the contributors to this volume seek to analyze texts in their entirety. The approach outlined in the introduction is "transgressive," crossing boundaries of canon and church set up by patriarchy. Although concentrating on the Christian New Testament, it moves outside the canon to those extracanonical writings produced by such "heretical" groups as Montanists and gnostics. Its hermeneutics of suspicion of texts that silenced and marginalized women (such as in an uncovering of the misogyny in The Book of Revelation) is powerfully completed by the shaping of the whole volume in the image of the "open, cosmic house of divine Wisdom." Thus, the volume's three sections extend the call of Wisdom into "Manifestations of Sophia," "Submerged Traditions of Sophia," and "Envoys of Sophia," including revelatory, epistolary, and biographical discourses. This volume deserves wide readership. Undergraduate; graduate; faculty; general.—*M. Lichtmann, Berea College*

WS-1161 BL458 93-35557 CIP
Sered, Susan Starr. **Priestess, mother, sacred sister: religions dominated by women.** Oxford, 1994. 330p bibl index afp ISBN 0-19-508395-4, $27.50

Sered (Bar-Ilan Univ., Israel) does a good job of answering the call of many to employ anthropological, sociological, and historical perspectives when writing in the social sciences. This broad perspective is what makes the author's study of female-dominated religions possible. Since relatively few religions fall into this category, it was necessary for Sered to cast wide her net. Sometimes the case studies overwhelm the reader with their diversity and detail. In the midst of multiple, complex case studies, it is possible to lose sight of the point Sered would make, though she is to be commended for her thorough efforts to back up her assertions. One might wonder if the religions she discusses are actually *dominated* by women or if they might be contextualized differently: religions within male-dominated religions where women occasionally play a leading role before a limited (female) audience. This book provides a broad view, made applicable by case studies, which will serve students who need examples and research to begin their own explorations of cultures within which women play important religious roles. Upper-division undergraduate and above.—*D. C. Samuels, SUNY at Stony Brook*

WS-1162 BS1235 93-572 CIP
Steinberg, Naomi. **Kinship and marriage in Genesis: a household economics perspective.** Fortress, 1993. 162p bibl indexes afp ISBN 0-8006-2703-2 pbk, $12.00

Steinberg uses the methodology of social anthropology in this highly productive analysis of the nature of kinship and marriage in the traditions of Gen. 11:10-50:26. She provides a detailed analysis of the three cycles of ancestral stories: the Sarah-Hagar cycle characterized by polycoity, the Rebekah cycle characterized by monogamy, and the Rachel-Leah cycle characterized by sororal polygyny. Differences in the understanding of kinship and inheritance in these cycles leads her to the tentative conclusion that the locus for the final redaction of these traditions was postexilic Israel. The editor of these traditions sought to establish the identity of the community and its role on the return to the land. Genealogical charts and a brief glossary enhance the usefulness of the work. Steinberg's precision in the use of sociological terminology and her ability to make informed cross-cultural comparisons set this study apart as one of the best treatments of kinship and inheritance in the Genesis traditions. This volume is a must for all libraries whose clientele includes biblical and social anthropology students and scholars. Advanced undergraduate through professional.—*H. O. Forshey, Miami University (OH)*

WS-1163 BP134 94-3968 CIP

Stowasser, Barbara Freyer. **Women in the Qur'an, traditions, and interpretation.** Oxford, 1994. 206p bibl index afp ISBN 0-19-508480-2, $29.95

This is both an analytical study of the first order and a vade mecum of information on women in the faith, the law, and the imagination of Sunni Muslims. Stowasser's extensive use of Arabic texts, whether fully translated or merely summarized, is at once rare and welcome. In part 1 she tells the story of sacred heroines, from Eve to Mary, who are renowned in Abrahamic scriptures prior to the Qur'an; in part 2 she examines Qur'anic references to the Prophet's wives, together with Hadith (traditions attributed to the Prophet Muhammad himself) on these same paragons of virtue. The author also surveys some modern Muslim interpretations of the Prophet's wives, including the egalitarian message of feminist interpreters such as the Moroccan sociologist Fatima Mernissi. One misses the Shi'i viewpoint, but that gap is due to the author's decision to focus on the Prophet's wives rather than on his daughters, since it is Muhammad's daughter and Ali's wife, Fatima, whose role for Shi'i Muslims exceeds that of all other women. See, for example, Ali Shariati's *Fatima is Fatima,* tr. by Lateh Bakhtiar (Tehran, 1981). Recommended for general readers, upper-division undergraduate and graduate students, and faculty at all levels.—*B. B. Lawrence, Duke University*

WS-1164 BX1912 93-41758 CIP

St. Pierre, Simone M. **The struggle to serve: the ordination of women in the Roman Catholic Church.** McFarland, 1994. 203p bibl index afp ISBN 0-89950-901-0, $27.50

St. Pierre takes a timely look at the ongoing debate over women's ordination within the Roman Catholic Church. This revised and updated 1991 master's thesis is clear, concise, yet broad in scope. It provides a balanced treatment of arguments for women's ordination embraced by Catholic feminists as well as the counterarguments issued by recent popes and members of the hierarchy. It even outlines the ways in which the report issued by Pope Paul VI's Pontifical Biblical Commission differed in perspective from the *Declaration on the Question of the Admission of Women to the Ministerial Priesthood* (1977) issued by the Sacred Congregation for the Doctrine of the Faith during the same pontificate. St. Pierre takes pains to address practical and pastoral concerns as well as scriptural and theological questions. This is a helpful volume for students, scholars, and anyone interested in sorting out the chronology and issues behind the Catholic women's ordination controversy. Both the essay itself and the appended annotated bibliography attest to the author's desire to promote an understanding of both sides of the issue that will lead to more fruitful conversations in the future than we have seen in the recent past. Undergraduate (all levels).—*D. Campbell, Colby College*

WS-1165 Brit. CIP

Toorn, Karel van der. **From her cradle to her grave: the role of religion in the life of the Israelite and the Babylonian woman,** tr. by Sara J. Denning-Bolle. JSOT Press, 1994. (Dist. by Sheffield Academic Press, 343 Fulwood Rd., Sheffield S10 3BP, UK) 151p indexes afp ISBN 1-85075-446-2 pbk, $18.50

This minimally revised translation of a 1987 Dutch original necessarily compresses chronology, geography, class distinctions, and the widely variegated experiences of real women to sketch an average Israelite woman's religious life. Van der Toorn's broad, socioculturally defined "religion" includes infant consecrations and their preoccupation with sexual polarity; table etiquette and its connection to purity; attitudes toward menstruation and fertility; attention to household gods; the possible relationship between fulfillment of vows and prostitution; necromancy; divination; prophecy; and the devotional practices of widows. Appropriately, he concentrates on folk piety and domestic worship rather than the state cult. The text, however, lacks sufficient attention to levirate marriage, polygamy, and involvement in sacrificial activity. Occasionally moving too

quickly from scant or ambiguous biblical references to general conclusions and from other ancient Near Eastern cultures (the "Babylonia" of the title is too narrow) to Israelite practice, and at times problematically essentializing women's nature, van der Toorn nevertheless offers both a helpful model based on the stages of a woman's life from birth to death for exploring the topic and excellent cross-cultural details by which to contextualize it. Undergraduate.—*A.-J. Levine, Vanderbilt University*

WS-1166 BX2347 91-15121 CIP

Wallace, Ruth A. **They call her pastor: a new role for Catholic women.** State University of New York, 1992. 204p bibl index ISBN 0-7914-0925-2, $44.50; ISBN 0-7914-0926-0 pbk, $14.95

Although the Roman Catholic hierarchy stands fast against allowing women into the ranks of the church's ordained ministry, in some places the shortage of priests has brought about the appointment of women as church administrators. The women "exercise overall responsibility in the parish for worship, education, pastoral services, and administration," according to Wallace's study of 20 such congregations. Nonresident male priests travel to the parishes to preside at Mass and other sacraments. Wallace describes the pastors, their parishes (mostly small rural churches), and parishioner response. Some of the women receive surprising support from bishops and male clergy, while others experience considerable overt and covert resistance. Wallace asserts that the point of greatest tension for the women is that they cannot totally minister to their parishioners. "Using the analogy of the shepherd," she says, "they can watch over their flock, but they must call on someone else to feed them." Wallace's work, a solid piece of sociological research, benefits from being clearly described and is free of academic jargon. Recommended for all women's studies and religion collections.—*S. H. Boyd, Regis University*

WS-1167 BS680.L25 90-35702 CIP

Wright, Christopher J.H. **God's people in God's land: family, land, and property in the Old Testament.** Eerdmans/Paternoster Press, 1990. 284p bibl indexes ISBN 0-8028-0321-0, $16.95

Wright posits the family as the primary link among the theological concepts of God, Israel (humanity), and land (the earth) in the Hebrew Scriptures and, by extension, the New Testament. This paradigm is helpful in distilling the ethical implications of legislation regarding land (property), which is thoroughly explored. The book is carefully crafted in the manner of a dissertation and replete with appropriate footnotes, biblical and author indexes, and extensive bibliography. It is a valuable source of information on social ethics in general (treatment of the poor, wives, children, and slaves) and land ownership in particular. About 50 pages are devoted to a discussion of the role of wives, which is very relevant to contemporary feminist interests. The review of the literature is rich, and the conclusions clearly underscore the danger of easy stereotypes.—*R. T. Anderson, Michigan State University*

WS-1168 BT650 90-46215 CIP

Zimdars-Swartz, Sandra L. **Encountering Mary: from La Salette to Medjugorje.** Princeton, 1991. 342p bibl index afp ISBN 0-691-07371-6, $24.95

During the past decade, popular and scholarly interest in Marian apparitions has increased dramatically, and literature on the subject has burgeoned. In *Encountering Mary*, Zimdars-Swartz provides a guide to the literature, as well as a balanced, comprehensive examination of the anatomy of a Marian apparition. Building upon the solid foundation laid by historical studies such as William A. Christian's *Apparitions in Late Medieval and Renaissance Spain* (1981) and Thomas Kselman's *Miracles and Prophesies in Nineteenth-Century France* (1983), Zimdars-Swartz adopts a phenomenological approach which seeks to establish the relationship between "apparitions as religious experience" and "apparitions as religious knowledge." Drawing upon her detailed analysis of the meaning of specific apparitions within local communities and the content of the messages from Mary reported in a wide variety of contexts, the author ends with a suggestive chapter on "modern apparition worldviews." *Encountering Mary* represents an important contribution to the ongoing scholarly effort to probe into the context and contours of popular religion in the modern era. Both public and academic libraries.—*D. Campbell, Colby College*

◆ SCIENCE & TECHNOLOGY

WS-1169   QC16   93-28136 CIP
Ajzenberg-Selove, Fay. **A matter of choices: memoirs of a female physicist.** Rutgers, 1994. 234p index ISBN 0-8135-2034-7, $40.00; ISBN 0-8135-2035-5 pbk, $18.00

Ajzenberg-Selove's book, the second in a series on the lives of women in science, is an important contribution to the still-inadequate corpus of literature relating the lives and experience of women scientists. Among the virtues of this book are its ready accessibility to a wider audience, its wealth of concrete detail, and the fact that it is about a contemporary woman physicist, of particular importance because (as the author points out) in the US fewer women work in physics than in any other scientific field. The author, who has lived a distinguished life both as a researcher and as a teacher (principally at Haverford College and the University of Pennsylvania), does a fine job of combining her life story with reflections on the status of women in science, why women choose or, more often, do not choose to become scientists, and the myriad explicit and subtle ways in which women suffer discrimination. Her candor about the nature of science itself and her willingness to be very open about her personal life make this book extremely valuable, and it will be helpful to young women considering science as a career. General; community college; undergraduate through faculty.—*M. H. Chaplin, Wellesley College*

WS-1170   QH45   94-3664 CIP
American women afield: writings by pioneering women naturalists, ed. by Marcia Myers Bonta. Texas A&M, 1995. 248p (Louise Lindsey Merrick natural environment series, 20) bibl afp ISBN 0-89096-633-8, $35.00; ISBN 0-89096-634-6 pbk, $15.95

American Women Afield, a collection of writings by 25 American women naturalists introduced by brief but helpful biographies by Bonta, is a distinct contribution to the growing body of literature on women scientists. All of the women included in this volume were lovers of nature: many were self-taught, most had to defy convention in order to do their field work, and each wrote with both scientific precision and great personal style about what she did, what it meant to her, and how she was perceived. Ornithologists, botanists, entomologists, ecologists, and one lone agrostologist, from scientists of the late 19th century to the nearly contemporary Rachel Carson, are represented here in articles written for popular journals, excerpts from books, letters to friends and family, and occasional field notes. Each naturalist is introduced by a brief biographical sketch, and there are suggestions for "further reading" as well as a short selected bibliography following their contributions. Since the selection was limited to those women who wrote successfully for the public, the collection is not inclusive; but the book provides a fascinating account of both some very interesting women and their significant contributions to natural history. General; undergraduate; graduate.—*M. H. Chaplin, Wellesley College*

WS-1171   TL521   93-61763 CIP
Bell, Elizabeth S. **Sisters of the wind: voices of early women aviators.** Trilogy Books, 1994. 206p bibl index ISBN 0-9623879-4-0 pbk, $14.95

Revealingly subtitled "Voices of Early Women Aviators," Bell's book derives from the diaries, journals, and published works of British and American women aviators in the 1920s and 1930s and those who wrote about them at that time, not decades later. This necessarily limits the number of voices included; nonetheless, the scope is wide enough to encompass such relatively unknown women aviators as Vilette De Sibour, Pauline Gower, and Dorothy Spicer, as well as the two most renowned aviators of the period, Amelia Earhart and Anne Lindbergh. It also includes the accounts of some early women passengers, since they brought a different perspective to the course of aviation in its early development by suggesting the accommodations the early commercial industry had to make to the notion of passenger flight. Because its main focus is the image these women aviators wished to convey, the book will disappoint those looking for a critical account, but it reads easily and conveys a wealth of information not readily available elsewhere. Heavily dependent on these autobiographical narratives, the book represents an interesting interdisciplinary blend of biography, literary crit-

icism, history, and feminist reflections. A helpful epilogue chronicles the course of these aviators' lives beyond what is recorded in their journals and books. General; community college; undergraduate.—*M. H. Chaplin, Wellesley College*

WS-1172   TL540   92-42486 CIP
Brink, Randall. **Lost star: the search for Amelia Earhart.** W.W. Norton, 1994. 206p index ISBN 0-393-02683-3, $25.00

Lost Star is not just another biography of Earhart, but a focused investigation of her disappearance in the South Pacific and the circumstances of her last flight. After a serious and exhaustive investigative effort, and with the benefit of the 1980 Freedom of Information Act, Brink has located and brought to light several documents and photographs. These are included in the book, which present new evidence: Brink makes a plausible case for the possibility that Earhart disappeared while on an espionage mission for the US government, concealed as one of the last legs of her round-the-world flight at the equator. The book is briskly written, well argued, and although journalistic in style, carefully constructed. Because there is a great deal of evidence presented that is not available elsewhere and because Brink, a former airline captain, is able to comment with authority on the design and capabilities of the aircraft used by Earhart, the book presents a compelling, albeit circumstantial, collection of testimony, photographs, and correspondence that argues strongly for its thesis. Helpful index; but no bibliography, perhaps because so much of the story rests on recent, original research. All levels.—*M. H. Chaplin, Wellesley College*

WS-1173   Q130   93-23026 MARC
Byrne, Eileen M. **Women and science: the Snark Syndrome.** Falmer, 1993. 208p index afp ISBN 1-85000-654-7, $85.00; ISBN 1-85000-655-5 pbk, $27.00

Byrne has studied the underlying reasons for the underrepresentation of women in all but the biological sciences and in technology. Her work is based on a five-year policy research project at the University of Queensland's Department of Education, but it takes full note of studies and research done in Europe and North America. The title derives from Byrne's belief that by dint of constant repetition, groundless assertions are taken as established fact as suggested by Lewis Carroll's "The Hunting of the Snark": "Just the place for a Snark! I have said it thrice: What I tell you three times is true." The "Snark Syndrome" is "the assertion of an alleged truth or belief or practice as the basis for policy making or for educational practice ...." For example, one of the particular findings of the book is that there appears to be no valid research that demonstrates that the mere increase of female staff in a given discipline results in an increase in female students in that discipline, making same-sex role modeling an ineffectual policy for increasing the number of women entering science as a career. The book is clearly written, with full chapter references. An incisive contribution to the understanding of women in science, for educators, policy makers, and all interested in changing the situation. Community college; undergraduate through professional.—*M. H. Chaplin, Wellesley College*

WS-1174   QA13   92-21619 CIP
Clewell, Beatriz Chu. **Breaking the barriers: helping female and minority students succeed in mathematics and science,** by Beatriz Chu Clewell, Bernice Taylor Anderson, and Margaret E. Thorpe. Jossey-Bass, 1993. 333p bibl index afp ISBN 1-55542-482-1, $29.95

A comprehensive and well-organized guide to intervention programs to help female and minority students in grades 4 through 8 succeed in mathematics and the sciences. The book has three major parts: (1) a description of the barriers to participation of female and minority students in mathematics and the sciences, and how to break these barriers in the middle school years; (2) a thorough and thoughtful examination of the strategies, structure, and operation of intervention programs for these students; (3) a conceptual and descriptive plan for developing, managing, evaluating, and disseminating programs; and a valuable list of programs and the materials available that describe curriculum or implementation methods. The authors also provide a review of the literature and research on the reasons why women and minorities are poorly represented in mathematics, science, and engineering. A clearly written, well-documented book, unique in its purpose. Most helpful to professional educators, curriculum specialists, and policymakers.—*M. H. Chaplin, Wellesley College*

WS-1175 Q141 94-41059 CIP
Creative couples in the sciences, ed. by Helena M. Pycior, Nancy G. Slack, and Pnina G. Abir-Am. Rutgers, 1996. 369p bibl index ISBN 0-8135-2187-4, $50.00; ISBN 0-8135-2188-2 pbk, $18.95

A collection of biographic studies of two dozen creative couples in the natural and social sciences, this book has an explanatory introduction that previews the contents and explains its inclusion in a series of volumes devoted to the lives of women in science. However, each essay is about a marriage in which both partners were successful scientists, and often the male member of the marital team is treated in as much detail as his spouse: the issues that are raised concern creative couples, not the women scientists alone. Insofar as these diverse essays have a common theme, they attempt to redress the almost consistently unequal balance of public recognition awarded to the male and the female members of the scientific couple and to address the nature of collaboration, particularly when it is both public and private, in scientific creativity. Although there has been a spate of fairly recent books on the lives of creative couples, this one is the first to focus exclusively on scientists and, as such, it is an important and valuable contribution to the field. The style and success of the essays varies, but they are all informative and clearly written. Undergraduates through faculty.—*M. H. Chaplin, Wellesley College*

WS-1176 GN365.9 90-8762 CIP
Haraway, Donna J. **Simians, cyborgs, and women: the reinvention of nature.** Routledge, 1991. 287p bibl index ISBN 0-415-90386-6, $55.00; ISBN 0-415-90387-4, $16.95

Haraway's wide-ranging collection of essays brings feminist theory to bear on such topics as human nature, the study of the behavior and social lives of monkeys and apes, and the interaction of women's nature and machines. As a whole, the book is a valuable and significant addition to the recent scholarship that argues for the social construction of nature. Haraway is an acknowledged authority on the history of scientific research on primates, and the book is thorough and probing in its analysis of primate studies. It is also provocative and original in its discussion of words such as "gender," "nature," and "experience." All of the ten essays that make up its contents have been revised from previous publication, but they are organized in a sensible and coherent fashion. Excellent bibliography; adequate index; a brief but helpful introduction. It is not an easy book: the language and the style make it most appropriate for upper-level and graduate courses in women's studies, epistemology, and feminist political theory.—*M. H. Chaplin, Wellesley College*

WS-1177 Q130 90-55724 CIP
Harding, Sandra. **Whose science? whose knowledge?: thinking from women's lives. Cornell, 1991.** 319p index afp ISBN 0-8014-2513-1, $34.50; ISBN 0-8014-9746-9 pbk, $12.95

Harding has written an important book for both natural and social scientists who are willing to look not only at their own methodologies and epistemological assumptions, but who are concerned also about the interrelationship between science and knowledge, on the one hand, and the social and political order, on the other. This is an ambitious book. It covers a lot of territory, including (though not restricted to) feminist construction of science, feminist epistemology, science in the First and Third Worlds, how the women's movement benefits science, critiques of western science as a model for both the natural and social sciences, science and race, sexual orientation, and social action. Harding writes demanding books: this one is no exception, but she has clarified her own earlier thought as well as explored new territory, and it emerges as the best statement of feminist epistemology and science that this reviewer is aware of. It is certainly required reading for people in the field; however, most undergraduates will find it difficult going. Would be much improved by the addition of a comprehensive bibliography.—*M. H. Chaplin, Wellesley College*

WS-1178 TL716 CIP
Holden, Henry M. **Hovering: the history of the Whirly-Girls: international women helicopter pilots.** Black Hawk, 1994. 254p bibl index ISBN 1-879630-95-8 pbk, $19.95

Apart from a brief introduction to the history of helicopter development, Holden's book is a series of biographical sketches, divided on the basis of how the

women learned to fly and what their professional careers have been. Many of the women had to establish themselves in a world that has been traditionally male, not an easy task. These sketches illustrate how successful these women were in overcoming strong bias in both the military and civilian arenas. The stories should stimulate both women and men interested in careers in fixed- and rotary-wing aircraft. Many of the women's lives are extremely interesting, but the sketches are often so brief that they are unsatisfactory. Recommended for those interested in the history of the gradual inclusion of women in the world of aviation. General.—*F. W. Yow, emeritus, Kenyon College*

WS-1179 QC175 92-28013 CIP
Keller, Evelyn Fox. **Secrets of life, secrets of death: essays on language, gender and science.** Routledge, 1993 (c1992). 195p bibl index ISBN 0-415-90524-9, $49.95; ISBN 0-415-90525-7 pbk, $15.95

A collection of essays by writer Keller, who has already achieved preeminence via her distinguished biography of Barbara McClintock, *A Feeling for the Organism* (CH, Jul'84), and the new classic *Reflections on Gender and Science* (CH, Jun'85). The thinking that shaped these previous works emerges here, but there is also a more detailed and probing account of the various relationships attending between language and gender, language and science, and, both beneath and beyond, gender and science. But the constant theme of the book is the role that language plays in our representation of the physical world. Its interest, however, is not exclusively epistemological: science as a social construction is looked at in various essays as it manifests itself in its sociopolitical and material affects. Although well written and equipped with an explanatory map of its intellectual terrain (in the author's introduction), it is demanding and sometimes quite dense. But the book is well worth the effort required to read it, and has important things to say about the meaning of science. Should be read by anyone interested in these questions. Advanced undergraduate through professional.—*M. H. Chaplin, Wellesley College*

WS-1180 Q191 92-21131 CIP
McGrayne, Sharon Bertsch. **Nobel prize women in science: their lives, struggles, and momentous discoveries.** Carol Publishing Group, 1993. 419p index ISBN 1-55972-146-4, $26.95

McGrayne sketches the lives of all nine women who have won Nobel prizes in science and of six who almost won. The sketches provide basic information about families and education, and insights into the personalities, life styles, friends, and social factors. All the women were tough, dedicated, and determined, yet many were also kind, generous, and "mothering." Some married and survived because of supportive husbands and families; others remained single. Some developed their "femininity" and even sophisticated elegance, while others ignored social conventions and dressed as they wished. What unites them is their passion for science and their desire to know more despite wars, unavailability of jobs or research funds, and other challenges. The biographies are well written, easy to read, and make the women come alive. Yet, each biography is short and therefore does not provide much detail about the scientific work. Inevitably, the focus on the Nobel-winning research will give some readers the impression that scientists work self-consciously toward the big Prize, or that it is necessary to work 80-hour weeks to succeed in science. In earlier years it may have been necessary for women to work harder and under more difficult circumstances than did men (though this may be changing), and this may begin to explain why there are only nine women Nobelists in science. For general audiences curious about science.—*J. Maienschein, Arizona State University*

WS-1181 T174 93-9447 CIP
Morgall, Janine Marie. **Technology assessment: a feminist perspective.** Temple University, 1993. 249p bibl index afp ISBN 1-56639-090-7, $39.95; ISBN 1-56639-091-5 pbk, $18.95

Morgall has written an important book that provides an analysis of how technology assessment relates to women's lives. The subject matter is, therefore, the process of identifying and evaluating the impact of technological change on women—in the workplace and in reproductive roles and, to a lesser extent, on their lifestyles. The author begins with a discussion of the evolution, organization, methods, and problems of technology assessment, and then proceeds to review the feminist literature on women and technology and the feminist scholarship already existing on technology assessment. She concludes with two examples: technology assessment of women in the clerical sector, and her own research on family planning, abortion, and technology assessment. Her style is straightforward; the writing is clear, concrete, and direct. A work to read with profit by scholars of women's studies, technology assessment, sociology, history of technology and culture, and labor. Fine bibliography; helpful index. All levels.—*M. H. Chaplin, Wellesley College*

WS-1182   Q130   95-20896 Orig
Morse, Mary. **Women changing science: voices from a field in transition.** Insight Books, Plenum, 1995. 291p index ISBN 0-306-45081-X, $27.95

Morse's examination of women's scientific careers and impact on the scientific enterprise is based on responses from both male and female scientists to inquiries posted on the Internet, 21 interviews with selected women, and extensive reading in the secondary literature. The anonymous responses and interviews are the heart of the book and offer a fascinating, sometimes stinging, often incisive analysis of science in the US today. Morse's commentary is well informed and well written. She gives a concise overview of feminist criticism of science, discusses women's experiences in scientific education and as career scientists, considers the possible effect of women on scientific styles and problems, and offers some recommendations for change. However, she stops short of confrontation with the central dilemma exposed by her research: as women enter the sciences in greater numbers and demand change to accommodate their needs and talents, the traditional infrastructure is already threatened by radical change as funding is reduced and social priorities shift. Morse's proposal that scientists seek other than traditional academic careers fails to address the complexity of the problem. Nevertheless, the book is well worth reading for its unique collection of individual perspectives from women in science. General readers, undergraduates.—*M. L. Meldrum, University of California, Los Angeles*

WS-1183   Q130   90-40018 CIP
The Outer circle: women in the scientific community, ed. by Harriet Zuckerman, Jonathan R. Cole, and John T. Bruer. W.W. Norton, 1991. 351p bibl index ISBN 0-393-02773-2, $24.95

This important sociological study of the recent history, participation, and rate of productivity of women (and men) in the scientific community is valuable not only because it presents new findings about the place of women in science, but also because it serves as a useful overview of recent scholarship in this field and illuminates about gender issues in general and our conceptual understanding of science. It has a distinguished list of contributors, and any of the essays would be valuable reading for an introductory course in women's studies or any studies on women in science. There is an excellent bibliography and a fine index; all of the essays are accessible to the general readers. The concluding essay breaks new ground in our understanding of why women publish approximately half as much as their male colleagues. The book belongs in every serious academic library.—*M. H. Chaplin, Wellesley College*

WS-1184   QB36   83-5290 CIP
Payne-Gaposchkin, Cecilia. **Cecilia Payne-Gaposchkin: an autobiography and other recollections,** ed. by Katherine Haramundanis. 2nd ed. Cambridge, 1996. 277p index ISBN 0-521-48390-5 pbk, $19.95

This new edition (1st ed., 1984) of Haramundanis's collection will be a very welcome addition to any library. Payne-Gaposchkin, one of the most important astronomers of the 20th century, is brought to life by a series of introductions and by her own words. Noted astronomer and author Virginia Trimble introduces the reader to Payne-Gaposchkin through a comparison with other women astronomers of her generation and more recent scientists. Contemporary Jesse Greenstein frames the scientific context of Payne-Gaposchkin's life and work, as well as adding personal recollections. Noted science historian Peggy Kidwell recounts the main events of Payne-Gaposchkin's life and career, while daughter Haramundanis gives a personal recollection of her mother and family. The bulk of the book is Payne-Gaposchkin's autobiography, "The Dyer's Hand," which explains her path to becoming an astronomer, the obstacles in her way, and how she integrated her roles as astronomer, woman, wife, and mother. She also gives the reader an important look at the Harvard College Observatory during the early and middle

part of this century. A must read for all astronomy enthusiasts and students, and highly recommended for all women interested in science.—*K. Larsen, Central Connecticut State University*

WS-1185   Q130   90-48085 CIP
Phillips, Patricia. **The scientific lady: a social history of women's scientific interests, 1520-1918.** St. Martin's, 1990. 279p bibl index ISBN 0-312-05685-0, $35.00

Phillips's book is a well-written and well-researched project. Its detailed review of women and the development of British science complements Margaret Alic's *Hypatia's Heritage* (CH, Mar'87). Drawn from unique primary sources, Phillips's discussions of hitherto unknown women in science and in overlooked formal and informal educational settings, media, and scientific associations are important contributions. Phillips's insistence on using the modern word "science" rather than the historically accurate "natural philosophy," while expanding the subjects covered (mathematics and accounting as well as the traditional empirical fields), inappropriately negates the classism, sexism, and conflict present in early and current scientific work. Phillips selected nice (and, as a result, too few) illustrations. This work is unfortunately not connected to current scholarship in history or theory of science or women's studies. Accessible to undergraduates.—*J. L. Croissant, Rensselaer Polytechnic Institution*

WS-1186   Orig
Rayman, Paula. **Pathways for women in the sciences,** by Paula Rayman and Annabelle Brett. Wellesley College Center for Research on Women, Wellesley College, 106 Central St., Wellesley, MA 02181, 1993. 177p (Wellesley report, part 1) bibl pbk $20.00

Rayman and Brett present here the final report of the first two years of the Pathways Project, a study designed to investigate factors that influence women of Wellesley College to pursue undergraduate studies in science and enter graduate programs and careers in science. The authors provide background information on the underrepresentation of women in science and a brief review of the literature on women and science. The project research focuses on two groups of women: a cohort of students, the Class of 1995, are followed through their first two undergraduate years to identify factors and key decision points that relate to choosing a major in science or math; and alumnae who majored in science or math from 1983 to 1991 are surveyed to identify factors that affect retention of women in those fields. The Pathways research indicates that interest in pursuing science or mathematics is developed before the college years; few women enter science if they have not shown prior interest, and thus women are not gained but lost from science by events during their college years. This on-going project involves a much needed longitudinal study of a cohort of women and helps identify events in their college careers that may affect their choice of major. Upper-division undergraduate through faculty.—*E. D. Kennedy, Albion College*

WS-1187   Q130   94-1883 CIP
Rose, Hilary. **Love, power and knowledge: towards a feminist transformation of the sciences.** Indiana, 1994. 326p bibl index ISBN 0-253-35046-8, $45.00; ISBN 0-253-20907-2 pbk, $18.95

Rose looks simultaneously back at her own substantial contributions to British critical science studies and forward to engage future feminists' critiques of contemporary science. She begins by discussing academic feminism and continues by outlining realist and postmodernist debates within feminist science theory. She reviews gendered ideologies of science and the struggles for the admission of women into science academies (such as Britain's Royal Society, founded in 1609) and analyzes female Nobelists and the problematics of "merit" in science. Rose also concisely overviews feminist critiques of contemporary biomedicine, and feminist science fiction. She unfortunately reasserts dualisms between realism and postmodernism, and she inadvertently frames gender as a matter of women and science. The book's disconnection from the mainstream of science studies neglects the contributions of new generations of feminists. Nonetheless Rose's outline of feminism as bringing love to the power/knowledge nexus is an important challenge to theories of science and society. Recommended for science studies and women's studies programs.—*J. L. Croissant, Rensselaer Polytechnic Institute*

WS-1188   Q181   89-28903 CIP
Rosser, Sue V. **Female-friendly science: applying women's studies methods and theories to attract students.** Pergamon, 1990. 159p bibl indexes afp ISBN 0-08-037469-7, $32.50; ISBN 0-08-037470-0, $12.95

Rosser not only accomplishes the task suggested by her subtitle, she also provides a comprehensive overview of the current feminist critiques of science as compared with critiques from African-American, Marxist, and non-Western perspectives. It is a well-written, informed, and authoritative discussion of the content and teaching of science at the college and university level, the critiques of this curriculum and instruction, and the alternative ways of knowing and teaching science. There is a very detailed subject index (as well as an author index), a list of references, and four supplemental bibliographies arranged by subject (since many of the titles listed fit into more than one category, not all readers will find this divided listing helpful). Since a severe shortage of US-trained scientists is predicted for the mid-1990s, and women and minorities are the most likely source of replenishment, this book is both timely and admirably executed.—*M. H. Chaplin, Wellesley College*

WS-1189   Q130   92-56445 CIP
Shepherd, Linda Jean. **Lifting the veil: the feminine face of science.** Shambhala, 1993. 329p bibl index afp ISBN 0-87773-656-1 pbk, $14.00

Shepherd examines contemporary explicit and implicit values in science from a feminist and Jungian point of view. An experimental scientist with a doctorate in biochemistry from Pennsylvania State University and deeply embedded in Jungian psychology, Shepherd believes science needs to be transformed by the "feminine" principle. In her view, science, as it is currently practiced, is held captive by "masculine values," and needs to be released by qualities one associates with the feminine. Along with being objective, logical, risk-taking, and competitive, scientists should recognize the value of being subjective, nurturing, receptive, intuitive, and cooperative. Shepherd discusses the work of Carol Gilligan and Mary Field Belenky, et al., as it is relevant to her position, but only mentions major authors in the gender and science field (Evelyn Fox Keller, Sandra Harding, Ruth Bleier, Ruth Hubbard) so that her discussion is limited to the link among Jungian psychology, feminism, and science. She presents, in easily accessible prose, a strong case for that link. Good index and bibliography. General; undergraduate; graduate.—*M. H. Chaplin, Wellesley College*

WS-1190   Q149   94-25219 CIP
Sonnert, Gerhard. **Gender differences in science careers: the Project Access study,** by Gerhard Sonnert with Gerald Holton. Rutgers, 1995. 187p bibl index ISBN 0-8135-2174-2, $50.00

Sonnert and Holton have prepared an important and informative book among the many in recent years that have tried to explain why there are fewer women than men in scientific careers, and why among the few who persist in science, even fewer attain the highest ranks. This monograph is a product of a large-scale research project organized to investigate the career paths of the men and women identified as promising scientists, mathematicians, and engineers by virtue of having been awarded a postdoctoral fellowship from the National Science Foundation, the National Research Council, or the Bunting Institute of Radcliffe College. The study was both quantitative and qualitative, so that the book includes a great deal of empirical data as well as some of the findings of open-ended interviews. As such, it is an indispensable contribution to the sociological literature and of immense value to those interested in the sociology of gender, women in science, and the sociology of science. The conclusions of this study tend to confirm other similar ones, but this book makes a real contribution by its wealth of information and the wide variety of its data. Undergraduate through professional.—*M. H. Chaplin, Wellesley College*

WS-1191   Q130   95-8598 CIP
Sonnert, Gerhard. **Who succeeds in science?: the gender dimension,** by Gerhard Sonnert with Gerald Holton. Rutgers, 1995. 215p bibl index afp ISBN 0-8135-2219-6, $49.00; ISBN 0-8135-2220-X pbk, $16.95

Sonnert's book could be aptly subtitled "How to Succeed in Science" because, in many ways, it is a manual of strategies on how to work the established social

system of science. The bulk of the book concentrates on the narration of life histories of ten male and ten female scientists; five in each group have had successful scientific careers, and five have had successful careers, but not as academic scientists. Although the focus is on gender differences, the life stories of these scientists reveal similar obstacles and difficulties (a few of the women also faced overt or covert discrimination). The major difference between male and female scientific careers is that the men had to contend with only one time clock, their own, whereas women had the challenge of synchronizing three: the female biological clock, their career clock, and the spouse's career clock. There is an interesting brief chapter on the implications of this study for policy makers. Incomplete and not very helpful index. Sociologists of science, gender study academicians, and policy makers will find much here of value. General; undergraduate through professional.—*M. H. Chaplin, Wellesley College*

WS-1192   Q130   90-28894 CIP
Women in science: token women or gender equality?, ed. by Veronica Stolte-Heiskanen et al. Berg/International Social Science Council/Unesco, 1992 (c1991). 256p bibl index ISBN 0-85496-742-7, $59.50

These essays report on women's activity in science, technology, and medicine in 12 countries on the European continent in the 1980s. Viewing women as valuable national scientific and technological resources, each article describes the situation in one particular country, as well as identifying general trends, obstacles impeding women's work, and opportunities and programs that promote it in those countries. For many reasons the book is valuable to upper-division undergraduate through postdoctorate researchers in sociology, science and society studies, women's studies, the sciences, political science, and international relations. It covers Eastern European and formerly communist countries (Yugoslavia, Hungary, Bulgaria) and other countries (such as Greece and Turkey) about which little is known concerning women's participation in science. The articles are well written, generally well researched, frequently draw information from unpublished government documents and independent surveys, and contain detailed statistical information (often presented in tabular form). Many selections append valuable bibliographies that list numerous elusive non-English sources. Highly recommended for all academic libraries.—*M. E. Webb, St. Francis College*

◆ History of Science & Technology

WS-1193   R692   91-20826 CIP
Bonner, Thomas Neville. **To the ends of the earth: women's search for education in medicine.** Harvard, 1992. 232p bibl index afp ISBN 0-674-89303-4, $34.95

Bonner's excellent book provides a new dimension to the chronicle of 19th-century women's quest for medical education. Notwithstanding surface appearances of separate but equal access to American medical education by mid-century, women's medical training in the US often was limited to second-rate institutions. Bonner documents women's determination to secure university medical education on a par with the training then available to men. That determination took thousands to Switzerland and France, where women found entry into the university schools. (By contrast, German and English universities remained closed to women longer.) American and European women took advantage of the Continental opportunities; in fact, the procession of foreign women into the schools of Paris, Zurich, Bern, and Geneva formed, according to Bonner, the largest historical migration of women for postgraduate education. Their story speaks of single-mindedness in spite of the burdens imposed by travel, study in a second language, impecunity, and often less than welcoming surroundings; the Russian chapter is particularly interesting. Bonner offers biographical sketches and lively anecdotes that make the book extremely readable. Recommended for women's studies and history of science and medicine collections in public and academic libraries.—*J. P. Brickman, United States Merchant Marine Academy*

WS-1194   CC115   90-23399 CIP
The ceramic legacy of Anna O. Shepard, ed. by Ronald L. Bishop and Frederick W. Lange. University Press of Colorado, 1991. 473p bibl index afp ISBN 0-87081-195-9, $41.95

This volume makes an important contribution to the fields of archaeology, archaeometry, history of science, and women's studies. Anna Shepard pioneered the field of archaeological ceramic analysis and authored the influential *Ceramics for the Archaeologist* (1956). In this collection, her research is assessed for both its specific contribution to Mesoamerican and southwestern American archaeology and to the archaeology of other regions. It contains 16 articles written by leading scholars who were personal acquaintances and/or colleagues with whom Shepard conducted her research; other articles are written by scholars whose current research was influenced by her. Together, they provide a rich, historical background to past and present ceramic studies. Finally, several of the articles contain important theoretical and methodological discussions. There is an extensive bibliography. Although there are few illustrations, the articles stand on their own merit. An essential resource for specialists, advanced undergraduates, and graduate students in archaeology and archaeometry. Scholars with interests in the history of science and women's studies will find this book an important resource as it documents the challenges of interdisciplinary research and the contributions of women to science.—*R. P. Wright, New York University*

WS-1195   QH365   94-26485 CIP
Charles Darwin's *The origin of species*: new interdisciplinary essays, ed. by David Amigoni and Jeff Wallace. Manchester, 1995. (Dist. by St. Martin's) 211p bibl index ISBN 0-7190-4024-8, $49.95; ISBN 0-7190-4025-6 pbk, $19.95

These essays examine the influence of Charles Darwin's *Origin of Species* on Western culture and how social thinkers and economists have appropriated his scientific ideas. In the introduction, Wallace discusses Darwin's thought process in writing and revising *Origin*. In "Science of Female Inferiority," Fiona Erskine suggests Darwin's introduction of the term "sexual selection" reflected his belief that women were subordinate, apparently unaware that Darwin invoked sexual selection because he felt natural selection alone could not account for structural and functional variations. She carefully chooses passages in Darwin's published and unpublished work that she feels demonstrate Darwin's antifeminism. In an intriguing article, Kate Flint compares *Origin* to Charles Dickens's *Great Expectations*, finding that both are obsessed with origins, wealth, and identification of parenthood. Harriet Ritvo's essay, "Classification and Continuity," analyzes the connection between taxonomy and evolution. A discussion of Darwin's scientific ideas by an evolutionary biologist would have considerably strengthened the collection; thus, it is strictly for academics in the humanities and social sciences. General readers will find it difficult, and biologists will be puzzled by some of its claims.—*J. S. Schwartz, CUNY College of Staten Island*

WS-1196   QH81   95-48024 CIP
Coming through the swamp: the nature writings of Gene Stratton Porter, ed. with introd. by Sydney Landon Plum. Utah, 1996. 172p bibl afp ISBN 0-87480-497-3, $55.00; ISBN 0-87480-498-1 pbk, $19.95

Indiana-born Gene[eva] Stratton-Porter (1863-1924) was a writer, photographer, and naturalist. The author of more than a dozen novels published between 1904 and 1927, she was perhaps best known for *A Girl of The Limberlost*, published in 1909. She began publishing articles on birds in 1900 and also published half a dozen nonfiction works about birds and nature, of which one, *Moths of the Limberlost* (1912), was reprinted four times between 1914 and 1926. Stratton-Potter also wrote a number of articles concerning birds and the out-of-doors, together with some poetry. At least four of her novels were produced by a movie company she incorporated in 1921. Editor Plum points out that many of Stratton-Porter's writings were efforts to look at nature through the eyes of particularly sensitive and observant children. Plum provides a useful introduction to Stratton-Porter's work, 12 excerpts (principally of her nature writing), a chronology of Stratton-Porter's life, and a comprehensive bibliography of her writings and of biographical and critical studies about her. A sampling of Stratton-Porter's black-and-white photos embellish this slim volume. A very useful introduction to the life and work of a largely forgotten author whose useful work was highly regarded by such contemporary critics as Theodore Roosevelt and William Lyon Phelps.—*K. B. Sterling, formerly, Pace University*

WS-1198   TL540   CIP
Holden, Henry M. **Her mentor was an albatross: the autobiography of pioneer pilot Harriet Quimby.** Black Hawk, 1993. 157p bibl index ISBN 1-879630-05-2, $17.95

An "autobiography" of Harriet Quimby, the first US woman to earn a pilot's license, to fly a monoplane, and to fly the English Channel, written from the point of view of the protagonist herself, by journalist and photographer Holden, who had access to her files. Virtually unknown until 1991 when the US Post Office issued a stamp in her honor, Quimby (born in 1875) lost her life participating at a Boston Air Meet on July 1, 1912, when she crashed with her airplane. This is the first book-length biography of her life and accomplishments, and Holden has made careful and extensive use of the written record, including many articles that Quimby wrote about herself. Focusing on her pioneering achievements as a woman and a pilot, Holden celebrates both. The book would be especially interesting to high school students and college undergraduates interested in the ways that women have broken through conventional barriers. The technical details of the design and features of the first airplanes are well explained for the general reader. Index of names. General; community college; undergraduate.—*M. H. Chaplin, Wellesley College*

WS-1199   TL139   93-42989 CIP
Jaros, Dean. **Heroes without legacies: American airwomen, 1912-1944.** University Press of Colorado, 1993. 265p bibl index afp ISBN 0-87081-312-9, $24.95

Although many Americans might recall the name of Amelia Earhart, especially after recent, speculative publicity surrounding her last flight in 1937, the role of women in US aviation remains largely unappreciated. Jaros's book not only serves as a reminder of the active role of women in the evolution of flight but also, and primarily, stands as an analytical study of journalistic and scholarly coverage of the subject itself. The first chapter summarizes the leading figures and their exploits; the seven remaining chapters examine contemporaneous coverage of their activities, the role of the Women Airforce Service Pilots (WASPs) who served mainly as ferry pilots during WW II, and critiques of relevant aspects of the history of women in US aviation. Jaros notes that the novelty of flight and the drama of WW II account for much of the attention given to women between 1912 and 1944. The lack of attention in the postwar years was apparently related to the tenor of the era, in which women were seen more favorably in traditional family roles. Recent interest in formal recognition for the WASPs has refocused attention on women and sparked commendable interest in publicizing both past and present activities. A thoughtful analysis. Graduate; faculty.—*R. E. Bilstein, University of Houston—Clear Lake*

WS-1200   Q130   90-50964 CIP
Mozans, H.J. **Woman in science: with an introductory chapter on woman's long struggle for things of the mind.** Notre Dame, 1991. 452p bibl index ISBN 0-268-01946-0 pbk, $14.95

Mozans (pseudonym for the Reverend John A. Zahn, C.S.C.) produced in *Woman in Science* a comprehensive survey of the role of women in intellectual society from ancient Greece up until the turn of the 20th century. His book is well written, easy to read, and only occasionally sounds as if it were published in 1913, the date of the original edition. The major thesis of this book—that women have not made greater contributions to science because of societal constraints, rather than because of inherent biological limitations (e.g.,smaller brains, lesser muscle mass, frailer stature)—was derived from J.S. Mill, but clearly it needed reiteration in the early part of this century, and recent feminist scholarship has had to examine this issue again today. Although Mozans vigorously champions the scientific potential of women, he nonetheless reveals a somewhat patronizing attitude, when he points out that educated women make intellectually sympathetic companions for their husbands. The most valuable part of the book is the long introductory chapter on women's struggle for intellectual liberation—the later chapters on women in science have been superseded by more recent scholarship. Brief bibliography of historical works cited. All levels of readers.—*M. H. Chaplin, Wellesley College*

WS-1201   QD22   94-43517 CIP
Quinn, Susan. **Marie Curie: a life.** Simon & Schuster, 1995. 509p bibl index ISBN 0-671-67542-7, $30.00

Quinn has written the first biography of Marie Curie that draws upon her own journal, written during the year after her husband died and only opened to researchers in 1990. Using this journal, as well as personal correspondence and conversations with family members and others who knew her intimately, Quinn presents a picture of Marie Curie that emphasizes scientific rigor, her exceptional abilities, and her dedication to work noted in other biographies of her. In addition, Quinn shows how Curie's passionate attachment to knowledge also manifested itself in passionate attachments to people. A significant section of the book describes her affair with a married colleague, a relationship that clearly helped her to recover from the devastating effect of her husband's premature death but also reveals her complexity and emotional needs. This fine and important biography does an excellent job of explaining both the significance of Marie Curie's scientific work and how she experienced herself, her husband, her colleagues, and the larger scientific community. For all levels of readers.—*M. H. Chaplin, Wellesley College*

WS-1202   TL540   93-14785 CIP
Rich, Doris L. **Queen Bess: daredevil aviator.** Smithsonian Institution Press, 1993. 153p bibl index afp ISBN 1-56098-265-9, $18.95

Despite her fame as one of the most fascinating figures in US aviation during the 1920s, the full story of Bessie Coleman's life and flying career has remained tantalizingly vague. In this short but pleasantly written and informative biography, Rich has performed an admirable service by preparing what is sure to be the definitive study of a remarkable young African American woman. Born in 1892 in Atlanta, Texas, Coleman came from a family that was poor in income and education, but rich in ambition. An attractive, ambitious, and free-spirited person keen on making a mark in life, she eventually moved to Chicago. She managed to get to France, earned a pilot's license there in 1921, returned to the US, and became a well-known figure in the air-show circuit until a fatal flying accident in 1926. Rich has done an outstanding job of tracking down will-of-the-wisp sources, including interviews and African American journals of the era, correcting the misinformation and rumors about an exceptional woman's unusual career.—*R. E. Bilstein, University of Houston—Clear Lake*

WS-1203   RG137   91-33682 CIP
Riddle, John M. **Contraception and abortion from the ancient world to the Renaissance.** Harvard, 1992. 245p bibl index afp ISBN 0-674-16875-5, $39.95

In this impressive historical detective work, Riddle discovers a wealth of ancient folk recipes that allowed women to control their reproduction. Discounting standard explanations of infanticide, famine, epidemics, sexual restraint, and the rhythm method to account for the demographic fluctuations from antiquity through the Middle Ages, the author argues persuasively that herbal contraceptives and abortifacients successfully curbed births. Riddle's central question asks how this panoply of knowledge became buried. How did knowledge become transmuted? Riddle asserts that once medical education became lodged in universities—by the 12th and 13th centuries—medical "knowledge" became severed from folk medicine. He speculates that with the onslaught of syphilis, women who understood effective herbal contraception may have withheld that information from their daughters for fear that sexual freedom would become a death warrant. Once the chain of knowledge was broken, even when the Renaissance sparked a revival of interest in classical medical texts, medical translators misread, misconstrued, and misconveyed reproduction recipes, leaving historians to assume that ancient contraceptives and abortifacients were ineffective. Riddle demonstrates consummate mastery of the ancient and early modern medical record. His impeccable scholarship will impress students of the subject. Graduate; faculty; professional.—*J. P. Brickman, United States Merchant Marine Academy*

WS-1204   QP81   88-24521 CIP
Russett, Cynthia Eagle. **Sexual science: the Victorian construction of womanhood.** Harvard, 1991. 245p index afp ISBN 0-674-80290-X, $25.00

Sexual Science is not so much about science as about how the Victorian world used science to justify an image of womanhood that viewed women as infe-

rior, both mentally and physically. Organizing her examination under four rubrics of 19th-century scientific thought—biogenetic law; sexual selection with its corollary, the greater variability of the male; the conservation of energy and the correlation of force; and (in social thought) the physiological division of labor—Russett presents a wealth of material in a clear, readable, and informative fashion. Much of her material can be found elsewhere, but she has done an admirable job of bringing it together, and this is a book that can be enjoyed by the general reader as well as by students of women's history, history of science, and gender studies. There are excellent notes and a good index, but no general bibliography.—*M. H. Chaplin, Wellesley College*

WS-1205   QP81   92-45026 CIP
Schiebinger, Londa. **Nature's body: gender in the making of modern science.** Beacon Press, 1993. 289p bibl index ISBN 0-8070-8900-1, $25.00

Schiebinger has written a fascinating account of how gender actively molded 18th-century science, particularly natural history. Proceeding from a historical situation in which the European scientists who wrote about nature were almost exclusively male, Schiebinger shows how they created for themselves a peculiar vision of nature in which Linnaeus's classification of plants was built on unarticulated notions of gender; his decision to name *mammals* as such (although he might equally well have chosen a characteristic of that class common to both sexes, such as hair, three ear-bones, or a four-chambered heart); and the "natural" division of humans into races based on a secondary sexual characteristic (the beard). Her book thus adds to the growing body of literature that makes explicit the social and political gender basis of much of modern science: how the nomenclature, the choice of problems to study, and the methodologies used were provided by men who, for the most part, saw women as a sexual subset whose chief function was to be reproductive. A carefully and extensively researched, well and clearly written book, with a full bibliography and index. For those working in general studies and in the history and sociology of science. General; community college; undergraduate through faculty.—*M. H. Chaplin, Wellesley College*

WS-1206   Q130   90-39668 CIP
Science and sensibility: gender and scientific enquiry, 1780-1945, ed. by Marina Benjamin. B. Blackwell, 1991. 295p index ISBN 0-631-16649-1, $42.95

This collection of essays centers around women's relationship with science over a period of nearly two centuries (1780-1945), and a substantive introductory essay by editor Benjamin. A scholarly, interdisciplinary, and innovative addition to the growing literature on women and science, it attempts to present, in some detail, three topics: the lives of three women practitioners of science, gender representation in science, and science and feminism. This is clearly a large order, and although each of the articles is rich and informative, the collection is less successful in establishing their interrelationship, partially because of limitations of space. Each article has its own useful bibliography, but there is no general bibliography, although there is a comprehensive index. Because there are nine authors, stylistic qualities vary, but the general tone is scholarly, detailed, and authoritative. An important book for academics interested in women's studies, women and science, feminist thought, and the history of science.—*M. H. Chaplin, Wellesley College*

WS-1207   QK21   95-12736 CIP
Shteir, Ann B. **Cultivating women, cultivating science: Flora's daughters and botany in England, 1760 to 1860.** Johns Hopkins, 1996. 301p bibl index afp ISBN 0-8018-5141-6, $29.95

Both science and science writing have a gendered history. Shteir chronicles a part of this history by focusing on women botanists and the cultural pressures on women who were interested in science during this hundred-year era. With substantial primary and secondary references, Shteir documents the shifts from women-centered, home-based herbal (and verbal) botanical tradition of the early 1700s to botany as "polite culture" in the late 1700s, in which it was appropriate for women to study to improve themselves as mothers, to the "professionalization" of botany around 1830 (which excluded women). The year 1760 marked the spread of the Linnaean classification system, a system that, in some ways, made botany accessible to many people. Because the Linnaean system puts sexuality and reproduction as central, the study of botany created cultural tensions about women, gender, and sexuality. Not only does this book provide fascinating insights into the lives of women botanists ("Flora's Daughters"), it also cogently analyzes the development of botany and the construction of gender in the 1700s and 1800s. For students of gender and science, history of science, and nature writing. Upper-division undergraduates, graduate students, and faculty.—*G. E. Stratton, Rhodes College*

WS-1208　　　　　　TL540　　　　　　93-9468 CIP
Ware, Susan. **Still missing: Amelia Earhart and the search for modern feminism.** W.W. Norton, 1993. 304p index ISBN 0-393-03551-4, $22.00

Ware's book is ostensibly a biography of Amelia Earhart, but is even more an examination of the social and cultural life of North America in the 1920s and 1930s, with a focus on the history of women during this period. Thus, Ware devotes a whole chapter to the topic "Popular Heroines/Popular Culture," summarizing the achievements of female movie stars, athletes, journalists, artists, and politicians in these two decades, noting their similarities (commitment to work over domesticity, homogeneity in terms of race, class, and religious background—white, middle-class, and Protestant—and, at least publicly, heterosexual). Amelia Earhart is portrayed as a pivotal figure in the development of modern feminism. Ware singles out for extended attention those aspects of her life and career that symbolized the new opportunities for women and that made her such a powerful role model. The book is easy reading, and although it does not have a bibliography, it is well researched, with extensive notes and a good index. The book's title is multiple in meaning: Earhart is still considered missing because (1) her remains have never been found; (2) her place in modern US history has been neglected; (3) her public career contributed to US feminism; and (4) the opportunities and equality she sought for women have yet to be found. All levels.—*M. H. Chaplin, Wellesley College*

◆ Biology

WS-1209　　　　　　SB470x　　　　　　92-53850 Orig
Bisgrove, Richard. **The gardens of Gertrude Jekyll.** Little, Brown, 1992. 192p index ISBN 0-316-09657-1, $45.00

Bisgrove provides an informative account of the motivating forces involved in the work of Jekyll and her important contributions to good garden planting throughout the world. The book is good companion work to Sally Festing's *Gertrude Jekyll* (CH, Nov'92); both works have been produced in time for the 150th anniversary of the birth of this woman who revolutionized the art of gardening. Bisgrove provides an excellent account of the selected best of Jekyll's planting plans, until now unpublished, and demonstrates that her ideas are relevant and fresh even for the present day. These are well expressed in both the text and in more than 100 full-color photographs and 45 watercolor planting plans, with full annotation. The text gives complete accounting of the plant materials, using both common and scientific names of a broad variety of materials for gardeners, horticulturists, and landscape architects interested in implementing the Jekyll style, so appropriate and adaptable for today's gardens—small or large. Appendixes include "Zone Ratings" and "List of Plans." Will appeal to a wide range of readers interested in gardening, landscape design, and the role of women in society. For every library with a gardening collection. All levels.—*K. T. Settlemyer, Lock Haven University of Pennsylvania*

WS-1210　　　　　　QH430　　　　　　92-10074 CIP
The Dynamic genome: Barbara McClintock's ideas in the century of genetics, ed. by Nina Fedoroff and David Botstein. Cold Spring Harbor Laboratory, 1992. 422p indexes ISBN 0-87969-422-X, $65.00

A tribute to McClintock, whose life (1902-92) almost spanned the history of genetics. Several of her published papers, including her 1983 Nobel lecture, are included, but reference should be made to *The Discovery and Characterization of Transposable Elements: The Collected Papers of Barbara McClintock* (CH, May'88) for a complete collection. In addition, the book under review

contains contributed review papers from many scientists who have discovered transposition in other organisms; reminiscences from colleagues; and papers from other scientists involved in aspects of genetics that McClintock pioneered. The book is similar in format and intent to *Phage and the Origins of Molecular Biology*, ed. by John Cairns, Gunther S. Stent, and James D. Watson (expanded ed., 1992, dedicated to Max Delbruck). The book's pagination is sometimes confusing; pages in contributed papers are numbered sequentially, but inserts of the McClintock papers have only the page numbers from their original publication. McClintock's work illustrates the power of description (cytogenetics) leading to experimentation, then a closer look at the chromosomal structure, and finally, formulation of new hypotheses to be tested. Valuable for senior undergraduates, and exciting reading for all interested in the history and intellectual methods of science. Advanced undergraduate through professional.—*M. L. Gilbert, Florida Southern College*

WS-1211　　　　　　SB470x　　　　　　Orig
Festing, Sally. **Gertrude Jekyll.** Viking, 1992 (c1991). 323p bibl index ISBN 0-670-82788-6, $25.00

Festing provides interesting insights to a woman far ahead of her time who should serve as an inspiration to all readers. Gertrude Jekyll was a master of many talents—superb artist and landscape painter, embroiderer, wood and metal worker, prolific writer, photographer, craftswoman, businesswoman, plantswoman, gardener, landscape architect, and designer. In her later years, her interests were intertwined and produced the sensitivity of design and craftsmanship embodied in her landscape work. Festing reveals many of the interactions with the people who surrounded and influenced Jekyll. She helps to dispel some of the myths and the distorted public impressions of the woman, and through biographical information, reveals "the contradictions of a single woman who overcame entrenched social and professional mores." The 47 black-and-white photographs, along with a number of line drawings, complement the interesting account of this remarkable woman. Includes full bibliographic citations for material quoted in the text and a select bibliography. Will appeal to a wide range of readers interested in gardening, landscape design, biography, and the role of women in society. A desirable addition to every library.—*K. T. Settlemyer, Lock Haven University of Pennsylvania*

WS-1212　　　　　　QL31　　　　　　93-22948 CIP
Galdikas, Biruté M.F. **Reflections of Eden: my years with the orangutans of Borneo.** Little, Brown, 1995. 408p ISBN 0-316-30181-7, $24.95

The orangutan is a unique animal: the only great ape in Asia (it lives today only on the Indonesian islands of Sumatra and Borneo, although in past times its range extended into central China). It is also the only higher primate to live nearly asocially: females remain with their offspring for many years, but adults of either sex seldom spend much time together. Thus, they are especially difficult to study, for the observer usually sees a single individual in a dense jungle, and that one orang may be trying to avoid detection. The longest semicontinuous field study of these apes has been carried out since 1971 by Galdikas, one of three women whose career in primatology was sponsored by the late Louis Leakey. She has concentrated equally on the study of wild orangs and on the rehabilitation and reintroduction of ex-captives, combined with efforts at conservation of their environment. Unfortunately, this book blends these scientific endeavors with a bit too much autobiography of her early years, leaving one wishing for more on the life of the orangs. Galdikas writes well, but she is far from generous to her colleagues. Despite her efforts, the orangutan remains more mysterious than its African cousins, the gorillas and chimpanzees. General; undergraduate through faculty.—*E. Delson, CUNY Herbert H. Lehman College*

WS-1213　　　　　　QL31.G58　　　　　　90-36974 CIP
Goodall, Jane. **Through a window: my thirty years with the chimpanzees of Gombe.** Houghton Mifflin, 1990. 268p index ISBN 0-395-50081-8, $21.95

Every college library and most public libraries should probably have a copy of this important and controversial book because it is likely that for many years it will remain the authoritative source for the nonspecialist in at least three areas: the behavior of wild chimpanzees, the autobiography of Jane Goodall's mature years, and a powerful statement for the animal rights movement regarding captive apes. The book also serves as a companion volume to Goodall's more technical *Chimpanzees of Gombe: Patterns of Behavior* (CH, Dec'86) and will assist undergraduates in visualizing the behavior patterns and accumulated data sets in that reference volume. Topics covered include infant and maternal behavior, social and sexual behavior of both males and females, and detailed accounts of dominance relations between the animals. Cognitive behavior and evolutionary strategies are briefly discussed, but memorable biographies of specific chimpanzees make up the bulk of the book. The autobiographical chapters on Goodall as a mature scientist are an important addition to studies of women ethologists, most of which concentrate on women in their younger years. Libraries should resist the attempts to label this book as "anti-science" because of its strong animal rights attitude, as these attitudes are taken very seriously by the public. Black-and-white and color photographs; useful index and appendixes on the care and conservation of apes. All levels of readers.—*T. C. Williams, Swarthmore College*

WS-1214   QK31   92-3664 MARC
Hellander, Martha E. **The wild gardener: the life and selected writings of Eloise Butler.** North Star Press of St. Cloud, 1992. 192p bibl index ISBN 0-87839-064-2 pbk, $19.95

Eloise Butler (1851-1933) was a science teacher and botanist best known for establishing The Wild Botanic Garden in Minneapolis, Minnesota. Part 1 of Hellander's account is a lovingly researched and written biography of a woman who defied conventional roles by pursuing a career in the male-dominated science of field botany. The second half is a selection of Butler's own writings, including brief native plant portraits and other short essays regarding the development of The Wild Garden. Eloise Butler's name may now be added to the growing list of largely unacknowledged American women naturalists of the late 18th and early 19th centuries, some of whom were documented in Marcia M. Bonta's *Women in the Field* (CH, Nov'91). Replete with very detailed chapter notes and an equally detailed index, Hellaner's handsome book is well illustrated with historic photographs and pen-and-ink drawings. Recommended for Midwestern libraries with a natural history specialty and for addition to history of American science and historic women's studies collections. General; undergraduate.—*G. D. Dreyer, Connecticut College*

WS-1215   QH428   94-44222 CIP
Keller, Evelyn Fox. **Refiguring life: metaphors of twentieth-century biology.** Columbia, 1995. 134p bibl index afp ISBN 0-231-10204-6, $20.00

The subtitle of Keller's book is a succinct description of these three essays, originally given at the University of California, Irvine, as part of the Wellek Library Lecture Series. These lectures address the biological discourse of gene action, the gene as the shaper and mover of life, and, finally, the transformation of the concept of the body itself by machines (most notably but not exclusively the computer). Throughout, Keller emphasizes that the guiding metaphors are both derived from and contribute to the biological processes being studied and the tools with which they are studied. It is not just that language shapes thought and research; the research and the creation of new technologies also shape and create new language and, in so doing, create new ways to experience and understand the body. This book does an excellent job of making manifest the close interaction between science and humanities and showing that the one is not embedded in the other, but that they are mutually interactive forces. Fine index. Recommended for all college and university libraries. Upper-division undergraduate through professional.—*M. H. Chaplin, Wellesley College*

WS-1216   QH31   92-39795 CIP
McCay, Mary A. **Rachel Carson.** Twayne, 1993. 122p (Twayne's United States authors series, 619) bibl index afp ISBN 0-8057-3988-2, $21.95

Although Carson gained fame for her thoughtful and evocative books about the sea, it was *Silent Spring* (1962), her extensively researched indictment of pesticide contamination that made her name synonymous with the beginning of the environmental movement. McCay's short, but detailed, biography of Carson includes the frustrations and challenges she met as a female scientist prior to WW II and afterward. Carson was an interpretive writer and McCay describes her books of "mythic proportion" and also her descriptions of wildlife refuges, bat radar, and others. As early as 1941, Carson described humans upsetting the bal-

ance of nature, and the final third of McCay's book describes Carson's research for *Silent Spring* and the conflict and controversy involved in the writing, publication, and aftermath. The book begins with a chronology of Carson's life, but inexplicably, a potentially useful bibliography is not arranged chronologically. Although McCay places Carson in the context of other naturalist authors, she does not fully recognize how much Carson's fame lives on today, or the fact that she still comes under attack from the pesticide companies that tried to suppress her book—a testimony to her remarkable foresight and influence. General; undergraduate; faculty; pre-professional; professional.—*J. Burger, Rutgers, The State University of New Jersey*

WS-1217   QL26   90-48043 CIP
Montgomery, Sy. **Walking with the great apes: Jane Goodall, Dian Fossey, Biruté Galdikas.** Houghton Mifflin, 1991. 280p bibl ISBN 0-395-51597-1, $19.95

Montgomery presents Dian Fossey, Jane Goodall, and Biruté Galdikas as models of empowered women revealing truths of primate behavior and striving to preserve our three closest relatives. This journalistic account provides titillating details of the women's private lives but is not reliable as a source of information on the animals. There are several black-and-white photographs and suggested reading, but no references or index. The book describes the lives of the three women, their relationships with Louis Leakey, with each other, and with the scientific establishment. Science libraries will find the work disappointing as it glorifies a mystic, shamanist view of primatology and is strongly anti-science. Both undergraduate and graduate libraries with an interest in the history, sociology, and anthropology of science may find the book useful as well as entertaining. The racist (black Africans are unfeeling savages, whites are compassionate) and sexist (only women are sensitive, patient observers) stereotypes suggest caution in use by unsophisticated readers. The books by Fossey (*Gorillas in the Mist*, CH, Dec'83) and Goodall (especially *Through a Window*, CH, Apr'91) are much superior. Advanced undergraduates and up.—*T. C. Williams, Swarthmore College*

WS-1218   QH26   92-22562 CIP
Norwood, Vera. **Made from this earth: American women and nature.** North Carolina, 1993. 368p bibl index afp ISBN 0-8078-2062-8, $37.50; ISBN 0-8078-4396-2 pbk, $17.95

Norwood's book defies easy categorization as it is simultaneously a history of US women who have written about or otherwise contributed to the knowledge of the natural world and a discussion of the role of women and women's understanding of the nature of ecology. It is an excellent book: informative, clearly written, accompanied by appropriate and helpful illustrations, and provided with a comprehensive bibliography and index. Although it covers a lot of territory—the contribution of women botanists in the early 1800s, 19th-century women illustrators of botanical subjects, landscape gardeners and ornithological photographers, and 20th-century environmental and animal researchers, with a thoughtful concluding chapter on ecofeminism—it avoids the superficial. Norwood has done a superb job of combining the narrative history of women naturalists with a reflective account of the role that women's values have played in this history. Both readable and scholarly it is the only available study that gathers together in coherent fashion this part of US history heretofore neglected. All levels.—*M. H. Chaplin, Wellesley College*

WS-1219   QP81   93-39793 CIP
Pool, Robert. **Eve's rib: the biological roots of sex differences.** Crown, 1994. 308p index ISBN 0-517-59298-3, $22.00

A reasonable, balanced, layperson's introduction to the biological (genetic and hormonal) component of average sex differences in abilities and behavior. Throughout, Pool cites work by specific researchers (most sex-difference investigators are women); his endnotes refer to text pages, not to numbers in the text. Topics include differences in spatial and verbal ability; hormonal and chromosomal effects on fetal development and on later behavior; experimental studies on other mammals; sexual orientation; sex differences in brain anatomy and lateralization; androgyny; and evolutionary roots of human sex differences. Pool also considers social, political, and educational implications of the nature/nurture battle and of the recognition of both biological and social input into average sex differences. He stresses that sex differences, whatever their source, are averages, that there is great individual variation and overlap between the sexes, that individuals should not be lumped together because of their sex, and that because of individual and average sex differences, teaching methods should be flexible. Pool writes well, knows his science, and deals with this controversial topic clearly and honestly. Though he feels biological factors must be recognized, he is not a biological determinist (e.g., "for most tasks, a woman's estrogen level will probably have less effect than what she ate for lunch"). The clear presentation, lack of technical terms, and thorough documentation make the book suitable for all levels, advanced high school through graduate school.—*E. B. Hazard, Bemidji State University*

WS-1220   QL31   95-40153 CIP
Poole, Joyce. **Coming of age with elephants: a memoir.** Hyperion, NY, 1996. 288p index ISBN 0-7868-6095-2, $24.95

Poole provides a wonderful look at both her development as a person and a scientist and the behavior of African elephants. In particular, she, along with Cynthia Moss, first discovered that male African elephants went through *musth* (an intoxicated state related to mating) as do Indian elephants. She provides an interesting account of both the person doing the science and the science. Poole's contributions are broadly important in understanding not only elephant behavior, but also behavior in general. She provides excellent descriptions of these contributions; readers will find them lucid and often fun to read. In addition, we see Poole's struggle to establish herself as a scientist and to deal with balancing a personal life with rigorous fieldwork. Readers will see the problems of sexism and resistance that many women face when working in male-dominated fields. She also raises important conservation and ethical issues regarding population control of elephants, sport hunting, and the difficult problems faced when questions of management arise. Readers will enjoy this well-written book on several levels: as biography, as science, and at times as both humor and tragedy. General; undergraduates; graduates.—*D. W. Kitchen, Humboldt State University*

WS-1221   HQ1154   92-36338 CIP
Rosser, Sue V. **Biology & feminism: a dynamic interaction.** Twayne, 1992. 191p index afp ISBN 0-8057-9770-X, $26.95; ISBN 0-8057-9755-6 pbk, $14.95

Rosser's excellent overview of the current status of women in science is a comprehensive review of feminist theories and of critiques of science as it has developed since the 19th century. The book, clearly written and readily accessible to anyone, provides much data to support Rosser's claim that the modern scientific method, purported to be objective and value free, is rooted in male values. These assumptions will come as no surprise to anyone who has been following recent discussions by Sandra G. Harding (*The Science Question in Feminism*, CH, Dec'86), Ruth Bleier, (*Science and Gender: A Critique of Biology and its Theories on Women*, CH, Oct'84), and Ruth Hubbard (in *Women Look at Biology Looking at Women*, ed. by R. Hubbard et al., CH, Mar'80) to mention only a few. Rosser is thoughtful and original in her essay on transforming the biology curriculum, and she has provided an extremely useful bibliographic essay by Faye Chadwell that speaks to science in general, not just to biology. A helpful, informed, and valuable book, of particular interest to those wanting to teach less gender-biased biology. Undergraduate through professional.—*M. H. Chaplin, Wellesley College*

WS-1222   QL737   92-56785 CIP
Small, Meredith F. **Female choices: sexual behavior of female primates.** Cornell, 1993. 245p bibl index afp ISBN 0-8014-2654-5, $26.95

Small provides an engaging and provocative account of female primate sexuality and mating strategies. Using sociobiological and feminist frameworks, she illustrates how female primates are sexual agents in decision-making processes that may ultimately affect their reproductive success. Small discusses the evolution of sexual reproduction and differences between male and female reproductive strategies. She then introduces the primate order and provides information on the female primate's life cycle. Historical and theoretical aspects of sexual selection theory and female choice are also presented, and Small makes it clear that the scientific community is currently changing its views on female sexual agency. She goes on to examine patterns of sexual behavior and mate selection in female primates; she suggests that females exhibit a great deal of variability in mate choice and that they seek novelty and variety in their sex lives. Humans are the focus of the final and perhaps most controversial chapter. Here Small

discusses how the human pair-bond evolved through reciprocity based on the need to raise highly dependent offspring, but that this pair-bond is in constant jeopardy due to both male and female desire for sexual variety. Small does an admirable job of describing difficult evolutionary principles. Highlighting each chapter is a pertinent drawing done by the author's sister. In addition, there are eight photographs of various nonhuman primates and a selective bibliography. Recommended for anyone with an interest in this topic. General through faculty.—*N. Krusko, Beloit College*

WS-1223   QH442   91-48168 MARC
Spallone, Pat. **Generation games: genetic engineering and the future for our lives.** Temple University, 1992. 343p bibl index ISBN 0-87722-966-X, $44.95; ISBN 0-87722-967-8 pbk, $16.95

Spallone examines biotechnology as it impacts developing nations, the environment, and women. She finds very little good in biotechnology; this stems from her broader opposition to the approach of Western culture to solving problems. She views the large, multinational corporations of the industrialized nations as seeking to exploit the environment, the Third World, and women as a result of their tendency to promote expensive technological solutions to problems, rather than less expensive solutions that are environmentally and culturally more acceptable. In 10 chapters, Spallone addresses the spectrum of current and future uses of biotechnology. After an introductory chapter, she examines two current uses of biotechnology, and then addresses issues of risk assessment, biotechnology and developing nations, patenting life, vaccines, diagnosis of genetic diseases, reproductive engineering, and biological warfare. Spallone spends little time explaining genetic engineering, although she does refer the reader to ample further reading. Some of her explanations simplify to the point of being misleading. This book will be persuasive to those who share the author's perspective on science and technology, but even those with opposing perspectives will find her discussions thought provoking. General; undergraduate.—*R. Seelke, University of Wisconsin-Superior*

WS-1224   QH506   94-48044 CIP
Spanier, Bonnie B. **Im/partial science: gender ideology in molecular biology.** Indiana, 1995. 207p index afp ISBN 0-253-32892-6, $29.95; ISBN 0-253-20968-4 pbk, $14.95

As a molecular biologist and women's studies director, Spanier's expertise and awareness of these two fields converge in her knowledgeable discussion of the formal representations of molecular biology and their inherent gender ideology. As both a "critic and friend" of molecular biology, she brings "healthy scientific skepticism" to her topic, which is of interest to scientist and nonscientist, feminist and nonfeminist. Using a feminist methodology, she questions the genderizing of nongendered beings in textbooks and other scientific writings by showing the cultural biases. She critiques the use of two sexes to describe molecular life by showing the limitations and distortions of this approach. This "biased construction of nature" creates false dichotomies in the centralized models used to study menstruation and DNA by separating the genetic from the nongenetic. Using numerous examples, Spanier discusses biologists' attempt to unify molecular biology through DNA technique and its negative consequence for cancer research. She concludes with a discussion on the need to acknowledge the political content of knowledge in molecular biology. Recommended for use in biology, general science, women's studies, and science and technology studies. Accessible to all.—*W. K. Bauchspies, Rensselaer Polytechnic Institute*

◆ Engineering & Technology

WS-1225   British CIP
Carter, Ruth. **Women in engineering: a good place to be?,** by Ruth Carter and Gill Kirkup. Macmillan, UK, 1990. (Dist. by New York University) 194p bibl indexes ISBN 0-333-45241-0, $35.00

As its title suggests, this book focuses on a specialized study of women engineers with a particular eye to the opportunities for women who have chosen this profession as well as the special problems created by their gender. Its methodology is based on interviews with 37 professional engineers in the US and the UK, ranging in age from 26 to 62. The book is intended for teachers of women's studies courses, feminists interested in issues relating to women and work, and engineering educators who are preparing women engineers. Although many books have been written about women and science, this is the first study to concentrate solely on women engineers, and as such, it makes a valuable contribution to an understanding of women's choices of nontraditional careers, the interplay of women's professional and personal lives, and the possible impact women may have on engineering and technology. The style is accessible to the general reader; the interview material is combined with an extensive knowledge of the literature on the subject; the bibliography is comprehensive and the index detailed.—*M. H. Chaplin, Wellesley College*

WS-1226   TA157   91-2050 CIP
McIlwee, Judith S. **Women in engineering: gender, power, and workplace culture,** by Judith S. McIlwee and J. Gregg Robinson. State University of New York, 1992. 248p bibl indexes ISBN 0-7914-0869-8, $54.50; ISBN 0-7914-0870-1 pbk, $17.95

McIlwee and Robinson have produced an important study of women in engineering and of the professional culture of engineers. They have an extensive knowledge of the theoretical work that has already been published on women engineers and scientists as well as the methodological expertise that permits them to undertake empirical research on the lives, work habits, family responsibilities, and attitudes of women in the engineering profession. The book focuses on the career patterns of women who entered engineering during the late 1970s and early 1980s (the first time they composed a significant minority). Although these women did well, they were not as successful as their male counterparts, and the authors contend that this is due to the interplay of gender role and the culture of engineering as expressed in its organizational and power structures. There are excellent tables, a subject and a name index, and a comprehensive bibliography. The book is clearly written, does a nice job of integrating theory and data, and is an extremely thoughtful and valuable book on this topic. Suitable for all levels of undergraduate readers, community-college level and up.—*M. H. Chaplin, Wellesley College*

WS-1227   T36   90-39330 MARC
Reconstructing Babylon: essays on women and technology, ed. by H. Patricia Hynes. Indiana, 1991. 206p index afp ISBN 0-253-32881-0, $35.00; ISBN 0-253-20622-7 pbk, $12.50

An excellent collection of essays, all relating to the topic of the impact of technology in the 20th century on women's health, specifically reproductive and biomedical technologies and environmental toxins. All four essay authors are established scholars in the field, and one of them, Gena Corea, is the author of the widely used and well-known text, *The Mother Machine: Reproductive Technologies from Artificial Insemination to Artificial Wombs* (CH, Oct'85). The level of discourse is high, well informed, and oriented toward changing social policy. Each of the 13 articles has its own bibliography; there is no general bibliography for the work as a whole. It belongs in every college and university library as it is a valuable reference source for both the theoretical construct, centered on women's right to dignity and autonomy, and the actual practices in the international world of control over women's reproductive rights.—*M. H. Chaplin, Wellesley College*

WS-1228   HQ1190   93-49043 CIP
Stabile, Carol A. **Feminism and the technological fix.** Manchester, 1994. (Dist. by St. Martin's) 184p bibl index ISBN 0-7190-4274-7, $59.95; ISBN 0-7190-4275-5 pbk, $19.95

The project here is to clarify the sources of tension between modern feminist theory and the structure of a technological world. Stabile (communication, Univ. of Pittsburgh) addresses a fundamental source of this tension in the dichotomy of female/nature/irrationality and male/culture/rationality and in the dominance of this dichotomy in feminist thought. She offers the notion that feminist technophobia reveals itself in feminist theorizing that clearly views the feminine as superior to the masculine and clearly values feminine technophobia over masculine technomania. She proposes that such theorizing closes the door on the possibility of redefining reality in feminist discourses and argues that feminist science must develop along lines that incorporate multiple sources of knowledge and that put distance between feminist scholarship and the single-issue politics that have

dominated feminism thus far. Stabile's vision of feminism in the 21st century emphasizes investigation of real life, depoliticization of feminist theory, and critical attention both to the persistent tendency of social sciences to exclude race and gender as central components of academic inquiry and to socially responsible and politically active arguments that privilege women's lives rather than continue to debate the primacy of either gender and its manifestations. Upper-division undergraduate and graduate collections.—*D. Van Ausdale, University of Florida*

WS-1229   T36   92-42054 CIP
Stanley, Autumn. **Mothers and daughters of invention: notes for a revised history of technology.** Scarecrow, 1993. 1,116p bibl index afp ISBN 0-8108-2586-4, $97.50

Stanley has written a pioneering work. There no other history and book-length studies of women inventors, and relatively few secondary sources that list, discuss, or, in any way, note the contribution made by women to the field of technology. In addition to the detailed and lengthy index, and the comprehensive (124-page) bibliography, the book is full of biographical, historical, and technical information. Its greatest value is as a sourcebook for women's inventions and their overall contribution to technological development. It is, in this respect, an indispensable reference tool, treating five different areas of human endeavor in technology: agricultural and food-related technology; health/medicine and related technology; reproductive technologies; machines; and computers. Although the sheer scope of the topics means that most women inventors and their inventions are only briefly discussed, there are several interesting interpretive essays on, e.g., early agriculture, the history of medicine, and antifertility technology. Stanley makes her central point well: because women have made significant contributions to technology, we need to rethink our definition of that field. Community college; undergraduate through faculty.—*M. H. Chaplin, Wellesley College*

WS-1230   HM221   91-18539 CIP
Wajcman, Judy. **Feminism confronts technology.** Pennsylvania State, 1991. 184p bibl index afp ISBN 0-271-00801-6, $28.50; ISBN 0-271-00802-4 pbk, $13.95

In a step forward for feminist thinking, Wajcman (University of New South Wales) presents an important study outlining major themes in scholarship on technology. This book places the analytic category of gender squarely into the foundations of the sociology of technology, in chapters outlining feminist critiques of science and technology, scholarship on technologies of production, studies of reproductive and domestic technologies, and works on the built environment and on technology as masculine culture. In claiming that feminist criticisms of science cannot "simply be translated into a feminist perspective on technology," Wajcman neglects other recent trends in the sociology of science and technology (which make science and technology distinctions problematic) and inconsistently applies ideas about technology and science as social relations. Nonetheless, because it is concise, well-referenced, balanced, and a much needed new approach, the book is important for upper-division undergraduates in women's studies, sociology, and science and technology studies programs.—*J. L. Croissant, Rensselaer Polytechnic Institute*

WS-1231   T36   94-15248 CIP
Women and technology, ed. by Urs E. Gattiker. Walter de Gruyter, 1994. 298p (Technological innovation and human resources, 4) bibl indexes afp ISBN 3-11-014307-0, $120.00

A collection of articles reflecting a multidisciplinary approach to key issues in the emergent field of women and technology, this book is well edited, well informed, and thoughtfully organized. It is particularly valuable because many of its findings correct and place in a larger context the earlier, well-known, and oft-quoted studies that emphasize almost exclusively the negative effects on women of the introduction of technology in the workplace. Although the articles differ in both their theoretical stance and their findings, several are more sanguine: one study, for example, shows that gender differences in network use disappear when the contextual factors are accounted for; and another concludes that empowerment for women will actually be helped with computer-mediated communication technology. The editor has written a helpful introduction and concluding summary; there are good indexes and many excellent bibliographies. An indispensable collection for scholars, organizational researchers, and public-policy decision makers. Undergraduate through professional.—*M. H. Chaplin, Wellesley College*

◆ Health Sciences

WS-1232 RA778 94-25289 CIP
Ammer, Christine. **The new A to Z of women's health: a concise encyclopedia.** 3rd ed. Facts on File, 1995. 562p index afp ISBN 0-8160-3121-5, $40.00

This third edition (rev. ed., 1991; lst ed., CH, Oct'83) of a very useful ready reference book for general readers has clear black-and-white drawings (e.g., breast self-examination) scattered throughout, many careful *see also* and *see under* cross references, charts (e.g., basal body temperature), boxed lists (daily calcium needs, principal vitamins, ovarian cancer stages, etc.), principal entries subject index (Appendix A), addresses (Appendix B), and even an extensive detailed index. The entries tend to be quite lengthy, considering the book's dictionary format, and certainly not focus exclusively on female issues (see, for example, patients' rights, impotence, chemotherapy, infertility, AIDS, male contraceptives, anabolic steroids, and varicose veins). There are new entries on alternative medicine, HIV, gene therapy, bone marrow transplants, cosmetic surgery, prenatal tests, Alzheimer's disease, uterine monitoring, Raynaud's syndrome, scleroderma, and more. Very highly recommended for all academic libraries. All levels.—*E. R. Paterson, SUNY College at Cortland*

WS-1233 RA418 93-18788 CIP
Angel, Ronald J. **Painful inheritance: health and the new generation of fatherless families,** by Ronald J. Angel and Jacqueline L. Angel. Wisconsin, 1994 (c1993). 264p bibl index ISBN 0-299-13960-3, $52.00; ISBN 0-299-13964-6 pbk, $19.95

This scholarly and thorough review of research largely from 1964 to 1990 includes many articles written or coauthored by Angel and Angel on single mothers, particularly poor unwed women and their children. The Angels raise concerns and attempt to answer very timely and challenging questions about the effects of race, Hispanic ethnicity, poverty, and father absence on the physical and mental health of minority women, children, and grandchildren. The authors carefully define the working poor, the underclass, the episodically and/or transitionally poor, and the chronically poor; gather comprehensive statistics; and suggest trends in births to adolescent mothers, immunizations, federal program cuts, state response by region, economic characteristics, and health status as reported by mothers compared to physicians' judgments. The new grandmotherhood discussion is perhaps the most interesting and unique in terms of multigenerational households, comorbidity of depression and chronic illness, stress, financial hardship, disability, drug abuse, and unemployment. A meticulously well referenced, readable, heavily footnoted, and nicely indexed book. Very highly recommended to graduate students, faculty, and professionals.—*E. R. Paterson, SUNY College at Cortland*

WS-1234 Orig
Berg, Frances M. **Health risks of weight loss.** [3rd ed.]. Healthy Weight Journal, 402 South 14th St., Hettinger, ND 58639, 1995. 157p bibl index ISBN 0-918532-44-2 pbk, $19.95

Frances Berg has done it again! This new edition (1st ed., CH, Nov'94) of *Health Risks of Weight Loss* is the single most valuable book available on the devastating impact of dieting. What makes it unique is that Berg looks at the scientific evidence in a field that is badly lacking in standards and controls. She brings clear and objective analysis to emotionally driven topics such as diet pills and gastric surgery. Every chapter is strong and packed with well-documented research. In the most stunning chapter, "Psychological Risks," Berg cites the well-known Minnesota experiment in human starvation, conducted in the mid 1940s, that showed clearly and unambiguously how harmful eating small amounts of food can be. No one would even suggest that these experiments be repeated because of ethical considerations. Yet, innocent dieters, often with the help of companies and products, replicate the results, which show, among many things, severe personality changes, food obsessions, and withdrawal from social activities. The chapter treating challenges for wellness and wholeness outlines the critical issues that need to be considered as work on decreasing the rates of obesity continues. Berg also argues that tolerance, respect, and appreciation of diversity—aspects of weight management that have been ignored or under-

rated—must be encouraged. Berg's strength is in consolidating research and communicating it in language accessible to public as well as professional audiences. Extensive and respectable bibliography. All levels.—*R. Kabatznick, Queens College, CUNY*

WS-1235 R692 94-12540 CIP
Briles, Judith. **The Briles report on women in healthcare: changing conflict to collaboration in a toxic workplace.** Jossey-Bass, 1994. 261p bibl index ISBN 1-55542-671-9, $25.00

Women in the healthcare workplace comprise a substantial number of working women in the US. Building upon a survey of women healthcare workers and previous works in this same area, Briles examines workplace "sabotage" among female healthcare workers. Using case studies in order to describe how and why sabotage occurs, she describes sabotaging behaviors in the chapter "Saboteurs, Bullies, Gossips and Other Toxic Co-workers." Drawing upon key management principles, including those aimed at managing conflict, strategies for managing and/or changing these destructive behaviors are proposed. These strategies are found in the chapters "Speak Up and Speak Out"; "Compete!"; "Eliminate Confrontophobia"; "Identify and Circulate the Unwritten Rules"; "Develop and Expand Teams"; "Cultivate Healthy Female Relationships"; "Banish Geisha Nursing (and Other Female Dominated Professions)"; "Abolish Sexual Harassment"; "Get a Mentor and Be a Mentor"; and "Embrace Change." Briles then concludes by emphasizing empowerment as the goal for women in the healthcare workplace. Recommended for professionals/practitioners, and upper-division and/or graduate students pursuing health care professions.—*M. Richardson, University of Washington*

WS-1236 RC81 94-37594 CIP
Consumer health USA: essential information from the federal health network, ed. by Alan M. Rees. Oryx, 1995. 543p indexes afp ISBN 0-89774-889-1, $49.50

This wonderful reference should be in every public and private library, especially in those with a focus on health concerns. It provides facts and information that all patients need in dealing with their medical or surgical needs. This impressive volume includes specific information on various ailments, so the patient and the care-provider should be able to understand their problems and to respond adequately to them. Discussed are AIDS and sexually transmitted diseases; allergies; blood diseases and disorders; cancer; contraception and reproduction; dental care and oral health; diabetes and other endocrine disorders; ear, nose, and throat disorders; eye disorders; gastrointestinal disorders; genetic disorders; heart disease and blood vessel disorders; infectious diseases; liver and gallbladder disorders; lung and respiratory disorders; mental and emotional health; neurological disorders; nutrition and weight loss; urogenital system disorders; women's health; and a miscellany that includes information on steroids, drugs and the brain, foot care, hyperthermia, pain control after surgery, nursing home care, and blood donations. Finally, there are addresses and phone numbers of health hotlines and state agencies on aging. A valuable reference work. General; professional.—*M. Kaufman, Westfield State College*

WS-1237 RA564 95-2401 CIP
Crook, Marion. **My body: women speak out about their health care.** Insight Books, Plenum, 1995. 304p bibl index ISBN 0-306-44943-9, $24.95

This book should be required reading for all medical students. Crook shares her invaluable community and public health nursing experiences, largely in Vancouver, northern Canada, and Washington State, and also wonderful, heartbreaking, and heartwarming family health care experiences of 54 diverse women aged 17 to 77. Reasonably organized, extremely readable, and nontechnical, this fine book is divided into 17 compact and concise chapters and then further subdivided into brief manageable sections. The author covers a range of topics and provides a good overview of such issues as the history of women doctors, the male model, quacks, alternative medicine, different needs during the life cycle, healing in different cultures, health information networks and systems, what women want from their doctors, why doctors do not provide health information, finding health information, and the next generation. There are many excerpts from interviews, quotations, and case studies shared throughout that clarify situations and make real the personal experiences of women. Excellent suggestions are offered and often specifically listed in outline form to help women improve their communication exchanges with physicians. All levels—*E. R. Paterson, SUNY College at Cortland*

WS-1238   R692   91-46383 CIP
Dakin, Theodora P. **A history of women's contributions to world health.** E. Mellen, 1991. 116p bibl indexes ISBN 0-7734-9624-6, $49.95

Dakin ably and concisely fulfills her goal to show that women throughout history have made enormous contributions to health care. No large number of women appear in any one period because of existing social, financial, political, legal, and gender barriers. The aggregate, however, documents that, despite multiple constraints, outstanding women emerged in all periods to become physicians, scientists, surgeons, nurses, and midwives, all of whom cared for people from birth to death. In the Middle Ages midwives held complete monopoly of women's care; men were barred by law from this specialty. Contributions covered many fields: anatomy, physiology, psychiatry, biochemistry, nutrition, and pharmacy. Along the way, Dakin provides an overview of medical history within the milieu characterizing each period. The content in this slim volume arouses the reader's interest and enthusiasm in pursuing more in-depth study. Recommended especially for those in the health professions, science, history, and women's studies.—*A. R. Davis, U.S. Public Health Service*

WS-1239   RA564   94-47498 CIP
Doyal, Lesley. **What makes women sick: gender and the political economy of health.** Rutgers, 1995. 280p bibl index ISBN 0-8135-2206-4, $50.00; ISBN 0-8135-2207-2 pbk, $15.95

Doyal's thoughtful compilation and insightful analysis of the status and measurement of women's health is prepared on a global perspective. Many statistics, facts and figures, and numerous comparisons of morbidity, mortality, and life expectancy rates are offered to contrast male and female, black and white, poor and rich, skilled and unskilled, developed and Third World, and different religious and cultural groups. Life expectancy for women in former communist eastern and central European countries has decreased by five to six years, but little data exists on these desocializing countries, so Doyal has concentrated on southern Asia, Africa, South America, Caribbean, Latin America, and the Pacific nations where heavy physical domestic labor, frequent childbearing, and undernutrition contribute to the chronic ill health of women. The most compelling parts of the book by far are the stories told by the women themselves from Third World and/or southern hemisphere countries, who face a high risk of dying in pregnancy or childbirth; reproductive deaths are an important indicator of the different health hazards that women face. Yet medical research and drug development continues to focus on men. Doyal ties together the economic, political, gender, and cultural issues that clearly show women to be at a distinct disadvantage in terms of their general well being and worth. Recommended, because of its global perspective, for university collections in public health, public policy, women's studies, and economics. Upper-division undergraduate through professional.—*E. R. Paterson, SUNY College at Cortland*

WS-1240   Can. CIP
Engel, June. **The complete breast book.** Key Porter Books, 1996. (Dist. by Firefly Books Ltd.) 274p bibl index ISBN 1-55013-748-4 pbk, $19.95

For reasons very personal to every woman, breast cancer or even a suspicion of it is a very traumatic experience. The premise of this concise, well-organized, well-written monograph is that "instead of reacting with terror it's better to know the facts." All aspects of breast cancer, ranging from the anatomy and physiology of the normal breast to alternative or unconventional therapies, are factually covered in an easy reading style in 20 relatively short chapters, but with enough detail. The writing is careful and consistent, so that at no time is the reader confronted with an unclear concept or medical term. There are no references given, but the number and credentials of the listed reviewers give authority. Highly recommended as one of the best books yet for any woman interested in breast cancer. The content is similar to but the style is different from *Cancer Sourcebook for Women* (CH, Jun'96) and the book is a good adjunct to *Breast Cancer: A Family Survival Guide* (CH, Nov'95). Directory of support and service organizations; selected reading list; glossary of medical terms. All levels.—*R. S. Kowalczyk, North Central Michigan College*

WS-1241   RC546   92-7113 CIP
Ettorre, Elizabeth. **Women and substance use.** Rutgers, 1993 (c1992). 204p bibl index ISBN 0-8135-1863-6, $37.00; ISBN 0-8135-1864-4 pbk, $15.00

Ettorre (sociology, Abo Akademi Univ., Finland) argues that most research in the substance field is insensitive to the needs of women, generally viewing them as a homogeneous category of stigmatized and marginalized addicts. She develops an alternative perspective that takes into consideration the experiences not of white, middle class Western males but of females of different races, cultures, classes, and sexual orientations. In so doing, she focuses on the substances of alcohol, minor tranquilizers, heroin, nicotine, and food. Although often providing valuable insights, Ettorre's critique of current explanations frequently appears flawed. For example, it would seem more plausible that Nestle's aggressive and effective marketing of infant formula in developing countries was an effort to increase its income rather than an attempt to undermine and devalue the role of women and women's bodies in the nurturing process. Ettorre suggests possible directions for a theory of substance use grounded in the experiences of women, with a diversity of useful ideas. Recommended for graduate libraries.—*D. J. Hanson, SUNY College at Potsdam*

WS-1242   RG103   95-32514 CIP
Evaluating women's health messages: a resource book, ed. by Louiselle Parrott and Celeste Michelle Condit. Sage Publications, CA, 1996. 445p index afp ISBN 0-7619-0056-X, $69.95; ISBN 0-7619-0057-8 pbk, $32.95

This book is unique in that it attempts to identify the gaps in both scientific and media health messages to women. There are six parts: historical, political, campaign agendas, fetal and maternal health, social support, and contemporary priorities. Chapters provide a critical summary of medical and/or social scientific research on the topic, and a descriptive and critical analysis of mass-mediated messages women receive about medical/scientific information. Thus, one may identify consistencies, inconsistencies, and gaps in the research, as well as incongruities in the translation of scientific literature to media messages. Topics include abortion, substance abuse, contraception, childbirth, prenatal care, reproductive and breast cancer, reproductive technology, menstrual health, and AIDS. An introductory chapter identifies major gaps in women's health, and a final chapter raises questions for future direction. Each chapter includes endnotes. There are biographical sketches of chapter authors. Appropriate for individuals interested in women's health issues, health care professionals, and those in public health, media, and journalism. Level: general; upper-division undergraduate through professional.—*M. Auterman, Augustana College (SD)*

WS-1243   RA564   92-49573 CIP
The Health of women: a global perspective, ed. by Marge Koblinsky, Judith Timyan, and Jill Gay. Westview, 1993. 291p index afp ISBN 0-8133-8500-8, $49.95; ISBN 0-8133-1608-1 pbk, $16.95

A work based on papers presented and discussions held at the 1991 National Council for International Health's Conference, "Women's Health: the Action Agenda." It covers such topics as female poverty, maternal morbidity/mortality, nutrition through the life cycle, reproductive-tract infections (mostly sexually transmitted diseases), family planning and contraceptive use, unsafe abortion, gender and morbidity/mortality, violence against women, mental health, inadequate access to quality care, and listening to poor and illiterate women speak about their bodies and needs. Written by anthropologists, epidemiologists, nutritionists, nurse-midwives, international public health specialists, policy advisers, and consultants, these essays are clearly for researchers and practitioners. The authors make many recommendations for health education programs and further research; they also provide invaluable international comparative statistics on gender differences in population, sexual crimes, domestic violence, prevalence of anemia, postpartum complications, etc. Extensive references and notes. Recommended especially for viewpoints from such areas as Southeast Asia, Africa, Central and South America, and the Caribbean. Graduate through professional.—*E. R. Paterson, SUNY College at Cortland*

WS-1244   HV1553   95-8958 CIP
Hooyman, Nancy R. **Feminist perspectives on family care: policies for gender justice,** by Nancy R. Hooyman and Judith Gonyea.

Sage Publications, CA, 1995. 418p (Family caregiver applications series, 6) bibl indexes afp ISBN 0-8039-5142-6, $55.00; ISBN 0-8039-5143-4 pbk, $25.95

Hooyman and Gonyea focus on the responsibility for caregiving of adult family members with chronic disabilities who require ongoing help with activities of daily living. The book begins with a brief overview of the feminist perspective and its advantages in analyzing the impact of family caregiving. Part 1 explores the impact of the changing US family structure, the changing economy and workforce, and changing health care needs and services, on families and women in particular. Part 2 discusses the social, political, and historical factors that affect both the nature and extent of caregiving. The invisible, unpredictable nature of care tasks helps frame the discussion of the burdens and benefits of caring. Part 3 provides a feminist critique of current policies and programs. The chapters in part 4 conclude with a feminist model for family care built on collective responsibility, gender equality, and family-responsive workplace intitiatives. Extensive bibliography. Particularly appropriate in the areas of family, gerontology, gender studies, and social work. Upper-division undergraduate through professional.—*M. Auterman, Augustana College (SD)*

WS-1245   RA418   94-37839 CIP

Hubbard, Ruth. **Profitable promises: essays on women, science and health.** Common Courage, 1995. 237p index ISBN 1-56751-041-8, $29.95; ISBN 1-56751-040-X pbk, $11.95

In this era of the human genome, Western society finds itself putting more and more credence in science, and particularly genetics, to explain and solve our problems. Bioethicists have long questioned the potential slippery slope of genetic research, manipulation, and its applications; fewer scientists have questioned their colleagues' activities. Hubbard (biology, Harvard) is one who has. These 16 essays, articles, book reviews, or lectures center on three general topics—genes, illness, and behavior; women, science, and power; and political understanding of science—which providing the organizing frameworks for the short, readable chapters. The overriding themes are a concern for the "medicalization and geneticization" of our lives and a request for responsibility in the scientific and technological communities. Hubbard promotes a sound public health philosophy by arguing against reductionistic methods for solving health problems. She instead encourages putting resources into understanding the massive social problems that lead to many current health problems. She also argues for a holistic interpretation of scientific findings, looking not only at "criminal" genes, for example, but the social, political, and environmental contexts in which criminal behavior occurs. Controversial, but appealing. General; undergraduate.—*M. A. Thompson, Saint Joseph College*

WS-1246   RA564   90-32946 CIP

Kane, Penny. **Women's health from womb to tomb.** St. Martin's, 1991. 209p bibl index ISBN 0-312-04635-9, $35.00

In this slim volume, Kane masterfully analyzes issues in women's health care from a comparative demographic viewpoint. In so doing, she consciously breaks the traditional boundaries of her subject by taking an international perspective, addressing women's entire life span (not just the reproductive years), and considering relevant differences in health concerns/treatment between the sexes. By comparing female and male patterns of illness prevention and improvements in health care and living conditions, she concludes that women and men have genuinely different patterns of health risk. Within this framework she explores such paradoxes as why women report more illness than men when, in fact, they are less vulnerable genetically and biologically. Many differences between the sexes arise from women's reproductive capacity as well as from their being statistically longer lived than men; they therefore require more health-related services over their lifetimes. By considering the larger social, biological, and cultural contexts of health care she is able to argue urgently that for women to get adequate health care and enjoy the old age they attain, the health-care establishment must realize they are not at risk for the same diseases as men. Through copious statistical data organized in tables, charts, figures, and a final thoughtful chapter, Kane allows readers to draw their own data-based conclusions about the invisibility of women's health issues and what is needed to get society to address them. Public and academic collections, lower-division undergraduate through graduate.—*D. J. Douglas, University of Wisconsin-Madison*

WS-1247   RA975   95-1123 CIP

Kauffman, Christopher J. **Ministry and meaning: a religious history of Catholic health care in the United States.** Crossroad, NY, 1995. 354p index ISBN 0-8245-1459-9, $29.95

Kauffman, a Roman Catholic professor of church history, generally succeeds in his two stated purposes: to sketch the historical development in the US of Catholic hospitals and to analyze the religious dimensions of the Catholic nursing experience. Essentially, this book best functions as a reference manual for persons interested in Roman Catholic institutional involvement in health care in the US: a Catholic health care history from its European origins to the mid-1990s. For persons interested in women's roles in American Catholicism, this is a rich resource; for those interested in the Catholic Church's institutional involvement in health care developments in the US, it is an equally rich resource. The Mayo brothers' clinical origins, for example, are described. For others, this will serve as the history of Catholic nursing in the US. The "meaning," interpretive aspect of the book is somewhat theologically clothed, e.g., comments like "the ecclesiology implicit in American Catholic health-care experience reflects the missionary-church dynamic: care givers and patients dwelling in the limit-situation of illness and forming a provisional community of faith." Faculty; professional.—*J. E. Allen, University of North Carolina at Chapel Hill*

WS-1248   RA564   92-12912 CIP

Mahowald, Mary Briody. **Women and children in health care: an unequal majority.** Oxford, 1993. 281p indexes afp ISBN 0-19-506346-5, $39.95

The concept of equality and its implementation for women and children in the health-care system are addressed in this very valuable and stimulating presentation. Mahowald, whose writings and research have addressed topics relevant to the conditions of women for over two decades, is a philosopher working in a clinical environment. From this perspective, based on case/care models of reasoning, she explores health issues that affect women and children. Her thesis is sharp, well thought out, and challenging, and covers the range of issues from sex roles and stereotyping in health care to abortion, fertility, fetal, newborn, and children's issues, the feminization of poverty, and the concept of the family's role in the kinds of health care women and children receive. These issues lie at the heart of many of the social controversies we are struggling with today. Stimulating reading for all those interested in women and children's health care issues. All levels.—*R. L. Jones, Pennsylvania State University, Hershey Medical Center*

WS-1249   RC889   95-35525 CIP

Marsh, Margaret. **The empty cradle: infertility in America from Colonial times to the present,** by Margaret Marsh and Wanda Ronner. Johns Hopkins, 1996. 326p bibl afp ISBN 0-8018-5228-5, $29.95

Marsh, a historian, and Ronner, a physician, are sisters who have here collaborated for the first time. The result of the two perspectives forms a comprehensive history of infertility in America, which should sweep away most of the myths so prevalent in popular thought. Infertility is not a new problem, nor is it proportionately any more of a problem than it was 200 years ago. Perhaps the major difference is the recognition that males are infertile as well as females, and that the ability to have an erection does not necessarily indicate fertility. Because of the emotions involved, physicians, particularly in the 19th century, resorted to invasive genital surgery on women, but for the most part their success rate was low. In spite of our greatly increased knowledge, the failure rate remains high. Interestingly, a small number of infertile couples in the past and even today suddenly get pregnant without any intervention. The book is a well-documented, comprehensive (including in vitro fertilization), understated rather than overstated commentary on a very human problem. General; upper-division undergraduates through professionals.—*B. Bullough, University of Southern California*

WS-1250   RA564   91-22711 CIP

Miles, Agnes. **Women, health and medicine.** Open University, 1991. 234p bibl indexes ISBN 0-335-09906-8, $75.00; ISBN 0-335-09905-X pbk, $27.00

Miles (sociology and social policy, University of Southhampton, UK) presents a broad view of many issues related to women as health care consumers and providers. This introductory work provides the foundation for study in a variety of topics described in seven independently constructed chapters. Chapters address the health and illness experiences of women, their interactions with health care providers, and their experiences as health care professionals. Although set primarily within the context of British society and health care, the text identifies research in the US and would be easily applicable to the American system of health care delivery. References are numerous and include classic medical sociology as well as recently published research. Occasional graphs highlight significant data within this easily readable volume. The information provided would be most useful to students of medical sociology and those with particular interest in the unique health experiences of women. Academic collections, lower-division undergraduate and up.—*M. P. Tarbox, Mount Mercy College*

WS-1251   RG580   94-42935 CIP
Mothers, babies, and cocaine: the role of toxins in development, ed. by Michael Lewis and Margaret Bendersky. L. Erlbaum, 1995. 397p bibl indexes afp ISBN 0-8058-1583-X, $79.95

In recent years there has been public awareness of the dangers inherent in and consequences of drug use during pregnancy; however not much of was it the consequence of scientific study. This work, although concentrating on a small subset of the overall problem, reveals the enormous difficulties confronting scientific study of such a problem. Two situations prominent among the many: women addictive to cocaine frequently use a variety of other drugs, e.g., alcohol, heroin, barbiturates (how does one separate the effects of cocaine from that of the other drugs?); after pregnancy, these women are likely to raise their children in an impoverished environment (how does one separate environmental effects from those brought on by cocaine use?). These and other aspects of the effects of cocaine use on child outcome, including methodological problems and human and animal study models, are examined in depth. Literature references are current. Overall, this is a good summary and overview of the knowledge in this area and the difficulties inherent in its gathering. Excellent in all respects. All levels.—*R. S. Kowalczyk, formerly, University of Michigan*

WS-1252   RA564.85   90-8383 CIP
Muller, Charlotte F. **Health care and gender.** Russell Sage Foundation, 1990. 258p indexes afp ISBN 0-87154-610-8, $34.95

Muller (director of health economics and professor at Mt. Sinai School of Medicine, who also teaches economics and sociology at the City University of New York Graduate School) examines different facets of the interaction of gender and health care, focusing on gender biases in relation to women. Chapters 1 and 2 discuss treatment issues and various aspects of health-care utilization by women. Working-age adults are the topic of Chapters 3 and 4, which explore financial concerns and the topic of women's increased need for health services. Chapter 5 focuses on the gender aspects of the health care needs of the elderly. The intricacies of federal/state programs are delineated in Chapter 6, providing statistics to validate many issues. Chapter 7 discusses reproductive care and the controversies surrounding this issue. The final chapter considers overall implications of gender in health care. Muller provides insights into gender issues and raises concerns that tend to remain unspoken. University and professional collections.—*J. B. Sherman, University of Arizona*

WS-1253   RG734   96-2445 CIP
Poppema, Suzanne T. **Why I am an abortion doctor,** by Suzanne T. Poppema with Mike Henderson. Prometheus Books, 1996. 266p index afp ISBN 1-57392-045-2, $25.95

Poppema introduces herself, provides clear, simple, and detailed descriptions of the daily operation of an abortion clinic, and comments throughout on political and social issues of feminism, patriarchy, violence against women, and the antichoice agenda. This family physician, wife, mother, teacher, speaker, and activist takes a bold stand in support of a woman's right to choose concerning her own body and specifically whether and how she will end a pregnancy. What is especially compelling is her strong reaffirmation of the important work done by her and her staff. Part of a chapter is devoted to her own decision to have an abortion; there are other chapters on Mifepristone or RU 486 as well as the much less known morning-after pill; there are three case studies in the appendix along with a consent form and survey. This is an extremely readable book despite the fact that few could relate personally to the author's early and steady academic suc-

cess from Catholic grade school to the University of New Hampshire and then Harvard Medical School. Highly recommended for all levels.—*E. R. Paterson, SUNY College at Cortland*

WS-1254   RA564   94-9745 CIP
Rosser, Sue V. **Women's health—missing from U.S. medicine.** Indiana, 1994. 213p bibl index afp ISBN 0-253-34991-5, $29.95; ISBN 0-253-20924-2 pbk, $14.95

Women's studies director and medical school professor Rosser very effectively critiques the male bias and clearly male-centeredness of clinical research and medical care in the US. Women are largely ignored in medical research, drug studies/trials, and in medical practice in other than heterosexually transmitted diseases, contraception, pregnancy, and child care issues. Rosser cites and discusses many excellent examples, including major heart disease studies and AIDS research. Medical school education has been especially resistant to change, despite growing numbers of female students. Racism, sexism, ageism, and homophobia are also examined in terms of medical practice, education, and research. The potential positive effects of having more women in medicine are outlined: they will focus on prevention, family, and older women and minorities and show concern for violence in the form of child and sexual abuse and incest. Rosser includes many statistics on women in medicine, and compares students to faculty. Each chapter is short, succinct, readable (with the possible exception of chapter 8 on feminist theory, difficult to comprehend), and well documented with anywhere from 50 to more than a hundred references; there is a selected bibliography on women and health. This fine critical analysis and thorough literature review of androcentrism in medicine is very highly recommended to all college, university, medical school, and medical research libraries. Upper-division undergraduate through professional.—*E. R. Paterson, SUNY College at Cortland*

WS-1255   Brit. CIP
Smyke, Patricia. **Women and health.** Zed Books, 1991. (Dist. by Humanities) 182p index ISBN 0-86232-982-5, $49.95; ISBN 0-86232-983-3 pbk, $15.95

Smyke has compiled an excellent, comprehensive, and readable review of the worldwide health status of women, particularly in developing nations. The author highlights statistical data from the UN Group on Women and Development report material. The volume addresses how the interrelated factors of economics, environment, culture, politics, and specific health disruptions influence the status of women and their health. Throughout the book women's compelling personal stories and excellent photographs support the book's goal to inspire advocacy and action toward improvement of the global health status of women. Appendixes offer specific suggestions for education with a useful resource list helpful for students in health or the social sciences. Although the book identifies many health problems of women and children, it does so in a positive, proactive way. Women's contributions to family, society, and national development are prized and heroically depicted. Recommended for undergraduate students in health care, health policy, public health, or women's studies. The book has general audience appeal also because of its important messages to women and policymakers alike.—*N. G. Snyder, University of Massachusetts*

WS-1256   RA778   89-36513 CIP
Spitzack, Carole. **Confessing excess: women and the politics of body reduction.** State University of New York, 1990. 200p bibl index ISBN 0-7914-0271-1, $44.50; ISBN 0-7914-0272-X, $14.95

Spitzack offers an interesting analysis of the components of dieting and health, ranging from cultural standards for female physical appearances, to body activities and the influences of others on one's body perception. The author examines all aspects of women's body reduction including motivational implications and the impact of personal relationships and the weight-reduction industry. The many variables of cultural intertwining are discussed as they relate to dieting and a life of thinness. The confessional metaphors evidenced in women's speech (temptation, accountability, deviance, and masochism) are also explored as are the dynamics of the dysfunctional family and romantic influences. Highly recommended for anyone interested in a sociocultural examination of weight control. A suitable addition to women's studies collections.—*P. H. Williams, William Paterson College of New Jersey*

WS-1257   R724   95-16274 CIP
Troubled bodies: critical perspectives on postmodernism, medical ethics, and the body, ed. by Paul A. Komesaroff. Duke University, 1996 (c1995). 241p index afp ISBN 0-8223-1676-5, $49.95; ISBN 0-8223-1688-9 pbk, $16.95

Editor Komesaroff argues that a new approach to medical ethics is needed. The traditional approach helped doctors analyze patient care issues from their own "scientific" view using the "agreed-upon" values of society. It was a paternalistic approach, which put the physician or the professional team in charge of making decisions that would maximize positive and minimize negative consequences for the patient. This approach fit the enlightenment beliefs that the advancement of science would bring a better life and the person best qualified to implement the ever-growing science of care was the expert doctor. Postmodernist philosophers have questioned the benign role of science and are less supportive of paternalism. They support the rights of individuals to make decisions about their own bodies. The contributors, all Australian scholars, discuss current ethical dilemmas, many of which relate to women's health care, and the writers uncover the lack of consensus not only among women but even among feminists. General; upper-division undergraduates through professionals.—*B. Bullough, University of Southern California*

WS-1258   R853   93-50549 CIP
Women and health research: ethical and legal issues of including women in clinical studies. v.1; v.2: Workshop and commissioned papers, ed. by Anna C. Mastroianni, Ruth Faden, and Daniel Federman. National Academy Press, 1994. 2v. 271, 247p index ISBN 0-309-04992-X, v.1, $34.95; ISBN 0-309-05040-5 pbk, v.2, $29.00

In 1992, the Committee on the Ethical and Legal Issues Relating to the Inclusion of Women in Clinical Studies, established by request of the National Institutes of Health, met to respond to public concern about underrepresentation of women, and racial and ethnic groups, in clinical studies. Volume 1 describes in detail the work of the Committee (16 professionals with backgrounds in such areas as clinical research, public health policy, behavioral sciences, and bioethics) who investigated drug development process; history of women's participation in clinical studies; scientific, legal, ethical, and social issues; and potential risks to women of childbearing age and their offspring. Volume 2 presents the workshop and commissioned papers by additional experts, who provided information to support the Committee's goals. Policies to include women in clinical studies were formulated in 1991. Committee recommendations support and direct the implementation of established policies, addressing study design, gender-specific differences, selection of study subjects, monitoring of policy implementation, and assurance of justice. Highly recommended for policy makers, researchers, ethicists, and health care professionals. Upper-division undergraduate through professional.—*A. R. Davis, Johns Hopkins University*

WS-1259   RA564   94-36836 CIP
Women's health care: a comprehensive handbook, ed. by Catherine Ingram Fogel and Nancy Fugate Woods. Sage Publications, CA, 1995. 744p bibl index afp ISBN 0-8039-7022-6, $89.95; ISBN 0-8039-7023-4 pbk, $54.95

Editors Fogel and Woods are well known in the areas of women's health and human sexuality. There are 27 contributors; most are recognized as authors whose writings provide comprehensive coverage of women's health care. Part 1 focuses on the connections between women's lives and women's health, including women in health occupations. Explored are sex differences in mortality, morbidity, use of health care, and factors influencing these differences. Various dimensions of health promotion are discussed using three age categories: young (menarche to 35 years), midlife, and older women (over 65). Part 2 explores women's experience as recipients of health care by examining sexism in health care, feminist theory and perspectives, well-woman assessment, and lesbian health care. Part 3 focuses on health promotion, including current theory and research, nutrition, exercise, fertility control, childbearing choices, mental health, and occupational health risks. Part 4 addresses a variety of common health problems: violence against women, high-risk childbearing, reproductive disorders, STDs, drug abuse, chronic illness, breast disorders, and reproductive technology. Undergraduate and graduate nursing students; professional nurses.—*M. Auterman, Augustana College (SD)*

WS-1260   RA778   91-12746 CIP
Women's health matters, ed. by Helen Roberts. Routledge, 1992. 200p indexes ISBN 0-415-06685-9, $69.95; ISBN 0-415-04891-5 pbk, $18.95

This scholarly and practical collection of essays contains contributions from female authors of different backgrounds. Studies take place in diverse locations of Glasgow, London, and Oxford and cover such varied issues as HIV, prostitutes, and intravenous drug use; midwifery; multiple births; breastfeeding; women and food; black West-Indian mothers and their children's health; and fatigue and morbidity. Because so little research is conducted by women about women and because women's health research often is not taken seriously nor readily funded, the authors share problems and make useful suggestions for futher study and funding. This assortment of contributions brings together researchers in nursing, midwifery, anthropology, epidemiology, sociology, and childbirth education and is therefore recommended for graduate-level social and health sciences collections, including those supporting women's studies courses and programs.—*E. R. Paterson, SUNY College at Cortland*

◆ Comparative & Historical Works

WS-1261   R722   93-31393 CIP
Allison, Mary Bruins. **Doctor Mary in Arabia: memoirs,** ed. by Sandra Shaw. Texas, 1994. 329p afp ISBN 0-292-70454-2, $42.50; ISBN 0-292-70456-9 pbk, $17.95

This fascinating book of memoirs is appropriate for any reader interested in medicine, the Mideast, or just plain adventure. Allison depicts graphically the medical practice of a dedicated woman physician, a missionary who handles more crises of every sort in one week than most of us experience in 10 years. Allison practiced medicine in Kuwait, Bahrain, Qatar, Oman, and India from 1934 to 1975. Her vignettes show a complex picture of the interaction of modern medical practices with the ancient mideastern political, social, and religious institutions of the area. She writes of daily medical emergencies whose resolutions—good or bad—are accepted by the people as the will of Allah. But she believes it is her faith in the Christian God that gives her the spiritual strength to continue in the face of ignorance and oppression. She struggles tirelessly with administrative problems, surgeries with no surgeon, epidemics, and women's health problems that are often due to the incredibly primitive treatment of women by those societies. Subtle themes, such as the competition between religions and the friction between medical personnel and evangelists, give body and depth to the overall picture. An excellent choice for anyone in health care or the social sciences, graduate or undergraduate, as well a general audience.—*D. J. Douglas, University of Wisconsin-Madison*

WS-1262   RA440   93-5822 CIP
Blustein, Bonnie Ellen. **Educating for health & prevention: a history of the Department of Community and Preventive Medicine of the (Woman's) Medical College of Pennsylvania.** Science History Publications/USA, 1993. 135p index ISBN 0-88135-184-9, $17.95; ISBN 0-88135-185-7 pbk, $11.95

In 1989, when Eddy Bresnitz became chair of the Department of Community and Preventive Medicine at the (Women's) Medical College of Pennsylvania, he commissioned Blustein to write this departmental history; a brave idea, well accomplished. In the 19th century, male physicians alloted to women physicians the job of disease prevention, not cure; to them it seemed woman's natural medical role. But social roles change, as do the goals of medical education. Throughout its history, the department was "trapped between the proverbial rock and a hard place: either medical education stressed cure rather than prevention (in which case the department was marginalized), or it stressed prevention in all fields (in which case the department was redundant)." Blustein tactfully includes departmental weaknesses as well as strengths. Her introduction places her work in the context of the history of preventive medicine, especially George Rosen's *Preventive Medicine in the United States, 1900-1975* (CH, Jul'76) (and its revision by Bonnie Bullough and George Rosen, *Preventive Medicine in the United States, 1900-1990*, CH, Jan'93), and Judith Walzer Leavitt, "Public Health and Preventive Medicine," in *The Education of American Physicians: Historical Essays*, ed. by Ronald Numbers (1980). Graduate; faculty; professional.—*T. P. Gariepy, Stonehill College*

WS-1263   Can. CIP
Comacchio, Cynthia R. **"Nations are built of babies": saving Ontario's mothers and children, 1900-1940.** McGill-Queen's, 1994 (c1993). 340p index afp ISBN 0-7735-0991-7, $44.95

Comacchio, a social historian who became interested in the scientific approach to child care while pregnant with her first child, addresses the role of maternal and parent education in improving the survival and health of infants and children. She traces the changes in the sociomedical definition of child welfare in Ontario from the late 1890s to the 1940s (prior to government health coverage). Discussion is clustered around four time periods: early 1990s, WW I, the interwar years, and the Great Depression. Her research reveals the complexity of factors that influenced the interrelationship between and among the professionals (medical, nursing, social work), society, state, and family. Specific topics explored include infant and childhood morbidity and mortality, heredity, maternal health, prenatal care, and delivery outcome; medicalization of parenting; regulation and regimentation of childhood and "habit training"; and strategies to promote favorable family response. Although the target of this historical review is maternal and child care in Ontario, the author identifies the parallels and occasional diversity of these trends in the remainder of Canada, Great Britain, France, and the US. A final chapter surveys outcomes in the 1940s. Figures and tables; nearly 90 pages of endnotes. Upper-division undergraduate through professional.—*M. Auterman, Augustana College (SD)*

WS-1264   RA564   93-32972 CIP
Finkler, Kaja. **Women in pain: gender and morbidity in Mexico.** Pennsylvania, 1994. 238p bibl index afp ISBN 0-8122-3243-7, $34.95; ISBN 0-8122-1527-3 pbk, $14.95

Finkler discusses the ways in which the lives of poor Mexican women are entwined with sickness and health. The book's concept is that of "life's lesions"— the bodily insults engendered by the adversities of existence, inimical social relationships, and unresolved tensions in the women's daily experiences. At the book's heart are the life histories of ten women drawn from a sample of 205 clinic patients with varied nonfatal symptomatologies. The life histories illustrate both the subjective nature of sickness and its embeddedness in material conditions and prevailing ideological currents. The sick women are compared with a sample of 54 healthy women from the same social strata and neighborhoods. Significantly, while most husbands of the healthy women hold stable jobs, most husbands of the sick women have transient sources of livelihood. The author posits that the more precarious economic resources of the latter households give rise to more adverse marital interactions, which in turn resonate on the wives' life lesions. Several theoretical chapters explore the connections between gender and sickness, and one deals with historical and contemporary perspectives on male-female relations and ideologies about women in Mexico. Upper-division undergraduate through professional.—*E. Wellin, University of Wisconsin—Milwaukee*

WS-1265   RJ102   92-34682 CIP
Klaus, Alisa. **Every child a lion: the origins of maternal and infant health policy in the United States and France, 1890-1920.** Cornell, 1993. 298p index afp ISBN 0-8014-2447-X, $36.95

Historian Klaus (Univ. of California, Santa Cruz) compares the efforts of France to decrease infant mortality with those of the US in the same era. Why France was chosen as a counterpart to the US is not explained, except that both countries were then almost simultaneously evolving, economically and politically, and both were strong military allies. The reader may assume from Klaus's analysis the following: In policies and efforts to prevent infant mortality, women were viewed primarily as mothers; women's rights were concerned with motherhood and child welfare and were best achieved through collective activism; the main source of activism was professional women; charitable activism bred professional activism, but also bureaucracy. The author shows that obstacles to women's and children's rights were, paradoxically, promoters of those rights: organized

religion, male-dominated politics, and lack of a sense of social responsibility by both males and females. According to this analysis, the greatest concern in child care was the single mother (no mention of the single father); social policy favored breast feeding and those who did so; and, infant mortality became an issue when population became an issue (national, class, cultural). A well-documented work, but no references, bibliography, or author index. Professional.—*V. L. Norman, University of North Dakota*

WS-1266   R141   92-49013 CIP
Practical medicine from Salerno to the Black Death, ed. by Luis García-Ballester et al. Cambridge, 1994. 402p index ISBN 0-521-43101-8, $69.95

In this outstanding collection of essays, noted medieval medicine scholars discuss the delineation and development of medicine during the critical period from the 11th century at Salerno until the mid-1300s. This period marked the transformation of medical education from the apprenticeship method to a university-based science, with its foundation in the classic writings of Hippocrates, Aristotle, Galen, Johannitius, Rhazes, and Avicenna, and the works of such contemporary medical writers as Guglielmo de Saliceto, Dino del Garbo, Lanfranco, and Guy de Chauliac. During this same period physicians, surgeons, and apothecaries, members of the "learned disciplines," refined the distinctions among them regarding scope of practice, and began to organize into fraternities and guilds to protect their livelihoods from those less well educated. One essay addresses the role of women practitioners. By the mid-14th century when the bubonic plague began to ravage the population of Europe, medicine and surgery were widely recognized as scientific disciplines, and medical education was firmly established in the great universities of Italy, Aragon, and France. Highly recommended. Graduate.—*A. R. Davis, Johns Hopkins University*

WS-1267   R154   94-66409 CIP
Rowland, Mary Canaga. **As long as life: the memoirs of a frontier woman doctor: Mary Canaga Rowland, 1873-1966,** ed. by F.A. Loomis. Storm Peak, 1994. 177p index ISBN 0-9641357-0-1 pbk, $11.95

This wonderful autobiography of a frontier woman doctor, Mary Canaga Rowland, demonstrates the difficulty an intelligent and educated woman had in entering and succeeding in what had once been only the domain of men. For 50 years, she served patients in the western states, always maintaining a sense of humor as well as concern for her fellow human beings. This book will interest medical historians and modern feminists as well as historians of the western states. General.—*M. Kaufman, Westfield State College*

WS-1268   R506   92-49007 CIP
Weiner, Dora B. **The citizen-patient in revolutionary and imperial Paris.** Johns Hopkins, 1993. 444p index afp ISBN 0-8018-4483-5, $48.50

Culminating decades of research, Weiner's book surveys medical reform and the politics of health care in Revolutionary and Napoleonic France. She eschews the famous "Paris hospital" and well-known developments in scientific medicine to focus instead on the "citizen patient" and efforts at national health care. In fine detail, the author traces the program for universal medical services initially sketched by the Poverty Committee of the National Assembly and the subsequent course of reform that variously affected nursing, midwives, pharmacy, medical students, hospitals, public health and hygiene, military medicine, and the creation of specialized facilities and treatments for the poor, the old, foundlings, the deaf, blind, and insane. Weiner successfully incorporates a previously invisible history of women into her larger story. By extending her scope to include the whole period, 1789-1815, she provides a more positive evaluation than previous accounts of medical reform in the French Revolution. Rooted in archival sources and handsomely illustrated, the book creates an evocative "you-are-there" quality for contemporary Paris. The 32-page bibliographic essay stands as a valuable guide to the history of medicine in the period. Given the great scholarly strengths of this book, its present-minded, normative element regarding debates over health care in democracies today seems unnecessary and out of place. Advanced undergraduate through faculty.—*J. McClellan III, Stevens Institute of Technology*

◆ Childbirth, Reproductive Health

WS-1269 HQ767 91-43021 CIP
Abortion, medicine, and the law, ed. by J. Douglas Butler and David F. Walbert. 4th ed.. Facts on File, 1992. 890p indexes afp ISBN 0-8160-2535-5, $65.00

Updating the third edition (CH, Feb'87), chapters in this work survey legal, medical, and ethical dimensions of abortion. The material on law covers state legislation, constitutional uncertainty, consequences of legal abortion, privacy (historical injustices against women remain), wrongful birth/life, fetal rights, and the world scene. A section on medicine covers prenatal development, personhood for embryos, RU486 (by developer Baulieu), availability of abortion, Alan Guttmacher on history, the abnormal fetus, fetal tissue research, and psychological aspects of unwanted pregnancy and abortion. The ethics section contains material on the rise and fall of the antiabortion movement in Congress (1973-83) by Senator Packwood; congressional action (1984-91); privacy (historically broader than previously believed); the ethics of abortion by Daniel Callahan, a Roman Catholic; fetal tissue transplants; and religion (a survey of pronouncements). Appendixes cover Dr. Everett Koop on health effects of abortion, fetal tissue research, a model Freedom of Choice bill, and Supreme Court pronouncements on Webster (Missouri) and Planned Parenthood of Southeast Pennsylvania. As the abortion debate "ranges even more heatedly," this volume will be of interest to a diverse readership. All libraries.—*H. O. Thompson, University of Pennsylvania*

WS-1270 RG652 95-5261 CIP
Borst, Charlotte G. **Catching babies: the professionalization of childbirth, 1870-1920.** Harvard, 1995. 254p index ISBN 0-674-10262-2, $39.95

Borst's book, based on her doctoral dissertation, provides a historically accurate and intimate look into the lives of immigrant midwives in four Wisconsin counties from 1870 to 1920. The blend of social science theory, with its emphasis on gender, social class, ethnicity and culture, and historical demography, affords the reader a rare opportunity to examine the move from midwife-attended to physician-attended childbirth in the US within the context of a particular community. Borst's emphasis throughout is what happened when midwives chose not to pursue midwifery as a professional role during the same era that physicians were pursuing professionalization. Each chapter highlights the reasons why midwives did not view themselves as professionals in spite of their formal training and their positive relationships with physicians. The author's understanding is that midwifery was viewed as a married woman's occupation and a neighborly act in the rural areas, as well as among the midwife entrepreneurs in the city. Well written, insightful, well documented, with 74 pages of endnotes and appendixes. An excellent work. All levels.—*J. E. Thompson, University of Pennsylvania*

WS-1271 Can. CIP
Burtch, Brian. **Trials of labour: the re-emergence of midwifery.** McGill-Queen's, 1994. 270p bibl index afp ISBN 0-7735-1141-5, $44.95; ISBN 0-7735-1143-1 pbk, $19.95

This book is part of a series sponsored by the Canadian Centre for Policy Alternatives to promote research on economic and social issues facing Canada. Burtch examines the history and reemergence of midwifery in Canada as a social movement (transformation). The strength of the book lies in the political, regulatory, and social analyses of factors that either contribute to or undermine the reemergence of community midwifery as a profession in Canada. Burtch's main premises are that campaigns against midwifery practice led to the near eradication of the lay midwife; that home birth, birth, and pregnancy have been redefined as "medical events" requiring supervision of physicians and use of technology; and that midwifery has been the subject of legal and state policies that work against it as a self-regulating profession. The book's weakness lies in trying to summarize centuries of midwifery practice and tradition along with the culture and customs of birth, using some incorrect interpretations and conclusions drawn from the selected data. Overall, the text is well written, insightful of Canadian midwifery, and supportive of the need for women to be actively involved in the choice of birth attendant and birth place. General; upper-division undergraduate through professional.—*J. E. Thompson, University of Pennsylvania*

WS-1272 RC280 95-36875 CIP
Cancer sourcebook for women: basic information about specific forms of cancer that affect women, featuring facts about breast cancer, cervical cancer, ovarian cancer..., ed. by Alan R. Cook and Peter D. Dresser. Omnigraphics, 1996. 524p (Health reference series, 10) bibl index afp ISBN 0-7808-0076-1, $80.00

The book's 49 chapters (made up of individual publications mostly from government sources such as the National Institutes of Health, Department of Health and Human Services, Centers for Disease Control, and the National Cancer Institute, but also from private sources such as the American Cancer Society and Y-Me) focus on various aspects of cancer of special concern to women. The 12 chapters of part 1 discuss different cancers, such as breast, cervical, uterine, ovarian, and vaginal. Part 2 (17 chapters) offers treatments, therapy, and coping; part 3 (nine chapters) presents prevention regimes, and part 4 (11 chapters) describes risk factors and current research. The availability under one cover of all these pertinent publications, grouped under cohesive headings, makes this certainly a most useful sourcebook. There is one shortcoming, however, in the introduction: the presentation of the basic aspects of cancer is inadequate. But, such a primer could serve as a unifying thread to put each chapter in a more comprehensible perspective for the intended lay reader. Of wider scope than, but equally interesting as, *Breast Cancer: A Family Survival Guide* (CH, Nov'95). All levels.—*R. S. Kowalczyk, North Central Michigan College*

WS-1273 RG186 94-11673 CIP
Coney, Sandra. **The menopause industry: how the medical establishment exploits women.** Hunter House, 1994. 370p bibl index ISBN 0-89793-161-0, $24.95; ISBN 0-89793-160-2 pbk, $14.95

As a journalist, Coney investigates the "industry" of medical care, which she contends is aimed at convincing mid-life women that menopause is a disease likely to require long-term treatment with hormones. This assumption evolves from her examination of published medical research and interviews with several women who describe their experiences with menopause and its treatment. Coney reveals details about the issues, treatments, opinions, and "politics" associated with menopause. She does not hesitate to emphasize that she presents an intentional point of view in questioning medical treatment for what she contends is a normal process experienced by midlife women, and one which does not usually warrant medical intervention. The book begins with a guide explaining the process used to gather data used in this examination. The book is well documented and includes illustrations of advertising used to entice women to seek treatment for menopause. Helpful glossary. General; professional.—*M. P. Tarbox, Mount Mercy College*

WS-1274 RG161 90-11178 CIP
Dan, Alice J., ed. **Menstrual health in women's lives,** ed. by Alice J. Dan and Linda L. Lewis. Illinois, 1992. 301p index afp ISBN 0-252-01784-6, $37.50; ISBN 0-252-06209-4 pbk, $16.95

For the most part, this collection is a successful attempt to enhance knowledge development in the general area of menstrual health. The editors, nursing academicians, bring together in one volume research studies from a number of disciplines. The major topics addressed are the premenstrual syndrome, change over the menstrual cycle, menopause, and contextual issues for menstrual health. Menstruation has an impact on all women biologically, psychologically, and culturally. This group of multidisciplinary authors is able to emphasize the normal experience of menstruation while acknowledging and describing with some rigor the multiplicity of interacting variables that make solid research in this area so challenging. This approach challenges the negative, largely unscientific, stigmatizing manner in which menstruation is dealt with throughout history and usefully recasts it as a bio-cultural event. As a result the authors explore the meaning of menstruation to individual women on a physiological, psychological, and social continuum throughout history and across cultures. With the help of basic research and relevant feminist theory we begin to understand menstruation in a neutral context, free from its shroud of mystery as a basic life experience for half the world's population. This volume should have relevance for a wide audience, but it will be especially relevant for those collections serving the health care professions and women's studies. Academic and public libraries.—*D. J. Douglas, University of Wisconsin-Madison*

WS-1275 RC280 93-43778 CIP
Feldman, Gayle. **You don't have to be your mother.** W.W. Norton, 1994. 256p ISBN 0-393-03640-5, $23.00

With experience as a journalist and book reviewer, Feldman approaches the topic of her own breast cancer with knowledge of previous writers' works and the response the general public has had to such accounts. Given the unique circumstances of her own illness, that of discovering the cancer in the eighth month of her pregnancy, Feldman maintains a hopeful outlook as she recounts the events that occurred in the months following the initial diagnosis. This autobiography of her experience with the health care system provides a valuable perspective for those who serve within that system on a daily basis. Because she experienced the death of her own mother from breast cancer at the age of 40, Feldman's account is particularly poignant in that she must deal with that experience not only as an adult child with the same disease but as a new mother who may well leave the same legacy to her unborn child. Feldman is candid about her relationships with her family members, friends, and health care professionals. She counts herself among those who have been both aided and encumbered by the system and shares a well-balanced view of her treatment and thoughts about the ordeal. All levels.—*M. P. Tarbox, Mount Mercy College*

WS-1276 RG186 94-16479 CIP
Furman, C. Sue. **Turning point: the myths and realities of menopause.** Oxford, 1995. 208p bibl index afp ISBN 0-19-508773-9, $19.95

Furman (anatomy and neurobiology, Colorado State Univ.) translates and interprets the medical literature related to menopause, including female reproductive hormones, the discomforts of menopause, osteoporosis, hysterectomies, and the hormonal impact on malignancies. Sound advice is given on diet, exercise, and avoiding smoking. Furman is obviously convinced of the efficacy of estrogen replacement therapy (ERT) and catalogs its usefulness not only for treating the symptoms related to menopause but also in preventing osteoporosis and cardiac fatalities. Since her primary audience is the ordinary woman, this would be a useful resource for students in a first- or second-year health course. However, the lack of references in the book limits its usefulness for nursing or other health science students because the research behind the generalizations cannot always be identified or evaluated, although there are chapter bibliographies. General; lower-division undergraduate.—*B. Bullough, University of Southern California*

WS-1277 94-69129 CIP
Gofman, John W. **Preventing breast cancer: the story of a major, proven, preventable cause of this disease,** ed. by Egan O'Connor. Committee for Nuclear Responsibility, 1995. 339p bibl index ISBN 0-932682-94-4 pbk, $15.00

It is argued that as much as two thirds of breast cancer is preventable by avoiding earlier ionizing radiation, primarily from medical sources. Gofman (molecular and cell biology, Univ. of California, Berkeley, emeritus) presents a detailed scientific study to evaluate this theory. Breast cancers induced by radiation received in a single year develop over many years. A variety of X-ray treatments, many of which have been abandoned, apparently play a role in the increasing incidence of this disease; these include therapies such as thymus irradiation, and mass screening for tuberculosis. Gofman remains concerned about the use of modern methods such as mammography, fluoroscopy, or treatment of skin disorders. He proposes that cooperation between radiologists and physicists is important to continue reducing the level of exposure to ionizing radiation. The public must be made more aware of this concern through the press. Excellent reference list; good index and glossary. Although not everyone will want to read the entire detailed analysis, most readers will gain important knowledge from perusing selected chapters. Upper-division undergraduate through professional.—*H. W. Wallace, University of Pennsylvania*

WS-1278 RG516 92-20160 CIP
Loudon, Irvine. **Death in childbirth: an international study of maternal care and maternal mortality, 1800-1950.** Oxford, 1993 (c1992). 622p bibl index ISBN 0-19-822997-6, $95.00

Loudon is a rare scholar: He is both a numbers cruncher and an urbane, insightful, and even occasionally witty writer. His subject is broad and his research extensive and meticulous. His aim is simply stated: "Although some notable histories of maternal care have been confined to a social-historical or feminist approach with

scarcely a statistic, let alone a statistical evaluation in sight, I believe that without rigorous statistical analysis the history of maternal care can easily become impressionistic, unreliable, and in the end unsatisfying." He uses his marvelous command of English to clarify the meaning of his numbers and to precisely define terms that seem to be simple. How, in fact, is "maternal mortality" to be defined? The answer he provides is technical, comprehensible, and elegant. The scope of this study is extraordinary: comparing maternal care and mortality in Britain, the Continent, the US, and Australia and New Zealand in a period when numbers were not always easily available. A reference book rather than a monograph to absorb in one or two sessions, it is a model of dispassionate scholarship and a book that should be in every college and university library. It is inconceivable that future scholars could ignore this book in any study of women's health and lifestyles of that period.—*I. Richman, Pennsylvania State University, Harrisburg*

WS-1279 RG67.G7 89-7076 MARC
Moscucci, Ornella. **The science of woman: gynaecology and gender in England, 1800-1929.** Cambridge, 1990. 278p bibl index ISBN 0-521-32741-5, $49.50

Moscucci's study intertwines two themes: changing medical practice of gynecology and changing views about woman's nature. Debates about use of the speculum, for example, considered both whether it afforded any medical advantage and whether its use involved "instrumental rape." Similarly, debates raged around whether ovariotomy was medically beneficial or whether it made women less feminine or even immoral. Drawing on records from two hospitals in London, Moscucci documents arguments about the legitimacy and practicality of specialized hospitals, what sorts of patients patronized them, how long the patients stayed, for what procedures, and what effect the balance of paying and charity patients had. She shows how the social construction of "femininity" shaped medical practice and how medical advances prompted revisions in social classifications as midwives, men-midwives, obstetricians, gynecologists, and general practitioners fought to define and divide up the turf surrounding woman's medicine. The story ends with the establishment of the Royal College of Obstetricians and Gynaecologists. This scholarly volume, which grew out of Moscucci's dissertation, is a valuable addition to the growing literature examining woman's medicine and its social context. University collections.—*J. Maienschein, Arizona State University*

WS-1280 RG51 94-19129 CIP
O'Dowd, Michael J. **The history of obstetrics and gynaecology,** by Michael J. O'Dowd and Elliot E. Philipp. Parthenon Publishing Group, 1994. 710p indexes ISBN 1-85070-224-1, $125.00

This monumental work could better be called an encyclopedia. Unlike traditional histories, its organization is primarily topical. A short historical overview is followed by detailed chapters on a wide range of topics related to women's bodies, the history of childbirth, and women's medicine. An unusual feature is the coverage of related medical specialties such as anesthetics, imaging, and radiotherapy, now essential tools of modern physicians in the field. Most chapters are followed by a chronology and bibliography. A final section includes short biographies of prominent historical figures. Detailed name and subject indexes are included. The illustrations are interesting but no match for those in Harold Speert's admirable *Obstetrics and Gynecology: A History and Iconography* (Iconographia Gyniatrica), 1994. Historical sections are anecdotal and a gold mine of information for those teaching in the field. Some sections are quite technical and require a medical education to fully understand, although they are clearly written. The book shows the cultural orientation of the authors, consulting gynecologists in Ireland and England respectively. They frequently point out that, although modern medicine has greatly reduced mortality in childbirth, not all changes have been improvements. In particular, modern technical medicine has often meant undesirable interference with normal childbirth. Essential for medical libraries and otherwise highly recommended. General; upper-division undergraduate through professional.—*M. Mac Arthur, University of Colorado at Denver*

WS-1281 RC280 94-37836 CIP
Pederson, Lucille M. **Breast cancer: a family survival guide,** by Lucille M. Pederson and Janet M. Trigg. Bergin & Garvey, 1995. 282p bibl index afp ISBN 0-89789-293-3, $59.95

Perhaps the greatest personal fear of any woman is getting breast cancer, and the greatest trauma any woman faces begins when she is told she has breast cancer. Both of these experiences are so unique that many books have been written by women who have had to face and cope with them, while many others have been written by husbands, relatives, doctors, psychiatrists, etc., who have had some close association with women with breast cancer. This book, based in part on direct interviews with nine women during their first year of adjusting to breast cancer and on written questionnaires from 45 other couples experiencing the trauma, as well as on a large literature survey, attempts to bring together under one cover informational guides that can be of benefit to both women and their families coping with the disease. All aspects of breast cancer are covered, including its medical basis; effects on the patient; and effects on husbands, children, and relatives. Names and addresses of sources of information are provided; glossary. Highly recommended. General; undergraduate through professional.—*R. S. Kowalczyk, formerly, University of Michigan*

WS-1282   93-61692 Orig
Stott-Kendall, Pamela. **Torn illusions: one woman's tragic experience with the silicone conspiracy.** New Horizon, NJ, 1994. 242p bibl ISBN 0-88282-090-7, $22.95; ISBN 0-88282-097-4 pbk, $13.95

Stott-Kendall presents a first-person account of the health problems experienced following silicone breast implants. The first two chapters provide the background of the events leading to her decision to receive breast implants and the five years of incapacitating and, at times, life-threatening illness until their removal. Several other chapters trace her struggle to regain health, her legal battle for compensation, and her search for understanding. The history of silicone use, research related to its physiological effects, and the safety of these devices are traced over a 30-year period. The role of the federal Food and Drug Administration regarding breast implants raises more unanswered questions about public advocacy. Closing chapters review other implantable devices containing silicone or with silicone coatings, a review of silicone risks, and questions about the future of these implants. The text contains a glossary of terms, extensive endnotes, and a list of support groups. The text is technical at times, hence the need for the glossary. For anyone interested in the controversy, from the general public to professionals. Not for the fainthearted.—*M. Auterman, Augustana College (SD)*

WS-1283   RD539   93-29670 CIP
Vasey, Frank B. **The silicone breast implant controversy: what women need to know,** by Frank B. Vasey and Josh Feldstein. Crossing, 1993. 153p index ISBN 0-89594-610-6, $20.95

For women, the concurrence of business interests, medical practices, and governmental regulation has proved on numerous occasions to be dangerous. The breast implant is a good example of a profit-generating threat to women's health. Vasey, a rheumatologist, has written a comprehensive, easily understandable, and well-documented handbook for women with breast implants, those who suffer from silicone-related disease, those who are considering implant removal, their families and spouses, and medical professionals. Medical facts regarding the spread of silicone throughout the body, its relationship to rheumatic disease, and its effects on the immune system are examined systematically and are supported by manufacturer's internal reports, general literature, and professional journals. Anecdotal accounts by dozens of Vasey's patients provide additional evidence regarding self-serving roles of manufacturers, inaction of the FDA, conflicting opinions offered by surgeons, and factors that persuaded more than a million women to use these devices for figure enhancement. In clear and informative writing, consumer advice and sources of additional information are provided. Highly recommended. General; community college; undergraduate; pre-professional; professional.—*L. G. Muzio, SUNY Empire State College*

◆ Nursing

WS-1284   RT82   94-46485 CIP
Fisher, Sue. **Nursing wounds: nurse practitioners, doctors, women patients and the negotiation of meaning.** Rutgers, 1995. 259p bibl index ISBN 0-8135-2180-7, $42.00; ISBN 0-8135-2181-5 pbk, $16.00

Fisher analyzed physicians' and nurse practitioners' encounters with female patients to compare how the providers gave care. A nurse-practitioner friend of the author had asserted that nurse practitioners address both physical and psychosocial problems (caring), while physicians deal only with physical problems (curing). Fisher concluded that major differences do exist in how the two providers talk with patients, and how they interpret the needs of women. Physicians had the patient undress first and stood looking down at the patient as the interview began. The nurse practitioner first talked with the patient dressed, both sitting face to face. Physicians conveyed to patients that they are not competent; nurses conveyed that women patients are competent, in their lives and in the encounter. These differences can influence whether, e.g., patients comply with prescribed regimens. However, both providers limited topics for discussion, albeit differently. Approaches show how best to interact with patients to assure maintenance of self-worth and greater compliance for recovery. The epilogue includes important implications for health policy. Highly recommended for providers at all levels, graduate faculty, and medical and nursing students. Upper-division undergraduate through professional.—*A. R. Davis, Johns Hopkins University*

WS-1285   RT37.N5   89-25949 CIP
Florence Nightingale and her era: a collection of new scholarship, ed. by Vern Bullough, Bonnie Bullough, and Marietta P. Stanton. Garland, 1990. 365p (Garland reference library of social science, 629) bibl afp ISBN 0-8240-6998-6, $50.00

This collection of 19 papers presented at an interdisciplinary conference represents new scholarship regarding the life of Florence Nightingale (8 papers) as well as other topics on nursing during the Nightingale era (11 papers). Much of the scholarship reflects research from primary sources such as correspondence between Nightingale and others; minutes and annual reports from the Hospital for Sick Children in Toronto, Canada; and papers and discussions recorded from the International Congress of Charities, Correction and Philanthropy, Chicago, 1893. The topics covered are among the most interesting facets of Nightingale's life and time, such as the establishment of the school of nursing at St. Thomas's Hospital in London, a health history of Nightingale, and Nightingale's relationship to the Sisters of Mercy during the Crimean War. Several papers examine women's issues that were significant during Nightingale's time and continue to be such as women's place in higher education, sexual harassment, and the women's movement. Most papers are well-written and well edited, although one or two contain distracting typographical errors. Academic and public library collections.—*A. H. Bishop, Lynchburg College*

WS-1286   RT120   93-27426 CIP
Foner, Nancy. **The caregiving dilemma: work in an American nursing home.** California, 1994. 190p bibl index afp ISBN 0-520-08359-8, $25.00

Caring: it is hard to define, yet one can readily identify when it does and does not occur. Caring is what everyone wants from health care providers. When a physician, nurse, or aide is uncaring, one blames them personally rather than examining the context in which the behavior occurs. Foner, an anthropologist, reverses that trend in her excellent in-depth analysis of work in a nursing home. Because aides provide the majority of care in nursing homes, Foner spent eight months observing and working with them in a single New York City facility. She describes the aides, the work they do, and the environment in which they do it. She accurately identifies the dilemma faced by these women: the expectation to provide compassionate care to the residents while meeting the various rules and regulations of the nursing home bureaucracy that actually rewards the efficient completion of tasks. Foner also outlines the aides' methods of adaptation, both positive and negative, to this dilemma. Individual chapters are devoted to the residents, the nursing hierarchy, the work culture, and family. Foner integrates theory related to bureaucracy, family, work, and gender to support and explicate her findings. This well-written book precisely describes the reality of nursing aide work in many nursing homes in the US. Highly recommended. General; undergraduate; graduate; technical/professional.—*M. A. Thompson, Saint Joseph College*

WS-1287   RT4   93-11137 CIP
Lewenson, Sandra Beth. **Taking charge: nursing, suffrage, and feminism in America, 1873-1920.** Garland, 1993. 333p (Development of American feminism, 1) index afp ISBN 0-8240-6897-1, $55.00

First in a new series, this book describes the evolution of nursing as a feminist profession. Lewenson describes the roles of early nursing leaders in shaping not only nursing but also feminism in the US. The ongoing struggles and accomplishments of these leaders are detailed throughout. The evolution of nursing organizations and formal nursing groups that crystallized nursing's role in health care are included. Chapter topics are presented in chronological order: "Formative Years," "Expanding Years," and "Taking Charge" cover the evolution of nursing concurrent with feminism. The exclusion of nursing from women's movement efforts is well described. Nurses' support for women's suffrage, and leadership efforts to improve the status of both the nursing profession and women in general, are elucidated. Tensions as well as cooperation between nursing and the women's movement are woven through the historical accounts. Photographs and appendixes embellish the text. Chapter notes provide extensive reference information to support the historical narrative. A fascinating and important book. All levels.—*S. Van Ort, University of Arizona*

WS-1288   DS559.8.W6   90-34487 CIP
Norman, Elizabeth M. **Women at war: the story of fifty military nurses who served in Vietnam.** Pennsylvania, 1990. 211p bibl index ISBN 0-8122-8249-3, $36.95; ISBN 0-8122-1317-3, $14.95

Norman reports a vital aspect of veterans' experiences in Vietnam—women's work as nurses. She tells a story of 50 women who entered the war zone for one year and returned home, bearing psychic scars. Like the combat soldiers, nurses suffered post-traumatic stress disorder, only their nightmares and guilt focused on the deaths they were unable to stay. The author highlights the strains and anguish of nurses' work in the war, the hallmarks of their service; the "emotional discipline" they had to muster (and the emotional toll that control took); the pace of the work; and the strong fellowship, professional autonomy, and personal confidence that developed. For many, in spite of the war's horrors, the year in Vietnam represented the peak of their nursing careers; never before or after did physicians give them the trust and the latitude that they enjoyed in Vietnam. But the narrative is often disconnected, stringing anecdotes that lack overarching themes, analytic framework, or strong contextual grounding in the war. Nevertheless, Norman highlights the pathos of the war and the valor of the vets, who now, in the collective memory, include women nurses. The book serves to redress a serious omission. Academic and general audiences.—*J. P. Brickman, United States Merchant Marine Academy*

WS-1289   RT86   94-33756 CIP
Roberts, Joan I. **Feminism and nursing: an historical perspective on power, status, and political activism in the nursing profession,** by Joan I. Roberts and Thetis M. Group. Praeger, 1995. 369p bibl index afp ISBN 0-275-94916-8, $65.00

Roberts and Group examine the feminist roots (1900-80) of the nursing profession. They note that the notion of "independent practitioner" assumes independent females. They maintain that ideas do not evolve from one point of time and progress in a linear fashion to a final conception; rather, nursing ideas of feminism, gender, race, class, and power are sculpted by the social context, shifting thought collectives, and multiple institutions such as hospitals, medicine, and business. The book begins, as it must, with Florence Nightingale. Her writing, philosophy, feminist ideas, and perceptions of nursing work are examined. The authors provide an exhaustive review of Nightingale scholarship, as well as a precise analysis of "the recognized founder of nursing." The chapters continue across time from the Progressive Era to the World Wars, the brash 1960s, and the conservative Reagan Era. The last chapter considers current relationships among gender, power, and leadership within nursing and the feminist future of professional

nursing. A thoughtful and well-written book with an impressive bibliography, appropriate for professional nursing students and nurse-scholars. General; undergraduate through professional.—*D. B. Hamilton, Western Michigan University*

WS-1290   RT84   93-28309 CIP
Selanders, Louise C. **Florence Nightingale: an environmental adaptation theory.** Sage Publications, CA, 1993. 38p (Notes on nursing theories, 9) bibl ISBN 0-8039-4859-X, $16.50; ISBN 0-8039-4860-3 pbk, $8.25

For over a century, Florence Nightingale has captured the minds of nurses and symbolized the hopes of the nursing profession. Selanders ventures to analyze Nightingale's thoughts from a 20th-century perspective and argues that her ideas serve "uniquely and brilliantly" as a model for current practice. Drawing from secondary sources such as Cook (1913), Woodham-Smith (1953), and Baly (1988), Selanders gives a brief overview of the life and the social context of Nightingale. Although faithful to existing facts, the descriptive portrayal of Nightingale is a somewhat flattering perspective that adds to her image as a heroine. The author analyzes Nightingale's ideas according to the well-accepted "concepts of nursing": person, environment, health, and nursing, and argues that Nightingale promoted a holistic view that encouraged the "environmental adaptation theory" currently accepted within nursing. The book does not include primary sources but has a complete listing of secondary sources. For community college, undergraduate, and graduate nursing students.—*D. B. Hamilton, University of Rochester*

WS-1291   RT120   94-22352 CIP
Zalumas, Jacqueline. **Caring in crisis: an oral history of critical care nursing.** Pennsylvania, 1995. 235p bibl index afp ISBN 0-8122-3255-0, $36.95; ISBN 0-8122-1510-9 pbk, $14.95

Zalumas's study explores the evolution and contemporary practice of critical care nursing through interviews with 25 experienced critical care nurses. The interviewees' comments about the evolution of the field should interest younger critical-care nurses, who are often unaware of how their specialty developed. However, the changes in health care delivery since the study was done in 1987-88 make her findings about the stresses and ethical issues in critical care relevant to nurses in other settings as well. The conflicts between nursing and hospital administration, the issue of death with dignity, and the increased use of technology that these critical care nurses identified are moving rapidly to noncritical care areas. Through the interviewees' discussions of their roles and values, student nurses at all undergraduate levels can learn what nursing is, what nurses do, the stresses in nursing, and the ethical issues they will face after graduation. The organization of the book makes it somewhat difficult to "dip" in to find specific types of information, and the index is of limited assistance. Extensive bibliography. Undergraduate through professional; two-year technical program students.—*M. Flickinger, Clark State Community College*

◆ Racial & Ethnic Issues

WS-1292   GR110   93-40560 CIP
Fontenot, Wonda L. **Secret doctors: ethnomedicine of African Americans.** Bergin & Garvey, 1994. 162p bibl index afp ISBN 0-89789-354-9, $49.95

Fontenot presents a rich descriptive account of African American medical beliefs and practices in rural Louisiana. Major focus is on the role of "secret doctors" or "treaters" obtained through oral histories. Chapters treat the history of the region and its multiple indigenous groups; general folk medicine practices of African Americans, with particular emphasis on rural Louisiana; the role of African American women in health care; religious influences; and plants utilized for medicinal purposes. Helpful maps and figures are included as well as an appendix, references, and an author index. This book is written in a comfortable style that fully engages the reader while providing comprehensive scholarly background to support its scientific credibility, as it describes an African American medical system distinct from and yet shaped by other cultural influences. An excellent example of quality ethnographic research and a most appropriate addition to libraries serving students and faculty in cultural anthropology, African American studies, public health, medicine, nursing, and the allied health professions. Upper-division undergraduate through professional.—*R. E. Darnell, University of Michigan*

WS-1293 RA564 95-4400 CIP
Health issues for women of color: a cultural diversity perspective, ed. by Diane L. Adams. Sage Publications, CA, 1995. 290p bibl indexes afp ISBN 0-8039-7311-X, $55.00; ISBN 0-8039-7312-8 pbk, $24.95

Issues related specifically to women's health, especially those of ethnic minority heritage, have been inadequately addressed in nursing and other health care books. This timely publication is a first in that it covers the health care needs of such a diverse group of women about whom little has appeared in the literature. The authors provide much needed information to help health care providers understand more fully the health needs of these groups, including Native American, Hispanic/Latina, Asian/Pacific Island, African American, and Arab-Middle Eastern American women. In addition, several chapters are devoted to health concerns of children homeless women of color. There is a chapter on ethical issues in research, and others on such issues as unequal access to care, unequal research treatment, and informed consent. The information provided has been well researched, and each chapter has an impressive list of current and relevant references. Essential reading for medical students and graduate nursing students preparing to serve as clinical nurse specialists or nurse practitioners. An excellent contribution. Upper-division undergraduate through professional.—*V. B. Byers, SUNY Health Science Center at Syracuse*

WS-1294 RC451 91-16538 CIP
Koss-Chioino, Joan. **Women as healers, women as patients: mental health care and traditional healing in Puerto Rico.** Westview, 1992. 237p bibl index afp ISBN 0-8133-8321-8 sc, $32.95

Koss-Chioino's eminently readable scholarly treatise offers conclusions broadly relevant to women. Her ethnographic study looks at women healers (part of the popular healing system in Puerto Rico known as *Espiritismo* She brings a unique view of healing, for she herself is a spiritist healer as well as being a skilled psychoanalyst. The Puerto Rican culture orients females toward pain, suffering, and caring for others early in life and many find self-definition by becoming healers. This study concludes that being female in that culture transcends different orientations and training. The author describes healing systems that are both complementary and overlapping; spiritists take up the slack in the traditional health care system by treating less severe illnesses in the "deferred and no diagnosis" categories. Koss-Chioino takes the approach that content and expression of any type of feelings can only be understood in the context of a set of culturally structured interactions that give them meaning. She discusses medical and psychological/psychiatric conditions and compares outcomes of physicians, mental health professionals, and spiritists. Although the systems of healing have different views of the body, the healing process, and the diagnosis, the outcomes are often similar. Her richly illustrative case studies show how the different expressions of malaise allow different healers to construct a diagnosis and treatment plan. Advanced undergraduate through professional.—*D. J. Douglas, University of Wisconsin-Madison*

WS-1295 RA564 95-35483 CIP
Race, gender, and health, ed. by Marcia Bayne-Smith. Sage Publications, CA, 1996. 210p (Sage series on race and ethnic relations, 15) bibl index afp ISBN 0-8039-5504-9, $49.95; ISBN 0-8039-5505-7 pbk, $24.00

A mostly readable and persuasive compilation of essays, this book is packed with statistical summaries and recommendations for improving the health care of minority women and children in the US. Current proposals in Congress are aimed at severely cutting financial assistance to these poor women and children. This book documents the limited access to health care for women of color as a result of race, class, gender, and culture. Western medicine based on the biomedical model has not served African American, American Indian and Alaska Native, Asian/Pacific Islander, nor Latina women well. These essays clarify the important connections between poor health and social problems such as violence, alcoholism, drug abuse, unemployment, poverty, and lack of health insurance. Poor women of color need to enhance their capacity for family planning,

job training, child care, drug treatment, and marketable skills. Western medicine needs minority primary-care physicians with an appreciation of cultural factors that contribute to the negative health status of the four diverse groups discussed. Extensive references; charts/graphs comparing white and nonwhite women by employment, income, insurance, education, death rates, abuse, etc.; helpful subject index. Recommended for health policy collections. Upper-division undergraduate through professional.—*E. R. Paterson, SUNY College at Cortland*

WS-1296 RA448 95-11310 CIP
Smith, Susan L. **Sick and tired of being sick and tired: black women's health activism in America, 1890-1950.** Pennsylvania, 1995. 247p bibl index afp ISBN 0-8122-3237-2, $34.95; ISBN 0-8122-1449-8 pbk, $16.95

Smith describes the black health movement in the US from the Civil War to 1950. She uses extensive resources to describe the efforts of the black health activists, with emphasis on the contributions of lay women to public health work. Recognizing that black women, both lay and professional, were the backbone of the health movement in the rural South, the author notes that women were also the primary targets of the movement, due to their influence on their families' health. This study identifies factors that influenced program development and implementation such as gender, class, and political dynamics. Tracing the history of public health through three chronological periods, Smith also interweaves the influence of epidemics, war, and racism on the efforts of health workers to improve the conditions of rural black families. The study is well documented with extensive notes and bibliography. The few pictures and the index are additional helpful resources. A unique historical view of health care for African Americans, and a reference for current health care reform. All levels.—*M. P. Tarbox, Mount Mercy College*

WS-1297 RA564 92-46308 CIP
Wings of gauze: women of color and the experience of health and illness, ed. by Barbara Bair and Susan E. Cayleff. Wayne State, 1993. 393p bibl index ISBN 0-8143-2301-4, $39.95; ISBN 0-8143-2302-2 pbk, $19.95

A very timely compilation of writings about the health experiences of African American, Native American, Latina, and Southeast-Asian American women of color. Of particular significance is the discussion of the way many minority women perceive themselves and their health experiences. These perceptions combined with their socioeconomic status influence the pursuit of professional help for health problems. The topics are all of current concern in women's health. Although this book will be of great value as a resource to educate all health-care providers regarding the health needs of minority women, there are some groups for whom it will hold special significance. Health care providers, including nurse practitioners, in geographical areas where these minority populations are concentrated, will find this book to be an invaluable resource. The essays are well documented with current and older references to aid in understanding the problems addressed. In addition, a special section includes an extensive listing of excellent references specific to developmental and health problems of minority women. This book should be required reading for all medical and graduate nursing students. General; graduate; faculty; pre-professional; professional.—*V. B. Byers, SUNY Health Science Center at Syracuse*

◆ Reproductive Technology

WS-1298 RG133 95-10455 CIP
Blank, Robert. **Human reproduction, emerging technologies, and conflicting rights,** by Robert Blank and Janna C. Merrick. CQ Press, 1995. 269p bibl index afp ISBN 0-87187-938-7 pbk, $19.95

Blank and Merrick, who teach political science and government relations, discuss policies and issues in reproductive health care in a balanced and well-informed manner. A thorough and accurate overview of the laws, regulations, and court decisions related to each of the issues is presented in a historical format that so it is possible to trace the development of current policies. Many of the policies seem to have developed in a state of near crisis because the emerging technology or rapidly changing societal norms brought the new issues forward at such a rapid pace. For example, the modern neonatal intensive care unit is now able to save infants who are severely brain damaged or have other disabilities that compromise their quality of life. Policy in this arena has moved from one extreme to the other as the various concerned participants and political forces lobbied for their favored directions. Other reproductive issues covered in detail include abortion, contraception, sterilization, embryo research, assisted reproduction, and surrogate motherhood. Undergraduate through professional; two-year technical program students.—*B. Bullough, University of Southern California*

WS-1299   RG137   89-13654 MARC
Developing new contraceptives: obstacles and opportunities, ed. by Luigi Mastroianni, Peter J. Donaldson, and Thomas T. Kane ... et al. National Academy Press, 1990. 193p bibl index ISBN 0-309-04147-3, $19.95

This report by a committee of distinguished scholars was initiated to study the slow pace at which new contraceptive products were being marketed. The need for continued development of these products is well documented by the large failure rates of certain contraceptives and the substantial number of abortions performed in the US because of contraceptive failure. The report points out the inadequacies associated with contraceptive products presently available and outlines how contraceptive failure is linked to the larger problems of population control, infant mortality, poverty, and general health. Other issues examined include new products likely to be available in the '90s; fascinating approaches to long-acting dosage forms with fewer side effects; values and attitudes toward contraceptives; product liability and how it affects research efforts; and organizations involved in the development of new contraceptives and their function and financing. The final chapter is an excellent review of obstacles and opportunities for contraceptive development. The volume contains approximately 25 pages of references and a glossary of terms. An important document for anyone seriously interested in contraceptives, population control, or family planning and counseling.—*A. M. Mattocks, University of North Carolina at Chapel Hill*

WS-1300   HD9995   91-41227 CIP
Grant, Nicole J. **The selling of contraception: the Dalkon Shield case, sexuality, and women's autonomy.** Ohio State, 1992. 223p bibl index afp ISBN 0-8142-0572-0, $29.95

After reading many clinical papers related to contraceptive research and subsequent women's choices, it was stimulating to read Grant's detailed sociological investigation of contraceptive devices from a feminist perspective. It is an excellent adaptation of Grant's research that presents events in a style that captures and holds the reader's interest. The development, promotion, and positive and negative consequences for women of one such method, the Dalkon Shield, are thoughtfully chronicled. This riveting reflection on a situation depicting women as both passive and active participants in controlling fertility, shaping current expectations of sexuality, and, ultimately, women's roles, are framed within a historical and social context. A particular strength of the work is a discussion of how events in the social-political arena impact societal views regarding contraception and sexuality. The promotion of contraceptives and the individuals involved who actually had personal interests in their acceptance are described. Analysis of ethical issues associated with seeming conflicts of interest and target marketing of devices is timely and enlightening. Grant illustrates many issues through compelling excerpts from personal interviews with women relating their experiences with the Dalkon Shield. These often poignant excerpts bring the reader close to this most intimate choice. Recommended for all academic and professional audiences.—*N. G. Snyder, University of Massachusetts*

WS-1301   RG133   92-9929 CIP
Issues in reproductive technology I: an anthology, ed. by Helen Bequaert Holmes. Garland, 1992. 449p (Garland reference library of social science, 729) indexes afp ISBN 0-8153-0035-2, $60.00

A remarkable collection of scholarly essays, philosophical discussions, and ethical arguments concerning reproductive choices not often described in research studies, i.e., RU486 plus prostaglandin, Norplant, cryopreservation, contraceptive vaccines, in-vitro fertilization, surrogacy, cervical caps, condoms, and male

contraceptives. Frequently discussed issues are also addressed, such as abortion, adoption, and infertility. Many qualified authors analyze research results, share US and international experiences, and make comparision between the US and Australia, Africa, Brazil, Britain, Canada, Denmark, and the Netherlands, all with a cross-disciplinary perspective. Some essays are less readable than others because of considerable use of technical terms, jargon, and acronyms, but there are also useful tidbits of information, like the use of the over-the-counter anti-ulcer medicine, Cytotec, as an abortifacient in Brazil. An extremely well-referenced work whose editor provides an extensive annotated bibliography on contract pregnancy as well as name and subject indexes. Highly recommended for graduate and professional audiences.—*E. R. Paterson, SUNY College at Cortland*

WS-1302   RG133   92-38060 CIP
Kaplan, Lawrence J. **Controlling our reproductive destiny: a technological and philosophical perspective,** by Lawrence J. Kaplan and Rosemarie Tong. MIT, 1994. 418p index ISBN 0-262-11176-4, $39.95

A carefully planned and illustrated interdisciplinary approach to complicated legal, ethical, biochemical, social, and philosophical principles involved in reproductive technologies, this book was compiled jointly by a biochemist (Kaplan) and a feminist philosopher (Tong). The book reflects the differing perspectives and attitudes of the authors and society, covering an impressive array of topics ranging from human reproduction, contraception, and sterilization to fertility/infertility and surrogate motherhood. Along the way controversial issues and cases are cited and explained, i.e., contra-gestational RU 486, sex education and school clinics, teen rights and parental notification, abortion, artificial insemination and sperm banks, and in vitro fertilization and surplus embryos as well as funding concerns. Technical terminology and medical acronyms and/or abbreviations are regularly introduced and defined, but a separate glossary would have been most helpful. Extensive notes and references; an appendix details basic biochemistry. Very highly recommended for its well-balanced and thorough coverage. Upper-division undergraduate through professional.—*E. R. Paterson, SUNY College at Cortland*

WS-1303   RG133   92-56139 CIP
Raymond, Janice G. **Women as wombs: reproductive technologies and the battle over women's freedom.** Harper San Francisco, 1993. 254p index afp ISBN 0-06-250898-9, $22.00; ISBN 0-06-250899-7 pbk, $10.00

Raymond (Univ. of Massachusetts) raises necessary, disturbing questions about the new reproductive technologies and all so-called technological-medical progress. She exposes manipulative definitions of "health" and "disease" that convince Westerners their infertility must be cured, thus allowing mass marketing of increasingly high-tech methods of conception, while at the same time promoting to the Third World infertility technologies, often rejected or banned in the West, such as forced sterilization, long-lasting, harmful contraceptives, sex predetermination, and female feticide. Notions of technological "success" and "progress" lose meaning as Raymond documents reports of highly inflated IVF success rates and demonstrates a spiraling cycle of "technological fixes" of problems created by the reproductive techniques themselves; the ultimate being the highly ironic "fetal reduction." And, frightening new definitions of motherhood and fatherhood have evolved, which emphasize genetic essentialism, exalt "ejaculatory fatherhood," and reduce women to "human incubators, allowing postmortem ventilation of brain-dead women and the terrifying prospect of "postmortem surrogacy." Raymond's discussion of international trafficking in women and children for sexual and reproductive purposes and in children and fetuses for organ donation stuns one's moral sense. This book is *must* reading for those concerned with women's human dignity and physical well-being.—*J. A. Kegley, California State University, Bakersfield*

WS-1304   RG133   95-13722 CIP
Reproduction, ethics, and the law: feminist perspectives, ed. by Joan C. Callahan. Indiana, 1996 (c1995). 427p index afp ISBN 0-253-32938-8, $39.95; ISBN 0-253-20996-X pbk, $24.95

Editor Callahan presents a fascinating look at the facts, facets, and legal effects of modern technology on reproduction. The feminist viewpoint of the issues is presented; however, it is pointed out that all feminists are not alike in their views, so a variety of opinions are examined. Each topic is explained scientifically, then anecdotal examples are presented, with the courts' historical and current stance, followed by a discussion of the sometimes differing feminist viewpoints. There are copious references with notes. The reader with some prior knowledge about in vitro methods will appreciate these intelligent discussions; those with no experience will find the discussions difficult to understand. It is an excellent eye-opener for researchers and physicians working in these exciting, relatively new reproductive frontiers. Some of the topics are quite complex, but the anecdotes keep the book readable. A work that provides insight on all issues concerning reproduction. Graduate through professional.—*J. A. Brown, University of Phoenix*

WS-1305   RG133   94-10154 CIP
Squier, Susan Merrill. **Babies in bottles: twentieth-century visions of reproductive technology.** Rutgers, 1995 (c1994). 270p index ISBN 0-8135-2116-5, $48.00; ISBN 0-8135-2117-3 pbk, $17.00

Squier, who teaches women's studies and English, has brought her interests together in a compilation of writings reflecting on the development of images in reproductive technology. Based on research started as a Fulbright Scholar in Australia, Squier proposes that a distinction is evident between sexuality and reproduction in the literature and images of modern and postmodern writers and illustrators. This distinction is further delineated in a historical review of the context of the shaping of such images through the work of scientific organizations and conferences as described throughout the book. Squier believes that both the image and the concept of reproductive technology are malleable and she relies on that proposition to further examine how the modern imaginative construction of reproductive technology shapes society's modern practices and awareness of issues that continue to repress contemporary views. The critical interpretations of feminist theorists regarding the literary representation of reproductive technology are also discussed in contrast to what Squier perceives as theorists' negative response to the actual implementation of reproductive technology in Western culture. Carefully written, supported by extensive research notes. Graduate through professional.—*M. P. Tarbox, Mount Mercy College*

WS-1306   RG133   94-30373 CIP
Van Dyck, José. **Manufacturing babies and public consent: debating the new reproductive technologies.** New York University 1995. 238p bibl index ISBN 0-8147-8785-1, $35.00

Van Dyck presents a well-researched and documented description of the status of public debate in the US and Great Britain about reproductive technology. In identifying five chronological stages of public debate, beginning with the birth of the first test tube baby in 1978, Van Dyck leads the reader through the discourse presented by medical scientists and feminists, who are the prime contenders in the debate about advances in and acceptance of reproductive technology. Science, journalism, and fiction are identified as the major elements that define the content and context of the public debate. In an effort to map this debate as it has evolved from controversy about reproductive technologies to general acceptance by the public, the author explores how arguments are posed and how facts are established. Power relationships, media maneuvers, technological strategies, and multiple interest groups are all examined for their influence on the methods and directions of the public debate on reproductive technology. Comprehensive list of notes and extensive bibliography. Upper-division undergraduate through professional.—*M. P. Tarbox, Mount Mercy College*

WS-1307   RG133   90-14148 CIP
Women and new reproductive technologies: medical, psychosocial, legal, and ethical dilemmas, ed. by Judith Rodin and Aila Collins. L. Erlbaum, 1991. 171p indexes ISBN 0-8058-0919-8, $29.95

Ten well-edited chapters examine perspectives of timely interest regarding women's health and reproductive technology. Contributors combine viewpoints on these issues from their respective disciplines in discussing medical, psychological, legal, ethical, cultural, and anthropological concepts related to recent technological advances or events. They discuss the impact and potential consequences of these events on the individual, family, and society. Sociopolitical ramifications are also suggested. Women's reproductive choices are thoroughly described and critically analyzed from a moral-ethical standpoint by experts in each field. This broad, thought-provoking review highlights the many controversies in this area. Unique to this presentation is the discussion of the interactive

nature of changes in reproductive options resulting in social change and vice versa. References cited are comprehensive and current. A volume well suited to upper-division undergraduate and gradute students in the health professions, women's studies, and other social sciences disciplines.—*M. A. Bright, University of Massachusetts at Amherst*

WS-1308   RG628   94-6363 CIP
Women and prenatal testing: facing the challenges of genetic technology, ed. by Karen H. Rothenberg and Elizabeth J. Thomson. Ohio State, 1994. 304p bibl afp ISBN 0-8142-0640-9, $75.00; ISBN 0-8142-0641-7 pbk, $17.95

This important book confronts some of the discomforting ramifications of reproductive genetic technology ignored in recent discussions of medical ethics: the ethical, psychological, social, and gender dynamics involved in the application of prenatal diagnostic technologies to pregnant women. Beyond the current literature, which focuses on the efficacy and safety of new procedures and abstract ethical dilemmas introduced by probing genetic materials before birth, the authors make women's concerns central to their inquiries. Genetic testing raises the specter of eugenics writ large and social control of women's lives, as women's private decisions fall under state scrutiny and social prescription. The authors demonstrate how reproductive technology imposes new burdens and responsibilities on women, often juxtaposing the interests of women and their fetuses. In such conflicts, the state looms as arbiter. Medical genetics raises new questions about the meaning of life, the responsibility of men and women to the life and well-being of unborn children, and the uneven burden that technology places on pregnant women. By contextualizing the conflicts introduced by prenatal diagnostic techniques in women's lives and psyches, the authors penetrate the depths of the ethical and moral questions raised by new science. For students of women's history and the history of medicine. Upper-division undergraduate through professional.—*J. P. Brickman, United States Merchant Marine Academy*

◆ Women & AIDS

WS-1309   RG580   90-14328 CIP
AIDS, women, and the next generation: towards a morally acceptable public policy for HIV testing of pregnant women and newborns, ed. by Ruth R. Faden, Gail Geller, and Madison Powers. Oxford, 1991. 374p index afp ISBN 0-19-506572-7, $39.95

Fine scholarly essays carefully examine legal, ethical, social, medical, and public policy issues regarding HIV testing of pregnant women and newborns. There is strong universal defense of confidentiality, privacy, and antidiscrimination protection in the essays as well as support for requiring informed parental consent for prenatal and newborn screening. Concern is expressed also for the rights of pregnant adolescents and for minority women and infants. Beginning chapters set the stage for later legal and policy discussions by providing a history of screening; covering medical knowledge of HIV infection and transmission in women and children; discussing obstetric and pediatric care of infected women and infants in light of intravenous drug use, poverty, and other social issues; and addressing issues of costliness, complexity, inaccuracy, and unavailability of present testing methods for infants. Extensive footnotes, detailed statistics, current research findings, prenatal/newborn screening statutes for the 50 states and DC provide ample background for position statements and comparisons of various programs. The technical language and frequent use of medical acronyms requires solid background in the topic. Highly recommended for university and professional collections in public health, law, and medicine.—*E. R. Paterson, SUNY College at Cortland*

WS-1310   RJ387   93-34761 CIP
Children, families, and HIV/AIDS: psychosocial and therapeutic issues, ed. by Nancy Boyd-Franklin, Gloria L. Steiner, and Mary G. Boland. Guilford, 1995. 334p bibl index afp ISBN 0-89862-147-X, $40.00; ISBN 0-89862-502-5 pbk, $19.95

The editors of this volume have worked since the mid-1980s in the Children's

Hospital of New Jersey, Newark, a city and community affected deeply by HIV/AIDS. Confronted daily by the challenges of the HIV epidemic, emphasis was initially placed upon the provision of basic medical services, but the mental health implications became evident as the enormity of the epidemic and its potential impact on women and families became evident. This book—the first to combine a psychosocial perspective with clinical case examples—focuses on the psychological and psychosocial issues of children and families. It introduces the Multisystems HIV/AIDS Model for the provision of effective service delivery and care of HIV/AIDS children and families. The model is family focused, culturally sensitive, and systems coordinated. The contributors offer a conceptual framework that orients the service provider to the medical, cultural, psychosocial, and mental health needs of HIV-infected infants, children, and adolescents; mothers and other relatives who are also infected with HIV/AIDS; and uninfected but nonetheless affected family members or other caretakers. Written by experts in the field, this volume is suitable for all libraries and should be included in every HIV/AIDS collection. All levels.—*J. M. Howe, VA Medical Library, San Francisco*

WS-1311 Orig
Gorna, Robin. **Vamps, virgins and victims: how can women fight AIDS?** Cassell, 1996. 398p index ISBN 0-304-32807-3, $60.00; ISBN 0-304-32809-X pbk, $16.95

Gorna's passionately written book describes issues women face regarding AIDS, primarily in the UK. She began as a volunteer for the Terrence Higgins Trust in 1986 and went on to attend numerous international meetings on AIDS. She very effectively points out important differences between the US epidemic and the contained numbers in the UK. She makes clear the risk distinctions between being the giver as opposed to the receiver of penetrative anal or vaginal intercourse. One must adjust to the repetition of vulgar words, but these are used deliberately and precisely for the purpose of clarity. Slang and medical terms are carefully defined and explained, i.e., incidence versus prevalence. The relative risks of specific activities are also debated and compared: French kissing, fellatio, cunnilingus, rimming, sex toys, intercourse during menstruation, needlestick injuries, and intravenous needle sharing. Acronyms are repeated throughout but listed only once in the beginning. Gorna painstakingly analyzes every shred of available evidence from research and case studies in order to document what is probable about the spread of AIDS, and recommends steps women can take to fight back. Very highly recommended. Upper-division undergraduates through professionals.—*E. R. Paterson, SUNY College at Cortland*

WS-1312 GN296 93-39065 CIP
Martin, Emily. **Flexible bodies: tracking immunity in American culture—from the days of polio to the age of AIDS.** Beacon Press, 1994. 320p bibl index ISBN 0-8070-4626-4, $25.00

Martin provides a sociological approach to the study of the human immune system. Rather than simply writing another science book, she approaches the question of disease (and the body's response to infection) through the role and impact of society's perceptions of illness, influenced to a significant degree by the media. Such is the theme of the first half of the book. The question of "flexible" is addressed in the latter portion of her book; the term addresses more society's perceptions and responses as much as the flexibility of the immune system itself. The author brings a decidedly feminist viewpoint to her work. This is not in itself a problem; most workers in the field were and are male. But the underlying theme here implies some bias in immune system research as a result. More importantly, though the book is ostensibly dealing with disease in general ("polio to AIDS"), Martin develops her approach primarily through the problem of AIDS (not surprising, given the author's association with ACT-UP, and the loss of friends to the disease). AIDS is arguably an excellent choice in addressing the cultural impact of disease, but as an enormously complex problem both for science and society, it is not necessarily an ideal "choice" of illness to fit the theme of the book. Undergraduate through professional; two-year technical program students.—*R. Adler, University of Michigan—Dearborn*

WS-1313 RA644 91-17428 CIP
Pearlberg, Gerry. **Women, AIDS, & communities: a guide for action.** Women's Action Alliance, Inc./Scarecrow, 1991. 129p bibl index afp ISBN 0-8108-2470-1, $27.50; ISBN 0-8108-2450-7 pbk, $19.50

This readable guide contains much more descriptive information and fewer listings than the standard directory/bibliography such as *AIDS*, ed. by D.A. Tyckoson (1985-89), *AIDS Information Sourcebook*, ed. by H.R. Malinowsky and G.J. Perry (3rd ed., 1991-92; 1st ed., CH, Jul'88), or Sarah B. Watstein and Robert A. Laurich, *AIDS and Women* (CH, May'91). Pearlberg offers many useful suggestions specifically targeted to community based programs, campus women's centers, and health and family planning clinics. The intent is to increase HIV/AIDS awareness in women by advising groups on ways to assess education needs and to plan prevention programs and activities that go beyond pamphlet and poster distribution. Risky behaviors are explained along with specific safer sex paraphernalia (condoms and dental dams). Also discussed are testing issues, crack use, rape, prostitution, pregnancy, care-giving concerns, and topics related to special audiences (e.g., children, adolescents, women in prison, older women, lesbians, physically challenged). The author is sensitive to cultural, ethnic, and language issues as well as to the age appropriateness of information, and she urges a diversity of approaches. Appendixes list educational materials; identify relevant organizations in New York, New Jersey, and nationally; provide sample assessment surveys; and cite references. Highly recommended for students and professionals in a variety of fields, such as public health, nursing, health education, social work, and medicine.—*E. R. Paterson, SUNY College at Cortland*

WS-1314 Orig
Wilton, Tamsin. **Antibody politic: AIDS and society.** New Clarion Press, 1993 (c1992). (Dist. by Paul & Company) 164p index ISBN 1-873797-05-2, $44.50; ISBN 1-873797-04-4 pbk, $16.95

Wilton lectures in health studies and women's studies (Univ. of Bristol, UK) and, indeed, this book discusses AIDS from a British perspective. The first aim of this book is to introduce AIDS to the nonspecialist reader, but as the author admits, concentration is on the social side of the epidemic. The second aim is to make an appraisal of what the risks are, to expose the political machinations that are largely responsible for ignorance and denial, and to indicate the personal and political strategies needed to bring the epidemic under control. Indeed, this volume is aptly titled "antibody politic" as the author provides many of her interpretations and opinions in her "campaign" against a variety of political and ideological ends. The third aim of this book is to try to make the world a less vicious and cruel place for people living with HIV/AIDS, a commendable goal; but the content might have been more credible to a larger audience if an objective analysis had been presented. Wilton, however, discusses some legitimate issues and provides provocative viewpoints. This volume will be particularly interesting to those who are looking for a feminist perspective of the AIDS epidemic in Great Britain. Advanced undergraduate.—*J. M. Howe, VA Medical Library, San Francisco*

◆ Mathematics & Physics

WS-1315 QC16 90-19560 CIP
Freeman, Joan. **A passion for physics: the story of a woman physicist.** A. Hilger, 1991. 229p index ISBN 0-7503-0098-1, $35.00

Because there are relatively few autobiographies by women scientists (who, in themselves, constitute a small group), Freeman has done us a favor in writing the story of her life. Her prose is lucid and factual; we are told about events and accomplishments, but little about the more personal details that might make for engrossing reading. The book has particular interest for those who would like to learn about the history of the stellar group of scientists who worked at the Cavendish Laboratory and the Atomic Energy Research Establishment, Harwell, UK. Scientific details are kept to a minimum, and the book is readily accessible to the general reader. Its underlying theme—that the important characteristics of a successful woman physicist are determination, an independent spirit, and a real enthusiasm for her subject—is clearly presented and may make it particularly valuable for young women considering a career in physics. This book fills a real gap in the scarce literature written by or about actual women scientists. It includes a fair number of photographs of physicists in this period and a good index. All levels of readers.—*M. H. Chaplin, Wellesley College*

WS-1316   QA27.5   89-49117 CIP
Mathematics and gender, ed. by Elizabeth Fennema and Gilah C. Leder. Teachers College, 1990. 214p index afp ISBN 0-8077-3002-5, $36.95; ISBN 0-8077-3001-7, $17.95

This collection of studies explores the reasons for the difference between females and males in the learning and amount of study of mathematics. The underlying theme of these articles is that there are pronounced differences in the way mathematics is taught to boys and girls with the result that, at the end of secondary school, males have learned more and different mathematics than have females. (All of the studies focus on elementary and secondary school education.) Some of the topics considered are spatial skills and gender, the interaction of teachers with students, internal influences, achievement, and motivation insofar as each of these factors affects male and female interest and performance in mathematics. Fennema and Leder have written extensively in this field and exhibit a comprehensive understanding of the existing literature. Each paper has its own detailed bibliography, and there are helpful indexes to both authors and subjects. This is an important reference tool for researchers in the field and can be read with profit by both undergraduate and graduate students and teachers in the fields of mathematics and women's studies.—*M. H. Chaplin, Wellesley College*

WS-1317   QC16x   Can. CIP
Rayner-Canham, Marelene F. **Harriet Brooks: pioneer nuclear scientist,** by Marelene F. Rayner-Canham and Geoffrey W. Rayner-Canham. McGill-Queen's, 1992. 168p bibl index afp ISBN 0-7735-0881-3, $29.95

A straightforward biography of a Canadian experimental physicist, for whom no other biography exists despite her significant contributions to the field of radioactivity—the identification of emanation (radon) and the discovery of the recoil of radioactive decay, among others. Although identified by Ernest Rutherford as "the most outstanding woman in the field of radioactivity," Brooks has been neglected in the history of science. This book fills a significant gap, not only in the contribution of women to science but for the accurate representation of the early history of the theory of the transmutation of elements. Despite the lack of source material chronicling Brooks's life, the authors have made a largely successful attempt to present her life, both in terms of her scientific career and in her particular position as a woman scientist at the turn of the century. There are detailed notes, a comprehensive biography, and an index. Particularly interesting to feminist scholars and sociologists of science is the final chpater on why Harriet Brooks was overlooked. All levels of readers.—*M. H. Chaplin, Wellesley College*

WS-1318   Orig
She does math!: real-life problems from women on the job, ed. by Marla Parker. Mathematical Association of America, 1995. 253p ISBN 0-88385-702-2 pbk, $24.00

A lively and engaging attempt to demonstrate to high school and beginning college students, especially women students, that mathematics is fun, friendly, and valuable in all manner of careers is provided by more than three dozen professional women (including psychologists, engineers, ophthalmologists, and mathematicians). They offer brief, career-oriented autobiographies and a selection of mathematics problems related to their work. The problems span an exceptionally broad range of fields; examples include calculating the necessary dioptric power for a pair of reading glasses, reliability analysis of a simple power line, and appropriate strategies for stock market investments. Only elementary mathematics is assumed. The writing displays an infectious enthusiasm for mathematics and technical subjects that, although aimed at women, should have broad appeal to all students. The book could be used either as a point of departure for classroom discussions in college-level quantitative literacy courses or to convince high school students to persevere with mathematics. A worthwhile resource for both general and academic libraries, and suitable for lower-division undergraduates and two-year technical program students.—*S. J. Colley, Oberlin College*

WS-1319   QC774   95-35246 CIP
Sime, Ruth Lewin. **Lise Meitner: a life in physics.** California, 1996. 526p bibl index afp ISBN 0-520-08906-5, $30.00

Sime has written an important book, not only because it is a detailed, comprehensive, and informative account of one of the most illustrious but little-known physicists of the 20th century, but also because it provides an insider's account of the discovery of fission and the treatment of Jewish intellectuals and scientists during the rise of Nazi Germany. Having access to a great many previously unpublished archival materials and Meitner's personal papers as well as having the scientific background to understand the physics involved, Sime has written a rich, well-documented, and illustrative biography. Her insights into the distortions of reality and the suppression of memory help to explain why this extremely talented and significant contributor to atomic physics has been neglected; the author's precise documentation and vast use of primary sources provide a very full account of both Meitner and the history of science in Germany under Hitler. Some descriptions of the science involved will be inaccessible to the nonscientist, but that should not deter anyone from reading this lucid, informed, and fascinating work. Excellent bibliography; fine index; interesting photographs. General; undergraduate through faculty.—*M. H. Chaplin, Wellesley College*

WS-1320   QC19   94-40095 CIP
Wertheim, Margaret. **Pythagoras' trousers: God, physics, and the gender wars.** Times Books/Random House, 1995. 279p bibl index ISBN 0-8129-2200-X, $23.00

Wertheim's sociocultural history of science attempts to demonstrate that the near-exclusion of women from the sciences is a direct result of science's long association with religion. Beginning with the mystical tradition in what we know of Pythagorean thought and concluding with "Einstein's recognition of a quasi-religious attitude to physics" she argues that the view of the scientist as "some sort of high priest" has repeatedly continued to militate against women's advancement in physics, her discipline of focus. She draws on the work of David F. Noble, *A World Without Women: The Christian Clerical Culture of Western Science* (1991). Written for the general reader, the book has the passion of advocacy and is readily accessible. One of its nice features is a concluding chapter on the status of women in physics in the 20th century that includes a good survey of research as well as some interesting case studies. It is Wertheim's contention that more women physicists would help to make physics more ethical, but she does not develop this argument. There is a fine index. General; lower-division undergraduate.—*M. H. Chaplin, Wellesley College*

◆ Sports & Physical Education

WS-1321   GV880   93-25049 CIP
Berlage, Gai Ingham. **Women in baseball: the forgotten history.** Praeger, 1994. 208p index afp ISBN 0-275-94735-1, $22.50

Berlage (Iona College) began this research long before the popular film *A League of Their Own* awakened public interest in the All American Girl's Professional Baseball League (AAGPBL), and women's baseball. Berlage presents important information on this significant aspect of women's history. Encompassing the late Victorian period to the present, two of the ten chapters cover AAGPBL and its players. Other topics include barnstorming teams; women's baseball in women's colleges, Little League, semiprofessional, and minor leagues; and Negro Leagues. Despite her wide range, Berlage often fails to make important connections. One mention of the strict AAGPBL rules against players smoking or drinking in public and/or in uniform appears on page 140; eight pages later appears a photo of the Racine Belles smoking and drinking in AAGPBL uniform at the infamous Sloppy Joe's Bar in Havana, Cuba. Berlage never mentions this photo. *Women in Baseball* is virtually identical to Barbara Gregorich's *Women at Play: The Story of Women in Baseball* (1993). Few significant individuals or organizations other than Victorian era women's colleges (Berlage) appear in either of these books. Berlage takes an academic approach, with chapters arranged around organizations, and includes end notes. Gregorich writes with greater flair and enthusiasm, organizes her chapters around individuals, but includes no documentation. Upper-division undergraduate through faculty.—*M. L. LeCompte, University of Texas at Austin*

WS-1322   GV886   94-30394 CIP
Blais, Madeleine. **In these girls, hope is a muscle.** Atlantic Monthly, 1995. 263p ISBN 0-87113-572-8, $21.00

Originating from an article in the *New York Times Magazine*, this book seemingly traces the path of a New England girls' high school basketball team through a season reminiscent of the movie *Hoosiers*. Pulitzer Prize-winning Blais (Univ. of Massachusetts at Amherst), however, weaves in a more complex narrative concerning past discrimination of girls and women not only in sport, but in society. The author, a self-proclaimed "sports virgin," does little to dispel this notion as she expertly records a season that culminates in a high school championship by a team that had previously lost in past playoff rounds. Blais notes young women having fun, being themselves, bonding, and building self as well as other psychosocial qualities that successful sport or "muscle" experiences have provided over time. The book is enjoyable reading and delivers a lucid message as to the status of contemporary women's continued struggle to gain an equal footing in the arena of life. General; upper-division undergraduate; graduate; professional.— *M. L. Krotee, University of Minnesota*

WS-1323   GV964   94-35584 CIP
Cayleff, Susan E. **Babe: the life and legend of Babe Didrikson Zaharias.** Illinois, 1995. 327p index afp ISBN 0-252-01793-5, $29.95

Cayleff (San Diego State Univ.) presents a feminist analysis of the life, sports career, and legacy of Mildred Ella "Babe" Didrikson Zaharias, the greatest woman athlete of all time. Utilizing previously ignored sources, as well as including Didrikson's family, associates, and physicians, Cayleff examines Babe's amateur athletic career from high school through the 1932 Olympics, as well as her professional and amateur golf accomplishments. Cayleff makes clear Didrikson's essential role in the creation and success of the Ladies Professional Golf Association (LPGA). However, Didrikson's self-promotional abilities, personality, gender-role conflicts, and carefully constructed heterosexual, feminine persona get most of the attention. *Babe* destroys Zaharias's facade of wedded bliss and insists that young golfer Betty Dodd, not George Zaharias, was Babe's real mate during the last six years of her life. The book is sure to fan flames ignited by recent controversy over lesbians and the LPGA. Despite efforts to set the record straight, there are errors, contradictions, and loose ends. Cayleff has incorrect information about Evelyn Hall in the Olympic high jump and the gender controversy about the late Stella Walsh, and she makes the confusion over the two Babe Didrikson awards even more bewildering. Although it will undoubtedly be controversial, *Babe* is a very important book about a unique and significant figure in US sports. Upper-division undergraduate through faculty.— *M. L. LeCompte, University of Texas at Austin*

WS-1324   GV966   94-27916 CIP
Crosset, Todd W. **Outsiders in the clubhouse: the world of women's professional golf.** State University of New York, 1995. 276p bibl index ISBN 0-7914-2489-8, $59.50

Crosset examines life on the LPGA tour or, as he states, the subworld of women's professional golf. As a sociologist, the author examines many issues from this perspective. The text is divided into four major topics: the social and historical context of the LPGA, inside the subworld, the ideological struggle over women's golf, and the LPGA as an agent of social change. Many of the author's conclusions are derived from observation and personal interviews with players and others involved with the LPGA tour, an elite occupation pursued by women golfers who work for themselves and are paid for performance only. Yet, they are outsiders who travel from club to club as they compete on the tour. Many quit the circuit after only three years, when the dreams of wins and big dollars do not come true. A revealing book. General; upper-division undergraduate through professional.— *J. Davenport, Auburn University*

WS-1325   SH421   95-30814 CIP
Foggia, Lyla. **Reel women: the world of women who fish.** Beyond Words, 1995. 294p index ISBN 1-885223-18-8, $24.95

This is the first comprehensive book on the history of women in fishing. Foggia argues that it is puzzling how the myth started that women did not fish; over the last 10 years, one-third of all anglers have been women. The book is divided into sections according to the type of angling: fly fishing, big-game saltwater

angling, and bass fishing, with a special chapter devoted to women who are in related areas of science and industry. The book contains more than 40 biographies of women prominent in angling, usually accompanied by a photograph of the personality. These stories elaborate on the many firsts accomplished by women, such as the first to describe the life cycles of insects from the angler's point of view, and the first to revolutionize fishing clothes and equipment so they would be comfortable and "user friendly" to women. The appendix, "The First Ever Women's Angling Resource Directory," contains detailed information ranging from a list of national and professional organizations to a compilation of books written by and for women. An excellent book for anyone interested in fishing, and especially for women who may be unaware of the rich legacy of women anglers. All levels.— *J. Davenport, Auburn University*

WS-1326   GV709   90-28692 CIP
Guttmann, Allen. **Women's sports: a history.** Columbia, 1991. 339p index ISBN 0-231-06956-1, $29.95

Guttmann (Amherst College), author of *From Ritual to Record* (CH, Oct'78) and *A Whole New Ball Game* (CH, Oct'88), offers the first comprehensive history of women's sports written by a single author. This ambitious work covers Western women's sport from ancient Egypt to the present time, with emphasis on Western Europe and North America. Using sources in languages other than English, it covers most social and ethnic groups, has cross-cultural comparisons, and also attempts to address relevant feminist issues. Despite ambitious aims, the book does fall short in certain respects. Guttmann seems at times to skip around and in some cases to leave loose ends. With a work of such enormous scope, there is obviously a lack of depth on some issues as well. Writing from a male perspective, Guttmann glosses over or ignores issues that have been of major concern to female athletes for more than a century, especially media bias and gender-orientation stereotyping. There is a bibliographical essay, an adequate index, copious notes, and good photos. Despite some problems, this is a major work that fills a huge void in the literature and will be the standard against which future books on women's sport history are measured.— *M. L. LeCompte, University of Texas at Austin*

WS-1327   GV709   95-44480 CIP
Hall, M. Ann. **Feminism and sporting bodies: essays on theory and practice.** Human Kinetics, 1996. 135p bibl index ISBN 0-87322-969-X pbk, $22.00

Hall overviews the feminist movement from its beginnings, with particular emphasis on the last 25 years when feminist studies and analysis of sport from the feminist perspective reached today's academic status. The author, a leading feminist scholar, presents an added dimension to the history of feminist theory by describing how she became involved in what is now called "second-wave feminism." The text is divided into six chapters, the title of each explaining quite succinctly its contents: "Research Odyssey of a Feminist"; "From Categoric to Relational Research"; "The Potential of Feminist Cultural Studies"; "The Significance of the Body"; "The 'Doing' of Feminist Research"; and "From Liberal Activism to Radical Cultural Struggle." A bibliography of feminist literature is included; many chapters cite the works of other active feminist scholars. Recommended for upper-division undergraduate and graduate students as well as faculty.— *J. Davenport, Auburn University*

WS-1328   Can. CIP
McFarlane, Brian. **Proud past, bright future: one hundred years of Canadian women's hockey.** Stoddart, 1994. (Dist. by Publishers Distribution Service) 206p index ISBN 0-7737-2836-8, $30.00

McFarlane, author of many popular hockey books, traces the history of women's ice hockey in Canada. He provides an excellent overview of the development at the collegiate, club, and league levels as well as the national and international competition levels. More than 100 photographs from various archives are included. McFarlane could have enhanced the contribution of this book by providing a bibliography of his interviews with various players and by listing the full citations of the archival and newspaper sources he used. The index is adequate but does not provide any cross-references for the players; for example, Margaret Smith Cater is listed under her maiden name Topp. Unfortunately, McFarlane omits any mention or discussion of women who officiate on the various levels. This title is by no means an academic treatise, and the author has a tendency to digress with personal stories. Still, with more than 100 years of participation in ice hockey and an Olympic medal sport in 1998, this groundbreaking resource assures recognition of Canadian women's historic role. Highly recommended for all sports collections.—*M. C. Su, Pennsylvania State University, Altoona Campus*

WS-1329 GV709 90-42698 CIP
Nelson, Mariah Burton. **Are we winning yet?: how women are changing sports and sports are changing women.** Random House, 1991. 238p index ISBN 0-394-57576-8, $20.00

What does it mean to be a female athlete in today's society? Nelson examines this question primarily by documenting stories of successful sportswomen, both professional and amateur, in diverse sports including body builders, race car drivers, dogsled racers, and the more familiar runners and tennis players. Issues of femininity, sexuality, and freedom attendant to women's venture into a previously male-dominated sports arena are forthrightly discussed. The author suggests a "new wave" partnership model for women's sport contrasted to the male military model. Nelson's attempts to make connections between mixed teams (coed) and the disabled as well an excessive digression to issues of sex orientation and rape are the most obvious faults in this otherwise well-written book, which presents readers with an interesting and forthright perspective of the changing role of women in the sports arena.—*M. A. Arrighi, University of Maryland at College Park*

WS-1330 GV464 95-90224 CIP
Simons, Minot. **Women's gymnastics: a history. v.1: 1966 to 1974.** Welwyn Publishing Company, P.O. Box 222475, Carmel, CA 93922-2475, 1995. 403p bibl ISBN 0-9646062-0-8, $35.00

Simons offers a worldwide history of gymnastics that involves all major competitions between 1966 and 1974, emphasizing the Olympics of 1968 and 1972. His book is a celebration and informative compendium of women's gymnastics, richly formatted and enhanced with dazzling photography. The biographies and behind-the-scenes stories bring alive the trials of defeat and glory, binding the technical aspects with the human drama of the sport. Anyone with a strong interest in gymnastics—performer, parent, or fan—will enjoy this book. It is written so the more serious can read every word, including a description of the routines, while the casual reader can skip these and concentrate on the stories and personalities. Instructors of the sport could enhance their teaching by offering inspiring examples and knowledge about individuals who endured during the toughest of times. Others can learn technique through the illustrations and diagrams of the moves describing the text. All levels.—*J. M. Fynewever, Michigan Technological University*

WS-1331 GV709 93-6510 CIP
Women in sport: issues and controversies, ed. by Greta L. Cohen.

Sage, 1993. 338p indexes ISBN 0-8039-4979-0, $46.00; ISBN 0-8039-4980-4 pbk, $23.95

Editor Cohen (Univ. of Rhode Island) is to be commended for her coordinating of all the material in this work. The book is divided into eight major sections covering such topics as gender issues, history, physiological and psychological aspects, and predictions for the future. The 31 authors have prepared excellent chapters coordinated with the major sections. The book is arranged in such a way that each chapter stands alone; students could use parts of the book in any sequence. Each chapter is supplemented by keywords used in the overview, discussion questions, and references. Excellent material for undergraduate and graduate students, to supplement courses in history and principles, women's studies, and issues involving women's sports. All levels.—*J. Davenport, Auburn University*

WS-1332 GV706 93-41211 CIP
Women, media and sport: challenging gender values, ed. by Pamela J. Creedon. Sage Publications, CA, 1994. 358p indexes ISBN 0-8039-5233-3, $48.00; ISBN 0-8039-5234-1 pbk, $23.95

This book investigates the "gendered value system of US culture that underlies and supports both sport and traditional sports media." A critical analysis is presented of the relationship of women, media, and sport from a feminist perspective. A new model for women's sports is proposed based on a different value orientation. The book appears to be well researched. Chapters by contributing authors enhance the breadth of the content both from a cultural and media perspective. Individuals interested in the history of women's sports and particularly in gender issues as related to varying media will find this volume informative. The feminist perspective pervades the entire text as the title clearly indicates. Upper-division undergraduate through professional.—*M. A. Arrighi, University of Maryland at College Park*

WS-1333 GV709 93-38013 CIP
Women, sport, and culture, ed. by Susan Birrell and Cheryl L. Cole. Human Kinetics, 1994. 408p bibl index ISBN 0-87322-650-X, $39.00

The editors call this volume a "boundary text," a collection of works from feminist-informed sports studies and from a feminist cultural studies perspective. These readings are intended to answer questions relating to gender, the body, and sport. The book is divided into five sections: "Women, Sport and Ideology"; "Gender and the Organization of Sport"; "Women in the Male Preserve of Sport"; "Media, Sport and Gender;" and "Sport and the Politics of Sexuality." The 24 pieces relate to these topics, e.g., "Gender and the Coaching Profession"; "A Postmodern Paradox? Cheerleaders at Women's Sporting Events"; "Gender Stereotyping in Televised Sports." Many of the chapters use technical feminist terms; thus, this book is recommended for upper-division undergraduates and graduate students in women's studies and women's sports.—*J. Davenport, Auburn University*

◆ SOCIAL & BEHAVIORAL SCIENCES

WS-1334   HV4708   94-21360 CIP
Adams, Carol J. **Neither man nor beast: feminism and the defense of animals.** Continuum, 1994. 271p bibl index ISBN 0-8264-0670-X, $24.95

Adams's *The Sexual Politics of Meat* (CH, Feb'91) introduced a new idea to the general public: that the eating of meat and the oppression of women are intimately connected. According to Adams, the patriarchal mind constructs both women and animals as "other," and sees them only in terms of their usefulness. Insofar as women participate in meat-eating, Adams argued, they are complicit in their own oppression. In this collection of her essays, Adams, a theologian, expands on those ideas, exploring a range of subjects: abortion rights and animal rights; connections between domestic violence and violence against animals; feminist ethics and vegetarianism; racism and animal oppression; and feminist-vegetarian theology. Although most of the essays were previously published, they have been largely inaccessible and so the collection is welcome. Some of the essays are geared to sophisticated academic audiences; most presume at least some acquaintance with feminist theory, but even general readers with an interest in animal rights will be intrigued by Adams's work. Her thinking is brilliant and original, and this volume belongs in every women's studies, theology, and environmental ethics collection.—*L. Vance, Vermont College*

WS-1335   HV4708   89-22338 MARC
Adams, Carol J. **The sexual politics of meat: a feminist-vegetarian critical theory.** Continuum, 1990. 256p bibl index ISBN 0-8264-0455-3, $22.95

Adams ranges widely through cultural anthropology, feminist theory, literary criticism, and history to build an argument that the consumption of meat supports sexism and male dominance. Women and animals, she contends, serve as the "absent referents" in the texts of patriarchal culture; by asserting that meat is the flesh of dead animals and by adopting vegetarian practices, women can signal a rejection of male violence and control. Ambitious and impassioned, the work is somewhat uneven in quality. Some of Adams's explorations of the links between feminism and vegetarianism are excellent and persuasive; her analysis of Mary Shelley's Frankenstein is particularly good. But in some portions of the book, her strong desire to find vegetarian traditions in feminism prompts her to advance tenuous connections. Still, as the first book to attempt to bring together feminist and vegetarian theory, Adams's work is a worthwhile acquisition. It will almost surely become a "bible" for feminist and progressive animal rights activists, and its claims are provocative enough to challenge women's studies faculty and students at all levels.—*L. Vance, Vermont College*

WS-1336   HV4711   95-17002 CIP
Animals and women: feminist theoretical explorations, ed. by Carol J. Adams and Josephine Donovan. Duke University, 1995. 381p bibl index afp ISBN 0-8223-1655-2, $54.95; ISBN 0-8223-1667-6 pbk, $17.95

Essays in this interdisciplinary, mostly radical collection urge feminist ecology to address issues of animal abuse and show how oppressions of women and nonhuman animals are interconnected. Part 1, "Sexism/Speciesism: Interlocking Oppressions," contains six philosophically outstanding essays; Joan Dunayer's "Sexist Words, Speciesist Roots," Maria Cominou's "Speech, Pornography, and Hunting," and Gary Francione's "Abortion and Animal Rights" are themselves worth the book's price. In part 2, "Alternative Stories," Linda Vance's "Beyond Just-So Stories" is engaging, Reginald Abbott's commentary on Virginia Woolf's "The Plumage Bill" (reprinted as an appendix) restores interesting history to contemporary discussions, and Susanne Kappeler's concluding "Speciesism, Racism, Nationalism" explores wider connections. Other essays discuss battering, lab research, chickens, wolves, fiction, and emotion. Of the growing number of works in ecofeminism, this reviewer knows of no other academic collection focusing on animals. Coeditor and contributor Carol Adams is well known for her books *The Sexual Politics of Meat* (CH, Feb'91) and *Neither Man nor Beast: Femi-*

nism and the Defense of Animals (CH, Jun'95). Every college library should welcome this fine addition to the literature of feminist ecology and animal liberation. All levels.—*C. Card, University of Wisconsin—Madison*

WS-1337   HQ1219   95-8994 CIP
Beauty queens on the global stage: gender, contests, and power, ed. by Colleen Ballerino Cohen, Richard Wilk, and Beverly Stoeltje. Routledge, 1996. 256p bibl index ISBN 0-415-91152-4, $55.95; ISBN 0-415-91153-2 pbk, $17.95

These essays address the intersections of beauty pageants, power, gender, ethnicity, and nationalism in a global context. Containing 13 ethnographic studies of beauty contests in locations as far-flung as Guatemala, Nicaragua, Andalusia, Texas, Minnesota, Thailand, Belize, Tonga, Russia, the British Virgin Islands, Liberia, the Philippines, and Tibet, the book treats subjects ranging from a local competition in the rural US to a "Moslem Philippine transsexual beauty queen contest." The editors advocate a cultural-studies approach to taking popular cultural phenomena seriously and see beauty contests as "places where cultural meanings are produced, consumed *and* rejected, where local and global, ethnic and national, national and international cultures and structures of power are engaged in their most trivial but vital aspects." Each essay outlines the history of the pageant in question and examines the significance of what happens both on- and offstage. Utterly unique among current scholarship on beauty culture and the body, the collection is a valuable contribution to gender studies, cultural studies, and anthropology.—*R. R. Warhol, University of Vermont*

WS-1338   HQ1233   92-36883 CIP
Ecofeminism and the sacred, ed. by Carol J. Adams. Continuum, 1993. 340p bibl ISBN 0-8264-0586-X, $24.95

In patriarchal religions, the earthly female body has been profaned while the transcendent (male) spirit has been sacralized. The consequences have been dramatic. Seen as evil at worst and insignificant at best, women, animals, and nature in general have suffered systematic degradation and oppression. What might happen, one wonders, if the physical, sensuous world were seen as sacred? In this outstanding new collection, a diverse group of feminist theologians, philosophers, and activists explores this central question. The 20 essays are grouped into three sections: the first offers feminist and womanist analyses of traditional religions; the second examines emergent ecofeminist spiritualities; and the third explores the ways such spiritualities might work in practice. Adams has done a remarkable job of bringing together contributors from a wide range of cultural and experiential backgrounds, giving voice to both the well-known (Rosemary Radford Ruether, Judith Plaskow, Charlene Spretnak) and the as yet unknown. The result is an engaging, passionate, and compelling book that should be in every theology, women's studies, and environmental ethics collection.—*L. Vance, Vermont College*

WS-1339   HQ1233   92-6598 CIP
Ecofeminism: women, animals, nature, ed. by Greta Gaard. Temple University, 1993. 331p index afp ISBN 0-87722-988-0, $44.95; ISBN 0-87722-989-9 pbk, $18.95

This admirable collection of 12 essays by academics and activists makes a significant contribution to the emergent ecofeminist literature. Arguing that the liberation of all oppressed groups must be addressed simultaneously, ecofeminists construct a theoretical bridge connecting environmentalism, animal liberation, and feminism. The editor's introduction skillfully erects the analytical foundation that frames the essays. Two essays describe ecofeminist theory, followed by three essays applying it. Two essays discuss the connections between animal liberation and ecofeminism, emphasizing the volume's unique focus on the centrality of all life on earth. The final four essays consider Western culture's perceptions of the woman-nature association and the cultural limitations of ecofeminism. Topics raised in the essays include green politics, the interpretation of history, ecofeminist praxis, and cultural imperialism. The writing style and structure of the essays are remarkably similar, making them accessible to students from the community college level up. A necessity for researchers in ecofeminism; appropriate for undergraduate and graduate students in the social sciences and humanities. Endnotes with each essay; extensive selected bibliography; adequate author/subject index.—*S. Cable, University of Tennessee at Knoxville*

WS-1340   HQ1823   91-16225 CIP

Eisenstein, Hester. **Gender shock: practicing feminism on two continents.** Beacon Press, 1991. (Dist. by Farrar, Straus & Giroux) 138p bibl index ISBN 0-8070-6762-8, $18.95

Eisenstein's highly readable occasional pieces offer accessible, thoughtful, well-documented reflection on implications of feminists' occupying major positions of power. Six essays compare feminist practice in Australia and the US, drawing on Eisenstein's experience as a US academic who spent 1980-88 in New South Wales's Department of Equal Opportunity in Public Employment as a "femocrat" (feminist bureaucrat—an Australian term that Eisenstein says has lost its derogatory connotations for feminists explicitly recruited for government jobs to implement feminist policies). Eisenstein, coeditor of *The Future of Difference* (1980) with Alice Jardin (interviewed here), claims that hiring "femocrats" is the Australian opportunity for feminist practice comparable to women's studies in the US. The last three pieces, also in comparative feminism, defend feminist optimism by drawing on Sara Ruddick's "maternal thinking," assess families as sites to meet needs for intimacy, nurturance, and reproduction, and examine the concept of gender in works by Catherine MacKinnon in law, Teresa de Lauretis in film, and Aihwa Ong on Malaysian factory workers. College, university, and public libraries.—*C. Card, University of Wisconsin*

WS-1341   HQ1181   95-5922 CIP

Feminism and social change: bridging theory and practice, ed. by Heidi Gottfried. Illinois, 1996. 286p index afp ISBN 0-252-02198-3, $39.95; ISBN 0-252-06495-X pbk, $14.95

In this interesting collection of essays, a group of well-known feminist social scientists (including Joan Acker, Heidi Hartmann, Judith Stacey, Dorothy Smith, and Verta Taylor) describe their experience in undertakings that were designed to change the world as well as to inform the academy. Their accounts of efforts to collect, generate, and use information for effective political advocacy and to facilitate women's ability to speak, mobilize, and act in their own behalf, demonstrate the variety of ways in which the emancipatory project has come to inform the best feminist research. However, it is often easier to imagine than to accomplish a social science that advances the interests of women. As these narratives reveal, the relation between researcher and informants in participatory research is particularly difficult, as one young scholar learned when she went "home" to study women as an insider but was treated as an outsider, and as an experienced researcher found when she had to tell less than the "whole" truth to avoid betraying her informants. The failures and dilemmas described here should help to inform the next generation of activist research. Both experienced researchers and their students will find this new contribution to the methodological literature compelling and provocative. All levels.—*N. B. Rosenthal, SUNY College at Old Westbury*

WS-1342   Orig

From Nairobi to Beijing: second review and appraisal of the implementation of the Nairobi Forward-Looking Strategies for the Advancement of Women, report of the Secretary-General. United Nations, 1995. 366p ISBN 92-1-130166-1 pbk, $25.00

This report of the UN Secretary General details women's societal position in cultures around the globe, delineating 11 areas of critical concern for women. An extensive review of political and demographic data presents an appraisal of progress made since the Forward-Looking Strategies for the Advancement of Women conference held in Nairobi. Although not as much progress has been achieved as activists would like, considerable advancement has been made toward increasing women's educational and economic opportunities and decreasing their exposure to violence and discrimination. A "new" issue facing women is a resurgence of war-related violence, exemplified by recent strife in the Balkan nations. The text makes an urgent call to women for increased participation in peace efforts. Another key area is women's unemployment in "transitional" economies, notably those now moving from communist/socialist to capitalist economies. Rates of female unemployment here are rising rapidly. Finally, poverty remains disproportionately a burden for women in all nations. Equitable distribution of development and opportunity does not appear to be forthcoming. Governments have not established mechanisms and policies for increasing equity, and there is little organized activity to create or support women's employment programs. Upper-division undergraduates and above.—*D. Van Ausdale, Valdosta State University*

WS-1343   HD9995   93-36105 CIP

Hicks, Karen M. **Surviving the Dalkon Shield IUD: women v. the pharmaceutical industry.** Teachers College Press (Columbia University), 1994. 197p bibl index afp ISBN 0-8077-6271-7, $38.00; ISBN 0-8077-6270-9 pbk, $17.95

Hicks's historical analysis treats violence against women, injustice, and victim empowerment. She meticulously documents corporate misconduct and greed amplified by legal and regulatory failure that result in public endangerment and injury. The author develops a detailed model for victim empowerment and for achievement of legal, political, and economic agendas. Procedures used by the author-participant-observer were remarkably effective counterattacks to the strategies of business interests and government designed to hinder, block, deceive, and thus prevent claims. Recommended for organizers of activist groups, undergraduates, pre-professionals, and professionals.—*L. G. Muzio, SUNY Empire State College*

WS-1344   Orig

Johnson, Pauline. **Feminism as radical humanism.** Westview, 1994. 168p bibl index ISBN 0-8133-2357-6, $49.95; ISBN 0-8133-2358-4 pbk, $17.95

Johnson's complex argument is that contemporary feminism is a form of humanism. Without recognition of this facet of itself, feminist scholarship runs aground on the paradox of its recognition of specificity and difference and its necessity to universalize claims-making in its commitment to social justice. Her treatment of contemporary humanist and postmodernist discourse, such as that of Habermas and Foucault, is thought provoking. Equally challenging are analyses of feminism's relations to Enlightenment and Romantic era thinking, the first providing the humanist universalizing tendency, the second the prototype of difference, although through a flawed masculinist, individualist subjectivity. The weaknesses of the book are its density, somewhat limited resources, and underdeveloped connections between sections. Expansion would have provided greater accessibility and clarified the contributions of radical humanism and feminism as possible responses to postmodernism. This book will be valuable for theorists and advanced students in sociology, political science, women's studies, and other fields interested in the politics of difference and identity illuminated by humanist, feminist, and postmodernist discourses. Upper-division undergraduate and graduate collections.—*J. L. Croissant, Rensselaer Polytechnic Institute*

WS-1345   HQ759   94-42159 CIP

Kahn, Robbie Pfeufer. **Bearing meaning: the language of birth.** Illinois, 1995. 441p bibl index afp ISBN 0-252-02171-1, $29.95

In her valuable study of the varieties of discourse and practice surrounding childbirth under capitalist and patriarchal systems, Kahn offers this prescription: "As childbearers, women have the most natural opportunity to be affected by the culture of the just born .... To preserve this potential of women makes the organization of childbearing practices so crucial .... Thus, the place and conduct of birth may become instruments of social change when the social structure supports a nonhierarchical expression of human agency." To make this point, Kahn weaves together four strands: the "attitudes towards birth in texts from Western tradition"; "the relationship between this tradition and current birth ... practices in the United States"; the "counterstories to the dominant ones" [found in "canonical" texts]; and "a personal narrative that interacts with the others." Although she grounds this subject matter within a longitudinal and broadly "human" perspective, she ignores the fieldwork-based, cross- and intracultural research of anthropologists such as Scheper-Hughes and Floyd-Davis. She also fails to address how her vision of the reorganization of childbirth practices can aid the desperate search to end infertility and/or teen pregnancy. All levels.—*K. S. Fine-Dare, Fort Lewis College*

WS-1346   HQ18   94-41559 CIP

Mavor, Carol. **Pleasures taken: performances of sexuality and loss in Victorian photographs.** Duke University, 1995. 171p bibl index afp ISBN 0-8223-1603-X, $47.95; ISBN 0-8223-1619-6 pbk, $17.95

Each of Mavor's three chapters focuses on a Victorian photograph collection: Lewis Carroll's girl-children; Julia Margaret Cameron's motherhood series; and the self-fashioning images of Hannah Cullwick. Mavor (Univ. of North

Carolina-Chapel Hill) means to read (and participate in) the desires and privations of her people. Because we share important Victorian fantasies (e.g., childhood as a "lost utopia"), Mavor argues, we fail to see their desires, which can be found in the "invisible sites of pleasure—sexuality and loss." To enable her to see the invisible, Mavor employs theory (significantly, that of Roland Barthes, Jacques Lacan, Maurice Merleau-Ponty, and Emmanuel Levinas), which suggests that she regards the photographs—her texts—as performances whose subjects are equally objects. Accordingly, Mavor herself is "neither in the text nor outside the text, but of the text." Fueled by theory, her estimable imagination sweeps the reader along on a journey of "haptic" associations as difficult to describe as to fault. The result is clearer: Mavor desanitizes the Victorians and reeroticizes their girl-children and women, fleshing them out in ways that render prevailing representations flat and bloodless by comparison. Excellent endnotes extend Mavor's performance. Good bibliography. Upper-division undergraduates and above.— *P. K. Cline, Earlham College*

WS-1347   HQ1181   93-33313 CIP
O'Barr, Jean Fox. **Feminism in action: building institutions and community through women's studies.** North Carolina, 1994. 301p index afp ISBN 0-8078-2129-2, $49.95; ISBN 0-8078-4439-X pbk, $16.95

Founding director of the Women's Studies Program at Duke University and editor of *Signs*, O'Barr has had a significant impact on the field. In this volume of essays she explores "building feminist institutions and community" through discussion of her endeavors in several realms: adult education, program development, fund-raising, journal editing, teaching women's studies, and consciousness-raising. Although "newly crafted" for the book, many of the chapters were originally designed as "talks"; some show their age, others the limitations of their audience. Too, O'Barr's experiences at Duke may have been rather too rarified to be generally applicable to other, less privileged, settings. Nonetheless, the book has considerable appeal. Cogent and compelling prose, creative integration of description and analysis, and clever approaches to problem solving make it useful to a number of constituencies both within and outside of women's studies. In the opinion of this reviewer, however, the book's value lies as much in its autobiographical as in its didactic elements, revealing a woman who wove the strands of necessity into the opportunity for both self-development and the empowerment of others. All levels.—*N. B. Rosenthal, SUNY College at Old Westbury*

WS-1348   Aust. CIP
Pettman, Jan. **Living in the margins: racism, sexism and feminism in Australia.** Allen & Unwin, 1992. 187p bibl index ISBN 1-86373-005-2 pbk, $19.95

Pettman's last line, "To be continued. . .," is a reassuring commitment. Her book attempts to consolidate years of conversations, conferences, and teaching experiences. It is, however, cursory, given the wide-ranging differences among women represented. Pettman furnishes readers with a map of many interstices of race and sex in Australia. She offers brief historical notes or examples. She also provides a basis for a feminist positioning with respect to race and sex and presents several theoretical models from which to view the construction of the "migrant" women and the "colonial encounter." Pettman probes the politics of representation and the construction of identities of aboriginal and "ethnic" women. This book, because of its over-determined language and lack of exposition, suits those who are already part of the conversations on sex, race, and power. It is of value to those who have joined these conversation from cultural studies, colonial studies, and feminist or women's studies' perspectives, although the multiple origins of the women "in the margin" and their positions in society are not adequately depicted. Excellent references. Advanced undergraduate; graduate; faculty.—*L. De Danaan, Evergreen State College*

WS-1349   HC79   92-45793 CIP
Seager, Joni. **Earth follies: coming to feminist terms with the global environmental crisis.** Routledge, 1993. 332p bibl index ISBN 0-415-90720-9, $27.50

Current global environmental problems, says Seager, are not so much caused by *human* acts as by *institutional* acts—those of government, industry, the military, and, increasingly, the "ecoestablishment." The culture of these institutions, she argues, relies on and perpetuates ideals of competition, abstraction, ratio-

nality, and hierarchical decision making. Such ideals operate to the detriment of women, the poor, and people of color, whose material conditions and exclusion from decision making means that they suffer the most direct and serious consequences of environmental degradation. Although she relies heavily on popular (and often partisan) secondary sources, Seager's ample use of statistics and case studies is impressive and her analysis of women's grass-roots movements is quite effective. She is somewhat unfairly dismissive of ecofeminism, however, caricaturing it as a spirituality based, personal transformation movement. Such a caricature does a disservice to both the burgeoning philosophical literature and the grass-roots activism that has emerged from ecofeminist ideals. Nonetheless, the book is a lucid, readable, and generally persuasive analysis of the impact of environmental decision making on women.—*L. Vance, Vermont College*

WS-1350   HQ1206   91-44545 CIP
Simonds, Wendy. **Women and self-help culture: reading between the lines.** Rutgers, 1992. 267p bibl index ISBN 0-8135-1833-4, $35.00; ISBN 0-8135-1834-2 pbk, $14.00

Simonds examines what the phenomenon of self-help reading reveals about gender relations in contemporary American culture. By interviewing women readers and editors of self-help books and by looking at bestsellers since 1963 (such as those offering advice about managing relationships, enhancing sexuality, developing self-esteem, becoming assertive, and improving spiritual life), Simonds argues that the genre's continued success is indicative of readers' search for meaning. Drawing on feminist theory and critical cultural studies, Simonds explores the appeal of self-help books and asks what readers are making of them. She looks at how these books affect the social construction, cultural consumption, and transmission of ideas about gender and the self. Simonds discusses readers' assessments of the meaning and effectiveness of self-help reading and the interaction between religious and therapeutic ideology in the activity of reading the genre. She also includes authors' and editors' views of their work. Simonds finds self-help books tend to recommend individual change that can validate caring and encourage a sense of community among women. General.—*M. Klatte, Eastern Kentucky University*

WS-1351   HQ1150   91-25057 CIP
Spain, Daphne. **Gendered spaces.** North Carolina, 1992. 294p bibl index afp ISBN 0-8078-2012-1, $39.95; ISBN 0-8078-4357-1 pbk, $14.95

An original combination of sociology and architectural design provides a convincing lesson on the association between gender stratification and spacial segregation. Spain examines the social institutions of family, education, and economy in the contexts of the spacial configurations of dwellings, schools, and workplaces, respectively. She reports preindustrial examples, using both ethnographies and Human Relations Area File data, and then presents qualitative historical data on the US for an industrialized example. Evidence uniformly indicates that the mutual influence of spacial segregation and gender inequality depends on the degree to which access to knowledge is structured by spacial location. From ceremonial men's huts to modern office buildings, variations in women's status are documented just as variations in spacial design are described and quite often illustrated. Both the quantitative and the qualitative findings focus on differential kinship power, inheritance rights, and control of labor and property to indicate the junction of gender, status, and space. Appendixes and bibliography are excellent, as are the tables and figures throughout the text. Truly interdisciplinary, this work will support studies in anthropology, sociology, architecture, design, and of course gender. College and university libraries.—*R. Zingraff, Meredith College*

WS-1352   HF6161   90-48686 CIP
Vinikas, Vincent. **Soft soap, hard sell: American hygiene in an age of advertisement.** Iowa State, 1992. 168p bibl index afp ISBN 0-8138-1788-9, $27.95

A well-researched study of advertising in popular periodicals. Vinikas seeks to evaluate the power of print advertising in American society from the 1900s to the 1980s. He examines advertisements for deodorant sprays and soaps, antiperspirants, mouthwashes, and cosmetic and hygiene products because they have become prominent in American everyday life. "By 1890," the author states, "advertisers had come to appreciate that women bought at least four-fifths of all consumer merchandise. Forty years later, women were buying 85 per cent of all the goods sold at retail." Through the use of negative advertising, sex-role stereotyping, and false advertising, companies learned that, in addition to a commodity, a company could also produce demands for a product. They found that ads could be used to fabricate novel diseases and unverifiable social symptomology in order to secure customers. Complements Carol Moog's *Are They Selling Her Lips?: Advertising and Identity* (CH, Jul'90), *Emotion in Advertising: Theoretical and Practical Explorations*, ed. by S.J. Agres, J.A. Edell, and T.M. Dubitsky (CH, May'91), and Trevor Millum's *Images of Woman: Advertising in Women's Magazines* (1975). Upper-division undergraduates and above.—*R. L. Ruben, Western Illinois University*

◆ Feminist Theory, Issues

WS-1354   HV6561   93-14800 CIP
Allison, Julie A. **Rape: the misunderstood crime,** by Julie A. Allison and Lawrence S. Wrightsman. Sage, 1993. 307p bibl indexes ISBN 0-8039-3706-7, $45.00; ISBN 0-8039-3707-5 pbk, $21.95

A comprehensive review of what is known about rape. The authors consider all forms of rape, including stranger rape, spousal rape, and acquaintance rape. Sections focus on attitudes toward rape and rape victims, reactions of rape victims, legal issues, treatment, and prevention. The scope of the book is broad and coverage of issues and topics is extensive and thorough. This study compares favorably with older comprehensive works, e.g., Manachem Amir's *Patterns in Forcible Rape* (CH, Feb'72); Ann Burgess and Lynda Holstrom's *Rape: Victims of Crisis* (1974); and Lorene Clark and Debra Lewis's *Rape: The Price of Coercive Sexuality* (1977). It is more comprehensive but gives less attention to theory than some recent works, e.g., *Acquaintance Rape: The Hidden Crime*, ed. by Andrea Parrot and Laurie Bechofer (1991); Lee Ellis's *Theories of Rape: Inquiries into the Causes of Sexual Aggression* (CH, Jan'90); and Linda Bourque's *Defining Rape* (CH, Dec'89). The book is well referenced and adequately indexed; the text is smooth and relatively easy to follow throughout. The authors have treated extensively aspects of the judicial process, with some attention to the dynamics of rape. Recommended for all levels.—*R. T. Sigler, University of Alabama*

WS-1355   HQ471   90-24125 CIP
Berger, Ronald J. **Feminism and pornography,** by Ronald J. Berger, Patricia Searles, and Charles E. Cottle. Praeger, 1991. 478p bibl index afp ISBN 0-275-93819-0, $39.95

This book offers a compact survey of recent scholarly and political reflection on contemporary issues relating to pornography. The authors assess a variety of feminist and libertarian positions, and they look at social science research that attempts—with no pretense at a consensus—to gauge pornography's causes and consequences. From the governmental commissions authorized by presidents Johnson and Reagan to recent municipal ordinances (in Minneapolis) and civil actions brought by private parties, they examine a range of social responses and public strategies. As an introduction, the book covers much ground. It is in the nature of such a survey that readers are presented with a wide spectrum of opinion rather than given a theme to follow, develop,and ultimately accept or reject. The terse format imposes didacticism. The effort to take no side is not always helpful, and judgments, such as "socialist feminism. . .is a theoretical framework capable of integrating the best of feminist thought," seem to leap out with inadequate support. Nevertheless, much useful information and up-to-date references make this an accessible introduction to a complex topic. All levels.—*J. T. Rosenthal, SUNY at Stony Brook*

WS-1356   HQ1190   93-40638 CIP
Braidotti, Rosi. **Nomadic subjects: embodiment and sexual difference in contemporary feminist theory.** Columbia, 1995 (c1994). 326p index afp ISBN 0-231-08234-7, $52.50; ISBN 0-231-08235-5 pbk, $15.50

Braidotti, an Italian Australian philosopher now based in the Netherlands, has assembled original work, revised essays, articles, and speeches into a coherent construction of a new feminist subject for the postmodern era: the nomad. Abandoning metaphors of exile made popular by earlier feminist thinkers, Braidotti

posits an identity that can shift intentionally between positions of language, class, ethnicity, race, gender, and sexual practice, rejecting both the fixed particular and the (falsely) homeless universal mode. From this transitory vantage point, the feminist subject can construct an ethical and political consciousness capable of resisting—even destabilizing—hegemonic thinking, and can create new modes of becoming. Braidotti demonstrates this nomadic subjectivity herself, traveling in different voices across a range of topics, calling on feminist theorists, on high and popular culture, on biomedical ethics, on European unity, and on American multiculturalism. Her lively writing is a wonderful blend of the personal and academic. Although beyond the grasp of most undergraduates, this book belongs in every library that serves graduate students and faculty in women's studies and philosophy.—*L. Vance, Norwich University*

WS-1357   HQ1206   95-12498 CIP
Carter, Pam. **Feminism, breasts and breast-feeding.** St. Martin's, 1995. 266p bibl indexes ISBN 0-312-12625-5, $35.00

Concern about women doing their motherly duty by breast-feeding their infants has been expressed repeatedly since the 18th century by a largely male health establishment. However, the question was rarely examined from the female point of view. Carter adopts a feminist perspective informed by poststructuralist thinking to explore this issue. She interviewed women's memories of feeding in a working-class neighborhood in a northern city in England from 1920 on, a time when a major decline in breast-feeding started. Carter found that women who failed to conform to normative expectations regarding infant feeding were not irrational and in need of change. Rather, they were expressing resistance to the dominant discourses of femininity within which infant feeding practices are framed. Women's experiences with breasts and breast-feeding have been controlled, shaped, and given meaning through the discourses of femininity, modesty, and heterosexuality. Attention to differences among women and to women's wishes to control their bodies reflects a need to expand women's choices regarding reproduction and sexuality, instead of limiting them to seemingly "natural" womanly behavior. Comprehensive bibliography. Upper-division undergraduates and above.—*C. Adamsky, University of New Hampshire*

WS-1358   HQ1190   94-3922 CIP
Colker, Ruth. **Pregnant men: practice, theory, and the law.** Indiana, 1994. 224p index afp ISBN 0-253-31371-6, $29.95; ISBN 0-253-20898-X pbk, $12.95

As lawyer, professor, and feminist theorist, Colker analyzes legal reasonings on reproductive rights. She considers the benefits of an equality based argument for reproductive choice over privacy based reasonings, which favor middle-class white women. The concept of "the pregnant man" is more than a counterfactual thought experiment; rather, it is a guideline for evaluating proceedings concerning men's reproductive choices. Assumptions about sexuality, pregnancy, and "woman" are mediated by race and class, and in general favor male authority. Thus the law disempowers poor women, most often women of color. Any interference in reproductive rights (e.g., waiting periods) becomes a matter of discrimination. Perhaps weakest in its analysis of the interplay of biology and culture, this work contains the outlines of a general theory of race, class, and gender in the legal system, but the narrative style leaves the theoretical possibilities obscure. For upper-division undergraduates and above; the descriptions of cases and decisions are especially useful.—*J. L. Croissant, Rensselaer Polytechnic Institute*

WS-1359   HQ1426   90-34999 CIP
Conflicts in feminism, ed. by Marianne Hirsch and Evelyn Fox Keller. Routledge, 1990. 397p index ISBN 0-415-90177-4, $49.50; ISBN 0-415-90178-2, $15.95

Like the feminist movement, the maturation of feminist theory has been accompanied by an increase in internal debates over substantive issues like pornography, race and class, reproductive technologies, and workplace equality, as well as over methodological approaches. In this collection of 20 essays by well-known academic theorists, editors Hirsch and Keller have successfully illuminated both the history of feminist theory in the context of feminism as a movement and the explicit sites of conflict. Their success is largely due to the fact that most of the essays were prepared specifically for this collection and thus address the topic of disagreement within the field in a focused way. However, the collection goes beyond simply mapping disagreement: most of the contributors responded to the editors' desire to consider a "model for a discourse of difference," one that would encourage the dynamic value of conflict while minimizing the potential for irreconcilable divisions. A unique contribution to a burgeoning discipline, this volume will be of great value to graduate students and faculty in women's studies, and belongs in any library collection of feminist theory.— *L. Vance, Vermont College*

WS-1360 KF9329 95-46944 CIP
Date rape: feminism, philosophy, and the law, ed. by Leslie Francis. Pennsylvania State, 1996. 186p bibl index afp ISBN 0-271-01428-8, $29.50; ISBN 0-271-01429-6 pbk, $13.95

Francis uses a set of short readings to investigate the feminist perspective on date rape. The volume begins with the republication of an article by Lois Pineau, which argues that for sex to be consensual a woman must communicate affirmatively that she wants to participate. If this communication did not exist, date rape has occurred. Counterpoints are offered by David Adams, Angela Harris, and Catharine Wells, feminists arguing a more moderate position. Pineau then responds to her critics. The volume concludes with a presentation and defense of the controversial Antioch College Sexual Offense Policy. Although philosophical and legalistic in some places, the text is clear and understandable, given the complexity of the issue discussed. The work is lightly referenced and adequately indexed. Suitable for libraries serving programs in criminal justice, sociology, psychology, or women's studies. Upper-division undergraduates and above.—*R. T. Sigler, University of Alabama*

WS-1361 HQ1233 93-39064 CIP
Diamond, Irene. **Fertile ground: women, earth, and the limits of control.** Beacon Press, 1994. 202p bibl index ISBN 0-8070-6772-5, $24.00

At a moment when certain articulations of feminism have come under attack from quarters across the political (and geographic) spectrum for what has been perceived as a universalizing and totalizing ideology, Diamond adds fuel to fire. She does so by questioning some of the major tenets of feminism, most notably, the issue of women's empowerment through control of fertility, reproductive functions, and sexuality. As a self-proclaimed ecofeminist and Green, she challenges both the language of "control" and the technologies that purportedly bring that control within reach. *Fertile Ground* is not an easy book; familiarity with the work of Michel Foucault and a grounding in some of the critical arguments that have surfaced in late 20th century feminist discourse (abortion, surrogacy, postcolonial theory) would certainly help readers. This difficult, challenging, and occasionally annoying work deserves serious attention from all who seek to understand better the connections between ecology and feminism, as well as some of the central tensions between the West and the rest of the world. Upper-division undergraduates and above.—*E. Broidy, University of California, Irvine*

WS-1362 Orig
Dirty looks: women, pornography, power, ed. by Pamela Church Gibson and Roma Gibson. BFI, 1993. (Dist. by Indiana) 238p index ISBN 0-85170-403-4, $40.00; ISBN 0-85170-404-2 pbk, $18.95

"For better or worse," observes Carol J. Clover in her introduction to this essential, critical volume, "pornography has become the feminist issue of the decade." The problem of pornography's meaning and ramifications has indeed polarized the feminist community. At one end of the spectrum are those who contend that pornography licenses rape and violence; on the other are those who view pornography as a meaningful text offering insight into the complex sexual behavior it represents. The former group seeks laws to prevent the sale and distribution of such sexual materials; the latter eschews this action as a form of censorship. This particular collection of 13 essays resists censorship and the fear of pornography's alleged consequences. Intelligently and intriguingly written, the various articles explore the nuances of theory and practice of pornography and violence, and scrutinize the delicate relationship between art and pornography. Overall, contributors "share in the conviction that there is no single right reading of pornography, and that even the most standard forms of heterosexual pornography confess a deeply complicated relationship to women and feminity, to men and masculinity, and to the terms of sexual difference that order our everyday lives." General readers, advanced undergraduates, and above.—*J. Boskin, Boston University*

WS-1363 HQ1421 94-7489 CIP
Farganis, Sondra. **Situating feminism: from thought to action.** Sage Publications, CA, 1994. 195p (Contemporary social theory, 2) bibl indexes ISBN 0-8039-4649-X, $36.00; ISBN 0-8039-4650-3 pbk, $16.95

Farganis (New School for Social Research) has written a concise study on the situation of feminist thought in relation to contemporary social controversies. She analyzes the Nussbaum (domestic violence and victimization), Baby M (motherhood and surrogacy), Sears (employment and affirmative action), and Hill/Thomas (race and sexual harassment) cases in a broad theoretical context. Farganis outlines major themes (e.g., difference and equality) and conflicts (e.g., essentialism versus cultural feminism) within feminist thought, illustrating how these played out in the resolution of the cases. Although insightful, the analyses are weak in details. This is exemplified in Farganis's reification of the "women's movement," which contradicts much of the pluralism in theory that Farganis outlines. Her goal is to make current issues in feminist philosophy and social theory broadly accessible. This is partially accomplished at the expense of detail and direction. For upper-division undergraduates and above.— *J. L. Croissant, Rensselaer Polytechnic Institute*

WS-1364 HQ1190 94-26606 CIP
Feminist nightmares: women at odds: feminism and the problem of sisterhood, ed. by Susan Ostrov Weisser and Jennifer Fleischner. New York University, 1994. 405p bibl index afp ISBN 0-8147-2619-4, $55.00; ISBN 0-8147-2620-8 pbk, $18.95

This collection of 18 essays questions the unproblematic ways that feminism has defined and used the notion of "sisterhood," in light of recent calls for diversity and recognition of differences on the part of feminists themselves. The essays range over several areas of social and literary texts, including scholarly research, the relationship among women in history, mother-daughter relations, and women in relation to men and to families. A major focus of these essays is the inequality among women of various races and classes, including ways in which women have oppressed other women. Differences among women are explored with the goal of clarifying how feminist theories and ideologies are related to social practices. The essays are well written, with copious notes. An important contribution to this new and controversial area of feminist criticism and politics. Upper-division undergraduates and above.—*B. Braendlin, Florida State University*

WS-1365 HQ1190 91-48337 CIP
Ferguson, Kathy E. **The man question: visions of subjectivity in feminist theory.** California, 1993. 236p bibl index afp ISBN 0-520-07939-6, $40.00; ISBN 0-520-07991-4 pbk, $13.00

In a creative analysis of praxis, cosmic, and linguistic feminisms, Ferguson (Univ. of Hawaii) discusses approaches to subjectivity, formulating an alternative to conventional ("modern") notions of self and subject in mobile subjectivities. Although mobile subjectivities need to be differentiated from prior nonessentialist formulations of standpoint theories (this reader would argue that they are not so different), Ferguson's book is nevertheless an important contribution. Ferguson recommends irony as the technique of choice for negotiating the contradictions of intellectual and daily life. However, an ironic voice often indicates a position of powerlessness, and this destabilizes Ferguson's recommendations. She provides a piece of exemplary scholarship and a critical opportunity to reframe major contentions in feminist theory in identity; in interactions of race, class, and gender; and in strategy. Highly recommended for students of political theory and women's studies. Well referenced. Graduate; faculty.—*J. L. Croissant, Rensselaer Polytechnic Institute*

WS-1366 HQ1237 95-3208 CIP
Gardner, Carol Brooks. **Passing by: gender and public harassment.** California, 1995. 256p bibl index afp ISBN 0-520-08187-0, $40.00; ISBN 0-520-20215-5 pbk, $16.00

Gardner insightfully examines the relationship between sex and public harassment—those "abuses, harryings and annoyances characteristic of public places." Public harassment is informal social control, another method of segregation, which can have long-lasting effects. Successful harassment is costly to women financially and psychologically in the form of cosmetic surgery, phobias, and constant self-monitoring. Public harrassment also differs, based on situational advantages, i.e., who has the power to define situations and the individuals involved. Though Gardner focuses on women and men, examining who participates in harassment, what behaviors are involved, and how behaviors are interpreted and dealt with, she reminds readers that women harass publicly as well as men. To ignore public harassment blinds people to discrimination that everyone tolerates and commits, and contributes to the continuation of a social order capable of repressing others. To rationalize any public harassment supports, justifies, and maintains the harassment of women, lesbians, racial and ethnic groups, and others. Gardner further notes that fear of rape must be understood by men if public harassment is to change. This book challenges readers to question what is taken for granted and rationalized as harmless behavior. Upper-division undergraduates and above.—*G. Rundblad, Illinois Wesleyan University*

WS-1367 HQ472 92-42237 CIP
The Invention of pornography: obscenity and the origins of modernity, 1500-1800, ed. by Lynn Hunt. Zone Books, 1993. 411p index afp ISBN 0-942299-68-X, $26.95

Hunt provides an instructive introduction to these nine papers, first presented at a scholarly conference in 1991. The basic theme is that pornography, apart from or in addition to its erotic appeal, has a strong political meaning. That the meaning is subversive to the conservative states of Europe, let alone to the France of the ancien regime, is almost self-evident. As Hunt says, pornography was "inherently subversive as a genre because it was based on materialist philosophy and often criticized priests, nuns, and aristocrats." With quick asides for Renaissance Italy and the Dutch Republic, the essays focus on France and England. The authors are in basic agreement on the interplay of modernity, individualism, the privatization of pleasure and the body, and the power of male fantasy and such myths as the virtuous courtesan and the libertine whore. However, the essays share so much common ground that readers move forward (in time and thematic development) slowly and with considerable repetition. A distinct lack of humor comes through (with some exceptions), and the dirty pictures are taken as seriously as Mercator's maps would be in a book on cartography. Advanced undergraduate and above.—*J. T. Rosenthal, SUNY at Stony Brook*

WS-1368 LC212.862 90-9478 CIP
Ivory power: sexual harassment on campus, ed. by Michele A. Paludi. State University of New York, 1991 (c1990). 309p index afp ISBN 0-7914-0457-9, $69.50; ISBN 0-7914-0458-7, pbk $21.95

This volume provides insights on harassment for students, faculty, staff, and administrators. The essays offer a thoroughly researched, theoretical approach to an occurrence whose frequency is documented as alarmingly high. Some may wish to ignore the issues of sexual and gender harassment on the nation's campuses. But anyone truly concerned with the victims' emotional and physical damage as well as with the lost "brain" power cannot underrate the presentation of facts. The reader is given views of male faculty *and* the impact of harassment on women students and faculty. Essays treat psychometric analysis, the legal aspects of harassment, clinical intervention for victims, and the establishment and maintenance of a task force on a campus. The book is intended to contribute to the transformation in the way a campus views sexual and gender harassment. A must for those truly interested in equality of both sexes and all colors in the academy.—*M. Klatte, Eastern Kentucky University*

WS-1369 KF3467 91-41340 CIP
Lindemann, Barbara. **Sexual harassment in employment law,** by Barbara Lindemann and David D. Kadue. BNA Books, 1992. 824p index ISBN 0-87179-704-6, $128.00

The authors' survey of rapidly developing case law on sexual harassment in employment was suggested by Lindemann's earlier *Employment Discrimination Law* (1976-). In traditional casebook format, summary and analysis of the law are integrated with major court decisions. Ostensibly, the intended audience is legal practitioners, but the book has wider appeal. A strength of the volume is the effort to connect sexual harassment law with other areas of the law. Coverage is thorough, although initial theoretical sections might have been improved by incorporating brief excerpts of essays and analyses of leading scholars such as Catharine MacKinnon. Two forewords by federal judges treat broader theoretical issues, but the viewpoints expressed are distinctly male, sug-

gesting the need for balance. Although this book will be a valuable addition to both law libraries and libraries serving upper-division undergraduate and graduate students, its fifth and final section considers special litigation issues and is of sole or primary interest to practitioners and legal scholars. Extremely helpful appendixes include Equal Employment Opportunity Commission (EEOC) Guidelines, appropriate sections of the EEOC Compliance Manual, an essay on sexual harassment law in Canada, and a sample antiharassment policy for employers.—*M. Hendrickson, Wilson College*

WS-1370 HQ471 92-41999 CIP
Making violence sexy: feminist views on pornography, ed. by Diana E.H. Russell. Teachers College Press (Columbia University), 1993. 302p bibl index afp ISBN 0-8077-6269-5, $46.00; ISBN 0-8077-6268-7 pbk, $19.95

Russell has edited a powerful feminist anthology dealing with nonviolent as well as violent pornography. Russell defines pornography as "material that combines sex and/or the exposure of genitals with abuse or degradation in a manner that appears to endorse, condone or encourage such behavior." From a feminist perspective, pornography is seen as a form of discrimination against women and a violation of women's civil rights. Part 1 is grounded in the concrete experience of victims and survivors of pornography. Part 2 offers selections on the meaning and significance of pornography for African American women, an African American man, gay men, and a personal account by a straight man. The selections on feminist research in pornography in Part 3 include two especially significant articles by the editor. "Pornography and Rape: a Causal Model" and "The Experts Cop Out." The collection concludes with articles on feminist strategies and actions against pornography. Advanced undergraduates and above.—*C. Adamsky, University of New Hampshire*

WS-1371 HQ1237 93-29383 CIP
Morris, Celia. **Bearing witness: sexual harassment and beyond—everywoman's story.** Little, Brown, 1994. 326p index ISBN 0-316-58422-3, $21.95

Morris's book is an urgent examination of sexual intimidation and breaks the silence that generations of women have been forced to keep. From factory lines to Capitol Hill, inner cities to universities and the upper echelons of media, law, and medicine, Morris brings to life the personal stories and solutions of women who suffer from some men's behavior. Here are the lewd remarks, the unwanted propositions, the wandering hands, and the specter of sexual violence that threaten women daily. Readers also discover women's newly found unity and their determination to fight back. A collection of stories *and* a road map of protest, the text explores the ways women have been crippled by ancient fears of female sexuality and examines the cultural heritage that has led to an imbalance of power between men and women. Arguing for equlity, at work and home, and for use of the collective "we," Morris invites sympathetic men to join a cause that can benefit them equally. Timely, impassioned, and frank, the book spotlights a national problem and issues a call to organize for justice. All levels.—*M. Klatte, Eastern Kentucky University*

WS-1372 HQ1075.5.U6 90-39262 CIP
Morrow, France. **Unleashing our unknown selves: an inquiry into the future of femininity and masculinity.** Praeger, 1991. 269p bibl indexes afp ISBN 0-275-93587-6, $42.95; ISBN 0-275-93837-9, $17.95

A major new contribution to feminist theory. Morrow presents a sophisticated revision of Freudianism, suggesting a model of the human mind that accounts for both the development of individual personalities and the evolution of culture. She posits that a child growing up in a patriarchal society develops two selves: a "majority self," the result of interaction with the maternal caregiver, and a "minority self," which is a product of relating to the father figure. Each self is achieved by a process of "accomplicity" with the given parent (reminiscent of symbolic interactionism in sociological theory). "Normal" boys and girls in patriarchal societies repress one of these selves in varying degrees, and retain and exhibit or react against stunted versions of the other. Feminist Freudians will probably see this book as a major stepping-stone to a summation of what is known about the mind. Useful as an outside reading for classes in personality theory, women's studies, social theory, and psychotherapy, lower-division undergraduate level and above.—*R. W. Smith, California State University, Northridge*

WS-1373 KF481 93-5723 CIP

The politics of pregnancy: policy dilemmas in the maternal-fetal relationship, ed. by Janna C. Merrick and Robert H. Blank. Haworth, 1994 (c1993). 247p index afp ISBN 1-56024-478-X, $39.95; ISBN 1-56023-047-9 pbk, $17.95

The 13 essays in this book demonstrate that pregnancy is more than a personal moral issue. Instead, reproductive questions are inevitably public policy concerns shaped by changing medical, technological, political, and legal forces. Written from a multidisciplinary perspective, this book raises numerous questions. For example, what are the respective rights of the fetus versus the mother, and how do workplace policies meant to protect the former conflict with the rights of the latter? What moral and legal duties do pregnant women have, and can they be prosecuted if they smoke, drink, take drugs, or fail to seek medical attention? Under what conditions, if at all, is in utero experimentation permitted, and how do recent state and federal court decisions affect not just abortion but surrogate motherhood, forced medical care for mothers, and workplace rights for pregnant women? The essays explore answers to these and other questions while also investigating major medical and biological issues often overlooked in the news. The result is a fascinating review of the debate surrounding reproduction in the US. All levels.—*D. Schultz, formerly, Trinity University*

WS-1374 HQ1090 90-45014 CIP

Seidler, Victor J. **Recreating sexual politics: men, feminism and politics.** Routledge, 1991. 311p bibl index ISBN 0-415-05853-8, $52.50

Seidler reexamines the impact of sexual politics on the relationships of men and women in society. He analyzes the theories of conservatism, liberalism, traditional Marxism, radical feminism, and social feminism as viewed in the 1990s. Seidler envisions a reformulation of social and political theory as essential in the transformation of masculinity. In the past decade, many books have addressed the misconceptions of masculinity. They include *Feminist Frameworks: Alternative Theoretical Accounts of the Relations Between Women and Men,* ed. by Alison M. Jaggar and Paula R. Struhl, (CH, Jun'78); James Doyle's *The Male Experience* (1st ed., CH, Feb'84; 2nd ed., 1989); Joe L. Dubbert's *A Man's Place: Masculinity in Transition* (CH, Oct'79); and Marc Fasteau's *The Male Machine* (CH, Feb'75). Seidler's book is another intellectual inquiry to complement those already in the library. Notes and bibliography assist in understanding the philosophical orientation of the content. Another source for considering the effects of social and political theory on the lives of women and men in the 1990s.—*G. M. Greenberg, emerita, Western Michigan University*

WS-1375 HV6558 90-43214 CIP

Sexual coercion: a sourcebook on its nature, causes, and prevention, ed. by Elizabeth Grauerholz and Mary A. Koralewski. Lexington Books, 1991. 240p bibl index afp ISBN 0-669-21786-7, $29.95

A collection that uses a relatively new conceptual framework—sexual coercion. Sexual coercion appears to be loosely defined in the introduction as unpleasant acts used by men to control women. The volume focuses on four sets of behavior that are held to fit within these parameters: rape, child sexual abuse, sexual harassment, and prostitution. The various essays treat definition, causality, and prevention. Individual contributions are well written, with good coverage of the specific topics. The authors range from established scholars to emerging professionals. There is an acceptable index and an excellent bibliography; the quality of the references varies from essay to essay. Recommended for libraries serving women's studies programs.—*R. T. Sigler, University of Alabama*

WS-1376 HQ472 94-40372 CIP

Strossen, Nadine. **Defending pornography: free speech, sex, and the fight for women's rights.** Scribner, 1995. 320p index ISBN 0-684-19749-9, $22.00

The "pornophobic" or procensorship feminists allege that pornography, as they choose to define it, is an attack on women. Led by Catherine MacKinnon and writer Andrea Dworkin (thus dubbed by Strossen as the "MacDworkinites"), they have been instrumental in American municipal and Canadian judicial efforts (viz. *Butler* v. *the Queen*) to control speech, publication, the media, and popular culture. Strossen argues that their efforts are a violation of free speech, that there is no accepted or demonstrated connection between "dirty books" and the deni-

gration of women or the incidence of heterosexual sex crime, and that the MacDworkinites are really working to foster the sweeping suppression of dissent, the persistence of sexism and homophobia, and conservative attacks on affirmative action and civil rights. Efforts to define, let alone to diminish, sexual harassment and the unequal treatment of women have only been hurt by the introduction of free speech issues. This is an important, readable, and casually erudite book (which combines popular treatment of controversy with law journal articles and court decisions). It is not a balanced, scholarly presentation; it is strongly biased in favor of the Bill of Rights of the US Constitution. All levels.—*J. T. Rosenthal, SUNY at Stony Brook*

WS-1377 HQ1870 90-43510 CIP

Third World women and the politics of feminism, ed. by Chandra Talpade Mohanty, Ann Russo, and Lourdes Torres. Indiana, 1991. 338p index afp ISBN 0-253-33873-5, $39.95; ISBN 0-253-20632-4 pbk, $14.95

Originally presented at an international conference, these papers focus on the recent debates over the development of feminist theory and politics by Third World women. Contributors discuss issues related to race, caste/class, gender and sexuality, colonialism and imperialism. The collection is divided into four sections. Section 1 examines questions of theory, culture, and the politics of representation in scholarly and literary texts and popular media. Section 2 focuses on political, economic, and ideological constructions of racialized womanhood in the context of the state. Section 3 presents differing views on the relation of nationalism and sexuality. Section 4 addresses issues related to identity and feminist practice. The contributors write from their own experience and from different perspectives. Though not comprehensive in coverage, these discourses provide challenging analyses. The editor emphasizes the need to rethink feminist theory and praxis within a cross-cultural/cross-national context. The essays are provocative and enhance knowledge of Third World women's issues. Highly recommended for upper-division undergraduate students and above.—*D. A. Chekki, University of Winnipeg*

WS-1378 HV6556 93-5693 CIP

Transforming a rape culture, ed. by Emilie Buchwald, Pamela R. Fletcher, and Martha Roth. Milkweed Editions, 1993. 467p indexes ISBN 0-915943-06-9, $23.95

Rape culture "is a complex of beliefs that encourages male sexual aggression and supports violence against women." Taking this as their starting point, the editors of this collection have gathered 35 essays that comment on one or another facet of verbal and physical aggression against women. The essays are organized into four sections: Living in a Rape Culture; Strategies for Change; Activism; and Visions and Possibilities. Some of the topics of the papers are: the churches and sexual violence; pornography; date rape; marital rape; sexual harassment in schools; and raising boys to have different and nonviolent attitudes toward girls. Contributors, mostly women, are active in rape crisis centers, violence prevention programs, lecturing on sexual assault, and educational programs. Most have also written widely on the problem. Though all of the essays had something important to say, this reviewer was particularly moved by Richard Orton's discussion of his work in a rape crisis center and the effect it had on him. Contributors hope that the volume will generate more public discussion of the problem and will lead to change. The collection would be quite useful in high school courses on sex education. General, community college, and lower-division undergraduate readership.—*D. Harper, University of Rochester*

WS-1379 89-18057 Orig

Walby, Sylvia. **Theorizing patriarchy.** B Blackwell, 1990. 229p bibl index ISBN 0-631-14768-3, $42.95; ISBN 0-631-14769-1, $14.95

Walby's multistranded project—to "provide a comprehensive overview of... explanations of women's subordination in contemporary society," to discuss "why recent changes have occured," and to develop a new theory for the analysis of gender relations—is contained within a short title, plain covers, and a thin volume. Her analysis is, however, both complex and dense. In the course of the book, she develops a three-dimensional taxonomy in order to construct a theory that conforms to what R.W. Connell (*Gender and Power*, CH, Jul'88) has called a "power analysis of gender" depicting men and women as "social blocks linked by a direct power relation." First Walby discusses what she invokes as the main theoretical prespectives on gender oppression (liberal feminist, Marxist feminist, radical feminist, and dual systems). Next she focuses on what each has to contribute to the understanding of what she calls the six structures of male domination and oppression (patriarchal relations in household production, paid work, culture, sexuality, use of violence, and the state). Finally, Walby reconstructs the historical transformations of patriarchy in each of these structures within a continuum of private to public "expropriation of women." The book should be of interest to faculty and students of feminist theory, upper-division undergraduate level and above.—*N. B. Rosenthal, SUNY College at Old Westbury*

WS-1380   HQ1190   95-11225 CIP
Whelehan, Imelda. **Modern feminist thought: from the second wave to 'post-feminism'.** New York University, 1995. 270p bibl index ISBN 0-8147-9299-5, $45.00; ISBN 0-8147-9300-2 pbk, $17.95

Whelehan's book should prove to be useful, if frustrating for feminists. Its central task is to examine contemporary conflicts and "crises" in feminism, including debates about sexuality, men's movements, postmodernism, postfeminism and the media, as well as theoretical and practical fissures within Marxist/socialist feminism, and black, lesbian, and radical feminisms. Embedded in the description of connections, themes, and genealogies is a weakness in theorizing about the causes of fragmentation. Some causes of feminist fragmentation are obvious, and Whelehan treats these insightfully, e.g., the neglect of black and minority women in a white middle-class-based movement, persistent heterosexism, or the perilous "academicizing" of feminist theory. But the role of the media, an institutionalized disregard of women's history, and the possibility for class- and capital-based interests to fragment the movement are only briefly implicated in the crisis and backlash. For those who have long experience with the movement and the literature, this book may be somewhat frustrating in its perspective; for younger students or those (re)discovering feminism and women's studies, Whelehan presumes a high familiarity. Nonetheless, the book is recommended for study of the history of "second-wave" feminist thought in the US. Upper-division undergraduates and above.—*J. L. Croissant, University of Arizona*

◆ Anthropology

WS-1381   F1261   95-32475 CIP
Alonso, Ana María. **Thread of blood: colonialism, revolution, and gender on Mexico's northern frontier.** Arizona, 1995. 303p bibl index afp ISBN 0-8165-1511-5, $45.00; ISBN 0-8165-1574-3 pbk, $19.95

Friedrich Katz argued 20 years ago that the Mexican Revolution of 1910 drew unique support from the *serrano* peasants of northwestern Chihuahua, whose communities were created in the late 18th century as military colonies to defend the region against Apaches. Alonso, an anthropologist, probes this hypothesis by examining the history of one of these communities, Namiquipa. She uses a variety of theoretical approaches, as well as local archival materials. In tracing the evolution of an ideology of resistance that she believes had a distinctively frontier component, Alonso focuses on gender and ethnicity, arguing that both were integral to the formulation of a code of honor essential to the reproduction of Namiquipa's way of life. The Porfirian state's assault on that system is the key to understanding Namiquipans' resistance. Most of Alonso's analysis focuses on the gendered formulation of honor and communal values. Although this book represents an innovative contribution to Mexican Revolution and frontier studies, a lack of attention to class and to Mexican colonial historiography raises questions about Alonso's claims of frontier egalitarianism, and the narrow geographical focus cautions against extending its conclusions. Upper-division undergraduates and above.—*S. M. Deeds, Northern Arizona University*

WS-1382   Orig
The Anthropology of breast-feeding: natural law or social construct, ed. by Vanessa Maher. Berg, 1992. 185p index ISBN 0-85496-721-4, $44.00

Seven essays by well-regarded social anthropologists focus on women rather than children, and several, especially those by editor Maher, take an unabashedly feminist perspective. Breastfeeding is viewed not so much as a "natural" phe-

nomenon, to be understood in terms of its biological, psychological, and nutritional effects on individuals, but as an aspect of culture, reflecting kinship, gender relations, age and class structure, economic and demographic realities, and notions of space and privacy. Examples of breastfeeding practices are drawn from contemporary Tunisia, Italy, Iran, and Nepal, and 17th- to 18th-century Iceland. The book is critical of the contemporary "medical model" of breastfeeding, supported by the (male-dominated) Western medical community and international aid agencies. Essays point out that lengthy breastfeeding may be unsafe for overworked, underfed, multiparous mothers; that exclusive breastfeeding has limited nutritional and protective advantages for babies past six months; and that bottle feeding transfers some of the cost of reproduction to men. By no means a comprehensive treatment of breastfeeding practices, the book is nevertheless a valuable addition to the excellent "Cross-cultural Perspectives on Women" series. Undergraduate through professional.—*M. A. Gwynne, SUNY at Stony Brook*

WS-1383   HQ1172   93-16206 CIP
Baker, Adrienne. **The Jewish woman in contemporary society: transitions and traditions.** New York University, 1993. 234p bibl indexes ISBN 0-8147-1210-X, $42.50; ISBN 0-8147-1211-8 pbk, $17.50

Baker's welcome study explores the experiences of American and British Jewish women. Baker considers the sometimes surprising shared experiences and attitudes of women from "secular," Reform, Orthodox, and other backgrounds, as well as the different attitudes and experiences of women from Sephardic and Ashkenazic communities. The presentation of cross-cultural material is inconsistent. Baker acknowledges some influences (e.g., Christianity's contribution to ending Jewish polygamy), but misses important parallels and patterns. For example, in discussing menstrual taboos, she dismisses pre-Judaic cultures as "primitive" and implies that Jewish women's positive feelings are unique. If there is a continuing theme, it is that more work is needed to reconcile the experiences that are common to women across the spectrum of Jewish practice. Baker has accumulated important new data. However, her inherently comparative research cries out for an analytical framework. The book bogs down in cultural particulars and skimps on synthesis. All levels.—*V. Alia, University of Western Ontario*

WS-1384   Orig
Baring, Anne. **The myth of the goddess: evolution of an image,** by Anne Baring and Jules Cashford. Viking, 1992 (c1991). 779p bibl index ISBN 0-670-83564-1, $40.00

Baring and Cashford apply a Jungian perspective to the myth of the goddess, arguing for the necessity of bringing together the images of the masculine and the feminine. Fortunately, they do not oversimplify a concept of one essential goddess in whom the others, from Demeter and Astarte to Eve, participate. The inclusion of a wide array of deities, as is found in this book, helps underscore the complexity, the profound differences and the similarities between one goddess and the next, but the unjustified exclusion of deities from Oriental and African traditions weakens the book. At times the lengthy background information overwhelms the analysis and duplicates what is already available in more usable form elsewhere. Although the analysis is supported by the work of such disparate scholars as Gimbutas and Lovelock, there are surprising gaps. For example, in the discussion of Greek gods there are no references to the work of Zeitlin or Vernant. Still, precisely because of the Jungian perspective, the extensive bibliography includes the unexpected and will prove valuable for a wide range of readers. Advanced undergraduate; graduate; faculty.—*J. de Luce, Miami University (OH)*

WS-1385   HD6113   95-46006 CIP
Bolles, A. Lynn. **Sister Jamaica: a study of women, work and households in Kingston.** University Press of America, 1996. 129p bibl afp ISBN 0-7618-0211-8, $32.50

Based on Bolles' fieldwork in 1978-79, this anthropological study links the national development strategies of "industrialization by invitation" to global economic issues, including the impact of the debt crisis and International Monetary Fund policies, and to the grassroots level of women's work and strategies of survival. Bolles pays particular attention to how poorly paid factory workers, who are primarily responsible for their families' livelihood, cope with poverty and insecurity, "making do" by stretching their wages through largely female networks of reciprocal support. Through such interdependence in their domestic economy they avoid total dependence on a single source of support, whether a male partner or a factory job. This study, which focuses chiefly on economic activities in the household, complements Helen Safa's more comparative *The Myth of the Male Breadwinner* (CH, Dec'95) about women and industrialization in Puerto Rico, the Dominican Republic, and Cuba, and Kevin Yelvington's more theoretical *Producing Power* (1995), which examines ethnicity, gender, and class in a Trinidadian factory. Bolles' conclusions about "African-Caribbean societies" are mostly true of Indian and Hispanic women factory workers, which suggests class and gender are more important than ethnicity. Recommended for women's studies and Caribbean studies collections. Upper-division undergraduates and above.— *O. N. Bolland, Colgate University*

WS-1386 GT525 91-15885 CIP
Dress and gender: making and meaning in cultural contexts, ed. by Ruth Barnes and Joanne B. Eicher. Berg, 1992. 293p index ISBN 0-85496-720-6, $59.95

This impressive collection emerged from 1989 workshop sponsored by the Centre for Cross-Cultural Research on Women, Oxford. Its 18 distinguished international authors work in anthropology, textile and design, art, cultural history, and ethnography. The 16 scholarly articles (footnotes and bibliographies) include textile traditions associated with women in headhunting Naga villages of mountainous northeast India; Buddhist communities of Thailand; Guatemalan Indian cultures; modern Israeli religious/nationalistic contexts; contemporary US quilting guilds; Venetian lacemaking institutions; 17th-century Japan; and Hindu customs of India. As a group, the essays show how dress as a cultural phenomenon defines personal identity geographically and historically; designates belonging to a community; and reflects social position, authority, and religious affiliation. Meaning may be incorporated into the construction process, clothing form, or cultural function. Two articles provide insight into European imperialism and African cultural assimilation through clothing. Overall, this excellent volume should serve as a useful resource. Undergraduate; graduate; faculty.— *B. B. Chico, Regis University (CO)*

WS-1387 HQ1752 95-9320 CIP
Fantasizing the feminine in Indonesia, ed. by Laurie J. Sears. Duke University, 1996. 349p bibl index afp ISBN 0-8223-1684-6, $49.95; ISBN 0-8223-1696-X pbk, $17.95

Clear, insightful, and rich in data, this volume is based on original fieldwork studies and contains much original thought and analysis. It centers on the formative elements and constraints of female behavior in 19th- and 20th-century Indonesia and looks at "tradition" as a cultural construct. Five main themes permeate the contributions: internal and external observations and participants' differing conceptions of femininity; change through historical time and the life cycle; interaction of the observer and observed; the need to reach beyond the bounds of contemporary feminist theories and analysis; and the development of a conscious awareness of the writer/observer's own thoughts, feelings, and emotions, including how the observer's life-cycle experiences, social positioning, and worldview affect observations and interpretations. The volume is accessible to readers who are not specialists in Indonesian or feminist studies. Black-and-white photos, selected bibliography, good index. Essential for all Indonesian and feminist collections; highly recommended for Asian collections. Upper-division undergraduates and above.— *L. A. Kimball, Western Washington University*

WS-1388 GN635 91-72229 MARC
Female and male in Borneo: contributions and challenges to gender studies, ed. by Vinson H. Sutlive. College of William and Mary, Borneo Research Council, P.O. Box 8795, Williamsburg, VA 23187-8795, 1991. 528p (Borneo Research Council monograph series, 1) ISBN 0-9629568-0-5, $32.50

Sutlive's provocative and fascinating work brings to the fore a crucial ethnographic realm. "Anthropological generalizations and comparisons have largely ignored research results from Borneo. . . . If considered, this research would require the reformulation of much anthropological theory." The papers in this skillfully edited, data-packed volume fully substantiate the need for such reformulation. Richly documented accounts based on extensive field studies analyze intrica-

cies of male-female relationships, sexuality, cosmology, female chieftianship, the complex actual and symbolic parallelisms and contrapositions of Iban's men's headhunting and women's weaving (including the interconnectedness of dream-questing, weaving, and power), life enculturation and roles, the demanding realities of survival, and the effects of modern times on Iban, Ngaju Dayak, Rungus Dusun, Kadayan, and European colonials. The sophisticated discussions combine historical, social anthropological, psychological, and other perspectives; they suggest the need for new theoretical constructs and approaches. The book is well written throughout, with many black-and-white photographs and diagrams, and a good bibliography but no index. Essential for all anthropological collections at all levels, all gender collections, and all Southeast Asian collections.— *L. A. Kimball, Western Washington University*

WS-1389 DT515 91-14182 CIP
Hausa women in the twentieth century, ed. by Catherine Coles and Beverly Mack. Wisconsin, 1991. 297p bibl index ISBN 0-299-13020-7, $19.95

With its focus on women, this volume is a welcome addition to the literature on Hausa people. The individual chapters, all based on original research, represent work from several academic disciplines (history, anthropology, economics, political science, African languages and literature). Since the editors did not impose a unified ideological position on the contributors, disparate viewpoints emerge. Throughout, the subject of women's participation in Hausa society is explored. Women's active roles are evident in a variety of circumstances—from royalty to prostitute, possession cult participant to radio program panelist. Historical and contemporary topics are investigated; elite and nonelite women are discussed; the urban context predominates. The excellent introduction relates the chapters and their respective themes to a larger social science literature on women. Thus, the book appeals to an audience well beyond Africanists; this is a valuable volume for readers interested in women's issues generally. By emphasizing context and the role gender plays in all Hausa relationships, the notion of universal gender asymmetry is called into question. Community college students and up.— *R. Ellovich, North Carolina State University*

WS-1390 BR1443 95-11563 CIP
Hoehler-Fatton, Cynthia. **Women of fire and spirit: history, faith, and gender in Roho religion in Western Kenya.** Oxford, 1996. 260p bibl index afp ISBN 0-19-509790-4, $45.00; ISBN 0-19-509791-2 pbk, $19.95

Around Lake Victoria's Kavirondo Gulf—where Bantu-speaking and non-Bantu-speaking Africans jostled for primacy during Kenya's administrative age—an indigenous Holy Spirit church of charismatic intensity and great staying power arose, even before WW I, strengthened in the 1920s and 1930s, and continued to flourish into the 1990s. It is the subject of this study, which complements earlier examinations by John Lonsdale, Okot p'Bitek, and Audrey Wipper. Hoehler-Fatton relies on the testimonies of a few long-lived and deeply involved informants, extensive nonpassive participant observation, and a review of the available archival and other documentary evidence. The first part of her book re-creates the history of the Roho Movement/Church and rightfully focuses on disputes over land and on conflicts between Luo- and Bantu-speakers, as well as those within the nascent Anglican church fostered by Archdeacon Walter Edwin Owen of the Church Missionary Society. The second half of the book deals with the critical role of women within the modern movement, as well as with the eschatological worldview of the Roho. This is a solid, if occasionally disjointed, monograph that adds detail and considerable texture to the study of indigenous religion in Africa. Two maps, good bibliography. Upper-division undergraduates and above.— *R. I. Rotberg, Harvard University*

WS-1391 HF3882 95-51427 CIP
Kapchan, Deborah A. **Gender on the market: Moroccan women and the revoicing of tradition.** Pennsylvania, 1996. 325p bibl indexes afp ISBN 0-8122-3155-4, $42.50; ISBN 0-8122-1426-9 pbk, $19.95

Kapchan's splendid ethnographic study of women's performance genres in Beni Mellal, Morocco, is an outstanding contribution to gender studies and to the understanding of Middle Eastern society. Its contribution to the already substantial literature on Morocco is greater than the book's title might imply. Through the idiom of social performances, Kapchan paints a vivid picture of the changing domains of household and family. In its examination of women's discourse, her study stands with Lila Abu Lughod's much acclaimed *Writing Women's Worlds* (CH, Apr'93). Kapchan's book offers a rare insight into changing public roles of women, as illustrated by the movement of women into previously male domains of the market and public performance. She focuses on the speech, aspirations, and behavior of female vendors, herbalists, and musicians—the *shikhat*. Through their voices, readers can sense the interplay of religion, family, and even the search for economic advantage. The writing is personal yet objective, and quite apart from the study's ethnographic substance, the reader gains an appreciation of the author's approach to fieldwork. This book will be useful to a broad audience, including those concerned with discourse analysis, the anthropology of gender, and the contemporary Middle East and North Africa. Upper-division undergraduates and above.—*D. G. Bates, CUNY Hunter College*

WS-1392   Brit. CIP
Knight, Chris. **Blood relations: menstruation and the origins of culture.** Yale, 1992 (c1991). 581p bibl indexes ISBN 0-300-04911-0, $45.00

Encyclopaedic in scope, this is a seminal work that will certainly stand as a classic example of the application of the Marxist anthropological model to an examination of the origin of human culture. Knight, trained in social and symbolic anthropology, proposes a parallel between the 20th century Marx-Engels perception of history as a struggle for freedom by producers of wealth (workers) from the owners of production and an Upper Paleolithic struggle for freedom by producers (females) from male dominance. This first human revolution rested on the ovulatory synchrony of female sodalities and the subsequent withholding of sexual favors from males to ensure their return from the hunt with their kill. Thus, culture is seen as starting with gender rather than husband-wife solidarity. For documentation, Knight draws on selected findings from sociobiology, paleoanthropology, ethnology, folklore (in particular, structuralist analysis), primatology, and feminist theory, from laboratory, field, and speculative studies, both pioneer and recent. The argument is closely reasoned and the style pleasant. Knight warns: "I fully expect my narrative to be vigorously contested" (p.5), and he is correct, for specialists in these fields will take issue with his position, as does this reviewer. Still, this is an important and stimulating contribution to studies on human cultural origins. The 31-page bibliography is a rich resource. Necessary reading for advanced undergraduates, graduate students, and professionals.—*P. Waterman, University of South Florida*

WS-1393   HN939   92-24045 CIP
Lockwood, Victoria S. **Tahitian transformation: gender and capitalist development in a rural society.** L. Rienner, 1993. 180p bibl index afp ISBN 1-55587-317-0, $35.00; ISBN 1-55587-391-X pbk, $15.95

An excellent, straightforward ethnographic account of the political economy of a Tahitian village on the island of Tubuai, French Polynesia. Lockwood is especially sensitive to world system theory; perhaps her major contribution is linking the closely observed village system to the larger regional and world political economy. This integration has been demonstrated before for Tahiti and other parts of the present and past French colonial world, but never with the richness of detail and consistent historical perspective of Lockwood's study. In a sense, she sustains the long-standing critique of colonial capitalism first suggested in theories of underdevelopment, i.e., whatever the cultural flows in this subsection of the world system, the people of Tubuai retain a peasant mode of production. But this account of underdevelopment is nuanced by specific treatments of French policies and plans in Tahiti and of the neocolonial politics that result. The study is also valuable for its presentation of political economy at the household level and of how it has altered over time to parallel changes in the world and regional systems. The changing nature of gender stratification and relations is a special feature of this look at household political economy. Advanced undergraduate; graduate; faculty.—*G. E. Marcus, Rice University*

WS-1394   BL2480   93-37980 CIP
Matory, J. Lorand. **Sex and the empire that is no more: gender and the politics of metaphor in Oyo Yoruba religion.** Minnesota, 1994. 295p bibl index afp ISBN 0-8166-2226-4, $49.95

This is a powerful detailing of gender relations following the collapse of the

old Oyo Empire and the beginning of British colonial rule in Nigeria. From her study of the history of Yoruba society and religion, the author, an African American anthropologist, presents evidence that calls into question the assumption that polar opposition between women and men is a dichotomy "naturally" based on the biology of the sexes. A close analysis of the context of cross-dressing in the Yoruba religions provides the author with much of the data for her finding that "gender is historical and is subject to transformation by reigning political and financial interests." Seven chapters and a series of appendixes set forth the interpretation and the data in impeccable fashion. This reviewer predicts that this book will become an ethnographic classic among professionals and students in the social and behavioral sciences. Advanced undergraduates and up.—*F. P. Conant, Hunter College, CUNY*

WS-1395   GT525   93-13886 CIP
On fashion, ed. by Shari Benstock and Suzanne Ferriss. Rutgers, 1994. 317p bibl index ISBN 0-8135-2032-0, $45.00; ISBN 0-8135-2033-9 pbk, $16.00

Film theory, literary criticism, intercultural analyses, and women's studies are merged in this compendium on fashion as fantasy, identity, and reflector of sexuality. Complemented by 63 illustrations, the 16 essays treat the body as fashion designer's territory; fashion as visual image; and fashion as political expression. The three political studies open cross-cultural horizons. Cheryl Herr (Univ. of Iowa), in "Terrorist Chic," reveals the schizophrenic state of Irish fashion from the conservative style of President Mary Robinson's suits to the paramilitary Provo uniforms of the terrorist Irish Republican Army in the North, and shows how feminine and terrorist fashions are fused in the outfits of IRA supporters. Barbara Brodman (Nova Univ.) joins 1992 Nobel Peace Prize winner Rigoberta Menchú in calling for human rights aid to Latin American Indians, particularly Guatemalan textile weavers, whose unique, high quality fabrics and designs have often been exploited by Euramerican fashion designers. Andrew Ross (Princeton Univ.) claims cooptation by contemporary designers of urban street styles derived from gangs in Los Angeles, New York, and London, and also exposes the paradox of dress that simultaneously resists and affirms the subordinate status of gang subculture. The collection offers many thought provoking ideas. All levels.—*B. B. Chico, Regis University (CO)*

WS-1396   NX456.5.P7   89-20375 CIP
Torgovnick, Marianna. **Gone primitive: savage intellects, modern lives.** Chicago, 1990. 328p bibl index afp ISBN 0-226-80831-9, $24.95

Torgovnick's collection of essays examines Western fascination with "primitive" cultures. The author suggests that the image of the "primitive"—as noble savage, as sexualized, as paradisal, as violent—is a Western invention, used to control countries outside of the West and minorities and women within it. The book elaborates on the feminist aspect of her thesis, arguing that primitivism provides a medium for asserting and naturalizing concepts of masculinity. She argues that the so-called primitive societies provides a "them" to define a Western unified, monolithic, and powerful "us." The power of the "us," however, is an illusion; and through her analysis Torgovnick suggests that Western culture must be revealed as fragmented along gender, class, national origin, race, and many other categories. Torgovnick limits her examples largely to 20th-century culture, examining the discourse of primitivism in modern art, literature, anthropology, and psychoanalysis as well as in texts such as photography, television, and travel literature. The book is well written and lively, and it injects a feminist perspective to the study of orientalism and Western dominance. It is illustrated with relevant and entertaining examples of "primitivism" and would be appropriate for both academic and nonacademic readers.—*A. Goldson, Brown University*

WS-1397   HQ1240   94-12466 CIP
Townsend, Janet Gabriel. **Women's voices from the rainforest.** Routledge, 1995. 212p bibl index ISBN 0-415-10531-5, $59.95; ISBN 0-415-10532-3 pbk, $17.95

Townsend attempts to address several issues concerning the lives of "pioneer women" in Mexico and Colombia and the work of outside researchers who study communities on the frontiers of colonization. Although Townsend is listed as the author, the book is presented as a collaborative effort by seven women trained in the fields of geography, nutrition, biology, sociology, socioagronomy, and literature from Britain and Latin America. Contending that the needs and perspectives of women pioneers have been ignored by outsiders, the authors move the reader from "etic" to "emic" insights, from a literature review to material gained from survey and life-history interviews collected during field visits to settlement communities. As part of this, they critique methodologies commonly used to assess development needs (indeed, the book is aimed at development specialists), make policy recommendations in support of pioneer women, and present "insider voices" through translations of some of the Mexican material. The subjects and messages are important, but the book reveals the difficulties involved in integrating work across disciplinary and geographical boundaries, as well as the problem of enabling "insiders" to have a considered say on policy recommendations that could affect their lives. Upper-division undergraduates, professionals.—C. Hendrickson, Marlboro College

WS-1398   DS646   93-10521 CIP
Tsing, Anna Lowenhaupt. **In the realm of the diamond queen: marginality in an out-of-the-way place.** Princeton, 1993. 350p bibl index afp ISBN 0-691-03335-8, $49.50; ISBN 0-691-00051-4 pbk, $14.95

Tsing's ethnography of Dayak people living in the Meratus hills on the island of Borneo spotlights several fascinating women and men who, through their activities as shamans, storytellers, and farmers, express their own marginality vis-à-vis the nation-state. Tsing emphasizes the marginal position of Meratus people in relation to Muslim lowlanders and government officials. She richly contextualizes her cases and stories in ongoing Meratus engagements with an environment under state-sponsored attack. Less emphasized are the ways in which residents of other highlands conceive of their cultural identities. Although Tsing relies on the notion of a "meratus" identity, the ideas, forms, and practices associated with this identity are less well described than are the fascinating inventions and border crossings of marginal individuals. Tsing deftly situates her own analysis in relation to the current competing accounts of marginality, subordination, difference, and resistance in the fields of cultural studies, social history, and cultural anthropology. Brilliantly and in a fluent prose style, Tsing uses these ethnographic insights to reflect on gendered politics and theory in Europe and North America. Advanced undergraduates and above.—J. R. Bowen, Washington University

◆ History, Biography & Theory

WS-1399   HQ1793   91-39685 CIP
Abu-Lughod, Lila. **Writing women's worlds: Bedouin stories.** California, 1993. 266p bibl afp ISBN 0-520-07946-9, $30.00

In this beautifully written book, Abu-Lughod, an Arab American anthropologist, presents stories, anecdotes, and reminiscences she recorded in the course of her research on women in a small Bedouin community in western Egypt. Collected from a handful of kinswomen, these diverse narratives are skillfully edited and rearranged by Abu-Lughod to illustrate the dynamics of such patriarchal institutions as patrilineality, polygyny, and arranged marriages and their impact on the lives of individual men and women. More than just providing the reader with a look into the private lives of Bedouin women, these stories are meant to demonstrate the shortcomings of anthropological and feminist theory and the politics of ethnograpic representation. These issues are fully addressed in the book's lengthy and skillfully argued introductory essay in which the author critically assesses the role of the anthropologist in creating and maintaining the myth of the culturally distinct "Other." An important contribution to the study of culture theory, gender ideologies, and Arab society. Advanced undergraduate; graduate; faculty.—A. Rassam, Queens College, CUNY

WS-1400   GN479.7   90-30497 MARC
Beyond the second sex: new directions in the anthropology of gender, ed. by Peggy Reeves Sanday and Ruth Gallagher Goodenough. Pennsylvania, 1990. 350p indexes ISBN 0-8122-8257-4, $36.95; ISBN 0-8122-1303-3, $16.95

In this collection of essays, a distinguished group of anthropologists, including Peggy Sanday, Igor Kopytoff, Sandra Barnes, Alice Schlegel, and Lila Abu-Lughod, provide ethnographic and theoretical insights into current issues of gender and power. The 11 essays emerged from a 1984 University of Pennsyl-

vania conference (three were published previously). All analysts share concerns with models that escape simplistic dichotomies of cultural/powerful males and natural/dominated women. Drawing on field materials primarily from Africa and Oceania, the authors explore context, nuances, and contradictions within gender ideologies and social actions. Although focusing on women's roles, many authors also reinterpret male ideology and behavior with a strong recognition of contemporary social and cultural changes. The writers also grapple with questions of theory and terminology, although a dialogue among articles rarely emerges. On the whole, this is a clearly written and interesting collection that elaborates concerns in J. F. Collier and S. J. Yanagisako's *Gender and Kinship* (1987) and M. Strathern's *Dealing with Inequality* (1987) while contributing to a central discussion of the contemporary social sciences. Undergraduates and up.—G. W. McDonogh, New College of the University of South Florida

WS-1401   Aust. CIP
First in their field: women and Australian anthropology, ed. by Julie Marcus. Melbourne, 1993. (Dist. by International Specialized Book Services) 189p bibl index ISBN 0-522-84466-9 pbk, $24.95

There is a special cultural context and quality in the essays that make up this volume having to do with white Victorian culture in Australia, on which contributors might have reflected more self-consciously. The dismissal and subordination of women anthropologists seemed particularly acute there, as did (and does) their resentment. As Marie de Lepervanche summarizes in the introduction, "The pattern of irregular work and interrupted careers experienced by these women is familiar to a number of women who entered the academy much later. There is also another pattern emerging from the biographies of these pioneering anthroplogists and that is the significance of male patronage or lack of it." The collection is composed of fascinating and engaging studies of Mary Ellen Murray-Prior, Daisy Bates, Jane Ada Fletcher, Ursula McConnel, Olive Pink, and Phyllis Kaberry. Lest one should think that because they were victimized and marginalized these women were necessarily more enlightened than their male colleagues and patrons, this volume demonstrates that these women mostly shared the same racist assumptions characteristic of the anthropology of their times. An important resource in the history of anthropology. General readers, advanced undergraduates, and above.—G. E. Marcus, Rice University

WS-1402   HQ1186   95-6078 CIP
Goldman, Anne E. **Take my word: autobiographical innovations of ethnic American working women.** California, 1996. 237p bibl index afp ISBN 0-520-20096-9, $40.00; ISBN 0-520-20097-7 pbk, $16.00

Goldman describes the manner in which working-class women have been denied autobiography. What they have actually been denied is the use of the conventional genre of autobiography as a literary form for self-presentation. These women have found other means, circuitous routes, to write about themselves. They have accomplished this through books marketed as cookbooks, "anonymous" (i.e., name erased by editor) oral histories, labor history, and ethnography. Goldman examines how these women situate themselves in their narratives and how they use them to present their very individual lives. The books under discussion (cookbooks by Hispanic and African American women, collaborative life histories of Hispanic and African American midwives and healers, and the stories of immigrant Jewish women active in the struggle to organize labor) were published as studies in the culinary arts, cultural studies, and labor history, yet, these remarkable women also told their own highly personal and fascinating stories. Despite its toilsome postmodernist jargon, Goldman's book offers important insights for literary and women's studies, and anthropology. Upper-division undergraduates and above.—F. J. Hay, Appalachian State University

WS-1403   GN345   91-24593 CIP
Wolf, Margery. **A thrice-told tale: feminism, postmodernism, and ethnographic responsibility.** Stanford, 1992. 153p bibl index afp ISBN 0-8047-1979-9, $29.50; ISBN 0-8047-1980-2 pbk, $10.95

Wolf addresses the postmodern and feminist critique of ethnography using three versions of a Taiwanese peasant woman's story. Wolf, a well-known ethnographer of Chinese family life, first presents a fictional account of a village woman. A young, poor housewife with no relatives in the village has a nervous breakdown. Her neighbors wonder if she is possessed by important spirits, but in the end decide she is "just" mentally ill. The second retelling consists of Wolf's fieldnotes of the village women's deliberations about the victim's condition. The third version is Wolf's academic article explaining the outcome—the unfortunate woman was denied the status of spirit-possession because of her peripheral role in the village kinship structure, as well as the anti-female bias of the culture. Along the way Wolf considers issues of postmodernism, reflexivity, and feminism in ethnography. How can one pretend to record objective "facts" when all understandings are contested and socially situated? How can one fail to expose the unequal distribution of power which subordinates women? This intelligent book concludes that the importance of telling the story so that the "natives" can understand it outweighs the importance of impressing academic elites with exotic erudition. Advanced undergraduate through professional.—*S. Plattner, National Science Foundation*

WS-1404   GN21   91-36288 CIP
Zumwalt, Rosemary Lévy. **Wealth and rebellion: Elsie Clews Parsons, anthropologist and folklorist.** Illinois, 1992. 360p bibl index afp ISBN 0-252-01909-1, $47.50

Elsie Clews Parsons was an interesting and active participant in the early development of anthropology and the study of folklore in the US. Born to wealth, Parsons pushed the social boundaries of her world and certainly of her family's expectations. She fulfilled the traditional female pattern in that she married within her social class and had a family, but armed with a doctorate from Columbia, she also taught at Barnard, and did field research on both Native Americans and African Americans. Using Parsons's private letters as well as manuscripts, Zumwalt gives the reader a glimpse into the life of this very modern, independent woman. In addition to Parsons's fieldwork, Zumwalt discusses Parsons's association with other leaders in the world of anthropology. This well-written, interesting biography is recommended to folklorists, historians, and anthropologists. General; advanced undergraduate; graduate; faculty.—*L. R. Metzger, University of Akron*

◆ Archaeology

WS-1405   GN799   93-47924 CIP
Barber, Elizabeth Wayland. **Women's work: the first 20,000 years: women, cloth, and society in early times.** W.W. Norton, 1994. 334p bibl index ISBN 0-393-03506-9, $23.00

Barber, author of *Prehistoric Textiles* (CH, Nov'91), is well equipped to study the interrelationships among women, society, and textiles from the Paleolithic to the Iron Age. She relies on a multidisciplinary approach to what evidence has survived, calling on the methods of archaeology, linguistic analysis, anthropology, and economics, among other disciplines. Her discussion of the difficulty of studying the perishable products of women's labor is especially informative. Herself a weaver, Barber brings to her study a scholar's and a practitioner's understanding of the craft of weaving; the details of cloth production are as valuable as the glimpses into the daily lives of women. Her analysis of mythology, however, is considerably less skilled and sophisticated than her analysis of archaeological evidence. Illustrations are all black-and-white and sometimes hard to discern. Since there are no reference numbers in the text to correspond to the sources listed at the end of the book, and no page numbers in that list to indicate where a particular source was cited in the text, the reader will be hard-pressed to locate discussions of Barber's sources. All levels.—*J. de Luce, Miami University (OH)*

WS-1406   E99   92-46737 CIP
Spector, Janet D. **What this awl means: feminist archaeology at a Wahpeton Dakota village.** Minnesota Historical Society, 1993. 161p bibl index afp ISBN 0-87351-277-4, $32.50; ISBN 0-87351-278-2 pbk, $15.95

A highly personal and imaginative treatment of how archaeologists can use information from living peoples as well as historic accounts to interpret archaeological sites. The book is based on the Little Rapids site, a 19th-century Eastern Dakota (Sioux) village near present day Minneapolis. Spector begins by describing how she became an archaeologist and the major influences in her professional life. She clearly distinguishes between her "emphathetic" style of archaeology and that practiced by many others. Spector presents her own fictional account of how

a particular artifact (an awl), may have been used by a Wahpeton woman, followed by a critical review of more conventional archaeological methods used to analyze such artifacts. Spector employs this technique to show how the values and beliefs of Native Americans and archaeologists can conflict. She also includes brief mention of some issues surrounding the repatriation of Native American artifacts. Finally, Spector uses historic sources to portray the Dakota way of life at the time Native Americans occupied the site, describes the excavation program, and highlights recovered materials. Community college level and above.—*T. A. Foor, University of Montana*

WS-1407   CC110   94-8818 CIP
Women in archaeology, ed. by Cheryl Claassen. Pennsylvania, 1994. 252p bibl index apf ISBN 0-8122-3277-1, $36.95; ISBN 0-8122-1509-5 pbk, $16.95

Slowly, the record is being set straight. Here is a fine collection of essays that help fill the gender gap in the history of archaeological practice. Most of the 41 women whose work is discussed were active in the US before 1940. Claassen observes that women have had to devise clever adaptations to participate, and survive, in archaeology. Few have been academics; many are contract workers, often linked to museums. Today, only 15 percent of archaeology professors in the top 30 academic departments are women. More encouraging is the fact that 50.9 percent of archaeology students are women. The essays reveal the complex relationship among class, ethnicity, and gender—women were mostly viewed as male scholars' students and helpmates, but were in dominant positions with respect to indigenous male "assistants." For example, Dorothy Popenow was said to have made "solo" expeditions—with a Spanish-speaking colleague; Frances Watkins wrote of a women's expedition with no men along, ignoring the crew of local men who worked with them. The next task is to uncover the hidden lives and contributions of these indigenous "assistants," still lost in the "Sherpa" mentality of archaeological history. General and academic readers at all levels.—*V. Alia, University of Western Ontario*

◆ Social/Cultural Anthropology

WS-1408   E98   91-11367 CIP
Allen, Paula Gunn. **Grandmothers of the light: a medicine woman's sourcebook.** Beacon Press, 1991. (Dist. by Farrar, Straus, Giroux) 246p bibl ISBN 0-8070-8102-7, $19.95

Gunn Allen begins this remarkable collection with a prayer whose first line "Look at us, hear us!" challenges the reader to put aside ideologies and preconceptions and reexamine the world through different eyes. In 21 beautifully told or retold stories, Gunn Allen shares a distinctly female universe of ritual and magic. Through the images that come alive in these tales gleaned from Mayan, Aztec, Navajo, and Cherokee sources, among others, the supernatural and the seemingly ordinary join together to form a tapestry of life that is both wonderfully spiritual and amazingly concrete. Introductory chapters provide a context for reading the stories and each individual story begins with a brief statement setting the scene or relating details about the history or lineage of the story. A glossary helps readers keep or find their way among the various goddesses and shamans, while a selective bibliography cites additional sources of myths and stories. Recommended for academic and public libraries. Especially recommended for libraries able to create a program or display around this "medicine woman's sourcebook."—*E. Broidy, University of California, Irvine*

WS-1409   GT3415   93-34877 CIP
Allison, Anne. **Nightwork: sexuality, pleasure, and corporate masculinity in a Tokyo hostess club.** Chicago, 1994. 213p bibl index afp ISBN 0-226-01485-1, $37.00; ISBN 0-226-01487-8 pbk, $14.95

Allison's very readable work is about hostess clubs—Japanese establishments whose service includes sexual talk between businessmen and hostesses. The author (Duke Univ.) compares businesses' justifications of their employees' use of these establishments ("opening up," relaxing, bonding with fellow workers) to the activities that really take place in them. Data came from three sources: observation and participation (the author worked in a Tokyo hostess club for four months);

interviews with customers, employees, and researchers of sex, family, and gender issues; and a detailed literature review of Japanese writings. The monograph has three parts. The first, a careful description of what takes place in a hostess club, provides readers with an in-depth understanding of the interpersonal relationships found there. Allison summarizes the club's physical setting and social context and explains how hostesses differ from prostitutes. In the second part, she describes what men do in the club, focusing on such highly formulaic activities as drinking, singing, joking with each other, and speaking to and about the hostesses in a specialized language. Third, Allison examines the role and scope of the women's services and explains how that relates to the goals of businesses and businessmen. Upper-division undergraduate and up.—*T. A. Foor, University of Montana*

WS-1410　　　HQ1745　　　95-31267 Orig
Bagwe, Anjali. **Of woman caste: the experience of gender in rural India.** Zed Books, 1995. 245p bibl index ISBN 1-85649-321-0, $59.95; ISBN 1-85649-322-9 pbk, $22.50

Bagwe, a US trained anthropologist, started fieldwork in her native village of Maharashtra with a research design using a questionnaire. The result of her five-year involvement is an analytical but deeply touching, well-written account of a researcher who moved from participant observer to marginal activist. Bagwe smoothly presents the story of four women who succeed in their small world by compromising, yielding, subverting, and transcending the traditional rural Indian system of male dominance. Their lives educate readers about how the monstrous mutations of caste and kinship-based patriarchy react to capitalism that brings in its wake a massive male migration for city jobs and a money-based economy. As a community organizer, Bagwe discovered that the women were more likely to be practical and less prone to ego hassles in public affairs. Bagwe demonstrates how the Malvani folk songs enabled women to transcend familial roles and find solidarity despite age differences (daughter-in-law versus mother-in-law). She also shows how the mechanization of agriculture has led to the feminization of rural poverty. All levels.—*N. N. Kalia, SUNY College at Buffalo*

WS-1411　　　E99　　　93-13176 CIP
Bahr, Diana Meyers. **From mission to metropolis: Cupeño Indian women in Los Angeles.** Oklahoma, 1993. 184p bibl index afp ISBN 0-8061-2549-7, $24.95

Bahr's brief work offers a glimpse into the lives of three generations of Cupeño Indian women residing in Los Angeles. The author asks to what extent Indian women have maintained their Indian identity in the urban milieu and how that identity is manifested. To answer this question, Bahr focuses not on technological or social aspects, but on what she refers to as *mentalité*, the ideas that people have about themselves and their lives. She chooses three aspects of *mentalité*—family, beneficence, and metaphysics—to explore. The discussion includes examples from the women's lives, examples of former and current Cupeño culture, and an analysis or comparison of the two. The continuation of ideas probably comes out most clearly and distinctly in the section concerning the women's attitudes toward deceased members of the family, who are still thought to be part of everyday life. The book is an important contribution to the growing literature on urban Indians and adds a new perspective, that of urban Indian women. Community college through graduate level.—*M. J. Schneider, University of North Dakota*

WS-1412　　　GN667　　　93-20568 CIP
Burbank, Victoria Katherine. **Fighting women: anger and aggression in Aboriginal Australia.** California, 1994. 250p bibl index afp ISBN 0-520-08307-5, $35.00; ISBN 0-520-08308-3 pbk, $16.00

Burbank presents a contemporary view of aboriginal daily life in the fictitiously named mission community of Mangrove, in the Northern Territory's Arnhem Land. Burbank's meticulous comparative scholarship leads to her compelling point, that anger and aggression are culturally constructed as behaviors and as ideas, and are experienced for diverse reasons and in diverse ways by women. The result is an "ethnotheory of aggressive behavior from the perspective of Aboriginal women." Burbank offers a broad discussion of the sources, meanings, and reasons for female aggression in a well-reasoned study of the cultural bases of behaviors related to power relationships. She concludes that anger and aggression are culturally constructed by all initiators and recipients. Genders are sys-

tems "in which unequal power relations are constructed, maintained, and challenged by mundane interactions between and among the sexes." Finally, she argues that aggression in the studied community "springs from a multiplicity of motives and represents a variety of strategies for both the situationally powerful and the situationally powerless." Recommended for upper-division undergraduates and above.—*S. R. Martin, Michigan Technological University*

WS-1413　　　RG518　　　92-402 CIP
Davis-Floyd, Robbie E. **Birth as an American rite of passage.** California, 1992. 382p bibl index afp ISBN 0-520-07439-4, $35.00

In this, her doctoral thesis in anthropology, Davis-Floyd argues that a woman during pregnancy and in giving birth is undergoing a "rite of passage," a series of rituals that signify she is moving from one status to another, that of "being a mother." Further, the medical establishment in its work on her as a "patient," engages in a series of actions (such as "prepping" her, giving her a hospital gown, medically inducing labor, giving medication to reduce labor pains, monitoring the fetus, doing an episiotomy), that physicians believe are necessary for successful birth, but are really technocratic rituals, i.e., behavior that typically has little or no instrumental use but that has great symbolic significance. Davis-Floyd attempts to document this from interviews with 100 pregnant women and with medical personnel. She reports that 70 per cent of the women interviewed accepted, to varying degrees, the use of the diverse medical procedures, and some women actively sought them. However, Davis-Floyd, like a number of others, rejects this pattern of birth and would replace it with a holistic experience free of medication, Cesareans, and the like. General; undergraduate; community college; professional.—*D. Harper, University of Rochester*

WS-1414　　　E184　　　94-5746 CIP
Donnelly, Nancy D. **Changing lives of refugee Hmong women.** Washington, 1994. 224p bibl index afp ISBN 0-295-97361-7, $30.00

In an ethnographic study of recent Hmong immigrant families in Seattle, Donnelly examines changing gender roles in both the economic and social spheres as Hmong women adapt to new social conditions and opportunities in the US. The author focuses specifically on changing patterns of courtship, marriage arrangements, and economic decision making in the household, and how women incorporate new values while attempting to retain elements of their Hmong identity. Through her description of Hmong textile marketing cooperatives in Seattle, Donnelly also provides a provocative analysis of "patronage" structures that characterize Euramerican relations with refugees in resettlement programs. An actor-based approach and inclusion of long passages in the Hmong women's own words make Donnelly's ethnographic presentation compelling and highly readable. Because of the recent political situation in Laos, the ethnographic fieldwork that would have illuminated traditional aspects of Hmong society is missing. However, the author uses oral histories and available written sources very effectively in attempting to provide historical and cultural contexts for the social and economic transformations wrought by immigration. All levels.—*L. L. Junker, Vanderbilt University*

WS-1415　　　　　　　Orig
Dorkenoo, Efua. **Cutting the rose: female genital mutilation: the practice and its prevention.** Minority Rights Publications, 1994. (Dist. by Paul & Company) 196p bibl index ISBN 1-873194-60-9, $24.95

Several recent studies have dealt with the subject of female genital mutilation (FGM)—some of these are essentially ethnographic, others more dramatic. Dorkenoo presents excellent coverage of the different operations; the physical, cultural, and psychological effects of such operations; and their medical and long-term implications. Originally limited to traditional societies, the practice has spread with the migration of refugees and immigrants to Western urban centers; the question now is whether to regulate or to abolish the practice. In many Western countries, individuals and immigrant communities pressure mothers to return "home" with a daughter to permit FGM to be performed. It is obviously easier to irradicate the practice in a Western environment than within a traditional society of the home country. Readers are presented with the rights of women, the rights of children (especially the girl-child), and the rights to good health and a "normal" sexual and reproductive life. These rights are the concern of a growing number of international initiatives, ranging from the UN and the World

Health Organization to a variety of nongovernmental groups. The author calls for continued involvement of grassroots feminist activities. Undergraduates and above.—*B. M. du Toit, University of Florida*

WS-1416   F1221   94-31546 CIP
Eber, Christine. **Women & alcohol in a highland Maya town: water of hope, water of sorrow.** Texas, 1995. 303p bibl indexes afp ISBN 0-292-72089-0, $40.00; ISBN 0-292-72090-4 pbk, $18.95

Eber's book is a historical and contextual ethnography of political and social relations surrounding gender and alcohol use and abuse. The study reports on detailed fieldwork carried out in San Pedro Chenalho, a Mayan town in highland Chiapas, during the late 1980s. The analysis attends carefully to the ways in which alcohol use has changed over time in relation to the intricacies of resistance to missionary zeal and ladino domination. Eber combines the strengths of feminist ethnography and its attention to difference with a broader political-economic perspective. The author successfully portrays the complex tensions that have arisen between alcohol's contradictory roles, as ritual and balm, in the community. This women-centered analysis focuses on the ways in which gender identities and relationships are reworked under the contemporary political economy and provides a nuanced reading of women's struggles and sources of power within rituals, households, and the community. The study has the potential buried within its ethnographic riches to make important contributions to understanding women's identities and power within a Native American society. All levels.—*V. A. Lawson, University of Washington*

WS-1417   HC138   93-48394 CIP
González de la Rocha, Mercedes. **The resources of poverty: women and survival in a Mexican city.** Blackwell, 1994. 311p bibl index afp ISBN 0-631-19223-9, $54.95

An original and elegant interpretation of how the daily lives of poor women in Mexico unfold within the context of urban poverty, this is by far the best account of their struggle for survival that this reviewer has read. González de la Rocha's in-depth analysis is uncommon even in an ethnographic work of this kind. Her profound understanding of the dynamic relationship between structural constraints and individual choices becomes evident when she notes, "choices and preferences do take place, even in the context of poverty." Readers glimpse the private but ever-changing lives of these women as they improvise coping strategies and develop adaptations that make possible their perseverance. As the author observes, relationships and their meaning and nature cannot be taken for granted as natural elements. "They are instrumental, built and cultivated." She argues that this social practice implies options and strategies, created by the poor. Those who succeed manage to survive and reproduce; those who do not sink into destitution, illness, and their own or their children's premature death. A compelling study that should be read by all those interested in Latin America, the Third World, poverty, the urban household, and women. All levels.—*E. Bastida, University of Texas—Pan American*

WS-1418   HB1071   95-31951 CIP
Inhorn, Marcia C. **Infertility and patriarchy: the cultural politics of gender and family life in Egypt.** Pennsylvania, 1996. 296p bibl index afp ISBN 0-8122-3235-6, $36.95; ISBN 0-8122-1424-2 pbk, $16.95

A companion volume to Inhorn's *Quest for Conception: Gender, Infertility, and Egyptian Medical Traditions*, this book discusses how the triple stigmata of femaleness, poverty, and barrenness serve to devalue and disempower women in contemporary urban lower-class Egypt. Based on research conducted in 1988-89 in Alexandria, Egypt's second largest city, the study examines the consequences of childlessness for poor women. Inhorn regards fertility as the most potent source of female power in this area. She combines individual case studies with a broader discussion about patriarchal Egyptian society (which contains the mandate of fertility). Her opening theoretical discussion is a useful summary of the large and still growing literature on Middle Eastern, Muslim, and Arab women. The role of Islam is also discussed. Although primarily written for specialists, the study can also serve as a general introduction to women's lives in poor sections of this area of the world. Notes, glossary, and some black-and-white photographs.—*L. Beck, Washington University*

WS-1419   DT159   95-18672 CIP
Jennings, Anne M. **The Nubians of West Aswan: village women in the midst of change.** L. Rienner, 1995. 177p bibl index afp ISBN 1-55587-570-X, $40.00; ISBN 1-55587-592-0 pbk, $17.95

Nubians are the most ancient people of the Nile valley of Africa. Their culture has been of particular interest to Western scholars after their relocation when the Aswan Dam Project was completed in 1962. Principally Muslim and relying mostly on subsistence farming and tourism, these people have preserved their traditional culture—including their own Nubian language—even while living and working within the dominant culture of Egypt. Nubian women are traditional Muslims who maintain private domiciles while their husbands, fathers, and brothers participate fully in the public sphere of community and nation. Yet, according to Jennings, women wield persuasive power and influence through their social networks, their contribution to building and maintaining households and homes, and by their participation in engagement, wedding, and funeral ceremonies. Jennings, an African American, lived twice in Nubian households, first in 1981 and later in 1986. Her ethnographic data yield rich insights into the social control that women's networks effect. She provides detailed information on the normative behaviors expected of women, men, and families, whose honor and community standing depend exclusively on their sons' and daughters' circumspect behavior and social interactions. All levels.—*A. S. Oakes, Idaho State University*

WS-1420   HQ1240   93-38862 CIP
Judd, Ellen R. **Gender and power in rural North China.** Stanford, 1994. 295p bibl index afp ISBN 0-8047-2295-1, $37.50

The culture of rural China is characterized by a pervasive devaluation of women that is constantly denied in everyday life. Women have always played a key role in agriculture, rural industry, commodity production, and the stratified and tight hierarchy of social relations in rural China, yet the contribution of women continues to be minimized and ignored even under the current decollectivization reform. In official circles, party hierarchy, and organizational structure, women are often effectively excluded from any role of public and social responsibility. Based on fieldwork in three Shangdong Province villages, this anthropological study focuses on household and interhousehold gender relationships, and on the current attempt by women to organize and change gender relationships in rural China. State power is invariably linked to gender politics, and in this case, state power also is invariably exercised through custom and customary practices that are reinforced by a pervasive and tenacious tradition. The enduring paradox perhaps underscores an overwhelming tenacity of tradition as much as a lack of state commitment to changes in gender relationships. Social changes are often the last link of revolutionary changes. Suitable for undergraduates and above.—*H. T. Wong, Eastern Washington University*

WS-1421   HT720   94-38588 CIP
Kapadia, Karin. **Siva and her sisters: gender, caste, and class in rural South India.** Westview, 1995. 269p bibl index afp ISBN 0-8133-8158-4, $50.00

Focusing on the experiences and attitudes of "untouchables" and women in Tamilnadu, Kapadia questions Louis Dumont's emphasis (in *Homo Hierarchicus*, 1974) on Hindu cultural consensus and the view that a "validation of hierarchic values is provided by lower-caste religion." Rather, Kapadia argues, "lower castes do not share upper-caste assumptions regarding ritual purity," and "the very understanding of what inauspiciousness and impurity are differs considerably between the Brahminical castes and the Non-Brahmins." Kapadia places her analysis of gender and caste firmly within the changing social contexts of kinship, marriage, ritual, and rural female labor, and she demonstrates the negative implications that class mobility may have for women in the rural economy. She concludes by noting that the "fall in women's status is, arguably, the most fundamental change taking place in the current transformation of rural Tamilnadu," and "it is in those impoverished castes in which very little economic differentiation has occurred ... that women's high status has, in large measure, remained intact." This meticulously researched, elegant analysis is highly recommended for upper-division undergraduates and above.—*B. Tavakolian, Denison University*

WS-1422 HQ1750 91-33340 CIP
Karim, Wazir Jahan. **Women and culture: between Malay Adat and Islam.** Westview, 1992. 255p bibl index afp ISBN 0-8133-8519-9 sc, $34.95

Karim examines differences of gender orientation between Malay customary law (*adat*) and Islamic religious law. Her thesis, that Malay *adat* and bilateral family organization have actively formulated the position of women vis-a-vis men in nonhierarchical ways, opposes the "universalist" argument of other authors that male dominance over females is "natural" because of biological differences in reproductive and child-nurturing roles. Karim sets the stage for analyzing the present-day interface between customary law and Islamic religious orthodoxy with a discussion of methods in culture history and ethnography, a historical sketch of how royal lineages combined with the bilateral social organization of traditional Malay societies to form early Malay states, and an in-depth discussion of how Malay customary law as ideology and practice has affected gender roles. Finally, she addresses the modern Malaysian situation in terms of the construction of power in political parties and voluntary movements, the interface between *adat* and Islam at the local community level, and the relationship between gender and power in the context of Islamic revivalism. She omits some historical details that would have strengthened her argument. Nonetheless, this book is an important anthropological and historical contribution to gender studies. Advanced undergraduate; graduate; faculty; professional.—*R. Provencher, Northern Illinois University*

WS-1423 DU740 93-8314 CIP
Lepowsky, Maria. **Fruit of the motherland: gender in an egalitarian society.** Columbia, 1994 (c1993). 383p bibl index afp ISBN 0-231-08120-0, $49.00; ISBN 0-231-08121-9 pbk, $17.50

Lepowsky (Univ. of Wisconsin, Madison) studied Vanitinai, an island southwest of New Guinea, in order to learn how social life could be organized without the assumption of male dominance. Vanitinai is no feminist paradise, simply a place where male and female roles largely overlap. It is reminiscent of nearby island societies (such as the Trobriand Islands) despite important differences in the structuring of gender and power. This book conveys a complex understanding of the orderliness of careers and social organization in such a place. It is informed both by detailed knowledge of the society and region and by critical awareness. Lepowsky deals evenhandedly with topics of primary concern to islanders—subsistence, life passages, sorcery, relations with the dead and with spirits, exchange, and power—presenting general analyses through specific incidents. This ethnography is important as a touchstone for accounts of Melanesian societies and for theories of gender relations. It is clearly written; however, so much information is provided that it will be demanding for advanced undergraduates. Graduate; faculty.—*J. Kirkpatrick, Community Resources, Inc.*

WS-1424 HQ1059 93-21379 CIP
Lock, Margaret. **Encounters with aging: mythologies of menopause in Japan and North America.** California, 1994 (c1993). 439p bibl index afp ISBN 0-520-08221-4, $38.00

Lock is known for her anthropological writings on Japan and medical anthropology, as well as on aging in women. This book is as much a discourse on gerontology in Japan as it is a study of menopause (*konenki*). It touches on Japanese national character, social change (e.g., the change from the extended household to the nuclear household), government policy, intergenerational relations, women's roles, and gender behavior. The first and major section of the book is more readable and concentrates on maturity and menopause among a large sample of Japanese women. The second section presents a historical perspective and traces "the making of menopause" and the influence of psychoanalytic theory on the medicalization of menopause. This study is the result of an extensive cross-sectional survey questionnaire administered in 1984 to 1,738 Japanese women, and subsequent interviews by Lock and Christina Honde with 105 women aged 45 to 50. One is struck by the intergenerational communication among Japanese women regarding *konenki*, the fact that there is no term for "hot flash," and that what is locally interpreted as a disturbance in the autonomic nervous system is primarily characterized by shoulder stiffness. Numerous verbatim biographical accounts illustrate each section. Some bibliographic errors. Graduate students and researchers.—*B. M. du Toit, University of Florida*

WS-1425 HQ1726 92-29104 Orig
Marcus, Julie. **A world of difference: Islam and gender hierarchy in Turkey.** Zed, 1992. 201p bibl index ISBN 1-85649-185-4, $49.95; ISBN 1-85649-186-2 pbk, $17.50

Marcus's book offers a general discussion of broad conceptual issues relating to women. Marcus conducted anthropological research on women in the Turkish city of Izmir; however, her book contains little information on Turkey or on Turkish women. She explores the notions that "gender inequality results from the practice of Islamic purity laws" and that "the moral community is based upon gender hierarchy and gender separation," but without presenting much actual data beyond a description of religious practices. She offers no wider view of women, their lives, and their place in Turkish society in general. Marcus effectively critiques images of the East ("orientalism") in the literature and discusses ethnographic research and writing. The book is more appropriate for gender studies than for Islamic, Middle Eastern, or Turkish studies, although the author would assert (correctly) that all of these are and should be interrelated. Much has been written in Turkish about the book's central issues, but Turkish sources (except four minor ones) are absent. Plates; short index. Graduate; faculty.—*L. Beck, Washington University*

WS-1426 Orig
Mir-Hosseini, Ziba. **Marriage on trial: a study of Islamic family law: Iran and Morocco compared.** I.B. Tauris, 1993. 245p bibl index ISBN 1-85043-685-1, $55.00

An excellent if very brief sketch of the Shari'a and its development introduces this clearly written comparative study of the relationship among Islamic law, modern legal codes, and social realities in contemporary Morocco and Iran. Mir-Hosseini (Girton College, Cambridge) calls her monograph a contribution to the anthropology of law; she did her fieldwork in the courts of the largest cities of each country—Teheran in Iran, and Casablanca, Rabat, and Salé in Morocco. The issue at the heart of her research is whether law shapes and controls human behavior and therefore social institutions, or whether it reflects prevailing social custom and the particular social order. To test these "not mutually exclusive" perspectives, the author focuses on personal status law, specifically on matters of marriage, divorce, and child custody. Interspersing summaries of individual cases in her analysis, the author takes into account such legal variables as the school of law (Maliki versus Shi'i), the court systems, and court procedures, and she examines closely the gender and socioeconomic status of the litigants. Mir-Hosseini reaches several paradoxical conclusions, among them the finding that in Iran, where the Shari'a is now enforced, women enjoy better status in law and in marriage than their counterparts in Morocco. Advanced undergraduates and above.—*L. M. Lewis, Eastern Kentucky University*

WS-1427 DT515 94-12014 CIP
Renne, Elisha P. **Cloth that does not die: the meaning of cloth in Bùnú social life.** Washington, 1995. 269p bibl index afp ISBN 0-295-97392-7, $40.00

If handwoven cloth is the mundane commodity it may seem, and if women rarely weave it anymore, why does it continue to play such a vital role in the lives of Bùnú women of Nigeria? In answering this intriguing question, Renne offers a marvelously nuanced study of how *things* can reveal the changing complexities of social life. Handwoven cloth for Bùnú is a key metaphor: "because of its skinlike proximity to the human body, cloth is intimately associated with the individual." The side facing outward projects an image to one's audience, "while an individual's private concerns and intentions are associated with its other side, facing inward." Cloth, then, mediates between self and circumstance. Handweaving has declined as industrially produced cotton fabrics have become increasingly available, attractive, and affordable. Christian dogma, British-style school uniforms, and other innovations have favored use of fabric, but still, through an "intentional, 'conspicuous archaism'" that allows Bùnú to "confound time," handwoven cloth is brought into present situations as medicine, value, a marker of identity and status, and a means to contemplate the "two-sided" ambiguities of contemporary life in a fast-paced world. All levels.—*A. F. Roberts, University of Iowa*

WS-1428   Orig

Rudie, Ingrid. **Visible women in east coast Malay society: on the reproduction of gender in ceremonial, school and market.** Scandinavian University Press, 1994. (Dist. by Oxford) 337p bibl indexes ISBN 82-00-21919-4, $45.00

Rudie has written a methodologically compelling study. Her fieldwork spans 20 years and encompasses three visits, anchoring her keen observations on change and continuity in Kelantanese villages. Rudie's interest in "thick description," her attention to the relationship between researcher and informant, her personal "history of making sense," and her reference to other ongoing conversations in anthropology make the work appropriate for graduate reading. Rudie also contributes to the study of gender in Malaysia. Her analyses of gender encompass the transformation of the family and the multiple constructions of marriage in changing economic circumstances. She is particularly effective in exploring the "interface between large-scale historical processes and small-scale biographical processes" and in examining her own relationship to data and interpretation. The book has an extensive bibliography. A good review of the literature of gender studies in Malaysia will be helpful to the serious reader. Upper-division undergraduates and above.—*L. De Danaan, Evergreen State College*

WS-1429   GT3251   90-40640 CIP

Seremetakis, C. Nadia. **The last word: women, death, and divination in inner Mani.** Chicago, 1991. 275p bibl index ISBN 0-226-74875-8, $45.00; ISBN 0-226-74876-6 pbk, $16.95

A compelling and complex (and occasionally diffuse) exploration of the female world of funerary ritual in Mani (Greece), *The Last Word* shows through powerful ethnography that women's engagement with death subverts simplistic binarisms such as those opposing death to life, or male to female. Seremetakis locates the hardening of such polarities in the twin phenomena of androcentric social theory and capitalism's imposition of positivism on a radically different cosmology. The evidence for female subversion of male power in earlier times sits awkwardly with this argument, and Seremetakis paradoxically conflates other, comparable studies of Greek societies in a generic national culture while nevertheless rightly insisting on the historical, local, and gender-based specificity of her own Maniat data. She has nonetheless provided a richly critical demonstration of the inadequacy of a dry theoretical binarism as opposed to a local and gendered sociology. She has crafted a finely contextualized ethnography in which her own involvement in the community and her engagement with local dream divination practices serve as restrained but powerful analytical tools rather than as the props of a merely self-indulgent autobiographical exercise. Although she sometimes asserts rather than demonstrates the force of her interpretations, the moving descriptions and often elegant writing carry the argument strongly. Advanced undergraduates and up.—*M. Herzfeld, Harvard University*

WS-1430   Aust. CIP

Sullivan, Norma. **Masters and managers: a study of gender relations in urban Java.** Allen & Unwin, 1995 (c1994). (Dist. by Paul & Company) 223p bibl index ISBN 1-86373-756-1 pbk, $24.95

Sullivan's book is a well-written ethnography of urban, lower-class Javanese women, constructed from a feminist perspective. Based on extensive fieldwork in 1979 and shorter stints throughout the 1980s, this community study of one neighborhood in the Javanese city of Yogyakarta covers several topics, including urban life and politics, stratification, and gender in the neighborhood and the nation. Sullivan describes neighborhood realities in detail; she also puts the neighborhood and its culture into a national context. Data from the study serve to challenge two widely held views: that Javanese state ideology promotes equality between men and women, and that Javanese rituals focus on and involve men only. Sullivan shows that, if anything, the government supports the statuses and roles of men as masters, of women as managers. She also indicates that prior scholarship—Javanese and other—on local rituals incorrectly overlooks the essential participation of women. Figures, charts, and tables appear throughout, presenting convincing evidence to support Sullivan's arguments about the importance of neighborhoods and neighbors for certain urban Javanese women and about the dominant-subordinate nature of gender relations in urban Java. Upper-division undergraduates and above.—*R. Ellovich, North Carolina State University*

WS-1431   DT443   94-27541 CIP

Swantz, Marja-Liisa. **Blood, milk, and death: body symbols and the power of regeneration among the Zaramo of Tanzania,** by Marja-Liisa Swantz with Salome Mjema and Zenya Wild. Bergin & Garvey, 1995. 158p bibl index afp ISBN 0-89789-398-0, $49.95

With the editorial assistance of Wild and the interspersed reminiscences and reflections of Mjema, Swantz (Univ. of Helsinki) has provided a sympathetic and informative account of the social and cultural life of the Zaramo people of coastal Tanzania. After a historical introduction detailing the excesses of both the colonial and independence regimes, which tested the resolve of these people to control their own destiny, the author considers in greater detail their ritual and symbolic life, with particular emphasis on the women in this traditional matrilineal society. In the process, Swantz considers birth, death, coming-of-age ceremonies, marriage, and, in addition, the tribulations of existence assumed to be brought on by witchcraft, sorcery, and spirit possession. The data are rich and the analysis sophisticated but lucid. This instructive work is essential for any anthropology and African studies library collection. All levels.—*W. Arens, SUNY at Stony Brook*

WS-1432   Orig

Taylor, Avril. **Women drug users: an ethnography of a female injecting community.** Oxford, 1993. 182p bibl index ISBN 0-19-825796-1, $35.00

Taylor's detailed "street ethnography" of Glasgow, Scotland, offers a thorough and somewhat surprising view of the daily lives of female drug addicts. In recent years, sociologists and anthropologists have overturned many stereotypes by spending time with groups whose customs are considered "deviant" and by examining in a detailed manner the "natural history" of life in that setting and broader context. By interspersing clear and concise generalizations among a wealth of well-organized direct quotations from the women themselves, Taylor demonstrates convincingly that these people are active, willing, intelligent, resourceful, and hard working, despite their deprecated status. She shows how they make a living (including sometimes—grudgingly—through prostitution); how they learn and are inducted into the culture of drug use; the elaborate social networks that develop; relations with others (e.g., men, "straight" relatives, neighbors, treatment personnel); and the special efforts they exert in trying their best to mother their children. Most have tried to quit using drugs, but only one has succeeded. The rational and pragmatic choices that are made by these women are epitomized in the logic of this as a "career" that often offers more than any plausible alternatives available to them. The book provides valuable insights into a grossly misunderstood segment of the modern urban scene. All levels.—*D. B. Heath, Brown University*

WS-1433   E99   94-38872 CIP

Voget, Fred W. **They call me Agnes: a Crow narrative based on the life of Agnes Yellowtail Deernose.** Oklahoma, 1995. 220p bibl index afp ISBN 0-8061-2695-7, $24.95

Voget, a well-respected anthropologist who has spent half a century studying the Crow Indians, has presented a fascinating story of the life of Agnes Yellowtail Deernose. The 14 narrative chapters are informative and heartwarming. They are replete with analogies dealing with intergroup, intragroup, and personal relations. Yellowtail Deernose makes clear the pre- and post-WW II dilemmas faced by a people in transition. One can only wonder how an elderly individual can remember so many minute details from past decades. This work has an excellent first chapter, entitled "Historic Crow and Reservation Culture," and an extensive bibliography. Those interested in ethnohistorical narrative accounts by Native American women might also read Margaret Blackman's *Sadie Brower Neakok, an Inupaig Woman* (CH, Sep'90) and Julie Cruikshank et al., *Life Lived Like a Story: Life Stories of Three Yukon Native Elders* (1990). Also recommended is Voget's *The Shoshoni-Crow Sun Dance* (CH, Mar'85). All levels.—*N. C. Greenberg, emeritus, Western Michigan University*

WS-1434   HD6194   91-41844 CIP

Wolf, Diane Lauren. **Factory daughters: gender, household dynamics, and rural industrialization in Java.** California, 1992. 323p bibl index afp ISBN 0-520-07072-0, $38.00

Wolf studied the lives of female factory workers in rural Java in 1982-1983 and again in 1986. Her book offers a wealth of important insights on changing gender roles in Southeast Asia, on the analysis of household economies, and on international processes of industrialization. She concludes that daughters who choose to work in nearby factories often do so without parental approval, and that, overall, factory work augments daughters' range of independent decision making. Wolf's finding undermines the notion that households make decisions as a single unit (with a single utility function) and reveals an important contrast between the relatively controlling patriarchies of East Asia and the greater possibiities for independent action within some Southeast Asian kinship systems. Wolf points to the independent role the kinship system plays in determining who decides to work where, and what is done with the wages. Wolf also traces the economic consequences of factory work over time, arguing that parents subsidize the factories by providing basic support to their daughters, but that factory work also serves as a cushion for farm families against illness or crop failure. Her attention to intrafamily dynamics and her subtle analysis of changing practices of marriage, labor, and spending should ensure this book a wide readership. Advanced undergraduate; graduate; faculty.—*J. R. Bowen, Washington University*

◆ Business, Management & Labor

WS-1435 HD6519 90-48929 CIP
Faue, Elizabeth. **Community of suffering & struggle: women, men, and the labor movement in Minneapolis, 1915-1945.** North Carolina, 1991. 295p bibl index afp ISBN 0-8078-1945-X, $39.95; ISBN 0-8078-4307-5 pbk, $14.95

Faue's study of women and the labor movement in Minneapolis from 1915 to 1945 raises important questions about the impact of gender on American institutions. In contrast to their male counterparts, female labor activists viewed their involvement in workplace struggles as an extension of their total lives rooted in their experiences as neighbors, mothers, or wives. The ambivalence of the trade union movement toward supporting women or fully including them in its ranks did not prevent the city's telephone operators, office workers, and garment workers from taking action on their own behalf. This gender-based form of local activism reached its height in the mid-1930s as both male and female wage laborers increasingly saw the labor movement as a vehicle to create real economic and political democracy in their community. The decline of the economy, the coming of war, and the increasingly bitter rivalry between the AFL and the CIO in the 1930s undercut community unionism and strengthened the trend toward a male-dominated, more bureaucratic form of labor organization. The author's unique and challenging hypothesis is not well served by her writing. The book reads as a series of short, interconnected essays rather than as a well-planned, logical monograph. Although a section on gender and language, for example, is fascinating, it is not well integrated into the book. Despite these limitations, the book merits attention from all concerned about the fate of the labor movement in general, and its female members in particular. Upper-division and graduate collections.—*H. Harris, Pennsylvania State University, New Kensington Campus*

WS-1436 HD6079.2.U5 90-1571 CIP
Gabin, Nancy F. **Feminism in the labor movement: women and the United Auto Workers, 1935-1975.** Cornell, 1990. 257p bibl index afp ISBN 0-8014-2435-6, $31.95; ISBN 0-8014-9725-6, $12.95

Thoroughly researched and thoughtfully conceived, Gabin's book, documents the struggles of United Auto Workers (UAW) women to achieve greater opportunity in the union, on the job, and ultimately in American society. Although the women never overcame segregated work and union hierarchies, they did make considerable inroads from the 1940s forward. Contrasting the ideology of the union with the reality of their place in the auto industry, women pressed for recognition through the formation of a Women's Bureau in the UAW. This Bureau became a training ground for women, some of whom went on to major roles within the Union and in the feminist movement. As the title indicates, the book addresses a host of important issues in women's and labor history. It offers a counterpart to the middle-class orientation of most 20th-century women's history. Most significantly, this monograph explores the "complex and contingent character of the mediation process between feminism and unionism within the UAW." Amply footnoted and carefully indexed; excellent bibliography. Gabin's fine book belongs in college and university libraries; it will be consulted frequently by modern American historians.—*D. Lindstrom, University of Wisconsin—Madison*

WS-1437 HQ1426 90-13309 CIP
Gordon, Suzanne. **Prisoners of men's dreams: striking out for a new feminine future.** Little, Brown, 1991. 324p bibl index ISBN 0-316-32106-0, $19.95

Gordon's book treats a particular aspect of change in women's lives, namely the increased emphasis on workplace achievement and on defining achievement by the number of hours dedicated to the job. Like Sylvia Hewlett (*A Lesser Life*, CH, Jul'86) Gordon is highly critical of equating women's emancipation with adoption of a male-defined, work-obsessed life-style, but unlike Hewlett, she is too realistic to blame feminists for the failure of American culture and politics to support alternatives. Gordon reviews a smattering of the research literature on work and family, reports interviews with an unsystematic sample of employed women (and a few men), and offers her own opinions passionately and often gracefully. The results are variable. There is a dreadful chapter on childcare that implies that the problem facing children are primarily of the yuppie, competitive kindergarten sort. But there is also an excellent chapter on successful self-described feminists who are reluctant to rock the boat for their less-advantaged sisters. Because she focuses only on women and the issue is individual achievement versus collective struggle, Gordon misses the opportunity to consider whether men also are overburdened by the US pattern of increasing work hours per week. This book popularizes a number of issues concerning the significance of paid work in women's lives, but does so with a noticeably upper-middle-class slant. General readers.—*M. M. Ferree, University of Connecticut*

WS-1438 HD6135 96-3351 CIP
Hakim, Catherine. **Key issues in women's work: female heterogeneity and the polarisation of women's employment.** Athlone, 1996. 257p (Conflict and change in Britain series—a new audit, 4) bibl indexes ISBN 0-485-80009-8, $70.00; ISBN 0-485-80109-4 pbk, $25.00

Sociologist Hakim has written a critique of popular misconceptions surrounding women's work patterns. Her main point is that much of the misunderstanding surrounding attempts to characterize women' work comes from not acknowledging the heterogeneity of the female workforce. Most of her examples and discussion concern the UK, but examples and work from other European countries and the US are often cited as well. Hakim's arguments are sometimes difficult to follow, since she quotes liberally even from those she disagrees with and oscillates between a looser and a more particular writing style depending on her degree of agreement with the points she presents. Although the author is quick to perceive bias in others, particularly those sympathetic to women's complaints, she does not acknowledge her own cultural biases. Some new evidence is produced regarding workforce segregation and work patterns, but most of the book critically reviews other research. Readers familiar with the issues Hakim discusses will not glean much new from this volume, and US students may find the discussion hard to follow, given its orientation toward particulars of the British situation and its focus on faulty empirical practice among sociologists. Most appropriate for research collections.—*J. P. Jacobsen, Wesleyan University*

WS-1439 HD6054 91-35889 CIP
Haslett, Beth J. **The organizational woman: power and paradox,** by Beth J. Haslett, Florence L. Geis, and Mae R. Carter. Ablex, 1992. 270p bibl indexes ISBN 0-89391-837-7, $55.00; ISBN 0-89391-845-8 pbk, $29.50

This volume presents a great deal of information on issues women face working in organizations. The writing style is academic, with frequent reference to research from many disciplines. Geared to educated readers and academic audiences, the book focuses on how work environments may make it more difficult for women to succeed. The authors present different ways of responding to and, at times, overcoming workplace difficulties. Coverage includes material on stereotypes, communication, power, leadership, and management style. Although none of this material is new, presenting it in one source is useful, particularly for use as a college text. The last part of the book contains a number of cases in which professional women face specific work-related problems and hurdles. For each case, the authors suggest several coping strategies. These cases are very well done and could be helpful not only to women but also to men facing similar problems in their working lives. Extensive, appropriate list of references. General and academic readers, advanced undergraduate through professional.— *F. Reitman, Pace University*

WS-1440　　　　HD6054　　　　93-4225 CIP
Karsten, Margaret Foegen. **Management and gender: issues and attitudes.** Quorum Books, 1994. 265p bibl index afp ISBN 0-89930-812-0, $59.95

Drawing on various areas of management theory and practice, Karsten focuses on those aspects of special importance to women. There is a great deal of well-documented, up-to-date information from professional, academic, and popular sources, presented in concise and readable fashion. The book supplements the traditional introductory management course by adding material about women often omitted or condensed, e.g., a chapter on women's contributions to management thought. Included are a number of interesting readings, discussion questions for each chapter, and several integrative cases. Subjects addressed are mainly those that women need to think about as they enter the workplace: career planning, mentoring, networking, discrimination, assertiveness, balancing career and family, stress management, international demands. Attention is paid to special problems of women of color. Although men have much to learn from the book about both men and women, the needs of men are addressed only tangentially. Advanced undergraduate.—*F. Reitman, Pace University*

WS-1441　　　　HD6053　　　　94-7518 CIP
Kwolek-Folland, Angel. **Engendering business: men and women in the corporate office, 1870-1930.** Johns Hopkins, 1994. 256p bibl index afp ISBN 0-8018-4860-1, $38.50

The origins and evolution of the structure of corporate offices along with their corresponding managerial and gender relationships are important, interesting, and complex topics. Since the organizational form and job segmentation of businesses can also largely define social as well as professional lives and opportunities, these topics provide some understanding as to how the American economy and society developed and defined itself. By examining the role of men and women within financial industries, Kwolek-Folland (history, Univ. of Kansas) explains much about a variety of individual, social, and commercial activities. This thorough, well-documented, and meaningful study follows the growth of the insurance and banking industries over an important era of American business and social history. It is a sweeping study that explores not only social, labor, and gender issues but also some broader issues such as the daily operations, physical environments, and architectural histories of several white-collar businesses. It is also an intriguing study because the author utilizes archival and other primary documents along with an array of public documents to provide insight into large national firms as well as smaller regional firms. Recommended for graduate students, researchers, and faculty.— *T. E. Sullivan, Towson State University*

WS-1442　　　　　　　　　　　　Orig
Leeming, E. Janice. **Segmenting the women's market: using niche marketing to understand and meet the diverse needs of today's most dynamic consumer market,** by E. Janice Leeming and Cynthia F. Tripp. Probus, 1994. 346p index ISBN 1-55738-561-0, $32.50

Rather than viewing the "women's market" as a single, homogeneous group with the same needs and wants, the authors of this book break it down into all its subcomponents, focusing on key market niches. They note, for example, that teenage girls are much more impulsive in their purchases and are obsessed about their hair (more than 80 percent shampoo and condition their hair every day). Twenty-somethings, on the other hand, are action-oriented and on the go, valuing leisure time more for the opportunity to have fun than to recharge their batteries. Thirty-somethings do not enjoy shopping as much anymore, but are required to buy for their families. Forty-somethings have more money to spend and are interested in looking good, fitness, and finance. The fifty-plus population is even more focused on these interests. Beyond age, other niche factors examined in the book include marital and economic status, race, and ethnicity. Sub-

jects are well covered and supported with numerous examples and statistics. Recommended for marketing professionals, researchers, faculty, and upper-division and graduate students.—*P. G. Kishel, Cypress College*

WS-1443　　　　HF5415　　　　93-30264 CIP
Nelson, Carol. **Women's market handbook: understanding and reaching today's most powerful consumer group.** Gale, 1994. 366p bibl index afp ISBN 0-8103-9139-2, $64.95

Marketers seeking to reach the women's market are well advised to read Nelson's informative and insightful book. Picking up where Freud left off, the author sets out to answer the question "What do women want?" She shows that the so-called "women's market" actually comprises many separate submarkets, or niches, each with its own needs and wants. For example, there is the active woman who is interested in physical fitness, sports, and nutrition; the traditional homemaker whose primary focus is hearth and home; the not-so-traditional homemaker who is balancing work and family needs; and a host of other women of varying ages, incomes, and interests. Each is looking for the products and services right for *her*. The one thing all women seem to have in common is time or, more specifically, the *lack* of it. Nelson points out that cosmetics giant Avon has recognized this and now, instead of relying on the bell-ringing "Avon Lady" to sell its products, makes it convenient for women to shop "by phone, fax, mail, and rep." The book contains numerous examples and photographs of actual ads. There is also a "Sourcebook" of consultants, organizations, publications, and other resources marketers can consult for additional information. Highly recommended for marketing professionals, researchers, faculty, students at all levels as well as the general public.—*P. G. Kishel, Cypress College*

WS-1444　　　　HD6061　　　　93-40664 CIP
Perlman, Richard. **Sex discrimination in the labour market: the case for comparable worth,** by Richard Perlman and Maureen Pike. Manchester, 1994. (Dist. by St. Martin's) 170p index ISBN 0-7190-3336-5, $59.95

Written by an American and a British academic economist, this book examines the causes of male/female wage disparity by starting from the effects of societal gender discrimination. Perlman and Pike conclude that the supply-side effects of societal conditioning of females prior to their entry into the labor market, which results in occupational crowding and therefore lower wages for women, are more important than the demand-side effects of discrimination in the labor market. There is an interesting comparison of the possible effects of affirmative action and comparable worth on reducing the male-female wage gap. The authors review the available empirical studies of implementing comparable worth policies in Australia, the UK, and the US. They conclude that the long-term effect of adopting comparable worth policies would be to reduce the male/female wage gap. Extensive references to both American and British sources. Although too technical for general audiences, this book is a valuable reference for researchers interested in sex discrimination and its effects on the labor market. Graduate; faculty; professional.—*E. P. Hoffman, Western Michigan University*

WS-1445　　　　KF300　　　　94-24940 CIP
Pierce, Jennifer L. **Gender trials: emotional lives in contemporary law firms.** California, 1995. 256p bibl index afp ISBN 0-520-20107-8, $48.00; ISBN 0-520-20108-6 pbk, $17.95

Although there are studies of token women who break into predominantly male occupations and of men who enter conventionally female jobs, Pierce's uniquely balance study looks at both processes simultaneously. Taking the "Rambo" masculinity of the lawyer who does litigation and the "supportive" femininity of the paralegal in the same firms as contrasting types, Pierce looks at the conventional and the cross-gendered incumbents of both roles and attempts to explain how gendering operates to constrain their choices and performances. By looking at litigators and paralegals in relation to each other, as well as in relation to the others in their own occupation, Pierce does an exceptionally clear job of demonstrating the effects of gender power and class hierarchy as structures, as well as showing the individual actors' efforts to conform and to resist these demands. The book also provides considerable insight into the emotional dimensions of both jobs, challenging stereotypes that see emotion work only when it is displayed by a gendered female. Useful for anyone interested in gender dimensions of occupations and occupational choice, or in the contemporary practice of law. All levels.—*M. M. Ferree, University of Connecticut*

WS-1446   Aust. CIP
Pink collar blues: work, gender & technology, ed. by Belinda Probert and Bruce W. Wilson. Melbourne, 1993. (Dist. by International Specialized Book Services) 173p bibl index ISBN 0-522-84520-7 pbk, $19.95

Pink Collar Blues is a compilation of seven chapters on gender and technology in the workplace authored by Australian, British, and American scholars and industrialists who participated in a 1992 conference. Technology (automation, information, and communication) and women in the workplace are discussed from a variety of informative perspectives, and the major theme addresses the important question of what women can do to realize the benefits of technological change. Topics of interest include the dominance of male versus female values in the design and application of technologies; gender inequality; the lack of recognition of women's contributions to technological development and women's multidimensional workplace skills, particularly organization and interpersonal skills; the absence of vocabulary to correctly identify women's workplace activities as skills and not personal attributes; women in trade union movements; and the concept of social versus technological determinism. The content is informative, current, and well documented with frequent references to international statistical surveys and research studies (Australia, UK, US, and Europe). Extensive bibliography. Recommended to undergraduate and graduate students of business, industrial relations, sociology, and feminist studies.—*R. Quinn, Bronx Community College*

WS-1447   HD6060.65.U5   90-31544 CIP
Reskin, Barbara F. **Job queues, gender queues: explaining women's inroads into male occupations,** by Barbara F. Reskin and Patricia A. Roos. Temple, 1991 (c1990). 388p bibl indexes afp ISBN 0-87722-743-8, $39.95; ISBN 0-87722-744-6, $16.95

The eight sociologists who wrote this book attribute the entry of women into previously male-dominated occupations to two major factors. First is the "occupational ghettoization" that results from the "de-skilling" of many occupations (often due to new technology), in which the job is broken down into simpler parts so that less training is required. Second is the formation of "job and labor queues." Individuals seeking employment rank the job openings available to them, applying first for those they rate best. Firms seeking employees act in a similar manner. The thesis of this book is that employers arbitrarily rank white males above females, thus forming labor queues biased by gender (and by race, though this factor is not emphasized). If men are able to move on to better occupations, employers have to reach further down the labor queues (where they have put women) to satisfy their need for employees. The volume contains case studies of 11 occupations, from blue collar to professional. Extensive list of references. Highly recommended for upper-division and graduate collections on labor studies or women's studies.—*E. P. Hoffman, Western Michigan University*

WS-1448   HD6053   90-8422 CIP
Rizzo, Ann-Marie. **The integration of women in management: a guide for human resources and management development specialists,** by Ann-Marie Rizzo and Carmen Mendez. Quorum Books, 1990. 206p indexes afp ISBN 0-89930-475-3, $40.00

Rizzo (Florida International University) and Mendez (Tennessee State University) examine gender-related issues in the workplace and focus on ways to promote women's role in management. The volume begins with a discussion of women in the workplace. This discussion includes some history, some consideration of sterotypes and their impact, and some theory and research (including feminist theory), which illuminate the issues. Following this, the authors discuss the integration of "outsiders" into an organization. Although reference is made to women and minorities, the material is applicable to all. The authors focus on helping employees contribute to organizations in ways that make work more satisfying. The third major topic is the presentation of specific cases, strategies, and workshop exercises to promote employee development and integration. These are described in sufficient detail for reader use. Rizzo and Mendez assume that organizations want to be the best they can be, and are therefore open to change. Chapter references. Professional and academic collections, upper-division and graduate.—*F. Reitman, Pace University*

WS-1449   HD6054   95-11808 CIP
Rosener, Judy B. **America's competitive secret: utilizing women as a management strategy.** Oxford, 1995. 230p index afp ISBN 0-19-508079-3, $25.00

Rosener addresses the issue of the underutilization of managerial career women in organizations and its implications for America's economic competitiveness. From the perspective of economic competitiveness, the author effectively integrates much of what has been written about familiar topics of management strategy, human resources, and workplace issues. The content is broad in scope, examining mindsets that contribute to this underutilization and why the situation exists (sexual static); discussing the issue of men's feelings in dealing with women in high-level managerial positions; identifying power, agenda setting, process, and benefits as areas where women make the most impact; and, most importantly, indicating approaches organizations can take to promote the effective use of female managerial talent. Of particular interest is an examination of the interactive leadership styles attributed to women versus the command-and-control style of men, and a most informative comparison of the underutilization of women in Japan, Britain, and European Union countries. Recommended for students of labor, economics, management, and sociology interested in a new treatment of gender differences in organizations.—*R. Quinn, CUNY Bronx Community College*

WS-1450   HD6067   94-40267 CIP
Samuels, Suzanne Uttaro. **Fetal rights, women's rights: gender equality in the workplace.** Wisconsin, 1995. 225p bibl index ISBN 0-299-14540-9, $32.50; ISBN 0-299-14544-1 pbk, $12.95

Samuels argues that fetal protection policies have allowed employers to bar women from jobs solely out of concern for fetal health and have thus imbued the fetus with rights independent of the mother, thereby undermining women's reproductive and employment rights. Such policies are almost always confined to male-dominated occupations, which pay more and provide better benefits and opportunities for advancement than female-dominated jobs. Moreover, these policies have placed at risk all employees' occupational safety and health by ridding the workplace of women instead of the hazards that prevent them from working there. By giving primacy to the fetus's "right" to be free from exposure to maternally transmitted harm, Samuels argues, such policies have reinforced similar arguments about fetal rights in the abortion debates. Samuels's straightforward presentation of fetal protection policies as undermining the intent of Title VII is both the strength and the weakness of the book. That feminists, as well as the New Right, sometimes hold similar positions complicates the discussion, but Samuels only alludes to this. She also inadvertently leaves the reader with the implication that sex segregation in the marketplace is a result of such fetal protection policies. The book addresses an important controversy, but begs for a fuller discussion. General readers; upper-division undergraduates and above.—*D. Kaufman, Northeastern University*

WS-1451   HF5547   91-19273 CIP
Strom, Sharon Hartman. **Beyond the typewriter: gender, class, and the origins of modern American office work, 1900-1930.** Illinois, 1992. 427p index afp ISBN 0-252-01806-0, $42.50

Did the emergence of office work provide new opportunities for women or simply an arena for more exploitation? Strom's answer is a definitive yes to both. Using massive quantitative and qualitative data, the author thoroughly examines the social conditions, prevailing ideologies, and individual responses involved. Diverse factors such as technology (typewriters, comptometers), expanding bureaucracies, and ideas such as "scientific management" and "women's place" combined to structure office work. Clerical workers increased 2.5 times from 1910-1930. Strom details both the demand and supply sides. Employers could get literate, high-school educated employees who would accept modest wages because the "marriage bar," exclusion from most occupations, middle-class office environment, and lower pay in other "women's jobs" made office work desirable. As did R. M. Kantor, in her classic work *Men and Women of the Corporation* (1977) Strom focuses on structural conditions rather than on gender per se. Weaknesses of the book include occasional dense writing and the lack of discussion of antidiscrimination efforts. Despite the latter, it is well recommended for advanced undergraduates, graduate students, and faculty.—*S. D. Borchert, Lake Erie College*

WS-1452 HD6054 93-27145 CIP

When the canary stops singing: women's perspectives on transforming business, ed. by Pat Barrentine; authors, Riane Eisler et al. Berrett-Koehler, 1993. 277p bibl index afp ISBN 1-881052-41-9, $24.95

Each essay in this collection by women contributes to developing a paradigm for the operation and management of organizations in this rapidly changing world. The proposed model is one that stresses a caring, supportive environment in which employees flourish and are enabled to function for the benefit of the organization, for their own benefit, and for the benefit of society. Each author describes an example from her own experience which shows how the model can be implemented and how it has been successful. Many essays contain discussions of spirituality not often found in management literature. The model is feminine in perspective as most of the values extolled are those stereotypically associated with women. The contribution of traditional masculine values is not ignored but is considered inadequate for today. Overall, the book calls attention to ideas and issues that merit consideration. Several of the essays are well written, some are very moving. However, there is considerable repetition of ideas and suggestions. References. General; advanced undergraduate through professional.—*F. Reitman, Pace University*

WS-1453 HD6054 91-14324 CIP

Womanpower: managing in times of demographic turbulence, ed. by Uma Sekaran and Frederick T.L. Leong. Sage, 1992. 286p index ISBN 0-8039-4105-6, $42.95; ISBN 0-8039-4106-4 pbk, $21.95

Based on discussion and papers presented at the 1989 Academy of Management Roundtable sponsored by the Women in Management Division, the eight individually authored chapters in this volume deal with the effective utilization of women in the workplace. Authors are respected management researchers, and each chapter contains conceptual analysis with extensive reference to the literature. Topics include the glass ceiling, managing diversity, work-family conflict, the entrepreneurial alternative, and global perspectives. The editors' introduction to the various parts and their concluding overview provide a cohesive whole. This publication extends earlier works in three important ways: (1) recommendations include practical solutions due in part to conference discussion by scholars and practitioners; (2) analysis of academic institutions and management education facilitates improved training for future professionals and managers; and (3) evaluation of the Anglo-American perspective of management theory and practice includes issues and differences for women of color and for white women. Complements Gary N. Powell, *Women and Men in Management* (CH, Dec'88) and *Women at Work*, ed. by Jenny Firth-Cozens and Michael A. West (CH, Jul'91). Upper-division undergraduate and graduate collections.—*K. C. Brannen, Creighton University*

WS-1454 HD6095 95-49853 CIP

Women and work: a handbook, ed. by Paula J. Dubeck and Kathryn Borman et al. Garland, 1996. 550p (Garland reference library of social science, 679) bibl indexes afp ISBN 0-8240-7647-8, $75.00

The stated objective of this handbook is the presentation of a broad overview of women's work experience in the US. The editors also intend this volume to serve as a reference tool, pointing the interested researcher to additional sources of information in the field of women and work. Organized into eight sections, the handbook has 150 essay entries authored by researchers selected or solicited by an editorial board. The sections cover women's labor force participation, approaches to analyzing women and work, women in diverse occupations, factors influencing occupational choice, legal factors, the organizational context of work, work and family, and cross-cultural and international issues. The volume reflects a sociological and institutionalist approach to women and work. The essays are relatively short, and each has its own references and bibliography. Comprehensive and useful subject and author indexes. A valuable reference tool for any women's studies or women and work collection. All levels.—*A. Bunton, Cottey College*

WS-1455 HD6054 93-23227 CIP

Women in management: a developing presence, ed. by Morgan Tanton. Routledge, 1994. 253p bibl indexes ISBN 0-415-09728-2, $65.00; ISBN 0-415-09729-0 pbk, $19.95

This volume contains papers first presented at a 1991 conference in the UK. The contributors are overwhelmingly British and female. In her introduction and first chapter on developing women's presence, Tanton sets the overall theme—the importance of, and problems in, integrating female experience into management practice. The subjects discussed are quite varied: women's development programs, women bosses, managing emotion, motherhood and management, female entrepreneurs, women-only management training. There is one contribution from a man—a personal reflection on management learning and the white male heritage—and one from two non-British women on women managers in Turkey. Personal experiences of the authors are integral to many of the papers. This collection's focus on the UK experience allows US readers to understand that the experiences of women in management in the two countries have been quite similar, although the steps to equality seem to be occurring later in the UK. The authors cite British and US literature. Upper-division undergraduate through professional.—*F. Reitman, Pace University*

WS-1456 Orig

Women in management: trends, issues, and challenges in managerial diversity, ed. by Ellen A. Fagenson. Sage, 1993. 342p (Women and work: a research and policy series, 4) index ISBN 0-8039-4591-4, $45.00; ISBN 0-8039-4592-2 pbk, $21.95

Five sections make up this contribution to the "Women and Work" series: Trends, Historical and Global Issues, Individual and Organizational Issues, Future Directions and Systemic Issues, and Challenges. Chapters are authored by recognized researchers of the topic. Although much of the literature reviewed will be familiar to those who track research on women in management, the analysis is placed within a useful gender-organization-system perspective. Systemic factors covered include laws, policies, sex role stereotypes, expectations, ideologies, cultural values, and histories. This volume contributes to the ongoing analysis of the interface between women's career aspirations and societal and organizational norms, assumptions, and values. Significant treatment is accorded the different perspectives and unique cultural dilemmas faced by women of color in management, and the legal and political realities including conservative court rulings and the 1991 Civil Rights Act. Extensive references. Advanced undergraduate through professional.—*K. C. Brannen, Creighton University*

WS-1457 Orig

Women in trade unions: organizing the unorganized, ed. by Margaret Hosmer Martens and Swasti Mitter. International Labour Office, 1994. (Dist. by ILO Publications Center, 49 Sheridan Ave., Albany, NY 12210) 205p ISBN 92-2-108759-X pbk, $26.00

This volume is largely a set of case studies about organizing women, a topic usually ignored by trade unions. An introductory essay discusses the main topics of the book: elements of the unorganized sector; women's unions or women in unions; domestic workers; homeworkers; rural workers; and workers in export processing zones. Although most of the case studies focus on activities in low-and middle-income countries such as Brazil, India, and Burkina Faso, organizing in developed countries is covered as well, especially with regard to homeworkers. The case studies describe successful and unsuccessful organizing activities, and circumstances faced by both the female workers and those attempting to organize them. For example, the legal environment varies with the country, and women in the low- and middle-income countries may be illiterate. The low wage received makes payment of union dues difficult for many women. The union for these women may need to offer a different set of services than normally made available to (male) workers all at one site. Some sections of the book have notes and/or a bibliography. Especially useful to those with practical concerns relating to women, work, and unions. Upper-division undergraduate through professional.—*J. E. Weaver, Drake University*

WS-1458 HD6060 91-2281 CIP

Work engendered: toward a new history of American labor, ed. by Ava Baron. Cornell, 1991. 385p index afp ISBN 0-8014-2256-6, $42.50; ISBN 0-8014-9543-1 pbk, $13.95

A collection of essays that highlights some of the most interesting work being done in the field of labor history today. By examining the ways in which sexual differences shape social roles, the authors provide important insights into the everyday behavior of ordinary working women and men. Just as gender largely determined work-force participation, it also played a key role in shaping the responses of both male and female workers to unfair or unsafe conditions on the job. Although all the essays are interesting, a number stand out. N. Hewitt's piece on Tampa cigar workers, D. Cobble's study of food service workers, and J. Dowd Hall's examination of Atlanta area textile workers illuminate little-known episodes in labor history while demonstrating the utility of analyzing such events through the lens of gender. An introductory theoretical essay by editor Baron lays out the intellectual framework around which the essays are built. Attempts by the authors to locate their research within this framework make for difficult reading at times. An important book for anyone interested in the ongoing evolution of the field of labor history. Upper-division undergraduate and graduate collections.—*H. Harris, Pennsylvania State University, New Kensington Campus*

◆ Comparative & International Studies

WS-1459　　　　HD6054　　　　95-9841 CIP
Napier, Nancy K. **Western women working in Japan: breaking corporate barriers,** by Nancy K. Napier and Sully Taylor. Quorum Books, 1995. 225p bibl index afp ISBN 0-89930-901-1, $59.95

In this research-based book, Napier (Boise State Univ.) and Taylor (Portland State Univ.) provide information on the experiences of Western women workers in Japan, examining the knowledge, skills, and behaviors associated with successful adjustment. Their research sample includes expatriates (only five to ten percent of the American businesswomen working in Japan), "independent job seekers," and "involuntary transferees." Among the topics covered by the authors: predeparture training and compensation packages of expatriates, variations in linguistic and technical ability, the role of relationships, and repatriation. In addition to 11 in-depth interviews, 91 survey responses were obtained from the Foreign Executive Women's Group and women members of the American Chamber of Commerce in Japan—an overall 32 percent response rate. Findings are presented within the context of existing research. Major parts of the book cover (a) the globalization environment; (b) demographics, job selection, the working environment, job adjustment, and outside work adjustment; and (c) recommendations for firms and for women, with a look to the future. Tables and figures; survey and interview instruments. The volume is particularly useful for women seeking work in Japan or firms sending women employees to Japan. For academic and professional collections supporting comprehensive international business collections.—*K. C. Brannen, Creighton University*

WS-1460　　　　HD6162　　　　93-247341 MARC
Pott-Buter, Hettie A. **Facts and fairy tales about female labor, family and fertility: a seven-country comparison, 1850-1990.** Amsterdam University, 1993. (Dist. by I.B.D., Ltd.) 370p bibl index ISBN 90-5356-045-9, $56.00

Pott-Buter's study compares the labor force experience of women in the Netherlands with that of women in six other countries (Great Britain, Belgium, Denmark, France, Germany, and Sweden) from 1850 to 1990. The purpose of the study is to determine why the measured labor force participation rate of Dutch women has been historically lower in many periods than the rate in the comparison countries. The book is densely written with quantities of data presented. It is well-organized with numbered sections, so that it would be relatively easy to use as a reference. In the final chapter the author admirably and completely sums up the facts that she has been able to substantiate as well as the commonly held misperceptions that she has been able to refute (the "fairy tales" of the title). Pott-Buter concludes that differences in participation rate between the Netherlands and the comparison countries are related to the Dutch family structure and high fertility rates. The book features good chapter-end summaries and a bibliography. A valuable research resource for women's labor market experience outside the US. Upper-division undergraduate through faculty.—*A. Bunton, Cottey College*

WS-1461　　　　　　　　　　British CIP
Saso, Mary. **Women in the Japanese workplace.** Hilary Shipman, 1990. (Dist. by Hawaii) 289p bibl index ISBN 0-948096-18-7, $45.00; ISBN 0-948096-19-5, $22.50

Saso's book presents information about Japanese women and their relationships to the workplace, and comparable material for women who work for Japanese companies in Britain and Ireland. The information comes from national statistics, research studies, and author's questionnaires and interviews at Japanese companies in the three countries, and from the knowledge and insights of the author, who has lived and worked in these countries. Postwar developments in legislation, education, unionization, child care, family support, and attitudes toward work and family are discussed. The focus is on the major occupational areas in which women work in Japan: the shop floor in large companies, small companies, family owned businesses, and self employment. Saso also describes work patterns of men in the three countries. Conditions in the US are not discussed. This study enhances an understanding of the similarities and differences in work patterns and work-family issues between Japan and the West. A bibliography includes Japanese and English references. Upper-division and graduate collections.—*F. Reitman, Pace University*

WS-1462　　　　HD6196　　　　95-4969 CIP
Stockman, Norman. **Women's work in east and west: the dual burden of employment and family life,** by Norman Stockman, Norman Bonney, and Sheng Xuewen. M.E. Sharpe, 1995. 232p bibl index ISBN 1-56324-708-9, $54.95; ISBN 1-56324-709-7 pbk, $21.95

This volume presents a comparison of women's paid and unpaid work patterns (and men and women's opinions about such patterns) for China, Japan, the US, and the UK. Its main contribution is to present results in English from the 1987 Sino-Japanese Working Women's Family Life Survey. Material on the US and UK is much less interesting and comprehensive than the coverage of Asian countries. The authors pose the question as to whether convergence is occurring as societies industrialize, and they answer in the negative, citing institutional differences as the cause for divergent paths. Chinese respondents were notably more likely than Japanese respondents to work full-time for pay, to believe that working full-time for pay was good or at least acceptable for married women, and to have husbands who performed a significant share of the housework. These differences are attributed to the socialist work structures in China and the accompanying child-care support system and ideological support for women's work. The book is well-written but not earthshaking in its theoretical structure or its conclusions. Lower-division undergraduate and up.—*J. P. Jacobsen, Wesleyan University*

WS-1463　　　　HD6206　　　　90-39662 CIP
Unesco. **Women in Arab society: work patterns and gender relations in Egypt, Jordan and Sudan,** by Seteney Shami et al. Berg/Unesco, 1991 (c1990). 217p ISBN 0-85496-724-9, $38.50

This book is a composite of three essays written by five Arab women scholars. They discuss the impact of social and economic changes brought about through contact with the modern economy on the lives of women in three different Arab societies. Shami and Taminian compare rural and urban patterns in their essay "Women's Participation in the Jordanian Labour Force"; Morsy's essay, "Rural Women: Work and Gender Ideology," studies the political and economic transformation of Egypt; and Bakri and Kameir, in "Women's Participation in Economic, Social and Political Life in Sudanese Urban and Rural Communities," examine a squatter community in the capital, Khartoum, and a village, in the Gezira as case studies. Taken together these essays (or, rather, these case studies based largely on empirical research) provide the reader with a better understanding of gender relations in three very different settings in the Islamic world. The picture that emerges is complex and the findings often surprising. For example, modern forces reinforce rather than disrupt traditional patterns and relations, and the introduction of modern, capitalist agriculture does not necessarily undermine small family holdings; sometimes it strengthens them. This is a book for those interested in the problems of development in the Islamic and Third World and especially the role women are playing in the process. Upper-division undergraduates and above.—*F. Ahmad, University of Massachusetts at Boston*

WS-1464   HD6182   93-10554 MARC
Women and work in South Asia: regional patterns and perspectives, ed. by Saraswati Raju and Deipica Bagchi. Routledge, 1994 (c1993). 282p bibl index ISBN 0-415-04249-6, $65.00

The 12 essays in this book are a valuable collection of studies by social geographers, economists, and anthropologists who have gone beyond aggregate statistics and gender stereotypes to document patterns of female labor participation in various South Asian nations. Through their efforts to look critically at much of the development research on women and work, the editors, Raju in particular, also provide a useful review of many of the theoretical complexities that characterize informal and "invisible" labor. Although the papers focus mostly on rural India, there are also discussions of women's work in Pakistan, Nepal, and Sri Lanka. Contributors are sensitive to issues of techno-environmental, ethnic, religious, and cultural diversity, and are also attentive to broader regional customs. The editors provide more comprehensive examinations of some of the general methodological and analytic difficulties in gathering and interpreting data on women's work, and they offer suggestions for future research, especially on women's work activities that take place in or around the home. Upper-division undergraduates and above.—*B. Tavakolian, Denison University*

WS-1465   HD6061   92-12157 CIP
Women's work and women's lives: the continuing struggle worldwide, ed. by Hilda Kahne and Janet Z. Giele. Westview, 1992. 324p index afp ISBN 0-8133-0636-1, $49.95

This collection of papers by authors from various social science disciplines focuses on women's paid employment in modernizing regions, socialist economies in transition, and industrialized economies. An introductory chapter provides a good overview of the status of women in the workforce around the world. A chapter on Japan shows that it is much harder for women there to combine marriage and a career than for women in the US, while a chapter on the Nordic countries indicates that it is easiest there. Another chapter provides good background on US governmental policies affecting the relationships between market work and support of family structure. Each chapter has an extensive bibliography, and many have statistical tables and charts. Suitable for academic libraries desiring a complete collection.—*E. P. Hoffman, Western Michigan University*

◆ Economics

WS-1466   HD6061   90-37561 CIP
Blum, Linda M. **Between feminism and labor: the significance of the comparable worth movement.** California, 1991. 249p bibl index afp ISBN 0-520-07032-1, $30.00; ISBN 0-520-07259-6 pbk, $11.95

In this monograph based on the author's PhD dissertation, Blum (sociology, University of Michigan, Ann Arbor) begins with a historical review of women's status in the American labor force, emphasizing the period since 1950. Then follow two case studies (with interesting anecdotal material) of the history of the implementation of comparable worth in the city of San Jose and in Contra Costa County, California. Unlike most economists, who are either critical of or neutral toward comparable worth, Blum is an advocate, claiming that women are "entitled to a just 'living wage,' regardless of the value the market places on their work." She proposes that the labor movement and the feminist movement should help politically mobilize working-class women through increased support of comparable worth. The volume contains limited statistical tables on women's status in the American labor force from 1950 to 1987 and has an extensive bibliography of recent material on women in the workplace. Appropriate for academic collections.—*E. P. Hoffman, Western Michigan University*

WS-1467   HD6073   94-282 CIP
Dangler, Jamie Faricellia. **Hidden in the home: the role of waged homework in the modern world-economy.** State University of New York, 1994. 225p bibl index ISBN 0-7914-2129-5, $49.50

Sociologist Dangler integrates her fieldwork on women in rural central New

York State doing industrial homework for electronics firms with a theoretical discussion of the social dynamics that sustain waged homework. Contrary to prior observers of the homework phenomenon who assumed it would die out as economies became more developed, she argues that it is a permanent structural feature of modern capitalism that can arise whenever particular conditions recur making its use possible. Dangler points out that the diversity of work in the informal sector obscures important dimensions along which industrial homeworkers differ from other informal sector participants, in particular class and gender differences (the workers in her sample are mainly lower-income women with primary responsibility for housework and child care, whose homework earnings are a fundamental contribution to family finances). This book successfully integrates diverse strands of literature concerning informal sector work in developing and developed economies and women's attempts to reconcile their double burden of paid work and family responsibilities. However, Dangler does not offer strong or concrete policy recommendations to either expand, formalize, or contract the role of homework in modern societies. Upper-division undergraduate through faculty.—*J. P. Jacobsen, Wesleyan University*

WS-1468   HD6060   91-14938 CIP
Kelly, Rita Mae. **The gendered economy: work, careers, and success.** Sage, 1991. 264p indexes ISBN 0-8039-4215-X, $42.00; ISBN 0-8039-4216-8 pbk, $18.95

Kelly, a political scientist, has written an interesting monograph on women's economic role in society. The history of laws affecting women, including the "protection" laws that limited the extent of women's work, introduces a chapter on the most recent antidiscrimination laws. There are several coauthored chapters dealing with such topics as women's employment stability; sexual harassment; male-female language, communication, and personality differences; and the characteristics of firms and industries more likely to employ women. There is a case study of the current legal and economic status of women in Arizona, including a consensus agenda from a conference on goals to improve that status. Kelly has produced other works on this topic, e.g., *Gender, Bureaucracy, and Democracy: Careers and Equal Opportunity in the Public Sector* co-edited with Mary M. Hale (CH, May'90), and *Comparable Worth, Pay Equity, and Public Policy*, co-edited with Jane Bayes (CH, Sep'88). Extensive references; short glossary; suggested readings. Appropriate for lower-division undergraduate through graduate level readers.—*E. P. Hoffman, Western Michigan University*

WS-1469   HQ834   90-19472 CIP
Morgan, Leslie A. **After marriage ends: economic consequences for midlife women.** Sage, 1991. 167p bibl index ISBN 0-8039-3548-X, $35.00; ISBN 0-8039-3549-8 pbk, $16.95;

This monograph, part of a series, "New Perspectives on Family," is published in cooperation with the National Council on Family Relations. Unlike most other similar studies, Morgan's work compares the economic status of separated, divorced, and widowed women both before and after their change in marital status. Using data from the National Longitudinal Surveys of Mature Women for the period from 1967 to 1982, the author considers how a woman's age, race, education, presence and age of children, and attitude toward working women affected the probability of her becoming separated, divorced, or widowed; of becoming poor; and of remarrying. The study finds that separated women suffered most in economic terms, having the highest poverty rates. The burdens society places on women in expecting them to fill the roles of both breadwinner and child-care provider are examined. Morgan advocates child-support reforms, particularly larger awards and stricter enforcement. Contains tables of statistical results. Complements *Women's Life Cycle and Economic Insecurity*, ed. by Margaret N. Ozawa (CH, May'90). Highly recommended for academic libraries serving upper-division and graduate students.—*E. P. Hoffman, Western Michigan University*

WS-1470   HQ1381   95-21629 CIP
Nelson, Julie A. **Feminism, objectivity and economics.** Routledge, 1996. 174p bibl index ISBN 0-415-13336-X, $45.00; ISBN 0-415-13337-8 pbk, $17.95

Part of a series "Economics as Social Theory," this monograph on feminist economic theory is not light reading. It contains many excerpts from, and expands on, Nelson's prior work. In part 1, she calls for fewer male-biased assumptions in economic theory, methods, and topic choices. She introduces a "gender-value compass"—a diagrammatic method to show the way gender relationships affect values. Part 2 consists of five application chapters: values in the history of the economics profession; a feminist theory of the family; household equivalence scales (the relationship of standard of living to income as family size varies); the family unit of taxation in the federal income tax, and the resulting "marriage tax"; and macroeconomics, including the value of unpaid housework (which is omitted from GDP) and how economists could better measure welfare. She particularly criticizes the new classical macroeconomics, which assumes all markets—including the labor market—clear, a theory which allows the conclusion that the unemployed have chosen leisure and are voluntarily unemployed. Part 3 is a reply to criticisms of feminist economics. The bibliography runs to 14 close-spaced pages. An essential reference for all libraries supporting graduate economics or women's studies programs.—*E. P. Hoffman, Western Michigan University*

WS-1471　　　　HD6061　　　　92-39227 CIP
Rhoads, Steven E. **Incomparable worth: pay equity meets the market.** Cambridge, 1993. 323p index ISBN 0-521-44187-0, $24.95

Rhoads (Univ. of Virginia) argues that programs to implement comparable worth are unsuccessful, having resulted in numerous labor market distortions and harmful effects both from a microeconomic and a macroeconomic viewpoint. A discussion of the theory of comparable worth as a mechanism for eliminating the wage differentials between men and women is admirably clear and presents both the pro and con viewpoints, although the author is clearly on the opponents' side. His analysis of Minnesota state and local governments' attempts to implement comparable worth is persuasive in its arguments that this system is plagued with problems and has not produced an acceptable method of reducing the effects of sex discrimination. Rhoads catalogs repeated instances where surpluses or shortages of labor cannot be eliminated when a system of comparable worth is in place. Examples drawn from the European Community, the UK, and Australia, while not as unequivocal as the Minnesota data, buttress his argument. This book will not please proponents of comparable worth; however, it is sobering in its warning of what can happen when markets are not allowed to determine wages, and for that reason it is a valuable piece of research. Lower-division undergraduate through faculty collections.—*A. Bunton, Cottey College*

WS-1472　　　　HD6095　　　　95-8589 CIP
Rose, Nancy E. **Workfare or fair work: women, welfare, and government work programs.** Rutgers, 1995. 263p index afp ISBN 0-8135-2232-3, $52.00; ISBN 0-8135-2233-1 pbk, $19.95

In this timely book Rose (California State Univ., San Bernardino) covers the history of welfare in the US, from the poorhouses of the Colonial period through the work programs of the Great Depression (which were mostly for white males), to the currently proposed reforms of Aid to Families with Dependent Children. The volume contains a very thorough study of the various federal training programs and government work programs from the 1930s through early 1995, focusing on the inadequacies of these programs for women receiving welfare. The author defines "workfare" as a requirement that an adult work in order to receive welfare payments, while "fair work" is working voluntarily in government created jobs. Rose argues that people have a right to socially useful work that pays above a poverty level income, and that welfare should be replaced by fair work. She favors federal rather than state control of welfare, and proposes expanding the Earned Income Tax Credit to include counting unpaid work in the home as equivalent to paid employment. Recommended for both undergraduate and graduate students.—*E. P. Hoffman, Western Michigan University*

WS-1473　　　　HQ536　　　　93-5441 CIP
Rubin, Rose M. **Working wives and dual-earner families,** by Rose M. Rubin and Bobye J. Riney. Praeger, 1994. 156p bibl indexes afp ISBN 0-275-94682-7, $49.95

Rubin compares the incomes, tax treatment, and Social Security benefits of one-earner and two-earner families in the US in the 1970s and 1980s. She provides an excellent discussion of the history of the "marriage tax," which is the extra federal income taxes that dual-earner married couples have to pay as compared to treating them as two single taxpayers. The pattern of women's labor force participation from 1890 to 1991 is shown, and statistical analyses are provided of the income, income distribution (showing inequality), assets, and expenditures of families with wives who do not work, work part-time, or work full-time outside the home. Economic models of household production and net earnings are presented and estimated. These models show that a working wife who earns the same amount as her husband adds at most 60 percent of her earnings to the family income. Contains many references to the ten-page bibliography. Good quality paper and binding. A very appropriate work for graduate students and faculty.—*E. P. Hoffman, Western Michigan University*

WS-1474　　　　HQ1870　　　　94-14949 Orig
Women in the age of economic transformation: gender impact of reforms in post-socialist and developing countries, [ed.] by Nahid Aslanbeigui, Steven Pressman, and Gale Summerfield. Routledge, 1994. 232p bibl index ISBN 0-415-10422-X, $65.00

This brief volume is an exceptional contribution to the economic and cross-cultural area of women's studies. Many studies of the impact of economic change on women are unable to distinguish between poverty issues and women's issues, and focus on the female-headed household. The studies in this work, most of them carefully done and well documented, examine the impact on women of different kinds of economic transitions in different kinds of societies, ranging from the postcommunist societies of East Germany, Poland, Romania, and the Soviet Union to the impact of World Bank policies on women in Zambia, to the effects of privatization in Chile, rapid economic development in Korea, and a change in economic structure in China. Most of these case studies interpret developments in a framework of gender equity in employment, child care and maternal leave, health care, entrepreneurial opportunities for women, and changes in the traditional male-female division of domestic and paid work opportunities. Virtually every study finds deteriorating conditions for women in terms of earnings, opportunities, and support services. A useful addition to undergraduate and graduate interdisciplinary collections in anthropology, women's studies, labor economics, and economic development.—*H. H. Ulbrich, Clemson University*

WS-1475　　　　HD4975　　　　91-13513 CIP
Workers and their wages: changing patterns in the United States, ed. by Marvin H. Kosters. AEI Press, 1991. 207p ISBN 0-8447-3747-X, $27.50

This collection of five papers, each with a commentary, results from a 1989 conference sponsored by the American Enterprise Institute. Highly qualified labor economists discuss the increase in the wage premium received for increased formal education (especially by college graduates relative to high school graduates) in the 1980s, which reversed the trend of the 1970s. One paper focuses on the slowness of the convergence of the wage premium between black and white *males*, but does not consider the cases of black and white *females*, or of females and males. Three papers consider the effects of gender; only one paper analyzes the data by both race and gender. Two papers consider the effects of international trade, technological change, and outsourcing of production operations on wages. Numerous figures, tables, and references. Appropriate for research libraries.—*E. P. Hoffman, Western Michigan University*

◆ History, Theory

WS-1476　　　　HQ1410　　　　90-48222 CIP
Amott, Teresa. **Race, gender, and work: a multicultural economic history of women in the United States,** by Teresa Amott and Julie Matthaei. South End, 1991. 433p index ISBN 0-89608-377-2, $40.00; ISBN 0-89608-376-4 pbk, $16.00

This wide-ranging study seeks to provide "liberatory knowledge," that is, to inform the public about the pervasiveness of gender, race, ethnic, and class oppression for most of American history. The volume is divided into three parts. It begins with a conceptual framework that highlights "three categories . . . —gender, race-ethnicity, and class—as interconnected, historical processes of domination and subordination." The bulk of the book is devoted to historical sketches of six groups of women: American Indian, Chicanas, European American, African American, Asian American, and Puerto Rican. After a three-stage analysis of capitalist development and women's work within it, the volume concludes with a call for "liberatory practice." Academics may find this book disappointing; it breaks little new ground. The authors do rework census data to offer a number of tables on labor-force participation rates, occupational distribution, and incomes. But those interested in a quantitative analysis would benefit more from Claudia Goldin's *Understanding the Gender Gap* (CH, Nov '90). Abundantly footnoted and amply indexed. Most appropriate for comprehensive collections.—*D. Lindstrom, University of Wisconsin-Madison*

WS-1477 HD6060 94-9072 CIP
Beasley, Chris. **Sexual economyths: conceiving a feminist economics.** St. Martin's, 1995 (c1994). 179p bibl index ISBN 0-312-12234-9, $49.95

"Sexual economyths," the title phrase, refers to "economic assumptions which exclude/marginalise women's experiences," according to Beasley. This short work purports to present the outline of a feminist economics. In fact, it is largely a review of others' work on feminist perspectives in economics, presenting only an overview of what might be contained in an economic theory that takes women as protagonist and women's private or unpaid work in the household as framework. The author provides a critique of Marxist and orthodox economists' attempts to incorporate a feminist economics, especially in the realm of the emotional portion of the work women do in the household. The book is written in a scholarly tone but is somewhat marred by excessive use of feminist and Marxist jargon, which may make it less accessible to the general reader. Still, it is a thoughtful treatment of the distinct framework of a feminist economic theory. Supplemental notes and bibliography. Graduate; faculty.—*A. Bunton, Cottey College*

WS-1478 HQ1190 92-40149 CIP
Beyond economic man: feminist theory and economics, ed. by Marianne A. Ferber and Julie A. Nelson. Chicago, 1993. 178p index afp ISBN 0-226-24200-5, $35.00; ISBN 0-226-24201-3 pbk, $12.95

This collection of essays by six feminist economists, with analytical discussions by four other economists (including a Nobel laureate), focuses on feminist economic theory. A recently developing field, feminist economics challenges the assumptions of the neoclassical rational choice model that individuals (with perfect information, certainty of outcome, and operating in perfect competition) make important life choices (concerning consumption, investment in education, and career field) to maximize their own utility. These authors criticize that model as being unrealistic because it ignores family responsibilities, principally the raising of children. They also consider previous attempts to incorporate the family into economic theory (called "the new home economics") to be a minimal improvement, as it assumes that the husband makes choices for the whole family. Unfortunately, the authors have not yet completed the development of any superior alternative theory. Nonetheless, this is an important work in the development of feminist economic theory. Essential for any library that maintains a collection in feminist economics.—*E. P. Hoffman, Western Michigan University*

WS-1479 HQ1381 93-8713 CIP
The Economic status of women under capitalism: institutional economics and feminist theory, ed. by Janice Peterson and Doug Brown. W. Elgar, 1994. 187p index ISBN 1-85278-894-1, $59.95

Peterson and Brown provide a collection of papers on the general topic of institutional economics as a framework for studying feminist perspectives on women, society, and economic change. Part 1 addresses the question of why institutional economics is an effective paradigm for feminist theory. Part 2 deals with other paradigms, including neoclassical economics and functionalism, and criticizes the perceived shortcomings or failures of these approaches in explicating the differential economic experience of women in a technologically developed society. Part 3 contains four essays that address particular aspects of women's experience: the former Soviet system, the effect of the women's movement, the dual career couple, and the status of Japanese women. Institutionalism and feminism are given a thoroughgoing treatment in which the major premises of these schools of thought are explained and their relationship discussed. A valuable primer for those wishing to avail themselves of the summarized treatment of theory and the fairly lengthy literature review in some essays. All essays are well documented, and each contains its own bibliography. Graduate; faculty.—*A. Bunton, Cottey College*

WS-1480 HD6061 92-900 CIP
England, Paula. **Comparable worth: theories and evidence.** Aldine de Gruyter, 1992. 346p bibl index afp ISBN 0-202-30348-9, $46.95; ISBN 0-202-30349-7 pbk, $22.95

The title of this book understates its scope and value. Although attuned to the controversial policy question of whether substantively different jobs can be determined to be of comparable worth to an employer and thus equally paid, the theoretical overview and empirical data that England presents are of more general relevance and interest. Essentially, England believes that to understand fully what is at issue in the comparable worth controversy, one needs to have a basic grasp of economic theories (both neoclassical and challengers), knowledge of the structure of the labor force (especially with regard to gender), and an informed perspective on US policy process, including court decisions about discrimination and wage-setting in general. The book provides all this background plus more: England's own integration of economic and social psychological theories into an original and persuasive "feedback model" of discriminatory effects, a reasonable effort to test this model with available data, and an argument for taking its policy implications seriously and addressing the devaluation of the work conventionally done by woman. Although she makes her own preferences apparent, England is exceptionally clear and even-handed in laying out all the positions in the debate. Advanced undergraduate; graduate; faculty; professional.—*M. M. Ferree, University of Connecticut*

WS-1481 HD4901 93-17207 CIP
Folbre, Nancy. **Who pays for the kids?: gender and the structures of constraint.** Routledge, 1994. 335p bibl index ISBN 0-415-07564-5, $65.00; ISBN 0-415-07565-3 pbk, $18.95

Folbre approaches the issue of the unfair distribution of the costs of social reproduction ("caring for ourselves, our children, and other dependents") from a theoretical framework informed by feminist scholarship and neoclassical institutionalist and neo-Marxian models of political economy. An important contribution of this approach is its explicit recognition of the interdependent nature of human behavior, specifically that individuals often act based on their collective identity and interests in chosen groups (such as the Sierra Club) or given groups (such as gender, age, or sexual preference). Each group an individual identifies with is structured by its own rules, norms, and preferences which have evolved over time. Folbre favors the concept of "structures of constraint" over the evolution of efficient social institutions (neoclassical institutionalists) or mode of production analysis (Marxists) as primary explanatory factors of the distribution of the benefits of economic development. She argues that collective action based on unfair structures of constraint helps explain how family labor became devalued. Using the structures of constraint framework, Folbre takes a bold new look at the her/his story of social reproduction in northwestern Europe, the US, and Latin America and the Caribbean. Her examination of the factors that have led to the persistence of, as well as destabilization of, structures of constraint (gender, age, sexual preference, race, class, and nation) and of the interaction of those structures with the process of economic development, is unprecedented and fills a gap in the literature. The book is written partly as a dialogue among a feminist economist, a neoclassical economist, and a Marxist economist, and Folbre often uses humor to get her point across. This well researched and heavily endnoted volume is immensely provocative and rewarding for the dedicated reader. Must reading for graduate students and faculty interested in the political economy of a participatory democracy.—*K. H. Larson, Elon College*

WS-1482 HD6061.2.U6 89-48812 CIP
Kessler-Harris, Alice. **A woman's wage: historical meanings and social consequences.** University Press of Kentucky, 1990. 168p (The Blazer lectures, 1988) index afp ISBN 0-8131-0551-X, $19.00

This book consists of five incisive lectures delivered by Kessler-Harris in 1988. Although instructive separately, together they represent a comprehensive dissection of the wage as a tool for social organization and social control. In "The Wage Conceived," prevailing notions about women's needs and their putative lifestyles are linked to the limits of their political resources, as symbolized by the wage. "Law and a Living" examines court rulings on the minimum wage as reflections of contradictory domestic and market forces. "Providers" is the most enriching chapter for feminist theory; it fruitfully questions the assumptions often made in women's studies about women's ways of perceiving, judging, and acting on their circumstances. "The Double Meaning of Equal Pay" and "The Just Price, The Free Market, and the Value of Women" analyze the ambiguities and risks associated with the equal pay and comparable worth controversies. The book is carefully documented and indexed, and it has value for all the social sciences.—*R. Zingraff, Meredith College*

WS-1483 HD4901 92-3371 CIP
Picchio, Antonella. **Social reproduction: the political economy of the labour market.** Cambridge, 1992. 193p bibl index ISBN 0-521-41872-0, $49.95

Picchio draws on her background in political economy and the history of economics as well as her research and previous publications in this area. This study is more political philosophy, mostly based on Marxist-feminist creeds, than careful economic analysis. She rejects most of the neoclassical, market-based, and capitalist frameworks of references inherent in contemporary empirical studies of economists. This interesting philosophical and political study is based on the relationship between the processes of production of goods and services and social reproduction of labor in the population. Since prices, including wage rates, are the mechanisms to allocate relatively scarce resources to the production of goods and services in the most productive and socially desired manner, the process of social reproduction is not well served by these capitalist and market settings according to the author. Thus, the Marxist notion of surplus value and labor theory of value along with "institutions and historical living standards" take a prominent place in Picchio's analysis. To get to this place, she attempts to reestablish the natural price of labor and takes readers through a regurgitation of the Poor Laws and the labor of women from a feminist perspective. Beginning students of economics are not ready for this discourse. A welcome addition to advanced undergraduate and graduate collections as an extension and addition to more wide-based readings in the history of economic thought.—*F. W. Musgrave, Ithaca College*

WS-1484 HD6300 89-25041 CIP
Potts, Lydia. **The world labour market: a history of migration,** tr. by Terry Bond. Zed Books, 1990. (Dist. by Humanities) 247p bibl index ISBN 0-86232-882-9, $55.00

Human groups have been exploiting each other shamelessly for as long as there are records on the subject, and probably long before that. This exploitation is particularly evident in the provision of labor at lowest possible cost, the bottom line for economic growth throughout most of the world's history. In this ambitious book, the author traces the patterns of labor migration from the European discovery of America to the present day, passing from slavery and the coolie system to European emigration to North America and the modern "brain drain." The work, misleadingly subtitled, owes little to conventional migration theory, is highly selective in the examples chosen, reflects a curiously stilted Marxist-Leninist view of sweeping historical events, and often bogs down in obscure discussions of recent German attempts to define such terms as "alien" and "guest workers." One of the more notable contributions is an unusual documentation of the sufferings endured by women in many migratory situations. In the tragic setting of forced migration, as in so many others, women have been more victimized than men. This is a book more fascinating for its historical details than for its theoretical contribution. Solid bibliography. Of interest mainly to scholars with a strong background in the history and economics of migration.—*J. R. McDonald, Eastern Michigan University*

WS-1485 HD87 94-35309 Orig
The strategic silence: gender and economic policy, ed. by Isabella Bakker. Zed Books/North-South Institute, 1994. (Dist. by Humanities) 170p bibl index ISBN 1-85649-261-3, $55.00; ISBN 1-85649-262-1 pbk, $17.50

This work combines a relatively new type of analysis of macroeconomic issues with a feminist frame of reference. Part 1 provides a theoretical criticism of how macro policies have ignored gender effects. The authors suggest new research strategies to overcome allegedly biased effects of macroeconomic policies and policies promoting structural change. The general idea is that supposedly gender-neutral policies have in fact unequal effects, which often are disadvantageous to women. Several essays in part 2 highlight policies in varied countries and societies to provide examples of macroeconomic policies and their impact on women in those societies. Contributors present a reasoned look at how macroeconomic

policies have a differential effect on women through feminization of the labor force, cutbacks in social services, and failure to recognize impacts on the "informal sector," for which women have traditionally been assigned responsibility. An understanding of basic economics and economic development is required to comprehend the arguments fully. A useful addition to economic development and macroeconomic collections. Upper-division undergraduate through faculty.—*A. Bunton, Cottey College*

WS-1486 HB74 95-7191 CIP
Women of value: feminist essays on the history of women in economics, ed. by Mary Ann Dimand, Robert W. Dimand, and Evelyn L. Forget. E. Elgar, 1995. 228p bibl index ISBN 1-85278-959-X, $79.95

In this collection of ten essays, the authors sketch American and British women's contributions to economics before 1960. Particular attention is given to the question of why these women's works received so little attention then and now. The first four essays survey the terrain identifying women economists, their institutional backgrounds, some of their networks, and their areas of expertise. The next five essays explore the lives of several prominent women in economics: Jane Marcet, Harriet Martineau, Harriet Taylor, Barbara Bodichon, Charlotte Perkins Gilman, and Mary Paley Marshall. The volume concludes with a critical analysis of two early 20th century British surveys of working women. Although somewhat idiosyncratic in the selection of women profiled either individually or collectively, this volume does provide a wealth of information both in the densely written essays and in the extensive bibliographies that accompany each contribution. *Women of Value* will be consulted frequently by feminist economists and historians of economic thought. Graduate; faculty.—*D. Lindstrom, University of Wisconsin—Madison*

◆ Comparative & International Studies

WS-1487 HD6167 95-19881 MARC
Bridger, Sue. **No more heroines?: Russia, women and the market,** by Sue Bridger, Rebecca Kay, and Kathryn Pinnick. Routledge, 1996. 220p bibl index ISBN 0-415-12460-3 pbk, $16.95

At first, this book appears to be nothing more than another depressing chronicle of Russian women's unenviable economic, political, and social conditions in the post-Soviet successor states. Beginning with the fourth chapter, however, the book becomes much more original and valuable. The authors interviewed the founders and some of the clientele (mostly highly educated, unemployed Moscow women) of three women's support organizations—Missiya, Guildia, and the Moscow Image Center. These case studies raise *No More Heroines?* above the level of most accounts of the impact of privatization in Russia. The authors admit to walking a tightrope: they want to record the successful survival strategies of individuals without losing sight of the bleak prospects for the vast majority of Russian women. For the most part, they succeed admirably in their balancing act. They emphasize the so-called "informal economy," and sensitively portray the severely limited opportunities and frustrated hopes of Russian women, while paying tribute to the stoicism and resourcefulness of their subjects. Of interest to scholars in women's studies, Slavic studies, and economics. Upper-division undergraduates and above.—*A. H. Koblitz, Hartwick College*

WS-1488 Orig
Eviota, Elizabeth Uy. **The political economy of gender: women and the sexual division of labour in the Philippines.** Zed Books, 1992. 212p bibl index ISBN 1-85649-109-9, $55.00; ISBN 1-85649-110-2 pbk, $19.95

Eviota's book provides a short but effective introduction to gender theory in the context of the political economy of world systems and then applies these two theoretical literatures to the specific case of the Philippines. The case study is enriched with a substantial overview of the political and economic history of the Philippines, making it possible for an otherwise uninformed reader to understand the context of recent economic developments. Eviota's history draws out the processes of colonialism, with unusually careful attention to both paid and unpaid work and how these forms of work have been transformed over time. The author provides a wealth of specific economic data on job segregation, wages, and state policies, especially rich in its depiction of historical changes in gender and ethnic segregation. One of the strengths of the book is that it offers more than a descriptive picture of women's place in the Philippine economy. Eviota develops a coherent theoretical analysis of the variety of forces that shape this place and hold women in it. Because of the attention to gender and class in both the ideological and structural dimensions, the book could be used to teach general courses on women and development, on political economy, or on gender stratification. Advanced undergraduate; graduate; faculty.—*M. M. Ferree, University of Connecticut*

WS-1489 Orig
George, Shanti. **A matter of people: co-operative dairying in India and Zimbabwe.** Oxford, 1994. 540p bibl index ISBN 0-19-563166-8, $29.00

In an informative critique of India's government-sponsored milk cooperative movement, George (Institute of Social Sciences, The Hague) accuses India's National Dairy Development Board (NDDB) of encouraging the development of dairy cooperatives using European models of dairying with little regard to the social and ecological context of the Indian villages involved. Moreover, the NDDB claims benefits for its dairy program that it does not provide. It does not bring together people of different castes or benefit the poor or empower women, as it claims. Often government-sponsored cooperatives divide castes, benefit the prosperous, and make women more dependent on men. George compares the NDDB's prototype Indian cooperative unfavorably with one near Serat City that has no government aid. She also compares the NDDB's program unfavorably with that of the Dairy Marketing Board (DMB) of Zimbabwe although the DMB's own programs have produced little milk and more failures than successes. This is because even in its failures, the DMB is more in tune with local circumstances and has achieved more local participation. George's book provides an interesting introduction to village life in India and Zimbabwe in addition to an analysis of dairy cooperatives. All levels.—*J. W. Webb, Eastern Kentucky University*

WS-1490 HC925 92-12784 CIP
Harris, Betty J. **The political economy of the southern African periphery: cottage industries, factories and female wage labour in Swaziland compared.** Macmillan, UK/St. Martin's, 1993. 296p bibl index ISBN 0-312-08471-4, $69.95

Written by an anthropologist from the University of Oklahoma, Norman, this book includes such broad topics as the spread of industrialization and the movement of international capital along with the minutia on wages paid to female workers in the different parts of the textile industry and the number of children they have. All of this is done in the context of southern Africa with emphasis on Swaziland (where Harris did field research in 1988-89). The growth of the textile industry in the region with its implications for women and development is a major concern, examined through the viewpoint of core-periphery relationships. This is an extensively noted book. The statements and conclusions of many authors are given without effectively tying the ideas together. Although recent growth of industry is the central focus, considerable time is spent on historical background and political issues. For those interested in southern Africa or the textile industry, this book may contain some useful detail. Broader implications of the situation are lacking. There are endnotes and references. Although suitable for advanced undergraduates, this work is likely to be valuable only for libraries that collect comprehensively on studies of southern Africa.—*J. E. Weaver, Drake University*

WS-1491 HD4904 94-40577 CIP
Investment in women's human capital, ed. by T. Paul Schultz. Chicago, 1995. 461p bibl index afp ISBN 0-226-74087-0, $67.00; ISBN 0-226-74088-9 pbk, $22.95

This useful conference volume mainly comprises econometric studies of fundamental issues regarding economic gender differences. While two studies concern the forces leading to changes in female participation in market work, most of the other studies discuss and measure gender differences in levels and rates of return on human capital investment, measured by various education and health indicators. The studies chiefly utilize nationally representative household interview data sets from several countries (including Brazil, Indonesia, Jamaica, the Ivory Coast, Malaysia, and Taiwan) for which little such data has been available until

recently (the samples mostly date from the mid to late 1980s). Familiarizing readers with some uses for these data is an important feature of this book. Other low-income countries discussed include Bangladesh, India, Kenya, Pakistan, and the Philippines; one article compares West Germany, the Netherlands, and Sweden. The book suffers from endemic conference volume drawbacks of weak coherence and nonoriginality: chapters are not well integrated, and much of the content (all of sections 2, 3, and 4, as well as the overview chapter) has already been published (in *Journal of Human Resources*, fall 1993). Upper-division undergraduate through professional.—*J. P. Jacobsen, Wesleyan University*

WS-1492 HD6223 94-41464 MARC
Mortgaging women's lives: feminist critiques of structural adjustment, ed. by Pamela Sparr. Zed Books, 1994. 214p bibl index ISBN 1-85649-101-3, $55.00

Sparr's collection of case studies addresses the impact of World Bank structural adjustment loans (SALS) on women in six economies—Egypt, Turkey, Ghana, the Philippines, Sri Lanka, and Nigeria. SALs set conditions requiring movement toward a deregulated market economy with a strong export sector, a smaller role for government, and more fiscal restraint. The case studies draw heavily on anecdotal and impressionistic evidence because of the limited availability of data on developing economies. Nevertheless, a clear pattern emerges: changes imposed as conditions of SALs impact negatively on women. In many cases women have more employment opportunities in the public sector and the informal sector than in production for export, so they tend to lose recent gains in employment, wages, and working conditions under SALS. Government retrenchment not only costs more women's jobs than men's, but also usually results in spending cuts focused in areas of special importance to women—education (where many women work and where girls often receive lower priority than boys), rural health care, and child care. A useful volume on a seldom explored topic intersecting feminist studies, economics, and development. Upper-division undergraduate through faculty.—*H. H. Ulbrich, Clemson University*

WS-1493 HD6138 89-26160 CIP
Pyle, Jean Larson. **The state and women in the economy: lessons from sex discrimination in the Republic of Ireland.** State University of New York, 1991 (c1990). 202p bibl index ISBN 0-7914-0379-3, $47.50; ISBN 0-7914-0380-7 pbk, $15.95

The Republic of Ireland provides an interesting case study for the analysis of women's status and paid employment because it has concentrated on the kind of economic growth that is usually associated with increases in women's employment and yet has not experienced this growth. Unlike other developing nations that rely on export processing for jobs, the Irish economy has not produced more jobs for women, and unlike other developed nations in the EEC, participation of Irish women in the labor force is not associated with access to better paying jobs. Pyle's book provides an intensive and fact-filled study that spells out the relevance of the Irish situation for a more general theory of women and economic development. Pyle's analysis highlights the role of a specific social policy intended to maintain "the family," by which the state explicitly means male dominance, and for shaping Irish economic development in general. The interrelationships between reproductive policy and employment policy are clarified, in part because the male domination of both is so blatant. This study could easily serve as a model for policy analysis in other less explicit or more controversial cases. Upper-division undergraduates and above.—*M. M. Ferree, University of Connecticut*

WS-1494 HD6114 94-47478 MARC
Safa, Helen I. **The myth of the male breadwinner: women and industrialization in the Caribbean.** Westview, 1995. 208p bibl index afp ISBN 0-8133-1211-6, $55.00; ISBN 0-8133-1212-4 pbk, $18.95

Safa's excellent study of the effects of industrial employment on women in Puerto Rico, the Dominican Republic, and Cuba is based on careful empirical research and explores broad issues of gender inequality. Comparisons of gender subordination in the workplace with gender relations in families and households show that state policies can have a rapid impact, but ideologies change slowly. Development strategies in Puerto Rico and the Dominican Republic are predicated on incorporating women as cheap labor in export-oriented industrialization. As men lose their traditional role of breadwinner, women take their place, but it is generally a hard, contested, and burdensome place. In Cuba, where the state supports women's equality in rights, pay, and household responsibilities, women gain greatly from educational opportunities and health and other services. However, patriarchal traditions die hard in the private and public spheres in all three places because some women still view themselves primarily as wives and mothers, and because men—at home, at work, and in the state—resist change and continue to benefit from women's subordination. A clearly organized and well-written study, highly recommended for women's studies, Caribbean studies, and comparative studies of industrialization. Upper-division undergraduates and above.—*O. N. Bolland, Colgate University*

WS-1495   F1565   94-16152 CIP
Tice, Karin E. **Kuna crafts, gender, and the global economy.** Texas, 1995. 232p bibl index afp ISBN 0-292-78133-4, $35.00; ISBN 0-292-78137-7 pbk, $14.95

Molas are the colorful and often imaginatively designed reverse-appliqué cloth panels that Kuna Indian women in Panama have worn on their blouses throughout this century; they have been popular as "folk art" for not quite half that time. This book is the first effort to describe molas in full sociocultural context—systematically dealing with their history, symbolism, production, distribution, and even linkages to politics and kinship, as well as economics. Tice is unusual in having spent considerable time in close, sustained contact with the Kuna, and her general description is often enhanced with vivid real-life vignettes. Key factors in the growth in production of molas include the shift from women making them as part of their own clothing (of which they are ethnically proud) to development of a cooperative that sells them mostly to tourists and dealers. With the coop have come a shift in sex roles (with women often having more cash than men, and now being politically outspoken), changes in diet, innovation, differentiation among the various island communities, and other repercussions. Tice is good in showing how regional, national, and even international events and processes influence diverse aspects of the local scene—a nice unselfconscious illustration of the world system in action. This book should equally interest those who care about gender studies, economic development, handicrafts, and Latin Amerian indigenous or peasant populations. Includes photographs, maps, tables, figures, glossary, a methodological appendix, discursive endnotes, and a good bibliography and index. Upper-division undergraduates and above.—*D. B. Heath, Brown University*

WS-1496   HC59   92-2873 CIP
Unequal burden: economic crises, persistent poverty, and women's work, ed. by Lourdes Benería and Shelley Feldman. Westview, 1992. 278p index afp ISBN 0-8133-8229-7, $52.95; ISBN 0-8133-8230-0 pbk, $15.95

An important addition to the growing body of empirical literature examining the impact of structural adjustment programs on various groups in society, particularly women and children. Specifically, the book focuses on how communities, households, and intra-household relations change to cope with the consequences of economic restructuring programs. Case studies from the Caribbean, South Asia, Italy, Bangladesh, Mexico, Bolivia, Nicaragua, and Tanzania are used to illustrate the diverse strategies that households use to cope with the economic and social stress of macroeconomic adjustment policies. The authors emphasize that successful household-level survival strategies depend on a country's overall political system and the role of the international financial system. *Unequal Burden* is accessible to undergraduate audiences but will also be a valuable resource for graduate students, faculty, and professionals in the field of development.—*K. H. Larson, Elon College*

◆ Women & Development

WS-1497   HQ1240   94-21082 CIP
African market women and economic power: the role of women in African economic development, ed. by Bessie House-Midamba and Felix K. Ekechi. Greenwood, 1995. 214p (Contributions in Afro-American and African studies, 174) bibl index afp ISBN 0-313-29214-0, $59.95

Most literature on women in African development discusses the role of women in West African societies. One of the principal virtues of this collection is that it examines women in West, East, and Southern Africa (but not in Central Africa as the editors allege). There are ten essays in all, many of them with useful tables and maps. The time frame encompasses the precolonial, colonial, and independent periods. Contributors highlight the many ways in which African women have adapted and changed over the decades as they have found new means to remain viable in the economies of their countries. These essays maintain that market women are essential in African economies and demonstrate how they have both expanded and adapted their roles in the national economies. In one of the most penetrating chapters, Catherine VerEecke focuses on Yola in northern Nigeria as she analyzes changes in the role of some Muslim Fulbe (Fulani) women who now participate actively in trading activities, which would not have been possible in earlier decades. All of the chapters deal with women in countries where English is the main European language. The comparative perspective would have been enhanced with offerings from francophone and lusophone areas. The selected bibliography and index are adequate. Upper-division undergraduates, graduate students, and faculty.—*R. A. Corby, University of Arkansas at Monticello*

WS-1498   HQ1240   91-31013 CIP
Gender analysis in development planning: a case book, ed. by Aruna Rao, Mary B. Anderson, and Catherine A. Overholt. Kumarian, 1991. 103p bibl afp ISBN 0-931816-61-0 pbk, $18.95

Women's impoverishment following the initial stages of modernization has been well documented. But few studies offer solutions or suggestions that serve to raise planners' awareness of the actual outcomes of development on women's daily lives. This book should be required reading for national development planners and practitioners, politicians, and social scientists interested in understanding the conditions of women (as well as of men and children) and the outcomes of development in five Asian countries: Bangladesh, India, Indonesia, the Philippines, and Thailand. The editors have purposely chosen Asian countries for their case studies because it is there that the gender inequality is the most severe. The volume provids rich raw materials that should enable students and planners to think about women's daily activities, their access to resources, and their control over the scarce commodities that sustain life. Although the case studies are descriptive and offer no solutions, the editors have included a gender analysis framework consisting of an activity profile, access and control profile, and key questions for project analysis.—*A. S. Oakes, Idaho State University*

WS-1499   HG1240   95-41235 CIP
Gordon, April A. **Transforming capitalism and patriarchy: gender and development in Africa.** L. Rienner, 1996. 218p bibl index afp ISBN 1-55587-402-9, $42.00; ISBN 1-55587-629-3 pbk, $19.95

Gordon contends that if Africa is to become a capitalist player in the world theater, it must overcome its deeply entrenched and socially embedded patriarchal practices, which both retard and sabotage capitalism. She rejects feminist theories that claim a direct correlation between capitalism and patriarchy. Instead, she uses empirical evidence and logical reasoning to argue that in Africa, patriarchal ideologies limiting women's social and political rights and roles undermine its chances to develop a capitalist economy that would ultimately improve its peoples' standard of living. Gordon shows, for example, that by restricting women's access to land ownership, male family members, who are often unable or unwilling to provide basic subsistence needs for family and household, continue to control women's roles in food production and in cash cropping. Her main argument is convincing: for Africa, capitalism cannot thrive, let alone coexist, with patriarchal social, economic, and political arrangements. Upper-division undergraduates and up.—*A. S. Oakes, Idaho State University*

WS-1500   HQ1240   95-13689 MARC

Jahan, Rounaq. **The elusive agenda: mainstreaming women in development.** University Press Limited/Zed Books, 1995. 144p bibl index ISBN 1-85649-273-7, $55.00; ISBN 1-85649-274-5 pbk, $17.50

Jahan's short but important book is "must" reading for anyone interested in women in development (WID) or gender and development (GAD). It addresses a familiar paradox: the relentless increase in the "feminization of poverty," especially in the developing world, despite heightened worldwide attention to women's issues. Unlike other recent treatments of the subject, this one identifies specific causes and offers reasonable recommendations. It reviews the efforts of four donor agencies (UNDP, World Bank, CIDA, NORAD) and two countries (Tanzania, Bangladesh) receiving aid to operationalize WID/GAD policies over the last 20 years. Jahan shows that progress has been mainly in areas that do not demand fundamental social-structural changes; goals requiring the dismantling of traditional gender hierarchies and redistribution of power and resources have generally not been met. The author sensibly recommends an "agenda-setting approach" involving changing institutional structures to enable women's greater participation in decision making, renewed emphasis on women's equality and empowerment, and decreased emphasis on operational measures. A useful adjunct to material emanating from the Fourth UN World ("Beijing") Conference on Women (September 1995). Upper-division undergraduates and above.—*M. A. Gwynne, SUNY at Stony Brook*

WS-1501   HD6060.65.D44   90-6460 CIP

Male bias in the development process, ed. by Diane Elson. Manchester, 1991. (Dist. by St. Martin's) 215p index ISBN 0-7190-2555-9, $49.95

A timely and important collection because most of the major international development agencies are in the process of moving from an approach emphasizing women in development to one that emphasizes an understanding of gender relations for development. The volume's carefully crafted analyses explain why the development process has been marked by male bias, operating in favor of men and against women. The six case studies represent urban and rural settings in Africa, Asia, and Latin America. Using economic, sociological, and anthropological perspectives, the authors demonstrate the hight cost to society of male bias in development theories and policies that have been presumed to be gender neutral. Data are drawn from agriculture, industry, and services. Examples from Nigeria and Peru demonstrate the preponderance of females in the informal sector, while a case study from Mexico indicates the negative impact on women of World Bank and IMF structural adjustment programs. The editor provides an excellent overview, and the conclusion offers many useful suggestions for overcoming male bias. Useful for students, policymakers, and practitioners involved in development.—*D. M. Warren, Iowa State University*

WS-1502   HQ1240   92-35076 Orig

Pankhurst, Helen. **Gender, development and identity: an Ethiopian study.** Zed Books, 1993 (c1992). 216p bibl index ISBN 1-85649-157-9, $49.95; ISBN 1-85649-158-7 pbk, $19.95

Pankhurst, a leading authority on Ethiopian society, explores within the context of Marxism and agrarian reform the relationships between the Ethiopian state and the peasantry, and between Ethiopian men and women. The study is based on fieldwork in the rural community of Menz conducted during 1988-89, with a return visit in 1992 after the fall of the Mengistu regime. Pankhurst addresses the intended impact of socialist state policies on the rural peasantry, particularly women. Despite Marxist rhetoric regarding liberation of oppressed persons such as women, the reality of male domination remained. The state's blindness to women emerges through empirical evidence presented on the rural household economy, marital relations, the life-cycle, and the influence of male-dominant religion. Using both ethnographic description and quantitative data, the author delineates how men and women perceive their relationships, and how women identify both the sources of their oppression and subordination, and of their power. This is a very important contribution to understanding of the forces of social change and continuity ranging from gender relationships to the household and the nation state. Two maps, six tables, and numerous notes, followed by three appendixes. Community college; undergraduate; graduate; faculty; professional.—*D. M. Warren, Iowa State University*

WS-1503   Orig

Ram, Kalpana. **Mukkuvar women: gender, hegemony and capitalist transformation in a South Indian fishing community.** Zed, 1992 (c1991). (Dist. by Humanities) 266p bibl index ISBN 1-85649-031-9, $57.95

An excellent book that details the everyday activities of a fishing caste in South India and, at the same time, points up the inadequacies of both economics and Indology as explanations for the organization of social life among the Mukkuvar. The book is also important in localizing feminist theory within a non-western context. The chapters on the "political economy of gender" and "the underground female economy" are particularly insightful in this respect. Ram, herself a Tamil-speaking Indian, conducted ethnographic field work among the Mukkuvar and participated in their daily lives. Her sense of identification with and difference from the Mukkuvar is one of the most interesting sub-texts in this work. The book is well written and will be easily accessible to a wide range of readers who have no specialized knowledge of India or of the issues of gender and capitalism with which it deals. It has a useful bibliography, an index, and glossary. There are also interesting and useful photos and illustrations.—*S. A. Tyler, Rice University*

WS-1504   HQ1240   94-22223 CIP

Scott, Catherine V. **Gender and development: rethinking modernization and dependency theory.** L. Rienner, 1995. 151p bibl index afp ISBN 1-55587-410-X, $35.00

Scott (political science, Agnes Scott College) effectively explores the influence of social constructions of gender differences in contemporary definitions of development, dependency, capitalism, and socialism, as reflected in both modernization and dependency theories. This critique of development theory and practice provides reconceptualizations of development from the standpoint of feminist theory, based on a systematic examination of how race, class, and gender structure people's lives. Although the geographical focus of the work is Africa and the development agency examined is the World Bank, this study has important implications for development in all Third World countries and for all development agencies. Essential reading for all development practitioners and professionals. Upper-division undergraduates and above.—*D. M. Warren, Iowa State University*

WS-1505   HQ1240   94-40205 MARC

Snyder, Magaret C. **African women and development: a history: the story of the African Training and Research Centre for Women of the United Nations Economic Commission for Africa,** by Margaret C. Snyder and Mary Tadesse. Witwatersrand/Zed Books, 1995. 239p index ISBN 1-85649-299-0, $55.00; ISBN 1-85649-300-8 pbk, $19.95

Snyder, founding director of the United Nations Development Fund for Women (UNIFEM), and Tadesse, until recently the head of the African Training and Research Centre for Women (ATRCW) at the UN Economic Commission for Africa, have written a compelling account of African women's role in development in both North and sub-Saharan Africa. Their history of the ATRCW provides valuable insights into "women in development" both on the African continent and within the global women's movement. The 12 chapters cover the history of women's movements, African women's initiatives in development, the development of women's policy concepts and legal statutes in Africa, and the growth of the African regional network of women leaders involved in influencing policy towards women. Also included is a survey of contemporary African women leaders who have been instrumental in establishing an African-oriented agenda to institutionalize improvement in the lives of women. This account traces the changing role of gender in development theories and strategies since the 1960s. The 20 appendixes provide the most recent data on women country-by-country, along with the key policy documents that are the legal basis for increased empowerment of African women. A must for development practitioners and persons with an interest in Africa and in gender relations. All levels.—*D. M. Warren, Iowa State University*

WS-1506   HQ1240   95-3457 CIP

Thomas-Slayter, Barbara. **Gender, environment, and development in Kenya: a grassroots perspective,** by Barbara Thomas-Slayter and Dianne Rocheleau et al. L. Rienner, 1995. 247p bibl index afp ISBN 1-55587-419-3, $49.95

Thomas-Slayter and Rocheleau (Clark Univ.) have collaborated with eight Kenyan colleagues to produce a vibrant set of case studies set in rural Kenyan communities. The cases explore the role of indigenous community institutions, particularly women's organizations, as they respond to changing resource conditions. Indigenous ecological knowledge is the foundation for gender-based strategies regarding the management of soil, water, and woodlands in the context of changing gender roles. The interrelationships of poverty, gender roles, indigenous knowledge, and environmental and resource management become the basis for development policy and practice. The case studies focus on water and soil resources, health and nutrition, agriculture and livestock, and agroforestry. Much of the fieldwork for the case studies used participatory rural appraisal methodologies. This is one of the first works available that explicates the importance of understanding gender-based knowledge within a community for sustainable approaches to development. Well written and highly readable, the study includes seven maps, a table, and 17 figures. An invaluable resource for students of culture change, gender relations, resource management, and development, not only in Kenya, but also as a model for use in many other parts of the world. All levels.—*D. M. Warren, Iowa State University*

WS-1507 HD6181 93-30881 CIP
White, Jenny B. **Money makes us relatives: women's labor in urban Turkey.** Texas, 1994. 190p bibl index afp ISBN 0-292-79077-5, $30.00; ISBN 0-292-79086-4 pbk, $12.95

Though the subtitle proclaims that this monograph is about "women's labor in urban Turkey," readers will find it is much more than that. In fact, White places the labor of Turkish women who work in the informal sector in the wider setting of an evolving social class, often described as the "lower middle class" of the petty bourgeoisie. This class, the result of massive rural migration into Turkey's cities and towns, plays a critical role in everyday life. White explains why working women from this class remain outside the structure of organized labor. She argues that the principal reason is social: the women are taught to see their "labor as leisure." White examines in detail the institutions and ideology that make this thinking possible: marriage in which brides are "taken" for their labor; and the relationship between husbands and wives, fathers and sons, fathers and daughters, and mothers and sons. She then places the structure of production in a sociocultural context, providing the reader with a vivid illustration of what may be described as the "modernity of tradition." Based on a variety of written sources as well as fieldwork and interviews, this fascinating and lively study illuminates an important and intriguing aspect of contemporary Turkey. It will interest anyone seeking to understand the development of capitalism in the Third World. Upper-division undergraduates and above.—*F. Ahmad, University of Massachusetts at Boston*

WS-1508 HQ1745 92-17852 MARC
White, Sarah C. **Arguing with the crocodile: gender and class in Bangladesh.** Zed Books/University Press, Dhaka, 1992. (Dist. by Humanities) 186p bibl index ISBN 1-85649-085-8, $49.95; ISBN 1-85649-086-6 pbk, $19.95

White challenges the traditional assumptions of developmental strategies designed by Western planners to chart and fund technological growth in the Third World. In this work based on her 1985-86 fieldwork in Kurimput ("the village of the crocodile"), Bangladesh, she seeks to counterbalance the male-oriented and Western-aid dominated discourse of class and power relations by taking readers into the lives of women from diverse background speaking for themselves. White's poignant portrayal of women's work, flowing with as well as against the daily currents of social interactions, shows how the bureaucratic planners and academicians have erred in artificially isolating "women's issues" from the broader social network of rural life. To correct this dangerous omission, White criticizes the major arguments in debates on women's work, questions how well the current donors represent the recipient's priorities, and how rural Bangladesh women themselves interpret what they do. Although academically rigorous, White's writing is lively and smooth. Highly recommended. General; advanced undergraduate; faculty; professional.—*N. N. Kalia, SUNY College at Buffalo*

WS-1509 HQ1240.5.D44 89-39055 CIP
Wignaraja, Ponna. **Women, poverty and resources.** Sage, 1990. 241p bibl index ISBN 0-8039-9624-1, $26.00

It is clear by now that underdevelopment affects poor women more than men. Wignaraja (currently coordinator, UN University Project on South Asian Perspectives and a former secretary-general of the Society for International Development) examines the interconnections between planned development and gender inequity by exploring the double burdens of being female and being poor. She argues that credit, by itself, does not alleviate poverty, particularly among Third World females. If the development process establishes no infrastructure for skills training, health care, social security, and repayment of loans, anomalies are created in which the availability of loans eventually erodes the dignity of the recipient and leads to an imprudent depletion of the local resources on which poor women have traditionally relied. For planners, Wignaraja recommends an action-research methodology to create strategies wherein the poor work toward change primarily by using indigenous resources and personal knowledge of the problems they face to create and evaluate solutions. Wignaraja believes this process should not be guided but, rather, expedited by the availability of credit. Based on a UNICEF study of finanical credit for both rural and urban poor females, the book also offers a useful summary of the lessons drawn for South Asia and, by implication, their relevance for Africa and Latin America. College and university libraries.—*N. N. Kalia, SUNY College at Buffalo*

WS-1510 HQ1240 92-24168 CIP
Women in developing economies: making visible the invisible, [ed. by Joycelin Massiah]. Berg/Unesco, 1993. 300p ISBN 0-85496-345-6, $69.95; ISBN 0-85496-346-4 pbk, $22.50

Examining women's work in Tunisia, Ghana, Colombia, India, and the Caribbean, the five essays in this collection explore why, after two decades of debate, women's work in developing societies continues to be handicapped by a benign neglect. In the Caribbean, the government continues to be reluctant to accept gender as a development issue. In predominantly agricultural Tunisia, males have appropriated the nobler rewards for themselves while the women slave at culturally devalued but labor-intensive chores of assistance. In Ghana, where most of the families can hardly survive without income generated by wives, sisters, or grandmothers, women engage mainly in petty trading in the nonmodern sectors of an export-oriented economy. In the urban economy of Colombia, women may be less discriminated against as individual laborers, but when industry expands, so do the gender differences in the domestic work. In India, most women work in the unorganized sectors so are systematically excluded from the contractual benefits available to their male colleagues in the unionized industrial sectors. The collection's strength lies in its evaluative synthesis of research data and its specific recommendations on how to fuse traditional modes of production with inevitable modernization by making women's work more visible, thereby increasing productivity and reducing poverty. Advanced undergraduate, graduate; faculty; professional.—*N. N. Kalia, SUNY College at Buffalo*

WS-1511 HD6053 90-31797 CIP
Women, employment and the family in the international division of labour, ed. by Sharon Stichter and Jane L. Parpart. Temple, 1990. 253p index ISBN 0-87722-739-X, $39.95

Within the larger context of international capitalist development, the editors and fellow scholars examine links between female productive and reproductive roles in the family and increasing female labor participation rates in the Third World. Using evidence from several developing countries, contributors argue that household structure is an underestimated determinant of female employment that helps to explain the widely varied nature and timing of female labor participation. These studies augment scholarship from the "household perspective" by integrating concepts from world system and feminist theories to explore how male-dominated employment structues and patriarchical state policies can interact with and mutually reinforce the exploitive demands of household and kin. Because researchers still know comparatively little about female labor profiles in developing countries, this research is a welcome contribution. The authors represent a full range of the social sciences and deliver a well-balanced, interdisciplinary perspective on a topic of enormous importance. The studies are consistently well written, although their depth and sophistication varies considerably. Upper-level undergraduates and above.—*B. Bullock, Randolph-Macon Woman's College*

WS-1512   HQ1240   94-1964 MARC
Women, the environment and sustainable development: towards a theoretical synthesis, by Rosi Braidotti et al. Zed Books/INSTRAW, 1994. 220p bibl index ISBN 1-85649-183-8, $49.95; ISBN 1-85649-184-6 pbk, $19.95

A revised and expanded version of a report compiled for INSTRAW (United Nations International Research and Training for the Advancement of Women) in 1990-92, this work explores the theoretical debates regarding women, the environment, and development (WED). It reviews feminist critiques of science (specifically with regard to dominant development models) and discusses the links between oppression of women and environmental crisis. Drawing on the work of Foucault, Haraway, and Harding, the authors argue that development research, theory, and practice must be sensitive to underlying issues of power among gender, geographic, political, and economic groups. Consistent with this approach, they situate themselves as writing from a relatively privileged academic perspective. The strengths of the study lie in special attention given to the shift in development theory from "women in development" to "gender and development"; alternative models of development such as DAWN (Development with Women for a New Era); deep ecology, social ecology, and ecofeminism. The authors also recognize and critique Western theories that maximize gender difference as well as approaches to sustainable development that idealize poor, southern, or Third World women. Upper-division undergraduates and above.—*S. K. Gallagher, Oregon State University*

WS-1513   HQ1240   92-29477 CIP
Young, Kate. **Planning development with women: making a world of difference.** St. Martin's, 1993. 187p bibl index ISBN 0-312-09090-0, $39.95

A convincing argument for the holistic GAD (gender and development) approach to development, the goal of which is development planning *with* rather than *for* women. Young charts theoretical swings in development thinking in the last 30 years, from early ethnocentric models of gender relations (which viewed women primarily as mothers), to a focus on women's role in basic needs provision, to the growth of feminist research and action with explicit attention to gender-based power structures. Three case-study chapters, examining women's agricultural role in Africa, factory employment in Asia, and work in the urban informal sector in Latin America, show that alleviating the symptoms of women's relative disadvantage (with training, access to credit, etc.) is only a first step toward women's "collective empowerment." Planners must also take into account the social structures and processes that underlie women's disadvantage (e.g., the ideology of male superiority, men's control of resources). This book cannot fail to sensitize development workers and students alike to the critical importance of taking women's roles into account in development thinking, planning, and implementation. All levels.—*M. A. Gwynne, SUNY at Stony Brook*

◆ Education

WS-1514   Can. CIP
Caplan, Paula J. **Lifting a ton of feathers: a woman's guide for surviving in the academic world.** Toronto, 1993. 273p bibl index afp ISBN 0-8020-2903-5, $45.00; ISBN 0-8020-7411-1 pbk, $18.95

This handbook provides valuable information, ideas, and perspectives for women not only on how to survive, but also to thrive, in higher education. Eight chapters cover such topics as the maleness of the academic world; the unwritten rules embedded in the culture of academia; myths about women and higher education; suggestions for graduate school; looking for jobs; writing the curriculum vitae; preparing for the interview; applying for contract renewal, promotion, and tenure; and becoming a full professor, chair, dean, or president. One invaluable chapter details a "Checklist for Women-positive Institutions." Questions for the reader to pose include questions for graduate students, questions to ask during recruitment and hiring, about working conditions, promotion and tenure, and questions to pose about the faculty association or union. The appendixes contain interesting statistical data on gender bias and guidelines for hiring, promotion, and tenure committees. Women well established in their academic careers will wish this book had been written at the commencement of their careers. This volume

will benefit not only graduate and undergraduate students but is a necessity for professors and administrators interested in promoting an inviting environment for women in academia.—*P. A. Cordeiro, University of Connecticut*

WS-1515   LC213   90-47055 MARC
D'Souza, Dinesh. **Illiberal education: the politics of race and sex on campus.** Free Press, 1991. 319p index ISBN 0-02-908100-9, $19.95

D'Souza contends that an "academic and cultural revolution" is under way at American universities. The revolution is being fought for minority victims of race and gender discrimination; its mission is to change bigoted attitudes toward minorities, rectify past and present inequities, and advance interests of minority victims. D'Souza concludes that US students receive an illiberal education, resulting in "closed-mindedness and intolerance." The evidence to support D'Souza's assertions comes from six case studies: the Berkeley admissions policy that favors "certified" minorities; the new multiculturalism at Stanford; protest at Howard over blacks' cultural status; censorship of remarks perceived as insensitive to minorities at Michigan; Duke's preferential hiring program for black faculty and radical scholarship in the humanities; and controversies over teaching race and gender at Harvard. In each case, D'Souza argues that a "tyranny of the minority" has cowed faculty and administrations into submission, and they now fail to support freedom of expression for all. A research fellow at the American Enterprise Institute, D'Souza's conservative attack on multiculturalism and "political correctness" is more systematic and better reasoned than Charles J. Sykes's *The Hollow Men: Politics and Corruption in American Higher Education* (1990). However, the argument is exaggerated to make the point. How many US college students attend Berkeley, Harvard, and Michigan? Instances of illiberalism can be found on many campuses, but D'Souza is wrong to suggest that the education most undergraduates receive is illiberal. His attack also deemphasizes the difficulty of making the college curriculum and professoriate responsive to changing domestic and global needs. Readers at all levels.—*G. A. McBeath, University of Alaska Fairbanks*

WS-1516   Orig
Darling, John. **Gender matters in schools: pupils and teachers,** by John Darling and Anthony Glendinning. Cassell, 1996. 132p bibl indexes ISBN 0-304-32803-0, $55.00; ISBN 0-304-32805-7 pbk, $17.95

This short book (121 pages of text) is part of a series dealing with contemporary issues in education, particularly in Scotland and the British Isles. The authors treat changes in the schools and curriculum since the Crowther Report in 1959, the Newsom Committee report in 1963, and the Sex Discrimination Act in 1975. They deal with the historical context of women's role in society and whether or not schools continue to be sexist. Small empirical studies are also included. The book treats some of the same issues as Myra Sadker and David Sadker's *Failing at Fairness* (CH, Sep'94) and Nancy Frazier and Myra Sadker's *Sexism in School and Society* (CH, Nov'73), but in a less personalized manner. *Gender Matters in Schools* is more academic and objective in its reporting style. The authors conclude that traditional patterns are still in place and that teaching young children is still seen as the domain of females. Both a "glass ceiling" and a "glass floor" remain. Academic readers, all levels.—*B. O. Pressley, California State University, Hayward*

WS-1517   British CIP
Evans, W. Gareth. **Education and female emancipation: the Welsh experience, 1847-1914.** University of Wales Press, 1990. (Dist. by Books International, Inc.) 332p bibl index ISBN 0-7083-1079-6, $45.00

An exceedingly well researched and carefully documented study of the expansion of education for women in Wales, 1847-1914. Evans places her subject in broader contexts of female emancipation in general and the overall growth of popular education in the period. She describes the impediments to improving the condition of women in Wales and how these barriers were eventually overcome by a combination of "strong-willed individuals, influential groups and societies as well as religious, social and economic determinants." Evans both connects and differentiates developments in Wales from more general trends in England. She also analyzes her subject on the basis of social class, differentiating the improvements in secondary and higher education that largely benefitted middle-class women from the expansion of popular education. Evans critically examines the general literature that deals with this subject. Appendixes and an excellent bibliography including Welsh sources. Recommended for collections that specialize in history of education or women's history. Upper-division undergraduates and above.—*S. Fishman, University of Wisconsin—Madison*

WS-1518   QA37   CIP
Gender and mathematics: an international perspective, ed. by Leone Burton. Cassell, 1991 (c1990). (Dist. by Publishers Distribution Center, P.O. Box C831, Rutherford, NJ 07070) 162p indexes ISBN 0-304-32279-2 pbk, $29.95

A gathering of researchers at the Sixth Annual Congress on Mathematics Education (1988) organized this volume on gender and the learning of mathematics. It was refreshing to hear from scholars outside the US although most of the contributions were from the English-speaking world. In spite of curricular differences unique to each country, these women encountered similar problems of gender differentiation in terms of achievement and attitudes in the mathematics classroom. One caveat about conference proceedings: an uncomfortable proportion of the studies do not have the rigor one would expect from a peer-reviewed volume. The weaknesses include very small sample sizes, no controls, and old data (e.g., 1983!), leaving the reader with a feeling that some of these studies could not have been published elsewhere. If read for flavor, however, rather than for empirically based conclusions, there is much to be tasted in this collection.—*R. F. Subotnik, Hunter College, CUNY*

WS-1519   LB2341   91-70325 Orig
Gillett-Karam, Rosemary. **Underrepresentation and the question of diversity: women and minorities in the community college,** by Rosemary Gillett-Karam, Suanne D. Roueche, and John E. Roueche. Community College Press, 1991. (Dist. by American Association of Community and Junior Colleges) 264p bibl ISBN 0-87117-225-9, $35.00

The authors of this book have all worked together in the Community College Leadership Program at the University of Texas, Austin. That program provided the impetus for this attempt to establish guidelines for improving the representation of women and minorities in leadership positions in community colleges across the country. The book is composed of somewhat disparate parts. The first two chapters define equality and diversity; Chapters 3 and 4 review the research literature about women and minorities in the academy. Chapters 6 and 7 highlight exemplary programs and quote leaders of such programs extensively. The final chapter concludes with recommendations for increasing representation and recognition for women and minorities in community colleges. This reviewer was bothered by the authors' somewhat grandiose expectations about what these institutions can accomplish to promote understanding of diversity in an educational system that, they readily acknowledge, tends to undervalue the community college. The book is strongest in its succinct review of the current literature about women and minorities in the academy generally and is useful for programs aimed at training administrators in higher education.—*A. J. Russ, Wells College*

WS-1520   LC225   95-8928 CIP
Henry, Mary E. **Parent-school collaboration: feminist organizational structures and school leadership.** State University of New York, 1996. 229p bibl index afp ISBN 0-7914-2855-9, $49.50

As educational administrators broaden their responsibilities to encompass participatory governance structures, they are often at a loss for models to create democratic learning communities. Henry's study, conducted in the Robertson School District in the northwest US, illuminates the boundaries and patterns of parental exclusion and inclusion. Using an ethnography informed by feminism, the author provides field-based answers to questions related to building, nurturing, and supporting collaborative school relationships. Henry contrasts traditional bureaucratic and patriarchal hierarchies with feminist organizational structures. Her feminist view centers on three key notions: (1) an ethic of care and connectedness; (2) collaboration and community-building; and (3) a focus on the core technology of teaching and learning. Advocating a context-specific approach to school leadership, Henry's findings are not prescriptive but rather make visible social and cultural practices that stress and enhance parent and school relationships. Henry's substantive work encourages those in educational administration to open schools

to parents. Essential for all those interested in school reform—general readers, upper-division undergraduates through faculty, professional educators.—*Karen I. Case, University of Hartford*

WS-1521   HQ1397   91-14334 CIP
The Knowledge explosion: generations of feminist scholarship, ed. by Cheris Kramarae and Dale Spender. Teachers College Press (Columbia University), 1992. 533p index afp ISBN 0-8077-6258-X, $65.00; ISBN 0-8077-6257-1 pbk, $25.95

These 44 contributions are an essential summary of women's studies. The first section recounts impacts of women's studies in various disciplines, including sociology, psychology, philosophy, engineering, musicology, sport science, and others. The second section reviews debates on topics that cut across disciplines, such as ecofeminism, sexual violence, families, pornography, reproductive technology, and sisterhood and racial/ethnic consciousnesses. Well edited, the volume demonstrates that the journeys of feminist research through the past 20 years, although traversing rough terrain, have been fruitful and show promise of abundance in the next 20 years. The collection is perhaps generation-specific, perhaps sacrifices depth for breadth, only touches on ambivalence about the academy, and examines only very briefly questions in the philosophy and sociology of knowledge raised by the explosion of feminist knowledge. Bibliographies with each contribution and comprehensive index. An exceptional resource.—*J. L. Croissant, Rensselaer Polytechnic Institute*

WS-1522   LB1756   94-44693 CIP
Levine, Susan. **Degrees of equality: the American Association of University Women and the challenge of twentieth-century feminism.** Temple University, 1995. 227p index afp ISBN 1-56639-326-4, $29.95

Aided by AAUW records, interviews with past board members, and related literature, Levine portrays the complexities and contradictions in this organization's growth during its second half-century. Amid differences with other women's organizations and among its own members over major social issues, the one unbroken thread is the organization's support for equal education for women. Initially, to assure that women's degrees were equal in quality to men's, AAUW served an accrediting function by maintaining a list of colleges whose women graduates could become members. To encourage women's participation in higher education, AAUW developed a fellowship program, which, for many members, has been the heart of its program. To assist faculty women in their fight for equity, it created the Legal Advocacy Fund. Finally, returning to the need to foster equality in education, it worked to achieve passage of Title IX and the Women's Educational Equity Act (WEEA). In developing her argument that AAUW always pursues issues central to feminism, Levine encourages readers to think about the meanings of terms like "women's organizations," "women's issues," "women's movement," and "feminism." This book can be read on many levels. Academic readers, all levels.—*R. W. Rohfeld, formerly, Syracuse University*

WS-1523   LC1752   91-14495 CIP
McClelland, Averil Evans. **The education of women: a guide to theory, teaching and research.** Garland, 1992. 227p (Source books on education, 23) indexes ISBN 0-8240-4842-3, $35.00

This volume was designed primarily as a handbook for researchers interested in exploring important historical trends and issues associated with the education of women and girls in America. Each of the three main sections is organized thematically and presented historically. Further, each chapter is introduced by a cogent essay that highlights some of the citations listed in the chapter reference list. The logic of whether a reference from a chapter's list appears in the essay is not clear, and sometimes the reader longs to have a bit more description for an intriguing title. Significant arguments or concepts are italicized for the benefit of readers who want to skim through selected sections. Although there exists in the literature far less scholarship on the education of nonmainstream women, McClelland appears to have made every attempt to include citations that describe the educational experiences of diverse groups of women. The development of opposing modern feminist philosophies and their implications for education are also judiciously presented. Recommended. Upper-division undergraduates; graduate students; practitioners; faculty.—*R. F. Subotnik, Hunter College, CUNY*

WS-1524 LD7212 94-31662 CIP
Palmieri, Patricia Ann. **In Adamless Eden: the community of women faculty at Wellesley.** Yale, 1995. 382p index afp ISBN 0-300-05529-3, $35.00

Palmieri's book is wonderful to read. Through prosopography she has recaptured a world virtually lost where a carefully selected group of white Protestant women, better educated than most of their peers, were able to educate generations of female undergraduates during 1875-1930. In an academic community that virtually denied entrance to women, these professors created an institution, influenced its governance system (Wellesley is the only women's college to have female presidents from the beginning), created a curriculum that contained not only the best of the liberal arts but incorporated the need for social responsibility and elements of what today is called multidisciplinary studies, and produced outstanding students whose accomplishments are well catalogued in documents such as (ironically) *Men of Science*. As women's colleges struggle to succeed in an academic arena dominated by the research university, it is well to note the unique quality of institutions such as Wellesley, and their importance for the history of education and the history of women. As a professor at a women's college, this reviewer applauds the foremothers whose careers are so powerfully recounted by Palmieri. All levels.—*A. J. Russ, Wells College*

WS-1525 LC3731 91-28833 CIP
Perspectives on minority women in higher education, ed. by Lynne Brodie Welch. Praeger, 1992. 163p bibl index afp ISBN 0-275-93742-9, $39.95

A compilation of articles resulting from the International Conference for Women in Higher Education at the University of Texas at El Paso. The primary focus is on African American and Hispanic women. The dearth of ethnic minority women is seen as a result of discrimination by white male dominated colleges and universities. The authors explore the problems created in terms of prejudice related to racial and gender issues. The difficulties in recruiting and retaining minority women are investigated and networking, mentoring, and other strategies that will create a more nurturing environment are emphasized. Encouragement is given to aid the campus community in better understanding diversity and education with regard to cultural awareness. Upper-division undergraduate and graduate students.—*B. O. Pressley, California State University, Hayward*

WS-1526 L82832 94-30861 CIP
Ruane, Christine. **Gender, class, and the professionalization of Russian city teachers, 1860-1914.** Pittsburgh, 1994. 258p (Pitt series in Russian and East European studies, 24) bibl index afp ISBN 0-8229-3864-2, $59.95

In this well-written, well-documented history of city teachers in Russia from 1860-1914, the author shows how demand for an educated citizenry in a modern state led to the emergence of a new class of teachers—a diverse group of men and women drawn from the intelligentsia, the old nobility, and peasants. There were conflicts within the ranks of this new professional class between men and women; between elementary school teachers drawn from the peasantry and upper class city-trained teachers; and between elementary teachers trained in a child-centered pedagogy and secondary teachers trained as subject specialists. And there were ongoing political conflicts between teacher groups demanding autonomy and an autocratic Czarist regime demanding submission. Of particular interest is the campaign to repeal a ban on married women as teachers, an example of successful political action and a heretofore unknown byway in gender studies. Especially valuable is a comparative lens interspersed throughout that illuminates the concept of professionalism in pre-Soviet Russia and in the US today. This book is highly recommended for historians, educators, gender study specialists, faculty, researchers, and general readers.—*E. S. Swing, Saint Joseph's University*

WS-1527 LC212 93-11586 CIP
Sadker, Myra. **Failing at fairness: how America's schools cheat girls,** by Myra and David Sadker. Scribner, 1994. 347p index ISBN 0-684-19541-0, $22.00

Myra and David Sadker are married, attended graduate school together, teach at American University, and have experienced sexism as graduate stu-

dents, as parents, and as professionals. Their personal experiences, and those of their daughters, led them to do research indicating that females' educational experience is inferior to that of males. According to the authors, the differential treatment of boys and girls is subtle and is overlooked or ignored by professionals who are unaware of the favoritism shown to boys. The authors run workshops on sexism in education and on sexual harassment, and many of the anecdotes they offer come from participants' stories told at these workshops. Examples of how girls' self-esteem is negatively affected by being ignored, having their ideas dismissed, and by being degraded are offered to support the authors' themes. Recommendations are made for parents to use their influence to ensure equity in children's education. The book will be best received by those who already believe that females are oppressed and by the general public who do not read much actual research in the social sciences. All levels.—*B. O. Pressley, California State University, Hayward*

WS-1528 LC212 93-20334 CIP
Streitmatter, Janice. **Toward gender equity in the classroom: everyday teachers' beliefs and practices.** State University of New York, 1994. 207p bibl index ISBN 0-7914-1803-0, $49.50

The lag between research and translation into school practice takes decades, an event that catches naive reformers by surprise since they may presume significant information will readily be accepted and incorporated into the classroom culture. Not so. Despite extensive data about inequity, academic environments continue to be inhospitable for girls. Streitmatter, reviewing relevant studies, breaks little new ground but does set up a philosophical framework for her descriptions and interpretations of educational practices. The author takes a small step in informing readers about what a sampling of teachers are doing to address equity issues. These modest, readable descriptions of eight randomly chosen educators (selected presumably on the basis of convenience rather than for exemplary performance) reveal an array of classroom activities—curricular, process-based, organizational—which highlight various aspects of responsive practice. This brief book would be most useful as a prompt to initiate discussions of equity/equality issues: it could accompany a comprehensive graduate educational text encompassing a broad range of recommended models that analyze, compare, and evaluate practices and structural patterns at all levels. Upper-division undergraduate; graduate; practitioner.—*B. H. Baskin, SUNY at Stony Brook*

WS-1529 Q181 94-44738 CIP
Teaching the majority: breaking the gender barrier in science, mathematics, and engineering, ed. by Sue V. Rosser. Teachers College Press (Columbia University), 1995. 264p bibl index afp ISBN 0-8077-6277-6, $50.00; ISBN 0-8077-6276-8 pbk, $22.95

Women are underrepresented in science. This collection summarizes this situation and suggests practical remedies for higher education. Despite recent gains in college enrollment, the percentage of women in science decreases along the professional pipeline; women constitute 45 percent of the workforce, 16 percent of employed scientists and engineers, but only four percent of living members of the National Academy of Sciences. The contributors provide examples of pedagogy to support women's participation and proposals to revise the dominant research paradigms for physics and engineering, chemistry, mathematics, computer science, and environmental science and geosciences. In her introduction, Rosser outlines a six-phase model to increase women's participation in science starting with a recognition of the issue, including identifying barriers and addressing them, and ending with redefining and restructuring science. A general theme is that subtle forms of discrimination and definition rather than a single factor lead to exclusion of women from science. The authors support more collaborative work, less male-dominated (and military-inspired) terminology, and recognition of the individual learning styles of all students. An excellent bibliography on women in science; chapter bibliographies. Upper-division through faculty.—*G. E. Hein, Lesley College*

WS-1530 HQ1181 90-37670 CIP
Transforming the curriculum: ethnic studies and women's studies, ed. by Johnnella E. Butler and John C. Walter. State University of New York, 1991. 341p index afp ISBN 0-7914-0586-9, $59.50; ISBN 0-7914-0587-7 pbk, $19.95

A collection of essays that address primarily the curricula of colleges and universities. Unlike much of what has appeared on these topics, this collection gets beyond pleas for fairness and the expressed anger of those who are oppressed or ignored. It deals with the complex experiences of the members of minority groups in the US, illustrating that all people of color do not think alike, nor are their experiences identical, or necessarily even similar. The experiences of first-generation Japanese women, or the "picture brides" of the early Chinese immigrants, are nothing like the experiences of African American women, or American Armenian women. Are Jewish studies to be considered ethnic? What of the attitudes of American Indians? The curriculum questions—what shall be substituted for what—are not addressed in detail, but the authors proposed that the curriculum be transformed radicaly—not only by greatly extending the Eurocentric content, but also by reexamining the very basis for identity. Instead of "cogito ergo sum," consider "I am we." New skills will be required of college teachers to present such material because it will provoke severe tensions among students. The whole field of ethnic and women's studies, as viewed by the authors of this collection, is just getting under way. It has not yet acquired a recognizable form that invites conherent research, however, these essays suggest the emergence of orderly scholarship. Upper-division undergraduate and graduate students.— A. W. Foshay, emeritus, Teachers College, Columbia University

WS-1531   LB2831   94-7301 CIP
Women leading in education, ed. by Diane M. Dunlap and Patricia A. Schmuck. State University of New York, 1995. 444p bibl index afp ISBN 0-7914-2215-1, $74.50

Dunlap and Schmuck's compilation of independent projects explores leadership styles and leadership patterns of women in education—primarily women teaching in K-12. Although the majority of public school teachers are female, women are underrepresented in administrative positions. There is little reliable data identifying the number of women administrators at the various levels. The authors examine conditions that are conducive to the entry of women into administrative positions and the elements that hinder women from making positive movement in school administration. Leadership, socialization of the genders, policy, management, and politics are investigated. The book was conceived in 1989 at the annual convention of the American Educational Research Association Special Interest Group on Research on Women in Education. It was written by women educators who believe that there will be continuing reform by and through women in education. Traditional theories of leadership and their influence in educational settings are noted, and numerous case studies demonstrating the effectiveness of mentoring, changing roles, cooperation, and collaboration are explored. Upper-division undergraduate through faculty; professional.—B. O. Pressley, California State University, Hayward

WS-1532   LB2837   Can. CIP
Women who taught: perspectives on the history of women and teaching, ed. by Alison Prentice and Marjorie R. Theobold. Toronto, 1991. 301p bibl afp ISBN 0-8020-2745-8, $45.00

This collection of ten essays on the history of female teachers in four English-speaking countries makes easily available some important articles that originally appeared in a variety of journals. Although the authors cover a broad geographic region (Australia, Britain, Canada, and the US), they concentrate on a relatively short time period, the mid-19th to mid-20th centuries. Common themes of feminization of teaching, development of women's secondary schools and colleges, and teacher organizations and unionism rising from universal discontent with low salaries and poor working conditions give the volume its cohesiveness. The essays are well written, some narrative, others analytical, all important enough to merit reproduction. A selective bibliography has been provided by Susan Gelman. Undergraduate libraries.—J. Raftery, California State University, Chico

WS-1533   HQ1180   92-30627 CIP
Women's studies in the 1990s: doing things differently?, ed. by Joanna de Groot and Mary Maynard. St. Martin's, 1993. 182p index ISBN 0-312-09122-2, $39.95

Coedited by a historian and a sociologist (both Univ. of York), who also contributed the first and last chapters, this collection contains six additional chapters written by a British economist, a Turkish journalist, two British women's studies scholars, a German political science professor, and a German historian. The impetus for the collection is entry into the third decade of "modern feminist scholarship and the practice of 'women's studies.'" Arrival in the third decade requires self-reflection, and the editors pose a set of useful challenges for this critique. Although each contribution is useful, several do not address the central questions: some describe a particular research project; another considers what "women-centered politics" might mean. Two very useful essays are those by Trev Broughton, who discusses her own transition from the Department of English to the Centre for Women's Studies, "lock, stock and typewriter" and that of Uta Schmidt, who analyzes the meaning, method, and theory of feminist history. Fatmagul Berktay raises the important question of how feminist scholarship will face the issue of pluralism. The conclusion poses a broad set of challenges that women's studies (i.e., feminist scholarship) will face in the 1990s. Each chapter concludes with extensive bibliography and notes. Graduate; faculty; professional.—S. Reinharz, Brandeis University

WS-1534   HQ1180   90-48653 CIP
Women's studies international: Nairobi and beyond, ed. by Aruna Rao. Feminist, CUNY, 1991. 349p afp ISBN 0-55861-031-6, $35.00; ISBN 0-55861-032-4 pbk, $15.95

Students will find this collection invaluable in understanding and appreciating women's roles as creative activists, teachers, and researchers cross-nationally. Of particular interest is the article describing how one functionally illiterate woman in India initiated the use of the video camera as a tool in training and organizing for development. Most of the authors go beyond merely describing the universally low status of women in their countries. They forthrightly describe issues (nearly universally involving access to education and training) research agendas, actions, and policy changes that must occur in each country to improve the harsh realities of women's lives. Researchers and methodologists can use this information to illustrate the links between research and action, and to show the contributions and gains where research is linked with policy. The second half of the volume includes a detailed listing of centers, institutes, groups, and organizations focused on research and teaching. A lengthy description of women's programs indicates the global relevance of women's issues. College and university libraries.—A. S. Oakes, Idaho State University

WS-1535   LB2332   92-34935 CIP
Working-class women in the academy: laborers in the knowledge factory, ed. by Michelle M. Tokarczyk and Elizabeth A. Fay. Massachusetts, 1993. 335p bibl index ISBN 0-87023-834-5, $45.00; ISBN 0-87023-835-3 pbk, $18.95

A collection of 20 eloquent and insightful testimonials by working-class female faculty about their experiences in academia. The essays focus on the problems and challenges that these women confront as they assimilate into the life of the predominantly middle-class academy. It shows how the overtly meritocratic academy, subtly and not so subtly, works to disengage faculty from working-class backgrounds. The stories of these working-class women are varied, but in the inevitable transformation to middle-class academics, most articulate a desire not to cast away their backgrounds. They do not want to become alienated from the friends and family of their youth, but to retain some part of the richness of working-class life. The essays, for the most part, maintain an effective conversational tone and blend nicely, each making a contribution to the reader's understanding of the dilemma of being working-class female by offering a slightly different perspective or focus. One or two entries attempt a more obtuse scholarly approach that is jarring in the context of the rest of the book. Recommended as general reading for academics. Undergraduate level on up.—N. E. Sacks, SUNY at Stony Brook

◆ History, Geography & Area Studies

WS-1536   JX1965   90-41683 CIP
Adams, Judith Porter. **Peacework: oral histories of women peace activists.** Twayne, 1991. 228p (Twayne's oral history series, 5) bibl index afp ISBN 0-8057-9106-X, $24.95

Because the history of women's lives and activities is so often missing from traditional archival sources, the use of oral history has become an important way to learn about those who were previously "hidden from history." This book is oral history at its best. Adams interviewed a generation of older women who have been peace activists throughout their lives and were members of two organizations: Women's International League for Peace and Freedom, and Women's Strike for Peace. Their backgrounds are different—some are Japanese-Americans interned during WW II or former resistance fighters in Europe. Some are socially conscious Quakers or African American civil rights activists; others had fathers who were members of the Ku Klux Klan. Some were identified as leaders, others remained in the shadows. Whatever their background, all shared a desire for peace and justice. And all were amazingly courageous, whether sitting down in front of a napalm factory, ferrying Vietnam resisters to Canada, or simply giving out leaflets day after day. Recommended to all readers who want to know "ordinary" women who shook the world.—*J. Wishnia, SUNY at Stony Brook*

WS-1537   JX1962   92-13755 CIP
Bacon, Margaret Hope. **One woman's passion for peace and freedom: the life of Mildred Scott Olmsted.** Syracuse, 1993. 394p index afp ISBN 0-8156-0270-7, $34.95

Bacon's biography of one of the first leaders of the Women's International League for Peace and Freedom (WILPF) benefits from the author's personal knowledge of the field, extensive research, and many interviews. Mildred Scott Olmsted was a moving spirit of WILPF for more than 60 years, through WW II, the Cold War, McCarthyism, and Vietnam. The history of the organization and of US and world pacifism are interwoven with the story of a woman whose personal relationships were troubled by her emotional isolation, her need for control, and even, Bacon suggests, by a deeply divided personality. Olmsted thought of herself as a pacifist, not a feminist. As Bacon explains, feminist analysis could have helped her to understand and perhaps resolve her conflicts with herself and others, but such a perspective was not available to her, nor would she have accepted it if it had been. Such insights enliven this solid biography; unfortunately, the pedestrian details of organizational and personal history at other points overwhelm the interesting narrative. A valuable contribution to women's history, peace studies, and the history of dissent. Many photographs; source notes. Advanced undergraduate; graduate; faculty.—*M. L. Meldrum, SUNY at Stony Brook*

WS-1538   UB418   94-29004 CIP
Gays and lesbians in the military: issues, concerns, and contrasts, ed. by Wilbur J. Scott and Sandra Carson Stanley. Aldine de Gruyter, 1994. 278p index afp ISBN 0-202-30540-6, $43.95; ISBN 0-202-30541-4 pbk, $21.95

This collection offers a broad range of perspectives on service in the US military by lesbian and gay people. The editors, both sociologists, attempt to provide a "balanced and scholarly presentation" that sets out the historical and cultural context and explores the dimensions of the current debates. All but one of the 17 papers are original for the book. Essays vary in scholarly quality, and topics range from an overview of recent lesbian and gay history (Cruikshank) to an excellent analysis of recent controversies, "Anatomy of a Panic" (Adam). This analysis provides an important balance to the article by Ray, which describes the debate on lifting the ban against lesbians and gay men as "one of the greatest crises" in American history. Scott and Stanley also include a very interesting section entitled "Evidence from the Militaries of Other Nations," i.e., Canada, Israel, Britain, and the Netherlands. The editors' introduction and conclusion are clear and helpful. The volume is a must for collections in military science and organization, military history, and gender studies, and is a good option for collections in social sciences, including public policy. General readers, upper-division undergraduates, and above.—*J. A. Brown, Connecticut State University*

WS-1539   HQ798   93-29651 CIP
The Girl's own: cultural histories of the Anglo-American girl, 1830-1915, ed. by Claudia Nelson and Lynne Vallone. Georgia, 1994. 296p bibl index afp ISBN 0-8203-1615-6, $45.00

Nineteenth-century Anglo-Americans assumed girls were the future wives and mothers of the race, the future shapers of culture and civilization. This collection describes some ways Anglo-American culture tackled problems of defining the "ideal girl" and dealing with a reality that was different and changing. Most successful are the essays on social reform, public life, artistic portrayals, the athletic student culture, and working. These illustrate tensions between ideals and realities, male images and female lives, and problems of definition. Mirroring the culture under study, the girls are those of the middle class with one exception. Mitchell's essay on working gives some consideration to class differentials. The editors and essayists assume that cultural differences between US and English society are small enough that descriptions and interpretations drawing on one also apply to the other, ignoring the much stronger egalitarian tradition in the US. Upper-division undergraduates and above.—*V. P. Caruso, Henry Ford Community College*

WS-1540   HD6079   94-19126 CIP
Jacoby, Robin Miller. **The British and American women's trade union leagues, 1890-1925.** Carlson Publishing, 1994. 238p (Scholarship in women's history, 7) bibl index afp ISBN 0-926019-68-6, $55.00

The series "Scholarship in Women's History" has produced the best of 921 previously unpublished dissertations in the field of women's history. Jacoby's study draws upon a wealth of primary sources to describe the different paths taken by these two labor organizations. Both began as cross-class reform leagues, but whereas the British came to highlight class, Americans emphasized gender. These preferences emerge clearly in crisply written comparative chapters that offer a wealth of empirical detail about the two Leagues' efforts to unionize, educate, and legislate. In highlighting the tensions between class and gender some 20 years ago, Jacoby anticipated one of the most fruitful directions women's history was to take. Since then both the topic and the approach have been subject to even closer scrutiny. See, for example, Vivien Hart, *Bound by Our Constitution* (CH, Mar'95), Elizabeth Anne Payne, *Reform, Labor and Feminism: Margaret Dreier Robins and the Women's Trade Union League* (CH, Nov'88), and Jenny Morris, *Women Workers and the Sweated Trades: The Origins of Minimum Wage Legislation* (1986). Footnotes. Recommended for upper-division undergraduate through faculty audiences.—*D. Lindstrom, University of Wisconsin-Madison*

WS-1541   BM729   91-10491 CIP
Jewish women in historical perspective, ed. by Judith R. Baskin. Wayne State, 1991. 300p index afp ISBN 0-8143-2091-0, $39.95; ISBN 0-8143-2092-9 pbk, $19.95

The 12 scholarly essays in this important collection deal with the role of women in Jewish history, from portrayals of women in the Hebrew Bible to the expressions of Jewish women's religious lives in the 20th-century US. The editor makes the point that insights gained by using gender as a category of analysis are invaluable in studying Jewish societies and cultures. Rabbinic Judaism assigned women to the realm of nature, as opposed to culture, and their activities were ideally confined to the private sphere of home, husband, and children. The reality of womens's lives, however, were quite often different from the rabbinic design. This discrepancy between the ideal and the reality is the major theme that connects the essays in this volume. In recent years, a number of books and articles have offered contemporary responses to traditional Jewish views of women's roles, obligations, and disabilities from the feminist perspective. Missing from this literature is the historical perspective. Few contemporary works have attempted to illuminate contemporary dilemmas and concerns by scholarly investigation of the lives and experiences of Jewish women in the past. This collection is intended to fill the vacuum. Should be read along with Judith Plaskow's *Standing Again at Sinai: Judaism from a Feminist Perspective.* Recommended for undergraduate and graduate students.—*J. Fischel, Millersville University*

WS-1542   HQ1172   89-72158 MARC
Kuzmack, Linda Gordon. **Woman's cause: the Jewish woman's movement in England and the United States, 1881-1933.** Ohio State, 1990. 280p bibl index afp ISBN 0-8142-0515-1, $39.50; ISBN 0-8142-0529-1, $16.95

Kuzmack's extensively researched study attempts to compare Jewish feminism in the US and England in the period 1881 to 1933. It documents a more widespread participation in national secular feminist movements by Jewish women than had generally been supposed. It also describes the development of a specifically Jewish woman's movement, involved in "welfare feminism" and in demands for a more equal role in the life of the Jewish community. Kuzmack states that her focus is on women who "directly affected the Jewish community." It is, therefore, surprising to see her exclude the women's Zionist movement and Eastern European immigrant radicalism. Certainly both had major impacts on the Jewish community. Nevertheless, this is an interesting and provocative work. The examination of the less well known British movement, with its aristocratic leadership and lack of working-class participation, is particularly valuable. Less sophisticated readers might not understand some of the references to feminist historical studies, but, as a whole, this would be an excellent addition to libraries with Jewish and women's studies collections.—*L. Mayo, County College of Morris*

WS-1543   PN682   91-27466 CIP
McLeod, Glenda. **Virtue and venom: catalogs of women from antiquity to the Renaissance.** Michigan, 1991. 168p bibl index ISBN 0-472-10206-0, $32.50

Catalogs of women appear in a variety of literatures. McLeod's work provides a badly needed and uniquely broad introduction to the study of such catalogs by looking at the tradition from Homer and Hesiod to Chaucer and Boccaccio to Christine de Pizan. The analysis raises as many questions as it answers about the accuracy with which the lists reflect cultural assumptions about women. The discussion of individual catalogs is inconsistent; background information varies considerably; and more substantial quotes, rather than the citation of individual words, would support the author's argument better. Inexplicable oddities frustrate and distract the serious reader. In the first chapter alone, for example, readers find Anthony and Cleopatra (not Antony); Hesiod's poem appears as the *Theogeny* (not *Theogony*) and Hesiod's home as Boethia (not Boeotia). These may not be serious errors, but they annoy the reader and raise doubts about the accuracy of the author's analysis elsewhere. The bibliography and notes, however, will prove invaluable to the general reader as well as the specialist.—*J. de Luce, Miami University (OH)*

WS-1544   HT1049   95-36096 CIP
More than chattel: black women and slavery in the Americas, ed. by Barry Gaspar and Darlene Clark Hine. Indiana, 1996. 341p bibl index afp ISBN 0-253-33017-3, $39.95; ISBN 0-253-21043-7 pbk, $18.95

This exciting collection demonstrates that "gendered relations and expectations" meant that "slave women experienced slavery quite differently from slave men." The collection begins with a fine historiographical piece by Claire Robertson on connections between African cultures and black women's experience in slavery in the Americas, focusing on family structure and gender divisions in labor. Eight essays on "Life and Labor" follow, most of them concerning slave women in the US or Brazil; these include notable work by Wilma King on women and their children, Robert Olwell on women and marketing, Mary Karasch on slave women on the Brazilian frontier, and Brenda Stevenson on gender identity among slave women in Virginia. Six essays on resistance and freedom deal chiefly with Caribbean milieus and feature contributions by Susan Socolow on free women of color in St. Domingue and by Barbara Bush on the debate surrounding slave fertility. The volume provides an excellent overview of the growing integration of the history of slavery and women's history, and is admirably suited for course work in those fields. Upper-division undergraduates and above.—*T. S. Whitman, Mount St. Mary's College and Seminary*

WS-1545   E184   95-18907 CIP
Nesaule, Agate. **A woman in amber: healing the trauma of war and exile.** Soho Press, 1995. 280p afp ISBN 1-56947-046-4, $24.00

Readers will find it difficult to put down this gem of a memoir about the suffering of a child and her family in WW II and their efforts as immigrants to rebuild their lives and psyches in America. Nesaule experienced the war as a young Latvian refugee. She went from a comfortable upper- middle-class life to the deprivations and horrors of wartime Germany. There she witnessed unspeakable torture, rape, and executions, even the creation of games among the corpses. Her mother was the glue that held the family together amid the terror, until one unforgettable, and almost unforgivable, moment of weakness. The author describes her experiences in displaced persons camps after the war. She also recounts the efforts of the Latvian community in Indianapolis to maintain its culture and, simultaneously, to assimilate. While succeeding admirably in many ways, Nesaule herself was unable to achieve genuine self-worth and to exorcise her personal demons until she told her story. This is a powerful, worthwhile, and ultimately inspiring book that adds to readers' understanding of the impact of war and emigration on families and individuals. All levels.—*L. Mayo, County College of Morris*

WS-1546   Can. CIP
Prang, Margaret. **A heart at leisure from itself: Carolina Macdonald of Japan.** UBC Press, University of British Columbia, 6344 Memorial Rd., Vancouver, BC V6T 1Z2, Canada, 1995. 346p bibl index afp ISBN 0-7748-0522-6, $39.95

North American Christian missions—to Japan in particular—were the preoccupation of Protestants, notably Presbyterians and Methodists, and once treated as hagiography. Recently, academics have rewritten the story. Prang's handsome and well-written book is an excellent example of such new academic interest. Caroline Macdonald was an Ontario Presbyterian who came to Japan in 1904 at age 30 to establish the YWCA in Tokyo. As she saw it, "women could reach women" in ways the church could not. She set herself first to learn Japanese. Without that, Macdonald argued, "we shall always be strangers in a strange land." After ten years as YWCA secretary, she started work on prison reform in Tokyo. Prang's work is particularly good on the integration of Macdonald's life with Japanese society, made more telling by her eventual fluency in the Japanese language. It shows what good scholarship can do with a once-arcane topic. The study reveals women and their work in the difficult circumstances of Japan from 1904 to 1930, and is made valuable by the author's sensitive attention to Japanese society, traditions, and politics. General readers; undergraduates.—*P. B. Waite, Dalhousie University*

WS-1547   GF50   93-10411 CIP
Rose, Gillian. **Feminism and geography: the limits of geographical knowledge.** Minnesota, 1993. 205p index afp ISBN 0-8166-2417-8, $44.95

An important book. The opening charge is that the "academic discipline of geography has historically been dominated by men." Although this is demonstrated in terms of the usual statistical indicators of employment, number of graduate degrees, and female participation rates in the corridors of academe, the principal concern is that geographical knowledge is "masculinist," i.e., a gendered view that excludes women's existence. Accordingly, Rose has three aims: to expose the masculinism of contemporary geographic discourse; to identify possible feminist strategies of resistance; to advocate a mode of inquiry in which women are knowledgeable about their own geographies. Following a discussion of the way geography is constrained by a complex series of "discursive positions, relations, and practices," she examines several substantive topics to demonstrate "masculinist" geography: time geography; the humanistic approach to place; landscape as "aesthetic masculinity." This is followed by a discussion of feminist geography. The book concludes with advocacy for a discipline that allows a more pluralist, sensitive, and dynamic understanding of space, place, and landscape, in which women geographers may particpate. Advanced undergraduates and above.—*B. Osborne, Queen's University*

WS-1548   GT610   95-1155 CIP
Severa, Joan L. **Dressed for the photographer: ordinary Americans and fashion, 1840-1900.** Kent State, 1995. 592p bibl index ISBN 0-87338-512-8, $60.00

Ordinary Americans, as revealed through their dress, are the subject of this extraordinary book. A lifetime of accumulated knowledge as costume curator (Wisconsin State Historical Society) coupled with extensive archival research

(New England to California) uniquely equip Severa to understand costume details recorded through various 19th-century photographic techniques. While historians of portraiture usually focus on artists, Severa stresses sitters' clothing. She is able to assign dates for many of the 272 photographs in this book, commenting extensively on women's hair styling, sleeve-cuts, length and fit of coats, collar shapes, trouser legs, etc. Because the photographs were taken over a period of 60 years for special events as well as for everyday activities and include diverse racial and ethnic groups, this hefty volume serves as an important statement on US social history and as a valuable reference tool for historical and academic institutions, museums, designers, and anyone who studies and interprets Americana. Each decade covered is introduced by a chapter describing contemporary fashion for women, men, and children according to published sources (mostly women's magazines) and personal diaries. Extensive bibliography and useful glossary for nonspecialists. All levels.—*B. B. Chico, Regis University*

WS-1549   HT149   95-43521 CIP
Smith, David A. **Third world cities in global perspective: the political economy of uneven urbanization.** Westview, 1996. 202p bibl index afp ISBN 0-8133-2998-1 pbk, $21.95

In this innovative book, Smith (sociology, Univ. of California-Irvine) attempts to connect the functioning of urban neighborhood communities to broader political and economic forces, using a case-study approach sensitive to historical change. His aim is to interpret, from a political economy perspective, the urban revolution sweeping across most of the developing world, and his focus is on global inequality and dependency. Many social scientists will find this approach controversial, but it presents intriguing conclusions and suggests some fascinating hypotheses for further investigation. It will be of special interest to devotees of postmodernist and social-theory paradigms in sociology, human geography, political science, and development studies. The first three chapters discuss contemporary theories of urbanization within the evolving world system. The next four treat empirical expressions via case studies based in West Africa and eastern Asia. The final chapter summarizes the central argument and recommends policies to ameliorate the negative consequences of uneven urban development. Although the bibliography is thorough and current, supporting figures are minimal, undercutting the effectiveness of the case-study presentations. Upper-division undergraduates and above.—*P. O. Muller, University of Miami*

WS-1550   HV5227   90-43246 CIP
Tyrrell, Ian. **Woman's world/woman's empire: the Woman's Christian Temperance Union in international perspective, 1880-1930.** North Carolina, 1991. 381p index afp ISBN 0-8078-1950-6, $45.00

Tyrrell (University of New South Wales) has given readers the first full study of the worldwide activities of the Women's Christian Temperence Union (WCTU) to the 1920s. Most accounts of the WCTU (e.g., Ruth Bordin's *Frances Willard: A Biography*, CH, Feb'87, and *Woman and Temperance*, 1981) have centered on Frances Willard's role; Tyrrell brings to the fore a number of other important leaders such as Mary Leavitt, Jessie Ackerman, and Lady Henry Somerset. In his very valuable but at times rather detailed account, Tyrrell emphasizes the WCTU link with evangelical Christianity. Surveying a broad setting in the US, Europe, Asia, and Africa, Tyrrell discusses WCTU activities against the use of alcohol and opium, and for prohibition, peace, feminism, Christianity, and the spread of Anglo-Saxon virtues and civilization. Admitting the ultimate worldwide failure of the world's WCTU, the author correctly asserts that the study of failure is important and that more international (rather than comparative) history is needed. Upper-division undergraduates and above.—*J. P. Felt, University of Vermont*

WS-1551   HQ1236   93-15275 MARC
Vickers, Jeanne. **Women and war.** Zed Books, 1993. 184p index ISBN 1-85649-229-X, $49.95; ISBN 1-85649-230-3 pbk, $17.50

Vickers looks at present-day wars and conflicts and their increasingly violent impact on civilians, as well as at defense policies, the arms trade, prospects for conversion from military to civilian production, and attempts by the UN to "turn swords into ploughshares" through international peacekeeping and peacemaking. She also brings into focus the relationships between disarmament and development and between peace and human rights. Vickers argues that it is important now and in the future for women to play a greater role in the peaceful resolution of disputes so that the 21st century may dawn with freedom from insecurity and fear, and contain the promise of a full and productive existence. Redirection to reduce militarism and violent resolution of conflict must be accompanied by development and by a more just and equitable world. According to Vickers women's contributions can make the difference. This book will aid recognition of the importance of women to this process. Advanced undergraduates and graduate students.—*M. Klatte, Eastern Kentucky University*

WS-1552   HQ653   92-52775 CIP
Watt, Jeffrey R. **The making of modern marriage: matrimonial control and the rise of sentiment in Neuchâtel, 1550-1800.** Cornell, 1993 (c1992). 302p bibl index afp ISBN 0-8014-2493-3, $39.95

Watt's statistical and anecdotal analysis of 4,100 court cases in a western principality of Switzerland is superbly bolstered by argument from contemporary theory and the impressive research on the family published over the past 20 years. The author juxtaposes the "Reformation and Seventeenth Century" with that of the 18th-century "Prussian Era," arguing convincingly "that the early modern period was decisive for the history of the family." Marriage in Neuchâtel evolved from a contract based on convenience to one of love and inclination. Watt divides cases brought before matrimonial courts and consistories into those concerning disputes over the formation of marriage (breach of contract, premarital and illicit sex, seduction) and those concerning the breakdown of marriage (divorce on the grounds of abandonment, desertion, adultery, cruelty). The adoption of Protestantism permitted greater leniency for the formation and dissolution of marriage, although "married couples were expected to stay married." Greater numbers of women sought and obtained separation and divorce on grounds of cruelty and incompatibility, which Watt concludes were signs of legal equality between the sexes and an anticipation of modern marriage laws. Undergraduate; graduate; faculty.—*J. E. Brink, Texas Tech University*

WS-1553   HQ1233   94-11691 CIP
Writing women and space: colonial and postcolonial geographies, ed. by Alison Blunt and Gillian Rose. Guilford, 1994. 256p index afp ISBN 0-89862-497-5, $40.00; ISBN 0-89862-498-3 pbk, $17.95

Essays in this fascinating volume are linked by a common interest in the engagement between gender and space. Unlike many edited collections, the contributions in this book are cohesive and of uniformly high quality, apparently the result of long discussion between the contributors and the editors. Essays range from several whose focus is the work of women travel writers in the British colonial period to a study of the interaction between the environmental movement and indigenous women in Australia. Also represented are studies from the US (WW II and women's increasing spatial spheres); Australia (suburbia and its accommodation of cultural diversity); South Africa (role of white women academics); and Ireland (nationalism, gender, and landscape). This list of regions covered does not do justice to the variety of approaches and exciting ideas here, nor does it capture the continuity which exists within the collection. Highly recommended. Upper-division undergraduates and above.—*S. Wurtele, Trent University*

WS-1554   HQ1121   90-49155 CIP
Writing women's history: international perspectives, ed. by Karen Offen, Ruth Roach Pierson and Jane Rendall. Indiana, 1991. 552p bibl index ISBN 0-253-34160-4, $37.50; ISBN 0-253-20651-0 pbk, $17.50

This collection of essays effectively illustrates the critical questioning of Western theoretical models that results when historians attempt to explain "gender hierarchies across cultural boundaries." Part 1, focusing on concepts and methods, considers the limitations of the traditional explanatory dichotomies of private/public, nature/culture, and feminine/masculine. Essays also analyze the problems of treating women's history as a separate field or as integrated into the "main body" of history, the privileged place given to "knowledge based on lived experience," and, finally, the important distinctions among women's history, feminist history, and gender history. Part 2 provides national historiograhies of the study of women and indicates the origins and the "state of the art" in 17 countries. There is also a useful bibliography on women, gender, and family in Russia and Central/Eastern Europe. A critical addition for both undergraduate and research libraries.—*M. J. Slaughter, University of New Mexico*

WS-1555   HQ1181   92-28707 CIP
Zinsser, Judith P. **History & feminism: a glass half full.** Twayne, 1993. 204p index afp ISBN 0-8057-9751-3, $26.95; ISBN 0-8057-9766-1 pbk, $14.95

Zinsser adds a critical feminist perspective to the growing number of works that attempt to document the history of history. She begins by describing efforts to alter the very substance, content, and definition of history, tracing the change from the movement to acknowledge women's experience (frequently referred to in women's history circles as the "add women and stir" method) to the more radical struggle to champion a reconceptualization and redefinition the very meaning of historical events and historical actors. In the second part of the book, Zinsser highlights the battles of women historians first to gain admittance to and ultimately to change the historical profession. This book should be required reading for academics across all gender and disciplinary lines. Zinsser neatly lays to rest the cherished myths of ungendered historical objectivity through her accounts of the struggles of feminist scholars to overcome the overt and covert sexism that dominated (and in certain instances still holds sway over) both the writing of history and the community of professional historians. Recommended for all academic library collections. All levels.—*E. Broidy, University of California, Irvine*

◆ Ancient

WS-1556   HQ1134   93-36217 CIP
Blundell, Sue. **Women in Ancient Greece.** Harvard, 1995. 224p bibl index ISBN 0-674-95473-4, $19.95

Blundell offers here an excellent, brief survey of women in archaic and classical Greek art, literature, and history. It is the sole comprehensive account in English of women in ancient Greece (as opposed to Greece and Rome). Blundell's reading is wide, her thought judicious, her prose clear, and her insight penetrating. She has a good bibliography, decent notes, and well-chosen illustrations. This reviewer particularly admires her restraint; she qualifies her statements when evidence is too weak to admit certainty, and she clearly indicates the exceptional nature of the Greek societies from which most evidence on women survives. Also noteworthy are her brief yet sensitive treatment of Sappho, her assertion that Athenian women had some power and autonomy in the domestic sphere, and her cautious analysis of infanticide. However, she relies too much on David Halperin's *One Hundred Years of Homosexuality* (1990) for information on pederasty, sexuality, and prostitution. David Cohen's *Law, Sexuality, and Society* (1991), overlooked in Blundell's notes, corrects Halperin at many points and also supports Blundell's account of the actual lives of women in classical Athens. She also neglects in text and notes the main ideas and books of Nicole Loraux (often difficult) and Eva Keuls (provocative but reckless and even silly.) This is still an impressive effort. Recommended for all college and university libraries.—*J. M. Williams, SUNY College at Geneseo*

WS-1557   HQ1130   95-30650 MARC
Brosius, Maria. **Women in ancient Persia, 559-331 BC.** Oxford, 1996. 258p bibl indexes afp ISBN 0-19-815009-1, $65.00

Brosius presents a thoughtful and illuminating examination of the status and influence of royal and nonroyal women in the first Persian Empire (559-331 BCE). She does not exaggerate in claiming that this is the first attempt to look seriously at these women from a new perspective. Even without her careful conclusions, the book provides an invaluable demonstration of intelligent and creative scholarship free of any unreflective acceptance of ancient or modern assumptions about Persian women. Brosius argues persuasively that the sensationalistic representations of women in the Greek sources derive in part from the political hostility between Greece and Persia, but also from Greek assumptions about the proper behavior of women. According to the author, to understand these women one must look carefully at the "historiographic and narrative pattern" within which any particular account of them appears. Brosius bases her examination on Persepolis Fortification texts, which provide complex portraits of these women. The specificity of her evidence, including linguistic evidence, is especially helpful, as is the extensive bibliography and the index of ancient sources. Upper-division undergraduates and above.—*J. de Luce, Miami University*

WS-1558   HQ1127   CIP
Clark, Gillian. **Women in late antiquity: pagan and Christian lifestyles.** Oxford, 1993. 158p bibl indexes afp ISBN 0-19-814675-2, $35.00

Clark examines various aspects of women's daily lives during "late antiquity," from the third to the sixth century CE. By so doing, she supplements the studies of Greco-Roman antiquity that stop somewhere around the late third century. The reader needs a persuasive discussion of what it means to be "pagan" and Christian at the very start, but Clark's overall approach is useful, particularly with her reminder of the nature and shortcomings of the evidence, most of which was written by men uninterested in women's lives. Clark also hints at continuities from "pagan" to Christian experience. Topics range from health, sexuality, marriage, and inheritance to asceticism and housekeeping. As with nearly all general discussions of women's lives in the ancient world, Clark says little about old women beyond suggesting the age of menopause. The depth of analysis varies, but invaluable citations of primary sources (particularly from Roman law) support every observation. The bibliography includes some useful citations, but the few black-and-white illustrations add nothing. Undergraduate and above.—*J. de Luce, Miami University (OH)*

WS-1559   HQ1134   93-39828 CIP
Demand, Nancy. **Birth, death, and motherhood in classical Greece.** Johns Hopkins, 1994. 276p bibl indexes afp ISBN 0-8018-4762-1, $39.95

Demand (Indiana Univ.) uses a constructionist approach to consider motherhood and childbirth in classical Greece; in doing so, she contributes significantly to previous efforts to understand the lives of women in Greece and Rome, e.g., Sarah B. Pomeroy's classic *Goddesses, Whores, Wives, and Slaves* (CH, Dec'75) and V. French's "Midwives and Maternity Care in the Roman World," in *Rescuing Creusa: New Methodological Approaches to Women in Antiquity*, ed. by Marilyn Skinner (1987). Relying primarily on Hippocrates' *Epidemics*, Demand considers a fifth-century gynecology that appropriated women's health folklore and (auguring Foucauldian theory) controlled female reproduction. She concludes by identifying those factors that may have led to the desire of the male-dominated polis to exert such control. Demand consistently considers issues of class and age in interpreting the evidence; she also draws analogies with modern Greek villages when a comparison can illuminate the ancient community. Better and clearer supporting visual evidence would be helpful; one plate even appears to be out of focus. The useful bibliography includes canonical as well as unexpected entries. General and academic collections at any level.—*J. de Luce, Miami University (OH)*

WS-1560   HQ1136   90-45259 CIP
Evans, John K. **War, women and children in ancient Rome.** Routledge, 1991. 263p bibl indexes ISBN 0-415-05723-X, $45.00

Evans focuses on the last two centuries of the Roman Republic, arguing that the ceaseless wars of the period led to a steady increase in the legal, social, and economic independence of Roman women. In this he differs from the two leading works in the field, Sarah Pomeroy's *Goddesses, Whores, Wives, and Slaves* (CH, Dec'75), and J.F. Gardner's *Women in Roman Law & Society* (CH, Dec'86). The evidence and arguments on both sides are presented clearly. A number of well-known passages and inscriptions are discussed in great detail, in effect constituting a series of model essays in interpretation. This is a lucid, learned, and forceful exposition of an original thesis, an important contribution to the social history of Antiquity. Evans's findings help to explain the leading role played by women in the early church. Evans is well known for his studies of Roman agriculture and peasant society, and in this work he shows himself a master of every aspect of social history. There are ten apposite illustrations, three useful indexes, and a splendid bibliography. Strongly recommended for all academic libraries, community college level up.—*R. I. Frank, University of California, Irvine*

WS-1561   DF228   94-1250 CIP
Henry, Madeleine M. **Prisoner of history: Aspasia of Miletus and her biographical tradition.** Oxford, 1995. 201p bibl index afp ISBN 0-19-508712-7, $29.95

The names of relatively few women living in Athens in the fifth century BCE are known; of them, Aspasia—courtesan, companion of Pericles, teacher of Socrates—may be the most famous. Henry's book is the first to examine Aspasia by considering how various sources have constructed her life. The book not only makes a welcome and significant contribution to the study of this particular woman, but Henry also contributes to a better understanding of the social and political culture of fifth-century Athens and women's positions in it. She challenges readers to consider not only how to tell a woman's life, but how the *bios* of Aspasia in particular has been constructed and reconstructed in classical and post-classical times, and to what end. Henry's analysis is rigorous and subtle; her examination of the original sources is meticulous. The extensive and sophisticated bibliography will prove as valuable to the specialist as the argument of the book itself. Upper-division undergraduates and above.—*J. de Luce, Miami University*

WS-1562   HQ472   90-43854 CIP
Pornography and representation in Greece and Rome, ed. by Amy Richlin. Oxford, 1992. 317p bibl index afp ISBN 0-19-506722-3, $45.00; ISBN 0-19-506723-1 pbk, $18.95

This volume belongs with other works of cultural studies. Contributors draw inspiration from Suzanne Kappeler's *The Pornography of Representation* (CH, Jan'87), although not always in agreement with its thesis. Moreover, the essays question Foucault's pronouncements on sexuality. The authors add significantly to the understanding of sexuality in Greece and Rome by applying feminist theory, among others, to their analyses. The volume is remarkable in part for its feminist authorship. Classics have been slow to move in this direction and collaborative feminist scholarship is still noteworthy. But it is also remarkable for the inclusion of material previously unavailable to the nonclassicist, for the variety and range of interpretations, and for the discussions of literary texts side by side with visual art. Chapters cover authors from the "canon," from the tragedians, and from Aristophanes to Livy and Ovid, as well as ancient romance novels and the products of pornographers. The 13 contributors represent some of the most recent and provocative work in classical scholarship to date. The handy timeline will help the general reader; the bibliography is particularly useful for the general reader and specialist alike. General; undergraduate; graduate; faculty.— *J. de Luce, Miami University (OH)*

WS-1563   HQ1137   92-38221 CIP
Robins, Gay. **Women in ancient Egypt.** Harvard, 1993. 205p bibl index ISBN 0-674-95468-8 pbk, $18.95

Best suited for the general reader, this book relies on artistic, archaeological, and written evidence to reconstruct the private and public lives of women in Egypt from approximately 3000 to 300 BCE. Thus, it provides an antecedent to such studies of women in Egypt as Sarah Pomeroy's *Women in Hellenistic Egypt* (CH, May'85). In the introduction, Robins analyzes particularly skillfully the challenges and problems inherent in her study, including the familiar problem of trying to reconstruct women's lives when scholars have maintained a persistent silence about them; evidence that may be fragmentary or derived from biased sources; evidence that often excludes entire classes of women; and modern prejudice that encourages errors in interpreting the evidence. Although the book contains a considerable number of illustrations, they are all black-and-white and are consequently often hard to discern. Moreover, the text does not adequately help the reader interpret the visual material, a fact that qualifies its effectiveness as evidence. The bibliography includes references that will interest the specialist as well as the general reader.—*J. de Luce, Miami University (OH)*

WS-1564   KJA3322   90-14170 CIP
Treggiari, Susan. **Roman marriage: *usti coniuges* from the time of Cicero to the time of Ulpian.** Oxford, 1991. 578p bibl indexes ISBN 0-19-814890-9, $120.00

Recent studies of Roman marriage are mostly to be found in works on the female's world, e.g., J. Balsdon's *Roman Women* (1963) and Jane Gardner's *Women in Roman Law & Society* (CH, Dec'86). Now Treggiari has explored all aspects of the institution, male as well as female, and also its legal, political, emotional, and class features. Treggiari (Stanford) is well known for her studies of freedmen and working women. Here she handles with expert assurance all the sources— Sanskrit cognates, poetry, satire, history, letters, and, above all, the *Digest*. Indeed, it is her close and continuous use of this mine of Roman legal thought that gives her work its special character and value. Comparative material is also used judiciously: there are glances at American prohibition, the double standard today, Edward VII's amours, and other contemporary matters to remind readers that the issues raised by Roman mores concern us as well. Notes give all the

relevant citations, the full bibliography is a veritable repertoire of modern scholarship on the subject, and use of the work is facilitated by three indexes-tests, persons, and subjects. This is a major contribution, indispensable to any collection dealing with ancient history, classical literature, or the social sciences.—*R. I. Frank, University of California, Irvine*

WS-1565   Orig
Walters Art Gallery (Baltimore, Md.). **Pandora: women in classical Greece,** by Ellen D. Reeder. Trustees of the Walters Art Gallery/ Princeton, 1995. 431p bibl ISBN 0-691-01125-7, $95.00; ISBN 0-691-01124-9 pbk, $35.00

This volume is the lavish catalog of the winter 1995 Walters Art Gallery exhibition. Among books about women in ancient Greece it is unique for the stunning array of visual evidence, fully documented and analyzed, and often in color. Authors of the interpretative essays that precede the illustrations include well-regarded scholars, although some of the articles will disappoint specialists. The essays tend to cover too familiar ground and do so with relatively little subtlety. Further, contributors appear reluctant to acknowledge outright the volume's debt to feminist scholarship. Pandora and Hesiod's economics were being discussed in the late 1960s, and the essay on women as animals inexplicably fails to cite Sherry Ortner's original article "Is Female to Male as Nature Is to Culture?" in *Woman, Culture, and Society*, ed. by M.Z. Rosaldo and L. Lamphere (1974). Ellen Reeder states at one point that the authors of Greek poetry were male; one wonders what happened to Sappho. Readers unfamiliar with feminist studies and classical scholarship over the past 25 years, however, will still find the book a provocative introduction. The bibliography includes useful references, but the real value of *Pandora* is the catalog itself. An accompanying video provides an engaging overview with an excellent narrative, but the visual material is inexpertly reproduced and can be hard to discern. All levels.—*J. de Luce, Miami University*

WS-1566   HQ1137   91-30599 CIP
Watterson, Barbara. **Women in ancient Egypt.** St. Martin's, 1992 (c1991). 201p bibl indexes ISBN 0-312-07538-3, $35.00

A handsome, easily read book about Egyptian women's lives during the pharaonic period, 3100-30 BCE. Most of the book focuses on peasant women; the final chapter emphasizes women of royalty. Watterson uses a fascinating array of evidence from tombs, statues, everyday objects, papyri, and historical records. The use of artistic sources (paintings, clay pots, poems) to reveal women's everyday lives is most interesting. Wonderful photographs illustrate the text very well. Some of the topics included are women's legal status and career possibilities, and women's domestic and personal lives—marriage, health, childbirth, household chores, clothing, and adornment. Throughout, Watterson draws strong parallels to and takes examples from modern Egypt, suggesting that the Egypt of today may reflect something of ancient times. This approach is methodologically questionable, as there have been vast changes in Egypt in the past 2000 years. Further, the references cited in the chapter notes do not necessarily correspond to the references cited for the chapter itself, making some sources difficult to trace. General.—*R. Ellovich, North Carolina State University*

WS-1567   DS62   93-5583 CIP
Whitehorne, John. **Cleopatras.** Routledge, 1994. 243p bibl index ISBN 0-415-05806-6, $49.95

Whitehorne (Univ. of Queensland) has compiled biographies of all the Cleopatras in Greek and Hellenistic history, beginning with the first, legendary namesake and ending with Cleopatra VII's surviving daughter, Cleopatra Selene, queen of Mauretania. Although he attempts to simplify the labyrinthine political and genealogical arrangements of the Hellenistic period, their sheer complexity is still a problem, especially for the inexperienced reader for whom this work is intended. Whitehorne also assumes that the reader already knows and understands the historical context of these political machinations. He uses primary sources quite skillfully. However, a surprising omission in the bibliography is Sarah Pomeroy's *Women in Hellenistic Egypt* (CH, May'85), a work that offers a contextual discussion of the role the Cleopatras played in Hellenistic Egyptian politics. Whitehorne's style is engaging, but his digressions, although fun to read, do not really contribute to one's understanding of the subject. Nonetheless, this is the first work devoted to Hellenistic queenship to appear for many years, and as such is valuable to anyone interested in the subject. Upper-division undergraduates and above.— *L. E. Mitchell, Alfred University*

WS-1568   HQ1127   90-24488 CIP
Women's history and ancient history, ed. by Sarah B. Pomeroy. North Carolina, 1991. 317p index afp ISBN 0-8078-1949-2, $39.95; ISBN 0-8078-4310-5 pbk, $13.95

This collection contributes as much to the study of women's lives in the ancient world as Pomeroy's *Goddesses, Whores, Wives, and Slaves* (CH, Dec'75) has since its publication. The 12 essays in the current volume provide a nearly unprecedented range of topics, from Sappho's poetry to Roman Asia Minor, from paganism to Judaism and Christianity, from Hellenistic queens to the redoubtable Fulvia. The chapters on health and science are particularly welcome. The reader will regret the authors' reluctance to discuss at greater length the entire life course of a woman, not just youth and maturity. In terms of methodology, individual chapters demonstrate both the use of the most traditional kinds of evidence and the application of promising multidisciplinary perspectives. The collection supplements nicely the third volume (including entries on women and family life) of *Civilization of the Ancient Mediterranean: Greece and Rome,* ed. by Michael Grant and Rachel Kitzinger (CH, Jan'89). The absence of a separate reference list will frustrate the serious reader, but many of the notes are invaluable to the specialist. All levels.—*J. de Luce, Miami University (OH)*

◆ Medieval & Renaissance

WS-1569   HQ759   91-16078 CIP
Atkinson, Clarissa W. **The oldest vocation: Christian motherhood in the Middle Ages.** Cornell, 1991. 274p bibl index afp ISBN 0-8014-2071-7, $24.95

Atkinson explores the history of the concept and institution of motherhood from the formation of the Christian medieval tradition to the epochal changes introduced by the Renaissance and Reformation. Two chapters treat early Christian attitudes toward motherhood and the survival of ancient theories about women's physiology. Another two investigate the monastic notions of "spiritual motherhood" that dominated the early Middle Ages and the new concept of theological motherhood expressed in the cult of the Virgin Mary that emerged in the high Middle Ages. Two more consider changing attitudes toward the family and female sanctity in the late Middle Ages and the decisive alteration of these late medieval views in the 16th century. A concluding chapter assesses the effect of changing concepts of motherhood on modern attitudes toward women. Atkinson argues that motherhood is not only a physiological phenomenon but a cultural construct as well, which alters over time: "Motherhood was never purely 'natural'; it has always been shaped by religious systems, power relationships, and material structures." An important contribution to the cultural history of the European family. College and university libraries.—*S. D. Sargent, Union College (NY)*

WS-1570   HQ18   93-6040 CIP
Baldwin, John W. **The language of sex: five voices from Northern France around 1200.** Chicago, 1994. 331p index afp ISBN 0-226-03613-8, $37.50

It is strangely refreshing among books that address issues of sexuality to find one whose title accurately describes the contents rather than having been chosen for sales appeal. Baldwin's does just that. The book describes and analyzes five different traditions of discourse about sex—Augustinian theological, Galenic medical, scholarly Ovidian, vernacular romantic, and fabliaux—using the writings of a single individual who lived around the turn of the 12th century in northern France to represent each tradition. The "sex" in Baldwin's title is intentionally ambiguous, for he is interested in exploring these authors' ideas about both sexuality and gender, and the interplay between the two. After introducing the five discourses, the body of the book compares the way the writers looked at a variety of topics, including the sexual body, desire, coitus, and children, and finds surprising areas of agreement and complementarity. In his conclusion, Baldwin stresses the negative impact of the recovery of Aristotle on what he terms a "privileged moment of gender symmetry in Western thought" around 1200, an assertion that will no doubt be challenged. The book will be helpful for anyone interested in ideas about women or gender and is free from poststructuralist jargon, though conversant with many contemporary theories of language and culture. Graduate; faculty.—*M. E. Wiesner, University of Wisconsin—Milwaukee*

WS-1571   HQ1143   91-12699 CIP
Bloch, R. Howard. **Medieval misogyny and the invention of Western romantic love.** Chicago, 1992 (c1991). 298p bibl index afp ISBN 0-226-05972-3, $45.00; ISBN 0-226-05973-1 pbk, $17.95

Returning to familiar ground in this fascinating and well-reasoned work, Bloch argues that Western notions of misogyny, developed from the writings of the early Church Fathers by the 4th century, profoundly influenced the invention of romantic love in the 12th century. He maintains that Christian writers created the *topoi* of woman as *simultaneously* the "Devil's gateway" and the "Bride of Christ" rather than as mutually exclusive alternatives. Since no individual woman was capable of being both, women were effectively "abstracted" from history. Locating the "core of the medieval discourse" on misogyny in writings on virginity, Bloch believes that William IX, the "antifeminist" and first "troubadour," transformed this misogynist theme of the Virgin Mary into a secular ideal of woman during his dispute with Robert d'Arbrissel, the "profeminist" founder of the monastery of Fontevrault. Specifically reacting to the improved economic and social position of women in southern France, which threatened to place women in the public sphere and hence in history, William embodied the fears of the nobility in an outpouring of courtly love poetry that reduced woman "to the status of a category. . .annihila[ting]. . .the identity of individual women." Bloch has used both textual evidence and recent studies (e.g., Herlihy and Goody) on family history to support his thesis. Highly recommended to supplement the work of C.S. Lewis, Georges Duby, Peter Brown, Penny Gold, and others. Upper-division undergraduates and above.—*C. W. Clark, St. Andrews Presbyterian College*

WS-1572   BF1583   94-39001 CIP
Brauner, Sigrid. **Fearless wives and frightened shrews: the construction of the witch in early modern Germany,** ed. by Robert H. Brown. Massachusetts, 1995. 164p bibl index afp ISBN 0-87023-767-5, $22.95

Brauner focuses on witchcraft, vernacular literature, and social change in early modern Germany. The book raises interesting questions about the genesis of the modern social problems of race, gender, and class oppression, and locates their roots in the early modern period. Brauner argues that witchcraft persecutions demonstrate that a dramatic social and economic restructuring was taking place, leading to dislocations and violence—often directed at women. She asks why women were targeted as witches, how the "witch" differed from the ideal urban housewife, and what effect the Reformation had on witchcraft persecutions and on the perception of women. To seek answers Brauner examines the Bible, 15th-century witchcraft "manuals," the writings of Martin Luther, and a variety of plays and stories, all of which spread the "learned concept of modern witchcraft" throughout Europe in the 16th century. She concludes the general belief was that within every housewife lived the wicked alter ago of the witch, waiting to "pounce on men" with her sexual voraciousness, her disobedience, her irrational emotionality. To keep the family intact, these urges (and therefore women themselves) had to be contained. Upper-division undergraduate and above.—*D. C. Samuels, SUNY at Stony Brook*

WS-1573   DA198   91-12692 CIP
Chibnall, Marjorie. **The Empress Matilda: queen consort, queen mother and lady of the English.** B. Blackwell, 1991. 227p bibl index afp ISBN 0-631-15737-9, $39.95

Thorough in research, judicious in its judgments, this excellent book is the first scholarly biography of Matilda since Oskar Rössler's *Kaiserin Mathilde* (Berlin, 1897). The great strength of Chibnall's study, other than meticulous scholarship, is its successful attempt to present Matilda as a whole figure. Chibnall shows that Matilda was not simply a blundering old dragon breathing fire into an England tormented by anarchy, but was an important figure in the histories of Normandy, Anjou, and of the Empire in the first half of the 12th century. The author draws a convincing picture of the Lady of the English as an astute and diligent, if not particularly successful, politician; good luck did not bless her very often. It is unlikely that any living scholar knows more about Matilda, her family, and her causes than does Chibnall, whose authority was established by her superb editing (e.g., *The Ecclesiastical History of Orderic Vitalis,* v.3, bks.V, VI: CH, Apr'73) and writing of history (e.g., *The World of Orderic Vitalis; Anglo-Norman England 1066-1166,* CH, Jul'85). The bibliography, index, and references are exemplary; the few black-and-white illustrations add little to the text. Upper-division undergraduates and above.—*J. W. Alexander, University of Georgia*

WS-1574   BV639   94-27864 CIP
Creative women in medieval and early modern Italy: a religious and artistic renaissance, ed. by E. Ann Matter and John Coakley. Pennsylvania, 1994. 356p indexes afp ISBN 0-8122-3236-4, $36.95

Growing out of a conference held at the University of Pennsylvania, this is a collection worthy of being in every academic library. In some ways it is a continuation of another fine collection, *The Crannied Wall: Women, Religion, and the Arts in Early Modern Europe*, ed. by Craig Monson (1992). It brings together the work of US and Italian scholars of history, literature, art history, music, philosophy, and religious studies, who examine women's creative expressions in the realms of religion and the arts. The collection as a whole is richly interdisciplinary, as are many of the individual essays, which interweave treatment of the arts with religion. Among these are Anne Schutte's fascinating comparison of Venetian "failed saints" with Italian women artists who painted self-portraits, and Carolyn Valone's examination of women's patronage of early Jesuit buildings. The essay by Gabriella Zarri (a highly influential Italian scholar whose work has rarely been translated) on the marriage of virgins is essential reading for anyone working on the Catholic Reformation or on female spirituality in any century. Upper-division undergraduates and above.—*M. E. Wiesner, University of Wisconsin—Milwaukee*

WS-1575   CB353   94-13063 CIP
The Cultural patronage of medieval women, ed. by June Hall McCash. Georgia, 1996. 402p bibl index afp ISBN 0-8203-1701-2, $60.00; ISBN 0-8203-1702-0 pbk, $25.00

In this collection, scholars in many disciplines explore a wide array of issues surrounding women's patronage from the sixth through the 15th century. Some of the essays focus on a single figure, such as Empress Theodora, Matilda of Scotland, Elizabeth de Burgh, or Isabel of Portugal, and some on groups of women, such as Plantagenet queens. Other essays examine one particular type of patronage over a broad sweep of time, such as women's literary patronage across 800 years in France or 300 years in England. Still others stress a particular issue, such as women's exact role in sponsoring literary and artistic projects, both sacred and secular. The subjects of these essays are married, widowed, or religious women, and cluster (as one would expect) largely at the top of the social scale, though Ralph Hanna's contribution uses Lollard trial records to examine the relationship of two peasant women to books in an innovative way. None of the essays is a simple recounting of patronage activities, but all consider complex questions surrounding patronage and provide extensive social and cultural context for these women's activities. The book is enhanced by multiple illustrations and a 50-page bibliography. Upper-division undergraduates and above.—*M. E. Wiesner, University of Wisconsin—Milwaukee*

WS-1576   BJ1600   90-43359 CIP
Dhuoda. **Handbook for William: a Carolingian woman's counsel for her son,** tr. and introd. by Carol Neel. Nebraska, 1991. 152p bibl afp ISBN 0-8032-1685-8, $30.00

A most welcome full English translation of a singular work—Dhuoda's handbook of consolation for her son is the only work written by a woman to have survived from the Carolingian period. Originally written in Latin, it was little studied until the French translation and edition of Pierre Riché in 1975 (on which this translation is based). It is one of the few sources written by a layperson of either sex from this early period, and gives the reader a perspective on Christianity not gained by reading the more common clerical works. Dhuoda relies most heavily on the Vulgate Bible, but adds her own insights in directing her son how to pray, how better to love God, and how to accept whatever fate God decrees. Not limiting herself to purely spiritual matters, she also discusses Frankish society and the role of a woman in its largely patriarchal organization. Neel's introduction is very useful, and her translation succeeds in capturing Dhuoda's "straightforward and emotionally laden" prose style. Recommended for all colleges offering medieval or women's history courses.—*M. E. Wiesner, University of Wisconsin—Milwaukee*

WS-1577   DD140   94-5289 CIP
The Empress Theophano: Byzantium and the West at the turn of the first millennium, ed. by Adelbert Davids. Cambridge, 1995. 344p index ISBN 0-521-45296-1, $59.95

Essays in this volume focus on Theophano, Byzantine wife of Emperor Otto II, premier ruler in Latin Christendom during the late tenth century. Until recently, scholars knew little about Theophano beyond her name and her status as a Byzantine princess; they had not even determined her blood relationship to the Eastern emperors. Nevertheless, historians had discovered some fascinating details about her, e.g., her love of luxurious clothes, her successful regency for her son Otto III, and her insistence on teaching her boy Greek. A collection of articles cannot provide a comprehensive study of Theophano. Contributors have chosen to describe aspects of the empress's world and to pose some key questions. Did this Byzantine empress help to stimulate the intellectual reawakening in western Europe c. 1000? Did her taste for luxury increase demand among Frankish noble women for silks, jewelry, and perfumes from the East? Did her presence in the West augment Byzantine influence on art and architecture in Frankish Europe? In sum, the volume is a step toward a definitive study of Theophano. Upper-division undergraduates; graduate students.—*T. S. Miller, Salisbury State University*

WS-1578   GT2465   90-24132 CIP
Gélis, Jacques. **History of childbirth: fertility, pregnancy and birth in early modern Europe,** tr. by Rosemary Morris. Northeastern, 1991. 326p bibl index ISBN 1-55553-102-4, $45.00; ISBN 1-55553-105-9 pbk, $15.95

The French title of Gélis's work, *L'arbre et le fruit*, provides a much more accurate description of both its style and its contents. This is not a narrative history of childbirth, but an extremely lively and impressionistic discussion of many of the beliefs and practices surrounding the female body, pregnancy, childbirth, and the care of young infants in premodern society—primarily in France, but with examples taken from other parts of Europe as well. Gélis draws on anthropology, folklore, and semiotics; his work is structured topically, with no sense of chronology. Gélis views premodern thoughts about the experience of conceiving and bearing children as closely linked to more general notions of analogies, nature, and time, with Christianity having little influence over beliefs that persisted for millenia. Some of the practices he describes still continue, though their meaning and symbolic context have been largely forgotten. The book is written in an almost poetic style that makes it very different from standard Anglo-American historical writing, but this, combined with the fascinating topic, make it a work for both academic and public libraries.—*M. E. Wiesner, University of Wisconsin—Milwaukee*

WS-1579   DK4249   91-61035 Orig
Halecki, Oscar. **Jadwiga of Anjou and the rise of East Central Europe,** ed. by Thaddeus V. Gromada. Social Science Monographs, 1991. (Dist. by Columbia) 400p (East European monographs, 308) indexes ISBN 0-88033-206-9, $43.00

This posthumous work by a great Polish historian has been carefully edited and seen through to publication by one of his former students. For Halecki, "East Central Europe" was a region with a distinctive character and mission in European history and culture. Here he focuses on the career of Jadwiga, daughter of the King of Hungary, ruler herself of Poland, and the wife of the Lithuanian prince who established the basis for the regional federation of Poland, Lithuania, Bohemia, and Hungary. Halecki argues that Jadwiga's role in bringing this about was crucial. His treatment of Jadwiga's life and times in the first two parts of this study provides rich detail and insight. Historians will find these sections an important scholarly contribution. In Part 3 of the book, Halecki offers a more reflective assessment of the way in which Jadwiga's principles and methods (defined as "the application of Christian ethics in politics") constitute a basis for resolving European problems. The editor observes that the events of the late 1980s in the former Soviet bloc would have confirmed Halecki in his belief that Jadwiga's message was still vital and relevant. College, university, and public libraries.—*P. W. Knoll, University of Southern California*

WS-1580   HQ1147   95-31506 CIP
Jochens, Jenny. **Women in Old Norse society.** Cornell, 1996 (c1995). 266p bibl index afp ISBN 0-8014-3165-4, $39.95

Most scholars interested in the European Middle Ages would have been thankful to Jochens if she had simply provided a survey of women's lives in medieval Iceland and Norway, because very little is available in English. She has certainly done that, discussing such issues as marriage, reproduction, leisure, and work from the late ninth to the middle of the 13th century. She has done much more, however; the book also provides sophisticated analyses of cultural interactions (e.g., Jochens's analysis of the pagan-Christian transition in gendered terms will be very useful for scholars of the spread of Christianity in other times and places) and presents fascinating new information. Among the latter is her investigation of the use of homespun cloth and coats (made by women) as a measure of value in Iceland and an item of trade for Icelandic men in their ventures beyond the island. One's view of "Vikings" does not often include their role as dealers in shaggy coats that became a fashion rage. Jochens's study is a model of interdisciplinary techniques and research; she carefully describes her sources—largely laws and sagas of various types—and their limitations, and then draws from them information, such as the etymology of key words ("wife," "husband"), possible only for a linguistic scholar of her caliber. All levels.—*M. E. Wiesner, University of Wisconsin—Milwaukee*

WS-1581   BX4220   90-45510 MARC
Johnson, Penelope D. **Equal in monastic profession: religious women in Medieval France.** Chicago, 1991. 294p bibl index afp ISBN 0-226-40185-5, $39.95

With this perceptive study, Johnson extends her research on women in medieval monasticism, an institution created as much by feminine monastics as by the masculine ones we have always read about. Based on deep readings—both qualitative and quantitative—of 11th- to 13th-century legal and economic charters that recorded the transactions and activities of monastic life, the focus is principally on some two dozen northern French nunneries. Not surprisingly, medieval nuns and abbesses were empowered by their spirituality and by their respected and very much nonsubordinate social leadership positions. Insofar as they shared with monks the gender-neutral family model of monastic life, the stereotype of passive or always reclusive nuns is quite misleading. But the symmetry between the two began to disappear as early as the 12th century, after which clerical reform and sclerotic societal changes combined to deform the primitive ideal of monastic life for the laity, male and female alike. Johnson provides lively and energetic guidance for this fascinating journey through three centuries of church history.—*R. J. Cormier, Wilson College*

WS-1582   DA330   90-25937 CIP
Jones, Michael K. **The king's mother: Lady Margaret Beaufort, Countess of Richmond and Derby,** by Michael K. Jones and Malcolm G. Underwood. Cambridge, 1992. 322p bibl index ISBN 0-521-34512-X, $59.95

An exemplary biography of Margaret Beaufort, thrice married to powerful political players of the 15th century, mother of Henry VII, founder of two Cambridge colleges, and political manipulator par excellence. The book illustrates the precarious power that could be wielded by a woman. It is a valuable contribution to women's history, while it also illuminates the political, religious, and social aspects of a confusing period of English history. The authors, well established authorities on this subject, smoothly integrate a wide range of archival and secondary documents into this sympathetic but objective and engaging biography. The "introduction" is actually a good historiographical essay. Jones and Underwood occasionally draw psychological conclusions that are beyond substantiation. Footnoting and bibliography are superb. Illustrations, genealogical tables, and appendixes are supportive. Advanced undergraduate; graduate.—*J.J. Butt, James Madison University*

WS-1583   HQ1148   91-19960 CIP
King, Margaret L. **Women of the Renaissance.** Chicago, 1991. 333p bibl index afp ISBN 0-226-43617-9, $45.00; ISBN 0-226-43618-7 pbk, $16.95

Building on her earlier work on humanist women, King has produced a more general survey of women in the Renaissance, focusing on women in the family, women in the church, and women in high culture. King includes material from 1350 to 1650 from all over Europe, although Italian and English examples are most common. One of the book's weaknesses is King's extrapolation from Italian examples. Another is lack of a strong chronological perspective; the work is perhaps more cultural anthropology than history, a sort of female counterpart to Jacob Burckhardt's *Civilization of the Renaissance in Italy* (1890). Despite these prob-

lems, King's book will be very useful for upper-division undergraduates or those starting research in the field because King has synthesized a great deal of material and provides nearly 40 pages of bibliography. Her writing is clear and elegant; the chapter on women and high culture is especially well done. The book requires some familiarity with European history, particularly in the section on religion, so it is not for beginning students. Recommended for all libraries with holdings in European or women's history.—*M. E. Wiesner, University of Wisconsin—Milwaukee*

WS-1584   KKH9851   91-13341 CIP
Kuehn, Thomas. **Law, family, & women: toward a legal anthropology of Renaissance Italy.** Chicago, 1992 (c1991). 415p bibl index afp ISBN 0-226-45762-1, $40.00

A collection of ten articles by Kuehn dealing with the three subjects that form his title; eight have appeared previously, though several of these have updated notes. All essays focus on Florence, so that the "Italy" of the subtitle is somewhat misleading. Kuehn's methodology and conclusions are highly suggestive, however, and will prove useful for those working elsewhere in Italy as well as in the rest of Europe. He is particularly interested in exploring cases in which legal theory and legal practices did not fit together, or, as he puts it, cases that "offer a poststructural space for the play of ambiguities." Kuehn challenges the conclusions of Christiane Klapisch-Zuber, Francis Kent, and others about the strength of patrilineage in Florentine society, using a huge variety of prescriptive and descriptive, public and private legal sources. His mastery of all types of legal sources is clearly evident and he has not neglected stories that illustrate and demonstrate his points in favor of pure analysis. This book can be read profitably by a wide range of Renaissance scholars, not simply those in legal history; it lapses into neither legal nor deconstructionist jargon while using the insights of both fields.—*M. E. Wiesner, University of Wisconsin—Milwaukee*

WS-1585   Orig
Leyser, Henrietta. **Medieval women: a social history of women in England, 450-1500.** St. Martin's, 1995. 337p bibl index ISBN 0-312-12934-3, $39.95

Leyser has gathered together the findings of a huge range of older and newer studies to provide a readable overview of women's lives in England over the 1000 years of the Middle Ages. The book's structure is partially chronological and partially topical, and includes information drawn from archeology and literature, as well as from more standard historical sources. The author is explicit about her sources, both primary and secondary, so that readers gain a good idea of *how* scholars have come to learn about medieval women as well as *what* they have learned. Readers themselves are encouraged to be historians by the inclusion of more than 50 pages of extracts from primary sources. The book contains chapters on the Anglo-Saxons and the impact of 1066 on women, then topical chapters for the period 1100-1500 on marriage and motherhood, work, widows, lay and religious women's spiritual lives, and women's literary interests. Highly recommended. General readers; high school students through undergraduates.—*M. E. Wiesner, University of Wisconsin—Milwaukee*

WS-1586   DP163   91-46645 CIP
Liss, Peggy K. **Isabel the Queen: life and times.** Oxford, 1992. 398p bibl index afp ISBN 0-19-507356-8, $30.00

Liss's lengthy biography of Isabel adds to the growing stack of books generated by the Quincentenary of Columbus. Directed to both a general and an academic readership, the work relies heavily on the rich and well-known chronicles of the reign; their vividness provides for a more successful treatment of Isabel's life than of her times. Particularly striking is the account of her adolescence, when she stood in the shadow of her brother Alfonso until his death and astutely manipulated aristocratic factions. Less convincing is Liss's evaluation of the mature queen. In the heady days of 1492 Liss detects a grand design of *la reina* to purify the realm, advance into the Atlantic and Africa, and to fulfill her destiny. Cast in terms of a sharp turn from medieval to modern, this assessment minimizes pragmatic and traditional qualities of the Catholic Kings. Although students wishing a succinct introduction in English to the reign should consult J. Hillgarth's *The Spanish Kingdoms, 1250-1516* (2 v., Oxford 1976-78), or F. Fernandez-Armesto's *Ferdinand and Isabella* (1975), this detailed study will be of interest to undergraduate libraries.—*S. P. Bensch, Swarthmore College*

WS-1587 HQ1143 89-20296 CIP
Medieval women and the sources of medieval history, ed. by Joel T. Rosenthal. Georgia, 1990. 384p index afp ISBN 0-8203-1214-2, $45.00; ISBN 0-8203-1226-6, $20.00

This collection is an invaluable resource for undergraduate and graduate students planning research on medieval women, or for more advanced scholars wishing to know what is available in other fields. It includes 14 essays, each of which focuses on one type of source (e.g., seals, coins, canon law, exempla or saints' lives) or on the sources available in a specific geographic region, or on sources that present particular interpretive problems (e.g., legal documents, obstetrical literature, or clerical tracts written by men hostile to women). Most of the contributors discuss the ways in which such sources have been used since the Middle Ages to elicit information on women, providing the reader with both positive and negative examples. They also make suggestions for future research. Each chapter ends with extensive notes and a bibliography of primary and secondary sources. The authors include many of the most prominent scholars in the field—Susan Stuard, James Brundage, Jane Schulenburg, David Herlihy, JoAnn McNamara—so that their discussions are based on their own archival experience. Learning that these major scholars also encountered difficulties will certainly be heartening for younger students. The inclusion of chapters on visual sources is particularly welcome. Highly recommended for all research libraries and for any undergraduate program that offers medieval history. Most of the essays are clearly written and accessible to any advanced undergraduate.—*M. E. Wiesner, University of Wisconsin—Milwaukee*

WS-1588 DF633 93-35728 CIP
Nicol, Donald M. **The Byzantine lady: ten portraits, 1250-1500.** Cambridge, 1994. 143p bibl index ISBN 0-521-45531-6, $39.95

With this slender volume, the eminent Byzantinist Donald M. Nicol follows in the footsteps of the famous Reformation scholar Roland H. Bainton and, as an emeritus professor, also produces a set of biographical sketches of prominent women from the culture with which he is so familiar. Bainton's work ultimately grew into the three volumes *Women of the Reformation in Germany and Italy* (CH, Apr'72), *Women of the Reformation in France and England* (CH, Jun'74), and *Women of the Reformation from Spain to Scandinavia* (1977). Nicol's subjects are all aristocrats and include several empresses; in many ways their life stories are quite similar, for most were used in diplomatic marriages inside and outside of Byzantium and found great comfort in religious devotion and activities. At times their devotion to religion put them at odds with male family members. The 13th-century nun and scholar Theodora Raoulaina, for example, was banished by her uncle the emperor for denouncing his religious policies. This is not a book that provides much analysis, but it certainly introduces all levels of readers to intelligent and competent women whose stories are largely unknown in the West and would be difficult to discover anywhere else for those who do not read Greek and Latin. General and academic readers at all levels.—*M. E. Wiesner, University of Wisconsin—Milwaukee*

WS-1589 DA229 94-31086 CIP
Parsons, John Carmi. **Eleanor of Castile: queen and society in thirteenth-century England.** St. Martin's, 1995. 364p bibl index ISBN 0-312-08649-0, $49.95

Parsons's study may be the best scholarly treatment of a medieval English queen yet written. Parsons looks at both Eleanor's role in 13th-century society and culture, and at *how* the myth of "good queen Eleanor" came to be constructed. In her 13th-century context, Eleanor emerges as a woman of intellectual interests, one with a keen appreciation for the use of network-building and a faithful retinue, a loyal and fertile wife, and a zealous seeker after land, wealth, and the power and status they connoted. After her death in 1290, perception of Eleanor had its ups and downs: the revered figure for whom Edward I built the famous Eleanor Crosses, the foreign she-devil of George Peele's *King Edward the First* (1593), and the saintly figure depicted in (and created by) Agnes Strickland's Victorian *Lives of the Queens of England from the Norman Conquest* (1840). Parsons has been writing about Eleanor for more than a decade; many of his trenchant findings about her insatiable quest for property, her match-making at court, and her elusive trail in her husband's counsels are no longer a surprise. His final comments on gender and the state are an appropriate conclusion to this short but definitive study. All levels.—*J. T. Rosenthal, SUNY at Stony Brook*

WS-1590 HQ1075 90-55736 CIP
Refiguring woman: perspectives on gender and the Italian Renaissance, ed. by Marilyn Migiel and Juliana Schiesari. Cornell, 1991. 285p index afp ISBN 0-8014-2538-7, $36.95; ISBN 0-8014-9771-X pbk, $12.95

A collection of 11 essays by historians, art historians, and literary scholars that grew out of a conference held at Cornell in 1988. Essays analyze visual and verbal representations of women in Renaissance Italy as well as women's role in the family and in civic life. Many of the essays offer revisions of revisionist views, nuancing the earlier works by Joan Kelly, Carolyn Merchant, and Christiane Klapisch that are now the backbone of feminist interpretations of the Renaissance. They explore both well-known and obscure texts; the inclusion of obscure texts by male as well as female authors is most welcome. The two essays by art historians also balance works that have previously been much discussed (representations of Judith) and those rarely mentioned (garden sculpture). The quality of the reproductions is very good, allowing the reader to see details important in the analysis. Most of the essays, especially the three by historians, are refreshingly jargon-free, though several of those by literary scholars presuppose familiarity with current psychoanalytical and new historicist criticism. Taken together, the collection demonstrates the complexity and ambiguity of gender in Renaissance Italy, and the importance of both women and men as creative agents. Upper-division undergraduates and above.—*M. E. Wiesner, University of Wisconsin—Milwaukee*

WS-1591 HQ1587 92-45709 CIP
Wiesner, Merry E. **Women and gender in early modern Europe.** Cambridge, 1993. 264p index ISBN 0-521-38459-1, $49.95; ISBN 0-521-38613-6 pbk, $14.95

Wiesner, well known for her numerous studies of early modern German women, has written a clear and stimulating textbook that introduces undergraduates and general readers to the topic of early modern European women and to the extensive literature available in English on various dimensions of their lives. Organized around the categories of body, mind, and spirit, the book includes discussions of male ideas about women, the female life cycle, women's economic role, literacy, women's role in the creation of culture, religion, witchcraft, and the relationship between gender and power, and reflects an impressive understanding of recent scholarship. Wiesner's command of this scholarship and the clarity of her analysis make this the best single volume on the topic. Although she analyzes women's role within the historical developments that traditionally have defined early modern Europe and shows the effects of these developments on women, Wiesner also explores women's private and domestic experiences and the period's gendered division between public and private power. Extensive bibliographies follow each chapter.—*J. Harrie, California State University, Bakersfield*

WS-1592 KD758 93-30673 CIP
Wife and widow in medieval England, ed. by Sue Sheridan Walker. Michigan, 1993. 221p index ISBN 0-472-10415-2, $39.50

Most of the essays in this collection deal with aspects of legal history, in particular the strategies widows and wives employed in claiming rights and property through litigation in both common law and ecclesiastical courts. Also included are valuable contributions on the political and socioeconomic experiences of medieval widows in England and Scotland. The authors of the essays have shared methodologies and approaches in ways that help the reader to consider these separate contributions as a unified whole. Some of the conclusions reached are more useful than others. Most compelling are Janet Loengard's and Sue Walker's works discussing dower litigation, Barbara Hanawalt's survey of how urban and rural widows used remarriage as only one of their options, and Richard Helmholz's discussion of the changing status of married women's wills. Most problematic is Cynthia Neville's article on the effects of rebellion on Scottish widows and wives, which suffers from a less measured and more polemical stance than the other essays. Nevertheless, each contribution provides important food for thought and grist for the continuing debate on the role of women in history. Highly recommended. Upper-division undergraduates and above.—*L. E. Mitchell, Alfred University*

◆ Africa

WS-1593   Orig

Barnes, Terri. **To live a better life: an oral history of women in the city of Harare, 1930-70,** by Terri Barnes and Everjoyce Win. Baobab Books, 1992. (Dist. by African Books Collective Ltd., The Jam Factory, 27 Park End St., Oxford OX1 1HU, UK) 230p ISBN 0-908311-35-4 pbk, $27.00

Barnes and Win have gathered interviews concerning life in Harare from 1930 to 1970. The focus is on women and women's voices, although information from and about men is also included. The words of 52 interviewees—41 women and 11 men—are quoted. Each interviewee is introduced with a very brief biography. As well, a six-page history section offers a context for the volume. Each of the 18 chapters has an introductory paragraph, after which Zimbabwean informants speak for themselves. No analysis is given; conclusions are left for the individual reader to draw. Topics covered range from the reason for urban migration, to girls' education in town, colonial pass laws, womens' voluntary associations, and prostitution. Some of the chapters are supplemented with material from newspaper clippings and instructive, old photographs of Harare. Written specifically with Zimbabwe O-level history students in mind, the book has very useful discussion questions and suggestions for oral history projects in Zimbabwe. General readers; community college students; lower-division undergraduates.—*R. Ellovich, North Carolina State University*

WS-1594   HD6212   91-23112 CIP

Berger, Iris. **Threads of solidarity: women in South African industry, 1900-1980.** Indiana, 1992. 368p bibl index afp ISBN 0-253-31173-X, $45.00; ISBN 0-253-20700-2 pbk, $18.95

With its complex combination of capitalism, Christianity, Western-style education and values, including racism—if not apartheid—South Africa has, since the 1940s and 1950s, provided a rich arena for research. To this Berger has added the gender component as a category of thought and catalyst for political action, together with its impact on women in South Africa's work force and labor unions. Dealing with white (Afrikaans), coloured, and black women, Berger traces their changing wage-labor functions and shifting roles from the turn of the century to the 1980s. Using complex data derived primarily from the Garment Worker's Union of the Transvaal and the Food and Canning Workers' Union and its African counterpart, Berger favors the "integrative approach," situating women in the combined context of work, family, culture, and community, as opposed exclusively to work-related phenomena. Demonstrating the increase of women in the work force, Berger shows the transformation from dependency and domesticity at the turn of the century, through the 1920s and '30s. By the 1940s and 1950s, wartime conditions combined with the exigencies of the apartheid state had transformed the structure of female wage-labor, bringing a flood of black women onto the industrial and domestic servant labor market. Events of the 1960s, '70s, and '80s culminated in repression and resistance. Berger shows that women were more inclined to become active union members when their participation could be centered around work-based and/or community-based culture and networks, or where unions had incorporated womens' concerns and informal community ties. Advanced undergraduate; graduate; faculty; professional.—*B. M. Perinbam, University of Maryland at College Park*

WS-1595   DT1058   91-9326 CIP

Bozzoli, Belinda. **Women of Phokeng: consciousness, life strategy, and migrancy in South Africa, 1900-1983,** by Belinda Bozzoli with the assistance of Mmantho Nkotsoe. Heinemann/J. Currey, 1991. 292p bibl index ISBN 0-435-08054-7, $45.00; ISBN 0-435-08056-3 pbk, $19.95

Based on interviews with 22 elderly Tswana women by a university-trained Tswana sociologist, this is fascinating social history. The book discusses the lives of these women during adolescence and retirement in the village of Phokeng near Rustenburg, Transvaal, as well as during the intervening years, many of them in the Johannesburg area where they worked as domestics. Although in some notable respects their lives are not representative of the whole black South African population, they do reflect the major changes that affected black people in the years from 1900 to 1983, as their traditional world felt the impact of an expanding industrial society. Bozzoli approached the project from a Marxist perspective but she

found that her subjects' attitudes toward their life experiences conformed neither to the Marxist model of capitalist oppression nor to the Africanists' paradigm of racial oppression. The women are shown to have developed a complex "ideology" that included traditionalism as well as nationalism, individualism as well as group consciousness. The author impressively sets her informants' reminiscences within a detailed historical context. The book will prove its usefulness in several disciplines. Recommended for all libraries supporting African studies.—*L. E. Meyer, Moorhead State University*

WS-1596   HQ1810   93-35396 CIP

Callaway, Barbara. **The heritage of Islam: women, religion, and politics in West Africa,** by Barbara Callaway and Lucy Creevey. L. Rienner, 1994. 221p bibl index afp ISBN 1-55587-253-0, $40.00; ISBN 1-55587-414-2 pbk, $19.95

Promising more than it delivers, this book deals primarily with Senegal and northern Nigeria (mainly Kano) with few significant references to Islamic communities elsewhere in West Africa. The historical introduction is disappointing. Comparisons—not justified in the discussion—between a state (Senegal) and a regional capital (Kano) call the overall conceptualization into question. A feminist paradigm is uncritically adumbrated, but the anthropology of Islam remains unexamined. These and other problems notwithstanding, the book provides useful insights. Treating a variety of topics such as Islamic law, education, and regional and local economies, as well as women within the political process, the authors arrive at partly predictable yet mainly interesting conclusions. Aside from the "progress" that is obviously "enhancing" women's education, political, and economic opportunities, the women of Senegal and, especially, women of Kano clearly continue to face obstacles. The discussion on Islam's redefinition of women's status is provocative. Although Islam provides individual rights, respect, inheritance privileges, property rights, and divorce regulations, the authors are correct in their judgment that its patriarchy largely suppressed freedoms and rights embedded in pre-Islamic norms. All levels.—*B. M. Perinbam, University of Maryland at College Park*

WS-1597   Orig

Cock, Jacklyn. **Colonels and cadres: war & gender in South Africa.** Oxford, 1994 (c1991). 253p bibl index ISBN 0-19-570706-0 pbk, $12.95

Proceeding from the premise that South Africa was at war during the 1980s, Cock (Univ. of the Witwatersrand, South Africa) endeavors to demonstrate that both black and white peoples' war experiences were crucially affected by gender relations. Through interviews with officers and common soldiers of both sexes and races, she effectively explores the separation of power between men and women and how, by exploiting long-established meanings of masculine and feminine, authorities prompted people to join the military effort. Based on research done between 1986 and 1990, most of it focused on the white community, this study reflects a reasonable feminist, antimilitary perspective that deserves attention. Cock, who clearly sees her analysis applying to other countries as well, found that on both sides in South Africa women were generally excluded from direct combat and from positions of leadership that would give them real power and authority over men. She identifies military experience with violence and aggression that men see as confirmation of their masculinity. This, she argues, would be eroded if females were fully integrated into the fighting services. Her conclusion is "that changing gender relations is necessary to reduce the risks of war." Though not always fully convincing, Cock's book is fascinating, provocative reading. It contains numerous excerpts from interviews and a good bibliography. Should be useful for courses in various disciplines. Lower-division undergraduate and up.—*L. E. Meyer, Moorhead State University*

WS-1598   Orig

Gender in Southern Africa: conceptual and theoretical issues, ed. by Ruth Meena. SAPES Books, 1993 (c1992). (Dist. by African Books Collective Ltd., The Jam Factory, 27 Park End St., Oxford OX1 1HU, UK) 201p index ISBN 0-7974-1162-3 pbk, $24.00

SAPES (Southern Africa Political Economy Series Trust), publisher of this collection, is a Zimbabwe-based organization that promotes research, teaching, and publication in southern Africa. The latter activity is particularly important given the problems that African scholars have in finding opportunities to publish their work. Essays in this volume come from the organization's Gender Planning Workshop. The collection includes six essays by African feminists who teach at four African universities. The authors charge that "mainstream" scholarship on development is dominated by Western and male biases and is unsuccessful in dealing with basic issues of poverty. Essays review feminist studies on Africa, research methodologies, the history of gender relations in southern Africa, economics and gender theory, sexualtiy, and AIDS. For feminists who want to know the views of African women scholars. Graduate; faculty.—*P. M. Martin, Indiana University-Bloomington*

WS-1599   DT510   95-34120 CIP
Greene, Sandra E. **Gender, ethnicity, and social change on the upper Slave Coast: a history of the Anlo-Ewe.** Heinemann/James Currey, 1996. 209p bibl index afp ISBN 0-435-08981-1, $60.00; ISBN 0-435-08979-X pbk, $23.95

Greene's study of gender and ethnicity among the Anlo-and Ewe-speakers of southeastern Ghana is an impressive contribution to an important field—impressive because in simultaneously conjugating gender and ethnicity, the author brings fresh perspectives to both. The chronological range is from the late 17th to the 20th century, when the region was affected by the Atlantic slave trade and the territory's social alchemy was changing in response to various in-migrations. Given these fluid dynamics, a range of ethnic-gender classificatory systems developed. Eschewing treatment of women exclusively as reactive "victims" of male dominance in these periods of rapid social change, the author instead locates her analysis in the much fuller set of institutional systems, including religious organizations. Her findings show that the external and internal forces of social modification—more than the drive from individual or collective human agency—contributed largely to the process that brought changes to both gender and ethnicity. In the process, women's interests were marginalized. On a broader level, Greene's work makes important contributions to the articulating nature of precolonial ethnicity and gender both within and outside the family, to the role of nonkin groups therein, and to a different understanding of the history of marriage in Africa. Upper-division undergraduates and above.— *B. M. Perinbam, University of Maryland College Park*

WS-1600   DT2990   91-9980 CIP
Mothers of the revolution: the war experiences of thirty Zimbabwean women, comp. and ed. by Irene Staunton. J. Currey/Indiana, 1991 (c1990). 306p afp ISBN 0-253-35450-1, $35.00; ISBN 0-253-28797-9 pbk, $12.95

Life histories are an increasingly popular genre in the study of women's experience in Africa (e.g., *Life Histories of African Women*, ed. by Patricia Romero, CH, Oct'88; *Three Swahili Women*, ed. by Sarah Mirza and Margaret Strobel, CH, Nov'89; and Jean Davison's *Voices from Mutira*, CH, May'90). These are significant sources when women's voices are "hidden," and even more significant in societies where lack of access to education gives women the highest illiteracy rate. The life histories of 30 Zimbabwean women have been collected by Staunton with the help of female Zimbabwean informants and translators. The women whose stories are documented were all engaged in the liberation struggle against the British in different ways: e.g., they were mothers of freedom fighters, provided food and other support to guerillas, lived in compulsory resettlement villages, dealt with colonial security forces. The accounts, which include their opinion of their situation in Zimbabwe since independence, are published unedited. Together, these stories are a powerful and eloquent tribute to the suffering and triumph of the Zimbabwean liberation struggle. Useful glossary and photographs of each woman. All levels.—*P. M. Martin, Indiana University-Bloomington*

WS-1601   Orig
Nigerian women in historical perspective, ed. by Bolanle Awe. Sankore/Bookcraft, 1992. (Dist. by African Books Collective Ltd., The Jam Factory, 27 Park End St., Oxford OX1 1HU, UK) 167p bibl ISBN 978-2030-07-4, $17.00

A collection of 11 short biographical accounts by Nigerian historians and writers on women. Together, they argue for the important role that women have played within patriarchal and male-dominated societies. The point is illustrated from different perspectives in time and space: the place of women in myths of origin; their

political and economic power in precolonial societies; the loss of power under British colonial rule and the efforts of women to counter this; and the influence of educated and elite women in contemporary society. An essay on a Muslim woman shows that Islam did not necessarily limit women's contribution to society. Through writing these accounts of individual women and placing them in a broad historical context, the writers also hope to point out the essential role that modern women should play in the development process. These well-researched and semipopular accounts are also highly readable, making them accessible to readers at many levels. It is especially useful to have a book written and edited by African women, and published in Africa.—*P. M. Martin, Indiana University-Bloomington*

WS-1602   DT2913   91-41251 CIP
Schmidt, Elizabeth. **Peasants, traders, and wives: Shona women in the history of Zimbabwe, 1870-1939.** Heinemann, 1992. 289p bibl index ISBN 0-435-08064-4, $45.00

Schmidt's book is an important addition to the literature on peasant studies in colonial Africa. Several historians have written on the impact of settler colonialism and capitalism on African farmers and on African responses in Southern Rhodesia (Zimbabwe), e.g., T.O. Ranger (*Peasant Consciousness and Guerilla War in Zimbabwe*, CH, Mar'86) and R. Palmer (*Land and Racial Domination in Rhodesia*, 1977). However, these scholars have neglected the critical role of women farmers in the formation of the peasantry and in resistance to proletarianization. Schmidt examines African patriarchy. She analyzes the alliance of African elders and European colonial authorities to control women and younger men, especially in regard to sexuality and reproductive powers, through legal constraints. She also discusses the attitudes toward missionaries toward women's roles and female initiatives in the face of the deteriorating status of women. The study is based on solid research and knowledge of feminist literature. Photographs; useful bibliography. Advanced undergraduate; graduate; faculty.—*P. M. Martin, Indiana University-Bloomington*

WS-1603   HD6212   CIP
Swaisland, Cecillie. **Servants and gentlewomen to the golden land: the emigration of single women from Britain to southern Africa, 1820-1939.** Berg/Natal, 1993. 186p bibl index ISBN 0-85496-745-1, $39.95

Swaisland describes the experience of an intrepid and small band of single British women—those who emigrated to South Africa. The Victorians focused their Malthusian fears of overpopulation on a presumed "surplus" of a million unmarried women. One response to that fear was the development of societies to promote and assist female emigration. After 1860, societies recruited only among the middle classes. Although later they embraced the imperialist agenda, migrants' motives, Swaisland shows, remained personal and vocational. Her data come mostly from the societies' records. Her account both closely follows their affairs and reflects their middle to upper middle class viewpoints. After broadly surveying her subject, Swaisland presents the particular experience of each occupation: domestics; children's nurses; governesses; teachers; and health professionals. Black South Africa is almost entirely outside her scope. So, too, is Afrikaner society. Rich in detail, the book lacks only the sturdier framework of issues raised in the scholarship on emigration. Swaisland (Institute for Social and Economic Research, Rhodes Univ.) started the book as a thesis at Oxford. Good bibliography. Advanced undergraduate; graduate.—*P. K. Cline, Earlham College*

WS-1604   HQ1800   91-139998 MARC
Women and gender in southern Africa to 1945, ed. by Cherryl Walker. D. Philip/J. Currey, 1991 (c1990). (Dist. by Indiana) 390p bibl index ISBN 0-85255-205-X, $35.00

With an excellent historical analysis of changing relations in southern Africa from the precolonial era to 1945, this study has moved the discussion on gender, class, and race in Africa forward. Going beyond "victim" analysis—demonstrating womens' subordination to men in precolonial and colonial Africa, as well as their declining socioeconomic status in the face of European colonialism—these essays discuss conclusions, from a highly selective database, that have a wider application for the rest of Africa. Presented by an interdisciplinary team of 12 white scholars (9 of whom are South African-based), the skillfully argued findings show, on the one hand, the extent to which some women became actively engaged with the invasive forces of domination (e.g., colonialism, capitalism, Christianity, racism, patriarchal and domestic ideologies), meeting them head-on. On the other hand, the essays demonstrate women's varied reactions, including incorporation and adjustment to imported values, resistance, changing roles in traditional homesteads, and the use of the home (private space, where the struggle and resistance to racial oppression either began or continued) for activities of public political significance. Although the conclusions resemble those of a "victim" analysis, the subtle, finely tuned discussion, looking for meaning from within southern African societies and cultures, results in a fresh approach to women's involvements in the African sociopolitical and economic processes in place for the last 100 years. College, university, and public libraries.—*B. M. Perinbam, University of Maryland at College Park*

WS-1605   HT1326   91-32722 CIP
Wright, Marcia. **Strategies of slaves & women: life-stories from East/Central Africa.** L. Barber/J. Currey, 1993. 238p bibl index ISBN 0-936508-27-2, $24.95; ISBN 0-936508-28-0 pbk, $12.95

Indigenous autobiography, especially of women during the early colonial period, is uncommon in East and Central Africa. Wright has employed life stories before, but this volume brings together in a convincing and fully contextualized manner the contrasting reminiscences of five women and a man who were intimately acquainted with the slave trade and with missionaries, from the mid-19th to the mid-20th century. Some of the stories were collected and contemporaneously "processed" by missionaries; another was recorded and edited by a son in the venacular. Wright sets those earlier narratives within a social historical framework of the slave trade, of domestic slavery, of internal displacement and migration, and of feminist consciousness. She satisfies the question of representativeness of the narratives by sampling early colonial frontier court records, but even if one remains skeptical about their evidentiary value, the six life stories are lively, illustrative, and very well woven by Wright into an overall reconstruction. Adequate bibliography, maps. Advanced undergraduate; graduate; faculty.—*R. I. Rotberg, Lafayette College*

◆ Asia & Oceania

WS-1606   Orig
Ali, Aruna Asaf. **The resurgence of Indian women.** Radiant, 1991. (Dist. by Advent Books) 264 index ISBN 81-7027-185-3, $30.00

Ali, who played a prominent role in India's struggle for independence, presents a detailed and lively account of India's women's movement as well as its freedom movement. The first part of the book surveys women's status within various religious traditions and provides the history of reformers and of the women's movement. The next part examines the role of Indian women in various struggles against British colonial rule, ranging from their participation in the agitation against the partition of Bengal in the 1900s to the "quit India" movement in the 1940s. The third and final section deals with social and economic changes in the post-independence period and discusses the obvious disparities in educational and economic opportunities between men and women, as well as among women themselves. Ali points out that as in development programs, in which gains have been appropriated largely by men and women of upper and middle classes, the women's movement has tended to reflect mainly the interests and concerns of the urban middle class. She argues that the women's movement needs to develop a broad base among the masses of women in India who live in urban slums and villages, where they still face the problems of poverty and illiteracy. The author's approach and conclusions are both provocative and informative. Excellent notes and index. Suitable for academic libraries at all levels and for public libraries.—*H. S. Jassal, SUNY College at Cortland*

WS-1607   Aust. CIP
Allen, Judith A. **Rose Scott: vision and revision in feminism.** Oxford, 1994. 331p bibl index ISBN 0-19-554846-9, $53.00

Widely published in her native Australia, Allen held there the first chair of women's studies. Very recently she became professor of history and director of woman's studies at Indiana University. In *Rose Scott* her purposes are revisionist. To that end, she rescues Scott (1847-1925) from gender studies' condescension, feminist theory's presentist agenda, and history's slights. Scott is a conservative choice. Modern feminism positions her as an "agent of bourgeois hegemony" and a hopeless puritan (rigidly opposed to mixed-gender swimming, for example). Her reputation is as a philanthropist and *salonière* (famous, like Gertrude Stein, because her friends were). To rescue Scott, Allen contextualizes her time, place, and circumstance. Dense description of Scott's complicated family, extensive illustration from her private and public writings, and candid assessment of women's experiences all situate Scott responding to a culture that represented women as "creatures of sex," first and foremost. Her public mission, "to challenge the degradation of women," made Scott old-fashioned by 1920; equality had captured the movement's agenda. Allen repositions Scott among feminism's foremothers. First-rate footnotes and bibliography. Upper-division undergraduate and up.—*P. K. Cline, Earlham College*

WS-1608   Orig
Basu, Aparna. **Mridula Sarabhai: rebel with a cause.** Oxford, 1996. 275p bibl index ISBN 0-19-563110-2, $24.95

Basu's book is a delightfully intimate journey into 20th-century Indian history. Born the privileged daughter of a wealthy industrial textile giant, Sarabhai was involved in several ways with the movement for freedom from British rule. Under Gandhi's influence, she became a full-time soldier in the Indian political war of independence. She did not marry, because she was afraid that marriage would bring bondage and possible restrictions on her activities and political opinions. Her opinions were different. Sarabhai was in prison for her political activities when her brother, a student at Oxford, fell seriously ill. The British offered to release her on parole, but that would have meant publicly accepting the principle of limited access in daily life. She demanded unconditional release, choosing not to see her dying brother. Basu has demonstrated Sarabhai's nonconformity well by detailing her support for Sheikh Abdullah on Kashmir. Sarabhai remains an important actor in Indian history, although she never held office. All levels.—*N. N. Kalia, SUNY College at Buffalo*

WS-1609   HD6197   91-30670 CIP
Brinton, Mary C. **Women and the economic miracle: gender and work in postwar Japan.** California, 1993. 299p bibl index afp ISBN 0-520-07536-6, $30.00

Brinton's book is about what its subtitle states: gender and work in postwar Japan. It is based on the study that the author, a sociologist, conducted in Japan in 1983-85 and 1987-88. Brinton draws on historical materials, survey and statistical data, and her own interviews. In the first two chapters, she compares the role of women and their work in the US economy with that of Japan's and compares human capital development in the two societies. The following three chapters are devoted to Japan. Brinton's analysis represents rather American and feminist views as chapter headings indicate: "Gendered system in employment," "Gendered work lives," and "Gendered education." The major strength of this book is the inclusion of numerous statistical data, though many of these are among data published by the Ministry of Labor and other government offices in Japan. Graduate; faculty.—*M. Y. Rynn, University of Scranton*

WS-1610   HQ1866   91-37965 CIP
Bulbeck, Chilla. **Australian women in Papua New Guinea: colonial passages, 1920-1960.** Cambridge, 1992. 327p bibl index ISBN 0-521-41285-4, $64.95

Australia became the colonial power in Papua New Guinea by gaining the southern part of the country from the British in 1905 and by capturing the northern sector from the Germans during WW I. Bulbeck's fascinating study focuses on the experiences of 19 single and married Australian women who lived in various environments in Papua New Guinea—among hospitals, schools, missions, plantations, and administrative headquarters—from 1920 to 1960, sometimes under very harsh and isolated conditions. Valuable chapters discuss the close connection between imperialism and racism, especially in matters involving sex. Bulbeck's thesis is that colonial mentality among Australians in Papua New Guinea differed very little from the social Darwinist thinking prevalent everywhere

Europeans governed nonwhite peoples. It is doubtful, however, that white women were more racist than white men, as has often been alleged. Well documented, with valuable appendixes and maps, this book is a sound contribution to understanding the workings of colonial government and the attitudes of colonial society. General; advanced undergraduate; graduate; faculty.—*W. W. Reinhardt, Randolph-Macon College*

WS-1611 HQ1743 92-6420 CIP

Calman, Leslie J. **Toward empowerment: women and movement politics in India.** Westview, 1992. 230p bibl index afp ISBN 0-8133-8103-7, $45.00; ISBN 0-8133-1695-2 pbk, $15.95

Calman's study is based on interviews with more than 30 participants in the Indian women's movement, analysis of statistical information and unpublished papers available at various research institutes in India, and examination of newspaper accounts of women's protest activities since the late 1970s. Calman, a political scientist, uses contemporary sociological perspectives on the "new social movements" (e.g., human rights, feminism, and environmentalism) to explain why a *women's* movement has arisen in India. She argues that a heightened consciousness about women's economic subjugation and social oppression (especially in the forms of rape and dowry death) has coincided with the Indian government's failure to protect and expand women's rights. Calman draws a distinction between the "rights wing," which emphasizes equality for women under the law, and the "empowerment wing" of the women's movement. The more activist and grassroots oriented empowerment wing has been more successful in attracting rural women and the urban poor because of the priority it has placed on their achievement of economic and social rights through land ownership, improved wages, political participation, self-determination, and increased self-confidence and assertiveness. Recommended. General; advanced undergraduate; graduate; faculty.—*B. Tavakolian, Denison University*

WS-1612 94-980912 Orig

Carter, Marina. **Lakshmi's legacy: the testimonies of Indian women in 19th century Mauritius.** Editions de l'Ocean Indien, 1994. (Dist. by African Books Collective Ltd., The Jam Factory, 27 Park End St., Oxford OX1 1HU, UK) 282p bibl ISBN 99903-0-168-9 pbk, $27.00

Carter is an accomplished scholar in the field of Mauritian studies. In this book she sets out "to penetrate the world of Indian women in indenture and to present new evidence of their experiences through a close analysis of the petitions and other verbal and written statements which they initiated." The result is a thorough investigation of conditions that influenced women to join the labor migration, of life at sea, of their living conditions in Mauritius, and—in many cases—of their escape or return to India. This information is gleaned from documents (registers, records, letters, and petitions written by or for Indian women) and other historical sources. In many cases Carter was able to put such historical documentary information into a case study with a photograph of the person in question. Scholars have tended to depict women as passive participants in the migration of men (their fathers, husbands, or brothers). This may be true in some cases, but readers find here the initiative and independence of Indian women as decision makers and actors. Graduate students and researchers.—*B. M. du Toit, University of Florida*

WS-1613 Orig

Chaudhuri, Maitrayee. **Indian women's movement: reform and revival.** Radiant, 1993. (Dist. by Advent Books) 210p bibl index ISBN 81-7027-163-2, $27.50

A timely and scholarly addition to the literature on the women's movement, covering the period from the 1850s to the late 1940s. Chaudhuri draws on historical sources in an attempt to construct the dominant discourse on the women's question in India and its critical encounter with colonialism. The women's movement is examined as an essential part of India's entry into modernity. The dominant discourse on women as influenced by various social reformers, Hindu resurgence, Islamic revivalism, and the national independence movement are presented. Chaudhuri evaluates the role of the middle class, the process of selection, rejection, assimilation, and modification of religious and secular ideologies, and the dominant trends within the women's movement as it shifted from reform to revival. The author also discusses women's issues, such as child

marriage, polygamy, widow remarriage, sati, purdha, education, and rights of inheritance. Unlike a feminist historiography, this richly documented study provides sociological analyses of the impact of socioeconomic and political forces on the status and roles of women, the dynamics of communal conflicts, politicization of religious identities, and women's movement in contemporary India. Advanced undergraduate; graduate; faculty.—*D. A. Chekki, University of Winnipeg*

WS-1614 Orig

Chowdhry, Prem. **The veiled women: shifting gender equations in rural Haryana, 1880-1990.** Oxford, 1994. 461p bibl index ISBN 0-19-563134-X, $29.95

Haryana, a state neighboring Delhi and bordering Punjab, was essentially a producer of low value food-cum-fodder crops during the British rule of India. The British perpetuated this kind of economy because it allowed Haryana to recruit workers from impoverished village youth. In this context, Haryanavi women were judged solely in terms of their reproductive capacity and their usefulness as agricultural laborers. This ideology was sustained because women were willing parties to their own exploitative marginalization through a gender conditioning that internalized inferiority as their legitimate evaluation. In independent India, the Haryanavi economy dramatically changed with the availability of irrigation, emphasis on cash crops, and mechanization of farming. Haryana today is the richest state of India. Chowdhry has produced an elegant piece of meticulous scholarship by combining a wide range of information from historical court records, census tracts, and gazetteers with proverbs and folktales. The result is a highly readable account in which hard data are intertwined with folk wisdom to illuminate the paradox of women's complicity in the maintenance of patriarchy. Graduate, faculty.—*N. N. Kalia, Buffalo State College*

WS-1615 Aust. CIP

Clarke, Patricia. **Life lines: Australian women's letters and diaries, 1788-1840,** by Patricia Clarke and Dale Spender. Allen & Unwin, 1992. 261p bibl index ISBN 1-86373-124-5 pbk, $22.95

It is possible to critize this volume of letters and diaries from early colonial Australia. Sometimes the introduction is a paraphrase of the material that follows. In other instances the excerpt presented is so short that it is unclear why the editors bothered to include it. In yet another case, in examining frontier medical practices the editors pass without comment the fact that a woman has unintentionally poisoned her husband and herself with a mercury salt. Yet if there are points to criticize, there are also points to admire. A large number of the letters and diaries are both beautifully written and very informative. The description of a journey from Sydney to the newly founded settlement at Bathurst by Elizabeth Hawkins and her family is particularly well done. What is more, the selections are true to the title. Here are women at the edge of the known world who desperately need a lifeline to those they have left. This book does a fine job of conveying their feelings. General; undergraduate.—*R. E. Schreiber, Indiana University at South Bend*

WS-1616 HQ684 92-31376 CIP

Ebrey, Patricia Buckley. **The inner quarters: marriage and the lives of Chinese women in the Sung period.** California, 1993. 332p bibl index afp ISBN 0-520-08156-0, $45.00; ISBN 0-520-08158-7 pbk, $16.00

An outstanding book by a leading authority on Chinese social history. Ebrey (Univ. of Illinois) effectively draws on a wide range of sources, narrative as well as expository, poetry and prose, to produce an account that relates the history of women to economic developments (increased urbanization and commercialization), to class and status, and to values and ideas (Neo-Confucian and other), many of them shared by women and men. Of the 15 chapters some deal with marriage as a social/economic institution (including an important discussion of dowries), others with women's roles (motherhood, widowhood, concubines), and there is one on adultery, incest, and divorce. This is an account too nuanced and complex to lend itself to easy summation, an account informed by the author's appreciation for the complexity of things and her sensitivity to the crosscurrents of history. Clearly written and well illustrated, it is essential reading for anyone interested in traditional China or in the comparative history of women. Advanced undergraduates and above.—*C. Schirokauer, City College, CUNY*

WS-1617   HQ1064   92-14990 CIP
Freed, Anne O. **The changing worlds of older women in Japan,** by Anne O. Freed with Yukiko Kurokawa and Hiroshi Kawai. Knowledge, Ideas & Trends, 1993 (c1992). 249p bibl ISBN 1-879198-10-X, $27.95; ISBN 1-879198-09-6 pbk, $17.95

Freed is a social work clinician/educator interested in gerontology, and has also done work on other societies. This book is based on her videotape interviews of 27 elderly Japanese women, aged 65 to mid-90s, all but three living in Tokyo. They were selected through senior centers, welfare offices, and nursing homes. The author wanted to learn how those women's lives were "transformed by the Sino-Japanese War [i.e., the conflict known as the "China Affair" or "incident" that merged into WW II], World War II, and westernization and urbanization." Each of chapters 5 to 21 covers one woman. Their stories are fascinating. The author's conclusion, however, remains rather pedestrian, as do the introductory chapters, which are not always accurate. The enormous amount of gerontological information and research materials readily available in Japanese are apparently not used at all. Freed's failure to follow the standard English translation of commonly used terms and events is regrettable and confusing. The case studies would have been better published simply as a collection of stories about some elderly Japanese women. Any reader unfamiliar with Japanese society should first read a standard work, such as Edwin Reischauer's *The Japanese* (CH, Nov'77).— *M. Y. Rynn, University of Scranton*

WS-1618   Aust. CIP
Freedom bound I: documents on women in colonial Australia, ed. by Marian Quartly, Susan Janson, and Patricia Grimshaw. Allen & Unwin, 1995. (Dist. by Paul & Company) 193p bibl index ISBN 1-86373-735-9 pbk, $22.95

WS-1618a   Aust. CIP
Freedom bound II: documents on women in modern Australia, ed. by Katie Holmes and Marilyn Lake. Allen & Unwin, 1995. (Dist. by Paul & Company) 208p index ISBN 1-86373-736-7 pbk, $22.95

These two interesting primary-source collections eavesdrop on the varied lives of Australian women in the 19th and 20th centuries. Letters to families and friends, journal entries, articles, and essays for newspapers speak to both paramount and peripheral issues. Volume 1 is in four parts (each containing 15 to 20 documents, each preceded by one or two contextual paragraphs): women in the convict society, 1788-1840; women in a masculine democracy, 1840-1860; women in urban and rural frontiers, 1860-1885; and women seeking social solutions, 1886-1901. Interesting documents include writings by an English lady discovering the natural wonders of New South Wales; a wife advising her husband on raising sheep; and an aboriginal woman's tale of mission life. Volume 2 is similarly divided, with parts on maternal citizenship, 1900-1920; the "Modern Desire for Pleasure and Freedom," 1921-1940; "Imagining Equality," 1941-1969; and "Liberation," 1969-1993. Documents in this section discuss the work of a woman in parliament, attacks on women workers, the art of marriage, affirmative action, the problems of an aboriginal mother, an interview with a lesbian, and a letter from a victim of sexual harassment whose life was reduced to a "zombie-like existence." The collection generally will enable readers to reflect more critically on the priorities and goals in Australian history, society, and culture, and to recognize the energy, bravery, and determination of Australian women who fought for rights and freedoms now largely taken for granted. All levels.— *W. W. Reinhardt, Randolph-Macon College*

WS-1619   HX546   94-24723 CIP
Gilmartin, Christina Kelley. **Engendering the Chinese Revolution: radical women, communist politics, and mass movements in the 1920s.** California, 1995. 303p bibl index afp ISBN 0-520-08981-2, $40.00

The Chinese Communist revolution has long been regarded as a man-centered phenomenon. Indeed, most of the existing studies of the Chinese Communist Party (CCP) focus on its male leaders and members. Female Chinese Communist revolutionaries, even revolutionary elites, seldom become central actors in a historical narrative of the revolution. By using gender as an important category of analysis in the study of the CCP, Gilmartin has made a significant contribution to understanding a less-studied dimension of modern Chinese history. Basing her work on extensive research of party documents and contemporary literature, supplemented by interviews with female revolutionary activists, Gilmartin pro-

duces a fascinating account of how women participated in the revolution, how the revolution's discourses challenged the patriarchal family structure and man-dominated social and legal practice in Chinese society, and how the CCP formed radical programs on gender transformation as part of its grand plans for transforming China. Gilmartin also reveals that despite its radical gender discourses, the CCP "reproduced and reinscribed central aspects of the gender system from the larger society within its own organizations." Consequently, "a patriarchal gender system that proved to be enduring grew within the body politic of the CCP." Those interested in China's modern history, the Chinese revolution, and women's studies will find this book highly valuable. Upper-division undergraduates and above.— *J. Chen, Southern Illinois University at Carbondale*

WS-1620   DS481   91-22174 CIP
Gupte, Pranay. **Mother India: a political biography of Indira Gandhi.** Scribner, 1992. 593p bibl index ISBN 0-684-19296-9, $30.00

For centuries Indians referred to their country as "Bharat Mata" or "Mother India," but recently the phrase has come to be associated with Indira Gandhi whose influence dominated India's politics from the death of her father Jawaharlal Nehru in 1964, to the death of her son Rajiv in 1991. This is a fine political biography and a lucid analysis of the factors that have influenced the course of contemporary Indian history. Gandhi is studied as a daughter of privilege and as a participant in the nationalist movement against the British Raj. Her valuable apprenticeship after 1947 led ultimately to her own election and to an amazing accretion of power through her own Congress(I) Party, to the Bangladesh War, and to the outrageous "transformation" of democracy during the two year "Emergency" from 1975 to 1977. The violent campaign by militant Sikhs in the Punjab to establish an independent "Khalisan" led to Gandhi's ordering a military assault on the Golden Temple and her own assassination. Her aid to the Liberation Tigers of Tamil or Eelam in Sri Lanka contributed not only to the continuing tragedy there, but also to the assassination of Rajiv by Tamil separatists. Gupte credits Gandhi with forwarding the noble ideas she inherited, but he is generally critical. Scholarly, well written, well documented with complete bibliography, this is a landmark study. All levels.— *W. W. Reinhardt, Randolph-Macon College*

WS-1621   HQ1391   90-28750 CIP
Heroic with grace: legendary women of Japan, ed. by Chieko Irie Mulhern. M.E. Sharpe, 1991. 326p index afp ISBN 0-87332-527-3, $39.95

The legendary women about which seven scholars of Japanese literature write in this collection lived from the proto-history of approximately the fourth century to the present day. The legends have evolved from the actual lives of women who were reigning empresses, writers, the widow of the first Minamoto shogun, a woman warrior, a reporter, and an actress. The two best essays—those on the warrior Tomoe and the actress Takamine Hideko—study a particular text in its historical context to illuminate both how women lived and how they have been remembered or wanted to be remembered. Some of the other chapters are less satisfactory as history. Controversial theories are reported as certain fact; a historical novel is the filter for reinterpreting the chronicles; and in the recent history there is carelessness about the names and dates. Nevertheless, the collection provides a welcome glimpse of how the Japanese themselves have crafted legends of women. Lower-division undergraduates, community college students, and general readers.— *S. A. Hastings, Purdue University*

WS-1622   D810   95-2162 CIP
Hicks, George. **The comfort women: Japan's brutal regime of enforced prostitution in the Second World War.** W.W. Norton, 1995 (c1994). 303p bibl index ISBN 0-393-03807-6, $25.00

Since 1991, when the first three Korean women brought suit against the Japanese government for their enforced prostitution during the Pacific War, "comfort women" have been much in the news. Bringing together Korean, Japanese, Dutch, and other documents, including some accounts by the victims themselves, Hicks describes not only the wartime experience of these women but also the process through which their stories have been brought to light. His materials, secured from various activists on behalf of the comfort women, are all the more valuable for his careful attributions and the bibliography at the end of the book. Unfortunately, Hicks's framing narrative fails to incorporate some of the insights his sources suggest. Perpetuating stereotypical views, he treats Asian women as an undifferentiated low-status group subject to patriarchal definitions of chastity and defilement, when in fact there was considerable variation in customs and values within East and Southeast Asia. Although Hicks notes that Korean feminists warn against making a simple dichotomy between professional Japanese prostitutes and innocent Korean draftees, he does so throughout the book.—*S. A. Hastings, Purdue University*

WS-1623   DS885   95-25165 CIP
Hopper, Helen M. **A new woman of Japan: a political biography of Katô Shidzue.** Westview, 1996. 304p bibl index afp ISBN 0-8133-8971-2, $49.95

Much about Hopper's study of Katô Shidzue will make it a welcome addition to the growing literature on women in modern Japan. Particularly valuable are its great wealth of detail and its attempt to cover all significant aspects of Shidzue's life, both in narrative synopses and in absorbing anecdotes of her encounters with Margaret Sanger, Agnes Smedley, and other leading figures of late-19th-and early-20th-century women's activism for family planning, birth control, and equality in home and workplace. Hopper begins with Shidzue's early family background and follows her through her varied and active career to the early 1990s. The text is amply documented and well indexed, making it especially useful to undergraduates in search of detailed material on aspects of modern Japan. Notably missing, however, are a rigorous analytical and critical treatment of central issues in Shidzue's life, and a sustained attempt to develop a theoretical dimension to the discussion. Although the story is engrossing and ably told, there is also at times a distracting "gee whiz" tone to the narrative voice. All levels.—*C. L. Yates, Earlham College*

WS-1624   DS481   93-10815 CIP
Jayakar, Pupul. **Indira Gandhi: an intimate biography.** Pantheon Books, 1993. 410p index ISBN 0-679-42479-2, $30.00

Indira Nehru Gandhi (1917-84) left an indelible impression on the history of India and the world for almost four decades. This biography is written by a person who knew her intimately for more than 30 years. The work is in eight parts. The first three sections deal with Indira's childhood; her spotty formal schooling; her adolescent years in the shadow of her father, Jawaharlal Nehru; her marriage to Feroze Gandhi; and her apprenticeship in the politics of the Congress party. Parts 4 to 8 form the most important segments of the work, treating Gandhi's career as prime minister, her splitting of the Congress party to liquidate the "Old Guard," her role in the liberation of East Pakistan (Bangladesh) in 1971, her assumption of authoritarian rule in 1975, her life in political wilderness during 1977-80, her return to power in 1980, and her tragic death at the hands of Sikh assassins in 1984. Straightforward and pleasantly written, Jayakar's account of Indira Gandhi is perhaps the best available biography. Jayakar has accomplished her task creditably in providing many insights into the complex character of her subject. What emerges is a captivating portrait of a great person of numerous paradoxes, a reluctant mover and shaker of the destinies of millions of Indians. All levels.—*B. G. Gokhale, emeritus, Wake Forest University*

WS-1625   HQ1767   94-1166 CIP
Ko, Dorothy. **Teachers of the inner chambers: women and culture in seventeenth-century China.** Stanford, 1994. 395p bibl index afp ISBN 0-8047-2358-3, $45.00; ISBN 0-8047-2359-1 pbk, $16.95

Focusing on gentry women of the prosperous lower Yangtze region, Ko shows how class, culture, and women's communities helped shape the construction of gender in late imperial China. In that era of rapidly growing commercial publishing, women were an important part of the reading—and writing—public, and women's literary clubs flourished. Although they did not question Confucian orthodoxy, women sometimes subverted it. Ko's account of women's reading of Tang Xianzu's late Ming play *The Peony Pavilion* in terms of Wang Yangming's neo-Confucian cult of *qing* (emotion, feeling, love) is an especially insightful and original examination of the values and culture of these women. Ko challenges simplistic depictions of women as victims and argues that within their social and cultural constraints, a women's literary culture developed that tran-

scended public and private spheres and redefined womanhood. Although admittedly limited to the minority of leisured and literate upper-class women, this multifaceted book is a breakthrough in the study of women as part of Chinese cultural and social history. Recommended for upper-division undergraduates and above.—*R. E. Entenmann, St. Olaf College*

WS-1626   Orig
Kumar, Radha. **The history of doing: an illustrated account of movements for women's rights and feminism in India, 1800-1990.** Verso, 1994 (c1993). 203p index ISBN 0-86091-455-0, $64.95; ISBN 0-86091-665-0 pbk, $19.95

Kumar, a feminist scholar, presents a well-organized, clearly written critical analysis of the women's movement in India. She shows how the movement initially emerged as part of the social reform movement and later became an important segment of the nationalist movement. Using old and new documents, excerpts from letters, and photographs, Kumar delineates the growing involvement of women and the development of the early women's organizations. The book's major contribution lies, however, in the examination of the dynamics of the women's movement in the postindependence period. Kumar provides a vivid description of the contemporary feminist movement, focusing on the campaign against dowry and dowry-related violence, and on the agitation against rape. Kumar's study demonstrates how socioeconomic and political issues, the role of feminist groups, and the relationships they have to party and mass-based organizations are intertwined. The concluding section raises some crucial questions about feminist movements in India and elsewhere regarding tradition and modernity, ethnic and religious identities, and nationalism. Upper-division undergraduates and above.—*D. A. Chekki, University of Winnipeg*

WS-1627   DS481.G23   90-49859 MARC
Malhotra, Inder. **Indira Gandhi: a personal and political biography.** Northeastern University, 1991 (c1989). 363p index afp ISBN 1-55553-095-8, $29.95

Malhotra, one of India's most influential journalists, has written a balanced book about one of modern India's most enigmatic leaders. This work does justice to the remarkable life, as well as the highly controversial career, of the pivotal female member of the "Nehru dynasty." Indira Gandhi, born in 1917, was the daughter of the first Prime Minister of India, Jawaharlal Nehru, the granddaughter of one of India's most wealthy lawyers, Motilal Nehru, and the mother of Rajiv Gandhi, prime minister of India from 1984 until 1989. She achieved great political power but her life was marked by loneliness and tragedy. Her mother died young and her father was often in prison during the fight for independence. Gandhi separated from her husband before his early death, and her youngest son, Sanjay, died in a plane crash. As prime minister from 1966 until 1977 and again from 1980 to 1984, she dominated India. Her assassination in 1984 gave a tragic end to a life providing ample material for the careful reconstruction and analysis this book offers. College, university, and public libraries.—*R. D. Long, Eastern Michigan University*

WS-1628   DS897   94-39864 CIP
Nakano, Makiko. **Makiko's diary: a merchant wife in 1910 Kyoto,** by Nakano Makiko; tr. with introd. and notes by Kazuko Smith. Stanford, 1995. 256p bibl index afp ISBN 0-8047-2440-7, $45.00; ISBN 0-8047-2441-5 pbk, $14.95

Kept for the year 1910 by the wife of a young pharmacist in Kyoto, this diary offers an inside view of women's work in a Japanese family. Nakano prepares meals, makes pickles, sews clothing, shops for gifts, supervises servants, and presides at household rituals. At the same time, one woman's methodical recording of the events of her own life tells much about urban men; her husband is constantly busy with professional associations, alumni groups, educational institutions, and cultural activities. The book includes more than 60 photographs of the Nakano family and the city of Kyoto. Kazuko Smith has provided a thoughtful introduction and rich annotations. The kinship charts, lists of frequently mentioned individuals, diagrams, and maps add to both the usefulness of the volume for experts on Japan and its accessibility to those for whom it will be an introduction to Japanese society. All levels.—*S. A. Hastings, Purdue University*

WS-1629   Orig
National Women's Education Centre (Japan), comp. **Women in a changing society: the Japanese scene.** Unesco, 1990. 218p pbk $25.00

This excellent volume is one of five publications by UNESCO on Women's Studies in the Pacific. Compiled by Japanese researchers from original studies and works translated from Japanese, the collection consists of five sections: general background of concern for women's status in Japan; the family; mass media; work; and socialization. The essays are short, and lack footnotes and correct citations, but there are adequate tables of data (without, however, tests of significance). Articles are readable and accessible, and contain some thought-provoking ideas. Among the best is an essay defining sexual discrimination in the Asian context. Other essays give interesting comparisons with Western materials (e.g., mass media, and proportions of articles devoted to ads versus other materials). The volume reflects concerns in Japan that center on women's dual roles in the family and work. However, it lacks a discussion of sexual violence, an important concern of North American women studies. Undergraduate readers.—*J. W. Salaff, University of Toronto*

WS-1630   HQ1762   90-11194 CIP
Recreating Japanese women, 1600-1945, ed. by Gail Lee Bernstein. California, 1991. 340p index afp ISBN 0-520-07015-1, $40.00; ISBN 0-520-07017-8 pbk, $14.95

Bernstein presents an excellent introduction establishing the historical background and social settings for these 13 studies and expertly integrates their diverse foci and approaches. Part 1 consists of essays on the division of labor in the household; the flexible and varied life cycle of farm women; the death of old women; women disciples of the Confucian school of Shingaku; poet-painter Ema Saiko; and a woman in the all-male sake-brewing industry. Part 2 contains essays on the Meiji State's policy toward women, guided by its objective of industrialization; Yosano Akiko, a poet and proponent of the "New Woman"; middle-class working women in the interwar years; growing consciousness of women in the Taisho textile industry; the independent-minded "Modern Girl"; motherhood and women's factory work in the 1930s and 1940s; and women in wartime films. There is some unevenness in content and analytical acuity but in general, this is a rich collection—essays are well researched, well written, and persuasively argued. Upper-division undergraduates and above.—*M. Hane, Knox College*

WS-1631   HQ1742   94-27345 CIP
Sahgal, Manmohini Zutshi. **An Indian freedom fighter recalls her life,** ed. by Geraldine Forbes. M.E. Sharpe, 1994. 167p index afp ISBN 1-56324-339-3, $46.50; ISBN 1-56324-340-7 pbk, $16.95

Sahgal's fascinating memoir, published in the "Foremother Legacies" series, intermingles the personal experiences of a member of the powerful Nehru household with many of the major events and patterns of the Indian struggle for independence. Among the chief additions it makes to the existing literature on women's participation in nationalist protest is the extent to which we learn about self-motivated and woman-directed political action and about disagreements and disappointments because of the course the movement took from the time of the Lahore Congress in 1929 (when Sahgal was 20 years old) until eventual independence for India in 1947. The frustrations of being overlooked, even directly opposed, by the Congress Party, despite her sacrifices as a freedom fighter, teacher, and social worker, leave Sahgal wondering if being a cousin of Jawaharlal Nehru was more an obstacle than an asset once India achieved independence. Although she ends her account with concerns about India's present and future, and questions about her own sacrifices having been in vain, Sahgal also emphasizes the very valuable role that women have played and should be encouraged to continue to play within Indian political life and social organization. Whether within the Ministry of Rehabilitation, as president of the Northern Railway Employee's Union, or president of the Family Planning Association of Delhi, the author has continued to look for opportunities to make a contribution to her country. Readable at any level.—*B. Tavakolian, Denison University*

WS-1632   GT3370   92-23468 CIP
Sati, the blessing and the curse: the burning of wives in India, ed. by John Stratton Hawley. Oxford, 1994. 214p bibl index afp ISBN 0-19-507771-7, $39.95; ISBN 0-19-507774-1 pbk, $15.95

This collection of essays and commentaries, a project of the Southern Asian Institute—Columbia University, admirably tackles many questions. Is sati (sometimes called suttee) a person, an event, or both? How long has it been in existence? Has it been an exception or a rule in Hindu life? What exactly do the brahmanical treatises prescribe? How does controversy over Roop Kanwar's 1987 sati unravel the contemporary mass perceptions of Sati in the independent and officially secular India? Bringing together a variety of perspectives, these erudite essays explore historical themes as well as current Indian feminists' reactions. To make the controversy intelligible and decipher the ambivalence, the contributors also explain the mind-set of those who wish to defend sati. Excellent glossary. General; graduate; faculty—*N. N. Kalia, Buffalo State College*

WS-1633   HQ1745x   Orig
Singh, Renuka. **The womb of mind: a sociological exploration of the status-experience of women in Delhi.** Vikas Publishing House, 1990. (Dist. by Advent Books) 240p bibl index ISBN 0-7069-4949-8, $35.00

Singh's study is based on interviews for a doctoral dissertation at Jawaharlal Nehru University in 1978-80. The author's approach generally is normative rather than empirical, and women are spoken of with little distinction as to caste, class, religion, or region. A "historical sketch of the position of Indian women" from 2500 BCE to 1947 occupies only five pages. Singh interviewed 200 predominantly Hindu and Sikh women in New Delhi, mostly of upper status. Protocols from two women described as "upper caste and upper class," living in posh circumstances, are superficially analyzed; they seem emotionally unstable, insecure, and unsettled in role or status. Singh says they have suffered "upheavals, anxieties. . .deprivations, brutishness. . .jealousies, betrayals, tyrannies. . ." and their marginal personality attributes in relation to traditional society seems clear. There follows a discussion of gypsy women living on the streets of Delhi who are said to "exude a sense of freedom, power, and pride"; the author fails to comment on the ironic contrast. A lengthy analysis of "Sita-consciousness" depicts the influence of the religious ideal on women's thought and behavior. A final chapter briefly assesses various feminist theories. Chapter notes.—*W. H. Harlan, Ohio University*

WS-1634   HD6073.T42   89-24325 CIP
Tsurumi, E. Patricia. **Factory girls: women in the thread mills of Meiji Japan.** Princeton, 1990. 215p bibl index afp ISBN 0-691-03138-X, $29.95

Tsurumi's meticulously documented account of the women who provided the bulk of the labor force in late 19th-century Japan continues the saga of the "underside" of Japanese history, introduced to scholars by Mikiso Hane in his *Peasants, Rebels, and Outcastes* (CH, Sep'82). In contrast to historians who have concentrated on Japan's success, Tsurumi shows that factory girls in silk and cotton mills were subjected to deceptive recruitment practices, low wages, poor food, crowded and unhealthy living environments, long hours, polluted air, sexual harassment, and lack of personal freedom. Enduring these hardships for the sake of their rural families, they suffered in different ways but probably no more than their sisters who remained in the village or who were contracted to weaving establishments or brothels. The author, who treats her subjects with dignity and compassion, emphasizes the women's pride in their work, their class consciousness, and their powerlessness. Although she confines her study to female workers, she explains their oppression in terms of class rather than gender. College, university, and public libraries.—*S. A. Hastings, Purdue University*

WS-1635   HQ1762   95-43512 MARC
Voices from the Japanese women's movement, ed. by AMPO, Japan Asia quarterly review. M.E. Sharpe, 1996. 207p index afp ISBN 1-56324-725-9, $54.95; ISBN 1-56324-726-7 pbk, $17.95

Japanese women's studies has produced large synthetic works and specialized analyses of women's activities in law, literature, politics, the sexual and entertainment businesses, and parenting. Further, there are now distinguished studies of individual women in their neighborhoods. The recent explosive growth of these materials in English translation makes feasible the construction of college and university courses on Japanese gender relations. This volume collects essays from the *Japan Asia Quarterly Review*, 24 about Japanese women with the remaining two representing the Korean and Ainu minorities. Topics vary widely, from "comfort women" to lesbianism, from the Equal Employment Opportunity Law to the subtleties of tea-serving obligations in the workplace, from the limited meaning of liberation for a woman on a declining farm to the exciting work with urban women at the Yokohama Women's Forum. Although the essays are short and the volume is disjointed, these authentic and sometimes eloquent voices deserve to be heard. Should be in all libraries that give attention to global women's issues, and in any collection that seeks to be current on Japanese social life. Upper-division undergraduates and above.—*R. B. Lyman Jr., Simmons College*

WS-1636   HQ243   92-30015 CIP
Warren, James Francis. *Ah ku* and *karayuki-san*: **prostitution in Singapore, 1870-1940.** Oxford, 1993. 433p bibl index ISBN 0-19-588616-X, $65.00

Through his imaginative use of coroner's records, photographs, and oral histories, Warren has succeeded, particularly in chapters 9 through 14, in shaping a social history that illuminates the role of Chinese and Japanese prostitutes in the history of Singapore. This fascinating material could have been presented much more concisely. More serious, Warren's focus only on Chinese (*ah ku*) and Japanese (*karayuki-san*) prostitutes, in a city that by his own account had Eastern European, Indian, and Malay women in the same profession, casts prostitution as an East Asian institution. His decision to treat the *ah ku* and the *karayuki-san* as one homogeneous subset of Singapore society not only obscures significant differences between China and Japan but also blurs the distinction between prostitution restricted to the majority Chinese population (the work of most *ah ku*) and prostitution patronized by the international community (the work of most *karayuki-san*). Although the words colonialism, gender, and race are scattered throughout his text, Warren's narrative fails to acknowledge how those concepts shaped both history and his sources. Graduate; faculty.—*S. A. Hastings, Purdue University*

◆ Europe

WS-1637   DL719   90-42995 CIP
Åkerman, Susanna. **Queen Christina of Sweden and her circle: the transformation of a seventeenth-century philosophical libertine.** E.J. Brill, 1991. 339p (Brill's studies in intellectual history, 21) bibl index afp ISBN 90-04-09310-9, $83.00

The background and motivations for Queen Christina of Sweden's abdication and subsequent conversion to Catholicism have long been a matter of scholarly debate by Scandinavian historians, specialists in religious ideas of the 17th century, and even modern practitioners of psychohistory. Akerman's book is no popular analysis of that episode, however, but rather an extremely dense work focusing on the 17th-century religious thinkers who came to have the greatest influence on this errant daughter of Gustavus Adolphus, whom the author characterizes as a "philosophical libertine." Originating as a doctoral dissertation in philosophy, this study advances new insights and fresh interpretations on the matter, drawing on a mass of obscure contemporary writing and rare manuscript sources. It may very well remain the "final word" on this complex issue in intellectual and theological history. It would undoubtedly be a most useful addition to any scholarly research library, but is hardly approachable by either lower-division undergraduates or the general reading public.—*K. Smemo, Moorhead State University*

WS-1638   BF1584   92-56410 CIP
Barstow, Anne Llewellyn. **Witchcraze: a new history of the European witch hunts.** Pandora, 1994. (Dist. by HarperCollins) 255p bibl index afp ISBN 0-06-250049-X, $25.00

There is no doubt that Barstow has read widely in the secondary literature on early modern witch hunting, especially in the English-language scholarship. Admittedly, too, she writes with a certain flair. But here she has simply gathered all the evidence that seems to support her militant feminist preconceptions. For Barstow, witch hunts were essentially "a war on women," in which women were "criminalized as a group" for the first time. Using impossibly fuzzy and weak reasoning, she tries to make a generally recognized aspect of many witch hunts into the key for any and all understanding. She seeks to shock readers with grotesque details of mutilations and executions of women carried out by a male clerical and legal establishment, and makes a pathetic effort to dance around incon-

venient findings, such as that in a few areas more men than women were accused. Barstow's diatribe against the misogyny of the witch hunts includes grossly naive efforts to find parallels with the European slave trade and with the Jewish Holocaust. If you belong to the Andrea Dworkin school of historical interpretation, you will appreciate this work. Otherwise, flee from it as from a demon. Not recommended.—*R. B. Barnes, Davidson College*

WS-1639   HQ1147   95-39296 CIP
Bitel, Lisa M. **Land of women: tales of sex and gender from early Ireland.** Cornell, 1996. 307p bibl index afp ISBN 0-8014-3095-X, $35.00

Anyone who wishes to write on women in medieval Christian Europe has to face the challenge of balancing the normative and mainly misogynistic dictates of "the fathers" against the realities of lived experience as it is seen in tales of courtship and love, economic relations, and domestic arrangements. When Ireland (mostly between 500 and 1000) is the case study, a vast body of heroic and historical literary material also has to be taken into account. Bitel juggles and juxtaposes these bodies of information, narration, and didacticism to argue that many roles and opportunities were open for *some* women, and that the male tellers of tales could both champion and condemn the bold females who transgressed the conventional bonds of hearth and of the dutiful obedience of daughter and wife. Men's ambivalence about their relations with "the other," as well as women's own conflicts about choice and destiny, are well delineated in this monograph. Bitel sometimes seems uncertain about which conclusion to drive home as her final word; this is to her credit given the diversity of sources, views, and historical and literary vignettes that enrich this complicated and thoughtful treatment. General readers; upper-division undergraduates and above.—*J. T. Rosenthal, SUNY at Stony Brook*

WS-1640   DK275   91-19720 CIP
Bonner, Elena. **Mothers and daughters,** tr. by Antonina W. Bouis. Knopf, 1992. 349p index ISBN 0-394-58761-8, $23.00

Bonner is most widely known in the West as the outspoken wife of the late physicist and former dissident, Andrei Sakharov. Perhaps some more knowledgeable Westerners recognize her as the author of the political memoir *Alone Together* (1986). Now, Bonner has produced a beautifully written (and beautifully translated) account of her childhood and youth. Bonner was born in 1923 and raised in a household whose central figures were her mother and stepfather (both staunch communists and highly-placed party members) and her maternal grandmother (an unrepentant bourgeoise who hated everything the Russian Revolution of 1917 represented). Mostly, the book chronicles Bonner's young life until her world came crashing down with the arrest of her parents in 1937. There are some sections that contain musings about the circumstances under which Bonner came to write the memoir, the war years, her life with Sakharov, and other post-1937 episodes. As history, this lyrical, haunting narrative has many flaws. As literature—as a memoir trying to make sense out of the present as much as the past—it makes compelling reading. General readers.—*A. H. Koblitz, Hartwick College*

WS-1641   HQ1593   94-5722 CIP
Burton, Antoinette. **Burdens of history: British feminists, Indian women, and imperial culture, 1865-1915.** North Carolina, 1994. 301p bibl index afp ISBN 0-8078-2161-6, $45.00; ISBN 0-8078-4471-3 pbk, $16.95

Burton here examines the collaboration of middle-class British feminists in justifying and furthering the cause of imperialism. The author argues that although feminists laid claim to individual and political self-representation, their project depended on the humanization of British womanhood. In the context of the imperial British state, this involved making "Britishness," more than sex, a precondition for rule. Using Edward Said's *Orientalism* (CH, Apr'79) as a point of departure, Burton asserts that Indian women were deployed as substitute "others" for their British "sisters." Her analysis of the language and rhetoric of feminist tracts and periodicals shows images of Indian women that were divorced from reality and framed to emphasize their condition as passive, enslaved, and brutalized. Describing themselves as crucial to the salvation of their abased "oriental" sisters, feminists simultaneously moved themselves from margin to center and became full participants in the ideological work of empire. The book will undoubtedly come in for some criticism of style, use of sources, and assertions about causality. Nonetheless, it is a provocative and interesting example of historical deconstruction. General, upper-division undergraduate, and above.—*N. B. Rosenthal, SUNY College at Old Westbury*

WS-1642   HD6060   94-46958 CIP
Downs, Laura Lee. **Manufacturing inequality: gender division in the French and British metalworking industries, 1914-1939.** Cornell, 1995. 329p bibl index afp ISBN 0-8014-3015-1, $39.95

Downs explores the dilemmas confronting French and British metal industries after 1914, when increased wartime demands (followed by sluggish postwar economies) compelled adoption of new technologies and production strategies, and simultaneously required adaptation of the workplace to women workers. She finds that employers relied on domestic analogies both to justify workplace gender inequities and to defend industrial employment of women. The result, as she notes, was the transformation and recodification of gender distinctions as integral to rationalized industrial restructuring. Underpinning these inseparable processes, according to Downs, is an "Aristotelian" logic of hierarchy built on beliefs of differences in social productivity inherent in gender differences. A brief bibliographic note and a list of the major archives are included; complete references are easily found in Downs's thorough footnotes. *Manufacturing Inequality* surely will prove invaluable and provocative to upper-division undergraduates and above, and will leave a clear impact on future scholarship.—*F. Burkhard, Morgan State University*

WS-1643   Orig
Hall, Catherine. **White, male and middle class: explorations in feminism and history.** Routledge, 1992. 307p index afp ISBN 0-415-90662-8, $49.95; ISBN 0-415-90663-6 pbk, $15.95

This collection of previously published essays from the coauthor of *Family Fortunes* (1987) may be compared in importance to Natalie Davis's *Society and Culture in Early Modern France* (CH, Mar'76). With the exception of the superbly crafted introduction, which offers an autobiographic sketch of the author's personal development within the broader context of professional and intellectual change since 1960, the ten pieces gathered here appeared only in forms limiting access and use. The daunting if catchy title disguises Hall's focus on England and its empire during the 18th and 19th centuries. Each essay probes events or debates that revealed evolving and frequently contradictory ideologies redefining class and gender, a paradigm expanded in the closing two essays to incorporate race and ethnicity as well. The absence of a bibliography is offset by thorough indexing and extensive chapter endnotes. This volume is an excellent addition to any collection and should attract considerable multidisciplinary use by researchers as well as graduate and undergraduate students.—*F. Burkhard, Morgan State University*

WS-1644   D802   95-38746 CIP
Hart, Janet. **New voices in the nation: women and the Greek resistance, 1941-1964.** Cornell, 1996. 313p bibl index afp ISBN 0-8014-3044-5, $39.95; ISBN 0-8014-8219-4 pbk, $16.95

Fundamentally an oral history, Hart's book is an important contribution to modern Greek studies. Hart persuasively argues that resistance against the Nazis and the rightists in the civil war liberated women, especially those in the National Liberation Front (EAM) and its youth organization (EPON), from traditional patriarchy. The book needs an early and deeper description of Greek patriarchy, especially an analysis of how men perceived women as social and political threats. Hart's insistence on styling her subject in dense and extensive theoretical dispositions distracts the reader and limits readership. The book's greatest contribution is in its oral interviews. Interviewees describe their activities, but this reviewer wonders if patriarchy also pervaded the Resistance. The tragic consequences of the civil war on politically engaged women (including executions) is a particularly significant section. Hart, an African American, is commended for her perseverance in learning Greek and in enduring racial prejudice during her research. Indeed, she recounts that many of the women she met identified with the African American struggle for civil rights. The text is enhanced by photographs. Upper-division undergraduates and above.—*P. C. Naylor, Marquette University*

WS-1645   HQ1121   91-34134 Orig
A History of women in the West: v.1: From ancient goddesses to Christian saints, ed. by Pauline Schmitt Pantel. Harvard, 1992. 572p bibl index afp ISBN 0-674-40370-3, $29.95

An important new series by the general editors of the *History of Private Life* (v.l: CH, Jun'87, v.3: CH, Oct'89). Rather than being organized chronologically, the 11 eclectic articles are arranged thematically. Part 1 deals with "Feminine Models of the Ancient World," Part 2 with "Traditional Rituals Women Share," and Part 3 with "Yesterday and Today." Almost all of the essays show the influence of the history of *mentalités* and of recent progress in anthropological studies. The essays capture new understandings of "gender" in representations of women as well as in women's experience in the ancient world. Inevitably repetitious, these studies nevertheless offer multifaceted glimpses into women's lives in antiquity. Especially valuable are the studies of Francois Lissarrague (who found no space especially reserved for women in her examination of representations of women on Athenian vases used for rituals of marriage, funerals, initiations, and sacrifices), and Claudine Leduc (who concluded that marriage patterns of "gift-giving" were intimately linked with political choices influencing the invention of the *polis*). One eagerly awaits the next four volumes. Valuable bibliography and helpful illustrations. Highly recommended. Undergraduate. General.—*C. W. Clark, St. Andrews Presbyterian College*

WS-1646   HQ1121   91-34134 CIP
A History of women in the West: v.3: Renaissance and Enlightenment paradoxes, ed. by Natalie Zemon Davis and Arlette Farge. Harvard, 1993. 595p bibl index afp ISBN 0-674-40372-X, $29.95

This is the third in a five-volume series (v.1, CH, Dec'92). Davis (Princeton Univ.) and Farge (Centre National de la Recherche Scientifique, Paris) have compiled 19 essays by American and European scholars. Focusing on paradoxes associated with women's lives from the 16th to 18th centuries, the material contrasts everyday activities and beliefs with examples of challenging traditions in a triad social view of women: conforming, maneuvering, and resisting. Traditional themes cover work (agricultural, domestic, industrial); family (virginity, marriage, motherhood, widowhood, spinsterhood); physical appearance; sexuality; education; religion; and political and legal theories regarding women's status. An intriguing iconographic study of 49 female images by Françoise Borin provides the transition, alluding to female subversion emerging during the Renaissance. Unusual examples include engravings by male artists; one depicts a nun with exposed breasts, another shows a brooding man wearing a voluminous cloak covered with depictions of women's faces. Within the category of female radicals or social deviants fall witches, prostitutes, criminals (guilty of parricides, infanticides, theft and pilfering), protestors (participants in mob riots), and the rare breed of 18th-century English and French female journalists. A few essays reflect original research; many are useful syntheses of recent scholarship produced on both sides of the Atlantic. Useful bibliography. All levels.—*B. B. Chico, Regis University (CO)*

WS-1647   HQ1121   91-34134 CIP
A History of women in the West: v.4: Emerging feminism from revolution to world war, ed. by Geneviève Fraisse and Michelle Perrot. Harvard, 1993. 640p bibl index afp ISBN 0-674-40373-8, $29.95

The fourth installment in a five-part series (v.1: CH, Dec'92; v.2: CH, Nov'93), this volume covers the crucial period 1789 to 1914 and consists of brief chapters by 18 distinguished French and American scholars. The format sacrifices consecutive narrative to examine specific themes and problems: the changes wrought by the French Revolution on the condition of women; women's productivity in the real and imaginary realms; their activity in the public and private spheres; and the development of feminism. Within these broad subject areas, contributors successfully embrace the variety of women's experiences. Separate treatments deal with Catholic, Prostestant, and Jewish variations and with women as workers, political activists, artists, wives, and mothers. A repeating motif, the changing perception of women, lends a degree of unity to the book's individual contributions. The final section presents two women whose lives bracketed the period—Madame de Staël and Frau Lou Salomé—to dramatize the changes in women's consciousness, the losses and gains, and the enduring conflicts in women's lives. The book is handsomely produced, with 47 well-chosen, unusual illustrations and an excellent bibliography. General readers, community college students and above.—*R. S. Levy, University of Illinois at Chicago*

WS-1648 HQ1121 91-34134 CIP
A History of women in the West: v.5: Toward a cultural identity in the twentieth century, ed. by Françoise Thébaud. Harvard, 1994. 713p bibl index afp ISBN 0-674-40374-6, $29.95

The overall emphasis in this collection of articles by a diverse group of scholars and writers is on the place, "condition," and cultural images of Western—primarily Western European—women. As in many collections, the quality of the articles varies considerably, as does the level of knowledge and sophistication required by the reader. There are extremely interesting and provocative discussions on the impact on women of WW I, the interwar period, the fascist and Nazi regimes, and recent demographic shifts in the nature of families. On the other hand, a particularly opaque philosophic summary, a muddled exposition of culture creation in France, and an ahistorical ideological attempt to reinterpret *all* progress as a male plot to increase domination are examples of other less sterling contributions. This volume would be a good addition to a women's history collection, to be dipped into judiciously rather than read cover to cover. Upper-division undergraduates and above.—*L. Mayo, County College of Morris*

WS-1649 HQ1147 95-33401 CIP
Jewell, Helen M. **Women in medieval England.** Manchester, 1996. (Dist. by St. Martin's) 210p bibl index afp ISBN 0-7190-4016-7, $59.95

Based largely on secondary sources, this history of women in post-Conquest England, roughly from 1000 to 1500, provides the general and student reader with a useful introduction to the subject. Jewell has divided the book into short chapters that depict the lives and activities of women in the countryside, in the urban centers, among the aristocracy, and in the church. Also included is an introduction that briefly discusses women in the Anglo-Saxon period. This is straightforward history; Jewell has not attempted to establish any particular methodological stance, nor has she seen fit to address in detail many of the controversies that have arisen in the historical community with respect to the issues of female participation in public life outside the family home and within the larger community. Although useful, this work would have benefited from a wider-ranging bibliography encompassing more current material, especially scholarship coming out of American presses in the last five years, as well as the kinds of primary sources, such as chancery and court records, the use of which Jewell admits has transformed the historical debates about women's lives and roles in medieval Europe. General readers through graduate students.—*L. E. Mitchell, Alfred University*

WS-1650 HQ1587 91-31639 CIP
Kaplan, Gisela. **Contemporary Western European feminism.** New York University, 1992. 340p bibl index ISBN 0-8147-4622-5, $40.00

A comprehensive and comparative survey of women's movements, primarily in the non-English speaking countries of Europe west of the Elbe River and from Scandinavia to the Mediterranean Sea. Focusing on the period from the 1960s to 1989, Kaplan considers the "possibilities and limits of protest," examines the degree of "change that has been fashioned by the movements," and measures women's status in the countries studied through the use of a wide range of variables. The first part of the book provides a comparative overview of the postwar European movements and of women's status and employment; Part 2 analyzes in greater detail the conditions and events in specific countries. Nations are arranged in four groups based on "theoretical paradigms" defined as progressive, conservative, marginal, and revolutionary. This book is more than a descriptive narrative of women's organizations and feminist activities; it also attempts to understand theoretical debates and variations in political strategies. Kaplan's efforts to be all-inclusive lead to some overgeneralizations, particularly when she attempts to summarize centuries of complex national histories. Especially useful is the extensive multilingual bibliography of secondary materials. General; undergraduate; graduate.—*M. J. Slaughter, University of New Mexico*

WS-1651 HQ186 96-19801 CIP
Karras, Ruth Mazo. **Common women: prostitution and sexuality in Medieval England.** Oxford, 1996. 221p bibl index afp ISBN 0-19-506242-6, $35.00

In this study of prostitution in England from 1348 to 1500, Karras examines issues of gender construction, commercialization, and power. In accordance with the "hydraulic" model of masculine sexuality, prostitution and marriage served as

safety valves for the release of pressure. Both institutions involved financial exchange; female sexuality was thus a commodity, and men were blameless in its purchase. Yet late medieval English culture had no conceptual category for women who engaged in sex for pay, perhaps because this precapitalist economy had a different attitude toward money and productive labor. What was significant was the tension between prostitution as a sexual outlet and the threat to male control that lurked in its background. In addition to a fine theoretical discussion, Karras presents some rich detail. Particularly striking is her account of John Rykener, a female impersonator who had a career as a street prostitute, and her discussion of what this implies about prostitutes' sexual acts. Analysis of literary and religious texts broadens Karras's examination of late medieval England's mental world. All levels.—*H. R. Lemay, SUNY at Stony Brook*

WS-1652 HQ1121 92-20411 CIP
Lerner, Gerda. **The creation of feminist consciousness: from the Middle Ages to eighteen-seventy.** Oxford, 1993. 395p bibl index afp ISBN 0-19-506604-9, $27.50

In this long-awaited sequel to *The Creation of Patriarchy* (CH, Oct'86), Lerner traces resistance to patriarchy and some of the searches for women's self-consciousness and self-expression from the 7th through the late 19th centuries CE. She examines the educational disadvantaging of women and their struggles for the right to possess public voices, notably through mystical reformulations of religious traditions. Lerner's reconstructed history of women analyzes examples of past struggles for empowerment through motherhood, education, self-authorization, supportive female clusters and networks, and quests for role models. Yet the early efforts to achieve a public voice were frequently smothered, leaving later attempts to escape women's isolation in the situation, in Lerner's apt phrase, of reinventing the wheel. This provocative and important work is highly recommended for the general public as well as for all college levels. The bibliography is extremely useful and well organized, and will be valuable for research and to guide library acquisitions.—*F. Burkhard, Morgan State University*

WS-1653 E184 92-20410 CIP
Linden, R. Ruth. **Making stories, making selves: feminist reflections on the Holocaust.** Ohio State, 1993. 191p bibl index afp ISBN 0-8142-0583-6, $39.50

In this brief and engagingly written book, Linden attempts to do three things, only one of which will interest more than a few people. She fashions a nonpositivist ethnography that will no doubt offend traditionalists in the discipline and may strike other readers as quite subjective. Her second—and major—subject is herself, her coming of age as a feminist and as a Jew, to which she devotes four of the first five chapters. However, Linden's changing consciousness and emerging reorientations are also the subtext of the book's third subject: the testimonies of Holocaust survivors. These she collected at the World Gathering of Jewish Holocaust Survivors in Jerusalem in 1983. Their continuing impact on her own identity, the uncertain nature of memory, the human importance of telling stories, the complex interaction of interviewer and witness, the "phenomenology of survival,"—all are issues about which the author has intelligent and sometimes provocative things to say. The longest chapter tells the life history of a single survivor, Leesha Rose, and makes for compelling reading. Nonetheless, in plumbing the meaning of survivors' testimonies unencumbered by private agendas, Lawrence L. Langer's *Holocaust Testimonies: The Ruins of Memory* (CH, Sept'91) remains a superior text. General; undergraduate; graduate; faculty.—*R. S. Levy, University of Illinois at Chicago*

WS-1654 DP269 95-18301 CIP
Nash, Mary. **Defying male civilization: women in the Spanish Civil War.** Arden Press, CO, 1996 (c1995). 261p bibl index ISBN 0-912869-15-1, $32.00; ISBN 0-912869-16-X pbk, $22.50

Nash's study opens with an excellent contextual overview of Spain's social and political developments from 1815 to 1936, and links these transformations to the changing social positions and gender debates surrounding women. Nash claims that in the early chaos of the Spanish Civil War an opportunity existed for pervasive gender transformation, symbolized in both the discursive images and the reality of the antifascist *milicianas*. Yet almost immediately, republican women were redirected toward traditional maternalist roles, their energies and aspirations channeled by organizations auxiliary to male-dominated political parties. While many individual women chose to struggle simultaneously against fascism and for social transformation, most readapted traditional roles to the urgencies of wartime survival. Nash argues that the revolutionary surge of the Spanish tragedy ended not with the 1937 crushing of anarchists and dissident Marxists, but with the earlier exclusion of women from the revolutionary process and agenda. The consolidation of the Franco regime led to even stricter legal impositions of exaggerated prewar gender stereotypes. Useful chronology and glossary; extensive bibliography. Upper-division undergraduates and above.—*F. Burkhard, Morgan State University*

WS-1655 DK189 95-38295 CIP
Russia—women—culture, ed. by Helena Goscilo and Beth Holmgren. Indiana, 1996. 386p bibl index afp ISBN 0-253-33019-X, $45.00; ISBN 0-253-21044-5 pbk, $24.95

What a treat this book is! The editors compare their effort to "project a more interdisciplinary, systematically inclusive view of women in Russian culture" to a house, with its "boudoir, bath, linen closet, kitchen, pantry, garden, and even the overdecorated parlor." Most of the articles, which span the disciplines of history, literature, and art, deal with aspects of domestic life, generally of women of comfortable means. Others discuss popular culture and women's art. With the exception of Nadya Peterson's moving piece on cleanliness, which discusses the fate of female prisoners in the Soviet Union, the book focuses on more pleasant sides of Russian and Soviet life than those Western readers have been accustomed to contemplate. The presence of articles that cover the Soviet period provides a useful sense of perspective on the continuities as well as the catastrophic breaks in Russian history. Naturally, the quality of 14 articles is uneven, not all make major contributions, and some are weakened by the lack of a comparative perspective. Nonetheless, this is a vital addition to studies of Russian/Soviet life, adding a dimension too often lost amid examinations of politics, labor, and oppression. All levels.—*J. Zimmerman, University of Pittsburgh*

WS-1656 HD6073 94-41738 CIP
Sayer, Karen. **Women of the fields: representations of rural women in the nineteenth century.** Manchester, 1995. (Dist. by St. Martin's) 201p bibl index ISBN 0-7190-4142-2, $69.95; ISBN 0-7190-4143-0 pbk, $24.95

Using the art and literature of the period, as well as various parliamentary reports on agricultural labor, Sayer (Univ. of Luton, UK) examines 19th-century imagery regarding rural Englishwomen and argues that these images were crucial in generating representations of femininity, domesticity, class, and nation. Dissatisfaction with aspects of advancing industrialization and capitalist relations led many contemporaries to perceive the countryside and its inhabitants as repositories of "true" Englishness and English virtues. Women, who represented especially nature and the pastoral, as opposed to male culture, served as indicators of the health of the nation and English culture. When "reality" and representation were perceived to be at odds, one or the other were manipulated to achieve conformity, through legislation or medical, moral, or imperial discourse. Rural women in the 19th century have been largely neglected by historians; Sayer's work and her interdisciplinary approach admirably contribute to filling this void. Upper-division undergraduates and above.—*J. Travers, SUNY at Stony Brook*

WS-1657 HQ1616 95-31953 CIP
Scott, Joan Wallach. **Only paradoxes to offer: French feminists and the rights of man.** Harvard, 1996. 229p index afp ISBN 0-674-63930-8, $27.95

Scott, author of numerous gender studies, continues to break new ground by rereading feminist history using the paradox of how, in their quest for full citizenship, women have claimed both their "equality" and their "difference." Through the experiences of four French feminists—Olympe de Gouges, Jeanne Deroin, Hubertine Auclert, and Madeleine Pelletier—and their specific campaigns for political rights, Scott poses the paradox for each historical period, noting that as they acted on behalf of women as a group, these feminists necessarily reinforced the differences they wanted to deny. Scott emphasizes that arguments made by these feminists are rooted in historical time: de Gouges claims citizenship for women, citing the language of the French Revolution; Deroin argues rights for women as workers and mothers in 1848; Auclert employs the scientific secular-

ism of the late 19th century to campaign for the vote; and Pelletier in the early 20th century contends that women are free individuals. Most important is Scott's thesis that the unsolvable tension between the affirmation of group identity and political equality does not hinder feminism, but adds to its political force. Undergraduates and above.—*J. Wishnia, SUNY at Stony Brook*

WS-1658 DD801 95-36465 CIP
Seymour, Bruce. **Lola Montez: a life.** Yale, 1996. 468p bibl index afp ISBN 0-300-06347-4, $30.00

Seymour reconstructs the life of Lola Montez, an Englishwoman who lived by her wits and scandalized 19th-century Europe and America. After a failed first marriage and in need of a way to support herself, Montez (née Eliza Gilbert) recreated herself as an exotic Spanish dancer and took to the stage. Her beauty, intelligence, and verve (more than her limited talent) brought her fame, fortune, interesting lovers, and ultimately, notoriety. A woman who defied convention and rejected bourgeois morality, Montez was as well known as a "celebrity" as she was as a dancer. Her freewheeling and high-handed ways, as well as her affair with the king of Bavaria, outraged yet entranced her contemporaries. Montez's manipulation of the press and the varied stories she told of herself have worked to obscure her true story until now. Seymour's achievement lies in his painstaking search for sources regarding Montez and his shaping of these sources into an intriguing biography of an amazing woman. All levels.—*J. Travers, SUNY at Stony Brook*

WS-1659 HV6046 95-37867 CIP
Shapiro, Ann-Louise. **Breaking the codes: female criminality in fin-de-siècle Paris.** Stanford, 1996. 265p bibl index afp ISBN 0-8047-1663-3, $45.00; ISBN 0-8047-2693-0 pbk, $15.95

Shapiro blends original research with insightful critical appropriations of recent scholarship to re-create the pervasive fascination with deviant and criminal women in the context of the social and political upheavals reshaping France before the Great War. She retraces the development of overlapping discursive and bureaucratic practices—in the press, the judicial system, the courtroom, in medicine, and in the daily cultural assumptions and acts of women and men themselves—and argues that "criminality" served as a reference point where French anxieties about their modern world were focused, encoded, and transformed into dramatic moral stories (re)expressing and (re)establishing social norms. Far from being simply passive victims and objects of masculine domination, women, as individuals and collectively, actively participated in the shaping of their culture. This work includes a thorough bibliography and extensive endnotes, and will prove fascinating reading for upper-division undergraduates and above. Among the most useful companion works exploring parallel materials and issues are Elinor Accampo's *Gender and the Politics of Social Reform in France* (1995) and Judith Walkowitz's *City of Dreadful Delight* (1992).—*F. Burkhard, Morgan State University*

WS-1660 HQ1692 96-36432 CIP
Spanish women in the golden age: images and realities, ed. by Magdalena S. Sánchez and Alain Saint-Saëns. Greenwood, 1996. 229p (Contributions in women's studies, 155) bibl index afp ISBN 0-313-29481-X, $55.00

Like many collections this one is very uneven, encompassing a broad range of disciplines and sources. Much of the pioneer work in early modern European women's studies has focused on religion, as a legitimate and reasonably well documented outlet for women during the Renaissance. Therefore, it is not surprising that the greatest strength of this volume is the essays in the first section, "Religion and Society." Essays in the second part, "Political Realms," attempt to demonstrate that women who were in a "key position to influence their royal spouse, brother, or son" actually did so. This is most convincingly argued concerning the reign of Charles II, a notoriously weak Habsburg monarch. The third and final section, "Female Identity," contains the most eclectic group of essays. It includes a brief but illuminating article about working women in Barcelona, various representations of women in literature and, finally, an analysis of melancholy expressed in the writings of female "intellectuals." The extensive bibliography represents the editors' dedication to provide the reader and researcher with additional resources. Graduate students and faculty will welcome this addition to their libraries.—*S. H. Burkholder, University of Missouri—St. Louis*

WS-1661   HQ1593   90-43509 CIP
Strobel, Margaret. **European women and the second British Empire.** Indiana, 1991. 108p bibl index afp ISBN 0-253-35551-6, $27.50; ISBN 0-253-20631-6 pbk, $8.95

Strobel's brief and mildly polemical book is an essay on the actions of (mainly) British women and their role in imperialism. Strobel shows them as explorers, wives of colonial officials, prostitutes, nurses, teachers, and missionaries. For these women the empire offered opportunities not available at home and for some, a chance to improve the lives of subject people (with mixed results). Limited as women were by sex roles and cultural patterns set by male domination, their efforts often tightened the grip of colonial control. The book aims to combat the "resurgence of colonial nostalgia." One myth of which Strobel disposes, in part, is the notion (even expressed by some modern scholars) that women were harmful to empire. As the argument went, married women distracted their husbands from imperial duties; they replaced indigenous mistresses from whom administrators had learned much about colonial society. Women in large numbers also made possible the creation of a more exclusive British group, distant from colonial subjects; and women's presence supposedly fueled the sexual appetites of indigenous men. The very complexity of empire makes any generalizations suspect, and Strobel's book is most useful in raising questions that would be better answered in more specialized works. Strobel recognizes this, but feels that a critical overview is now called for. The documentation is full. College and university libraries.—*P. T. Smith, Saint Joseph's University*

WS-1662   HQ1154   91-35739 CIP
Ware, Vron. **Beyond the pale: white women, racism and history.** Verso, 1992. (Dist. by Routledge, Chapman & Hall) 263p index ISBN 0-86091-336-8, $59.95; ISBN 0-86091-552-2 pbk, $18.95

Combining personal insights with more traditional journalistic and historical approaches to her material, Ware has produced a pathbreaking book on the interplay of ideas about white women, feminism, racism, and colonialism. Ware analyzes the complicity of political movements and ideologies that attempted to enlarge the scope of women's opportunities and freedom in upholding regimes that restricted such opportunities for people of color. She argues that this approach is a means of understanding "the links between racism and male dominance so that being against one form of oppression involves the possibility of being against the other, with nothing taken for granted." Beginning with an examination of contemporary feminists' failure to recognize the function of race in the fashioning of white femininity, Ware moves to historicize the intricate interplay of gender, race, and class by looking at the politics of antislavery, the role of English women in social reform movements in India, and the relationship between the British anti-lynching and anti-imperialist campaigns. Only *Western Women and Imperialism*, ed. by Nupur Chaudhuri and Margaret Strobel (1992), seeks to address the issues Ware has raised. All levels.—*S. K. Kent, University of Florida*

WS-1663   BF1582   95-13470 CIP
Williams, Gerhild Scholz. **Defining dominion: the discourses of magic and witchcraft in early modern France and Germany.** Michigan, 1995. 234p bibl index afp ISBN 0-472-10619-8, $39.50

Williams has incorporated earlier research into this study of the discourses of magic. Using texts from the period 1400-1650, including Jean d'Arras's *Melusine* and well-known works on magic or witchcraft by Paracelsus, Kramer, Weyer, Bodin, and Pierre de Lancre, she argues that magic as an intellectual and cultural language was used by Europeans to explain the unknown, including witchcraft, the discoveries of the New World, and religious diversity. It was also applied to women, aliens, religious dissenters, and heretics, in an effort to control them by marginalizing them. Williams views such groups as "objects acted upon by those who presumed power over them" rather than as historical actors who constructed their identities. Central to her analysis is Kramer's *Malleus Maleficarum* (1486)—a text Williams believes underestimated by historians Norman Cohn and Erik Midelfort—because of its importance in shaping the discourse on women. Methodologically, the book is informed by George Lakoff's notion of experiential realism and other contemporary theories of cultural discourse. Its conceptual framework and dense prose make it of greatest interest to advanced students and specialists in literature and gender studies.—*J. Harrie, California State University, Bakersfield*

WS-1664   HD6053   90-41551 CIP
Women's work and the family economy in historical perspective, ed. by Pat Hudson and W.R. Lee. Manchester, 1990. (Dist. by St. Martin's) 299p index ISBN 0-7190-2377-7, $59.95

This collection delivers precisely what the title advertises: ten empirically grounded investigations into the complex interrelationships between women's work and the family economy. Organized chronologically, the book spans some 300 years, beginning with early protoindustrial settings and concluding with mature industrialization. All of the essays are based upon northern and western European sources; half of them center upon England alone. As the superb introduction emphasizes, these essays draw upon recent feminist historiography to shape the issues, methods, and selection of materials. This constitutes both the book's strength and its weakness. Carefully marshaled empirical evidence enables several authors to challenge overarching generalizations typical of developing fields. But some essays become mired in detail. As much as the editors strive to empower women, their lives—within the family and the economy—offer variations upon comparative powerlessness. The product of a series of seminars sponsored by the University of Liverpool, this footnoted volume will be consulted by graduate students in women's and European history.—*D. Lindstrom, University of Wisconsin-Madison*

◆ Europe
Biography

WS-1665   HQ1593   90-139703 MARC
Bennett, Daphne. **Emily Davies and the liberation of women, 1830-1921.** A. Deutsch, 1991 (c1990). (Dist. by Trafalgar Square/David & Charles) 279p bibl index ISBN 0-233-98494-1, $39.95

Bennett's study is the first authoritative biography of Emily Davies, founder in 1869 of Girton College, the first institution of higher learning for women in Britain. Using Davies's personal correspondence and papers, Bennett vividly recounts the struggles Davies overcame in the fight for a women's college at Cambridge. Bennett argues that Davies was correct in believing that political rights for women had to follow educational equality. Davies has not received due credit for her achievements, Bennett maintains, because she placed the diploma before the vote, opposed the violent suffragettes, and shunned public recognition. Bennett's insights are clear and sharp. Davies is revealed as a tenacious, farsighted figure at the forefront of the women's movement. This is a fine biography of an important Victorian, as well as an informative book on Victorian education and the women's movement in late 19th-century Britain. College and university libraries.—*G. M. Stearns, University of Cincinnati*

WS-1666   DA555   90-24757 CIP
Charlot, Monica. **Victoria: the young queen.** B. Blackwell, 1991. 492p index ISBN 0-631-17437-0, $29.95

Charlot's biography of Queen Victoria has three great strengths. First, it makes extremely good use of previously underutilized archival material. Second, it offers new insight into the relationship between Victoria and the Prince Consort, presenting both of them as very strong characters and revealing significant tensions within their undoubtedly extremely loving marriage. And third, probably because the book was written first in French and thus in some sense from the "outside," Charlot is careful throughout to set the biographical information in a broad, understandable context. The hierarchical arrangements of the British nobility are explicated clearly, for example; and such issues as the Chartist movement, the Irish famine, or the Eastern Question are explained in a way that makes them comprehensible even to the uninitiated reader. At the same time, the Victorian specialist will appreciate the thorough treatment of such relatively arcane subjects as "the Kensington system," the educational method employed by the mother of the young Princess Victoria. Very attractively written (although surprisingly somewhat sloppily edited), this work should be part of any research collection and is valuable for an undergraduate library.—*M. M. Garland, Ohio State University*

WS-1667 Brit. CIP
Clarke, Kathleen. **Revolutionary woman: Kathleen Clarke, 1878-1972: an autobiography,** ed. by Helen Litton. O'Brien Press, 1991. 240p index ISBN 0-86278-245-7, $33.00

Many firsthand accounts have been published about events in Dublin during the Easter Week uprising against the British in 1916. Clarke's memoir makes a significant contribution to the genre. Clarke came from a prominent Irish revolutionary family. Her uncle, John Daly, was a celebrated leader of the Fenian movement. Her brother Ned and husband, Tom Clarke, president of the short-lived "Republic" established in 1916, were executed by the British. Clarke herself played a key role in the Irish struggle for freedom. In the 1920s she was elected to the Dublin Corporation and in 1939 became the first woman Lord Mayor of Dublin. Her memoir is peopled with rich personalities like Eamon de Valera and the Countess Markievicz, with whom she was imprisoned for almost a year. The book sheds light on the relationship between activists in Ireland and sympathizers in the US who contributed money and weapons to the cause. Details of Clarke's personal life and the role of women in a revolutionary situation are also evocatively portrayed. All levels.—*J. H. Wiener, City College, CUNY*

WS-1668 Orig
Conley, Verena Andermatt. **Hélène Cixous.** Toronto, 1992. 153p bibl index ISBN 0-8020-2879-9, $45.00; ISBN 0-8020-7387-5 pbk, $16.95

Hélène Cixous serves as a generative figure for feminist theory. Conley has produced a substantive study, although one might wonder how a writer of such significance can be represented in so brief a work. Conley writes of Cixous as cultural theorist, as an author addressing "broad issues of cultural change through the medium of writing." She traces chronologically the changes in Cixous's genre-crossing work, and the influences from Marx, Freud, Heidegger, and Clarice Lispecter, among others. Conley details Cixous's genesis of women's writing as a subversive medium concerned with embodiment, birth, death, and passion. With Cixous's moving text and world as a site of poetic and political struggle, Conley does not fully develop the literary or historic context, nor does she deliver on the analysis of Cixous as cultural theorist; rather, she presents a unitary, although emergent, subject. Nonetheless this is a significant companion to Cixous's work and to feminist literary and cultural theory generally. Graduate; faculty.—*J. L. Croissant, Rensselaer Polytechnic Institute*

WS-1669 DA958 90-26393 CIP
Côté, Jane McL. **Fanny and Anna Parnell: Ireland's patriot sisters.** St. Martin's, 1991. 331p bibl index ISBN 0-312-06089-0, $69.95

Côté, who has previously written on European and Canadian economies, has produced a well-crafted study of Charles Stewart Parnell's two notable sisters. The book begins with a multigenerational history of the Irish-American Tudor-Stewart-Parnell family, which provides an essential context for Fanny and Anna's generation. The focus of the study, however, is on the Ladies' Land League, which the sisters founded and led in the early 1880s. Côté makes clear that the two women were very important figures in both Ireland and the US and that the Ladies' Land League was far more than an auxiliary to the men's organization. On the contrary, it took center stage in the face of the Coercion Act. Of particular interest is the betrayal of the women's movement by C.S. Parnell and Michael Davitt, and Anna's response in her history, *A Tale of the Great Sham* (reprint ed., 1988). Of interest to students of modern Irish history and feminism at all levels. Illustrations, extensive notes.—*C. W. Wood Jr., Western Carolina University*

WS-1670 CT788 93-45728 CIP
Creighton, Louise. **Memoir of a Victorian woman: reflections of Louise Creighton, 1850-1936,** ed. with introd. and annot. by James Thayne Covert. Indiana, 1994. 187p bibl index afp ISBN 0-253-31469-0, $29.95

Covert (Univ. of Portland) found Creighton's MS autobiography while doing research for a projected dual biography of Creighton and her husband, Mandell, an Oxford don, later Bishop of London. It is valuable women's and social/intellectual history on its own; and women historians may want to look at the full MS, given Covert's description of his editing and deletions. Noteworthy aspects are Creighton's intelligence (she was a prolific biographer and historian) and perspective. Termed here a "Victorian," she lived through the changes of the Edwar-

dian and interwar years and was an unusually frank observer and commentater from family relations to religion to sociopolitical affairs. Creighton eventually supported women's suffrage (in a note Covert wrongly identifies the determinedly Constitutionalist Millicent Fawcett with the avowedly militant "suffragettes"). While writing of a conventional, nannied upbringing (one of a dozen children), she notes her family's basic un-Englishness. Her accounts of her life as mother of seven and as vicar's and bishop's wife are far from the usual platitudes, and her friendships at varying points on the religious continuum—from Mary (Mrs. Humphry) Ward to Maude Royden—provide fascinating reading for students of the role of women in the Anglican church. Upper-division undergraduate and graduate collections.—*V. Clark, Choice*

WS-1671 HX313 91-33752 CIP
Elwood, R.C. **Inessa Armand: revolutionary and feminist.** Cambridge, 1992. 304p bibl index ISBN 0-521-41486-5, $49.95

Armand (1874-1920) was arguably, as R.C. Elwood claims, "one of the most important women in the pre-revolutionary Bolshevik Party and second only to Aleksandra Kollontai in the ranks of early Soviet feminists." However, what little recognition Armand receives among scholars more often concerns her possible role as Lenin's mistress than her contributions to revolutionary ideology and praxis. Elwood's biography is an attempt to lift Armand out of the shadow of more prominent Bolshevik personalities and to portray her as a capable and seasoned publicist as well as a feminist. At times, Elwood succeeds in conveying a sense of Armand's beliefs, accomplishments, and personality; the chapter on her brief stint as director of Zhenotdel is interesting and well done. In general, though, the biography contains too many speculative arguments and scantily supported claims (e.g., Armand's 20-year commitment to feminism is several times averred but not satisfactorily demonstrated). Moreover, the book suffers from uneven writing and repetitious phrasing. Although at present it is the most comprehensive English-language treatment of Armand available, it is likely soon to be superseded. Advanced undergraduate; graduate; faculty.—*A. H. Koblitz, Hartwick College*

WS-1672 DC137.1 90-45488 CIP
Erickson, Carolly. **To the scaffold: the life of Marie Antoinette.** W. Morrow, 1991. 384p index ISBN 0-688-07301-8, $22.95

The tragic life of Marie Antoinette, Queen of France, has been told and retold many times in the almost 200 years since her death during the French Revolution. Few historians, however, have recounted her life with such vivid detail and close attention to the personal aspects of the Queen's everyday activities as this author. Erickson devotes almost two thirds of the book to Marie's life up to the outbreak of the French Revolution: she covers Marie's early years in Vienna under the influence of her mother, the Empress Maria Theresa, and the Hapsburg court; her betrothal to the Dauphin of France; and her becoming Queen when her husband, Louis XVI, ascended the throne in 1774; the birth of her children; the scandalous "Affair of the Diamond Necklace"; and her growing unpopularity in France by 1789. The final third of Ericson's study traces Marie's role during the Revolution and leads to the overthrow of the monarchy and her death on the guillotine in 1793. Beautifully written and thoroughly researched, this balanced account is history at its best. An excellent introduction to this leading figure in French history. Highly recommended for all levels.—*G. C. Bond, Auburn University*

WS-1673 CT788 94-12343 CIP
Frank, Katherine. **A passage to Egypt: the life of Lucie Duff Gordon.** Houghton Mifflin, 1994. 399p bibl index ISBN 0-395-54688-5, $27.50

Frank, noted for biographies of Mary Kingsey (CH, Feb'87) and Emily Brontë (CH, May'91), has produced an interesting and well-written account of the life of another extraordinary 19th-century British woman. Duff Gordon, translator of a number of scholarly works, is best known as the author of *Letters of Egypt*, which has been reissued periodically since its original publication in 1865. At the age of 40, Duff Gordon left behind her family and her friends (including John Stuart Mill, Thomas and Jane Carlyle, and Caroline Norton) to live in Egypt, hoping that a more propitious climate would improve her delicate health. Her letters home, some of which are reproduced in this volume, are witty, perceptive, and full of love for her adopted country and its inhabitants. Frank's study, although not a critical biography of Duff Gordon's life and work, makes good use of previously unpublished or bowdlerized family correspondence and documents, and it improves on earlier biographies written by various family members. Although Frank's source notes are awkward, her portrait of the unconventional Lucie Duff Gordon is engaging. Accessible to general readers and undergraduates.—*J. Travers, SUNY at Stony Brook*

WS-1674 DA3 91-33675 CIP
Hill, Bridget. **The Republican virago: the life and times of Catharine Macaulay, historian.** Oxford, 1992. 263p index ISBN 0-19-812978-5, $55.00

An interesting, perceptive work that attempts to resurrect the reputation of a remarkable woman whose contributions to 18th-century radical, republican thought have largely been forgotten. Stimulated by her interest in women's history, Hill's study is the first biography of Macaulay. Hill's task has been complicated by the absence of family papers or collections that offer anything more than anecdotal and fragmentary evidence about her subject. Consequently, she has had to rely primarily on a limited number of secondary works and the published observations of Macaulay's contemporaries, many of whom were critical of her controversial political ideas and personal behavior. A warm supporter of both the American and French Revolutions and a central figure in the Wilkite agitation of the 1760s and 1770s, Macaulay, Hill argues convincingly, overcame the gender-inspired condescension of her age to play an important role in the shaping of a republican, revolutionary ideology in Britain and America. Her influence was based on a small number of political treatises and her eight-volume *History of England* (1764). Indeed, the strength of Hill's book is its analysis of Macaulay's ideas in the context of the radical politics of the age. For graduate students and scholars in political and women's history.—*R. A. Soloway, University of North Carolina at Chapel Hill*

WS-1675 DK125 90-12288 CIP
Hughes, Lindsey. **Sophia, Regent of Russia, 1657-1704.** Yale, 1991 (c1990). 345p bibl index ISBN 0-300-04790-8, $29.95

Hughes's "purpose" in this book is to help "the Pious Tsarevna' and her era to emerge from the shadow cast over them by Peter the Great ." Her purpose is achieved very well. Thoroughly in command of the literature and sources, including unpublished material, Hughes (London University) provides both lucid narrative description and insightful analysis of the career of a ruler who played a key role in Russia's transition from old to new. The book has three main parts; the first concludes with a discussion of the rebellion of 1682, perhaps the clearest account of the Khovanshchina in print. The middle section includes detailed discussions of the three areas in which Sophia did most to effect a transiton to a new era: religious affairs, culture, and foreign policy. The final section makes clear Peter's role in his sister's fall, and briefly describes Sophia's final years in the Novodevichy Convent. The "postscript" is a very thorough discussion of the historiography of the subject. Well-chosen illustrations contribute to the success of the book, which is accessible to relative beginners while satisfying the needs of scholars.—*J. T. Flynn, College of the Holy Cross*

WS-1676 Orig
Lewis, Gifford. **The Yeats sisters and the Cuala.** Irish Academic, 1994. (Dist. by International Specialized Book Services) 199p bibl index ISBN 0-7165-2525-9, $39.50

Susan Mary "Lily" Yeats (1866-1949) and Elizabeth Corbet Yeats (1868-1940) were eclipsed in life and afterward by their illustrious older brother, William Butler Yeats, as well as by a younger brother, Jack Yeats, a distinguished painter, and by their eccentric artist father, John Butler Yeats. Nevertheless, the sisters were themselves significant Anglo-Irish cultural figures. Lily Yeats, trained in William Morris's embroidery workshop, became a skilled practitioner of this craft. Elizabeth, educated as a kindergarten and art teacher, published admired brushwork manuals. Between 1909 and 1940, the sisters together managed Cuala Industries of Dublin, producers of fine crafts and books. Cuala Press, operative until 1946, published handsome limited editions of the works of W.B. Yeats, Lady Gregory, Douglas Hyde, Lord Dunsany, and many other Irish authors, as well as Jack Yeats's earthy *Broadsides* of 1908-15. Lewis's readable study, based on archival sources, is informative on Yeats family relationships and the pre-WW I Dublin artistic world. It covers similar ground, but from a different perspective, as does William M. Murphy's *Prodigal Father: The Life of John Butler Yeats, 1839-1922* (CH, Nov'78). All levels.—*D. M. Cregier, University of Prince Edward Island*

WS-1677 DA585 91-546 CIP
Morgan, Janet. **Edwina Mountbatten: a life of her own.** Scribner, 1991. 489p index ISBN 0-684-19346-9, $27.50

A definitive biography of an important, fascinating woman. Using the private diaries and letters of the Mountbatten family as well as letters and interviews with their intimates, Morgan creates a rich, detailed tapestry of Edwina Mountbatten's life, family, and relationships with the wealthy, royal, and famous. She is portrayed as a multifaceted person—a globe-trotting socialite and as a private free spirit whose independence initially strained but ultimately strengthened her marriage to Lord Louis Mountbatten. The author illuminates Mountbatten's transition from an indulged millionairess of the interwar years to the hard-working, devoted campaigner for health care and public causes during WW II and thereafter, until her death in 1960. Morgan credits her, as the last Vicereine of India, with assisting the smooth transfer of power, building friendships between Muslim and Hindu leaders, and developing a reciprocated spiritual friendship with Nehru. This perceptive biography entertains and enlightens. Recommended for those also interested in Lord Mountbatten. All levels.—*G. M. Stearns, University of Cincinnati*

WS-1678 Orig
Rose, June. **Marie Stopes and the sexual revolution.** Faber & Faber, 1992. 272p bibl index ISBN 0-571-16260-6, $22.95

Although Rose clearly admires Marie Stopes, she refuses to romanticize her subject. She offers instead a frank portrait of a complex and driven woman, who insisted that sexual fulfillment was possible and desirable for women as well as men, yet experienced deep frustration and unhappiness in her own relationships. Rose has made extensive use of Stopes's personal papers in writing this biography. She attempts to use new material to make a critical assessment of several of Stopes's assertions regarding her own life and its relation to her work, most notably Stopes's famous claim that her first husband never consummated their marriage. Despite such interesting revisions, the book is overall very similar in scope and interpretation to Ruth Hall's longer biography, *Passionate Crusader* (CH, Mar'78), even using many of the same quotations from Stopes's extensive correspondence. The possibility suggested by the title, that Stopes's life will be integrated with contemporary change in social attitudes and mores, is not fully realized. Included are an interesting selection of photographs from the collection of Stopes's son, notes, a chronology, and a select bibliography. A good short biography for the general reader; useful as background for the specialist in women's history or the history of sexuality.—*M. L. Meldrum, SUNY at Stony Brook*

WS-1679 DC146 CIP
Roudinesco, Elisabeth. **Théroigne de Méricourt: a melancholic woman during the French revolution,** tr. by Martin Thom. Verso, 1991. 284p index ISBN 0-86091-324-4, $34.95

Roudinesco, a psychoanalyst, successfully uses the roots of modern feminism, the history of insanity from 1792 to 1841, and a historiographical essay to rehabilitate one of the Revolution's most controversial, enigmatic, and tragic figures. From her obscure and debauched youth in the Austrian Netherlands, Théroigne de Méricourt suddenly appeared to play a dramatic and partly mythical role in Paris and Vienna during the first five years of the Revolution. Roudinesco is meticulous in separating fact from legend, using extensive records in Viennese and Parisian archives to recreate the political career of this victim of melancholia. A supporter of the Girondins and an advocate for women's rights, de Méricourt was publicly flogged during the Terror, later arrested, offically declared "mad," and incarcerated in asylums for the last 23 years of her life. This thorough and riveting book now restores de Mérincourt to her rightful place in the history of the Revolution. Illustrated, notes, chronology. All levels.—*J. E. Brink, Texas Tech University*

WS-1680 HX244 92-16656 CIP
Seymour-Jones, Carole. **Beatrice Webb: a life.** I.R. Dee, 1992. 369p bibl index afp ISBN 1-56663-001-0, $30.00

In the cottage industry that has sprung up around Beatrice Webb, another biography may seem unnecessary. Deborah Nord's *The Apprenticeship of Beatrice Webb* (CH, Sep'85), Lisanne Radice's *Beatrice and Sydney Webb* (CH, Feb'85), Barbara Caine's *Destined to be Wives: The Sisters of Beatrice Webb* (CH, Oct'87) and *The Diary of Beatrice Webb*, ed. by N. and J. MacKenzie (1982), and *The Letters of Sidney and Beatrice Webb*, ed. by N. MacKenzie (1978) have provided much information about this key Victorian and Edwardian figure. Upper-class social reformer and Fabian socialist, Webb experienced the difficulties and contradictions facing autonomous, independent women who sought to effect social and political change. Seymour-Jones does a nice job in illuminating the psychological price exacted for her rebellion against convention and for her renunciation of personal fulfilment. General; undergraduate.—*S. K. Kent, University of Florida*

WS-1681   Can. CIP

Stone, James S. **Emily Faithfull: Victorian champion of women's rights.** P.D. Meany, 1994. 336p bibl index afp ISBN 0-88835-040-6, $38.00

The late 19th century women's movement in Britain has drawn attention from historians in recent years, including Caine, Herstein, and Rendall. Until now, however, Emily Faithfull's role has been largely ignored. Faithfull was a member of the Langham Place Circle, which launched the women's movement in the 1860s. For four decades, she worked energetically to advance women's causes, such as higher education, training for jobs, equitable property laws, and voting rights. Above all, she was a gifted journalist who founded the Victoria Press and edited the *Victoria Magazine*, an influential women's journal. Faithfull was shunned by reformers for many years because of her involvement in the Codrington divorce scandal of 1864, with its overtones of adultery and lesbianism. Stone's ponderous book offers a wealth of information about Faithfull and resurrects her as a person of significance. Yet, it is a catalog of facts rather than a biography and will be of little general interest to historians.—*J. H. Wiener, CUNY City College*

WS-1682   BP585   91-24462 CIP

Taylor, Anne. **Annie Besant: a biography.** Oxford, 1992. 383p bibl index ISBN 0-19-211796-3, $59.00

Annie Besant was one of the most remarkable British women of the 19th century. A leading freethinker and socialist, she was a pioneer in the struggle for birth control and women's rights. She edited important journals like the *Link* and *Our Corner*, led the London match girls in a famous strike in 1888, and advocated Irish Home Rule and Indian independence. During the final decades of her life she championed Theosophy and helped to popularize Hindu mysticism in the West. Several biographies of Besant have been published, but Taylor's balanced, comprehensive study is the best by far. It chronicles her personal life in detail, depicting her as a self-willed, obsessive woman who overcame an unhappy marriage and the legal separation from her children to achieve remarkable goals. Her close relationships with Shaw, Gandhi, Charles Bradlaugh, W.T. Stead, and Madame Blavatsky, among others, are impressively delineated. Taylor views Besant's commitment to Theosophy, generally regarded as a wrong turning in her career, as consistent with it. Advanced undergraduate; graduate; faculty.—*J. H. Wiener, City College, CUNY*

WS-1683   HQ1595   94-12757 Orig

Thompson, Ruby Alice Side. **Ruby: an ordinary woman,** ed. by Bonnie Thompson Glaser and Ann Martin Worster. Faber & Faber, 1995. 274p ISBN 0-571-19858-9, $24.95

Although Ruby Thompson's life may have appeared ordinary, her diary, edited by A.M. Worster and by Thompson's granddaughter, B.T. Blaser, reveals her to have been a singular and free-thinking women. Begun in 1909 when she was 25, the diary recounts Thompson's rage over the restraints placed on her by motherhood, and by marriage to an inflexible and traditional man. It also offers her thoughts (surprisingly familiar to a late 20th century reader) on such topics as Catholicism, sexuality, literature, and relations between men and women. The reader is beguiled by Thompson's passion and intelligence, and sympathetic with her inability to make her life conform to her beliefs and wishes. Because access to the inner lives of ordinary people is usually limited, the preservation of one women's voice is welcome and informative, especially for scholars of social and women's history. The volume ends in 1938; this reviewer looks forward to the continuation of Thompson's story. All levels.—*J. Travers, SUNY at Stony Brook*

WS-1684   Brit. CIP

Ward, Margaret. **Maud Gonne: Ireland's Joan of Arc.** Pandora, 1990. (Dist. by HarperCollins) 211p bibl index ISBN 0-04-440583-9 pbk, $16.95

To Ward, feminist and social democrat, Maud Gonne is the "last of the romantic nationalists," an exotic heroine who expanded political opportunities for women while inspiring greater resistance to British rule. Her commitment to the cause of Irish independence, enhanced by her social position and her charismatic symbolic value, advanced the movement in vital ways. Her most productive contribution was her agitation on behalf of prisoners. But despite Ward's sympathetic treatment, Gonne sometimes appears as an upper-class English lady dabbling in Irish nationalism. Flouting contemporary social convention, Gonne often allowed her tangled personal affairs and her sensitivity to public opinion to push her into hypocrisy. Examples are her insistence before her marriage to Major John MacBride that her illegitimate daughter by the French nationalist Millevoye was her "niece," and her refusal to use her married name until after MacBride's execution by the British transformed him into a republican hero. The book is useful as a brief introduction to Gonne's life.—*H. T. Blethen, Western Carolina University*

◆ Europe
Britain

WS-1685   JQ1593   93-18896 CIP

Banks, Olive. **The politics of British feminism, 1918-1970.** E. Elgar, 1993. 149p bibl index ISBN 1-85278-108-4, $49.95

Banks (sociology, emeritus, Leicester Univ.) has sketched an overview of her subject. Because it is based entirely on secondary sources, the book is nearly a bibliographical essay. Banks describes the important political issues for women in the half-century between the decline of ardent, equal-rights feminism of the suffragettes and the quite sudden emergence in the 1960s of a feminism that again was about independence and equality. During the period Banks describes, feminism largely concerned women as wives and mothers because the political parties so decided, and most feminists bent to their view. Banks focuses on the traditional topics at the center of contemporary debate; family endowment and marriage bars figure prominently, but abortion rights are little discussed. A much less ambitious book than Martin Pugh's excellent *Women and the Women's Movement in Britain, 1914-1959* (CH, Dec'93), of which Banks has made extensive use, Banks's book should find favor among college teachers looking to assign a brief account of a generally unexplored period in British feminism. Good bibliography. Undergraduates.—*P. K. Cline, Earlham College*

WS-1686   HQ1593   91-47945 CIP

Barker-Benfield, G.J. **The culture of sensibility: sex and society in eighteenth-century Britain.** Chicago, 1992. 520p index afp ISBN 0-226-03713-4, $49.95

Closely reasoned and extensively documented, this work on the origins and evolution of sensibility traces the movement's rise and transformations in 18th-century England. Sensibility—a term used to explain how the senses operate to determine one's "psychoperceptual" view of the world—came to be seen as a way to liberate both sexes from society's bonds and from conventional behavior. Sensibility's characteristics and contradictions are thoroughly examined, documented, and explicated by summarizing numerous philosophical tracts, memoirs, various forms of popular culture literature, and "sentimental" novels, which proved to be the movement's most effective means of expression. These widely read novels usually revolved around one to three sets of couples whose feelings and senses determined their personal and social relationships, and whose personalities and actions exemplified the strengths and weaknesses of the movement. Sensibility's proponents hoped to improve human behavior and to influence contemporary political, social, and economic issues. Its critics, particularly males, discredited the movement for its excesses in personal lives and its proposals for radical social reforms. This debate eventually focused on the private life and public pronouncements of Mary Wollstonecraft Godwin, who became the symbol of the rebellious female, the most famous advocate of sensibility, and an early leader for women's rights. Advanced undergraduate; graduate; faculty.—*R. T. Matthews, Michigan State University*

WS-1687 HO18 91-2751 CIP
Barret-Ducrocq, Françoise. **Love in the time of Victoria: sexuality, class and gender in nineteenth-century London,** tr. by John Howe. Verso, 1991. 225p bibl ISBN 0-86091-325-2, $29.95

Though much narrower in content and scope than its inflated title suggests this book, which first appeared in French in 1989, is nevertheless an interesting if modest contribution to the burgeoning fields of Victorian sexuality and women's studies. It is a largely anecdotal survey of case histories of seduction and illegitimacy in the mid-19th century, drawn from the detailed and often fascinating interviews and questionnaires required by foundling hospital officials before they would accept the children of unmarried mothers. Barret-Ducrocq argues that the picture of female working-class sexuality that emerges from these dossiers disproves Victorian middle-class assumptions that their social inferiors were excessively licentious and depraved. The author makes little effort to re-create a statistical profile from these sad stories, but is content to present short excerpts interlaced with judicious and balanced commentary rather than extensive social analysis. The result is a short, readable, well-documented study in social history. Upper-division undergraduates and above.—*R. A. Soloway, University of North Carolina at Chapel Hill*

WS-1688 HQ1595 91-24220 CIP
Caine, Barbara. **Victorian feminists.** Oxford, 1992. 284p bibl index ISBN 0-19-820170-2, $39.95

Another work on Victorian feminism might appear redundant, but Caine's study, although revisiting familiar ground and familiar individuals, does so on the basis of the most current historical and theoretical scholarship. Caine examines the connection between women's experiences and their analyses of women's oppression, and places both within the context of discursive practices that informed the Victorian era. Many of the themes she treats—sexuality, the nature of femininity and masculinity, the question of equality versus difference—are not new; they have been dealt with at length in a number of works, e.g., Philippa Levine's *Victorian Feminism, 1850-1900* (London, 1987); David Rubenstein's *Before the Suffragettes: Women's Emancipation in the 1890s* (1986); Sandra Stanley Holton's *Feminism and Democracy* (CH, Jun'87); and Susan Kent's *Sex and Suffrage in Britain, 1860-1914* (CH, Nov'87), to cite just a few. Caine draws on a vast amount of secondary literature to make sense of the relationship between discourse and experience, and thus provides a mature synthetic treatment of an important topic in women's and British history. Undergraduate; graduate; faculty.—*S. K. Kent, University of Florida*

WS-1689 HD8390 93-50835 CIP
Clark, Anna. **The struggle for the breeches: gender and the making of the British working class.** California, 1995. 416p bibl index afp ISBN 0-520-08624-4, $35.00

Clark (Univ. of North Carolina) has written a pioneering study of the role of gender in British working-class history that serves as an antidote to E.P. Thompson's male orientation in *The Making of the English Working Class* (CH, Jul'64) and Barbara Taylor's narrow study of gender in the Owenite movement, *Eve and the New Jerusalem* (CH, Sep'83). Clark concentrates on the late 18th century and first half of the 19th century, and her work clearly indicates the need for a similar study of the late Victorian era. For her analysis she uses artisans and textile workers in Glasgow, Lancashire, and London; thus, her view is British rather than solely English. She introduces gender into such topics as domestic life, the emerging factory system, radical political philosophy, popular culture, politics, and proletariat organizations, e.g., the Chartists. Clark demolishes the myth of domestic bliss before industrialism, traces the conflict of gender during industrialization, and demonstrates that the fatal flaws of misogyny and patriarchy muted the radicalism of the working class. The book is well researched and generally well written. It provides valuable insight into a misunderstood and neglected aspect of British social history. Illustrated. Upper-division undergraduates and above.—*W. J. Hoffman Jr., Hiram College*

WS-1690 HV6949 93-40060 CIP
Dolan, Frances E. **Dangerous familiars: representations of domestic crime in England, 1550-1700.** Cornell, 1994. 253p index afp ISBN 0-8014-2901-3, $37.95; ISBN 0-8014-8134-1 pbk, $15.95

Using the household as an analogue for the Commonwealth, Dolan examines domestic violence as represented in ballads, pamphlets, and plays to demonstrate the political "threat" posed to the established order by "dangerous familiars"—servants and (mostly) women who murdered their masters or husbands, committed infanticide, or were accused of witchcraft. That early modern English justice was biased against women and the lower orders is well known to historians, whose work Dolan uses more extensively than many critics. Her arguments, carefully related to recent literary and historical scholarship, are sophisticated and deserve attention. No doubt society did perceive murderous females as threatening social stability; and Dolan is right to emphasize, for example, that husband-murder was by law petty treason, while wife-murder was merely homicide. Her notion that both popular and canonical literature reflect anxiety about female threats to social order is plausible, though she perhaps exaggerates the extent of patriarchal paranoia. Dolan's contention that literary representations of domestic violence became less hostile to women after the civil war ought to prompt more research. Her discussion of witchcraft adds literary evidence to the widely accepted picture of witches as marginalized women. Clichés abound, however, and these detract from a useful study. Upper-division undergraduates and above.—*W. B. Robison III, Southeastern Louisiana University*

WS-1691 PR1110 91-16313 CIP
English women's voices, 1540-1700, ed. by Charlotte F. Otten. Florida International, 1992. (Dist. by University Press of Florida) 421p bibl index afp ISBN 0-8130-1083-7, $49.95; ISBN 0-8130-1099-3 pbk, $22.95

A useful and, at times, exciting collection of primary materials. Women's voices, speaking about lived experience in contrast to those of women in creative literature, are not easy to come by. Otten has culled the materials—many unpublished since the 17th century and a few still in manuscript—to give readers glimpses of informed and sensitive comments on gender, status, and sex. The volume's eight sections deal with abuse, persecution and prison life, political statements, love and marriage, health care, childbirth and death, prayer, and the right to preach. Short introductions explain the selections with each section, and a bibliography of women writers, 1540-1700, is of value. The accounts wherein women describe courtship, joys and pains of requited love, devotion to children and the frequent death of offspring, and their urge to be taken as full members of Christ's flock, are valuable materials, made accessible here to students and teachers. Some excerpts are very powerful; others are somewhat overlong. An occasional omission in chapter bibliographies and the need for more comparisons with male experience are minor flaws. An unusually timely, thoughtful, useful volume. Upper-division undergraduates and above.—*J. T. Rosenthal, SUNY at Stony Brook*

WS-1692 HQ1075 95-21565 CIP
Fletcher, Anthony. **Gender, sex and subordination in England, 1500-1800.** Yale, 1995. 442p bibl index ISBN 0-300-06531-0, $37.50

Fletcher draws a map on which readers can trace the changing ideologies, strategies, and discourses that men, in their patriarchal guise, constructed and used over the course of three centuries to explain and maintain their sexual and gendered dominance of society. He has done this by using contemporary sources, along with modern scholarship that rests largely on literature, books of manners, educational treatises, and such personal materials as diaries and letters. In the early 16th century the humoral tradition and classical arguments still held sway; woman was an imperfect male—in physiological as well as moral and intellectual terms. As new modes of explanation came into vogue, she was variously viewed as different but unequal (a hierarchical model) and, by the time of the Enlightenment, as a creature of sensibility who could be shaped to internalize such virtues as meekness and chastity, which she had to learn and display. This richly argued study summarizes much current work and, gently but firmly, makes no bones about how resolutely male-voiced society erected barrier after barrier, hurdle after hurdle, lest sisters, wives, and daughters break into the open. All levels.—*J. T. Rosenthal, SUNY at Stony Brook*

WS-1693 KD754 95-7637 CIP
Frost, Ginger S. **Promises broken: courtship, class, and gender in Victorian England.** University Press of Virginia, 1995. 241p bibl index afp ISBN 0-8139-1610-0, $35.00

In a carefully researched examination of breach of promise lawsuits in Victorian England, historian Frost identifies some of the ambiguities and contradictions contained within power relationships based on gender and class. Frost maintains that breach of promise suits "lay at a crossroads of legal, social, and cultural values." Her close scrutiny of 875 specific cases, mostly occurring between 1850 and 1900, provides rich information on the confluence of late-Victorian gender and class stereotypes, romantic ideals in popular drama and fiction, courtship rituals and broken engagements, premarital sex and sexual assault, class-based moral codes, and legal institutions and processes. Most significantly, Frost's practice-oriented analysis demonstrates important areas of social life in which women were ironically enabled by the structural and ideological characteristics of a patriarchal and highly class-conscious society to act in their own material and social interests. Although the victims of legal restrictions, social stigmas, and severely limited economic opportunities, working-class and lower-middle-class women of "good character" were often able to use core beliefs and values of a masculinist and paternalistic society as a basis for claiming their own rights as dependent, exploited, and betrayed victims of male suitors and seducers. All levels.—*B. Tavakolian, Denison University*

WS-1694 DA355 92-37725 CIP
Frye, Susan. **Elizabeth I: the competition for representation.** Oxford, 1993. 228p bibl index afp ISBN 0-19-508023-8, $35.00

Frye's excellent monograph is a study of the "conscious and unconscious strategies through which [Elizabeth I] worked to create an identity beyond accepted gender definitions." Frye is thus at pains to restore what she calls "agency" to the last of the Tudors. As the subtitle indicates, she avers that Elizabeth encountered "competition" for representation from male-oriented contemporaries who sought to define her—and all women—as passive, weak, and in need of defense. Frye explores the contest for representation by examining three episodes in the queen's reign: the London coronation entry of 1559, the Kenilworth entertainments of 1575, and the "tension" evinced by courtiers and artists in the last phase of the queen's life (c.1590). The truth of Frye's central argument, that Elizabeth succeeded in fashioning her own image for posterity, is asserted rather than demonstrated. Although laden with feminist and historicist jargon, the book draws on a multitude of original sources and succeeds in recontextualizing Elizabeth and the allegory that proved her most effective means of self-representation. Advanced undergraduates and above.—*D. R. Bisson, Belmont University*

WS-1695 HQ1593 95-2958 CIP
Giles, Judy. **Women, identity and private life in Britain, 1900-50.** St. Martin's, 1995. 189p bibl index ISBN 0-312-12624-7, $39.95

Giles (Univ. College of Ripon and York St. John) rescues British working-class women from the condescension and mythologizing of middle-class welfare workers (male and female) and feminist writers. The latter, following Virginia Woolf's lead, describe working-class women as "lacking an inner life," and generally disdain its substitutes: domesticity, materialism, and "respectability." More sympathetic, Giles explores what private life and home, frequently examined for middle-class women, actually meant to working-class women. She finds they meant relationships, in which gender, class, generation, education, and wealth played overlapping and contradictory roles. Understanding one relationship (adolescent servant and her mother) requires understanding the others on which it impinges and depends (father and mother, servant and mistress, etc.). Giles's interviews of 21 northern English women form her principal window into private lives that were not heroic, as feminists have wished, but scarred by poverty's deprivations and brutalities. She also uses autobiography, contemporary journalism, and fiction. Her data are modest, but the analysis is intelligent and intellectually engaging. Although Giles's prose is often dense, the reader's reward is a sophisticated template for tracing meaning in the inner lives of Woolf's servants. Upper-division undergraduates and above.—*P. K. Cline, Earlham College*

WS-1696 HQ1596 95-17959 CIP
Gleadle, Kathryn. **The early feminists: radical Unitarians and the emergence of the women's rights movement, 1831-51.** Macmil-lan, UK/ St. Martin's, 1995. 266p bibl index ISBN 0-312-12861-4, $59.95

For those interested in the origins of feminist theory and the women's rights movement, Gleadle's book argues that the British movement of the second half of the 19th century drew much of its ideology and strength from the Radical Unitarian feminists of the 1830s and 1840s. Radical feminist ideas about marriage and women's rights emerged from a Unitarian belief in freedom, communalism, and egalitarian family life. While recognizing the need for changing laws that hindered women's equality, these Unitarians emphasized the need for a more basic transformation of society, which they thought could be achieved through education and the dissemination of literature. A most interesting section discusses their analysis of the "slavery" of women and the dispute with the Chartists, who saw only wage labor as slavery and hence did not support suffrage for women. Despite the nod to Owenism and early socialists, Gleadle makes it appear as if Unitarians were the true intellectual founders of British feminism. Most annoying to this reviewer is the author's constant repetition that she did research others had neglected or had gotten wrong. Upper-division undergraduates and above.—*J. Wishnia, SUNY at Stony Brook*

WS-1697 HD6135 89-70180 CIP
Glucksmann, Miriam. **Women assemble: women workers and the new industries in inter-war Britain.** Routledge, 1990. 325p bibl index ISBN 0-415-03196-6, $52.00; ISBN 0-415-03197-4, $15.95

Seeking to locate the origins of the sexual division of labor in present-day manufacturing industries, Glucksmann focuses on the development of mass consumer production in the interwar period. Because women were regarded by employers as preferable to men in semiskilled positions, they entered into factory employment in significant numbers. Women constituted, in fact, the central labor force within industries generating the main source of British wealth at the time. Almost immediately, these industries became rigidly segregated by sex. Concurrently, the existence of the "ideal home" run by the "ideal housewife"—concepts that became current during the interwar period—depended on middle-class women consumers of the goods being produced by women assemblers. Thus, Glucksmann argues, women became implicated in the operations of the capitalist economy to a much greater extent than ever before, from two positions: that of worker and that of consumer. As a result, "a qualitatively different social relation was created between production consumption. . . ." Glucksmann does not show the impact of this change on women's status within the working classes, within society as a whole, or within British politics. Despite this weakness, the book is an important contribution to the literature of the interwar period. Upper-division undergraduates and above.—*S. K. Kent, University of Florida*

WS-1698 HQ1236 93-15079 CIP
Graves, Pamela M. **Labour women: women in British working-class politics, 1918-1939.** Cambridge, 1994. 271p bibl index ISBN 0-521-41247-1, $59.95; ISBN 0-521-45919-2 pbk, $19.95

This important and timely study sheds considerable light on both the labor movement and feminism in interwar Britain. Graves argues effectively that women's choice of separate-but-equal status within the labor movement after enfranchisement in 1918 structured not only the way in which labor women could develop their political issues, but also the way in which they could participate in labor politics. Despite being marginalized by male labor politicians, and contributing to their own diminished effectiveness, labor women developed a full-fledged social democratic health and welfare campaign, which was successful in local government activities and legislation. Another important theme analyzed cogently is the split between middle-class feminists and working-class labor women, which undermined a more unified political voice for women. Based on sound research, especially contextualized interviews with 50 women and 50 men active in the movement, this is a fascinating study that all four-year college and university libraries should have.—*M. J. Moore, Appalachian State University*

WS-1699   HQ18   94-28904 CIP
Harvey, A.D. **Sex in Georgian England: attitudes and prejudices from the 1720s to the 1820s.** St. Martin's, 1994. 205p index ISBN 0-312-12418-X, $45.00

Once a neglected field, the history of sexuality is now attracting a flood of scholarship. Harvey's contribution carefully distinguishes sexual attitudes from the more problematic matter of sexual practices in 18th-century England. Other scholars have already raked over many of his themes, such as the emerging myth of women's sexual passivity. Harvey does offer, however, some provocative and original comments on the links between changing sexual prejudices and shifts in sartorial fashion. His attempts to establish such connections reflect his recognition that changes in sexuality cannot be isolated from other components of social development. In general, though, he eschews grand theories of the type associated with philosopher-historian Michel Foucault in favor of a descriptive approach. Where Harvery does tentatively essay the connections between class and sexual attitudes, his analysis suffers from an overly schematized conception of social structure. The book is thoroughly researched: literary sources find a place alongside judicial records and the latest findings of social historians. Harvey writes with gusto, avoiding both the jargon that afflicts his field and the linguistic shackles of political correctness. Endnotes; no bibliography. General and academic readers, undergraduate and up.—*J. Sainsbury, Brock University*

WS-1700   HQ1593   90-38582 CIP
Horn, Pamela. **Victorian countrywomen.** B. Blackwell, 1991. 281 index ISBN 0-631-15522-8, $36.95

Horn's readable and informative account of Victorian rural women—a hitherto ignored topic—supplements her study, *The Changing Countryside in Victorian and Edwardian England and Wales* (CH, Jun'86). On the surface, Victorian villages were masculine, and this is how historians have viewed them. Horn (Oxford Polytechnic University) gently but persuasively corrects this imbalance by analyzing the role and daily lives of women in rural society, including females of various classes and occupations, and their changing status throughout the century. Despite increasing economic and social pressures to confine rural women to their homes, the professionalization of women as midwifes, nurses, and teachers in the late 19th century enhanced their independence and prominence in rural society. Through an adept blending of sources, Horn presents a revisionist and unforgettable account of the lives of rural females. The book is well researched, well organized, and well written, and includes significant statistical appendixes. Detailed bibliography; average index. College, university, and public libraries.—*W. J. Hoffman Jr., Hiram College*

WS-1701   LC41   92-25847 Orig
Hughes, Kathryn. **The Victorian governess.** Hambledon, 1993. 256p bibl index afp ISBN 1-85285-002-7, $40.00

In an era when proper young ladies were not supposed to work outside the home, what would happen when a gentlewoman's family, through death or some other misfortune, could no longer support her? With few occupational options open to them, thousands of these young women became governesses. Upper-class families had traditionally sent their boys off to boarding schools but girls, like "delicate flowers," were to be educated at home, guided by governesses to be morally correct young ladies with just enough knowledge to attract suitable husbands. By the mid-19th century, the rapidly growing middle class also hired governesses, finding them socially prestigious and cheaper than tuition at private schools. It is estimated that at that time there were 25,000 governesses. Hughes has written a fascinating and very readable study of these women, who constantly experienced the tensions and anomalies of gentlewomen without support. They were neither family members nor servants, motherly yet childless, teachers but without much training, well-dressed but not chic, ladies but not suitable for a proper marriage. Many were successful teachers and some went on to marry, but most, dependent on the good will of employers, were underpaid, lonely, and without a future, and ended their days in poverty. All levels.—*J. Wishnia, SUNY at Stony Brook*

WS-1702   HQ18.G7   89-77936 CIP
Hyam, Ronald. **Empire and sexuality: the British experience.** Manchester, 1990. (Dist. by St. Martin's) 234p bibl index ISBN 0-7190-2504-4, $59.95

Hyam's able and pioneering study of the relationships among imperial authority, experience, and environments, and the sexual behavior of Europeans in British colonies, is both the fullest and best book to date on sexuality within an imperial context. Though evidence is, by the nature of the subject, often anecdotal, Hyam (Cambridge) provides both a sound argument and more than adequate documentation to that argument. He explores homosexuality, concubinage, prostitution, the role of regimental brothels in India, and tastes in sexual practices throughout the empire, with some emphasis on Africa, South Asia, and New Zealand. Sexual demands made by male figures in administrative authority or made within a heirarchical environment such as the military are compared to those made—often for chastity and purity—within the quite different authoritarian environment of missionary activity. The entire inquiry is seen within the context of changing attitudes within Britain toward sexual matters, largely in the high Victorian age. Hyam makes, often in passing, interesting observations concerning the ineffectiveness of feminist studies in throwing light on his subject, the role of pornography in society, concepts of masculinity, and pseudo-Freudian speculation, for which he has little patience. The book belongs in all college libraries because of the wide range of applicability of its findings.—*R. W. Winks, Yale University*

WS-1703   HQ1075   93-18776 CIP
Kent, Susan Kingsley. **Making peace: the reconstruction of gender in interwar Britain.** Princeton, 1994 (c1993). 182p bibl index afp ISBN 0-691-03140-1, $24.95

Kent has made an important contribution to the literature reinterpreting war in terms of gender. Her focal point is WW I, and her objective is to understand why British feminists who had fought for gender equality before 1914 emerged from the war accepting notions of separate spheres for men and women. Kent's main thesis is that the experiences of the war are represented through the language of sexuality and gender, that sex, war, and death are intertwined in the public mind. Hence peace is symbolized by the end of the sexual disorder of the war. The concept that men wanted to return to "normalcy," with marriage and maternity for women seen as antidotes to wartime sexual and economic freedom, is certainly correct. Despite the power of the sexual language, however, it is still hard to understand why feminists accepted this social construct. Nor is Kent's argument that war finds its "most vivid" representation in metaphors of sex and gender completely convincing. Mangled bodies and mud are quite vivid; at one point, Kent notes that men caught in the terrible carnage of the battlefield are also pawns and victims. These misgivings aside, Kent's book is recommended as a stimulating analysis of the meshing of language, gender, and war. Upper-division undergraduates and above.—*J. Wishnia, SUNY at Stony Brook*

WS-1704   92-85445 Orig
Kunze, Bonnelyn Young. **Margaret Fell and the rise of Quakerism.** Stanford, 1994. 327p bibl index afp ISBN 0-8047-2154-8, $39.50

Kunze's revisionist study of early Quaker history gives more weight to the role of Margaret Fell, wife of George Fox. Because of her well-born status and strength of mind, Fell exercised crucial leadership in the early days from her base at the family estate. Correspondence, account books, and meeting minutes suggest that Fell influenced Fox's theology, helped organize important women's meetings that established marriage criteria, and oversaw a substantial economic enterprise. Rather than being just a dutiful helpmeet, Fell wrote many original works challenging current patriarchal notions. She was far from perfect, often domineering and at times not very ethical. And despite egalitarian pronouncements of fellow Quakers, Fell, Fox, and William Penn were well aware of class distinctions and treated others accordingly. The book is a needed corrective to sympathetic histories of the past. It may be, as Kunze believes, that much dissension was suppressed or covered up to present a unified and orderly picture of early Quaker history. Although Kunze is very appreciative of Fell's role, she does not romanticize it. The organization of the book—divided into Fell's "worlds"—is questionable, as are a few of the author's speculations, but overall this is an important work of scholarship. Undergraduates and above.—*B. Lowe, Florida Atlantic University*

WS-1705   HQ1599.E5   89-18577 CIP
Levine, Philippa. **Feminist lives in Victorian England: private roles and public commitment.** B. Blackwell, 1990. 241p bibl index ISBN 0-631-14802-7, $49.95

Like the debate that engendered it, this work combines both intellectually provocative and analytically trivial elements. Levine's aim is to rescue early activists for women's rights (first-wave feminists) in Britain from charges that they were bourgeois conservatives by linking their backgrounds to their political choices. Her revision comes in two parts. The first part, "Private Roles," attempts a group biography (prosopography) of "women active in women-centered campaigns" during the second half of the 19th century; the second, "Public Commitment," reexamines four campaigns that engaged the energies of these pioneers in "women-centered politics." Unfortunately the prosopographical section of the work is almost entirely useless because Levine seems to have almost no understanding of data analysis. Fortunately, the second section of the work—a reconstruction and reframing of feminist political ideas—redeems the work. Levine shows how opposition to the Contagious Diseases Acts and the protective legislation movement, on the one hand, and activism on behalf of the Married Women's Property Acts and women's access to higher education, on the other, point to a distinct feminist politics "cognizant of the effects of class stratification" but different from all other contemporary movements in a collective, sex-based perspective that involved the "meshing of public and private" spheres. Upper-division undergraduates and above.—*N. B. Rosenthal, SUNY College at Old Westbury*

WS-1706   90-71680 Orig
Lewis, Jane. **Women and social action in Victorian and Edwardian England.** Stanford, 1991. 338p bibl indexes afp ISBN 0-8047-1905-5, $39.50

Lewis uses the lives and work of five women to illuminate late 19th and early 20th century British approaches to philanthropy. Demonstrating that in the late Victorian period care of the poor was viewed as gendered work appropriately carried out by middle-class women as an extension of their family responsibilities, Lewis extends understanding of the beginnings of the British welfare state. Historians have often emphasized those processes that led to the growth of public, state-managed, male-directed welfare systems, ignoring more private, individualistic approaches traditionally used by women. With the development of a professional social work model, middle-class women lost an arena for valuable activity and working-class welfare recipients lost contact with individuals who cared about their moral and spiritual as well as their physical needs. Lewis's subjects are Mary Ward, Beatrice Webb, Octavia Hill, Helen Bosanquet, and Violet Markham. The first two have been extensively studied by historians, but not from Lewis's perspective; she is more sympathetic to Ward than most recent writers have been. Because the other three figures have been comparatively neglected, this treatment is most welcome. Important for any woman studies, social work, or general graduate history collection.—*M. M. Garland, Ohio State University*

WS-1707   HF5813   93-46094 CIP
Loeb, Lori Anne. **Consuming angels: advertising and Victorian women.** Oxford, 1994. 224p bibl index afp ISBN 0-19-508596-5, $29.95

Loeb (Univ. of South Carolina) takes a fresh look at late-Victorian advertisements and the rise of hedonistic consumerism. She argues that by the 1880s, when political democracy seemed assured, the British middle class began to turn away from its traditional values of hard work, thrift, and self-help to pursue a democratic materialism. She examines how advertisers were able to use "celebrity" endorsements to promote a democratic view of individual distinction, explores how ads help reconstruct notions of community, and challenges the Veblenesque perspective that the consumer revolution was fueled by social emulation. Loeb's argument about the impact of consumerism on women's status is most compelling. Although ads did not challenge the ideology of separate spheres, the commercial ideal of women as commanding and sensual was at odds with the Victorian feminine ideal. Loeb concludes that consumerism, and advertisers' targeting of women as the primary consumers, empowered women as women's role of family purchaser acquired greater importance. Fascinating and richly illustrated, this work is a welcome addition to social and women's history. Upper-division undergraduates and above.—*J. Travers, SUNY at Stony Brook*

WS-1708   HQ1236   92-41371 CIP
Lovenduski, Joni. **Contemporary feminist politics: women and power in Britain,** by Joni Lovenduski and Vicky Randall. Oxford, 1993. 388p bibl index afp ISBN 0-19-827738-5, $48.00; ISBN 0-19-878069-9 pbk, $16.95

In this thoughtful and thought-provoking study, two scholars of and partici-

pants in the British women's movement examine its evolution, successes, and failures since the late 1970s. To organize their research, the authors identify five key themes emerging from Women's Liberation Movement congresses between 1970 and '78: equality at work, health and reproductive rights, motherhood and child care, sexuality and violence, and women's citizenship and political representation. Their use of self-critical social science methodologies is given life through the extensive interviews with activists at all levels of involvement. Among other conclusions, they point to the professionalization and institutionalization of the movement along with the broad acceptance of its goals, but also to the growth of conflicts within the movement leading to its fragmentation. A must for all students of women's movements and issues and for theorists of the new social movements, this study includes an excellent bibliography and will be an acquisition valuable to all levels of readers.—*F. Burkhard, Morgan State University*

WS-1709   HV541   94-30052 CIP
Luddy, Maria. **Women and philanthropy in nineteenth-century Ireland.** Cambridge, 1995. 251p bibl index ISBN 0-521-47433-7, $64.95; ISBN 0-521-48361-1 pbk, $27.95

An important contribution to the recent historical scholarship on women's roles in philanthropic work, Luddy's study is both comprehensive and engaging. Luddy (Univ. of Warwick) reveals the crucial role religion played in the formation of Irish philanthropic organizations. Sectarian concerns determined not only who should receive charity but also who were appropriate caregivers. Luddy argues further that sectarianism divided Catholic and Protestant philanthropists, and that this division worked against the development of a political critique of poverty and resulted in a duplication of services to Ireland's poor and outcast. Finally, Luddy's work underscores the extent of women's involvement in providing charitable services throughout the 19th century, and emphasizes the social power exercised by women, whose standards weeded out the "truly needy" from those who were "morally unfit" to receive aid. Upper-division undergraduates and above.—*J. Travers, SUNY at Stony Brook*

WS-1710   HQ32   94-16822 CIP
Mason, Michael. **The making of Victorian sexual attitudes.** Oxford, 1995 (c1994). 256p bibl index afp ISBN 0-19-812292-6, $29.95

In a continuation of his *The Making of Victorian Sexuality* (CH, Jan'95), Mason argues that the sexual attitudes commonly identified as "Victorian" (e.g., prudery, repression) found support most often among radicals, feminists, and others usually seen as progressives. Additionally, he claims that mainstream morality restricted sex to marriage while tolerating occasional lapses, and that Evangelicalism, and religion generally, contributed little to stricter attitudes. Major topics include prostitute rescue, Owenism, and George Drysdale's *The Elements of Social Science*, but the range of material is broad indeed. Moreover, Mason is aware that the century is not all of a piece, but he fails to identify smaller periods adequately. His complex and occasionally convoluted presentation does not help in the understanding of this difficult, often contradictory, material. The reader may well conclude that Victorian sexual attitudes were too varied and complex for easy generalization. Nevertheless, Mason's two books lay a wealth of material before readers interested in Victorian sexuality. Graduate; faculty.—*A. Horstman, Albion College*

WS-1711   HQ18   93-28824 CIP
Mason, Michael. **The making of Victorian sexuality.** Oxford, 1994. 338p bibl index afp ISBN 0-19-812247-0, $25.00

In this dense but provocative monograph, Mason (English literature, University College, Univ. of London) has undertaken a history and critique of the conventional notion of Victorian prudishness. Drawing on a variety of contemporary literary, demographic, and philosophical sources, he maintains that Victorian sexual behavior and attitudes were more varied, complex, and contradictory—over time and between social groups—than has traditionally been believed. Did Victorians deny female sexual response? Hard to reconcile, Mason argues, with the frequently encountered belief that ovulation was contingent on female orgasm. Did they limit sex to marriage? Hard to reconcile with the high rates of bridal pregnancy found in English market towns at the height of Victoria's reign. Given the mass of material the author attempts to cover, it is inevitable that the reader is at times left dazed and confused. Such problems notwithstanding, Mason succeeds in conveying the complex environment in which sexual discourse and conduct intersect, or more generally fail to do so. Upper-division undergraduate; graduate; faculty.—*M. Gordon, University of Connecticut*

WS-1712   HQ29   94-22957 CIP
Matus, Jill L. **Unstable bodies: victorian representations of sexuality and maternity.** Manchester, 1995. (Dist. by St. Martin's) 280p bibl index ISBN 0-7190-4347-6, $69.95; ISBN 0-7190-4348-4 pbk, $24.95

In these essays, Matus (English, Univ. of Toronto) examines printed works on such topics as motherhood, prostitution, wet-nursing, infanticide, and insanity, seeking to show that British Victorians had several, often contradictory, views of the sexual and maternal aspects of women. Although her sources from the period 1840-70 include medical works and literary criticism, most of the book is an analysis of eight novels, all written by women. The author locates much material relating to sexuality and motherhood in these works from the high Victorian age, and, inspired by Foucault, she also finds ambiguities and contradictions everywhere en route to a conclusion attacking what is, by now, the straw man of monolithic Victorianism. Parts of the book have been previously published in periodicals, the chapters vary in their integration of medical and literary views, and repetition, even of quotes, occurs. Jargon, pervasive at first, occasionally distractive later, helps make the theoretical aspects of the book accessible only to scholars, but the literary analysis can be understood by upper-division undergraduates.—*A. Horstman, Albion College*

WS-1713   DS61   91-32433 MARC
Melman, Billie. **Women's Orients, English women and the Middle East, 1718-1918: sexuality, religion and work.** Michigan, 1992. 417p bibl index ISBN 0-472-10332-6, $39.50

Moving beyond the generally recognized symbiosis between Orientalism and Western imperialism, this stimulating and well-researched book shows how women not only perceived the Middle East differently from their male contemporaries but also used their travels to reflect on their own subordination in English society. Their rare 18th-century travel accounts (especially Lady Mary Wortley Montagu's) rather envy what they take to be the economic and sexual liberty—paradoxically facilitated by the veil—of upper-class Ottoman women. The more numerous accounts by middle-class Victorian women tended to desexualize the harem and see in it woman's natural domestic sphere, to which they were accustomed back home. Toward the end of the century, evangelical missionary activity opened new opportunities for married and single Englishwomen alike. Amelia Edwards and others contributed to the development, outside the academic establishment, of archaeology and Egyptology. The writings of Lady Anne Blunt on her travels with her husband, Wilfred Blunt, in Arabia reveal both an empathy for bedouin society and the complex hierarchical husband-wife relationship of this aristocratic Victorian couple. Advanced undergraduate; graduate; faculty.—*D. M. Reid, Georgia State University*

WS-1714   HT1163   91-45790 MARC
Midgley, Clare. **Women against slavery: the British Campaigns, 1780-1870.** Routledge, 1993 (c1992). 281p bibl index ISBN 0-415-06669-7, $69.95

Written out of a "desire to realize the radical potential of women's history" this doctoral thesis investigates the connection between abolitionism and feminism in Britain. As such, Midgley's study parallels Jean Yellin's research for *Women & Sisters: The Antislavery Feminists In American Culture* (CH, Nov'90) and is part of a larger reexamination of the British abolition movement best symbolized by David Turley's *The Culture of English Antislavery, 1780-1860* (CH, Apr'92). Although women occasionally had a supporting role in the larger London-based movement designed to lobby parliament, it was the creation in 1825 of the Female Society for Birmingham that brought women activists to center stage. By 1830, local women's societies made up one third of all the abolition organizations in Britain and they raised 20 percent of all the funds expended in that long campaign. After the British Emancipation Act of 1832, the women's organizations survived into the 1860s to support American emancipation and, gradually, to take up other reform causes, particularly those relating to women. Midgley has written an interesting history of "proto-feminism," with much biographical detail

on the women involved. The book is as much a social history of the 19th-century British women's movement as it is of abolition. General; undergraduate; graduate; faculty.—*R. T. Brown, Westfield State College*

WS-1715   PR468   95-10929 CIP
Mitchell, Sally. **The new girl: girls' culture in England, 1880-1915.** Columbia, 1995. 258p bibl index afp ISBN 0-231-10247-X pbk, $17.50

Mitchell's provocative study joins the growing number of books that revise understanding of girls and their literature at the turn of the century (see also Shirley Marchalonis's *College Girls: A Century in Fiction* and Shirley Foster and Judy Simons's *What Katy Read: Feminist Re-readings of "Classic" Stories for Girls*, both CH, Nov'95). Mitchell (Temple Univ.) proposes that around the turn of the century working- and middle-class girls "increasingly occupied a separate culture." Turning to books, magazines, clothing styles, clubs, sports, schools, and memoirs for evidence, Mitchell defines this culture as a "provisional free space" where girls were no longer children but not yet gendered or sexualized. She pays special attention to the writer L.T. Meade, the literature of girls' schools and pioneering experiences at Cambridge and Oxford, and the culture surrounding scouting; the approach is largely descriptive, leaving the field open for further analysis. In the most innovative chapter, "Reading Feelings," Mitchell attempts to move from an understanding of the fiction most often cited by girls as "addictive" to some understanding of their interior world and the connections between the act of reading and daydreaming and fantasy. Mitchell's conclusion traces the demographic and political influences (including WW I) that restricted the culture after 1920. An excellent bibliography and 30 illustrations enhance the text. Recommended for collections in women's studies, children's literature, and British history at all levels.—*E. R. Baer, Gustavus Adolphus College*

WS-1716   DA320   94-1035 CIP
Orlin, Lena Cowen. **Private matters and public culture in post-Reformation England.** Cornell, 1994. 309p bibl index afp ISBN 0-8014-2858-0, $41.50

Applying "new historicist" techniques of analyzing an event through its various textual manifestations, Orlin uses the 1551 murder of upstart landowner Thomas Arden by his wife to explore the relationship between private and public realms. Indicting historical research for not problematizing the past or finding social constructions in the archives, Orlin, borrowing from Geertzian anthropology and deconstruction, views texts themselves as events, and offers a "thick description" that attempts to uncover signs and metaphors encoded in written words. Works examined range from political treatises to chronicles, but most are plays; there is a fascinating chapter on Shakespeare's *Othello*. Orlin suggests that during this period of emerging capitalism the domestic realm became feminized, abandoned by men, and separated from the patriarchal professional world. The redacted texts expose confusion and fear, with Arden's fate symbolic of how domestic life could be held responsible for spouse murder. This is a thoughtful, mostly convincing analysis, although Orlin's writing is sometimes cryptic and esoteric. She may be trying too hard to read certain conclusions into the texts. Historians will find her methods questionable and muddy, while literary scholars may see her subtle nuances as exemplary and as necessarily inconclusive. It is a work of astonishing, if controversial, erudition. Graduate; faculty.—*B. Lowe, Florida Atlantic University*

WS-1717   HQ1599   94-42382 CIP
Perkin, Joan. **Victorian women.** New York University, 1995 (c1993). 264p bibl index ISBN 0-8147-6624-2, $45.00; ISBN 0-8147-6625-0 pbk, $17.95

Perkin's comprehensive account of the lives of 19th-century English women, from birth to old age, is a useful addition to the growing literature on this subject. Eschewing secondary studies, Perkin relies exclusively on memoirs, letters, and other contemporary accounts to explicate the quality of everyday life during a period of immense social change. Among other things, she examines the status of women with reference to work patterns, marriage, sexuality, and education. Her analysis of class and gender differences is striking; she makes clear that working-class women suffered greater disabilities in almost every area. Likewise, her discussion of the inequalities of English law is poignant. Through direct testimony, Perkin recounts instances of divorced and separated women being permanently barred from seeing their children, and of married women entirely stripped of financial means by their husbands. Yet, her assessment is judicious; although warmly sympathetic to the plight of women she never overstates the case. All levels.—*J. H. Wiener, CUNY City College*

WS-1718   HQ1593   92-24099 CIP
Pugh, Martin. **Women and the women's movement in Britain, 1914-1959.** Paragon House, 1993 (c1992). 347p bibl index ISBN 1-55778-592-9, $44.95

Pugh skillfully guides his readers through the historical record and current debates, arguing that "substantial achievements of the women's movement after 1918 were not inconsistent with the formal decline of feminist organizations"— an argument familiar to students of British radical movements. He examines the sudden and rapid waning, after 1918, of a feminism of independence and equality, and the reorienting of the women's movement toward issues of wives and mothers. The new feminism is set in the context of economic, political, and social changes in women's lives. Especially good are Pugh's analyses of women's experience of the world wars, the movement's evolving leadership, the parties' triumph over nonparty organizations, the political behavior of women voters and MPs, and the viewpoint of women's publications. He also explores the Conservatives' success in mobilizing women's support and women's allegiance to a cult of domesticity. There is a good bibliography. Pugh (Newcastle Univ.) is best known for *The Making of Modern British Politics, 1867-1939* (CH, Nov'82) and *The Tories and the People, 1880-1935* (CH, Jul'86). Undergraduate and above.—*P. K. Cline, Earlham College*

WS-1719   HQ759   92-40849 CIP
Ross, Ellen. **Love and toil: motherhood in outcast London, 1870-1918.** Oxford, 1993. 308p bibl index afp ISBN 0-19-503957-2, $55.00; ISBN 0-19-508321-0 pbk, $19.95

Ross's long-awaited book blends individual stories and statistics with forceful argumentation to reveal the role played by urban mothers in modernizing Britain. Ross's emphasis on mothers as providers and preservers challenges the interpretations of administrative or intellectual histories such as Gerturde Himmelfarb's *Poverty and Compassion* (CH, May'92), which also examine the shift from Victorian individualism to the origins of the welfare state in an urban setting. Ross (Ramapo College) focuses on mundane yet crucial subjects such as shopping; selection of marital partners; bearing and rearing children; caring for the sick; and fending off those who threaten mothers and children, from fathers to radical interventionists. Such unremarked and unnamed concerns are difficult to research. If "toil" is more obvious than "love" in the book, this is driven by the nature of the sources on which Ross relies; court cases and autobiographies of children may distort the typical mother's story. *Love and Toil* will be a controversial but standard text in British history and women's studies. Extensive notes; bibliography limited to primary sources. Recommended for advanced undergraduates and above.—*M. Baer, Hope College*

WS-1720   HD8396   91-9082 CIP
Schwarzkopf, Jutta. **Women in the Chartist movement.** St. Martin's, 1991. 337p index ISBN 0-312-06213-3, $49.95

Schwarzkopf's book adds an important gender dimension to the understanding of Chartism by considering the role of working-class women in the movement. With very few exceptions, female Chartists did not address specifically feminist issues at all, either by examining the question of male domination of women, or by acting in their political lives in ways that would challenge Victorian assumptions about respectable female behavior. Even the Female Chartist Associations, local "ladies' auxiliaries" to the larger Chartist movement, were almost always organized by male leaders, who continued to serve as the main speakers for such groups and to develop their agendas. Schwarzkopf argues that the fundamental project of Chartism was to resist the massive societal changes imposed by industrialization, and that a large part of that resistance involved the reinforcement—indeed, perhaps even the creation—of a clearly delimited sexual division of labor. Women could thereby create domestic havens in which males could exercise some authority in what was otherwise a very oppressive world. Strengths of the book include an excellent introductory chapter on changes in the living conditions of early 19th-century working-class women and a thoughtful analysis of

ways in which middle-class feminine values influenced, but did not create, working-class feminine values. Useful in any research library, especially one with strength in women's studies, Victorian history, or class history.—*M. M. Garland, Ohio State University*

WS-1721   HQ1599   91-43786 CIP
Shiman, Lilian Lewis. **Women and leadership in nineteenth-century England.** St. Martin's, 1992. 263p bibl index ISBN 0-312-07912-5, $35.00

Shiman examines the part women played in some of the key reform movements in 19th-century England. She is interested in how women overcame legal and social barriers to exercise public roles on the platform and in the press. As Shiman shows, female speakers were taunted and sometimes physically threatened because of their "unladylike" behavior. Yet by a slow accretion of activities (the Victorian equivalent of networking), they helped to advance the cause of reform. Shiman covers a spectrum of controversial issues in her generally solid survey, including the suffrage question and repeal of the Contagious Diseases Acts. However, her major focus is on evangelical religion and temperance reform, where women made major breakthroughs, and on connections with the US, where women were generally freer to engage in public activities. Much of the terrain of this book is familiar. But it is an engrossing study that helps to explain the position of women in 19th-century England and the movement for their emancipation. Graduate; faculty.—*J. H. Wiener, City College, CUNY*

WS-1722   KD1500   93-590 CIP
Spring, Eileen. **Law, land, & family: aristocratic inheritance in England, 1300 to 1800.** North Carolina, 1993. 199p index afp ISBN 0-8078-2110-1, $29.95

Spring's significant and highly original study of inheritance among the aristocracy and gentry from the late Middle Ages is a work of social as well as legal history. Spring, an independent researcher, places legal practices within the context of family values. As a consequence, the devices employed by land-owning families to deal with problems presented by the common law principle of primogeniture—entail, use, and strict settlement—are significantly reinterpreted. The concern of landed families was not simply to tie up their estates but to make secure provisions for all family members. Most specifically, they worked to exclude women from land holding and to nullify the common law rules of inheritance that would have allowed 40 percent of land to be inherited by females. Spring also critiques the historical literature on land law and family history, including the work of Lawrence and Jean Stone, J.C. Holt, Lloyd Bonfeld, and Alan McFarlane, from her new perspective. Her study is a truly important contribution to both fields and is highly recommended for academic libraries interested in British history, women's studies, and legal history. Advanced undergraduates and above.—*C. W. Wood Jr., Western Carolina University*

WS-1723   PN5124   95-30310 MARC
Tinkler, Penny. **Constructing girlhood: popular magazines for girls growing up in England, 1920-1950.** Taylor & Francis, 1995. 209p bibl index ISBN 0-7484-0285-3, $75.00; ISBN 0-7484-0286-1 pbk, $24.95

Tinkler's highly partisan monograph shows in detail how popular magazines for girls in Britain served the interests of patriarchy and capitalism from 1920 to 1950. Arguing that gender differences are socially determined, the author demonstrates how magazines such as *Girls' Own Paper* and *Miss Modern* exploited girls as consumers and taught them to accept their subordinate position in work and marriage. Tinkler claims that readers of these magazines ought not to be viewed as passive or easily manipulated, but the thrust of the argument remains conspiratorial. Publishers deliberately excluded from their pages the possibilities of lesbian relationships; their target audience was "invariably white"; during WW II girls were "expected to join the Services which enabled men to fight and kill." These magazines especially served patriarchal interests by their preoccupation with female appearance and their insistence on the importance of motherhood. Though Tinkler details seminal changes during this turbulent period in British social history, her analysis stresses the continuities of "cultural management." Whether her arguments manifest an admirable theoretical sophistication or unintended anachronism remains a complicated issue. Upper-division undergraduates and above.—*D. L. LeMahieu, Lake Forest College*

WS-1724   D639   93-20667 CIP
Woollacott, Angela. **On her their lives depend: munitions workers in the Great War.** California, 1994. 241p bibl index afp ISBN 0-520-08397-0, $38.00; ISBN 0-520-08502-7 pbk, $15.00

Despite the frequency with which their experience is invoked by scholars debating the transitory nature of the marked upsurge in female employment during WW I, there has not been a full-scale study of women munitions workers in England. Woollacott's new book would be valuable enough on that score alone, but it is doubly welcome for approaching its subject on its own terms. Seeking to comprehend what munitions work meant to its female participants at the time, Woollacott provides a wide-ranging analysis of labor and leisure, set within the complex interrelationship of class and gender. Although she is aware of the diversity of the women involved and of the persistence of patriarchy in the workplace and society at large, the author celebrates the growing sense of female solidarity and the ineradicable self-confidence that munitions work fostered. For many women, Woollacott shows, such opportunities provided emancipation not from bored idleness but from the drudgery and meager wages of domestic service. Moreover, the munitions workers demonstrated a justifiable pride in their service to the war effort in the face of dangers, which if not strictly comparable to those endured by men at the front, were both prevalent and severe (such as TNT poisoning or explosions). Well written and clearly organized, Woollacott's study can be recommended to a wide readership. General readers; upper-division undergraduates and above.—*F. Coetzee, George Washington University*

WS-1725   HV9649   92-136980 MARC
Zedner, Lucia. **Women, crime, and custody in Victorian England.** Oxford, 1992 (c1991). 364p bibl index ISBN 0-19-820264-4, $72.00

In this excellent contribution to Victorian social history, Zedner reminds readers that gender, as much as social class, was a topic of intense interest to Victorians. She shows how the prevailing social values and concerns toward women shaped the view of the criminal woman. The female criminal contravened moral codes but, in doing so, betrayed the accepted ideals of womanhood. Female deviance in the earlier Victorian age was regarded as moral deficiency, perhaps aided by a poor environment. By the turn of the century female crime was seen as not so much the deliberate flouting of social norms, but rather the result of innate deficiencies. Drunkenness, "feeble-mindedness," insanity, and irrationality were the result of a disordered constitution. Zedner also deals with penal theory and policy, and demonstrates how daily life in local and national prisons for women was less regimented than in similar men's facilities. Her sweep is broad; in a clear style, she does an excellent job of summarizing crime trends, penal theory, and perceptions of women. A fascinating work from start to finish. All levels.—*P. T. Smith, Saint Joseph's University*

◆ Europe
France

WS-1726   DC373   91-2689 CIP
Berenson, Edward. **The trial of Madame Caillaux.** California, 1992. 296p index afp ISBN 0-520-07347-9, $25.00

Drawing on a vast array of sources, Berenson reconstructs a dramatic moment in the history of the Third Republic: the trial of Henriette Caillaux. His work is a critique of French society during the Belle Epoque with emphasis on the role of gender and social class. By focusing on this sensational trial, the author examines the mores of French society. Charged with the murder of Gaston Calmette (editor of *Le Figaro*), a crime Madame Caillaux readily admitted at her trial, she was able literally to get away with murder because she successfully exploited the all-male court's condescending feelings toward women. Claiming typical female instability and weakness as a consequence of Calmette publishing her husband's love letters to a mistress, Caillaux argued that her act was a crime of passion. Although Berenson provides an innovative perspective on this affair, some of the issues in this case were also examined in Rudolph Binion's pioneering work, *Defeated Leaders: The Political Fate of Caillaux, Jouvenel and Tardieu* (1960), which Berenson cites. Berenson's book is notable because it is informed by feminist literature, giving it an appropriate contemporary flavor. College, university, and public libraries.—*J. Szaluta, United States Merchant Marine Academy*

WS-1727   DC801.B853   90-41861 CIP
Carles, Emilie. **A life of her own: a countrywoman in twentieth-century France,** by Emilie Carles, as told to Robert Destanque; tr. by Avriel H. Goldberger. Rutgers, 1991. 271p ISBN 0-8135-1641-2, $19.95

Carles presents vignettes and themes from her life in graphic stories and descriptions of peasant work and life. The harshness, the isolation, the community, the poverty, the power of authority are all here. Compulsory education opened Carles's eyes to a wider world, empowering her to make her life her own, a life that included marriage to the man of her choice (a pacifist who voted communist) and a teaching career dedicated to empowering students and armoring them against alcoholism, chauvinism, and authority. After retirement she became an activist to defend her region from despoliation by highway intrusion. This is no bland memoir. The translation ensures Carles's presence. Her story has both intellectual value, as direct narrative of country life in 20th-century France, and emotional wallop, as the successful struggle of an unusual woman to make and enjoy a life of her own. Buy it, read it, get your students to read it. This is the kind of source historians rarely get.—*V. P. Caruso, Nazareth College*

WS-1728   RC532   91-55063 CIP
Evans, Martha Noel. **Fits and starts: a genealogy of hysteria in modern France.** Cornell, 1991. 268p bibl index afp ISBN 0-8014-2643-X, $24.95

Evans's book is primarily an intellectual history that traces the "theories and treatments of hysteria in France from the inception of modern psychiatry in the late 19th Century to the present." Its originality rests not just on the subject matter, but also on the author's intent to show that hysteria (and perhaps other diseases) is both an illness *and* a verbal construction. Additionally, by describing the "history" of hysteria as behavior and myth in France, the author demonstrates that medical histories have a national dimension. The strength of the book lies in the detailed discussion of theoretical positions and debates, ranging from those of late 19th-century Jean-Martin Charcot to contemporary French feminists, and the demonstration that their "truths" often represent individual "interests and inclinations." Less effective are descriptions of the "observable" history of French women, provided to help explain the existence of and discourse on hysteria. The book could be useful reading for those with special backgrounds and interests in the history of medical theory and sexuality. It also provides excellent examples of the ways in which feminist theory may challenge accepted knowledge.—*M. J. Slaughter, University of New Mexico*

WS-1729   DC715   93-16756 CIP
Farge, Arlette. **Fragile lives: violence, power and solidarity in eighteenth-century Paris,** tr. by Carol Shelton. Harvard, 1993. 314p (Harvard historical studies, 113) bibl index ISBN 0-674-31637-1, $49.95; ISBN 0-674-31638-X pbk, $17.95

Farge, a scholar at the CNRS in Paris, has written a remarkable work. In some ways, Farge's study is comparable to David Garrioch's *Neighbourhood and Community in Paris, 1740-1790* (CH, Jun'87)—both were originally published the same year, both used police records, and both covered similar topics: the family, work, and crowds. Garrioch, however, focuses more on the social bonding and support offered within the community, while Farge analyzes individuals—the hapless, wretched, and guilty, and their relation to the police. Through a series of vivid vignettes, such as the abduction of children in the 1750s, declarations of pregnancy, workshop disputes, arrest lists of gang members, accident reports at the time of Marie Antoinette's marriage celebration, and the reported pregnancy of a 9 year old, Farge seeks to cast aside traditional wisdom and to make a fresh examination of human behavior. She also documents the efforts of the police to spy on and to control the lower classes. Reflecting a special sensitivity to women's roles, this book remains social history at its best: real people, thoughtful analysis, and archival research. Highly recommended. General; advanced undergraduate, and above.—*D. C. Baxter, Ohio University*

WS-1730   D810   91-4010 CIP
Fishman, Sarah. **We will wait: wives of French prisoners of war, 1940-1945.** Yale, 1992 (c1991). 253p bibl index afp ISBN 0-300-04774-6, $35.00

In an original approach to the French national trauma during WW II, Fishman adds a new dimension to understanding the experiences of the French people. Fishman studies the "passive" actors in history, women and children, as opposed to those who are considered to be the "active" shapers of history, namely, statesmen, soldiers, and intellectuals. In 1940, well over one-and-a-half million French soldiers were captured by the German army. Approximately half the prisoners were married men, and most of them had children. In this collective biography of the wives of these POWs, Fishman poignantly and thoughtfully portrays the wives' plight and the myriad problems they faced, such as raising children without fathers, having inadequate financial resources, and being lonely. Their problems were compounded by a societal ambivalence toward them: they were pitied but they were also suspected of being adulterous. And at a time when married women with children were facing new responsibilities and seeking employment, the paternalistic Vichy regime passed laws limiting them from working outside the home. Fishman profiles the prisoners too, and the trauma of their lengthy captivity. Their ordeal did not end with repatriation; they were regarded as defeated soldiers. The heroes in France were those who had joined the resistance. This highly readable book is recommended to readers at all levels.—*J. Szaluta, United States Merchant Marine Academy*

WS-1731   HV1448   91-29887 CIP
Fuchs, Rachel G. **Poor and pregnant in Paris: strategies for survival in the nineteenth century.** Rutgers, 1992. 325p bibl index ISBN 0-8135-1779-6, $45.00; ISBN 0-8135-1780-X pbk, $18.00

Fuchs's study explores poor women's control of reproduction, pregnancy, and childbirth in Paris between 1830 and WW I, through a mixture of individual portraits, statistical summaries, and policy debates. Fuchs focuses on mothers—single and married—constrained by minimal wages and precarious social positions. She documents significant shifts from rules, prior to 1870, based in public morality, patriarchy, and the "traditional" family to the medicalization and fears of depopulation that promoted systematic government intervention in reproduction and postpartum welfare thereafter. Although the data are interesting and well researched in hospitals and courtrooms, they often overpower more general and coherent arguments about gender, policy, and poverty. Furthermore, the fragmentary nature of the data provides only speculative if intriguing clues about practices of abortion and infanticide as they appeared in public documents. On the whole, poor women's lives, knowledge, and networks are eclipsed in this work by policy, institutions, and elite debates. Nevertheless, an excellent and provocative resource for comparative studies in history, gender, and health. Graduate, faculty.—*G. W. McDonogh, Bryn Mawr College*

WS-1732   HD3334   90-55726 CIP
Furlough, Ellen. **Consumer cooperation in France: the politics of consumption, 1834-1930.** Cornell, 1991. 311p bibl index afp ISBN 0-8014-2512-3, $37.95

The cooperative movement is generally seen as a practical, almost populist, low-level alternative to capitalism. The well-known case is Scandinavia, where cooperative enterprises prevented foreign penetration of home markets and kept national ties cohesive. Little has been written about French co-ops until Furlough's research. Here the cooperatives took root in reaction to the extremely competitive individualism of French capitalism. For every Bon Marché, there were dozens of cooperative retail outlets by the 1850s and 1860s. How successful they were in providing jobs and low-cost alternatives is not made altogether clear, but as a political/economic ideal everyone from associationists to socialists embraced the concept. After legalization in 1867, co-ops continued as important avenues of self-help, but also provided financing of strikes and labor militancy. These philosophies were institutionalized in two rival cooperative organizations and continued well into the 20th century. Much of the latter half of the book deals with women's roles within the movement. Faculty, graduate students, and upper-division undergraduate students.—*R. W. Kern, University of New Mexico*

WS-1733   Orig
Gemie, Sharif. **Women and schooling in France, 1815-1914: gender, authority and identity in the female schooling sector.** Keele University Press, Keele University, Staffordshire ST5 5BG, UK, 1995. 240p bibl index afp ISBN 1-85331-151-0, $56.00

As Gemie (Univ. of Glamorgan) acknowledges, the study of women's

education in France is rapidly exploding with newly published research, perhaps best represented by Jo B. Margadant's award-winning *Madame le professeur* (1990). By attempting to reconstruct the ambivalent perceptions of the schoolmistresses and their students toward education, Gemie, an established scholar in French studies, approaches the topic in a novel fashion. To reconstruct their experiences, Gemie uses Habermas's theoretical framework of the public sphere to explore the rapidly evolving educational world as a subsector of French culture during the 19th century. Written in a fluid and lively style, this work is a careful and tender examination of the challenges confronting women moving into the "public" sphere during this era of heated political and gender debates. Of particular interest are the two student diaries appended to Gemie's work; in these, readers glimpse the anxieties and enthusiasms of the students themselves. Although the book will interest graduate student and scholarly researchers primarily, it is also accessible to the educated general public. Solid bibliography and endnotes.—*F. Burkhard, Morgan State University*

WS-1734   HX546   91-32529 CIP
Grogan, Susan K. **French socialism and sexual difference: women and the new society, 1803-44.** St. Martin's, 1992. 249p bibl index ISBN 0-312-07250-3, $45.00

Grogan examines three strands of early French socialist thought that centered on ending women's subordinate position and using the "new" woman to transform society. These ideas formed a coherent trinity, since each set—those of Charles Fourier, of Henri Comte Saint-Simon and his followers, and of French feminist Flora Tristan—stressed the "special nature" of women. For Fourier, however, the unique feminine attribute was her powerful libido, and the full expression of women's passions would help drive his ideal society. Tristan, on the other hand, emphasized the moral superiority of women; her world would be based on the "feminine virtues" of love, altruism, and moral integrity. The Saint-Simonians held a variety of intermediate positions, emphasizing to degrees women's sexual or maternal roles. Grogan clearly shows how these early socialist theories were rooted in the idea of sexual complementarity and thus stressed "equality in difference." Challenging the idea of category by gender proved impossible for these early socialists. The book's clarity and evenhandedness make it very valuable for both upper-division undergraduate and graduate collections.—*G. P. Cox, Air University, USAF*

WS-1735   DC158   91-30118 CIP
Gutwirth, Madelyn. **The twilight of the goddesses: women and representation in the French revolutionary era.** Rutgers, 1992. 440p bibl index ISBN 0-8135-1787-7, $39.95

Gutwirth provides an important analysis of the complex interplay of factors surrounding women and their changing status in pre-Revolutionary, Revolutionary, and post-Revolutionary France. Among these factors were sexual antagonism, male rage, "republican" ideological claims, fear of female sexuality and intelligence, relegation of women to a narrowly delineated sphere within the family, and visual and literary representations in the service of politics. Gutwirth's work ought to inspire scholars to attempt interdisciplinary studies of other revolutions. Ample and often revealing illustrations can be difficult to discern because they are reproduced only in black-and-white, one-quarter to half-page in size, but the reader can see well enough to get the point. Readers must be alert to follow the occasionally unsatisfying citation method, and the diffuse style needs editing. The bibliography will be useful to general readers and specialists. General; advanced undergraduate; graduate; faculty.—*J. de Luce, Miami University (OH)*

WS-1736   PQ653   91-16792 CIP
Kadish, Doris Y. **Politicizing gender: narrative strategies in the aftermath of the French Revolution.** Rutgers, 1991. 197p bibl index ISBN 0-8135-1708-7, $35.00

An enthusiastic semiotic reading of the links between femininity and revolution in ten English and French novels and two French paintings from 1789 to 1872. Kadish teases out meaning from allegories and discovers palimpsests to argue that gender is politicized through the literary and artistic renderings of females. Women are shown in a variety of guises and roles, from property owners, to asssassins, to lesbians, to seemingly submissive wives and mothers. Kadish's analysis covers a wide political spectrum in the novels of Balzac, Chateaubriand, Dickens, Shelley, de Stael, Bronte, and Sand, and in the paintings by David and Anne-Louis Girodet. Aided by an appendix of semiotic elements that appear in the works, the reader is the beneficiary of an intriguing and forceful argument for cultural and symbolic political gains by women in the wake of post-Revolutionary economic and legal restraints. Upper-division undergraduates and above.— *J. E. Brink, Texas Tech University*

WS-1737　　　　　HQ1616　　　　　92-42841 CIP
Moses, Claire Goldberg. **Feminism, socialism, and French romanticism,** by Claire Goldberg Moses and Leslie Wahl Rabine. Indiana, 1993. 371p bibl index afp ISBN 0-253-33889-1, $39.95; ISBN 0-253-20818-1 pbk, $19.95

Moses and Rabine assess the French feminists of the 1830s—their lives, their writings, and their significance for feminists today. The work focuses mainly on the *Saint-Simoniennes*, though Flora Tristan is also discussed. The book has several parts: a coauthored introduction; a historical essay by Moses; a literary analysis by Rabine; excerpts from the writings of Suzanne Voilquin, Claire Démar, and Flora Tristan; letters from several *Saint-Simoniennes*; and selections from the feminist periodical *Tribune des femmes*. The authors argue convincingly that the *Saint-Simoniennes* illustrate a different kind of feminist path, and that previous chroniclers of women's movements have distorted history by portraying modern feminism exclusively as a linear descendant of Anglo-Saxon women's rights movements of the mid-19th century. The collaboration of Moses and Rabine is not entirely successful; at times they contradict each other, and on occasion, they seem to be vying to produce the most arcane and jargon-laden passages. (Rabine wins!) This is, nevertheless, an important book, of interest to scholars of 19th-century social, literary, and political movements as well as to researchers in women's studies. Graduate; faculty.—*A. H. Koblitz, Hartwick College*

WS-1738　　　　　HQ1613　　　　　90-2963 CIP
Proctor, Candice E. **Women, equality, and the French Revolution.** Greenwood, 1990. 210p (Contributions in women's studies, 115) bibl index afp ISBN 0-313-27245-X, $39.95

This is a revision of Proctor's 1982 dissertation, a well-written explication of the debate over full citizenship for women during the French Revolution. Although not acknowledged, the book proceeds from Terry Smiley Dock's *Women in the Encyclopedie: A Compendium* (1979). Drawing primarily on treatises, pamphlets, and published speeches of revolutionary elites between 1789 and late 1793, the author complies an impressive array of arguments on the greatest failure of the Revolution to meld principles with practices. Proctor is careful to place the theories for female emancipation in the centuries-old quarrel over the nature of women, and then obliquely guides the reader through the Revolution's zeal for liberty, equality, and, ultimately, fraternity to the moment when the Jacobins denied "any and all assertions of sexual equality." There are some noteworthy limitations here, not all of them the fault of the author. Careless copy editing and a very limited bibliography, especially of recent and impressive scholarship on women in the Revolution, do not present the book in the light it deserves. Suitable for advanced students.—*J. E. Brink, Texas Tech University*

WS-1739　　　　　HQ1075　　　　　93-26899 CIP
Roberts, Mary Louise. **Civilization without sexes: reconstructing gender in postwar France, 1917-1927.** Chicago, 1994. 337p index afp ISBN 0-226-72121-3, $48.00; ISBN 0-226-72122-1 pbk, $18.95

In this, her first monograph, Roberts (Stanford Univ.) demonstates why she is rapidly emerging as a leading and innovative scholar. Exploring the cultural crisis that demoralized the French after the Great War, Roberts argues that the frequently heated discussions surrounding female identity provided the French with an accessible way to discuss the meaning of everyday social and cultural changes. Using popular and specialized contemporary literatures, periodicals, and archival materials, she examines how debates on women worked on literal as well as symbolic levels and enabled the French to redefine their lives. Roberts emphasizes three central images—the modern woman with short hair and hemline, the mother, and the single woman—to bring the impassioned postwar debates into brilliant focus. Although the thorough endnotes will enthrall researchers, the inclusion of a select bibliography would have enhanced this study's value as a teaching tool for advanced undergraduates. All libraries.—*F. Burkhard, Morgan State University*

◆ Europe

Germany

WS-1740　　　　　HQ759　　　　　90-21164 CIP
Allen, Ann Taylor. **Feminism and motherhood in Germany, 1800-1914.** Rutgers, 1991. 299p index ISBN 0-8135-1686-2, $42.00

Like the heroines of her book—19th-and early 20th-century German feminists—Allen in this stimulating study departs from tradition. She rejects the image perpetuated by some German historians of a German feminist movement imbued with an illiberal or authoritarian ideology. Through well-chosen comparative examples (primarily from the works of historians of the American feminist movement) and a thoughtful examination of the lives of several middle-class German women from all faiths, Allen demonstrates how German feminists independently developed their own sense of self based on the idea of motherhood ("spiritual motherhood" rather than a necessarily biological concept). Education, particularly the role of the kindergarten, figures prominently in her discussion of the ways in which Germany's feminists sought to wean the nation away from its reliance on "paternalistic discipline" and toward a maternal and more progressive impulse. Readers also learn about the legal discrimination against German women, feminists' attitudes towards German unification, and the feminist community in general. In taking the mystique out of German feminism, Allen has helped to place it in the mainstream of German history and in so doing, has opened up new avenues for research. Upper-division undergraduates and above.— *M. S. Coetzee, Yale University*

WS-1741　　　　　DS135　　　　　90-45234 CIP
Kaplan, Marion A. **The making of the Jewish middle class: women, family, and identity in Imperial Germany.** Oxford, 1991. 351p bibl index afp ISBN 0-19-503952-1, $39.95

Until the appearance of this book, the history of Imperial German Jewry has been one based almost exclusively on the experiences of men. Kaplan redresses this imbalance with her fine account of the everyday lives of German Jewish women in the late 19th and early 20th centuries. Although she follows in the tradition of recent scholars of German women (e.g., A. Taylor Allen, Ute Frevert), who use gender as a building block, Kaplan constructs her history on the foundations of ethnicity, religion, and class as well. Based on memoirs, newspapers, organizational literature, and statistical records, Kaplan's account primarily documents the daily routines and associational activities of the Jewish, middle-class, urban housewife, yet the author does devote some attention to the lives of the independent, academically inclined, and career-minded young women of that generation. Arguing along lines similar to those stressed by Allen in her *Feminism and Motherhood in Wilhelmine Germany, 1800-1914* (1991) Kaplan demonstrates how Jewish women, consigned by Judaism to a largely domestic role, became cultural and spiritual mediators to their own families and helped acculturate them to German society. All levels.—*M. S. Coetzee, Yale University*

WS-1742　　　　　D811　　　　　92-42097 CIP
Owings, Alison. **Frauen: German women recall the Third Reich.** Rutgers, 1993. 494p index ISBN 0-8135-1992-6, $24.95

This collection of approximately 30 interviews with German women who lived through the Third Reich is an extraordinarily rich historical source, both exhilarating and exasperating, moving and, occasionally, hilarious. Owings asks tough questions, has a fine eye for telling gestures, and chooses her subjects from all walks of life. The book presents the experiences of women on the home front as they remembered them a half-century later. Although the time lapse may distort the past, these altered realities are valuable in themselves. The women's responses to probings about the Holocaust, membership in the party or its auxiliary organizations, and treatment at the hands of the Russians and Americans are full of surprises. Unregenerate antisemites, self-effacing heroines of the resistance, and everything in between make their appearances in lengthy, sometimes multiple, sessions. This book enriches readers' understanding of what it was like to be alive in Hitler's Germany and how some Germans have come to terms with their past. An excellent work. All levels.—*R. S. Levy, University of Illinois at Chicago*

WS-1743   HQ1623   94-39348 CIP
Reagin, Nancy R. **A German women's movement: class and gender in Hanover, 1880-1933.** North Carolina, 1995. 322p bibl index afp ISBN 0-8078-2210-8, $49.95; ISBN 0-8078-4525-6 pbk, $18.95

In the theoretical debates concerning German feminism, Reagin carves out a middling position for herself and defends the necessity of analyzing class as well as gender to explain why the German women's movement shifted to the right, particularly after 1918. She chooses the city of Hanover to test her thesis because it represents the more typical manifestations of grass-roots membership than do the radical extremes of Berlin, Bremen, or Hamburg. Reagin demonstrates convincingly that ideology within the movement was not so important as class in determining its politics. Ostensibly the Hanoverians were *überparteilich*, seeking to establish themselves as "mothers of the community" analogous to "city fathers." They were largely successful in expanding the public role of women in Hanover because they appeared to be efficient workers for the common good and because were able to take advantage of personal relations with the male governing elite. But Reagin sees the pose of being "above politics" for what it is—an extremely "partisan neutrality." The bourgeois members of the movement consciously inculcated bourgeois values among working-class women while working against Social Democratic influence over them. This is a sophisticated work of feminist and urban history. All levels.—*R. S. Levy, University of Illinois at Chicago*

WS-1744   DS135   90-389 CIP
Spiel, Hilde. **Fanny von Arnstein: a daughter of the Enlightenment, 1758-1818,** tr. by Christine Shuttleworth. Berg, 1991. 368p bibl index ISBN 0-85496-179-8, $59.95

Fanny von Arnstein, "the fair Hebrew," wrote little that has survived. Next to nothing is known about her childhood or early married years in Vienna. "What she did and experienced, whom she visited and received, what public occasions she attended and what journeys she made" are the subject of a good deal of airy hypothesizing. Repeatedly, readers are told what von Arnstein "must have felt" about the important events and personalities of her day. Fortunately, the value of this book does not rest on speculation about its elusive heroine. Spiel has much of interest to say about the court life of Vienna and Berlin, the doings of a small circle of wealthy Jews in those two towns, and what they experienced as they struggled to enter into the mainstream of European life. Spiel also discusses von Arnstein's one legitimate claim to fame, the salon she established in Vienna where the interchange of ideas, cultivated conversation, and the socializing of talented people from many backgrounds could take place. As a painless introduction to the social and cultural life of Vienna and Berlin in the Age of Enlightenment, this book succeeds well. College and university libraries.—*R. S. Levy, University of Illinois at Chicago*

WS-1745   HQ766   91-40106 CIP
Usborne, Cornelie. **The politics of the body in Weimar Germany: women's reproductive rights and duties.** Michigan, 1992. 304p bibl index ISBN 0-472-10368-7, $42.50

Usborne (Roehampton Institute, London) expands her PhD dissertation into a comprehensive discussion of Weimar Germany's turbulent attention to abortion and population control. In analyzing agendas across the political spectrum, as well as considering a broad variety of feminist organizations and professional groups, Usborne finds many common denominators: anxiety about eroding traditional family values, shifting birth rates, and wide support for strong state intervention. What divided these groups was the extent of their willingness to see women attain true reproductive freedom with unlimited access to contraception and abortion. Although Weimar women did make some gains, economic crises and the growing eugenics movement stimulated collective action in the name of the *Volk*, a trend the Nazis carried to extremes after 1933. Appendixes include translations of pertinent German anti-abortion and birth control legislation, parliamentary motions, and reform proposals from 1871 to 1976. Based on extensive archival research and primary sources, and with a comprehensive bibliography, this work, despite some confusing British legal terminology, is strongly recommended for all undergraduate and graduate libraries with holdings in 20th-century German and women's history.—*D. R. Skopp, SUNY College at Plattsburgh*

WS-1746   PT2377   90-36156 CIP
Zucker, Stanley. **Kathinka Zitz-Halein and female civic activism in mid-nineteenth-century Germany.** Southern Illinois, 1991. 264p bibl index afp ISBN 0-8093-1674-9, $39.95

Kathinka Zitz-Halein (1801-1877) was a little-known German writer and social activist who flourished in Mainz during the period of the 1848 Revolutions and the following two decades. She participated intensively in the uprisings of 1848-1850, and was accused of high treason (the charges were subsequently dismissed). Zitz-Halein left behind a quantity of poetry and prose, much of which touches on themes of political and social interest. The quality of her writing was rather mediocre, and Zitz-Halein herself does not appear to have been a particularly attractive personality. Nevertheless, her story is fascinating, not least because of the light it sheds on the mid-19th-century political and social scene in Hessian Germany. Zucker's biography of Zitz-Halein (published posthumously) is somewhat unevenly written. At its best, however, the book provides an engrossing portrait of women's activism around the time of the 1848 Revolutions, and expands knowledge of midcentury debates on women's rights and variants of feminism. The book belongs in any library with good collections in German or 19th-century European history on women's studies.—*A. H. Koblitz, Hartwick College*

◆ Europe
Italy & Spain

WS-1747   HX925   90-42665 CIP
Ackelsberg, Martha A. **Free women of Spain: anarchism and the struggle for the emancipation of women.** Indiana, 1991. 229p index afp ISBN 0-253-30120-3, $39.95; ISBN 0-253-20634-0 pbk, $14.95

Acklesberg's account of *Mujeres Libres*, the Spanish anarchist women's organization, details the founding and development of that organization and its significance within the broader context of Spanish history and politics from the late 19th century through 1939. The work not only fills a gap in knowledge of women's radical politics, but also addresses current concerns of feminist scholars. Among these concerns are the importance of women's communities and gender-specific experience as the basis for women's entry into public politics; the relationship of that political participation with women's goals and visions; and the ways in which commonalities and differences in women's experience serve to both unify and divide women in their public activism. The work requires background knowledge of anarchism and Spanish history, and would be a useful resource for advanced undergraduate and graduate courses in political theory, the history of women's politics, and modern Spanish history.—*M. J. Slaughter, University of New Mexico*

WS-1748   HQ1638   91-8901 CIP
De Grazia, Victoria. **How fascism ruled women: Italy, 1922-1945.** California, 1992. 350p index afp ISBN 0-520-07456-4, $29.95

A welcome and vital addition to undergraduate and graduate libraries. De Grazia's sophisticated but accessible treatment of women under Italian fascism portrays the experiences of women as they went about their daily lives during Mussolini's dictatorship. It places fascism's policies on women within a broad chronological and geographical context and it demonstrates the complex interaction of fascist goals and women's complicity in and resistance to the establishment and implementation of its program. As Mussolini and his followers sought to negotiate the contradictions between the requirements of the modern state and the deep-seated desire to recreate traditional (patriarchal) authority in the aftermath of WW I, they produced a paradoxical situation for women. The fascist regime prohibited women's participation in suffrage, in the labor force, and in decision-making affecting reproductive life. Yet fascist efforts to mobilize mass politics, to rationalize social services, and to prepare for war in the 1930s often produced some of the emancipatory developments they decried by eroding traditional roles and relationships for and between men and women. A must-read for students of European history. Undergraduate; graduate.—*S. K. Kent, University of Florida*

WS-1749 BF1815.L46 89-20607 CIP

Kagan, Richard L. **Lucrecia's dreams: politics and prophecy in sixteenth-century Spain.** California, 1990. 229p bibl index afp ISBN 0-520-06655-3, $24.95

An original and imaginative work firmly grounded in documents produced during the lengthy Inquisition trial of a 16th-century Spanish prophet. At issue was the source and content of dreams that echoed secular criticism of Philip II's domestic and foreign policies. Through a judicious analysis of oral testimony and dream transcriptions, Kagan examines the close relationship between politics and prophecy in 16th-century Spain and, through Lucrecia, provides a glimpse of the political and economic injustices of Philip's reign. This well-organized and well-written presentation adroitly places Lucretia's prophecies and trial within the context of court and inquisitorial politics, the dream culture of Renaissance Spain, and the broader historical context of Philip's reign. All college and university libraries should purchase this book. Upper-division undergraduates and above.—*S. H. Burkholder, Westminster College*

WS-1750 HV847 92-35169 CIP

Kertzer, David I. **Sacrificed for honor: Italian infant abandonment and the politics of reproductive control.** Beacon Press, 1993. 252p bibl index ISBN 0-8070-5604-9, $25.00

An engaging, deeply researched history of institutionalized infant abandonment in 19th-century Italy. Kertzer combines local studies with statistical generalizations and ably places them in sweeping comparative and historical perspective. The book complements John Boswell's *The Kindness of Strangers* (1988) and Michel Foucault's *Discipline and Punish: The Birth of the Prison* (CH, May'78). Kertzer (Brown Univ.) explores social norms and ideologies through the prism of the "the Wheel"—a device linking the foundling home and the outside world, contrived so as to permit anonymous abandonment of infants. He wisely notes several causes for institutionalized infant abandonment, but stresses the Catholic Church's overriding concerns for family honor and the infant's soul as distinct from its welfare; hence the book's forceful but overly pointed title. Of special interest is the discussion of efforts to cope with unintended consequences and perverse incentive effects in the system of "reproductive control." An epilogue suggests that this history sheds fresh light on current controversies over reproductive rights and policies in the US. General; advanced undergraduate; graduate; faculty.—*J. Alcorn, Trinity College*

WS-1751 DP269 94-29752 CIP

Mangini, Shirley. **Memories of resistance: women's voices from the Spanish Civil War.** Yale, 1995. 226p bibl index afp ISBN 0-300-05816-0, $25.00

English-language scholarship on the historical experiences of Spanish women is quite rare; thus, Mangini's work is most welcome. Her focus is on the women of Republican and Civil War Spain, many of whom, in the hostile and often brutal environment of Franco's regime, spent years in prison or in exile. Rather than writing a historical monograph of gendered experience in those years, Mangini uses what she terms "outlawed memory texts" to build "a protest rally from the past." Relating not only what the women told, but also *how* they told their stories, Mangini "conjures up a past that has been erased." Those whose words and experiences are examined range from well-known political figures to lesser known women representing a variety of class backgrounds and political affiliations. The texts Mangini uses include memoirs, diaries, autobiographies, fiction and semifictional accounts, and transcribed oral histories. By moving beyond the heroic to look at the meaning and legacy of prison and exile, Mangini has made a significant contribution to theoretical understanding of the memory and meaning of war. An important addition to any library. All levels.—*M. J. Slaughter, University of New Mexico*

WS-1752 GT2762 90-24575 CIP

Martín Gaite, Carmen. **Love customs in eighteenth-century Spain,** tr. by Maria G. Tomsich. California, 1991. 204p bibl index afp ISBN 0-520-07043-7, $34.95

In 18th-century Spain, aristocratic married women were frequently courted by men other than their husbands. These escorts, or *cortejos*, fulfilled an important role in the daily lives of women as companions, flatterers, gift-givers, and sta-

tus symbols. This recent translation of a book originally published in 1972 thoroughly explores the origin and development of the *cortejo* custom, the specific nature of the companion relationship, and the mixed reaction to its popularity. Although the information presented provides some fascinating insights into love customs in 18th-century Spain and, more broadly, the inner contradictions of Spanish society, the inclusion of numerous lengthy quotations (there are few pages free of them) detract from the author's sensitive analysis. Martín Gaite, a contemporary novelist, is an excellent linguist and commentator who draws on a broad range of primary and secondary sources. Her book contributes to the expanding knowledge of women in 18th-century Europe. Upper-division undergraduates and above.—*S. H. Burkholder, Westminster College*

WS-1753 HD6073.R482 90-9581 CIP

Zappi, Elda Gentili. **If eight hours seem too few: mobilization of women workers in the Italian rice fields.** State University of New York, 1991. 396p bibl index afp ISBN 0-7914-0481-1, $59.50

A history of female rice workers—specifically, rice weeders—in turn-of-the-20th-century Italy may suggest a certain narrowness in contemporary social/labor history. Perhaps so, given the alarming lack of general historical knowledge in the public mind, but this study ably avoids such criticism by stressing that rice was the most expensive crop in Italy; that women almost exclusively handled the job of weeding; and that the mobilization of these agricultural workers well preceded that of male industrial workers, making them the earliest group to take collective action in Italy's modernization, so becoming a pioneering focus of Socialist organizing efforts. Agricultural women seldom received such early political aid in Europe; Spanish female farm workers, for instance, received far less attention, although their numbers were much larger. In general, so little attention has been paid to women workers in European agricultural history that this work fills an important slot in our knowledge. Useful in economic, social agricultural, and women's studies courses at the upper-division and graduate levels.—*R. W. Kern, University of New Mexico*

◆ Europe
Eastern & Central Europe, Russia

WS-1754 HD6167 94-20199 CIP

Bobroff-Hajal, Anne. **Working women in Russia under the hunger tsars: political activism and daily life.** Carlson Publishing, 1994. 326p (Scholarship in women's history, 3) bibl index afp ISBN 0-926019-64-3, $60.00

Bobroff-Hajal's well-researched study examines industrial workers in the central industrial region of Russia at the time of the 1917 revolutions. She discusses women's roles in food riots, street fighting, and political organizations, posing the issue of why so much activism was ultimately ineffective and why these Russian women were unable to form continuing organizations to better their lives. The explanation is somewhat repetitive: women were socialized through rituals and folklore to be tied to husbands and children rather than to each other, thus inhibiting any tendencies toward a natural interest group. More interesting, however, are the author's descriptions of working-class family and gender patterns, including childhood socialization, adolescence, courtship and wedding ritual, and communal living arrangements, which paradoxically managed to reinforce separation of nuclear families. Bobroff-Hamal uses fascinating folkloric, newspaper, memoir, and oral history sources not readily available in English to paint a vivid picture of the lives of these Russian women. A valuable addition to collections in Russian and women's history. Upper-division undergraduates and above.—*L. Mayo, County College of Morris*

WS-1755 HV9772 94-10627 CIP

Constante, Lena. **The silent escape: three thousand days in Romanian prisons,** tr. by Franklin Philip. California, 1995. 257p afp ISBN 0-520-08209-5, $22.00

Winner of the 1992 Prix Européen of the Association des Ecrivains de Langue Française, Constante's prison memoir presents a sequence familiar to readers of political incarcerations. Constante was in continuous solitary confinement for 3,000 days. Her narrative ends when, after more than eight years, she was moved to a cell with other women (Constante says, "my three-and-a-half years of communal life are really a whole other story"). One is impelled to ask: How is it possible to live for 3,000 days separated from human contact? And how does one recall such a time? This compelling text is an answer—and it is also a monument to human will, invention, and ingenuity. Constante bemoans the "loss" of the 300-odd days she cannot recall, and enumerates the days periodically where her memory fails to serve. What she does remember is remarkable; she not only served 12 years and more in prison but also relived it from 1977 to 1985 as she wrote. How does one repair clothes? How to write without a pencil? How to make a comb? Above all, how to keep your sanity? And how did she remember? She asks, "What can I do to recall it more precisely?" She accomplishes this by summoning feeling first: "Once again the same anxiety, the same rebellion ...." Then the cell appears: "The darkness. The obstructed window. The shutters ...." Finally, the sounds: " ... G. had summoned me to the (cell) wall (by knocking). We were going to be leaving." As Constante "returns" to her solitude she takes readers along and wonderfully, frighteningly, invites them to feel and see and hear. All levels.—*E. J. Zimmermann, Canisius College*

WS-1756   HQ1610   93-4301 CIP
Corrin, Chris. **Magyar women: Hungarian women's lives, 1960s-1990s.** Macmillan, UK/St. Martin's, 1994. 312p bibl index ISBN 0-312-10689-0, $49.95

Corrin draws on her ethnographic research to present a descriptive account of Hungarian women's experiences since the end of WW II. This book is difficult to assimilate because it lacks the structure of a theoretical perspective and the author tends to draw conclusions about causes and outcomes of women's social, economic, and political status without providing documentation. Nevertheless, Corrin provides an overwhelming amount of new information about Hungarian culture and the socioeconomic and political transformations of its citizens' public and private lives. The chapter on health care and Hungarian women's health emphasizes the hardships of pregnancy because of inadequate equipment and shortages of physicians. Moreover, Corrin debunks the idea that participation in paid work liberalizes women in socialist nations. She accomplishes this by showing the extent to which Hungarian women work in monotonous and often dangerous occupations for lower wages than their male counterparts, while doing double duty in the household as well. Graduate; faculty.—*A. S. Oakes, Idaho State University*

WS-1757   HQ1590   93-34898 MARC
Einhorn, Barbara. **Cinderella goes to market: citizenship, gender and women's movements in East Central Europe.** Verso, 1993. 280p index ISBN 0-86091-410-0, $59.95; ISBN 0-86091-615-4 pbk, $17.95

Einhorn's book is both a progress report and an analysis of the status of women in postcommunist East Central Europe. Readers should not be put off by the jargon-laden introductory section: once into the body of the work, Einhorn clears up her prose and delivers her information with uncommon intelligence. Like editors Nanette Funk and Magda Muellers in their collection *Gender Politics and Post-Communism* (1993), Einhorn sees contemporary Eastern European women as oppressed by the resurgence of patriarchal traditions and by the repudiation of even the valuable aspects of the Marxist regimes. Thus, a "women's liberation" that was misconceived in the first place and never adequately implemented has been rejected. Women today are losing reproductive rights, being excluded from the political sphere, and bearing the brunt of the economic dislocation of transition in regimes that seek to confine them to their reproductive role. Einhorn expresses some hope that this situation is temporary and that women who once had jobs and some privileges will not long acquiesce to being relegated to an impoverished, rightless private sphere. All levels.—*J. Zimmerman, University of Pittsburgh at Greensburg*

WS-1758   HQ1662   93-31191 CIP
Engel, Barbara Alpern. **Between the fields and the city: women, work, and family in Russia, 1861-1914.** Cambridge, 1994. 254p index ISBN 0-521-44236-2, $59.95

Engel's new book brings together a decade's research on the experiences of Russian peasant women as their society belatedly underwent large-scale industrialization. Despite the profound shift in subject matter, this book resembles her earlier

Mothers and Daughters (CH, Sep'83) in some important ways. It is not an analytic monograph, but a series of essays dealing with women in different localities and in different work situations (peasant women whose husbands migrated; women in rural factories; women in the capitals; prostitutes). Although Engel has attempted to use quantitative material where it is available, both the scattershot nature of Russian sources and, no doubt, her own predilections, have led her to concentrate on the individual and the anecdotal. She has used court records of divorce proceedings to especially good effect, and through them readers hear the voices of villagers, husbands, and women as they argue over women's duties and expectations in a changing world. With its readable prose and its emphasis on the life experiences of individual, poor women, this book makes an excellent introduction to its subject. All levels.—*J. Zimmerman, University of Pittsburgh at Greensburg*

WS-1759   KLA540   92-47481 MARC
Goldman, Wendy Z. **Women, the state and revolution: Soviet family policy and social life, 1917-1936.** Cambridge, 1993. 351p (Cambridge Russian, Soviet and post-Soviet studies, 90) index ISBN 0-521-37404-9, $59.95; ISBN 0-521-45816-1 pbk, $18.95

Goldman focuses on subjects that have been largely ignored in early Soviet history. Nearly 14 percent of the book covers the ideological origins of the Bolshevik vision on the woman question and the "withering away" of the traditional family. The remainder is devoted to the Soviet state's efforts to address issues of central importance to Russian women: de facto marriage, contraception, abortion, and divorce. Goldman's feminist perspective in tracing what she sees as the betrayal of the libertarian commitment to individual freedom inherent in the woman question and the end of the patriarchal family through the 1936 policy for a repressive strengthening of the family unit might impress some as controversial. Yet the book is a valuable investigation of issues central to the Soviet regime's claim for seven decades of liberating women and fostering freer, more equal relations between the sexes. Based on solid archival research, the absence of a bibliography is an unfortunate shortcoming. The book should be read by all serious students of the Soviet period. Upper-division undergraduates and above.—*G. E. Snow, Shippensburg University of Pennsylvania*

WS-1760   HQ1715.5   89-32120 MARC
Jancar-Webster, Barbara. **Women & revolution in Yugoslavia, 1941-1945.** Arden Press, CO, 1990. 245p bibl index ISBN 0-912869-09-7, $26.50; ISBN 0-912869-10-0, $16.95

One of a series of volumes edited by Jane Slaughter and Richard Stites intended to examine "the function of sex/gender systems in the revolutionary process" as well as women's roles in 20th-century revolutions. The goals of the series are highly sophisticated; however, this book does not measure up to them. A primary problem appears to be the fragmentary and anecdotal nature of Jancar-Webster's sources, which do not lead themselves easily to analytic treatment. Second, she appears to have been hampered by her effort to adhere closely to editorial guidelines and to explore the topic in too brief a work. Nevertheless her book does address the lack of attention to women in revolutionary struggles in that it informs the Western reader of the major role that women played in the partisan struggle in Yugoslavia. Jancar-Webster also arrives at sensible if somewhat depressingly familiar conclusions in regard to women's actual status and functions in the partisan effort and the gains they achieved. A useful introduction to a fascinating subject, but far from the last word. Upper-division undergraduates and above.—*J. Zimmerman, University of Pittsburgh at Greensburg*

WS-1761   DK219.3   89-23073 CIP
Maxwell, Margaret. **Narodniki women: Russian women who sacrificed themselves for the dream of freedom.** Pergamon, 1990. 341p bibl index afp ISBN 0-08-037462-X, $36.00; ISBN 0-08-037461-1, $14.50

Maxwell's book is a rather amateurish popular work on the lives of Russia's terrorist women. The first part of the work, which deals with the 19th century, offers nothing new for the scholar; the material on the 20th century is somewhat more informative. Maxwell has used autobiographical and journalistic accounts to provide anecdotal narratives of the activities of women who are not nearly so well known as Perovskaia and Zasulich, although in the case of Spiridonova they clearly should be. Nonetheless, the work never rises above the level of anecdote and hagiography. Maxwell deals with neither the personalities of the women nor the difficult issues raised by terrorism until the very end, and then in a cursory way. She does not manage to disentangle revolutionary politics. This book might be of some use in introducing undergraduates to the subject, but the 19th century is much better served by Barbara Engel and Clifford Rosenthal's *Five Sisters: Women Against the Tsar* (CH, Dec'75); readers will have to wait for a satisfactory work on Soviet revolutionary women.—*J. Zimmerman, University of Pittsburgh at Greensburg*

WS-1762   D792   94-1301 CIP
Noggle, Anne. **A dance with death: Soviet airwomen in World War II.** Texas A&M, 1994. 318p afp ISBN 0-89096-601-X, $29.95

As Christine A. White points out in her introduction, women have long been involved in military as well as civilian aviation in Russia and the USSR. In 1935 women constituted 19 percent of pilots in the USSR (as compared to three percent in the US in the same year). During WW II numerous Soviet women served as combat pilots, navigators, gunners, and flight mechanics in both the special women's regiments and the regular men's units. The women's units were in fact more productive, efficient, and highly decorated than their male counterparts, and it is a great shame that their history is not better known today. From 1990 to 1992, Noggle (Univ. of New Mexico and a WW II Women Airforce Service Pilot herself) interviewed the world's first women combat fliers and some of their support personnel. The brief published interviews, translated with the help of a teacher at the Moscow Military Academy, appear here along with current photographs of more than 60 of the women. The wealth of details and stories makes for fascinating reading, at times almost overwhelming; it might have been better to highlight a few women rather than include all interviews. Also, one could have hoped for more information on the women's relationships with male units, and on what happened to the women after the war. The book is, however, an amazing, inspiring account. It is an invaluable resource for researchers, yet could be read with interest by undergraduates.—*A. H. Koblitz, Hartwick College*

WS-1763   HQ1662   90-37203 CIP
Russia's women: accommodation, resistance, transformation, ed. by Barbara Evans Clements, Barbara Alpern Engel, and Christine D. Worobec. California, 1991. 300p index afp ISBN 0-520-07023-2, $45.00; ISBN 0-520-07024-0 pbk, $14.95

Consisting of scholarly articles by 15 different historians, this collection is a welcome demonstration that the subspecialty of Russian women's history has indeed been established. The articles range in period from medieval history to the 1930s (with an afterword by Clements summarizing trends to the present). For the most part, the articles are examinations of social history, and most deal with women of the lower classes. This reviewer was particularly impressed by David Ransel's essay on differences in infant mortality among 19th-century Russian and Tatar peasants, and by Wendy Goldman's essay on abortion law and practice in Soviet Russia. Given the wide scope of the volume's contents, it is hardly surprising that the collection does not present a coherent image of women's life in Russia. Most of the articles do not represent startling new approaches or data; rather, this is a good summary of current work that fills in gaps and helps bring the Russian experience into perspective. Undergraduate libraries.—*J. Zimmerman, University of Pittsburgh at Greensburg*

WS-1764   HQ1662   91-30488 CIP
Women and society in Russia and the Soviet Union, ed. by Linda Edmondson. Cambridge, 1992. 233p index ISBN 0-521-41388-5, $54.95

A collection of ten papers first presented at the 1990 World Congress for Soviet and East European Studies. The chapters span a time period from approximately 1870 to the first years of glasnost and perestroika, and are written by historians, political scientists, and Slavicists. The topics addressed include the treatment of women in popular and high culture, women as political and scientific figures, the fate of the women who defended the Provisional Government during the October Revolution, prostitution in the early Bolshevik period, and the gendered impact of glasnost and perestroika. Individual contributions are somewhat uneven in quality (one or two of the literary pieces seem particularly weak), and the volume lacks uniform coverage of all aspects of women in society, in all time periods from 1870 to the present. Moreover, the rapid pace of economic and social deterioration in the post-Soviet successor states has meant that much of the information in the contemporary chapters is already somewhat out of date. Nev-

ertheless, the volume contains much that is topical, valuable, interesting, and well written; no library should be without this important resource. General; undergraduate; graduate; faculty.—*A. H. Koblitz, Hartwick College*

WS-1765   HQ1665   94-17273 CIP
Women in Russia: a new era in Russian feminism, ed. by Anastasia Posadskaya and others at the Moscow Gender Centre; tr. by Kate Clark. Verso, 1994. 203p ISBN 0-86091-487-9, $65.00; ISBN 0-86091-657-X pbk, $19.95

Some of the economic, cultural, and social catastrophes that followed the collapse of the Soviet Union have received considerable coverage; however, the worsening situation of women has rarely been studied. In these essays, Russian women scholars (most of them researchers at the Moscow Centre for Gender Studies) address the increasing gender segregation of the labor force, legal discrimination against women, violent pornography and other forms of misogyny in the post-Soviet press, myths concerning women's status in Soviet and post-Soviet society, the lesbian culture, and prospects for women's movements. Like most collections, this one is uneven and occasionally repetitious. Moreover, some of the writers are distressingly idealistic about the state of women's rights movements in the West, and ignorant about many aspects of their own country's rich feminist traditions (especially in the period 1865-1936). The best essays, however, are impressive both for the sophistication of their theoretical framework and for their wealth of detail; those by Klimenkova, Khotkina, and Lipovskaya are particularly powerful. Clark's translation is skillful, nuanced, at times even elegant. Of interest to Slavicists, economists, political scientists, historians, and women's studies specialists; required reading in courses on present-day Russia. All levels.—*A. H. Koblitz, Hartwick College*

WS-1766   HQ1665   93-15181 MARC
Women's glasnost vs. naglost: stopping Russian backlash, by Tatyana Mamonova with Chandra Niles Folsom. Bergin & Garvey, 1994. 184p index afp ISBN 0-89789-339-5, $49.95

For those unfamiliar with Russian, "*naglost*" means something like boldness or brazenness. Mamonova uses the term in a somewhat nonstandard fashion to signify the calls for women's return to the kitchen, rampant pornography, commodification of women, and other antifemale manifestations of what she characterizes as the post-soviet "maleocracy." The work is divided into numerous chapters, only a few of which (mainly four of Mamonova's own essays—about 20 percent of the book) have direct relevance to the title. Mamonova is provocative and entertaining as always, though perhaps more self-contradictory than usual. Her essays lead readers through the depressing post-soviet world of misogyny and female poverty and helplessness, though she offers some hope in the form of the numerous small women's organizations that have sprung up in the wake of glasnost. The essays provide something of interest to everyone, from the specialist in Slavic or women's studies to the general reader. Somewhat disappointing, however, are the repetitious and tedious interviews that make up most of the volume. Contrary to statements in the foreword, the interviews do not present a "wide cross section" of society—*all* 17 women are intelligentsia or white collar.— *A. H. Koblitz, Hartwick College*

WS-1767   HN530.R87   90-41811 CIP
Worobec, Christine D. **Peasant Russia: family and community in the post-emancipation period.** Princeton, 1991. 257p bibl index afp ISBN 0-691-03151-7, $39.50

Worobec offers a fascinating, rich account of peasant households, families, and economic strategies in post-emanicpation Russia. Worobec convincingly argues that only by understanding the normal functioning of peasant society prior to the modernization drives of the late 19th and 20th centuries can one fully appreciate "the resilience of peasant customs and institutions." She provides a wealth of detail and case studies to support her contention that peasant custom and law were reasonably successful in fighting natural conditions, government interference, and outside pressures for modernization. Worobec's book is notable for its sensitive discussion of women's roles and opportunities in and varied accommodations to the extreme patriarchy of Russian peasant society. The book can be profitably (and enjoyably) read by upper-division undergraduates in Russian and East European history and women's studies, as well as by specialists. A must for university libraries, and for college libraries with strong collections in these areas.—*A. H. Koblitz, Hartwick College*

◆ Latin America & the Caribbean

WS-1768   HQ1236   92-20274 CIP
'Viva': women and popular protest in Latin America, ed. by Sarah A. Radcliffe and Sallie Westwood. Routledge, 1993. 270p bibl index ISBN 0-415-07312-X, $55.00; ISBN 0-415-07313-8 pbk, $16.95

Yet another collection seeking to enhance understanding about the similarities and differences surrounding gender within Latin American societies. Contributors represent a broad cross section of the scholars working on issues related to gender, class, and ethnicity in Latin America. The editors seek to externalize knowledge of women's movements and to "contextualize women's protest not only in terms of pre-existing political organizations, socio-economic structures and reproductive responsibilities, but also to uncover some of the 'internalities' of political protest." Their intellectual framework for this project is the work of the European deconstructionists. Although this context offers a richer framework, it also makes for a denser analysis, one likely to be daunting for most undergraduates. However, this worthwhile volume is a valuable addition for those interested in the heterogeneity of Latin American society and in gender, and is a valiant attempt to intellectualize beyond a *traditional* Eurocentric understanding of the continent. Graduate; faculty.—*A. J. Russ, Wells College*

WS-1769   HQ1542   95-23353 CIP
Besse, Susan K. **Restructuring patriarchy: the modernization of gender inequality in Brazil, 1914-1940.** North Carolina, 1996. 285p bibl index afp ISBN 0-8078-2252-3, $39.95; ISBN 0-8078-4559-0 pbk, $16.95

Besse offers a detailed and insightful analysis of the impact of modernization and political change on Brazilian women during the interwar years. She focuses on the formulation of public policy concerning gender relations. Besse sees this issue as a critical part of the larger political conflicts of the era, conflicts that involved the definition of the state and its role in Brazilian life. Brazil did not prove a propitious laboratory for women's causes: the organized feminist movement collapsed in 1937, as the author notes, with the rise of a reactionary intellectual climate and the establishment of a dictatorship. Besse's study is based on a wide array of primary and secondary sources, and complements and adds to earlier work done by June Hahner, Eva Blay, Dain Borges, and Helieth Saffioti. It is clearly written and contains an extensive bibliography of sources in English and in Portuguese. Recommended for readers in women's studies, gender studies, and Latin American history. Upper-division undergraduates and above.—*R. M. Levine, University of Miami*

WS-1770   HV6322   93-41428 CIP
Bouvard, Marguerite Guzman. **Revolutionizing motherhood: the Mothers of the Plaza de Mayo.** Scholarly Resources, 1994. 278p bibl index afp ISBN 0-8420-2486-7, $45.00; ISBN 0-8420-2487-5 pbk, $15.95

Bouvard's book is an tale of incredible bravery. This documentary account is full of genuine heroes whose lives were transformed by the brutal excesses of the military junta that ruled in Argentina from 1976 to 1983. All the mothers whose children were "disappeared" by the military government during those years, supposedly because they were "subversives," had to confront their roles as women in Latin American society, conduct individual quests to find their loved ones, and deal with the sorrow of losing children. Bouvard traces the increasing involvement of some of these mothers in the public sphere, specifically in public demonstrations in plazas. The book has three themes: chapters 1-5 trace the history of the junta and the development of the mothers' resistance to the regime; chapters 5 and 6 treat the ways in which the conservative forces in the government mollified the military by absolving some of the worst offenders after the junta fell and the mothers continued to protest. The last three chapters describe the new model developed by the Mothers of the Plaza de Mayo for human rights struggles, for understanding feminism in the Latin American context, and the schisms these developments caused within the group. For the purist, Bouvard's personal involvement may limit some of her conclusions regarding the rightness of this cause. For this reviewer, it validated the cause and gave heart and meaning to the scholarship. Highly recommended for general readers, upper-division undergraduates, and above.—*A. J. Russ, Wells College*

WS-1771   HV1448   94-47497 CIP
Dias, Maria Odila Silva. **Power and everyday life: the lives of working women in nineteenth-century Brazil,** tr. by Ann Frost. Rutgers, 1995. 221p bibl index afp ISBN 0-8135-2204-8, $45.00; ISBN 0-8135-2205-6 pbk, $15.95

Written by a leading social historian, this monograph deals with the lives of ordinary women in 19th-century Brazil. Dias (Univ. of São Paulo) concentrates on female social roles. Her subjects are black, white, Indian, and mixed-race women of the "oppressed classes." They lack protection or support from others, and include slaves, single women, single mothers, women unmarried or whose husbands had died or abandoned them—all providers for their children and, in many cases, the mainstay of emerging industrial growth. The book concludes with a chapter entitled "The Magic of Survival," describing the ways in which these women coped and struggled and, in the process, came to terms with the changing, urbanizing world. Dias's analysis draws on an array of statistics, travelers' accounts, and archival documentary sources. The tight writing style and level of specificity makes it mainly suitable for specialists in Latin American history. Contains 17 illustrations, tables, and nearly 40 pages of endnotes and citations. Upper-division undergraduates and above.—*R. M. Levine, University of Miami*

WS-1772   HV1448   91-15140 CIP
Golden, Renny. **The hour of the poor, the hour of women: Salvadoran women speak.** Crossroad, NY, 1991. 207p index ISBN 0-8245-1088-7, $19.95

The war in El Salvador has bound that small Central American Republic to the US. Conditions drove more than ten percent of the nation's population North in search of peace. Today, at least 500,000 Salvadorans live in the US, with the greatest number residing in the Los Angeles area. As in the case of most refugees, the majority will stay in this country, forming an El Salvador *afuera* (outside) that nation's borders. Golden's book concentrates on the lives of Salvadoran women who struggled to preserve their lives and community. They tell their own stories of homeless, landless, and unemployed women who enter into the process of national liberation. Golden does an excellent job of intertwining the influences of Jesuit priests who spread the gospel of liberation theology. The glue in this movement is the national martyrs: Archbishop Oscar Romero, the six Jesuits, and common folk. It is an intense account of the struggle of a people to survive, and of the creation of a "new woman" who organizes and administers refugee communities such as Segundo Montes. The work indicates why Salvadoran women in Los Angeles are at the vanguard of the labor movement, forever shattering the myth of the docile Latina. Excellent sources and good index. Highly recommended for libraries at all levels.—*R. Acuña, California State University, Northridge*

WS-1773   HQ170   91-8664 CIP
Guy, Donna J. **Sex & danger in Buenos Aires: prostitution, family, and nation in Argentina.** Nebraska, 1991. 260p bibl index afp ISBN 0-8032-2139-8, $35.00

Guy has assembled valuable evidence on prostitution in the Argentine capital from the 1860s to 1954. There is information on white slavery, police policies, and public health problems, especially venereal disease. Primary sources used include manuscripts, journals, and newspapers. Portions of the book have appeared in Guy's pervious publications. Because her subject is restricted to prostitution and its ramifications, there is a tendency to exaggerate its importance as a causal factor in the political and economic sphere. James R. Scobie's *Argentina: A City and A Nation* (2nd ed., CH, Mar'72) and his *Buenos Aires: Plaza to Suburb, 1870-1910* (CH, Feb'75) offer a more comprehensive, balanced view of multiple, complex issues in national and urban history. Suitable for institutions with graduate programs in gender studies.—*D. M. Flusche, Eastern Michigan University*

WS-1774   HQ1532   95-2729 CIP
Lavrin, Asunción. **Women, feminism, and social change in Argentina, Chile, and Uruguay, 1890-1940.** Nebraska, 1995. 480p (Engendering Latin America, 3) bibl index afp ISBN 0-8032-2897-X, $60.00

Feminism in the Southern Cone developed as an extension of what both women and men regarded as women's central role: maternity. Concern for the well-being of mother and child was the prime motivation of feminists during the half-century examined here. Lavrin, editor of *Latin American Women: Historical Perspectives* (CH, May'79) and *Sexuality and Marriage in Colonial Latin America* (CH, Sep'90), in this book examines the educational, social, legal, and political dimensions of various reform movements. She situates Latin American feminism in the heart of a patriarchal society, where it found allies in the socialist, anarchist, and populist movements, as well as in the struggles for reform of labor and university codes. Living the reality of a sexual double standard, feminists fought not for women's sexual liberation but for a legal base from which they could defend their dignity as mothers and dedicate their earnings to the care of their children. The battle for legal equality had to be fought country by country, and on premises different from those prevailing in the US. There is assuredly much for northern feminists (and patriarchs) to learn from this book. Highly recommended. Upper-division undergraduates and above.—*J. L. Elkin, University of Michigan*

WS-1775   F2537   95-4352 CIP
Levine, Robert M. **The life and death of Carolina Maria de Jesus,** by Robert M. Levine and José Carlos Sebe Bom Meihy. New Mexico, 1995. 162p index ISBN 0-8263-1648-4 pbk, $15.95

Child of the Dark propelled Carolina Maria de Jesus from obscurity and poverty to recognition as a best-selling author. Translations have enabled her work to reach a worldwide readership. Black, female, illegitimate, and poor, she received more acclaim abroad than at home in Brazil and was seen as a symbol of a rigid class system and racism in a society where women (especially black) were marginalized and the poor and destitute were degraded. For foreigners, hers was the voice of the underclass. For Brazilians, she—and not the social injustices she revealed—was the focus of attention. She was not adopted by the literary establishment or the women's movement; her work did not provoke national debate. Although de Jesus wrote three more books, poems, short stories, and memoirs, hers was a meteoric rise and fall. Levine (Univ. of Miami) has collaborated with a well-known Brazilian scholar to devise a research strategy based on de Jesus's writings, library research, and interviews. Their reconstruction of her life story is compelling reading. The authors' major contribution has been to place de Jesus and her work in the social, political, economic, and cultural context of modern Brazil, especially the São Paulo of the late 1950s and early '60s. The resulting work clarifies issues raised in *Child of the Dark* and is an indispensable guide to modern Brazil. Strongly recommended. General, undergraduate.—*A. J. R. Russell-Wood, Johns Hopkins University*

WS-1776   HQ1465   92-39037 CIP
LeVine, Sarah. **Dolor y Alegría: women and social change in urban Mexico.** Wisconsin, 1993. 239p bibl index ISBN 0-299-13790-2, $37.50; ISBN 0-299-13794-5 pbk, $12.95

LeVine's highly readable study of 15 mestizo women from the ages of 19 to 73 illustrates how urbanization and rapid social change—particularly massive expansions in the educational and health care systems—have affected the lives of working-class Mexican women. Spanning the period from the 1920s to the 1970s, their stories are skillfully interwoven within the context of Mexico's dynamic postrevolutionary history. Their histories are organized around the themes of early childhood; adolescence (including sexual development); courtship and marriage; pregnancy, childbirth, motherhood and child rearing (including birth control, health care and schooling); widowhood and old age. Although they are not self-consciously feminist in any sense, nor aware of or connected to the women's movement of middle-class Mexican women, the younger women in this study seem less willing to accept traditional roles and relationships with husbands, other authority figures, and even their own children. All levels.—*E. Hu-DeHart, University of Colorado at Boulder*

WS-1777   HQ1017   91-9737 CIP
Nazzari, Muriel. **Disappearance of the dowry: women, families, and social change in São Paulo, Brazil (1600-1900).** Stanford, 1991. 245p bibl index afp ISBN 0-8047-1928-4, $35.00

Nazzari provides well-researched explanations for the disappearance of the dowry in Brazil that will have implications for other regions. Using *inventarios*, Brazilian judicial processes of settlement of estates, Nazzari traces the changes in dowry custom from 1600 to 1900. She combines this research with an analy-

sis of legal and economic changes to draw her conclusions. In the early 17th century all daughters of property owners in Nazzari's sample received a substantial dowry. By the mid-19th century, 75 percent of women from the same class married without a dowry. This change was accompanied by a reversal of family priorities that favored endowing daughters in the 17th century with large bequests to provide the basis for conjugal family wealth to those that favored providing sons in the 19th century with equal wealth and more opportunities for education to prepare for life in a capitalistic society. Nazzari concludes that the marriage bargain altered over the years in such a way that the dowry was no longer the link in a patriarchal society among propertied families. She also notes that migration, urbanization, and entrepreneurial adventures created an independent source of wealth for young males. Upper-division undergraduates and above.—*D. Baldwin, University of Arkansas at Little Rock*

WS-1778   HQ1467   94-44006 CIP
Randall, Margaret. **Our voices/our lives: stories of women from Central America and the Caribbean.** Common Courage, 1995. 213p index ISBN 1-56751-047-7, $29.95; ISBN 1-56751-046-9 pbk, $12.95

Randall's book consists of six essays that include life stories of a feminist from the Dominican Republic and a woman from Belize, descriptions of encounters between different women's groups in Gautemala, Nicaragua, and Cuba, and a personal essay about the author's experiences in Chile. No single theme dominates the book, and the brevity of the pieces is frustrating. The most interesting sections are either too short or are offhand references that go unexplained. The author's own life serves only as subtext, though it might be the most interesting story in the collection. The work's strength emerges when it is read as a whole; readers unfamiliar with Central America and the Caribbean can get a sense of the historical, social, and ethnic complexity of these two regions. Simultaneously, through examples, Randall makes a persuasive argument for an inclusive definition of feminism. The essays have a strong contemporary tone, especially those about Nicaragua and Cuba. How they will endure over time is not clear. General; undergraduate.—*J. Rosenthal, Columbia University*

WS-1779   HX546   93-10819 CIP
Randall, Margaret. **Sandino's daughters revisited: feminism in Nicaragua.** Rutgers, 1994. 311p ISBN 0-8135-2024-X, $47.00; ISBN 0-8135-2025-8 pbk, $16.95

An ardent supporter of Latin American social movements who spent 20 years in Mexico, Cuba, and Nicaragua in cultural and political solidarity work, Randall does not mask her sympathies for the Sandinistas. However, she is sharply critical of the male-dominated Sandinista leadership—and by extension, of other social revolutions in Latin America—for their failure to integrate a feminist analysis into revolutionary work. In this book, which is a sequel to the much acclaimed *Sandino's Daughters* (CH, Jun'82), a series of interviews with female revolutionaries in Nicaragua during the anti-Somoza struggle of the 1970s, Randall returns a decade later to revisit with some of these same women, as well as to introduce additional women active in Nicaraguan government and society when the Sandinistas were in power during the 1980s. Representing social backgrounds ranging from working-class to elite, these 13 compelling voices recount their personal histories of political awakening, including the process of engagement with women's issues and feminism, thereby collectively shedding light on the problematic relationship between feminism and socialist revolution. All levels.—*E. Hu-DeHart, University of Colorado at Boulder*

WS-1780   HQ1501   91-4013 CIP
Senior, Olive. **Working miracles: women's lives in the English-speaking Caribbean.** University of the West Indies, Institute of Social & Economic Research/ J. Currey/Indiana, 1992 (c1991). 210p bibl index ISBN 0-253-35136-7, $35.00; ISBN 0-253-28885-1 pbk, $14.95

Based on data and interviews generated by the Women in the Caribbean Project (1979-1982) and without pretense of being the "last word," *Working Miracles* attempts to provide an understanding of the realities of the lives of women in the English-speaking Caribbean. Senior uses a multidisciplinary women-centered approach, but claims no major theoretical advances. The book covers specific topics, such as gender roles, within the broad themes of childhood, family, livelihood, public and political participation, and relationships with men, while shortchanging other topics such as health, aging and sexuality, spirituality, and religion. It is, unfortunately, not cross-cultural within the context of the Caribbean and focuses almost exclusively on one class and one race in the English-speaking Caribbean—poor and working class Afro-Caribbean women. Much statistical and other hard data can render the text dry, but the voices of the women themselves extracted from the interviews make this at times a rich and readable book. Upper-division undergraduates and above.—*E. Hu-DeHart, University of Colorado at Boulder*

WS-1781 HQ1507 95-11827 CIP
Smith, Lois M. **Sex and revolution: women in socialist Cuba,** by Lois M. Smith and Alfred Padula. Oxford, 1996. 247p bibl index afp ISBN 0-19-509490-5, $39.95; ISBN 0-19-509491-3 pbk, $16.95

According to the authors, this book "is an examination of one nation's efforts to conceptualize, prioritize, and implement sexual equality, and it offers an assessment of the successes, failures, and dilemmas of that process." Smith and Padula made this assessment by examining official sources, primarily those produced by the Federation of Cuban Women and in interviews with its director, Vilma Espin—the estranged wife of Cuba's second most powerful man, Raul Castro—and a few other women in key official posts. Thus, the emphasis of the study is on the history of Cuban revolutionary social policy as it this applies to elite women and how it has been implemented—or failed to be implemented—during 30 plus years of revolutionary rule. The quality of the chapters varies with the availability and sources of data. For example, one learns much more about women in prerevolutionary Cuba (chapter 1) from a reading of chapter 2, which documents the struggle against the Batista dictatorship as remembered by a few of the women who are today high government officials. Chapters 3 and 4 provide a wealth of data on the Federation of Cuban Women. The chapter on health could have been strengthened by concrete comparative data instead of vague generalizations about Third World health. The same may be said about the chapter on education. Finally, there is little in the book that would prepare readers to understand the recent surge of prostitution in Cuba. The strength of this study lies in reminding readers that knowledge of Cuba is seriously limited by the lack of rigorous data collection on the actual experiences and opinions of the Cuban people. Undergraduates and above.—*E. Bastida, University of Texas—Pan American*

WS-1782 HQ1236.5.M6 89-77883 CIP
Soto, Shirlene. **Emergence of the modern Mexican woman: her participation in revolution and struggle for equality, 1910-1940.** Arden Press, 1990. 199p bibl index ISBN 0-912869-11-9, $26.50; ISBN 0-912869-12-7, $16.95

In this well-researched addition to English-language studies of Latin American women, Soto examines Mexican women's continual efforts to gain political, social, and economic equality. She explores their attempts at industrial unionization and their extensive and varied roles in the Revolution. Soto focuses especially on the pioneering work of the Yucatecan Ligas Feministas in raising women's political consciousness. Under the leadership of Elvia Carrillo Puerto and her brother, the state's governor, Yucatan led the fight for women's rights in general and their enfranchisement in particular. Despite the insistence of all Mexican feminists that, as citizens, women deserved equal political rights, the national government delayed granting their demands until 1953. Foremost among the justifications offered was the fear that women were so fanatically religious, as illustrated by their involvement in the Cristero Revolt, that the church would completely control their vote. Soto expands beyond narrow political limits, however, to provide enlightening pictures of the individual women involved and to lament the lack of recognition accorded them. The excellent bibliography makes this a valuble tool for students and faculty alike.—*K. M. Butler, Colgate University*

WS-1783 F1221 91-8904 CIP
Stephen, Lynn. **Zapotec women.** Texas, 1992 (c1991). 316p bibl index afp ISBN 0-292-79064-3, $35.00; ISBN 0-292-79065-1 pbk, $14.95

From seven years of research—fieldwork and historical documentation—Stephen is able to draw on firsthand insights gleaned during an important period of economic growth and cultural change in the Zapotec community of Teotitlan. The uniqueness of this community is well described. Stephen notes that Teoti-

tlan is a place caught between a rapidly advancing future in export production and a long-entrenched ethnic past anchored in ongoing institutions. Within this structural and institutional setting, the author presents a careful analysis of the role of gender in indigenous peasant communities. Stephen uses the concept of social reproduction as a way of relating cultural and economic spheres to demonstrate the multiple ways in which male and female roles are linked to specific social relationships and institutions. Her approach is fresh and appealing, particularly as it relates to three areas of her analysis. First, she distinguishes the different types of ethnic identity manifested by the community, depending on the nature of the social exchange. Second, discussion of class differentation is especially important and informative. Finally, she does not dichotomize gender roles by their "private" or "public" social locations. Instead, Stephen describes gender roles by examining the ways in which they operate in conjunction with other social institutions to reproduce significant social relations, particularly those tied to productive and cultural functions. Strongly recommended.—*E. Bastida, University of Texas—Pan American*

WS-1784 HQ1075 94-39349 CIP
Stern, Steve J. **The secret history of gender: women, men, and power in late colonial Mexico.** North Carolina, 1995. 478p bibl index afp ISBN 0-8078-2217-5, $29.95

Stern assiduously avoids the trap of reductionism that so often limits complex realities to a formula dictated by theory. His work undermines notions of a single Latin American gender culture, dominated by tyrannical patriarchs with complicity from submissive women. Rather, he finds a world peopled by patriarchs at all levels, from family to state, whose dominance is constantly challenged by nonsubmissive women who refuse to accept the dissipations and dalliances of the men. The ways in which they do this become the subject of female "gossip" and occasional male banter, but the historical record is clear in criminal court cases found in Mexico City, Oaxaca, and Morelos. Stern makes a compelling claim for a universality of these case studies. He provides a fascinating chapter on the ways in which this colonial reality is still clearly visible in the present, despite the major upheavals of a socialist revolution in the 20th century. At the same time, he is also careful to point out the discontinuities with the present Mexican system. Upper-division undergraduates and above.—*A. J. Russ, Wells College*

WS-1785 HQ1236 90-48182 CIP
Stoner, K. Lynn. **From the house to the streets: the Cuban woman's movement for legal reform, 1898-1940.** Duke University, 1991. 242p bibl index afp ISBN 0-8223-1131-3, $42.50; ISBN 0-8223-1149-6 pbk, $16.95

Stoner's fascinating, delightfully written, and impressively researched account of the women's movement in Cuba nicely dovetails with the tumultuous history of the republic between the war of independence in 1898 and the passage of the important constitution in 1940. Stoner focuses attention on the remarkable careers of a handful of determined feminists such as Mariblanca Sabas Alomá, Ofelia Rodríguez Acosta, María Collado, Loló de la Torriente, and Ofelia Domínguez Navarro, and their success in getting contradictory family and gender goals incorporated in the constitution of 1940. In this context, she deftly manages to incorporate insightful observations on politics, social class, race, and the process of modernization in Cuba that persuasively explain why the social legislation of 1940 placed Cuba in the forefront of reform in the Americas, despite lack of unanimity among Cuban feminists. A very useful addition to Cuban and Latin American historiography, and Latin American women's history. All levels.—*F. W. Knight, Johns Hopkins University*

WS-1786 Orig
Surviving beyond fear: women, children and human rights in Latin America, ed. by Marjorie Agosin. White Pine, NY, 1993. 217p bibl ISBN 1-877727-25-3 pbk, $14.00

Possibly the first volume published in English to focus on two neglected groups in the field of human rights in Latin America: women and children. Because perpetrators of human rights abuse and violence have primarily been males (representing the military or the state), it has often been presumed that the victims have also been men. To correct such misperception, this collection of essays by US and Latin American scholars and human rights activists highlight how ordinary women in various Latin American countries have created "political space" by mobilizing around human rights, particularly the issue of their "disappeared" loved ones. They share excruciating stories of women political prisoners subjected to unimaginable sexual torture, and publicize the plight of children of political prisoners, many of whom were forcibly removed from their parents only to be adopted by their parents' torturers. A must-read for those interested in expanding their understanding of human rights abuses in Latin America, especially the critical role of women in the ongoing struggle against these abuses. All levels.—*E. Hu-DeHart, University of Colorado at Boulder*

WS-1787 HD8290 92-40484 CIP
Wolfe, Joel. **Working women, working men: São Paulo and the rise of Brazil's industrial working class, 1900-1955.** Duke University, 1993. 312p bibl index afp ISBN 0-8223-1330-8, $45.00; ISBN 0-8223-1347-2 pbk, $17.95

Wolfe's superbly written book is a revisionist history of São Paulo's labor movement, focusing on its textile workers (mostly unskilled women) and metal workers (mostly skilled men), their struggle to improve their lives, and their bold but violent confrontations with industrialists, repressive government officials, and professional labor bosses (*pelegos*). Workers in São Paulo had organized informal workplace committees well before formal unions were set up and manipulated by anarchists, communists, and government-controlled *pelegos*. These factory "commissions" became the harbinger for union democracy. The commissions, or shop-floor groupings, gave women workers the power to organize their movements without interference from men. Industrialists, union organizers, and leftist radicals often collided over the control of the commissions. For four decades and against all odds, factory commissions prevailed as the articulators for rank-and-file demands. Wolfe's book is a triumph of a good social history, free of ideological rhetoric but full of new exciting interpretations. It is highly readable and packed with new facts solidly backed up by sound analyses. Advanced undergraduates and above.—*E. Pang, Colorado School of Mines*

WS-1788 HQ1240 93-422 CIP
Women & change in the Caribbean: a Pan-Caribbean perspective, ed. by Janet Momsen. I. Randle/Indiana/J. Currey, 1993. 308p index ISBN 0-253-33897-2, $35.00; ISBN 0-253-33896-4 pbk, $16.95

A collection of 18 essays on many aspects of women's lives in the contemporary Caribbean, specifically, in Jamaica, Curacao, Montserrat, Barbuda, Dominica, Guadeloupe, Guyana, Suriname, Nevis, Puerto Rico, Barbados, Grenada, Trinidad, and Cuba. Momsen, a geographer, provides an introduction. Four essays are concerned with women in the domestic domain and the community, and five with the intersection of reproduction and production. The other nine essays focus on women's changing economic roles in rural and urban employment. Common themes include the interaction of race, class, and gender differentials, the multiplicity of women's work, and the contradiction between the public activities of women and the patriarchal ideology that restricts them to domestic roles. The topics are diverse, but the essays consistently meet a high standard of research and clarity. Although each essay has a list of references, a comprehensive bibliography would have been useful. Highly recommended, alongside Olive Senior's *Working Miracles* (CH, Sep'92) for multidisciplinary Caribbean and women's studies collections at the upper-division undergraduate and graduate levels.—*O. N. Bolland, Colgate University*

WS-1789 HQ1462 94-10179 CIP
Women of the Mexican countryside, 1850-1990: creating spaces, shaping transitions, ed. by Heather Fowler-Salamini and Mary Kay Vaughan. Arizona, 1994. 253p index afp ISBN 0-8165-1415-1, $35.00; ISBN 0-8165-1431-3 pbk, $15.95

Exploring women as historical actors in the 20th century, the editors and contributors question the marginality with which they are depicted in revolutionary iconography. Through a series of interdisciplinary articles, the authors overcome the difficulty of investigating this group of women by drawing creatively upon research in Mexican community studies, gender studies, and rural history. The chronological focus in 1850 to 1990, a time period when families were negotiating the transition from an agrarian to an industrial society. Articles can be divided into three topical sections: the process of state formation, 1850 to 1910; the socioeconomic effects of revolution and state consolidation, 1910 to 1940; and

the confrontation with urbanization and industrialization, post-1940. New insights are offered into women's income-producing capacity before modern capitalist growth and the regional factors that shaped this activity, women's role in industrial developments, and the social differentiation accompanying land tenure changes. However, the authors' most significant contribution is their effort to understand the interaction between historical agency at the micro level and macrostructural forces. This important work in an understudied field is essential reading for anyone interested in Mexican history or gender issues. All levels.—*D. Baldwin, University of Arkansas at Little Rock*

WS-1790 HQ1460.5 89-77866 MARC
Women, culture, and politics in Latin America, by Emilie Bergmann et al.; Seminar on Feminism and Culture in Latin America. California, 1990. 269p bibl index afp ISBN 0-520-06552-2, $38.50

This collection reflects the authors' "fundamental commitment to collaborative intellectual activity...[and] collective practice as the key to efforts to mediate among literary studies, history, politics, area studies, feminist theory, and Europe and the Americas." Their methods include looking at traditional texts from new perspectives and giving "serious attention" to obscure texts, some of which were uncovered in the course of their work. The resultant volume reflects both the strengths and weaknesses of such collaborative efforts. In a somewhat scattered historical approach the material covered ranges from "Latin American Feminism and the Transitional Arena" in the period from 1910 to 1955, to Sor Juana Inéz de la Cruz, 1648 to 1695, to three chapters on bibliography (Chapters 10, 11, and 12). Clearly, chronology was not the organizing issue used. The authors conclude that the "history of women's participation in literary culture and political life in Latin America is a history still in the making [and that] a feminist critique of society arose out of the distinctive experience of the Latin American women themselves, rather than out of European or United States influences." Thereby, they refute the charge that Latin American feminism is a colonial or neocolonial phenomenon. Although the volume has limited general use, it would be of value to feminist and/or Latin American collections.—*A. J. Russ, Wells College*

◆ Middle East & North Africa

WS-1791 HQ1784 91-26901 CIP
Ahmed, Leila. **Women and gender in Islam: historical roots of a modern debate.** Yale, 1992. 296p index afp ISBN 0-300-04942-0, $30.00

Ahmed's engaging book is both the only currently available survey of the history of women in Middle Eastern societies and a polemical work articulating a revisionist feminist view of women and gender in Islam. Ahmed examines the status of women in ancient Mesopotamia, Egypt, and pre-Islamic Christian societies before moving on to topics more familier to Islamists, e.g., the status of women in pre-Islamic Arabia, the attitude of Muhammad to his wives, the treatment of women in Islamic law, modern controversies over the veil. This sweeping historical framework presages the author's principal argument: that in its attitude toward and treatment of women, Islamic civilization is the heir of more ancient Middle Eastern (and European) traditions. She identifies an "ethical" streak in Islam that stresses equality and respect for women, a tendency obscured by a misogyny inherited from ancient, classical, and Christian civilizations. Many historians will object to a number of the book's conclusions. The force of Ahmed's argument occasionally outpaces balanced historical judgment, but that argumentative streak is also the source of much of the book's insight and interest. This book will both spark debate among specialists and become a staple of undergraduate courses.—*J. P. Berkey, Mount Holyoke College*

WS-1792 HQ1784 92-33583 MARC
Arab women: old boundaries, new frontiers, ed. by Judith E. Tucker. Indiana, 1993. 264p index afp ISBN 0-253-36096-X, $35.00; ISBN 0-253-20776-2 pbk, $14.95

The disparate articles in this volume cover feminism, Islam, gender conflict, economics, nationalism, politics, and change. Contributors are drawn from many disciplines and the quality of the essays is generally rather high. The editor however, seems unable to draw a connecting theme linking the contributions. Is it "Arabness," language, cultural similarity, social structural resemblance, subsistence, location, religion, all of these? Tucker is successful in showing why none of these criteria alone suffice, but is less effective in synthesizing an effective operational paradigm for the collection. As a result, it is hard to see why "Arab" women should have been the focus of the collection, rather than Middle Eastern and North African women generally. Some contrasting material on "Arab" non-Muslim women might have helped to define the subject better. Alternatively, choosing one aspect of women's life might have brought more coherence. Nevertheless, the collection is useful, insightful, and well documented. All levels.—*L. D. Loeb, University of Utah*

WS-1793   HQ1793   94-19055 CIP
Badran, Margot. **Feminists, Islam, and nation: gender and the making of modern Egypt.** Princeton, 1995. 352p bibl index afp ISBN 0-691-03706-X, $35.00

Badran has written a detailed historical study of the Egyptian feminist movement in the first half of the 20th century, based on primarily women's sources— their memoirs, essays, letters, journalistic articles, fiction, and oral histories gathered by the author and others. Translator and editor of *Harem Years*, a biography of Egypt's foremost feminist, Huda Sha'rawi (CH, Nov'87), Badran uses her extensive research on modern Egyptian history to challenge the notions that feminism is only a Western creation and that it is incompatible with Islam. In focusing on the gendered nature of nationalist, Islamic, and imperialist discourses, Badran covers issues concerning family law, education, work, prostitution, voting rights, and women's political action on Palestine. More scholars have written about women in Egypt than any other area of the Muslim world, with the exception of Iran; this new study will be respected for its high level of scholarship and its sophisticated analysis. Badran includes an excellent bibliography and 65 pages of notes. Graduate; faculty.—*L. Beck, Washington University*

WS-1794   HQ1793   93-27067 CIP
Baron, Beth. **The women's awakening in Egypt: culture, society, and the press.** Yale, 1994. 259p index afp ISBN 0-300-05563-3, $27.50

From 1892 to 1920, a flourishing women's press, supported by authors from ethnically and religiously diverse Egyptian communities, appeared in Arabic in Egypt for circulation throughout the Arab world. Baron, a social historian, examines 30 women's periodicals as sources for Egyptian cultural and social history. She includes a section on the production (with special attention to the backgrounds of the women writers), dissemination, and consumption of this press and another section on the texts themselves and their social contexts. The periodicals served as a forum for issues relating to marriage and divorce, veiling and seclusion, education, and work; they also provided domestic instruction and entertainment. Baron concludes that a close relationship existed between a culture of literacy and social transformation, between the production of female intellectual elite writers and change in the lives of middle- and upper-class women during the three decades preceding the 1919 revolution. A useful comparative work is Judith Tucker's *Women in Nineteenth-Century Egypt* (CH, Oct'86). Detailed footnotes with references. Graduate; faculty.—*L. Beck, Washington University*

WS-1795   Orig
Hart, Ursula Kingsmill. **Behind the courtyard door: the daily life of tribeswomen in northern Morocco.** Ipswich, 1994. 166p ISBN 0-938864-18-1 pbk, $11.95

WS-1795a   HQ1791   94-6193 CIP
Lazreg, Marnia. **The eloquence of silence: Algerian women in question.** Routledge, 1994. 270p bibl index afp ISBN 0-415-90730-6, $59.95

Despite being politically powerless, women have emerged as a pivotal group in the struggle in contemporary Algeria between Islamic fundamentalists and the secular military government. It is not a new role. Lazreg, both an Algerian and a trained sociologist, notes that "in another but more deadly replay of their past, women have emerged as symbols of cultural integrity, Islamic or secular,

and conflicting interests between men." To paraphrase the book's well-chosen title, women have always served by the eloquence of their silence as focal points of Algerian society, "ruled by men but not *of* them." Lazreg develops this theme in historical sequence, from the mainly unrecorded precolonial period through the denigration of women (*and* men) under French colonialism, women's active role in the independence struggle, and their deteriorating status under the socialist government. It is a tragic story told well, with minimal sociological jargon. In a work on women in neighboring Morocco, Hart describes in faithful and interesting detail her life with her anthropologist husband among the Moroccan Rifian Ait Waryaghar tribe. Among studies comparable with Lazreg's and Hart's, Leila Ahmed's *Women and Gender in Islam* (CH, Oct'92) is more broad-gauged and essentially historical. Fatima Mernissi's *Beyond the Veil* (1975), like Hart's book, deals with Morocco. Mernissi focuses on the veil as image and ignores its natural and social usage for Muslim women. Overall, *Behind the Courtyard Door* seems more a combination travelogue and personal memoir than a profound scholarly study. *The Eloquence of Silence* is both personal and scholarly, probing deeply into the subconsciousness of Algerian women caught in the crossfire of secular politics and Islam. Hart's book is suitable for general readers and lower-division undergraduates; Lazreg's is recommended for upper-division undergraduates and area specialists.—*W. Spencer, formerly, Florida State University*

WS-1796   BP135   90-47404 CIP
Mernissi, Fatima. **The veil and the male elite: a feminist interpretation of women's rights in Islam,** tr. by Mary Jo Lakeland. Addison-Wesley, 1991. 228p index ISBN 0-201-52321-3, $24.95

In some predominantly Muslim countries like Turkey, which have established a tradition of secularism, women's rights have come under increasing pressure from Islamists, who argue that such rights are alien to Islam and are the result of westernization that has weakened and undermined Islamic society. Opponents of this thesis, especially some Muslim feminists like Mernissi, have begun to fight the Islamists with their own weapons—the Quran and the traditions of the Prophet Muhammad—to argue that Islam gave rights to women and never sanctioned their oppression. This essay by a Moroccan sociologist—a brilliant analysis of classical Islamic sources undertaken in a historical context—shows that the Prophet wanted to create an egalitarian society based on individual responsibility but that the male elite subverted his efforts to retain privileges sanctioned by pre-Islamic tribalism. The author emphasizes that women, especially those in the Prophet's household, played an active and creative role in the politics of the new society. Made accessible by a felicitious translation, this work will help to correct the widely held misconceptions about Islam and women and therefore deserves the widest audience. All levels.—*F. Ahmad, University of Massachusetts at Boston*

WS-1797   HQ1726   92-37454 CIP
Moghadam, Valentine M. **Modernizing women: gender and social change in the Middle East.** L. Rienner, 1993. 311p bibl index afp ISBN 1-55587-346-4, $40.00; ISBN 1-55587-354-5 pbk, $17.95

One of the best studies of women and social change in the Middle East ever to be published. In this scholarly analysis of the impact of change on women's roles and statuses and of women's responses to and involvement in the processes of change, Moghadam provides a detailed account of political (especially of Islamist movements and revolutions), economic, social, and cultural factors as they relate both to the modern Middle East as a whole and to specific countries. She focuses on middle-class women who play pivotal roles as agents of change. Comparative data from other parts of the world greatly enhance the book's usefulness. Moghadam uses Iran and Afghanistan as case studies. She draws her data from a wide reading of the literature and from her own research and experience in the Middle East. Describing herself as a Marxist-feminist sociologist, Moghadam does not treat Islam or "culture" as determining factors in women's roles and statuses, unlike many other writers on Middle-Eastern women. Her study is a superb resource for scholars and students interested in gender, the Middle East, and development and social change. It contains 40 pages of detailed notes, a bibliography that includes the most current publications, photographs (that ought to be identified by place and date), tables, and a figure. Graduate; faculty.—*L. Beck, Washington University*

WS-1798 HQ1735 93-47024 CIP
Moghissi, Haideh. **Populism and feminism in Iran: women's struggle in a male-defined revolutionary movement.** Macmillan, UK/St. Martin's, 1995 (c1994). 217p bibl index ISBN 0-312-12068-0, $59.95

Even though the women's movement in Iran played a role in the overthrow of the shah, Moghissi, a feminist political activist and a founder of the National Union of Iran, argues that "women have been the main losers of the 1979 Revolution." In a critical and important study of the revolution, she shows that the left sacrificed women's rights, a fundamental part of the struggle for democracy and individual liberties, on the alter of anti-imperialism and populism, and abandoned the leadership of the revolution to the Islamists. The hegemony of the Shiite/Iranian cultural tradition in which women are expected to be subordinate made the struggle even harder. These themes are explored first within the context of Iranian history and Shiite religious discourse and then within the framework of the secular revolutionary movement. Moghissi's discussion is particularly engaging when she analyzes the policies of the Fedayeen, the principal leftist body in the revolution. Not only did the men retain "a patriarchal and gender hierarchy and sexual division of labour in politics," but women in the movement also shared similar perceptions. The lesson of this failure is that Iranian feminists must become autonomous, define their own goals, set their own priorities, and formulate their own strategies. Only then is there a chance of success in the future. Upper-division undergraduates and above.—*F. Ahmad, University of Massachusetts at Boston*

WS-1799 HQ1728 94-41373 Orig
Moors, Annelies. **Women, property and Islam: Palestinian experiences, 1920-1990.** Cambridge, 1995. 274p (Cambridge Middle East studies, 3) bibl index ISBN 0-521-47497-3, $59.95; ISBN 0-521-48355-7 pbk, $19.95

Moors' study examines the experience of Palestinian Arab women. Palestinian women appear to have adopted the same sorts of socioeconomic strategies used by other Arab women, often trading potential inheritance of land to strengthen kinship bonds with brothers and other agnates. Patterns may differ by type of settlement, e.g., urban versus rural, and have been modified by women's achievement of higher levels of education and entrance into "productive" labor and by the personal and society-wide consequences of Palestinian/Israeli interaction. The data were obtained mainly through interviewing women from differing socioeconoimc levels in locales in and around the West Bank city of Nablus. The author chose to include very little participant-observation in support of her ideas, depriving the reader of a critical perspective on the social context examined. Do the women's testimonies jibe with observable interaction? What are men's views of the circumstances described? Despite these concerns, this is a well-written, engaging study—useful to social scientists, Middle East scholars, and specialists in gender studies. General readers; upper-division undergraduates and above.—*L. D. Loeb, University of Utah*

WS-1800 HQ1236 94-16062 CIP
Paidar, Parvin. **Women and the political process in twentieth-century Iran.** Cambridge, 1995. 401p bibl index ISBN 0-521-47340-3, $59.95

Paidar's work is an analytical discussion of gender relationships, women's activities, and the impact of the state on women in 20th-century Iran, with focus on three political discourses relating to modernity, revolution, and Islamization. Previously writing under the name Nahid Yeganeh, the Iranian-born author draws on both secondary and primary sources to investigate Iranian women's efforts to construct political discourses, institutions, and processes, often under difficult circumstances. Much of Paidar's treatment of the early and middle 20th century is directed toward her analysis of women's actions during the 1978-79 revolution and subsequent creation of the Islamic Republic. Her coverage of Iran is necessarily restricted by the general lack of primary and secondary sources about women outside the capital of Tehran and outside the middle-to-upper socioeconomic classes. Her use of material from Persian-language newspapers, journals, and magazines is helpful for readers who lack knowledge of Persian. The study is best compared with Valentine Moghadam's excellent *Modernizing Women: Gender and Social Change in the Middle East* (CH, Oct'93). Some photographs; useful bibliography. For readers who lack any prior knowledge of Iran and for specialists.—*L. Beck, Washington University*

WS-1801 DS80 90-25824 CIP
Peteet, Julie M. **Gender in crisis: women and the Palestinian resistance movement.** Columbia, 1991. 245p bibl index afp ISBN 0-231-07446-8, $37.50

Peteet analyzes organization and representation of women in the early phase of the resistance movement (1921-29); evolution of a political consciousness among them; the process of mobilizing them; the role of ideas and gender in the national movement; activism and domesticity; and the loss of autonomy and the transformation of gender. The study is based on Peteet's field work during the period 1968-82. Ranging from illiterate to educated, the women interviewed resided mainly in Lebanese refugee camps. The work presents an intimate portrait of change in gender relations during an intense and sustained crisis and is unique in its portrayal of "ordinary" women and political activists, beginning with the pre-1948 years. Peteet relates in forthright and lucid language the various forms of political consciousness that evolved under adverse conditions following the brutalization of women and girls by the Stern gang in 1948, in the wake of the Dayr Yasin massacres. She describes what became a "culture of resistance" during exile and an enforced lifestyle bordering on desperation. The author also examines the Palestinian National Movement's conception and exercise of power as it relates to the question of sex and shows how women's roles evolved from passivity to active political involvement in the resistance movement. The work is well annotated, enhanced by a relevant select bibliography, and aided by a useful index. A first-rate study. All levels.—*C. E. Farah, University of Minnesota*

WS-1802 HQ1784 91-10866 CIP
Shaaban, Bouthaina. **Both right and left handed: Arab women talk about their lives.** Indiana, 1991 (c1988). 242p afp ISBN 0-253-35189-8, $35.00; ISBN 0-253-20688-X pbk, $12.95

Shaaban is a Syrian feminist who teaches English literature at Damascus University. In her words, this book "is not a sociological study. . .It is a personal book." In this reviewer's opinion, that is the book's great strength and appeal. Written in an engaging style, the book relates the struggles of Arab women from various social classes and differing generations in four Arab countries. In Syria, the state guarantees many civil rights, but Syrian women describe how they have to struggle against their fathers, husbands, and brothers for the right to be treated equally and with dignity. In Lebanon, women are engaged in a similar struggle amidst a cruel civil war, which, happily, has ended since the book was written. In Palestine, women fight for individual rights and statehood at the same time; and in Algeria, rights that were won during and after the national liberation war against French colonialism are endangered as Islamists challenge the power of the secular government. Shaaban allows women to speak of their frustrations and their hopes, and what emerges is a composite picture, not just of the plight of women but of four societies engaged in battle against tradition and outmoded mentalities. All levels.—*F. Ahmad, University of Massachusetts at Boston*

WS-1803 DS135 91-35675 CIP
Simon, Rachel. **Change within tradition among Jewish women in Libya.** Washington, 1992. 221p bibl index afp ISBN 0-295-97167-3, $30.00

Simon examines the Jewish community in a Muslim country between the latter half of the 19th century and 1967, when most of the remaining Jews emigrated. The book offers rare insight into Libyan Jewish women—both rural and urban—at a time when they were affected by both local Muslim and international factors. Through chapters on women's status, family life, work, education, and participation in public life, the author describes changes from the Ottoman through the Italian and British periods, up to Libyan independence. Painstaking research in limited and uneven sources enabled Simon to present data that show that although the Jewish community and its leaders felt bound by traditional ways, some Libyan Jews were adopting different and new modes of operation. Because of economic exigencies, some Jewish women were allowed to work outside the home and to recieve a secular education. European and Zionist models served as motivators of change in this context. Of particular interest to those concerned with North African history, Jewish studies, and women's studies. Advanced undergraduate; graduate; faculty.—*R. Ellovich, North Carolina State University*

WS-1804   HQ1728   91-42410 CIP
Strum, Philippa. **The women are marching: the second sex and the Palestinian revolution.** Lawrence Hill Books, 1992. (Dist. by Independent Publishers Group) 345p index ISBN 1-55652-122-7, $29.00; ISBN 1-55652-123-5 pbk, $16.95

Strum (political science, Brooklyn College), member of the executive committee of the board of directors of the ACLU and author of *Louis D. Brandeis* (CH, Sep'84) has written a sympathetic yet critical, hopeful but realistic analysis of the role of women in the intifada and of the impact of the intifada on the status of women. Based on numerous interviews with largely urban middle-class Palestinian women and on extensive meetings with women's committees in towns and villages throughout the West Bank, Strum suggests that "the Intifada and the women's committees have changed the roles of women" but "most peoples' *perception* of women's roles have not been altered." The underlying theme of this well-written and stimulating book is the question of whether contemporary changes in women's activities will outlive the intifada. Strum is particularly concerned with the apparent clash of fundamentalism and feminism. Recommended for all libraries, not merely those specializing in Middle Eastern or women's studies. General; undergraduate; graduate; faculty.—*B. Harris Jr., Occidental College*

WS-1805   HQ1728.5.Z8   89-13852 MARC
Warnock, Kitty. **Land before honour: Palestinian women in the occupied territories.** Monthly Review Press, 1990. 199p bibl index ISBN 0-85345-809-X, $33.00; ISBN 0-85345-810-3, $13.00

While teaching political theory and the history of ideas at Birzeit University in the West Bank, Warnock interviewed at length some 50 Palestinian women of various ages and social classes. She does not claim that her interlocutors were "representative' of more than themselves," but she uses material gathered from them to explore various facets of their lives. Following a brief introductory history of Palestine, Warnock devotes chapters to the traditional position of women, the forms and contexts of social change, education, work in agriculture and industry, politics, and women's organizations. The Islamic revival, resistance to Israeli occupation, and the "national struggle" are issues that pervade these chapters. One of the signal virtues of this work is its use of long excerpts from the interviews; these excerpts allow the women to come alive as individuals and reveal varied responses to their shared cultural and political ordeals. Since December 1987 the intifada has made manifest the importance of women to the Palestinian national movement. Warnock concludes, however, that new roles for women in current abnormal conditions provide no assurance against the future restoration of patriarchal attitudes. A fascinating study accessible to readers at all levels.—*L. M. Lewis, Eastern Kentucky University*

WS-1806   HQ1726   91-19665 CIP
Women in Middle Eastern history: shifting boundaries in sex and gender, ed. by Nikki R. Keddie and Beth Baron. Yale, 1992 (c1991). 343p index afp ISBN 0-300-05006-2, $35.00

Women in the Muslim World ed. by Lois Beck and Nikki Keddie (CH, Mar'79) featured five articles that provided a historical perspective for other case studies. This new collection, on the other hand, is a sustained effort to examine the role that women played in different historical periods of Islamic history and may well be the first scholarly collection to do so. A masterly introduction by Keddie on "deciphering Middle Eastern women's history" and a paper on Islam and patriarchy in comparative perspective provide a framework for the other essays. These are followed by three essays on the first Islamic centuries, another three on the Mamluk period in Egypt (1258-1517), four essays on modern Turkey and Iran (though one is actually on the late Ottoman Empire 1800-1914), and five essays on the modern Arab world (three on Egypt and one each on Palestine and Algeria). Given the problem of sources, which tend to be male-oriented, as is the case with most other regions of the world, the authors have been remarkably creative in reclaiming the history of Middle Eastern women. This volume in which almost every study is rich in fresh interpretation will be a model for any further research on this important topic. Upper-division undergraduates and above.—*F. Ahmad, University of Massachusetts at Boston*

WS-1807   HQ1793   91-3408 CIP
Zuhur, Sherifa. **Revealing reveiling: Islamist gender ideology in contemporary Egypt.** State University of New York, 1992. 207p bibl index ISBN 0-7914-0927-9, $47.50; ISBN 0-7914-0928-7 pbk, $15.95

Zuhur's monograph complements Soha Abdel Kader's *Egyptian Women in a Changing Society 1899-1987* (CH, Jun'88), Fatima Mernissi's *The Veil and the Male Elite* (CH, Feb'92), and Bouthaina Shaaban's *Both Right Handed and Left Handed* (CH, May'92). Although Zuhur covers virtually the same ground as Abdel Kader, her approach is refreshingly different. Zuhur writes as a feminist and a Muslim (though not an "Islamist") and consciously places "Islamist gender ideology" in political and socioeconomic context. She notes that the Islamist response tends to be colored by political opposition to the secular state as well as by the class characteristics of the Islamists. One of the principal aims (and successes) of this study is to test the correlation between socioeconomic background and religiopolitical belief. The author's methodology and assumptions are set out in the first two chapters; Ch. 3 provides the historical/political background necessary to understand gender politics. Zuhur then turns to her interviews and allows mainly women, both Islamists ("veiled") and secular ("unveiled"), to relate their experiences and worldviews. The result is a masterly essay that demolishes some myths and stereotypes and enhances understanding of the predicament of Muslim women in the contemporary world. All levels.—*F. Ahmad, University of Massachusetts at Boston*

◆ North America

WS-1808   JK3495   90-30867 CIP
Baker, Paula. **The moral frameworks of public life: gender, politics, and the state in rural New York, 1870-1930.** Oxford, 1991. 251p bibl index afp ISBN 0-19-506452-6, $29.95

Examining rural New York counties, Baker (University of Massachusetts, Amherst) exploits a multitude of local sources (newspapers; letters and diaries; club, lodge, and church records; local government documents; voting and referendum returns; yearbooks; and speeches) to create a brilliant synthesis of transitions in American public life from the 19th to the 20th centuries. Although Baker is most interested in the changing public roles of rural men and women, which she believes became less distinctive over time, her book is significant for the way it links and explicates the entire range of social, economic, and political changes occurring in rural America in this period. By skillfully developing historical context, Baker shows not only why women's public roles changed but also why women could still remain marginalized in the larger society. An important, integrative work, this is essential reading for serious students of the Gilded Age and Progressive Era. Upper-division undergraduates and above.—*P. F. Field, Ohio University*

WS-1809   E185   94-31761 CIP
Black women in America, ed. by Kim Marie Vaz. Sage Publications, CA, 1995. 396p bibl index ISBN 0-8039-5454-9, $52.00; ISBN 0-8039-5455-7 pbk, $24.95

This interdisciplinary collection offers discussions of black women in history (particularly as historical activists), in literature and media, in self-images, and in contemporary social situations. Contributions vary considerably in quality and level of scholarship. The better articles include historical examinations of black women in female antislavery societies and in Renaissance Spain; a description of the developing "rape complex" in the post-Civil War South; a thoughtful discussion of public perceptions and policies toward single mothers; and a provocative analysis of life satisfaction in a small group of older women. A few other essays suffer from a distressing lack of scholarly rigor and a tendency to substitute slogans for analysis. As a whole, however, the volume can be helpful in stimulating questions and discussion for students in African American studies, American studies, and women's studies.—*L. Mayo, County College of Morris*

WS-1810 HQ1419 93-1316 CIP
Bolt, Christine. **The women's movements in the United States and Britain from the 1790s to the 1920s.** Massachusetts, 1993. 390p index ISBN 0-87023-866-3, $45.00; ISBN 0-87023-867-1 pbk, $15.95

Bolt's comparative history of women's rights and suffrage organizing provides a useful overview of an extensive monographic literature. Her account centers around the life and times of spearhead organizations and their leaders, from movement beginnings until the vote was achieved. As with most historical surveys, much of what is recounted here is not new to scholars. In this case, the work is most original and the comparison most engaging when it touches on the interaction and cross-fertilization between the movements in the US and Britain; it is at its most pedestrian when recounting the separate history of each movement. Bolt ably shows how activists "read each other's works, watched each other's progress, exchanged visits and even labored in each other's campaigns," all the while maintaining their national identity, tactical distinctiveness, and unique ideology. The major drawback of the book is its lack of a bibliography, a serious flaw in a work that is, in fact, largely a review of the literature. Undergraduates.—*N. B. Rosenthal, SUNY College at Old Westbury*

WS-1811 E99 95-9264 CIP
Boyd, Loree. **Spirit moves: the story of six generations of native women.** New World Library, 1996. 436p afp ISBN 1-880032-59-7 pbk, $16.95

Boyd has written an engaging, accessible history of the women in her family. Her text is without flourish, and the gifts of her predecessors' lives are never romanticized. They are based on family memories, legends, and personal narratives. The story begins with her great, great grandmother, Bird Song. Born in 1886, "Ten years after the battle of Little Big Horn," Bird Song was a Blackfoot traded to a French trapper at age nine. From this incident, Boyd chronicles the challenges faced by her forebears, progeny of the Blackfoot Nation, as they walk their sometimes tragic, always difficult pathways. The book celebrates Boyd's heritage and a renewed grasp of the significance of Native roots and values. Her stories are layered with complexities of family lives and shaky relationships. These difficulties are particularly compelling when she explores family members' multiple loyalties and identities as they seek to establish themselves in communities that reject their skin color and ancestry. The book is written in a straightforward style and represents, stylistically, the perspectives and speech of the women Boyds depicts. The cover and text feature illustrations by the author's mother, Silversong, whose work is discussed in some of the concluding chapters. General readers.—*L. De Danaan, Evergreen State College*

WS-1812 E184 91-39227 Orig
Building with our hands: new directions in Chicana studies, ed. by Adela de la Torre and Beatríz M. Pesquera. California, 1993. 246p index afp ISBN 0-520-07089-5, $45.00; ISBN 0-520-07090-9 pbk, $14.00

This collection by leading Chicana scholars is useful in gauging the state of Chicana studies. The articles are not connected by discipline or theme, which is both the strength and weakness of the volume. Essays are, however, excellent examples of gender analysis and how it is applied to add dimensions to traditional research. Exceptional is Vicki Ruiz's "'Star Struck' Acculturation, Adolescence, and the Mexican American Woman, 1920-1950," in which historian Ruiz reconceptualizes early 20th century Chicano history with a feminist focus. Deena J. González and Angelina Veyna's essays on Colonial New Mexico also challenge popular stereotypes of earlier works. Along with Emma Pérez and Antonia Castañeda, these scholars represent a critical group of Chicana historians. Other authors from varied disciplines contribute, as the title implies, to building the foundation of a distinctly Chicana analysis. Each essay has good endnotes, and the collection has a good index. General; community college; undergraduate.—*R. Acuña, California State University, Northridge*

WS-1813 HQ1410 90-30323 CIP
Castro, Ginette. **American feminism: a contemporary history,** tr. by Elizabeth Loverde-Bagwell. New York University, 1990. 302p bibl index afp ISBN 0-8147-1435-8, $55.00; ISBN 0-8147-1448-X, $12.50

American feminism has made unique contributions to the political process by showing the interrelationship of theory and practice by advancing the concept that the political and the personal are intertwined. Nevertheless, most historians of American feminism ignore the theoretical aspects of the movement especially neglecting the early radical theorists who raised so many basic questions about patriarchal institutions. This book attempts to fill that vacuum. The early writers of the movement are carefully and quite brilliantly analyzed. Clearly for Castro it is the radicals who made the most important contributions to early feminist theory. But if the analysis of theory is the book's greatest strength, it is also its weakness. Theory dominates and it is the theory of the late 1960s and early '70s. Moreover, theory is separated from practice. Only the last quarter of the book discusses recent developments in the movement, such as the struggle for reproductive rights and the establishment of rape crisis centers, shelters for abused women, and child care centers. Hence the book is excellent as a reminder of the early vitality of the radical theorists of the movement but it cannot be read as a complete history of contemporary feminism. College, university, and public libraries.—*J. Wishnia, SUNY at Stony Brook*

WS-1814 E628 94-39218 CIP
Clinton, Catherine. **Tara revisited: women, war, & the plantation legend.** Abbeville, 1995. 240p bibl index ISBN 1-55859-491-4, $27.50

Clinton seeks to "relocate the legend [of Tara] in a complex interweaving of myth and memories" by focusing on the "the actual impact of the [Civil] war upon ... Southern plantation women ... black and white." Her lavishly illustrated presentation combines deft sketches of notables such as Mary Chestnut, Susie King Taylor, and Sallie Tompkins with distillations of recent scholarship on 19th-century plantation women. Clinton does not deal with poor white women or free people of color; instead, she concentrates on the big plantations, to link that wartime South with its later mythic reconstruction. Women's fostering of Confederate nationalism, contradictions of gender roles wrought by women's volunteerism or plantation management, and the unhinging effect of slave resistance on the Confederacy are all discussed. Subsequent chapters recount the postwar "campaign to recreate the past," stressing the role of the United Daughters of the Confederacy, then turning to the enduring cultural appeal of the southern belle and the faithful mammy, as exemplified in *Gone With the Wind*. This book is first-rate cultural history, for general readers and specialists alike.—*T. S. Whitman, Mount St. Mary's College and Seminary*

WS-1815 E78 91-4791 CIP
Devens, Carol. **Countering colonization: Native American women and Great Lakes missions, 1630-1900.** California, 1992. 185p bibl index afp ISBN 0-520-07557-9, $30.00

Focusing on Ojibwa, Cree, and Montagnais-Naskapi women, Devens analyzes the gender-specific responses to Christian missionary activity. In the 17th century, Jesuit efforts to convert Native Americans to Catholicism and to a "male-dominated nuclear family" social structure usually elicited a unified community rejection. In the early 19th century, Methodist missionaries preached a similar dual message of the Protestant gospel and "female domesticity." This time, however, either the community accommodated or it divided sharply along gender lines, with women either outwardly (but grudgingly) conforming or actively opposing not only the proselytizers, but the male Indian converts as well. Therefore, Devens, argues, the emergent divisive gender relations in the Great Lakes witnessed by early 20th century anthropologists were not traditional patterns but, rather, the results of Euroamerican colonizing efforts. Devens is most persuasive when she restricts her discussion to Native American communities that had accepted the presence of missionaries, and when she assesses the corrosive power of the fur trade in shaping a predominant male pattern of accommodation to Christianity. Nevertheless, her assessment of women's responses is an important counter to the tendency in most other studies to generalize Native American responses from male-generated documents. Advanced undergraduate; graduate; faculty.—*R. L. Haan, Hartwick College*

WS-1816 F596 95-21682 CIP
Dunlap, Patricia Riley. **Riding astride: the frontier in women's history.** Arden Press, CO, 1996 (c1995). 193p bibl index ISBN 0-912869-17-8, $26.50; ISBN 0-912869-18-6 pbk, $18.95

Dunlap argues that although some women on the 19th-century American western frontier escaped the restrictions of their eastern industrial gender roles, mos migrating women considered those roles desirable. However, even the migrating white women who attempted to live up to the ideals of the "cult of true womanhood" failed to transplant those familiar roles to their new homes in the rural West. Dunlap believes that "real, revolutionary change" occurred only when a second generation of western women, unschooled in eastern ideals, sought political and social equality. The book omits much of the debate over gender roles in the far West, familiar to readers of the new western history or feminist scholars, and recounts the lives of African American and Native American women in isolated chapters. General readers will find the book entertaining. Those who saw the movie *The Ballad of Little Joe* will enjoy reading about women who dressed as men, and especially "Little Joe" Monaghan, whose legend served as the basis for the film about a woman who worked as a ranch hand and eventually established her own homestead in Idaho while dressed as a man. General readers; lower-division undergraduates.—*L. Sturtz, Beloit College*

WS-1817 HQ1438 91-31410 CIP
Fink, Deborah. **Agrarian women: wives and mothers in rural Nebraska, 1880-1940.** North Carolina, 1992. 242p bibl index afp ISBN 0-8078-2019-9, $34.95; ISBN 0-8078-4364-4 pbk, $12.95

Fink explores the lives of farm women in Boone county, Nebraska in this anthropological study. Though she relies heavily on oral interviews, letters, and diaries, Fink also interprets court records, wills, deeds, and census materials to form a historical context. Although an agrarian ideology permeated conversations among Nebraska men, Fink found that Jeffersonian agrarianism did not offer Nebraska women the same independence. She argues against the notion that a rural, frontier existence liberated women from the problems their urban sisters faced. Women's roles in production on the farm helped them gain control of their lives, but the organization of labor within the nuclear family detracted from its liberating potential. The work women and children did freed men; though women participated in political and social activities, they did not enjoy the same opportunities as men. For example, women who were active in Farmers' Alliance groups more often discussed matters directly related to their husbands' work rather than to their own or to other women's issues such as suffrage and prohibition. Illustrated with maps, tables, and photographs. College and university libraries.—*E. Kuhlman, University of Montana*

WS-1818 HQ1172 92-47003 CIP
Fishman, Sylvia Barack. **A breath of life: feminism in the American Jewish community.** Free Press, 1993. 308p index ISBN 0-02-910342-8, $22.95

Fishman offers readers a good summary of the uneasy marriage between feminism and Judaism. Jewish women, who are the subject of this study, have been leaders and followers of feminism since the movement gained momentum in the 1960s. For many Jewish women, the challenge has been to reconcile the individualistic goals of liberal feminism with the social ideals of Judaism. Clearly, there are factors, other than feminism, that have contributed to the growth of interfaith marriage among Jewish women and men, the rise in the single population, and the decrease in the size of the Jewish family. But feminism has affected the way Jewish women view themselves and their adult destinies. Fishman has summarized the discussion effectively and deserves a large audience. All communities that try to harmonize traditions born in other times with all modernisms, including feminism, can learn from this study. General; undergraduate; graduate; faculty.—*J. Sochen, Northeastern Illinois University*

WS-1819 E99 95-7652 CIP
Flood, Renée Sansom. **Lost Bird of Wounded Knee: spirit of the Lakota.** Scribner, 1995. 384p bibl index ISBN 0-684-19512-7, $25.00

Flood recounts the tragic story of Lost Bird, an infant survivor of the 1890 Massacre at Wounded Knee, South Dakota, adopted by non-Indian parents, Leonard and Clara Colby, as an example of how intercultural adoptions can go wrong. The primary focus of the book is on the Colbys, neither of whom was parent material. Leonard Colby acquired leadership in the military and was appointed assistant attorney general of the US, but he was also an opportunist and womanizer. Clara Colby was an internationally known suffragist and publisher of a women's newspaper, a career woman with little time to raise a daughter. In adolescence Lost Bird became depressed and rebellious, traits that Flood attributes

to rearing a child with a Lakota "cultural imprint" in a non-Lakota society, although non-Indian children develop similar behavioral problems. Lost Bird died at age 30, her adult life a failing struggle against poverty and poor health. The issue of intercultural adoption is very current and this book provides a unique, although not unbiased, perspective on the subject. It also serves social history by depicting the darker side of upper middle class, turn-of-the-century society. All levels.—*M. J. Schneider, University of North Dakota*

WS-1820 HD6509 92-46311 CIP
Forged under the sun: the life of María Elena Lucas, ed. with introd. by Fran Leeper Buss. Michigan, 1993. 314p afp ISBN 0-472-09432-7, $32.50; ISBN 0-472-06432-0 pbk, $13.95

This is an oral history of a 47-year-old Chicana farmworker. Based largely on interviews, it also includes Lucas's diary entries and her poetry. Lucas's story begins and ends in South Texas. Her life, however, is centered in Onarga, Illinois, a small town south of Chicago. The narrative takes readers through her involvement with the Farm Labor Organizing Committee as well as the United Farm Workers. Lucas's admiration for César Chávez personally touches her life. *La Güerita* (the Blond One), María Elena, always has a cause giving purpose to her life. Her family life, however, is as tragic as her poverty, including losing a son to drugs. The *Güerita* helps the workers around her, those with and without documents, but is unable to connect with her nuclear family. A cultural conflict drives a wedge between her and her siblings. Lucas's life is the struggle of a woman whose feminism is instinctive. One of the best oral histories on Chicanos to date. Good index. Highly recommended for general readers, undergraduates, and above.—*R. Acuña, California State University, Northridge*

WS-1821 F128 95-6566 CIP
Friedman-Kasaba, Kathie. **Memories of migration: gender, ethnicity, and work in the lives of Jewish and Italian women in New York, 1870-1924.** State University of New York, 1996. 242p bibl index afp ISBN 0-7914-2761-7, $59.50

Friedman-Kasaba attempts to analyze whether immigration created conditions that enabled women to free themselves from Old World social constraints. She compares Russian Jewish and Italian women in subordination, empowerment, and adaptation to their changing environments. Using historical studies, memoirs, letters, unpublished documents, and fiction written by immigrant women or their offspring, she tries to synthesize the perspectives of feminists and "historical structuralists" (who focus on dynamics of labor market forces and relations in the receiving country). She questions the conclusions of "assimilationists," who assume that migration ultimately and inevitably led to greater economic or social self-determination on the part of immigrant women. Instead, the author describes far more complex and paradoxical experiences that vary with ethnicity, marital status, and family interactions, as well as with world economic forces and American reactions. Despite fascinating material in chapters on young single immigrant women and wives and mothers, however, there is far too much repetition of basic premises. The book is also so bogged down in sociological jargon that the scholar and certainly the average student will find it difficult to plow through.—*L. Mayo, County College of Morris*

WS-1822 JV6601 94-5613 CIP
Gabaccia, Donna. **From the other side: women, gender, and immigrant life in the U.S., 1820-1990.** Indiana, 1995 (c1994). 192p bibl index afp ISBN 0-253-32529-3, $29.95; ISBN 0-253-20904-8 pbk, $12.95

A complement to the many books describing, analyzing, and celebrating "the world of our fathers," this is a most welcome contribution to the history and sociology of American immigrant life. Gabaccia, a historian with a particular interest in the Sicilian migration, provides a wide-angle view of those who came from the other side of the sea—or in the case of Mexicans, the river—to the new land. Although she discusses many issues, there is a distinct and double-edged leitmotif captured in the title of the middle section: "Foreign and Female." Gabaccia notes in her introduction that "Demographically and culturally, women immigrants closely resembled men of their own backgrounds...[at] work, at home and in their communities, however, their lives diverged from the men's: regardless of their exact origin, women's and men's responsibilities were more often complementary than shared." She demonstrates that the sharing not only of responsibilities but also of thoughts and feelings and, often, ways of coping were quite gender-specific. Gabaccia's final section—two chapters and a conclusion dealing with race, ethnicity, class, feminism, and a number of other variables influencing the lives of immigrant women and their progeny—is followed by one of the most useful parts of the book: an excellent bibliographic essay that provides a trove of materials for further study, example, and inspiration in what many have claimed is a neglected field. All levels.—*P. I. Rose, Smith College*

WS-1823   DS148   94-37932 CIP
Hyman, Paula E. **Gender and assimilation in modern Jewish history: the roles and representation of women.** Washington, 1995. 197p bibl index afp ISBN 0-295-97425-7, $30.00; ISBN 0-295-97426-5 pbk, $14.95

In this highly important, lucidly written study, Hyman (Yale), a pioneer of the contemporary Jewish women's movement, reconsiders central themes of modern Jewish history from a gendered perspective. Carefully distinguishing the "process" of assimilation from the "project" of assimilation, and western Jewry, from East European Jewry, she argues that in each case men and women met modernity's challenges differently, transforming in the process both gender roles and the way women and Judaism are represented. In her chapter "America, Freedom, and Assimilation," Hyman brilliantly synthesizes recent literature, weakening only in her discussion of synagogue life and in her analysis of the origins of sisterhoods. Her provocative final chapter, "The Sexual Politics of Jewish Identity," is more speculative and less persuasive. Concern over declining manliness, for example, needs to be placed in comparative perspective; it is by no means confined to Jews and antisemites alone. No student of modern Jewry can ignore this work. Even if some of its points are disputed, its central thesis "that to be valid an examination of the processes of Jewish assimilation in the modern and contemporary periods must include women and gender in its design" is masterfully proven. All levels.—*J. D. Sarna, Brandeis University*

WS-1824   E85   89-23503 MARC
The Indian captivity narrative: a woman's view, comp. by Francis Roe Kestler. Garland, 1990. 588p (Women's history and culture, 2) bibl index afp ISBN 0-8240-4247-6, $85.00

The value of this collection is that a number of captivity narratives written or dictated by the women who experienced captivity are gathered in one volume. The account of Mary White Rowlandson, captured in 1675, is the first. Narratives of 16 other women captives are included in this work; the last is that of Josephine Meeker, captured by the Utes in 1878. The narratives are organized in eight chronological chapters with a brief introduction to the general historical background of the times and biographical information about the women. Unfortunately, there is little historical analysis or interpretation. Indeed, the perspective is seriously outdated; the compiler presents a Eurocentric view of the meeting of two cultures, casting the white woman as heroically surviving her "ordeal" and the Native American largely as the cruel perpetrator of that "ordeal." The bibliography is equally out-of-date. There is no mention of any work done in the last decade; the omission, or neglect, of the work of William Cronon and of James Axtell (especially regarding the women who chose to stay with their "captors") is inexplicable.—*C. M. McGovern, University of Vermont*

WS-1825   HQ1904   95-35974 CIP
Jeansonne, Glen. **Women of the far right: the mothers' movement and World War II.** Chicago, 1996. 264p index afp ISBN 0-226-39587-1, $29.95

Jeansonne has written a scary book. He describes articulate and intelligent women who forcefully proclaimed antisemitism and anticommunism as their creed and who tirelessly worked to prevent the US entry into WW II. None of these leaders are familiar today, but in the 1930s and '40s, the *Chicago Tribune* and the Hearst newspapers gave them regular coverage. Elizabeth Dilling, for example, a native Chicagoan, became a virulent anticommunist in the 1920s who feared a Bolshevik takeover of the US. Her book *The Red Network: A "Who's Who" and Handbook of Radicalism for Patriots* (1934) combined her fear of communists and her hatred for Jews. The National Legion of Mothers of America and the Women's National Committee to Keep the US out of the War, led by Cathrine

Curtis, joined Dilling, Bund members, German sympathizers, and Lyrl Van Hyning's We the Mothers Mobilize for America in opposing the Lend Lease Act and FDR's 1940 reelection. That women could, and did, support causes that enforced hateful stereotypes requires historians and all citizens to acknowledge that women come in as many ideological forms as men do, a sobering thought. Recommended. All levels.—*J. Sochen, Northeastern Illinois University*

WS-1826   HQ1410   90-49165 CIP
Jensen, Joan M. **Promise to the land: essays on rural women.** New Mexico, 1991. 319p index ISBN 0-8263-1247-0, $27.50

Following Jensen's *With These Hands: Women Working on the Land* (CH, Apr'81) and *Loosening the Bonds: Mid-Atlantic Farm Women, 1750-1850* (CH, Nov'86), this volume continues her 20-year study of rural women and their role in American economic development. Essays range from the professional/academic to the personal. Employing biography, autobiography, demography, and iconography, Jensen creates a portrait that emphasizes the interdisciplinary nature of her sources. She states that the essays "do not form a pattern. . .and reflect her lower middle class preoccupation" with how farm women survive and why they work as they have. Jensen includes two essays on her own family history, a memoir, and, in the introduction, a sweeping survey concerning rural women in US history. Additional essays treat Native American and slave women, and women from the American Midwest, Southwest, and Mid-Atlantic. Throughout, the author provides thorough research apparatus that may be read in part or as a whole, depending on the needs of the reader. Of interest for women studies, history, and, most, particularly, economic history collections. All levels.—*M. Klatte, Eastern Kentucky University*

WS-1827   TT835   92-43108 CIP
Kansas quilts & quilters, by Barbara Brackman et al. University Press of Kansas, 1993. 206p index afp ISBN 0-7006-0584-3, $40.00; ISBN 0-7006-0585-1 pbk, $22.50

Presented here is a portion of the material gathered as part of the Kansas Quilt Project. Organized in 1986, the Project has focused on collecting information about Kansas quilts and quiltmakers, encouraging the preservation and proper care of quilts, and heightening public appreciation of the art of quiltmaking. Like similar projects across the US, one goal of the Kansas Project was to produce a richly illustrated volume about quilting in Kansas. Contributors explore the role of quilts in the historical as well as contemporary life of the state, examine types of quilts associated with specific groups of Kansas residents or that are particularly popular in Kansas, and trace the impact of certain individuals on the art and practice of quiltmaking in Kansas as well as the country as a whole. Well researched and well written, the volume represents an important contribution to quilt history as well as to the history of American women. It is also an excellent example of how the analysis of material culture can enhance the understanding of an area's historical experience. All levels.—*P. Melvin, Loyola University*

WS-1828   HD6079   90-44367 CIP
Kirkby, Diane. **Alice Henry: the power of pen and voice: the life of an Australian-American labor reformer.** Cambridge, 1991. 254p bibl index ISBN 0-521-39102-4, $44.50

Alice Henry's strength as a reformer was in speaking and writing clearly and in supporting her points with information, skills honed as a journalist and reformer in Australia. Committed to reform, especially for women workers, Henry worked 20 years in the Women's Trade Union League (WTUL) bringing Australian perceptions regarding the state and labor legislation to the US. Kirkby's presentation of Henry and the WTUL as they saw themselves, with goals of legitimizing women's work and women's public roles as independent persons with a power base equal to men's, is valuable for American readers. Chapters 5 and 6 on Henry's work with the WTUL journal (*Life and Labor*), WTUL's training schools, and her relationships with WTUL president Margaret Dreier Robins, present an insightful picture of the tensions and problems of the WTUL. Kirkby faced a monumental archival task because records—mostly public rather than personal—were scattered over two continents and numerous libraries. Footnotes and bibliography of secondary literature. Upper-division undergraduates and above.—*V. P. Caruso, Nazareth College*

WS-1829 HX696.O9 89-45416 CIP

Kolmerten, Carol A. **Women in utopia: the ideology of gender in the American Owenite communities.** Indiana, 1990. 209p bibl index afp ISBN 0-253-33192-7, $29.95

Although there have been exceptions, the attempts to establish utopian societies either in practice or as literary models have usually been concerned with the equality of participants. Kolmerten is a scholar who has devoted much of her professional career to analyzing the status of women in utopian communities; although her book concerns only the American Owenite communities, the material summarizes a broader context. Women have not usually been afforded the same privileges, power, and esteem as men in communal experiments. Aside from Kolmerten's findings on gender differences, her study provides a history of Owenism with enough context from English and American social history to make the specific case meaningful. The work also includes a brief biography of Frances Wright, an early feminist at New Harmony and elsewhere, and insightful comments about the legacy of Owenism. This historical approach to feminism and utopia nicely complements recent analyses of current feminist thinking about utopia in such works as Frances Bartkowski's Feminist Utopias (CH, Apr'90). Extensive bibliography. College and university libraries.—*E. J. Green, Prince George's Community College*

WS-1830 HQ1410 90-46014 CIP

Krause, Corinne Azen. **Grandmothers, mothers, and daughters: oral histories of three generations of ethnic American women.** Twayne, 1991. 231p (Twayne's oral history series, 6) bibl index afp ISBN 0-8057-9105-1, $24.95

Krause's book clearly demonstrates the usefulness of oral history for learning about the lives of "ordinary" people who make up the fabric of society. The book follows three generations of Italian, Jewish, and Slavic women in Pittsburgh; it is through their relationships and the changes in their lives that readers learn about ethnic America in the 20th century. Some of the women had lives of economic ease, some achieved professional success, while others struggled for the bread on their tables. Yet despite class and ethnic differences almost all the women shared two characteristics—pride in their ethnicity and love of family. Krause shows enormous changes over time. The first generation suffered the shocks of immigration, had arranged marriages, and worked hard inside and outside the home. The second generation experienced depression and war, married for love, and stayed home with children when it was economically feasible. The third generation experienced feminism, married (and divorced) for love, and combined careers and motherhood. This fascinating book shows readers on all levels the importance of gender, class, and ethnicity in determining the lives of American women.—*J. Wishnia, SUNY at Stony Brook*

WS-1831 F358 91-26844 CIP

Lagerquist, L. DeAne. **In America the men milk the cows: factors of gender, ethnicity, and religion in the Americanization of Norwegian-American women.** Carlson Publishing, 1991. 255p (Chicago studies in the history of American religion, 12) bibl index afp ISBN 0-926019-49-X, $50.00

A first-rate scholarly contribution to the relatively unplowed field of immigrant women's history in general, and of Norwegian Lutheran immigrant women in particular. Lagerquist's well-annotated study relies heavily on original source materials in the form of letters, diaries, interviews, and contemporary publications, demonstrating, as her subtitle implies, the manner in which ordinary Norwegian American women of the Lutheran faith became Americanized in their first, second, and third generations in this country. Lagerquist concludes that although their churches had no place for them as leaders, many of these women nonetheless found personal satisfaction and growth through participation in women's societies. She further argues that their church mediated the ways in which they became Americanized "modern" women. Originally a doctoral dissertation, this study is highly readable for a general audience as well as a work of persuasive scholarship. It is replete with personal incidents and anecdotes that give a "feel" for the lives of these women and the challenges they often faced. It is also a remarkable combination of "grass roots" and women's history within the particular parameters of ethnicity, gender, and religion, which the author effectively addresses. Highly recommended for public libraries, especially in the Scandinavian regions of the Midwest, as well as for undergraduate and graduate libraries.—*K. Smemo, Moorhead State University*

WS-1832 F158 90-41311 CIP

Lane, Roger. **William Dorsey's Philadelphia and ours: on the past and future of the Black city in America.** Oxford, 1991. 483p index afp ISBN 0-19-506566-2, $29.95

William Dorsey (1837-1923) was one of Philadelphia's most prominent citizens, and its first African American historian. During his adult life he kept numerous scrapbooks, focusing on black issues of local and national interest. Using these newly discovered scrapbooks as his primary source, Lane has woven an interesting account of the vitality and optimism of African American life in the urban north during the late 19th century. Lane blends the events chronicled by Dorsey into the sweep of American history, producing a first-rate account. Of equal importance, Lane juxtaposes Dorsey's Philadelphia with today's African American community. Lane finds that the changes in black urban society are many and varied, but that there is one abiding truth: African Americans, despite their gains and progress, are still disadvantaged. Lane recognizes his liberal bent (indeed, he writes of his family's volunteer work in Harlem, including his own involvement). Of perhaps greatest importance, he ends on a hopeful note, arguing that dramatic improvement is within reach. College, university, and public libraries.—*D. R. Jamieson, Ashland University*

WS-1833 F347 93-25041 CIP

Letters from Forest Place: a plantation family's correspondence, 1846-1881, ed. by E. Grey Dimond and Herman Hattaway. University Press of Mississippi, 1993. 512p index afp ISBN 0-87805-653-X, $30.00

Dimond and Hattaway have skillfully edited more than 230 letters written between 1846 and 1881 by members of the Thomas A. Watkins family, who resided at Forest Place in Carroll County, Mississippi, where they farmed 15,000 acres with about 75 slaves. These letters provide an intimate picture of the relationships that developed among members of the family and the slaves. A majority of the letters are written by Watkins's wife, Sarah, who attempted in vain to facilitate relations between Letitia, the oldest daughter, and her father. He wanted Lettie to marry into a family that he considered "good enough." She chose otherwise, and married William Walton, a lawyer. The couple removed to Austin, Texas; Watkins angrily told them never to return. A second daughter, Mary, attended finishing school in Maryland but left in the spring of 1861 when war started. She came home, taught school, and engaged with her mother in charitable wartime enterprises. However, inflation destroyed the basis of plantation life and most of the slaves were sold or ran away. Mary eventually married Jefferson McLemore, a Confederate soldier. Sarah died in March 1865. With inflation, the loss of slaves, and increased federal control, Thomas Watkins moved to Austin to live near his daughter Letitia until he died 17 years later. Photographs; maps; appendix. General and academic readers, community college level and above.—*J. D. Born Jr., Wichita State University*

WS-1834 F394 95-32451 CIP

López-Stafford, Gloria. **A place in El Paso: a Mexican-American childhood.** New Mexico, 1996. 212p ISBN 0-8263-1687-5, $24.95; ISBN 0-8263-1709-X pbk, $16.95

Based on the author's experiences growing up in the "Gateway City" during the 1940s and '50s, López-Stafford's memoirs take readers on a tour of one of the Mexican Americans' most historic barrios. What follows is the delightful tale of Gloria, raised by her single father in a household with a brother and loving grandfather. Because of the family's dire poverty, she is sent to live with a neighborhood woman and then to well-to-do godparents. The tension of a mixed blood union adds to the account. Gloria's experiences resurrected forgotten memories of this reviewer's own childhood. "In the Segundo Barrio during the 1940s, people spoke Spanish .... In South El Paso [this Spanish] was formal and polite. People apologized if they said a word like *estupido*." It was a time when people were rural, and the tensions of urban life and technology had not eroded traditional courtesies. It was a time when children still said "good morning" and excused themselves when leaving. The reader will quarrel with definitions of some terms, such as "macho," but this is a tale of another time, sprinkled with popular Mexican *refranes*, sayings that add spice to the tale. The book is literally the salsa in Chicana/o history. All levels.—*R. Acuña, California State University, Northridge*

WS-1835   CT275   95-14156 CIP
Madaline: love and survival in antebellum New Orleans, ed. by
Dell Upton. Georgia, 1996. 366p bibl index afp ISBN 0-8203-1758-6,
$29.95

Madaline Selima Edwards lived in Tennessee, Mississippi, Alabama, and
Louisiana; married and separated; lived with another man; engaged in an affair
with a married man in New Orleans; and died in California. Beginning in 1843,
she kept a diary and produced letters, essays, and a few articles. Her papers
eventually found their way to the Southern Historical Collection at the University
of North Carolina, where Upton found them and recognized their importance in
preserving unique observations of mid-19th century social life. Edwards was a
woman on the fringe of a society in which women depended on men for subsistence. Her poor choice for a husband and her decision to leave him led to her subsequent attempts to support herself. Her relationship with her married lover
was partially based on economics; her dependence eventually ended their affair.
Upton maintains that Edwards's story is useful in understanding the relationship between the structures of society and the individuals who live within them.
The limits of society might have made Edwards economically dependent, but
her thoughts soared far beyond her time and place. All levels.—*J. P. Sanson,
Louisiana State University at Alexandria*

WS-1836   E169   92-24760 CIP
**The Madonna connection: representational politics, subcultural
identities, and cultural theory,** ed. by Cathy Schwichtenberg.
Westview, 1993. 336p index afp ISBN 0-8133-1396-1, $55.00; ISBN 0-
8133-1397-X pbk, $17.95

In recent years, few if any performers have so galvanized attention or polarized society as Madonna. Within a short span of time, she has achieved an icon-
ical status and become the most significant woman performer since Mae West created havoc with her independent, flaunting pose and prose. And no performer, not
even Elvis Presley or Muhammad Ali, has so tantalized the academic profession. As Schwichtenberg asserts, Madonna has forced the academy "to think seriously about the politics of popular culture." The result is this intriguing volume, a collection that delves into the Madonna phenomenon while it also grapples
with the problem of how to approach the complexities of mass popular culture.
This collection of 13 essays plus an introduction is divided into four sections, each
of which focuses on a different cultural and theoretical dimension of the Madonna
presentation: race and audiences; reception and interpretations within the gay community; conceptions of feminist theory and praxis; and the ideological power of
commodity culture. Overall, the issues posed by the essays are provocative,
wide-ranging in their design and approach, and varying in style and content.
Although highly theoretical, the volume's strength lies in the construction of a cultural map of Madonna's connection to American society by a diverse group of
scholarly topographers. General; advanced undergraduate; graduate; faculty; professional.—*J. Boskin, Boston University*

WS-1837   HQ1392   91-47518 CIP
Matthews, Glenna. **The rise of public woman: woman's power and
woman's place in the United States, 1630-1970.** Oxford, 1992.
297p index afp ISBN 0-19-505460-1, $25.00

Despite the explosion of scholarship in the field of women's history, there are
only a handful of books that attempt to cover all of US history. This is a welcome
addition to the body of such books, which can be used in the classroom or simply read for knowledge and pleasure. Matthews does not attempt a complete
history but concentrates instead on her major theme—the struggle of women to
attain public space and public power. Using the latest scholarship, she shows how
religious introspection and women's domestic culture initiated the development
of women's public consciousness; how 19th-century changes in employment,
transportation, and, most critically, literature, continued the process; and finally
how women entered the political arena. There is a heavy reliance on examples
of individual heroines, which gives the book a personal appeal but frequently hinders analysis. Discussing African American achievers does not substitute for a
full discussion of the public role of African American women. Because so many
books tend to glorify white, middle-class feminists, Matthews's chapters on
working women and the political Left are most informative. The end of the
Cold War should encourage a reevaluation of the influence of left-wing politics
on women's public role. All levels.—*J. Wishnia, SUNY at Stony Brook*

WS-1838   BF1576   90-37581 CIP
McMillen, Persis W. **Currents of malice: Mary Towne Esty and her
family in Salem witchcraft.** P.E. Randall, 1990. 603p bibl indexes
ISBN 0-914339-31-1, $25.00

In overwhelming detail and with little analysis McMillen describes the background, court proceedings, and conclusion of the 1692 outbreak of witchcraft at
Salem, Massachusetts. Assuming that the reader knows nothing about the event,
the author feels compelled to retell the story in a frequently rambling, disorganized
manner. Despite its 500-plus pages organized into 46 short, choppy chapters,
the book contains neither new information nor a new interpretation of New England witchcraft. McMillen reduces the origins of Salem witchcraft to inter-
minable descriptions of boundary disputes and other minor conflicts between
the Towne and Putnam families. The Puritan ministry, especially Cotton Mather,
is singled out for moralistic condemnation. In light of Chadwick Hansen's
excellent narrative history, *Witchcraft at Salem* (CH, Mar'70); accessible collections of primary sources such as *What Happened at Salem?*, ed. by David Levin
(2nd ed., 1960) and *Salem-Village Witchcraft*, ed. by Paul Boyer and Stephen Nis-
senbaum, (1972); and the recent spate of sophisticated studies on New England
witchcraft such as John Demos's *Entertaining Satan* (1982) and Carol F. Karlsen's
The Devil in the Shape of a Woman (CH, Jun'88), there is no discernable reason
why college libraries should acquire this book. Not recommended.—*E. W. Carp, Pacific Lutheran University*

WS-1839   E747   94-27833 CIP
Morin, Ann Miller. **Her excellency: an oral history of American
women ambassadors.** Twayne, 1995. 315p (Twayne's oral history
series, 14) bibl index afp ISBN 0-8057-9118-3, $27.95; ISBN 0-8057-
9142-6 pbk, $16.95

Morin's collection of 15 oral histories of US women ambassadors ably fills
a gap in both studies of women's careers and of the history of the US Foreign Service and the Department of State. Wife of a Foreign Service Officer and educator in schools overseas, Morin brought the specific experience to her interviews
that enabled her to connect with her subjects and to interpret the significance of
their stories. The life histories Morin selected for the book illustrate a diversity of
backgrounds and experiences. Eight came up through the ranks of the Foreign
Service and seven were political appointees. She includes the earliest women
ambassadors along with the first African American and Hispanic women. Her
choices range from the well-publicized service of Anne Armstrong at the coveted
post of the Court of St. James in London and the controversial role of Jeane
Kirkpatrick at the UN to the first husband and wife career ambassadors, Jane Abell
and Carleton Coon, in Bangladesh and Nepal, respectively. Morin's conclusions discuss the contributions of women to this male-dominated field and list the
first 44 women ambassadors up to 1993. The oral histories are compelling and
the analysis succinct. General readers and undergraduates.—*P. W. Kaufman, University of Massachusetts at Boston*

WS-1840   E185   90-20701 CIP
Morton, Patricia. **Disfigured images: the historical assault on Afro-
American women.** Greenwood, 1991. 173p (Contributions in Afro-American
and African studies, 144) bibl index afp ISBN 0-313-27296-4, $45.00

Morton (Trent University, Canada) is a major figure in the revisionist history
of African American women. Morton thoroughly reviews the depiction of black
women in historical writing and in the literature of the other social sciences, from
the 19th century to the present. She finds a mostly negative portrait, e.g., sexual
promiscuity, poor mothering, matriarchal pathology, and emasculating dominance
of African American males. The partial exception to the negative image is the
stereotyped white portrait of the tough, jolly, warm black Mammy so popular in
the movies and on pancake boxes. Sexism is mixed with racism in the black
woman's portrait. The list of authors, white and black, accepting these stereotyped
images in whole or in part reads like a who's who of American social science: Robert
Park, Daniel Moynihan, Nathan Glazer, Eugene Genovese, E. Franklin Frazier,
Charles Johnson, Kenneth Stampp, Stanley Elkins, Thomas Pettigrew, and Abraham Kardiner. Morton presents a detailed analysis of how, and to a lesser extent
why, these negative images of African American women have predominated in
social science articles and books, almost all of which have been written by men.
Concluding chapters deal with new research on black Americans and the women
of Africa. Selected bibliography. All levels.—*J. R. Feagin, University of Texas*

WS-1841   E85   92-31235 CIP
Namias, June. **White captives: gender and ethnicity on the American frontier.** North Carolina, 1993. 370p index apf ISBN 0-8078-2079-2, $39.95; ISBN 0-8078-4408-X pbk, $16.95

Namias here employs historical and literary methodology in analyzing the literature on white captives of Native Americans from 1607 to 1870. She identifies the male and female archetypes of the genre and explains how these served the political needs of nation building and conquest, and the sociocultural ideologies of "true womanhood" and the domestic sphere. In two fascinating case studies—Mary Jemison (1758-1833) and Sarah Wakefield (1862)—Namias shows how capitivity narratives contained the potential for subversion of these dominant constructions in the personal confrontation of two "others," woman and Indian. Namias also deals with artistic representations, integrating this discussion well with the literary analysis. She also includes some ethnologic material in the Jemison story. There are some awkward passages that should have been more carefully edited, but the book is a valuable and absorbing contribution to several areas of American studies. Highly recommended for students at all levels. Includes a complete list of captivity narratives and comprehensive endnotes.—*M. L. Meldrum, SUNY at Stony Brook*

WS-1842   HD8083   94-45185 CIP
Nelson, Daniel. **Farm and factory: workers in the Midwest, 1880-1990.** Indiana, 1995. 258p index afp ISBN 0-253-32883-7, $29.95

Nelson's study suggests the unique elements of simultaneous agricultural and industrial development in Ohio, Indiana, Illinois, Michigan, Wisconsin, Minnesota, and Iowa while also stressing a commonality of experience. Nelson (Univ. of Akron) is the author of *American Rubber Workers and Organized Labor, 1900-1941* (CH, Nov'88) and *Managers and Workers: Origins of the New Factory System in the United States, 1880-1920* (CH, May'76). American labor histories have highlighted such industries as the steel works at Gary and automobile manufacturing in and around Detroit, but most have failed to include the Midwest as an industrial sector. In the Midwest, Nelson accurately suggests, the "simultaneous growth of agriculture and industry" was "a feature that produced notable patterns of individual mobility and that left a distinctive and inescapable heritage." Nelson revises a more traditional view of women's work in both farm and factory, and argues that in agriculture "the quality of women's work materially affected the success of the farm family." A Cleveland clothes factory in the late 19th century offered women employees "special training and counseling and, if successful, promotions to supervisory posts." The idea of race hovered about the industrial scene into the 20th century, affecting the labor movement, and, as might be expected, African Americans bore the brunt of white hostility. Complements Leo Marx's *Machine in the Garden* (CH, Feb'65) and Allen Bogue's *From Prairie to Cornbelt: Farming on the Illinois and Iowa Prairies* (1963). Notes. All levels.—*P. D. Travis, Texas Woman's University*

WS-1843   HQ1075   95-43791 CIP
Norton, Mary Beth. **Founding mothers & fathers: gendered power and the forming of American society.** Knopf, 1996. 496p index ISBN 0-679-42965-4, $35.00

Norton provides a wealth of information on the formative years of New England society, 1620-1670, emphasizing spousal, family, and sexual connotations and the interactive connections between family and community. At the forefront of these connections is the status of women. The book is considerably weakened by Norton's interpretation of the New England experience as a conscious attempt to implement the patriarchal-hierarchical system expounded by Sir Robert Filmer and the views of John Locke (whose relevant writings were published 20 years after the period with which Norton deals) and by his adherence to a thesis of "gendered power." Comparative analysis of English legal development, which the early settlers had recently experienced, is all but totally excluded. Although the study is for the most part thoroughly researched, the author could have drawn more on manuscript church and court records. Nevertheless this work is enlightening, well written, and a valuable resource. All levels.—*H. M. Ward, University of Richmond*

WS-1844   PS570   95-17850 CIP
Pacific Northwest women, 1815-1925: lives, memories, and writings, ed. by Jean M. Ward and Elaine A. Maveety. Oregon State, 1995. 349p bibl index afp ISBN 0-87071-387-6, $27.95

The 30 women who wrote these letters, stories, and poems were "recorders and keepers of stories," of history, and of the effects of the region. The collections are arranged in four sections based on the themes emerging repeatedly: "Connecting with Nature"; "Coping: Learning by Doing"; "Caregiving: Family and Community"; and "Communicating: From Private to Public." The stories—many delivered in the natural, unvarnished language of pioneers—offer firsthand accounts of Indian raids, marriages, childbirth, and burial customs. They very frankly reveal the brutalities involved in settling virgin territories, hence they are not meant for the squeamish reader (settlers killed pet dogs for food, and at times indulged in cannibalism). One believes that these women are prototypes for those whose stories remain untold. Yet, as is often the case in feminist anthologies, there is an unmistakable defensiveness here. Frederick Jackson Turner is called to task for the "virtual absence of women of all ethnicities" in his frontier sagas. Further, all American Indian women are stereotyped as "drudges" and Anglo-Saxon women as "Saints in Sunbonnets." The editors (both Lewis and Clark College) are justified in believing that the exclusion of women's perspectives from historical writing "creates unreality." Yet this reviewer wonders if the women in this book would appear more heroic if grouped with male contemporaries instead of being placed in a territory of their own. Upper-division undergraduates; graduates.—*J. A. Dompkowski, Canisius College*

WS-1845   F358   95-9849 CIP
Pickle, Linda Schelbitzki. **Contented among strangers: rural German-speaking women and their families in the nineteenth-century Midwest.** Illinois, 1996. 311p index afp ISBN 0-252-02182-7, $49.95; ISBN 0-252-06472-0 pbk, $14.95

Pickle's analysis adds an important ethnic dimension to the rapidly growing literature on frontierswomen. While demonstrating considerable variation in individual experiences through rich examples, Pickle highlights patterns in family strategy, cultural tradition, and gender roles that enabled the successful adaptation of German speakers to midwestern farm life. A strong chapter on premigration gender patterns in German-speaking communities in Europe serves as a firm basis for the discussion of cultural continuity and change. Pickle carefully makes her case for the role of ethnicity in shaping the immigrants' experience, providing examples of both conservatism and flexibility, and acknowledging factors that were not unique to German speakers. In a chapter on "special groups" (Volga Germans, Saxon Old Lutherans, the Amana, Communia, and Bethel colonists, and German-speaking nuns), the impact of ethnicity is blurred by religious and social agendas. Although an interesting sidenote, the unique qualities of these groups make their experiences an awkward addition to the text. Despite this weakness, Pickle's work is a significant contribution to studies of German immigration and women on the frontier. Useful appendixes provide a discussion of sources and a statistical profile. All levels.—*E. M. Eisenberg, Willamette University*

WS-1846   E159   91-46604 CIP
Reclaiming the past: landmarks of women's history, ed. by Page Putnam Miller. Indiana, 1992. 232p index afp ISBN 0-253-33842-5, $35.00

The question "Who owns the past?" has been an important stimulus for reexamining the nation's definition of what constitutes national historic landmarks. The National Historic Landmark Program identifies and, by so doing, defines which sites possess exceptional value for understanding American history. *Reclaiming the Past* is an attempt by the Women's National Historic Landmark Project to make women's history part of the public perception of what is considered historically important. The seven essays included in this volume focus on women in architecture, the community, education, the arts, politics, religion, and work. These essays bring recent scholarship on women's history together with knowledge of the historic sites associated with women's experience and contributions. The authors have taken special care to identify sites associated not only with famous or extraordinary women but also with those more representative of the general patterns associated with women's experience. The volume provides a useful model for future thematic studies and enriches understanding of the American experience. Should be included on the shelves of libraries at all levels.—*P. Melvin, Loyola University*

WS-1847　　　　GV199.9　　　　89-14717 CIP
Robertson, Janet. **The magnificent mountain women: adventures in the Colorado Rockies.** Nebraska, 1990. 220p index afp ISBN 0-8032-3892-4, $21.95

The Colorado Rocky Mountains have attracted myriad fascinating women since the gold-rush days of the 1850s. Robertson uses a biographical approach to chronicle the resilient, independent women homesteaders, botanists, physicians, recreationists, and trail guides who have climbed, skied, and reveled in Colorado's backcountry from 1858 to the present. The contributions the mountain women made are as varied as their individual backgrounds. The suffragist Julia Archibald Holmes came to Colorado with her gold-seeking husband and became the first white woman to ascend Pikes Peak. Susan Anderson, MD, settled in the isolated mountain village of Fraser, Colorado, where she found people to be more accepting of a female doctor. Coral Bowman Wilber became enamored of rock climbing in Colorado, where she established the first American school of technical climbing for women in the 1980s. All of the women in Robertson's book created an awareness and appreciation of mountain splendor through their work, writings, and the lives they lived. Useful maps, photos, and a glossary of mountaineering terms. General readers.—*E. Kuhlman, University of Montana*

WS-1848　　　　HQ1904　　　　91-10979 CIP
Scott, Anne Firor. **Natural allies: women's associations in American history.** Illinois, 1992 (c1991). 242p index afp ISBN 0-252-01846-X, $29.95

Scott provides an overview of all-female voluntary associations from the early days of the Republic through the Progressive era. The voluntary association offered women a vehicle through which they could exercise a public agenda, despite the social and political constraints placed on them in society's male-dominated institutions: churches, political offices and bodies, and higher education. The associations covered in this study vary, from liberal, conservative, and radical political interests to social justice concerns and religious issues. The evolution of these groups is charted through changing political climates both locally and nationally, showing how women effected change both within the associations themselves and within society at large. *Natural Allies* is not a "contribution" or an "oppressed" women's history. The author does not attempt to show how women's associations contributed to a patriarchal society, or how men oppressed women. Instead, she argues that these associations were central to American social and political development. Scott makes it clear that a comprehensive history of the US can no longer be written wihout an analysis of women's associations. *Natural Allies* is a lesson in grass-roots, participatory democracy. Photographs. All levels.—*E. Kuhlman, University of Montana*

WS-1849　　　　HQ520　　　　91-32770 CIP
Spigel, Lynn. **Make room for TV: television and the family ideal in postwar America.** Chicago, 1992. 236p index afp ISBN 0-226-76966-6, $42.00; ISBN 0-226-769667-4 pbk, $15.95

Spigel's book is a cultural history that focuses on how popular culture, especially women's magazines, helped define the adoption and use of television in US homes from 1948-55. In addition to extensive network archival sources, Spigel studied articles, photographs, cartoons, and advertisements for this time period in *Better Homes and Gardens, American Home, House Beautiful,* and *Ladies' Home Journal* to ascertain the way those sources implicitly or explicitly suggested how television could/should be incorporated into home decor and family life. Societal expectations were that television would be a unifying force in the family while simultaneously preserving the traditional gender roles being stressed during the postwar period. Spigel points out the tension arising from those expectations and documents through examples how these expectations were addressed in women's magazine ads and articles. In 1955, NBC advertised in two major women's magazines, instructing women how to watch daytime television while continuing to do household chores. This book corrects the heretofore pervasive marginalization of women in the writing of television history. The notes—35 pages—are excessive; the absence of a bibliography limits inexcusably the book's usefulness. Advanced undergraduate; graduate; faculty.—*S. H. Hildahl, Wells College*

WS-1850　　　　F755　　　　90-25338 CIP
Swetnam, Susan Hendricks. **Lives of the saints in southeast Idaho: an introduction to Mormon pioneer life story writing.** Idaho/Idaho State Historical Society, 1991. 188p bibl index ISBN 0-89301-144-4 pbk, $12.95

Basing her work on a collection of biographies of Mormon settlers in southeastern Idaho and informed by wide reading in the theoretical literature of biography, Swetnam provides an introduction to the pioneer life narrative. After outlining her methodology, the author considers everyday life, orthodox story patterns, the miracle narrative, examples of those who questioned orthodoxy, patterns of women's narratives, and some examples of the stylistically best narratives. The book is well written, and the examples chosen for the study seem representative. All of the narratives are housed at Idaho State University and at the Idaho State Historical Library. Because the examples were selected to fit particular categories, other potential questions are not addressed. In addition, the introduction contains some dubious interpretations of Mormon doctrine. The bibliography lists all of the narratives in the collection as well as primary and secondary works used. Adequate index. For libraries with collections on the westward movement, Idaho history, Mormonism, women's studies, and biography. Upper-division undergraduates and above.—*T. G. Alexander, Brigham Young University*

WS-1851　　　　F290　　　　94-40961 CIP
Tokens of affection: the letters of a planter's daughter in the Old South, ed. by Carol Bleser. Georgia, 1996. 403p bibl index afp ISBN 0-8203-1727-6, $45.00

Attics can provide exciting treasures from time to time. The attic that hid and then released the letters of Maria Bryan is certainly among them. Written between 1824 and 1844 by a plantation woman, the letters poignantly depict the rhythms of the central Georgia community of Mt. Zion. With most frequent references to Augusta, Georgia, but with evidence of both regional and national connections including New Orleans, an Alabama plantation, and Newport, Rhode Island, the letters provide commentary on the lives of women, child-rearing patterns, political developments, and religion. The letters are also a marvelous source for those who would understand the 19th-century South and, more particularly, the perspective of women on the range of issues that helped to define the South. The editor has included informative notes that help to fill in the chronological gaps, as well as essential genealogical information. Indeed, editorial emphasis is much more on the personal than on the larger context. Missing from the editorial notes is a sense of larger political and economic concerns that surrounded the world represented in the letters. Nevertheless, publication of these letters represents an important contribution to the documentary literature of the 19th-century South. All levels.—*T. F. Armstrong, Texas Wesleyan University*

WS-1852　　　　HQ1236　　　　95-11197 CIP
Tyler, Pamela. **Silk stockings and ballot boxes: women & politics in New Orleans, 1920-1963.** Georgia, 1996. 323p index afp ISBN 0-8203-1790-X, $40.00

Feminine activists in New Orleans are the subject of this political study. In the early 20th century, upper-class women sought the vote through the Portia Club, the Era Club, and the Louisiana Woman Suffrage Association. After women's suffrage was granted in 1920, women were not politically organized until Hilda Phelps Hammond and the Louisiana Women's Committee began crusading against Huey P. Long. Nonpartisan activities for better government were pursued by Martha Gilmore Robinson and the Woman Citizens' Union, and the League of Women Voters. The Independent Women's Organization got involved in backing candidates. During the Civil Rights Movement (1950s-1960s) Rosa Freeman Keller was the best-known white woman who championed this cause. Tyler discusses characteristics of these women. They did not view themselves as liberals or feminists; most reflected the racial views of their region. After WW II, the women's organizations they had formed broadened in membership to include other ethnic groups and classes. A vivid, well-written narrative on a facet of New Orleans politics never before discussed in such detail, this book is a welcome addition to urban studies on women. Illustrations; footnotes. All levels.—*J. Jackson, Southeastern Louisiana University*

WS-1853　　　　HQ1058　　　　91-15289 CIP
Wilson, Linda. **Life after death: widows in Pennsylvania, 1750-1850.** Temple University, 1992. 215p index afp ISBN 0-87722-883-3, $34.95

Wilson's examination of widows in early Philadelphia and Chester County, Pennsylvania delineates their efforts to forge new lives, to hold their families together, and to provide for their own welfare and that of their children. In the process, Wilson illuminates, among other things, inheritance laws and practices, estate management, and relief procedures. She demonstrates that husbands' provisions and relief programs related to widows generally were more flexible and humane than the law admitted. Wilson maintains that historians must reassess the concept of "domesticity" with "its presupposition of gender-defined 'spheres' and female incompetence in the public domain." Pennsylvania widows were not restricted by traditionally held concepts of proper female behavior. Whether seeking the best way to make do with reduced income, adjusting to being on relief, or managing their husbands' estates, family considerations, much more than either gender or home perspectives, shaped their responses to widowhood. Concentrating primarily, though not exclusively, on facets of widows' lives extrapolated from probate records, Wilson's fine study challenges previous works on early American women in important respects. Upper-division undergraduates and above.—*G. S. Rowe, University of Northern Colorado*

WS-1854   E185   94-7418 CIP
Winegarten, Ruthe. **Black Texas women: 150 years of trial and triumph,** consulting editors, Janet G. Humphrey and Frieda Werden. Texas, 1995. 427p bibl index afp ISBN 0-292-79087-2, $60.00; ISBN 0-292-79089-9 pbk, $24.95

Winegarten, a prolific and competent independent scholar of Texas history, enriches understanding of the Lone Star State with this long-needed and well-done study of the African American women of Texas, from the Spanish colonial era to the present. Although the book lacks a thesis, the theme of progress-despite-adversity is present on nearly every page as the author traces the stubborn efforts and accomplishments of individual black women in Texas and the organizations they founded. Beginning in the domestic labor ghetto as child and home care workers, black women lifted themselves by their apron strings and thus also lifted their community. Some distinguished themselves in business, others in education or the dangerous politics of protest. Many, less visibly, contributed to essential community-building by founding nurseries, homes for the elderly, hospitals, churches, lodges, and more. Winegarten's narrative about these people and their accomplishments, drawn from limited secondary literature and many primary archival sources, is enhanced by several hundred period photographs as well as by reproductions of key documents, all beautifully formatted by the publisher to complement the text. This is as good a state study as Darlene Clark Hine's *When the Truth Is Told: A History of Black Women's Culture and Community in Indiana, 1875-1950* (1981). All levels.—*H. Beeth, Texas Southern University*

WS-1855   HQ1438   94-30150 CIP
Wolfe, Margaret Ripley. **Daughters of Canaan: a saga of southern women.** University Press of Kentucky, 1995. 281p index afp ISBN 0-8131-1902-2, $37.50; ISBN 0-8131-0837-3 pbk, $14.95

In a work that lays bare myriad myths and stereotypes while presenting true stories of ambition, grit, and endurance, Wolfe offers the first professional historical synthesis of southern women's experiences across the centuries. In telling their stories she considers many ordinary lives, among them Native American, African American, and white women from the Tidewater and Appalachia, to the Mississippi delta, to the Gulf coastal plain. These women, whose varied economic and social circumstances resist simple explanations, include wives, mothers, pioneers, soldiers, suffragists, politicians, and civil rights activists. The author contends that the specter of race has haunted all southern women, and though gender is a common denominator, it does not transcend race, class, or point of view. Wolf argues that the region's females have born the full weight of southern history, mythology, and legend. Drawing on two decades of study and reflection and a lifetime of experience and observation, she has produced an insightful, vivid, frequently startling, and sometimes shocking work of revisionist feminine history. All levels.—*M. Klatte, Eastern Kentucky University*

WS-1856   E98   95-5903 CIP
Women and power in native North America, ed. by Laura F. Klein and Lillian A. Ackerman. Oklahoma, 1995. 294p bibl index afp ISBN 0-8061-2752-X, $24.95

Using detailed analyses of women's roles in 11 contemporary North American tribes, Klein and Ackerman seek to answer questions concerning the power

of Native American women to control their own and others' lives. Specifically, the authors want to know what kind of autonomy native women have today. In presenting their findings the authors not only bring native women into clearer focus in terms of specific cultures but also underscore the variations that exist. The final chapter offers a comparative and theoretical summary. Despite differences in approach—some chapters are more historical than others—all chapters maintain the general focus and are short, descriptive, and clearly written. The book provides a ready reference on native women in different regions. By showing how these women have adapted to the modern situation, especially to work outside the home, the book demonstrates the differences between present and former tribal life. More important, the book moves away from popular polemics about native women as "equal" or "oppressed" and provides actual examples of women's abilities to control their lives. All levels.—*M. J. Schneider, University of North Dakota*

WS-1857   HX653   92-10609 CIP
Women in spiritual and communitarian societies in the United States, ed. by Wendy E. Chmielewski, Louis J. Kern, and Marlyn Klee-Hartzell. Syracuse, 1993. 275p index afp ISBN 0-8156-2568-5, $39.95; ISBN 0-8156-2569-3 pbk, $17.95

As its title indicates, this collection of original essays focuses on women in the American utopian experience for the past two centuries. The editors argue that more attention needs to be paid to the roles of females in this unusual setting. The range of coverage is extensive and includes articles about females in such well-studied groups as the Shakers, Mormons, and Perfectionists, as well as essays on more obscure groups, for example, the Woman's Commonwealth of Texas, and later, the District of Columbia. The editors also added two excellent, first-hand accounts of female life in contemporary communes—the religious Hutterite colonies and the secular Twin Oaks (Virginia) Community. Common to this genre of edited work, some essays are much better than others. Fortunately, the editors wisely provided an overview essay and short introductory pieces to the various topics discussed. The volume is further enhanced with good illustrations, appropriate scholarly notes, and a comprehensive index. Advanced undergraduate; graduate; faculty; professional.—*H. R. Grant, University of Akron*

WS-1858   HQ1438   95-21715 CIP
Women of the commonwealth: work, family, and social change in nineteenth-century Massachusetts, ed. by Susan L. Porter. Massachusetts, 1996. 240p index afp ISBN 1-55849-004-3, $45.00; ISBN 1-55849-005-1 pbk, $15.95

Essays in this collection explore the experience of women in 19th-century Massachusetts. In her introduction, the editor makes a compelling case for an entire volume on this topic: not only did the century witness drastic economic and political change, but the emerging ideology of separate spheres and burgeoning industrial presence in the state had a special impact on women. The first half of the volume examines the nature of women's work, the tie (whether waged or unwaged) that bound all women during this time. Five essays cover myriad subjects, including specific female professions such as teaching and social work, as well as the effect that marital status and ethnic and social class had on working women. The later half of the collection focuses on the experiences of women who "broke new ground" either in participating in their profession or in their advocacy on behalf of other working women. By embracing a wide range of women's experiences, from elite African Americans to Irish American political reformers and working-class whites, the volume serves as a useful portrait of Massachusetts women during a century of great change. Upper-division undergraduates and above.—*J. M. Lewis, University of Arkansas at Little Rock*

WS-1859   PS430   90-21070 CIP
Women's comic visions, ed. and introd. by June Sochen. Wayne State, 1991. 238p afp ISBN 0-8143-2307-3, $34.95; ISBN 0-8143-2308-1 pbk, $14.95

A collection of essays focusing on women's humor. Although the book limits its subject largely to the American experience, its range is otherwise broad. The first three essays are theoretical, examining, for example, why there has been so little recognition of women humorists and women's humor; how women have dealt with their peripheral position in male-dominated society by "carnivalizing" language; and how humor has functioned to bond women. The second section explores and analyzes the work of various American women humor writers (and cartoonists) from the 19th and 20th centuries; the third section concentrates on women performers, from vaudeville, stand-up comedy, television, and film. The work of black and white women, and lesbian and heterosexual women is examined. Written from diverse disciplinary perspectives (e.g., literary theory, psychology, history, and American studies), the essays are clear and well referenced, and they provide a comprehensive overview of a subject rarely discussed.— *A. Goldson, Brown University*

WS-1860 HX656 91-24490 CIP
Wunderlich, Roger. **Low living and high thinking at Modern Times, New York.** Syracuse, 1992. 259p bibl index afp ISBN 0-8156-2554-5, $34.95

Modern Times was an experimental community established on Long Island, NY, in the middle of the 19th century by Josiah Warren. This is the first book-length study of the community and its residents, a notable collection of free thinkers and eccentrics. Modern Times came to be identified with the free love movement and eventually changed character and name, becoming the town of Brentwood, after a 13-year existence. Unlike most communal societies, individual sovereignty was a prime value there. Wunderlich reinforces this theme by an unusual structure that mixes mini-biographies of residents with the chronological development of the community, but readers will need time to adjust to this form of presentation. Occasionally, the text also is mired down with minutiae of land deed and real estate transactions that do little to move the story forward. Nevertheless, Wunderlich's book will be the standard reference on Modern Times for years to come. Adequate index and bibliography. General; undergraduate; graduate; faculty.—*E. J. Green, Prince George's Community College*

WS-1861 HQ1423 89-16540 CIP
Yellin, Jean Fagan. **Women & sisters: the antislavery feminists in American culture.** Yale, 1989. 226p index afp ISBN 0-300-04515-8, $25.00

"Am I not a woman and a sister?" The answer in the 1830s and '40s was clearly "No," because black slave women and the white women who braved the platform and entered the public arena in the abolitionist cause discovered that American society reinforced its existing cultural expectations with an opposing dialogue. The symbol of the fettered supplicant black woman offered for sale in the public arena became the icon for the movement of white women into public argument. Yellin (English, Pace University) uses this most effectively as the thematic connection to explore the writings of the antislavery feminists in their attempt to employ public discourse and popular fiction to change women's roles. In the political arguments and fictional accounts of Angelina Grimke, Maria Child, Sojourner Truth, and Harriet Jacobs, the figure of the enchained female slave was used to illustrate such themes as sexual control, racial harmony and union, and gender equality. Symbols provide compelling messages and the photographs in this volume strengthen and support the arguments in the text. *Women and Sisters* is a powerful book; it is made so by the author's ability to link ancient and modern symbols of oppression to the varied rhetoric of abolitionism and its accompanying theme, women's liberation. Yellin's writing is clear and concise; the topic fits collections of US women's history and sociology. College, university, and public libraries.—*V. T. Avery, Northern Arizona University*

◆ North America
Biography

WS-1862 F656 90-36047 CIP
Bachelor Bess: the homesteading letters of Elizabeth Corey, 1909-1919, ed. by Philip L. Gerber. Iowa, 1990. 462p index afp ISBN 0-87745-302-0, $42.50; ISBN 0-87745-303-9, $14.95

For a vibrant firsthand account of homesteading in South Dakota in the early 20th century, Bess Corey's letters are unexcelled. The immediacy of the difficulties, the helpfulness of neighbors, the determination and effort needed simply to stay even, and the simple pleasures of homemade entertainment are all here. So is the struggle to earn enough money by teaching to hang onto the land and the constant need for more training to stay certified to teach as standards were raised.

The letters give life and color to discussions of women on the frontier in works such as Sandra L. Myres's *Westering Women and the Frontier Experience, 1800-1915* (CH, May'83). Gerber's lengthy and detailed introduction places the letters and Corey's life in a context that is helpful. The letters are presented basically as written, with little editorial cleanup. Where there are gaps in the sequence, Gerber has provided a brief summary of what Corey was doing then. Wayne Franklin provides a brief afterword that summarizes Corey's last years. Upper-division undergraduates.—*V. P. Caruso, Nazareth College*

WS-1863 LD7212 92-46863 CIP
Bordin, Ruth. **Alice Freeman Palmer: the evolution of a new woman.** Michigan, 1993. 314p bibl index ISBN 0-472-10392-X, $49.50

Bordin explores the concept of the late 19th century "New Woman"—defined as a woman who exercised control over her own life—in this biography of Alice Freeman Palmer (1855-1902), a leader in women's education, an administrator in the Massachusetts public schools, and a dean at the University of Chicago. Bordin suggests that creation of the middle-class, college-educated "New Woman" was an evolutionary process and uses Palmer's life to demonstrate. Palmer attended the coeducational University of Michigan and became Wellesley's president at 26, but renounced her position at marriage. Bordin argues Palmer became an "independent New Woman" when she shirked economic responsibility for her siblings and father, not when she emerged from receiving parental support. Yet marriage proved a turning point that shaped Palmer's professional options. Ultimately, she was able to mold higher education for women and men in her position at the University of Chicago. Sources used include letters, college archival material, and secondary literature about women's education. General; undergraduate; graduate; faculty.—*L. Sturtz, Beloit College*

WS-1864 HQ1413 90-50769 CIP
Brown, Ira V. **Mary Grew, abolitionist and feminist, (1813-1896).** Susquehanna University, 1991. (Dist. by Associated University Presses) 214p bibl index afp ISBN 0-945636-20-2, $35.00

In 19th-century abolitionist and woman's-rights documents, the name of Philadelphian Mary Grew turns up repeatedly as organizer, officer, reporter, and speaker. Supported by an independent income, Grew was a lifelong activist in these two crusades. Well acquainted with such luminaries as Garrison, Phillips, Mott, Stone, and Whittier (who wrote an ecomium urging others to grow as Mary Grew) she labored patiently and dutifully in the second rank. In this straightforward chronologically organized biography, Brown makes extensive use of Grew's antislavery reports and of her correspondence, found in a variety of collections. He often quotes or paraphrases, usually staying close to her writing. Unfortunately, he stays too close, declining to entertain questions on matters such as Grew's motivation, relative standing, emotional life, Boston marriage, and chronic illness, or on such things as the mechanics of living a rather privileged woman's life in the 19th century. The result, one must say with regret, is a dull book. Recommended only for graduate libraries or those aspiring to complete collections in abolitionism or woman's rights.—*A. Graebner, The College of St. Catherine*

WS-1865 HX84 94-43829 CIP
Camp, Helen C. **Iron in her soul: Elizabeth Gurley Flynn and the American Left.** Washington State, 1995. 396p bibl index afp ISBN 0-87422-105-6, $40.00; ISBN 0-87422-106-4 pbk, $28.00

Camp (Pace Univ.) has maintained a longtime interest in the life of Flynn. She writes sympathetically of her subject's early introduction to radicalism and to street speaking through the socialist activism of her Irish American parents. Camp traces Flynn's family history and the streak of Irish militancy they possessed. She chronicles Flynn's own activities, from her early public speaking days to joining the Industrial Workers of the World (IWW) in 1906; her work with the Workers Defense Union and the infamous Sacco and Vanzetti case; and her eventual membership in the American Communist Party in 1926. Flynn's arrest and trial under the Smith Act in 1951 cover an entire chapter, and her period of federal imprisonment (1955-57) is also well noted. The book discusses Flynn's later years in the Communist Party and her death in Moscow in September 1964. Camp tells a good story—interesting, readable, and even exciting at points, unusual for a historical biography. Extensive endnotes, good bibliography.—*S. K. Hauser, University of Wisconsin—Milwaukee*

WS-1866 PS2506 91-32599 CIP
Capper, Charles. **Margaret Fuller: v.1: An American romantic life.**
Oxford, 1992. 428p index afp ISBN 0-19-504579-3, $39.95

The first of a two-volume biography of Margaret Fuller, America's premiere female Romantic intellectual. Capper exploits heretofore unexplored letters, diaries, and journals in this work. Three influences helped shape Fuller's remarkable career: her relationship with her overbearing father, her gender, and the intellectual culture of early 19th-century New England. Capper delves gingerly into psychohistory as he analyzes Fuller's attachment to her father. As a woman, Fuller had a choice of two careers: teacher to young upper-class women, or writer; these were the only acceptable occupations for unmarried women. Fuller maintained both roles with a great deal of success. Capper contextualizes three important influences on Fuller's intellectual development: Unitarianism, Romanticism, and Transcendentalism. Too often, his narrative becomes mired in the pedigree of the young aristocratic Bostonians with whom Fuller shared her ideas. Though the work is almost 400 pages in length, Capper's creation of the intellectual climates within which Fuller operated is often inadequate. Photographs. Graduate; faculty.—*E. Kuhlman, Washington State University*

WS-1867 HQ1413 91-33106 CIP
Clifford, Deborah Pickman. **Crusader for freedom: a life of Lydia Maria Child.** Beacon Press, 1992. 367p bibl index ISBN 0-8070-7050-5, $30.00

New England author and reformer Lydia Maria Child (1802-1880) came to public adulation in 1824, when women writers were yet a rarity. After her marriage to the hapless David Child, she was drawn into the abolitionist cause and in 1833 published an important tract that cost her reputation in polite society. While her husband was engrossed in hairbrained schemes, she lived a largely separate life, unconventional for a married woman, making a precarious living editing reform periodicals and turning out books that ranged from a study of religion to city sketches to advocacy of Indian rights to maternal advice. Clifford's book, which supplants earlier biographies, is appropriately compact, fully documented, and sensible in interpretation. Although he describes the problems David Child caused his wife, Clifford avoids the lure of making Maria's husband the villain of her life, and warns readers not to oversimplify or conventionalize a complex, contradictory, and sometimes prickly woman. Clifford discusses the literary and reform context of Child's work and outlines the themes of Child's writing, but her focus is resolutely biographical. Recommended for all libraries. Consider, too, as source volume *Lydia Maria Child, Selected Letters, 1817-1880*, ed. by Milton Meltzer and Patricia Holland (1982).—*A. Graebner, The College of St. Catherine*

WS-1868 E807 87-40632 CIP
Cook, Blanche Wiesen. **Eleanor Roosevelt: v.1: 1884-1933.** Viking, 1992. 587p bibl index ISBN 0-670-80486-X, $27.50

Eleanor Roosevelt is best known as Franklin D. Roosevelt's helpmate. In this first volume of a projected two-volume biography, Cook confirms and amplifies the conventional widsom concerning Roosevelt's life. The book's value and strength, however, lie in its attention to the extraordinary journey of a woman caught between the Victorian conventions with which she grew up and the realities of 20th-century America. Cook's Roosevelt was no plaster saint, but a person who struggled to balance her family obligations with her deep concern for improving life for her fellow Americans, most especially women and children. Readers familiar with the Roosevelts will expect and find new insights on Eleanor's complicated partnership with FDR and her difficult relations with mother-in-law, Sara Delano Roosevelt. Even more impressive are Cook's narrative accounts of Eleanor's surprisingly rich if periodically troubled childhood and adolescence, her impressive range of political and journalistic activity in the 1920s, and her intimate relationships with Earl Miller and Lorena Hickock, which friends, family and many writers have chosen to ignore or dismiss. In its depth of research, deft prose, and empathy for its subject, this biography is a model. Cook has produced a classic. All levels.—*M. J. Birkner, Gettysburg College*

WS-1869 E472.9.C33 89-24403 CIP
Coryell, Janet L. **Neither heroine nor fool: Anna Ella Carroll of Maryland.** Kent State, 1990. 177p bibl index afp ISBN 0-87338-405-9, $22.00

An unusual figure among 19th-century American women, Anna Carroll rejected women's rights arguments but attached herself to politicians and made her way as publicist, pamphleteer, and lobbyist. She gained most public attention for her claim that she originated the military strategy used by Grant in the Tennessee valley. This biography, originally a dissertation, reexamines Carroll's life, work, and claims, revealing the author's conclusions in its title. Coryell follows the history of Carroll's posthumous reputation, but neither that nor Carroll's life are of sufficient stature in this telling to make book-length treatment essential for most libraries. Recommended only for graduate libraries and others with special emphasis on women's or Civil War history.—*A. Graebner, The College of St. Catherine*

WS-1870 HX843.7.G65 89-10967 CIP
Falk, Candace Serena. **Love, anarchy, and Emma Goldman.** Rev. ed.. Rutgers, 1990. 388p bibl index ISBN 0-8135-1512-2, $45.00; ISBN 0-8135-1513-0, $14.95

In the earlier edition of this work (CH, Mar'85), Falk had used hundreds of Goldman's personal letters, particularly those written to her lover/associate Ben Reitman, to examine the interconnection between her love life and her public persona. The current book tightens the focus by eliminating repetitive personal correspondence and adding helpful historical analysis. The result is a provocative portrait of this fascinating radical leader. Goldman's vulnerability in love relationships contrasts with her daring and bravado in political ideology and personal safety. Issues of sexuality, gender, and individual self-realization, as well as radical politics, are illuminated in this impressionistic biography of an anarchist and feminist giant. Highly recommended to all libraries interested in women's studies and/or radical politics.—*L. Mayo, County College of Morris*

WS-1871 E185 95-38775 CIP
Fisher, Ada Lois Sipuel. **A matter of black and white: the autobiography of Ada Lois Sipuel Fisher,** by Ada Lois Sipuel Fisher with Danney Goble. Oklahoma, 1996. 204p index afp ISBN 0-8061-2819-4, $19.95

As a recent graduate of Langston University and an aspiring law student, Fisher was the plaintiff in *Sipuel* vs. *University of Oklahoma* (1948), one of the Supreme Court cases (along with *McLaurin* vs. *University of Oklahoma*, 1950) that opened state-supported graduate and professional education to African Americans and paved the way for the *Brown* decision of 1954. Argued in state and federal courts by Thurgood Marshall of the NAACP, *Sipuel* was the first case in which Marshall raised the point that separate was inherently unequal, a crucial precedent for *Brown*. About 40 percent of the narrative is a valuable and fascinating account of Sipuel's growing up in the 1920s and '30s in Chickasha, a town of about 15,000 in southwest Oklahoma. The daughter of a Pentecostal minister, Sipuel was acutely aware of the impact of segregation. Another 40 percent of the book describes the *Sipuel* case from the plaintiff's view, including the ludicrous efforts of the state to avoid complying with the Supreme Court decision. The rest of the book covers her career as an attorney, a teacher, and administrator at Langston, and eventually as a regent of the University of Oklahoma. Written with charm and grace, the book should appeal to readers at all levels.—*T. H. Baker, University of Arkansas at Little Rock*

WS-1872 CT275 93-34693 CIP
Funigiello, Philip J. **Florence Lathrop Page: a biography.** University Press of Virginia, 1994. 310p bibl index ISBN 0-8139-1489-2, $29.95

Funigiello offers readers an interesting insight into the life of an upper-class woman at the turn of the 20th century. Page was born in 1858 into a wealthy family and raised in Elmhurst, Illinois, a small town near Chicago. She married Henry Field, a brother of Marshall Field, one of Chicago's great entrepreneurs, and bore two daughters before her husband's untimely death left her a widow in her early 30s with two small children. After a brief widowhood, she married Thomas Nelson Page, a novelist and lawyer from the South. Her life with Page in Washington and then in Rome, where he served as US Ambassador during WW I, made her an eyewitness to some of the major events in the US and the world. Funigiello places Page's life into the larger context of women's and social history. He compares her experiences with those of other women of her class, and generally finds her to be typical of them. Page was not a reformer or an overt critic of the woman's role in society. Rather, she displayed strength and independence through proper channels. General readers; upper-division undergraduates and above.—*J. Sochen, Northeastern Illinois University*

WS-1873 HV28 95-4134 CIP
Gollaher, David. **Voice for the mad: the life of Dorothea Dix.** Free Press, 1995. 538p bibl index ISBN 0-02-912399-2, $28.00

In standard American hagiography, Dorothea Dix is the altruistic crusader responsible for asylum care of the insane. Having worked through the large Dix collection at Harvard, Gollaher is less interested in demythologizing than in understanding a complex personality. To explain Dix's emergence as a reformer he emphasizes anger stemming from the misery of her early life, as well as English precedents. He sketches the context of New England reform and Dix's substantial contribution, but he is also alert to how Dix used, rather than challenged, prevailing ideas of femininity to carve out a powerful, if lonely, place for herself in 19th-century society. Gollaher also follows Dix's extraordinary myopia regarding slavery, the administrative style that made her ill-suited to Civil War bureaucracy, and the compulsive, restless self-denial that surely was based in more than altruism. The book's length may reduce its accessibility for some readers, but, as the author recognizes, knowledge of Dix's work and ideas have a particular relevance at a time of acute debate about forms and financing of society's care for those who cannot care for themselves. All libraries.—*A. Graebner, College of St. Catherine*

WS-1874 Z720 91-18499 CIP
Guerrier, Edith. **An independent woman: the autobiography of Edith Guerrier,** ed. by Molly Matson. Massachusetts, 1992. 154p bibl index ISBN 0-87023-756-X, $27.50

During the final years of the 19th century, settlement houses emerged as one response to the challenges associated with increased urbanization, industrialization, and immigration. Rather than providing minimal relief and bracing words to cure the problems associated with poverty and social disorganization, settlement workers simultaneously attacked urban problems and promoted opportunities for individual growth. Women, in particular, found settlement houses congenial environments in which to develop careers. Such was the case for Edith Guerrier. Her autobiography provides a glimpse into the world of the early 20th century single woman. Once introduced to the settlement environment and the supportive female network that flourished there, Guerrier found not only an income but a life. In the process, she developed from a relatively shy and inexperienced young woman into the founder of an art pottery and a pioneer in the emergent library profession. An excellent contribution to scholarship on women, urban reform, and the Progressive era. All levels.—*P. Melvin, Loyola University*

WS-1875 E99 92-56816 CIP
Hale, Janet Campbell. **Bloodlines: odyssey of a native daughter.** Random House, 1993. 187p ISBN 0-679-41527-0, $18.00

The subtitle of *Bloodlines* indicates that this is something different from the usual autobiography. Because the book deals with the efforts of a Native American woman to surmount poverty and family problems, it is similar to other recent autobiographies by Indian women. But unlike those other books, Hale's account is not about reservation or Indian life. Hale provides only selective details of her ancestry and life, preferring instead to record her feelings about some of the events that have shaped her life and her work. In one chapter the author explores the relationship between autobiography and writing, explaining how she uses her own experiences to bring characters to life. Other chapters deal with the abusive treatment she received from her mother and older sisters, her relationship with her father, and an examination of her grandmother's life for answers to other questions. Because this small, eloquent book does not have the sometimes counterproductive, strident tones of other recent autobiographical works, it is suitable for ethnic studies, literature, sociology, and family classes. General; community college; undergraduate; graduate.—*M. J. Schneider, University of North Dakota*

WS-1876 HX84.H43 89-28394 CIP
Healey, Dorothy. **Dorothy Healey remembers a life in the American communist party,** by Dorothy Healey and Maurice Isserman. Oxford, 1990. 263p index afp ISBN 0-19-503819-3, $22.95

Scholars are beginning to examine more objectively the inner workings of the Communist Party USA. Without denying its subservience to Soviet control, Isserman is interested in examining generational conflict and change, specifically, how the party was shaped by events within the US. Although oral history purists might fault his rewrite methods, Isserman's research is solid, his style felicitous, and his subject's story worth telling. Since joining the Young Communist League at age 14 (her mother was a Communist party charter member who weaned her children on Upton Sinclair's novels), Healy was in the forefront of organizational drives, labor struggles, civil rights crusades, and intraparty warfare. She was the object of red-baiting witch hunts and spent time underground and in jail for her political beliefs. Coming of age during the "Popular Front" years, Healey, California's most prominent Communist, rejected the party doctrine of "democratic centralism," which forbade questioning of existing policies. She defended the 1939 Stalin-Hitler Pact and the 1956 Hungarian invasion, but she spoke out against the 1968 Czechoslovakian invasion. Barely tolerated by Gus Hall and the New York party hierarchy, Healey resigned from the party in 1973 (her last service to the party was the Angela Davis defense campaign) but remained active in other radical movements. Harboring little bitterness toward her estranged colleagues, Healey retained a vision of socialism with freedom and a hatred of capitalism. Recommended for general and academic readers, upper-division undergraduate level and above.—*J. B. Lane, Indiana University Northwest*

WS-1877 HQ1413 90-46851 CIP
Huckle, Patricia. **Tish Sommers, activist, and the founding of the Older Women's League.** Tennessee, 1991. 282p bibl index afp ISBN 0-87049-691-3, $28.95

Written with warmth and compassion, Huckle's book is more a tapestry of reminiscences and reflections than a traditional history or biography. The book is the story of a life traced from early childhood through political awakenings in the late 1930s and '40s, reflecting the avant-garde world of dance and theater, describing relations and marriages, and showing resistance to, preparation for, and acceptance of death as a meaningful part of life. Huckle chronicles Sommers's lasting contribution to the struggle of all people for dignity, respect, and empowerment, a word repeated frequently by Sommers and those around her. Although the title refers to the founding of the Older Women's League (OWL), a relatively small portion of the book focuses exclusively on this organization. Instead, Huckle involves the reader in Sommers's intricate journey of discovery, a journey that led to her profound understanding of the economic and social position of older women. Sommers played a key role in women's history; Huckle has brought that role to life.—*E. Broidy, University of California, Irvine*

WS-1878 E99 91-12326 CIP
Jeffrey, Julie Roy. **Converting the West: a biography of Narcissa Whitman.** Oklahoma, 1991. 238p (The Oklahoma western biographies, 3) index afp ISBN 0-8061-2359-1, $24.95

Narcissa Whitman and her husband Marcus traveled to Oregon Territory in 1836 as pioneer missionaries to the Cayuse Indians. The second Great Awakening, which she experienced as a child in New York, had fueled Narcissa's missionary zeal, and she eagerly sought converts to her Christian spirituality among the Indians. Narcissa's efforts were frustrated by the cultural barriers that separated her from the Cayuse. Undaunted, she developed a receptive congregation among other whites in the Territory. After 11 years of missionary work, Narcissa and her husband became victims of conflicts between whites and Indians. Violence erupted as more easterners pushed westward, and the Cayuse ultimately took revenge on the Whitmans. Both white and Native American perspectives are told in this well-balanced narrative, revealing the cultural constraints that worked against human understanding between the two cultures. Jeffrey presents a compelling biography based on sources not exploited by previous scholars. This is a book for anyone interested in the cultural exchange between white and native populations, in women in the West, and in 19th-century evangelical movements. Maps and photographs.—*E. Kuhlman, University of Montana*

WS-1879   PS2719   94-21064 CIP
John, Angela V. **Elizabeth Robins: staging a life, 1862-1952.**
Routledge, 1995. 283p index ISBN 0-415-06112-1, $25.00

Students of women, theater, and Anglo-American culture will appreciate John's carefully and thoroughly researched biography of a self-supporting woman who was born during the American Civil War and lived to the 1950s. Robins's first career was acting. John illustrates her family's varied responses, working conditions in both the US and England, difficulties in getting parts, and successes with Ibsen's plays in England. She describes well Robins's gradual transition to theater management and then to authorship. John gives a clear account of Robins's role in the English women suffrage movement, her service on the WSPU Committee, and resignation from the Committee in October 1912. Here readers see the uses of "influence" and "connections." Robins's feminism after suffrage was expressed in her concern for women's health issues, of which John provides examples. From the early 1900s on, writing was increasingly Robins's means of support; John links Robins's life experiences to her writings. Although never married, there were significant others in Robins's life. Readers feel some of the texture of her relationships with family, friends, and companions. All levels.—*V. P. Caruso, Henry Ford Community College*

WS-1880   HQ1413   94-9151 CIP
Karcher, Carolyn L. **The first woman in the republic: a cultural biography of Lydia Maria Child.** Duke University, 1994. 804p bibl index afp ISBN 0-8223-1485-1, $37.95

Karcher's authoritative biography argues compellingly that Lydia Maria Child, 19th-century reformer, novelist, and author of works for housewives and children, merits serious literary study. Karcher (Temple Univ.) demonstrates how Child, although aware of society's stress points, was able to imagine creative alternatives to the violence, racism, religious intolerance, and patriarchy that seemed inevitable to most. Punished for her presumption in embracing interracial marriage, the equality of religions, and the empowerment of women, she faced proscription, except in radical circles, throughout her lifetime. Even in the 20th century, scholars have had difficulty fitting her into standard paradigms in literature or history. Karcher's exhaustive scholarship in primary and secondary sources places Child firmly within her culture, analyzes all her writings, and demonstrates the uniqueness of her vision by comparing her work to contemporary writers struggling with the same themes. Much more thorough and psychologically compelling that Deborah Clifford's *Crusade for Freedom* (CH, Dec'92), this should become the standard biography of a noteworthy writer and belongs in all academic libraries. Illustrations, chronology, and a complete list of Child's works. All levels.—*P. F. Field, Ohio University*

WS-1881   HV40   91-26623 CIP
Kemplen, Tilda. **From roots to roses: the autobiography of Tilda Kemplen,** ed. by Nancy Herzberg. Georgia, 1992. 176p bibl afp ISBN 0-8203-1412-9, $24.95

Kemplen's book provides readers with a concrete and personal account of growing up in the mountains of eastern Tennessee in a poor coalminer's family. Kemplen credits her parents for giving her sound values and a deep commitment to helping others. Her home always sheltered needy relatives, orphans, and neighbors. This parental example became her guide for her adult behavior. Although she never attended high school—the nearest one was more than 20 miles away from her home and there was no transportation available—Kemplen always wanted to pursue her education. After marrying and having two children, she began the difficult task. She attended college, became certified to teach, eventually obtained a master's degree, and in 1973, founded the Mountain Communities Child Care and Development Center, a multipurpose facility serving the mountain counties in her area. Autobiography introduces an exceptional person to large audiences as well as offering a glimpse of many representative lives. Kemplen's story is an exemplary model of the genre. General; undergraduate; graduate; faculty; community college.—*J. Sochen, Northeastern Illinois University*

WS-1882   HQ1455x   Can. CIP
Kinnear, Mary. **Margaret McWilliams: an interwar feminist.** McGill-Queen's, 1991. 210p bibl index afp ISBN 0-7735-0857-0, $34.95

Kinnear broadly defines feminism as concern for women's place within a

socially constructed role in relation to equality with males and identification with other women as a social group. Using McWilliams's life as an example, Kinnear creates a prism for understanding what early 20th-century Canadian feminists did after women won the vote. McWilliams's public life melded the two strands of prewar feminism: women as persons responsive to the "family claim" and as persons in their own right. Her career in voluntary organizations such as the Canadian Federation of University Women, in local politics as alderman for Winnipeg, and service on advisory commissions illuminates the development of McWilliams's political thinking. Because McWilliams left few personal papers Kinnear has relied on public records such as newspapers, interviews, and McWilliams's published works. Thoroughly researched, the book would be useful to programs in Canadian studies, and to women's studies with a comparative orientation.—*V. P. Caruso, Nazareth College*

WS-1883   E467   92-50717 CIP
Leckie, Shirley A. **Elizabeth Bacon Custer and the making of a myth.** Oklahoma, 1993. 419p bibl index afp ISBN 0-8061-2501-2, $26.95

Leckie's biography of Elizabeth Bacon Custer (EBC) includes a personal history of her marriage to George Armstrong Custer and a description of life as an army wife, 1864-76. Leckie uses diaries and letters effectively, integrating well secondary works on women, family, and the military. Controversies over the Battle of the Little Big Horn are presented as an arena in which EBC protected her husband's reputation as she had furthered his career, because she thought both were a wife's role. Thinking it unwomanly to discuss military tactics, EBC persuaded men to defend her husband militarily, while she defended his private life zealously in her writing. Present difficulties in separating myth and fact illustrate her success at promoting her husband as a noble hero. She ignored his gambling and his fondness for women, and minimized the factions within the 7th cavalry under his command. Readers learn about Victorian marriage and widowhood, army life for women, and the power of social convention with which the "general's widow" safeguarded his reputation and her status. All levels.—*V. P. Caruso, Western Michigan University*

WS-1884   HD6509   92-43028 CIP
Leeder, Elaine J. **The gentle general: Rose Pesotta, anarchist and labor organizer.** State University of New York, 1993. 212p bibl index afp ISBN 0-7914-1671-2, $49.50

Using personal papers, diaries, and published works, Leeder has chronicled Rose Pesotta's rise from Russian immigrant to leadership in the International Ladies' Garment Workers' Union (ILGWU). Her work fostered close friendships with numerous leftists, such as Emma Goldman, and these associations provide intriguing insights into the complex character of American radicalism. Unfortunately, Leeder's biography has several problems, especially with contradictory assertions. For example, she describes Pesotta's pain in losing her deported lover to another women, but a few pages later tries to characterize Pesotta as an anarchist who believed "in sexual varietism (nonexclusive sexual relations)." This and other inconsistencies stem in large part from Leeder's failure to make a convincing case for her thesis, that of Pesotta's anarchism. Pesotta knew many anarchists and most certainly studied their ideas, but as Leeder's protagonist, she instead comes across as a practical institutionalist, a pioneering woman in the American trade union movement. Still, this should be interesting reading for those interested in labor, women's, and leftist history. General readers, advanced undergraduates, and above.—*R. F. Zeidel, University of Wisconsin-Stout*

WS-1885   E185   93-9370 CIP
Mabee, Carleton. **Sojourner Truth: slave, prophet, legend,** with Susan Mabee Newhouse. New York University, 1993. 293p bibl index afp ISBN 0-8147-5484-8, $35.00

Interest in the African American past has encouraged development of a heroic mythology that includes the activities of individuals from Crispus Attucks, to Nat Turner, to Sojourner Truth. This work is both the definitive biography and the demythologization of Truth. The writing required painstaking research in newspapers and correspondence, and was complicated because Truth, herself, was illiterate. The authors force readers to rethink Truth's life and to consider whether abolitionist rhetoric exaggerated the importance and often the reality of Truth's activities. Their portrait also shows the inner workings of the abolitionist movement and the postwar civil rights campaigns. The authors depict a woman who was remarkable for her articulation of freedom and her efforts in the cause of civil liberty for African Americans and women, and whose accomplishments were all the more notable because her illiteracy forced her to depend on friends for financial support and written expression. The authors, however, reveal a woman who was sometimes less than a heroine. For all of the strengths of the book, a querulous tone detracts from its readibility. General; undergraduate; graduate.—*T. F. Armstrong, Francis Marion University*

WS-1886　　　　E99　　　　95-6891 CIP
McBride, Bunny. **Molly Spotted Elk: a Penobscot in Paris.** Oklahoma, 1995. 360p bibl index afp ISBN 0-8061-2756-2, $24.95

Based on diaries, letters, newspaper clippings, and interviews, this book chronicles the life of Mary Alice Molliedell Nelson, one of many Native Americans who found jobs as stage and screen performers during the early decades of this century. Although born and raised a Penobscot on Indian Island, Maine, Nelson was exposed to both Indian and non-Indian music and dance, and as a youngster she did housework in exchange for ballet lessons. Later, under the name of Molly Spotted Elk, she had an international career as a dancer and actress. While performing in France she fell in love with Jean Archambaud, and they had a daughter. Her husband's death during WW II left her with few resources; there was no work for an aging dancer, and she eventually suffered a nervous breakdown. She worked at many odd jobs before returning to Indian Island, where she died in 1976. The book introduces the little-known topic of Native American stage and screen performers, but, because of the focus on Molly's life, it touches only briefly on other performers, the history of their work, and the problems these performers faced. All levels.—*M. J. Schneider, University of North Dakota*

WS-1887　　　　E748　　　　91-28230 CIP
Miller, Kristie. **Ruth Hanna McCormick: a life in politics, 1880-1944.** New Mexico, 1992. 339p bibl index ISBN 0-8263-1333-7, $24.95

In a first-rate political biography, journalist Kristie Miller presents the life of her grandmother, Ruth Hanna McCormick. This Illinois politico was involved in a number of female firsts: first elected to the US House as member-at-large; first nominated by a major party for the Senate; first to manage a campaign for a presidential nomination. In the 1920s, McCormick was the most successful woman politician in the US. Miller's study is well grounded in McCormick's papers (owned by Miller) and in the Hanna-McCormick family papers at the Library of Congress. The study is illuminating on a number of matters, e.g., the role played by McCormick's father, Mark Hanna, in the presidencies of William McKinley and Theodore Roosevelt; the McCormick publishing empire; the Byzantine intricacies of Illinois politics; and the 1940 and 1944 presidential bids of Thomas E. Dewey, among other events. Minor errors include listing Henry Cabot Lodge among the irreconcilables; Elihu Root as secretary of state in 1930; Senator Gerald P. Nye as Hitler's strongest Senate defender. Upper-division undergraduates and above.—*J. D. Doenecke, New College of the University of South Florida*

WS-1888　　　　HQ1413　　　　93-12223 CIP
Miller, Sally M. **From prairie to prison: the life of social activist Kate Richards O'Hare.** Missouri, 1993. 261p index afp ISBN 0-8262-0898-3, $29.95

Miller has written a long overdue history of an important 19th-century woman activist. Kate Richards O'Hare's life represents both the conventional female sphere of acceptable public involvement (temperance and social service) and more radical forms of antiwar activism considered unladylike in Victorian America. Born into a homesteading family in populist Kansas, O'Hare, on her discovery of the Socialist party, quickly began moving in unconventional circles. In the tradition of Kansas populists, she developed a reputation for fiery oratory. By 1917, she was arrested and imprisoned for her violation of the Espionage Act. Like most women activists, O'Hare's primary personal concern was striking a balance between home, family (she bore four children), and work. Miller successfully exploits O'Hare's correspondences and publications for this insightful biography. Useful bibliographic essay; photographs. All levels.—*E. Kuhlman, Washington State University*

WS-1889　　　　HV8023　　　　95-16780 CIP
Myers, Gloria E. **A municipal mother: Portland's Lola Greene Baldwin, America's first policewoman.** Oregon State, 1995. 232p bibl index afp ISBN 0-87071-386-8, $26.95

In this biography, Myers, a freelance researcher and historical writer, persuasively argues that Lola Baldwin was the first US policewoman. In 1908 Baldwin was sworn in "to perform police service" for the city of Portland, Oregon. Her role was restricted primarily to working with women and young girls as they came into contact with the law. This was part of the Progressive Era's redefinition of the role of women in society. Myers clearly portrays some of the paradoxes of feminism and social reform during this time and in Baldwin's career. This book started off as Meyers's master's thesis, but has been considerably revised and expanded. She has done a substantial amount of primary research to support her contention that Baldwin is truly America's pioneer policewoman. In telling Baldwin's story, the author is also exploring the broad social and cultural impulses of the time that gave rise to the idea of women in police work. Written clearly and concisely, the book should interest general readers as well as students and faculty in criminal justice and women's studies programs.—*P. Horne, Mercer County Community College*

WS-1890　　　　E621　　　　93-38830 CIP
Oates, Stephen B. **A woman of valor: Clara Barton and the Civil War.** Free Press, 1994. 527p index ISBN 0-02-923405-0, $27.95

Readers familiar with Oates's previous work will recognize many of his trademarks: this book is meticulously researched, minutely detailed, and beautifully written. Oates places a larger-than-life character in the midst of a dramatic historical event, sprinkles in a little light psychoanalysis, and lets the story unfold as dramatically as possible. Unlike his other books, however, this one does not attempt a full, definitive biographic treatment of its subject. And unlike his other subjects, this one is a woman. Both of these exceptions are problematic. Concerned only with the Civil War years, Oates recounts Barton's battlefield nursing experiences, but readers get little prewar background and nothing about her long career after the war's end. The narrow focus leaves readers with numerous unanswered questions about Barton's motivations and personality, as well as the context of her activities. Women's historians are likely to find frustrating the "great woman" approach of this biography, and most undergraduates will find the length prohibitive. Recommended for general readers who like heavy doses of military history.—*E. C. Green, Sweet Briar College*

WS-1891　　　　E185　　　　94-44317 CIP
Rollins, Judith. **All is never said: the narrative of Odette Harper Hines.** Temple University, 1995. 261p index afp ISBN 1-56639-307-8, $39.95; ISBN 1-56639-308-6 pbk, $16.95

Rollins, a sociologist, recorded the life story of Odette Harper Hines and prepared this narrative. Hines describes her family and neighborhood in the Bronx, where she became acquainted with people of many races and many famous African Americans, e.g., Bojangles Robinson, cousin Lester Granger (later head of the National Urban League), Mary McLeod Bethune, Marcus Garvey, and Paul Robeson. She came of age in the 1930s, but her middle-class family was not seriously affected by the Depression. Like others, however, she was drawn toward the Left politically. She worked on the Writers Project for the WPA and then joined Walter White at the NAACP. She served as a Red Cross worker in Europe during WW II, and returned to mary a doctor in Alexandria, Louisiana. There she "meddled" in efforts to register and vote, to obtain jobs, and to desegregate public facilities. She also housed several CORE workers (the author was one) who came to Alexandria in 1964. Hines overcame various setbacks in her life and has found meaning in helping others. Rollins describes her work as biography and history. It is much more the former than the latter, but historians will appreciate this African American woman and her views on race, class, and gender. General readers; undergraduates.—*L. H. Grothaus, Concordia Teachers College*

WS-1892　　　　E748　　　　91-17186 MARC
Scobie, Ingrid Winther. **Center stage: Helen Gahagan Douglas, a life.** Oxford, 1992. 369p index afp ISBN 0-19-506896-3, $24.95

Researched extensively in public and private papers; in oral interviews with

Helen Gahagan Douglas (HGD), her family, and friends; and in the secondary literature, Scobie's study places Douglas where she wanted to be, on center stage. Although Scobie covers Douglas's childhood, her Broadway and operatic careers, and her post-1950 life, 60% of the book discusses HGD's political career, beginning in 1937-8 with her involvement in migrant farm labor issues and her recruitment by Eleanor Roosevelt into Democratic Party politics around 1940. Sympathetic to problems of balancing family and career, Scobie focuses on Douglas's public life. Especially important is her presentation of the 1950 senatorial campaign between Douglas and Nixon, the first to make the Douglas campaign central. The reference notes are very complete and include mini-bibliographic essays. The index is good. Scobie does an excellent job placing HGD in the context of issues, gender, and politics—both national and state—in the 1940s. Undergraduate; graduate; faculty; general.—*V. P. Caruso, formerly, Nazareth College*

WS-1893 F220 93-8509 CIP
Segrest, Mab. **Memoir of a race traitor.** South End, 1994. 274p index ISBN 0-89608-475-2, $30.00; ISBN 0-89608-474-4 pbk, $15.00

Segrest's memoir is at once almost physically painful to read and close to impossible to put down. As she recounts her struggles both as a grassroots political organizer and as a white daughter of the South, she exposes the most intimate details of her life, sparing neither herself nor her family, and revealing information most people would hide: the father who spoke eloquently and worked tirelessly for segregated private schools rather than see his community's schools integrate; the relative who, in 1965, shot a black man to death in the Tuskegee bus station; the scores of other Segrests whose world was circumscribed by their whiteness and straightness. Circumstances both personal and political forced Mab Segrest to break away. She developed at an early age a political consciousness. She became an activist, a trait she paradoxically attributes to her father, the activist segregationist. Most significantly, she came out as a lesbian. The difficulty, for author and reader alike, is the realization that her treason is, first and foremost, to her own people, her own family. This brave and poetic memoir, however, turns treachery into the highest calling. Highly recommended to readers at all levels.—*E. Broidy, University of California, Irvine*

WS-1894 HQ1413 94-22725 CIP
Sklar, Kathryn Kish. **Florence Kelley and the nation's work: the rise of women's political culture, 1830-1900.** Yale, 1995. 436p bibl index afp ISBN 0-300-05912-4, $35.00

Florence Kelley (1859-1932) is best known as general secretary of the National Consumers' League, an important women's agency in Progressive reform. Sklar's book, the first volume in her long-awaited biography of Kelley, uses Kelley's life as framework for an extraordinarily illuminating exploration of women's public place before 1900. Kelley was the granddaughter of Philadelphia abolitionists, confidante of her Congressman father, Cornell graduate, rebellious daughter who married disastrously abroad, Marxist and translator of Engels, divorced mother, Hull House resident, and an Illinois factory inspector. Sklar explains with admirable clarity how Kelley and other women like her, though excluded from the electoral process, gave a particular shape because of that exclusion to American consideration of the state and of the proper relationship between state and economy. In this, Sklar places women as central to Progressivism. One hopes that Sklar's concluding volume (in progress) includes a fuller appreciation and evaluation of Kelley's presence and complex personality. This volume should be purchased by every library with substantial holdings in American history All levels.—*A. Graebner, College of St. Catherine*

WS-1895 E449 91-7435 CIP
Sterling, Dorothy. **Ahead of her time: Abby Kelley and the politics of antislavery.** W.W. Norton, 1992 (c1991). 436p bibl index ISBN 0-393-03026-1, $22.95

Sterling's fascinating biography exhumes the life and achievements of Abby Kelley, whose energetic leadership in the abolitionist and women's suffrage movements has been largely forgotten. Although Kelley was one of the earliest women to speak in public for the abolition of slavery, her participation was hotly debated in the early 1840s by the male movement leaders. Her work as organizer and propagandist became a role model for women such as Lucy Stone and Susan B.

Anthony. The story of her marriage to the reformer Stephen Foster reveals that the struggle to balance the demands of work and family is not a new dilemma for women. But she was relegated to oblivion by abolitionist historians because she challenged the stereotype of male leadership and by suffrage historians because she accepted the post-Civil War decision to give priority to African American suffrage over women's suffrage. Sterling's meticulous research from original sources and lively style restore Kelley to her rightful place and present an illuminating portrait of a woman who refused to accept the invisible barriers erected to constrain her gender. Thorough notes, selected bibliography, and a fine group of photographs. Recommended for everybody.—*M. L. Meldrum, SUNY at Stony Brook*

WS-1896 E185 94-14577 CIP
Stetson, Erlene. **Glorying in tribulation: the lifework of Sojourner Truth,** by Erlene Stetson and Linda David. Michigan State, 1994. 242p bibl index afp ISBN 0-87013-337-3, $28.95

Although she was an extraordinarily effective 19th-century speaker on religion, race relations, and gender, Sojourner Truth lacks a scholarly biography. Conflicting sources partially explain the deficiency. An illiterate former slave, Truth is known only through what contemporaries said she said or did; unfortunately they seldom agree. By reconstructing and analyzing the contexts in which others saw and heard her, however, Stetson (Indiana Univ.) and David (an independent scholar) have produced an alternative to biography, a "lifework," which examines people's perceptions of Truth as an example of how she had influenced them. The authors demonstrate that Truth's illiteracy was intentional, a way of distancing herself from Euro-American culture; and they show the sophistication of her techniques for swaying audiences, which made her more than a match at times for such reformers as William Lloyd Garrison, Elizabeth Cady Stanton, and Frederick Douglass. This clear and well-written analysis of a woman who had a compelling vision of the relationships among race, class, gender, and power belongs in college and university libraries collecting in women's and African American studies.—*P. F. Field, Ohio University*

WS-1897 E99 91-50306 CIP
St. Pierre, Mark. **Madonna Swan: a Lakota woman's story,** as told through Mark St. Pierre. Oklahoma, 1991. 209p index afp ISBN 0-8061-2369-9, $19.95

During a six-year period, St. Pierre interviewed Madonna Swan Abdalla, a Lakota woman born on the Cheyenne River Reservation in 1928. The resulting account of her life was arranged by St. Pierre, who enhanced her interviews with information about the land and history of the Cheyenne River people. The relationship between St. Pierre and Swan remains close; she related to him much about her way of life, both the happy times and the fearful times, such as the seven years in Sioux Sanitorium where she survived tuberculosis. As a child Swan was sent to Immaculate Conception Mission School and the memories of her childhood mix the pleasures of being with her family and the reluctance to go away from them to school. She tells of her puberty ceremony and Lakota religion, and of the Catholicism that her grandmother successfully integrated with traditional praying with the pipe. This life story is interesting because it demonstrates the constant impingement of the outside world on the reservation—Christianity, WW II, alcoholism, and violence. Against all odds, Swan survived her illness and began working at the sanitorium. After many years away, Swan returned to the reservation and in 1966 she began working for the Head Start Program. This is a straightforward account of one woman's life during a time of momentous change for the Lakota people. St. Pierre provides useful notes to supplement the text and inform readers of the significance of ceremonies and political events.—*G. M. Bataille, Arizona State University*

WS-1898 HQ1413 94-35499 CIP
Swain, Martha H. **Ellen S. Woodward: New Deal advocate for women.** University Press of Mississippi, 1995. 275p bibl index afp ISBN 0-87805-756-0, $40.00

Swain's biography details the professional life of a prominent southern woman in the administrations of Presidents Franklin D. Roosevelt and Harry S. Truman. As director of women's work relief programs in New Deal agencies and later as a member of the Social Security Board, Woodward was part of the inside group of Democratic women connected with Eleanor Roosevelt and Molly Dewson. A native of Mississippi, Woodward received her training in the state's women's club movement where she was active in "municipal housekeeping." The death of her husband Albert propelled her into Democratic politics when she was elected to complete his term in the Mississippi legislature. Her subsequent work for the Women's Division of the Democratic Party led to her 20 years of government service in Washington, where she was a strong advocate for programs helping women and their families. Her life story demonstrates once again how women's organized volunteer work for social welfare, coupled with their ability to enlist support at the grass-roots level, was translated into the social programs of the New Deal. Complements Susan Ware's *Partner and I: Molly Dewson, Feminism, and New Deal Politics* (CH, Feb'89). General readers; upper-division undergraduates and above.—*P. W. Kaufman, University of Massachusetts at Boston*

WS-1899   E748   95-4288 CIP
Wallace, Patricia Ward. **Politics of conscience: a biography of Margaret Chase Smith.** Praeger, 1995. 245p bibl index afp ISBN 0-275-95130-8, $24.95

On June 1, 1950, Senator Margaret Chase Smith stood on the floor of the US Senate and delivered her famous "Declaration of Conscience" excoriating the political paranoia, vicious smear tactics, and guilt by association that had quickly become known as "McCarthyism." This truly courageous act by the freshman liberal Republican from Maine represented Smith's "finest hour and arguably her only hour." What does one make of a 32-year congressional career that produced no legislation but rests proudly on the record of roll-call votes answered and thousands of constituent letters addressed on the day they were received? How does one evaluate a professional life motivated by no overarching cause (certainly not feminism)—"my job is my life"—or principle, save that of looking for or holding on to an exceptional personal and political opportunity? Whatever one may think about the heroism that propelled Margaret Chase Smith into the firestorm of Joseph McCarthy's anticommunist crusade, this is the chronicle of a suspicious, occasionally reclusive political maverick whose survival owed more to expert handling and seniority than to the brief moment of courage for which she is remembered. General.—*E. M. Tobin, Hamilton College*

◆ North America
Canada

WS-1900   F597   95-1826 CIP
Bennett, John W. **Settling the Canadian-American West, 1890-1915: pioneer adaptation and community building,** by John W. Bennett and Seena B. Kohl. Nebraska, 1995. 295p bibl index afp ISBN 0-8032-1254-2, $50.00

Bennett (anthropology, Washington Univ.), author of the standard *Northern Plainsmen: Adaptive Strategy and Agrarian Life* (1969) and additional studies on settlement and adaptation, teams again with Kohl (Webster Univ.), author of *Working Together: Women and Family in Southwestern Saskatchewan* (1976). This "binational" research focuses on how homesteaders adapted to an erratic, difficult environment "on both sides of the border" in the late 19th and early 20th centuries. Using local history books along with pioneer recollections, Bennett and Kohl merge history with anthropology to create a readable and sometimes pathos-ridden account of homesteading in this sector of North America. In so doing, they add to the knowledge of "adaptive settlement" described in Walter P. Webb's *The Great Plains* (1931). The plight of pioneer women and their strength to persevere in face of personal hardships is most moving: at the age of 16 Sarah was married to a man who would "spank me until I could hardly sit ... tie me up in an old cave in cellar where there were spiders, bugs and lizzards; he'd put dust down the back of my neck and pour water on top of it ...." For those with interests in anthropology, the American West, social history, and Americana, Bennett and Kohl's *Settling* is a must read. Illustrations, notes. All levels.—*P. D. Travis, Texas Woman's University*

WS-1901   F1089   94-28442 CIP
Chong, Denise. **The concubine's children.** Viking, 1995 (c1994). 266p afp ISBN 0-670-82961-7, $21.95

Chong's book is an excellent complement to more scholarly, and therefore less accessible, examinations of Canadian west coast Chinatowns. Because the view from within these communities is still relatively unexplored, Chong offers a fresh and insightful perspective. In addition to providing details of life in several British Columbia Chinatowns, this book also documents the transition that occurs between generations as the process of cultural adaptation takes place. The story, however, is not rooted only in Canada, but also explores family connections between China and North America. Chong accomplishes this by focusing on the concubine's children, some of whom were left in China and one who was born and raised in Canada. Chong, the concubine's granddaughter, reconstructs the family's experiences through collections of letters, photographs, and oral histories. Her book offers a window on a world long considered as one to be hidden from the view of outsiders. General readers; undergraduates.—*S. Wurtele, Trent University*

WS-1902   Can. CIP
Errington, Elizabeth Jane. **Wives and mothers, schoolmistresses and scullery maids: working women in Upper Canada, 1790-1840.** McGill-Queen's, 1995. 375p bibl index afp ISBN 0-7735-1309-4, $55.00; ISBN 0-7735-1310-8 pbk, $22.95

For this well-written and copious book, Errington has used published and unpublished primary materials, such as court records, newspapers, letters, memoirs, and diaries, as well as secondary publications on early Canadian social history and Canadian women, including Katherine M.J. McKenna's *A Life of Propriety: Anne Murray Powell and Her Family, 1755-1849* (CH, Jan'95). In discussing lower-class women, however, she had to rely on information from their wealthy employers or on upper-class observers of their lives. Errington details elaborately and well the accomplishments and hardships of women, and occasionally emphasizes the subtle powers of the oppressed—adaptations, adjustments, and accommodations analogous to those found in the literature of slavery, e.g., Eugene Genovese's *Roll, Jordan, Roll* (CH, Nov'75) Errington's narrative is sometimes reminiscent of Julia C. Spruill's *Women's Life and Work in the Southern Colonies* (1938), with its enumeration of occupations filled by women, and she reintroduces well-known conclusions by recent historians of US women's life in the early 19th century. Nevertheless, this is a valuable and needed addition to Canadian history. Upper-division undergraduates and above.—*E. R. Fingerhut, California State University, Los Angeles*

WS-1903   Can. CIP
Fairclough, Ellen Louks. **Saturday's child: memoirs of Canada's first female cabinet minister.** Toronto, 1995. 179p index afp ISBN 0-8020-0736-8, $35.00

Ellen Fairclough was the first woman to hold a cabinet post in Canada's federal government. In this era of gender history's ascendancy, that is clearly enough to justify the publication of her memoirs. There is, unfortunately, little else to justify publication; this book makes only the smallest of contributions to Canadian political history. A member of the Conservative Party, Fairclough won election to Parliament in 1950 and, when John Diefenbaker formed a government in 1957, she became Secretary of State, a relatively minor job. Her memoirs add little if anything to what is already known of Diefenbaker and his government, her account of her work in government in the three portfolios she held is barebones, and she says all but nothing about the climactic events that brought the government down in 1963. As the autobiography of a politician, then, this is thin gruel. Fairclough's prepolitical life is more interesting in the way it is presented here. She came from modest origins and made her way upward with hard work and native wit. She was a joiner, seeking out clubs and organizations, and Fairclough made herself into a skilled accountant. No militant feminist, she nonetheless set an example by working even though she had a child, much to the horror of some, and her supportive husband gets and deserves praise. General readers, faculty.—*J. L. Granatstein, York University*

WS-1904   Can. CIP
Frager, Ruth A. **Sweatshop strife: class, ethnicity, and gender in the Jewish labour movement of Toronto, 1900-1939.** Toronto, 1992. 300p (The Social history of Canada, 47) bibl index afp ISBN 0-8020-5968-6, $60.00; ISBN 0-8020-6895-2 pbk, $19.95

Historians are showing an ever-increasing interest in the links between class, ethnicity, and gender. Frager's chronicle of the Jewish labor movement in Toronto's garment industry illustrates the benefits of such an integrated approach. This thoroughly researched study draws on English and Yiddish sources from both oral and written records. Yiddish sources are not widely accessible to historians, and Frager's use of them adds substantial weight to her study. In addition to examining the evolution of working-class activism within the Jewish community, Frager assesses the importance of ethnic identity to this process. The main emphasis of her book, however, is on the often-ignored role of Jewish women in the labor movement. Frager combines an analysis of the social constraints faced by Jewish women in Canada with consideration of union policies. This provides the basis for detailed biographical profiles of four Jewish women who were active in the garment worker's labor movement. Frager's densely packed study will be of particular interest to labor historians. Advanced undergraduate; graduate; faculty.—S. Wurtele, Queen's University

WS-1905   Can. CIP
Hallett, Mary. **Firing the heather: the life and times of Nellie McClung,** by Mary Hallett and Marilyn Davis. Fifth House, 1993. (Dist. by Toronto) 336p index ISBN 1-895618-20-7, $26.95

Early 20th century prairie author, suffragist, and social reformer, Nellie McClung, is often relegated to the margin of Canadian consciousness. This collaborative biography, with an explicitly feminist perspective, redresses that assessment and reestablishes McClung's place as activist and writer. Ontario born and Manitoba raised, McClung established an independent role in her traditional framework, achieving national fame with the best-selling *Sowing Seeds in Danny* (1908). From a platform as a popular lecturer, she campaigned for the interlinked programs of prohibition and women's suffrage, later serving in the Alberta Legislature and on the board of the CBC. The chapter reassessing McClung's writings in the light of feminist criticism is particularly strong; it revises "long-accepted attitudes" and advances a "new interpretation of texts long thought of as unarguable." Short on pure literary criticism, this rereading highlights McClung's social conscience, writing to lift the burden of her prairie contemporaries, and emphasizes her edge of cynicism and realism as opposed to the usually perceived rosy romanticism. Well written and documented, this book is a first-rate addition to any Canadian or women's studies collection. Readily accessible to all readers at the undergraduate level and stimulating for those beyond.—W. E. Eagan, Moorhead State University

WS-1906   Can. CIP
McKenna, Katherine M.J. **A life of propriety: Anne Murray Powell and her family, 1755-1849.** McGill-Queen's, 1994. 327p bibl index afp ISBN 0-7735-1175-X, $34.95

McKenna's study well balances the traditional institutional and male-oriented political and economic histories of the founding of Upper Canada. Its first third is a chronologically organized life story that assimilates many new insights of recent gender analysis. Its last two thirds is devoted to Powell's family. There are seemingly not enough sources for a full-length discussion of her; therefore several sections are devoted to the life events of her siblings, children, and grandchildren. The book thus rambles across Upper Canada to England and even to the northern US. This latter part also repeats some events considered in the first, chronological section. However, these shortcomings are minor compared to the important new approach McKenna takes and the fresh way Powell's story is told, going far beyond the limited feminist analyses of the first part. The author relies and expands on recent feminist historical literature and theory to explain her considerations of inter-gender and same-gender relations. The details of genealogical relationships and the relations among the leading women of Upper Canada may boggle some readers, but these affairs are no more intricate than some of the shifting business partnerships and political factions that befuddled readers of male-oriented histories for many generations. In spite of its organizational limitations, this will be a standard for feminist literature in Canadian, if not general English-language North American history. Upper-division undergraduate; graduate.—E. R. Fingerhut, California State University, Los Angeles

WS-1907   R462x   Can. CIP
Mitchinson, Wendy. **The nature of their bodies: women and their doctors in Victorian Canada.** Toronto, 1991. 474p index afp ISBN 0-8020-5901-5, $60.00; ISBN 0-8020-6840-5 pbk, $22.95

Mitchinson's survey of the female patient-doctor relationship in the second half of the 19th century in English Canada is soundly based on doctors' medical records, medical texts and professional journals, and appropriate archival and secondary sources. Her themes are not unfamiliar to historians of Victorian era women. She demonstrates the power of cultural biases about women and their bodies that were reinforced by the male-dominated medical profession, which used science to advance its social position and confirm preconceived gender roles. Mitchinson begins by surveying gender attitudes and women's health problems, and describes how medical men, in invasive fashion, fitted their cultural assumptions about sex and gender into their prescriptive activities. She shows how women's health matters—puberty, menstruation, menopause, abortion, childbirth, birth control, and gynecology—were addressed, and ends by examining the treatment of female insanity. The first of its kind for Canada, this important and much needed study is recommended for all collections in women's studies, health, and North American social history.—M. J. Moore, Appalachian State University

WS-1908   HV6535x   Can. CIP
The Montreal massacre, ed. by Louise Malette and Marie Chalouh; tr. by Marlene Wildeman. Gynergy Books, P.O. Box 2023, Charlottetown, Prince Edward Island, Canada C1A 7N7, 1991. 177p ISBN 0-921881-14-2 pbk, $12.95

An uneven collection consisting of personal reflections, letters to newspaper editors, personal correspondence, and analysis of the assassination of 14 women by a man in a classroom of the Ecole Polytechnique in Montreal, Canada, on 6 December 1989. These selections reflect the editors' three intentions: to expose misogyny, to raise consciousness, and to express rage. Most fruitful are "Buryin Women's Words"; "Violence, Fear, Feminism"; and "Where are the 49%. . .?", which offer insightful feminist analysis of the massacre and response to it. A knowledge of Quebec provincial politics is helpful. No illustrations; and references appear only in the analytical pieces. Undergraduate readers.—V. P. Caruso, Nazareth College

WS-1909   Can. CIP
Potter-MacKinnon, Janice. **While the women only wept: loyalist refugee women.** McGill-Queen's, 1993. 199p index afp ISBN 0-7735-0962-3, $34.95

In this thoughtful case study of the Loyalist experience, Potter-MacKinnon focuses on the women who settled in the region of present-day Kingston, Ontario. Confronted with a cohort who left only a handful of diaries, letters, and petitions, the author creatively limns sources such as land grants, Patriot committee reports, and official British records. Primarily subsistence farmers from New York's northern frontier, her subjects often participated in counterrevolutionary activity; moreover, they typically shared or carried the full weight of maintaining their farms and raising their families. Harried from their homes and temporarily exiled to camps in Quebec, these women encountered a patriarchal power system wherein they had little option but to appeal to British paternalism in order to survive. Although Potter-MacKinnon draws a lively and graphic picture, her assertion that Patriot women fared better as a result of changes in American society falters somewhat because she does not develop the other half of the comparative equation with the verve and documentary support that she employs with the Loyalists. Nevertheless, the work succeeds in restoring Loyalist women to their rightful place in the historical record. Advanced undergraduate and above.—S. W. See, University of Vermont

WS-1910   Can. CIP
Sangster, Joan. **Earning respect: the lives of working women in small-town Ontario, 1920-1960.** Toronto, 1995. 333p bibl index afp ISBN 0-8020-0518-7, $45.00; ISBN 0-8020-6953-3 pbk, $19.95

Sangster's study makes a valuable contribution to the ever-growing literature examining constructions of gender in the field of labor history. Sangster examines women's work, family, and community lives, beginning with the education and socialization of girls that prepare them for entry into the paid labor force. She then documents and analyzes the experiences of women who, by choice or necessity, undertake work outside the home. Her analysis includes an excellent discussion of the evolution and nature of a distinct women's workplace culture. Union activity is explored, covering both formal and informal protest efforts. Sangster concludes with an assessment of the post-WW II era. Here she considers women's negotiation of, and experience with, changing societal views of the family. Her analysis integrates traditional archival research techniques with extensive use of oral histories. Inclusion of the voices of the women she studies adds tremendous depth, strength, and sensitivity to this excellent book. Although her research focuses on one small Canadian locale, her approach and findings will be of value for anyone studying labor history, women's history, or local history. All levels.—*S. Wurtele, Trent University*

WS-1911 Can. CIP

Strange, Carolyn. **Toronto's girl problem: the perils and pleasures of the city, 1880-1930.** Toronto, 1995. 299p bibl index afp ISBN 0-8020-0598-5, $50.00; ISBN 0-8020-7203-8 pbk, $22.95

Strange deals with the problem of the young single girl who migrates to the big city, looking for work. She examines Toronto in the 50 years after 1880, roughly the date when the Toronto police force shifted its attention from curbing drunkenness and petty crime to public morality, which included the morals of women. Single women were considered dangerous and, at the same time, endangered. Opportunities for them were limited. Right-thinking people, who composed Toronto's growing middle class, considered domestic service the most respectable and safest employment. They could not comprehend why girls preferred jobs as sales clerks, typists, and factory workers, which paid quite poorly but gave them time off. The same people saw no connection between the low wages these girls earned and the attraction of prostitution. This fine book is largely untouched by feminist ideology. Only in one place is Strange uncomfortable with her evidence: the case of Clara Ford in 1894. Ford, a black women in her 30s, had confessed to killing a white teenage man, and was acquitted by a jury of white males after a deliberation of only a half hour. Strange interprets the verdict as evidence of male indulgence, an aspect of masculine dominance. However, the case against Clara Ford was flawed, and the white male jury probably acquitted her simply because they were unconvinced of her guilt. A book for both the student of social history and the general reader. Upper-division undergraduates and above.—*J. A. S. Evans, University of British Columbia*

WS-1912 GT2713x Canadian CIP

Ward, Peter. **Courtship, love, and marriage in nineteenth-century English Canada.** McGill-Queen's, 1990. (Dist. by Toronto) 219p index afp ISBN 0-7735-0749-3, $24.95

Ward's study actually covers the period from the 1780s to about 1914. "Because of insufficient sources, Prince Edward Island and Newfoundland receive short shrift," and the 19th-century Canadian West is excluded from Ward's account. The author explains that "Two great themes lie at the heart of this inquiry. One is the community's ongoing interest in the reproduction and defence of the family as a social institution. The other is the couple's search for privacy and intimacy in the face of public intrusiveness." Ward (University of British Columbia) based his research on such family papers as "diaries and letters written and read by ordinary men and women." His range is vast. The thread running through the narrative is the troubled courtship and marriage of George Stephen Jones and Catherine Eleonore-Honorine Tanswell, both of Quebec City. An incidental contribution of the work is the author's clarification of the problem of class structure, which is by no means as clearly defined as neo-Marxist historians would have readers believe. Ward also reveals the improving status of women during the period. He does admit, however, that his sources reflect the top strata of society. Eight tables and one figure largely deal with age at marriage. Six illustrations describe a fictional account of "the role of sleighing in courtship," and one shows an early valentine. The documentation is thorough and the index excellent. College, university, and public libraries.—*J. J. Talman, University of Western Ontario*

◆ North America
Colonial & 18th Century

WS-1913 HD6073.H842 90-31349 CIP

Boydston, Jeanne. **Home and work: housework, wages, and the ideology of labor in the early republic.** Oxford, 1990. 222p bibl index afp ISBN 0-19-506009-1, $29.95

Boydston, in her quiet, analytical way, delivers suggestive or unconventional ideas at about one per page. Set securely within a Marxist framework, her study surveys unpaid labor of both working- and middle-class women in the Northeast during the antebellum period. Boydston perceives the family as a central force in the emergence of a factory society. Making shrewd and imaginative use of court records, diaries, and fiction, she rejects the contention that antebellum housework was not onerous or time consuming for these women. Although women were subordinate to men before the 1800s, Boydston observes, their home chores were recognized and usually appreciated. Though the tasks remained unchanged, recognition of them waned with the region's industrial transformation. By the 1820s and '30s, economic life and labor had become privatized, and women's homework became ideologically separated from the "productive" labor of men. Describing women's manifold household chores and responsibilities, the impact of new technology on housewifery, and the emergence of a new urban poverty attendant on industrialization, Boydston demonstrates the distinctive cultural spin that gender relations gave to factory labor and the manner in which woman as "goodwife" was displaced by woman as mother and "nurturer." Brief, brilliantly complex, consistently engaging, her book will influence scholars of the subject for years to come.—*M. Cantor, University of Massachusetts at Amherst*

WS-1914 F2230 95-38417 CIP

Breslaw, Elaine G. **Tituba, reluctant witch of Salem: devilish Indians and Puritan fantasies.** New York University, 1996. 243p (The American social experience, 35) index afp ISBN 0-8147-1227-4, $24.95

Breslaw reexamines the role of Tituba, household slave of Samuel Parris, accused of witchcraft in Puritan Salem in 1692. Examining the accusations and confession in social context and in light of multicultural influences, Breslaw discusses Tituba's role as a scapegoat or as a manipulator of Puritan fears. "In the process of confessing to fantastic experiences, she (Tituba) created a new idiom of resistance against abusive treatment and inadvertently led the way for other innocents accused of ... witchcraft." Breslaw makes a strong circumstantial case that Tituba was not an African, as is often assumed, but rather a South American Indian. This well-researched and well-written study is a new approach to understanding New England life, emphasizing the syncretic cultural exchange between Puritans and nonwhites. Tituba's mental images of altered states of consciousness, dreams, spirits, possession—all of which came from her origin in the Caribbean—were translated by the New Englanders to mean she was a witch. Tituba's mental world and religious beliefs would have been strange to the Puritans, just as their world was alien to her. Undergraduates and above.—*D. C. Samuels, SUNY at Stony Brook*

WS-1915 F187.C5 90-41099 CIP

Calvert, Rosalie Stier. **Mistress of Riversdale: the plantation letters of Rosalie Stier Calvert, 1795-1821,** ed. by Margaret Law Callcott. Johns Hopkins, 1991. 407p index afp ISBN 0-8018-4093-7, $34.95

In 1794, at age 16, Rosalie Stier came to the US with her wealthy aristocratic Belgian family. In 1799, she wed George Calvert, ancestor of the Fifth Lord Baltimore and master of Mount Albion tobacco plantation. Her family returned to Belgium abruptly in 1803, leaving Rosalie and her husband in charge of their Riversdale estate just outside the nation's new capital. Callcott presents the politically insightful, socially revealing letters she wrote to her Belgian family. Translated from the French, her correspondence records the investments she made with her father's money, political events that affected those investments (an ardent Federalist, Mrs. Calvert lambasted Thomas Jefferson and his 1807 Embargo Act), and the social and cultural life of the new nation. Hew busy life involved bearing nine children (five survived), tutoring her children, maintaining the European art collection her father kept at Riversdale, and managing the plantation's house-keeping slaves. She neglects to mention perhaps the most revealing aspect of the Calverts' lives: George Calvert's "other" family, consisting of his black mistress and their offspring. Illustrated with maps and photos. All levels.—*E. Kuhlman, University of Montana*

WS-1916   KF223   93-17290 CIP
Cameron, Jean. **Anne Hutchinson, guilty or not?: a closer look at her trials.** P. Lang, 1994. 239p (American university studies. Series IX, history, 146) bibl afp ISBN 0-8204-2227-4, $45.95

In yet another look at the 1637 Antinomian crisis, Cameron assesses the legality of Anne Hutchinson's civil and ecclesiastical trials. Cameron is, at best, only partially successful. Not until chapter 8 does she get to the actual trials; the first seven chapters are devoted to biographical, theological, and legal back-grounds. The civil trial gets two chapters, the ecclesiastical one, and an epi-logue sums up Hutchinson's later life. Regarding Hutchinson's guilt, Cameron hammers away throughout the essay that she most certainly was not guilty, and that the real culprit was her mentor, John Cotton, who abandoned her for his own personal safety. There really is not much to quarrel with regarding Cameron's position, although it is not particularly new. Assuming, somewhat naively, that the innocent go free, friends are loyal, and power is used humanely, Cameron seems not to appreciate that when cornered, one fights back with everything avail-able. In desperate need of good editing, eccentrically documented, and without an index, the book can be recommended only for those libraries that strive for com-plete holdings on the Hutchinson trials.—*H. R. King, Eastern Michigan University*

WS-1917   KFC3691   95-20116 CIP
Dayton, Cornelia Hughes. **Women before the bar: gender, law, and society in Connecticut, 1639-1789.** North Carolina, 1995. 382p bibl index afp ISBN 0-8078-2244-2, $49.95; ISBN 0-8078-4561-2 pbk, $18.95

Dayton's pioneering study adeptly serves as a creative lynchpin convening the subfields of American legal history, women's studies, and social history. Her thor-oughly researched analysis of women's participation in and treatment by pre-19th century Connecticut courts provides one of the richest and most insightful accounts of early American legal culture in years. Through her textured blending of indi-vidual case studies and quantitative analysis, Dayton depicts the transition from 17th-century Puritanism to 18th-century republicanism as one of lost rights, disempowerment, and status declension for New Haven women. Her survey of 150 years of legal actions regarding debt, divorce, sexual assault, adultery, and slander reveals that the New Haven legal system regressed from serving as an inclusive and egalitarian community forum for Puritan women to a hardened and exclusive patriarchal bureaucracy by the 1740s. Dayton's book successfully stations the study of the American legal system at the epicenter of the history of gender and social change in New England. This well-written work is recommended to all serious students of early American history. Upper-division undergradu-ates and above.—*R. J. Lettieri, Mount Ida College*

WS-1918   F158   90-14260 CIP
Drinker, Elizabeth Sandwith. **The Diary of Elizabeth Drinker,** ed. by Elaine Forman Crane. Northeastern University, 1991. 3v. 2,398p indexes afp ISBN 1-55553-093-1, $210.00

A major source of information on life in Revolutionary and the early national US. Elizabeth Sandwith Drinker (1735-1807) was the wife of Henry Drinker, one of the great Quaker merchants of Philadelphia. Her diary, begun in 1758 and extending to her death, chronicles affairs both great and small, ranging from the relations of a mistress to her servants to the problems of the Loyalist-leaning Philadelphia Quakers during the American Revolution. An acute observer of pub-lic affairs, Elizabeth Drinker was not reluctant to comment on people and events. Her diary is worth reading for the glimpses it offers of a remarkable mind and per-sonality and for its rich chronicle of life in Philadelphia for half a century. Crane's editing is painstaking but unobtrusive, and the work concludes with an impressive set of biographical notes on those mentioned in the text. Recommended for all graduate and undergraduate collections, and for all readers with interests in women's, religious, or early national history.—*T. D. Hamm, Earlham College*

WS-1919   E322   92-7860 CIP
Gelles, Edith B. **Portia: the world of Abigail Adams.** Indiana, 1992. 227p bibl index afp ISBN 0-253-32553-6, $24.95

Concerned that Abigail Adams's numerous biographers have depicted her from a narrowly masculine perspective, Gelles seeks to examine Adams both as a unique individual and as representative of women's world in 18th-century America. Min-ing the extensive Adams family correspondence and drawing on a range of insights gleaned from psychology, anthropology, sociology, and literary theory, the author describes Adams's evolving ties with her husband during the Revolu-tionary struggle; charts manifestations of her "Domestic Patriotism" during the war years; explores the epistolary connections she maintained for a time with James Lovell and Thomas Jefferson; and analyzes her relationships with her sister and her daughter, Abigail Adams Smith. In the process, Adams's strength, courage, and wit (as well as her bouts of depression and gender conservatism) emerge more fully than they have in any previous work. Although Gelles has a tendency at times to belabor the general concepts she uses to understand her subject (for example, her overelaboration of the nature and meaning of gossip), she has succeeded in providing a well-rounded portrait of a remarkable figure. The book belongs in every college library. General; community college; undergraduate; graduate; fac-ulty.—*J. K. Somerville, SUNY College at Geneseo*

WS-1920   KFN5200   92-7680 CIP
Narrett, David E. **Inheritance and family life in Colonial New York City.** Cornell/New York State Historical Association, Cooperstown, 1992. 248p index afp ISBN 0-8014-2517-4, $41.50

Narrett's examination of inheritance practices among the Dutch and English in Colonial New York City—the first such study of an Anglo-American urban cen-ter—is an important addition to the literature of inheritance and the early fam-ily. The sanctioning of community property within marriages, the encouragement of mutual wills by spouses, and the practice of dividing property equally among all offspring, typical under Dutch law, generally faded by the late 17th century under the unsystematic encroachment of English common law. Narrett carefully traces the transference of property at death among the Dutch, reveals the pro-cess by which English practices increasingly became the norm after 1664, and relates these developments to family custom to demonstrate how women lost impor-tant legal rights over time. His discussion of widows' rights, executor and guardian selection, intestacy law and practices, and the bequeathing of property by par-ents to their children not only illuminates the Colonial family, but also casts light on the early legal rights of women, and on Colonial New York history. This will become a standard work. Advanced undergraduate; graduate; faculty; professional.—*G. S. Rowe, University of Northern Colorado*

WS-1921   HQ835   91-5061 CIP
Smith, Merril D. **Breaking the bonds: marital discord in Pennsylvania, 1730-1830.** New York University, 1992 (c1991). 225p bibl index afp ISBN 0-8147-7934-4, $40.00

Smith's study treats a hundred-year period during which the old patriarchi-cal tradition of marriage as the ideal changed to an attitude of "companionate" marriage. These disparate views of marriage frequently resulted in new ways of dealing with marital strife. Smith's thesis is "that women and men were influ-enced both by the new ideals about marriage concerning how wives and husbands should behave, and by traditional patriarchal notions about men being the head of the household, especially in terms of earning and controlling the money to sup-port the family." Conflicts occurred when couples could not reconcile expecta-tions with reality. Smith argues that the result was a family life that was much more a "communicative world" in which neighbors, family, and friends dis-cussed and aided those involved in marital strife, rather than becoming more private, an opinion expressed by many historians. Although in some ways this is a new look at an important aspect of social and family history, the work also has several flaws. First, because of the paucity of sources, it appears at times to be little more than a recitation of one incident after another. Second, there is little concern for historical development, because the analysis jumps back and forth between the early 18th-, mid-19th-, and turn of the century. Upper-division undergraduates, graduate students, and faculty.—*G. W. Franz, Pennsylvania State University, Delaware County Campus*

◆ North America
19th Century

WS-1922 E449 93-42427 CIP
The Abolitionist sisterhood: women's political culture in ante-bellum America, ed. by Jean Fagan Yellin and John C. Van Horne. Cornell, 1994. 363p index afp ISBN 0-8014-2728-2, $42.50; ISBN 0-8014-8011-6 pbk, $16.95

This collection tackles the difficult concept of political culture, but nowhere defines it. The essays are organized into three major groups: the female anti-slavery societies of New York, Boston, and Philadelphia; the action of black women in creating a political culture allied with but separate from white women's; and the strategies and tactics of the abolitionist movement. The third section comes closest to defining political culture, for it examines power, influence, resource allocation, and participation—all political questions. All the essays are informative and insightful on women navigating many complex and conflicting pressures—domesticity, separate spheres, moral responsibility, the social/economic/political environment, and public action on racism and slavery—while building and operating female and mixed gender organizations to address those issues. The last two sections contain the most nuanced and interesting essays. Kathryn Kish Sklar's coda, which discusses the importance of class divisions in Britain in fostering a different political environment and culture for British women in the antislavery movement, is noteworthy as well as being the only cross-national paper. Upper-division undergraduates and up.—*V. P. Caruso, Henry Ford Community College*

WS-1923 E625 93-30098 CIP
Bacot, Ada W. **A Confederate nurse: the diary of Ada W. Bacot, 1860-1863,** ed. by Jean V. Berlin. South Carolina, 1994. 199p index ISBN 0-87249-970-7, $29.95

At the beginning of the Civil War Ada Bacot was a young, childless widow living on a plantation in South Carolina. Imbued with Confederate fervor and resenting the dependence of widowhood, she volunteered as a nurse at a hospital for South Carolinians in Charlottesville, Virginia. Her diary reports her efforts to secure approval for the trip and her adventures in Virginia from December 1861 until she returned home in January 1863. With an eye for readability, Berlin, an editor of Sherman's correspondence, has selected text (60 to 75 percent was cut) and annotated all references to people and places. The diary is quite good, providing insights on varied topics: relationships between nurses and doctors, race relations, the inner workings of southern hospitals, daily life in wartime, state rivalries within the Confederacy, and, above all, the ambivalent feelings of a woman striving to be both traditional and independent. A preface and epilogue supply additional information on Bacot; there is also an excellent index. Highly recommended for libraries collecting in women's history, the Civil War, and southern history. All levels.—*P. F. Field, Ohio University*

WS-1924 HQ1418 94-17649 CIP
Bartlett, Elizabeth Ann. **Liberty, equality, sorority: the origins and interpretation of American feminist thought: Frances Wright, Sarah Grimké, and Margaret Fuller.** Carlson Publishing, 1994. 184p (Scholarship in women's history: rediscovered and new, 1) bibl index afp ISBN 0-926019-62-7, $40.00

Bartlett has written an intellectual history of these three prominent 19th-century feminists' thought. She argues in the introductory chapter that these women's philosophies are not derived solely from male Enlightenment thinkers, but her analytical chapters on each thinker belie the generalization. Although each woman surely brought her own experience and perspective to her thought, each also was heavily influenced by English and Scottish Enlightenment thought, moral philosophy, and radical sectarianism (in the latter case, Sarah Grimke only). Because this dissertation was written in 1981, it has not benefited from the rich scholarly work done in the 1980s and '90s, particularly Charles Capper's biography of Margaret Fuller (CH, Apr'93) and Jean Fagan Yellin's study of antislavery feminists, *Women and Sisters* (CH, Nov'90). Recommended only for libraries with extensive collections in women's studies.—*J. Sochen, Northeastern Illinois University*

WS-1925 HQ1438 94-22983 CIP
Bartlett, Virginia K. **Keeping house: women's lives in western Pennsylvania, 1790-1850.** Historical Society of Western Pennsylvania/Pittsburgh, 1994. 178p bibl index afp ISBN 0-8229-3854-5, $39.95; ISBN 0-8229-5538-5 pbk, $19.95

Bartlett has written a lively and engaging study of everyday life in western Pennsylvania from 1790 to 1850. Do not be misled by the title; Bartlett casts a wide net in discussing all facets of domestic life in the region and their impact on both genders. She begins with migration into western Pennsylvania and early frontier households, then focuses on the development of the region and its impact on society through urbanization, improved purchasing power, and time devoted to religion and leisure. The net effect is a detailed portrait of life in an area experiencing dynamic change. Brimming with primary source evidence such as quotes, pictures, and recipes, this study should be of immense value to anyone who interprets the past at historic sites and museums. Aimed at a popular audience, the book relies on an introduction by Jack Warren to place the topic in historical perspective. Although Bartlett's generous use of primary source material is applauded, readers need to watch for the occasional authoritative quote from 20th-century works of fiction that can present a misleading and incorrect view of the past. All levels.—*J. M. Lewis, University of Arkansas at Little Rock*

WS-1926 HD6073 91-55077 CIP
Blewett, Mary H. **We will rise in our might: workingwomen's voices from nineteenth-century New England.** Cornell, 1991. 221p bibl index afp ISBN 0-8014-2246-9, $35.00; ISBN 0-8014-9537-7 pbk, $11.95

Blewett adds another title to her numerous contributions in New England labor and women's history with this documentary work based on selections from diaries, letters, and other materials written by the women themselves. The introduction describes preindustrial shoemaking (in which male and female shoemakers each had separate, distinct roles) and the shift from home and artisan's shop production to the new factories. The factory system set in motion many changes, including a reevaluation of the role and status of women in the social as well as the economic sense. Although women were as much industrial workers as men, they were still unequal and considered merely supplemental wage earners in a family-based economic unit, even though many women were the sole breadwinners. A reluctant revolution in prevailing attitudes toward women as co-industrial workers was in order, but was not easily achieved. As a result, women undertook an active role in 19th-century labor and reform movements to protect their interests as wage earners. Each step from exploited cottage workers to the continuing drive for recognition on a level equal to that of male industrial workers is described by the women themselves, which makes this enlightening and highly personal reading. All levels.—*M. J. Butler, University of Massachusetts—Dartmouth*

WS-1927 HQ1438 94-16767 CIP
Boatwright, Eleanor Miot. **Status of women in Georgia, 1783-1860.** Carlson Publishing, 1994. 184p (Scholarship in women's history, 2) bibl index afp ISBN 0-926019-63-5, $50.00

Boatwright's masters' thesis from the 1930s is one of a series of "rediscovered" works in women's history. Neglected until now, Eleanor Boatwright should have been linked with her better known peers, such as Julia Cherry Spruill and Guion G. Johnson. A fine biographical sketch of the author, which places the book firmly in the context of the field of women's history, introduces the monograph (and is arguably the most important part of the book). This study of women in antebellum Georgia certainly deserves recognition for being a pioneering work in women's history. Much of its material and methodologies, however, has been superseded by recent scholarship. Although the book is gracefully written and filled with insightful observations, Boatwright's views on race were not so advanced as her views on gender. Most likely to be of use to specialists.—*E. C. Green, Sweet Briar College*

WS-1928 CT274 95-2417 CIP
Bonfield, Lynn A. **Roxana's children: the biography of a nineteenth-century Vermont family,** by Lynn A. Bonfield and Mary C. Morrison. Massachusetts, 1996 (c1995). 267p bibl index afp ISBN 0-87023-972-4, $50.00; ISBN 0-87023-981-3 pbk, $19.95

Although centered around the lives of Roxana Brown Walbridge Watts (1802-62) and her descendants, this thoroughly researched, well-written biography of a farm family is as much a social history of village life in 19th-century Vermont, specifically, the town of Peacham. Two institutions—Peacham Congregational Church and Caledonia County Grammar School, otherwise known as Peacham Academy—shaped village life and the lives of the Walbridge-Watts family in particular. Married to Daniel Walbridge at 19, Roxana was left widowed with six children at 32. She subsequently married Lyman Watts, a widower with two young sons and bore three more children. In accounts that are unsentimental yet often poignant, Bonfield, an archivist, and Morrison, a writer and teacher, trace the lives of each of these children, as well as that of a grandson raised by Roxana. Three settled in the Midwest; three went to California during the gold rush; six eventually settled permanently in Vermont. Throughout her life, Roxana Walbridge Watts remained the central figure of this scattered clan. She had insisted that all her children—girls as well as boys—receive a formal education. It was this shared literacy that held the family together. Its engaging personal histories have been drawn from c.300 letters and 30 diaries preserved among its descendants. Bonfield and Morrison use these sources to discuss social change and movement in American life generally. Among other topics, the authors consider the westward migration, increasing rate of divorce, movement from rural agricultural labor to urban industrial work, and the opportunities open to versus the expectations of women during this period. Endnotes; bibliography of manuscript as well as printed sources. Highly recommended for all levels.—*H. M. MacLam, Choice*

WS-1929   F279   92-23308 CIP
Brevard, Keziah Goodwyn Hopkins. **A plantation mistress on the eve of the Civil War: the diary of Keziah Goodwyn Hopkins Brevard, 1860-1861,** ed. by John Hammond Moore. South Carolina, 1993. 137p index ISBN 0-87249-841-7, $21.95

Keziah Brevard, a childless widow in her late 50s, had her hands full running two large South Carolina plantations, a smaller farm, and a house in nearby Columbia. Nevertheless, she was a successful businesswoman and planter who managed to increase her land, slave holdings, and agricultural production during the 1850s. Her daily involvement with her overseer, slaves, and crops necessarily occupied her thoughts and many pages of her diary, but she did comment occasionally on the political rumblings in South Carolina (especially in early 1861), usually expressing foreboding about the coming storm. More comfortable on her farms than in the social whirl of Columbia, Brevard looked at the secession crisis from the periphery rather than from the center (unlike two more famous women diarists, Mary Chesnut and Emma Holmes). A genealogical chart identifying the many people mentioned in the diary, a map, photographs, and two appendixes complement the editor's excellent introduction, explanatory footnotes, and epilogue. Advanced undergraduate; graduate; faculty.—*R. G. Lowe, University of North Texas*

WS-1930   HQ1438   91-33851 CIP
Bynum, Victoria E. **Unruly women: the politics of social and sexual control in the old South.** North Carolina, 1992. 233p bibl index afp ISBN 0-8078-2016-4, $34.95; ISBN 0-8078-4361-X pbk, $12.95

Although women in the Old South could not vote for the region's lawmakers, Bynum (Southwest Texas) argues that their relationship to the state is still worth examining. Drawing on records of women who appeared in courts in three counties of the North Carolina Piedmont to seek redress against abuse or to answer charges of disorderly behavior, she anlyzes how courts attempted to enforce ideals of domesticity and how deviant women resisted. The study focuses on unmarried but sexually active free black and poor white women. Bynum carefully delineates the varied strands of race, class, kin group, and marital status that shaped a woman's place in the eyes of the patriarchal state. Bynum continues the study through the Civil War, demonstrating how the scarcities of wartime spread unruly behavior and focused women's attention on the protection of livelihood and family. A sophisticated but lively account of the lives of a subset of women whose experiences reflect importantly on the nature of southern society, the book is recommended for undergraduate and graduate collections in southern, women's, and Civil War history.—*P. F. Field, Ohio University*

WS-1931   F73   90-52582 CIP
Cabot, Elizabeth Rogers Mason. **More than common powers of per-**

ception: the diary of Elizabeth Rogers Mason Cabot,** ed. by P.A.M. Taylor. Beacon Press, 1991. 357p index ISBN 0-8070-5104-7, $25.00

Cabot's writings provide the reader with a panoramic view of 19th- and early 20th-century Boston from the perspective of a woman of wealth and social standing. Information about Cabot's values, thoughts, and relationships comes from the diary itself as well as from letters and other supporting material related to the Cabot family housed at the Massachusetts Historical Society and the Schlesinger Library at Radcliffe. Although the diary is filled with the raw data concerning the impact of Catholicism on Boston society, antebellum social reform activities, education for young women, marriage and the hazards of childbirth, and the bonds of female friendship, editor Taylor's analysis tends to treat these issues as peripheral to identifying Cabot's circle of family and friends, a major drawback of the volume. An introduction to each chapter and endnotes that made better use of modern critical studies would have vastly improved this work. Graduate level.—*A. M. Andrew, Beloit College*

WS-1932   HD6073   92-39119 CIP
Cameron, Ardis. **Radicals of the worst sort: laboring women in Lawrence, Massachusetts, 1860-1912.** Illinois, 1994 (c1993). 229p index afp ISBN 0-252-02013-8, $36.95

"Excellent," "enlightening," and "moving" describe this story of the women of Lawrence, Massachusetts, the driving force in the 1912 strike that shut down the mills of that city. Consigned to the edge of poverty by the notoriously low wages of the textile industry, ignored by the male-oriented labor movement, and faced with impending wage cuts, women workers acted to defend their precarious economic position. Despite opposition from male workers and unions, the laboring women of Lawrence walked out, and by using female neighborhood networks, successfully held their ground. Women, not men, played the dominant role in this strike. They attacked not only economic exploitation, but also gender discrimination in the mills. The shocking militance of these women ran counter to the prevailing belief that a woman's place was in the home, a belief that ignored the fact that women were as much a part of the American permanent industrial work force as men. Nevertheless, driven to desperation, Lawrence's working women, in "unladylike" fashion, struck the mills. What makes this particular book outstanding is that Cameron debunks the myth of women's domain as exclusively domestic and confronts the sad reality of the increasing number of deliberately underpaid female industrial workers. A significant addition to American labor, social, and cultural and women's studies. All levels.—*M. J. Butler, University of Massachusetts—Dartmouth*

WS-1933   JK1896   94-20242 CIP
Camhi, Jane Jerome. **Women against women: American anti-suffragism, 1880-1920.** Carlson Publishing, 1994. 328p (Scholarship in women's history, 4) bibl index afp ISBN 0-926019-65-1, $60.00

The 19th-century suffragists' most vociferous opponents were women. Camhi outlines antisuffragists' ideas about women's nature, theories of government, and women's moral influence. She argues that they believed they were defending the republic by opposing women's suffrage, but they were not "operating out of unreasonable fear and hysteria." Antisuffragists' organizational structure and tactics, their allies, their congressional battle, and the effect they had on the strategies of the suffragists, are each given chapters. Suffragists assumed the power behind oppostion groups came from men, when it actually orginated with women. Ida Tarbell is taken as a case study, though she apparently was not a typical antisuffragist. Camhi emphasizes that antisuffragists and the "anti" sentiment are increasingly unpopular and have been ignored by historians. She provides an honest view of their concerns and their efforts to keep families—and mothers (disinterested and political only in their moral influence)—at the center of American civilization. Camhi concludes by looking briefly at an "explanatory hypotheses" on feminism and antisuffrage thought. A good introduction to the dynamics of suffrage, particularly for students at undergraduate level.—*D. C. Samuels, SUNY at Stony Brook*

WS-1934   E605   91-2161 MARC
Dawson, Sarah Morgan. **The Civil War diary of Sarah Morgan,** ed. by Charles East. Georgia, 1991. 626p index afp ISBN 0-8203-1357-2, $34.95

An abbreviated version of Morgan's diary appeared in 1915 as *A Confederate*

Girl's Diary, edited by her son, Warrington Dawson. In 1960 the diary was reissued with a new introduction and notes by James I. Robertson. Now Charles East, former director of Louisiana State University Press, has published the diary's full text for the first time. Accompanying the new text (double the length of the old) are new notes and a 25-page essay commenting on the Morgan family and on the diary's significance. Morgan was the 19-year-old daughter of a recently deceased, wealthy attorney in Baton Rouge in 1862, when the diary begins. The diary has long been recognized as an excellent account of refugee life during the war. The new version adds little to the account of the war but much to an understanding of Morgan. A talented writer prone to philosophize, she loved to comment on the human interactions she observed. The diary is rich in accounts of social life, courtship, and the relations between soldiers and civilians. Morgan's attempts at adolescent self-definition return repeatedly to themes of gender and class. The book is especially important for undergraduate and graduate libraries collecting in southern, women's, and social history.—*P. F. Field, Ohio University*

WS-1935   F213   90-50640 CIP
The diary of Caroline Seabury, 1854-1863, ed. with introd. by Suzanne L. Bunkers. Wisconsin, 1991. 148p bibl index ISBN 0-299-12870-9, $30.00; ISBN 0-299-12874-1 pbk, $10.95

Caroline Seabury was a single Massachusetts woman who in 1854 went to Columbus, Mississippi, to teach at a girls' academy. Keeping a diary from the time she left New York, she wrote more about her travel impressions and the nursing for which she volunteered than about her pedagogical duties in Columbus. Caught in the Confederacy by the Civil War, Seabury found her position increasingly difficult. Finally, in 1863, she was able to slip through the lines in a trip that was filled with tension and discomfort, and that gave her an idea of the effects of the war on the Confederate poor. Informed, but no abolitionist, she appears to have been a conscientious reporter and a thoughtful observer, slow to make damning judgments. Her diary will be of interest to libraries with very strong holdings in women's and Civil War history, but it is too slight to be considered by most libraries serving chiefly undergraduates or the general public.—*A. Graebner, The College of St. Catherine*

WS-1936   E443   95-14154 CIP
Discovering the women in slavery: emancipating perspectives on the American past, ed. by Patricia Morton. Georgia, 1996. 320p bibl afp ISBN 0-8203-1756-X, $40.00; ISBN 0-8203-1757-8 pbk, $20.00

Recognizing that women's history and slave history cannot be separated, this collection of essays is part of the literature that attempts to insert women's experiences into the analysis of slavery. The primary aim of the essays is to end the historical silence about slave women, to deepen the understanding of the slave woman's everyday life of work and family. The most interesting contributions, however, focus not on the "usual" but on the diversity of the slave world. Not all slave women worked on large plantations; there are fascinating studies of the experiences of urban women, both slave and free. Other studies deal with the ways slave women showed their resistance and individuality through religion, disobedience, and even by the way they dressed. Specialists will note that some of the material, e.g., the analysis of the difficult relationships between white and black women, has been treated by other historians, but since the volume is clearly meant to appeal to a wide readership, those discussions are useful. For those who wish to know more about slave history, an excellent introduction analyzes the major studies of slavery published in the last 30 years. All levels.—*J. Wishnia, SUNY at Stony Brook*

WS-1937   KF299   92-38987 CIP
Drachman, Virginia G. **Women lawyers and the origins of professional identity in America: the letters of the Equity Club, 1887 to 1890.** Michigan, 1993. 290p index afp ISBN 0-472-10305-9, $49.50

The Equity Club, founded in Ann Arbor by University of Michigan law students in 1886, lasted only four years and after its founding never had another general meeting; its membership barely exceeded 30. But it is known to historians by the letters participants wrote for circulation within the club as a condition of membership. These letters afford a fine insight into the situation of early women lawyers. The letters are reproduced here, preceded by Drachman's helpful introduction and followed by biographical sketches of club members. The letters are a good

reminder of the wide variety of motivations, support networks, and experience of these pioneers. These women differed about whether they were women who happened to be lawyers or lawyers who happened to be women. They discussed strategies to build a successful practice, how to combine marriage and career, women's health, and appropriate professional dress—remarkably contemporary in topic if not content. At least some of the women were keenly aware of their sisters in medicine, and of the essential support their ambitions in law received from men. Throughout, the letters give tantalizing glimpses of independent personalities. Recommended for libraries with particular interest in the law, history of the professions, and women's history. Advanced undergraduates and above.—*A. Graebner, The College of St. Catherine*

WS-1938   HD6096   93-40054 CIP
Dublin, Thomas. **Transforming women's work: New England lives in the industrial revolution.** Cornell, 1994. 324p bibl index afp ISBN 0-8014-2844-0, $35.00

Dublin (SUNY-Binghamton) makes gender the focus for this study of industrialization in 19th-century New England. Rather than retread worn steps in industrial history by merely "adding" women, Dublin casts his contribution in a feminist mold, acknowledging influences by Gerda Lerner (*The Majority Finds Its Past*, CH, Mar'80) and Joan Wallach Scott (*Gender and the Politics of History*, 1988). Animating this detailed reinterpretation of urban industrial development is the alarming parallel that Dublin sees between women's roles in the wage-based economy then emerging and the backlash against women's gains now. Both eras provide examples of potential economic and social independence for women that instead becomes transformed into a "major constitutive element in the dependence of women within patriarchal families" in American history, thus undermining the very independence such economic transitions promise. Dublin provides a snapshot of this process by detailed comparisons of working women at mid-19th century with those of 1900. By century's end, they were "older, more likely to be married or widowed, and more integrated into a family wage economy" than their earlier counterparts. They were ethnically, but not racially, more diverse. Dublin notes that as early as 1860, "black women had even fewer [wage] opportunities than did immigrants," a pattern that intensified over time. He closes his study by asking whether we will permit women full equality in the workplace or will once again subvert the process. Advanced undergraduate; graduate; faculty.—*J. Kleiman, University of Wisconsin Center*

WS-1939   JK1911.O7   89-8824 CIP
Edwards, G. Thomas. **Sowing good seeds: the Northwest suffrage campaigns of Susan B. Anthony.** Oregon Historical Society, 1990. 355p bibl index afp ISBN 0-87595-192-9, $22.50

Susan B. Anthony made three trips to the Northwest. In 1871, she traveled 13,000 miles in three months, delivered 170 speeches, and set the stage for the coalition of the eastern-dominated national woman suffrage organizations and suffragists in the Northwest. Her trip in 1896 was of shorter duration, but equally important for the impetus she brought to the revived suffrage efforts of that decade and for the politically astute way she handled the growing dissatisfaction emerging around the tactics of Abigail Scott Duniway. In 1905, at the age of 85, Anthony was present at the annual meeting of the National American Woman Suffrage Association in Portland, Oregon, in the role of venerable leader. Edwards's use of secondary sources is rather limited, but he has combed the newspapers of the region during the years of Anthony's visits, especially the 1871 visit. Thus the debates surrounding the question of woman suffrage appear full blown in Edwards's account and a dissension within the movement—a dissension that seldom reached the public eye—is laid out clearly. A sound contribution to local suffrage history and to the telling of the full story of Susan B. Anthony. College, university, and public libraries.—*C. M. McGovern, University of Vermont*

WS-1940   HQ800   92-39514 CIP
An Evening when alone: four journals of single women in the South, 1827-67, ed. by Michael O'Brien. University Press of Virginia, 1993. 460p index ISBN 0-8139-1440-X, $35.00

O'Brien (Miami Univ.) has in this volume edited four journals of single women that chronologically span the middle period of US history. O'Brien, author of such well-received works as *The Idea of the American South, 1920-1941* (CH, Nov'79) and *Rethinking the South: Essays in Intellectual History* (1988), focuses on the writing of four disparate women: Elizabeth Ruffin, Jane Caroline North, Ann Lewis Hardeman, and an unnamed "Selma Plantation Diarist." An excellent 46-page substantive introduction places these women within the broader context of their time. All four journals are compelling and are likely to be unfamiliar to all but specialists in the field. This reviewer's favorite was the North account, written in an often breezy or chatty manner. Hardeman, however, clearly had the greatest trials and tribulations of the quartet. A devout women, she raised her sister's children while suffering from what was probably acute mastoiditis. Genealogical charts are most helpful; the ten illustrations are germane; the copious notes are a model of their type. Advanced undergraduates and above.—S. G. Weisner, Springfield Technical Community College

WS-1941 F499.B4 90-35046 CIP
Farm wife: a self-portrait, 1886-1896, ed. by Virginia E. McCormick. Iowa State, 1990. 243p index afp ISBN 0-8138-1212-7, $22.95

Literary excellence or coverage of dramatic historical events such as wars or pioneering normally justify the publication of diaries. In contrast, Margaret Gebby's journal, written when she was in her fifties and caring for a family of six, record in a plain, unemotional style the daily routines of farm life in northwestern Ohio a century ago. Editor McCormick, who has a varied background in cooperative extension and home economics, has enlivened the journal for modern readers by topically arranging Gebby's entries in 20 different categories, ranging from crops and housekeeping to transportation and excursions. McCormick offers extensive commentaries in the text and notes, which explain and expand on the frequently cryptic entries; her research in primary and secondary sources has been prodigious. The result is an enlarged understanding of a changing rural world and of women's roles in that world. For collections in Midwestern agriculture, Victoriana, and women's history. Upper-division undergraduates and above.—P. F. Field, Ohio University

WS-1942 E628 95-8896 CIP
Faust, Drew Gilpin. **Mothers of invention: women of the slaveholding South in the American Civil War.** North Carolina, 1996. 326p bibl index afp ISBN 0-8078-2255-8, $29.95

Long ignored in Civil War histories, women's experiences have increasingly become a focus of interest to historians. Drawing on the diaries, letters, memoirs, and creative works of the South's slaveholding class, Faust (Univ. of Pennsylvania) adds fresh and provocative insights and nuances to the Southern female experiences most comprehensively described in George C. Rable's *Civil Wars: Women and the Crisis of Southern Nationalism* (CH, Nov.'89). With clarity, imagination, and skill, she uses categories of race, gender, and class to explain in highly readable prose how her privileged subjects felt victimized by the war, how they responded to its challenges in areas as diverse as managing plantations and planning wardrobes, and above all, how their reconstructed selves still managed to incorporate assumptions based on class and race. Profoundly stimulating in its ability to impart larger meanings to the daily activities of the female half of the Southern master class in wartime, this book belongs in academic and public library collections in women's, Civil War, and Southern history. All levels.—P. F. Field, Ohio University

WS-1943 E445 92-39173 CIP
Fox, Tryphena Blanche Holder. **A northern woman in the plantation South: letters of Tryphena Blanche Holder Fox, 1856-1876,** ed. by Wilma King. South Carolina, 1993. 280p bibl index afp ISBN 0-87249-850-6, $34.95

An edited collection of 81 letters (out of a total of 187 in the Mississippi Department of Archives and History), written by Tryphena Holder Fox (1834-1912), who left her native Pittsfield, Massachusetts, in 1852, moved to the Southwest to become a plantation tutor, and remained in the South for the rest of her life. In 1856 she married a physician and moved to Louisiana. The letters in this volume, most addressed to her mother, recount the details of her life in an isolated settlement in Plaquemines Parish. Although the 20 years covered in Fox's correspondence (1856-76) encompassed tumultuous events in southern history, she has little to say about the Civil War or about the larger sectional crisis that preceded it. Nor are there reflections, unguarded or otherwise, about slavery. In fact, one surprising thing about Fox is how quickly she adopted the prejudices and attitudes toward

slaves and abolitionists held by native southerners. However, Fox's letters are exceptionally valuable for the light they shed on daily activities, family relationships, and childrearing. Because her family came from the middling social class, Fox's correspondence is a corrective to the social history more often written from the perspective of wealthier planters. The editing is quite helpful and not obtrusive. Illustrations and maps. Advanced undergraduate; graduate; faculty.—J. M. Matthews, Georgia State University

WS-1944 JK1898 91-31177 CIP
Frost, Elizabeth. **Women's suffrage in America: an eyewitness history,** by Elizabeth Frost and Kathryn Cullen-DuPont. Facts on File, 1992. 452p bibl index afp ISBN 0-8160-2309-3, $45.00

A useful and interesting compendium of primary source materials on the women's suffrage movement, 1800-1920. The 14 short essays and "Chronicles of Events" for each period frame well-chosen excerpts from letters, memoirs, speeches, press accounts, petitions, court decisions, and other contemporary sources. Contemporary illustrations accompany the text. Related topics such as abolition, women of color, temperance, women's war work, and the women's labor movement are also covered. Two useful appendixes provide the texts of the key documents and legislation, and biographies of the most important figures. The primary excerpts are drawn from a variety of published works, which are listed in a bibliography. The only question that might be raised about this admirably edited and absorbing volume is whether it adds significantly to the extensive primary source literature and anthologies already available on the suffrage movement. As an introduction to the subject and a convenient reference source for course assignments, it will be helpful to undergraduates; general readers will also find it accessible and illuminating.—M. L. Meldrum, SUNY at Stony Brook

WS-1945 F761 92-1206 CIP
George, Susanne K. **The adventures of the woman homesteader: the life and letters of Elinore Pruitt Stewart.** Nebraska, 1992. 218p bibl index afp ISBN 0-8032-2141-X, $25.00

Elinore Pruitt Stewart's *Letters of a Woman Homesteader* appeared in 1914 and was reprinted most recently in the 1980s for a market that has prized her engaging picture of a resiliant and self-reliant Great Plains woman. George has collected extant Stewart letters and manuscripts, interviewed Stewart's children, located individual published pieces, and combed the public record. In this volume she presents a large sampling of Stewart's writing—especially that not previously published—chiefly from the period between Stewart's brief public notice and her death in 1933. George introduces and connects the pieces with explanatory sections; the book's subtitle is accurate. One is better able to appreciate the quality of Stewart's optimism and courage given the details George provides about economic reverses and unrelenting hard work. Photographs and a helpful bibliography are included, as is an afterword with some shrewd comments about Stewart as a writer. The result is a modest, useful, and appealing companion to Stewart's *Letters*. General; undergraduate; graduate; faculty.—A. Graebner, The College of St. Catherine

WS-1946 HQ1418 89-24930 CIP
Ginzberg, Lori D. **Women and the work of benevolence: morality, politics, and class in the nineteenth-century United States.** Yale, 1990. 230p index afp ISBN 0-300-04704-5, $25.00

Ginzberg (Pennsylvania State University) undertakes to explain the significance of the changes that occurred in the ideology and practice of formal benevolence by women during the 19th century. Critically examining a multitude of private writings by benevolent ladies, scores of biographies, and the growing number of secondary works on particular causes and organizations, Ginzberg constructs a highly sophisticated argument explaining how gender and class considerations interacted to shape benevolent activity. Ginzberg observes that the ideology of female difference and moral superiority to men, while it contained the potential to undermine male authority and redefine middle-class values, actually masked behavior by women that suggested shared values with men and indicated both were often pursuing class interests. Eventually ideology mirrored reality, and reform became linked to social efficiency rather than tenderhearted concern for the unfortunate. The book is extensively footnoted but lacks a bibliography. Some may question Ginzberg's categories of analysis and her eastern, urban orientation, but this is a significant scholarly work, appropriate for upper-division undergraduates and above. Essential for institutions with strong women's studies programs.—*P. F. Field, Ohio University*

WS-1947   PS2018   94-20240 CIP
Grant, Mary H. **Private woman, public person: an account of the life of Julia Ward Howe from 1819 to 1868.** Carlson Publishing, 1994. 268p (Scholarship in women's history, 5) bibl index afp ISBN 0-926019-66-X, $55.00

In scholarship and scope this book reads like what it is, a doctoral dissertation that pounds home a thesis with the enthusiasm of a young scholar but lacks the contemplative finesse of further revision. Grant presents the reader with a portrait of Julia Ward Howe, an intellectual and a gifted female writer who, similar to other geniuses, had difficulty following the 19th-century's dictates for women. In particular, Howe failed to embody successfully "the cult of true womanhood," mainly the roles of wife and mother, sometimes to dysfunctional degrees. With a husband who wanted a totally devoted wife and who kept her subordinate to him through pregnancy, motherhood, frequent moves, and threats of divorce, Howe was an unhappy and frequently depressed prisoner in her own home. When she found the conservative cause of suffrage (unlike the more radical cause of Elizabeth Cady Stanton and Susan B. Anthony) in 1868, all her troubles miraculously disappeared, according to Grant. Despite the success of the "Battle Hymn of the Republic" and Howe's work (with her husband) for the cause of abolition, suffrage in essence finally made the "private woman" a "public person." All levels.—*J. M. Lewis, University of Arkansas at Little Rock*

WS-1948   E628   92-17204 CIP
Hall, Richard. **Patriots in disguise: women warriors of the Civil War.** Paragon House, 1993. 224p bibl index ISBN 1-55778-438-8, $21.95

As indicated in the title, Hall's patriots are women. He begins with a discussion of the roles women could play in the Civil War without violating societal norms: nurse, spy, sutler (supplier), and daughter of the regiment. He then focuses on women who violated societal norms by disguising themselves as men to serve as soldiers and presents a variety of anecdotes about these women. There are detailed narratives and careful analyses of two women combatants. Sara Emma Edmonds, who enlisted as Franklin Thompson in the 2nd Michigan Volunteers and served for three years, receives detailed examination. So does Loreta Janeta Velaquez, who claimed to have served as Lt. Harry T. Buford with the Confederacy. The "Mountain Charley" legend is also related and examined. In appendixes B and C Hall discusses his sources and his efforts to verify Edmonds's and Velaquaz's claims. Hall's work reflects persistent digging for records and memoirs, and careful comparison and collation of information to substantiate the women's stories. No more hunting in obscure places for information on women as combatants in the Civil War. The information is here. General; community college; undergraduate.—*V. P. Caruso, formerly, Nazareth College*

WS-1949   E449   92-40310 CIP
Hansen, Debra Gold. **Strained sisterhood: gender and class in the Boston Female Anti-Slavery Society.** Massachusetts, 1993. 231p bibl index afp ISBN 0-87023-848-5, $30.00

The first thorough study of the influential Boston Female Anti-Slavery Society (BFASS). Although short-lived (1833-40), the organization provided crucial funding for the antislavery movement, distributed scores of antislavery tracts and books, and offered a rare, racially integrated forum for some of the most dynamic female abolitionists in New England. Hansen places the history of the BFASS in the context of Boston's changing social and economic order, and finds that the growing divisions so evident in Boston's social structure were duplicated by the BFASS's membership. Although the breakup of the society traced the path followed by the male-dominated American and Massachusetts Anti-Slavery Societies, the author details how the divisions in the BFASS membership distinguished it from other similar societies. Most important, *Strained Sisterhood* recounts the divergent definitions of womanhood that helped drive the BFASS apart and serves as a useful corrective to those studies that promote the idea of "women's solidarity based upon gender alone." Advanced undergraduates and above.—*D. Yacovone, Massachusetts Historical Society*

WS-1950   F782   93-19432 Orig
Harris, Katherine. **Long vistas: women and families on Colorado homesteads.** University Press of Colorado, 1993. 216p bibl index ISBN 0-87081-288-2, $24.95

Harris (Univ. of Colorado, Boulder) challenges interpretations of western historians, whom she labels "mythmakers" and "realists." Rather than continue the debate on the success/failure interpretations of homesteading in Colorado, she presents stories of women's experiences in late 19th and early 20th century Colorado. Her work supplements and enriches various existing interpretations, such as John Faragher's *Women and Men on the Overland Trail* (CH, May'80), J.R. Jeffrey's *Frontier Women* (1979), Glenda Riley's *The Female Frontier* (CH, Jan'89), and S.L. Myres's *Westering Women and the Frontier Experience, 1800-1915* (CH, May'83). Harris appropriately links her work to that of Paula Petrik (*No Step Backward*, CH, Jul'88) and Sarah Deutsch (*No Separate Refuge*, CH, May'88). She, too, focuses on a specific, small group of women: those who filed homestead claims in Colorado for themselves. A fine writer, Harris does well in limiting statistical data, making this book a pleasure to read. Recommended especially for those interested in western or women's history. General, undergraduate.—*N. J. Hervey, Luther College*

WS-1951   F44   93-19716 CIP
Heffernan, Nancy Coffey. **Sisters of fortune: being the true story of how three motherless sisters saved their home in New England and raised their younger brother while their father went fortune hunting in the California Gold Rush,** by Nancy Coffey Heffernan and Ann Page Stecker. University Press of New England, 1993. 289p index afp ISBN 0-87451-650-1, $40.00; ISBN 0-87451-651-X pbk, $15.95

Gathered here is correspondence between Lizzie, Annie, and Charlotte Wilson of Keene, New Hampshire, from 1847 to 1864 and their father James Wilson, Jr., who, for most of this period, sought his fortune in California. The 300 letters in this volume, culled from the manuscript collection of the Wilson Papers lodged in the New Hampshire Historical Society, create a personal narrative of the women's lives that borders on autobiography. The correspondence will be valuable to historians and students for the historical light it sheds on private emotions, family concerns, women's issues, child rearing, and public events. To a remarkable degree the Wilson family's concerns—debts, private ambitions, education, religious practices, treatment of servants, friendship, marriage, childbirth, and illness—intersected with major public events like the Gold Rush, the slavery issue, and the Civil War. By adding a scholarly narrative between letters and sections, in the fashion of *The Diary of Martha Ballard, 1785-1812,* ed. by Robert and Cynthia McCausland (1992), the editors have constructed an exceptionally unified and illuminating collection of primary documents. Recommended for all university and college libraries.—*E. W. Carp, Pacific Lutheran University*

WS-1952   HQ146   92-6558 CIP
Hill, Marilynn Wood. **Their sisters' keepers: prostitution in New York City, 1830-1870.** California, 1993. 434p bibl index afp ISBN 0-520-07834-9, $35.00

With this work, Hill, currently visiting scholar at Harvard-Radcliffe, adds to a growing literature on the interaction of class and gender inequalities that created urban prostitution in the 19th century. Her study complements Christine Stansell's *City of Women: Sex and Class in New York, 1789-1860* (CH, Apr'87) by including the higher echelons of prostitutes rather than focusing exclusively on streetwalkers. Hill's research is impressive. Compiling lists of prostitutes from police records, brothel guides, reform publications, and newspapers, she has created profiles of these women from census, tax, and House of Refuge records. She has even analyzed letters by prostitutes published in the lurid penny press. Systematically demolishing the common stereotypes of prostitutes, Hill shows that some "fallen" women still had opportunites, had supportive friends, could use the law to protect themselves, and were an integral part of the urban community. A balanced, carefully qualified analysis on a controversial topic, this work should be acquired by libraries collecting in urban history and women's studies. Advanced undergraduate; graduate; faculty.—*P. F. Field, Ohio University*

WS-1953 HQ1236 94-44083 CIP
Hoffert, Sylvia D. **When hens crow: the women's rights movement in antebellum America.** Indiana, 1995. 153p index afp ISBN 0-253-32880-2, $25.00

Using speeches, pamphlets, newspaper reports, editorials, and personal papers, Hoffert discusses how ideology, language, and strategies of early women's rights advocates influenced a new political culture that resisted, though included, women as participants. The result is a testimony to the control that men traditionally had over public discourse and, by extension, over public life. The book provides a highly readable survey that is compact and comprehensible in its treatment of the early women's rights movement in the US. Hoffert describes the impact of republicanism, natural rights, utilitarianism, and the Scottish Common Sense School, to show how early activists moved beyond the limits these philosphies placed on them, e.g., the idea of Republican Motherhood bestowed the privilege of training future republican leaders after giving birth to them, while denying women opportunities to participate in the republican process. The book also shows the work of the penny press in spreading the demands of women's rights advocates to a wide audience, establishing the competence of women to contribute to public discourse and life. The text reveals the power of rhetoric, and explains practical decisions made in the face of strident opposition, while telling a good story. Undergraduates; graduate students.—*M. Klatte, Eastern Kentucky University*

WS-1954 LD7062 93-39509 CIP
Horowitz, Helen Lefkowitz. **The power and passion of M. Carey Thomas.** Knopf, 1994. 526p index ISBN 0-394-57227-0, $30.00

Horowitz has used current methodologies in biographical writing to illuminate an all but forgotten important figure in the history of US higher education. After serving briefly as dean at Bryn Mawr, M. Carey Thomas became president of the college (1894 to 1922). She was among the first women to graduate from Cornell University (1877) and one of the first American women to obtain a doctorate (University of Zurich). Thomas's stalwart conviction that women should/could receive precisely the same kind of higher education that men obtained at elite private institutions, in order to perform the same useful roles in society, made her unique in the lexicon of leaders for women's higher education in the late 19th and early 20th century. Horowitz's book helps scholars and students understand why the mature Thomas was untouched by the ambiguities of this issue experienced by so many of her peers in women's colleges. Horowitz weaves a fascinating tale of WASP culture in the northeast and of this complex women's place in that society. As with her earlier works on higher education (*Alma Mater*, CH, Feb'85, and *Campus Life*, CH, Dec'87) She has made a solid contribution with this biography. General readers, undergraduates, and graduate students.—*A. J. Russ, Wells College*

WS-1955 F666 91-41361 CIP
Kellie, Luna. **A prairie populist: the memoirs of Luna Kellie,** ed. by Jane Taylor Nelsen. Iowa, 1992. 188p bibl afp ISBN 0-87745-368-3, $22.95; ISBN 0-87745-369-1 pbk, $9.95

A very interesting portrait of the life of a farm woman and her family in Nebraska from the 1880s to the turn of the century. In both a personal and political memoir, Kellie describes life in a sod house with a growing family (she had 11 children). Further, through Kellie's detailed description of the unpredictable weather conditions, the unfair railroad rates, the high cost of borrowing, and the never-ending cycle of debt faced by farmers, the late 20th century reader recaptures the precarious life on the frontier. Kellie was both typical and unusual for her time and place. Many farm women shared her experiences, but she was among the few who became politically active in the Farmers Alliance and the Populist Party. She served from 1894 to 1901 as editor and publisher of the *Prairie Home*, a newspaper dedicated to Alliance politics. Particularly in the 1890s, she worked for women's suffrage and a middle-of-the-road position for the Populist party, a position in which the Populists stayed independent of both dominant parties. However, by 1901, her efforts seemed to bear no fruit and she returned to private life, cultivating her chickens and garden, and raising her large family. Advanced undergraduate; graduate; faculty; general.—*J. Sochen, Northeastern Illinois University*

WS-1956 HQ1413 92-6159 CIP
Kerr, Andrea Moore. **Lucy Stone: speaking out for equality.** Rutgers, 1993 (c1992). 301p bibl index ISBN 0-8135-1859-8, $43.00; ISBN 0-8135-1860-1 pbk, $15.95

Lucy Stone (1818-93) has not deserved the degree of historical anonymity that has befallen her. Kerr's lively biography will help reestablish Stone as one of the three most important feminists of the 19th century. Kerr provides the most complete record to date of Stone's career in the woman's rights movement, and gives special attention to her tireless efforts to advance feminism after the Civil War. Equally important, Kerr offers the most thorough analysis of Stone's personal life, especially her strained and unorthodox marriage to Henry Blackwell, that is ever likely to be written. Unfortunately, the author does not analyze Stone's ideas and largely ignores her antislavery career. Kerr's failure to digest the large body of antislavery historiography has led to several glaring errors of fact and apparent inconsistences in interpretation. General; undergraduate; graduate; faculty.—*D. Yacovone, Massachusetts Historical Society*

WS-1957 HQ800 92-12216 CIP
Kitch, Sally L. **This strange society of women: reading the letters and lives of the Woman's Commonwealth.** Ohio State, 1993. 391p bibl index afp ISBN 0-8142-0579-8, $39.50

Founded in Belton, Texas, in 1867, the Woman's Commonwealth was an intentional community of 20-25 women, mostly mothers and daughters, devoted, on religious grounds, to celibacy. They replaced economic dependence on men with collective operation of their own businesses. Seeking to still intergenerational conflict, the Commonwealth removed to Washington, DC, in 1898. In 1983 Kitch (Ohio State Univ.) obtained the group's correspondence when the last survivor died. Mostly concentrated in the period of the move to Washington, the letters form the basis for Kitch's analysis of the history of the group, the relationships among its members, and the use of language by the women to define their own unique perspectives. Although the Commonwealth touched relatively few women and was atypical of most women's experiences in the late 19th century, Kitch believes it is valuable for understanding how individual women have used ideology and unusual social arrangements to control and better their lives. A final chapter assesses the feminist character of the movement. Well written and drawing from a rich feminist perspective, this work is an essential choice for women's studies collections. Advanced undergraduate; graduate; faculty.—*P. F. Field, Ohio University*

WS-1958 E601 90-25762 CIP
Lee, Elizabeth Blair. **Wartime Washington: the Civil War letters of Elizabeth Blair Lee,** ed. by Virginia Jeans Laas. Illinois, 1991. 552p bibl index afp ISBN 0-252-01802-8, $39.95

Laas (Missouri Southern State College) has done an outstanding job of editing the Civil War letters of Elizabeth Blair Lee. Laas has judiciously selected 368 letters, roughly one-third of the total available, for inclusion in this handsomely produced volume. The "treasure" was first discovered by Lee's descendants in a hayloft of a barn on family property and was later deposited at the Princeton University library. Copious and meaty notes enhance the value for scholar and general reader alike. Lee came from a politically active family. Her father held a seat in Andrew Jackson's "kitchen cabinet." She was an "attractive, slender and vivacious young woman." Lee promised to write to her husband, naval officer Samuel Philips Lee, every day. Her letters abound with keen insights on the people and politics of wartime Washington. Publisher's claims in the jacket blurb that the book is the "equivalent of the celebrated diaries of Mary Boykin Chestnut" are exaggerated, but this effort nevertheless stands in its own right as a very important work that most libraries will want to acquire. All levels.—*S. G. Weisner, Springfield Technical Community College*

WS-1959 F292 94-17033 CIP
Leslie, Kent Anderson. **Woman of color, daughter of privilege: Amanda America Dickson, 1849-1893.** Georgia, 1995. 225p bibl index afp ISBN 0-8203-1688-1, $29.95

Born a slave, Amanda Dickson became extremely wealthy when she inherited the estate of her white father in 1885. Dickson was brought up in his household, where her mother was housekeeper. Her childhood foreshadowed a lifelong crossing of racial boundaries. She first married a white man, but remarried a person of color; some of her children presented themselves as white, others as black. Leslie sees Dickson's search for personal identity as "bounded by her sense of class solidarity with her father, ... her gender role as a lady, and her racial definition as a person to whom racial categories did not apply." Lacking letters or memoirs written by Dickson, Leslie constructs her story from documents of the white Dicksons and from an oral history maintained by the African American Dicksons, fleshed out with sociohistorical analysis of 19th-century Hancock County and Augusta, Georgia, the two places where Amanda Dickson lived. Leslie overcomes the limitations of his sources to provide new insights on the intersection of race, class, and gender in the postbellum South, through the life of this remarkable woman. Upper-division undergraduates and above.—*T. S. Whitman, Mount St. Mary's College and Seminary*

WS-1960 E415 92-5871 CIP
The Letters of Jessie Benton Frémont, ed. by Pamela Herr and Mary Lee Spence. Illinois, 1993. 595p bibl index afp ISBN 0-252-01942-3, $39.95

Daughter of Thomas Hart Benton, senator from Missouri, Jessie Benton Frémont (1824-1902) married explorer, soldier, politician, and entrepreneur John C. Frémont at 17. Accustomed to moving in elite circles, she used her formidable abilities agressively in behalf of her husband's career, most notably in his western reports, his presidential bid in 1856, and his Missouri command in 1861. She often worked to the outer edges of what convention allowed a 19th-century wife, but she never openly scorned that convention. Of her 800 letters extant, this thick volume reproduces 271. The letters are presented in a handsome format, enhanced by meticulous scholarly apparatus and 50 pages of admirable introductions, virtually a biography in themselves. Frémont's letters are often lively, but they are usually not particularly revealing about intimate aspects of her life, nor about whatever private reflections she had regarding her position as a gifted, ambitious woman married to a difficult man who never gained the success they sought. Libraries with strong interest in western Americana will want this book as a matter of course. Advanced undergraduate; graduate; faculty.—*A. Graebner, The College of St. Catherine*

WS-1961 F865 89-78223 CIP
Levy, JoAnn. **They saw the elephant: women in the California gold rush.** Archon Books, 1990. 265p bibl index afp ISBN 0-208-02273-2, $25.00

The phrase "seeing the elephant" symbolized for '49 gold rushers the exotic, the mythical, the once-in-a-lifetime adventure, unequaled anywhere else but in the journey to the promised land of fortune: California. Most western myths promoted by writers, filmmakers, and other artists generally depict an exclusively male gold rush. Levy's book debunks that myth. Here a variety of women travel, work, and write their way across the pages of western migrant history. Some crossed plains and mountains with husbands and families in prairie schooners; others crossed the Panamanian Isthmus on their way to California on their own. Some women worked alongside men at the gold mines; others set up and kept homes, raised children, and ran boarding houses. As with other frontiers, the gold mining West allowed women a variety of working options: acting, teaching, shopkeeping, and preaching. Charley Parkhurst drove a stagecoach for Wells, Fargo and Company. On her death, it was discovered that "Charley" had disguised herself as a man so she could work to make her dream of buying a cattle ranch come true. Such were the women of the American West. For college and public libraries.—*E. Kuhlman, University of Montana*

WS-1962 E312 91-4797 CIP
Lewis, Nelly Custis. **George Washington's beautiful Nelly: the letters of Eleanor Parke Custis Lewis to Elizabeth Bordley Gibson, 1794-1851,** ed. by Patricia Brady. South Carolina, 1991. 287p bibl index ISBN 0-87249-754-2, $24.95

The adopted daughter of George and Martha Washington (her father was Martha's son by Martha's first marriage), Eleanor Parke Custis Lewis maintained an extensive correspondence with her Philadelphia friend, Elizabeth Bordley Gibson, from her days as a Virginia belle in post-Revolutionary America to shortly before her death in 1851. Throughout her life, Lewis moved in elite circles; her letters contain brief references to hundreds of prominent political and diplo-

matic figures, planters, merchants, military officers, lawyers, physicians, and their wives and families. Mostly, however, Lewis's exchanges chronicle her preoccupation with friends and relatives, especially her children and grandchildren. Although it offers some insights into the concerns and experiences of an upper-class southern woman before the Civil War, the collection makes for excruciatingly dull reading. Not a "must" purchase for any library, though libraries with strong southern history sections may wish to acquire it.—*J. K. Somerville, SUNY College at Geneseo*

WS-1963 HQ1438x 89-64484 Orig
Lindgren, H. Elaine. **Land in her own name: women as homesteaders in North Dakota.** North Dakota Institute for Regional Studies, 1991. 300p index ISBN 0-911042-39-3, $25.00

Lindgren has gathered documents on more than 300 women to tell the remarkable story of those who claimed land on the Great Plains in the late 19th and early 20th centuries. Modifications of the 1862 Homestead Act and relaxed government requirements encouraged nontraditional settlers, including single women, to claim land. This changed policy coincided with increased immigration from Scandinavia, Southern and Eastern Europe, and the Middle East. The homesteaders represented a group of adventurous women from a wide range of backgrounds and experiences. Many of the women in Lindgren's study were immigrants or daughters of immigrants; a few were African American. Most combined their homesteading with paying jobs, "working out" as teachers, nurses, domestics, and seamstresses to support their land. Lindgren has provided a marvelously detailed appendix with information on the women's ethnicity, their age at the time of the initial land transaction, their marital status, and the location of their claim. As an added bonus, the book is chock-full of illustrations—photographs of the homesteaders and their "shacks." For students of women's history and Western history, and for general readers as well.—*J. Raftery, California State University, Chico*

WS-1964 F213 94-42013 CIP
Louisa S. McCord: political and social essays, ed. by Richard C. Lounsbury. University Press of Virginia, 1995. 510p bibl index ISBN 0-8139-1570-8, $45.00

Daughter of South Carolina leader Langdon Cheves, close friend of Dixie diarist Mary Boykin Chesnut, and conservative Confederate essayist, Louisa Sarah McCord earned, through her political and social essays and other writings, a place among the leading lights of the antebellum southern intelligentsia. This worthy collection of her writings on political economy, the role of women in society, the racial and cultural context of slavery, and the politics of southern particularism displays a sparkling wit and linguistic agility far superior to that of John C. Calhoun, George Fitzhugh, and Edmund Ruffin, but it also reveals the same crabbed intellectual vision that led the region inexorably toward Appomattox. A literary legacy forgotten until recently, McCord's work should be assured with this exemplary volume—and with a forthcoming companion volume of her memoirs, correspondence, poetry, and drama—an honored place in the pantheon of a brilliant, if doomed, circle of antebellum Dixie reactionary thinkers. Recommended for college and university libraries, and for all public libraries in the South.—*R. A. Fischer, University of Minnesota—Duluth*

WS-1965 JK1911 93-846 CIP
McBride, Genevieve G. **On Wisconsin women: working for their rights from settlement to suffrage.** Wisconsin, 1994 (c1993). 352p bibl index ISBN 0-299-14000-8, $43.00; ISBN 0-299-14004-0 pbk, $19.95

Beginning with statehood in 1848, several important events in Wisconsin's history occurred simultaneously with significant moments in the movement for female emancipation. McBride situates her analysis of Wisconsin-specific activities in the context of larger, nationwide crusades for temperance and suffrage. The work, however, is most successful when the narrative centers on Wisconsin. McBride's discussion of the role several key women played in publishing and editing local newspapers underscores the significance of the press for an increasingly literate populace. This local focus, however, is also one of the study's greatest weaknesses. The book is a lengthy local history that at times assaults the reader with a barrage of personal and place names that become a confusing litany for those not well versed in Wisconsin history, politics, and geography. Even with that caveat, however, the study is recommended for libraries supporting collections in women's studies and US social history. Upper-division undergraduates and above.—*E. Broidy, University of California, Irvine*

WS-1966 F273 94-16869 CIP
McCurry, Stephanie. **Masters of small worlds: yeoman households, gender relations, and the political culture of the antebellum South Carolina Low Country.** Oxford, 1995. 320p index afp ISBN 0-19-507236-7, $39.95

McCurry's study of ten low-country antebellum South Carolina political districts, stretching from the Atlantic Ocean to the fall line, examines the yeoman and planter classes of that geographic area and explains the complex nature of their relationship while recognizing the influence of an enslaved African American majority on both white groups. McCurry analyzes the role of evangelical Protestantism as early 19th century revivals created a closer relation between white yeoman and planters while simultaneously influencing the slaves. She also explains the impact of gender, however subtle. Chapter 5, "Household of Faith," introduces the familial concept that set forth teachings and practices that reinforced subservient roles for white females, and increased legitimacy for the power of male yeomen and planters. When the Nullification Crisis occurred, the ideas promulgated in South Carolina by evangelicalism and popular politics simply served to manipulate yeoman political power to gain a movement for "southern Christian conservatism," which culminated in South Carolina's secession by 1860. Tables; appendix; photograph. Upper-division undergraduates and above.—*J. D. Born Jr., Wichita State University*

WS-1967 KF223 90-23045 CIP
McLaurin, Melton A. **Celia, a slave.** Georgia, 1991. 148p bibl index afp ISBN 0-8203-1352-1, $19.95

Although McLaurin respects the historiographical trend toward "agency" studies of slavery, which emphasize slaves' abilities to affect their treatment in processes of active dialogue with their masters (e.g., Eugene D. Genovese's *Roll, Jordan, Roll*, CH, Nov'75, and Charles W. Joyner's *Down by the Riverside*, CH, Feb'85), but he does not see it in operation often, and especially not in this account of black female powerlessness. The Missouri courts of 1855 style her only "Celia, a Slave." Owned by Robert Newsome in Callaway County, Missouri, Celia was repeatedly raped by her widowed master, who bought her in 1850 when she was 14, expressly for concubinage. She bore two children, one surely and the other likely Newsome's. Sometime in 1855 she fell in love with George, another of Newsome's slaves, who insisted that Celia break things off with the master. Celia attempted to do so by asking help of Newsome's white daughters, but this ploy failed. During another attack by Newsome, she killed her master. In a trial in which a legal team led by respected local statesman and minister John Jameson argued that any woman had the right to defend herself against rape, Jameson's team tried to extend the "any woman" of Missouri law to include slave women. They failed and Celia was hung, but the events and the trial involve complexities well worth examination and discussion. Informed by theory, the book is not thesis-ridden and it may be used easily by scholars of any perspective. All levels.—*J. Roper, Emory and Henry College*

WS-1968 SF274 94-12093 CIP
McMurry, Sally. **Transforming rural life: dairying families and agricultural change, 1820-1885.** Johns Hopkins, 1995. 291p index afp ISBN 0-8018-4889-X, $39.95

Most readers know of the work of Gilbert Fite and other agricultural historians, but few may be aware of more recent studies with divergent themes, such as Mary Neth's *Preserving the Family Farm: Women, Community, and the Foundations of Agribusiness in the Midwest, 1900-1940* (CH, Jul'95). McMurry (Pennsylvania State Univ.), author of *Families and Farmhouses in Nineteenth-Century America* (CH, Feb'89), focuses on the movement from farm-made cheese in Oneida County, New York, to the development of a post-Civil War industry that brought vast social changes affecting rural women and family life. "The intent here," McMurry states, "is to reconstruct the cultural history of agriculture ...." She achieves this purpose and weaves local history into broader themes. *Transforming Rural America* is a good read for those with interests in agricultural, economic, social, cultural, family, and women's history. Notes; essay sources. Upper-division undergraduates and above.—*P. D. Travis, Texas Woman's University*

WS-1969 BX9789 92-20920 CIP
Mother's first-born daughters: early Shaker writings on women and religion, ed. by Jean M. Humez. Indiana, 1993. bibl index afp ISBN 0-253-32870-5, $39.95; ISBN 0-253-20744-4 pbk, $17.50

Growing from remarks on quaint celibacy and plain aesthetic, studies of the Shakers have become steadily more complex and sophisticated. In this volume of primary sources, Humez makes readily available writings by Shaker women through the 1840s. She supports the documents with extensive notes and long interpretive essays. Humez's aim is to demonstrate women's contributions to Shaker religion during what she terms the foundational stage of the movement. She includes women's recollections of Mother Ann Lee, correspondence of Lucy Wright, letters from missionary sisters in the Midwest, and women's ecstatic outpourings in the revivalism of the 1830s and 1840s. Humez judiciously finds much in Shakerism that is feminine—but not necessarily feminist. She is especially helpful in pinpointing paradox and contradiction regarding Shaker women, their status and roles. This is a useful collection for those with special interest in American religion, feminist theology, and communitarianism. Thanks in large part to Humez's introductions, the volume is certainly accessible to upper-division undergraduates, but few are likely to find it essential.—*A. Graebner, The College of St. Catherine*

WS-1970 F391 90-85476 CIP
Myers, Lois E. **Letters by lamplight: a woman's view of everyday life in South Texas, 1873-1883.** Baylor University, 1991. 222p bibl index afp ISBN 0-918954-53-3, $23.95

Myers, assistant director of the Baylor Institute for Oral History, presents a monograph illustrated by fragments of correspondence, not a collection of letters. She has skillfully woven a tale that offers historical background of the era, family history, and a vivid picture of the daily chores and struggles of a young couple on the Texas frontier after the Civil War. The detail provided is not unlike that in the Laura Ingalls Wilder stories, although this is an adult work. As it proceeds, Myers paraphrases more frequently. Some letter fragments are not dated, leaving the reader somewhat confused about what is actually included in which letters. Racial prejudice, financial realities, and significant health problems, all common to the time and place, are clearly portrayed. This book differs considerably from other works based on letters from frontier women, e.g., C.J. Foote's *Women of the New Mexico Frontier, 1846-1912* (CH, Oct'90), E. Cory's *Bachelor Bess* (CH, Jul'91), M.J. Mayer's *Klondike Women* (CH, May'90) and A.K. Grierson's *The Colonel's Lady on the Frontier* (CH, Jun'90) but is similar to E.C. Fisk's *Lizzie* (CH, Nov'89) in which most of the writing is also that of the author. Recommended for Texas libraries of all types and for collections that emphasize frontier and/or women's history.—*N. J. Hervey, Luther College*

WS-1971 HQ1438 90-41814 CIP
Osterud, Nancy Grey. **Bonds of community: the lives of farm women in nineteenth-century New York.** Cornell, 1991. 303p bibl index afp ISBN 0-8014-2510-7, $42.50; ISBN 0-8014-9798-1 pbk, $14.95

Osterud's monograph is about the meaning of gender for women of rural New York State after 1850. It is based on diaries, letters, and interviews supplemented by church and census records. Specific exploration is on the balance and interaction between men and women at home, at work, in the community. The Nanticoke Valley of Broome County is rich in primary resources and public records. Osterud concludes that gender divided womens' lives into male and female spheres, yet integrated them too, so that they had both male and female support systems. Single and aged women did not escape restrictions imposed by gender but neither were they isolated. Women worked alongside men in the fields yet retained distinct roles. Men's records were based on credits and debits, leading to the conclusion that women's work lacked value. Yet, women were not at risk in this capitalistic economy. Social organizations were usually integrated as well. In Nanticoke Valley, women provided alternatives to male dominance. This is a fine study that complements and supplements many works, including Elizabeth Bott's *Family and Social Network* (1957), Mary Ryan's *Cradle of the Middle Class* (1981), C.D. Johnson's *Islands of Holiness* (CH, Mar'90), and Jon Gjerde's *From Peasants to Farmers* (CH, Oct'85). Highly recommended for all academic libraries.—*N. J. Hervey, Luther College*

WS-1972   BX8695   91-20686 CIP

Romney, Catharine Cottam. **Letters of Catharine Cottam Romney, plural wife,** ed. by Jennifer Moulton Hansen. Illinois, 1992. 317p bibl index afp ISBN 0-252-01868-0, $32.50

This collection of more than 170 letters written between 1873 and 1917 provides insight into the life of a plural wife, mother, and colonist. The second of five wives of polygamist Miles Romney, Catharine Cottam married Miles Romney when she was 18. Written from Utah, eastern Arizona, and northern Mexico, her letters document the ways in which one woman dealt with religion, economic struggle, birth, death, loneliness, motherhood, and Mormon "sisterhood." In addition to serving as a corrective to the Turner notion that life on the frontier was beneficial for women as well as for men, the book has value for the new historiography of emotions because it clearly demonstrates that modern sensiblities about marriage, monogamy, sexuality, and love are cultural constructs limited by time and place. As with many collections of primary source material, this volume's value for an undergraduate library would probably be limted to historical studies. However, it offers a fascinating story whose readership could and should be broader.—*A. J. Russ, Wells College*

WS-1973   E164   92-5076 CIP

The selected letters of Mary Moody Emerson, ed. by Nancy Craig Simmons. Georgia, 1993. 622p index afp ISBN 0-8203-1462-5, $65.00

In this lengthy volume, Simmons has collected 334 of Emerson's 900 extant (and mostly unpublished) letters. Known as the aunt who greatly influenced Ralph Waldo Emerson, she was a gifted writer and intellect in her own right. Having chosen not to marry, she created an independent and (for women of her time) unconventional existence for herself. Emerson lacked extensive formal training, but gave herself a rigorous education in the humanities and became a writer, using the genres open to early 19th century women—letters and diaries. The selected letters were written from 1793 to 1862. They are organized chronologically in six parts, an arrangement that accents the growth of her maturity, her intellect, and her letter-writing skills. The letters describe events in her daily life, her reactions to her readings, the intellectual grapplings of her correspondents, and her own theological and philosophical ideas. Simmons has made these challenging letters accessible through meticulous editing and illuminating introductions to each part of the collection. Her footnotes are conveniently located at the bottom of each letter. They identify people, events, quotations, and book to which Emerson refers in the letters. Advanced undergraduate; graduate; faculty.—*B. P. Smaby, Clarion University of Pennsylvania*

WS-1974   HQ1413   94-29913 CIP

Sherr, Lynn. **Failure is impossible: Susan B. Anthony in her own words.** Times Books/Random House, 1995. 382p bibl index ISBN 0-8129-2430-4, $23.00

Sherr uses her considerable skills as an ABC correspondent to recapture for modern audiences the qualities that made Susan B. Anthony the most cherished symbol of women's quest for equality. With a reporter's eye for the passages that most reveal Anthony's character and thought, she has sifted through the microfilm edition of Anthony's papers, scrapbooks, and reminiscences to select for this documentary history items as short as a single line or as long as several pages. The resulting work is divided into 27 topical chapters, ranging from those that reveal Anthony's causes (slavery, temperance, women's rights) to those that show her personality (attitudes toward money, her friends, the media, travel). Reactions to Anthony by reporters and political friends and foes dot the text, as do photographs and anecdotes. Sherr introduces each chapter with a page or two placing the subject in context. Most documentary collections are aimed at researchers and include complete texts, scholarly commentary, and numerous annotations. This should not be confused with such works, although readers introduced to Anthony by this engaging book may soon be hooked on women's history. Recommended for undergraduate and public libraries.—*P. F. Field, Ohio University*

WS-1975   E668   93-18626 CIP

Silber, Nina. **The romance of reunion: northerners and the South, 1865-1900.** North Carolina, 1993. 257p bibl index afp ISBN 0-8078-2116-0, $34.95

Silber uses the image of romance—"gendered," heterosexual, urban, and mid-

dle-class romance—between *strong man* and *good girl* to apprehend developing northern attitudes toward the defeated South from the end of the Civil War to the end of the century. Once, northerners use gendered images to insult southern enemies by ascribing "feminine" qualities of weakness to a feared Confederate rival. By the 1890s, however, as northern industrial society matured and consequently developed huge problems of dislocation and no little dispute about proper roles for men and women, the continuities of gender roles in the South become attractive, even enviable. In many stories and journalists' reports the theme appears of the strong Yankee wedding the dependent southern belle who *knows her place* and supports her man in his place. Thus, in the language of reconciliation crucial to economic integration of the postbellum nation and vital to the ideological reunification in the Spanish-American War of 1898, northern choice of metaphors for praise revealed a chauvinism as profound, if different, as the older choice of metaphors. Moreover, "[o]ne of the most noteworthy features of the reunion process was the transformation in white northerners' racial outlook .... This new orientation [of southern gender roles] paved the way for northern acceptance of some of the most virulent forms of racism which American society had ever produced." Only Paul Buck's classic *Road to Reunion* (1937) previously examined northern images of reconciliation, and his concerns are hardly with gender. Silber's book is a study with broadest implications and is accessible at all levels of study.—*J. Roper, Emory and Henry College*

WS-1976   F596   89-22549 CIP

So much to be done: women settlers on the mining and ranching frontier, ed. by Ruth B. Moynihan, Susan Armitage, and Christiane Fischer Dichamp. Nebraska, 1990. 325p bibl afp ISBN 0-8032-3134-2, $32.50; ISBN 0-8032-8165-X, $12.95

Thanks to the detective work of many historians, including the three editors of this collection, scholars now realize how essential women and families were and how diverse were their experiences and reactions in the opening and settling of the American West. This carefully chosen collection graphically illustrates the active roles of women. The three sections—California and Nevada, 1849-80; High Plains and Rocky Mountains, 1870-90; Southwestern Desert, 1863-1900—highlight the differences within each subregion and over time. The editors provide a general introduction—one for each section and one for each letter/diary entry. Such a balanced collection offers rich primary source materials to students of the American West and women's history. Common themes emerge, but individuality is also preserved. An important addition to the literature.—*D. Campbell, United States Military Academy*

WS-1977   HQ1458   91-45750 Orig

Southern women and their families in the 19th century, papers and diaries. Series A, Holdings of the Southern Historical Collection, University of North Carolina, Chapel Hill [microform], consulting editor, Anne Firor Scott. University Publications of America, 1992 (c1991). 3 pts. 49 microfilm reels (pt.1: 25 reels; pt.2: 18 reels; pt.3: 6 reels. Each pt. with guide.) ISBN 1-55655-294-7 pt.1, $2,570.00; ISBN 1-55655-295-5 pt.2, $1,855.00; ISBN 1-55655-296-3 pt.3, $620.00

A collection of primary materials generated by 19th-century southern women is now available in microfilm. These documents will enhance scholarship and widen research opportunities on southern culture and gender issues. There are three parts to this collection. Parts 1 and 2 focus on the diaries and correspondence written by members of southern families. Part 3 consists of the documents of several families living primarily in Louisiana and Mississippi. All of the materials reflect the cultural and social norms of southern elites before, during, and after the Civil War. Inventories accompanying all three parts provide biographical and other information about each correspondent. An introductory essay by Scott illuminates the broader historic, social, and cultural context of the collection. Scott focuses on the importance of social appearances and propriety in southern society, and the intrusion of reality these women experienced as revealed by the documents: marital infidelity, unruly children, and the loneliness and burden of managing plantations for absentee husbands. Many of the reels contain letters and diary entries that are difficult to read because of faded and illegible writing. The editors assure the viewer that every attempt was made to produce a high-quality reproduction. Filming for the collection conforms to standards for the filming of archival records. The set is of tremendous value to southern and women's historians. All levels.—*E. Kuhlman, Washington State University*

WS-1978 HD6073 91-11900 MARC
Turbin, Carole. **Working women of collar city: gender, class, and community in Troy, New York, 1864-86.** Illinois, 1992. 231p bibl index afp ISBN 0-252-01836-2, $39.95

In 1864, a group of largely Irish shirt-collar laundresses formed the first US women's labor organization in Troy, New York. Collar workers remained active in the labor movement for the next 20 years. In this work Turbin, a sociologist at Occidental College, tries to explain why this early example of women's labor activism occurred. Painstakingly analyzing the few surviving statements of collar workers for clues about their lives and ideologies, and comparing Troy's female labor force to their counterparts in other industries and communities, Turbin describes how community, gender, class, ethnicity, and religion shaped female workers' strategies for their lives. Turbin decries prior analyses for oversimplifying working women's actions by contrasting their behavior too rigidly to men's. In her view, women were often more skilled and committed to a trade than they were credited as being; concern for families did not make women necessarily more conservative. Turbin's study is cogent, thought-provoking, well-written, and an obvious choice for any undergraduate or graduate library collecting in women's or labor history.—*P. F. Field, Ohio University*

WS-1979 HQ1413 94-49519 CIP
Underhill, Lois Beachy. **The woman who ran for president: the many lives of Victoria Woodhull.** Bridge Works, 1995. 347p bibl index ISBN 1-882593-10-3, $23.50

Notorious in the US of the 1860s and '70s, Victoria Woodhull spoke out agressively on many causes, especially free love and women's rights. Her newspaper was the first in the US to reprint *The Communist Manifesto*, and the first to publish details of Henry Ward Beecher's philandering. She infuriated her enemies and alarmed her friends. Then, perhaps secretly subsidized (to uncomplicate Commodore Vanderbilt's estate), she left for England in 1877, where she married a wealthy banker and died as a respectable figure in 1927. Underhill's book puts all this in readable form. The author has used archival material, most productively for Woodhull's years in England, though documentation is minimal. Pointing out that Elizabeth Stanton and Susan B. Anthony overshadowed Woodhull, Underhill seeks to reestablish her. This book is unlikely to do so, however, largely because the author spends so little time assessing Woodhull's influence. Though Underhill has filled in additional background, it is still unclear that Woodhull was much more than an opportunistic, charismatic adventuress. Essential only for comprehensive women's history collections.—*A. Graebner, College of St. Catherine*

WS-1980 94-76283 Orig
Wakeman, Sarah Rosetta. **An uncommon soldier: the Civil War letters of Sarah Rosetta Wakeman, alias Private Lyons Wakeman, 153rd Regiment, New York State Volunteers,** ed. by Lauren Cook Burgess. Minerva Center, 1994. 110p bibl index ISBN 0-9634895-1-8, $25.00

Among the several million people who served in Civil War armies and navies were several hundred women disguising themselves as men. Embarrassed family members often concealed the women's service, preventing their unique stories from being told. Now Burgess, a university administrator and Civil War reenactor, has edited the letters of Sarah Rosetta Wakeman, an independent-minded, teenage farm girl from New York who joined the army for patriotic and financial reasons. Remaining undetected, even after her death from chronic diarrhea in 1864, she led the life of a typical soldier, experiencing combat several times in Banks's Red River campaign. Several dozen letters remain. Written to her family and quite revealing of her emotional state and reactions to her situation, they have been carefully edited and annotated. Burgess also supplies maps, photographs, a history of Wakeman's regiment, a family genealogy, and, most significantly, an introduction summarizing what is currently known about female Civil War soldiers. Important, because of the unique subject matter, for all libraries collecting in women's history, military history, and the Civil War.—*P. F. Field, Ohio University*

WS-1981 HQ1906 90-26748 CIP
Wedell, Marsha. **Elite women and the reform impulse in Memphis, 1875-1915.** Tennessee, 1991. 191p bibl index afp ISBN 0-87049-704-9, $21.50

By choosing to examine in some detail the stirrings of social responsibility

among upper-class women in Memphis, Wedell (Memphis State University) has illuminated both the promise and limitation of the women's movement in the American South. Building on the work of Anne Firor Scott and Jean Friedman, Wedell organizes her study around the activities of several important and hitherto neglected figures in the urban history of the South. She documents their activities in organizing a women's network and giving it expression in the Memphis Women's Christian Association, the Memphis WCTU, and the Nineteenth Century Club. Noting that these Gilded Age and Progressive Era women were too accepting of the "ideology of liberal capitalism" and of "a male-dominated hierarchy," Wedell credits them with creating "a public record and presence" and an "autonomous realm," which, though limited in scope, provided a modest step toward more independence for southern women. Clearly written and well organized, Wedell's study is an important contribution to southern urban history. Upper-division undergraduates and above.—*J. P. Felt, University of Vermont*

WS-1982 HQ1439 94-36540 CIP
Whites, Lee Ann. **The Civil War as a crisis in gender: Augusta, Georgia, 1860-1890.** Georgia, 1995. 277p index afp ISBN 0-8203-1714-4, $35.00

Whites (Univ. of Missouri, Columbia) focuses on the role of women in Augusta, Georgia, during the Civil War and Reconstruction. Her work, like *Divided Houses*, ed. by Catherine Clinton and Nina Silber (1992), Celine Garcia's *Celine: Remembering Louisiana* (CH, Sep'88), and Catherine Clinton's *Tara Revisited* (CH, Oct'95), has as its primary base journals and letters of planter-class women. Whites links women's lives during the Civil War with those of women during WW I and WW II, shifting from home to community and work, from dependency to independence, and back again when these wars were over. After the Civil War, men were restored to positions of power and status in their homes, a substitute for the economic and political power previously held. Whites's work joins a massive volume of research documenting the contributions and sacrifices of Confederate women. Her far-ranging conclusions represent fine writing of the feminist school. However, she neglects the significant role played by women in a plantation economy. Her interpretations invite additional, comparative research. Recommended for academic institutions, specifically those with collections in the Civil War, Southern history, and women's history. Upper-division undergraduates and above.—*N. J. Hervey, Luther College*

WS-1983 HV5232 94-43878 CIP
Willard, Frances E. **Writing out my heart: selections from the journal of Frances E. Willard, 1855-96,** ed. by Carolyn De Swarte Gifford. Illinois, 1995. 474p bibl index afp ISBN 0-252-02139-8, $29.95

Frances Willard (1839-1898), central figure in the Women's Christian Temperance Union, kept an extensive journal, rediscovered in 1982. Gifford has sampled judiciously and annotated extensively; she connects sections with helpful introductions, and includes photographs. Although Willard did not keep her journal during most of her WCTU years, Gifford's book is far more than chinking at the edges. It provides a remarkable window on late-19th-century women's lives. Willard struggled to make her family's Methodism her own; she was also devastated by early deaths in her family. She fell deeply in love with Mary Bannister (among other women), but had to repress those feelings when Mary became her sister-in-law. Willard became engaged to a man she subsequently decided she admired but did not love; she apparently gave up another man because of the possessive love of her closest woman companion at the time. Willard searched, sometimes despairingly, for a satisfactory career. Through it all she wrote with remarkable candor and detail to produce a document that, enriched by Gifford's editing, will be invaluable to both faculty and students.—*A. Graebner, College of St. Catherine*

WS-1984 E445 94-5968 CIP
Wood, Betty. **Women's work, men's work: the informal slave economies of lowcountry Georgia.** Georgia, 1995. 247p index afp ISBN 0-8203-1667-9, $45.00

Wood is an able scholar whose study *Slavery in Colonial Georgia, 1730-1775* (CH, Oct'84) made a valuable contribution that is now extended with this thoughtful examination of slave life. Covering the period 1750-1830, Wood makes a compelling case for strength of quasi-independent economies wherein slaves exacted rights as producers and consumers in their own market. She illustrates the decidedly different roles of slave men and women in this informal economic structure, but stresses that it was the welfare of the slave family that primarily motivated people in bondage to work in this semiautonomous economy. Some recent scholars have argued that, because it blunted their will to resist, such limited economic empowerment served only to keep slaves more firmly under their masters' authority. Wood recognizes this interpretation, but places greater emphasis on how such modest economic empowerment strengthened slave families and provided African Americans with a degree of human dignity in coping with the rigors of bondage. This work is carefully researched and fully documented, and includes 44 pages of notes from primary and secondary accounts. Highly recommended for university and public libraries with specialized collections on the pre-Civil War South and slavery. Upper-division undergraduates and above.—*R. Detweiler, California State University, Dominguez Hills*

WS-1985   E449   91-24795 CIP
Yee, Shirley J. **Black women abolitionists: a study in activism, 1828-1860.** Tennessee, 1992. 204p bibl index afp ISBN 0-87049-735-9, $34.95; ISBN 0-87049-736-7 pbk, $17.95

Black women, North and South, helped to destroy the "peculiar institution," especially those who gambled their lives as operatives in the Underground Railroad—of whom only Harriet Tubman has attained adequate recognition. The story of their deeds is integral to knowledge of the antislavery impulse; unfortunately, that story remains to be told. Instead, Yee has fashioned a narrative burdened by self-limits and by the reigning vogue in deconstructionist feminist ideology. Focusing primarily on exemplars of free African American Victorian society up North, active in antislavery work when more pressing demands of family and status permitted, Yee has concentrated on a group that collectively freed fewer slaves than did Tubman on a single odyssey into the Chesapeake. Even this story, interesting and peripherally relevant in its own right, is smothered by theoretical homage to the deconstructionist triad of race, class, and gender, exemplified by such essays as "Black Women and the Cult of True Womanhood." Thus, the volume contributes to feminist historiography, but provides little more than an appetizer for students of the African American struggle for liberation. Advanced undergraduate; graduate.—*R. A. Fischer, University of Minnesota—Duluth*

◆ North America
20th Century

WS-1986   F547   94-4176 CIP
Adams, Jane. **The transformation of rural life: southern Illinois, 1890-1990.** North Carolina, 1994. 321p bibl index afp ISBN 0-8078-2168-3, $49.95; ISBN 0-8078-4479-9 pbk, $19.95

"Little Egypt," as Southern Illinois has been known since 1816, is the regional context of a series of seven farm case studies woven together by Adams to illustrate how farming and farm life has changed over the past century. Drawing information from a broad range of primary sources—especially extended personal interviews with older residents—Adams, an anthropologist, creates a detailed profile of life on Union County farms. Women's roles in supporting the agricultural enterprise is a central theme, as are changes in rural social life after WW II. Although the farm wife's responsibilities differed from one ethnic group to another—the region's settlers included Yankees, Germans, and Upland South Scotch-Irish—most farm women not only participated in field work, but also engaged in several small-scale activities to supplement family income and diet. Most women raised chickens for eggs and meat, raised and milked cows, produced vegetables and fruits, and made family clothing. These activities not only supplied much of the family diet, but surplus commodities sold in town stores and markets provided household income. The book includes period photographs, graphs, and diagrams. Recommended for college and university libraries.—*K. B. Raitz, University of Kentucky*

WS-1987   E807   95-23500 CIP
Black, Allida M. **Casting her own shadow: Eleanor Roosevelt and the shaping of postwar liberalism.** Columbia, 1996. 298p bibl index afp ISBN 0-231-10404-9, $29.95

Eleanor Roosevelt spent the years before her husband's presidency overcoming her innate shyness and feelings of inferiority, and learning how to use her abilities to support social programs in which she developed interests. She continued to expand her influence during her years as first lady, sometimes prodding her husband to take actions that she thought were necessary but that he deemed politically unwise. Black's book focuses on the post-White House years of her life, when she became an imposing presence in American politics in her own right. In many ways, Eleanor Roosevelt became the conscience of the Democratic party and the country, pleading for fair wages and diversity, working against segregation, racial violence, McCarthyism, and reactionary forces, and also convincing timid Democrats to join in her crusades. Black studied Roosevelt from the perspective of political history, and not pure biography. The resulting blend is a useful portrait of a woman who became a successful liberal power broker. Using numerous primary and secondary sources, Black carefully recounts the intricacies of postwar liberalism without losing sight of Mrs. Roosevelt's enormous contributions to the development of that creed. Upper-division undergraduates and above.—*J. P. Sanson, Louisiana State University at Alexandria*

WS-1988   NX180   93-485 CIP
Blair, Karen J. **The torchbearers: women and their amateur arts associations in America, 1890-1930.** Indiana, 1994. 259p index afp ISBN 0-253-31192-6, $29.95

Building on her *The Clubwoman as Feminist* (CH, Feb'81), Blair focuses on Progressive Era women's organized support for the arts. Stressing that 19th-century Americans allocated culture to the woman's sphere, Blair notes that women were expected to be appreciative consumers, but not professionals. Blair offers a typology of club development and devotes separate chapters to the support that women's organizations gave to music, the visual arts, pageantry, and theater. Her final chapter treats the emphasis on edifices widespread in the 1920s, a development, the author asserts with too little evidence, that helped bring the high years of women's clubs to a close. Using little-known sources, Blair cites a number of remarkable women who played an important part in raising awareness of the arts. An appreciative but not uncritical historian of this movement, Blair describes class and racial bias, and recognizes a variety of motivations and varying levels of feminism. She keeps her attention resolutely on her club women, rarely venturing into the more explicit feminism of the period or into perplexing—and rewarding—questions about the specific shape the women's amateur groups gave to middle-class cultural life. With its valuable bibliography, this book should be an essential purchase for most libraries. All levels.—*A. Graebner, The College of St. Catherine*

WS-1989   HQ767   92-39693 CIP
Blanchard, Dallas A. **Religious violence and abortion: the Gideon Project,** by Dallas A. Blanchard and Terry J. Prewitt. University Press of Florida, 1993. 347p bibl index afp ISBN 0-8130-1193-0, $39.95; ISBN 0-8130-1194-9 pbk, $16.95

Blanchard and Prewitt provide what may be one of the most important case studies in the abortion stalemate. Using a variety of data sources, the book highlights the controversy surrounding the bombing of three abortion clinics in Pensacola, Florida, in 1984, code-named, by those involved, "The Gideon Project." The book begins with an examination of the national context of abortion in the early 1980s as well as the local conditions that fostered conflict over this issue in Pensacola. Following this, detailed transcripts of the arrest and subsequent trial of the "Pensacola Four" underscores the religious pragmatism that rationalized the destruction of "property" as a means to ending abortion. The final section demonstrates the relevance of this research, particularly for understanding the theological and sociological factors that promoted the use of violence within the most radicalized wing of the "anti-abortion" movement. These factors include biblical and historical justification for religious violence, at least for radical fundamentalists; the perceived, though tacit, support of the Reagan administration for abortion-related violence; and the apparent failure of the anti-abortion movement to effect significant change. The book is well written and documented. All levels.—*C. M. Hand, Lenoir-Rhyne College*

WS-1990   HS2330   90-11287 CIP
Blee, Kathleen M. **Women of the Klan: racism and gender in the 1920s.** California, 1991. 228p index afp ISBN 0-520-07263-4, $24.95

In this sociological study Blee (University of Kentucky) uses the concept of gender to analyze the role of women in the Ku Klux Klan of the 1920s. Examining women and morality as symbols, the paths by which women entered the Klan, and the activities of the half-million strong women's Klan, Blee concludes that women were vital to the work of the Klan, particularly in sustaining campaigns of ostracism and economic boycotts against minorities. Blee shows the compatibility of the Klan's racist message with the seemingly progressive notion of women's rights, and effectively demonstrates how the Klan developed its mass appeal. The book is solidly based in newspaper and archival research and includes analysis of interviews with former Klanswomen and their victims. The strong Indiana Klan made up the core of the original research; other areas are less well covered. Intelligent and well written, this work is important for undergraduate and graduate collections in women's studies and right-wing political movements.—*P. F. Field, Ohio University*

WS-1991   F645   95-5742 CIP
Calof, Rachel. **Rachel Calof's story: Jewish homesteader on the Northern Plains,** ed. by J. Sanford Rikoon. Indiana, 1995. 158p index afp ISBN 0-253-32942-6, $20.00; ISBN 0-253-20986-2 pbk, $12.95

In clear and compelling language, Calof tells her story of hardship and perseverance, from her childhood in Russia to her struggles as a Jewish homesteader in North Dakota. Calof's memoir is frank and sometimes shocking, recording abuse at the hands of her stepmother in Russia and by her in-laws in America. Her account of her homesteading years poignantly conveys the perils—both psychological and physical—of the isolated northern farmer. Two essays frame the memoir and place Calof's story in historical context. First, J. Sanford Rikoon, editor of the volume, locates Calof's experience among the various efforts to settle Jews as farmers in America's heartland. Although Rikoon fails to assess the significance of these settlers' origins in shaping their decision to farm, his coverage of Jewish farming activity is thorough and well documented. Next, Elizabeth Jameson uses Calof to challenge popular stereotypes of the West, emphasizing recent revisions of Western history that recognize the roles played by women and immigrants. Taken together, the memoir, an epilogue by Calof's son, and the essays provide a vivid account and the necessary context for understanding a Jewish farm experience in the US. General readers, undergraduates.—*E. M. Eisenberg, Willamette University*

WS-1992   HQ1426   90-43457 CIP
Chafe, William H. **The paradox of change: American women in the 20th century.** Oxford, 1991. 256p bibl index afp ISBN 0-19-504418-5, $22.95

The *Paradox of Change* is an interesting insider's book; that is, it is written for those who are knowledgeable about women's history and who have read Chafe's *The American Woman* (CH, Feb'73). The latest book is a thoughtful reevaluation of the same themes and issues first faced in the earlier study. Chafe has benefited from the rich scholarship that has been produced in the field in the past 20 years. His argument has become more nuanced as a result. For example, he originally argued that the large numbers of women in the work force insured value change in the near future, but reality has required him to alter that judgment. Job segregation for the majority of women workers has become the norm. Similarly, the diversity in ideology, class, and race among women has made the forward movement of women as a single mass unattainable. Much chastened, Chafe foresees an immediate future of some gains and some losses, a very human conclusion to a synthesis of women's history in this century. Upper-division undergraduates and above.—*J. Sochen, Northeastern Illinois University*

WS-1993   HD6072   94-14415 CIP
Clark-Lewis, Elizabeth. **Living in, living out: African American domestics in Washington, D.C., 1910-1940.** Smithsonian Institution, 1995 (c1994). 242p index afp ISBN 1-56098-362-0, $26.00

Clark-Lewis has done an assiduous job of gathering the memories of African American women who served the homes of whites in Washington, DC in the early

20th century. Her characterizations and their recorded remembrances reveal the credibility and dignity of these strong women. Recounted through extensive quotations, the story reveals the nature of the migration from the South, the symbolism of the hated uniforms, the pride of moving from living in to working out, the preparation for doing good housework, the special role of the laundress as cultural facilitator, and the work ethic of proud women who had to be servile. This basic study will be a foundation for broader subsequent interpretations of urban labor, women, and African American history. Recommended reading for scholars of these fields of history and for householders who have employed house workers or domestic servants, Clark-Lewis's book offers eloquent insight into those who cleaned "no crystal stair."—*J. H. Smith, Wake Forest University*

WS-1994   D769   91-16921 CIP
Dear boys: World War II letters from a woman back home, ed. by Judy Barrett Litoff and David C. Smith. University Press of Mississippi, 1991. 253p index afp ISBN 0-87805-521-5, $37.50; ISBN 0-87805-540-1 pbk, $15.95

While doing work for their other two splendid books based on the homefront in WW II—*Miss You* (1990) and *Since You Went Away* (CH, Mar'92)—historians Litoff and Smith discovered a gem. *Dear Boys* contains edited excerpts from the bimonthly wartime column published in *The Bolivar (Mississippi) Commercial*. The strengths of these columns resides in Mrs. Keith Frazier Somerville's exuberant style—her interest in every person and everything, her eye for colorful detail, her ear for the telling anecdote. Surprisingly and refreshingly, she made a systematic effort to include women, African Americans, and ethnics in her coverage, in a fair-minded and always enthusiastic manner. For Somerville, WW II was an all-American, community-wide project. High morale was essential to this goal, and judging by the countless letters of gratitude written back to her, Somerville's columns did an excellent job of upholding morale. *Dear Boys* is greatly enhanced by a fascinating and informative biographical essay by historian Martha Swain on Somerville, a well-bred onetime school teacher. The book includes extensive editorial footnotes. *Dear Boys* will trigger memories and add context for the general public who remembers small-town rural America during the war and will prove invaluable to students and scholars who wish to study the war's impact on everyday citizens.—*D. Campbell, Indiana University*

WS-1995   VB324   92-39963 CIP
Ebbert, Jean. **Crossed currents: Navy women from WWI to Tailhook,** by Jean Ebbert and Marie-Beth Hall. Brassey's (US), 1993. 321p bibl index ISBN 0-02-881022-8, $25.00

Ebbert and Hall's work fills a substantial void in women's military history by providing an authoritative and comprehensive study of Navy women since WW I. Until now, chroniclers of women's naval history could consult only Jeanne Holm's general work, *Women in the Military: An Unfinished Revolution* (CH, Jun'83) or several autobiographies, including Joy Hancock's *Lady in the Navy* (1972) and LouAnne Johnson's *Making Waves* (1986). Through direct experience (Ebbert is a former officer) and indirect knowledge (both authors are married to retired Navy captains) combined with archival research and oral histories, the authors thoroughly explore the dimensions of women's naval service. They highlight the expansion of women's positions and address current issues, including Tailhook's aftermath and women's future in combat roles. Although sometimes short on analysis, the book succeeds as a record of women's struggle for and eventual acceptance in America's Navy. Military and women's historians will find this monograph invaluable. Advanced undergraduates and above.—*J. A. Luckett, United States Military Academy*

WS-1996   JK1896   91-2073 CIP
Ford, Linda G. **Iron-jawed angels: the suffrage militancy of the National Woman's Party, 1912-1920.** University Press of America, 1991. 299p bibl index ISBN 0-8191-8205-2, $47.50; ISBN 0-8191-8206-0 pbk, $24.50

Ford's book provides knowledgeable readers with illuminating information about the 168 suffrage women who chose jail rather than comply with the law that forbade their disruptive suffrage demonstrations. This study, which began as a doctoral dissertation, is an example of the second generation of scholarship in women's history. It studies a period and an organization that has already received a lot of attention, but it adds more detail and a different interpretation to the subject. Although the National Woman's Party, and Alice Paul, its leader, have generally been viewed as the more militant wing of the suffrage movement, Ford takes this view a step further and suggests that their militancy was based on nonviolent principles of protest and that these suffragists were also feminists who explored the deeper meanings of feminism through their militant actions. Recommended for libraries with extensive collections in women's history.—*J. Sochen, Northeastern Illinois University*

WS-1997   HQ1419   91-16843 CIP
Gender, class, race, and reform in the Progressive Era, ed. by Noralee Frankel and Nancy S. Dye. University Press of Kentucky, 1991. 202p index afp ISBN 0-8131-1763-1, $24.00

What role did women play in the Progressive Era of the 1890s-1920s? How did various social classes and ethnic groups regard values and reform measures, i.e., "protective legislation," prohibiting child labor and minimum wage? The 12 studies in this collection address these questions. Although they vary in style and level of analysis, common themes emerge. Ethnicity and class divide women, although they share a common desire for reform. In Tampa, Anglo women side with cigar manufacturers; Latinas, working with male kin, strike for better wages. African American women struggle for increased school monies and antilynching laws. One of the best articles concerns the Children's Bureau, which established a beachhead for women in the federal government and successfully advanced child welfare. Fighting child labor, however, destroyed the coalition between working and middle class. Most essays are interesting and well written, but a chapter summarizing the advances and limitations of this era would have provided a more integrated volume. Overall, however, the collection is recommended for upper-division undergraduates and above.—*S. D. Borchert, Lake Erie College*

WS-1998   HD6073.C62   90-1557 CIP
Glenn, Susan A. **Daughters of the Shtetl: life and labor in the immigrant generation.** Cornell, 1990. 312p index afp ISBN 0-8014-1966-2, $29.95

A sophisticated study of the working lives of young Jewish women who, between about 1880 and WW I, left Eastern Europe for the US and found work in the needle trades of New York and other cities. Glenn's analysis is satisfyingly nuanced and multilayered: ethnicity, religion, class, gender, technology, and geography all are gathered in a complex pattern. The author is especially thought-provoking in connecting the experience and outlook of these women with their East European roots and with developments in the US garment industry. In doing so she contests the static and culturally isolated image of the shtetl; she also argues vigorously with scholars such as Leslie Tentler (*Wage-Earning Women*, CH, Jan'80) who downplay industrial employment as force for or expression of change in women's lives. Glenn takes particular pains to consider why young women who assumed their wage work was only temporary were nevertheless such vigorous participants in efforts to improve working conditions. This exceptionally fine book should be automatically purchased by libraries with strengths in women's history, labor history, or ethnic studies, and should be considered by other libraries as well.—*A. Graebner, The College of St. Catherine*

WS-1999   HD6072   92-44921 CIP
Gray, Brenda Clegg. **Black female domestics during the Depression in New York City, 1930-1940.** Garland, 1993. 201p bibl index afp ISBN 0-8153-1013-7, $51.00

Gray examines several intersecting themes significant in 20th-century African American history. She explores the effect of the Depression on northern, urban, working-class black women, their status and treatment as workers, racism, the urban black family, and the relationship between working women and the black community. Gray focuses on domestic work because it "has been the primary source of employment of black women in the United States" in this century. She illustrates how these women came to play a dominant role in the black working-class community and, indeed, became a vital force in the community's struggle to overcome numerous race, class, and, in the case of this group, gender obstacles. The author uses African American newspapers, Urban League papers,

census materials, and most important, oral histories of more than 100 black women. She also adds a brief postscript tracing domestics and the changing job environment in the decades following the 1930s. Haphazard editing and topical circumscription, however, mar this work. Despite some demographic significance to labor and African American scholars, the book is recommended only for specialists and graduate libraries.—*K. Edgerton, Washington State University*

WS-2000   F899   93-29485 CIP
Haarsager, Sandra. **Bertha Knight Landes of Seattle, big-city mayor.** Oklahoma, 1994. 334p bibl index afp ISBN 0-8061-2592-6, $28.95

Bertha Knight Landes became the first woman mayor of a major US city in 1926. In this compelling biography, Haarsager traces the making of a female politician during the Progressive era. Acquiring her political skills through participation in women's clubs, Landes won followers during her tenure on the Seattle City Council. She adopted the feminist plea to make the city of Seattle into a "larger home." She promoted zoning laws and city planning ordinances, regulated dance halls, and improved public safety and health programs. Landes belonged to an environmental advocacy group, bringing environmental concerns and goals to her mayoral agenda. Haarsager uses the theoretical approaches of Michel Foucault and Victor Turner to explore issues of gender and power during an era when both men and women were leery of a woman in a powerful, public position. Her sources, skillfully adopted, include oral histories, the Bertha Knight Landes Papers, and numerous narrative and theoretical monographs. Illustrated with photographs. Upper-division undergraduates and above.—*E. Kuhlman, Washington State University*

WS-2001   F217   90-22168 CIP
Hiscoe, Helen B. **Appalachian passage.** Georgia, 1992 (c1991). 321p afp ISBN 0-8203-1354-8, $29.95

In 1949, Hiscoe arrived in a small coal mining company town in southwestern West Virginia to join her husband, physician Bonta Hiscoe, who had been hired as town doctor. This book recounts that experience, as seen through the eyes of a woman who, although college educated, was an outsider who frequently found it difficult to understand the local people and their culture. The doctor was paid through a union-approved miner's payroll deduction, but had to furnish all drugs and equipment, and was required to make house calls. Hiscoe expresses dismay at living conditions and at the general well-being of the miners and their families. Literacy was very low; many miners signed their company store bills with an x. Sanitation was primitive, children played barefoot and regularly developed intestinal worms. The birth rate for women aged 13 to 40 was high, and families commonly had up to a dozen children living in a two-or three-room uninsulated shack with no running water. Rumors and lies formed the core of what people accepted as reality. This book provides useful insight into how outsiders perceived a postwar Appalachian mining community. For public libraries and Appalachian collections.—*K. B. Raitz, University of Kentucky*

WS-2002   HD6073   92-46352 CIP
Jellison, Katherine. **Entitled to power: farm women and technology, 1913-1963.** North Carolina, 1993. 217p index afp ISBN 0-8078-2088-1, $39.95; ISBN 0-8078-4415-2 pbk, $13.95

Jellison presents a fascinating, multilayered account of the introduction of technology on midwestern farms from the Progressive era to the postwar years. She makes insightful use of USDA records, farming journals, and advertisements to explain how government and industry appealed to the farm woman for support of their modernization goals while remaining within the traditional patriarchal structure of the farm, and to demonstrate how the women responded. Although farm women often did support the acquisition of technology, they sought by doing so to enhance their power in the farm family and to maintain their roles as producers and contributors in the farm business. They refused to accept the role of full-time homemaker, to which agricultural reformers sought to consign them, and continued to "have a part in the farming," though often unrecognized even within their families. Of interest to graduate students and scholars of American agriculture, technology, and women's history. Supplemented by interesting photographs, tables, and notes.—*M. L. Meldrum, SUNY at Stony Brook*

WS-2003 TR647 92-33000 CIP
Kirsh, Andrea. **Carrie Mae Weems,** by Andrea Kirsh and Susan Fisher Sterling. National Museum of Women in the Arts, 1993. (Dist. by Northeastern University) 116p bibl ISBN 0-940979-21-7 pbk, $29.95

Published as a catalog for a 1993-95 National Museum of Women in the Arts touring exhibition, this retrospective of the photographic art of Carrie Mae Weems reflects both the reigning vogue in postmodern minority art as political deconstruction and an immense talent belying such tokenism. Introductory remarks by NMWA Director Rebecca Phillips Abbott and essays by curator-editors Kirsch and Sterling belabor the racial, gender, and class clichés of political correctness. Weems's art, however, stands on its own. Full of human insights and anger channeled into wry irony, the more than five dozen Weems works on display evoke a gritty but rich exploration of modern African American life. Recommended for academic and public libraries with strong collections in the fine arts and/or African American culture. General; advanced undergraduate; graduate.—*R. A. Fischer, University of Minnesota—Duluth*

WS-2004 D811 93-38919 CIP
Kochendoerfer, Violet A. **One woman's World War II.** University Press of Kentucky, 1994. 211p afp ISBN 0-8131-1866-2, $25.00

The fiftieth anniversary of WW II has spawned the publication of numerous wartime memoirs. Kochendoerfer's work, however, is notably different from other accounts as she served with both the Women's Army Auxiliary Corps (WAAC) and the Red Cross. Based on journal entries, her tale is unmarred by present-mindedness and provides a wealth of detail about wartime Europe. The author's experiences in Britain, France, and Germany are unique. As a Red Cross director she traveled with the 17th and 82nd Airborne Divisions during the war's last months. She preceded military women into the divisions' areas of operation, and her access to senior personnel enabled her to explore the characters of such leaders as generals James M. Gavin and Dwight D. Eisenhower. Other observations include description and analysis of the American occupation and of Europe's postwar conditions. Augmented by photos, this monograph is extremely useful to undergraduates and above, especially students of military and social history.—*J. A. Luckett, United States Military Academy*

WS-2005 HV741 93-9926 CIP
Ladd-Taylor, Molly. **Mother-work: women, child welfare, and the state, 1890-1930.** Illinois, 1994. 211p index afp ISBN 0-252-02044-8, $39.95

Ladd-Taylor's elegant, richly textured narrative combines the political and cultural insights of Progressive Era/pre-New Deal historiography with an even-handed synthesis of contemporary work in feminist theory and women's studies. The result is a crisply written examination of the politicization of women's traditional work of childrearing—*mother-work*—and the establishment of early 20th century child welfare services. Because motherhood was a central organizing principle of early 20th century American political culture, Ladd-Taylor focuses attention on three representative organizations: the "traditional maternalists" in the National Congress of Mothers and Parent-Teacher Associations (PTA) who sought to professionalize motherhood by bringing science and education into the home; the "progressive maternalists" of the Children's Bureau who emphasized women's obligation to the state to raise "citizen-workers"; and the feminists of the National Woman's Party, who asserted women's right to pursue marriage and career. Although these groups enjoyed a somewhat uneasy alliance before ratification of the Nineteenth Amendment, as evidenced by their successful support for mothers' pensions and the Sheppard-Towner Act, their post-suffrage activities prefigured the bitter divisions over the Equal Rights Amendment and the growing rift between private lives and public policy. General readers.—*E. M. Tobin, Hamilton College*

WS-2006 F868 95-23508 CIP
Lemke-Santangelo, Gretchen. **Abiding courage: African American migrant women and the East Bay community.** North Carolina, 1996. 217p bibl index afp ISBN 0-8078-2256-6, $29.95; ISBN 0-8078-4563-9 pbk, $14.95

Lemke-Santangelo's study is a seminal work. Writing with an unambiguous purpose—to examine the migration and community-building efforts of African American women who moved from the South to the East Bay cities of Califor-

nia during WW II—the author presents, in an endearing style, the experiences of women about whom little has been written. A riveting introduction sets the stage for a journey involving "economic autonomy, hard work, education, worship, family ties, charity, and independent self-help institutions," which readers share. What makes this story so poignant is that it is told by 50 women who actually lived the experiences Lemke-Santangelo recounts. With chapter titles such as "It Was Just Like Living in Two Worlds," "To Make the Two Worlds One," "I Never Thought I'd Have to Create All That," "I Always Desired Independence, Never Wealth," "I Never Denied Where I Came From" and "If We Didn't Do It, It Just Wouldn't Get Done," Lemke-Santangelo unfolds a unique history of the lives of a segment of the US population. Feminists as well as nonfeminists will find the book a welcome respite from the lives of mainstream women. All levels.—*R. Stewart, SUNY College at Buffalo*

WS-2007 Orig
The Lillian Wald papers [microform]. Research Publications, CT, 1992. 2 units 45 reels ea. 35mm microfilm. Guide to reels. Complete collection: $8,550.00; Individual units: $5,030.00

Lillian Wald is one of the most intriguing figures in recent US history. Nurse, social worker, philanthropist, and social activist, Wald was a prominent actor in turn of the century humanitarian reform movements. She founded New York's Henry Street Settlement House and the Visiting Nurse Service. This collection, consisting of correspondence, office files from Henry Street Settlement House, and such hard-to-find materials as newspaper clippings, photographs, and fliers, provides a wealth of primary data crucial for scholars working in urban studies, labor and suffrage movements, and women studies. The public Lillian Wald is well represented here. Researchers interested in a more intimate view of Wald may find that these materials raise more questions than they answer. Although the set provides a window into a range of pressing social and political issues, letters to, rather than correspondence from, Wald offer limited access to key elements of her own life and motivations. In spite of this limitation, the collection is highly recommended for large academic and public library collections, with one caveat: the unbound reel guide provided to this reviewer seems to use the terms reel and box interchangeably and leaves something to be desired.—*E. Broidy, University of California, Irvine*

WS-2008 Orig
Lou Henry Hoover: essays on a busy life, ed. by Dale C. Mayer. High Plains, WY, 1994. 156p index ISBN 1-881019-04-7, $23.50

Long obscured by the towering shadow of Eleanor Roosevelt, Lou Henry Hoover has appeared, by contrast, as a traditional wife and pleasant, if unimportant, First Lady. This collection of essays attempts to revive the historical reputation of the wife of President Hoover. Based on her recently opened papers in the Hoover Library, essayists chronicle Hoover's early life, interest in the Girl Scouts, support of women's amateur sports, and encouragement of the arts. The several historians involved in this project have made extensive use of the Hoover papers (and make frequent plugs for the Hoover Library), but seldom address current issues in the secondary literature. For example, one writer asserts that Hoover's activism should be seen as a more conservative form of feminism, but does not mention any of the raging historical debates about the varieties and definitions of feminism. More a contribution to Hoover hagiography than to women's history, the essays are quite uncritical of their subject: every act of charity is faithfully recorded, no harsh words were ever spoken. Although the collection may "serve as a catalyst for further studies on" Hoover, they do not confirm "her unique place in women's history."—*E. C. Green, Sweet Briar College*

WS-2009 HQ1236 92-7978 CIP
Lynn, Susan. **Progressive women in conservative times: racial justice, peace, and feminism, 1945 to the 1960s.** Rutgers, 1993 (c1992). 218p index ISBN 0-8135-1867-9, $40.00; ISBN 0-8135-1868-7 pbk, $15.00

Lynn's excellent and illuminating book is based on dozens of interviews with women involved in civil rights and peace activism, primarily through the American Friends Service Committee and the Young Women's Christian Association, during the "conservative times" following WW II. Lynn supplements these personal accounts with other primary sources to belie the idea that the feminine mystique held all American women captive during this era. Her discussion enriches understanding of the nature, dimensions, potential, and limitations of feminism as a social and political force. Her work also adds much to knowledge of the persistence of feminist and leftist traditions through mentoring and generational interaction. The story of the YWCA's transformation into a truly interracial organization and the comparison of women's roles in the mixed-sex AFSC and the women-only YW are particularly interesting. A valuable companion to the work of Nancy Cott, and of Leila Rupp and Verta Taylor on feminist history, this is a useful book for serious students of the American Left and the postwar era. Notes and a list of interviews. Advanced undergraduate; graduate; faculty.—*M. L. Meldrum, SUNY at Stony Brook*

WS-2010 HQ766 93-42738 CIP
McCann, Carole R. **Birth control politics in the United States, 1916-1945.** Cornell, 1994. 242p bibl index afp ISBN 0-8014-2490-9, $29.95

Did birth control advocates in the early 20th century abandon women's rights for the sake of respectability? McCann (Univ. of Maryland, Baltimore County) contends they had little choice given massive opposition. Although botched abortions accounted for 25-30 percent of maternal mortality, the Comstock Law prohibited the sale and distribution of contraceptives; most Americans viewed women as mothers; eugenicists equated poverty with inferiority; organized medicine fought birth control and public health measures; and even women's rights groups such as the National Women's Party fled from the ideas of financially and sexually independent women. McCann argues that, for pragmatic purposes, Margaret Sanger conceded to the medical profession's demand for control, "racial betterment," and the economic rationale of child spacing. It worked; by 1945, some 800 independent clinics existed. The costs, however, included women's loss of authority and patronizing service to poor, immigrant, and African American women. Although the book is fairly well written, it could have used another rewrite to cut academic prose. Recommended for specialists who are interested in the wars among different birth control organizations and with a hostile environment.—*S. D. Borchert, Lake Erie College*

WS-2011 UA565 89-600225 CIP
Morden, Bettie J. **The Women's Army Corps, 1945-1978.** Center of Military History, United States Army, 1990.(For sale by U.S. GPO) 543p index $30.00; $25.00

Morden completes the study of the Women's Army Corps begun by Mattie Treadwell in (1954). She superbly summarizes Treadwell's work on the WW II WAC and extends the history of the Corps from 1945 through its disestablishment in 1978. Morden, a retired officer recalled to active duty in 1974 to prepare this monograph, relies on an extensive collection of original documentary material. Numerous tables, charts, and illustrations furnish invaluable information about the personnel, training, and utilization of Army women. Meticulously documented, this account is the most complete extant source for women in the Army. It combines personal reminiscences and lore with rigorous scholarship to chronicle policy decisions and changes that brought women from serving in an ancillary agency to becoming an integrated mainstay in today's Army. An essential source for women's studies and military history collections. All libraries.—*J. A. Luckett, United States Military Academy*

WS-2012 HX843 92-31335 CIP
Morton, Marian J. **Emma Goldman and the American left: "nowhere at home."** Twayne, 1992. 183p bibl index afp ISBN 0-8057-7794-6, $26.95; ISBN 0-8057-7795-4 pbk, $13.95

Emma Goldman's political career in her adopted homeland has been the topic of social and intellectual historical scholarship since her death in 1940. Relying heavily on Goldman's autobiography, *Living My Life* (1931), Morton shows that although Goldman perceived herself as a political exile "nowhere at home," in reality she had deep and lasting ties, politically and personally, to the American Left. The friendships and sexual relationships she cultivated always centered around radical politics, binding her to the leftist American political context of her time. Morton's book functions not only as a biography of Goldman, but also as a primer of radical political thought in the early 20th-century US. Yet Goldman's Jewish immigrant past persisted: although the most deterministic event

in her life was the 1886 Haymarket riot, her intellectual life nevertheless awakened in Russia. Goldman's life in the US, Soviet Russia, and Europe allows Morton to explore the varying faces of anarchism—individualist, communist, and anarcho-syndicalist. Photographs and bibliographic essay. General; advanced undergraduate; graduate; faculty.—*E. Kuhlman, Washington State University*

WS-2013 HV741 90-38389 CIP
Muncy, Robyn. **Creating a female dominion in American reform, 1890-1935.** Oxford, 1991. 221p index afp ISBN 0-19-505702-3, $28.00

Muncy seeks to provide an explanation for the continuity of white, middle-class, American female reformers between the Progressive Era and the New Deal. She finds it in the interlocking organizations and agencies dominated by women reformers who provided the philosophy, leadership, and constituency for child welfare policy during this period. In chapters devoted to Hull House, the Children's Bureau, the School of Social Service Administration at the University of Chicago, the Sheppard-Towner Maternity and Infancy Act, and New Deal child welfare policy, Muncy traces the rise and fall of the female dominion. This is an oft-told story. What is new is Muncy's feminist argument that the female dominion constituted a professional culture distinct from that of men, one that stressed reform, service, popularizing scientific knowledge, and cooperation. Muncy's gendered analysis is provocative but exaggerates the differences between female and male reformers and the pervasiveness of female professional culture. Her work should be supplemented by older studies with a broader scope such as Clarke A. Chambers's *Seedtime of Reform* (1963) and Roy Lubove's *The Professional Altruist* (CH, Sep'65). Upper-division undergraduates and above.—*E. W. Carp, Pacific Lutheran University*

WS-2014 HN79 94-21695 CIP
Neth, Mary. **Preserving the family farm: women, community, and the foundations of agribusiness in the Midwest, 1900-1940.** Johns Hopkins, 1995. 347p index afp ISBN 0-8018-4898-9, $39.95

Neth (Virginia Polytechnic Univ.) takes her place alongside Sally McMurry (*Transforming Rural Life*, CH, Jul'95) and with other historians who offer knowledgeable and creative approaches to understanding farming in the US. Through oral histories and conventional sources, Neth attacks the "patriarchal order-farmer as principal actor and male head of household ..." and reveals "gender, family, and community at the center of the story ... using them as a lens to reexamine agricultural history and policy." Neth's women shed the historical image of passivity to forge lives for themselves and their families even as agribusiness grew and consumed rural America. Those with interests in agricultural, economic, family, and women's history will treasure reading *Preserving the Family Farm*. Upper-division undergraduates and above. Notes; bibliographical note.—*P. D. Travis, Texas Woman's University*

WS-2015 HD6079 94-24544 CIP
Orleck, Annelise. **Common sense & a little fire: women and working-class politics in the United States, 1900-1965.** North Carolina, 1995. 384p bibl index afp ISBN 0-8078-2199-3, $39.95; ISBN 0-8078-4511-6 pbk, $15.95

Orleck's intelligent work reminds readers of a time when workers fought valiantly for the right to be represented by a union. Focusing on the lives of four remarkable women—Fannia Cohn, Clara Lemlich Shavelson, Pauline Newman, and Rose Schneiderman—Orleck weaves a complex and compelling story of class and ethnic tensions, the struggles for workers' rights, internecine warfare, and above all, the extremely gendered nature of both politics and work. Using the term "industrial feminists," borrowed from Mildred Moore's 1915 tract on the Women's Trade Union League, Orleck describes a uniquely class-based feminism, defined by the shop floor, the family, and the community; a feminism, in the words of Rose Schneiderman, that demanded bread and roses, too. Although the stories of the struggles for equality are compelling, it is Orleck's probing yet respectful examination of the personal as political that makes this such a remarkable work. For three of the four women whose collective biography is told here, relationships with other women were the focal point of their lives and their work. Their stories, as related in this tightly written, fascinating work, reveal whole new layers to the history of women and the working-class struggle. Highly recommended. All levels.—*E. Broidy, University of California, Irvine*

WS-2016   D810   92-24084 CIP
Putney, Martha S. **When the nation was in need: blacks in the Women's Army Corps during World War II.** Scarecrow, 1992. 231p bibl index afp ISBN 0-8108-2531-7, $35.00

Putney, a historian and a former servicewoman, has written the most comprehensive survey to date of the experiences of African American WACs who served in WW II. Illustrations complement and supplement her narrative and graphically portray the segregation of black women (but not other ethnic women, including Japanese Americans) and the range of roles they played. Although forced segregation kept some young African American women from joining, the rumor of sexual promiscuousness—the "prostitution thing"—was a greater deterrent to recruitment. The Army had a 10 percent ceiling but black women never exceeded 6 percent. The Navy refused to allow black women to join until almost the end of the war, when President Roosevelt needed African American votes to secure his fourth term. Racism and sexism are twin themes of this book. Following 150 pages of text valuable appendixes list black women officers by name and the camps where the WACs served. All levels.—*D. Campbell, Austin Peay State University*

WS-2017   HV5089   95-4396 CIP
Rose, Kenneth D. **American women and the repeal of prohibition.** New York University, 1996. 215p (The American social experience series, 32) index afp ISBN 0-8147-7464-4, $40.00

The Women's Christian Temperance Union assumed a special affinity between women and the fight against alcohol, claiming the campaign as women's special right and responsibility because its goal was to protect the home—woman's sphere. Support for that view helped ensure the passage of the 18th amendment—the only amendment to be repealed. Rose argues that women were also central in the repeal movement. Repeal women, personified and led by the aristocratic Pauline Sabin, presented a vastly more fashionable and secular image than Prohibitionist women. But, strikingly, instead of employing the principle of individual liberty, Repeal women fell back on the same kind of maternalist logic as Prohibitionists: women had a special responsibility to protect the home—in this case, by repeal because Prohibition had turned out to be a threat to the home. Even among women of the 1920s, who were unalarmed by changes in social mores, conservative definitions of women died slowly. Rose stresses the independence from male control of the Women's Organization for Prohibition Reform. He makes his case with clarity—and temperance. Upper-division undergraduates and above.—*A. Graebner, College of St. Catherine*

WS-2018   HQ1906   94-18184 CIP
Roth, Darlene Rebecca. **Matronage: patterns in women's organizations, Atlanta, Georgia, 1890-1940.** Carlson Publishing, 1994. 207p (Scholarship in women's history, 9) bibl index afp ISBN 0-926019-70-8, $55.00

Roth's 1978 dissertation, now published as part of Carlson's series of "re-discovered" scholarship in women's history, is a fascinating look at the women's organizations of Atlanta between 1890 and 1940. In an innovative methodology, Roth analyzes the patterns of development of the female associational world, examining both black and white, conservative and progressive, religious and secular collectively. The book is brimming with insightful observations (such as the recognition that "women as individuals profited from the professionalization of welfare work by being able to find employment in a new career, but women's organizations per se did not.") Writing before Linda Kerber, Roth wrestles with defining women's nontraditional activities; Kerber described "republican motherhood," Roth discovered "matronage." Writing before Nancy Cott, Roth clearly illuminates the shortcomings of the label "social feminism." And writing before Cynthia Neverdon-Morton, Roth uncovers the rich and complex network of black women's associations and incorporates it into the larger story of women's organizational activism. Of particular interest to scholars of southern women, but useful for anyone interested in women's history, southern history, the Progressive Era, or social welfare history. All levels.—*E. C. Green, Sweet Briar College*

WS-2019   HQ1438   91-26105 CIP
Schackel, Sandra. **Social housekeepers: women shaping public policy in New Mexico, 1920-1940.** New Mexico, 1992. 213p bibl index ISBN 0-8263-1324-8, $29.95

The state of New Mexico has proved a vibrant laboratory for the close examination of women's political participation during the Great Depression and the New Deal. Focusing on the intersections of race, class, and gender, Schackel explores the evolution of public policy, specifically in the areas of infant health and welfare, that became the special preserve of both professional and volunteer social workers and reformers. Ostensibly an examination of New Mexico, the book complements similar investigations of female progressive politics, for example, Robin Muncy's *Creating a Female Dominion in American Reform, 1890-1935* (CH, Jul'91). This is particularly true of Schackel's discussion of the central role of female-centered social organizations, the tensions between the largely Anglo, middle-class reformers and the populations they "served," and the function of the federal government in initiating and promoting social welfare programs. Community studies often afford a detailed look at the development, implementation, and effect of policy decisions that range far beyond the community (or state) in question. The concept of social housekeeping illuminates an important feature of maternal politics. Highly recommended for all academic and large public libraries.—*E. Broidy, University of California, Irvine*

WS-2020   HQ1419   92-22588 CIP
Schneider, Dorothy. **American women in the Progressive Era, 1900-1920,** by Dorothy Schneider and Carl J. Schneider. Facts on File, 1993. 276p bibl index afp ISBN 0-8160-2513-4, $24.95

The Progressive Era marked the beginning of a resurgence of democratic values in American politics and society. Upper- middle-class white women found opportunities to formulate their own revisioning of an America that awarded women political equality, commencing with the right to vote. Drawing from their past works on women's roles in the military, the Schneiders devote two chapters of this work to female pacifists and WW I supporters. Other chapters highlight women's working lives, both inside and outside the home. A chapter entitled "Black Women on the Move" merely adds a minority voice, rather than integrating women of color within US women's history. (Chicana, Hispanic, Asian, and Native American women are not included at all.) Based on secondary source materials, this book is a largely descriptive history, offering little that is new in the way of theoretical background or methodology. Illustrated with lively photographs. General; community college; undergraduate.—*E. Kuhlman, Washington State University*

WS-2021   D639   90-50751 CIP
Schneider, Dorothy. **Into the breach: American women overseas in World War I,** by Dorothy and Carl J. Schneider. Viking, 1991. 368p bibl index ISBN 0-670-83936-1, $29.95

The first full-length treatment of approximately 25,000 middle-class, well-educated women who combined duty with adventure to serve overseas during the Great War. White women and a few African American women took advantage of the loosely structured environment to create their own contribution as Red Cross or "Y" workers; physicians; nurses, "Hello Girls"; reporters or novelists. Some even tried to engineer a peace settlement. An appendix lists numbers of women by organization and occupation; the bibliographic essays are extensive. More than 348 of these women died overseas; hundreds or thousands more contracted illnesses related to their wartime service. Yet few women, even those in uniform (Army and Navy nurses, "Hello Girls"), were able to obtain medical treatment or veteran's pensions without extensive lobbying efforts. Americans quickly forgot the experiences of these women. Consequently, in WW II, women volunteers were forced to begin from scratch, which took precious time and repeated any of the same mistakes. The authors conclude war "was no epiphany, but it did broaden minds and open vistas." This well-written, well-researched book is indespensable for public libraries and university collections.—*D. Campbell, Indiana University*

WS-2022   D810   90-20639 CIP
Since you went away: World War II letters from American women on the home front, ed. by Judy Barrett Litoff and David C. Smith. Oxford, 1991. 293p bibl index afp ISBN 0-19-506795-9, $22.95

Other scholars of WW II have published letters written home by servicemen, but this is the first collection sampling the letters written by sisters, sweethearts, wives, and mothers, saved by thousands of servicemen. Chapters are organized around themes that were important to these women: courtship, marriage, motherhood, work, sacrifices. Editors provide background information on each letter writer and recipient. The editors also made special efforts to include letters from all regions, classes, and a variety of ethnic groups (letters from African Americans have been the hardest to secure). This well-crafted book should be available in public libraries for readers who remember WW II as being "only yesterday" and for their children and grandchildren who want to understand what the war meant to these women on the homefront. It will also be a valuable addition to high school and college libraries. Finally, what women tell readers in these letters about their concerns and their wartime feelings will cause historians to rethink what has been written about the homefront.—*D. Campbell, Indiana University*

WS-2023   DS920   94-8382 CIP
Soderbergh, Peter A. **Women marines in the Korean War era.** Praeger, 1994. 167p bibl index afp ISBN 0-275-94827-7, $45.00

Relying on the personal reminiscences of 80 participants, Soderbergh seeks to elucidate the contributions of women Marines during the Korean War era (1948-55). He describes women Marines' roles against the backdrop of 1950s America and the Korean War. His primary sources include both his own war recollections and those of the women Marines with whom he corresponded to gather data for this study. Soderbergh's book includes 24 photographs and a useful bibliography that enumerates all major women's military and Korean War sources. Soderbergh's monograph supplements the only other work that treats women Marines in this period, Mary V. Stremlow's official study, *A History of the Women Marines, 1946-1977* (1986). *Woman Marines* provides insight into the values, attitudes, and motivations of servicewomen, but it lacks the incisive analysis and interpretation characteristic of a graduate-level work or research source. Best suited for lower-division undergraduates and comprehensive military collections.—*J. A. Luckett, United States Military Academy*

WS-2024   D769   91-47594 CIP
Soderbergh, Peter A. **Women marines: the World War II era.** Praeger, 1992. 189p bibl index afp ISBN 0-275-94131-0, $39.95

Soderbergh's book is an outgrowth of a biographical study of Germaine Catherine Laville, an alumna of Louisiana State University (LSU) killed during WW II while serving in the US Marine Corps Women's Reserve (MCWR). In preparing the biography, Soderbergh, an ex-Marine and professor of education at LSU, interviewed 146 of Laville's women marine friends and collected a wide range of data on them, including their reasons for joining, jobs held during wartime service, and long-term implications of wartime service. Chapter titles are titles of hit tunes of the 1940s. The result is a large collection of well-selected quotes that are woven together in an interesting narrative. This book adds flesh to the historical skeletons of the administrative histories such as Pat Meid's *Marine Corps Women's Reserve in World War II* (1964) and Mattie Treadwell's *The Women's Army Corps* (1954). General; undergraduate.—*D. Campbell, Austin Peay State University*

WS-2025   HV1447   90-46559 CIP
Stadum, Beverly. **Poor women and their families: hard working charity cases, 1900-1930.** State University of New York, 1992. 235p index ISBN 0-7914-0751-9, $49.50; ISBN 0-7914-0752-7 pbk, $16.95

In this poignant book Stadum analyzes 300 records of poor families who sought assistance from the Minneapolis Charity Organization Society between 1900 and 1930. She focuses on local services and women's work as mother, homemaker, paid wage earner, wife, and charity recipient. In each role, tension existed between societal expectations and a woman's resources. The records show that women accepted social workers' standards of homemaking, turned to others for help, earned cash at home, had to work at very low wages, reacted vehemently to abusive treatment within marriage (conjugal harmony was rare), and were torn between fear for their safety and a practical need for men's earning ability. Focusing on three lives, Stadum shows that because of class differences, poor women were criticized by the very social workers who were supposed to help. The women sacrificed themselves and when even that was not enough, they relinquished their children. Stadum deals with the first third of this century, but the situation of the female grandchildren of these women has not changed substan-

tially although the wealth of this country has increased dramatically. Thoroughly documented with 18 tables, 63 pages of notes. All levels.—*S. Reinharz, Brandeis University*

WS-2026   E99   90-22003 CIP
Stockel, H. Henrietta. **Women of the Apache nation: voices of truth.** Nevada, 1991. 198p bibl index afp ISBN 0-87417-168-7, $24.95

Stockel discusses Chiricahua Apache women by mentioning such historical figures as Lozen and Dahteste and then by focusing on four contemporary Apache women—two from Mescalero, New Mexico, and two from Fort Sill, Oklahoma. Elbys Naiche Hugar, the great-granddaughter of Cochise, is the curator of the Mescalero Apache Cultural Center and coauthor of a Mescalero Apache dictionary used in the schools to maintain the Apache language. Kathleen Smith Kanseah, the descendent of a captured Mexican woman, is another Mescalero Apache woman committed to passing on Apache tradition. Mildred Imach Cleghorn, who in 1989 was tribal chair of the Fort Sill Apache, was a prisoner at Fort Sill the first four years of her life and rose to become a leader at the same place she was imprisoned. Ruey Haozous Darrow, a Fort Sill Apache woman with a Master's degree in microbiology, works for the Indian Health Service, a job that routinely takes her miles from her Oklahoma home. All four women retain strong ties to tradition and in their conversations with Stockel refer frequently to Apache history and tradition. The book ends with descriptions of a Mescalero Apache puberty ceremony, Mescalero Apache Heritage Day (1989), and the celebration of Fort Sill Apache 75th Anniversary of Freedom. A popular account of Apache life written from the point of view of a woman who is eager to communicate the spirit of these Apache women. Undergraduate and general readers.—*G. M. Bataille, Arizona State University*

WS-2027   HQ1413   91-14089 CIP
Stokes, Rose Pastor. **"I belong to the working class": the unfinished autobiography of Rose Pastor Stokes,** ed. by Herbert Shapiro and David L. Sterling. Georgia, 1992. 173p index afp ISBN 0-8203-1383-1, $30.00

Rose Pastor Stokes achieved fame at the turn of the 20th century because of her marriage, the wedding of a "poor little Jewish factory worker" to James Graham Phelps Stokes, a scion of a wealthy, aristocratic New York family. It was the essence of the American dream, female version. However, Stokes remained committed to the working class, women's rights, and radical politics. Although her husband, originally an active Socialist, returned to conventional politics in the pressures of WW I, she ultimately rejected the war and became a founding member of the American Communist party. Although written through her later "red-colored" glasses, her unfinished autobiography eloquently conveys her passion, dedication, and a feeling for the appalling conditions of the poorest immigrant workers. An illuminating introduction and extensive footnotes are helpful in providing context and descriptions of the early 20th-century radicals involved in the same struggle. A valuable addition to collections in labor, radical, and women's history. All levels.—*L. Mayo, County College of Morris*

WS-2028   JX1965   93-16801 CIP
Swerdlow, Amy. **Women Strike for Peace: traditional motherhood and radical politics in the 1960s.** Chicago, 1993. 310p bibl index afp ISBN 0-226-78635-8, $45.00; ISBN 0-226-78636-6 pbk, $19.95

Swerdlow adds an important chapter to the history of 20th-century women's political action. Her account of the Women Strike for Peace (WSP) provides an excellent summary of the activities of one particular organization as well as a window into a range of often-conflicting political ideologies and activities. Speaking as both scholar (implying detachment) and activist (Swerdlow was a founding member of the organization), Swerdlow offers an insider's glimpse of the internal dynamics of WSP while not shying away from the historian's duty to contextualize and critique those same dynamics. She grapples with the issues raised by WSP's articulation of a decidedly maternalist politics. Her analysis of this stance, and of WSP's one-issue orientation, adds significantly to the understanding of female political participation between the first and second wave of feminism and helps explain the tensions occasioned by the rise of a distinctly different feminist and racial politics in the mid-1960s. Highly recommended for general readers, advanced undergraduates, and above.—*E. Broidy, University of California, Irvine*

WS-2029   HQ1236   91-13069 CIP
Thomas, Mary Martha. **The new woman in Alabama: social reforms and suffrage, 1890-1920.** Alabama, 1992. 269p bibl index afp ISBN 0-8173-0564-5, $29.95

Thomas's book fills an important niche in southern and women's history. The first half treats the rise of African American and white women's organizations in the late 19th century. Urban middle-class women, while remaining closely tied to the traditional domestic sphere, gained experience in the public arena, acquiring organizational skills, knowledge about the art of politics and lobbying, and techniques for arousing community support for public programs. These talents were put to use as women joined in the Progressive movement, working for child labor laws, temperance, educational improvements, abolition of the convict lease system, and numerous other reforms. The second half of this work traces the struggle for woman suffrage in Alabama and the integration of women into the political process after adoption of the 19th amendment. By the 1920s, the role of women had changed significantly. A "new woman" who could comfortably and effectively work in the public arena had emerged. This well-written, balanced work is solidly based on a wide variety of secondary and primary sources. General; undergraduate; graduate.—*K. R. Johnson, University of North Alabama*

WS-2030   E184   94-24110 CIP
Tomita, Mary Kimoto. **Dear Miye: letters home from Japan, 1939-1946,** ed. with introd. and notes by Robert G. Lee. Stanford, 1995. 400p index afp ISBN 0-8047-2419-9, $45.00

Tomita, a Japanese American from California, was stranded in Japan following the bombing of Pearl Harbor. She struggled during her exile to overcome the loss of citizenship and the cessation of correspondence with, and financial and emotional support from, family and friends in the US. In despair, Tomita entered into an arranged, loveless, and disastrous marriage. In letters written mostly to her childhood friend, Miye Yamasaki Nishita, and to Kay Oda, another Japanese American stranded in Japan, the young Nisei woman chronicled her efforts to survive, physically, emotionally, and psychologically. The letters cover three periods: the prewar years (1939-41); the war years (1941-45); and the postwar years (1945-46), during which Tomita worked as a civilian employee for the US occupation forces pending her repatriation. As an "Indelibly American" woman, she describes the conflict of competing political loyalties, gender role expectations, and ethnic identity in a voice of immediacy and authenticity that make these intensely personal, un-selfconscious letters a valuable contribution to "countermemory" in the face of the erasure of Japanese American wartime history. All levels.—*M. Sood, SUNY at Stony Brook*

WS-2031   F347   92-17772 CIP
Trials of the earth: the autobiography of Mary Hamilton, ed. by Helen Dick Davis. University Press of Mississippi, 1992. 259p afp ISBN 0-87805-579-7, $25.00

This autobiography of a Delta country pioneer woman is a unique addition to the history of the Mississippi lumber industry. Set in the late 19th and early 20th century, it is the account of Mary Hamilton, wife of a mysterious Englishman, Frank Hamilton, who came into the Delta as a lumberman. Hamilton details life in lumber camps where she was usually the only woman cooking for dozens of her husband's workers. She married at 18 and followed her husband from Arkansas into Mississippi, with the dream of owning a home. During the turbulent years of her marriage, Hamilton lost four of nine children and her beloved farm; lived through a flood; experienced wolves, panthers, and bears in the surrounding woods; and saw her husband falsely accused of murder. A true gem of regional history, Hamilton's narrative was written in the 1930s and rediscovered in the 1990s. With the eloquence of a novel, this true story should appeal to scholar and novice alike. All levels.—*J. Jackson, Southeastern Louisiana University*

WS-2032   F897   95-31253 CIP
Watkins, Marilyn P. **Rural democracy: family farmers and politics in western Washington, 1890-1925.** Cornell, 1995. 239p index afp ISBN 0-8014-3073-9, $42.50

Renewed interest in US rural/agricultural history speaks well of those with specialties in women's and family history who have brought new insights from these disciplines to bear on farm history. Watkins's book gives greater attention to "women and the issues of gender" in farm organizations of the late 19th and

early 20th centuries. Farm women have not been presented as "prominent political players" in earlier studies of the Populists, Grangers, and Farmer's Alliance. Watkins (Institute of the North American West, Seattle) sets the record straight by suggesting that the Populists, for example, "grew out of a community-based voluntary association that included men, women, and children" and "transcended politics as usual." Watkins focuses on "a portion of south-central Lewis county" (Washington), a region that provided farm women "access to partisan politics at a time when it was generally considered a male domain ...." She stresses that "rural men and women shared an ethic that valued hard work and recognized farming as a family way of life to which all contributed ...." Intelligently written and meticulously researched, this study is for those with interests in agricultural/rural history, women's studies, family history, or social history. List of illustrations; tables; notes. All levels.—*P. D. Travis, Texas Woman's University*

WS-2033   D810.W7   89-71489 CIP
Weatherford, Doris. **American women and World War II.** Facts on File, 1990. 338p index afp ISBN 0-8160-2038-8, $29.95

Weatherford's study of the multiple roles played by American women in WW II deals in succession with nurses (too briefly), servicewomen, women in war work, and women on "the home front." No aspect of women's war participation, from WAC to widow, is excluded from this survey. Using personal accounts and contemporary journalistic coverage, Weatherford compiles a wealth of detail and anecdote that makes absorbing reading, and she corrects commonly held misconceptions (e.g., that the drafting of women was considered unthinkable before the Equal Rights Amendment of the 1970s). The illustrations are excellent. There are ample footnotes and a useful bibliography note. The book is perhaps of greatest interest and value to undergraduates in 20th century women's studies and to general readers. It could also be mined by graduate students, but the latter will find much familiar material here. Weatherford's conclusions about changes in women's roles and expectations following wartime experiences are interesting but are scattered throughout in a less than cogent fashion. However, her telling facts and quotations are "a wonderful read."—*M. L. Meldrum, SUNY at Stony Brook*

WS-2034   JK1896   92-27412 CIP
Wheeler, Marjorie Spruill. **New women of the New South: the leaders of the woman suffrage movement in the southern states.** Oxford, 1993. 280p bibl index afp ISBN 0-19-507583-8, $45.00; ISBN 0-19-508245-1 pbk, $19.95

The blossoming of women's history has generated numerous case studies of women suffragists and state suffrage campaigns, but overviews have generally focused on the successful national campaign for the Nineteenth Amendment. Now Wheeler (Univ. of Southern Mississippi) presents a regional synthesis of women's suffrage efforts where reform was least popular: the South. Focusing on the lives and ideologies of 11 of the region's leading suffragists, Wheeler explains how these women hoped to exploit white southern males' devotion to racism and states' rights to win votes for women. She explores the difficulties inherent for southern suffragists in trying to be both traditional and pathbreaking, true both to the white South's conservatism and to progressive ideals. Wheeler foreshadows many of the divisions in the postsuffrage women's movement. Her manuscript research is impressive but her analysis stops short of the grassroots suffrage movement, the political situation in many southern states, and the suffrage efforts of African American women. Important for libraries collecting in the South, progressivism, and women's history. Advanced undergraduates and above.—*P. F. Field, Ohio University*

WS-2035   HD6509   90-24460 CIP
Wieck, David Thoreau. **Woman from Spillertown: a memoir of Agnes Burns Wieck.** Southern Illinois, 1992. 280p index afp ISBN 0-8093-1619-6, $32.50

Born (1892) and raised in a coal town, Agnes Burns Wieck lost her mother at age ten and helped to rear her younger brothers while her coal miner father eked out an uncertain living. She left southern Illinois for Chicago in 1915 and received formal training in labor organizing by the Women's Trade Union League. Still later, she married a coal miner, Ed Wieck, gave birth to a son, and wrote for the *Illinois Miner*. In 1933, Wieck became the leader of the short-lived Women's Auxiliary of the Progressive Miners of America. David Thoreau Wieck, author and editor of this work, uses his mother's speeches, letters, and other primary sources to recreate her life as well as to set her activities into a larger cultural context. The problems of union organizing, of the Depression, as well as the role of women in working families all receive treatment in this rich historical account. Wieck also gives attention to the difficulties experienced by reformers within the United Mine Workers. Recommended for all libraries with holdings in US labor history, social history, and women's history.—*J. Sochen, Northeastern Illinois University*

WS-2036   HQ1413.B39   90-12699 CIP
A woman making history: Mary Ritter Beard through her letters, ed. by Nancy F. Cott. Yale, 1991. 378p bibl index afp ISBN 0-300-04825-4, $35.00

Mary Ritter Beard stands out as a true pioneer in the effort to "write women back into history." Frequently overshadowed by her more famous and controversial husband, Beard's own accomplishments were largely ignored, even in reviews of texts in which her contributions equaled those of her husband. Cott's edition of Mary Beard's letters should serve to undo much of that neglect. Cott skillfully selected letters designed to illustrate Beard's "character, activities, and intellectual interests," including letters documenting her work for woman suffrage, her efforts to establish a Woman's Archive, and her antiwar activities. The letters are fascinating, providing invaluable insights into some of the most critical moments in 20th-century US women's history. Beard was truly a historian who made, as well as recorded and interpreted, history. Cott's introductory essay offers important biographical information as well as thoughtful analysis of Mary Beard's life and accomplishments. Cott ties the letters together with historical or interpretative comments, which turn personal correspondence into logical and sequential history. Highly recommended for all college and university libraries.—*E. Broidy, University of California, Irvine*

WS-2037   HQ1438   88-72049 CIP
Women of New Mexico: Depression era images, comp. and ed. by Marta Weigle. Ancient City, 1993. 129p bibl ISBN 0-941270-55-6, $29.95; ISBN 0-941270-54-8 pbk, $17.95

A wonderfully engaging depiction of the life of some New Mexican women in the 1930s. Weigle selected these images from the collection of Farm Security Administration (FSA) photographs, with accompanying texts drawn from manuscripts produced by the Federal Writers' Project. Juxtaposed texts and images provide an opportunity for the reader to compare the language of each, as each deepens understanding of the other. The images are sharp and detailed, and each reflects the "fresh and original ... view" for which FSA photographers such as John Collier, Jr. and Dorothea Lange became well known. There is nothing romantic here in the narratives of women plastering houses, making soap (and nearly everything else they needed), coaxing seedlings, and enjoying an occasional song or dance. Carefully produced and beautifully organized, these glimpses of rural women living their lives also reveal their productive roles. women. Excellent notes and references to the works chosen for reproduction; biographical sketches of photographers and writers represented. All levels.—*L. De Danaan, Evergreen State College*

WS-2038   F869   94-40397 CIP
Yung, Judy. **Unbound feet: a social history of Chinese women in San Francisco.** California, 1995. 395p bibl index afp ISBN 0-520-08866-2, $45.00; ISBN 0-520-08867-0 pbk, $15.95

Historian Judy Yung's work fills a big void in Asian American and women's studies literature. She focuses on Chinese women in San Francisco, from their time of entry into the US in the late 19th century through WW II. Working from dual outsider/insider perspectives as a trained historian but also as daughter of one of her subjects, Yung skillfully documents, retells, and analyzes the life experiences of these women as immigrants and as daughters and wives of immigrants, marginalized by their race, class, and gender statuses. Interwoven into the sociohistorical text and analysis are numerous mininarratives and personal testimonies of three generations of Chinese women spanning more than 50 years of collective memory. Their stories demonstrate expected hardships and heartbreaks, but above all, the pragmatic behavior of these mostly ordinary yet often remarkable women to adapt and survive in the US. Educated, middle-class women, their views on gender roles and relations were mainly influenced by Chinese nationalism, Christianity, and acculturation into American ways of thinking and doing. All levels.—*E. Hu-DeHart, University of Colorado at Boulder*

◆ Political Science

WS-2039   HQ1190   90-26835 CIP
Biehl, Janet. **Rethinking ecofeminist politics.** South End, 1991. 181p index ISBN 0-89608-392-6, $25.00; ISBN 0-89608-391-8 pbk, $10.00

Recently, Greens and ecofeminists have had sharp political disputes at conferences and in the media. Here Biehl, a Green, takes aim at several popular ecofeminist books and anthologies, attacking them for sins ranging from irrationality, to poor scholarship, to failure to embrace the "social ecology" versions of history and science put forth by Biehl's mentor, Murray Bookchin. And indeed, the popular writings she condemns often do demonstrate disregard for scholarship and for generally accepted social and natural fact, urging instead ersatz goddess worship, cosmic unity, the essentialism of the woman/nature connection, and so on. Unfortunately, Biehl ignores the considerable body of ecofeminist theory that has appeared in scholarly journals, theory that itself advances responsible critiques of ecofeminist "excesses." And ironically, Biehl's own work is academically shoddy, being alternately undocumented or supported by dated, obscure, or secondary sources. Although Biehl's vitriolic putdowns of ecofeminism may delight some of her Green and social ecology cohorts, the book contributes little to any serious debate about environmental ethics or ecofeminism.—*L. Vance, Vermont College*

WS-2040   JA74   94-24068 CIP
Brown, Wendy. **States of injury: power and freedom in late modernity.** Princeton, 1995. 202p index afp ISBN 0-691-02990-3, $39.50; ISBN 0-691-02989-X pbk, $12.95

In this rich and thought-provoking book, Brown (women's studies, Univ. of California at Santa Cruz) interrogates the state-centered, emancipatory politics of contemporary feminists like Catharine MacKinnon, Christine Williams, Carole Pateman, Barbara Ehrenreich, and Frances Fox Piven to demonstrate how "feminism operating with unreconstructed liberal discourse is ... trapped." She argues that by formulating "unfreedom" as socially injurious practices that need to be redressed through state intervention, the feminist political projects (and those of the political Left) inadvertently perpetuate and strengthen the power of the masculinist liberal state and capitalism, although the state and the capitalist economy are the sites of domination. She suggests alternate discourses of freedom be formulated that "exploit and subvert" the "diffuse and subtle" masculinism of the postmodern state and refashion democratic politics. *States of Injury* should be required reading in graduate and upper-division undergraduate courses in liberalism, modern political theory, feminist theory, and critical legal theory. Strongly recommended for libraries that serve faculty, graduate, and upper-division undergraduate students.—*S. R. Bald, Willamette University*

WS-2041   K644   92-3465 CIP
Feminist jurisprudence, ed. by Patricia Smith. Oxford, 1993. 628p afp ISBN 0-19-507397-5, $35.00

Smith's collection offers a wide range of selections of path-breaking work by noted feminist theorists, such as Andrea Dworkin, Catharine A. MacKinnon, Martha Minnow, and Deborah Rhode. Sections cover issues relating to equality, justice, adjudication, freedom, human dignity, and legal theory. Each section contains a helpful, albeit brief, introductory analysis. An introduction to the book, which discusses various feminist theoretical perspectives (Marxist, socialist, liberal, radical, postmodern, relational), suggests the diversity and scope of feminist thought, but necessarily provides only a cursory analysis of complex issues. The volume demonstrates the transformative nature of feminist analyses of law. In both the specific critiques of legal issues, such as reproductive freedom, pornography regulation, and legal responses to violence against women, and the broader theoretical articles, the provocative challenges of feminist theorists to traditional legal analysis is evidenced. From various feminist perspectives, the authors challenge the assumptions that legal reasoning is neutral and that "objective" standards of legal decision making are possible or desirable. As the editor of the volume suggests, "The norm for judges is white and male, and this norm is mistaken for perspectiveless objectivity." Advanced undergraduate through professional.—*M. Hendrickson, Wilson College*

WS-2042   HQ1236   95-30132 CIP
Gender power, leadership, and governance, ed. by Georgia Duerst-Lahti and Rita Mae Kelly. Michigan, 1995. 305p bibl index afp ISBN 0-472-09610-9, $47.50

The editors make a comprehensive effort to chart the course of "gender power" as an organizing concept implicit in or addressed directly by political science. The editors hope to review empirical and evaluative research as these apply to the process of government and to present their own integrative approach. They argue that gender as a political dynamic should be approached in multiple institutional contexts using a variety of methodologies. Besides the editors (who wrote four chapters), contributors are K.L. Tamerius, N. Norton, M.A. Newman, L. Kathlene, and M.E. Gay. All chapters focus on institutional leadership and governance and apply organizational theory to congressional committees and other nonexecutive agencies. Basic premises include the following: human interaction is inherently gendered; gender is expressed ideologically as "masculinism" and "feminism"; gender power is the result of the ideological expression of behavior and social constructs; masculinism is the constitutive ideology of leadership and governance and of academic efforts to evaluate their effectiveness. Every chapter cites existing studies, comparing feminist scholarship and the state of the art in political science. Bryan D. Jones's *Leadership and Politics* (1989), a major text, is singled out for ignoring gender. Upper-division undergraduates through faculty.—*J. V. Scott, Eastern Michigan University*

WS-2043   95-79554 Orig
The Human Rights Watch global report on women's human rights, by the Human Rights Watch, Women's Rights Project. Human Rights Watch, 1995. (Dist. by Yale) 458p ISBN 0-300-06546-9 pbk, $15.00

This volume is a compilation of investigations by the Women's Rights Project of Human Rights Watch, a respected international group monitoring human rights abuses around the world. It includes detailed reports on rape used as a weapon of war and of political repression in Somalia, Haiti, India, and Peru, as well as the more publicized cases in Bosnia. In addition, it provides an extensive and eye-opening examination of sexual abuse of women prisoners in the US. Other sections provide accounts of forced prostitution and sexual traffic in women, abuses of female domestic workers, domestic violence against women in Brazil and South Africa, forced virginity exams in Turkey, and abortion restrictions in Ireland and Poland. The combination of fact-finding and advocacy is powerful witness against abuses of women that governments, including that of the US, are reluctant to define as real infringements of human rights. The great strength of this book lies in how it assembles women's voices and places them in a context that affirms women as truly human beings. A valuable global perspective for courses on sexual violence, and an essential reference compendium. All levels.—*M. M. Ferree, University of Connecticut*

WS-2044   KF387   93-31233 CIP
Law in everyday life, ed. by Austin Sarat and Thomas R. Kearns. Michigan, 1993. 285p index afp ISBN 0-472-10441-1, $39.50

Sarat and Kearns (Amherst College) have edited a truly marvelous work on the impact of the law on daily life and vice versa. In a particularly thoughtful and cogent introductory essay, the coeditors set forth the analytic framework of the volume's subsequent chapters by critiquing the "instrumentalist" and "constitutive" paradigms of the law and everyday life and proposing a reconciliation between them that attends "to particular practices and concrete, historically situated examples of law and social relations." The remaining six essays provide these examples in their examination of an 18-century woman's approach within the context of the legal system and her own religious beliefs to the sexual abuse by her husband of their daughter (Hartog), the subordination of women by legally protected pornography (MacKinnon), the development of legally mandated education programs for disabled children in six families (Engel), personal journeys through law and everyday life (Williams, Kennedy), and a challenge to rethink the meaning of the everyday in law (Marcus). With exception of the MacKinnon essay, which continues her previously pubished one-note, anti-civil liberties tune familiar to most members of this volume's target audience, the essays are all exemplary, thought-provoking works worthy of a long, contemplative read by scholars, lawyers, and judges alike. Graduate; faculty, professional.—*M. W. Bowers, University of Nevada, Las Vegas*

WS-2045   JC328   92-39228 CIP
Mason, Andrew. **Explaining political disagreement.** Cambridge, 1993. 170p bibl index ISBN 0-521-43322-3, $44.95

In this revision of his dissertation, Mason reviews the pertinent literature with regard to political and moral disagreement, noting that such disagreement is persistent and intractable. Analyzing the "contestability" and "imperfection" theses, he offers a hybrid of the two that he labels "essential contestedness." This perspective suggests that disagreements are not merely a function of those who occupy different positions failing to understand one another (imperfection) nor the value ladenness of concepts (contestability). Instead, disagreement arises because of a mix of rational and nonrational factors. The models of Gilligan and Chodorow are used to illustrate how and why fundamental disagreement arises. Because of the gender differences in child rearing in modern capitalist societies, girls/women are more apt to employ an "ethics of care" while men/boys are more likely to use an "ethics of rights" in their moral and political decision making. Such an example thus demonstrates the intractability of political and moral disagreements. The volume contains a reasonable survey of the literature but still reads like a dissertation. The Chodorow/Gilligan illustration might be more effective if incorporated beyond one isolated chapter. Recommended for graduate students and faculty.—*L. Bowen, John Carroll University*

WS-2046   K675   89-77702 CIP
Mason, J.K. **Medico-legal aspects of reproduction and parenthood.** Dartmouth (UK), 1990. 367p index ISBN 1-85521-015-0, $53.95

Mason (University of Edinburgh) offers a manual on the uncertain area of reproductive law. Although this study focuses on Britain, it also draws on the law and practices of the US and the Commonwealth for clarification and suggested alternative solutions. Ambitious in scope, the volume begins with a discussion of sex and marriage and ends with a chapter on child abuse. Between these issues Mason includes chapters on contraception, abortion, fetal rights, infertility, experimentation, and infanticide. The book has two main strengths. First, this holistic approach enables Mason to show that these issues are so interconnected that policy decisions in one area affect those in other areas as well. Second, although writing in a rapidly changing field, the author offers a surprisingly up-to-date survey. There are, however, two disappointments. First, rather than drawing more heavily on his experiences and insights as a physician, Mason leans instead toward a legalistic approach. Second, the book is limited by its exploration of reproduction within the confines of the traditional family. A list of cases and a table of statutes are included. Appropriate for graduate school collections.—*S. Behuniak-Long, Le Moyne College*

WS-2047   Aust. CIP
Naffine, Ngaire. **Law and the sexes: explorations in feminist jurisprudence.** Allen & Unwin, 1991 (c1990). (Dist. by Paul & Company, c/o PCS Data Processing, Inc., 360 West 31 St., New York, NY 10001) 170p bibl index ISBN 0-04-442210-5 pbk, $19.95

Drawing on critical legal studies and feminist jurisprudence, Naffine argues that the "abstract individual" of the Anglo-American legal tradition is in fact a white, middle-class man. Therefore, any claims that the legal system might make to neutrality and objectivity are inherently false. This leads to a central contradiction, because the legitimacy of law, by its own definition, depends on its objectivity. Although this is not an original argument, Naffine's handling of it is exemplary. Her prose is crisp and unburdened by technical jargon, making legal philosophy accessible even to undergraduates. Her summaries and analyses of feminist jurisprudence in England, the US, and Australia are succinct and comprehensive. Most significantly, she extends the feminist critique of white-male-as-norm to class and masculinity, demonstrating how the criminal justice system, in particular, enforces a very specific gender and class ideal. An excellent addition to both social science and women's studies collections. College and University libraries.—*L. Vance, Vermont College*

WS-2048   HQ1236   90-27912 CIP
Phillips, Anne. **Engendering democracy.** Pennsylvania State, 1991. 183p bibl index ISBN 0-271-00783-4, $28.50; ISBN 0-271-00784-2 pbk, $13.95

Phillips's book is relevant to those concerned with the relationship of feminism to politics and government on both sides of the Atlantic. Phillips (London

Polytechnic University) discusses various political models in detail to determine which model best makes possible participation by the largest number of citizens, especially women, who have been mostly excluded over the centuries. Phillips draws on the expositions of both male and female political scientists and subjects them to a minute analysis from a feminist perspective. The book, however, has a quite practical component, as, for instance, when Phillips discusses participatory democracy. In theory, this should involve the greatest number of individuals in decision-making, but because most people just do not attend meetings, it becomes in practice decision-making by an unrepresentative few. Phillips concludes that with all of its inadequacies, liberal democracy and one person, one vote, is the most promising approach to government. A brief but closely reasoned book that is more analysis than advocacy. Upper-divison undergraduates and above.—*E. Cassara, emeritus, George Mason University*

WS-2049 Orig
Wetzel, Janice Wood. **The world of women: in pursuit of human rights.** Macmillan, UK, 1993. (Dist. by New York University) 228p bibl index ISBN 0-333-55030-7, $45.00; ISBN 0-333-55031-5 pbk, $20.00

Wetzel's book is about linkages forged on behalf of the world's women. It is a book about human-rights policies and programs that incorporates knowledge for therapeutic practices. Wetzel is concerned with making grass-roots projects more accessible and celebrates the work of women in the developing world while honoring the efforts of those in industrial societies. She focuses on women who are poor, but recognizes issues common to all. Clearly oriented to problems of gender, Wetzel also acknowledges the negative impact of ethnicity, class, age, sexual preference, disability, and other differences of people. Although the content focuses on problems of women, the book makes clear that their strength, endurance, and resourcefulness offer hope for the world. It is written to influence educators and members of the professions to direct their efforts to the global conditions of women from a human-rights perspective. Wetzel provides a comprehensive resource for achieving human rights for women as well as resources for all who wish to learn by sharing the expertise of women in the developing world. General; undergraduate; graduate; faculty; professional.—*M. Klatte, Eastern Kentucky University*

WS-2050 HQ1236.5.U6 90-8381 MARC
Women, politics, and change, ed. by Louise A. Tilly and Patricia Gurin. Russell Sage Foundation, 1990. (Dist. by CUP Services, P.O. Box 6525, Ithaca, NY 14851) 670p bibl indexes afp ISBN 0-87154-884-4, $45.00

Tilly and Gurin have gathered together the usual suspects in this edited volume. Indeed, the usual suspects, including Kristi Andersen, M. Nancy Cott, Patricia Fernandez-Kelly, Nancy Hewitt, M. Kent Jennings, Rebecca Klatch, Jane Mansbridge, etc., form a veritable who's who in feminist research. Thus in some ways the strength of this book is its weakness. It is timely and the authors are all first-rate scholars in their respective fields. Moreover, an anthology such as this, which brings together important minds, is a valuable addition to feminist research. However, volumes of this nature may contribute to the making of a new feminist canon, as it becomes too easy to see these eminent scholars as gatekeepers, in a negative sense, of their own fields. Hence, this volume would have been applauded more enthusiastically had Gurin and Tilly used their own status in the field to publish younger and less established voices. Nonetheless, most libraries will wish to own this collection. Upper-division undergraduates and above.—*I. E. Deutchman, Hobart and William Smith Colleges*

◆ Comparative Politics

WS-2051 HQ1236.5.T9 88-45715 CIP
Arat, Yesim. **The patriarchal paradox: women politicians in Turkey.** Fairleigh Dickinson, 1989. 162p bibl index afp ISBN 0-8386-3347-1, $26.50

The paradox of patriarchy in the title of this revised doctoral dissertation is that women politicians in Turkey entered into electoral politics because of the encouragement of patriarchal husbands or fathers and yet were hindered in numbers and success by patriarchy as a cultural and structural value. In short, patriarch encourages female political involvement but also inhibits and constrains it. Arat interviewed a representative sample of 16 female parliamentarians and 12 female members of municipal councils. Her interviews addressed questions of social economic status (upper-middle-class), father and husband support in entering politics, and ultimate male discrimination in not achieving the pinnacles of politics. The explanation of the paradox and the smallness of numbers of female politicians is said to rest in the fact that Kemal Attaturk, the great modernizer of Turkey, mandated gender equality, thereby preventing feminism from emerging as a separate militant phenomenon. The result is a degree of attenuated and constrained female political involvement. The volume contains a lengthy appendix of names of all female parliamentarians with education and professions plus the text of the interview questions. Recommended for all four year college collections.— *L. J. Cantori, University of Maryland, Baltimore County*

WS-2052 HG1236 91-44884 CIP
Basu, Amrita. **Two faces of protest: contrasting modes of women's activism in India.** California, 1992. 308p bibl index afp ISBN 0-520-06506-9, $35.00

Studies of political activism in the developing world overwhelmingly focus on class relations. Basu's book offers a welcome and fascinating example of how to incorporate ethnic and gender relations into such analysis. Using two case studies, of the Communist party (CPI-M) in West Bengal, and the Shramik Sangathana in Maharashtra, Basu presents a subtle comparison of their divergent approaches, strategies, and dilemmas. By contrasting the reformism and hierarchical leadership of the CPI-M with the militant grass-roots activism of the Shramik Sangathana, Basu is able to evaluate the two movements and to offer a compelling argument for understanding the interaction of caste, gender, and class in Indian politics. The study is founded on rich field research, relying on numerous interviews and weaving together the levels of village study with centralized elite analysis. The attempt to view political activism "through the lens of women's experience" is particularly important for those interested in peasant movements, leftist politics, and women's protest. Extensive endnotes, glossary, and bibliography. Useful for undergraduate and graduate collections.—*A. E. MacLeod, Bates College*

WS-2053 HQ1236.5.T28 90-8605 CIP
Chou, Bih-Er. **Women in Taiwan politics: overcoming barriers to women's participation in a modernizing society,** by Chou Bih-er, Cal Clark, and Janet Clark. L. Rienner, 1990. 207p bibl index ISBN 1-55587-106-2, $30.00

A liberal-feminist case study of women in politics in the Republic of China on Taiwan. Rapid economic development and industrialization have transformed the role of women in politics in Taiwan. The authors point to the key element in the electoral system, the "reserved-seats system"—10 of the assembly seats are reserved for women—and argue that it is analogous to the women's movement in the West; both are extremely effective vehicles for promoting women's entrance into governmental positions. The study discusses the inadequacies of modernization theories which insist that the worldwide gross underrepresentation of women in politics is a transitory stage in the eventually egalitarian process of economic development. The authors also examine feminist theories that focus on the continued, and perhaps increased, subjugation of women under capitalist development, which remains overtly patriarchal. Coming down in the middle of the debate, the authors argue that with institutional change (e.g., the "reserved-seats" model) and with organized efforts, rapid change can and does happen. Upper-division undergraduates and above.—*I. Infante, Alverno College*

WS-2054 Orig
Fisher, Jo. **Out of the shadows: women, resistance and politics in South America.** Latin America Bureau, UK, 1993. (Dist. by Monthly Review) 228p bibl index ISBN 0-906156-77-7 pbk, $15.00

Fisher has written an informative and provocative new study of how the changing political situations in four South American nations (Chile, Paraguay, Argentina, and Uruguay) have affected women's lives. Based on several years of extensive field research, Fisher's study uniquely integrates the personal testimonies of women with the broader political and social context of each nation. Her study explores ways women have responded to repressive authoritarian governments, political liberalizations, and newly democratizing regimes. The result of this study is to show how women in different countries and from different classes have dealt with the issues of political repression, sexism, and economic hardship. From grassroots working-class women's organizations' fight for basic services to middle-class women's struggle for political rights, Fisher demonstrates that women have not stood idly by as political transformations have taken place in their countries. Rather, her study provides a human face to the larger political and economic changes which are now taking place in South America. Recommended for all academic levels.—*L. Chen, Indiana University at South Bend*

WS-2055 Can. CIP
Gender and politics in contemporary Canada, ed. by François-Pierre Gingras. Oxford, 1995. 273p index afp ISBN 0-19-541011-4 pbk, $28.00

Gingras's collection of 12 essays examines how Canadian women fare in political parties and in public policy and how gender is portrayed in the media and in scholarship, and includes empirical studies and broader theoretical analyses. One question addressed is whether a larger number of women in political leadership would contribute to increased support for feminist goals. Two studies of leaders find that the gender gap on most issues is small. A third essay argues that a feminist theory of representation must go beyond sex parity. Two essays that review national gender policies and pay equity legislation point out the shortcomings of an equal rights approach that does not emphasize role changes. The ambivalent relationship between feminism and nationalism is examined in two essays on Quebec. Interviews with homeless women in Halifax provide a critique of the neoconservative policy agenda. Two essays on the media find sex-role stereotyping. Limitations of survey research are explored in two essays. A concluding essay draws lessons about effective strategies for feminists, finding more of an emphasis on mainstreaming than on disengagement but stressing the complementarity of both strategies. A well-balanced collection, recommended for upper-division undergraduates through faculty.—*J. G. Everett, University of Colorado at Denver*

WS-2056 K1781 94-1052 CIP
Hart, Vivien. **Bound by our Constitution: women, workers, and the minimum wage.** Princeton, 1994. 255p index afp ISBN 0-691-03480-X, $35.00

Another volume in the superb "Princeton Studies in American Politics: Historical, International, and Comparative Perspectives" series, this book explores minimum wage politics and practices in Great Britain and the US over the past century or so. The comparison is instructive: both movements arose as part of women reformers' campaign against sweated industry. But once they hit the political maw the paths diverged; Great Britain speedily enacted a law that covered few trades, but the US struggled for some 30 years. American state efforts to mandate minimum wages for women were struck down by the Supreme Court, redirecting effort from gender-based remedies to the ultimately successful class-based Fair Labor Standards Act. Since then the American law has become more inclusive, covering virtually every worker, whereas the British abolished minimum wages in 1993. This review's sketchy summary cannot do justice to this thoroughly researched, tightly written, and conceptually rich study. Its thesis, that the US Constitution "explains" much of the divergent history, puts this book firmly within the "new institutionalism." Abundantly footnoted, *Bound by Our Constitution* will be widely consulted by scholars in the social sciences and humanities, particularly those in history, political science, law, and women's studies. Upper-division undergraduate; graduate; faculty.—*D. Lindstrom, University of Wisconsin-Madison*

WS-2057 JA75 94-8989 CIP
Kelly, Petra K. **Thinking green!: essays on environmentalism, feminism, and nonviolence.** Parallax, 1994. 167p ISBN 0-938077-62-7, $18.00

This is the last book in English of the nonviolent world political leader and German Green Party founder Petra Karin Kelly (1947-1992). It follows her *Fighting for Hope* (1984), *The Anguish of Tibet*, which she edited (1991), and *Nonviolence Speaks to Power* (1992). She addresses issues that have brought recognition to her as one of the 20th century's most influential personalities. These include women and power, ecology and economy, new Green politics, the madness of arms races, nonviolent social defense alternatives, the inviolability of human rights, the missed opportunities in German reunification, ways out of the Old/New World Order, and the planetary life-saving imperative. Overall she sets forth "a green agenda for the ecological and nonviolent transformation of society". A foreword by Peter Matthiessen and afterwords by Mark Hertsgaard, Charlene Spretnak, and Eleanor Mulloney Lecain help to make this book the most current single source of knowledge about Petra Kelly's life, thought, and action. Petra Kelly's truthful, compassionate, down-to-earth commitment will engage and educate readers of all ages and walks of life.—*G. D. Paige, emeritus, University of Hawaii at Manoa*

WS-2058 JQ5854 93-217014 MARC
Making policy not tea: women in Parliament, ed. by Arthur Baysting, Dyan Campbell, and Margaret Dagg. Oxford, 1994 (c1993). 205p ISBN 0-19-558275-6 pbk, $29.95

During the 60 years since 1933, 36 women have been elected to the New Zealand Parliament. This slim volume contains a series of sometimes lengthy quotations by these women on such topics as starting out, family life, lifestyle, housework, and gender politics. Their relationship with male colleagues, whose chauvinism they often encountered, and with other female legislators of their own and the other political party; support or otherwise from spouses; hardship on their young children; the distance between home and capitol—these are problems with which women members of the American Congress or the British House of Commons are only too familiar. Criticism of the rules and behavior of the New Zealand Parliament is frequently similar to criticism about Washington, and so are some of the comments regarding the opposite party. Includes biographical sketches and photos. An index, however, is sorely missed. A glossary of terms pertaining to parliamentary and New Zealand politics and perhaps a political map of the country would greatly enhance the usefulness of this anecdotal and very readable book.—*W. S. G. Kohn, emeritus, Illinois State University*

WS-2059 K1824 94-44875 CIP
Protecting women: labor legislation in Europe, the United States, and Australia, 1880-1920, ed. by Ulla Wikander, Alice Kessler-Harris, and Jane Lewis with Jan Lambertz. Illinois, 1995. 379p bibl index afp ISBN 0-252-02175-4, $49.95; ISBN 0-252-06464-X pbk, $19.95

Rarely do edited books have the coherence found here. Each of the 11 chapters on specific countries (plus an introduction and a chapter on international conferences) was written by a resident expert from that country. Protective legislation for women originated primarily between 1880 and 1920. In some countries the motivating factors were to preserve the dominance of men in the workplace and maintain women's social function in the family. In other countries, there was some hope that protective legislation for women would be a wedge leading to labor legislation to enhance the work life of men as well as women. In other cases, states enacted protective legislation to ensure future population by equating women with perpetual motherhood. Regardless of the rationale, the effect of such protective labor legislation was to further disadvantage women in the workplace. In most countries feminists were divided over the wisdom of protective legislation. For nonfeminists, women were almost always viewed as a group defined by motherhood. The richness of this book allows exploration of the issues in many contexts and adds considerably to more general works on the origins of the welfare state. Upper-division undergraduates through faculty.—*C. Shrewsbury, Mankato State University*

WS-2060 KTL517x Orig
Putting women on the agenda, ed. by Susan Bazilli. Ravan, 1992 (c1991). 290p ISBN 0-86975-422-X pbk, $24.95

With this collection it is clear that the feminist movement is asserting itself in South Africa. Because many African traditions denigrate the role of women, the authors assert the need for constitutional guarantees in a "new South Africa." The volume grew out of a series of conferences on Women and the Constitution, the final one in Johannesburg in November 1990, organized by Lawyers for Human Rights. All but one of the contributors are women, and all are either academics or lawyers. Most of the concerns expressed in these essays have parallels worldwide: rape, sexual harassment, and political and legal discrimination against women. With major constitutional changes occurring, the women stress the need for a gender-neutral constitution. They write that this will happen only if women fight for their rights and become significant actors in the political arena. Affirmative action for women is also a topic for several contributors. Bazilli's introduction accurately surveys the themes of the other authors. Advanced undergraduate; graduate.—*J. J. Grotpeter, St. Louis College of Pharmacy*

WS-2061   Orig
Rose, Kalima. **Where women are leaders: the Sewa movement in India.** Zed Books, 1993 (c1992). 286p index ISBN 1-85649-083-1, $55.00; ISBN 1-85649-084-X pbk, $19.95

Rose's work is a journalistic account of a nonprofit, grassroots organization named SEWA (Self-Employed Women's Association) in India. The characteristics of SEWA and the insightful observations of the author make this book valuable reading for people interested in women's issues, grassroots participation, social movements, local management, and labor-capital relations. SEWA, with a membership of 30,000, is an organization of women for women by women. SEWA's emergence, scope, style, leadership, and struggle are the focal points of Rose's study. Rose discusses, in particular, the relationships between banking, credit, medicine, and landownership on one hand and the empowerment of women on the other. Rose succeeds in giving us a powerful case study; however, the study starts and ends with the case in question. The author neither attempts nor pretends to link her observations with broader issues and theories. In brief, this is a realistic account of SEWA and strategies that work. From this point of view alone, the book is useful for practitioners and scholars alike.—*R. Khator, University of South Florida*

WS-2062   JC599   93-48349 CIP
Tula, María Teresa. **Hear my testimony: María Teresa Tula, human rights activist of El Salvador,** tr. and ed. by Lynn Stephen. South End, 1994. 240p ISBN 0-89608-485-X, $30.00; ISBN 0-89608-484-1 pbk, $14.00

Tula'sl book is an excellent example of the first-person testimonial genre, which has been popularized in Latin American and Third World literature and may be favorably compared to such well-known testimonies as Rigoberta Menchú's *I, Rigoberta Menchú, An Indian Woman in Guatemala* (CH, Jan'85) and Dorothy Jeffree's and Roy McConkey's *Let Me Speak: Domitila Chungarro, A Woman of the Bolivian Mines.* Through the collaborative mediation of Lynn Stephen, María Teresa Tula, a human rights and women's rights activist in El Salvador, vividly depicts the struggle of the courageous women of CO-MADRES, a Salvadoran human rights group which labored to secure humane treatment and accountability for political prisoners and the disappeared. María's story is of her own political and social awakening as she searches for her husband imprisoned for his union activism, and it is also the story of the grassroots revolutionary struggle for justice in El Salvador. As with the personal testimonies of Menchú and Domitila, María's struggle represents an integral part of the growing feminist movement in El Salvador, which fought to end the unequal work burdens of women in the home, their political marginalization, and sexual repression. A very readable book from an activist and progressive perspective, recommended for all readership levels.—*W. Q. Morales, University of Central Florida*

WS-2063   Can. CIP
Vicker, Jill. **Politics as if women mattered: a political analysis of the National Action Committee on the status of women,** by Jill Vickers, Pauline Rankin and Christine Appelle. Toronto, 1993. 347p bibl index afp ISBN 0-8020-5850-7, $50.00; ISBN 0-8020-6757-3 pbk, $19.95

This book analyzes the institutionalization of a "parliament of women" amid the linguistic and ethnic diversity of Canada from 1972-88, utilizing documentary evidence and interviews. Canada's National Action Committee on the Status of Women (NAC), which affiliated more than 600 organizations at last count,

struggled over the breadth of its women's agenda over three significant stages of organizational life. Clearly and accessibly written, the authors make conceptual and theoretical advances in their linkage of feminist movements, conventional politics, and the state, and in their insistence that institutionalization is healthful rather than mere co-optation. This rich, in-depth case study is a relevant goldmine for international audiences, for the authors continually draw comparative insight with the US and Europe and their contrasting political cultures and feminist strategies. The book is a useful counterpart to edited collections: Sue Ellen Charlton, et.al, *Women, the State, and Development* (1989), on the degree to which women engage with the state in different world regions, and Kathleen Staudt' *Women, International Development and Politics* (1990), on how institutionalization fares in different contexts. Useful for general and academic libraries, undergraduate and graduate.—*K. Staudt, University of Texas at El Paso*

WS-2064   HQ1236   94-1147 CIP
Women and government: new ways to political power, ed. by Mim Kelber. Praeger, 1994. 229p bibl index afp ISBN 0-275-94816-1, $59.95

We hardly know everything we need to about women in politics. Unfortunately, however, Kelber's book does little to advance our knowledge. Hers is not a serious academic endeavor; indeed it feels as though it was put together quickly with little care. For example, neither the editor nor any of the contributors are identified by academic or professional affiliation. There is no theoretical question which guides this book. A series of brief essays on the status of women in government in the countries of Norway, Sweden, Finland, Denmark, Iceland and Germany are offered with no explanation as to why these countries were selected. Judging from the last chapter on what American women can do to win political equality, perhaps these other countries are to serve as models for the US. However, that is mere speculation as the editor does not develop such an argument. The essays themselves are basic, offering little to the serious researcher. As befits such a superficial introduction, the bibliography itself is a scant four pages. Serious comparative work on women in politics is needed. This book does little to advance that need. Only libraries with intense budget surpluses need order it.—*I. E. Deutchman, Hobart and William Smith Colleges*

WS-2065   HQ1236   94-18706 CIP
Women and revolution in Africa, Asia, and the New World, ed. by Mary Ann Tétreault. South Carolina, 1994. 456p index ISBN 1-57003-016-2, $39.95

Tétrault's collection is packed with illuminating theoretical essays and substantive chapters of 20th-century revolutions in 16 countries. Revolution is broadly defined to include socialist, religious, nationalist, and capitalist/modernizing efforts as they intersect with women and families. Although revolutions generally broaden the political agenda (to include topics such as wife beating, unpaid heavy labor, and bridewealth exchange) or to construct new female symbolism, gains for women are mixed and nowhere is equality achieved. Readers will find coverage of those revolutions with a sparse literature, such as North Korea and Afghanistan, especially useful. Tétrault's collection, *the* probable classic on the topic for the 1990s, provides greater conceptual breadth and country-level depth than the 1980s classics *Promissory Notes: Women in the Transition to Socialism*, edited by Sonia Kruks, Rayna Rapp, and Marilyn Young (CH, Dec'89), and *Women, the State, and Development*, edited by Sue Ellen Charlton, Jana Everett, and Kathleen Staudt (CH, May'90). Highly recommended for undergraduate, graduate, and general reader libraries.—*K. Staudt, University of Texas at El Paso*

◆ International Relations

WS-2066 Orig

Bunch, Charlotte. **Demanding accountability: the global campaign and Vienna Tribunal for women's human rights,** by Charlotte Bunch and Niamh Reilly. Center for Women's Global Leadership, Rutgers University/United Nations Development Fund for Women (UNIFEM), 1994. (Dist. by Women Ink) 169p ISBN 0-912917-29-6 pbk, $14.95

Bunch (founder of *Quest: A Feminist Quarterly*), and Reilly describe the strategies, global campaigning, networking, and coordination employed by women's NGOs to ensure that the topic of gender-based violence occupied a central place at the 1993 UN World Conference on Human Rights. The authors focus on the Global Tribunal that preceded the World Conference, where 33 women from 25 countries gave compelling accounts of gender-based violations of their human rights. Weaving together these testimonies, the statements of the presiding judges, and their own observations and analysis, Bunch and Reilly compellingly underscore the universality and indivisibility of women's human rights. They leave no doubt that these stories influenced the wording and easy passage of the Vienna Declaration at the World Conference. A valuable appendix quotes extracts of important documents from the global campaign and the Tribunal, the Vienna Declaration, and an extensive list of global resources and contacts. An excellent companion to *Human Rights of Women: National and International Perspectives*, ed. by Rebecca Cook (CH, Feb'95), highly recommended for undergraduates, graduates, general readers, and political activists.—*S. R. Bald, Willamette University*

WS-2067 HQ1233 92-43416 CIP

Enloe, Cynthia. **The morning after: sexual politics at the end of the Cold War.** California, 1993. 326p bibl index afp ISBN 0-520-08335-0, $38.00; ISBN 0-520-08336-9 pbk, $15.00

Enloe's question is "Where are the women?" in analyses of militarization. Examining global politics in the post-Cold War era, she convincingly argues that the "omission of gender ... risks not only a flawed political analysis but also perpetually unsuccessful attempts to roll back militarization." Thus, Enloe displays the best of feminist scholarship in linking theory and reality. Popular images are used effectively to make her argument. The book is timely, containing many powerful observations about the debate on gays in the military, women in combat, the Tailhook scandal, and how such issues inform our understanding of other domestic issues. That she does all this without suggesting that gender or militarization are constructed but one way gives the analysis its rigor. She demonstrates the complexity of gender relations and global military politics, and that not everything can be attributed to the US military-industrial complex. Instead, she says, while "every public power arrangement has depended on the control of femininity as an idea," the particulars will vary depending upon the economic and social context of the nation-state in question. Thus, masculinity and femininity will be constructed to serve that country's national security. Highly recommended.—*L. Bowen, John Carroll University*

WS-2068 JX1391 91-14471 CIP

Gender and international relations, ed. by Rebecca Grant and Kathleen Newland. Indiana, 1991. 176p index ISBN 0-253-32613-3, $42.50; ISBN 0-253-21265-0 pbk, $15.95

A good introduction to the emerging study of gender theory applied to international relations. The collection of readings represents one of the first attempts to analyze the gendered biases of traditional international relations theory and their implications for women. The articles go beyond a simple critique of "fitting women in" where they have historically been left out to a complex deconstruction of how concepts of the state, power, war, and peace have reified existing western notions of male dominance and female subordination. The articles on theories and programs of "women in development" provide a much needed critique of the biases inherent in development aid policies applied to the Third World. Should be read by anyone interested in international relations theory, development studies, and women's studies.—*L. Chen, Indiana University at South Bend*

WS-2069 K644 94-20682 CIP

Human rights of women: national and international perspectives. Pennsylvania, 1994. 634p index afp ISBN 0-8122-3261-5, $54.95; ISBN 0-8122-1538-9 pbk, $21.95

Edited by Rebecca Cook, this collection of 22 excellent papers is the outcome of the Consultation on Women's International Human Rights Law at the University of Toronto in 1992. The scholars, drawn from South Asia, Africa, Latin America, Australia, UK, the Netherlands, Canada, and the US, provide rich data and analysis to highlight societal and national differences in the interpretation and implementation of women's human rights. The postcolonial scholars in particular maintain the importance of not "universalizing" women's experiences; instead they insist that differences be recognized in developing effective legal strategies for promoting women's human rights both inside and outside their homes. The multiple perspectives offered by this collection of eminently readable and interesting papers makes it a valuable resource for upper-division classes in women's studies, international relations, and international law. Recommended for upper-division undergraduates, graduate students, faculty, general readers, and political activists.—*S. R. Bald, Willamette University*

WS-2070 HQ1240 90-39963 CIP

Pietila, Hilkka. **Making women matter: the role of the United Nations,** by Hilkka Pietila and Jeanne Vickers. Zed Books, 1990. (Dist. by Humanities) 177p index ISBN 0-86232-968-X, $49.95; ISBN 0-86232-969-8, $15.00

This volume elucidates the various UN actions about women, especially the Decade for Women, 1975-1985. The authors make internal UN documents accessible by translating "UN-ese" into readable material. A particularly useful chapter outlines the Forward-Looking Strategies for the Advancement of Women in Africa. . . (1984), the unanimously adopted final document from the celebrated Nairobi conference that closed the decade. Practical, useful appendixes add to this slim narrative volume, such as the UN Convention on the Elimination of All Forms of Discrimination Against Women (1979); programs on women in development of UN-affiliated organizations; and "A Practical Guide: How to Prepare a Resolution for a UN Conference," among others. This volume could have gone further in making a Byzantine system and its bureaucratic politics more understandable, but it is a generous beginning to widening awareness of gender in international organizations. Useful for college and university students and for general readers.—*K. Staudt, University of Texas at El Paso*

WS-2071 JF848 94-33981 CIP

Suffrage and beyond: international feminist perspectives, ed. by Caroline Daley and Melanie Nolan. New York University, 1995 (c1994). 368p bibl index ISBN 0-8147-1870-1, $55.00; ISBN 0-8147-1871-X pbk, $19.95

These 16 papers from an August 1993 conference in Wellington, New Zealand, discusses the achievements and impact of women's suffrage campaigns through case studies focusing on New Zealand, Australia, the Pacific Islands, Japan, South America, France, Germany, the US, and Great Britain. The authors reject the "gift" argument (that men gave women the vote) and call for revisions in the "standard model" (based on the US and British experience) of when and how suffrage was achieved in order to incorporate the diverse experiences of various nations. Several authors examine racism and internationalism in the suffrage movements. The collection offers useful information about women's struggles for political rights in a number of nations. Australia and New Zealand are particularly well covered. The essays are uneven, however, the editors provide a good thematic introduction which makes the case for the value of suffrage history for understanding women's citizenship. Upper-division undergraduate; graduate; faculty.—*J. G. Everett, University of Colorado at Denver*

WS-2072 HQ1190 93-10251 CIP

Sylvester, Christine. **Feminist theory and international relations in a postmodern era.** Cambridge, 1994. 265p (Cambridge studies in international relations, 32) bibl index ISBN 0-521-39305-1, $54.95; ISBN 0-521-45984-2 pbk, $16.95

Sylvester (Northern Arizona Univ.) has written a tour de force challenging both international relations specialists and feminist scholars to converse with each other. In very witty prose spiced with sharp critiques of long-standing international relations sacred cows, Sylvester comes closer than any other authors currently writing on gender and IR questions to applying various feminist theoretical lenses to international relations theory and theorizing. She organizes her text by reviewing the long-standing debates in international relations starting with the realist/idealist debate, then the scientific/traditional debates, and on to the modern/post modern debate. Sylvester weaves into her analysis various feminist theories whose relevance to IR debates she convincingly demonstrates. She makes a case that ignoring feminist epistemological concerns has left the field of IR theory isolated from the very real and necessary cross-cultural perspectives of women, and that these omissions have been detrimental to international relations. The last part of her book entails two brief examples of how some women in England and some others in Zimbabwe have through their own actions disrupted long-held, cherished notions of the male-centric discipline of international relations. Recommended for upper-division undergraduates, graduate students, and faculty.—*L. Chen, Indiana University at South Bend*

WS-2073   JX1391   92-11103 CIP
Tickner, J. Ann. **Gender in international relations: feminist perspectives on achieving global security.** Columbia, 1992. 180p bibl index afp ISBN 0-231-07538-3, $30.00

Beginning with women's absence from the theory and practice of international relations, Tickner unmasks a hegemonic masculinity that defines national security in narrow terms inadequate for understanding the complexities of global problems and politics today. Economic and ecological security would become a more central part of international relations if a more gendered perspective were taken to the discipline. Carefully drawing on previous feminist critiques, Tickner's tightly reasoned argument concludes with notes towards a nongendered perspective. Among the concepts Tickner rethinks are national security, citizenship, the state, rationality, development, and state power. Tickner also considers other critics of the dominant realist school in international relations, demonstrating how attention to gender could enrich their perspectives, too. She avoids the simplistic opposition of women to men, also noting how hegemonic masculinity neglects other views of masculinity and men, as well as excluding all women. Although not giving attention to many major perspectives in international relations, Tickner does set the stage for what should be a widely contested discussion. Advanced undergraduate through faculty.—*C. Shrewsbury, Mankato State University*

WS-2074   HQ1154   94-26018 CIP
Whitworth, Sandra. **Feminism and international relations: towards a political economy of gender in interstate and non-governmental institutions.** St. Martin's, 1994. 184p bibl index ISBN 0-312-12311-6, $49.95

Whitworth (York Univ.) argues that international relations are shaped by particular notions of gender roles. She provides a useful overview of various feminist theories and extends this literature with insights from international political economy and critical theory. Her empirical chapters explore the links between ideas, material conditions, and institutions as exemplified by the International Planned Parenthood Federation (IPPF) and the International Labor Organization (ILO). Whitworth explains the causes and consequences of IPPF's early decision to downplay connections between birth control and women's empowerment, and to emphasize instead the goals of family, social, and international stability. She also examines how and why the ILO initially focused on gender differences only when women's childbearing and nurturing roles were involved. Her detailed analysis makes a valuable contribution; she demonstrates how actors can mobilize to promote or contest particular conceptions of gender roles embodied in organizations, conceptions that have tremendous impact on the life conditions of common people throughout the world. Upper-division undergraduate through faculty.—*N. W. Gallagher, Wesleyan University*

WS-2075   HQ1236   93-28668 CIP
Women and politics worldwide, ed. by Barbara J. Nelson and Najma Chowdhury. Yale, 1994. 818p index afp ISBN 0-300-05407-6, $50.00; ISBN 0-300-05408-4 pbk, $25.00

This work is the first of its kind to include essays on countries from North America to Nepal, Kenya to Korea. It sets the standard for future international and comparative research on women and politics. A monumental work coedited by a US and a Bangladeshi scholar, it provides the first ever collection of incisive articles about women in politics in 43 countries, each chapter written by a

woman scholar, activist, or official in that country. Each chapter first presents a useful snapshot of political, demographic, educational, and economic data on women; handy summary tables provide easy comparison across countries in each topical area. However, chapters are not written in cookbook style; rather, each author addresses the unique historical and current political issues most salient to women in her country, from rural development to democratization, health to headscarves. The editors give excellent orientations to the conceptual framework, research design, methodology, and data collection procedures. The framework introduces important concepts in the field, such as nationalism, international economic forces, the women's movement, formal and informal politics, women's issues, and women's gender ideologies and action strategies. A lively, accessible work. Undergraduate through faculty.—*M. A. Saint-Germain, University of Texas at El Paso*

WS-2076   K644   94-15775 CIP
Women's rights, human rights: international feminist perspectives, ed. by Julie Peters and Andrea Wolper. Routledge, 1995. 372p index afp ISBN 0-415-90994-5, $65.00

Thirty-six international contributors in this collection map "the directions the movement for women's human rights is taking." An introductory section describes the emergence of the movement and its strategies to transform human rights discourse and practice, in particular its success at the 1993 Vienna Conference. Country- and issue-based sections analyze gender-based oppression in nine countries and the topics of violence and health, socioeconomic development, and silencing. Sections on the public/private distinction and cultural relativism in international law offer a feminist critique of human rights concepts as based on male experience and interpreters. One of several recent collections at the intersection of women's studies and international affairs, this volume's strength is conceptual. It articulates arguments made by women's human rights advocates that human rights practice should include domestic violence and women's marginalization, and sketches out methodologies for using existing human rights machinery and maintaining connections to grassroots women's activism. Some of the country reports do not cover new ground, and the essays are uneven, but on the whole they are stimulating. Undergraduate through faculty.—*J. G. Everett, University of Colorado at Denver*

WS-2077   HQ1190   94-15857 CIP
Women, gender, and world politics: perspectives, policies, and prospects, ed. by Peter R. Beckman and Francine D'Amico. Bergin & Garvey, 1994. 250p bibl index afp ISBN 0-89789-305-0, $59.95

Women, Gender, and Politics is designed as a supplementary text for introductory international relations courses. Beckman (Hobard and William Smith Colleges) and D'Amico (Cornell) have assembled a collection of short essays that introduces debates among feminist scholars and between feminists and mainstream theorists about the relationship between gender and international relations. Contributors include J. Ann Tickner, Jean Bethke Elshtain, Nuket Kardam, Anne Sisson Runyan, and many newer names in the field. As an edited volume, the book has more depth and diversity but less coherence than alternative introductory texts, such as Spike Peterson and Anne Sisson Runyan's *Global Gender Issues* (1993) or Cynthia Enloe's *Bananas, Beaches & Bases* (1990). It includes chapters on third world feminist perspectives, (Hamideh Sedghi), development (Nuket Kardam), and international political economy (Geeta Chowdhry). The bibliography is varied and up-to-date. For those who want more detailed information about women as actors in international politics, Beckman and D'Amico have also edited a companion volume, *Women in World Politics* (1995). All levels.—*N. W. Gallagher, Wesleyan University*

WS-2078   HQ1240   89-35794 CIP
Women, international development, and politics: the bureaucratic mire, ed. by Kathleen Staudt. Temple, 1990. 320p afp ISBN 0-87722-658-X, $39.95

Staudt's superbly edited book encapsulates the serious debates among feminists—particularly Third World feminists—about the exigencies, logistics, and probable outcomes of an historically entrenched system of resistance and exclusion known as "the bureaucracy." When institutionalized in the massively technical world of development politics, the bureaucracy depowers more than one half of the world's population—women. The contributors are individually and collectively founts of development experience and wisdom, and their state-of-the-art analyses are astute, pertinent, and, most importantly, not marked with the stains of cooptation and accommodation. The essays have substantive bibliographies and references and, in addition to being a necessary addition for an academic library, should be required reading for all those in development work. Graduate students and faculty are the most likely academic audience.—*I. Infante, Alverno College*

WS-2079   HQ1170   90-40855 CIP
Women, Islam and the state, ed. by Deniz Kandiyoti. Temple University, 1991. 276p index ISBN 0-87722-785-3, $44.95; ISBN 0-87722-786-1 pbk, $18.95

An interesting and valuable contribution to a growing literature concerned with the relationship of the status of women and the state, this book examines the connection between Islam, the form and essence of state projects, and the status of women in eight Middle Eastern and South Asian nations. The authors address the difficulty scholars have had in "conceptualizing the role specificity of Islam in relation to the status of women." Kandiyoti discusses the emanicipation of women in Turkey, often thought to be distinguished among Muslim nations for its comprehensive reforms, but points out that the decisive actions of Kemalism were partly due to the specific historical circumstances of the struggle for Turkish national independence. S. Joseph compares Iraq and Lebanon: Iraq with its homogeneous ruling elite and disciplined political party has pursued a state policy seeking to shift the allegiance of the population away from the large family, ethnic, tribal groups, while in Lebanon, the state has been controlled by a heterogeneous, factionalized, competitive ruling elite with few disciplined politicial parties that has supported sectarian loyalties at the expense of national unity. Iraq has used the state as an agent of legal reform; the minimalist Lebanese state has left authority over women and the family to the private sector. Other case studies on Iran, Pakistan, Bangladesh, Egypt, and Yemen contribute to an empirical base from which further comparative and theoretical work on women, religion, and the state can be built. Undergraduate collections.—*C. J. Riphenburg, College of Dupage*

◆ Political Theory

WS-2080   Can. CIP
Brown, L. Susan. **The politics of individualism: liberalism, liberal feminism and anarchism.** Black Rose Books, 1993. (Dist. by Toronto) 198p bibl index ISBN 1-895431-79-4, $38.95; ISBN 1-895431-78-6 pbk, $19.95

Brown cleverly sketches the theoretical overlappings between anarchist and liberal political philosophy. Both are inspired by what she calls the ideals of "existential individualism," the belief in the full and free development of the individual striving for a world in which subjects are self-determining and autonomous—free from domination and coercion. But she argues that liberalism's commitment to instrumental individualism (the belief in property in one's own person and a system of private property) is inherently competitive, producing social and economic inequality and relations of domination, and ultimately undermines the goal of personal autonomy and self-development. For Brown anarchism offers "the most coherent critiques of power," a theory of free and voluntary association and, if supplemented by existentialism's theory of free will and ethical responsibility, is best suited to direct the liberation of individuals. Brown's failure to confront contemporary challenges to her anarchist project (her theorization of power, her existential notion of free will, and assumptions regarding universal emancipation) is a serious shortcoming in an otherwise interesting work. All levels.—*E. Stavro-Pearce, Trent University*

WS-2081   HQ1236   92-9372 CIP
Chapman, Jenny. **Politics, feminism and the reformation of gender.** Routledge, 1993. 315p bibl index ISBN 0-415-01698-3, $79.95

Chapman's brilliant and unconventional book deserves a wide readership. She argues, first, that women's representation among political elites depends largely on the extent to which women have the resources that men in that par-

ticular system value; second, that women also have a distinctive role in reproduction and thus a distinctive voice and set of interests underrepresented in any system designed around men's role, voice, and interests; third, that these interests are themselves divided, because women want both shared parenting and support for women's single parenting; fourth, that women attempting to achieve political influence are caught in various double binds, not only that of assimilation or self-assertion, but also that of which of women's divided interests to represent and how. Chapman musters an impressive range of evidence, from the differences in the opportunity structure for men in political systems as diverse as Scotland and the former Soviet Union as explanations for the marginalization of women, to critical analysis of the political programs of the women in the Green party in Germany, the Woman's List in Iceland, and the Norwegian Parliament, to a reconsideration of classic feminist theorists from De Beauvoir and Mead to Firestone and Rich. There is wild profusion of theoretical insight, comparative empirical evidence, and practical strategic considerations. Scholars in the field of gender politics, widely understood, should consider this essential reading. Advanced undergraduate; graduate; faculty; professional.—*M. M. Ferree, University of Connecticut*

WS-2082   HQ1190   90-55730 CIP
Di Stefano, Christine. **Configurations of masculinity: a feminist perspective on modern political theory.** Cornell, 1991. 206p index afp ISBN 0-8014-2534-4, $29.95; ISBN 0-8014-9765-5 pbk, $10.95

"Western political thought is a historical and canonical discourse located predominantly among white European men, and produced by such men for themselves." With this introduction, Di Stefano (University of Washington) joins the ranks of feminist theorists who reread the political tradition with an eye to uncovering gendered meanings. The use of psychoanalytic theory distinguishes this book from Susan Moller Okin's *Women in Western Political Thought* (CH, Jun'80), Jean Bethke Elshtain's *Public Man, Private Woman* (CH, Jun'82), and Linda Nicholson's *Gender and History* (CH, Jun'86). While these authors explore how philosophers have treated women, Di Stefano focuses on how the canon is gender-specific in its assumption of the male as norm. Drawing on object relations theory, she illustrates how modern masculinity operates as ideology. Surfacing as heroic masculinity in Thomas Hobbes, productive masculinity in Karl Marx, and disciplinary masculinity in John Stuart Mill, all three variations of this ideology banish the (m)other in their accounts of social reality. It is therefore ironic that in crafting such an original reading, Di Stefano casts aside her own voice in favor of the language of the male-dominated discipline. Recommended for graduate libraries.—*S. Behuniak-Long, Le Moyne College*

WS-2083   Brit. CIP
Equality politics and gender, ed. by Elizabeth Meehan and Selma Sevenhuijsen. Sage, 1991. 200p index ISBN 0-8039-8482-0, $55.00; ISBN 0-8039-8483-9 pbk, $19.95

This book takes the sameness/difference debate as a point of departure to analyze the concept of equality (or more precisely equality of opportunity), a useful premise for an edited volume given current debates among feminist scholars. Issues such as procedural versus material equality are addressed, informing readers not only about gender but about theories of state, the meaning of justice, etc. The book's greatest strength, constituting its contribution to the field, is its inclusion of analyses of equality of opportunity in a variety of political and economic systems; it thus illuminates the varying conceptualizations of equality. Readers can draw inferences about the meaning of equality in liberal/capitalist societies versus more communitarian systems. At the same time, the promise of comparative analysis is not always acknowledged (especially in the introduction) making the volume appear more a series of individual discussions than an integrated whole. Recommended for upper-division undergraduates and graduate students.—*L. Bowen, John Carroll University*

WS-2084   K644   90-8743 CIP
Feminism and Legal Theory Conference. **At the boundaries of law: feminism and legal theory,** ed. by Martha Albertson Fineman and Nancy Sweet Thomadsen. Routledge, 1991. 368p bibl ISBN 0-415-90305-X, $49.50

Fineman, a law professor, and Thomadsen, a philosopher, have edited a provocative and highly readable volume on the relationship between feminist thought and legal discourse. The book is not excessively jargonistic but is accessible to a wide readership and thus is truly feminist in its orientation. The essays emphasize the significance of understanding and listening to the entirety of women's experiences. Providing a challenge to feminist inquiry, the authors stress seeming gaps between feminist ideals and most women's lives (e.g., most women marry and have children and make daily decisions that may seem antifeminist but are key to survival). Legal discourse provides a useful conceptual framework to demonstrate this gap between theory and reality while allowing the contributors to analyze the extent to which feminism can transform the law or whether the law is inherently male-oriented. Contributors examine the utility of "difference" as a point of reference in a legal system organized around sameness, rights, and equality. The essays are insightful and challenging and the volume provides a useful complement to C. MacKinnon's *Toward a Feminist Theory of the State* (1989) and to S. Okin's *Justice, Gender, and the Family* (1989). Very highly recommended for all collections.—*L. Bowen, John Carroll University*

WS-2085   HQ1075   90-21084 CIP
Ferguson, Ann. **Sexual democracy: women, oppression, and revolution.** Westview, 1991. 293p bibl index afp ISBN 0-8133-0746-5, $42.50; ISBN 0-8133-0747-3 pbk, $15.95

A gathering of articles, some previously published, focusing on a feminist and democratic socialist vision of society. Ferguson opens with a personal odyssey through the Civil Rights Movement, the New Left, and feminism, revealing how each article emerged from her engagement with the critical issues of the day. Each chapter offers a compelling and lucid philosophical "sorting through" of issues ranging from race and gender to the political economy of motherhood. Unified by a theory of "multisystems feminist materialism," the book critiques the Marxist failure to theorize sex, while arguing for a feminism that does not forget history or social class. In an era when cultural feminism confronts postmodernism, the strong case made here for a feminism that analyzes "modes of sex/affective production" is an important contribution to feminist thought. Parallel to this thesis is a critique of essentialist versions of lesbianism and perhaps the best-developed review of lesbian identity written to date. Comprehensive bibliography. All levels.—*B. D. Adam, University of Windsor*

WS-2086   KD734   95-102 CIP
Law and body politics: regulating the female body, ed. by Jo Bridgeman and Susan Millns. Dartmouth, 1995. (Dist. by Ashgate) 304p bibl index ISBN 1-85521-515-2, $59.95

This collection of 11 essays by feminist law faculty, based on a 1993 conference at the University of Liverpool, explores ways in which "law and the female body make contact and with strategies through which the nature and meaning of that contact can be reformulated" so that women's voices can be heard. In spite of references to Foucault and French feminists, this is not an effort at legal deconstruction; rather, it offers a feminist practitioner's perspective on rights discourse. Essays on pregnancy, new reproductive technologies, abortion, anorexia, and sterilization of developmentally disabled women address the power of the medical profession in defining women's legal positions. Essays on "bodyrights," battered women, and rape look at how women are constructed in legal discourse. Essays on genital mutilation and human rights raise issues of essentialism and difference. A strength of this collection lies in the discussion of recent British case law (a list of cases and statutes is included) relevant to feminist legal politics. Weaknesses include the lack of a comprehensive introduction to frame the essays, unevenness in the essays, and a lack of clarity in the discussion of strategies of change. Upper-division through faculty.—*J. G. Everett, University of Colorado at Denver*

WS-2087   HQ1190   93-19490 CIP
Phillips, Anne. **Democracy and difference.** Pennsylvania State, 1993. 175p index afp ISBN 0-271-01096-7, $30.00; ISBN 0-271-01097-5 pbk, $14.95

Phillips, in this interesting collection of articles written between 1984-93, reflects on her transition from socialist feminism to a radical democratic pluralist feminism. She weaves her way through contemporary Anglo-American debates on democracy relying on feminists (Fraser, Gilligan, Young, Mendus, Pateman), antifoundationalists (Rorty, Walzer), and more mainstream theorists (Dahl, Rawls, MacIntyre, and Sandel). These theorists are confronted in terms of the

insights they offer and limitations they pose for radicalizing the democratic project. Phillips does not see democracy as presently realized; the underrepresentation and marginalization of women and racial and ethnic minority groups challenge political equality. She is suspicious of consociationalism (elite accommodation of difference) and traditional forms of pluralism that do not understand the systematic political exclusion of women and minorities. Instead she calls for active and equal participation of all citizens, the unfulfilled promise of democracy. Her unwillingness to fully endorse postmodernism with its relativist implications, and her reluctance to jettison socialist insights regarding how economic powerlessness threatens democratic equality, makes this a timely reflection. General through faculty.—*E. Stavro-Pearce, Trent University*

WS-2088   JC176   91-38426 CIP
Sapiro, Virginia. **A vindication of political virtue: the political theory of Mary Wollstonecraft.** Chicago, 1992. 366p bibl index afp ISBN 0-226-73490-0, $53.00

Since the publication of *A Vindication of the Rights of Women* in 1792, Mary Wollstonecraft has been variously eulogized, vilified, forgotten, and reclaimed. In recent years, feminists have enthroned her as an important theoretical foremother; both her polemic and the story of her unconventional life have become standard elements in the basic women's studies syllabus. But in her own time she was well known for other literary and political writing that is largely ignored. In this elegant intellectual biography, Sapiro offers a rereading of Wollstonecraft's life and work that portrays her as a "thoughtful and complex" writer on politics and society. The author freely admits to a desire to affect tradition and to reveal the Wollstonecraft's ideas as worthy of considerably "more than a footnote in the general history of political theory." This historically nuanced analysis claims a place for Wollstonecraft's thought within the modern tradition of political theory, arguing that her work ought to be studied as a critical contribution to the ongoing political conversation of the last three centuries. A must for all undergraduate libraries with strength in political science and women's studies. General; undergraduate; graduate; faculty.—*N. B. Rosenthal, SUNY College at Old Westbury*

◆ U.S. Politics

WS-2089   KF478   83-22527 CIP
Baer, Judith A. **Women in American law: v.2: The struggle toward equality from the New Deal to the present.** Holmes & Meier, 1991. 350p indexes afp ISBN 0-8419-0920-2, $39.95; ISBN 0-8419-0921-0 pbk, $19.95

The second volume of a set in which the first volume had the subtitle *From Colonial Times to the New Deal* (1985) and presented a compendium of documents with commentary. A full-blown textbook, Baer's work examines the status of women under statutory and case law of the US in the context of scholarship of women and politics and women's studies. Simply stated, Baer argues that societal sex roles still unjustly assign women unpaid domestic responsibilities in addition to the rights they now enjoy (in the abstract) equally with men under the law. Sex roles thus demonstrate "the law's inadequacy as an instrument of change," a conclusion not inconsistent with the strides Baer shows women have made in employment, family law, reproduction, education, and the legal system itself. Baer is sensitive to differences among women in relation to race, class, and sexuality. Firmly grounded in legal and feminist scholarship, her writing style is nevertheless refreshingly direct and accessible. Informative and provocative, her book is highly recommended for all levels, from general readers to graduate students and faculty.—*D. L. Fowlkes, Georgia State University*

WS-2090   KF3464   90-10176 MARC
Belz, Herman. **Equality transformed: a quarter-century of affirmative action.** Transaction, 1991. 320p (Studies in social philosophy & policy, 15) ISBN 0-88738-882-5, $32.95; ISBN 0-88738-393-9, pbk $19.95

Belz (University of Maryland) offers a detailed, scholarly, and highly critical analysis of affirmative action since the early 1960s. He argues that while Title VII of the 1964 Civil Rights Act was intended to provide individuals with equal employment opportunites without regard for race, over time, practices by public and private employers that benefit certain groups on the basis of race or gender have become widespread. Instead of viewing employment discrimination as an injury suffered by identifiable individuals, policies now stress disparate impacts that employment practices may have on racial groups. Legislators, judges, regulatory agencies, and activists have replaced the goal of color-blind equal opportunity with that of equal results across racial groups regardless of the personal histories of individual members. Consequently, Belz believes that some individuals who suffered no personal injuries benefit; some who inflicted no injuries suffer; some who need help but belong to the wrong group fail to get it; and all members of the preferred group are stigmatized. The book is timely in light of recent Supreme Court decisions that increase the burden of proof faced by employees alleging employment discrimination. Contemporary congressional debates about quotas, race-norming of tests, and related concerns promise to be key campaign issues. Belz cites some supporters of affirmative action whose works could balance his own. Extensive endnotes and a useful chronology are supplied. Recommended for upper-division undergraduates and graduate students.— *J. A. Melusky, Saint Francis College*

WS-2091   KF3467   92-42906 CIP
Blank, Robert H. **Fetal protection in the workplace: women's rights, business interests, and the unborn.** Columbia, 1993. 225p bibl index afp ISBN 0-231-07694-0, $29.50

In this volume, Blank (Univ. of Canterbury, New Zealand) applies his expertise in biomedical ethics to the study of workplace fetal protection policies (FPPs). His unique approach neither ignores the burden that FPPs have on working women nor minimizes the risk that exposure to hazardous substances has on developing fetuses. Challenging the dichotomy of pitting women's interests against those of their fetuses, this work criticizes the shortsighted policies that result from this construction of the issue. Blank contends that policy choices are not limited to protecting women through exclusion, or opting not to protect reproductive health at all. Instead, he presents alternatives to FPPs that safeguard reproductive health while respecting women's need to work. These include: job transfers, maternity and paternity leaves, screening programs, and guaranteed access to prenatal care. This study also finds balance in examining both legal and scientific scholarship and offers a comprehensible discussion of both. Recommended for upper-level college collections.—*S. Behuniak-Long, Le Moyne College*

WS-2092   HQ1391   93-36098 CIP
Boxer, Barbara. **Strangers in the Senate: politics and the new revolution of women in America,** by Barbara Boxer with Nicole Boxer. National Press Books, 1994. 256p index ISBN 1-882605-06-3, $23.95

Boxer was elected to the US Senate from California in 1992 after serving in the House of Representatives for ten years representing the San Francisco Bay area. Nicole Boxer, her daughter, is in the film industry. The book is a well-written, readable account of the author's personal "real-life" political experiences. The foreword by Hillary Rodham Clinton on the political activism of women along with Boxer's chapter on the history of women in the Senate establishes a working historical perspective. The book begins with an account of the pressure brought by women in the House on the Senate to investigate the sexual harassment allegations of Anita Hill against Clarance Thomas, an event which Boxer believes significantly changed voter's attitudes and more than tripled the number of women in the Senate in one year. This is not a bipartisan account; nor is there any suggestion that the author intended it to be. Boxer makes frequent reference to her Democratic women colleagues and their support of the Democratic agenda with only occasional mention of Republican women. Anyone, regardless of personal political preference, interested in the changing role of women in American politics, will find the book exceptionally interesting and instructive. Women, Boxer believes, are not better than men in politics—only different, and their different perspectives are crucial to our democratic society. All levels.—*D. F. Bletz, Wilson College*

WS-2093   HD6060   92-22871 CIP
Clayton, Susan D. **Justice, gender, and affirmative action,** by Susan D. Clayton and Faye J. Crosby. Michigan, 1992. 152p bibl index ISBN 0-472-09464-5, $34.50

Clayton and Crosby provide a useful application of social psychological scholarship to enhance affirmative action theory and justify its continued use in soci-

ety. They introduce relative deprivation and an equity framework to raise the gender-bias consciousness necessary for collective action and public policy advocacy. The volume provides well-informed discussion of affirmative action operations in the context of fairness and justice. The work is not in the tradition of justification based on compensatory justice. The authors outline gender bias as a significant unit of analysis for effective affirmative action plans. They provide insightful case-study and long-overdue discussion of the white female perspective and associated innovative characteristics of effective affirmative action plans: expanded definition of qualifications, nontemporary plans, and nontraditional approaches to problems. Excellent references. Required reading for undergraduate and graduate students and professional practitioners.— *A. A. Sisneros, Sangamon State University*

WS-2094   KF3771   91-46603 CIP
Colker, Ruth. **Abortion and dialogue: pro-choice, pro-life, and American law.** Indiana, 1992. 179p index afp ISBN 0-253-31393-7, $29.95; ISBN 0-253-20738-X pbk, $12.95

This is feminist scholarship at its best: interdisciplinary, passionate, personal, and political. This book is more original than its title suggests. Although other works, e.g., Laurence Tribe's *Abortion: The Clash of Absolutes* (CH, Dec'90), Faye Ginsberg's *Contested Lives: The Abortion Debate in an American Community* (1989), Mary Ann Glendon's *Abortion and Divorce in Western Law* (CH, Feb'88), and *Rights Talk* (1991), have noted how the absolutism of the abortion debate thwarts the discovery of common ground, none have so sensitively appreciated the concerns of both sides and so eloquently suggested an alternative theory as Colker (Tulane Univ.). She crafts a feminist-theological perspective based on the conception of an authentic self that moves toward the aspirations of love, compassion, and wisdom. When these aspirations are applied to abortion politics, problems within both movements are revealed. How can pro-choicers be so disrepectful of concerns for life? How can pro-lifers ignore the realities of women's lives? Colker then shows a way out of the thicket by utilizing an equality framework guided by the three aspirations. Both controversial and inspiring, this volume is highly recommended for all libraries.—*S. Behuniak-Long, Le Moyne College*

WS-2095   HQ767   92-25268 CIP
Cook, Elizabeth Adell. **Between two absolutes: public opinion and the politics of abortion,** by Elizabeth Adell Cook, Ted G. Jelen, and Clyde Wilcox. Westview, 1992. 236p bibl index afp ISBN 0-8133-8286-6, $45.00; ISBN 0-8133-8287-4 pbk, $14.95

In this examination of public opinion on abortion in the US, the authors analyze abortion from three perspectives: abortion politics as normal, as dysfunctional, and as empowerment. Because abortion politics has generated greater political participation and because voters are paying greater attention to it and some citizens are even voting according to a politician's view on this single issue, abortion is a salient public policy topic to study. The two most important reasons why people differ on the issue of abortion are their beliefs about human life and their attitudes toward sexual morality. Religion, in particular, is an important determinant of abortion attitudes. Catholics and evangelical Protestants are equally likely to support restrictions on legal abortions, but mainline Protestants are more supportive of legal abortion than evangelicals or Catholics. Of the religious groups discussed in this book, American Jews were the most supportive of legal abortion. Still a slight majority of Americans favor access to legal abortions in some circumstances, but reject access in others. In conclusion, the authors speculate about what would happen should *Roe* v. *Wade* be overturned. The debate between two absolutes—right to life versus right to choose—will continue. Academic and public library collections.—*R. A. Strickland, Appalachian State University*

WS-2096   HQ1236   91-39293 MARC
Costain, Anne N. **Inviting women's rebellion: a political process interpretation of the women's movement.** Johns Hopkins, 1992. 188p index afp ISBN 0-8018-4333-2, $28.00

With the women's movement poised to enter a third stage, it has become increasingly important to understand the rise and decline of the second wave of feminism. While most of the literature has attempted to explain the movement by using mass society or resource mobilization theories, this book is similar to Ethel Klein's *Gender Politics* (CH, Mar'85) in its adoption of the political process approach. Costain (University of Colorado) employs interviews and empirical data to study the organizational strength of the movement, the political opportunities presented by the government, and the psychological changes reflected in public opinion. The data suggest that rather than obstructing the women's movement, the US government "invited women's rebellion," but Costain contends that a price was exacted for this invitation. The feminist political agenda was unduly controlled by government officials who favored equality issues (e.g., ERA) over special-needs issues such as child care. How to apply the lessons learned is the focus of the final chapter. Of special interest to feminists, this book will appeal to anyone interested in movement politics and serves as an excellent example of how to give life to empirical data. Recommended for all college libraries.—*S. Behuniak-Long, Le Moyne College*

WS-2097   KF481   93-4102 CIP
Daniels, Cynthia R. **At women's expense: state power and the politics of fetal rights.** Harvard, 1993. 183p index afp ISBN 0-674-05043-6, $19.95

Daniels examines the legal assault on women's rights that is being conducted in the name of the fetus. But this is not a book about abortion. Instead, Daniels (Rutgers Univ.) traces some of the unplanned and, until now, largely overlooked consequences of *Roe* v. *Wade*. Ironically, instead of strengthening women's position in society and politics, legalized abortion creates an atmosphere where all women are suspected of devaluing motherhood. Within this clime, the state uses its power to force a pregnant woman to act in ways that subordinate her interests to those of the fetus she carries to term. Three well known cases involving Angela Carder (court ordered medical treatment), Johnson Controls (protective fetal policies in the workplace), and Jennifer Johnson (prosecution of a pregnant drug addict) are analyzed to show the tenuous nature of woman's citizenship when she dares to challenge the cultural ethic of selfless motherhood. While the analysis is fascinating, the argument is diminished by reliance on three cases in which women's rights eventually prevailed. Inclusion of an updated survey of cases would show the threat to be more widespread than these examples might indicate. Recommended for all levels.—*S. Behuniak-Long, Le Moyne College*

WS-2098   HQ1237   93-23836 CIP
Eisenstein, Zillah R. **The color of gender: reimaging democracy.** California, 1994. 277p index afp ISBN 0-520-08338-5, $45.00; ISBN 0-520-08422-5 pbk, $15.00

Eisenstein suggests that the belief in rugged individualism that characterized and permeated politics in the 1980s was particularly hostile to the values of equality, diversity, and inclusiveness. She argues for a revisioning of democracy that is inclusive of women of color and crosses economic lines. Her thesis is framed in the language of rights. She contends that the most fundamental of these are rights of privacy, bodily integrity, and reproductive rights. To achieve equality, these rights must be viewed as connected with other issues such as health care, economic justice, and, in general, the need for affirmative government services. Eisenstein considers, but rejects, the notion that liberal democracy cannot be made receptive to the needs of those who are not politically powerful. She does not aim or manage to discuss the probability for change, or, in any depth, the mechanisms for achieving a revisioned democratic system. Her principal accomplishment is to point conceptually in the direction of a revisioned democracy, premised on rights that reflect the complexity of human experience and the diversity among women. Recommended for undergraduate and graduate collections.—*M. Hendrickson, Wilson College*

WS-2099   KF874   92-53618 CIP
Epstein, Lee. **The Supreme Court and legal change: abortion and the death penalty,** by Lee Epstein and Joseph F. Kobylka. North Carolina, 1992. 417p bibl index afp ISBN 0-8078-2051-2, $45.00; ISBN 0-8078-4384-9 pbk, $16.95

Often in literature on the US Supreme Court, it is argued that changes in personnel produce swift legal doctrine shifts. To answer the question, "Why does the law, as interpreted by the US Supreme Court, sometimes change abruptly?" the authors examined the influence of three factors—the Court itself, the prevailing

political environment during the time of its rulings, and the pressure groups lobbying the Court—on abrupt legal doctrine changes in the policy areas of capital punishment and abortion. It is argued that the shift from *Furman* v. *Georgia* (1972) to *Gregg* v. *Georgia* (1976) happened because an activist, pro-death-penalty Nixon administration plus a faulty understanding of Court logic by the Legal Defense Fund led to *Furman*'s reversal. What happened from *Roe* v. *Wade* (1973) to *Webster* v. *Reproductive Health Services* (1989)? In addition to the emergence of a countermovement of pro-lifers who emulated the strategies used by the pro-choicers, legal doctrine shifts on abortion were precipitated by personnel changes on the Court, an aggressively antiabortion Reagan Justice Department, and a stagnated pro-choice grass-roots movement. From their two case studies, the authors concluded that legal and political factors are the forces that condition abrupt legal change. Advanced undergraduate through faculty collections.—*R. A. Strickland, Appalachian State University*

WS-2100   HQ767.5.U5   90-2228 CIP
Faux, Marian. **Crusaders: voices from the abortion front.** Carol Publishing Group, 1990. 289p index ISBN 1-55972-020-4, $19.95

The story chronicled by Faux in *Roe v. Wade: The Untold Story* (CH, Dec'88) is continued here as the focus shifts to the political aftermath of the legalization of abortion. Loosely organized around the 1989 Webster case, the book sketches portraits of six activists: Frank Susman, who represented Reproductive Health Services of St. Louis before the court; B.J. Isaacson-Jones, director of the same Missouri clinic; Terry Randall, founder of Operation Rescue; "Moira," an activist in Operation Rescue; Vernice Miller of the Center for Constitutional Rights, which filed a friend of the court brief emphasizing women of color; and Frances Kissling, executive director of Catholics for a Free Choice. It is an odd assortment in that activists within leading organizations such as the National Abortion Rights Action League, the Planned Parenthood Federation, and the National Right to Life Association are excluded. Although the six profiles provide some fascinating background to the Webster case, these are clearly Faux's observations with no pretense of objectivity or of a scholarly stance. This book is best used either as a casual read or as a companion to more theoretically rigorous studies of abortion grass roots activism such as Faye Ginsburg's *Contested Lives* (1989) or Kristin Luker's *Abortion and the Politics of Motherhood* (CH, Feb'85).—*S. Behuniak-Long, Le Moyne College*

WS-2101   KF4755   91-33695 CIP
Fiscus, Ronald J. **The constitutional logic of affirmative action,** ed. by Stephen L. Wasby. Duke University, 1992. 150p index afp ISBN 0-8223-1206-9, $17.95

Hard-hitting yet sensitive to those who oppose quotas, this book can be considered a guide for avoiding excessive white sacrifices. It analyzes individual fairness in concrete yet complex terms, makes realistic assumptions despite initial appearances, and confronts controversial concepts (e.g., innocent persons, group perspectives, seniority). Fiscus refutes criticisms of distributive justice as a balanced approach by which to address the affirmative action debate, and responds to questions that require revisitation raised by R.K. Fullinwider (*The Reverse Discrimination Controversy*, CH, Feb'81)—e.g., the quality of "logic" and "human judgment" currently represented on the Supreme Court. He considers leading affirmative action theory (best exemplified by K.M. Sullivan, comment, "Sins of Discrimination," *Harvard Law Review* 100 [1986]: 78) as a point of departure in developing the principle of proportionality. Fiscus cites all relevant Supreme Court decisions, challenges society to reconfirm or abandon commitment to Title VII and the Constitution, forces the question of why and how much longer society can profit from racism, and presents a new paradigm for legitimate quotas. Excellent endnotes but no bibliography. Graduate level.—*A. A. Sisneros, Sangamon State University*

WS-2102   HQ1391   95-37651 CIP
Foerstel, Karen. **Climbing the hill: gender conflict in Congress,** by Karen Foerstel and Herbert N. Foerstel. Praeger, 1996. 201p bibl index afp ISBN 0-275-94914-1, $39.95

The Foerstels provide an excellent account of the battle of the sexes in Congress. They demonstrate that the method of access for most women prior to and following Jeanette Rankin's first tenure in Congress was to succeed a deceased incumbent, usually a spouse. Following this, the 1990s are put into an appropriate framework of analysis. In spite of the record electoral gains witnessed in recent years, women still account for less than 11 percent of the House and Senate combined, and their inferior status in both chambers is still very much a fact. Women are not key players on the standing committees, nor are they entrenched in the leadership of either party. Yet women are important to the success or failure of congressional members in their staff roles, as they account for about 60 percent of all staff (although they still serve disproportionately in the lower-paying jobs). The prognosis for women in this book is not overly optimistic, but it is realistic. Women are still "climbing the hill," and will be doing so for decades in their attempt to rival men in political power. Upper-division undergraduates through faculty.—*B. L. Fife, Ball State University*

WS-2103   KF475   90-34876 CIP
Forer, Lois G. **Unequal protection: women, children, and the elderly in court.** W.W. Norton, 1991. 256p index ISBN 0-393-02949-2, $22.95

Forer, a retired trial judge, has written a compelling account of how the seemingly "neutral" law disadvantages the "disempowered" in US society. The stories she tells clearly illustrate the implications of binding judges to precedent despite changes in social structures and thus in litigants. The law of the "reasonable man" is the basis of the Anglo-American legal tradition, yet citizenship and access to the legal process now extend beyond "reasonable" (i.e., white, middle-aged, property-owning) men. As Forer details so well, children, women, and the elderly are held to the reasonable-man standard in the name of equality, but may ultimately be disadvantaged because of differences in experiences. Drawing on the analysis of Carol Gilligan, Forer is really calling for a more feminist jurisprudence that relies on difference. Yet she says in her introduction that she does not want fundamental change in the law, just a few reforms. It would appear that if common and constitutional law are both male, then more radical changes may be in order. Still, the personal stories provide a powerful introduction to the law, particularly in the trial court setting, which is an aspect of the judicial process too often neglected by scholars. Highly recommended for undergraduate collections and general readers.—*L. Bowen, John Carroll University*

WS-2104   HQ1236   91-10605 CIP
Fowlkes, Diane L. **White political women: paths from privilege to empowerment.** Tennessee, 1992. 255p bibl index afp ISBN 0-87049-717-0, $38.95; ISBN 0-87049-718-9 pbk, $14.95

Fowlkes's goal is to understand political women. As a self-identified feminist scholar and political scientist, she set out to challenge the conclusions drawn about women by her white male colleagues. She designed a study to learn how white middle-class political women understand their worlds and their places in them. To overcome misconceptions about the "universal woman" in American politics, Fowlkes interviewed 27 women who had been active in politics in the Atlanta metropolitan area. The subjects ranged in age from 79 to 22; they were engaged in electoral politics as Democratic or Republican party activists and/or officeholders, or participated in counter-culture political activities. Their stories, when studied together, dramatize white women's political development from a wide variety of white women's perspectives, ranging from radical feminism to racist, conservative antifeminism. As a result of the study, Fowlkes recommends further areas of investigation, including a study of politically active women of color. Extensive reference list and bibliography. Upper-division undergraduates and above.—*R. L. Ruben, Western Illinois University*

WS-2105   KF3771   90-20709 CIP
Freedman, Warren. **Legal issues in biotechnology and human reproduction: artificial conception and modern genetics.** Quorum Books, 1991. 229p indexes afp ISBN 0-89930-635-7, $55.00

The law regulating medically assisted reproduction is a morass resulting from the many types of technologies, the variety of state laws, and the number of parties claiming legal rights. It is therefore remarkable that Freedman (retired liability counsel and assistant secretary for Bristol-Myers Squibb Corp.) offers a work that is as cogent as it is comprehensive. Artificial insemination, in vitro fertilization, and surrogate motherhood are among the technologies studied within a framework that identifies potential legal problems as well as solutions. The inter-

ests and obligations of all the parties, from the parents to the government, are considered. This volume distinguishes itself by offering legal guidance based on a survey of existing statutes, policies, contracts, and cases. Freedman also appreciates that the "new families" created by the technologies will not be confined to infertile couples alone since single people and homosexual partners have a stake in reproductive law as well. Only one aspect of Freedman's analysis needs strengthening—his assumption that the law governing birth control, abortion, and sterilization creates a constitutional right to use procreative technologies. Recommended for libraries at all levels.—*S. Behuniak-Long, Le Moyne College*

WS-2106   KF3771   93-8231 CIP
Garrow, David J. **Liberty and sexuality: the right to privacy and the making of Roe v. Wade.** Macmillan, 1994. 981p bibl index ISBN 0-02-542755-5, $28.00

With over 200 pages of endnotes, Garrow provides a detailed and carefully crafted historical examination of the right to privacy and ultimately the 1973 watershed Supreme Court decision in *Roe* v. *Wade*. From the closing down of birth control clinics in Waterbury, Connecticut to the famous *Griswold* v. *Connecticut* Supreme Court decision which created a constitutional right to privacy, the stage was set for the march toward abortion rights. Garrow examines the activities of early abortion rights activists who from 1933 to 1967 generally sought to legalize therapeutic abortions. Although only three states—North Carolina, Colorado and California—had reformed their abortion laws by 1967 to allow for abortions under narrowly defined circumstances, the stage was set for legislative battles across the country. The clash of interest groups over abortion law repeal from 1967 to 1969, the ultimate attack upon the constitutionality of the Texas abortion statute, and the Supreme Court's handling of the *Roe* and *Doe* cases receive comprehensive coverage. The politics and controversy surrounding abortion and sexual privacy rights since *Roe* are discussed as the clash between pro-life and pro-choice advocates continues. All levels.—*R. A. Strickland, Appalachian State University*

WS-2107   KF478   93-20926 CIP
Goldstein, Leslie Friedman. **Contemporary cases in women's rights.** Wisconsin, 1994. 339p index ISBN 0-299-14030-X, $49.50; ISBN 0-299-14034-2 pbk, $19.95

This work increases the number of textbooks about women and the law written at a level appropriate for undergraduate students. It breaks no new ground but is characterized by a focus on privacy rights, especially as applied to abortion and to parenthood; on sex discrimination, primarily in employment; and on sexual violence and pornography. The text provides a survey of each topic. The typical chapter traces the development of the law through commentary on the line of cases that has shaped the current interpretation of constitutional law in the areas reviewed. Each section includes the text of the opinions in exemplary cases. A list of standard questions for discussion follows. One appendix includes a brief discussion of how the Supreme Court works. Undergraduate.—*C. Shrewsbury, Mankato State University*

WS-2108   HQ767   95-25448 CIP
Graber, Mark A. **Rethinking abortion: equal choice, the Constitution, and reproductive politics.** Princeton, 1996. 244p bibl indexes afp ISBN 0-691-01142-7, $29.95

By summarizing the pro-life, pro-choice, and anti-*Roe* v. *Wade* arguments, Graber calls into question the usefulness of the "fetal life versus procreative choice" debate. In chapter 3 ("Equal Choice"), this "rethinking" of abortion policy results in an impassioned argument for legal abortions based on the principle that attempts to limit abortion access lead to capricious law enforcement practices, random legal interpretation by physicians, and discrimination. The author further notes that abortion access is most equal when the law either permits abortion on demand or forbids all abortions. In chapter 5 ("Realizing Equal Choice"), Graber argues that the optimal tactic for keeping abortion legal is to reinforce a New Deal party system in which both parties are "evenly balanced" on abortion. Under this system, neither party is particularly interested in abortion policy, and each is more likely to fight over economic issues. Thus, traditional politicians would be more likely to ignore abortion-policy proposals and would preserve the status quo, which keeps abortions legal. Although Graber acknowledges the philosophical allure of pro-life arguments, he contends that as long as some women have the ability to choose abortion and others do not, abortion restrictions are hypocritical. General readers; upper-division undergraduates through faculty.—*R. A. Strickland, Appalachian State University*

WS-2109   KF4758   90-40553 CIP
Hoff, Joan. **Law, gender, and injustice: a legal history of U.S. women.** New York University, 1991. 525p bibl index afp ISBN 0-8147-3467-7, $39.50

Hoff (history, Indiana University) has written what will surely be a controversial work on the legal history of women in the US. A discussion of women during the Colonial period is followed by a legal history of women through five identifiable periods: constitutional neglect (1787-1872), constitutional discrimination (1872-1908), constitutional protection (1908-1963), constitutional equality (1963-1987), and the current constitutional period beginning in 1987. Hoff's basic premise is that advances in the rights of women have come in a "too little, too late" pattern, recognizing civil rights for women only when those rights are no longer valued by the male hierarchy (e.g., voting rights, employment rights). Taking on both conservatives and liberals, Hoff argues that the liberal legal system will not resolve the problem and a more radical approach is necessary, one that pursues not equality for women but equity. Otherwise, women in the US "will continue to become progressively more liberated by male standards without being effectively emancipated." This radical approach must, she argues, put women into the Constitution on female and not male terms. This work is further bolstered by extensive endnotes and six appendixes that list various acts, litigation, constitutional amendments, and declarations relating to the progress of women's rights over the course of US history. Upper-division undergraduate and graduate students.—*M. W. Bowers, University of Nevada, Las Vegas*

WS-2110   HV9950   95-41817 CIP
Martin, Susan Ehrlich. **Doing justice, doing gender,** by Susan Ehrlich Martin and Nancy C. Jurik. Sage Publications, CA, 1996. 270p (Women and the criminal justice system, 1) bibl indexes afp ISBN 0-8039-5197-3, $38.95; ISBN 0-8039-5198-1 pbk, $17.95

Synthesizing literature from women's studies, law, and criminal justice studies, the authors highlight ways in which organizational norms and societal expectations shape obstacles to full acceptance of women as police officers, correctional officials, and lawyers. Martin and Jurik demonstrate from the literature the effects of the "double bind" on women in these fields. Women police officers who adopt the traditional male style may be criticized as overly aggressive and unfeminine, whereas women using a feminine style will be viewed as incompetent in an occupation that rewards macho attitudes and behavior. As social "outsiders," women in law enforcement often find their career advancement blocked by lack of access to informal networking. Yet women's opportunities in criminal justice are also expanding, and women may bring to their roles attributes that reformulate the role of police and correctional officers. For example, women officers tend to be more sensitive in handling interactions with citizens. The integration of women may, therefore, advance the reputations and performance of police. While the book informs admirably concerning women in several male-dominated occupations, it treats very minimally the subject of women as criminal defense lawyers (and does not address women as prosecutors). Recommended for all collections.—*M. Hendrickson, Wilson College*

WS-2111   F391   91-25644 CIP
Morris, Celia. **Storming the statehouse: running for governor with Ann Richards and Dianne Feinstein.** Scribner, 1992. 325p index ISBN 0-684-19328-0, $25.00

The gubernatorial campaigns of Richards (Texas) and Feinstein (California) rank among the most conspicuous and fascinating races involving women candidates to date. This book is based primarily on interviews with campaign participants. Both campaigns were costly, close, and depended on coalitional support of women and people of color. The author compares and contrasts the two campaigns, including the factors influencing the outcome of each. However, much of the book consists of generally rich and thorough case studies of the two campaigns, with particular attention paid to the candidates' characters and personalities. While the book offers insights about the barriers encountered by women in politics, Morris does not explicitly bring into her analysis much of the schol-

arly work on voting behavior or women's role in politics. Nonetheless, her book is savvy and does provide some useful insights into the organization and management of statewide campaigns. It is an appropriate acquisition for undergraduate libraries and will serve as a useful resource for students writing research papers on women in state politics. Recommended for undergraduate libraries and general readers.—*M. Hendrickson, Wilson College*

WS-2112   JK2495   91-8604 CIP
Nelson, Albert J. **Emerging influentials in state legislatures: women, Blacks, and Hispanics.** Praeger, 1991. 157p bibl indexes afp ISBN 0-275-93829-8, $39.95

In this ambitious statistical study exploring the influence of women, blacks, and Hispanics in state legislatures, Nelson argues these groups must not only be elected but must become fully incorporated into the legislative bodies before their influence can be felt. The longitudinal study involves analysis of partisan control in 135 legislatures over the 1982, 1984, and 1986 elections. Nelson argues, for example, that to assume that a Democratic chamber 18 per cent of whose members are women is an indicator of influence neglects the fact that a large proportion of the women will be Republicans. Some findings: (1) Democratic women have more clout because their party controls more state legislatures; (2) black Democrats, like female Democrats, do better in metropolitan states where Democratic organizations are weak or in decline and there are fewer Roman Catholics; (3) non-black and non-Hispanic females slightly increased their representation in their respective parties; (4) representation of blacks and Hispanics declined slightly, 1983-87; (5) the expectation that minority influence would be exercised to increase funding for education, social welfare, and mental health and hospitals was not borne out. Nelson suggests further research, including interviews with individual minority representatives, to augment the quantitative findings. Upper-division undergraduate and graduate students.—*L. L. Duke, Clemson University*

WS-2113   KF8745   95-33987 CIP
Race, gender, and power in America: the legacy of the Hill-Thomas hearings, ed. by Anita Faye Hill and Emma Coleman Jordan. Oxford, 1995. 302p afp ISBN 0-19-508774-7, $25.00

This edited volume analyzes in detail the impact and context of Anita Hill's testimony at the Senate confirmation hearings of Supreme Court Justice Clarence Thomas. The intersections of race, gender, class, and status are deconstructed by an impressive array of legal and political scholars and practitioners, including several participants in Hill's hurriedly assembled "defense" team. Some of the essays focus on the Hill testimony and its impact, critiquing the role of Hill's lawyers during the hearings (portrayed as a flawed pseudotrial of Hill herself), evaluating the impact of Hill's revelations on sexual harassment law and policy, analyzing the role of the Hill-Thomas hearings on the elections of 1992 (dubbed the "Year of the Woman"), and considering ways of promoting community education about gender relations and sexual harassment. The richest, most provocative essays consider in historical and contemporary terms the status of African American women (and men) and the ways in which status, history, and culture shaped the perceptions and treatment of Hill. An essay by Hill posits that the absence of a sponsor and her single marital status adversely affected the way her demeanor and testimony were interpreted. In a complex and troubling essay, "The Crisis of Gender Relations among African Americans," Orlando Patterson considers the role of slavery and racial discrimination in "poisoning" gender relations among black men and women. Several essays aptly pull together the book's diverse themes. A powerful, thoughtful book for all levels of readers.—*M. Hendrickson, Wilson College*

WS-2114   KF3464   90-37995 CIP
Rosenfeld, Michel. **Affirmative action and justice: a philosophical and constitutional inquiry.** Yale, 1991. 373p bibl index afp ISBN 0-300-04781-9, $30.00

In this important and timely book, Rosenfeld (law, Yeshiva University) seeks to integrate philosophical and constitutional approaches to affirmative action policies. He includes a thorough analytical review of literatures in philosophy, social and political theory, law, and social science. The book is divided into three parts. An opening section critically analyzes and assesses four liberal conceptions of justice—libertarian, contractarian, utilitarian, and egalitarian. A second section skillfully describes and critiques the Supreme Court's ambiguous and inconsistent legacy on affirmative action and considers relationships between philosophical conceptions of justice and Court doctrine. A final section attempts to construct an alternative conception of affirmative action, based on what Rosenfeld describes as the "dynamic relationship between equality as identity and equality as difference." Rosenfeld develops a provocative philosophical defense of affirmative action based on a principle of "justice as reversible reciprocity." He argues that deficiencies in liberal positions can be overcome through recourse to a dialogical process involving a "reversal of perspectives" and the suppression of power-dominated strategic communication. This solid and detailed study may be read productively with more general treatments of the law and politics of difference, such as Martha Minow's *Making All the Difference* (CH, Mar'91), and Iris Marion Young's *Justice and the Politics of Difference* (1990). Recommended for upper-division undergraduate and graduate students.—*M. Kessler, Bates College*

WS-2115 KF220 93-10125 CIP
Schuetz, Janice. **The logic of women on trial: case studies of popular American trials.** Southern Illinois, 1995 (c1994). 257p bibl index afp ISBN 0-8093-1869-5, $34.95; ISBN 0-8093-1926-8 pbk, $16.95

Employing what the author describes as a "rhetorical analysis" of the events and circumstances surrounding the highly publicized trials of Rebecca Nurse, Mary Surratt, Lizzie Bordon, Margaret Sanger, Ethel Rosenberg, Yvonne Wanrow, Patricia Hearst, Jean Harris, and Darci Pierce, Schuetz contends that each one implicated specific questions of gender, justice, and values that defined the roles of women in society during their time. These cases involve women from different areas and demographics and cover diverse issues ranging from the Salem witch trials to the assassination of Abraham Lincoln, espionage, urban terrorism, and battered woman's syndrome. Yet the author sees all of them linked by gender issues, including the historical definitions and conceptions of womanhood that helped define the circumstances surrounding the crimes and the prosecution and media coverage of the trials. The result is that each trial reveals the specific legal narratives, paradigms, and stereotypes that influenced the logical structure and outcomes of the trials of these women. Despite the absence of a concluding chapter better tying the gender issues in these nine trials together, this is a good companion to collections on women's studies, history, and the law.—*D. Schultz, University of Minnesota*

WS-2116 KF228 91-14129 CIP
Sobol, Richard B. **Bending the law: the story of the Dalkon Shield bankruptcy.** Chicago, 1991. 408p index afp ISBN 0-226-76752-3, $29.95

As an attorney with 25 years' experience in federal litigation, Sobol has the background necesary to write this case study of the Dalkon Shield bankruptcy litigation. The author presents the results of attending the key hearings in this landmark case along with interviews with the primary litigants. He outlines how the A.H. Robins Company used US bankruptcy law to halt thousands of lawsuits throughout the country and then to secure two major court rulings that limited both the number of women eligible to receive compensation and also the liability of Robins. Sobol suggests that damage awards are often a product of interplay among the goals and values of the judge, the skills of the attorneys, and the resources that the warring parties are able to bring to the courtroom. This case study resembles Peter H. Schuck's *Agent Orange on Trial* (CH, Dec'86). The text is clearly written and easy to follow, and Sobol does a good job of carefully documenting the facts of the case. Graduate students and faculty.—*R. A. Carp, University of Houston*

WS-2117 HQ1236 93-4264 CIP
Thomas, Sue. **How women legislate.** Oxford, 1994. 205p bibl index afp ISBN 0-19-508507-8, $35.00; ISBN 0-19-508508-6 pbk, $14.95

The election of 1992 produced the 103rd US Congress, in which the number of women in the Senate rose from two to six and the number of woman in the House jumped from 29 to 47. The timely question of what difference, if any, women make in legislatures is the subject of Thomas's book. Her answer should interest those who study representational theory, women and politics, minority politics, and research methodology. She persuasively argues that the presence of women does matter, not only symbolically but in terms of policy outcomes

as well. Drawing on original survey and interview data, Thomas documents the policy goal differences that exist between male and female legislators, and suggests why changes in legislative procedures have yet to occur. There are recent collections that study women in political office (e.g., Dorothy Cantor and Toni Bernay's *Women in Power: The Secrets of Leadership*, 1992; *The Year of the Woman: Myths and Realities*, ed. by Elizabeth Adell Cook, Sue Thomas, and Clyde Wilcox, 1994; Debra Dodson's *Gender and Policymaking: Studies of Women in Office*, 1991; and *Women in Politics: Outsiders or Insiders?*, 1993, ed. by Lois Lovelace Duke) but this book is distinctive in its singular and thorough focus on measuring gender impact on legislatures. Notes, appendixes. Recommended for all levels.—*S. Behuniak, Le Moyne College*

WS-2118 KF228.J64 90-39646 CIP
Urofsky, Melvin I. **A conflict of rights: the Supreme Court and affirmative action.** Scribner, 1991. 270p index ISBN 0-684-19069-9, $22.95

Anyone who seeks an understanding of the complexities and dilemmas inherent in the practice of affirmative action programs could find no better primary source than Urofsky's superb account of the origin, trial, appeal, and the final decision in the case of *Johnson* v. *Transportation Agency, Santa Clara County, California* (1987). An illuminating view of the political and cultural milieu of the Supreme Court is woven through the narrative of the six-year legal battle fought by Paul Johnson, whose promotion was reversed in favor of a female, Diane Joyce, as a result of an affirmative action program. Urofsky skillfully disentangles the often bewildering elements of the US legal process and integrates them into a comprehensive whole. Especially noteworthy is his insightful analysis of the attorneys preparing themselves and their briefs for oral argument, the questioning from the bench during the hearing, the use of amicus curiae briefs, the role of public interest groups in litigation, and the internal procedures of the Supreme Court. This book is free of technical jargon and will be rewarding reading for the general public as well as for undergraduate students of the judiciary. Appendix contains the complete Supreme Court decision in the *Johnson* case. Careful documentation and good index.—*R. J. Steamer, emeritus, University of Massachusetts at Boston*

WS-2119 HQ1391 93-14615 CIP
Witt, Linda. **Running as a woman: gender and power in American politics,** by Linda Witt, Karen M. Paget, and Glenna Matthews. Free Press, 1993. 330p index ISBN 0-02-920315-5, $22.95

In this important addition to research on women and politics, the authors summarize a scattered literature on the subject and offer new insights as a result of their extensive original interviews with women political leaders. The authors' diverse disciplinary backgrounds (history, journalism, political science) enable them to merge historical with contemporary perspectives. Social scientific research findings are incorporated, such as in the thought-provoking chapter "What Difference Does Difference Make?" Purported differences in women's political agendas, their perspectives as outsiders, and their characteristics and qualities act as a double-edged sword, the research suggests. These differences may make women appealing political candidates due to their images as agents of much needed change and reform. Alternatively, ascribing shared characteristics to women qua women may reinforce stereotypes of sexual differences that restrict women's participation in a male-dominated field. The text does contain some minor flaws. For example, far too much emphasis is placed on Anita Hill as the force behind women's relative success in the 1992 elections, when voters' enthusiasm for change better explains increased interest in women candidates. A useful, interesting, and comprehensive work. General; undergraduate; graduate.—*M. Hendrickson, Wilson College*

WS-2120 JK2482 91-9035 CIP
Women and men of the states: public administrators at the state level, ed. by Mary E. Guy. M.E. Sharpe, 1992. 273p bibl index afp ISBN 1-56324-051-3, $42.50; ISBN 1-56324-052-1 pbk, $17.50

The topic of this volume is the status of women in managerial positions in state government. It is the second book to emerge from a comparative state project, the first being *Gender, Bureaucracy, and Democracy* edited by Mary M. Hale and Rita Mae Kelly (CH, May'90). The eight authors, all women, combine forces to write the volume's ten chapters, each authored by one or two. Chapters are woven together nicely, all drawing on a survey of 1,289 managers conducted in six states for the project, but also reviewing in detail the relevant findings of other scholars. Principal themes include position and salary inequities, barriers to advancement, informal networks, collateral family obligations, mentoring, sexual harassment, gender traits in management, and gender differences on attitudes toward reform policies. The book's findings include some surprises, e.g., women enter management at younger ages and with more privileged backgrounds than men; and white women report more sexual harassment than nonwhite women. The chapter on gender and management style is particularly probing. We have here an integrated, thoughtful, scholarly, timely, and committed work—absolutely top drawer! Advanced undergraduate through professional collections.—*C. T. Goodsell, Virginia Polytechnic Institute and State University*

WS-2121   HV95   90-50089 CIP
Women, the state, and welfare, ed. by Linda Gordon. Wisconsin, 1991 (c1990). 311p index ISBN 0-299-12660-9, $35.00; ISBN 0-299-12664-1, $12.95

Although Diana Pearce coined the term "feminization of poverty" a decade ago (e.g., Women and Children, 1981), much of the scholarship on the welfare state has not reflected a new understanding of the gendered nature of the welfare state. Hence, Gordon's book is a welcome attempt to fill this void. Gordon (University of Wisconsin) is well known for her work on birth control and domestic violence. In this edited volume she brings together 12 essays by well-known experts on women and welfare. Her own contribution merits particular attention as do the pieces by Virginia Sapiro, Barbara Nelson, Nancy Fraser, Frances Fox Piven, and Diana Pearce. Although most of the essays have been published elsewhere, bringing them together in a single volume makes an important contribution. Gordon's book deserves serious consideration by scholars of social welfare in the US because of its challenge to take the gendered nature of the welfare system more seriously. Valuable as a supplementary text in courses on American politics, urban politics, and the history of US social welfare. Undergraduate collections.—*I. E. Deutchman, Hobart and William Smith Colleges*

◆ Psychology

WS-2122   HQ1090   92-56801 CIP
Allen, Marvin. **In the company of men: a new approach to healing for husbands, fathers, and friends,** by Marvin Allen with Jo Robinson. Random House, 1993. 235p afp ISBN 0-679-42287-0, $21.00

With the contemporary emphasis on liberation, Allen and Robinson's examination of social conditioning and its effect on males and females is worthy of recommendation. Allen uses his personal experiences along with his discoveries in individual and group therapy with dysfunctional men to clearly and compassionately inform the reader of successful techniques in psychotherapy. The negative effects of the male socialization process are documented through the use of case histories and therapy sessions. Extremely readable, the book is filled with excellent narratives and dialogues that makes processes used and conclusions derived available to the general public as well as to professionals in psychotherapy. A book without technical jargon that provides men and women with greater insights and understanding necessary for individual growth. General; community college; advanced undergraduate through professional.—*G. M. Greenberg, emerita, Western Michigan University*

WS-2123   BF408   92-43634 CIP
Creativity, ed. by John Brockman. Simon & Schuster, 1993. 221p ISBN 0-671-78926-0 pbk, $12.95

Although this book is the work of many, there is a theme throughout focusing on creativity as evidenced in the work of famous scientists and artists of the "modern era." The same litany of names appears throughout the chapters: Einstein, Darwin, Freud, Picasso, Galileo. Only two women are even mentioned, dancer Martha Graham and writer Virginia Woolf. If women have not reached the high level of creativity represented by Einstein, Darwin, etc., something

needs to be said about why not. Scientific research can no longer overlook half of the population, and when a book such as this omits women or members of minority groups, some explanation should be given. For example, if women have lacked high levels of cognitive skills or motivation this should be documented since women and some minority groups were denied admission to most Western universities and art academies until the 20th century, this surely limited their roles as creators of modern science and the modern arts. More extensive treatments of the topic of creativity can be found in *Creative People at Work*, ed. by Doris B Wallace and Howard E. Gruber (CH, May '90), and in Mark A. Runco's forthcoming "Creativity Research Handbook" (1993). General; community college; undergraduate through faculty.—*F. Smolucha, Moraine Valley Community College*

WS-2124   HQ1206   92-13206 CIP
An ethic of care: feminist and interdisciplinary perspectives, ed. by Mary Jeanne Larrabee. Routledge, 1993. 310p bibl index ISBN 0-415-90567-2, $49.95; ISBN 0-415-90568-0 pbk, $16.95

Larrabee (philosophy, DePaul Univ.) brings together key contributions from many disciplines to the debate engendered by Carol Gilligan's *In a Different Voice* (CH, Oct '82). Challenging established developmental theory, Gilligan argued that women's moral reasoning stems from an ethic of care, supplementing the model of justice. These essays, many previously published in *Signs*, address methodological issues, review current research, offer historical perspectives, and raise questions concerning the cross-cultural appropriateness of either the ethic of care or the ethic of justice. Part 1 succinctly reviews the psychological and philosophical issues, and Part 2 widens the discussion historically and culturally. Part 3 reviews pertinent data, and includes Lawrence Walker's comprehensive summary of major studies on the subject. Part 4, which includes Gilligan's reply to critics, extends the discussion into the territory of feminist ethics and the consideration of caring as one expression of a highly individualistic development of self-identity. The final chapters lay the groundwork for a feminist theory of female development that holds promise of integration with theories of male development, with both perspectives sensitized to historical and cultural dimensions. Chapter notes. Advanced undergraduate through professional.—*L. M. C. Abbott, California State University, Fresno*

WS-2125   HQ79   92-28488 CIP
Gamman, Lorraine. **Female fetishism,** by Lorraine Gamman and Merja Makinen. New York University, 1995 (c1994). 236p bibl index afp ISBN 0-8147-3071-X, $45.00; ISBN 0-8147-3072-8 pbk, $16.95

Is there such a phenomenon as female fetishism or is sexual fetishism always associated with men, as commonly believed since the time of Freud? To answer this question, Gamman and Makinen first seek to define fetishism by analyzing different types: anthropological, consumer, and sexual. Of interest is their discussion of the history of the concept of consumer fetishism and the process of "disavowal." In a complex and fascinating argument, they deconstruct Freudian and Lacanian psychoanalytic thought on fetishism, which centers on the male's use of the fetish to assuage castration fears. But as the literature and interviews show, women also make use of fetishes. Why? To find the answer, Gamman and Makinen explore the close relationship between sexual fetishism and food fetishism or bulimia. They regard women as sexually active, rather than as perverts or merely as passive objects of the male gaze. Finding the theories of Freud and Lacan inadequate to explain female sexual fetishism and bulimia, they conclude that a more apt explanation lies in the wider cultural/historical contexts in which fetishism exits as a process of disavowal and a separation of meanings. Upper-division undergraduates and above.—*K. M. Weist, University of Montana*

WS-2126   BF408   92-56172 CIP
Gardner, Howard. **Creating minds: an anatomy of creativity seen through the lives of Freud, Einstein, Picasso, Stravinsky, Eliot, Graham, and Gandhi.** Basic Books, 1993. 464p bibl indexes ISBN 0-465-01455-0, $30.00

Gardner presents a portrait of the "Exemplary Creator" (or "E.C.") based on the biographies of seven creators of the modern era, each of whom represents one of the multiple intelligences identified by Gardner: Freud (intrapersonal), Einstein (mathematical), Picasso (visual), Stravinsky (musical), T.S. Elio (linguistic), Martha Graham (kinesthetic), and Gandhi (interpersonal). According to Gardner, the "E.C." (referred to as "she") typically comes from a middle class home on the periphery of the intellectual mainstream, a home that encouraged learning but is not a particularly warm environment. The "E.C." typically endures a period of social isolation where "her" talents are not appreciated by members of her discipline, with few close confidants. Since Gardner only included one woman in his sample, his use of the pronoun "she" when describing the "Exemplary Creator" is purely gratuitous. The extent to which this profile fits other creators of the modern era remains to be demonstrated, as well as the applicability of this profile to creators in other cultures and historical periods. It is also interesting that Gardner, who is one of the most outspoken critics of treating intelligence as being monistic (as IQ), should present a monistic theory of creative thinking. Appropriate for public libraries.—*F. Smolucha, Moraine Valley Community College*

WS-2127   BF697   95-11812 CIP
Hesse-Biber, Sharlene. **Am I thin enough yet?: the cult of thinness and the commercialization of identity.** Oxford, 1996. 191p bibl index afp ISBN 0-19-508241-9, $25.00

Hesse-Biber makes one of the most powerful and compelling arguments about the cult of thinness: it is often akin to the obsessions and ritualistic behavior found among members of cults. Salvation is the reward for those who attain ideal bodies. The author, a sociologist, skillfully draws this parallel through interviews with women (and some men) with eating disorders, ranging from compulsive eating to anorexia, using their own stories and insights. What is so refreshing is that these people are not made into "cases." Rather, it is a literary and psychological pleasure to track their discovery of a different path of self-acceptance and self-love based on their own internal standards. Social activism, therapy, spirituality are all included as potential healing agents. Unlike many other books in this area, there is a particular sensitivity to multicultural issues such as the combination of racism and the beauty myth. Extensive references; many informative notes and comments. Highly recommended for upper-division undergraduates and graduate students, as well as two-year technical program students.—*R. Kabatznick, Queens College, CUNY*

WS-2128   BF692   93-39206 CIP
Johnson, Robert A. **Lying with the heavenly woman: understanding and integrating the feminine archetypes in men's lives.** Harper San Francisco, 1994. 101p afp ISBN 0-06-251065-7, $15.00

What is the reason for the recent popularity of Jungian psychology and therapy? Is it the quest for meaning of relationships between men and women that created a market for works like this one? Through this small book, Johnson translates some arcane concepts into simple, understandable ideas and provides the reader with insights into the feminine elements of male being. The use of myths, tales, and spirituality introduces a starting point for those who question their role in society. The emphasis on the conceptualization of the anima and the need for men to be consciously aware of their femininity is carefully developed throughout the book. Since there is no bibliography, professionals of analytical psychology may appreciate reading M. Esther Harding's *Woman's Mysteries, Ancient and Modern* (1971) and Warren Steinberg's *Masculinity: Identity, Conflict, and Transformation* (CH, Apr'94).—*G. M. Greenberg, emerita, Western Michigan University*

WS-2129   BF201   94-10786 CIP
Morawski, Jill G. **Practicing feminisms, reconstructing psychology: notes on a liminal science.** Michigan, 1994. 276p bibl index afp ISBN 0-472-09481-5, $39.95

Morawski has produced what she characterizes as an extended essay exploring the history and current status of feminist psychology and posing challenges for its future development. She critiques especially a feminist empiricist approach to psychology and offers instead a social epistemological analysis. In three major sections devoted to objectivity, subjectivity, and validity, Morawski analyzes the roles of investigator, subject, and their relation to one another. Drawing upon extensive sources from philosophy, history, literary criticism, and feminist theory, among others, she urges the adoption of more self-conscious, reflexive, democratic, and personal research methods by psychologists. She high-

lights the way in which an examination of gender as a category in psychological research, by feminists and nonfeminists alike, still reflects the dominance of the discipline's attributions to individual, cognitive causes rather than social, contextual ones. A difficult and thought-provoking book, for a very specialized audience with considerable background in feminist theory, or history and philosophy of science and social science. Graduate through professional.—*K. S. Milar, Earlham College*

WS-2130   BF323   94-38111 CIP
Nichols, Michael P. **The lost art of listening.** Guilford, 1995. 251p afp ISBN 0-89862-267-0, $19.95

Nichols examines the importance of listening and the covert assumptions, emotional defensiveness, and unconscious needs that inhibit good listening. He suggests ways to break through to others when listening has broken down and to control emotional reactions so that we may be better heard. He argues that the essence of good listening is empathy, achieved by suspending preoccupation with self to enter the experience of others. Practical suggestions are offered for handling interruptions, moving beyond assumptions, and defusing anger. A tendency to stereotype jobs and gender roles is distracting: men complain about not being appreciated at work, women about being overwhelmed taking care of house and children; women apply for jobs, men hire them; women are "Indians," their bosses "Chiefs"; and in describing the pretense of listening, Nichols takes an unwarranted shot at "state funded bureaucrats on autopilot." Written in a readable, clear style, the topic of listening is covered extensively. An index or bibliography would have been helpful to those interested in further research. Recommended for undergraduates, professionals in counseling, and the general public.—*A. L. Deming, Trinity College (DC)*

WS-2131   HQ1206   92-8806 CIP
Polster, Miriam F. **Eve's daughters: the forbidden heroism of women.** Jossey-Bass, 1992. 206p bibl indexes afp ISBN 1-55542-464-3, $24.95

Locating herself within a widespread feminist movement, which has emphasized both the politics of representation and the politics of interpretation, and which has foregrounded the ways in which words of power (both exaltatory and denigratory) have been used throughout history to privilege some groups and individuals, and to marginalize or depreciate others, Polster, a professor of psychiatry and co-director of the San Diego Gestalt Training Center, seeks to free the potent word *hero* from its traditional connotations, and to open it up for application to a range of figures, who would never, under the traditional and archaic dispensation, have been characterized as heroes. Her splendidly written and argued exposition may eventually enable all of us to see the single mother working a job and going to night school, the Anita Hills who expose and challenge sexual harassment in even the most august institutions of society, and many others as heroes. A fascinating little book accessible to both general readers and professionals, and that deserves the widest readership.—*B. Kaplan, Clark University*

WS-2132   HQ1206   92-8642 CIP
Psychology of women: a handbook of issues and theories, ed. by Florence L. Denmark and Michele A. Paludi. Greenwood, 1993. 760p index afp ISBN 0-313-26295-0, $115.00

American Psychological Association past president Denmark and Hunter College colleague Paludi have assembled the definitive current reference work on the psychology of women. In 18 well-referenced chapters, two appendixes, and a bibliographic essay, they and the other authors, all eminent psychologists, have produced a major resource summarizing research findings, addressing methodology, reviewing contemporary knowledge on lifespan development, and assessing issues of work, health, victimization, and societal sexism. An extraordinary review of contemporary knowledge, the work expands that base with original contributions to theory, methodology, and clinical practice. Denmark and Fernandez's introductory historical overview of the psychology of women is authoritative and comprehensive, clarifying the relationships among intertwined strands of theoretical legacy. Rabinowitz and Sechzer advance theory with their perspectives on research methods, exploring the impact of "nonequivalence" of the genders in the interpretation of gender differences. Fitzgerald and Ormerod's essay on sexual harassment and Etaugh's on midlife and later years offer definitional clarification, new information, and research summaries of immense practical significance. Extensive chapter references. Advanced undergraduate through professional.—*L. M. C. Abbott, California State University, Fresno*

WS-2133　　　　　　RC451　　　　　　94-38395 MARC
Russell, Denise. **Women, madness and medicine.** Polity, 1995. (Dist. by Blackwell) 196p index afp ISBN 0-7456-1260-1, $49.95

Russell focuses on biological psychiatry and how it impacts women. She argues that it is women, primarily, who are the negative benefactors of the discipline. Russell, a respected philosopher, argues that this aspect of psychiatry produces more harm than good—a provocative argument that she triumphantly makes throughout this book. The most interesting chapter treats epistemological problems with the dominant medical psychiatric perspective. Russell takes on schizophrenia and eating disorders as examples of bias in psychiatry and how a "string of unsubstantiated theories" have emerged. What is worse, however, is that women remain subordinated and diminished in a covert way. Although Russell does not make this point directly, it certainly leaves one wondering how many professionals conveniently project their sexism onto theories that support it—making it both easy and popular to avoid examining one's own attitudes towards women. Her book beautifully integrates Phyllis Chelser's seminal work, *Women and Madness* (CH, Mar'73). Russell recommends a new line of research and theories to come to grips with human distress. Must reading for upper-division undergraduates, graduates, and professional practitioners in all fields relating to women's health.—*R. Kabatznick, Queens College, CUNY*

WS-2134　　　　　　HQ1206　　　　　　92-13751 CIP
Seldom seen, rarely heard: women's place in psychology, ed. by Janis S. Bohan. Westview, 1992. 459p afp ISBN 0-8133-1394-5, $60.00; ISBN 0-8133-1395-3 pbk, $19.95

Bohan has gathered articles from 1968 to 1991 that address the place of women in psychology as participants and as subjects. She suggests that social constructionism can provide a framework for re-placing women in the discipline. Bohan's prologue provides the reader with an understanding of constructionism. She builds a model incorporating a feminist critique of science, constructionism, and an historical examination of the place of women in psychology, which is then instantiated by the readings she collects. The four parts of the book, each ably introduced by Bohan, examine (1) women's place in psychology historically; (2) psychology's construction of gender (re-viewing women); (3) the re-shaping of theory, method, history, and therapeutic practice (re-placing women); and, (4) what a woman-inclusive psychology might be. This final section points out that a constructionist view demands that feminist psychologists analyze the potentially anti-feminist consequences of deconstruction. A thought-provoking volume, suitable for advanced undergraduates and above.—*K. S. Milar, Earlham College*

WS-2135　　　　　　BF175　　　　　　95-41726 CIP
Smith, J.C. **The castration of Oedipus: feminism, psychoanalysis, and the will to power,** by J.C. Smith and Carla Ferstman. New York University, 1996. 316p index afp ISBN 0-8147-8018-0, $55.00; ISBN 0-8147-8019-9 pbk, $18.95

This is a provocative experiment in theory. Smith and Ferstman wondered what would happen if postmodernism, feminism, and psychoanalysis were forced into a synthesis. If the key element of each approach were retained, how would we find ourselves thinking about men and women? The resulting book is a loose compendium of ideas drawn from Nietzsche, Freud, Lacan, Derrida, and leading feminist psychoanlysts. The myths of Oedipus, Dionysus, Medusa, and others are reinterpreted in light of these perspectives to suggest new possiblities for discourse and action. Contemporary concepts of desire, meaning, masochism, and fantasy are explained. At the theoretical level, the experiment leads to the conclusion that psycoanalysis must transcend its fixation on patriarchal models of psychic development, as exemplified by the Oedipus complex. Similarly, feminism must abandon its attachment to the liberal notion of equality and move toward a Nietzschean appreciation of power and its dynamics. Although the argument lacks clarity and depends excessively on quotes from the masters, readers will find much to ponder in this volume. Graduates; faculty.—*T. Sloan, University of Tulsa*

WS-2136　　　　　　HQ1206　　　　　　91-26030 CIP
Unger, Rhoda. **Women and gender: a feminist psychology,** by Rhoda Unger and Mary Crawford. Temple University, 1992. 706p bibl indexes ISBN 0-87722-897-3, $39.95

Unger and Crawford, experienced psychology faculty, present a book with value beyond the classroom. The chapters on commitments and relationships, violence against women, and sex, status, and power deserve a broad audience. From feminist and cross-cultural perspectives the authors analyze the impact of gender at the individual, interpersonal, and cultural levels. The work, which includes several chapters written from developmental, social psychological, and clinical perspectives, is a persuasive critique of androcentric knowledge, as well as a broad-ranging survey of emerging scholarship. Four themes appear throughout: knowledge as a source of power; the importance of language and naming; the diversity of women's lives; and most centrally, the treatment of gender as a social construction. In addition to research reports, anecdotes, and interview material, there are suggested readings by chapter as well as references. Undergraduates and up; interested general readers.—*L. M. C. Abbott, California State University, Fresno*

WS-2137　　　　　　　　　　　93-083774 Brit. CIP
Women and AIDS: psychological perspectives, ed. by Corinne Squire. Sage Publications, 1993. 196p index ISBN 0-8039-8587-8, $55.00; ISBN 0-8039-8588-6 pbk, $19.95

An edited collection focusing on different elements in women's experience with AIDS. The introductory chapter (by editor Squire) is a highly politicized overview; readers should concentrate on the eight wonderful chapters that follow. The two on HIV and women's reproductive rights (by Hortensia Amaro and Lorraine Sherr) are well worth the price of the book. Both present balanced, clear information on pregnancy, counseling, and HIV testing. Later chapters on HIV transmission, women's experiences in delivering AIDS-related services to others, and portrayals of women during the AIDS crisis are also quite well done. Cindy Patton's brief chapter on HIV risk and women builds on and extends her earlier work (with Janis Kelly, *Making It: Woman's Guide to Sex in the Age of AIDS*, 1987; *Sex and Germs: the Politics of AIDS*, 1985). An important book for all general readers, pre-professional and graduate students, and psychology and medical faculty and professionals who have any responsibility or interest in the area of women and AIDS.—*A. C. Downs, formerly, University of Houston-Clear Lake*

◆ History, Theory

WS-2138　　　　　　BF201　　　　　　95-18570 CIP
Bringing cultural diversity to feminist psychology: theory, research, and practice, ed. by Hope Landrine. American Psychological Association, 1995. 465p bibl indexes afp ISBN 1-55798-292-9, $40.00

Developed in response to the atheoretical nature of much research on ethnic differences, this collection represents forward movement in the search for an explicit theoretical framework for rendering coherent a multiplicity of sociocultural variables. Although the collected articles represent many, at times conflicting, viewpoints, they fulfill the 1990-91 mandate of APA's task force on cultural diversity, creating a resource work for serious scholars. Given the sheer numerical proportion of women of color in the world, this contribution to overcoming their marginality as a topic in feminist psychology is long overdue. Landrine, Klonoff, and Brown-Collins's chapter on methodology argues for change, offering reasons for generalizing anthropology's emic and etic approach to feminist research. Several chapters include important recommendations for those researchers concerned with diversity, and most discuss the confounding variable of power. Attention is drawn to areas where further research is sorely needed, such as the omission of ethnicity in studies of gender socialization. The generalizability problem presented by the concept of the socially constructed self is given attention, as is cautious support to the framework of contextual behaviorism. Extensive chapter bibliographies, supplemented by tables, charts, and an appendix. Upper-division undergraduate through professional.—*L. M. C. Abbott, California School of Professional Psychology*

WS-2139 BF692 90-11196 CIP
Christen, Yves. **Sex differences: modern biology and the unisex fallacy,** tr. by Nicholas Davidson. Transaction, 1991. 141p bibl index ISBN 0-88738-869-8, $29.95

A logical treatise that purports to answer the question of whether or not women and men are essentially different. Simone de Beauvoir's assertion that "one is not born, but rather becomes a woman" (1949) serves as the fulcrum for Christen's argument through 12 short chapters that focus primarily on issues friendly to sociobiological explanations of observed sex differences. His skill as a science writer is evident as he (over)simplifies complex issues to arrive at his conclusion that de Beauvoir's ". . .premise is incorrect but the conclusion is accurate" (p.113); biological determinism or predisposition is augmented by the social context into which one is born. Christen celebrates the resulting differences between the sexes and maintains that these differences become validating for both men and women. Appropriate for community college students and up, as well as informed general readers.—*B. Ayers-Nachamkin, Wilson College*

WS-2140 BF1408 94-26269 CIP
Greer, Mary K. **Women of the Golden Dawn: rebels and priestesses.** Park Street Press, 1995. 490p bibl index ISBN 0-89281-516-7, $29.95

Greer has prepared a joint history of four women seeking independence from convention in the years just before and after 1900: Mina Bergson, Florence Farr, Maude Gonne, and Annie Horniman. They shared membership in and devotion to a mystical cult termed the Golden Dawn, and the history of this movement is also the topic of the book. Two of the four were especially significant in the life and work of a literary figure: Florence Farr with George Bernard Shaw (mostly before and while he was writing his first play), Maud Gonne with W.B. Yeats. Mina Bergson's career is of at least marginal interest for students of her distinguished brother Henri. Maude Gonne's participation in the movement for Irish independence is rather fully treated. It is startling to find that Greer appears to grant the role of the planets in the subjects' lives the same reality that their astrological beliefs and rituals led them to. But this does not seem to interfere with her ability to treat the mundane influences on their lives. The sources of information are annotated in great detail. Graduate; faculty.—*I. L. Child, Yale University*

WS-2141 HQ1206 91-58602 CIP
Kaschak, Ellyn. **Engendered lives: a new psychology of women's experience.** Basic Books, 1992. 265p bibl index ISBN 0-465-01347-3, $25.00

Kaschak employs a heuristic blend of sociocultural and psychotherapeutic analyses to inform her exploration of the psychology of women/the reality of women's lived experiences. She begins with a useful and unusually lucid comparison of traditional male-centered and feminist (postmodern) epistemologies and their impacts on (especially) psychotherapies. Following a brief discussion of the social psychological construction of gender based on the illusion of anatomical dichotomy, Kaschak introduces a thought-provoking feminist interpretation of the Oedipal myth using as female counterpart to Oedipus not Electra but Oedipus' daughter-sister, Antigone. The resulting model of female-male relationships in patriarchal society, a model that emphasizes seeing and knowing rather than sexuality, is used in subsequent chapters to explain the development of a sense of self, self-esteem, and specific psychological outcomes of learning to be a woman (e.g., depression, and eating and dissociative disorders). Kaschak concludes with suggestions for applying her model to the development of feminist psychotherapy. Those with an interest in feminist psychology/sociology should find this book intellectualy stimulating, a treat. Highly recommended for academic libraries serving upper-division undergraduates, graduate students, and professionals.—*B. Ayers-Nachamkin, Wilson College*

WS-2142 HQ1075 89-38800 CIP
Making a difference: psychology and the construction of gender, ed. by Rachel T. Hare-Mustin and Jeanne Marecek. Yale, 1990. 212p index afp ISBN 0-300-04715-0, $18.95

Hare-Mustin and Marecek, along with Bernice Lott, Rhoda K. Unger, and Jill G. Morawski, have authored a series of six chapters devoted to what gender means, how feminist scholarship is advanced (and impeded), and strategies for feminist-based inquiry. All of the authors raise extremely important questions of how or if feminist research can or should be integrated into, be superordinate to, or coexist with current psychological theory and research. Hare-Mustin and Marecek introduce useful vantage points for this debate and successfully argue for newer empirical language, including alpha and beta bias, which are tendencies to exaggerate or minimize research differences, respectively. Although mainstream psychologists and graduate students have historically closed off or minimized input from feminist scholars, this book deserves to be read, and reread, especially by those most resistant to feminist thought and ideology. Earlier texts such as those by S.G. Harding, *The Science Question in Feminism* (CH, Dec'86) and A.H. Eagly, *Sex Differences in Social Behavior* (CH, Oct'87) raised similar, but preliminary questions. However, the present book easily surpasses those earlier works. The gauge of genuine scholarship is the ability of a work to generate critical and empirical debate and to foster change. This new book does so, clearly and with power.—*A. C. Downs, University of Houston—Clear Lake*

WS-2143 HQ755 94-7245 Orig
Murdock, Maureen. **The hero's daughter.** Fawcett Columbine, 1994. 250p bibl index ISBN 0-449-90962-X, $23.00

Jungian therapist Murdock here undertakes to describe the difficult and costly path from being a father's daughter to establishing separate identity. Part 1 explores the overidentification with the father and masculine definitions of success, and the rejection of the mother and feminine values that characterize the favored father's daughter in childhood. Part 2 details the resultant losses—in her feminine nature, spirituality, creativity, and relational abilities. Part 3 presents the journey of individuation, acceptance of the father as mortal man, and reclamation of female identity and power. Autobiographical material is supplemented with legends, literary figures, and clinical case vignettes to illustrate this journey, with all its material successes, its personal price, and its alienation. One of the strongest contributions of the work is its development of the psychological profile of a father's daughter: shared behaviors and characteristics highlighting her relationship with power and spirituality, as well as with other men in her life. The author finds widespread evidence that these characteristics typify most women in patriarchal cultures. Chapter notes. All levels.—*L. M. C. Abbott, California School of Professional Psychology*

WS-2144 BF692 93-11508 CIP
The psychology of gender, ed. by Anne E. Beall and Robert J. Sternberg. Guilford, 1993. 278p index afp ISBN 0-89862-286-7, $28.95

Beall and Sternberg's collection is comprehensive and readable. Sternberg's introductory chapter concisely treats the issue of biological versus environmental determinants of gender. The contributions include analyses of gender in relation to thought and behavior, various theoretical perspectives, life-span and cross-cultural viewpoints, and a final integrative chapter. Of particular note, Florence Geis reviews the literature on self-fulfilling prophecies and demonstrates how stereotypes reinforce the status quo of gender inequity. In an especially well-written essay, Bernice Lott and Diane Maluso examine the social learning of gender and its relevance to feminist thought. Biologically based approaches are dealt with by Douglas Kenrick and Melanie Trost, who carefully distinguish between simple biological determinism and the complexities of evolutionary factors in shaping gender differences. Many contributors deal extensively with the social implications of studying gender, especially with respect to gender differentials in power. For advanced undergraduates, graduate students, and faculty in psychology, sociology, and gender studies.—*H. L. Minton, University of Windsor*

WS-2145 HQ1206 89-25083 CIP
Theoretical perspectives on sexual difference, ed. by Deborah L. Rhode. Yale, 1990. 315p index afp ISBN 0-300-04427-5, $25.00

Without hesitation, this reviewer judges Rhode's book as the best ever written on the issues of sex, gender, and sex differences. No fewer than 21 brilliant scholars, ranging from N.Chodorow to E.B. Freedman, pose "cutting edge" questions concerning theory, research, philosophy, ethics, history, biology, ethology, social sciences, law, politics, and social policy concerning sexual differences. All of the authors raise, delineate, and defend often extremely complex issues, and each author fosters and focuses debate on most of the issues pertinent to current feminist scholarship. Although this book addresses current issues, it will undoubtedly be cited by researchers and theorists for years to come. It raises issues previously ignored and offers fresh perspectives on old debates. All readers will discover something in this volume to which they will object, but those objections will insure more precision in arguments regularly entertained by feminists. All of the authors write at a level that is likely to be decipherable and understandable only to professionals, faculty, and advanced students. Nonetheless, this book should unquestionably be in every library with any holdings on women's studies, feminist scholarship, social sciences of sex roles and sex differences, and legal studies.—*A. C. Downs, University of Houston—Clear Lake*

WS-2146   RC451   91-32410 MARC
Ussher, Jane M. **Women's madness: misogyny or mental illness?** Massachusetts, 1992 (c1991). 341p bibl indexes ISBN 0-87023-786-1, $47.50; ISBN 0-87023-787-X pbk, $16.95

Ussher, a clinical psychologist who has resigned from active therapeutic practice on ideological grounds, attempts to deconstruct various theoretical explanations of behavior that is considered abnormal and ultimately condemns both mainstream and feminist therapies. Her discourse encompasses a very broad range of issues including the relationship between witchcraft and madness; the 19th-century movement to subsume psychological processes within the medical domain; psychoanalytic, positivist, humanist, and feminist theories of psychological functioning, and more. Certain themes recur throughout this treatise: patriarchally-biased labeling as self-fulfilling prophecies, feminity as synonymous with madness, and the separation of women from their own experiences, all subsets and evidence of the deleterious effects of pervasive misogyny and patriarchal oppression within society. Ussher concludes by calling for reform of our institutions and offers some relatively practical suggestions for how this might be accomplished, many of them focusing on the empowerment of women. Extensive and useful bibliography. Unlike many works that adopt a deconstructionist approach, this one is highly accessible as well as interesting and informative.—*B. Ayers-Nachamkin, Wilson College*

WS-2147   RC451   94-40877 CIP
Wenegrat, Brant. **Illness and power: women's mental disorders and the battle between the sexes.** New York University, 1995. 217p index afp ISBN 0-8147-9282-0, $29.95

Are certain mental disorders more common among women then men? History would substantiate this, according to Wenegrat. He examines anxiety, depression, multiple personality disorders, eating disorders, and what was once known as hysteria. His premise is that one reason women are at higher risk for these disorders is their lack of social power. When looking at mental disorders, Wenegrat writes, clinicians need to understand the larger social picture—economic, cultural, and sociological conditions—that helps to mold and define the symptoms. Wenegrat presents data that indicate that women are largely disadvantaged because they shoulder most of the responsibility for taking care of children, making them economically dependent on others. He also offers a historical view of mental disorders as illness roles, examining how particular illnesses met women's needs during the late 1800s. Wenegrat presents multiple personality disorders and eating disorders as two modern-day epidemics, supporting his view with statistics and historical information. An evolutionary, cross-cultural view of women's social power is presented through examination of results from research studies dealing with social power of both men and women. He concludes stating that as women gain social power, the difference in the frequency of mental disorders between men and women will decrease. Upper-division undergraduate through professional.—*M. A. Gillis, Elmira College*

◆ Body Image, Eating Disorders

WS-2148   RC552   91-42850 CIP
Controlling eating disorders with facts, advice, and resources, ed. by Raymond Lemberg. Oryx, 1992. 218p index afp ISBN 0-89774-691-0 pbk, $29.50

A compilation of 25 chapters by professionals in the field of eating disorders. Three primary sections deal with causes, symptoms, and effects of eating disorders; personal, social, and cultural issues; and treatment of eating disorders. The last two sections offer a directory of facilities and selected resources, including books, journals, and other materials. The chapters are lightweight—each is about three pages long and summarizes generally rather than developing current thinking in this field. Much of the book discusses people who have eating disorders, but there are several technical chapters on the disorder. Although it tries to cover a substantial topic in a much too superficial way, the book's feminist orientation is strong, powerful, and very important. The resource lists cover a wide range of materials, including newsletters and audio materials. Recommended for general readers and lower-division undergraduates.—*R. Kabatznick, Queens College, CUNY*

WS-2149   RC552   94-3801 CIP
Dolan, Bridget. **Why women?: gender issues and eating disorders,** by Bridget Dolan and Inez Gitzinger. New updated ed. Athlone, 1994. 145p bibl indexes ISBN 0-485-11450-X, $45.00; ISBN 0-485-12106-9 pbk, $15.00

The eating disorders field is not at a loss for books; many of these say the same thing. It is a pleasure that Dolan and Gitzinger explore some interesting new topics regarding gender issues and eating disorders. Anorexia in boys, a sex education program for women with eating disorders, and eating patterns and unwanted sexual experiences are three that are particularly interesting. The authors are primarily clinicians with some psychoanalytical perspective. The book has as its origins information exchanged at a meeting of the European Council on Eating Disorders, the goal of which was to address specific gender issues, primarily: why women? Each chapter has its own references, some more complete than others. Recommended for all undergraduates.—*R. Kabatznick, Queens College, CUNY*

WS-2150   RC552   93-23951 CIP
Feminist perspectives on eating disorders, ed. by Patricia Fallon, Melanie A. Katzman, and Susan C. Wooley. Guilford, 1994. 465p index afp ISBN 0-89862-180-1, $36.95

Just the title alone is thrilling, but an entire edited collection of feminist writings on eating disorders is enough to make one cry out in sheer joy. Considering the numbers of books, papers, and conferences devoted to this complex subject, the feminist presence has been surprisingly scarce—a chapter here, a presentation there. This book, edited by three respected psychologists, is an important milestone in the field. The material is divided into the following sections: "A Gendered Disorder: Lessons from History"; "A Place for the Female Body"; Treatment Issues: a Feminist Reanalysis"; Reconstructing the Female Text"; and "Possibility." Any of the chapters would make an excellent basis for a graduate seminar. The chapters "The Politics of Prevention" and "Still Killing Us Softly: Advertising and the Obsession with Thinness" are particularly strong and important. Each chapter has a complete and helpful bibliography. The entire book is essential reading for graduate students, researchers, faculty, professionals, and practitioners.—*R. Kabatznick, Queens College, CUNY*

WS-2151   BF697   93-48225 CIP
The good body: asceticism in contemporary culture, ed. by Mary G. Winkler and Letha B. Cole. Yale, 1994. 247p index afp ISBN 0-300-05628-1, $27.50

This book examines our obsessions with the "good body" in the contexts of contemporary culture and of ancient ascetic practices of self-denial. It is divided into four parts: religious and moral implications; authority and cultural constructions, interpretive narrative, and cultural ideals. The contributors include a wide range of experts who participated in an interdisciplinary conference that explored the relationship between the current cultural ideal of control and the rise in eating disorders. Many diverse topics are covered: Psychologist and researcher Mary Brown Parlee argues that the biomedical version of premenstrual syndrome is incontestable, not because it is necessarily true, but because of the way science is structured. Other writers discuss the effects of child abuse and other forms of sexual victimization on body image. There is an elegant article on Flannery O'Connor's "celebration of embodiment" in her last novel. On the whole, this book elevates the field of eating disorders by reaching beyond current psychological theory and pop sociology. It links in a larger historical context attitudes and behaviors that associate certain physical characteristics with moral and aesthetic superiority. Recommended. Upper-division undergraduate; graduate; professional.—*R. Kabatznick, Queens College, CUNY*

WS-2152 BF697 93-46941 CIP
Johnston, Joni E. **Appearance obsession: learning to love the way you look.** Health Communications, 1994. 232p ISBN 1-55874-270-0 pbk, $9.95

Johnston sends a clear, almost personal message to readers about the impact of physical attractiveness and appearance in our culture. After an introduction to appearance issues, she writes in a way general readers will appreciate and understand. Her presentation of media portrayals of appearance is quite good, although her referencing system and lack of footnotes are confusing for those wanting to study these works. Of special note is the fact that she identifies and discusses the impact of appearance obsession on both women *and* men, thus challenging earlier gender-biased notions about the cultural importance of appearance. Johnston elects to focus on family messages about appearance and unfortunately spends little time discussing peer messages. The final seven chapters focus on dealing with one's appearance, including weight and dieting, exercising, clothing, social factors involving appearance, self-esteem, and body image. These chapters represent the best parts of the book, and readers concerned with altering their perceptions about appearance and/or their actual appearance will find ample, concrete suggestions for improvement. Most appropriate for general readers.—*A. C. Downs, formerly, University of Houston-Clear Lake*

WS-2153 RC552 93-7246 CIP
MacSween, Morag. **Anorexic bodies: a feminist and sociological perspective on anorexia nervosa.** Routledge, 1993. 273p bibl indexes ISBN 0-415-02846-9, $74.50

In this intelligent analysis of anorexia nervosa, MacSween moves beyond theoretical approaches that ignore social structure to a historically and politically situated conceptualization of the disorder. This conceptualization recognizes the body as a social construction and shows how the socioeconomic organization of a given culture shapes its members' understandings of the body. Important to her analysis is MacSween's attention to the relevance of gender distinctions for social meanings of the body, particularly because meanings of the female body are fraught with contradictions. Rather than conceptualizing anorexia as an intensification of these contradictions (including desire and control, dependence and autonomy), MacSween argues that anorexia transforms the categories through which female experience is created. This transformation, she argues, is an attempt to resolve at the level of the body the conflicting demands of individuality and femininity that all women face in a patriarchal bourgeois culture. Recommended. Undergraduate and above.—*D. Gimlin, SUNY at Stony Brook*

WS-2154 BV4596 95-16206 CIP
Manlowe, Jennifer L. **Faith born of seduction: sexual trauma, body image, and religion.** New York University, 1995. 225p bibl index afp ISBN 0-8147-5517-8, $40.00; ISBN 0-8147-5529-1 pbk, $16.95

Manlowe's provocative work with a theological overlay ties together sexual abuse and eating disorders in women. Several things separate Manlowe's scholarship from some of the more impressionistic journalism sometimes found at the popular levels of feminism. Manlowe defines her terms, describes her sample of interviewees (middle-class Christian women), and anchors her work in behavioral science (e.g., psychiatric nosology). She then moves into the spiritual realm, deconstructing misogynous themes in Christian discourse and discussing the politics of 12-step groups. The appendixes include the methodological specifics, and there are also extensive references and an index. This book definitely belongs in libraries serving graduate programs in religious studies, women's studies, counseling, and social work.—*T. L. Brink, Crafton Hills College*

WS-2155 GN298 93-37997 CIP
Many mirrors: body image and social relations, ed. by Nicole Sault. Rutgers, 1994. 346p bibl index ISBN 0-8135-2079-7, $45.00; ISBN 0-8135-2080-0 pbk, $16.00

This unusual collection is based on research projects intended to explore the connection between social relationships and the human body. Contributors are anthropologists, sociologists, and human service workers residing in Canada, Jordan, and the US. The people whose bodies are discussed include members of small tribes in various parts of the world, American teenagers, women professionals, women in recovery programs, female body-builders, and persons from a wide variety of other groups. Some chapters focus on talk, others on meaning, behavior, adornment, and cosmetics. The collection is also exceptional in that the chapters refer to one another, as if there were a conversation going on among authors. The research methods used are fine examples of interviewing, participant observation, and discourse analysis. The analyses are refreshing and original, in most cases. Contributors argue convincingly that there is a profound connection between the social world and the way people shape their bodies. Although the introduction and anthropologist Peggy Reeves Sanday's foreword present the issue on theoretical grounds, it is the studies themselves that prove the point. Undergraduates and above.—*S. Reinharz, Brandeis University*

WS-2156 RC552.E18 90-40323 CIP
Matthews, John R. **Eating disorders.** Facts on File, 1991. 168p bibl index ISBN 0-8160-1911-8, $21.95

Part of a new and creative series, "Library in a Book," the goal of which is to provide all the essential research tools needed to begin one's own research in an area. This book supplies a lopsided view of eating disorders, since it is slanted more toward popular weight-related books than it is toward scholarly books and journals. On the other hand, it contains an interesting "chronology of important events" that includes entertaining facts, such as the date when a man was convicted of mail-order charges for selling weight reduction plans based on clients' handwriting samples. It also covers "legal issues relating to eating disorders"—a topic one rarely reads about. Organizations are listed alphabetically with names, addresses, telephone numbers, and a brief description of their purpose and focus. The address for Weight Watchers International is five years out of date. The sections on the history and treatment for obesity, anorexia, and bulimia provide a concise overview of these disorders. Recommended for lower-division undergraduates, community college students, and general readers.—*R. Kabatznick, Queens College, CUNY*

WS-2157 RC552 91-19478 CIP
Moorey, James. **Living with anorexia and bulimia.** Manchester, 1992 (c1991). 144p ISBN 0-7190-3368-3, $24.95

A sophisticated book about anorexia and bulimia written to reach a wide audience ranging from professional to family and friends. Although parts may be too detailed and technical for the latter, it is a concise and up-to-date presentation of these painful and disruptive eating disorders. Moorey writes in a very warm and supportive style and is careful not to judge or blame patients or parents. He encourages patients to take responsibility for their healing. Although personal responsibility lies at the heart of recovering from these disorders, it is rarely emphasized in treatment books. In that sense, this approach sets this book apart from others. It is refreshing to see the focus on empowerment rather than on victimizing patients using condescending labels and descriptions. Moorey also encourages parents to "look after yourselves and your marriage," which is a polite way of telling caregivers not to become so overly involved that they lose (and disempower) themselves. Unfortunately, there is no index; however, there is a brief list of suggested readings. Recommended. Undergraduate; general.—*R. Kabatznick, Queens College, CUNY*

WS-2158 RC552 92-16188 CIP
Robertson, Matra. **Starving in the silences: an exploration of anorexia nervosa.** New York University, 1992. 101p bibl index ISBN 0-8147-7434-2, $30.00; ISBN 0-8147-7435-0 pbk, $12.95

This short book is not easy reading. Robertson assumes a fairly sophisticated audience with considerable background in French structuralist philosophy and feminist theory. She presents her own feminist perspective on anorexia nervosa intertwined with interpretations of selected theories of Foucault, Lacan, Irigary, and other great thinkers and writers. She also provides brief cultural history of such varied and yet related topics as fasting, health food, vegetarianism, diet, eating, hunger strikes, force feeding, anemia, holy anorexia, and sexual fears. Robertson helped this reviewer to better understand the female self-starver, a term she promotes over "anorexic" because the former exercises control over her own body while the latter suffers passively from a psychiatric illness from which she may not recover. Robertson's message is a very important one—that the self-starver needs to speak and write for herself in order to express her own pain, oppression, loneliness, etc. and not let the male-dominated medical profession describe her behavior and prescribe her treatment. Extensive bibliography and index; recommended to graduate students, researchers, and faculty in women's studies, and to mental health professionals.—*E. R. Paterson, SUNY College at Cortland*

WS-2159 HQ1219 90-49983 MARC
Wolf, Naomi. **The beauty myth: how images of beauty are used against women.** W. Morrow, 1991. 348p bibl index afp ISBN 0-688-08510-5, $22.00

Wolf argues that the cult of female beauty has emerged as a formidable political weapon in resistance to the considerable economic, social, and political gains women in the "First World" have made recently. With the exception of some statistical information, Wolf presents almost nothing new on the subject of the beauty myth, leaving the enormous potential of her thesis undeveloped. The book's power derives primarily from the exuberant passion of its author. Would that an editor had encouraged Wolf to define her terms more precisely, to forego poorly supported and sweeping generalizations, and to distinguish between description and the genuine analysis of a phenomenon and its effects. Wolf also needs to reconsider her ahistorical posture: it is simply not true that the beauty myth is peculiar to the late 20th century. The references cited in the text vary in their relevance and usefulness, but the bibliography, although incomplete in some areas, will provide the reader with most of the classics on this issue. Community college level and up.—*J. de Luce, Miami University (OH)*

◆ Clinical/Applied Psychology

WS-2160 RC451 92-48733 CIP
Bernstein, Anne E. **The psychodynamic treatment of women,** by Anne E. Bernstein and Sharyn A. Lenhart. American Psychiatric, 1993. 670p bibl index afp ISBN 0-88048-368-7, $45.00

An examination of Bernstein and Lenhart's work will demonstrate its significance to the professional literature in the understanding of the contemporary scene and, especially, the unique problems experienced by women. The authors' expertise as psychiatrists makes this a valuable contribution that provides insights into the complex issues related to the psychodynamic treatment of women. In a well-organized and documented fashion, each issue is presented through a historical review, an exploration of a variety of clinical models and theories, specific case histories, and the processes used in the psychodynamic intervention for a particular conflict in the life cycle of women. Each of the seven chapters has extensive notes. In addition, the appendixes, bibliography, and supplemental readings prove the careful scholarship involved in developing this important work. Professionals who want to explore the problems within the social and cultural context that are specific to women will be rewarded by reading this book. Graduate through professional.—*G. M. Greenberg, emerita, Western Michigan University*

WS-2161 HV6250 92-30005 CIP
Burstow, Bonnie. **Radical feminist therapy: working in the context of violence. Sage, 1992.** 302p bibl index ISBN 0-8039-4787-9, $45.00; ISBN 0-8039-4788-7 pbk, $22.95

Burstow's book should prove very useful as a resource for practitioners working in a wide variety of areas dealing with violence against women. Among the issues Barstow discusses are childhood sexual abuse, abuse by partner, self-mutilation, troubled eating, drinking problems, psychiatric survivors, and clients

who consider ending their lives. Other topics include working with lesbians, Native American women, African American women, Jewish women, immigrant women, and women with disabilities. The first part of the book presents the theoretical foundations; the remaining 12 chapters integrate theory and practice. Written from a well-articulated radical feminist position, the text is grounded in structuralist theory that situates problems in living within the systematic oppressions of classism, sexism, and racism. Respect for women and for their right to make their own decisions in therapy permeates the text. Advanced undergraduate; graduate; faculty; professional.—*C. Adamsky, University of New Hampshire*

WS-2162 RC533 90-10434 CIP
Feminist perspectives on addictions, ed. by Nan Van Den Bergh. Springer, 1991. 222p index ISBN 0-8261-7350-0, $32.95

Using a feminist perspective to analyze the conditions that nourish the addictions of "at-risk" women, this anthology provides a different approach to the causes and cures of addictive behavior. Part 1 provides excellent working definitions as a basic foundation for the contents of the book. Parts 2 and 3 include articles by recognized authorities experienced in a broad range of disorders (e.g., substance abuse, eating disorders, workaholism, gambling, and disorders of older women and lesbians). Each topic is written as a discrete unit with a similar format: it covers the essential information that defines the addiction, reviews the research, and suggests successful treatment and therapy. Through this anthology, mental health professionals can become more knowledgeable about the influence of cultural, social, and psychological factors that may create conditions that affect women's lives. In addition, the expertise of the book's contributors bring together the ways in which theory and practice can be used in individual and group therapy. Advanced undergraduates and up.—*G. M. Greenberg, emerita, Western Michigan University*

WS-2163 RC467 91-25284 CIP
Gender issues in clinical psychology, ed. by Jane M. Ussher and Paula Nicolson. Routledge, 1993 (c1992). 245p indexes ISBN 0-415-05485-0, $64.50; ISBN 0-415-05486-9 pbk, $16.95

As suggested by its title, this collection highlights the need to recognize and incorporate dimensions of gender and power involved in (particularly) the delivery of clinical psychological services. The ten chapters range from discussions of sexism in professional organizations, the impact of logical positivism on clinical practice, and discrimination in diagnostic labeling to some very interesting practical applications of feminist approaches in a variety of settings: a neighborhood-based psychotherapy service that extends the definition of therapy to include empowering involvement in social action projects, and a consultation service on child sexual abuse that also promotes interagency networking, family, and individual therapies. Although the book is clearly aimed at a British audience of clinical psychologists and those in allied professions, a broader, international audience might find the practical models of heuristic value. Faculty; professional.—*B. Ayers-Nachamkin, Wilson College*

WS-2164 RC537 91-15472 CIP
Jack, Dana Crowley. **Silencing the self: women and depression.** Harvard, 1991. 256p bibl indexes afp ISBN 0-674-80815-0, $19.95

In this significant work, therapist Jack (Western Washington University) reexamines traditional views of depression from the perspective of depressed women clients and study participants themselves. Building on the substantial recent body of research that stresses the centrality of relationships to women's self-esteem and development (see, for example, D. Belle, "Stress of Caring" in *Handbook of Stress*, ed. by L. Goldberger and S. Breznitz, CH, Jun'83; J. Bowlby, *Attachment and Loss*, 3 v.; v.1, CH, Feb'70; v.2, CH, May'74; J. B. Miller, *Toward a New Psychology of Women*, 2nd ed., CH, Jul'87; and C. Gilligan, *In a Different Voice*, CH, Oct'82), she finds the etiology of depression not in dependence, but in the experience of women in unequal relationships. In a futile quest for intimacy, her participants have censured their authentic selves, silenced their perspective, and "lost" themselves in compliant behavior designed to achieve and maintain relationships. In internalizing the broader culture's devalued and sexualized assessment of women, they experience first a divided self, then hopelessness as the authentic part is disconfirmed and denied a voice. Those participants who have progressed in therapy regain a perspective that confirms both their relational selves and the moral themes that arise from the interdependent, rather than the autonomous (or male) self. In addition to the author's "Silencing the Self Scale," the volume includes synoptic data on longitudinal study participants, tables, and extensive chapter notes.—*L. M. C. Abbott, California State University, Fresno*

WS-2165   HV6570   93-39239 CIP
Jacobs, Janet Liebman. **Victimized daughters: incest and the development of the female self.** Routledge, 1994. 209p bibl index afp ISBN 0-415-90626-1, $49.95; ISBN 0-415-90922-8 pbk, $15.95

Jacobs (Univ. of Colorado, Boulder) views incest through a feminist, rather than a child protection, lens and focuses on the impact of incest on the daughter's sense of self. This study integrates feminist psychological theory with interviews with 50 women sexual abuse survivors. Jacobs begins by discussing the destruction of the mother-daughter bond in incestuous families. Her analysis then moves to complex issues involving the daughter's relationship with the perpetrator. The daughter may idealize or identify with the incestuous father; frequently she empathizes with and cares for him. Jacobs discusses consequences of these processes for the daughter in the form of revictimization, powerlessness, dissociation, and denial of her body. The final chapter describes the process of "change and transformation" some victims achieve, over time, with therapy. This short book is enriched with appropriate quotations from the informants. However, the complexity of the feminist developmental and therapeutic theories will be difficult for undergraduates without considerable background. Although it appears easy to read, it is actually quite demanding. Highly recommended for libraries serving graduate programs in psychology, social work, or feminist studies as well as therapists who treat women.—*M. E. Elwell, Salisbury State University*

WS-2166   RC560.I53   89-43302 MARC
Meiselman, Karin C. **Resolving the trauma of incest: reintegration therapy with survivors.** Jossey-Bass, 1990. 320p bibl indexes afp ISBN 1-55542-219-5, $24.95

Another entry into the burgeoning literature on incest. Meiselman, a clinical psychologist, has a private practice in California. The book is aimed first at psychotherapists, second at other professionals (teachers, attorneys, etc.), third at graduate students in relevant areas, and finally at people with incest in their background. Using the now common terminology of incest "victim" or "survivor," the author sketches traumas described by therapy patients, discusses psychoanalytic defense mechanisms (repression, denial, etc.) of such patients, and describes in useful terms an eclectic treatment program she calls reintegration therapy. Meiselman's previous book, *Incest: A Psychological Study of Causes and Effects with Treatment Recommendations* (1978) and several journal articles written by her demonstrate her knowledge of the field. She appears to be a warm, insightful clinician. Useful for graduate students in various human service areas, and for any readers suffering after effects of incest.—*R. W. Smith, California State University, Northridge*

WS-2167   RC569   93-47203 CIP
Miller, Dusty. **Women who hurt themselves: a book of hope and understanding.** Basic Books, 1994. 280p bibl index ISBN 0-465-09220-9, $22.00

Violence against women has been an increasingly popular topic for the media and publishers. Miller brings to our attention an important component of this issue by examining the complex factors inherent in the behaviors of women who inflict harm upon themselves. As an experienced therapist who has worked with women who mutilate their bodies (because of being abused, violated, and neglected as children), she has developed a treatment approach that carefully examines the history of childhood and the subsequent pattern of behavior in adulthood. The first part details the ways in which childhood traumas create the Trauma Reenactment Syndrome (TRS). The second part describes the author's approach to working with TRS women and demonstrates through case studies how this therapy can assist the patient in acquiring the skills to resolve early painful relationships. A clear discussion of various psychotherapies that failed provides the professional with a better understanding of the complexity of this problem. These successful approaches make this book a valuable contribution to the literature. Undergraduate; graduate; professional.—*G. M. Greenberg, emerita, Western Michigan University*

WS-2168   RC489   93-36036 CIP
Shore, Lesley Irene. **Tending inner gardens: the healing art of feminist psychotherapy.** Haworth, 1995. 194p bibl index afp ISBN 1-56024-885-8, $39.95; ISBN 1-56023-856-9 pbk, $14.95

Shore's use of metaphors to describe the process of psychotherapy makes this small book a unique diversion from other works. Her approach provides both experienced and inexperienced psychotherapists with some thought-provoking ideas. It is obvious that Shore has been able to combine scientific knowledge with the art of therapy when she describes the process of nurturing a person through the use of language and its relationship to the seasons in a garden. The simplicity with which this book is written gives the reader an opportunity to comprehend the interacting factors of mind and body as well as the complex realities of society's significance in patterns of individual growth. This is a timely book for therapists who want to learn how to use space and time in probing men's and women's inner conflicts. The references and bibliography are excellent sources for expanding one's own horizons as well as integrating special tools in working with clients. Graduate; professional.—*G. M. Greenberg, emerita, Western Michigan University*

WS-2169   RC488   91-2554 CIP
Women and power: perspectives for family therapy, ed. by Thelma Jean Goodrich. W.W. Norton, 1991. 288p index ISBN 0-393-70117-4, $32.95

An excellent, provocative collection of 24 feminist essays, focusing on issues of power in "family therapy" settings; the papers range from abstract theoretical discussions, involving such figures as Foucault and Lukes, to brief illustrations of therapeutic interventions in concrete cases. Formally organized in five unequal parts (The Social and Psychological Context, Romance, Story and Ritual, Family Therapy, and Clinical Practice), the essays collectively combine an admirable mix of theoretical argument and exhibitions of practice. Among the essayists are editor Goodrich ("Women, Power, and Family Therapy: What's Wrong With This Picture"); Jean Baker Miller ("Women and Power: Reflections Ten Years Later"); Linda Webb-Waton ("The Sociology of Power"); Deborah Anna Luepnitz ("Foucault, Feminism, and Prosecuting Daddies"). Of considerable value to all those interested in "family therapy" but especially to those practitioners who have taken for granted current concepts and categories pertaining to family therapy. References appended to each article. Advanced undergraduates and up.—*B. Kaplan, Clark University*

WS-2170   RC489   94-5534 CIP
Women in context: toward a feminist reconstruction of psychotherapy, ed. by Marsha Pravder Mirkin. Guilford, 1994. 502p bibl index afp ISBN 0-89862-095-3, $44.95

The range and specificity of examples in this edited collection raises awareness of the life contexts of diverse women in psychotherapy, even for readers who regard themselves as enlightened. The diversity addressed includes gender, race, class, sexual lifestyle, and combinations. Unique to this volume are sections on the sociopolitical aspects of life cycle issues, health issues, and of problems presented in psychotherapy. No particular feminist theory is evident; the "reconstruction of psychotherapy" seems to mean the changes assumed to follow when service-delivery practitioners caringly attend to women's full situations. The power of this volume lies in its authors' readable, nonstrident, respectful evocation of women struggling with social forces that often are invisible to their would-be helpers. Pertinent social policy, human development, psychology, and psychotherapy literatures are addressed in each chapter. Appropriate for gender studies as well as psychotherapy and mental health programs. Undergraduate through professional.—*C. T. Fischer, Duquesne University*

WS-2171   RC451   94-10840 CIP
Women of color: integrating ethnic and gender identities in psychotherapy, ed. by Lillian Comas-Díaz and Beverly Greene. Guilford, 1994. 518p bibl index afp ISBN 0-89862-371-5, $44.95

In tone and framework, this mainstream academic work is thoroughly referenced, and largely adopts the language of variables, factors, and interaction effects. Nevertheless, it also succeeds in vividly evoking the "confluence of racial, gender, and ethnocultural factors in the psychotherapeutic treatment of women of color." The editors have assured that awareness of this confluence, unacknowledged in most training and practice settings, will remain with readers. Similarly, the book successfully reminds us of individuals' diversity within groups. The psychotherapy context, "clinical management" problems, and many concrete instances bring the volume to life and assure its utility. Part I addresses issues in provision of mental health services to a sample of ethnic women: African American, Native American, Asian and Asian American, Latina, West Indian, and Indian subcontinent. Part 2 addresses women of color in the context of therapeutic systems: psychodynamic, cognitive-behavioral, family, feminist, integrative, and psychopharmacological. Part 3 addresses a sample of special groups of women of color: professional, lesbian, battered, mixed race, and Southeast Asian American refugee. A major resource for all clinicians and human services professionals—psychologists, physicians, nurses, educators, counselors; suitable for gender studies programs. Undergraduate through professional—*C. T. Fischer, Duquesne University*

WS-2172 RC489 91-30785 CIP
Worell, Judith. **Feminist perspectives in therapy: an empowerment model for women,** by Judith Worell and Pam Remer. Wiley, 1992. 380p bibl index ISBN 0-471-91860-1, $44.95

A systematic work, the first of its kind—an integrated compilation of studies and conceptual articles on feminist issues as they bear on psychotherapy and counseling. The authors methodically overview socialization issues; therapy and assessment approaches compatible with feminist therapy; life-span issues in counseling women; working cross-culturally and with lesbian and ethnic minority women; ethical and other professional issues; and give a model of training. Many chapters begin and end with personal belief questionnaires to raise and change consciousness. Teaching devices include careful repetition of themes, suggested readings and exercises, charts and lists, and cases for illustration and discussion. The authors present their model of feminist therapy as one of empowerment for women through changing both person and society. This change is pursued via respecting uniquely women's characteristics, and via challenging assumptions and roles. This book is very North American in its practicality and its emphasis on social psychology. There are some references to the social construction of reality and to the position that "the personal is political." Unlike feminist work from other continents, however, this one is independent of postmodern philosophy, psychoanalysis, Marxism, and deconstructionism. Recommended for graduate programs in counseling and psychology.—*C. T. Fischer, Duquesne University*

◆ Developmental Psychology

WS-2173 HQ798 90-30819 CIP
Emma Willard School (Troy, N.Y.). **Making connections: the relational worlds of adolescent girls at Emma Willard School,** ed. by Carol Gilligan, Nona P. Lyons, and Trudy J. Hanmer. Harvard, 1990 (c1989). 334p afp ISBN 0-674-54040-9, $25.00; ISBN 0-674-54041-7, $10.95

Essays in this collection were originally published by the Emma Willard School, where girls' psychological development was studied between 1981 and 1984. Psychologist Carol Gilligan added a prologue, preface, and epilogue concerning the possibility of a "musical language for psychology." This expanded edition places the Emma Willard School studies within the context of other research on adolescent girls. It makes the case that the years between 11 and 16 are particularly important for girls and revolve around the "crisis of relationship." The essays are written by a variety of individuals whose biographies are briefly presented at the beginning of the volume. The methods used by researchers varied widely from psychological testing to more free-ranging conversation and observation. Each essay contains a methodology section explaining how the study was done, and concludes with a brief bibliography. Several pages of the volume are printed in a different color to highlight examples of how girls talk about a particular issue. In the penultimate chapter, teachers discuss their experience as members of this study, and in the final chapter, Gilligan and her colleagues reflect on developmental theory, and research methodology, particularly sentence stem completion. The collection is written in an engaging, expansive manner, with literary references and personal reflections. Public and academic libraries, community college level up.—*S. Reinharz, Brandeis University*

WS-2174 HQ1206 90-13923 CIP
Gustafson, Sigrid B. **Female life careers: a pattern approach,** by Sigrid B. Gustafson and David Magnusson. L. Erlbaum, 1991. 221p (Paths through life, 3) bibl indexes ISBN 0-8058-0948-1, $49.95

In the mid-1960s, David Magnusson (University of Stockholm) began a longitudinal research project concerning individual development titled "Paths Through Life." During the past three years, Gustafson (Virginia Polytechnic Institute and State University) has participated in the project. This volume is the third to emerge from the study: the first (*Individual Development from an Interactional Perspective*, 1988) dealt with theory and methods used in the project as a whole; the second (Hakan Stattin and Magnusson, *Pubertal Maturation in Female Development*, 1990) "presented a biosocial model of female development in adolescence." The current volume subdivides the population of Swedish adolescent girls into various types, or "patterns," which account for different "developmental streams" or "expected, differential processes of development over time." The authors give each pattern a specific name (e.g., High-Aspiring Theoreticals; Gifted, Moderately Low-Adapted Achievers). The book presents findings about specific patterns and demonstrates a methodology and a theoretical argument about how developmental research should be done. The study is directed exclusively to research psychologists and contains extensive tables, figures, and statistical information. There are four appendixes of measures, six pages of references, and separate subject and author indexes.—*S. Reinharz, Brandeis University*

WS-2175 BF723 94-45864 CIP
Kerr, Barbara. **Smart girls two: a new psychology of girls, women, and giftedness.** Ohio Psychology, 1995 (c1994). 270p index ISBN 0-910707-25-1 pbk, $18.00

As suggested by its title, this book is in part a 20-year follow-up study of a small group of women identified as gifted and whose education from grades 5-12 was predicated on that label. This group provides an initial context for the extended discussion of more general issues related to the self-actualization of gifted women. Using an inclusive, contemporary definition of giftedness, Kerr reviewed biographies of 33 women who distinguished themselves in their chosen fields and includes brief profiles of nine (e.g., Maya Angelou, Marie Curie, Katharine Hepburn), identifying 14 elements common to the majority (e.g., time alone, voracious reading, same-sex education, mentors, integration of roles). Several chapters are devoted primarily to the results and implications for women of seven research projects ranging from Terman's classical studies (e.g., L.M. Terman and M. Oden, "The Gifted Child Grows Up," in *Genetic Studies of Genius, Vol. 4*, 1947), to the more contemporary work of D.C. Holland and M.A. Eisenhart, *Educated in Romance: Women, Achievement, and College Culture* (1990) and L.M. Brown and C. Gilligan's *Meeting at the Crossroads* (1992). Concluding chapters describe typical developmental characteristics of gifted females and make concrete recommendations for ways parents, professionals, and the gifted themselves may nurture their potential for excellence. Throughout, Kerr makes clear the deleterious effects of conventional gender role expectations and urges that gifted girls be taught "... to demand equality in the classroom and to create equality in their own families." All levels.—*B. Ayers-Nachamkin, Wilson College*

WS-2176 HQ759 92-34612 CIP
Musick, Judith S. **Young, poor, and pregnant: the psychology of teenage motherhood.** Yale, 1993. 272p bibl index afp ISBN 0-300-05353-3, $27.50

Most adolescent mothers have themselves been raised by families whose poverty limited their capacity to provide good child rearing. Thus, girls raised in poverty are at risk of being "encumbered with psychological burdens that result in self-limiting choices and self-defeating behaviors." Musick, a developmental psychologist with the Ounce of Prevention Fund, contends that no intervention into the growing problems of adolescent pregnancy and parenthood will succeed unless it focuses on enhancing psychological competencies and self-concepts. Musick draws extensively from the experiences of young women served by the Fund's various programs. The book examines a range of family and environmental influences on development and their relationship to premature motherhood, and describes the special challenges faced by these young parents. A concluding chapter delineates the interrelated domains in which these young women must be helped toward positive change: education, work, parenthood, and relations with men. Highly recommended for policymakers and the range of professionals who work with adolescents.—*B. A. Pine, University of Connecticut*

WS-2177 HQ778 91-3320 CIP
Singer, Elly. **Child-care and the psychology of development,** tr. by Ann Porcelijn. Routledge, 1992. 180p bibl indexes ISBN 0-415-05591-1, $55.00

Singer develops a philosophical and historical approach to the issue of child care. She traces the development of child care centers over the last two to three centuries, in light of such social and cultural changes as urbanization, the separation of workplace from home, the nuclear family ideal, mothers working outside the home, the influence of two world wars, and the "War on Poverty." She also considers influences on the care of children from broad philosophical movements such as romanticism, the Enlightenment, and a more recent emphasis on science. Though the purposes and practice of child care centers have varied from age to age, Singer points out major issues that have remained constant. One is the role of the mother in the cognitive and emotional development of the child. Is separation from mother a good or bad thing for the child? Can a mother satisfy her own needs and still be a good mother? Is close contact with a mother essential for development? In this well-written book, Singer convincingly asserts that how we view such issues today is shaped by the history of the child care center. Though there are other historical approaches such as Theresa R. Richardson's *The Century of the Child* (CH, Feb'90), Singer offers more engaging, metacognitive explanations for otherwise dry facts. She attempts to answer "why," not just "what." "Must" reading for child care professionals. All collections.—*K. L. Hartlep, California State University, Bakersfield*

WS-2178 HQ798 95-36209 CIP
Taylor, Jill McLean. **Between voice and silence: women and girls, race and relationship,** by Jill McLean Taylor, Carol Gilligan, and Amy M. Sullivan. Harvard, 1995. 253p bibl index afp ISBN 0-674-06879-3, $22.00

The latest in a series of longitudinal studies carried out by the Harvard Project on Women's Psychology and Girls' Development, this research shifts focus from the voices of the privileged (see *Making Connections: The Relational Worlds of Adolescent Girls at Emma Willard School*, ed. by Carol Gilligan, Nona Lyons, and Trudy Hanmer, CH, Nov'90) to the voices of girls from an urban public high school. A total of 26 working-class girls from African American, Caribbean, Portuguese, Latina, Irish, and Italian backgrounds, designated as at risk for early motherhood and school dropout, were interviewed four times over a three-year period. The girls responded to questions about themselves in and out of school, their relationships with their mothers and another important person in their lives, acting in the face of conflict, decisions about sex, and the future. Commentary on and excerpts from these interviews are interspersed with reflections on a series of retreats on women and race for the adult women involved in the study. Although the effects of race on development are noted, the basic emphasis of the study is on the reaffirmation of the project's view that the essential adolescent female developmental challenge is finding voice in relationship. All levels.—*K. M. McKinley, Cabrini College*

WS-2179 HQ1206 94-35574 CIP
Women growing older: psychological perspectives, ed. by Barbara F. Turner and Lillian E. Troll. Sage Publications, CA, 1994. 282p index ISBN 0-8039-3986-8, $46.00; ISBN 0-8039-3987-6 pbk, $23.95

Current research on older women is related to theoretical themes in the psychology of adult development and aging in an effort to stimulate theory development. The eight distinguished authors "adopt a stance of theoretical pluralism" in exploring various issues, with an introductory chapter that reviews recent scholarship and identifies avenues for further exploration. The following seven chapters focus on particular aspects. Motivational frameworks direct examination of life-span development of women in the Terman Study of the Gifted and the social clock project based on Mills College graduates. Another chapter explores how three models—trait, socioculture, and social cognition—apply to a study of stereotypes of women of different age and race. Psychodynamic theories are used to examine creativity, attachment across three generations, and gender identity in midlife. A final chapter considers a life-span approach to older women's social relations and causal mechanisms. The chapters combine reviews and presentation of fresh empirical data. A valuable compilation. Upper-division undergraduate through faculty.—*E. Scarborough, Indiana University at South Bend*

WS-2180 HQ1206 91-12093 CIP
Women's growth in connection: writings from the Stone Center, by Judith V. Jordan et al. Guilford Press, 1991. 310p bibl index afp ISBN 0-89862-562-9, $40.00; ISBN 0-89862-465-7, pbk $18.95

This clear series of working papers, carefully illustrated with clinical case examples, presents key elements of the model of women's development that has evolved over the last decade at Wellesley College's Stone Center. In contrast to traditional models of development that describe a process of separation and achievement of autonomy, this model describes growth as it takes place within and through relationship. The authors, each of whom blends academic and clinical experience, explore women's relational sense of self, the developmental origins and implications of empathy, and the relational path of women's development, as well as complex and unresolved issues such as power, anger, work, eating patterns, and the effectiveness of traditional and more empathic therapeutic methods with women clients. Extending the work of David C. McClelland (*Power: the Inner Experience*, CH, Sep'76) and Carol Gilligan (*In a Different Voice*, CH, Oct'82), these papers describe how cultural denigration of relational qualities and objectives has restricted women's effectiveness, and even their development, with depression a frequent result. Although it poses more questions than answers, this compilation makes a significant contribution to enriching our model of human nature and development. Advanced readers.—*L. M. C. Abbott, California State University, Fresno*

◆ Psychoanalytic Works

WS-2181 BF109 92-53237 CIP
Appignanesi, Lisa. **Freud's women,** by Lisa Appignanesi and John Forrester. Basic Books, 1993 (c1992). 563p bibl index ISBN 0-465-02563-3, $30.00

A beautifully written, careful book of wide scope and a welcome addition to writings about Freud's circle and the work of its members. The English authors successfully challenge the myth that the female founders of psychoanalysis were puppets of the master. Here, the women spring into life, from Anna Freud to Lou Andreas Salome, from Muriel Gardiner to Marianne Kris, from Karen Horney to H.D. to Sabina Spielrein. Their worlds and ideas emerge vivid and significant, at times as wild and speculative as those of Freud (e.g., the essays of the Princess Marie Bonaparte). Their interwoven lives are considered, their friendships, their notorious rivalries, and their conflicts with Freud. Throughout, there is an elegant examination of Freud's paradoxical attitudes towards women and how they became manifest with female collaborators, his family, and the horizon of his theory of femininity. There is a section about the first female patients. No short review can possibly do justice to this fine and balanced work, which includes a modern appraisal of the relation of feminism to psychoanalysis. Not only a must for all students of psychoanalysis, but should be of great interest to programs in women's studies, historians of ideas, and the intellectual general public. All levels.—*R. H. Balsam, Yale University*

WS-2182 BF175 93-39481 CIP
Chodorow, Nancy J. **Femininities, masculinities, sexualities: Freud and beyond.** Kentucky, 1994. 132p bibl index afp ISBN 0-8131-1872-7, $20.00

Chodorow's latest book reflects further the influence of her psychoanalytic training on her well-established credentials as feminist sociologist. Since the era of her groundbreaking *The Reproduction of Mothering* (CH, Nov'78), her interests have widened to intrapsychic detail, and she here suggests a new direction in thinking about "sexualities." The intention is to avoid the problems arising from a monolithic theory of generic "man" and "woman." These papers were delivered at the University of Kentucky in 1990 as the Blazer Lectures. The first section is an excellent critique of Freud's views about women. Through the lenses of woman as subject (e.g., case reports) and woman as object (theory), she finds differences, the former being more complex than the infamous theory itself. The next two sections are more confusing: she argues against contemporary psychoanalytic writers for overly dwelling on the "homosexualities" at the expense of heterosexuality. She finds them at once too individual and too general in their approach. Her recommendation is for individualized "constructions of gendered experience," with emphases on cultural factors. Chodorow's book will interest feminists, cultural theorists, and psychoanalysts, especially those following her thought since the seventies. General; undergraduate through professional.—*R. H. Balsam, Yale University*

WS-2183　　　　　HQ29　　　　　Orig
Deutsch, Helene. **Psychoanalysis of the sexual functions of women,** ed. by Paul Roazen; tr. by Eric Mosbacher. Karnac Books, 1991. (Dist. by Brunner-Mazel) 132p bibl index ISBN 0-946439-95-8, $27.95

Publication of this book preceded the publication of Deutsch's more frequently cited two-volume work, *The Psychology of Women* (1946-47), by nearly 20 years, but was clearly the foundation upon which the latter was based. It was also the first book focused on women to emerge from the psychoanalytic tradition. As such, it expanded on the Freudian view of "normal" women as inherently masochistic and passive. Appearing here for the first time in English translation, academicians and the educated public will find this book accessible, owing in part to competent translation and skillful, though somewhat positively biased, editing. The editor, a professor of political science, introduces each of the 12 chapters (ranging from infantile sexuality to menopause) providing both theoretical overview and cultural-historical context. Most appropriate for college and university collections.—*B. Ayers-Nachamkin, Wilson College*

WS-2184　　　　　RC451　　　　　91-6761 CIP
Deutsch, Helene. **The therapeutic process, the self, and female psychology: collected psychoanalytic papers,** ed. by Paul Roazen; tr. by Eric Mosbacher et al. Transaction, 1992. 271p index ISBN 0-88738-429-3, $39.95

Editor Roazen (a researcher of Freud and psychoanalysis) reviews many writings of Helene Deutsch to bring together this collection of 22 psychoanalytic papers. The reader is introduced to a chronological history of the background and experiences that made Deutsch an influential pioneer in psychoanalysis. Each paper is very brief, with theoretical analyses, clinical observations, and reference notes, covering psychology of women, therapeutic practices, neurosis, psychiatry, and identification. Many feminists of today might question Deutsch's formulation in the psychology of women; however this book can provide stimulating discussions when presented together with the ideas of Karen Horney in *Feminine Psychology* (CH, Feb'68). The book under review will interest scholars of women's studies and the psychology of women. In light of the current research on adolescent girls by Carol Gilligan (*Making Connections*, ed. by C. Gilligan, N.P. Lyons, and T.J. Hammer, CH, Nov'90), the ideas of psychosexual development may again be reexamined along with the ideas of Deutsch. Graduate; faculty; professional.—*G. M. Greenberg, emerita, Western Michigan University*

WS-2185　　　　　BF175　　　　　92-36505 CIP
Doane, Janice. **From Klein to Kristeva: psychoanalytic feminism and the search for the "good enough" mother,** by Janice Doane and Devon Hodges. Michigan, 1993 (c1992). 101p bibl index ISBN 0-472-09433-5, $29.95

Doane and Hodges try to reconcile feminist views of working mothers not tending their children so continuously as did the at-home working mother of past eras. Frankly, their efforts fail to do so to a large degree. Psychoanalysts who wrote about the "good enough mother" and the "good breast" did not assume that the father or someone else could serve as a substitute at almost any time. They all thought mother-to-child bonding and child-to-mother attachment were very important and happened because of the interaction between the mother and the child. The authors discuss the works of three important female analysts: Melanie Klein, Nancy Chodorow, and Julia Kristeva. Of these, Chodorow makes the most sense for today's mentality. An interesting book, easy to read, that should appeal to upper-division, pre-professional, and graduate students in psychology and social work.—*R. J. Howell, Brigham Young University*

WS-2186　　　　　BF692　　　　　91-14406 CIP
Elliot, Patricia. **From mastery to analysis: theories of gender in psychoanalytic feminism.** Cornell, 1991. 244p index afp ISBN 0-8014-2546-8, $33.95; ISBN 0-8014-9780-9 pbk, $10.95

Assuming at the outset that a liberating feminism requires a critical theory of gender and that an adequate psychoanalytic understanding of the subject can contribute significantly to such a critical theory, Elliot, using a Lacanian typology of forms of discourse, expounds, criticizes, and evaluates—in terms of their promotion of a discourse of Analysis as contrasted with discourses of the Master, the Bureaucrat or the Hysteric—the theorizing of such well-known, psychoanalytically informed feminist writers as Juliet Mitchell, Jacqueline Rose, Dorothy Dinnerstein, Nancy Chodorow, Luce Irigaray, and Julie Kristeva. Although contestable and certain to be contested, the author's representations and critical assessments of the discourses of these feminist-psychoanalytic theorists are relatively clear and accessible even to culture critics who do not share the terministic screens of the author or the subjects of her discourse. A worthwhile contribution to ongoing debates over "gender," the politics of engendering, the forces of gender oppression, and instrumentalities needed to eliminate such oppression. Graduate level.—*B. Kaplan, Clark University*

WS-2187　　　　　BF1566　　　　　91-58949 CIP
Faber, M.D. **Modern witchcraft and psychoanalysis.** Fairleigh Dickinson, 1993. (Dist. by Associated University Presses) 191p bibl index afp ISBN 0-8386-3488-5, $29.50

Faber, a professor of English, directs this study primarily at understanding modern-day witchcraft as a religious cult, sometimes known as Wicca. For clues, he appeals to anthropological research, to studies of Western cultural history, to Bettelheim's interpretations of fairy tales, and to psychiatric theory and case studies (with an emphasis on object-relations versions of psychoanalysis, and on Jungian analysis of symbolism). This varied background is applied very successfully to pertinent factual data, obtained in interviews with cult members, attendance at a coven meeting, and reading printed matter representative of the cult. The unifying thread in Faber's interpretation is the theme of seeking a magical return to early childhood dependence on maternal omnipotence, accompanied by fantasies of personal omnipotence. Underlying this theme is the ubiquity of conflict between desires for separation and for union; in a final chapter Faber aims to show the relevance of this conflict to much else in present-day culture. He thus returns, by implication, to his initial suggestion that the witchcraft cult has a special appropriateness to our times. Advanced undergraduate through faculty.—*I. L. Child, Yale University*

WS-2188　　　　　BF175　　　　　89-35686 CIP
Freud on women: a reader, ed. with an introd. by Elisabeth Young-Bruehl. W.W. Norton, 1990. 399p index ISBN 0-393-02822-4, $25.00

In this first collection of Freud's writings on women, Young-Bruehl (Wesleyan University) provides a definitive anthology. Her informative introduction chronicles the emergence and revisions of key concepts in Freud's understanding of women's psychology, and presents these ideas in the context of important developments in his life and clinical practice. Key subjects, such as hysteria and masochism, are traced in abridged and annotated selections from *The Standard Edition of The Complete Psychological Works of Sigmund Freud*, ed. and tr. by James Strachey (1953-74). The chronological selections are complemented by an annotated bibliography covering the most significant Freud studies, and subsequent psychoanalytic works in the major conceptual area covered by his writings on women. Both of the major feminist critiques of Freud are briefly presented in the introductory essay, and work in the increasingly important area of child psychoanalytic studies is mentioned both here and in the annotated bibliography. A detailed index facilitates comparison of early and later writings on central concepts, and a brief chronology of Freud's life adds historical context. Although psychoanalytic consensus has developed concerning women in the years since Freud, this volume makes a significant contribution by clarifying his thoughts, their evolution, and the investigative approach to his clinical cases that gave rise to these ideas. All levels.—*L. M. C. Abbott, California State University, Fresno*

WS-2189 BF723 91-35415 CIP
Furman, Erna. **Toddlers and their mothers: a study in early personality development.** International Universities, 1992. 414p bibl indexes ISBN 0-8236-6555-0, $49.50

Furman summarizes a psychoanalytic study of toddlers and their mothers at the Hanna Perkins School. The first third of the book describes the school, the toddler, the program, the staff, the methods of observation, and the child-parent pairs who participated. A Toddler Assessment Profile, developed for the study, is reprinted and described in some detail and may interest professionals in the field. The remainder of the book describes the clinical findings about the toddler and his or her relationships with parents, teachers, and peers. It points out what developmental tasks seem to be most important for this age group, what circumstances may foster or hinder development, and what therapeutic interventions might be useful. Though readable, the age span is quite narrow, basically a single year of life. Those who wish a psychoanalytic approach over a greater age range might better consult Greenspan and Pollock's four volume series, *The Course of Life* (v.1, CH, Apr'90; v.2, CH, Oct'90; v.3, CH, Sep'91; v.4, CH, Jul'92). Advanced undergraduate; graduate; faculty; professional.—*K. L. Hartlep, California State University, Bakersfield*

WS-2190 BF109 92-48252 CIP
Gilman, Sander L. **Freud, race, and gender.** Princeton, 1993. 277p index afp ISBN 0-691-03245-9, $24.95

Gilman synthesizes the work of psychoanalysts, Freud biographers, literary critics, and historians to provide this impressive new reading of the meanings of "race" and "gender" in Freud's time. With admirable scholarship, the author tackles numerous assumptions about the manner in which Freud's Jewish male identity shaped his scientific stance in and against antisemitic culture. Since many of Freud's key concepts, particularly those about women, take on new dimensions in light of Gilman's analysis, this is an essential book for fin-de-siècle cultural studies, Jewish studies, and the history of psychology and medicine. The book also has great relevance to contemporary debates on multiculturalism. Excellent notes and index. Advanced undergraduate through faculty.—*T. Sloan, University of Tulsa*

WS-2191 HD6054 94-46292 CIP
Harris, Anita M. **Broken patterns: professional women and the quest for a new feminine identity.** Wayne State, 1995. 220p bibl index afp ISBN 0-8143-2550-5, $39.95; ISBN 0-8143-2551-3 pbk, $17.95

Harris, a journalist and president of a media consulting firm, interviewed 30 professional women in law, corporate management, science, and medicine. She weaves these personal histories together with the history of working women and homemakers in the US. Focusing mainly on the 20th century, Harris uses a psychoanalytic framework to argue that the central struggle of a woman's life is to be unlike her mother yet retain connection with her. The more daughters identified with mothers they saw as downtrodden, the more they wished to escape that fate; the more they rebelled against "traditional" women's roles, the more conflicted they became. Now at midlife, not sure about the wisdom of their choices, many of these women wonder how they can be more like their mothers. Harris claims that during historical or personal times of crisis or confusion, we seek the all-powerful mother of our infancy from whom we once ran in fear. The number of historians, sociologists, and psychologists quoted is prodigious, the footnotes and citations are impressive and informative. Yet, somehow—perhaps because Harris attempts too much interpretation with too little original data—the book provides few new insights. General readers; undergraduates.—*K. M. McKinley, Cabrini College*

WS-2192 BF175 94-39464 CIP
Kurzweil, Edith. **Freudians and feminists.** Westview, 1995. 222p bibl index afp ISBN 0-8133-1420-8, $59.00; ISBN 0-8133-1421-6 pbk, $17.95

This new work by Kurzweil (*The Freudians: A Comparative Perspective*, CH, Jul'90) traces the long and often quarrelsome history of relations between proponents of Freudian psychoanalysis and feminists and suggests a symbiotic rather than antagonistic interpretation of that history. Kurzweil, editor of *The Partisan Review*, writes with authority about the political and sociological context in which Freud's thinking about women developed, and she provides a detailed summary of most of the major points of intersection between psychoanalytic

and feminist theory in Freud's original circle and in the English, US, French, and German psychoanalytic communities during the 50 years since Freud's death. Kurzweil's argument distinguishes between a "First Wave"—modernist, empirical—and a "Second Wave"—postmodernist, Lacanian—feminism. She is consistently critical of the latter, and one value of her book will be as a stimulus to discussion of postmodern feminist theory. The bibliography is quite thorough for a work of this length, and both early theorists such as Horney, Deutsch, and Klein, and recent ones such as Kristeva, Cixous, and Irigaray are interestingly summarized and evaluated. Upper-division undergraduate through faculty.—*D. A. Davis, Haverford College*

WS-2193 RG161 92-39668 CIP
Lupton, Mary Jane. **Menstruation and psychoanalysis.** Illinois, 1993. 228p bibl index afp ISBN 0-252-02012-X, $34.95; ISBN 0-252-06315-5 pbk, $14.95

Lupton claims a greater centrality for menstruation, and reactions concerning the phenomenon in both women and men, than psychoanalysis has granted. She has many ideas about why women's monthly bleeding has been subjected to repression in clinical practice, in theory, and in the literature of studies of gender differentiation. Her careful and scholarly reference covers the period between the Freud/Fliess correspondence in the 1890s up to the present. Her coverage of the early Freudians is especially good. Lupton's recovery and assessment of attitudes to menstruation is informed by the thesis that menstrual flow has signaled negative gender responses, focused on female taboo, exclusion, and denigration in society. Lupton formulates menstruation as *the* central bodily difference she perceives in locating gender difference applicable to psychoanalytic theorizing. She asserts a positive, life-affirming force in the menstrual condition, an aspect largely unexplored, due to psychoanalytic and societal inhibition. Suitable for all psychoanalytic scholars, sociologists, historians of ideas, philosophers of science, and those in gender and women's studies. Advanced undergraduate through professional.—*R. H. Balsam, Yale University*

WS-2194 BF175 93-32444 CIP
Neumann, Erich. **The fear of the feminine and other essays on feminine psychology,** tr. by Boris Matthews et al. Princeton, 1994. 296p (Essays of Erich Neumann, 4) index afp ISBN 0-691-03474-5, $39.95; ISBN 0-691-03473-7 pbk, $12.95

In the past 20 years, Jungian psychology has become increasingly popular. For those interested in analytical psychology, this compilation of five essays, by a noted Jungian, examines the need for a synthesis of the feminine and masculine in order to rectify the misunderstanding of patriarchal Western civilization. However, the emphasis on mysticism, spiritual forces, and mythology may seem arcane to psychotherapists who view change as essential in this contemporary world. Since these essays were written prior to 1960, one should examine new interpretations of Jungian psychology. Warren Steinberg's *Masculinity: Identity, Conflict, and Transformation* (CH, Apr'94) and Loren E. Pedersen's *Dark Hearts: The Unconscious Forces that Shape Men's Lives* (1991) should be valuable in a contemporary analysis of the female and male archetype and how men and women today integrate these concepts into the process of unifying the self. Graduate through professional.—*G. M. Greenberg, emerita, Western Michigan University*

WS-2195 HQ1090 93-46057 CIP
Ross, John Munder. **What men want: mothers, fathers, and manhood.** Harvard, 1994. 242p bibl index afp ISBN 0-674-95080-1, $29.95

Ross presents a psychoanalytic study of male development by focusing on a boy's early identification with his mother, his ambitions to become a father, the aggression and generational rivalry of father-son relations and, finally, the development of romantic, erotic passion for a woman. Throughout this discussion, Ross emphasizes the complexity and uncertainty of manhood that are the result of the interaction between the feminine underside of a man's basic nature and the inherent risk involved in the assertion of stereotypical masculine virility. Detailed reinterpretations of the Oedipus myth, with a special focus on King Laius, the father of Oedipus, and of the classic case of Little Hans, provide illustrations of Ross's arguments. These reanalyses are supplemented with case studies from his research/clinical experiences. The discussion of Freud's reluctance to confront adult sexuality and passionate love is especially interesting, and the conclusion that womb envy is no less a factor in the inner life of men than penis envy is in the psychology of women is certain to stir thought in any reader. Upper-division undergraduate through professional.—*R. B. Stewart Jr., Oakland University*

WS-2196   BF109   91-18644 MARC
Sayers, Janet. **Mothers of psychoanalysis: Helene Deutsch, Karen Horney, Anna Freud, Melanie Klein.** W.W. Norton, 1991. 319p bibl index ISBN 0-393-03041-5, $24.95

Through biographical analysis of the mothering experience of Helene Deutsch, Karen Horney, Anna Freud, and Melanie Klein, Sayers attempts to trace the transformation of psychoanalysis from father and phallo-centered to mother-centered. Although having the biographies of these "mothers" in one volume is attractive, they are so limited in scope as to be less useful to the reader than fuller treatments found in available full-length biographies, i.e., Elisabeth Young-Breuhl's excellent biography, *Anna Freud* (1988). With the exception of the psychoanalytic writings of her subjects, Sayers uses very few primary sources. Further, she obliquely refers to conflicts and relationships among these women and between some of them and Sigmund Freud, but fails to clearly delineate the nature of these relationships and conflicts. Psychoanalytic jargon makes for difficult reading. Of limited appeal even to graduate students and faculty.—*K. S. Milar, Earlham College*

WS-2197   BF175   89-39688 CIP
Sprengnether, Madelon. **The spectral mother: Freud, feminism, and psychoanalysis.** Cornell, 1990. 264p bibl index afp ISBN 0-8014-2387-2, $24.95

Sprengnether has done a scholarly reassessment of the psychological and literary sources that attempt to theorize about the nature of women. There is an examination of object relations theory, Lacanian theory, and poststructuralism, along with concepts based on a philosophical and historical point of view. The issues are clearly focused and the author manages to elicit the flaws and ambiguities of Freud's theory related to the preoedipal mother. This is a valuable contribution to the ongoing debate of the influence of the patriarchal social order and its effect upon women. Sprengnether does an excellent job of bringing together Freud's ideas through the use of biographies, major case studies, and literary theory. There are sufficient documentations and citations to satisfy the serious scholar. A good supplement to this book is *Psychoanalysis and Women: Contemporary Reappraisals*, ed. by Judith L. Alpert (1986). These challenging ideas can add significantly to the current discussion by theorists and practitioners in a better understanding of psychology, feminism, and psychoanalytic thought.—*G. M. Greenberg, emerita, Western Michigan University*

◆ Social Psychology

WS-2198   CIP
Butler, Sandra. **Feminist groupwork,** by Sandra Butler and Claire Wintram. Sage, 1991. 200p bibl index ISBN 0-8039-8209-7, $55.00; ISBN 0-8039-8210-0 pbk, $19.95

Butler and Wintram are government social workers in the UK, one serving in an inner city, the other in a rural area. They describe what North Americans call group therapy, with diverse women some would call disadvantaged. The authors are attuned explicitly to socioeconomic-political dimensions of women's lives and to patterns of oppression in which women participate. Although the book appears to be grounded in deconstructionism and social constructionism, there is little jargon or militancy. Rather, the chapters form a helpfully detailed handbook on the logistics, language, techniques, and ups and downs of doing feminist group work. Numerous quotations from group members reflect their social class and education, their being caught in their own stereotypes and truncated vision, and their gradual liberation to new visions and hopes about themselves and the larger world. Transformation occurs through group interaction, conflict, solutions, sharings, and breakthroughs, not from indoctrination. Definitely a fresh con-

tribution to readers interested in women's studies, group dynamics, group "therapy," the politics of knowledge, and social change. Appropriate for undergraduates through faculty in social sciences and human service fields.—*C. T. Fischer, Duquesne University*

WS-2199   HD6054.3   89-20539 CIP
Freeman, Sue Joan Mendelson. **Managing lives: corporate women and social change.** Massachusetts, 1990. 262p index afp ISBN 0-87023-716-0, $35.00; ISBN 0-87023-717-9, $13.95

Freeman, a practicing psychologist and professor of education and child study at Smith College, uses a phenomenologic approach to study a sample of 40 women sent by their employers for management training. These are women who advanced largely on the basis of on-the-job training from clerical to management positions. An ethnographic research approach was used in constructing and conducting the interviews. Based on the premise that individual development affects and is affected by social change, the study challenges customary assumptions about women. Parts 1 and 2 examine personal and professional development and document revised thoughts and feelings as well as behavior and the synergism among them. The reports lend support for a more contextual view of personality formation as opposed to fixed personality traits. Part 3 traces the interaction between individual psychological development and social change within the context of work and the larger sociopolitical environments. Frustrating for its lack of any summary statistics. Extensive bibliography. A useful qualitative supplement to the study of women at work. University collections.—*K. C. Brannen, Creighton University*

WS-2200   HQ1206   90-8181 CIP
McCollum, Audrey T. **The trauma of moving: psychological issues for women.** Sage, 1990. 310p (Sage library of social research, 181) bibl indexes ISBN 0-8039-3699-0, $36.00; ISBN 0-8039-3700-8, $17.95

Using a core sample of 42 women interviewed in depth over a two-year period, supplemented with additional feedback from more than 100 women in network groups, McCollum explores women's subjective experience of moving. The setting for her study is "Northland," a rural northern New England community whose excellent small university, major medical center, and several high-tech industries attract many movers annually. McCollum, a psychotherapist and former newcomer to the area, has not attempted to generalize findings from her limited sample to the overall US population. Rather, her intent is "to bring into focus the psychological issues that confront women who move." The issues McCollum examines are the psychosocial obstacles to women making genuine and responsible choices about moving; loss; the meaning of "home" and its re-creation; the longing for intimacy and concomitant need to initiate friendships; renewal of inner conflicts; and conjugal relationships. The author discusses "the myth of the transportable homemaker," i.e., the assumption by many women that they can re-create and maintain "home" anywhere, and shows that many unrecognized factors determine how successfully this can be done. One of McCollum's most significant findings is that "the development of a realm of work—paid or not—commanding recognition outside the home" is critical to feelings of positive connection in the community. The book is well organized, well written, and the issues are clearly defined. Highly recommended for sociology and women's studies collection.—*H. M. MacLam, Choice*

WS-2201   HV6626   94-15637 CIP
No safe haven: male violence against women at home, at work, and in the community, ed. by Mary P. Koss et al. American Psychological Association, 1994. 344p bibl indexes ISBN 1-55798-237-6, $39.95; ISBN 1-55798-244-9 pbk, $24.95

Koss and her five collaborators offer comprehensive coverage of female victimization by men. Violence is broadly defined, thus psychological abuse and sexual harassment are included in addition to physical abuse and rape. The consistent focus on women as victims comes at the expense of full consideration of the interactive nature of some forms of violence in an intimate setting. Published by the American Psychological Association (APA) and written by leading and respected researchers in this area, the book is the most recent product of the APA Task Force on Male Violence Against Women. The book is well written, has an adequate index, and is well referenced, citing most of the work with a psychological focus on these issues. These references produce an extensive bibliography. Recommended for libraries serving graduate and upper-division undergraduate programs in psychology.—*R. T. Sigler, University of Alabama*

WS-2202   95-69789 Orig
Tseëlon, Efrat. **The masque of femininity: the presentation of woman in everyday life.** Sage Publications, CA, 1995. 152p bibl index ISBN 0-8039-8806-0, $65.00; ISBN 0-8039-8807-9 pbk, $19.95

In this readable though complex analysis of the social construction of femininity (with examples ranging from the 12th century through the present, and from an orientation subsuming symbolic interactionism, semiotics, and dialectical interpretation), Tseëlon draws on the writings of Freud, Aries, Elias, Goffman, Lacan, Baudrillard, and other scholars, always in nonpolemical tones even when taking a stance. She explicitly avoids an ideological position, in favor of acknowledging "uneven surfaces." The author is a social and cultural psychologist at Leeds Metropolitan University, UK, where her empirical research at times combines statistical techniques with qualitative analyses of questionnaires, interviews, and discussions with participants. These refreshing studies of "the presentation of woman in everyday life," particularly through dress, respect the multidimensionality, seeming contradictions, and dynamic paradoxes of how women participate in their cultures. Throughout, Tseëlon explores the fall-out from the dynamics of social constructions of feminine essence and standards for women's appearance. Upper-division undergraduate through faculty.—*C. T. Fischer, Duquesne University*

◆ Sociology

WS-2203   HQ1059   95-2151 CIP
Apter, Terri. **Secret paths: women in the new midlife.** W.W. Norton, 1995. 347p bibl ISBN 0-393-03766-5, $25.00

Apter explores the midyears of a generation of women who participated in a social revolution that changed women's roles. The middle phase of women's lives has been largely ignored, although for most of the women Apter studied, crisis at midlife was a normal developmental stage. A central question asked by the women in her sample is "Why did it take so long for me to trust myself?" Apter found that women in midlife have more power, relative to men, than they had in their youth, because they take charge and are self-assertive. Women at 40 are able to challenge the social construction of their identity. Unlike Germaine Greer and Gale Sheehy, Apter sees menopause as only one reference point for midlife women, rather than the center of midlife development. In her sample of 80 women between the ages of 39 and 55, she identified four types of women: *traditional*, i.e., those who stayed within the conventional feminine framework; *innovative*, those who set out to pioneer in a "man's world"; *expansive*, women who expanded their horizons beyond the conventional; and *protesters*, energetic women who lack direction. Friendship with other women also plays a significant role in their lives. General readers; upper-division undergraduates and above.—*C. Adamsky, University of New Hampshire*

WS-2204   HQ1190   95-16865 MARC
Assiter, Alison. **Enlightened women: modernist feminism in a postmodern age.** Routledge, 1996. 164p index ISBN 0-415-08338-9, $45.00; ISBN 0-415-08339-7 pbk, $14.95

Assiter's effort to put postmodernist theories to rest is laudable. Although this reviewer still sees much of value in postmodern theories, Assiter's cogent critiques of contradictions and weaknesses in the works of postmodern scholars (Lyotard, Derrida, Irigaray, and Foucault, among others) indicates the limits of such theories in emancipatory agendas such as feminism. This is a clear text, directed at an undergraduate audience. But the selection of this readership is a disservice to the complexity of the subjects of her book and to Assiter's own arguments. For example, postmodernism is portrayed as a flight from universals, yet the author avoids the question of characterizing postmodernity. The book is constrained by a poorly researched and poorly argued critique of constructivist approaches to sexuality, and is bereft of insights from feminist science studies on postposi-

tivist (but not antirealist) epistemologies. Some elements of postmodern and poststructuralist theories do not work well for feminists and others with emancipatory agendas, and Assiter does a good job articulating these. Nonetheless, corrections do not entail a retreat to Enlightenment universals, foundational epistemologies, and biological determinism.—*J. L. Croissant, University of Arizona*

WS-2205   HQ1233   91-29875 CIP
Bacon-Smith, Camille. **Enterprising women: television fandom and the creation of popular myth.** Pennsylvania, 1992. 338p bibl index afp ISBN 0-8122-3098-1, $39.95; ISBN 0-8122-1379-3 pbk, $17.95

A scholarly contribution to understanding the alternative popular culture produced by women fans of *Star Trek* and other science fiction television programs. Fans focus not on celebrity stars but on the characters they portray. Fandom refers to the fiction, art work, newsletters, conventions, and other works produced by fan writers using some characters from *Star Trek* and other programs. There are several genres of this fiction, which is shared *informally*, always on a nonprofit basis, among other interested members of the fan community, locally, nationally, and internationally. The sharing of fan fiction and other art constitutes a major basis for the social organization networks among fans. For half these fans, this constitutes a hobby; for others, it approaches their principal social community or worldview. Bacon-Smith's many years of skillful ethnographic research and lucid prose help nonfans understand the cultural and the theoretical significance of the fan-produced fiction, artwork, and social relations that make fandom so cohesive and critically essential to its members. Excellent bibliography, poor subject index. Both males and females in communications, sociology, ethnography, psychology and women's studies benefit from this fine book. All levels.—*S. H. Hildahl, Wells College*

WS-2206   HV6561   96-4426 CIP
Bergen, Raquel Kennedy. **Wife rape: understanding the response of survivors and service providers.** Sage Publications, CA, 1996. 179p (Sage series on violence against women, 2) bibl index afp ISBN 0-8039-7240-7, $42.00; ISBN 0-8039-7241-5 pbk, $18.95

Bergen reports the findings of her research, which includes a national survey of managers of organizations offering services to abused women, 37 of whom were interviewed intensively; interviews of 40 victims of spousal rape; and 18 months of participant observation at a battered woman's center. Chapters focus on the trauma of victimization, methods for victims to cope with this trauma, and provision of services to victims of spousal rape by existing agencies. Although this book lacks the depth of works such as David Finkelhor and Kersti Yllo's *License to Rape: Sexual Abuse of Wives* (1985) or Diana Russell's *Rape in Marriage* (CH, Jan'83), it supplies further documentation on the impact of domestic and sexual abuse, and on the delivery of services to victims of forced sexual intercourse in marriage within the population of abused women. About a third of the book is devoted to appendixes that identify resources and describe the instruments Bergen used to gather data. Upper-division undergraduates and above.—*R. T. Sigler, University of Alabama*

WS-2207   BF575   92-53240 CIP
Campbell, Anne. **Men, women, and aggression.** Basic Books, 1993. 196p index ISBN 0-465-09217-9, $22.00

Why are men more aggressive than women? That question posed by Campbell forms the central inquiry in this study. The author argues that gender differences lie in the social psychology of socialization and in how men and women form opinions about their own aggression. Data used by Campbell to answer this question include many interviews with men and women, gang members, juveniles and adults awaiting trial, and a review of the research literature. In a unique manner, Campbell analyzes both aggression and gender differences. Although the book has many strong points, one overarching strength is the impressive range of literature covered by Campbell and her ability to maintain a tight focus on the assumptions and conclusions regarding her thesis. The reader may gain much from Campbell's argument and from the supporting evidence that women believe their aggression results from a *loss* of self-control, while men see their behavior as *gaining* control over others. Highly recommended for gaining insight into the relationship between gender differences and aggression. Undergraduate; graduate; faculty.—*P. J. Venturelli, Valparaiso University*

WS-2208 HQ1064 92-8679 CIP

Chatman, Elfreda A. **The information world of retired women.** Greenwood, 1992. 150p (New directions in information management, 29) index afp ISBN 0-313-25492-3, $39.95

Chatman's book presents an in-depth study of the informational and social worlds of older women in a southeastern retirement community. In particular, Chatman is interested in the contextual setting in which these women seek out and receive information. Social network theory provided the conceptual framework for investigating this process and ethnography the method for data collection. Between 1987 and 1989, Chatman conducted open-ended interviews with 55 women; all but one respondent (Latino) were white and the modal age was 82. Chatman skillfully narrates significant elements in the lives of her respondents, in particular their loneliness and their shared view of death as a liberating force. There is little, if any, networking among these women and no close friendships, a finding in contrast to that of other works written about older women. Perhaps this is partly explained by the advanced age of the women. If this is the case, Chatman has touched on an important area that needs to be explored further. Although it was explicitly stated that network theory would provide the theoretical framework for this analysis, there is little reference to that theory past its initial discussion in one of the early chapters. Chatman could have strengthened her study by directly applying the theory throughout the presentation. In spite of this drawback, the book is worth recommending to those interested in aging and older women. Undergraduate; graduate.—*E. Bastida, University of Texas—Pan American*

WS-2209 KF535 94-1335 CIP

Chused, Richard H. **Private acts in public places: a social history of divorce in the formative era of American family law.** Pennsylvania, 1994. 234p bibl index afp ISBN 0-8122-3202-X, $32.95

Chused has made it his task to gather together a range of literature that would otherwise be more difficult to survey. Tracing the historical transitions among private, legislative, and judicial release from matrimonial bonds and focusing particularly on Maryland, Chused also defines the changing contours of child custody and divorce grounds. It seems to have been difficult for him to squeeze generally useful conclusions from the historically specific material. The book is a resource richer in its footnotes and appendixes than in its minimally adequate bibliography. Though not difficult to read, it is more likely to be of interest to scholars and researchers. However, it is accessible to all interested readers from undergraduates on up.—*A. P. Bober, Southern Connecticut State University*

WS-2210 HQ1064 90-26598 CIP

Day, Alice T. **Remarkable survivors: insights into successful aging among women.** Urban Institute, 1991. 314p afp ISBN 0-87766-492-7, $42.75; ISBN 0-87766-491-9 pbk, $24.50

Day's book is a thoughtful analysis of markers of successful aging among women. The author, trained at Smith and Columbia, uses data from 589 older American women surveyed in 1978 and 1987 to examine how opportunities for independent activity and intimate social interactions affect aging. The study opens with brief vignettes contrasting two models of successful aging, discusses theoretical modeling, and describes data collection, study design, and sample characteristics. In the following two chapters, Day traces common patterns in life transitions among diverse women (i.e., living arrangements, social support, functional capacity) to uncover similarities related to successful aging, examining the relationships the women developed to maintain support. Day also analyzes three pivotal variables (perceived well being, capacity for independent activity, and private safety net) associated with successful aging. Remaining chapters discuss markers of successful versus oppressive aging, late-life adaptation to new roles, and guidelines for action. Developing conceptual models from empirical data, an extremely difficult task, is accomplished convincingly in this book. An excellent addition to the literature that complements *Women As They Age: Challenge, Opportunity, and Triumph*, ed. by J. Deanne Garner and Susan O. Mercer (1989).—*L. A. Baumhover, University of Alabama*

WS-2211 HQ1206 95-13906 CIP

Dean, Jodi. **Solidarity of strangers: feminism after identity politics.** California, 1996. 219p index afp ISBN 0-520-20230-9, $40.00; ISBN 0-520-20231-7 pbk, $16.00

In attempting to move beyond the rigidities of identity politics, Dean proposes a way to conceive of "we" without labels, a way that enables people to think about differences in a new light, overcoming the competing duality's of us/them, male/female, white/black, straight/gay, public/private, general/particular. Rather than solidarity built on a we/they model, the author proposes one based on the respect of differences. Reflective solidarity is defined as the mutual expectation of a responsible orientation to relationship. In the first chapter, Dean argues that reflective solidarity provides spaces for differences because it upholds the possibility of a universal, communicative "we." She then shows how the debate over identity politics leads to reflective solidarity and proposes a model of civil society based on multiple, interconnecting, discursive spheres. Dean looks at the institutionalization of reflective solidarity, focusing on the role of law in transmitting solidarity. The final chapter discusses the opposition between difference and universality. Basically, Dean argues that reflective solidarity refers to the need to respect and take responsibility for others. Graduate; faculty.—*C. Adamsky, University of New Hampshire*

WS-2212 BR560 91-39181 CIP

Demerath, N.J. **A bridging of faiths: religion and politics in a New England city,** by N.J. Demerath and Rhys H. Williams. Princeton, 1992. 358p bibl index afp ISBN 0-691-07413-5, $29.95

Using a wide range of methods, Demerath and Williams analyze the changing social organization of Springfield, Massachusetts over a 300-year period. Their particular focus is on the decline in prominence and power of the Congregational Church and the rise of the Catholic Church after WW II as the major religious force in Springfield. The core of the book is an examination of the influence of religious institutions on the political process and the civic culture of Springfield. Although most citizens subscribe to the doctrine of separation of church and state, Demerath and Williams demonstrate that a much closer relationship exists than the formal governmental structure suggests. Perhaps more important, they reveal that Springfield residents consider this relationship appropriate. The authors use three case studies to examine in detail the dynamics of the relationship between church and state. Demerath and Williams are obviously familiar with the Springfield community study and other relevant literature, but they are sparing with footnotes and references, which contributes to the enjoyment of reading their book. This work belongs in the grand tradition of community studies and should be included in any collection on contemporary urban social organization. General, undergraduate; graduate; faculty.—*J. R. Hudson, Pennsylvania State University, Harrisburg*

WS-2213 HV9475 95-16255 CIP

Díaz-Cotto, Juanita. **Gender, ethnicity, and the state: Latina and Latino prison politics.** State University of New York, 1996. 480p index afp ISBN 0-7914-2815-X, $74.50

Díaz-Cotto argues that minority and female prisoners are treated more harshly in US prisons than are white males. She attempts to document this in a detailed history of the recent experiences of Spanish-speaking prisoners in New York State prisons. This is a history of prison overcrowding, riots, punitive responses, litigation, and occasional reforms. Díaz-Cotto concludes that in the complex and convoluted Attica prison riot, Latinos played a significant role—some as rioting prisoners, others as outside negotiators. At the Green Haven Correctional Facility there were post-Attica prison reforms, e.g., the hiring of female and minority guards, which were resisted by white male guard staff, who continued subtle discrimination against minority prisoners, and especially against Latinos. Emerging from this were various underground prisoner groups and coalitions that were seen by authorities as making prison administration difficult. All of this is told in 13 chapters, each supplemented by extensive footnotes containing a large number of references. For those who are close newspaper readers, little of this is new; however, brought together in book form this information may be useful to some criminologists and to those interested in ethnic relations. Upper-division undergraduates and above.—*D. Harper, University of Rochester*

WS-2214 BX4220 92-8035 CIP

Ebaugh, Helen Rose Fuchs. **Women in the vanishing cloister: organizational decline in Catholic religious orders in the United States.** Rutgers, 1993. 191p bibl indexes ISBN 0-8135-1865-2, $35.00, ISBN 0-8135-1866-0 pbk, $15.00

The demise of the long-standing institution of Catholic convents in the US is the topic of this book. Ebaugh focuses on religious orders of women within the US and provides an in-depth case study of one order. The author hopes to contribute to the growing literature on organizational decline and draws a parallel between the growth and decline of religious orders and that of American business organizations. Ebaugh argues that the process of decline in religious orders does not follow the model of decline described in the literature. She cites several contributing factors, e.g., change in the structure and mission of religious orders (though not their relationship to the larger church), and the environment produced by the Second Vatican Council, which resulted in an organizational form that rejected the model of cloister and substituted identification of members with the outside world. Ebaugh develops a process model of exogamous factors that have led to the decline of these religious orders of women. Advanced undergraduate; graduate; faculty.—*M. Klatte, Eastern Kentucky University*

WS-2215   HQ759   95-7692 MARC
Eyer, Diane. **Motherguilt: how our culture blames mothers for what's wrong with society.** Times Books/Random House, 1996. 317p index ISBN 0-8129-2416-9, $25.00

Eyer strongly criticizes the "ideology of motherhood" that has developed since the Industrial Revolution of the 1840s. The concepts of "maternal instinct" and "maternal bonding" are seen as invented by "experts" and "scientists" influenced by their "unexamined assumptions about what makes a Good Mother." Eyer accuses US policy makers of "racist and sexist scapegoating." Giving a historical overview and citing numerous sources, the author substantiates her premise that blaming mothers for society's problems is unfounded and diversionary. She stresses that "the real crime" in America lies in the damage being done to children in today's "unregulated, unsubsidized patchwork of care" and proposes alternate models of child care found in other countries. The author concludes that "motherblame" can be stopped in the following ways: by a recognition that mothers are not the primary cause of the problems of American children; a retraining of experts and scientists; an emergence of "New Fathers" who share with mothers the responsibility of nurturing and providing for their children; a genuine family-friendly workplace; and family governmental supports, particularly "a first-rate subsidized, regulated, child care system." Eyer's broad generalizations of identified groups as responsible for "mother guilt" may be questioned, but she does offer a fascinating presentation of the current phenomenon of "motherblame." She also identifies possible solutions to improve the plight of children. Highly recommended for students, policy makers, and human service providers.—*M. O. McMahon, East Carolina University*

WS-2216   HQ77   95-33421 CIP
Feinberg, Leslie. **Transgender warriors: making history from Joan of Arc to Rupaul.** Beacon Press, 1996. 212p bibl index ISBN 0-8070-7940-5, $27.50

"Transgender" describes a person of either sex, defined by anatomy, who has "transed the gender barrier" to play the role opposite that suggested by anatomy. Such terminology takes a bit of getting used to, but this book quickly becomes engrossing. A cross-cultural and historical overview of sex and gender, copiously illustrated and referenced, and peppered with personal insights, it argues that "male" and "female" are points on a continuum rather than poles, resulting in multiple possibilities for sexual orientations and gender roles. Feinberg (an anatomical female living as a male) is hardly objective, and some of the historical and anthropological "facts" presented are at best speculative, but the book's main points are well taken. Feinberg shows that transgender people were honored in some early societies, but that more often, they have been ostracized as antisocial or comic. The author asserts that their oppression is historically and culturally linked with other forms of discrimination based on race, class, and religion; that they have played important roles in social movements throughout history; and that the contemporary movement for "trans liberation" is deeply indebted to the recent women's and gay liberation movements. This is a consistently absorbing, clearly written, and cogently argued book. All levels.—*M. A. Gwynne, SUNY at Stony Brook*

WS-2217   HD9993   93-1993 CIP
Formanek-Brunell, Miriam. **Made to play house: dolls and the commercialization of American girlhood, 1830-1930.** Yale, 1994 (c1993). 233p index afp ISBN 0-300-05072-0, $25.00

For anyone who has wondered about the origin of the "Barbie" doll as a gender representation of women, this book provides the beginning of the answer. Formanek-Brunell persuasively argues that the history of dolls in America (their creation, marketing, and use) documents the struggle of women and girls to gain cultural control of representations of their gender identity. For instance, female and male dollmakers prized highly different characteristics in the products they designed and made. Women emphasized soft and pliable dolls that felt real to their owners, while men were interested in technologically advanced (and often hard and heavy) dolls that could walk and talk. Not surprisingly, the dolls inspired different types of play on the part of their owners, too. The supple dolls got cuddled like real babies, while the active dolls sometimes frightened their owners and provided them with an example of a gender role that stressed conformity rather than creativity. Formanek-Brunell uses an impressive array of sources, from collector's encyclopedias to current works on gender and progressivism, and even the dolls themselves. The downside is that she tries to cover too much in too few pages. General readers; advanced undergraduates and above.—*J. M. Lewis, University of Arkansas at Little Rock*

WS-2218   HQ1154   92-43433 CIP
Frankenberg, Ruth. **White women, race matters: the social construction of whiteness.** Minnesota, 1993. 289p bibl index afp ISBN 0-8166-2257-4, $44.95

How does race affect white women's lives? This crucial question focuses readers' attention on how people perceive, think about, and act on presumed racial differences. Frankenberg examines how whiteness, gender, and social class converge, through interviews with 30 white women. She looks at segregated communities, worldviews, and intimate associations. Unfortunately, most of the women have great difficulty articulating "whiteness" because it is normative and thus invisible. The author presents three stages of racial "discourse": "essential racism," or biological inferiority; "color and power evasiveness"; and "race cognizance," or pluralism. Frankenberg is on target observing how society is still responding to essential racism; she also has a keen ear in hearing the women's many contradictions. Nevertheless, the book fails for three reasons: lack of clarity regarding whiteness; academic prose; and the failure to clearly link the material rewards of racism with cultural ideas. Efforts such as the video series "Eyes on the Prize" are more effective in conveying the latter. Not recommended.—*S. D. Borchert, Lake Erie College*

WS-2219   HV8978   95-49171 CIP
Freedman, Estelle B. **Maternal justice: Miriam Van Waters and the female reform tradition.** Chicago, 1996. 458p index afp ISBN 0-226-26149-2, $34.95

Well known in reform circles of her day, Miriam Van Waters (1887-1974) did not lead a national movement, but instead exercised her considerable gifts as superintendent of the Massachusetts Reformatory for Women at Framingham. By all accounts a charismatic personality, she was most successful working with individual inmates. Freedman's biography is a salutary caution against easy periodization and categorization in 20th-century American women's history. In the 1940s, Van Waters was still drawing from the roots of the social gospel that flourished in the early years of this century. Amid the post-WW II stress on motherhood, she was motivated by the maternalist attitudes from her youth, which, ironically, were by the '40s a liability. When threatened by Cold War politics Van Waters was able to call successfully on the support of middle-class women's voluntary organizations with no special reputation for courage. She gained much personal solace from an enduring, intense relationship with heiress-reformer Geraldine Thompson, yet did not consider herself lesbian. Blessed by extraordinarily rich sources, Freedman has written an admirable biography, one that does not claim more than deserved for her subject. Upper-division undergraduates and above.—*A. Graebner, College of St. Catherine*

WS-2220   HQ1154   92-705 CIP
French, Marilyn. **The war against women.** Summit Books, 1992. 223p ISBN 0-671-66157-4, $20.00

In this accessible book French makes the case for her assertion that there is a global systematic offensive by men against women, motivated by greed and laziness, and by lust that is willfully ungoverned, but motivated most persistently and deeply by hatred and a raging need to control. In chapters on economic exploitation, on religious dogma and practice, on science and professions, ideological control, and on one-on-one male violence against women, French assembles information that many feminists will find familiar but that a wider audience badly needs to hear. She documents this grim picture persuasively, drawing on feminist sources and on the mainstream media. French's style is more journalistic than academic, but there are passages (e.g., on "fundamentalism") that dig into deeper analysis. Her treatments of Africa and the Middle East have a certain exoticism about them, and although vectors of race and class are present, their handling is not particularly sophisticated. Even so, the book will be useful to a broad readership. Undergraduate; general.—*M. Frye, Michigan State University*

WS-2221   HM22   93-27763 CIP
Gender and the academic experience: Berkeley women sociologists, ed. by Kathryn P. Meadow Orlans and Ruth A. Wallace. Nebraska, 1994. 266p index afp ISBN 0-8032-3558-5, $35.00; ISBN 0-8032-8606-6 pbk, $14.95

Orlans and Wallace collected memoirs from 16 women graduates of the Berkeley Sociology Department from 1952-1972, when the program was ranked first in the nation. Contributors include sociologists such as Dorothy Smith, Arlie Russell Hochschild, Jacqueline Wisemann, and Arlene Kaplan Daniels. They illustrate the convoluted paths to sociological experience, including nonacademic careers, from various backgrounds and through diverse family lives and social movements, emphasizing luck, unexpected turns of events, and the support of mentors. The editors supply a brief introduction and epilogue, but even with this the memoirs stand decontextualized and "unsociological." This reader was left wondering about the three-quarters of entering women (and two-thirds of the men) who did not complete their doctorates. The "gentle, positive, and nostalgic" character of the contributions indicates that this is an insider's text—a non-Berkeley sociologist reads it as a voyeur. Nonetheless, the book is recommended because of who made it and how. Readers are richer for having shared this journey and for the work these occasionally reluctant pioneers have done in refiguring sociology. Upper-division undergraduates and above.—*J. L. Croissant, Rensselaer Polytechnic Institute*

WS-2222   HQ800   93-36034 CIP
Gordon, Tuula. **Single women: on the margins?** New York University, 1994. 224p bibl index ISBN 0-8147-3063-9, $40.00; ISBN 0-8147-3064-7 pbk, $14.95

Unmarried women have traditionally been marginalized by a family-oriented society. In an attempt to understand the lives of these women and to answer the question of whether they are still marginalized, Gordon interviewed women in London, San Francisco, and Helsinki. The book begins with a rather superficial historical analysis, but the interviews yield much useful information. Work is central to the lives of unmarried women; they work as hard as men, but they get paid less. Most value their independence and freedom, but recognize that this can mean loneliness and a difficult social life. Although the image of the "old maid" is diminishing, traditional views of sexuality are still prevalent: one is considered deviant if one is sexually active, but also if one is celibate. Gordon concludes that even though single women are still somewhat marginalized, they are successfully constructing their lives. She acknowledges that not all women are alike and is sensitive to differences of race, class, and sexual orientation. Nevertheless most of those interviewed were comparatively higher paid professionals; not enough attention was given to poorer women, especially those with children, or to rural women. All levels.—*J. Wishnia, SUNY at Stony Brook*

WS-2223   E185   95-34416 CIP
Hemmons, Willa Mae. **Black women in the new world order: social justice and the African American female.** Praeger, 1996. 289p bibl index afp ISBN 0-275-95208-8, $59.95

Hemmons offers a detailed, macro and micro examination of the mutually reciprocal functions and interdependent relationships of social institutions (politics, economy, education, social services, family, health, and criminal justice) detrimental to black women in the US under the "New World Order." She provides a view of the multidimensional disadvantage, through institutionalized racism and sexism, that black women disproportionately face. The macro-level data is

very insightful, especially when presented with comparative data for black men and white women and men. Other strengths include discussion of the often unacknowledged advantages that the privileged receive ("legacies" in colleges and universities, Social Security income, "standardized" tests for educational placement) and the extensive use of court cases to illustrate how the status quo is maintained. Limitations of Hemmons's work include poorly integrated case-study examples and failure to develop implications of the "New World Order." This book is disheartening because, Hemmons notes, as "minorities" become more numerous in society and as the economy continues to be based on service occupations (i.e., low-pay, low-skill, part-time work with few benefits), the institutionalized suppression of black women will intensify. Upper-division undergraduates and above.—*G. Rundblad, Illinois Wesleyan University*

WS-2224   Aust. CIP
Horsfall, Jan. **The presence of the past: male violence in the family.** Allen & Unwin, 1991. 167p bibl index ISBN 0-04-442326-8 pbk, $19.95

Horsfall, a part-time community health center counselor and a senior lecturer in community health, posits that "patriarchal power" promotes and encourages male violence toward women and children. According to Horsfall, four issues are "patently missing" from the literature —the male perpetrator; males taking responsibility for being violent; dysfunctional fathers; and the use and intergenerational transfer of patriarchal power—and it is not accidental. The concept of conspiratorial use of patriarchal power informs her discussion of the above issues. Women researchers such as Suzanne Steinmetz and others are accused by Horsfall of contributing to male-dominated research. Richard Gelles and Murray Strauss's research is rejected as "superficial, bloodless, distant and perpetrator-less." However, Horsfall uses their data when she wants to present empirical evidence to support her issues. This brief book is a disappointment. It fails to explore adequately the scope of the issues, diminishing the credibility of the work. It contains first person, emotional, sexist language. Except to express an opinion from a feminist perspective, this work makes little contribution to the body of theory or empirical research already present in family sociology, or to the discipline of social work.—*R.C. Myers, Central Washington University*

WS-2225   LC2607   96-127672 Orig
Jejeebhoy, Shireen J. **Women's education, autonomy, and reproductive behaviour: experience from developing countries.** Oxford, 1996 (c1995). 306p bibl index afp ISBN 0-19-829033-0, $65.00

Jejeebhoy's study is a long awaited follow-up to S.J. Cochrane's *Fertility and Education: What Do We Really Know?* (CH, Jan'80). Using findings from world fertility surveys, demographic and health surveys, and anthropological studies, Jejeebhoy evaluates the link between women's formal education, autonomy (knowledge source, decision making, emotional, economic/social, and self-reliance), and fertility behaviors (age at marriage, parity, timing, breast-feeding, contraception, postpartum abstinence, child and maternal mortality). The well-documented inverse relationship between education and fertility, long presumed to be relatively simple, proves to be more complex. The influence of women's education operates differentially on fertility, depending on the stage of development and magnitude of the gender gap. Jejeebhoy assesses the various complex pathways by which education affects fertility-inhibiting and stimulating behaviors, and discusses policy implications of various critical pathways. Well researched, well documented, and well written, this monograph is a must for students of demography, family, gender inequality, and development. Contains detailed chapter endnotes, useful glossary, detailed appendixes, subject/author index. Bibliography is extensive and current. Upper-division undergraduates and above.—*D.W. Hastings, University of Tennessee, Knoxville*

WS-2226   KF4758   89-28509 CIP
Kaminer, Wendy. **A fearful freedom: women's flight from equality.** Addison-Wesley, 1990. 250p index ISBN 0-201-09234-4, $18.95

Kaminer's work is a far-reaching essay on the contradictions in present American feminism and the public's confused, largely disparaging attitude toward it. Her title is misleading; the book actually concerns women who fought for equality, rather than fled from it in fear. Kaminer makes good use of her background as a lawyer. She employs historical and legal materials to demonstrate that women need justice that the courts frequently deny. Her book brims with expressions that crystallize her argument, e.g., "feminists ought not to be blamed for the failures of the system they're attacking." The 13 central chapters deal with theories of rights; constitutional standards of equality; a history of protectionism; a history of protective labor laws, equality and the sexual revolution; equality in the workplace; equality in education; federal resistance to expanding civil rights; pregnancy, child care, and the workplace; equality in divorce, child custody, and surrogacy; equality and reproductive choice; and equality in criminal justice. Her insight on each topic warrants an entire monograph. Kaminer successfully integrates contemporary and historical materials but is less successful in integrating material among the chapters. There are 20 pages of endnotes and an 11-page author-subject index. College, university, and public libraries.—*S. Reinharz, Brandeis University*

WS-2227 H35 90-28754 CIP
Krieger, Susan. **Social science and the self: personal essays on an art form.** Rutgers, 1991. 273p bibl ISBN 0-8135-1714-1, $37.00; ISBN 0-8135-1715-X pbk, $14.95

Krieger's unusual book consists of many parts: autobiography, analysis of the writings of Georgia O'Keeffe, discussion of the art of Pueblo potters, epistemological discussion, interview narratives from other social scientists, and a previously published article by the author. This experimental form is one expression of Krieger's attempt to find a voice for the individual self of the social scientist in his/her writings. The author poses the eternal question—how can we know?—and abides by the eternal dicta—"to thine own self be true," and "know thyself." Particularly important are Krieger's preinterview notes, the community responses, and her own subjective experience of interviewing. All of Krieger's heartfelt reevaluations of her teaching, writing, and research make this book a carefully written, sobering, and courageous undertaking. Illustrations of an O'Keeffe painting and Pueblo pots might have enhanced the book. Notes. Upper-division undergraduates and above.—*S. Reinharz, Brandeis University*

WS-2228 CS2389 89-43654 CIP
Kupper, Susan J. **Surnames for women: a decision-making guide.** McFarland, 1990. 147p bibl index afp ISBN 0-89950-496-5, $19.95

Kupper had women who had married but used surnames other than those of their husbands fill out questionnaires asking about their experiences with using nontraditional surnames. This select sample was composed of 362 women (and 70 husbands) and was mostly urban/suburban and well educated. Chapters are devoted to various aspects of the surname choice. These include identity, family ties, feminism, pragmatism, feelings, opinions of others, and the law with regard to women and to children. Drawing from the responses, Kupper presents illustrative quotes from and interpretations of the reactions of women who have had difficulties and successes in using the surname they wish. Among the verbatim comments, some are serious; some, amusing. One of the amusing ones points out that when the husband and wife have separate surnames, they are likely to get two batches of junk mail! The chapters on law will be especially useful for women contemplating keeping their birth names or planning to change their surnames or those of their children. Strongly recommended for the women's issues and social sciences areas. All levels.—*E. D. Lawson, SUNY College at Fredonia*

WS-2229 British CIP
Laws, Sophie. **Issues of blood: the politics of menstruation.** Macmillan, 1990. (Dist. by New York University) 244p bibl index ISBN 0-333-48233-6, $35.00

Laws asks the pointed questions about the social construction of menstruation in middle-class British culture. Centered on reports and conversations of men, *ssues of Blood* is a lively text discussing the politics of sexual access as well as perspectives of the medical profession in describing this biological process. Laws argues that women's experiences are defined by male culture, that the "etiquette" of menstruation constrains women, and that most analyses have romanticized interpretations of non-Western cultural constructions of menstruation. These are somewhat tenuous claims, in part because Laws has taken the bold but inopportune step of rebelling against the feminist norm of including women's voices. Although insightful, especially in its critique of gynecological interpretations of premenstrual tension and pain, Laws's book does not meet the standards set by Emily Martin's *The Woman in the Body* (1987) for sophistication or for

methodology in analyzing cultural representations of reproduction. Recommended as a resource for programs in women's studies, anthropology, or sociology.—*J. L. Croissant, Rensselaer Polytechnic Institution*

WS-2230 HQ1075 93-14927 CIP
Lopata, Helena Znaniecka. **Circles and settings: role changes of American women.** State University of New York, 1994. 325p bibl index afp ISBN 0-7914-1767-0, $54.50

Lopata's book is a very readable, densely packed discussion of women's roles in the US. Using a "symbolic interactionist form of social role theory," Lopata outlines the roles women fulfill in society and how these are influenced and changed—from "traditional" times, through "transitional" periods, to the "modern" era—not only by larger ideological, social, and cultural factors, but also by more micro-interactions between people in women's social circles and the women themselves. Lopata provides a systematic survey of the complex influences on women's roles and how these factors affect the way women play out roles. Although the book tends to be much more heavily weighted toward women's domestic and familial roles, occupational roles and other extrafamilial roles (i.e., student, friend, neighbor, and community member) also receive insightful, though sparse, attention. Lopata does provide a systematic survey of past research on social roles, but the book would be enhanced if she had given respondents from her more recent research a more explicit voice to illustrate the theoretical issues on which she is focusing. Extensive bibliography, but the index lacks detail. Upper-division undergraduates and above.—*G. Rundblad, Illinois Wesleyan University*

WS-2231 HQ1058 95-35750 CIP
Lopata, Helena Znaniecka. **Current widowhood: myths & realities.** Sage Publications, CA, 1996. 251p bibl index afp ISBN 0-8039-7395-0, $44.00; ISBN 0-8039-7396-9 pbk, $21.95

In this book Lopata assembles research on widowhood in America and adds the theoretical framework of symbolic interactionism and concepts such as "support systems" to cross-cultural and historical perspectives. Her purpose is to extract realities of widowhood from the myths surrounding it, and to counter, where appropriate, the limiting view of widows found in contemporary society. Lopata concludes that American society lacks a distinctive, lasting role of "widow." She analyzes the processes by which wives become widows, problems in transition (e.g., change in kin roles, especially that of mother), and the effect of being widowed on friendships. She explores the complex networks in which these changes must be viewed and the cultural expectations associated with them, and also examines regional, class, racial, and ethnic variations. A major theme in Lopata's study is the relationship of modernization to the roles of widowhood. Perhaps the hardest *reality* reported is that older widows are devalued in American society, stigmatized by the view of the elderly as unproductive and of women as dependent, despite programs, both financial and social, available for widows. This book should be read by all those coping with widowhood; those studying gender, aging, or social roles; and those providing services to widows. All levels.—*M. M. Denny, St. Joseph College*

WS-2232 HQ1181 94-23288 CIP
Luebke, Barbara F. **Women's studies graduates: the first generation,** by Barbara F. Luebke and Mary Ellen Reilly. Teachers College Press (Columbia University), 1995. 207p bibl afp ISBN 0-8077-6275-X, $46.00; ISBN 0-8077-6274-1 pbk, $22.95

Women's studies developed as an interdisciplinary field in the mid-1970s and is now offered at hundreds of colleges and universities throughout the US. Many individuals have majored in women's studies, yet very little is known about their postgraduation careers. Luebke and Reilly (Univ. of Rhode Island) studied the attitudes and experience of 89 such graduates, chosen by program directors. Their research represents the first of its kind and dispels some hostile myths. The authors provide two chapters on their methods and an overview of their findings. Subsequent chapters offer long descriptions by graduates of their careers, divided into categories: "Potpourri"; health, social, and human services; education and library services; and law and government. The book concludes with "advice from the experienced" and "what we [the researchers] learned from the first generation." Readers positively inclined toward women's studies are likely to be moved by the graduates' impassioned statements; skeptics probably will not be convinced because the study has an advocacy perspective. The researchers urge current students to overcome their hesitations and declare women's studies as their major. There is a one-page list of resources to aid involvement with women's studies. This book just begins to fill the information void about women studies graduates—many more studies are needed, particularly given the current hostile political environment. Undergraduate and above.—*S. Reinharz, Brandeis University*

WS-2233   HQ798   90-12655 CIP
McRobbie, Angela. **Feminism and youth culture: from 'Jackie' to 'Just seventeen.'** Unwin Hyman, 1991. (Dist. by HarperCollins) 255p index ISBN 0-04-445910-6, $49.95; ISBN 0-04-445911-4 pbk, $16.95

In this lively and instructive collection of essays, McRobbie explores the lived experience of teenage, largely working-class girls in Birmingham and London. Earlier work in the sociology of youth has focused almost exclusively on boys, or used a structuralist approach that tended to obliterate the subjects under study. McRobbie seeks in this book to redirect the sociological enterprise back to real subjects, to correct the deficiencies of youth studies by bringing girls into the picture in a central rather than marginal way, and "to see how teenage girls interpreted some of the structural determinations of age, class, and gender in the context of their own lived experience." Her investigations of popular culture take her from an ethnographic study of teenage girls' perceptions of school, home, and family, to cultural analyses of the popular girls' magazines *Jackie* and *Just Seventeen.* McRobbie concludes that *Jackie*'s message of the 1970s—that girls must find and hold onto a boy as a measure of their success and economic survival—has, in the 1980s of *Just Seventeen,* given way to one that projects a more self-confident, more independent, more exciting female subject. An important, rewarding book. College and university libraries.—*S. K. Kent, University of Florida*

WS-2234   Can. CIP
Mies, Maria. **Ecofeminism,** by Maria Mies and Vandana Shiva. Fernwood Publications/Zed Books, 1993. (Dist. by Humanities) 328p index ISBN 1-85649-155-2, $55.00; ISBN 1-85649-156-0 pbk, $19.95

Mies and Shiva, internationally respected feminist activists and writers, have put together a book that forcefully demonstrates the ways in which ecological destruction disproportionately affects women, and particularly women in the developing world. This is not mere coincidence, they argue; the oppression of women and the degradation of nature spring from the same ideological roots. Although this is hardly a new argument, the book's value lies in its application to questions of international development, which both authors contend is merely a furtherance of the colonial projects of an earlier age. What is really needed, they claim, is a return to local self-governance with an emphasis on subsistence production, both in the developing South and the industrialized North. For Mies and Shiva, consumer liberation movements, women's cooperatives, and grassroots activism all offer models for an ecologically sustainable and women-friendly future. Readers looking for an introduction to principles of ecofeminism, or for sustained philosophical analyses will not find them here, but the book would still be a good addition to environmental studies and ecofeminist collections. General readers; undergraduates.—*L. Vance, Vermont College*

WS-2235   KF478   94-47019 CIP
Mothers in law: feminist theory and the legal regulation of motherhood, ed. by Martha Albertson Fineman and Isabel Karpin. Columbia, 1995. 398p bibl afp ISBN 0-231-09680-1, $65.00; ISBN 0-231-09681-X pbk, $16.50

This collection of essays is drawn from papers presented at two conferences on motherhood, feminism, and legal theory. The range of the essays, however, is broader and more appealing than the provenence or the title might suggest. Topics covered include pictures of mothers in novels and autobiographies, the social construction of "Ideal Mother" and "Ideal Breadwinner," and political discourse about "welfare mothers," as well as specific analysis of laws affecting mothers in the Canadian First Nations, black pregnant teens, and lesbian mothers. Powerful articles discuss provision of legal representation to mothers charged with child abuse and the tensions between dependence and independence for mothers as workers, caregivers, and care recipients in old age. Although the collection has its weaknesses (e.g., its entire section on regulating mothers focuses on racism and black mothers), its strengths far outweigh them. This excellent contribution to women's studies literature on mothering intentionally defines moth-

ering as more than just a burden on women seeking emancipation or a feminine essence that women seek to express; it sees struggle and practical difficulty interwoven with social ideology and legal practices. Strongly recommended. All levels.—*M. M. Ferree, University of Connecticut*

WS-2236   HQ1206   91-12245 CIP
Mulqueen, Maggie. **On our own terms: redefining competence and femininity.** State University of New York, 1992. 221p bibl index ISBN 0-7914-0951-1, $44.50; ISBN 0-7914-0952-X pbk, $14.95

Mulqueen proposes a theory of "balancing," in which women are enabled to make more or better life choices through a process of redefining competence and femininity. Competence, a "male" value, is seen as incompatible with "femininity," creating conflict for women who value both. This dilemma is addressed by redefining competence as a gender-free trait and femininity as the recognition that what is female is feminine. By resolving the dilemma between achievement and femininity (balancing), a positive sex-role image and sense of competence may be achieved. Although acknowledging that socialization and enculturation can never be fully eliminated, Mulqueen argues that the capacity to question norms enables a woman to construct her life with greater self-determination. Analyses of case studies of competent women illustrate the processes of generalizing, diversifying, and integrating involved in balancing. The author has provided a cogent critique of the effects of traditional cultural and psychological concepts on women's self-esteem. General, advanced undergraduate; graduate; community college; professional.—*C. Adamsky, University of New Hampshire*

WS-2238   HQ1420   93-26987 CIP
Not June Cleaver: women and gender in postwar America, 1945-1960, ed. by Joanne Meyerowitz. Temple University, 1994. 411p afp ISBN 1-56639-170-9, $49.95; ISBN 1-56639-171-7 pbk, $19.95

This volume is part of an ongoing revisionist endeavor to dispel the myth of women in the 1950s that conjures images of the quintessential white, middle-class housewife who stayed at home to rear children, clean house, and bake cookies. Each of the 15 essays explores a different piece of postwar US women's history. Several essays focus on women in the labor force and in activist organizations. Others examine cultural constructions of gender and subcultural challenges to them. The writers point first to the diversity among women and the multifarious activities in which they engaged. It is demonstrated that women's sense of themselves included not only gender identity, but also their interrelated class, racial, ethnic, sexual, religious, occupational, and political identities. The contributors also suggest that postwar public discourse on women was more complex than often portrayed. They address the postwar domestic stereotype and its meanings, how and where it was produced, and the manifold ways that women appropriated, transformed, and challenged it. They investigate the competing voices within the public discourse on women and the internal contradictions that undermined and destabilized the domestic stereotype even as it was constructed. Upper-division undergraduates and up.—*M. Klatte, Eastern Kentucky University*

WS-2239   HQ1206   92-13770 CIP
O'Connor, Pat. **Friendships between women: a critical review.** Guilford, 1992. 228p bibl index afp ISBN 0-89862-976-4, $44.95; ISBN 0-89862-981-0 pbk, $17.95

Friendship is an understudied topic because social science is affected by sexist and homophobic attitudes, as is the rest of society. O'Connor draws attention to the importance of studying female friendship in her well-written, carefully argued overview of the literature. She devotes one chapter to theoretical perspectives; one each to friendships among married women, single women, and elderly women; one to a comparison of female friendships with kin relationships, work-based friendships, and lesbian relationships; and a concluding chapter on directions for future research. O'Connor challenges conventional views, including the belief that female friendships complement marital relationships. Each chapter contains detailed vignettes and concludes with a useful starting point for new research. O'Connor's most provocative revelation is that the study of friendships has also been hampered by ageism, reflected in the fact that the female friendships that are personally and socially most meaningful can be found among elderly women, at least in contemporary Western societies. Advanced undergraduate; graduate; faculty.—*S. Reinharz, Brandeis University*

WS-2240   Can. CIP
Rethinking restructuring: gender and change in Canada, ed. by
Isabella Bakker. Toronto, 1996. 292p bibl afp ISBN 0-8020-0702-3, $55.00;
ISBN 0-8020-7651-3 pbk, $22.95

This collection focuses on the impact of globalization on women in the labor
force. What is the nature of socioeconomic and political restructuring in Canada?
How is the gender order being transformed? The authors evaluate the changing
role of the welfare state and the restructuring process by examining some of the
concerns raised by the new feminist politics. Policy areas related to the labor market, fiscal policy, trade, and citizenship and differential impacts
on women and men are highlighted. Part 1 examines the feminization of the
labor force, the problems of home-based and part-time women workers, federal
government training, and labor-market policies. It shows how the livelihoods
of women are being profoundly affected and new structures of gender inequality created. Part 2 looks at the relationships among states, markets, and individuals in the context of national policies and the notion of social citizenship, and
identifies the extent of gender bias in welfare state policies. Part 3 considers
the challenges and opportunities posed by global restructuring, and in light of a
global feminist movement, presents alternative strategies aimed at gender equality. An important contribution to international economics and gender studies.
Graduate; faculty.—*D. A. Chekki, University of Winnipeg*

WS-2241   HQ1240   95-43943 CIP
Sachs, Carolyn E. **Gendered fields: rural women, agriculture, and
environment.** Westview, 1996. 205p bibl index afp ISBN 0-8133-2519-
6, $54.95; ISBN 0-8133-2520-X pbk, $19.95

Sachs' work is a superb review of material about contemporary women working in agriculture across the globe. Three chapters cover the theoretical and
historical background of women in relation to the land. They discuss the feminist
approach, and the complexity and impossibility of generalizing across race,
nationality, ethnicity, and sexual preference. Specific chapters treat women's connectedness to the land, plants, and animals. A special chapter is devoted to the
roles of women on family farms in the US, Africa, and Latin America. A final discussion places women in the context of current global processes of agricultural
restructuring. Each chapter is replete with national or cultural-specific references
to past research. Sachs, author of *Invisible Farmers: Women in Agricultural
Production* (CH, Dec'83), is a rural sociologist who has done research in this area
for more than 15 years. *Gendered Fields* brings together the findings of her
research with those of other feminist and rural researchers in England, Europe,
Latin America, and Africa. It contains an excellent integration of primary and secondary data, with more than 260 citations to relevant work. Essential for those
who seek an understanding of the significance of gender in rural society. All
levels.—*D. P. Slesinger, University of Wisconsin—Madison*

WS-2242   HC110   CIP
Scanlon, Jennifer. **Inarticulate longings: the Ladies' Home Journal,
gender, and the promises of consumer culture.** Routledge, 1995.
278p index ISBN 0-415-91156-7, $59.95; ISBN 0-415-91157-5 pbk, $16.95

In this revealing study, Scanlon explores the relationship between white, middle-class women and the emerging consumer culture of the 1910-1930 period. She
focuses on the *Ladies' Home Journal*, the top circulating women's publication
of the era, to examine how women's roles were simultaneously defined, expanded,
and restricted by the purveyors of mass consumption. Contradictions abounded
in the messages transmitted by the magazine, as it promoted both traditional
"woman's values" and immersion in the consumer society. Thus, the *Ladies'
Home Journal* spoke of housekeeping as "women's only true work," but also helped
to challenge barriers by reporting on "women's paid work." Unfortunately,
Scanlon observes, this resulted in attempts by some to become superwomen, who
attempted to do it all. The magazine also conveyed other messages, including feminist attitudes involving suffrage and an early hint of what Betty Friedan later
referred to as the feminine mystique. Indeed, these inarticulate longings purportedly resulted in a "powerful base" for this leading women's magazine. Although
an often richly textured work, the book contains verbiage that is sometimes off-
putting and relies a little too heavily on contemporary parlance. Highly recommended for both general and academic libraries. All levels.—*R. C. Cottrell,
California State University, Chico*

WS-2243   HQ1240   94-22223 CIP
Scott, Catherine V. **Gender and development: rethinking modernization and dependency theory.** L. Rienner, 1995. 151p bibl index
afp ISBN 1-55587-664-1 pbk, $16.95

Scott's book is a feminist critique of development theory. The author argues
that both the modernization and the dependency theoretical frameworks are
grounded in gender differences that reflect male centeredness. Simply including women as actors in the political development of Third World countries is inadequate because the theories themselves are, at their core, biased. Scott's review
of the theoretical frameworks is sophisticated and compelling. The author treats
Southern Africa as a case in point to explicate the sources and implications of theory that locates the position of women as part of the definition of "traditional"
in modernization terms, and of "underdeveloped" in the dependency framework. Although a somewhat difficult approach to the theory of political development, this book will appeal to students of Third World development and change,
as well as feminist political theory. Upper-division undergraduates and above.—
A. A. Hickey, Western Carolina University

WS-2244   HQ1190   94-32900 CIP
Shugar, Dana R. **Separatism and women's community.** Nebraska,
1995. 216p bibl index afp ISBN 0-8032-4244-1, $30.00

Shugar analyzes the complexity and contradictions of feminist separatism
and the work of building communities accomplished by its rhetorics and practices.
Separatism is not necessarily essentialist or lesbian, is paradoxical, and simultaneously enables and fractures feminist collectivities. Struggles to authenticate membership and govern groups become exclusionary, and prevent collectives from successfully managing internal conflict, as evident in archives and publications of
business and land collectives, as well as in feminist fiction. In autobiographical
interstices, Shugar recounts her experience of an unanticipated conflict between
collectives during her research; these segments creatively play out the thesis of her
book. Because she has not used anthropological methodology, Shugar is limited to
textual resources. What do women in or formerly in collectives make of separatism,
and Shugar's research? She suggests, but does not fully articulate, the ways in
which debates about pornography and sexuality, which currently trouble feminist theory and practice, as well as continuing problems with race and class mirror conflicts over separatism. Recommended for upper-division undergraduate and
graduate students in women's studies, gay and lesbian studies, and those interested
in alternative communities.—*J. L. Croissant, University of Arizona*

WS-2245   HQ1075   95-39468 CIP
Sigel, Roberta S. **Ambition & accommodation: how women view
gender relations.** Chicago, 1996. 240p bibl index afp ISBN 0-226-
75695-5, $48.00; ISBN 0-226-75696-3 pbk, $16.95

Based on quantitative (telephone survey) and qualitative (nondirective focus
group) research, Sigel's goal is to discover how individuals today, particularly
women, subjectively experience gender relations. Drawn from a New Jersey sample, her findings show that ordinary American women recognize and are unsettled
by their "second-class" status, yet choose individual coping strategies rather
than collective, political avenues to address their sense of relative deprivation.
Sigel, a political scientist, argues that these women have a "minority consciousness," not a "group consciousness." As the importance of male partnership and
family outweigh sisterhood, her data indicate that women share a "common situation" but are not part of a "common cause." Sigel's research provides valuable insights as to why these women are ambivalent about feminism and, less
overtly, how the women's movement has not responded to their ways of being and
knowing. Exceptionally well written, Sigel's study is both theoretically and methodologically a model of scholarly research. Her book is rich in women's and men's
voices and statistical data. It is as much a map of gender relations today as it is
a superb example of using complementary research methods. All levels.—
P. E. Herideen, Northeastern University

WS-2246   HV1445   95-50177 CIP
Whalen, Mollie. **Counseling to end violence against women: a
subversive model.** Sage Publications, CA, 1996. 166p bibl indexes
afp ISBN 0-8039-7379-9, $37.00; ISBN 0-8039-7380-2 pbk, $17.95

Whalen presents a specific and grounded subversive counseling model for battered women, i.e., subversive in that it rejects the individual and pathology-ori-

ented images of battered women in favor of a political and social change model. This theoretical work is based on research, along with the author's extensive background in the area of feminist interventions with battered women. Whalen shows her ability to synthesize and demonstrates her knowledge of this literature with a typology of women's movement ideologies and their associated views of gender. Perhaps the most influential feminist for Whalen is Leonore Walker (*The Battered Woman*, 1979). Whalen also builds on Ellyn Kaschak's essay "Feminist Psychotherapy," in *Female Psychology*, ed. by Sue Cox (1976). Whalen is mindful of the connection between theory or ideology and practice in counseling. Her intent is to join the client and counselor to agitate for change in social institutions and to increase access of battered women to, among other things, material resources, safety, personal power, and women's collective strength. The references are well selected, and there are both subject and author indexes. This well-done work is a must for libraries. Upper-division undergraduates and above.—*Y. Peterson, Saint Xavier University*

WS-2247   HQ1426   93-25975 CIP
Wolf, Naomi. **Fire with fire: the new female power and how it will change the 21st century.** Random House, 1993. 373p bibl index ISBN 0-679-42718-X, $21.00

According to Wolf, the primary obstacles that block the path to women's equality are within the women's movement rather than part of the external social structure or institutions, and can be overcome if women have the desire and the determination. Ignoring the diversity of feminism within the current and historical women's movement, Wolf dichotomizes feminism into two categories: "victim feminism" and "power feminism." Victim feminism, the "appeal for status on the basis of female specialness instead of human worth," is characterized by fighting "underhandedly"; power feminism is based on the "overarching premise, 'More for women'." Wolf optimistically feels that worldly power is shifting into female hands, sufficiently so that women's jokes about men's power now qualify as "sexism." Men, she writes, have lost their authority and realize that women have already begun to "win." In the tradition of liberal feminism Wolf emphasizes the power of individual voices over collective action. Countering Audre Lorde's philosophy that the master's tools will not destroy the master's house, Wolf contends that only the master's tools are relevant. Written in an easily accessible style, the book will undoubtedly stimulate many useful discussions. General readers; undergradautes.—*C. Adamsky, University of New Hampshire*

WS-2248   HQ1421   90-7175 MARC
Women's progress: promises and problems, ed. by Jeanne Spurlock and Carolyn B. Robinowitz. Plenum, 1990. 258p index ISBN 0-306-43422-9, $39.50

The editors of this collection asked a number of psychiatric practitioners to address frequently neglected topics concerning women's lives. Although the particular subjects of these essays reflect the nature of the lives of women these practitioners meet in their daily rounds, the overall effect of the volume is to correct the traditional ways of perceiving women, especially women under stress. Discussions range from familiar topics like working women and battered women to those that seldom appear in the literature—foster mothers, adoptive mothers, mothers of exceptional children, lesbian mothers, criminal offenders, and transsexuals. Serving as a "model to encourage researchers. . .to investigate other areas of women's lives, areas rife with problems but largely denied or ignored," this volume will be of use to practitioners, especially those who do not specialize in these areas but who occasionally come into contact with such clients or patients. The nontechnical language and extensive bibliographies make it also useful to a broader audience—those engaged in women's studies and all the women who live the lives described.—*C. M. McGovern, University of Vermont*

WS-2249   HQ766   94-17171 CIP
Women's studies manuscript collections from the Schlesinger Library, Radcliffe College. Series 3. Sexuality, sex education, and reproductive rights [microform]: Pt. A: Family planning oral history project; Pt. B: The papers of Mary Ware Dennett and the Voluntary Parenthood League. University Publications of America, 1994. Pt. A: 3 reels; Pt. B: 36 reels. ISBN 1-55655-502-4, Pt. A, $355.00 with guide; ISBN 1-55655-510-5, Pt. B, $4,290.00 with guide

The Schlesinger Library has made available in microfilm two significant manuscript collections relating to the history of sexuality, contraception, and reproductive rights in the US. Part A, the Family Planning Oral History Project, consists of transcripts of interviews with 23 women and two men who worked to improve women's knowledge about and access to contraception. The interviews, conducted in the 1970s by historians James W. Reed and Ellen Chesler and Schlesinger director Jeanette Cheek, include explanatory introductions and indexes. They range from Grant Sanger's reminiscences of his mother in the early years of this century to lawyer Sarah Weddington's account of acting as counsel to *Roe* v. *Wade* (1973) and her presidency of the National Abortion Rights Action League (NARAL). Although the interviews were not intended to be comprehensive (some are as short as 32 pages), there is much interesting and provocative material here, and most of the subjects come vividly to life. The interviews are typed, well organized, and clearly legible in this format. The finding guide includes an introduction by Linda Gordon, a clear, precise, and indexed listing for each interview, and a general subject index.

Part B, the Papers of Mary Ware Dennett and the Voluntary Parenthood League, consists of Dennett's personal papers, which incorporate office files of the VPL (1919-41) and its predecessor, the National Birth Control League (1915-19). Dennett (1872-1947), founder and first director of both organizations, was not only a birth control activist but a worker in leather crafts, suffragist, pacifist, and advocate of sex education as well. Although a crucial figure in the birth control and sex education reform period of the 1920s and '30s, Dennett has been eclipsed by her charismatic contemporary, Margaret Sanger. The Dennett papers are rich resources, not only for the history of activism in contraception and sexuality, suffragism, pacifism, and the arts and crafts movement, but also for the history of women's activism and its different themes and strategies. The papers have been carefully processed by the Schlesinger and are divided into five series, comprising nearly the whole of Dennett's life: Personal, Arts and Crafts, Suffrage, Birth Control and Sex Education, and Other Organizations and Causes. Most of the material is clearly legible on microfilm (there are some handwritten documents that are hard to read) and each new set of frames is marked with a filmed copy of the appropriate page from the file listing, to assist the reader. The finding guide includes an introduction by Linda Gordon, a brief biography and scope and content note, clear and precise reel by reel index, a correspondent index, and a subject index. Upper-division undergraduates and above.—*M. L. Meldrum, University of California, Los Angeles*

WS-2250   HQ1154x   Orig
The World's women, 1970-1990: trends and statistics. United Nations, 1991. 120p (Social statistics and indicators. Series K, 8) ISBN 92-1-161313-2 pbk, $19.95

The UN proclaimed 1976-85 as the "Decade for Women," and focused on issues pertinent to women: equality, development, peace, the family and reproduction, economic life, and participation in economic and political decision-making. The text of this report features an experimental and innovative approach that provides a highly usable collection of indicators on these areas. The report is the most complete description available of the condition of women in the world, compiled by a credible international organization. The format lends itself to presentation of a wide range of social and human development indicators. Each indicator is represented through a descriptive text, illustrative charts, and an assembly of data. Every attempt is made *not* to offer a preconceived picture, but to allow evidence to speak for itself. It is the intention of the UN that the report become a useful tool for promoting equality and for changing attitudes toward women's work, worth, and responsibilities. Of interest to policymakers and to anyone striving to promote the status of women through legislation or development strategies and effective lobbying. Upper-division undergraduates and above.—*M. Klatte, Eastern Kentucky University*

◆ History, Research, Theory

WS-2251 HV9105 94-47525 CIP
Alexander, Ruth M. **The "girl problem": female sexual delinquency in New York, 1900-1930.** Cornell, 1995. 200p bibl index afp ISBN 0-8014-2821-1, $29.95

Alexander's historical study documents the experience of female sexual delinquents from 1900 to 1930. Working-class adolescents and young adults were severely sanctioned for failing to obey Victorian moral standards. These "delinquent" girls were usually incarcerated in state reformatories. Alexander analyzes records of 100 female residents of institutions in Bedford Hills and Albion, New York. Working from case examples, she illustrates the actions that defined young women as delinquent, their reformatory experiences, and their struggles to reenter society. She reconstructs interaction among young women facing changing cultural standards, their frightened families, and the legal system of courts and reformatories. Alexander's interest is in the process of identifying a new social issue, "the girl problem," and in the 20th-century redefinition of adolescence. Rebellious lower-class young women who experimented sexually were severely handled, while middle-class girls received understanding or therapy for similar behavior. Case examples and archival photographs enhance the historical, theoretical material. This thoroughly researched book includes a helpful bibliographic essay and extensive notes. Upper-division undergraduates and above.— *M. E. Elwell, emerita, Salisbury State University*

WS-2252 HM22.U6 90-34390 CIP
Bannister, Robert C. **Jessie Bernard: the making of a feminist.** Rutgers, 1991. 276p bibl index ISBN 0-8135-1614-5, $27.95

Bannister (Swarthmore) has produced a well-written biography of Jessie Bernard (1903-), an important figure in American sociology. He describes Bernard's life from childhood, through a turbulent marriage, single parenthood, and into the mid-1980s, tracing the development of an intellectual in a troubled landscape of anti-Semitism, conflicting feminisms, and, later in her career, growing skepticism of "positivistic" social sciences. The text cites the scholars influencing Bernard's work and portrays an important perspective on the workings of American sociology in 1920-60s and on feminism in the '60s and '70s. Bannister's study is a good example of credible and sensitive scholarship, bringing out various critical perspectives on Bernard and documenting ambivalences toward gender, race, politics, and the social sciences in her work. Although not a social history of feminism, Bannister's book is informed by feminist issues. It will make a contribution to sociology programs as well as to those in women's studies, for undergraduate through graduate readers.—*J. L. Croissant, Rensselaer Polytechnic Institution*

WS-2253 HV6626 93-12897 CIP
Barnett, Ola W. **It could happen to anyone: why battered women stay,** by Ola W. Barnett and Alyce D. LaViolette. Sage, 1993. 186p bibl index ISBN 0-8039-5309-7, $38.95; ISBN 0-8039-5310-0 pbk $18.95

A good introduction for newcomers to the topic. Despite the authors' claim of an eclectic approach, the work is essentially theoretical, which is the predominant mode of explanation in this literature. The question of why battered women stay is not new and was answered by Leonore Walker (*The Battered Woman*, 1979). Walker introduced the concept of learned helplessness, used here in conjunction with learned hopefulness. Barnett and LaViolette also use the role of fear, the battered women's syndrome, and the newly pervasive concept of post-traumatic stress to answer the question. This book is similar in its empathy and readability to Mildred Daley Pagelow's *Woman-Battering* (1981). The interspersed vignettes of battered women's lives are convincing. The bibliography is of good quality and includes classic studies as well as more modern sources. Overall, an enlightening book for the uninitiated about the complex processes involved in why battered women stay. General, community college, and undergraduate readership.—*Y. Peterson, Saint Xavier University*

WS-2254 HQ1180 90-43508 CIP
Beyond methodology: feminist scholarship as lived research, ed. by Mary Margaret Fonow and Judith A. Cook. Indiana, 1991. 310p index afp ISBN 0-253-32345-2, $37.50; ISBN 0-253-20629-4, pbk $14.95

A stellar cast of authors discuss and describe feminist research, reflecting the state of feminist discourse in sociology. Their 15 informative pieces (both quantitative and qualitative, some reprinted from journals and some written especially for the collection) cover a variety of topics. But all share a focus on epistemological and methodological issues that confront a feminist-oriented sociology: the difference a feminist perspective makes to the scholarly enterprise, and the responsibilities that feminist scholars have to their community, to their subjects, and to themselves. Among the notable contributions: Verta Taylor and Leila Rupp discuss how contradictions between convictions and findings reshaped their understanding of feminism as a historical process; Liz Stanley and Sue Wise describe the complex interaction between research and theory as their community activism subjected them to a series of obscene phone calls. These were transformed into a research project that had a dramatic impact on their lives and their views. Although the volume demonstrates that feminism has had less transformative impact on sociology than on other disciplines, its high quality makes it a must in sociology and women's studies collections.—*N. Rosenthal, SUNY College at Old Westbury*

WS-2255 HQ1687 90-26144 CIP
Bok, Sissela. **Alva Myrdal: a daughter's memoir.** Addison-Wesley, 1991. 375p index ISBN 0-201-57086-6, $22.95

Bok has written a memoir, a biography, and a eulogy of her mother while trying to understand her mother. Alva Myrdal made and kept a life of her own against great odds and under a variety of circumstances. Readers see her development from a girl determined to get an education and make a difference to her recognition as a Nobel Prize winner. They gain insight into the child of famous activist parents and how marriage, children, career, and public policy activism could be combined in Sweden in an earlier generation. The "us" of Alva's journals, letters, and publications, plus Bok's own memories, reflections, and journals give great immediacy to a reflective narrative. A personal look at an early superwoman, the book is delightful and enthralling. All levels.—*V. P. Caruso, Nazareth College*

WS-2256 HV1448 91-36251 CIP
Cohen, Sherrill. **The evolution of women's asylums since 1500: from refuges for ex-prostitutes to shelters for battered women.** Oxford, 1992. 262p bibl index afp ISBN 0-19-505164-5, $39.95

The 16th and 17th centuries in Catholic Europe witnessed the growth of new institutions designed to house repentant prostitutes and girls and women at risk of becoming prostitutes. This little-known surge in institution building arose out of the Catholic reform movement and the Counter-Reformation. Cohen presents a portrait of life in three such institutions for women, in the Italian cities of Florence and Pistoia. In Western societies from the 16th century onward, far more types of gender-specific institutions have been created for women than for men. The institutions for women served many social functions, usually including control of women's sexuality. Representing a new residential option for women beyond those of marriage or convent, these institutions were "asylums" in a dual sense, operating as both sites of internment and shelters from harm. Cohen demonstrates how the multifunctional women's institutions of the early modern era served as the prototypes for a variety of asylums for women that emerged in later centuries, e.g., hostels, homes for unwed mothers, and battered women's shelters. In a major revision of the historiography of social institutions, Cohen argues that the women's institutions of early modern Europe played a pioneering role in developing techniques and institutional forms in the fields of corrections and social welfare. All levels.—*M. Klatte, Eastern Kentucky University*

WS-2257 HQ1236 90-45845 CIP
Fauré, Christine. **Democracy without women: feminism and the rise of liberal individualism in France,** tr. by Claudia Gorbman and John Berks. Indiana, 1991. 196p bibl index afp ISBN 0-253-32155-7, $29.95

For several reasons, this translation of Fauré's work on the development of the liberal idea of the abstract individual and the relations between that idea and feminist thought is most welcome. It brings to English-language readers a very different perspective from that provided by Anglo-American scholars. Fauré, a French feminist sociologist, integrates well-known texts by male authors such as Montaigne, Bodin, Montesquieu, Rousseau, and Condorcet with lesser-known texts by male and female authors such as Marie de Gourney and Théroigne de Méricourt, and sets intellectual developments clearly within the context of political change in France. Fauré covers a broad time frame—from Christine de Pizan to Napoléon—and also brings in non-French thinkers such as Locke, Kant, and Mary Wollstonecraft. This is essential reading for anyone exploring issues of gender and power, the public/private dichotomy, or women and political life in any time period, and belongs in all libraries with women's studies collections. It is written in sprightly style, translated well, and reassures readers that not all French feminists have given up political analysis in favor of deconstruction. Upper-division undergraduates and above.—*M. E. Wiesner, University of Wisconsin-Milwaukee*

WS-2258   HQ1180   89-24200 CIP
Feminist praxis: research, theory and epistemology in feminist sociology, ed. by Liz Stanley. Routledge, 1990. 282p indexes ISBN 0-415-04186-4, $52.50; ISBN 0-415-04202-X, $15.50

Stanley (Manchester University) has edited a fine and unique collection. The introductory chapters are good discussions of the theories, methodologies, and politics of feminist sociological research. Later chapters relate contributors' experiences as researchers and activists from some of the various "standpoints," but the collection does not include the full range of perspectives expected from the espoused agenda of avoiding "monolithic feminism." The volume is more than an anthology of the trials and tribulations of qualitative sociological research, and invites readers to think critically about research method and process, researcher biography and experience, and analysis. The essays are engaging, personal, and consistent, although not all chapters fulfill a promise of extraordinary quality or depth. The index could be more comprehensive, but with its bibliographic quality this collection is a valuable resource on British feminist scholarship for libraries supporting undergraduate or graduate students in sociology or women's studies.—*J. L. Croissant, Rensselaer Polytechnic Institution*

WS-2259   HQ146   91-45024 CIP
Gilfoyle, Timothy J. **City of eros: New York City, prostitution, and the commercialization of sex, 1790-1920.** W.W. Norton, 1992. 462p bibl index ISBN 0-393-02800-3, $24.95

The 19th century was marked by rapid increase in the growth of cities. The development of industry, which was largely responsible for this phenomenon, spawned cities in which young men were on their own. Perhaps as a response to this population, the 19th-century city was also known for its vice—in particular, for prostitution. Red light districts were common and were found in virtually all cities. Gilfoyle examines commercialized vice in New York City. He brings the tools of the social historian to the task and analyzes the topic from virtually every conceivable side. The author avoids both sensationalism and dullness. This is a well-written, well-documented work that focuses on what can only be described as the lower depths of society. The book takes its place alongside older works, such as Gunther Barth's *City People* (CH, Jan'81) and recently published studies, such as Kenneth Scherzer's *The Unbounded Community* (CH, Jan'93). General; advanced undergraduate; graduate; faculty; professional.—*I. Cohen, Illinois State University*

WS-2260   HV699   94-18800 CIP
Gordon, Linda. **Pitied but not entitled: single mothers and the history of welfare, 1890-1935.** Free Press, 1994. 433p index ISBN 0-02-912485-9, $22.95

Especially during rancorous debate over the nation's welfare system and women's place in it, many libraries should acquire Gordon's excellent book. How, she asks, did aid to single mothers come to be constructed so that it now generates such dissatisfaction? Her answer, sobering for feminists, is that ADC was designed by women activists. It turned out to be unsatisfactory because its early advocates, despite relative personal freedom from gender constraints, were guided by maternalist definitions of women, and because the alliances they made, however understandable, helped guarantee a division between welfare and

entitlement programs such as old age insurance. The resulting system was easily overwhelmed by subsequent social changes. Gordon's work is advocacy of expanding welfare, but her approach is characterized by a fair-minded, thoughtful refusal to settle for too easily dichotomized judgments of the past. She painstakingly dissects what she properly insists was a shared gender system, and she looks unblinkingly at racism in its manifold guises. A full summary restatement of Gordon's argument might have made the book more accessible to a broader audience. As it is, this sophisticated, engaged history puts demands on readers but is exceptionally rewarding. Upper-division undergraduate and graduate collections.—*A. Graebner, The College of St. Catherine*

WS-2261   HM131   91-15786 CIP
Heskin, Allan David. **The struggle for community.** Westview, 1991. 195p bibl index afp ISBN 0-8133-8338-2 pbk, $24.85

Heskin's clear, well-written, and well-organized book provides undergraduates with a good introduction to ethnographic and participatory research in the social sciences. Heskin's case study of a Los Angeles community of 500 tenant households describes residents' successful fight against being displaced from their rented homes and analyzes their subsequent empowerment as a collective. Given Heskin's participation in the group, the book is testimony to his commitment to praxis, the intersection of practice and theory. He is concerned not only with organizing people to gain power but also with identifying what people must do with power once they obtain it. Each chapter ends with a summary and notes. Heskin includes an excellent chapter on the role of working-class and Third World women in community development. He has constructed an extensive bibliography on community empowerment, development, and organizing. Good subject-author index. Useful to graduate and undergraduate students and faculty in sociology, anthropology, social work, urban planning, and history.—*S. Cable, University of Tennessee at Knoxville*

WS-2262   HM22   91-33223 CIP
Hoecker-Drysdale, Susan. **Harriet Martineau, first woman sociologist.** Berg, 1992. 190p bibl index ISBN 0-85496-645-5, $25.50

Poet, novelist, essayist, traveler, translator, social activist, and journalist, Martineau (1802-1876) was one of the most prolific of the 19th-century British women writers. Her work was probably more widely read than that of any other woman of her time yet is little known in ours. Hoecker-Drysdale attempts, in this brief intellectual biography, to claim Martineau as one of the early masters of sociological thought. Martineau orginally gained fame as the author of a series of short stories illustrating the principles of classical political economy and, this biographer argues, these and later nonfiction works on the subject were key to popular acceptance of the doctrine. Moreover, her journey to the US and the resulting three-volume work, *Society in America* (1837), contemporaneous with Tocqueville's *Democracy in America* (1835) remains one of the "most thorough sociological studies of a society in the nineteenth century." Finally, Martineau was one of the early followers and popularizers of Auguste Comte; she produced the first translation of his work into English, publishing a condensed version of his *Cours de philosophie positive* in 1853. Hoecker-Drysdale's presentation of this complex woman and of her career is an intriguing portrait of an early advocate of the moral sciences. Undergraduate; graduate; professional.—*N. B. Rosenthal, SUNY College at Old Westbury*

WS-2263   Orig
Inside/out: lesbian theories, gay theories, ed. by Diana Fuss. Routledge, 1991. 426p bibl ISBN 0-415-90236-3, $55.00; ISBN 0-415-90237-1 pbk, $15.95

A wonderfully diverse collection of original papers dealing with issues and questions relating to lesbians, gays, and sexuality in late 20th-century Western society. Editor Fuss teaches English at Princeton; if the volume can be said to have a perspective it is one informed by postmodern literary criticism. This means that the uninitiated will have to wade through a fair amount of jargon, but the effort is worth making. The collection is divided into five sections and contains papers on gender identity, the arts, the body, AIDS, and education. Virtually all of the papers question conventional wisdom and many offer acute, irreverent, and, occasionally, angry points of view. It is difficult to single out particular contributions, but Carole-Anne Tyler on "The Politics of Gay Drag," Judith Mayne on lesbian authorship, Ellis Hanson on gays viewed as modern vampires, and Cindy Patton on pornography and safe sex should serve as a good sample. This collection will be required reading for those in gay and lesbian studies and for anyone else interested in nontraditional perspectives on sexuality.—*M. Gordon, University of Connecticut*

WS-2264 HQ1419 93-47666 MARC
Jackson, Margaret. **The real facts of life: feminism and the politics of sexuality, c1850-1940.** Taylor & Francis, 1994. 206p bibl index afp ISBN 0-7484-0099-0, $75.00; ISBN 0-7484-0100-8 pbk, $25.00

Jackson details the contentious debate over control of women's sexuality that developed in the 19th century, and she convincingly argues that the personal was already understood as political by feminists over a century ago. Jackson also explores the emergence of sexology as a "science" and as a form of antifeminist backlash that actively tried to depoliticize issues of sexual autonomy and sexual pleasure. She looks in detail at the contributions of important individuals on both sides, for example, Elizabeth Blackwell and Havelock Ellis. Although she does not gloss over important differences within the feminist camp at the turn of the century, she clearly favors those who held the more politicized view of relations between men and women (which she calls female sexual autonomy) over those who advocated "free love" as human liberation. This book will be useful both for those who would understand the historical roots of today's flourishing debates over prostitution, pornography, lesbianism, single mothers, and "family values" and for those interested in the politics of social science (particularly students in family studies, marriage counseling, sexology, and psychosexual adjustment). However, the focus on British feminist politics makes it less useful for American students, and the level of detail will probably appeal most to graduate students and research historians.—*M. M. Ferree, University of Connecticut*

WS-2265 Can. CIP
Knowledge, experience, and ruling relations: studies in the social organization of knowledge, ed. by Marie Campbell and Ann Manicom. Toronto, 1995. 288p bibl index afp ISBN 0-8020-0720-1, $55.00; ISBN 0-8020-7666-1 pbk, $17.95

For those following sociologist Dorothy Smith's work, this collection is a welcome addition to feminist methodologies and standpoint theories. The case studies—which include the institutional ethnographies and constructions of AIDS discourse, multiculturalism, international relations, domestic violence, school policy and practice, clerical and social work, photographs, adolescent sexuality, nursing, local land use policy, and literacy—articulate the conceptual and practical implications of Smith's sociology. Editors Campbell and Manicom, with the other colleagues of Smith represented here, expand the original concept of a sociology viewed from women's perspective to one applicable to many kinds of institutional and discursive subordination. Despite powerful analyses and the collective enterprise that Smith's work has engendered, problems remain. For example, whose standpoint should take priority when mothers and teachers are both disfranchised by school discourse, yet mothers are also dismissed by teachers? Because the feminist theoretical and epistemological implications of the framework are not engaged, theory remains unchallenged and many contributions lose the support of a formal explanation. Nevertheless, the volume is highly recommended for women's studies, sociology, and the sociology of knowledge. Upper-division undergraduates and above.—*J. L. Croissant, University of Arizona*

WS-2266 HV700 93-10013 CIP
Kunzel, Regina G. **Fallen women, problem girls: unmarried mothers and the professionalization of social work, 1890-1945.** Yale, 1994 (c1993). 264p bibl index afp ISBN 0-300-05090-9, $27.50

Unmarried mothers: Are they seduced and abandoned victims, sex delinquents, or neurotics? In this fascinating history of illegitimacy and maternity homes, Kunzel (history, Williams College) traces the reconstruction of out-of-wedlock pregnancy from a moral to a sociological and, ultimately, psychological problem. This is also a history of professionalism. The maternity home was a key arena in which women in the new, scientifically based profession of social work attempted to distance themselves from earlier "Lady Bountiful" approaches to helping. Kunzel documents the struggle between women whose religious calling was to save their "fallen sisters" through shelter and reform, and social workers who, wanting to "de-gender" helping and professionalize benevolence, ultimately gained control of services, casting pregnant girls as clients and defining their behavior as pathological and even criminal. Also part of the struggle to define unmarried pregnancy were the mothers themselves; two of the six chapters draw from extensive case records to document their experiences. Highly recommended for scholars and students in social work, feminist studies, sociology, and social history. Upper-division undergraduates and above.—*B. A. Pine, University of Connecticut*

WS-2267 HQ1154 93-29360 CIP
Lehmann, Jennifer M. **Durkheim and women.** Nebraska, 1994. 173p bibl index afp ISBN 0-8032-2907-0, $30.00

A feminist critique of one of sociology's "founding fathers" was almost inevitable, but Lehmann's approach is far from predictable and shows Durkheim to be both a brilliant analyzer and a partial victim of his cultural milieu. The first and last chapters of the work respectively place Durkheim squarely in the swirling modernist controversies of his time and the equally bedeviling postmodernist controversies of ours. Lehmann's last chapter is particularly provocative; she combines an impassioned and trenchant indictment of the oppressive links between late capitalism and neoliberalism with an argument to incorporate Durkheim's valuable legacy in a social theoretical stance she names "post-poststructuralism" or "critical structuralism." The intervening chapters carefully trace and critically dissect the ambiguous and contradiction-riddled place of women in the "master's" monumental oeuvre. The work is thoroughly researched and well documented, and it should do much to renew interest in Durkheim as a cogent if imperfect observer of the human condition. Upper-division undergraduates and above.—*W. P. Nye, Hollins College*

WS-2268 HV700 92-39087 CIP
Morton, Marian J. **And sin no more: social policy and unwed mothers in Cleveland, 1855-1990.** Ohio State, 1993. 183p bibl index afp ISBN 0-8142-0602-6, $39.50

In this brief but valuable study, Morton traces the development of public and private health-care policies for single mothers in Cleveland from the mid-19th century to the present. Focusing on the history of Cleveland's public hospital and five private maternity homes, *Sin No More*'s primary contribution lies in its comprehensive investigation of Protestant and Catholic institutions as well as those sheltering black and white women, in a single city. Contrary to many historians, Morton denies the importance of public policy and public institutions to understanding the 20th-century welfare state, insisting instead that private agencies are central to that task. Morton also rejects historians' emphasis on the secularization of social welfare. She convincingly argues that throughout the 20th century private maternity agencies retained their explicit evangelical purpose of reclaiming sinful women and continued older policies of institutionalization and of instructing unwed mothers in women's work. Supplements Rickie Solinger's recent work, *Wake Up Little Susie: Single Pregnancy and Race Before Roe v. Wade* (CH, Oct'92). Advanced undergraduate; graduate; faculty; professional.—*E. W. Carp, Pacific Lutheran University*

WS-2269 HQ27 95-13185 CIP
Odem, Mary E. **Delinquent daughters: protecting and policing adolescent female sexuality in the United States, 1885-1920.** North Carolina, 1995. 265p bibl index afp ISBN 0-8078-2215-9, $39.95; ISBN 0-8078-4528-0 pbk, $14.95

Odem's important book provides a model for the study of state institutions and issues of social control. Odem focuses on multiple efforts to define and regulate adolescent female sexuality in the US between 1885 and 1920. Beginning with national campaigns to reform "age of consent" laws, the author illustrates enforcement of those laws by examining court records from Los Angeles and Alameda Counties (California). In addition to readability, the beauty of this book is, first, its careful interweaving of sexual ideologies, the moral norms of reformers, and the development and application of regulatory laws. Second, and perhaps more important, is Odem's careful treatment of all the protagonists in the story—state officials, middle-class moral reformers, the girls, and their families. The relationships among these groups of individuals are never static, their aims and goals not always in agreement, and, above all, the consequences of their actions often unintended. Always taking into account class, ethnic, and racial differences and using examples of these whenever possible, Odem reassesses working-class moral codes and family relations. The complexity and the clarity of argument, the detailed research, and the compelling narrative make this a book that could, and *should*, be read by the beginner and the expert in a variety of fields.—*M. J. Slaughter, University of New Mexico*

WS-2270 HQ1180 91-27838 CIP
Reinharz, Shulamit. **Feminist methods in social research.** Oxford, 1992. 413p bibl index afp ISBN 0-19-507385-1, $39.95; ISBN 0-19-507386-X pbk, $19.95

Reinharz has written a valuable and wide-ranging survey of feminist projects in the social sciences, the methods employed, and the value of the work produced. Each chapter outlines a particular strategy for collecting information (interview, ethnography, survey, experiment, cross-cultural comparison, oral history, content analysis, case study, action research), describing its actual use by academic feminists. Though the work is not exhaustive, it provides broad representation for much current scholarship while avoiding what Annette Kolodny has called the "minefield"—the rancorous debates about the essential nature of men and women, not to speak of the sometimes devastating explosions of hostility over postmodernist theory and practice that have fragmented feminism in the academy. Preferring to examine the feminist project in terms of unities rather than divisions, Reinharz describes the range of methods that feminist researchers use and neatly sidesteps the thorny issue of whether they have transformed disciplinary methods and paradigms or have been swallowed by them. In so doing, she depicts an umbrella that encompasses diversity and shelters a variety of perspectives, approaches, and modalities. Students and faculty alike should find the descriptions of research agendas, problems, and methodological solutions informative, exciting, and suggestive.—*N. B. Rosenthal, SUNY College at Old Westbury*

WS-2271 HQ1075 91-17418 CIP
Rose, Sonya O. **Limited livelihoods: gender and class in nineteenth-century England.** California, 1992. 292p bibl index afp ISBN 0-520-07478-5, $39.95

Rose (sociology, Colby College) proceeds from the increasingly familiar argument that work and home life, economic relations and family relations are not separate spheres but are intimately connected in lived experience. For example, labor legislation and workplace management construct relations among classes, but they also often define what is masculine or feminine and construct relations between the genders. The spheres, Rose convincingly demonstrates, are connected at many points. A consequence is that class and gender relations are often constructed simultaneously. Rose focuses on legislation, factory management, "homework" for married women, trade union development, and gender antagonism in certain industries. Her extensive bibliography includes government documents, private papers, trade union and business association archives, newspapers, and an impressive list of secondary works. Readers will readily discern Rose's differences with the Marxists on the formation of class relations and appreciate that she does not oversimplify complexity but may wish her argument had a sharper outline. In contrast, Rose simplifies English society and culture—especially "industrial capitalism"—sometimes distorting them. A more important measure is that the book virtually compels scholars to revisit the past with an eye to connecting the sphere of work with that of home life and to discovering the connections between the construction of gender and of class relations. Upper-division undergraduates and above.—*P. K. Cline, Earlham College*

WS-2272 HN28 89-10961 CIP
Smith, Dorothy E. **Texts, facts, and femininity: exploring the relations of ruling.** Routledge, 1990. 247p bibl indexes ISBN 0-415-03231-8, $35.00

Smith (Ontario Institute for Studies in Education) has added another notable work to her already extensive porfolio of sociological scholarship. The first five sections of this book develop theory and methods for sociological practice. Based on ethnomethodological foundations of Garfinkel and Schutz, perhaps Smith's most important theoretical contribution is a description of subjectivity, influenced heavily by Marx. Borrowing generously form Foucault's formulation of discursive practice, her interpretation of power relations in the materials is somewhat undeveloped. Only the sixth chapter, "Femininity as Discourse,"

takes an explicitly feminist focus—on the construction of femininity in mainstream Canadian and US media. More analyses such as this would have fulfilled the promise of the title. Well written and provocative, Texts, Facts, and Femininity is unfortunately beyond the reach of all but the most advanced undergraduates. An important resource for programs is sociology, anthropology, and women's studies.—*J. L. Croissant, Rensselaer Polytechnic Institution*

WS-2273 Orig
Tal, Kalí. **Worlds of hurt: reading the literatures of trauma.** Cambridge, 1996. 296p (Cambridge studies in American literature and culture, 95) index ISBN 0-521-44504-3, $54.95; ISBN 0-521-56512-X pbk, $18.95

Tal's brilliant idea is that survivors of trauma create a literature of hurt that contributes to the dominant culture's self-understanding. Tal (Univ. of Virginia, Charlottesville) writes an excellent introductory chapter on "reading the literature of trauma," a good essay on Holocaust literature, and two serviceable chapters on Vietnam veteran syndrome. Half the book focuses on her main interest, the extensiveness and depth of sexual abuse of women by men. Throughout she demonstrates methodological strength in informative and enlightening close textual analyses. Her analysis of the collective trauma women suffer is excellent, but in agreeing with Andrea Dworkin that the collective hurt of women suffered at the hands of men outweighs the hurt suffered by victims of the Nazi holocaust she sets up a strong need for a concluding chapter that pulls together all the literatures of hurt and defends her excellent premise. Instead, she stops, saying she could not write a suitable conclusion. This leaves a big hole, but the individual chapters are so good that libraries collecting literary theory and women's studies should have it. There are excellent notes.—*Q. Grigg, Hamline University*

WS-2274 HQ1593 94-27195 CIP
Tebbutt, Melanie. **Women's talk?: a social history of 'gossip' in working-class neighbourhoods, 1880-1960.** Scolar, 1995. 206p bibl index ISBN 1-85928-026-9, $59.95

The popular image of gossip as the activity of nasty and feckless women is overturned in this intelligent and careful analysis of British working-class women's neighborhood talk as a source of community strength. The denigration of all women's talk as useless gossip is seen as an attempt to silence women, to maintain their isolation in the home, and to deny women the power they have in the public sphere of the doorstep and neighborhood shop. "Gossip" has helped to create a public life for housebound women: it has been used to gather information vital to the survival of the family, to set moral standards for a stable and respectable life, and above all, to help women create a community. Of course, the moral standards set by neighborhood gossip could also lead to harsh criticism of poor housekeeping, overt sexuality, and to behavior judged by appearances and "what the neighbors would think." The book ends in 1960 with the move from terrace houses and tenement closes to housing estates and a more privatized life, making doorstep gossip part of "world we have lost." It would be interesting to have a new study of women's gossip in the age of television and the working mom. General readers; upper-division undergraduates and above.—*J. Wishnia, SUNY at Stony Brook*

WS-2275 HQ1190 92-27886 CIP
Theory on gender/feminism on theory, ed. by Paula England. Aldine de Gruyter, 1993. 377p index afp ISBN 0-202-30437-X, $51.95; ISBN 0-202-30438-8 pbk, $23.95

A first-rate collection of commissioned essays. Each essay offers an overview of how a specific theoretical perspective (from orthodox Marxism to ethnomethodology) works to explain gender, a self-critique of the theory's limitations from a feminist perspective, and a sketch of the potential for future developments along more feminist lines. Because the contributors are adherents of the theories presented, the outlines of how each respective theory works are sympathetic, but the self-critiques are sometimes half-hearted. This potential failing is offset by including other essays that critique these theoretical pieces and by allowing their advocates space for rejoinders. Thus the volume as a whole is a model of inclusive feminist dialogue. The collection could serve as a solid introduction to sociological theory, as tested by the application of these theories to a core issue. The volume could also be used as an introduction to the empirical literature on gender, as made relevant by diverse theoretical positions. The essays are not without jargon, but the attempt to speak to adherents of different theoretical schools along with the critical dialogue means that most of the terms are defined. The collection has the potential to "mainstream" feminist concerns into sociological theory. Advanced undergraduate; graduate; faculty.—*M. M. Ferree, University of Connecticut*

WS-2276   HQ146   94-16168 CIP
Tong, Benson. **Unsubmissive women: Chinese prostitutes in nineteenth-century San Francisco.** Oklahoma, 1994. 300p bibl index afp ISBN 0-8061-2653-1, $24.95

Tong has studied Chinese prostitutes in 19th-century San Francisco by using a social historian's tools, tracing geographical location and socioeconomic conditions. This is possible since prostitution was considered a job and prostitutes declared their profession as did other workers. He finds basic differences between the first half of the century, when the West was in social flux, prostitutes were able to become entrepreneurs, and there was freer competition in the trade, and the second, after the Chinese Exclusion Act, when gangs organized commercial sexual exploitation and government discriminated against Chinese and marginalized prostitutes. Such a book is best when comparative, and Tong's greatest contribution is his comparison of the living conditions of Chinese and Caucasian prostitutes. Caucasian women had more choice in entering their field and were more able to earn enough to buy property. As time went on, women in both groups began to work in nonsexual professions; the age of prostitutes declined over time. (Fewer married Chinese than non-Chinese prostitutes remained in the profession.) Tong sees the Chinese prostitutes as displaying the "powers of the weak," as active, opposing their oppression. This book would have been even more useful had Tong also compared Chinese to other nonwhite women, such as Mexicans. Although the nature of the historical materials of marginalized people tends to make it impossible for the author to control his material, Tong is to be congratulated for using such a wide range of materials to arrive at sensitive conclusions. Both general and academic readers at all levels.—*J. W. Salaff, University of Toronto*

◆ Comparative & International Studies

WS-2277   HQ766   91-6973 CIP
Ahmad, Alia. **Women and fertility in Bangladesh.** Sage, 1991. 184p bibl index ISBN 0-8039-9682-9, $27.50

Social scientists have come to realize that the social and economic status of women and the social roles available to them have extremely important impacts on their fertility aspirations and behavior. Ahmad examines this and related issues in Bangladesh. The combination of extreme, widespread poverty, and deep-rooted patriarchy conspires to severely limit both the status and roles available to women, which, in turn, support the traditional high fertility evident today in Bangladesh. Add to this a national goverment that has been unable or unwilling to alter the objective circumstances of women. Drawing on official Bangladeshi statistics and a series of in-depth interviews with both urban and rural women, the author does a good job of fleshing out the sometimes complicated effects of socioeconomic structure, cultural institutions, and government policies on the reproductive behavior of Bangladeshi women. Ahmad's conclusions are not optimistic; the resource constraints and priorities of the national government make it unlikely that her sensible policy recommendations—which focus on changes in the education, employment, and health spheres—will be implemented any time soon. The few bright spots in this account rest on the actions of such nongovernmental organizations as the Grameen Bank. Demographers and development sociologists and economists will find this study informative. Upper-division undergraduates and above.—*K. Hadden, University of Connecticut*

WS-2278   Orig
Arora, Anand. **The women elite in India.** Radiant, 1991 (c1990). (Dist. by Advent Books) 201p index ISBN 81-7027-154-2, $32.50

As the literacy rate among women in India has risen (from 0.6 per cent in 1901 to 24.88 per cent in 1981) so has occupational mobility among women. Arora's study investigates the problems and predicaments faced by Indian women who occupy decision-making roles in government, education, and medicine. It is based on interview data collected from women working in higher positions in these fields in the states of Haryana and Punjab, and from their male colleagues, including their senior officers and their subordinates. The study concludes that Indian women can handle positions of responsibility and decision-making. However, their minority status in such positions and age-old prejudices still stand in their way and pose problems and difficulties in their careers. Overall, Arora concludes that women in India are on the move. A useful work for students and professional social scientists interested in comparative studies of working women. Upper-division undergraduates and above.—*R. P. Mohan, Auburn University*

WS-2279   Can. CIP
Balakrishnan, T.R. **Family and childbearing in Canada: a demographic analysis,** by T.R. Balakrishnan, Evelyne Lapierre-Adamcyk, and Karol J. Krótki. Toronto, 1993. 329p bibl index afp ISBN 0-8020-2856-X, $60.00; ISBN 0-8020-7356-5 pbk, $19.95

Canada made its first national study of the determinants of fertility behavior in 1984. This accessible (i.e., well written, nontechnical) volume reports the results of that survey. In most respects, the Canadian Fertility Survey resembles similar studies carried out earlier in most other developed nations. It differs primarily in its heavy emphasis on change in the institution of the family as the major determinant of reproductive behavior. A great deal of information was collected—and is reported in this book—about attitudes and behavior concerning cohabitation, marriage, divorce/separation, and intergenerational family relationships. The authors conclude that Canadian women (all respondents were women) are reassessing the centrality of marriage, family, and childbearing. Accordingly, the birth rate has declined and is likely to remain low, as in the US and other developed countries. Contraception and abortion are also discussed at length. Many tables and figures. An excellent addition to collections in demography and sociology. Undergraduates and above.—*K. Hadden, University of Connecticut*

WS-2280   HB1050   91-36547 CIP
Basu, Alaka Malwade. **Culture, the status of women, and demographic behaviour.** Oxford, 1993 (c1992). 265p bibl index ISBN 0-19-828360-1, $49.95

Basu focuses on regional cultures and demonstrates a significant relationship between the status of women and demographic behavior. The author presents empirical evidence from a multicultural slum in the city of Delhi that suggests a close link between culture and fertility, child mortality, and gender differences in physical welfare. Based primarily on qualitative observations and interpretations, Basu's study reveals that women's demographic behavior is influenced by the extent of women's exposure and interaction with the nonfamilial outside world, and the extent of female autonomy in decision making. Basu found important regional cultural differences in fertility-related variables. Throughout her book, Basu stresses the role of economic independence for women as one of the key factors in reducing fertility and increasing gender equality, and concludes with a discussion of some of the policy implications. Well written and well organized, this work makes an important contribution to social demography and women's studies. Advanced undergraduate; graduate; faculty.—*D. A. Chekki, University of Winnipeg*

WS-2281   HQ1465   92-5588 CIP
Behar, Ruth. **Translated woman: crossing the border with Esperanza's story.** Beacon Press, 1993. 372p ISBN 0-8070-7052-1, $25.00

Behar's engaging and insightful work can be read at many different levels. It is, most obviously, a tale of human survival against heavy odds. The subject, Esperanza, is a Mexican market woman. The earlier part of the book details her long life as daughter, wife, and mother, a biography marked by tribulation, pain, and rage. But Esperanza is also an unconventional heroine. Not, in the author's words, "the exemplary feminist heroine for whom Western women are always searching," but rather a person who in the process of self-construction achieves the power to rename and rework the world into which she was born. Behar insists that readers recognize the authority of stories such as Esperanza's, representations that fit neither the stereotype of the long-suffering Latin woman nor the projections of First-World activism. The book also takes readers deep into a cross-cultural encounter, different worlds of class, age, and background—in itself a microcosm of the vexing, complex, interwoven, and contradictory universe that everyone, to some degree, inhabits. Behar, a Cuban American herself caught in the intersection of different systems, has written a valuable and subtle book. General; community college; undergraduate; graduate; faculty.—*O. Pi-Sunyer, University of Massachusetts at Amherst*

WS-2282   HQ1453   95-3611 CIP
Billson, Janet Mancini. **Keepers of the culture: the power of tradition in women's lives.** Lexington Books, 1995. 476p bibl index ISBN 0-02-903512-0, $25.00

Billson interviewed 250 Canadian native, minority, and/or immigrant women for this study of women's attitudes toward themselves and their lives. Seven different cultures—Iroquois, Blood, Inuit, Jamaican, Mennonite, Chinese, and Ukranian—are represented. In two historically oriented sections, Billson sets the scene for the interviews, which are organized into sections titled "Love, Marriage, and Divorce," "Challenges Confronting Women," and "Toward the Twenty-First Century." The final chapters analyze the results of the interviews, ending with comments from interviewees on the book. Appendixes present Billson's methodology. Although Billson employs a feminist sociological philosophy that regards women as oppressed, the book is so solidly based on research that the philosophy does not intrude. In fact, she suggests that her research indicates a wide range of personal and cultural variations in female/male relationships. The scholarship is impeccable. This will become a classic example of the interrelationship of theory, research, and analysis. Extensive chapter bibliographies. All levels.—*M. J. Schneider, University of North Dakota*

WS-2283   H8662   92-20487 CIP
Brochmann, Grete. **Middle East avenue: female migration from Sri Lanka to the Gulf.** Westview, 1993. 199p bibl index afp ISBN 0-8133-8617-9, $38.50

Brochmann's study combines data collected during five months of field work with analyses of secondary national and international data in describing the causes and consequences of Sri Lankan women's migration to the Gulf. Although the use of cross-sectional data means that many of the findings are inferred rather than observed, this book helps to fill a significant gap in previous literature on migration. Early chapters offer an overview of macrosocial (political and economic) forces that provide the context for women's migration, as well as microsocial factors (gender ideology, inequality, and decision making) that both constrain and facilitate women's migration. The process of initiating migration, the legal and economic status of women in Sri Lanka, and women's experience as contracted laborers in the Gulf form the central part of the analysis. Greater use of qualitative data would have enriched this study, particularly in discussions of the motivations and consequences of women's migration for communities, households, and individuals. Nevertheless, this multilevel analysis makes a solid contribution to migration studies, women's labor, and the world economic system. Advanced undergraduates and above.—*S. K. Gallagher, Gordon College*

WS-2284   Can. CIP
Carbert, Louise I. **Agrarian feminism: the politics of Ontario farm women.** Toronto, 1995. 255p bibl index afp ISBN 0-8020-2931-0, $50.00

In *Agrarian Feminism*, Carbert provides a comprehensive analysis of the political force of farm women in one region of Ontario. However, she takes readers far beyond Huron and Grey counties by including an expertly researched framework of national women's agrarian movements, most notably those originating in the West. A discussion of the Women's Institutes, which are predominantly local in orientation, completes her presentation of the context of farm women's involvement in politics. Carbert's empirical analysis is based on in-depth interviews drawing on elements of both political science and sociology. She is particularly interested in the degree to which gender relations within marriage affect farm women's involvement in community organizations. Such involvement is further explored to determine the extent to which it influences political attitudes and political activism. This study, with its multiple levels of analysis, provides very good insight into the diversity of agrarian women's experiences with feminism. It is of particular importance because it allows access to the world of rural farm women, a world that is all too frequently hidden from the view of a predominantly urban society. Upper-division undergraduates and above.—*S. Wurtele, Trent University*

WS-2285   HD6101   90-36942 CIP
Chant, Sylvia. **Women and survival in Mexican cities: perspectives on gender, labour markets, and low-income households.** Manchester, 1991. (Dist. by St. Martin's) 270p bibl index ISBN 0-7190-3443-4, $49.95

Chant examines women's work and household structure among the poor in three of Mexico's fastest growing cities: Leon, a shoe production center; Queretaro, a major manufacturing center; and Puerto Vallarta, a thriving tourist resort. Each of these communities represents an important aspect of the contemporary Mexican economy. Within this context, the author explores the interrelationship between female employment and household organization. Particular emphasis is given to the ways in which female employment and household structure are influenced by local patterns of labor demand. Chant writes a provocative narrative in which she creatively weaves together existing knowledge on the interrelationship between female employment and household structure in Third World economies with her own fact-finding explorations in the three noted Mexican cities. In this manner, Chant provides a comparative view of female employment, not only in Mexico—the setting of her work—but also throughout other Third World nations. The comprehensiveness of her bibliography gives the newcomer a superb resource in further exploring the role of women in a comparative perspective. This book is important not only to those interested in Latin America, but also to those interested in women's issues, sociology, social anthropology, human geography, and the politics and economics of the Third World.—*E. Bastida, University of Texas—Pan American*

WS-2286   Orig
Corrêa, Sonia. **Population and reproductive rights: feminist perspectives from the South,** by Sonia Corrêa with Rebecca Reichmann. Zed Books/Kali for Women/DAWN, 1994. 136p bibl index ISBN 1-85649-283-4, $49.95; ISBN 1-85649-284-2 pbk, $17.50

Written before the 1994 Cairo International Conference on Population and Development, this book revisits a number of issues that gained press attention during that conference. But it differs from other similar treatises on women's right to reproductive self-determination (e.g., Dixon-Mueller 1993) in its discussion of issues such as polygyny, female genital mutilation, and bride price of particular concern to women in southern ("developing") countries. Corrêa reviews fertility management policies dictated by religious and nationalist interests, sketches the history of the women's reproductive rights agenda within the human rights movement, describes southern women's efforts to construct an internationally recognized "framework"—not yet a fully articulated platform—to interpret women's issues within the context of human rights legislation and policy, and calls for a "virtual revolution in prevailing gender systems and development models." This is a concise, readable, well-documented presentation, less strident and more reasonable in tone than some others. Especially timely in view of the forthcoming Fourth International Women's Conference (Beijing, 1995), it will be of particular interest to development specialists and policy makers.—*M. A. Gwynne, SUNY at Stony Brook*

WS-2287   HQ1590   94-25155 CIP
Family, women, and employment in Central-Eastern Europe, ed. by Barbara Łobodzińska. Greenwood, 1995. 315p (Contributions in sociology, 112) bibl index afp ISBN 0-313-29402-X, $65.00

This collection of essays is one of the first to attempt a systematic and statistically grounded examination of the situation of women and the family in the postsocialist states of Bulgaria, the Czech Republic, Slovakia, the former German Democratic Republic, Hungary, Poland, Romania, and former Yugoslavia. Each contributor discusses changes that have occurred in legislation, the economy, social and family services, political participation, employment, income, educational priorities, agriculture, health care, and attitudes. There is much specified detail here that will interest the specialist. However, for those who have been monitoring postsocialist deterioration and disintegration of society, little will seem particularly new or surprising. Moreover, the collection has several drawbacks. The editor and some of the authors appear wedded to archaic "totalitarian" models and hypotheses, and the writing is occasionally turgid and jargon-laden. In addition, the editor fails to reconcile the data on the deteriorating situation of women since 1989 with her hypothesis that the successor states are constantly evolving toward true democracy.

The obvious incongruity between the contributors' data and the editor's theoretical framework makes for a volume that seems at times mired in self-contradiction. Graduate; faculty.—*A. H. Koblitz, Hartwick College*

WS-2288 Orig
Gandhi, Nandita. **The issues at stake: theory and practice in the contemporary women's movement in India,** by Nandita Gandhi and Nandita Shah. Kali for Women, 1992 (c1991). (Dist. by South Asia Books) 347p bibl ISBN 81-85107-22-X, $22.00

In this realistic assessment of the Indian women's movement, Gandhi and Shah—both women—spent a decade of research, participant observation, and extensive travel all over India to cover the grass-roots feminism practiced by a variety of voluntary organizations. Following discussion of the evolutionary phases of the Indian women's movement, the authors deal with sexual harassment, domestic conflicts, organizational dilemmas of centralized versus decentralized structures, predicaments of aligning with conservatives (who are otherwise staunchly opposed to general liberation) against pornography, and foreign funding of indigeneous social movements. Using an activist perspective to demonstrate how women are subjected to the kind of everyday violence men seldom face, Gandhi and Shah also provide a comprehensive analysis of rape and dowry as policy issues in the Indian context. Excellent reading for students of feminism in the Third World. General; advanced undergraduate; graduate; faculty.—*N. N. Kalia, SUNY College at Buffalo*

WS-2289 HQ1742 89-27840 CIP
Gender and the household domain: social and cultural dimensions, ed. by Maithreyi Krishnaraj and Karuna Chanana. Sage, 1990 (c1989). 264p (Women and the household in Asia, 4) index ISBN 0-8039-9635-7, $26.00

A collection of nine papers from a 1985 conference of Indian, Bangladeshi, and American anthropologists and sociologists. Part 1 begins with an introduction by the editors on cultural settings of women's roles; Part 2 with an introduction on aspects of women's health and education. An Ahmedabad study of low-status households confirms the "differential socialization" of boys and girls. From rural Bangladesh comes a report on attitudes toward sex characteristics and clothing of children. An excellent South Indian study describes a small landowning subcaste whose women spend their entire lives within a small fortress; extreme seclusion is considered an "index of caste superiority." Research in 28 villages in Kerala and Tamil Nadu indicates that the degree of women's autonomy varies with class level; lower-class women are severly constrained, but among landowning families women may "control the purse strings" and participate in managing agricultural activities. Part 2 opens with a Punjab study of the higher survival rate of male children, attributed to the "fatal neglect" of female infants. A Bangladesh study shows large differences in health, education, and nutrition of men and women, attributed to negative religious and cultural attitudes toward women. Finally, a vividly detailed report on rural women and childbirth in Bangladesh focuses on problems resulting from the practice of purdah, and offers lengthy case studies of three "barefoot obstetricians." Bibliography for each chapter. Upper-division undergraduates and above.—*W. H. Harlan, Ohio University*

WS-2290 HQ1240 93-50628 CIP
Gender, work & population in sub-Saharan Africa, ed. by Aderanti Adepoju and Christine Oppong. International Labour Office/J. Currey/Heinemann, 1994. 245p bibl index ISBN 0-435-08953-6, $45.00

African women, their work responsibilities, and their reproductive lives are the subjects of this collection. Throughout the 13 chapters, factors such as rural and urban living, education, ethnicity, and religion are considered in relation to reproduction, child nursing, child spacing, and child rearing (including child fostering). All of these variables are weighed against women's work and women's work schedules. The introductory chapter does a good job of presenting the conceptual intricacies of these issues. Unfortunately, there is little indication of who various contributors are: disciplinary backgrounds and work affiliations are not noted for the most part. Several excellent chapters (3-6) show that the overall quality of the available data on African women is poor; the idea of women's work is inadequately conceived, making much of it invisible; and the concept of household has not been appropriately defined and applied consistently. These chapters make

specific suggestions that would rectify such shortcomings and, by so doing, assist in the improvement of agricultural, economic, and family planning policies. Graduate; faculty; professional.—*R. Ellovich, North Carolina State University*

WS-2291 HQ1170 95-4925 CIP
Gerami, Shahin. **Women and fundamentalism: Islam and Christianity.** Garland, 1996. 178p (Women's history and culture, 9) bibl index afp ISBN 0-8153-0663-6, $29.00

Most of the material for this study came from personal interviews conducted by Gerami in her native country of Iran, where women's role has been conditioned by the space they occupy in the first fundamentalist Islamic state. The study consists of six chapters that treat the gender role paradigms that form the basis of her research orientation; the gendered vision of religious fundamentalism; a comparison with American women's stand on the New Christian Right; Egyptian women's response to discourse on fundamentalism; the fundamentalist state and middle-class Iranian women. Gerami concludes with a discussion of Iranian women leaders who spoke to the author and on whose authority she constructed her findings on the family, power, and feminism generally. The study is well illustrated, with some 43 tables providing a quantitative analysis of Gerami's conclusions. An excellent work that contributes significantly to understanding Middle Eastern women's perceptions of their role in the interlocking relationship between state, faith, and family. Should be must reading for all students of women's issues. Upper-division undergraduates and above.—*C. E. Farah, University of Minnesota*

WS-2292 HV8023 92-25902 CIP
Heidensohn, Frances. **Women in control?: the role of women in law enforcement.** Oxford, 1993 (c1992). 283p bibl index ISBN 0-19-825255-2, $52.00

Heidensohn's book is the first in-depth, comparative study of women and law enforcement in Britain and the US. The book examines women's role in the control of crime and disorder. It is based on a series of open-ended interviews with British and US policewomen and explores their experiences in dealing with crime, vice, and everyday incidents, as well as dealing with the hostility and harassment of their male colleagues. This study not only highlights women's role in law enforcement in two societies but also analyzes the importance of gender in social control. Although the primary focus here is on British policewomen, the book is nevertheless very valuable for interested American readers. Heidensohn's study is the most significant work about policewomen since Susan E. Martin's *On The Move: The Status of Women in Policing* (1990) and Patricia Lunneborg's *Women Police Officers: Current Career Profiles* (1989). Heidensohn (Univ. of London) has made an important contribution to the literature on women in policing. Good bibliography. Advanced undergraduate; graduate; faculty; professional.—*P. Horne, Mercer County Community College*

WS-2293 HQ1236 93-12 CIP
Heitlinger, Alena. **Women's equality, demography and public policies: a comparative perspective.** Macmillan, UK/St. Martin's, 1993. 383p bibl index ISBN 0-312-09638-0, $69.95

As some developed countries fall below replacement-level fertility (2.1 children per woman) and others approach it, voices of concern, if not alarm, have been raised. The specters of a declining population and labor force, a shrinking domestic consumer market, and, especially, an aging population are at the heart of such concerns. When national interests are seen to be threatened by such trends, immigration is one potential response. Although Heitlinger considers immigration, her major purpose is to explore the establishment of governmental policies that would simultaneously encourage fertility and enhance women's equality. Because of the seeming incompatiblilities between motherhood (and, to a lesser degree, fatherhood) and career, much of the discussion focuses on work-related issues: high-quality, affordable childcare; flexible working hours, maternal or family leave; and gender equality in pay. The real strength of this book lies in its thorough discussion of all of these issues and more, in Canada, Britain, and Australia; US and international situations are also occasionally discussed. Because of the emphasis on governmental structures and policies and on the organization of women's rights movements in these three countries, this work may be of limited interest to Americans. It is, however, recommended to students and scholars with an interest in the sociology of work and of the family and in comparative women's studies. Advanced undergraduates and above.—*K. Hadden, University of Connecticut*

WS-2294   HQ1233   93-28018 CIP

Identity politics and women: cultural reassertions and feminisms in international perspective, ed. by Valentine M. Moghadam. Westview, 1994. 458p index afp ISBN 0-8133-8691-8, $59.00; ISBN 0-8133-8692-6 pbk, $17.95

Contributors to this volume discuss cultural reassertions—primarily religious fundamentalisms—and women's identities and activism. The first section considers world economic change, historic precedents for women's collective action, and movements for religious and ethnic identity. The second section consists of case studies of country and regional identity politics, with heavy emphasis on Islamic fundamentalism, but including Orthodox Judaism, Hinduism in India, Zionism, and the US New Right. The case studies suffer from uneven writing, but nevertheless provide valuable materials for understanding relationships between ethnic and gender identities. The third section presents contradictory impulses and strategies for change, closing with a statement by the UN Division for the Advancement of Women on the necessity of bringing international laws, and through them religious codes, into accord with UN declarations for equality. The statement notes that religious fundamentalism does not necessarily violate UN principles, but its current manifestations do not provide equality in education, employment, and legal protection for women. Advanced undergraduates and above.—*J. L. Croissant, Rensselaer Polytechnic Institute*

WS-2295   Orig

International migration policies and the status of female migrants: proceedings of the United Nations Expert Group Meeting on International Migration Policies and the Status of Female Migrants, San Miniato, Italy, 28-31 March 1990, [prep.] by the Department for Economic and Social Information and Policy Analysis, Population Division. United Nations, 1995. 300p bibl ISBN 92-1-151281-6 pbk, $35.00

Given the scant attention to females in the literature, one would not guess that almost half of all international migrants are women. Their economic roles have also been underrated. All too often female migrants are viewed—especially by national migration and employment policies—as mere dependents of men. As a result of these and other factors, female migrants are often discriminated against, segregated, and isolated. In spite of these negative features, growing numbers of women are turning to international migration as a means of improving their status and their life chances. These and many other issues confronting female migrants are addressed in this report. The volume consists of the report and recommendations of the meeting, along with a selection of 16 papers presented, which make up most of the volume. A few of the papers are sufficiently general to be of broad interest to demographers, women's studies specialists, and migration and employment policy makers. Most, however, include so much detail that they are likely to interest only a rather narrow group of scholars.—*K. Hadden, University of Connecticut*

WS-2296   HQ1762   92-24871 CIP

Iwao, Sumiko. The Japanese woman: traditional image and changing reality. Free Press, 1993. 304p index ISBN 0-02-932315-0, $24.95

Iwao's interesting overview of middle-class women's place in Japanese society might be subtitled "women trying to redefine their roles," or "the quiet revolution." Iwao's treatment of marriage distinguishes generational change and unmarried from married women, and traces the changes to women's views over the life cycle. Iwao describes women's and men's attitudes and behavior in sweeping terms. Because much of the data come from surveys by others, as well as from articles in the press and popular magazines, she cannot do subtle cross tabulations. This leaves many important sociological questions unanswered; there is also a lack of depth in the case studies of the women cited because of the secondary analysis of material. Iwao sees an incremental alteration in women's roles, to which men, and ultimately the system, will respond. A fascinating chapter on women activists describes women joining the "Daily Life Party," part of the "citizen's movement." Iwao expects that ground swells like these will ultimately increase women's participation and lead to the feminization of work and politics. General; undergraduate; community college; professional.—*J. W. Salaff, University of Toronto*

WS-2297   HQ18   94-49589 CIP

Kon, Igor S. **The sexual revolution in Russia: from the age of the czars to today,** tr. by James Riordan. Free Press, 1995. 337p index ISBN 0-02-917541-0, $25.00

Sociologist Igor Kon was one of the first Soviet scholars to turn his attention to questions of sexual practice. As Kon puts it, "since the mid-1960s, I have been the organizer of or a participant in virtually all Soviet undertakings concerned with the study of gender and sexuality, as well as functioning as the most important conduit of information about Western research and ideas on these subjects for my country. Thus, my memory, for all its shortcomings, is perhaps a better source of information about Soviet sex research than any journalistic report." Kon is in no sense being immodest here. His personal reminiscences and horror stories about the sorry state of Soviet and post-Soviet sexology will fascinate general readers as well as specialists in Slavic studies and sexuality research. The book contains an annoying number of typographical errors, and the translation in parts is awkward or misleading. There are far too many footnotes and academic digressions for the work to be easily understood by nonspecialists, and historical sections are too disorganized and sketchy to satisfy scholars. Moreover, Kon underplays the violence and misogyny of most post-Soviet erotica and pornography. Nevertheless, this is an important attempt to chronicle the history of sexuality in the USSR and the post-Soviet successor states. A valuable addition to any library.—*A. H. Koblitz, Hartwick College*

WS-2298   HQ759   91-36797 CIP

Leira, Arnlaug. **Welfare states and working mothers: the Scandinavian experience.** Cambridge, 1992. 200p bibl index ISBN 0-521-41720-1, $54.95

In this timely theoretical and empirical study Leira, a Norwegian researcher, makes significant contributions to the understanding of Scandinavian child-care policies and economic policies relative to the employment of women. Leira compares and contrasts child-care policies in Norway, Sweden, and Denmark. Her comprehensive analysis dispels the widely held belief that these three countries have similar approaches to social welfare policies concerning the needs of women in the work force. Rather, she shows that in Norway, where mothers have been slower to join the labor market, there are important differences, the most significant of which is that Norway did not actively create policies to support the employment of mothers. The author examines this fact and offers several hypotheses as explanation. She further considers the strategies that employed Norwegian mothers developed to meet their child-care needs and shows how these mothers, through everyday practices, are reconstructing the role of motherhood in postwar Norwegian society. Advanced undergraduate; graduate; professional.—*F.J. Vecchiolla, Springfield College*

WS-2299   HQ1793.29.C35   90-2435 CIP

Macleod, Arlene Elowe. **Accommodating protest: working women, the new veiling, and change in Cairo.** Columbia, 1990 (c1991). 206p bibl index afp ISBN 0-231-07280-5, $32.00

Women in the Muslim World, ed. by Lois Beck and Nikki Keddie (CH, Mar'79), broke new ground and laid a foundation for Islamic women's studies. Scholars like Macleod have built on this foundation. Macleod shows Cairo as seen through the eyes of "lower-class women" as they leave the traditional household to enter the new work force and cope with a society in the process of radical change. Basing her work on a close association with 28 lower-middle-class households and on informal interviews with about 60 working women, Macleod describes, often in their own words, the lives of these women. She articulates their predicament, caught as they are between traditional values, which a working life has forced them to question (and often abandon), and modern, secular values, which still seem alien to them. Their story is told with critical sympathy and understanding, qualities that enable Macleod to challenge Western stereotypes of relations between men and women in the Muslim world. She observes that Islam "is the language in which all social encounters are conducted." This book will fascinate anyone the least interested in working women and social change, especially in the Third World. All levels.—*F. Ahmad, University of Massachusetts at Boston*

WS-2300   HQ76   92-6309 CIP

Miller, Neil. **Out in the world: gay and lesbian life from Buenos Aires to Bangkok.** Random House, 1992. 365p ISBN 0-679-40241-1, $22.00

Miller's previous book, *In Search of Gay America* (1989), won the 1990 ALA prize for lesbian and gay nonfiction. This new book is Miller's journalistic description of the homosexual people he met while traveling in 13 countries around the globe. Although he did not visit any truly isolated societies, the places he did go to were sufficiently off the Euramerican beaten track to qualify as decidedly culturally different from the locations usually portrayed by sociology texts that depict homosexualty. Further, the common sexual behaviors and societal responses in those places were also quite often unlike those as interpreted by ethnocentric Western theories. For example, in China, Japan, Thailand, and Egypt, many men have sex with other men, but the Euroamerican concept of a "gay identity" is virtually nonexistent. Miller's observations generally support a social construction theory of gay identity as arising, in some societies, from a more basic panhuman, omnisexual biological matrix when the societies have achieved four conditions: personal freedom and social tolerance; sufficient economic development to allow independence and social mobility; relatively high status for women; and a decline in the power of those family or religious institutions that define and limit every facet of one's life. All levels.—*R. W. Smith, California State University, Northridge*

WS-2301   DS432   92-22147 CIP
Minturn, Leigh. **Sita's daughters: coming out of purdah: the Rajput women of Khalapur revisited,** by Leigh Minturn with Swaran Kapoor. Oxford, 1993. 371p bibl indexes afp ISBN 0-19-507823-3, $45.00; ISBN 0-19-508035-1 pbk, $19.95

Minturn has provided a comprehensive description of the social changes in Khalapur, India, from 1955 to 1975. If the focus were merely on changes in women's attire, the title would be somewhat misleading. But as the author clearly demonstrates, purdah is more than a behavior or fashion: it includes a set of beliefs about women's sexual nature, a set of attitudes about appropriate behavior for women, and a set of perceptions about the social consequences of not following tradition. Purdah is based on religious and social prescriptions that include the lifelong cloistering of women to the extent that wives' faces often are unknown to their spouses. The value of this work is that it traces the social processes that have led to a decline in the numbers of men who want or expect wives to practice purdah. Minturn also describes the consequences of its decline for social relationships between wives and mothers-in-law, wives and brothers, wives and husbands, and wives and other women. Education as well as modern technological advances in agriculture and the transformation of the Indian economy (from a barter to a cash economy) are the antecedents of purdah's decline. It becomes clear that laws in support of women's right to own land or in opposition to dowry payments and practices as *sita* are less effective as change agents than education. Advanced undergraduate and above.—*A. S. Oakes, Idaho State University*

WS-2302   HQ1745   90-19387 CIP
Mitter, Sara S. **Dharma's daughters: contemporary Indian women and Hindu culture.** Rutgers, 1991. 198p bibl index ISBN 0-8135-1677-3, $32.00; ISBN 0-8135-1678-1 pbk, $12.95

Indian women experience constant readjustment to the forces of modernity in order to maintain continuity in traditional values, customs, traditions, and roles. This is the subject matter of Mitter's book, which debunks some of the myths surrounding the status and role of women in Indian society. Mitter's work is based on her many visits to India and a year's stay in the metropolis of Bombay, the site for this study. As a participant-observer, she sketches detailed portraits of the lives of urban women, ranging from construction crew laborers to middle-and upper-middle class women. Mitter explains the plight of Indian women caught between the forces of tradition and modernity and shows how religious mythology allows for the incorporation of and adjustment to alien and unorthodox ideas. This book is an interesting addition to the literature on the status of women in a Third World patriarchial society. Upper-division undergraduates and above.—*R. P. Mohan, Auburn University*

WS-2303   HQ1525   94-24809 MARC
Reddock, Rhoda E. **Women, labour & politics in Trinidad & Tobago: a history.** Zed Books, 1994. 346p bibl index ISBN 1-85649-153-6, $60.00; ISBN 1-85649-154-4 pbk, $25.00

This thoroughly researched and clearly written study of women in colonial

Trinidad and Tobago between the early 19th century and 1962 focuses on the women's work and political activities. Reddock's historical sociology reveals new information and also deepens understanding of broader social dynamics. The division of labor by gender and ethnicity during the periods of slavery and indentureship, the colonial ideology of "women's place," and the politics of sex, race, and class provide the essential background for the analysis of women's role in the labor movement and nationalist politics. Women's contributions to social change differed because, despite their common gender, they were divided by race and class. Thus, middle-class African women were more involved in social work and politics than their Indian counterparts, while working-class Indian and African women participated in labor organizations. However, in this patriarchal society, trade unions and political parties were dominated by men, most of whom were middle-class. Many works cited are omitted from the bibliography, but this is essential reading for Caribbean and women's studies, along with Olive Senior's *Working Miracles* (CH, Sep'92) and Janet Momsen's *Women & Change in the Caribbean* (CH, Apr'94). Upper-division undergraduates and up.—*O. N. Bolland, Colgate University*

WS-2304   HN350   94-8488 MARC
Scott, Alison MacEwen. **Divisions and solidarities: gender, class and employment in Latin America.** Routledge, 1994. 265p bibl index ISBN 0-415-01849-8, $59.95; ISBN 0-415-01850-1 pbk, $18.95

Latin American specialists will welcome this empirical study of social and occupational mobility in Peru during the 1970s, a period of rapid industrialization in that country. Several features distinguish this fine work. First, Scott has made substantial use of existing social theory to frame her empirical analysis. The review of theories that apply to social processes in Third World countries is itself reason enough to read the book, but there is more! The author uses detailed economic data from the 1940, 1961, and 1972 Peruvian censuses, along with 172 case studies, to revise current theory while adding substantially to the understanding of how class and gender interact in systems of inequality. In particular, Scott argues for a reformulation of the concept of class to include subjective as well as objective experiences. Finally, this work is one of the few that treats women's and men's experiences in formal as well as informal economic sectors. As a result, many conventional assumptions about the nature and consequences of work in the informal sector are challenged and found either to be incorrect or imprecise for Peru. Upper-division undergraduates and above.—*A. S. Oakes, Idaho State University*

WS-2305   HQ16   94-36929 CIP
Sexy bodies: the strange carnalities of feminism, ed. by Elizabeth Grosz and Elspeth Probyn. Routledge, 1995. 303p bibl index ISBN 0-415-09802-5, $59.95; ISBN 0-415-09803-3 pbk, $17.95

A daringly experimental entry in the latest phase of sexuality studies, this collection makes no claims of unity or coherence among its eclectic contents. Avoiding a stable definition of "sex," the editors (whose previous work includes Grosz's *Volatile Bodies*, CH, Feb'94, and Probyn's *Sexing the Self*, CH, Dec'93) argue that "sex, and for that matter queer, could function as *verbs* rather than as *nouns* or adjectives.... They could be fully conceived as activities and processes, rather than objects or impulses, as movements rather than identities." Accordingly, the 15 essays in the collection—written by scholars and creative writers in Australia, the UK, Canada, and the US—explore "what is fundamentally weird and strange about all bodies, all carnalities," both heterosexual and gay. The interdisciplinary essays draw on literature, cultural studies, critical theory, psychoanalysis, postcolonial and antiracist studies, history, queer theory, and feminist theory. Containing pieces by writers as different as Angela Davis, Nicole Brossard, and Sabina Sawhney, the book represents an important step toward opening up a dialogue between feminist theory and queer theory. A significant addition to any research collection.—*R. R. Warhol, University of Vermont*

WS-2306   HQ1728   94-32264 CIP
Sharoni, Simona. **Gender and the Israeli-Palestinian conflict: the politics of women's resistance.** Syracuse, 1995. 199p bibl index afp ISBN 0-8156-2643-6, $29.95; ISBN 0-8156-0299-5 pbk, $14.95

Sharoni, an Israeli feminist, peace activist, and academic, analyzes how gender permeates and is unrecognized in the hostility between Palestinians and

Israelis and discusses how gender informs resistance. Her study includes 19 photographs of negotiators, demonstrators, professionals, etc., effectively illustrating gender issues. Themes are treated in a balanced way, leading to an examination of cooperation between women on both sides. On the other hand, Sharoni does not presume a symmetry between the groups. She is innovative in showing connections between the struggle for peace and the struggle for gender equality within each group, and she is bold in demonstrating how the peace accord was based on negotiations among men. Her book suffers, however, from repetition and from occasional sweeping arguments based on a small set of examples. Although timely, the book deals primarily with the period 1987-93. Clearly much has changed in the Middle East since then; gender relations, however, have changed very little. General readers; upper-division undergraduates and above.—*S. Reinharz, Brandeis University*

WS-2307   HQ1075   93-6923 CIP
Sunder Rajan, Rajeswari. **Real and imagined women: gender, culture and postcolonialism.** Routledge, 1994 (c1993). 153p index ISBN 0-415-08503-9, $59.95; ISBN 0-415-08504-7 pbk, $16.95

A dominant state, highly stratified social structures, and severe conflicts between tradition and modernity serve as the backdrop for Sunder Rajan's six essays on gender in India today. Through a content analysis of Indian media advertisements, and Indian as well as non-Indian films and fiction, Sunder Rajan uncovers the taboos that reinforce socially sanctioned violence against women to answer such questions as: How do the cultural mechanics of gender-appropriate silence justify the killing of females as fetuses and young brides? Why do so many women give the kind of death-bed testimony that enables their husbands and their families to remain unpunished even when they clearly drove these women to suicide or murdered them? How can one explain the rise and acceptance of Indira Gandhi as a leader in a predominately patriarchal culture? To interpret the subtexts of self and society Sunder Rajan goes beyond the sensationalist portrayal of suttee to explore the issues involved in grassroots protests by the women's groups at local levels. The author also investigates the subjectivity of body in pain in suttee experienced as a woman burning alive, rather than focusing on the finality of death. Sunder Rajan excels in presenting complex ideas in a lucid style. Valuable to both the professional and the general student of feminist theory. Excellent footnotes.—*N. N. Kalia, SUNY College at Buffalo*

WS-2308   HQ1206   92-890 CIP
Veeder, Nancy W. **Women's decision-making: common themes . . . Irish voices.** Praeger, 1992. 159p bibl index afp ISBN 0-275-94354-2, $42.95

The experiences of three generations of women from Northern Ireland, including 22 women aged 65 and over, their 40 daughters, and 38 granddaughters, provide the evidential base for this book on female decision-making and authority in the family. Veeder, an American, initiated the project, developed the questionnaire, and analyzed the results. The study was carried through by Northern Irish students, who assembled the snowballing sample of respondents from among their relatives and friends and conducted the hour-long interviews. The descriptive material selected by Veeder confirms that this group of women has often made decisions even while appearing not to, that family welfare was a primary concern for them, and that their actions empowered them in subtle ways. The same passages also indicate that the respondents have generally had a narrow range of options and poor control over outcomes. Because Veeder takes an essentialist view of female personality structure, she is less interested in power differentials within and among families than in showing how commonalities in the component elements of women's decision-making articulate with a distinct female style in the conduct of interpersonal relations. Undergraduate; community college; preprofessional.—*N. B. Rosenthal, SUNY College at Old Westbury*

◆ Gender, Sexuality

WS-2309   KJC8377   93-44510 CIP
Abortion in the new Europe: a comparative handbook, ed. by Bill Rolston and Anna Eggert. Greenwood, 1994. 312p bibl index afp ISBN 0-313-28723-6, $75.00

The struggle over abortion rights in the US and the changing politics of the former communist nations of Eastern Europe make this collection an extremely valuable source of information for anyone interested in current politics and women's rights. Essays cover the present laws and political climate of most European countries, from the most restrictive (Ireland and Portugal) to the most liberal (Sweden, the Netherlands, and the Czech Republic.) Except for Ireland and Portugal, abortion rights are generally accepted in Europe. In fact, the problem in many Eastern European nations is that lack of sex education and contraception makes abortion the major form of birth control. On the other hand, because of its extensive contraceptive education, the Netherlands, which has the most liberal laws, also has the lowest proportion of abortions in Europe. Essays also demonstrate that when abortion is restricted, women travel to countries with more liberal laws. Thus "abortion tourism" flourishes in Ireland and now in Poland, where laws are becoming less liberal. Although religious and right-wing forces express their opposition to abortion in many countries, nowhere is there the extremism (and violence) that one finds in the US—a comparison to ponder. All levels.—*J. Wishnia, SUNY at Stony Brook*

WS-2310   HQ1206   89-46322 Aust. CIP
Bacchi, Carol Lee. **Same difference: feminism and sexual difference.** Allen & Unwin, 1991 (c1990). (Dist. by Paul & Company, c/o PCS Data Processing, Inc., 360 West 31 St., New York, NY 10001) 330p bibl index ISBN 0-04-442152-4 pbk, $19.95

Bacchi combines a richly detailed review of the debates within feminism with a revealing inventory of actual policies and judicial rulings to evaluate the sociopolitical and cultural costs of how women are perceived. Are they the same as or different from men? She argues convincingly that this ubiquitous question invariably masks the more significant policy issues. Her illustrations of the ways in which vision is impaired by the sameness/difference framework include debates about maternity benefits, wages, occupational health, affirmative action, rape, divorce, pornography, and even the essence of womanhood. Bacchi draws on British, American, and Australian developments to demonstrate that socially responsible and inclusive policies are associated with and may depend on escaping the limits of sameness/difference thinking. The writing is at times tedious and may deter the novice, but the thoroughness of this research will satisfy any reader with a serious interest in gender studies. The extensive bibliography and well organized index make this book a particularly valuable resource. College, university, and public libraries.—*R. Zingraff, Meredith College*

WS-2311   HQ117   94-27897 CIP
Barry, Kathleen. **The prostitution of sexuality.** New York University, 1995. 381p index afp ISBN 0-8147-1217-7, $24.95

Barry's work is courageous, insightful, and disturbing. Not simply a book about prostitution, Barry's study significantly challenges the taken-for-granted understanding of sexual relations between males and females (highlighting the personal as political) as well as the general comprehension of "consent," "forced," and "free" sexual relations. Barry broadly defines sexual exploitation as "a practice by which person(s) achieve sexual gratification, or financial gain, or advancement, through the abuse of a person's sexuality by abrogating that person's human right(s) ...." In international coverage of sexual exploitation she uses both macro- and microsociological approaches to show how sexual exploitation becomes "normalized" in societies through industrialization of sex, trafficking, pimping, and patriarchal laws. Barry carefully distinguishes among prohibitionist, (neo)regulationist, and abolitionist movements and also illuminates the centrality of men's patriarchal role in sexual exploitation and the processes of transforming women into objectified, sexed bodies. The dearth of social support for eliminating sexual exploitation of women (even in the UN) and for providing women with economic alternatives is disheartening. However, Barry discusses some grassroots groups organized to address the commodification of women. Upper-division undergraduates and above.—*G. Rundblad, Illinois Wesleyan University*

WS-2312   HQ111   93-5447 CIP
Bell, Shannon. **Reading, writing, and rewriting the prostitute body.**
Indiana, 1994. 229p bibl index afp ISBN 0-253-31166-7, $35.00; ISBN 0-253-20859-9 pbk, $12.95

Bell's work is a postmodernist study of the prostitute, more specifically, the prostitute's body. Bell argues that, in the ancient world, prostitutes "produced discourses" on prostitution. Over the past 2,000 years, however, such discourses have been suppressed and marginalized. Bell points out that in the modern West, prostitution has been associated with sickness and perversion; in the ancient world, it had a sacred and healing function. Bell takes it as her task to construct a "genealogy" of the prostitute body that will "disturb, destabilize, and undermine" the "philosophical foundations" of the Western world. She attempts this through examining ancient texts written by prostitutes, using "the presence of postmodern prostitute discourse," and by exploring (and taking part in) "performance art" relating to women's—and men's—bodies. In her study, Bell makes an absolutely crucial point: the exchange of sex for pay "has no inherent meaning" and is "signified differently in different discourses." On the other hand, she exaggerates the centrality of prostitution to female gender roles and the importance of postmodernism specifically, and intellectual academic discourse generally, to society, culture, and political life. Graduate; faculty.—*E. Goode, SUNY at Stony Brook*

WS-2313   HQ77   92-32030 CIP
Bullough, Vern L. **Cross dressing, sex, and gender,** by Vern L. Bullough and Bonnie Bullough. Pennsylvania, 1993. 382p index ISBN 0-8122-3163-5, $51.95; ISBN 0-8122-1431-5 pbk, $16.95

In this informative book, the Bulloughs introduce the multiple forms transvestitism and cross-gendered behavior have taken historically and cross-culturally, as well as the wide variation in meanings these activities have had. The authors' findings show that traditionally, female transvestites have come from the lower social classes and have dressed as men to gain access to more powerful social positions. Conversely, men have cross-dressed for what have been considered "erotic" reasons deriving from psychopathological drives. Unlike female cross-dressers, male transvestites have tended to come from the upper classes. In effect, the status loss inevitably brought about by taking on a female appearance has been mediated for these men by membership in the highest social echelons. The authors' work also examines the medicalization of transvestitism, which explains cross-dressing as originating from traumatic childhood experiences, the organization of heterosexual transvestitism beginning in the 1950s, and the research focusing on this movement and its membership. All levels.—*D. Gimlin, SUNY at Stony Brook*

WS-2314   HQ76   92-8622 CIP
Cruikshank, Margaret. **The gay and lesbian liberation movement.** Routledge, 1992. 225p bibl index afp ISBN 0-415-90647-4, $49.95; ISBN 0-415-90648-2 pbk, $14.95

Cruikshank approaches her "personal interpretation" of the gay and lesbian liberation movement as a sexual liberation movement, a political movement, and a movement of ideas. She uses these perspectives to trace the historical roots of the movement, to elaborate on its successes and failures, and to provide some insights into its possible future development. Charting the history of the gay and lesbian liberation movement is not an easy task given both the movement's struggles against an array of external forces and conflicts within its own ranks. Cruikshank does not shy away from either front; she documents the attack on lesbians and gays and also delineates the difficulties inherent in a multiracial, multicultural movement comprising women and men. Although one can applaud Cruikshank for her efforts to bring the gay and lesbian liberation movement into focus, the book often reads like a text. Her attempt to illuminate so much complex history results in oversimplification and an occasionally pedantic tone. In addition, Cruikshank's obvious admiration for San Francisco as the capital of gay/lesbian life serves to diminish the contributions of other regions. In spite of these reservations, the book is highly recommended. General; undergraduate.—*E. Broidy, University of California, Irvine*

WS-2315   HQ1075.5U6   90-43381 CIP
Gender differences: their impact on public policy, ed. by Mary Lou Kendrigan. Greenwood, 1991. 249p (Contributions in women's studies, 121) bibl index afp ISBN 0-313-24875-3, $42.95

Kendrigan's previous book, *Political Equality in a Democratic Society* (CH, Sep'84) urges policy analysts to assess gender inequality by measuring outcomes. This idea holds that a system is gender fair if the results, not the opportunities, are equitable. These essays by professors of social work, and sociology, political scientists, and policy analysts in private practice, plus an introduction and conclusion by Kendrigan, continue her argument for "equality of results." The chapters concern compensation for crime victims (women are undercompensated), various forms of job loss (women are disadvantaged because of family responsibilities), job training programs, taxation, tourism policy (women are trivialized), veterans' benefits, and the role of care-taker (women are expected to be care-takers). Invidious sexism permeates these policies and institutions in a way that renders ineffective the good intentions of individuals to avoid institutional sexism and racism. Essays both display hidden forces that promote gender inequality and suggest ways to remedy the situation. Endnotes, abstracts, select bibliography, integrated subject/author index, and identifying information for each contributor. Upper-division undergraduates and above.—*S. Reinharz, Brandeis University*

WS-2316   HV6250   94-3057 CIP
Graham, Dee L.R. **Loving to survive: sexual terror, men's violence, and women's lives,** by Dee L.R. Graham with Edna I. Rawlings and Roberta K. Rigsby. New York University, 1994. 321p bibl index afp ISBN 0-8147-3058-2, $24.95

Graham and her coauthors have written either a completely biased analysis of the destructiveness of male domination or one of the most provocative analyses of this subject to date. Beginning with the example of the "Stockholm syndrome" (a situation in which hostages adopted the viewpoint of their captors), the authors provide illuminating connections among this syndrome, the causes of feminine behavior, and the concept and development of heterosexuality. The authors' strengths include a tightly knit feminist perspective on sexual terror, men's violence, and women's lives coupled with rich coverage of current feminist research on these topics. Because the research is so well documented and the discussion is so provocative, this reviewer believes the lack of contrary research on the feminist position advanced throughout this volume to be only a minor weakness. Like Susan Brownmiller's groundbreaking *Against Our Will: Men, Women and Rape* (CH, Feb'76), this book is essential reading for scholars and undergraduate and graduate students of gender and sexuality, feminist theory, and social psychology.—*P. J. Venturelli, Valparaiso University*

WS-2317   HQ76   92-417933 CIP
Herdt, Gilbert. **Children of horizons: how gay and lesbian teens are leading a new way out of the closet,** by Gilbert Herdt and Andrew Boxer. Beacon Press, 1993. 290p index ISBN 0-8070-7928-6, $25.00

An interesting addition to the growing body of literature on lesbian and gay experience. *Children of Horizons* examines "coming out" both as an individual decision and as a more complicated process of becoming part of a larger community. The book focuses on "youth" (as they are consistently, and sometimes annoyingly, labeled throughout the text) participating in adult-facilitated support groups run through a Chicago lesbian and gay community services center. Herdt and Boxer spent two years meeting with facilitators, interviewing the "youth," and observing a wide range of social and support functions at the center. Although certain key issues such as race would have benefited from a more critical analysis, Herdt and Boxer present a unique perspective on the complex set of social relations that face all young people. The lesbian and gay youth studied here experience many of the same conflicts as their straight classmates; however, their homosexuality necessitates an even more self-reflective look at questions of identity and community. Recommended for any academic library supporting sociology, women's studies, or a lesbian and gay studies program.—*E. Broidy, University of California, Irvine*

WS-2318   HQ1075   91-2396 CIP
Jeffreys, Sheila. **Anticlimax: a feminist perspective on the sexual revolution.** New York University, 1991 (c1990). 359p bibl index ISBN 0-8147-4179-7, $40.00; ISBN 0-8147-4180-0 pbk, $11.95

Jeffreys is an English lesbian who argues vigorously that everything in the sexual revolution—from Kinsey, to Masters and Johnson, to transsexual surgery—is designed to keep women powerless. She asserts that sex therapists who said it is all right for wives to have orgasms are part of a male conspiracy to keep women defenseless. It is also a plot to say it is okay for unmarried women to have sex. Claims that noncoital positions are acceptable are also part of the conspiracy. Women who founded women's groups have been duped; gay males are in complicity. Pornography (apparently even pictures of solitary naked men, designed for homosexual males) is always antifemale. Even many lesbian-feminists have been fooled. Jeffreys argues that sexual behavior, as presently socially constructed, necessitates dominance and submission, with the sole intention of keeping women helpless both in and out of the bedroom. She selects passages from various sex writers that support her case. Good bibliography and index. Undergraduate level.—*R. W. Smith, California State University, Northridge*

WS-2319 HQ125 92-43845 CIP
Jenness, Valerie. **Making it work: the prostitutes' rights movement in perspective.** Aldine de Gruyter, 1993. 150p bibl index afp ISBN 0-202-30463-9, $37.95; ISBN 0-202-30464-7 pbk, $17.95

Jenness constructs an interesting account of the evolution of the National Task Force on Prostitution, also known as COYOTE (Call Off Your Old Tired Ethics), the most visible organization in the prostitutes' rights movement. Using archival and interview data, she documents the moral, legal, feminist, and medical debates that shaped the organization's claims-making activities across a 20-year period. Her findings demonstrate how changes in the dominant arena of social problems discourse framed and altered COYOTE's efforts to disclaim its deviant status and redefine prostitution as a legitimate work occupation. On a more theoretical level, Jenness shows how the social constructionist framework can be used to connect the study of social movements with the normalization of deviance. The book contains a useful bibliography and is well written, although it occasionally lapses into academic jargon. Upper-division undergraduates, graduate students, and professionals interested in such topics as social movements, deviance, sexuality, women's studies, and the sociology of culture should find the research interesting and useful. Recommended.—*J. Lynxwiler, University of Central Florida*

WS-2320 HQ1075 93-31479 CIP
Kipnis, Aaron. **Gender war, gender peace: the quest for love and justice between women and men,** by Aaron Kipnis and Elizabeth Herron. W. Morrow, 1994. 300p bibl index ISBN 0-688-11924-7, $23.00

In this work Kipnis and Herron examine the roots of gender division and conflict, offer techniques for healing the anger and hurt men and women feel toward each other, and suggest a reconstruction of contemporary gender relations. *Gender War, Gender Peace* offers these insights while recounting the story of a camping trip attended by a group interested in building integration, empathy, and interdependence between men and women. Within this context, the authors discuss group members' personal experiences of gender conflict and connection; at the same time they make reference to theoretical work dealing with these issues. In addition, the authors emphasize the importance of both ancient and contemporary images of masculinity and femininity and point out the ways in which cultural symbols influence individuals' enactment of gender in everyday life. As part of the healing process suggested here, the authors urge a reconsideration and reformation of idealized notions of gender, and recommend that men and women make an effort to form gender partnerships and gender peace. General readers.—*D. Gimlin, SUNY at Stony Brook*

WS-2321 HQ29 94-6378 CIP
McCormick, Naomi B. **Sexual salvation: affirming women's sexual rights and pleasures.** Praeger, 1994. 284p bibl index afp ISBN 0-275-94359-3, $22.95

Feminist sex researcher, educator, and psychotherapist, McCormick attempts to reconcile the contrasting views of radical and liberal feminists on the nature of women's sexual experience. She examines the changing nature of women's sexual scripts, not only for the narrow range of women covered by much popular media but also for the culturally diverse, older women, lesbians, and bisexuals. Differences in how men and women deal with intimacy and love are explored. In her chapter on prostitution, she recognizes sexual slavery but also investigates the economic and personal issues that lead some women to choose prostitution as an occupation. The chapter on sexual victimization provides some

special insights into sexually coercive males and the sexual victimization of women while finding aspects of pornography that are of value to women's sexual experiences. A successful attempt to integrate information based on research with more adversarial feminist literature to arrive at a more objective appreciation of women's sexuality. General; upper-division undergraduate; graduate; professional.—*W. P. Anderson, University of Missouri—Columbia*

WS-2322 HQ27 90-20580 CIP
Nathanson, Constance A. **Dangerous passage: the social control of sexuality in women's adolescence.** Temple University, 1991. 286p bibl index afp ISBN 0-87722-824-8, $34.95

Written by a population specialist at Johns Hopkins, this provocative monograph examines attempts to control the sexual behavior of female adolescents from the 19th century through the 1980s. Nathanson's concern is more with the ideology that underlies various policies than with the policies themselves. A central thesis is that there has been a fundamental transformation in the conceptualization of adolescent female sexual behavior. Formerly construed as something having the potential to interfere with the orderly transition from the role of daughter to those of wife and mother, adolescent sexuality is now perceived as something that may create problems in regard to a woman's economic independence, e.g., becoming a single mother on AFDC. The roots of this problem have also been redefined as emphasis has shifted from moral, to political, to medical, to economic analyses. Irrespective of their ideology, however, reformers have been much more willing to blame "the failings of individuals rather than the inadequacies of social institutions." Nathanson explores the motivation of all those involved in the creation of policy. For example, both feminists and conservative politicians are seen as having their own agendas that may come into conflict with the larger interests of sexually active young women. Of interest to social policy analysts as well as to students of adolescent sexual behavior. Graduate level.—*M. Gordon, University of Connecticut*

WS-2323 Can. CIP
Ross, Becki L. **The house that Jill built: a lesbian nation in formation.** Toronto, 1995. 357p bibl index afp ISBN 0-8020-0460-1, $50.00; ISBN 0-8020-7479-0 pbk, $19.95

Lesbian studies has been interpreted largely through an American lens. Although Ross's book adds considerably to the expanding horizons of lesbian studies, her most significant contribution is in her focus on Canada, specifically Toronto, as a site of important lesbian activity. After setting some historical context for an emerging Canadian lesbian and gay rights movement in the early 1970s (and, in the process, describing a range of tensions that made organizing around issues of sexuality both difficult and painful), Ross turns her attention to LOOT, the Lesbian Organization of Toronto. Although LOOT existed as an organization for less than four years, its ambitious program to provide a wide range of social, cultural, and political services to Toronto's lesbian community, coupled with the fact that its short life coincided with some of the most bitterly contested debates in both the gay liberation and feminist movements, makes it an important topic for a community study. Drawing on a variety of sources, including interviews with key members of the group, Ross paints a vivid picture of life in a prominent sector of the Toronto lesbian universe. Some of the book is slow going, but it is well worth the effort, both for the story it relates about one specific community and as a significant contribution to international lesbian studies. All levels.—*E. Broidy, University of California, Irvine*

WS-2324 HQ767 92-33303 CIP
Sachdev, Paul. **Sex, abortion and unmarried women.** Greenwood, 1993. 321p (Contributions in womens studies, 133) bibl index afp ISBN 0-313-24071-X, $49.95

Sachdev reports the findings of a study of 70 volunteer unmarried Canadian women between the ages of 18 and 25, who had a first pregnancy terminated by abortion during the year prior to the study. The author, a professor of social work at Memorial University, interviewed the women and explored their sexual histories, their experience with contraception, the decision to abort, the abortion itself, and its aftermath. The findings are reported in straightforward fashion and their policy implications are discussed. Sachdev provides a useful review of abortion legislation in Canada and the US. Although he concludes that "serious psychological reactions to abortions are low and transient," he feels that emphasis should be placed on the development and provision of improved contraceptive technology. This book will be of most interest to specialists in the field of family planning.—*M. Gordon, University of Connecticut*

WS-2325   HQ1403   89-32594 CIP
The Sexual liberals and the attack on feminism, ed. by Dorchen Leidholdt and Janice G. Raymond. Pergamon, 1990. 244p indexes afp ISBN 0-08-037458-1, $35.00; ISBN 0-08-037457-3, $16.95

Articles in this genuinely revolutionary collection began mostly as presentations to a 1987 conference on sexual liberalism, defined as the politicized view that sexual expression is natural and essentially liberating, even if it includes exploitation of women. Contributors take issue with this perspective on male and female sexuality. They provide reasoned arguments that modern sexuality, however "liberal and free," is socially constructed and reflects society's patriarchal values, including the degradation of women. Contributors consist of leading feminist writers and thinkers, including Catharine A. MacKinnon (*Sexual Harassment of Working Women*, 1979), Sheila Jeffreys, Phyllis Chesler, Andrea Dworkin, and John Stoltenberg (*Refusing to Be a Man*, CH, Dec'89). Many controversial issues are dissected, such as pornography, abstention from marital and other intercourse, homosexuality, lesbianism, pedophilia, and autoeroticism. The most basic argument is with those civil libertarians, including most (male) leaders of the ACLU, who defend the pornographers' degradation and exploitation of women in the name of free speech. These authors radically disagree, posing the cogent and well-articulated argument that protecting pornographers in the name of free speech itself violates the much more fundamental right of women to nonexploitation and gender equality, to protection from sexual subordination through pictures and words, through sexual traffic in women such as prostitution, and through male sexual violence. This collection should be purchased by all libraries.— *J. R. Feagin, University of Florida*

WS-2326   Orig
Siann, Gerda. **Gender, sex and sexuality: contemporary psychological perspectives.** Taylor & Francis, 1994. 200p (Contemporary psychology series, 9) bibl index ISBN 0-7484-0185-7, $75.00; ISBN 0-7484-0186-5 pbk, $24.95

Siann solidly overviews historical, theoretical, and empirical work on gender, sex, and sexuality. She manages to touch on most of the relevant psychological, cultural, anthropological, and sociological issues in a mere 177 pages. The seven chapters cover much ground: (1) definitions of gender, sexuality, sex, and sexual orientation; (2) an overview of psychoanalytic views; (3) biological determinants of sex and sexual orientation; (4) developmental research and prominent developmental theories, such as gender schema theory; (5) evidence of sex differences; (6) feminism and status issues; and (7) gender stereotypes and the impact of stereotypes on gender-differentiated behavior, including violence. Siann's scholarship and balanced presentation of earlier work is evident throughout these chapters. Her book will find its greatest utility as an excellent overview source to guide readers to original source materials. Despite a high price for a volume its size, this book is well worth reading. Undergraduate and graduate students, practitioners, professionals, and researchers.—*A. C. Downs, formerly, University of Houston—Clear Lake*

WS-2327   HQ767   95-19055 CIP
Simonds, Wendy. **Abortion at work: ideology and practice in a feminist clinic.** Rutgers, 1996. 262p bibl index afp ISBN 0-8135-2244-7, $48.00; ISBN 0-8135-2245-5 pbk, $16.95

Simonds observed and interviewed workers at a feminist clinic, 1990-1992, asking the question "how do feminist ideals translate (or not translate) into the daily routines of health care provision," i.e., client care and the way in which health care workers interact. Her analysis shows how women who provide abortions think about them ("Feminists Working"); her analysis of the environment in which abortion is provided ("Working Feminism") helps readers understand women's choices in a new way. Workers handled feelings about late-term abortions (defending a woman's right to define viability) by rejecting the medicalized model of "pro-choice" advocates and by placing women's choices in a context of constraining social forces that "anti-abortion" advocates fail to recognize. Providing an empathetic but balanced portrayal and analysis of interviewees' responses, Simonds

also draws on the theory and research of other sociologists to help interpret her data. Her analysis addresses why value-free approaches to the position of "pro-choice" and "antiabortion" make the ideal of anti-abortion tenable; how to define a feminist health care practice and distinguish it from traditional medical practice; how a feminist defense of abortion should be constructed; where feminism and bureaucracy can coexist; how conflicts among feminists indicated the intransigence of racism, and the demise of collectivism in a feminist community. An excellent resource for those interested in abortion and in the women's health care movement, the book's insights and applicability go well beyond the important question of providing health care to women. All levels.—*M. M. Denny, St. Joseph College*

WS-2328   HQ1426   90-52587 CIP
Uncertain terms: negotiating gender in American culture, ed. by Faye Ginsburg & Anna Lowenhaupt Tsing. Beacon Press, 1990. (Dist. by Farrar, Straus, Giroux) 338p ISBN 0-8070-4612-4, $24.95

This collection begins with an intriguing section challenging the idea that there is a common female experience. Articles by Katie Stewart, Carol Gilligan, Rayna Rapp, and Carol Stack (author of *All Our Kin*, CH, Sep'74) reject the white middle-class standard of feminism and explore how race, ethnicity, and class differentiate women's experiences. A section with contributions by Faye Ginsburg, Susan Harding, Carole Vance, Judith Stacey, and Elizabeth Gerard explores the impact that feminist thinking and New Right thinking have had on each other. A third section, with essays by Kath Weston, Cynthia Saltzman, Sandra Morgan, and Patricia Fernandez Kelley, examines the relationships among the modern workplace and productivity, female solidarity, and family commitments. The fourth section, with articles by Ellen Lewin, Joyce Canaan, Suzanne Carothers, and Riv-Ellen Prell, examines stereotypes and the everyday lives of women. A final section, with articles by Sharon Thompson, Irma McClaurin-Allen, Emily Martin, and Anna Tsing, looks at the construction of women's responses to a variety of marginal situations, including teenage mothering and suicide. Although too diverse to describe in a short review (and its disconnectedness is a weakness), this volume is an important addition to the literature on the status and experience of women in US society. Perhaps most important is the serious attention given to racial, ethnic, and class differences in the ways women experience and respond to sexism. It would have been improved however, by an overview for the uninitiated reader offering a road map through the various issues considered. Chapter notes. Upper-division undergraduates and above.—*J. R. Feagin, University of Florida*

WS-2329   HQ29   93-20712 CIP
Wyatt, Gail Elizabeth. **Sexual abuse and consensual sex: women's developmental patterns and outcomes,** by Gail Elizabeth Wyatt, Michael D. Newcomb, and Monika H. Riederle. Sage Publications, CA, 1993. 250p bibl indexes ISBN 0-8039-4733-X, $24.95

A team of psychologists supervised a telephone interview survey of 248 women—126 African Americans and 122 European Americans—age 18 to 36, residing in Los Angeles county, concerning their sexual lives past and present. The results are presented in what the authors refer to as a "Structual Equation Model" (or SEM) Analysis. Perhaps the most crucial finding of this study is that "childhood sexual victimization had a significant impact on women's sexual behaviors throughout the life course." Women who had been subject to the most severe abuse—whether by a family or a nonfamily member—especially a number of times over an extended period of time, were as adults more likely to become the victims of rape and to have multiple sexual partners. They were also likely to engage in sexual behaviors that exposed them to the risk of contracting sexually transmitted diseases, including HIV and unwanted pregnancy. Implications of the findings are discussed; the authors recommend developing "a climate of sexual health in the home." This book is not a pleasant reading experience. It is highly technical and quantitative, and is therefore recommended only to a small number of professionals.—*E. Goode, SUNY at Stony Brook*

◆ Marriage & the Family

WS-2330   HQ76   93-37935 CIP
Andrews, Nancy. **Family: a portrait of gay and lesbian America.**
Harper San Francisco, 1994. unpaged afp ISBN 0-06-250011-2 pbk,
$25.00

Stereotypes about lesbians and gay men abound. Three of those most frequently uttered characterize homosexuals as Caucasian; unable to sustain long-
term relationships; and found only in large urban areas. In this compilation of por
traits of the real gay and lesbian America, Andrews has shattered every single one
of these stereotypes. The photographs and accompanying text (part author introduction to the subjects of the photographs, part the words of the lesbians and
gay men themselves) portray an amazingly rich and diverse cross-section of the
US. Andrews photographed and interviewed lesbian Elvis impersonators, HIV/AIDS
activists, grandmothers, muralists, poets, rodeo riders, Holocaust survivors, and
government officials, to name but a few. The Americans in this book come
from many different regions of the country and represent a vast array of racial, ethnic, and class backgrounds. Although some people have been photographed alone,
others are shown with partners, children, parents, pets. Herein lies this book's
greatest strength. Andrews is saying something more profound than "we are family." She has documented the far more complex and meaningful reality that lesbians and gay men have family, in all the complicated ways one might define
that term. Strongly recommended for college, university, and public libraries.—
E. Broidy, University of California, Irvine

WS-2331   HQ778   92-50388 CIP
Berry, Mary Frances. **The politics of parenthood: child care,
women's rights, and the myth of the good mother.** Viking, 1993.
303p bibl index ISBN 0-670-83705-9, $22.50

The idealized "traditional" family in which mothers have primary responsibility for children is a modern invention, more fiction than fact. It is, however,
a view of women's roles and responsibilities that persists despite unprecedented
rates of labor force participation among mothers and the widely acknowledged
stress they bear in fulfilling their dual roles as parents and employees. In this book,
historian and lawyer Berry (Univ. of Pennsylvania) argues persuasively that fathers
and mothers must be, and be seen as, equally responsible for child care. Anything
less deprives women of equal opportunities and undermines child care assistance strategies aimed at helping parents balance work and family roles. Berry
shows how and why the earlier tradition of fathers as primary caregivers gradually gave way to that of mother care. Later chapters provide an incisive analysis of sociopolitical forces and events that have shaped current child care and family policy, and lay out an agenda for change based on challenging existing gender
relations and patriarchy. Highly recommended for policymakers, advocates,
and scholars in family and related studies, as well as for the informed general
reader.—*B. A. Pine, University of Connecticut*

WS-2332   HQ75   92-53818 CIP
Burke, Phyllis. **Family values: two moms and their son.** Random
House, 1993. 233p ISBN 0-679-42188-2, $21.00

Both heterosexuals and homosexuals can benefit from reading Burke's compelling narrative of her own lesbian family. She portrays their experience with
great integrity and, at times, an almost painful honesty that conveys the idea
that "the personal is political." Her use of irony and humor makes the telling of
this story fresh and illuminating. Burke describes the process and feelings involved
in her partner's decision to give birth, with all its legal, social, and psychological dimensions. The stages of pregnancy, birth, and early months of life are
discussed in highly personal terms, as well as the role of a support group of
other pregnant lesbian women and their partners. Burke discusses the obstacles
she faced in a procedure, eventually successful, to adopt at age three the son whom
she had come to love long before his birth to her partner. She relates the daily joys
and chores of parenthood in a manner that any parent will find poignant and
recognizable. This book also includes a penetrating analysis of the activist gay
and lesbian community in San Francisco during 1990-92. Burke writes vividly
about important demonstrations in 1991 against the making of the film *Basic
Instinct* in that city. Activists sought to alter the negative and violent portrayal
of lesbians in that film. Fair-minded people will be informed and enriched by read-

ing this fine book. The absence of an index and bibliography is regrettable but
understandable, given the book's narrative purpose. All levels.—*S. H. Hildahl,
Wells College*

WS-2333   HQ759   93-34798 CIP
Burns, Ailsa. **Mother-headed families and why they have increased,** by Ailsa Burns and Cath Scott. L. Erlbaum, 1994. 217p bibl
indexes afp ISBN 0-8058-1440-X, $49.95

Burns and Scott (Macquarie Univ., Australia) review the literature on mother-
headed families and then propose an explanation for this phenomenon, which they
call the decomplementary view. Nations surveyed in their study include the US,
Sweden, the former Soviet Union, and Japan. The first four chapters describe
trends in mother-headed families and briefly discuss the historical, social, and economic contexts within which changes occurred. Chapters six through eight treat
existing theories of such households, e.g., biosocial theories, selected demographic
arguments, and feminist views. In contrast to these theories, the authors offer their
"decomplementary view," which states that men and women have lost much of
their social reasons for being together. Given that women now are able to earn
wages, contraceptive methods reduce the chances of accidental pregnancy, unmarried motherhood is socially tolerated, and welfare services provide a safety net
in emergencies, women are now able to avoid marriage and its inegalitarian
domestic roles. Although not identical to the feminist perspective, the decomplementary argument is compatible with basic feminist premises and represents
an expansion of the ideology advising female independence from the traditional
institution of marriage. General readers; undergraduates.—*T. E. Steahr, University of Connecticut*

WS-2334   HQ800   90-26212 CIP
Chandler, Joan. **Women without husbands: an exploration of the
margins of marriage.** St. Martin's, 1991. 178p bibl ISBN 0-312-06107-
2, $29.95

Written by a British sociologist, this book surveys information about women
in five different relationships to husbands: women who are widowed, divorced,
separated, who have absent husbands, or who cohabit. Taken together, the author
considers women in these groups to be on the "margins of marriage" rather than
"not married." This is because the institution of marriage is so strong in Western societies that the lives of these women outside of conventional marriage are
influenced by marriage itself. Therefore, Chandler claims that there should not be
a "legally sharp divide between those women who are married and those who
are not." Although this is an interesting idea, the author does not provide fresh
research but, rather, reiterates the work of others. The writing is somewhat
tedious and quite repetitious. (In this reviewer's copy of the book, the bibliography ended with the letter M, indicating an error in the book production.)—
S. Reinharz, Brandeis University

WS-2335   HQ535   91-59009 CIP
Coontz, Stephanie. **The way we never were: American families
and the nostalgia trap.** Basic Books, 1992. 391p index ISBN 0-465-
00135-1, $27.00

Coontz attempts to debunk "white, middle-class myths," or stereotypes,
about families of the past and present. Her main objective is to reduce what she
perceives as anger and guilt that today's family members experience as they try
to live up to stereotypes of the perfect "Leave It to Beaver" family. Coontz's
assumption seems to be that today's families are burdened by legacies of families that have accepted and have perpetuated the stereotypes foisted onto the
public. The 11 chapters deal with various family-life issues from a historical social
perspective. There are good documentation and endnotes for each chapter. The
book is weakened by its allegiance—sometimes strident—to feminist dogma (especially in Chapter 7). In view of Coontz's stated objectives and political overtones,
her work will probably help those people who have fairly liberal views about family life and can easily accept alternative lifestyles. The historical vignettes are
interesting and, though geared to prove Coontz's points, are still informative. Adequate subject index. General; advanced undergraduate.—*R.C. Myers, Central
Washington University*

WS-2336 HD6055 91-11815 CIP
Dinnerstein, Myra. **Women between two worlds: midlife reflections on work and family.** Temple University, 1992. 223p bibl index afp ISBN 0-87722-884-1, $34.95; ISBN 0-87722-885-X pbk, $16.95

People born between the late 1930s and early '40s were a transitional generation; their lives were affected by broad changes in women's paid work opportunities and in gender ideologies. This case study of 22 middle-class women describes differences: some were traditional college students, others were nontraditionalists; some adapted well to being homemakers with children, others felt stuck and suffered depression; some persuaded their husbands and children to share responsibilities, others capitulated to their families' demands. But they shared a common dilemma: when they chose to depart from the ideal stay-at-home-and-reproduce-babies role, it was solely up to them—on their own—to devise strategies and techniques to make it all work. Having decided to combine families and careers, these women were guaranteed success by their social and economic advantages. In a real sense, they had it all. They attended college, married, had children, stayed home for a time, and then resumed careers either by increasing their credentials or by simply re-entering the job market. Although the women in this study do not reflect the experiences of women of all colors and social classes, their stories of advantaged lives indicate that social change has not been as revolutionary as one would like to believe. General and undergraduate readers.—*A. S. Oakes, Idaho State University*

WS-2337 HQ1075 93-51060 CIP
Fraad, Harriet. **Bringing it all back home: class, gender and power in the modern household,** by Harriet Fraad, Stephen Resnick, and Richard Wolff. Pluto, 1994. 172p bibl index ISBN 0-7453-0707-8, $66.50

In this work, Fraad, Resnick, and Wolff present a compelling application of Marxist/feminist theory to issues of class (i.e., where surplus labor is produced, appropriated, and distributed) and gender (i.e., differentiated meanings regarding sex) processes from within the household. Their discussion of how gender and class depend on and continually change one another in the household is very clear and detailed. The authors also provide two "application" chapters, one of which treats the influence of the Reagan-Bush years on the household. The other chapter, which addresses anorexia nervosa, is more loosely connected to their theoretical foundation but is still quite valuable. The real gem of this book, however, is the chapter dedicated to critiques of the authors' scheme by Stephanie Coontz, Zillah Eisenstein, Nancy Folbre, Heidi Hartmann, Julie Matthaei, and Kim Lane Scheppele, and the authors' responses to their critiques. This is academic work at its best, enabling readers a rare opportunity to witness the give and take of scholarship. Graduate; faculty.—*G. Rundblad, Illinois Wesleyan University*

WS-2338 HQ759 95-2998 CIP
Gabor, Andrea. **Einstein's wife: work and marriage in the lives of five great twentieth-century women.** Viking, 1995. 341p bibl index afp ISBN 0-670-84210-9, $22.95

Einstein's Wife (the title is misleading) is actually the story of the careers and marriages of not one but five successful 20th-century women. The subjects of this book—Mileva Maric Einstein, Lee Krasner, Maria Goeppert Mayer, Denise Scott Brown, and Sandra Day O'Connor—were chosen because they all had enduring marriages (two of them were even happy) as well as significant accomplishments in their respective fields: science, art, physics, architecture, and jurisprudence. Gabor makes the point that despite the wide differences in their backgrounds and interests, they all accepted marriage as the defining aspect of their lives, and each measured her own success as a person not primarily by her career achievement but by her marriage. In addition, all of them encountered prejudice in the workplace, and all of them felt the tension between their work aspirations and their home aspirations; their husbands had to contend with no such obstacles. Nonetheless, these women all made significant contributions in their fields. This book is extremely well researched and contains copious notes and an excellent index. It is also very interesting reading with much personal detail—a real contribution to the field of gender studies. General; undergraduate through professional.—*M. H. Chaplin, Wellesley College*

WS-2339 HQ536 91-15452 CIP
Goldscheider, Frances K. **New families, no families?: the transformation of the American home,** by Frances K. Goldscheider and Linda J. Waite. California, 1991. 303p bibl index afp ISBN 0-520-07222-7, $34.95

Based on the National Longitudinal Survey data, this book examines the process of social change, focusing on the effects of marriage and divorce on the family. In the context of the development of egalitarian gender roles, the authors ask whether trends in nonmarriage, nonparenthood, and divorce are leading to a future of "no families" or whether the family can become a sharing partnership thereby forming "new families." The book is a systematic assessment of family patterns that have emerged in the 1970s and 1980s as a result of increased employment of women, divorce, nonfamily living, and declining fertility. Detailed analyses of marriage, parenthood, divorce, the division of household labor, husbands' and children's share in household tasks, and the role of husbands, wives, and children in the domestic economy are provided. Family differences by race, region, and community size are also indicated. In light of broader social and demographic processes that affect the family, future trends, e.g., an increasing number of dual career families and alternative families, are projected. Highly recommended.—*D. A. Chekki, University of Winnipeg*

WS-2340 Aust. CIP
Goodnow, Jacqueline J. **Men, women, and household work,** by Jacqueline J. Goodnow and Jennifer M. Bowes. Oxford, 1994. 224p bibl index ISBN 0-19-553572-3 pbk, $19.95

Goodnow and Bowes studied the division of household work among a nonrandom sample of 50 heterosexual Australian couples who were identified as "couples who did things differently, ... not following the conventional pattern of men's work, women's work." The authors categorize four styles of sharing housework: adopting a nonstereotyped speciality; doing most jobs on a fluid basis; eliminating jobs from the list; and assigning jobs on the basis of the principle "to each their own." Couples negotiate the division of housework either "with few words" or with open discussion. Issues of fairness and the importance of maintaining a good relationship are the most important goals for sharing that these couples express. Time availability, competence, preferences, and standards are also examined. Regarding outside influences, the majority of the couples say they have different patterns than their parents; and women respondents are more likely than men to cite the influence of friends and the women's movement. The high degree of detail and its list-like generalizations do not make this book a good choice for undergraduates; however, the attention it provides to the negotiation process as well as the meanings attached to sharing and the goals motivating it will be of interest to specialists in family and gender. Graduate; faculty; professional.—*J. Wilkie, University of Connecticut*

WS-2341 HQ1410 92-3421 CIP
Johnston, Carolyn. **Sexual power: feminism and the family in America.** Alabama, 1992. 413p bibl index afp ISBN 0-8173-0583-1, $36.95

According to Johnston, the perspective that informs her study of American feminism from the Colonial period to the 1990s insists that American women have been empowered by being wives and mothers. She does not deny a measure of entrapment by stereotypical roles, but prefers to stress empowerment, derived either through authority explicitly granted women in specific roles or through the contrast between that putative authority and the available means to exercise such authority. This, rather than victimization, lies at the roots of feminism. She argues that family issues have been crucial since the beginnings of American feminism. The ideas are not novel, but in any event, stating a thesis, even repeating it at intervals, does not prove it. Johnston asserts and discusses, but her discussion is usually description (not always with a fine eye) rather than careful argument. Johnston provides a discriminating bibliographic essay and a helpful bibliography, but these do not rescue this book. Libraries striving for comprehensive collections in women's history will buy this title. Those forced to be more selective should pass it up for more penetrating and interesting analyses of American feminism.—*A. Graebner, The College of St. Catherine*

WS-2342　　　　HQ75　　　　92-54977 CIP
Lewin, Ellen. **Lesbian mothers: accounts of gender in American culture.** Cornell, 1993. 233p bibl index afp ISBN 0-8014-2857-2, $34.95; ISBN 0-8014-8099-X pbk, $13.95

Are lesbian mothers significantly different from heterosexual mothers? Through 135 in-depth interviews with lesbian and straight women, the author answers no. Lewin contends motherhood supersedes sexuality. Although single mothers acquire greater autonomy, they struggle with economic insufficiency, tenuous ties with the children's fathers, and conflicts with friends, extended families, and employers. Social support systems are crucial for both groups. According to Lewin, lesbian mothers differ from heterosexuals only in three areas: motherhood is more intentional and rebellious; staying closeted is frequently necessary to maintain child custody and jobs; and there are higher and frequently unfulfilled expectations of their partners. This is an interesting study that demonstrates the centrality of motherhood, stressing the extent to which individuals negotiate reality. The book is clearly written. It downplays, however, the unique experiences of lesbian mothers and their offspring. Lewin also underestimates the substantial changes in family behavior in the US. Recommended. General; undergraduate.—*S. D. Borchert, Lake Erie College*

WS-2343　　　　HQ536　　　　95-3336 CIP
Mackey, Richard A. **Lasting marriages: men and women growing together,** by Richard A. Mackey and Bernard A. O'Brien. Praeger, 1995. 185p bibl index afp ISBN 0-275-95075-1, $55.00

Mackey and O'Brien interviewed 120 nonclinical respondents who had experienced long-term marriages. They used a qualitative, phenomenological approach based on grounded theory to examine marital adjustment and marital satisfaction. The study's greatest contribution is the insight it provides into individual subjective evaluations of the marital experience by African American, Mexican American, and Jewish couples, which made up more than one-half of the sample (about 70 percent). The primary focus was on the effect of gender difference on marriage, but Mackey and O'Brien also considered differences among racial, religious, and socioeconomic groups. The authors selected from the data issues that affected the longevity of the marriages, such as intimacy, decision making, parenting, conflict, and marital satisfaction. Unfortunately, there was no in-depth discussion of some complex issues. The reviews of the existing literature that prefaced most chapters were painfully brief, and in almost every chapter, the authors either failed to explain or simply abbreviated their discussion of how their findings fit into the literature. In these times of austere library budgets, this book is too expensive for what it offers.—*R.C. Myers, Central Washington University*

WS-2344　　　　HQ755　　　　95-5761 CIP
Mahony, Rhona. **Kidding ourselves: breadwinning, babies, and bargaining power.** Basic Books, 1995. 277p bibl index ISBN 0-465-08593-8, $23.00

Arguing that sexual division of labor in the home is the key to understanding gender inequality, Mahony successfully employs an exchange model to explain intrafamilial negotiations over who will perform child care and chores. Rich in examples, sophisticated in analysis, theoretically eclectic, this book is a must read for anyone concerned with the social conditions that make for the inequities of everyday life. Although the book could stand alone as a clear, nontechnical application of sociological and economic theory to a fundamental problem, it is doubly useful for the provocative solutions proposed by the author to battles raging in homes across the country. Changes in social policy are discussed, but Mahony places more emphasis on exhorting women to marry men of lower status, train in professions that pay high wages, and relinquish claims to child rearing expertise, allowing their spouses "solo time" with the baby. This, she optimistically concludes, will lead to enough stay-at-home dads to tip cultural norms in the direction of the disestablishment of the home-mother connection. Libraries at all levels.—*K. M. Daley-McKinley, Cabrini College*

WS-2345　　　　HQ777　　　　94-19995 CIP
McLanahan, Sara. **Growing up with a single parent: what hurts, what helps,** by Sara McLanahan and Gary Sandefur. Harvard, 1994. 196p index afp ISBN 0-674-36407-4, $19.95

McLanahan (Princeton) and Sandefur (Univ. of Wisconsin—Madison) doc-

ument the negative impacts of growing up with a single parent. Working with four large existing surveys, they compare children from single-parent families with children from intact biological families on four measures predicting degree of adult success: high school graduation, entrance into and graduation from college, steady employment, and early unwed motherhood. Their analysis finds that compared with youth from intact families, young adults living apart from birth parents (including never married, widowed, divorced, or remarried parents) are twice as likely to drop out of high school or become single parents and one and half times as likely to be unemployed. Further analysis demonstrates that single-parent families have less income, less parental involvement and supervision, and less "social capital"—defined as community connection and support. The concluding chapter of this short, clearly written book suggests sensible policy directions for the support of single-parent families by noncustodial parents, governments, and communities. A strength of this book is the clarity of the analysis in easily understood bar graphs and charts. Highly recommended for undergraduate libraries; accessible to general readers; useful to professionals.—*M. E. Elwell, Salisbury State University*

WS-2346　　　　HQ759　　　　95-16209 CIP
McMahon, Martha. **Engendering motherhood: identity and self-transformation in women's lives.** Guilford, 1995. 324p bibl index afp ISBN 1-57230-002-7, $32.50

Drawing on and extending the symbolic interactionist perspective on identity, McMahon argues for the character-transforming and engendering effects of mothering. Using data from interviews with 31 middle-class and 28 working-class employed Toronto women with preschoolers, she skillfully weaves the mothers' words with a sophisticated social-psychological analysis. McMahon equally adeptly integrates structuralist concerns with power and inequality with interactionists' attention to identity and meanings. She claims that the gendered effects of women's mothering maintain gender inequalities, yet her data reveal that women speaking for themselves define mothering as morally transformative. She resolves this contradiction by privileging the meanings women give to their lives, yet maintaining an awareness of the impact of class and life situation. She offers a true sociological challenge to the much more psychologically based work on gender identity. In McMahon's model, women give birth, then behave in ways they interpret as transformative, drawing on culturally available models of connectedness and responsibility. In so acting, they redefine themselves as "better" women. This is a book to be read for its contribution to sociological theories of gender and family. Recommended for graduate students and professionals.—*K. M. McKinley, Cabrini College*

WS-2347　　　　HQ759　　　　92-17494 CIP
Miller, Naomi. **Single parents by choice: a growing trend in family life.** Insight Books, 1992. (Dist. by Plenum) 239p index ISBN 0-306-44321-X, $24.95

Miller focuses on well-educated, financially stable single women who choose to become biological parents or to raise children. She explores briefly subtopics such as single, transracial, international, agency, and independent adoptions and presents a short overview of parents who adopt infants, older children, and handicapped children. Divorced parents and their childrens' perspectives are treated, as are those of gay and lesbian parents. Miller also includes some comparisons with Sweden, Britain, and Israel. The author's purpose is to raise the potential for considering single parenthood normative. Conclusions drawn from existing studies, along with interviewees' statements concerning their decisions, are well done, enjoyable, and easy reading. This reviewer is unaware of any recent book that combines the many subtypes of single parenting and adoption with clinical sensitivity and clear writing style. As sociologist David Popenoe writes on the cover, "While it is too early for major findings, [Miller] carefully describes the lay of the land and does the work necessary for future research." General; undergraduate; community college; preprofessional.—*Y. Peterson, Saint Xavier College*

WS-2348　　　　HQ759　　　　91-21509 CIP
Nice, Vivien E. **Mothers and daughters: the distortion of a relationship.** St. Martin's, 1992. 258p bibl index ISBN 0-312-06764-X, $35.00

In this book, a British social worker, feminist, and mother/daughter offers a passionate defense of motherhood, taking on the psychoanalytic establishment and its tendency to identify mothers and mothering as the source of problems for both children and adults. Nice sets her polemic in the context of a literature review. Surveying both the psychoanalytic literature and feminist accounts of relations between mothers and daughters, the author takes the position that psychoanalytic theory, at base misogynist, distorts the character of motherhood and of mothering relations. Her book focuses on motherhood as "a developmental process," and is centered around what might be called "the mother's view," examining the mother-daughter relation in terms of its potential for offering "the basis of supportive, affiliative growth for women." The combination of substantive review and critical perspective that this book presents makes it ideal for undergraduate courses in women's studies. Also, the book is well and clearly written, despite the limitations of the survey style. The book has one minor flaw (but to this reviewer, irritating and perhaps revealing): a consistent misspelling of Nancy Chodorow's name throughout. All levels.—*N. B. Rosenthal, SUNY College at Old Westbury*

WS-2349 HQ759 93-44717 CIP
Ragoné, Helena. **Surrogate motherhood: conception in the heart.** Westview, 1994. 215p bibl index afp ISBN 0-8133-1978-1, $55.00; ISBN 0-8133-1979-X pbk, $17.95

Ragoné has made one of the first systematic studies of surrogate motherhood. Formal interviews with surrogate mother program directors, surrogate mothers, and commissioning couples (fathers and adoptive mothers) provide a context for understanding the complex interrelationships among the parties involved in the surrogate process. The scope of this investigation is broad and includes an examination of open and closed surrogate mother programs, surrogates' and couples' motivations for selecting surrogacy, and the influence of surrogacy on conventional notions of kinship and family. The author provides an insightful critical analysis of surrogate motherhood as a nontraditional means of achieving the traditional goals of parenthood and family. Strategies such as developing social bonds between the surrogate mother and adoptive mother, emphasizing social motherhood over biological motherhood, and creating a sense of shared pregnancy between both mothers normalize surrogacy. Included in this book is an interesting collection of appendixes with examples of biographical sketches of surrogate mothers, contracts, surrogate mother and couple application forms, and semen specimen instructions. A valuable addition to current knowledge on kinship and family. All levels.—*L. Heuser, Willamette University*

WS-2350 94-68659 Orig
Ribbens, Jane. **Mothers and their children: a feminist sociology of childrearing.** Sage Publications, CA, 1995 (c1994). 236p bibl index ISBN 0-8039-8834-6, $65.00; ISBN 0-8039-8835-4 pbk, $19.95

Deconstruction of the "malestream" interpretation of childrearing is well underway. Ribbens contributes to this effort through the generation of typologies based on an interpretation of the meanings mothers give to their experience of childrearing. Critiquing the value judgments implicit in psychological conceptions of the "good mother" and the sociological tendency to see family as effect rather than cause, Ribbens sets out to construct a framework for a feminist sociology of childrearing. This edifice is built upon an analysis of what 24 white, middleclass mothers, living outside London, have to say about how they bring up children. The structure imposed on this data gives rise to a typology of perspectives on children (natural innocents, little devils, or small people), of maternal responses (adaptive, directive, or negotiative), of central preoccupations (time, control, and independence), and of ways mothers mediate between the boundaries of public and private worlds (weak or strong boundaries crossed with high or low assertiveness). Though the empirical data is not able to support such a construction, there is no doubt that Ribbens raises important theoretical issues that should be considered by those working for a sociology of childrearing. Upperdivision undergraduates and above.—*K. M. Daley-McKinley, Cabrini College*

WS-2351 HQ834 89-36065 MARC
Riessman, Catherine Kohler. **Divorce talk: women and men make sense of personal relationships.** Rutgers, 1990. 276p index ISBN 0-8135-1502-5, $37.00; ISBN 0-8135-1503-3, $13.00

Divorce is the outcome of nearly one half of marriages in the US today; it is therefore important to understand how divorces occur. Riessman's book contributes to that understanding through the use of special techniques developed by sociologists who study language and narratives. Riessman carefully studied what people say and how they say it. This approach enabled her to see that divorced men and women mourn different dreams, and that they no longer feel attached to those dreams. As a result, "the divorced say it isn't all bad." The numerous transcripts in this book help readers to interpret the author's data. Although she deals with individual lives, the overall focus of her work is on general social psychological principles and their combined social effect. A 5-page preface gives the author's background; the book concludes with 37 pages of notes, 7-page combined author/subject index, and an important 9-page methodological appendix. General and undergraduate readership.—*S. Reinharz, Brandeis University*

WS-2352 HQ611 91-32062 MARC
Seccombe, Wally. **A millennium of family change: feudalism to capitalism in Northwestern Europe.** Verso, 1992. (Dist. by Routledge, Chapman & Hall) 343p bibl index ISBN 0-86091-332-5, $59.95

Seccombe challenges Peter Laslett's paradigm of the nuclear family structure as prevalent in northwestern Europe from pre-industrial times through the transition to industrial capitalism. This work of historical sociology employs Marxist analysis that is bolstered by feminist critiques of "malestream" scholarship. Seccombe combines a clear theoretical perspective with a synthesis of numerous studies in social history. His key theoretical contribution is to expand the concept of mode of production to include reproduction and thus to place family structures within the center of the social relations of production. He then traces changing family forms from the late Roman Empire into the 19th century. Seccombe's discussions range from Jesus's criticism of "family values" to the resiliency of patriarchy into the age of capitalism. He has provided a gracefully written and analytically critical countermodel to the dominant literature on the historical family. It is a must for students of the family, whether historical or contemporary. Extensive endnotes; references limited to works in English and French. Advanced undergraduate; graduate; faculty; professional.—*P. G. Wallace, Hartwick College*

WS-2353 HQ755 93-24570 CIP
Sharpe, Sue. **Fathers and daughters.** Routledge, 1994. 184p bibl index ISBN 0-415-10301-0, $59.95; ISBN 0-415-10302-9 pbk, $16.95

Sharpe, a freelance writer, presents an interesting view of the father-daughter relationship as experienced by a nonrandom sample of British respondents. Data were gathered through interviews and analysis of letters sent in by respondents. Chapters cover childhood, approval and achievement, dominance and violence, sexuality, fathering styles, aging, and fathers' effects upon daughters' relations with other males. The chapters on dominance/violence, fathering styles, and aging offer little new information. Sharpe has not cited any research journal articles in her bibliography, although a brief search of the *Journal of Marriage and the Family* showed that articles on the father-daughter relationship do exist. Also noticeably missing are books by major US academics, e.g., Suzanne Steinmetz and Richard Gelles. Sharpe's qualitative methodology uses excerpts from her interviews and letters to illustrate and support her points and assertions rather than letting her subjects simply speak for themselves from the interviews and letters. Tom Koch's *A Place in Time* (CH, Sep'93) is a good example of letting one's subjects speak for themselves and gives a much better treatment of caring for parents (including father-daughter relations). Chapter notes are adequate; subject index is rather spartan. General readers.—*R.C. Myers, Central Washington University*

WS-2354 HQ809 93-37021 CIP
Stacey, William A. **The violent couple,** by William A. Stacey, Lonnie R. Hazlewood, and Anson Shupe. Praeger, 1994. 182p bibl index afp ISBN 0-275-94698-3, $49.95

The third in a trilogy on family violence, this follows Stacey and Shupe's *The Family Secret: Domestic Violence in America* (CH, Jan'84), which focused on abused women, whereas Shupe, Stacey, and Hazlewood's *Violent Men, Violent Couples* (CH, May'87) emphasized abusive men. *The Violent Couple* now carefully shifts the emphasis from woman as victim to mutual combat, a perspective introduced by Lenore E. Walker in *The Battered Woman* (1979) but used here with more optimism than in Walker's portrayal. The specific sample includes 86 couples in the Austin, Texas, area, but Stacey, Hazlewood, and Shupe have worked with hundreds of domestic disturbance reports and interviewed police, counselors, women's advocates, and other interventionists. The explanatory framework is the commonly used social learning approach, based on quantitative and qualitative data. Multiple interventions are presented in the context of a systemically integrated framework for reducing both men's and women's violence in relationships. The work ends with a brief chapter on the broader societal context of family violence. The format is standard, the tables clear, and the selected bibliography limited but fairly representative. Another strand in the evolution of the literature on violence reduction among American couples. Upper-division undergraduate; graduate; professional.—*Y. Peterson, Saint Xavier University*

WS-2355 HQ59 94-2807 CIP
Thurer, Shari L. **The myths of motherhood: how culture reinvents the good mother.** Houghton Mifflin, 1994. 381p bibl index ISBN 0-395-58415-9, $24.95

Much as Betty Friedan, in *The Feminine Mystique* (1963), debunked the myth of the mystical experiences of housewifery, Thurer sets out to challenge the 20th-century myths of motherhood. To delegitimate the guilt-inducing modern myths about the nurturing, all-giving, at-home mother, she presents a discursive and selective history of Western mother-child relationships from the Neolithic era to the present. Intending to demonstrate the historical variability of mothering and mother-child relationships, the book covers topics from Phoenician and Greek infanticide to the Virgin Mary to wet nursing to modern psychological theories. Thurer stops short of radical cultural relativism, however, claiming without any evidence or even argumentation, that mother love is natural and that sexual inequality, patriarchy, and misogyny are responsible for such distortions of the mother-child relationship as child abuse and infanticide. A psychoanalytically trained psychologist, Thurer offers Freudian interpretations parenthetically throughout the book; and as her history becomes more contemporary, she deals less with mothering behavior and more with psychological theorists. Unfortunately the book lacks a clear theoretical focus and offers little more than a compilation of secondary-source historical materials. It may be useful for its overview of historical writing on motherhood. General readers.—*K. M. Daley-McKinley, Cabrini College*

WS-2356 HQ1206 95-6647 MARC
VanEvery, Jo. **Heterosexual women changing the family: refusing to be a 'wife'!** Taylor & Francis, 1995. 165p bibl index ISBN 0-7484-0283-7, $75.00; ISBN 0-7484-0284-5 pbk, $24.95

Feminists and family scholars will find much in this book to challenge their thinking about how child care and household maintenance work can be restructured to make "family" life pleasurable and the division of labor equitable. The research reported here is feminist in orientation. It consists of interviews with a self-selected sample in Britain who have rejected the conventional family structure: single mothers by choice, voluntarily childless heterosexual couples, heterosexual couples with children in role-reversal situations, heterosexual couples with children with shared roles, and multiple-adult arrangements. The interpretive analysis of VanEvery's data includes controversial conclusions at best. She states that women must control male access to them as a way of empowerment. This separatist approach may take several forms, from having nothing to do with men to having close relationships but not sharing living quarters. The author predicts that as people engage in antisexist living arrangements, work organizations will encounter increasing demands for more flexible work schedules to meet the needs of workers who parent and those who manage households. Upper-division undergraduates and above.—*A. S. Oakes, Idaho State University*

WS-2357 HQ759 91-32331 CIP
Walters, Suzanna Danuta. **Lives together/worlds apart: mothers and daughters in popular culture.** California, 1992. 295p bibl index afp ISBN 0-520-07851-9, $25.00

An exceptional study of the cultural representations that depict the relationship between mothers and their daughters in the US. Walters examines 50 years of discursive practices found in popular movies, television shows, women's magazines, psychoanalysis, feminist writings, and expert literature to isolate the development of a unified cultural narrative. Her analysis pieces together an ideology of the mother-daughter relationship that is grounded in a psychology of separation and conflict. The author then demonstrates how this ideology has been incorporated into current feminist critiques as well as into pro-family poli-

tics. The problems of this dominant narrative are discussed along with an alternative reading that emphasizes the rich variations found in the lived experiences of women. Walters has produced a first-rate analysis of how a society's symbolic practices emerge and coalesce to establish a unified cultural reading that not only defines, but also becomes, mundane reality. The book is well written and thoroughly researched. It should appeal to those interested in mass media, feminism, popular culture, and the mother-daughter relationship. Advanced undergraduate; graduate; faculty; professional.—*J. Lynxwiler, University of Central Florida*

WS-2358 HQ728 89-17996 CIP
Whyte, Martin King. **Dating, mating, and marriage.** Aldine de Gruyter, 1990. 325p bibl index ISBN 0-202-30415-9, $44.95; ISBN 0-202-30416-7, $24.95

A comparative analysis of the dating and marital experiences of three cohorts of American women who married between 1925 and 1984. Based on in-depth, retrospective interviews conducted with a sample of 459 Detroit-area women, the findings of this study challenge a number of common beliefs about the impact of premarital behavior on marriage. For example, although the data confirm a rising level of premarital sexual activity in recent decades, they also reveal that intimacy before marriage is not related to subsequent marital choices or patterns. Framed by thoughtful and well-written introductory and concluding chapters, seven substantive chapters offer a systematic assessment of the interaction among mating, dating, marriage, and remarriage. An unusually clear description of the study's research methods is also presented in the text and appendixes. An exemplary model of an empirical report about changing courtship patterns and marriage, this work is highly recommended for libraries serving upper-level undergraduates, graduate students, and professionals in social sciences and human services.—*K. R. Broschart, Hollins College*

WS-2359 HQ1240.5.I5 90-32924 CIP
Williams, Linda B. **Development, demography, and family decision-making: the status of women in rural Java.** Westview, 1990. 157p bibl afp ISBN 0-8133-8020-0, $26.00

Williams's study is based on data gathered from a survey of more than 500 households in four villages in rural Central Java. Williams investigates intergenerational dynamics involved in the process of mate selection, the influence of migration on the ability of women to make major household decisions once they are married, and the impact of women's autonomy on contraceptive use and overall fertility. The detailed analysis of data reveals that among the major predictors of a spouse's ability to influence the marriage decision are education of both spouses' fathers; marital duration; years of schooling; and residence in a large urban center. Residential mobility and infrequent contacts with parents on both sides are found to play a major role in increasing a woman's status within her household. The author's finding that women with high levels of status within their households are less likely to use any form of contraceptive challenges family planning programs in Indonesia. This well-written and carefully documented book is an important contribution to the literature on demography, the role of women, and modernization. Policymakers, development researchers, planners, and international aid agencies will benefit from the implications of the study. Figures, tables, appendix. Highly recommended for upper-division undergraduates and above.—*H. S. Jassal, SUNY College at Cortland*

WS-2360 HQ778 94-45703 CIP
Wrigley, Julia. **Other people's children.** Basic Books, 1995. 177p index ISBN 0-465-05370-X, $21.00

Wrigley's discussion of child care by in-home workers is based on more than 150 interviews with parents and caregivers in New York and Los Angeles. Some parents emphasize class differences by hiring minority women, often new immigrants, who usually provide housework as well as child care. Other parents opt for social class similarity, hiring trained nannies or college students who do not do housework and are likely to share parents' child-care philosophies. Wrigley's analysis is built on themes emerging from her interviews. Her sociological perspective highlights social class difference and conflict between employers and caregivers. As employers, parents often compete for control over their children's care with caregivers who do not share their values, but are essential to parents in realizing their personal and career goals. Women who provide in-home child care are often lonely and frustrated. This readable, brief study is useful for families making child-care choices as well as for students of family, social class, and child-care policy. Weaknesses involve questions of whether child-care concerns in New York and Los Angeles are nationally applicable, and Wrigley's failure to analyze the policy issues raised. General readers and undergraduates.—*M. E. Elwell, emerita, Salisbury State University*

◆ Race, Class, Ethnicity

WS-2361 E184 90-28075 CIP
Blea, Irene I. **La Chicana and the intersection of race, class, and gender.** Praeger, 1992. 167p bibl index afp ISBN 0-275-93980-4, $45.00

Blea's political position deserves the respect of the Chicano intellectual community and provides the underlying theme of most of her work. This most recent book reflects Blea's commitment to a Chicano feminism. Blea, author of *Toward a Chicano Social Science* (CH, Mar'89), provides the reader with a good introduction to many of the social issues affecting Chicano women today (e.g., teen pregnancy, high fertility rates, role of older women, poverty, school dropouts). Particularly appealing is the author's emphasis on historical events and figures, e.g., Blea's discussion of the role of the Adelitas during the Mexican revolution and of the intellectual legacy of Sor Juana Ines de la Cruz and that of other noted Mexican and Chicano women. Although Blea does an excellent job in bringing to the surface important issues that have been either ignored or not significantly addressed in the social science literature (e.g., violence in humor, dated paradigms, lesbians), she analyzes these issues only superficially. Other minor—but irksome—details are the spelling of the Spanish Dolores as Delores, and the datedness of many of the references. The latter shortcoming is particularly important when discussing contemporary concerns such as health, the elderly, and crime. In sum, the book is recommended as an introduction to the broader topic of Chicano culture and social reality, and to the somewhat narrower topic of Chicano women.—*E. Bastida, University of Texas—Pan American*

WS-2362 HT1521 91-22025 CIP
Essed, Philomena. **Understanding everyday racism: an interdisciplinary theory.** Sage, 1991. 322p (Sage series on race and ethnic relations, 2) bibl index ISBN 0-8039-4255-9, $39.95; ISBN 0-8039-4256-7 pbk, $19.95

Essed's book is a rewarding though stylistically dense admixture of scholarly review, intellectual explorations, and empirical study of black women in the US and The Netherlands. The author addresses the question of everday racism—the processes of interaction that reaffirm and reproduce the ideology of racial subordination. She asks how black women acquire their knowledge of racism and how this socialization leads to their comprehension of racist events as well as their response to such events. The study design also permits Essed to identify cultural differences between the two groups of women. For example, "none of the Surinamese women were socialized at home to understand racism," while the opposite seemed true for American women who "lived under segregation." Other cultural differences appear in the women's knowledge and theories of racism. Essed ends strongly with a discussion of "problematizing those who problematize racism," sharply depicting the societal pattern of both denying racism and delegitimizing those who refuse to be indifferent to racism. College and university libraries.—*H. J. Ehrlich, formerly, University of Iowa*

WS-2363 E185 92-6954 Orig
hooks, bell. **Black looks: race and representation.** South End, 1992. 200p bibl ISBN 0-89608-433-7, $12.00

In her introduction, hooks tells the reader that her collection of 12 essays are "gestures of defiance. They represent my political struggle to push against the boundaries of the image, to find words that express what I see, especially when I am looking in ways that move against the grain, when I am seeing things that most folks want to believe simply are not there." Hooks does just that in a vol-

ume that is passionately personal but continues the articulate critique found in her previous books like *Ain't I a Woman* (CH, Apr'82) and *Talking Back* (1989). *Black Looks* will generate a wide variety of responses, but hooks's keen insight and cutting analysis need to be heard in present discussions of racism, sexism, and multiculturalism. The essays cover a wide range of subjects, but all focus on contemporary images. One essay discusses Oscar Micheaux's films, another looks at Jennie Livingston's film, *Paris is Burning* and a third, "Madonna," reflects on distinctions between cultural appropriation and cultural appreciation. Her essays not only expose the persistent blindness of what she calls "white supremacist capitalist patriarchy," but also affirm resistance to destructive images. Essays "Living Blackness as Political Resistance" and "The Oppositional Gaze" offer insights into both the structure of racism and ways of combating it. Recommended for all levels.—*C. Hunter, Earlham College*

WS-2364 E185 95-6395 CIP
hooks, bell. **Killing rage: ending racism.** H. Holt, 1995. 277p bibl afp ISBN 0-8050-3782-9, $20.00

Humanities scholar bell hooks is one of the finest analysts of American race relations writing today. This new book is a collection of interrelated essays probing many aspects of racial struggle in the US, with a particular accent on providing a voice for African American women. The author offers deep insights, e.g., her point that "racism" is not the right term for the problem in the US; a better term is "neo-colonial white supremacy." For change in white dominance to come, everyone in the society must engage in counterhegemonic antiracist action "that is fiercely and passionately calling for change." The author probes the depth and importance of black rage, and how that rage can be both pathological and liberating for African Americans. She does not pull back from problems within the black community, but digs deeply into the meaning of sexism in black life and ways to challenge that sexism. The book covers many other topics, including teaching resistance to white supremacy, white racism in the media, internalized racism and the white beauty standard, Eurocentric Christianity and black Islamic fundamentalism, and the role of love in creating a multiracial society. This is a proactive work in the tradition of books like James Baldwin's *The Fire Next Time* (1963). All levels.—*J. R. Feagin, University of Florida*

WS-2365 HM146 93-6064 CIP
Jackman, Mary R. **The velvet glove: paternalism and conflict in gender, class, and race relations.** California, 1994. 425p bibl indexes afp ISBN 0-520-08113-7, $38.00

Jackman, distinguished survey researcher, sociologist, and author with Robert Jackman of *Class Awareness in the United States* (CH, Nov'83), here explores how racial, gender, and class stratification are viewed by dominant and subordinate groups. Arguing from survey data that traditional social science views of hostility and conflict as the heart of oppressive relations are incorrect, she suggests that "velvet glove" ideologies are used as less openly hostile ways of rationalizing expropriation. Paternalism, in which dominant groups come to believe they "know best" for subordinate groups, is one major velvet-glove ideology. Even while exploiting subordinates, dominants may profess love and affection and give praise to their victims. Whether in male-female, black-white, or employer-worker relations, paternalistic ideologies surround actions seen by dominants as benevolent. There is much that is original in this book, but it is limited by a too heavy reliance on one research data set for the year 1975. In addition to being somewhat dated, the findings are based on very short answers to short questions and do not lend themselves well to the intensive, probing, and philosophical analysis Jackman attempts. Excellent bibliography and footnotes. Upper-division undergraduates and above.—*J. R. Feagin, University of Florida*

WS-2366 UB418 95-32467 CIP
Moore, Brenda L. **To serve my country, to serve my race: the story of the only African American Wacs stationed overseas during World War II.** New York University, 1996. 272p bibl index afp ISBN 0-8147-5522-4, $24.95

Moore explores the effect of racial and gender policies during WW II by examining the experiences of African American women assigned to the 6888th Central Postal Directory Battalion. Using a detailed survey and interviews of 51 participants, Moore delineates the institutional and personal factors that shaped these women's lives. She describes the decision to recruit and train African American women for military service, the conduct of their training, their deployment overseas, and their postwar experiences. Moore studies the detriments to service, racial and gender discrimination, and the tangible and intangible benefits of service. Employing sociological theory, Moore also analyzes the unit in terms of social cohesion, social conflict, and phenomenology. A fine study of military sociology and group interaction, this work adds to a slender corpus of scholarship concerning African American women in the military. With the exception of privately published books and a few memoirs, the only other scholarly monograph is Martha Putney's *When the Nation Was in Need* (CH, Jul'93). Moore's work includes solid documentation, a useful bibliography, and several helpful tables. Suitable for undergraduate and graduate collections.—*J. A. Luckett, United States Military Academy*

WS-2367 KF8745 92-54119 CIP
Race-ing justice, en-gendering power: essays on Anita Hill, Clarence Thomas, and the construction of social reality, ed. with introd. by Toni Morrison. Pantheon Books, 1992. 475p ISBN 0-679-74145-3 pbk, $15.00

Published on the first anniversary of the Clarence Thomas Supreme Court confirmation hearings, this remarkable collection includes an exquisitely written introduction by Toni Morrison, in which she frames the discourse contained in the 18 essays that follow. The Thomas hearings forced onto center stage the interrelated issues of race, gender, and multiculturalism. The essays, contributed by African Americans—a federal judge, novelists, and scholars of history, literature, law, philosophy, women's studies and African American studies—address these issues. The quality of the essays is amazingly consistent; they are all well written and original. Especially impressive are Leon Higginbotham's evaluation of Thomas's qualifications and capabilities; Michael Thelwell's indictment of Yale's decision to concentrate on recruitment and integration of only the brightest and most promising black students in lieu of establishing a course of study in African American culture and history; Cornel West's review of the failure of black leadership and racialist reasoning; and Paula Giddings's historical insights into African American sexism. This is an important volume on a timely subject. Highly recommended for all libraries and all readers.—*F. J. Hay, Harvard University*

WS-2368 HQ1421 94-20592 CIP
Racism in the lives of women: testimony, theory, and guides to antiracist practice, ed. by Jeanne Adleman and Gloria M. Enguídanos. Haworth, 1995. 385p bibl index afp ISBN 1-56024-918-8, $49.95; ISBN 1-56023-863-1 pbk, $17.95

The 31 contributors to this collection are women who reflect great diversity in terms of ethnicity, race, age, sexual orientation, and even size (e.g., one article is titled "The Full-Figure Black Woman: Issues of Racism and Sizeism"). These women also represent a wide variety of professional backgrounds, among them, law, anthropology, social work, and women's studies, but a probable majority engages in one or another of the mental health professions. The articles vary significantly in style, tone, and depth of scholarship, but the collection should be of considerable interest to those concerned with the complex convergence of sexism and racism. The volume is well organized and well edited. Useful index.—*W. P. Nye, Hollins College*

WS-2369 E185 90-48068 CIP
Scott, Kesho Yvonne. **The habit of surviving: black women's strategies for life.** Rutgers, 1991. 208p bibl ISBN 0-8135-1646-3, $19.95

In this highly readable book Scott (Grinnell), author of *Tight Spaces* (1987), winner of a 1988 American Book Award, presents four in-depth interviews with successful black women, together with her own autobiography. These women, each in her own chapter, describe their lives as daughters, mothers, wives, workers, and community activists. They reveal themselves as troubled and provocatively thoughtful, and their pained comments contradict stereotyped notions of black women. Committed to antiracist and nonsexist human relationships, these "hidden" feminists demonstrate in oral histories how they carry on the struggle to survive the rewards and punishments of upward mobility,

the internal "colorism" within the African American community, the hiding of intelligence behind sacred mothering, the male-centeredness of work and family, and the psychic costs of trying to "have it all" and "keep the revolution going" at the same time. This is a serious treatment of the double cancer of racism and sexism that is growing at the center of US society. Notes. All levels.—*J. R. Feagin, University of Texas*

WS-2370 DD78 91-17061 Orig
Showing our colors: Afro-German women speak out, ed. by May Opitz, Katharina Oguntoye, and Dagmar Schultz; tr. by Anne V. Adams. Massachusetts, 1992. 239p ISBN 0-87023-759-4, $40.00; ISBN 0-87023-760-8 pbk, $13.95

The frank accounting here of the social consequences of interracial sexual liaisons in Germany demonstrates how prejudice and stereotypical thinking persists in spite of the increased education and modernization associated with European societies. Socially oppressed and politically marginal, the women who contributed their stories speak openly of their explicit rejection by German natives. These women also describe difficulties relating to peoples with whom they have never lived but with whom they share a genetic heritage—African natives. Afro-German women's particular status makes the problems of accepting their own skin color and racial identification doubly traumatic. Most of the women quoted in this collection grew up in homes with loving parents who, too, struggled with the social stigma of interracial relationships. These Afro-German women verbalize the inner struggles they experienced in the process of defining their self-concepts and in identifying the social group to which they belong. Their accounts reveal the dignity and courage with which they approach the status conferred on them by a society in which racial identification has too long been a political issue. College, university, and public libraries.—*A. S. Oakes, Idaho State University*

WS-2371 HD6054 92-3988 CIP
Sokoloff, Natalie J. **Black women and white women in the professions: occupational segregation by race and gender, 1960-1980.** Routledge, 1992. 175p bibl index ISBN 0-415-90608-3, $49.95; ISBN 0-415-90609-1 pbk, $16.95

Sokoloff's carefully researched book explodes numerous myths about women and minorities displacing white men in the professions. She examines government data (1960-80) and concludes that although women and nonwhite men did gain greater access to professional/technical positions, white men maintained their dominance in the most desired professions. White women made some gains further down the ladder in professions, such as accounting, once dominated by white males; black men and women made lesser gains in the same areas. Some professions became integrated by gender and racial group, but most of the 30 professional/technical arenas studied did not. Some professional groups, such as physicians, grew so fast that the number of black/female professionals did increase, although usually in less well paid subsectors. White male representation grew faster, however, so white men had an even greater dominance of these fields by 1980. White men have *not* been displaced in most professions but have continued to be the overwhelming majority in the most desirable occupations. The "twofer" myth about black women is refuted: black women have not gained parity with black (or white) men in the professions. Given 1980s myths about white men being displaced by female/minority workers, this book's well-documented refutations are a breath of fresh air. General; advanced undergraduate through professional.—*J. R. Feagin, University of Florida*

WS-2372 HQ999 91-25068 CIP
Solinger, Rickie. **Wake up little Susie: single pregnancy and race before Roe v. Wade.** Routledge, 1992. 324p bibl index ISBN 0-415-90448-X, $25.00

Solinger surveys public policy, community attitudes, and private responses to illegitimate pregnancy, maternity, and the children that structured these mothers' experiences. The author demonstrates how female sexuality, fertility, and the single mother have been used as proving grounds for theories of race, gender, and social stability. Solinger provides the first published analyses of maternity home programs for unwed mothers, 1945-65, as well as examining how nascent cultural and political constructs such as the "population bomb" and the "sexual revolution" reinforced racially specific public policy initiatives. Such initiatives encouraged white women to relinquish their babies, spawning a flourishing adoption market, but subjected black women to social welfare policies that assumed they would keep their babies and aimed to prevent them from having more. Incorporating responses of social service and political professionals of this era to the "crisis" of out-of-wedlock pregnancy with letters, poems, and statements from the women themselves, this book offers an arena to explore the intersection of female biology and social constructions of gender, race, and class. All levels.—*M. Klatte, Eastern Kentucky University*

WS-2373   HQ1185   95-10653 MARC
Unrelated kin: race and gender in women's personal narratives, ed. by Gwendolyn Etter-Lewis and Michéle Foster. Routledge, 1996. 229p index ISBN 0-415-91138-9, $55.00; ISBN 0-415-91139-7 pbk, $16.95

Essays on women's multiple identifications and experiences make up most of this work. Breaking with the prevailing emphasis on women of color, the collection focuses instead on First World women. The volume's theme suggests that women cannot and should not be perceived as a homogeneous mass, experiencing their lives in similar ways. Instead, contributors rely on the oral histories of women across cultures in First World nations to illustrate how previous works have neglected the variety of women's cultural experiences. The volume does not ignore women of color. Several essays treat their experiences, embedding their narratives into the larger context of international perspectives. However, no attempt is made to represent the women's life stories and oral histories as the "standard" for all women everywhere. Instead, contributors offer more in-depth analysis of a cross-section of women, embracing each individual's racial/ethnic/national cultural identity without privileging or comparing. Etter-Lewis and Foster present their study of the women's narratives as voices of "authority." This places women at the center of their own cultures rather than relegating them to the periphery of society. All levels.—*D. Van Ausdale, Valdosta State University*

◆ Social Movements, Social Change

WS-2374   HQ1391   91-10784 CIP
Astin, Helen S. **Women of influence, women of vision: a cross-generational study of leaders and social change,** by Helen S. Astin and Carole Leland. Jossey-Bass, 1991. 203p bibl index afp ISBN 1-55542-357-4, $25.95

The ideas about leadership examined in this book are based on interviews with three generations of women who played significant organizational and intellectual roles in the development of the women's movement in and around higher education between the mid-1950s and mid-1980s. The model of leadership that emerges stands in contrast to social movement research that emphasizes positional resources and formal organizational structures. The 77 women "influentials" who form this snowball sample provide support for a view of leadership constructed instead on the basis of outcomes—leadership defined as that which actually moves a group of people to change something significant—and hence suggests process rather than personality. Unfortunately, much of the book is organized around the personalities of these leaders, their backgrounds, and their individual obstacles. This fits better with the secondary goal of the book, i.e., celebrating the accomplishments of these founding mothers, than it does with the purpose of clarifying leadership-as-empowerment as a process. Nonetheless, the interview material provides much suggestive data, the chronologies are useful, and the theoretical suggestions stimulating. A worthwhile addition to any library.—*M. M. Ferree, University of Connecticut*

WS-2375   HQ1426   89-49083 CIP
Buechler, Steven M. **Women's movements in the United States: woman suffrage, equal rights, and beyond.** Rutgers, 1990. 258p bibl indexes ISBN 0-8135-1558-0, $37.00; ISBN 0-8135-1559-9, $14.00

Buechler offers a comparative analysis of the woman suffrage movement (1848-1920) and of the contemporary women's movement (1960s to the present), dis-

cussing in turn their origins; their embodiments in networks, communities, and formal organizations; ideologies; attempts to transcend racial and class barriers; opposing forces and countermovements; and "endings and futures." He draws on an extensive knowledge of contemporary literature on feminism and social movement theory (including his own work) and on other relevant primary sources. As an introduction to the study of women's movements the book is informative and thought provoking, and for that reason alone is valuable; the bibliography is excellent. In its conclusions regarding women's movements and social movements in general, it is less than satisfying. Buechler falls short of his stated goal of using the women's movements to illuminate social movement theory; he clearly demonstrates that these movements challenge current models, but his comparative framework prevents him from developing a more meaningful analysis.—*M. L. Meldrum, SUNY at Stony Brook*

WS-2376   Can. CIP
Challenging times: the women's movement in Canada and the United States, ed. by Constance Backhouse and David H. Flaherty. McGill-Queen's, 1992. 335p index afp ISBN 0-7735-0910-0, $49.95; ISBN 0-7735-0919-4 pbk, $19.95

Statements by women in the US about "the women's movement" are often ethnocentric and neglect the extent to which the women's movement is thriving in other countries. Based on a 1989 conference organized by the Centre for American Studies (which studies the US from a Canadian viewpoint) and the Centre for Women's Studies and Feminist Research, this volume examines the women's movements in both Canada and the US in terms of their accomplishments and future challenges. The uniformly excellent and informative essays are divided into eight sections following a superb introduction by coeditor Backhouse. These sections treat the origins of the movement in Canada and the US; developments since the 1960s; interrelationship of academic and activist feminism; racism; violence; women and the economy; reproductive rights; and alternative visions. Taken as a whole, the volume meets its objectives while emphasizing that much remains to be done. Taken individually, these essays would make excellent additions to women's studies course syllabi. General; advanced undergraduate; graduate; faculty.—*S. Reinharz, Brandeis University*

WS-2377   HQ1426   94-2718 CIP
Feminist organizations: harvest of the new women's movement, ed. by Myra Marx Ferree and Patricia Yancey Martin. Temple University, 1995. 474p bibl index afp ISBN 1-56639-228-4, $49.95; ISBN 1-56639-229-2 pbk, $22.95

This in-depth and detailed study of feminist organizations addresses the fundamental questions of how and why so many have managed to endure. The text reveals what price these organizations have paid: what effects have they had; and what promises they hold. Essays consider four issues that feminist organizations maintain for survival and effectiveness. One is institutionalization, i.e., the development of regular and routinized relationships with other organizations, and what institutionalization means for feminism. Some essays challenge the claim that institutionalization necessarily leads to deradicalization, and raise questions about the political learning that goes on within movement organizations. The second issue is the relationship of feminist organizations to the (feminist) movement. Third is the tension arising from the multidimensional nature of feminist politics, which takes different forms at different times, in different areas of the country, within different socioeconomic and political contexts, among women of diverse racial, ethnic, class, and age groups. Last, these organizations are the outcome of specific situational and historical processes that contribute to the plenitude of women's movement organizations of all sizes, shapes, and orientations. Upper-division undergraduates and above.—*M. Klatte, Eastern Kentucky University*

WS-2378   HQ767.5.U5   90-40541 MARC
From abortion to reproductive freedom: transforming a movement, ed. by Marlene Gerber Fried. South End, 1990. 317p index ISBN 0-89608-388-8, $30.00; ISBN 0-89608-387-X, $14.00

Fried's important collection grounds the discussion about abortion in the lives of a broad spectrum of women, including minority groups and Third World women. Essays move from a defense of abortion into a demand for the full range of reproductive rights. The 47 contributions are clustered in 4 sections: the politics of the abortion rights movement; speaking out for women: choosing ourselves; defending abortion rights: confronting threats to access; and expanding the agenda: building an inclusive movement. Entries range from poems, to statements of political programs, to personal narratives, to descriptions of services. Some essays are excerpted from books, e.g., Angela Davis's *Women, Race, & Class* (CH, May '82), or from articles, e.g., Alice Walker's "What Can the White Man Say?" (*The Nation*, May 22, 1989); others were written especially for this volume. Particularly helpful are a listing of key US Supreme Court abortion cases, a compilation of data on abortion and sterilization in the Third World, and on US women who have abortions. Editor Fried's overarching essay synthesizes the argument for transforming the movement. The volume concludes with a brief statement about each of the 46 contributors and a 4-page integrated subject/author index. Chapters that cite literature provide references in endnotes. All levels.— *S. Reinharz, Brandeis University*

WS-2379   JX1974   91-55538 CIP
Krasniewicz, Louise. **Nuclear summer: the clash of communities at the Seneca women's peace encampment.** Cornell, 1992. 259p bibl index afp ISBN 0-8014-2635-9, $34.50; ISBN 0-8014-9938-0 pbk, $13.95

In the summer of 1983, a group of women purchased land near the Seneca Army Depot in upstate New York and planned a summer encampment to protest nuclear arms deployment and the patriarchal society that they perceived as supporting and fostering militarism and oppression. Krasniewicz has undertaken an anthropological study of the interactions and conflicts within the camp and between the encampment women and the people of the nearby communities. She employs several theoretical tools, including Geertz's concept of "thick culture," Turner's "liminal period," deconstruction of texts and symbols, and a variety of narrative techniques, including a "textual collage." Both the events described and Krasniewicz's approach are interesting, but she is ultimately unable to offer much in the way of fresh interpretation or provocative analysis. Some of her material deserves much fuller discussion, e.g., how the lives of women attending the camp were changed. This is a fine case study that offers useful material for scholars of radical feminism and of social change and conflict in late 20th-century America. Excellent photographs, good bibliography. General; undergraduate; graduate; faculty.— *M. L. Meldrum, SUNY at Stony Brook*

WS-2380   HQ1190   94-13416 CIP
Marshall, Barbara L. **Engendering modernity: feminism, social theory and social change.** Northeastern University, 1994. 197p bibl index ISBN 1-55553-212-8, $37.50; ISBN 1-55553-213-6 pbk, $14.95

Marshall (Trent Univ., Canada) seeks to reposition social theory in a way that allows gender its proper role. Gender divisions underlie such massive social developments as industrialism and capitalism. For this reason, gender is not to be treated as one analytical variable on a par with many others; to allow such treatment is to allow feminism to become just one of the many voices in a postmodern pluralism. Modern social theory has emphasized the public/private distinction and has linked other important distinctions to it, all of which prevents social theory from treating difference adequately. The way to better theorizing is to historicize such dualisms as individual/society and family/economy. Along the way the author makes insightful comments on a great many topics, on other feminist writers, and on Marx, Habermas, Giddens, and other influential theorists of modernity. Upper-division undergraduate and graduate collections.— *J. W. Meiland, University of Michigan*

WS-2381   HQ1426   92-91 CIP
Ryan, Barbara. **Feminism and the women's movement: dynamics of change in social movement, ideology and activism.** Routledge, 1992. 203p bibl index ISBN 0-415-90598-2, $49.95; ISBN 0-415-90599-0 pbk, $16.95

Within a framework of resource mobilization, Ryan provides a succinct analysis of women's movements within the US. The research is based on participant-observation, oral history, and documentation of formal organizations for women's liberation activities, starting with a summary of suffrage activities from the opening decades of this century through movement resurgence in the 1960s and into the 1980s. Ryan's analysis balances the concerns of structural characteristics of movements with emotional and ideological meanings. She does not thoroughly examine the resources used by feminist organizations, but does well describing the complexity of the movement. There are problematic implicit judgments of the efficacy of positions and strategies, e.g., lesbian separatism or civil disobedience in relation to the formal legal and public struggles. Still, Ryan is attentive to the multiple meanings within the movement and to the conflicts that have troubled and renewed women's activities. A useful book for women's studies, and a source and example for sociologists and political scientists. General; advanced undergraduate; graduate; professional.— *J. L. Croissant, Rensselaer Polytechnic Institute*

WS-2382   HQ1426   91-8619 CIP
Simon, Rita J. **Women's movements in America: their successes, disappointments, and aspirations,** by Rita J. Simon and Gloria Danziger. Praeger, 1991. 171p bibl index afp ISBN 0-275-93948-0, $39.95

Simon and Danziger here review the achievements and frustrations of American women's movements in the areas of suffrage, political participation, education, employment, marriage, and family life. Each of the three major chapters includes a historical review, pertinent quotations, statistical tables illustrating the extent of change or lack of change, and public opinion polls examining the views of the American public in general. There is a brief concluding chapter suggesting strategies for future change. The book provides some interesting information but is ultimately unsatisfying to the serious reader. Both factual material and analysis lack depth, originality, and even conviction; one cannot avoid the impression that the writers themselves were not really very interested in the project. Several minor errors of fact and syntax, suggesting inadequate copy editing, detract further from the overall quality. The book is a convenient resource for its statistical tables and poll data; the bibliography is also useful. It has otherwise little to recommend it to the scholar or student.— *M. L. Meldrum, SUNY at Stony Brook*

WS-2383   HQ767   90-23877 CIP
Staggenborg, Suzanne. **The pro-choice movement: organization and activism in the abortion conflict.** Oxford, 1991. 229p bibl index afp ISBN 0-19-506596-4, $27.50

Concerned more with organizational than with ideological factors, Staggenborg examines the antecedents and history of today's "pro-choice" movement, its development "from a small band of entrepreneurs to a strong social movement consisting of professional leaders and formal organizations as well as grass roots activists," and the circumstances that conditioned its single-issue and countermovement orientation. Moving between national and local focal points, from organizations centered in Washington, DC to both independent and nationally linked groups and activities in the state of Illinois and the city of Chicago, Staggenborg shows that although the movement actually garnered grass-roots support and financial resources in times of defeat as well as victory, the galvanizing presence of anti-abortion forces rather than the ideological proclivities of activists require a single-issue orientation. Highly recommended for college, university, and public libraries.— *N. B. Rosenthal, SUNY College at Old Westbury*

WS-2384   HQ1154   94-26260 CIP
Whittier, Nancy. **Feminist generations: the persistence of the radical women's movement.** Temple University, 1995. 309p index afp ISBN 1-56639-281-0, $49.95; ISBN 1-56639-282-9 pbk, $18.95

Like many other university communities in the late 1960s and early '70s Columbus, Ohio, was a hotbed of political and cultural activism. A resurgent women's movement—especially its radical feminist element—flourished in this environment. Whittier located and talked with 34 women who were the "core" of the radical feminist community in Columbus. Her informants' descriptions of their work in the movement, accounts of organizational success and failure, portraits of other activists, and recollections of debates, fights, and splits provide the basis of her reconstruction of their collective history. Whittier argues that these self-portraits reveal key differences in the collective identities and aims of women who entered the movement at different times. Using the "generational perspectives" of successive cohorts of activists, she theorizes about transformation and persistence in insurgent ideology and the continuation of social movements even through periods when activism and resources decline. The analysis of intracohort tensions is particularly interesting because almost two-thirds of her informants are lesbians. This intelligent and well-written book is highly recommended for its significant contribution to women's studies and social movements. All levels.—*N. B. Rosenthal, SUNY College at Old Westbury*

WS-2385 HQ1236 89-78129 CIP
Women and social protest, ed. by Guida West and Rhoda Lois Blumberg. Oxford, 1990. 406p bibl index afp ISBN 0-19-506118-7, $49.95; ISBN 0-19-506517-4, $18.95

West and Blumberg open their excellent collection on women's participation in social protest with a theoretical introduction that states their goals of creating feminist theory by using feminist methodology. The 17 chapters bring together previously published and new research on 19th- and 20th-century women who have protested for the rights of various groups, e.g., blacks, tenants, welfare recipients, workers, women in general, and lesbians. Other protests concern peace, ecology, and political change. Although the focus is on the US, chapters also deal with Europe, China, Israel, Latin America, and Nigeria. The editors categorize this diverse range of materials into four types of social concerns: economic, nationalist or racial/ethnic, humanistic/nurturing, and rights of women. Each part of the book is devoted to one of the types, introduced by a brief essay by the editors. Chapter notes; single, integrated bibliography; combined subject/author index; and a biographical paragraph about each contributor. Some of the chapters contain quantitative material and most contain interesting historical vignettes. An important contribution to sociology, political science, and women's history. College, university, and public libraries.—*S. Reinharz, Brandeis University*

◆ Social Problems

WS-2386 HV741 95-34682 CIP
Armstrong, Louise. **Of 'sluts' and 'bastards': a feminist decodes the child welfare debate.** Common Courage, 1995. 344p ISBN 1-56751-067-1, $29.95

The author of *Kiss Daddy Goodnight* (1978) continues her theme of protection for women and children. This time her attention is on protective services and foster care. Armstrong skillfully blends voices from the poor, agency personnel, and feminists. Her focus is on the bureaucratic oppression of the poor, through professional worldviews and language that transform poor women from social victims to perpetrators of crimes against children. She illustrates the importance of conformity to officialdom, because noncompliance, even to ill-defined standards, can result in involuntary removal of children. Although Armstrong does not claim her sample is representative, her arguments are compelling and relentless. This book is not as dispassionate, comprehensive, or theoretical as Ross A. Thompson's *Preventing Child Maltreatment through Social Support* (CH, Feb'96). However, it strongly challenges the current system to self-consciously do more for children and their families. Notes are appropriate, although not voluminous. Especially important reading for the helping professions and the general public because it reveals the pseudoscientific character of bureaucracy. All levels.—*Y. Peterson, Saint Xavier University*

WS-2387 HV5132 91-27765 CIP
Asher, Ramona M. **Women with alcoholic husbands: ambivalence and the trap of codependency.** North Carolina, 1992. 223p bibl index afp ISBN 0-8078-2028-8, $29.95; ISBN 0-8078-4373-3 pbk, $12.95

Asher's study of women with alcoholic husbands is a well-balanced ethnography in the symbolic interactionist tradition. According to Asher, the codependency label used to organize treatment for such women is not so much a description of an objective illness as it is the outcome of a social process that involves constructing a medical reality. The data for this contention are drawn from a series of interviews with 50 women whose experiences before, during, and after coming to treatment highlight the interplay of structured role assumptions and negotiated definitions. Asher carefully documents how the emergence of alcoholism in her subjects' lives creates contradictory expectations with regard to mar-

riage, husband-wife roles, problem drinking, and self-image. The analysis maps the definitional work and management strategies that are central to the lived experiences of these women and their struggle to make sense of self, spouse, and situation. Asher's findings suggest that codependency is a problematic concept that has been reified by the therapeutic community in its attempt to control definitions of and treatment for alcoholism. A well-written book that will appeal to advanced undergraduates, graduate students, and readers who are interested in alcohol treatment programs, women's issues, and deviant behavior.—*J. Lynxwiler, University of Central Florida*

WS-2388 HV1445 94-43371 CIP
Berrick, Jill Duerr. **Faces of poverty: portraits of women and children on welfare.** Oxford, 1995. 214p index afp ISBN 0-19-509754-8, $25.00

Berrick's informative report on poverty is actually more than the title implies. In addition to providing richly detailed explanations of five women's lives, describing how they became welfare dependent, and what later became of them, the book offers very readable summaries of macro stratification research. Because of the effective mixture of aggregate and individual data, the relevance of welfare policy debates for the personal choices "welfare mothers" must make is magnified and illustrated through compelling biography. As a counter to much of the public's antagonism about AFDC payments in particular, Berrick documents how essential the program has been as a path to recovery from personal economic catastrophe. Five chapters that are distinctive case studies are sandwiched between an introduction to the myths and realities of welfare at the beginning and a concluding assessment of assorted proposals for policy reform at the end. Because the policy options are evaluated in the context of real women's struggles instead of hypothetical women's motives, they have a pragmatic appeal that should interest readers regardless of political affiliation. All levels.—*R. Zingraff, Meredith College*

WS-2389 HV31 92-6861 CIP
Bryson, Lois. **Welfare and the State: who benefits?** St. Martin's, 1992. 270p bibl index ISBN 0-312-08054-9, $45.00

Bryson's concise, skillful volume deserves the attention of scholars, including those familiar with (and a bit fatigued by) the continuing avalanche of welfare state literature. She argues for broadening the discourse surrounding the welfare state to include tax expenditures, private labor-market mechanisms, and household care, and particularly for apprehending the continuing exploitation of women and minorities within the welfare state so understood. A detailed, wide-ranging assessment of cross-national trends in light of a decade of neoconservative policy dominance in OECD nations, the analysis includes the usual specific comparisons of the US, UK, and Sweden, but also much information about Australia and, to a lesser extent, Japan. On all counts, Bryson provides a feminist perspective that adds considerable substance to other analyses, e.g., *The Welfare State East and West*, ed. by Richard Rose and Rei Shiratori (CH, Apr'87). Concluding chapters demonstrate the ways in which the system of public, market, and household social provisions offer little challenge to patriarchal prerogatives even in the most "progressive" societies. Bryson recommends that analysts recast studies of the welfare state in terms of varying state intervention in an era of global capital mobility. Valuable bibliography includes references for less familiar welfare states. Recommended for graduate students and advanced undergraduates interested in social policy.—*D. B. Robertson, University of Missouri-St. Louis*

WS-2390 HV6250.4.H66 90-47126 CIP
Comstock, Gary David. **Violence against lesbians and gay men.** Columbia, 1991. 319p bibl index afp ISBN 0-231-07330-5, $35.00

A skillful combination of empirical data and theoretical analysis mark this interesting and important study. Beginning with a chapter that sets the historical framework for a discussion of violent anti-lesbian/gay behavior, Comstock presents data on both victims and perpetrators. Although Comstock analyzes the data presented for both victims and perpetrators, he wisely focuses more attention on perpetrators. The actions of judges, testimony of witnesses, and comments of the perpetrators themselves help to place violence against lesbians and gay men in a larger social, cultural, and political context. Comstock effectively builds on this in his analytical chapter, "Understanding Anti-Gay/Lesbian Violence." The concluding chapter, "A Biblical Perspective" combines theology and social science in an attempt to further illuminate the problem. Although the combination of dry statistics and a theological orientation may not suit all readers, the book makes a valuable contribution to lesbian and gay studies and also provides critical information frequently missing from criminology texts. College, university, and public libraries.—*E. Broidy, University of California, Irvine*

WS-2391 HV9956 94-1582 CIP
Daly, Kathleen. **Gender, crime, and punishment.** Yale, 1994. 338p bibl index afp ISBN 0-300-05955-8, $37.50

Daly's analysis of crimes prosecuted and punishments pronounced in a metropolitan felony court represents a compelling contribution to literature on gender, crime, and the interpretation of social science data. She compares the records of women and men, examining both their respective "pathways" to criminality and the punishments received. The differences that may be attributed to gender are smaller by far than what most previous scholarship suggests, yet the distinctions Daly does discover are highly credible, thanks to her painstaking logic and analytical acumen. This work contrasts the findings of an aggregated quantitative data analysis with the results of a detailed qualitative inquiry about pairs drawn from the same sample. Gender gaps that appear to be persistent under statistical controls tend to dissolve in the deeper scrutiny of qualitative comparisons. One important result for feminist scholarship is how these findings challenge expected paternalism, on the one hand, and "evil woman" effects, on the other, in criminal justice judgments. Daly's writing makes accessible differing philosophies about sentencing and varying semantics about crime and punishment. The best works in several disciplines that address gender, crime, and punishment are instructively noted throughout this book, and the bibliography is outstanding. Upper-division undergraduates and above.—*R. Zingraff, Meredith College*

WS-2392 HV1444 90-36628 CIP
The Feminization of poverty: only in America?, ed. by Gertrude Schaffner Goldberg and Eleanor Kremen. Greenwood, 1990. 231p (Contributions in women's studies, 117) index afp ISBN 0-313-26421-X, $45.00

A politically astute collection of essays that compare five capitalist (US, Canada, Sweden, France, and Japan) and two socialist (Poland and the USSR) countries to determine whether there is a universal clustering of poverty among females. The authors, most of whom teach at Adelphi University, organize materials for each country into four categories: labor market factors; policies that promote labor market equality of women; social welfare benefits or government income transfers; and demographic factors. Each of these has been shown to have some influence on the economic status of women. Each chapter is filled with data, tables, notes, and lengthy bibliographies explaining the conditions in that particular country. The volume concludes with a discussion of universal patterns, national differences, and changing trends, and illustrates that the situation for women, in the US in particular, is more economically precarious than in other countries. There is a nine-page subject/author index and information on contributors. Although the writing is dry, the essays are cohesive and the material is extremely valuable. Upper-division undergraduates and above.—*S. Reinharz, Brandeis University*

WS-2393 HV6250 94-16362 CIP
Flowers, R. Barri. **The victimization and exploitation of women and children: a study of physical, mental and sexual maltreatment in the United States.** McFarland, 1994. 240p bibl index afp ISBN 0-89950-978-9, $25.95

Flowers reviews the information available about ways in which women and children are abused or sexually exploited. This book is broader in scope but less detailed than works such as *Sexual Coercion*, ed. by Elizabeth Grauerholz and Mary A. Koralewski (1991); *Domestic Violence in Context*, by Robert T. Sigler (CH, Feb'90); or *No Safe Haven: Male Violence Against Women at Home, at Work, and in the Community*, by Mary Koss et al. (CH, Jan'95). It is also broader than earlier works by Flowers, e.g., *Children and Criminality: The Child as Victim and Perpetrator* (CH, Mar'87) and *Woman and Criminality: The Woman as Victim, Offender, and Practitioner* (CH, Jan'88). This book covers child abuse, pornography, prostitution, rape, spouse abuse, and sexual harassment. The writing is straightforward and relatively easy to follow; use of tables is effective. Although most of the information reported is relatively current, the author on occasion fails to note that incidence and prevalence rates he reports are based

on data collected in the 1960s and 1970s. The work is adequately referenced and indexed. Recommended for libraries serving undergraduate programs in the social sciences.—*R. T. Sigler, University of Alabama*

WS-2394 HV4493 90-49624 CIP
Harris, Maxine. **Sisters of the shadow.** Oklahoma, 1991. 252p bibl index afp ISBN 0-8061-2324-9, $19.95

Written by a psychotherapist, this book argues that there are human archetypes that exist in all individuals as "shadows" that people do not acknowledge as part of themselves. In their effort to deny their shadow elements, some poeple have projected them onto others, thereby creating new human identities, e.g., "witches." Harris claims that four shadows have existed for women: the predator; the rebel; the victim; and the exile. These shadows are currently projected with a vengeance onto homeless women, who accept them unwittingly because of their own psychological makeup. Although economic and sociological changes must occur to prevent and alleviate the problems of homeless women, Harris aruges that through psychotherapy and other forms of support, homeless women can stop accepting the responsibility of bearing these shadows. This book uses numerous historical and contemporary examples from many cultures and an extensive set of myths and stories to make its case. Unfortunately, not enough space is given to the stories and words of homeless women themselves. Harris writes clearly, concisely, and respectfully, but some of her examples provide insufficient information to support her argument. Although there are nine pages of endnotes, their format provides inadequate detail to locate specifically the sources of Harris's ideas. There is an interesting six-page bibliography and an integrated subject/author index.—*S. Reinharz, Brandeis University*

WS-2395 HV6250 91-34912 CIP
Hate crimes: confronting violence against lesbians and gay men, ed. by Gregory M. Herek and Kevin T. Berrill. Sage, 1992. 310p ISBN 0-8039-4541-8, $38.00; ISBN 0-8039-4542-6 pbk, $18.95

A first-rate interdisciplinary collection: beautifully organized, highly readable, informative, multicultural, and attentive to feminist concerns. The 18 papers, written in many styles by 16 authors, discuss the concept of "hate crime," recent trends, contexts of violence, the AIDS impact, research methodology, perpetrators (adult and juvenile), survivors, and responses by lesbians and gay men, with special attention to 1980s organizing in New York City, San Francisco, and on campuses. The collection offers a nice balance of analysis, empirical research, and political perspective. A third of the essays were contributed by the editors. The volume also includes a dozen NIMH conference papers published in the *Journal of Interpersonal Violence* (v.6, no. 3: 1990). Added are four hair-raising survivor narratives (two by lesbians; two by gay men). Papers are well documented and there are good notes on editors and contributors. A major source on recent US developments, together with Gary Comstock's *Violence Against Lesbians and Gay Men* (CH, Sep'91), this volume is a "must read" for anyone in law enforcement, health care, or social services, as well as for educators, social scientists, and lesbians and gay men everywhere. All levels.— *C. Card, University of Wisconsin*

WS-2396 HV1569 92-50714 CIP
Hillyer, Barbara. **Feminism and disability.** Oklahoma, 1993. 302p bibl index afp ISBN 0-8061-2500-4, $27.95

Hillyer is a lesbian, feminist theorist, and mother of Jennifer, a retarded daughter, now 27 years old, who lives in a supervised setting. This poignant, personal book is an attempt to understand the challenges of Hillyer's daughter's disability for feminist theory. In the process, Hillyer covers a very broad range of topics and reaches a new understanding of herself. The first chapter was written in 1979 and reflects on Jennifer's possibilities. Hillyer then considers women with disabilities *and* the women who care for them. In a particularly useful chapter, she describes the gamut of politically charged terms. Her literature review is massive and well integrated. Hillyer comments on the ways in which biographies and autobiographies have been written concerning people with disabilities. Among other issues, she discusses "pace and time" for people with disabilities in contemporary American culture; grief; mother-blaming; denial and normalization; technologies; caregivers and difference; and recovery programs (they have a great deal to offer and can be reworked so as to not be sexist). Sensitively written and very brave, this book contributes to the growing body of literature on women and disabilities, and will be helpful to anyone working on these issues personally, professionally, or as an advocate.—*S. Reinharz, Brandeis University*

WS-2397 HQ71 91-46253 CIP
Johnson, Janis Tyler. **Mothers of incest survivors: another side of the story.** Indiana, 1992. 162p bibl index afp ISBN 0-253-33096-3, $20.00; ISBN 0-253-20737-1 pbk, $9.95

Johnson's book is based on six ethnographic interviews of mothers of incest victims. As is typical of this genre, the work is very readable. The approaches used in analyzing the women's lives are sociological, feminist, and symbolic interactionist. The book is more descriptive and less analytical than S. Forward and C. Buck's *Betrayal of Innocence: Incest and its Devastation* (1978). Similarities and differences among the women, demographically and behaviorally, are presented. Johnson also discusses the impact of keeping and revealing the secret, as well as the mothers' responses. She offers explanations and some conclusions but the small sample raises questions about whether these can be generalized. The book is part of the author's doctoral dissertation in social work, begun in the late 1970s. The endnotes do not include year and publisher, forcing the reader to consult references. Bibliography and index are standard. General; undergraduate.—*Y. Peterson, Saint Xavier College*

WS-2398 HV6626 93-24630 CIP
Jones, Ann. **Next time, she'll be dead: battering & how to stop it.** Beacon Press, 1994. 288p index ISBN 0-8070-6770-9, $22.00

Yet another addition to the burgeoning field of family violence. The philosophical assumption underlying this work is that all women have an absolute right to freedom from bodily harm, even at home. Legal cases, however, are cited that support the frequent failure of the system to protect women from assault. The author, having experienced domestic violence in childhood, explores its nature and addresses the frequently raised question of why women stay in abusive relationships. This work, written by a knowledgeable journalist, is more direct and less structured than Dean D. Knudsen and JoAnn Miller's anthology *Abused and Battered* (CH, Oct'91). The latter also deals with social and legal responses to domestic violence. It is perhaps even more engaging reading than Ola Barnett and Alyce LaViolette's *It Could Happen to Anyone* (CH, Jan'94). Jones's very readable book includes an index of sources and topics. The chapter notes are solid and placed in the back, resulting in less distraction. General readers; undergraduate students.—*Y. Peterson, Saint Xavier University*

WS-2399 HV4506 92-39453 CIP
Liebow, Elliot. **Tell them who I am: the lives of homeless women.** Free Press, 1993. 339p bibl index ISBN 0-02-919095-9, $24.95

Liebow, author of *Tally's Corner* (1967), undertook this participant observation study shortly after he was diagnosed with cancer, retired from his job, and began to volunteer in a soup kitchen in the Washington, DC, area. Befriending women in the shelter, he decided to write a book that would tell the story of their lives. The somewhat disjointed result is a combination of Liebow's story and those of numerous homeless women. After a preface concerning methodology and an introduction entitled "The Women, the Shelters and the Round of Life," chapters are divided into two major parts: "Problems in Living" and "Making It: Body and Soul." Footnotes contain additional information, not just bibliographic citations. The book concludes with five appendixes. This reviewer found the "Life Histories" appendix particularly intriguing and disheartening at the same time. The information Liebow provides is valuable for policymakers, social service providers, and the general public concerned with the pervasiveness of homelessness in America. As a book, however, the work reads as a series of continuous beginnings, rather than an integrated whole, an uncanny yet appropriate parallel to the fits and starts of these women's lives. General readers, advanced undergraduates, and above.—*S. Reinharz, Brandeis University*

WS-2400 HV6046 95-15374 CIP
Mann, Coramae Richey. **When women kill.** State University of New York, 1996. 215p bibl index ISBN 0-7914-2811-7, $59.50

Are female killers more deceitful than male killers? Do gender-based dif-

ferences really exist in this type of crime? Mann addresses these questions in comprehensive and exhaustive detail. Sources she consulted for this study include uniform crime reports (UCR); National Center for Health Statistics (NCHS); prison studies; "anecdotal" studies; and city studies, among others, covering the years 1958-67, 1968-77, 1978-87, and 1988 to the present. Mann uses selected demographics on the study cities—Atlanta, Baltimore, Chicago, Houston, Los Angeles, and New York—in describing crime scenes. She analyzes the murder victims of the female homicide offenders, highlighting three distinct approaches; she also analyzes other homicide victims and murder circumstances, and criminal justice data (prior arrest, history of victims, amount of bond, and detention status). She concludes with a summary of the research findings and a synoptic profile of the contemporary female criminal homicide offender. The focus of this last chapter details the motives of female offenders, largely through case studies. Strongly recommended. Upper-division undergraduates and above.—*P. J. Venturelli, Valparaiso University*

WS-2401 HQ759 95-2084 CIP
Mulroy, Elizabeth A. **The new uprooted: single mothers in urban life.** Auburn House, 1995. 188p bibl index afp ISBN 0-86569-038-3, $55.00

What are the daily stresses of trying to survive as a poor mother, alone in a mostly hostile society, raising children in unsafe and insecure environments? In this book, Mulroy (social work, Univ. of Hawaii) contributes greatly to the understanding of the experiences of single mothers, particularly those living in urban areas, and provides the reader with a wealth of demographic and statistical data. In the women's own voices, she tells of their struggles to meet three basic needs: personal safety and security from abuse; shelter in the form of affordable and decent housing for their families; and employment that provides a living wage. An important aspect of Mulroy's book is her focus on the interdependence of these needs and her recommendations for public actions. Highly recommended for policy makers, scholars, students of public policy, and the informed general public. All levels.—*B. A. Pine, University of Connecticut*

WS-2402 HV4493 95-19319 CIP
Ralston, Meredith L. **"Nobody wants to hear our truth": homeless women and theories of the welfare state.** Greenwood, 1996. 202p (Contributions in women's studies, 153) bibl index afp ISBN 0-313-29292-2, $55.00

Ralston's book assesses the "welfare system" by comparing excerpts from interviews, conducted with 20 homeless women receiving welfare, with a set of neoconservative, neoliberal, and feminist theories of the welfare state. The lives of these women encompass an endless series of abuse (sexual, physical, emotional, economic) from childhood through adulthood (drug addiction, alcoholism, prostitution, and criminality). Varied in race and age, the women are articulate about how they became homeless. The only theories that might illuminate their experience are feminist analyses of patriarchy, racism, and sexism. Although the book is concise and well argued, it suffers from its presentation of the women only in one-paragraph excerpts rather than as whole case studies. The theories are also presented in a didactic manner, sometimes bordering on listing one item after the other. Ralston demonstrates that the political rhetoric dominating the left and the right are ineffectual in reducing homelessness among addicted women. Only a strategy addressing the dynamics of these families, including their destructive impact on the self-esteem of children, will make a difference. Upper-division undergraduates and above.—*S. Reinharz, Brandeis University*

WS-2403 HQ759 92-9821 CIP
Ravoira, LaWanda. **Social bonds and teen pregnancy,** by LaWanda Ravoira and Andrew L. Cherry. Praeger, 1992. 175p bibl index afp ISBN 0-275-94179-5, $45.00

Each year an estimated 240,000 babies are born to runaway or homeless teenagers. Most of these children—about 190,000—live with their adolescent mothers on the street or in shelters. This book explores the double jeopardy of homelessness and adolescent pregnancy and parenting. It reports findings of a study of 369 teenaged, mostly pregnant or parenting homeless women residing in three shelters in the South and one in New York. The first four of the book's eight chapters provide an overview of issues and concepts relevant to these dual problems. Chapters 5 through 8 give details of the study and its findings. Unfortunately, the chapters are uneven; some of the themes are neither well developed nor integrated. In particular, social bond theory—a construct of social control, attachment, and problem-behavior theories developed by Cherry, which was to have served as a conceptual framework for the discussion of prevention and intervention strategies—falls short of the authors' promise. The last chapter, containing some of the young women's personal stories, succeeds in telling their plight and makes the book worth reading. Community college; professional.—*B. A. Pine, University of Connecticut*

WS-2404 HV6561 90-5865 MARC
Sanday, Peggy Reeves. **Fraternity gang rape: sex, brotherhood, and privilege on campus.** New York University, 1990. 203p bibl afp ISBN 0-8147-7902-6, $19.95

Sanday, author of *Female Power and Male Dominance* (CH, Nov'81), presents "an anthropological case study and analysis of group rituals and male bonding on a college campus." The case study focuses specifically on an event reported to Sanday in 1983 by a student victim of an activity known, in fraternity lore, as "pulling train" and correctly termed as gang rape by Julie Ehrhart and Bernice Sandler in their report, Project on the Status and Education of Women (1985). Termed the "XYZ Express," this event is the rubric for Part 1, in which the author describes the institutional context that made this gang rape seem natural and expected. She also tells the story from the point of view of two female students, describes the reaction of the fraternity brothers and the university, and details cases on other campuses to demonstrate that this is a national phenomenon. Part 2 presents data and arguments in support of the putative thesis that "pulling train" is a form of "phallocentrism"—sex employed as a symbol of masculine social power and dominance. It is male students, especially some fraternity brothers, who are socialized into such practices. Although this is a rather conventional notion, it is supported here more by ideological than by empirical data. Still this is a worthwhile book. Community college, undergraduate, and general readers.—*P. M. Wickman, SUNY College at Potsdam*

WS-2405 HV6046 90-6432 CIP
Simon, Rita J. **The crimes women commit, the punishments they receive,** by Rita J. Simon and Jean Landis. Lexington Books, 1991. 136p bibl index afp ISBN 0-669-20236-3, $22.95

Althought the title has changed, this is a second edition of Simon's *Women and Crime* (CH, Nov'75). It presents current data on women's criminality, criminal justice experiences, demographic characteristics, and socioeconomic profiles. One chapter identifies four dominant themes used to explain female crimes and punishments: masculinity, opportunity, economic marginalization, and chivalry. Subsequent chapters offer an abundance of descriptive detail (more than 50 tables) that confirms the persistence of trends Simon identified in her first edition: women are increasingly involved in property and minor white-collar offenses, but not in violence; courts continue to exhibit some leniency toward women; and some improvements in the management of female corrections are apparent. This edition is valuable because of its scope as a current report. As an investigation into the impact of the women's movement on female crime and social control, however, it is only suggestive. Without multivariate analysis it cannot resolve the theoretical disputes. Nonetheless, it is a clearly written and instructive revision that will be useful for all pertinent undergraduate studies.—*R. Zingraff, Meredith College*

WS-2406 Can. CIP
Thorne-Finch, Ron. **Ending the silence: the origins and treatment of male violence against women.** Toronto, 1992. 394p bibl index afp ISBN 0-8020-5989-9, $55.00; ISBN 0-8020-6923-1 pbk, $19.95

Not just another book about men who batter, this work fulfills its promise with a solid and critical overview of psychological, physiological, and social theories on abuse. A survey of the frequency of abuse against women is followed by an assessment of the effects of male violence on women. Although reminiscent in style of Mildred D. Pagelow's *Family Violence* (1984), Thorne-Finch's book has a more narrow focus. It is also less technical than *Abused and Battered*, ed. by D.D. Knudsen and J.L. Miller (CH, Oct'91). Thorne-Finch critiques treatment approaches and the state's response to violent men. The author's male perspective and typology invite men to compare their responses to their own

and other men's violence. Concrete methods for intervention and treatment are given. The author takes an advocacy position that is both therapeutically and sociologically well informed and solidly documented. Standard references are provided. This book is well worth reading for interveners, students of family violence and men in general. Undergraduate; professional; general.—*Y. Peterson, Saint Xavier College*

WS-2407 HT361 91-31209 CIP
Wilson, Elizabeth. **The sphinx in the city: urban life, the control of disorder, and women.** California, 1992 (c1991). 191p bibl index afp ISBN 0-520-07850-0, $35.00; ISBN 0-520-07864-0 pbk, $14.00

Wilson presents an interesting if unusual postulate: cities, or urban life, have given women more opportunities to be liberated than they have given men. Cities provide women with increased chances of living fuller lives and of finding other women who share their feelings and values, and provide women an arena in which to explore the several dimensions of their sexuality. Wilson pursues this investigation by examining both European and American cities from the historical perspective of the last 100 years. She is not naive in underestimating the social costs of urban life that many women have experienced, nor does she believe that the current crop of urban problems are being solved or even adequately addressed. One of her salient points is that much urban reform and urban planning has been overly patriarchal and therefore not only incomplete but also inadequate and irrelevant for women. What is needed, she proclaims, is a "new vision, a new ideal of life in the city—and a new 'feminine' voice in praise of cities." This book is addressed to a general audience, but could be added with profit to courses on urban social organization and urban problems. All levels.—*J. R. Hudson, Pennsylvania State University, Harrisburg*

WS-2408 HV132 91-11740 CIP
Wiseman, Jacqueline P. **The other half: wives of alcoholics and their social-psychological situation.** Aldine de Gruyter, 1991. 297p bibl index afp ISBN 0-202-30382-9, $39.95; ISBN 0-202-30383-7 pbk, $19.95

Wiseman studied wives of alcholics in the US and Finland, comparing the problems they face in defining their husbands as problem drinkers. She also investigated the approaches these wives used to get their husbands to curb excessive drinking, the search for successful treatment, and the effects of alcholic husbands on the women and their marriages. Using a symbolic-interactionist framework, Wiseman refreshingly analyzes the situation from the wives' perspective, bringing a new dimension to the understanding of the family situation. Her study reveals how little power wives have to control their husbands' drinking on their own, although the expectation is that they should. A fascinating and informative work, the book is lucidly written by an expert in the field, and is accessible to a wide variety of readers. Extensive references.—*C. Adamsky, University of New Hampshire*

WS-2409 HV6626x 90-84733 Orig
Woman battering: policy responses, ed. by Michael Steinman. Academy of Criminal Justice Sciences/Anderson Publishing Company, 1991. 264p ISBN 0-87084-807-0 pbk, $15.95

Written specifically for this volume, most of these articles report results from contemporary research. The focus on system responses to woman battering includes issues of measurement, police policies and programs, and intervention programs. The contributing authors are recognized for their work in this area and have produced an excellent group of essays. The quality of the referencing varies from chapter to chapter. There is effective use of selected tables and illustrations. The writing is fairly consistent and readable at an advanced level. Recommended for libraries serving programs in women's studies, sociology, psychology, social work, counseling, or criminal justice. Upper-division undergraduates and above.—*R. T. Sigler, University of Alabama*

◆ Women & Work

WS-2410 HD4904 93-31949 CIP

Apter, Terri. **Working women don't have wives: professional success in the 1990s.** St. Martin's, 1994 (c1993). 280p bibl index ISBN 0-312-09675-5, $19.95

A thorough, timely revision of Apter's *Why Women Don't Have Wives* (CH, Dec'85). Written for a popular audience, the book nonetheless takes readers through the academic literature on balancing careers and families in a way that represents fairly the complexity of the conclusions of the research, criticizes the limitations of the questions that have been asked, and reflects the best of contemporary gender theory. Although Apter used intensive interviews with a small sample of American and British working mothers to develop her perspective, the interview materials themselves do not dominate the book. Instead, Apter has digested their concerns and conflicts and worked them into a coherent narrative of structures and choices. The perspective she offers holds a vivid awareness of the economic underpinnings and social patterns that constrain people who are acting with the best will in the world. She blends this into a more complex picture in which motives are not always pure, constraints are never absolute, and male power is real but not all-determining. A balanced, useful, nuanced look at a vexing issue that, as Apter clearly shows, will not just go away. This book will be very useful for many women who are struggling with the choices and constraints she describes. All levels.—*M. M. Ferree, University of Connecticut*

WS-2411 HD2336 93-11104 CIP

Boris, Eileen. **Home to work: motherhood and the politics of industrial homework in the United States.** Cambridge, 1994. 383p indexes ISBN 0-521-44370-9, $59.95; ISBN 0-521-45548-0 pbk, $17.95

Industrial homework is factory or office work that is contracted by employers to be done in the home. Developing alongside the factory system from the early 19th century on, outwork has been an integral, although largely invisible part of production in the US. In this thorough, wide-ranging, and well-crafted history of homework, Boris asserts that its regulation has proved to be a remarkably obdurate problem, largely because of its gendered context. Despite changes in products and demographics, it has almost always been poorly paid piece work, done almost exclusively by women. Far from diminishing in recent years, outwork has actually expanded as an integral component of the electronic revolution. Boris details the ongoing political struggle over outwork from the 1870s on, describing the way in which the constituencies who engaged in debate—employers, trade unionists, reformers, state and federal legislatures, and the courts—framed the issues. She argues convincingly that because the language of motherhood provided the rhetorical frame for all parties in the struggle, the outcome not only reinforced dominant cultural understandings, but facilitated the persistence of underpaid and unregulated waged work for women in the home. General readers, upper-division undergraduates, and above.—*N. B. Rosenthal, SUNY College at Old Westbury*

WS-2412 HD6060 91-2736 CIP

Cockburn, Cynthia. **In the way of women: men's resistance to sex equality in organizations.** ILR Press, 1991. 260p (Cornell international industrial and labor relations report, 18) bibl index ISBN 0-87546-700-8, $36.00; ISBN 0-87546-701-6 pbk, $16.95

How are men and the organizations they dominate responding to sex equity efforts in the work force? Cockburn examines four different organizations in England: a major retail company; a white collar, elite, national public bureaucracy; a Left, labor, local authority; and a trade union with a predominately low-skilled membership. She painstakingly compares the myriad reasons why and the conditions under which men are either favorable or opposed to women's advancement. What becomes clear is that neither men nor women are consistent and the results of seeking equity are mixed. Male leaders are happy to advance a few women, but balk at the great cost of generally improving positions and pay. Women workers most appreciate improved maternity and child care benefits, but this reinforces traditional domestic roles. Cockburn briefly compares discrimination by sex, ethnicity, social class, and disability. She also explains theoretical ideas as male hegemony, and describes the limits of socialism for feminism, effectively integrating discussion with case studies. Although this work

is somewhat densely written, it is highly recommended because of its detailed research, action steps, and international comparisons. Upper-division undergraduates and above.—*S. D. Borchert, Lake Erie College*

WS-2413 HD6079 92-52747 CIP

Cook, Alice H. **The most difficult revolution: women and trade unions,** by Alice H. Cook, Val R. Lorwin, and Arlene Kaplan Daniels. Cornell, 1992. 300p bibl index afp ISBN 0-8014-1916-6, $46.50; ISBN 0-8014-8065-5 pbk, $14.95

This comparative sociological study of issues surrounding gender, unions, and governmental practices was prepared by the same research team that released *Women and Trade Unions in Eleven Industrialized Countries* (CH, Jul'84). Emphasis is placed on efforts to increase the decision-making presence of women within unions and to achieve workplace and social-policy changes in key areas such as health and safety, pay equity, training, and hours. Despite a rather pessimistic tone, the investigation is perhaps most interesting because of its constant comparisons of labor practices and legal measures affecting gender and family issues in four other nations—Britain, Germany, Austria, and Sweden—with the historical and contemporary situation of working women in the US. Topics range widely from discussions of microlevel programs to increase women's participation within unions to macrolevel attempts to influence social policy formulation through political parties, activism, and interest group alliances. Advanced undergraduate; graduate; faculty; professional.—*F. Burkhard, Morgan State University*

WS-2414 HD6060 94-32845 CIP

Gender inequality at work, ed. by Jerry A. Jacobs. Sage Publications, CA, 1995. 438p bibl index ISBN 0-8039-5696-7, $46.00; ISBN 0-8039-5697-5 pbk, $23.95

Written by academics from the field of sociology, this collection of articles on gender issues at work, is diverse, including studies on compensation, authority, career processes, and occupational segregation. Many insights on the measurement, status, and explanations of male/female inequality are provided. Each contribution presents a well-researched, -written, and -referenced study. The sociological approach is paramount. Material from economics, particularly the human capital approach, is often discussed and debated, and management literature is cited. Introductory and concluding chapters help tie the material together, but each study is independent. Several chapters address occupational/job segregation and resegregation. Specific studies on managers, television writers, sociology professors, and computer workers are included, as is a chapter on sex segregation internationally. The influence of social forces on outcomes is stressed. Evidence that the gender gap is closing is presented; however, the authors do not foresee equality soon. A good volume for researchers in the field. Graduate; faculty.—*F. Reitman, Pace University*

WS-2415 HD6095 92-19837 CIP

Glazer, Nona Y. **Women's paid and unpaid labor: the work transfer in health care and retailing.** Temple University, 1993. 273p bibl index afp ISBN 0-87722-979-1, $39.95

Glazer examines two areas of work that have changed in important but often unrecognized ways since mid-century: retail sales and nursing. Both types of work have undergone what Glazer terms "work transfer," in which some labor previously done as waged work is shifted into unpaid but profitable labor, i.e., is transformed into "housework," women's unpaid, unrecognized, domestic responsibilities. Glazer details the nature of this transformation and what it has meant for both waged workers (sales clerks and nurses) and unpaid family workers who now are doing much of the shopping and nursing care. The emergence of the "supermarket" and the decline of home delivery are parts of the "self-service" revolution that changed retailing. Sending patients home "quicker and sicker" has not only been a means of hospital cost management, but a boon for home health technology companies. In both cases, the kind of labor done without pay, primarily by women, has been a source of profits for companies that dominate these industries. The wealth of descriptive detail is a great strength of this book. Anecdotal and statistical evidence are woven together throughout the work to give a comprehensive view of changes that are part of daily life but are rarely noticed as sociologically significant. Advanced undergraduates and above.—*M. M. Ferree, University of Connecticut*

WS-2416   HD6054   93-37848 CIP
Jacobs, Jerry. **Professional women at work: interactions, tacit understandings, and the non-trivial nature of trivia in bureaucratic settings.** Bergin & Garvey, 1994. 144p bibl index afp ISBN 0-89789-380-8, $47.95

Jacobs's study is a qualitative assessment of how routine, largely ignored aspects of work (what the author calls "trivia") affect the work experience. The opening two chapters present Jacobs's argument that sociology's partiality for quantitative analyses has led to the neglect of a central aspect of work: the routine, or trivial nature of the work process itself. Five of eight chapters are devoted to analyses of open-ended interview data with five professional women. Particular attention is paid to these women's career paths, career development, social interaction, burnout, and strategies for coping with and/or resisting the bureaucratic characteristics of work. While successful at providing a rich description of the work experience, this book does little to link these particular women's experiences to important theoretical, conceptual, and public policy issues that are being addressed elsewhere in the literature on women's employment. Nevertheless, this monograph provides a convincing argument for the need for qualitative analyses of the taken-for-granted characteristics of work. Advanced undergraduate; graduate.—*S. K. Gallagher, Oregon State University*

WS-2417   HQ759   92-56789 CIP
Lamphere, Louise. **Sunbelt working mothers: reconciling family and factory,** by Louise Lamphere et al. Cornell, 1993. 330p bibl index afp ISBN 0-8014-2788-6, $39.95; ISBN 0-8014-8066-3 pbk, $15.95

An extension of the interesting research on working-class women previously pursued separately by Lamphere (*From Working Daughters to Working Mothers*, CH, Dec'87) and Patricia Zavella (*Women's Work and Chicano Families*, CH, Feb'88). The current data is new and consists of qualitative interviews with 53 Anglo and Mexican American women in Albuquerque and a chapter of quantitative data on the industrial shifts in this particular labor market. Research issues these anthropologists address include a variety of significant differences among women: those based on ethnicity, marital status, extended family network, economic role in the family, and workplace situation. The former three concerns are relatively common in the work-and-family literature. This book makes its most substantial contribution by relating shop-floor management strategies (hierarchical or participative) to the women's work experiences broadly understood, and by considering the work histories of both husbands and wives in shaping the perceived role women's earnings play in the family. By looking at the structure of opportunity and constraint these women are negotiating, the authors move away from individualistic analyses of women's "choices" and do much to mitigate stereotypes of working-class women as particularly "traditional." Advanced undergraduates and above.—*M. M. Ferree, University of Connecticut*

WS-2418   HQ759.48   90-25897 CIP
Lerner, Jacqueline V. **Employed mothers and their children,** by Jacqueline V. Lerner and Nancy L. Galambos. Garland, 1991. 295p (Reference books on family issues, 17) index afp ISBN 0-8240-6344-9, $33.00

A collection of articles describing research relating to child development and parental employment. Issues studied include the effects of day care on children, child self-care, household labor of children, and employment of parents, with particular emphasis given to maternal employment. The authors stress the need for "a larger sense of community responsibility for children, whoever their parents are." The collection serves as a contemporary source of sound data on families and employed parents, particularly mothers. Each chapter includes an annotated bibliography of relevant reference materials. The volume may be used as a resource for advanced research and policy relating to the needs of children today. A valuable reference for parents, pediatricians, social workers, and students in the fields of child development and child welfare. All levels.—*M. O. McMahon, East Carolina University*

WS-2419   HD6475.A2   90-2003 MARC
Lubin, Carol Riegelman. **Social justice for women: the International Labor Organization and women,** by Carol Riegelman Lubin and Anne Winslow. Duke University, 1991 (c1990). 328p index afp ISBN 0-8223-1062-7, $45.00

A straightforward narrative of what the International Labor Organization is

and what it has done for women, this book follows the chronology of events and organizational changes in the ILO from its founding in 1919 to 1990. The account is rich in detail, including short biographical sketches of most of the women who have played influential roles in the organization or in related trade unions, employer association, or national government agencies throughout this entire 70-year span. Actions and recommendations are meticulously dated and the major players are identified. Conclusions about outcomes are often advanced as well, but very modestly, and few generalizations about organizational processes are offered. Highly controversial debates—such as the battle between advocates of protective legislation for women and defenders of equal treatment for both sexes—are reported briefly, with no hint of the passions that raged in these struggles, or why they did. Similarly, the highly charged issues around appropriate policies for women in developing countries receive mention but little analysis. In sum, a specialized descriptive study, most useful for those concerned with individuals and discrete events in international policy and labor history.—*M. M. Ferree, University of Connecticut*

WS-2420   HD6053   89-25673 CIP
Lunneborg, Patricia W. **Women changing work.** Greenwood, 1990. 210p (Contributions in women's studies, 112) bibl index afp ISBN 0-313-26843-6, $42.95; ISBN 0-89789-214-3, $12.95

Designed for the general reader, this book on women employees in ten occupations explores the ways in which nontraditional workers, in this case women, change their once exclusionary work worlds. Very little research has examined how women have changed traditional male work worlds. Lunneborg, a retired professor of psychology and adjunct professor of women's studies at the University of Washington, has previously authored numerous publications, including some on working women. In this book, she speaks explicitly to women and wishes to encourage women workers to get into nontraditional work usually reserved for men. Drawing on in-depth interviews with women employees, Lunneborg asks five broad questions: How do you approach your job differently than men do? What subtle differences do you notice in the way you do your job relative to men? How do male/female value differences in your occupation affect the way work is done? What are the strengths of women for your occupation? How would increasing the numbers of women in your occupation change your job and workplace? These probing questions generated important answers, including the basic finding that women relished managing and organizing people, data, and things. The women employees' style rejected the traditional male hierarchical, competitive, controlling style for one accenting more sharing, consensus-building, tolerance, support, and openness to change. Although Lunneborg's writing sometimes reads like a first draft, the material is extraordinarily important and thoughtfully analyzed.—*J. R. Feagin, University of Florida*

WS-2421   Can. CIP
Martin, Michèle. **"Hello, Central?": gender, technology, and culture in the formation of telephone systems.** McGill-Queen's, 1991. (Dist. by Toronto) 219p bibl index afp ISBN 0-7735-0830-9, $34.95

A feminist history of women workers of the Canadian Bell Telephone system. Martin contends that women may contribute to the distribution of a technology despite their underrepresentation in its development. She attempts to show also the link between the development of a new technology and the political-economic and cultural-ideological conditions within which it grew. Martin dwells on how Bell manipulated these women workers to maximize its profit. The author's excessive use of Marxist terminology, however, makes the book sound like a piece of propaganda. Despite the heavy political undertone, there is much useful and interesting information on women operators of Bell Telephone in Canada—how they were trained, what was expected of them, and how they changed functionally and normatively through the years. Comparative data on male workers as well as on women garment workers are missing, hence, the reader is encouraged to consult a good source on economic history or industrial sociology, e.g., *Man, Work, and Society*, ed., by S. Nosow and W.H. Form (1962). Upper-division undergraduates.—*M. Y. Rynn, University of Scranton*

WS-2422   HQ759   91-36728 CIP
Moen, Phyllis. **Women's two roles: a contemporary dilemma.** Auburn House, 1992. 172p bibl index afp ISBN 0-86569-198-3, $45.00; ISBN 0-86569-199-1 pbk, $16.95

Although numerous books and articles have described the stresses and strains experienced by employed women and their families, this book contains new, relevant information. With a sense of urgency, Moen identifies differences in women's approaches to combining work and family roles by examining, among other issues, the diversity of their work commitment. Moen argues that employed women with families generally fit one of four topologies: "captives," "conflicted," "copers," and "committed." Trend analysis, a technique that receives considerable attention throughout her book, reveals that captives (working women whose family cares make them unwilling employees) are declining while committed workers (well-educated career women whose family plans are often delayed) are increasing. Moen brings new information and insights into the costs for women and for young chldren of mothers' combining two roles. Finally, this book includes logical arguments for transforming the structure of work and for reconfiguring the patterns of education-work-retirement over women's—as well as men's—life course. Advanced undergraduate; graduate; faculty.—*A. S. Oakes, Idaho State University*

WS-2423 HV8023 94-42841 CIP
Schulz, Dorothy Moses. **From social worker to crimefighter: women in United States municipal policing.** Praeger, 1995. 175p bibl index afp ISBN 0-275-94996-6, $55.00

Schulz offers a solid social history of the roles women filled in policing American communities from the 1820s through the 1980s. Her approach is primarily descriptive, characterized by outstanding documentation that showcases the individual careers of specific women and charts the changes in custom, law, and law enforcement that have transformed the nature of women's work and influence. As a focused study of gender and occupation, the book establishes how women who pioneered entry into police work were overwhelmingly more qualified in education and training than their male peers, and it explains how the equalization of standards has involved requiring less of women rather than more of men. Implications here for the study of occupational restructuring in general as well as for the professionalization of law enforcement in particular are worth serious reflection. This book also contains significant historical detail regarding the development of social work as a profession and its impact on the functions designated as "policing" during the turbulence of the Depression years, the war years, and the years of civil unrest leading up to the famous Kerner Commission Report. Not intended to be a theoretical or analytical treatment of either gender or law enforcement, it offers interesting narrative and presents with appropriate praise many actual women who faced high risks and high challenge as they sought first to improve policing and then to gain equal footing on patrol. All levels.—*R. Zingraff, Meredith College*

WS-2424 HD6060 91-36332 CIP
Shelton, Beth Anne. **Women, men and time: gender differences in paid work, housework and leisure.** Greenwood, 1992. 182p (Contributions in women's studies, 127) bibl index afp ISBN 0-313-26512-7, $39.95

The division of household labor has been much studied in recent years, with most studies concluding that women do considerably more housework and childcare than men and have much less leisure time. Shelton's book reaffirms these basic findings with a reanalysis of quantitative time-use data collected in 1975, 1981, and 1987. The point of the analysis is to examine change over time, but the use of different samples restricts this to aggregate-level changes between groups and therefore limits the potential for understanding the specific dynamics of change within individuals or households. The analysis is relatively uninspired and the findings thus mostly contribute to confirming patterns found in other studies with less representative samples or less recent data. Specialists will probably want to quibble with some of the specific decisions about the data analysis and interpretation, but on the whole, the author offers a competent, dissertation like presentation of findings. Graduate.—*M. M. Ferree, University of Connecticut*

WS-2425 HD6065 92-21874 CIP
Vogel, Lise. **Mothers on the job: maternity policy in the U.S. workplace.** Rutgers, 1993. 202p ISBN 0-8135-1918-7, $34.00; ISBN 0-8135-1919-5 pbk, $16.00

Vogel examines how the equality/difference debate within feminism has been played out in pregnancy policy in the US. The first half of the book explores

the history of this policy—and feminist responses to it—with particular attention to race and class in determining who has benefited from policies based on "difference." The second half of the book addresses ideological, strategic, and theoretical issues that have emerged from the pregnancy policy debate. Refusing to choose between difference and equality, Vogel argues that theories, and policies based on them, must begin to incorporate cultural heterogeneity as well as structural relations of power. Policies founded on such "differential consideration" can affirm women's capacity to bear children within a broader conceptualization of equality that takes into account a range of specificities. This is a well-written, important book that will be of interest to all those with interests in public policy (both historical and current), culture, theory, and practice. Advanced undergraduate; graduate; faculty; professional.—*S. K. Gallagher, Rutgers, The State University of New Jersey New Brunswick*

WS-2426 HD6073 90-25829 CIP
Wilson, Fiona. **Sweaters: gender, class, and workshop-based industry in Mexico.** St. Martin's, 1991. 224p bibl indexes ISBN 0-312-06110-2, $65.00

Wilson writes: "I wanted to explore rural industrialisation not only from the perspective of what was good or profitable for capital, I also wanted to examine the processes and transformations at work in the context of a particular locality (in Mexico) and see these through the eyes of the people most actively involved." Wilson realizes this double objective very well. She pays close attention to local manifestations of gender and class relations both in the past and present, and focuses on the actions of particular groups in local society. Her analytical emphasis then moves to a more abstract discussion underlining important general points and drawing conclusions from the Mexican example that may be applied in the construction of a theoretical model of workshop-based production. Throughout, Wilson explores local social and economic changes as seen through women's eyes, comparing the worlds of contemporary workshop workers with that of their mothers and grandmothers. Material on the histories, actions, and opinions of people from a small town in Mexico is presented together with an interpretation of the structures in which their lives are set. Strongly recommended for upper-division undergraduates and above.—*E. Bastida, University of Texas—Pan American*

WS-2427 HT687 91-13905 CIP
Witz, Anne. **Professions and patriarchy.** Routledge, 1992. 233p bibl indexes ISBN 0-415-05008-1, $69.50; ISBN 0-415-07044-9 pbk, $17.95

Witz (University of Exeter) offers a broad framework for understanding the relationship between professions and patriarchy. She outlines strategies for professionalization, such as exclusion and demarcation by gender, based on neo-Weberian concepts of closure and power. The first part of the study establishes a foundation, reviewing patriarchy, capitalism, gender relations, work, and the basic theories of the professions. The second part is composed of chapters on gender and medical professionalization generally, and brief but detailed historical studies of British obstetrics and midwifery (late 19th century), nurse registration (late 19th-early 20th century), and radiography (1920s). This is a useful construct for understanding the institutionalization of male power and masculine values. The studies are well selected, although the thesis clearly needs to be tested on other professions. The book has an extensive bibliography, but Witz's writing inhibits her analytic vigor. Of interest to sociology and women's studies programs. Upper-division undergraduates and above.—*J. L. Croissant, Rensselaer Polytechnic Institute*

WS-2428 HD6053 90-33854 CIP
Women at work: psychological and organizational perspectives, ed. by Jenny Firth-Cozens and Michael A. West. Open University Press, 1990 (c1991). (Dist. by Taylor & Francis) 214p indexes ISBN 0-335-09253-5, $59.00; ISBN 0-335-09252-7, $21.00

This collection examines the psychological and organizational work environment of women. Chapters are individually authored and present a carefully documented examination of the topic by reviewing past and current research, considering practical implications, and proposing changes in individual and organizational behavior. The book is divided into three parts. The first part covers general issues such as types of work assigned to women; the power-based relations of gender that impact the activities of job assessment and selection; equal opportunity policies; and women's training needs. Part 2 examines problems working women face, including sexual harassment; women's reproductive health in the context of work; reproductive hazards at work; and women returning to the workforce after a career break. Part 3 examines women in middle-class careers—entrepreneurs, doctors, computer professionals, managers, and politicians. The overall perspective of this collection challenges the status quo, such as the resistance to suggestions for changing the organization of work, and addresses the issues of working women as related to politics and power. Upper-division and graduate collections.—*K. C. Brannen, Creighton University*

WS-2429   Can. CIP
Women, work, and coping: a multidisciplinary approach to workplace stress, ed. by Bonita C. Long and Sharon E. Kahn. UBC Academic Women's Association/Canadian Centre for Policy Alternatives, Ottawa/McGill-Queen's, 1993. 332p indexes afp ISBN 0-7735-1128-8, $49.95; ISBN 0-7735-1129-6 pbk, $17.95

This collection of 14 scholarly essays derived from a 1991 University of British Columbia workshop advances considerably the understanding of challenges and coping strategies employed by North American women facing work-related stress. The initial overview presents solid statistics documenting the nature and extent of the increase of women's workforce participation while acknowledging the lack of corresponding changes in the unpaid labor associated with home and family responsibilities. The stressors that women must cope with include a hostile, gendered work environment, an unsupportive home environment, social disapproval, and confusion and conflict in self-concept and role appraisal. Among the useful explorations is Judi Marshall's essay, which develops a four-tiered model of coping strategies used by women managers, ranging from denial to creative reshaping of the cultural context in the workplace. Similarly, Craig Smith looks at responses to the disparate sources of stress and develops a model of appraisal, stress, and emotion with diagnostic and predictive utility. A concluding essay integrates many of the contributing themes within a transactional model of stress and coping. Extensive chapter references and diagrams. Advanced undergraduate through professional.—*L. M. C. Abbott, California School of Professional Psychology*

Name Index

Index entries refer to review numbers.

~ A ~

Abromowitz, Jennifer. Women outdoors. WS-0171

Abu-Lughod, Lila. Writing women's worlds. WS-1399

Ackelsberg, Martha A. Free women of Spain. WS-1747

Acker, Ally. Reel women. WS-0119

Acker, Bertie, tr. Iphigenia. WS-0691

Adair, Christy. Women and dance. WS-0957

Adams, Alice E. Reproducing the womb. WS-0176

Adams, Carol J. Neither man nor beast. WS-1334

Adams, Carol J. The sexual politics of meat. WS-1335

Adams, Carol J., ed. Animals and women. WS-1336

Adams, Carol J., ed. Ecofeminism and the sacred. WS-1338

Adams, Diane L., ed. Health issues for women of color. WS-1293

Adams, Jane. The transformation of rural life. WS-1986

Adams, Judith Porter. Peacework. WS-1536

Adaskina, Natalia L. Popova. WS-0228

Adelman, Janet. Suffocating mothers. WS-0318

Adepoju, Aderanti, ed. Gender, work & population in sub-Saharan Africa. WS-2290

Adleman, Jeanne, ed. Racism in the lives of women. WS-2368

Adler, Kathleen. Perspectives on Morisot. WS-0244

Adler, Leonore Loeb, ed. International handbook on gender roles. WS-0166

Aercke, Kristiaan, ed. Women writing in Dutch. WS-0621

Agosín, Marjorie, ed. A dream of light & shadow. WS-0677

Agosín, Marjorie, ed. Surviving beyond fear. WS-1786

Agosín, Marjorie, ed. What is secret. WS-0703

Ahmad, Alia. Women and fertility in Bangladesh. WS-2277

Ahmed, Leila. Women and gender in Islam. WS-1791

Aiken, Susan Hardy. Dialogues/Dialogi. WS-0718

Ajzenberg-Selove, Fay. A matter of choices. WS-1169

Åkerman, Susanna. Queen Christina of Sweden and her circle. WS-1637

Alayeto, Ofelia. Sofía Casanova (1861-1958): Spanish poet, journalist and author. WS-0667

Alcott, Louisa May. A long fatal love chase. WS-0793

Alcott, Louisa May. Louisa May Alcott unmasked. WS-0794

Alcott, Louisa May. Moods. WS-0795

Alegría, Claribel. Fugues. WS-0668

Alencar, José de. Senhora: profile of a woman. WS-0669

Alexander, Paul. Rough magic: a biography of Sylvia Plath. WS-0876

Alexander, Ruth M. The "girl problem." WS-2251

Ali, Aruna Asaf. The resurgence of Indian women. WS-1606

Allan, Tuzyline Jita. Womanist and feminist aesthetics. WS-0319

Allen, Ann Taylor. Feminism and motherhood in Germany, 1800-1914. WS-1740

Allen, Carolyn. Following Djuna. WS-0729

Allen, Judith A. Rose Scott: vision and revision in feminism. WS-1607

Allen, Marvin. In the company of men. WS-2122

Allen, Paula Gunn. Grandmothers of the light. WS-1408

Allgood, Myralyn F. Another way to be. WS-0671

Allison, Anne. Nightwork: sexuality, pleasure, and corporate masculinity in a Tokyo hostess club. WS-1409

Allison, Jenene J. Revealing difference. WS-0622

Allison, Julie A. Rape: the misunderstood crime. WS-1354

Allison, Mary Bruins. Doctor Mary in Arabia. WS-1261

Almeida, Irène Assiba d'. Francophone African women writers. WS-0411

Alonso, Ana María. Thread of blood. WS-1381

Alston, R.C. A checklist of women writers, 1801-1900. WS-0083

Alvarez, Ruth M. Katherine Anne Porter: an annotated bibliography. WS-0107

Alwes, Karla. Imagination transformed. WS-0492

Amell, Alma. Rosa Montero's odyssey. WS-0670

Amert, Susan. In a shattered mirror. WS-0712

Amigoni, David, ed. Charles Darwin's The origin of species. WS-1195

Ammer, Christine. The new A to Z of women's health. WS-1232

Ammons, Elizabeth. Conflicting stories. WS-0282

Amoia, Alba della Fazia. Women on the Italian literary scene. WS-0706

Amott, Teresa. Race, gender, and work. WS-1476

Anderson, Alice. Human nature: poems. WS-0877

Anderson, Amanda. Tainted souls and painted faces. WS-0493

Anderson, Bernice Taylor. Breaking the barriers. WS-1174

Andrew, Joe. Narrative and desire in Russian literature, 1822-49. WS-0713

Andrews, Nancy. Family: a portrait of gay and lesbian America. WS-2330

Angel, Jacqueline L. Painful inheritance. WS-1233

Angel, Ronald J. Painful inheritance. WS-1233

Anglesey, Zoe, tr. Mouth to mouth. WS-0687

Appelle, Christine. Politics as if women mattered. WS-2063

Appignanesi, Lisa. Freud's women. WS-2181

Apter, Terri. Secret paths: women in the new midlife. WS-2203

Apter, Terri. Working women don't have wives. WS-2410

Arat, Yesim. The patriarchal paradox. WS-2051

Arbuckle, Elisabeth Sanders, ed. Harriet Martineau in the London Daily News. WS-0509

Arcana, Judith. Grace Paley's life stories. WS-0878

Ardis, Ann L. New women, new novels. WS-0320

Arebi, Saddeka. Women and words in Saudi Arabia. WS-0412

Arico, Santo L. Contemporary women writers in Italy. WS-0708

Armitage, Susan, ed. Women in the West. WS-0033

Armitage, Susan. So much to be done. WS-1976

Armitt, Lucie, ed. Where no man has gone before. WS-0353

Armstrong, Louise. Of 'sluts' and 'bastards.' WS-2386

Arnold, Marilyn, ed. A readers companion to the fiction of Willa Cather. WS-0111a

Arora, Anand. The women elite in India. WS-2278

Aroutunova, Bayara. Lives in letters. WS-0723

Asher, Ramona M. Women with alcoholic husbands. WS-2387

Ashley, Douglas. Music beyond sound. WS-1002

Aslanbeigui, Nahid, ed. Women in the age of economic transformation. WS-1474

Assiter, Alison. Enlightened women. WS-2204

Astin, Helen S. Women of influence, women of vision. WS-2374

Aston, Elaine. An introduction to feminism and theatre. WS-1031

Atkinson, Clarissa W. The oldest vocation. WS-1569

Aufderheide, May. American women composers. WS-1001

Awe, Bolanle, ed. Nigerian women in historical perspective. WS-1601

~ B ~

Babbitt, Susan E. Impossible dreams. WS-1068

Bacchi, Carol Lee. Same difference. WS-2310

Bach, Steven. Marlene Dietrich: life and legend. WS-0967

Bachmann, Ingeborg. Malina: a novel. WS-0607

Backhouse, Constance, ed. Challenging times. WS-2376

Backscheider, Paula R. Spectacular politics. WS-1032

Bacon, Margaret Hope. One woman's passion for peace and freedom. WS-1537

Bacon-Smith, Camille. Enterprising women. WS-2205

Bacot, Ada W. A Confederate nurse. WS-1923

Badran, Margot. Feminists, Islam, and nation. WS-1793

Baechler, Lea, ed. Modern American women writers. WS-0112

Baer, Judith A. Women in American law. WS-2089

Bagwe, Anjali. Of woman caste. WS-1410

Bahr, Diana Meyers. From mission to metropolis. WS-1411

Bai, Hua. The remote country of women. WS-0427

Bailey-Mershon, Glenda, ed. Jane's stories. WS-0907

Bair, Barbara, ed. Wings of gauze. WS-1297

Bair, Deirdre. Anaïs Nin, a biography. WS-0879

Baird, Joseph L., tr. The letters of Hildegard of Bingen, v.1. WS-1130

Baker, Adrienne. The Jewish woman in contemporary society. WS-1383

Baker, Paula. The moral frameworks of public life. WS-1808

Bakker, Isabella, ed. Rethinking restructuring. WS-2240

Bakker, Isabella, ed. The strategic silence. WS-1485

Balakrishnan, T.R. Family and childbearing in Canada. WS-2279

Balch, Trudy, tr. Women writers of Latin America. WS-0678

Baldauf-Berdes, Jane L. Women musicians of Venice. WS-1003

Baldwin, John W. The language of sex. WS-1570

Ballaster, Ros. Seductive forms. WS-0440

Bammer, Angelika. Partial visions. WS-0284

Banks, Olive. The biographical dictionary of British feminists. WS-0058

Banks, Olive. The politics of British feminism, 1918-1970. WS-1685

Bannister, Robert C. Jessie Bernard: the making of a feminist. WS-2252

Bar On, Bat-Ami, ed. Engendering origins. WS-1077

Bar On, Bat-Ami, ed. Modern engendering. WS-1095

Barbauld, Anna Letitia. The poems of Anna Letitia Barbauld. WS-0441

Barber, Elizabeth Wayland. Women's work: the first 20,000 years. WS-1405

Bardes, Barbara. Declarations of independence. WS-0732

Barickman, Richard B. Academic and workplace sexual harassment. WS-0154

Baring, Anne. The myth of the goddess. WS-1384

Barker-Benfield, G.J. The culture of sensibility. WS-1686

Barnes, Ruth, ed. Dress and gender. WS-1386

Barnes, Terri. To live a better life. WS-1593

Barnett, Ola W. It could happen to anyone. WS-2253

Barney, Natalie Clifford. Adventures of the mind. WS-0285

Baron, Ava, ed. Work engendered. WS-1458

Baron, Beth, ed. Women in Middle Eastern history. WS-1806

Baron, Beth. The women's awakening in Egypt. WS-1794

Baron, John H., ed. The remarkable Mrs. Beach, American composer. WS-1016

Barr, Marleen S. Lost in space. WS-0356

Barranger, Milly S. Jessica Tandy. WS-0120

Barranger, Milly S. Margaret Webster. WS-0121

Barreca, Regina. Untamed and unabashed. WS-0286

Barreca, Regina, ed. Fay Weldon's wicked fictions. WS-0553

Barrentine, Pat, ed. When the canary stops singing. WS-1452

Barret-Ducrocq, Françoise. Love in the time of Victoria. WS-1687

Barrett, Jacqueline K., ed. Encyclopedia of women's associations worldwide. WS-0010

Barry, Kathleen. The prostitution of sexuality. WS-2311

Barstow, Anne Llewellyn. Witchcraze: a new history of the European witch hunts. WS-1638

Barth, Else M. Women philosophers. WS-0136

Bartholomeusz, Tessa J. Women under the Bō tree. WS-1113

Bartkowski, Frances. Travelers, immigrants, inmates. WS-0357

Bartlett, Anne Clark. Male authors, female readers. WS-0442

Bartlett, Elizabeth Ann. Liberty, equality, sorority. WS-1924

Bartlett, Virginia K. Keeping house. WS-1925

Basham, Diana. The trial of woman. WS-0287

Baskin, Judith R, ed. Jewish women in historical perspective. WS-1541

Baskin, Judith R., ed. Women of the world. WS-0316

Basu, Alaka Malwade. Culture, the status of women, and demographic behaviour. WS-2280

Basu, Amrita. Two faces of protest. WS-2052

Basu, Aparna. Mridula Sarabhai: rebel with a cause. WS-1608

Bataille, Gretchen M., ed. American Indian women. WS-0003

Bataille, Gretchen M., ed. Native American women: a biographical dictionary. WS-0021

Battersby, Christine. Gender and genius. WS-1069

Bauer, Dale M., ed. Feminism, Bakhtin, and the dialogic. WS-1079

Baym, Nina. American women writers and the work of history, 1790-1860. WS-0733

Bayne-Smith, Marcia, ed. Race, gender, and health. WS-1295

Baysting, Arthur, ed. Making policy not tea. WS-2058

Bazilli, Susan, ed. Putting women on the agenda. WS-2060

Beach, Cecilia, comp. French women playwrights before the twentieth century. WS-0084

Beach, Cecilia, comp. French women playwrights of the twentieth century. WS-0004

Beall, Anne E., ed. The psychology of gender. WS-2144

Beard, Mary Ritter. A woman making history. WS-2036

Bearor, Karen A. Irene Rice Pereira: her paintings and philosophy. WS-0195

Beasley, Chris. Sexual economyths. WS-1477

Beasley, Faith E. Revising memory. WS-0623

Beasley, Maurine H. Taking their place. WS-0255

Beckman, Peter R., ed. Women, gender, and world politics. WS-2077

Beer, Frances. Women and mystical experience in the Middle Ages. WS-1114

Beere, Carole A. Sex and gender issues. WS-0159

Behar, Ruth. Translated woman. WS-2281

Behn, Aphra. The rover; The feigned courtesans; The lucky chance; The emperor of the moon. WS-0443

Belcher, Gerald L. Collecting souls, gathering dust. WS-0236

Belcher, Margaret L. Collecting souls, gathering dust. WS-0236

Bell, Betty Louise. Faces in the moon. WS-0880

Bell, Elizabeth S. Sisters of the wind. WS-1171

Bell, Linda A. Rethinking ethics in the midst of violence. WS-1070

Bell, Maureen. A biographical dictionary of English women writers, 1580-1720. WS-0085

Bell, Robert E. Women of classical mythology. WS-0137

Bell, Shannon. Reading, writing, and rewriting the prostitute body. WS-2312

Bell-Scott, Patricia, ed. Life notes. WS-0912

Belli, Gioconda. The inhabited woman. WS-0672

Belz, Herman. Equality transformed. WS-2090

Ben-Zvi, Linda. Women in Beckett. WS-1066

Bendroth, Margaret Lamberts. Fundamentalism & gender, 1875 to the present. WS-1115

Benedict, Barbara M. Framing feeling. WS-0444

Benería, Lourdes, ed. Unequal burden. WS-1496

Benjamin, Marina, ed. Science and sensibility. WS-1206

Bennett, Betty T. Mary Diana Dods, a gentleman and a scholar. WS-0494

Bennett, Daphne. Emily Davies and the liberation of women, 1830-1921. WS-1665

Bennett, John W. Settling the Canadian-American West, 1890-1915. WS-1900

Bennett, Joy. Mary McCarthy: an annotated bibliography. WS-0097

Bennett, Paula. Emily Dickinson: woman poet. WS-0796

Bennington, Geoffrey. Virginia Woolf and the madness of language. WS-0555

Benstock, Shari, ed. On fashion. WS-1395

Berenson, Edward. The trial of Madame Caillaux. WS-1726

Berenstein, Rhona J. Attack of the leading ladies. WS-0968

Berg, Frances M. Health risks of weight loss. WS-1234

Bergen, Raquel Kennedy. Wife rape. WS-2206

Berger, Iris. Threads of solidarity. WS-1594

Berger, Ronald J. Feminism and pornography. WS-1355

Bergman-Carton, Janis. The woman of ideas in French art, 1830-1848. WS-0196

Bergmann, Emilie. Women, culture, and politics in Latin America. WS-1790

Berlage, Gai Ingham. Women in baseball. WS-1321

Berlin, Jean V., ed. A Confederate nurse. WS-1923

Berliner, Louise. Texas Guinan: queen of the nightclubs. WS-1033

Berliner, Michael S., ed. Letters of Ayn Rand. WS-0773

Bernadac, Marie-Laure. Louise Bourgeois. WS-0189

Bernstein, Anne E. The psychodynamic treatment of women. WS-2160

Bernstein, Gail Lee, ed. Recreating Japanese women, 1600-1945. WS-1630

Berrick, Jill Duerr. Faces of poverty. WS-2388

Berrill, Kevin T., ed. Hate crimes. WS-2395

Berry, Mary Frances. The politics of parenthood. WS-2331

Berry, Paul. Vera Brittain: a life. WS-0546

Besse, Susan K. Restructuring patriarchy. WS-1769

Besser, Gretchen Rous. Germaine de Staël revisited. WS-0624

Biehl, Janet. Rethinking ecofeminist politics. WS-2039

Bigwood, Carol. Earth muse. WS-1071

Billson, Janet Mancini. Keepers of the culture. WS-2282

Bindocci, Cynthia Gay. Women and technology. WS-1231

Bingham, Shereen G., ed. Conceptualizing sexual harassment as discursive practice. WS-0256

Binstock, R.C. Tree of heaven. WS-0830

Birch, Sarah. Christine Brooke-Rose and contemporary fiction. WS-0547

Birkett, Jennifer, ed. Determined women. WS-0365

Birrell, Susan, ed. Women, sport, and culture. WS-1333

Birtha, Becky. The forbidden poems. WS-0881

Bisgrove, Richard. The gardens of Gertrude Jekyll. WS-1209

Bishop, Ronald L., ed. The ceramic legacy of Anna O. Shepard. WS-1194

Bitel, Lisa M. Land of women. WS-1639

Black, Allida M. Casting her own shadow. WS-1987

Blackmer, Corinne E., ed. En travesti: women, gender subversion, opera. WS-1009

Blair, Karen J. The torchbearers. WS-1988

Blais, Madeleine. In these girls, hope is a muscle. WS-1322

Blanchard, Dallas A. Religious violence and abortion. WS-1989

Blank, Robert H. Fetal protection in the workplace. WS-2091

Blank, Robert. Human reproduction, emerging technologies, and conflicting rights. WS-1298

Blea, Irene I. La Chicana and the intersection of race, class, and gender. WS-2361

Blee, Kathleen M. Women of the Klan. WS-1990

Bleser, Carol, ed. Tokens of affection: the letters of a planter's daughter in the Old South. WS-1851

Blewett, Mary H. We will rise in our might. WS-1926

Bloch, R. Howard. Medieval misogyny and the invention of Western romantic love. WS-1571

Bloemink, Barbara J. The life and art of Florine Stettheimer. WS-0197

Blum, Linda M. Between feminism and labor. WS-1466

Blumberg, Rhoda Lois. Women and social protest. WS-2385

Blundell, Sue. Women in Ancient Greece. WS-1556

Blunt, Alison, ed. Writing women and space. WS-1553

Blustein, Bonnie Ellen. Educating for health & prevention. WS-1262

Boatwright, Eleanor Miot. Status of women in Georgia, 1783-1860. WS-1927

Bobo, Jacqueline. Black women as cultural readers. WS-0177

Bobroff-Hajal, Anne. Working women in Russia under the hunger tsars. WS-1754

Bodenheimer, Rosemarie. The real life of Mary Ann Evans. WS-0495

Boehm, Philip. Malina: a novel. WS-0607

Bohan, Janis S., ed. Seldom seen, rarely heard. WS-2134

Bohls, Elizabeth A. Women travel writers and the language of aesthetics, 1716-1818. WS-0358

Bok, Sissela. Alva Myrdal. WS-2255

Boland, Eavan. Object lessons. WS-0548

Bolen, Jean Shinoda. Crossing to Avalon. WS-1116

Bolles, A. Lynn. Sister Jamaica. WS-1385

Bolt, Christine. The women's movements in the United States and Britain from the 1790s to the 1920s. WS-1810

Bombal, María Luisa. House of mist; and, The shrouded woman. WS-0673

Bonaparte, Felicia. The gypsy-bachelor of Manchester. WS-0496

Bond, Terry. The world labour market. WS-1484

Bonfield, Lynn A. Roxana's children. WS-1928

Bonner, Elena. Mothers and daughters. WS-1640

Bonner, Thomas Neville. To the ends of the earth. WS-1193

Bonney, Norman. Women's work in east and west. WS-1462

Bonta, Marcia Myers, ed. American women afield. WS-1170

Boone, Joseph A. Engendering men. WS-0327

Bordin, Ruth. Alice Freeman Palmer. WS-1863

Boris, Eileen. Home to work. WS-2411

Borst, Charlotte G. Catching babies. WS-1270

Bostridge, Mark. Vera Brittain: a life. WS-0546

Botstein, David, ed. The Dynamic genome. WS-1210

Bourgeois, Louise. Louise Bourgeois: the locus of memory, works, 1982-1993. WS-0198

Bouvard, Marguerite Guzman. Revolutionizing motherhood. WS-1770

Bove, Cheryl. Iris Murdoch: a descriptive primary and annotated secondary bibliography. WS-0089

Bowes, Jennifer M. Men, women, and household work. WS-2340

Bowlby, Rachel. Virginia Woolf and the madness of language. WS-0555

Boxer, Andrew. Children of horizons. WS-2317

Boxer, Barbara. Strangers in the Senate. WS-2092

Boyd, Loree. Spirit moves. WS-1811

Boyd-Franklin, Nancy, ed. Children, families, and HIV/AIDS. WS-1310

Boydston, Jeanne. Home and work. WS-1913

Bozzoli, Belinda. Women of Phokeng. WS-1595

Brackman, Barbara. Kansas quilts & quilters. WS-1827

Brady, Kristin. George Eliot. WS-0497

Brady, Patricia, ed. George Washington's beautiful Nelly. WS-1962

Braham, Jeanne. Crucial conversations. WS-0735

Braidotti, Rosi. Nomadic subjects. WS-1356

Braidotti, Rosi. Women, the environment and sustainable development. WS-1512

Brauner, Sigrid. Fearless wives and frightened shrews. WS-1572

Brecher, Deborah, comp. The Women's information exchange national directory. WS-0035

Breen, Jennifer. In her own write. WS-0359

Brennan, Shawn, ed. Women's information directory. WS-0034

Brennan, Shawn. Resourceful woman. WS-0005

Breslaw, Elaine G. Tituba, reluctant witch of Salem. WS-1914

Brett, Annabelle. Pathways for women in the sciences. WS-1186

Brevard, Keziah Goodwyn Hopkins. A plantation mistress on the eve of the Civil War. WS-1929

Bridgeman, Jo, ed. Law and body politics. WS-2086

Bridger, Sue. No more heroines? WS-1487

Brienzo, Gary. Willa Cather's transforming vision. WS-0831

Brightman, Carol. Writing dangerously. WS-0882

Briles, Judith. The Briles report on women in healthcare. WS-1235

Brink, Randall. Lost star. WS-1172

Brinton, Mary C. Women and the economic miracle. WS-1609

Britton, Andrew. Katharine Hepburn: star as feminist. WS-0969

Brivic, Sheldon. Joyce's waking women. WS-0361

Brochmann, Grete. Middle East avenue. WS-2283

Brockman, John, ed. Creativity. WS-2123

Broe, Mary Lynn, ed. Silence and power. WS-0941

Broomfield, Andrea, ed. Prose by Victorian women. WS-0532

Brophy, Elizabeth Bergen. Women's lives and the 18th-century English novel. WS-0445

Brosius, Maria. Women in ancient Persia, 559-331 BC. WS-1557

Broude, Norma, ed. The Power of feminist art. WS-0227

Brown, Gillian. Domestic individualism. WS-0362

Brown, Ira V. Mary Grew, abolitionist and feminist, (1813-1896). WS-1864

Brown, Janet. Taking center stage. WS-1035

Brown, Julie, ed. American women short story writers. WS-0731

Brown, L. Susan. The politics of individualism. WS-2080

Brown, Penny. The captured world. WS-0498

Brown, Robert H., ed. Fearless wives and frightened shrews. WS-1572

Brown, Wendy. States of injury. WS-2040

Brownmiller, Sara. An index to women's studies anthologies. WS-0006

Brownstein, Rachel M. Tragic muse. WS-1036

Brownstone, David. The women's desk reference. WS-0011

Broyles-González, Yolanda. El Teatro Campesino: theater in the Chicano movement. WS-1037

Bruccoli, Matthew J., ed. Modern women writers. WS-0113

Bruckner, Matilda Tomaryn, ed. Songs of the women troubadours. WS-0661

Bryson, Lois. Welfare and the State. WS-2389

Buchwald, Emilie, ed. Transforming a rape culture. WS-1378

Buck, Claire, ed. The Bloomsbury guide to women's literature. WS-0086

Buckley, Thomas, tr. Duras. WS-0665

Budick, Emily Miller. Engendering romance. WS-0736

Buechler, Steven M. Women's movements in the United States. WS-2375

Bulbeck, Chilla. Australian women in Papua New Guinea. WS-1610

Bullock, Alan. Natalia Ginzberg: human relationships in a changing world. WS-0707

Bullough, Bonnie. Cross dressing, sex, and gender. WS-2313

Bullough, Bonnie. Florence Nightingale and her era. WS-1285

Bullough, Vern L. Cross dressing, sex, and gender. WS-2313

Bullough, Vern L., ed. American nursing: a biographical dictionary, v.2. WS-0052

Bullough, Vern L., ed. Prostitution: a guide to sources, 1960-1990. WS-0169

Bullough, Vern. Florence Nightingale and her era. WS-1285

Bunch, Charlotte. Demanding accountability. WS-2066

Bunkers, Suzanne L., ed. Inscribing the daily. WS-0302

Bunkers, Suzanne L., ed. The diary of Caroline Seabury, 1854-1863. WS-1935

Burbank, Victoria Katherine. Fighting women. WS-1412

Burgan, Mary. Illness, gender, and writing. WS-0549

Burgard, Peter J., ed. Nietzsche and the feminine. WS-1096

Burgess, Lauren Cook, ed. An uncommon soldier. WS-1980

Burgin, Diana Lewis. Sophia Parnok: the life and work of Russia's Sappho. WS-0715

Burke, Carolyn. Becoming modern. WS-0832

Burke, Phyllis. Family values. WS-2332

Burney, Fanny. The Early journals and letters of Fanny Burney: v.2: 1774-1777. WS-0446

Burns, Ailsa. Mother-headed families and why they have increased. WS-2333

Burns, E. Jane. Bodytalk: when women speak in Old French literature. WS-0625

Burstow, Bonnie. Radical feminist therapy. WS-2161

Burtch, Brian. Trials of labour: the re-emergence of midwifery. WS-1271

Burton, Antoinette. Burdens of history. WS-1641

Burton, Leone, ed. Gender and mathematics. WS-1518

Buss, Fran Leeper, ed. Forged under the sun. WS-1820

Butler, Deborah A. American women writers on Vietnam. WS-0099

Butler, J. Douglas, ed. Abortion, medicine, and the law. WS-1269

Butler, Johnnella E., ed. Transforming the curriculum. WS-1530

Butler, Sandra. Feminist groupwork. WS-2198

Byars, Jackie. All that Hollywood allows. WS-0970

Bynum, Victoria E. Unruly women. WS-1930

Byrne, Eileen M. Women and science. WS-1173

~ C ~

Cabot, Elizabeth Rogers Mason. More than common powers of perception. WS-1931

Cadden, Michael. Engendering men. WS-0327

Caine, Barbara. Victorian feminists. WS-1688

Callahan, Joan C., ed. Reproduction, ethics, and the law. WS-1304

Callaway, Barbara. The heritage of Islam. WS-1596

Callen, Anthea. The spectacular body. WS-0199

Calman, Leslie J. Toward empowerment. WS-1611

Calof, Rachel. Rachel Calof's story. WS-1991

Calvert, Rosalie Stier. Mistress of Riversdale. WS-1915

Cameron, Ardis. Radicals of the worst sort. WS-1932

Cameron, Jean. Anne Hutchinson, guilty or not? WS-1916

Camhi, Jane Jerome. Women against women. WS-1933

Camp, Helen C. Iron in her soul. WS-1865

Campbell, Anne. Men, women, and aggression. WS-2207

Campbell, Jill. Natural masques. WS-0447

Campbell, Marie, ed. Knowledge, experience, and ruling relations. WS-2265

Camper, Carol, ed. Miscegenation blues. WS-0591

Canning, Charlotte. Feminist theaters in the U.S.A. WS-1038

Canton, Katia. The fairy tale revisited. WS-0959

Caplan, Paula J. Lifting a ton of feathers. WS-1514

Capper, Charles. Margaret Fuller: v.1: An American romantic life. WS-1866

Carbert, Louise I. Agrarian feminism. WS-2284

Card, Claudia, ed. Feminist ethics. WS-1080

Card, Claudia. Lesbian choices. WS-1072

Carles, Emilie. A life of her own. WS-1727

Carr, John C. Sex differences and learning. WS-0043

Carr, Robert, tr. House/garden/nation. WS-0698

Carrier, Jeffrey L. Jennifer Jones: a bio-bibliography. WS-0122

Carrier, Jeffrey L. Tallulah Bankhead. WS-0120a

Carson, Anne. Goddesses & wise women. WS-0138

Carson, Diane, ed. Multiple voices in feminist film criticism. WS-0991

Carter, Alison. Underwear, the fashion history. WS-0200

Carter, Mae R. The organizational woman. WS-1439

Carter, Marina. Lakshmi's legacy. WS-1612

Carter, Pam. Feminism, breasts and breast-feeding. WS-1357

Carter, Ruth. Women in engineering. WS-1225

Carter, Sarah. Women's studies: a guide to information sources. WS-0007

Carter, Susanne, comp. Mothers and daughters in American short fiction. WS-0100

Carter, Susanne. War and peace through women's eyes. WS-0101

Cary, Elizabeth. The tragedy of Mariam, the fair queen of Jewry. WS-0448

Cashford, Jules. The myth of the goddess. WS-1384

Castellanos, Rosario. Another way to be. WS-0671

Castiglia, Christopher. Bound and determined. WS-0737

Castillo, Ana. So far from God. WS-0883

Castillo, Debra A. Talking back. WS-0674

Castle, Terry. The apparitional lesbian. WS-0322

Castro, Ginette. American feminism. WS-1813

Cayleff, Susan E. Babe: the life and legend of Babe Didrikson Zaharias. WS-1323

Celant, Germano. Laura Grisi. WS-0240

Ch'en, Hsüeh-chao. Surviving the storm. WS-0428

Chadwick, Whitney. Women, art, and society. WS-0201

Chafe, William H. The paradox of change. WS-1992

Chalouh, Marie, ed. The Montreal massacre. WS-1908

Chanana, Karuna. Gender and the household domain. WS-2289

Chandler, Joan. Women without husbands. WS-2334

Chant, Sylvia. Women and survival in Mexican cities. WS-2285

Chapman, Jenny. Politics, feminism and the reformation of gender. WS-2081

Charlot, Monica. Victoria: the young queen. WS-1666

Charnon-Deutsch, Lou. Narratives of desire. WS-0675

Chatman, Elfreda A. The information world of retired women. WS-2208

Chaudhuri, Maitrayee. Indian women's movement. WS-1613

Chaudhuri, Una. Staging place. WS-0738

Chekhov, Anton Pavlovich. Stories of women. WS-0716

Chernaik, Warren. Sexual freedom in restoration literature. WS-0449

Cherry, Andrew L. Social bonds and teen pregnancy. WS-2403

Cherry, Kelly. The exiled heart. WS-0884

Cheung, King-Kok. Articulate silences. WS-0739

Chibnall, Marjorie. The Empress Matilda. WS-1573

Chmielewski, Wendy E., ed. Women in spiritual and communitarian societies in the United States. WS-1857

Chodorow, Nancy J. Femininities, masculinities, sexualities. WS-2182

Chong, Denise. The concubine's children. WS-1901

Chou, Bih-Er. Women in Taiwan politics. WS-2053

Chowdhry, Prem. The veiled women. WS-1614

Choy, Elsie. Leaves of prayer. WS-0429

Christen, Yves. Sex differences. WS-2139

Christine, de Pisan. The book of the duke of true lovers. WS-0626

Christine, de Pisan. The writings of Christine de Pizan. WS-0627

Chughtai, Ismat. The crooked line. WS-0430

Church, Joseph. Transcendent daughters in Jewett's *Country of the pointed firs*. WS-0797

Chused, Richard H. Private acts in public places. WS-2209

Cima, Gay Gibson. Performing women. WS-1039

Citron, Marcia J. Gender and the musical canon. WS-1005

Citron, Stephen. Noel and Cole. WS-1006

Cixous, Hélène. The book of Promethea—Le livre de Promethea. WS-0629

Cixous, Hélène. "Coming to writing" and other essays. WS-0628

Claassen, Cheryl, ed. Women in archaeology. WS-1407

Clardy, Andrea Fleck. Words to the wise. WS-0065

Claridge, Laura. Out of bounds. WS-0341

Clark, Anna. The struggle for the breeches. WS-1689

Clark, Cal. Women in Taiwan politics. WS-2053

Clark, Gillian. Women in late antiquity. WS-1558

Clark, Janet. Women in Taiwan politics. WS-2053

Clark-Lewis, Elizabeth. Living in, living out. WS-1993

Clarke, Deborah. Robbing the mother. WS-0833

Clarke, Kathleen. Revolutionary woman: Kathleen Clarke, 1878-1972. WS-1667

Clarke, Micael M. Thackeray and women. WS-0499

Clarke, Norma. Ambitious heights. WS-0500

Clarke, Patricia. Life lines. WS-1615

Clayson, Hollis. Painted love. WS-0202

Clayton, Susan D. Justice, gender, and affirmative action. WS-2093

Clements, Barbara Evans, ed. Russia's women. WS-1763

Clewell, Beatriz Chu. Breaking the barriers. WS-1174

Clifford, Deborah Pickman. Crusader for freedom. WS-1867

Clinton, Catherine. Tara revisited. WS-1814

Clover, Carol J. Men, women, and chain saws. WS-0971

Clyman, Toby W., ed. Women writers in Russian literature. WS-0728

Cock, Jacklyn. Colonels and cadres. WS-1597

Cockburn, Cynthia. In the way of women. WS-2412

Code, Lorraine. What can she know? WS-1073

Coger, Greta M.K. McCormick, ed. New perspectives on Margaret Laurence. WS-0592

Cohen, Beth, ed. The Distaff side. WS-0601

Cohen, Colleen Ballerino, ed. Beauty queens on the global stage. WS-1337

Cohen, Greta L., ed. Women in sport. WS-0174

Cohen, Paula Marantz. Alfred Hitchcock: the legacy of Victorianism. WS-0972

Cohen, Paula Marantz. The daughter's dilemma. WS-0363

Cohen, Sherrill. The evolution of women's asylums since 1500. WS-2256

Coiner, Constance. Better red. WS-0740

Cole, Eve Browning, ed. Explorations in feminist ethics. WS-1078

Coles, Catherine, ed. Hausa women in the twentieth century. WS-1389

Colker, Ruth. Abortion and dialogue. WS-2094

Colker, Ruth. Pregnant men. WS-1358

Collins, Aila, ed. Women and new reproductive technologies. WS-1307

Comacchio, Cynthia R. "Nations are built of babies." WS-1263

Comas-Díaz, Lillian, ed. Women of color: integrating ethnic and gender identities in psychotherapy. WS-2171

Comstock, Gary David. Violence against lesbians and gay men. WS-2390

Condé, Maryse. I, Tituba, black witch of Salem. WS-0630

Cone, John Frederick. Adelina Patti: queen of hearts. WS-1007

Coney, Sandra. The menopause industry. WS-1273

Conger, Syndy McMillen. Mary Wollstonecraft and the language of sensibility. WS-0450

Conley, Verena Andermatt. Hélène Cixous. WS-1668

Connor, Kimberly Rae. Conversions and visions in the writings of African-American women. WS-0741

Constante, Lena. The silent escape. WS-1755

Cook, Alan R., ed. Cancer sourcebook for women. WS-1272

Cook, Alice H. The most difficult revolution. WS-2413

Cook, Blanche Wiesen. Eleanor Roosevelt: v.1: 1884-1933. WS-1868

Cook, Elizabeth Adell. Between two absolutes. WS-2095

Cook, Judith A., ed. Beyond methodology. WS-2254

Cook, Rebecca J., ed. Human rights of women. WS-2069

Cook, Susan C., ed. Cecilia reclaimed. WS-1004

Coontz, Stephanie. The way we never were. WS-2335

Copeland, Edward. Women writing about money. WS-0290

Copeland, Rebecca L. The sound of the wind. WS-0431

Corbett, Mary Jean. Representing feminity. WS-0501

Corey, Elizabeth. Bachelor Bess. WS-1862

Cornell, Sarah, tr. "Coming to writing" and other essays. WS-0628

Corrêa, Sonia. Population and reproductive rights. WS-2286

Corrin, Chris. Magyar women: Hungarian women's lives, 1960s-1990s. WS-1756

Coryell, Janet L. Neither heroine nor fool. WS-1869

Cosslet, Tess. Women writing childbirth. WS-0291

Costa, Marie. Abortion: a reference handbook. WS-0160

Costain, Anne N. Inviting women's rebellion. WS-2096

Costin, M. Georgia. Priceless spirit. WS-1118

Côté, Jane McL. Fanny and Anna Parnell. WS-1669

Cott, Nancy F. A woman making history. WS-2036

Cottle, Charles E. Feminism and pornography. WS-1355

Coultrap-McQuin, Susan, ed. Explorations in feminist ethics. WS-1078

Coultrap-McQuin, Susan. Doing literary business. WS-0742

Covert, James Thayne, ed. Memoir of a Victorian woman. WS-1670

Craft-Fairchild, Catherine. Masquerade and gender. WS-0452

Crane, Elaine Forman, ed. The Diary of Elizabeth Drinker. WS-1918

Crawford, Mary. Women and gender. WS-2136

Creedon, Pamela J., ed. Women in mass communication. WS-0279

Creedon, Pamela J., ed. Women, media and sport. WS-1332

Creevey, Lucy. The heritage of Islam. WS-1596

Creighton, Louise. Memoir of a Victorian woman. WS-1670

Crook, Marion. My body. WS-1237

Crosby, Christina. The ends of history. WS-0324

Crosby, Faye J. Justice, gender, and affirmative action. WS-2093

Crosland, Margaret. My life. WS-1026

Crosset, Todd W. Outsiders in the clubhouse. WS-1324

Cruikshank, Margaret. The gay and lesbian liberation movement. WS-2314

Cudjoe, Selwyn R. Caribbean women writers. WS-0288

Cullen-DuPont, Kathryn. The encyclopedia of women's history in America. WS-0008

Cullen-DuPont, Kathryn. Women's suffrage in America. WS-1944

Cullingford, Elizabeth Butler. Gender and history in Yeats's love poetry. WS-0502

Curry, Jane Kathleen. Nineteenth-century American women theatre managers. WS-1041

Curry, Jane. Marietta Holley. WS-0800

Curtis, Penelope. Barbara Hepworth: a retrospective. WS-0203

Cutting-Gray, Joanne. Woman as "nobody" and the novels of Fanny Burney. WS-0453

Cypess, Sandra Messinger. La Malinche in Mexican literature from history to myth. WS-0676

~ D ~

D'Acci, Julie. Defining women. WS-0257

Dakin, Theodora P. A history of women's contributions to world health. WS-1238

Daley, Caroline, ed. Suffrage and beyond. WS-2071

Daly, Brenda O., ed. Narrating mothers. WS-0305

~ E ~

Emma Willard School (Troy, N.Y.). Making connections. WS-2173

Ender, Evelyne. Sexing the mind. WS-0366

Engel, Barbara Alpern. Between the fields and the city. WS-1758

Engel, June. The complete breast book. WS-1240

Engel, Madeline H. Female detectives in American novels. WS-0103

England, Paula, ed. Theory on gender/feminism on theory. WS-2275

England, Paula. Comparable worth. WS-1480

Enloe, Cynthia. The morning after. WS-2067

Epstein, Lee. The Supreme Court and legal change. WS-2099

Erickson, Carolly. To the scaffold. WS-1672

Ericson, Margaret D. Women and music. WS-0123

Errington, Elizabeth Jane. Wives and mothers, schoolmistresses and scullery maids. WS-1902

Essed, Philomena. Understanding everyday racism. WS-2362

Esteves, Carmen C. Green cane and juicy flotsam. WS-0299

Esteves, Carmen C., tr. Happy days, Uncle Sergio. WS-0894

Estrin, Mark W. Critical essays on Lillian Hellman. WS-0885

Etter-Lewis, Gwendolyn, ed. Unrelated kin. WS-2373

Ettorre, Elizabeth. Women and substance use. WS-1241

Evans, Augusta Jane. Beulah. WS-0807

Evans, Augusta Jane. Macaria, or, Altars of sacrifice. WS-0808

Evans, John K. War, women and children in ancient Rome. WS-1560

Evans, Martha Noel. Fits and starts. WS-1728

Evans, Robert C., ed. "My name was Martha." WS-0473

Evans, Robert C., ed. "The muses females are." WS-0475

Evans, W. Gareth. Education and female emancipation. WS-1517

Evasdaughter, Elizabeth N. Catholic girlhood narratives. WS-0293

Everett, Patricia R. A history of having a great many times not continued to be friends. WS-0854

Eviota, Elizabeth Uy. The political economy of gender. WS-1488

Eyer, Diane. Motherguilt: how our culture blames mothers for what's wrong with society. WS-2215

Ezell, Margaret J.M. Writing women's literary history. WS-0454

~ F ~

Faber, M.D. Modern witchcraft and psychoanalysis. WS-2187

Faden, Ruth R., ed. AIDS, women, and the next generation. WS-1309

Fagenson, Ellen A. ed. Women in management. WS-1455

Fairclough, Ellen Louks. Saturday's child. WS-1903

Falk, Candace Serena. Love, anarchy, and Emma Goldman: (Rev. ed.). WS-1870

Fallon, Patricia, ed. Feminist perspectives on eating disorders. WS-2150

Farganis, Sondra. Situating feminism. WS-1363

Farge, Arlette. Fragile lives. WS-1729

Farrell, Michèle Longino. Performing motherhood. WS-0634

Fast, Cathy Carroll. The women's atlas of the United States. WS-0060

Fast, Timothy H. The women's atlas of the United States. WS-0060

Faue, Elizabeth. Community of suffering & struggle. WS-1435

Fauré, Christine. Democracy without women. WS-2257

Faust, Drew Gilpin, ed. Macaria, or, Altars of sacrifice. WS-0808

Faust, Drew Gilpin. Mothers of invention. WS-1942

Faux, Marian. Crusaders: voices from the abortion front. WS-2100

Favret, Mary A., ed. At the limits of Romanticism. WS-0321

Fay, Elizabeth A. Eminent rhetoric. WS-0260

Fedorko, Kathy A. Gender and the gothic in the fiction of Edith Wharton. WS-0836

Fedoroff, Nina, ed. The Dynamic genome. WS-1210

Feiler, Lily. Marina Tsvetaeva: the double beat of heaven and hell. WS-0719

Feinberg, Leslie. Transgender warriors. WS-2216

Felber, Lynette. Gender and genre in novels without end. WS-0367

Feldman, Gayle. You don't have to be your mother. WS-1275

Feldman, Paula R., ed. Romantic women writers. WS-0345

Feldman, Shelley, ed. Unequal burden. WS-1496

Feldstein, Josh. The silicone breast implant controversy. WS-1283

Feminism and Legal Theory Conference. At the boundaries of law. WS-2084

Fennema, Elizabeth. Mathematics and gender. WS-1316

Fenster, Thelma S., tr. The book of the duke of true lovers. WS-0626

Ferber, Marianne A., ed. Beyond economic man. WS-1478

Fergus, Jan. Jane Austen: a literary life. WS-0504

Ferguson, Ann. Sexual democracy. WS-2085

Ferguson, Kathy E. The man question. WS-1365

Ferguson, Moira, ed. The Hart sisters. WS-0301

Ferguson, Moira. Colonialism and gender relations form Mary Wollstonecraft to Jamaica Kincaid. WS-0554

Ferguson, Moira. Eighteenth-century women poets. WS-0789

Ferguson, Moira. Jamaica Kincaid. WS-0889

Ferree, Myra Marx, ed. Feminist organizations. WS-2377

Ferrell, Nancy Warren. Barrett Willoughby: Alaska's forgotten lady. WS-0837

Ferrer, Daniel. Virginia Woolf and the madness of language. WS-0555

Ferstman, Carla. The castration of Oedipus. WS-2135

Festing, Sally. Gertrude Jekyll. WS-1211

Fido, Elaine Savory. Out of the Kumbla. WS-0307

Fineman, Martha Albertson, ed. Mothers in law: feminist theory and the legal regulation of motherhood. WS-2235

Fineman, Martha Albertson. At the boundaries of law. WS-2084

Fink, Deborah. Agrarian women. WS-1817

Finke, Laurie A. Feminist theory, women's writing. WS-0368

Finkler, Kaja. Women in pain. WS-1264

Finn, Geraldine. Why Althusser killed his wife. WS-1081

Finnegan, Mary Jeremy. The women of Helfta. WS-1122

Finson, Shelley Davis, comp. Women and religion. WS-0139

Finucci, Valeria. The lady vanishes. WS-0709

Firth-Cozens, Jenny. Women at work. WS-2428

Fisch, Audrey A., ed. The Other Mary Shelley. WS-0530

Fiscus, Ronald J. The constitutional logic of affirmative action. WS-2101

Fisher, Ada Lois Sipuel. A matter of black and white: the autobiography of Ada Lois Sipuel Fisher. WS-1871

Fisher, Jo. Out of the shadows. WS-2054

Fisher, Sue. Nursing wounds: nurse practitioners, doctors, women patients.... WS-1284

Fishman, Sarah. We will wait: wives of French prisoners of war, 1940-1945. WS-1730

Fishman, Sylvia Barack, ed. Follow my footprints. WS-0748

Fishman, Sylvia Barack. A breath of life. WS-1818

Fister, Barbara. Third World women's literatures. WS-0067

Fitzsimmons, Richard. Pro-choice/pro-life. WS-0164

Flaherty, David H., ed. Challenging times. WS-2376

Flakoll, D.J., tr. Fugues. WS-0668

Fletcher, Anthony. Gender, sex and subordination in England, 1500-1800. WS-1692

Fletcher, John. Iris Murdoch: a descriptive primary and annotated secondary bibliography. WS-0089

Flint, Kate. The woman reader, 1837-1914. WS-0294

Flood, Renée Sansom. Lost Bird of Wounded Knee. WS-1819

Florence, Penny, ed. Feminist subjects, multi-media. WS-0179

Flowers, R. Barri. The victimization and exploitation of women and children. WS-2393

Foerstel, Herbert N. Climbing the hill. WS-2102

Foerstel, Karen. Climbing the hill. WS-2102

Fogel, Catherine Ingram, ed. Women's health care. WS-1259

Foggia, Lyla. Reel women: the world of women who fish. WS-1325

Folbre, Nancy. Who pays for the kids? WS-1481

Foner, Nancy. The caregiving dilemma. WS-1286

Fonow, Mary Margaret, ed. Beyond methodology. WS-2254

Fontenot, Wonda L. Secret doctors. WS-1292

Forbes, Geraldine, ed. An Indian freedom fighter recalls her life. WS-1631

Ford, Charles. Così. WS-1010

Ford, Linda G. Iron-jawed angels. WS-1996

Forer, Lois G. Unequal protection. WS-2103

Formanek-Brunell, Miriam. Made to play house. WS-2217

Forrester, John. Freud's women. WS-2181

Foster, Frances Smith. Written by herself. WS-0749

Foster, Gwendolyn Audrey. Women film directors: an international bio-critical dictionary. WS-0124

Foster, Shirley. What Katy read. WS-0295

Fowler, Virginia C. Nikki Giovanni. WS-0891

Fowler-Salamini, Heather, ed. Women of the Mexican countryside, 1850-1990. WS-1789

Fowlkes, Diane L. White political women. WS-2104

Fox, Sandi. Wrapped in glory. WS-0238

Fox, Tryphena Blanche Holder. A northern woman in the plantation South. WS-1943

Fox-Genovese, Elizabeth, ed. Beulah. WS-0807

Fracasso, Evelyn E. Edith Wharton's prisoners of consciousness. WS-0838

Frager, Ruth A. Sweatshop strife. WS-1904

Fraiman, Susan. Unbecoming women. WS-0369

Fraisse, Geneviève, ed. A history of women in the West: v.4: Emerging feminism from revolution to world war. WS-1647

Francis, Leslie, ed. Date rape: feminism, philosophy, and the law. WS-1360

Franck, Irene. The women's desk reference. WS-0011

Francke, Lizzie. Script girls. WS-0973

Franits, Wayne E. Paragons of virtue. WS-0208

Frank, Katherine. A passage to Egypt. WS-1673

Frankel, Noralee, ed. Gender, class, race, and reform in the Progressive Era. WS-1997

Frankenberg, Ruth. White women, race matters. WS-2218

Frankiel, Tamar. The voice of Sarah. WS-1123

Franklin, Caroline. Byron's heroines. WS-0505

Fraser, Wayne. The dominion of women. WS-0587

Frawley, Maria H. A wider range. WS-0506

Frederics, Diana. Diana: a strange autobiography. WS-0556

Freed, Anne O. The changing worlds of older women in Japan. WS-1617

Freed, Eugenie R. "A portion of his life." WS-0455

Freedman, Diane P., ed. Millay at 100. WS-0856

Freedman, Estelle B. Maternal justice. WS-2219

Freedman, Warren. Legal issues in biotechnology and human reproduction. WS-2105

Freeman, Barbara Claire. The feminine sublime. WS-0370

Freeman, Joan. A passion for physics. WS-1315

Freeman, Sue Joan Mendelson. Managing lives. WS-2199

Fregoso, Rosa Linda. The bronze screen. WS-0974

French, Marilyn. The war against women. WS-2220

Freud, Sigmund. Freud on women. WS-2188

Fried, Marlene Gerber. From abortion to reproductive freedom. WS-2378

Frieden, Sandra, ed. Gender and German cinema. WS-0975

Friedman, Marilyn. What are friends for? WS-1082

Friedman, Susan Stanford, ed. Signets. WS-0864

Friedman, Susan Stanford. Penelope's web. WS-0839

Friedman-Kasaba, Kathie. Memories of migration. WS-1821

Fromm, Gloria G. Windows on modernism. WS-0579

Frost, Elizabeth. Women's suffrage in America. WS-1944

Frost, Ginger S. Promises broken: courtship, class, and gender in Victorian England. WS-1693

Frost-Knappman, Elizabeth. The ABC-CLIO companion to women's progress in America. WS-0012

Frye, Ellen. Amazon story bones. WS-0892

Frye, Joanne S. Tillie Olsen: a study of the short fiction. WS-0893

Frye, Susan. Elizabeth I: the competition for representation. WS-1694

Fuchs, Miriam, ed. Marguerite Young, our darling. WS-0919

Fuchs, Rachel G. Poor and pregnant in Paris. WS-1731

Fuderer, Laura Sue. The female bildungsroman in English. WS-0068

Funigiello, Philip J. Florence Lathrop Page. WS-1872

Furlong, Monica. Visions & longings. WS-1124

Furlough, Ellen. Consumer cooperation in France. WS-1732

Furman, C. Sue. Turning point. WS-1276

Furman, Erna. Toddlers and their mothers. WS-2189

Furtado, Ken. Gay and lesbian American plays. WS-0125

Fuss, Diana, ed. Inside/out. WS-2263

Futterman, Marilyn Suriani. Dancing naked in the material world. WS 0962

~ G ~

Gaar, Gillian G. She's a rebel. WS-1011

Gaard, Greta, ed. Ecofeminism. WS-2234

Gabaccia, Donna. From the other side. WS-1822

Gabin, Nancy F. Feminism in the labor movement. WS-1436

Gabor, Andrea. Einstein's wife. WS-2338

Gainor, J. Ellen. Shaw's daughters. WS-0371

Galambos, Nancy L. Employed mothers and their children. WS-2418

Galdikas, Biruté M.F. Reflections of Eden. WS-1212

Gallagher, Bernice E. Illinois women novelists in the nineteenth century. WS-0809

Gallagher, Catherine. Nobody's story. WS-0456

Gallop, Jane. Around 1981. WS-0372

Gamman, Lorraine. Female fetishism. WS-2125

Gander, Forrest, ed. Mouth to mouth. WS-0687

Gandhi, Nandita. The issues at stake. WS-2288

Garb, Tamar. Sisters of the brush. WS-0209

Garber, Linda. Lesbian sources. WS-0165

García Pinto, Magdalena. Women writers of Latin America. WS-0678

García Ramis, Magali. Happy days, Uncle Sergio. WS-0894

García-Ballester, Luis, ed. Practical medicine from Salerno to the Black Death. WS-1266

Gardaphé, Fred L. Italian signs, American streets. WS-0750

Gardiner, Judith Kegan, ed. Provoking agents. WS-1100

Gardner, Carol Brooks. Passing by: gender and public harassment. WS-1366

Gardner, Howard. Creating minds. WS-2126

Gardner, Vivien, ed. The New woman and her sisters. WS-1053

Garner, Shirley Nelson, ed. Shakespearean tragedy and gender. WS-0485

Garrison, Stephen. Edith Wharton, a descriptive bibliography. WS-0104

Garrow, David J. Liberty and sexuality. WS-2106

Garton, Janet, ed. Contemporary Norwegian women's writing. WS-0608

Garvey, Ellen Gruber. The adman in the parlor. WS-0262

Gasper, Barry, ed. More than chattel. WS-1544

Gatens, Moira. Feminism and philosophy. WS-1083

Gates, Henry Louis, ed. Zora Neale Hurston: critical perspectives past and present. WS-0875

Gates, Joanne E. Elizabeth Robins, 1862-1952. WS-0296

Gättens, Marie-Luise. Women writers and fascism. WS-0180

Gattiker, Urs E., ed. Women and technology. WS-1231

Gavin, Christy. American women playwrights, 1964-1989. WS-0105

Gebby, Margaret Dow. Farm wife. WS-1941

Geis, Florence L. The organizational woman. WS-1439

Gélis, Jacques. History of childbirth. WS-1578

Gelles, Edith B. Portia: the world of Abigail Adams. WS-1919

Gemie, Sharif. Women and schooling in France, 1815-1914. WS-1733

Genini, Ronald. Theda Bara: a biography of the silent screen vamp, with a filmography. WS-0976

George, Shanti. A matter of people. WS-1489

George, Susanne K. The adventures of the woman homesteader. WS-1945

Geraghty, Christine. Women and soap opera. WS-0263

Gerami, Shahin. Women and fundamentalism. WS-2291

Gerber, Philip L. Bachelor Bess. WS-1862

Gerhart, Mary. Genre choices, gender questions. WS-0373

Germaine, Max. A Dictionary of women artists of Australia. WS-0047

Gerry, Thomas M.F. Contemporary Canadian and U.S. women of letters. WS-0106

Gessen, Masha, ed. Half a revolution. WS-0720

Gethner, Perry, ed. The lunatic lover. WS-0649

Ghorayshi, Parvin, comp. Women and work in developing countries. WS-0142

Gibbons, Sheila J. Taking their place. WS-0255

Gibbs, Liz, ed. Daring to dissent. WS-0551

Gibson, Pamela Church, ed. Dirty looks. WS-1362

Giele, Janet Z., ed. Women's work and women's lives. WS-1465

Gifford, Carolyn De Swarte, ed. Writing out my heart. WS-1983

Giglio, Virginia. Southern Cheyenne women's songs. WS-1012

Gilbert, Miriam. Love's labour's lost. WS-1045

Giles, Judy. Women, identity and private life in Britain, 1900-50. WS-1695

Gilfoyle, Timothy J. City of eros. WS-2259

Gill, Pat. Interpreting ladies. WS-0457

Gillett-Karam, Rosemary. Underrepresentation and the question of diversity. WS-1519

Gilligan, Carol. Between voice and silence. WS-2178

Gilligan, Carol. Making connections. WS-2173

Gilman, Charlotte Perkins. A journey from within. WS-0842

Gilman, Charlotte Perkins. Benigna Machiavelli. WS-0840

Gilman, Charlotte Perkins. The diaries of Charlotte Perkins Gilman: v.1: 1879-87; v2: 1890-1935. WS-0841

Gilman, Sander L. Freud, race, and gender. WS-2190

Gilmartin, Christina Kelley. Engendering the Chinese Revolution. WS-1619

Gilmore, Leigh. Autobiographics. WS-0374

Gingras, François-Pierre, ed. Gender and politics in contemporary Canada. WS-2055

Ginsburg, Faye. Uncertain terms. WS-2328

Ginzberg, Lori D. Women and the work of benevolence. WS-1946

Gitzinger, Inez. Why women? WS-2149

Gladney, Margaret Rose, ed. How am I to be heard? WS-0868

Glanville, Philippa. Women silversmiths, 1685-1845. WS-0239

Glaser, Bonnie Thompson, ed. Ruby: an ordinary woman. WS-1683

Glassman, Deborah N. Marguerite Duras. WS-0637

Glazer, Nona Y. Women's paid and unpaid labor. WS-2415

Gleadle, Kathryn. The early feminists. WS-1696

Glendinning, Anthony. Gender matters in schools. WS-1516

Glenn, Susan A. Daughters of the Shtetl. WS-1998

Glickman, Sylvia, ed. American women composers. WS-1001

Glück, Tereze. May you live in interesting times. WS-0895

Glucksmann, Miriam. Women assemble. WS-1697

Godwin-Jones, Robert. Romantic vision. WS-0638

Goellner, Ellen W., ed. Bodies of the text. WS-0958

Gofman, John W. Preventing breast cancer. WS-1277

Goldberg, Gertrude Schaffner. The Feminization of poverty. WS-2392

Goldberger, Avriel H., tr. Delphine. WS-0662

Golden, Eve. Platinum girl. WS-0977

Golden, Renny. The hour of the poor, the hour of women. WS-1772

Goldensohn, Lorrie. Elizabeth Bishop. WS-0896

Goldman, Anne E. Take my word: autobiographical innovations of ethnic American working women. WS-1402

Goldman, Dorothy. Women writers and the great war. WS-0557

Goldman, Wendy Z. Women, the state and revolution. WS-1759

Goldsborough, Jennifer Faulds. Women silversmiths, 1685-1845. WS-0239

Goldscheider, Frances K. New families, no families? WS-2339

Goldsmith, Elizabeth C., ed. Going public: women and publishing in early modern France. WS-0639

Goldstein, Leslie Friedman. Contemporary cases in women's rights. WS-2107

Golemba, Beverly E. Lesser-known women. WS-0013

Gollaher, David. Voice for the mad. WS-1873

Gonyea, Judith. Feminist perspectives on family care. WS-1244

González de la Rocha, Mercedes. The resources of poverty. WS-1417

Goodall, Jane. Through a window. WS-1213

Goodenough, Ruth Gallagher. Beyond the second sex. WS-1400

Goodman, Katherine R., ed. In the shadow of Olympus. WS-0614

Goodman, Susan. Edith Wharton's women. WS-0843

Goodnow, Jacqueline J. Men, women, and household work. WS-2340

Goodrich, Thelma Jean, ed. Women and power. WS-2169

Gordon, April A. Transforming capitalism and patriarchy. WS-1499

Gordon, Linda. Pitied but not entitled. WS-2260

Gordon, Linda. Women, the state, and welfare. WS-2121

Gordon, Lyndall. Charlotte Brontë: a passionate life. WS-0507

Gordon, Suzanne. Prisoners of men's dreams. WS-1437

Gordon, Tuula. Single women. WS-2222

Gorna, Robin. Vamps, virgins and victims. WS-1311

Gorrell, Lorraine. The nineteenth-century German Lied. WS-1013

Gorsky, Susan Rubinow. Femininity to feminism. WS-0508

Goscilo, Helena, ed. Lives in transit: a collection of recent Russian women's writing. WS-0724

Goscilo, Helena, ed. Russia—women—culture. WS-1655

Gossett, Suzanne. Declarations of independence. WS-0732

Gottfried, Heidi, ed. Feminism and social change. WS-1341

Gould, Lewis L., ed. American first ladies: their lives and their legacy. WS-0002

Gourse, Leslie. Madame Jazz. WS-1014

Gourse, Leslie. Sassy: the life of Sarah Vaughan. WS-1015

Graber, Mark A. Rethinking abortion. WS-2108

Graham, Dee L.R. Loving to survive. WS-2316

Grambs, Jean Dresden. Sex differences and learning. WS-0043

Grant, Judith. Fundamental feminism. WS-1084

Grant, Mary H. Private woman, public person. WS-1947

Grant, Nicole J. The selling of contraception. WS-1300

Grant, Rebecca, ed. Gender and international relations. WS-2068

Grattan, Virginia L. American women songwriters. WS-0126

Grauerholz, Elizabeth. Sexual coercion. WS-1375

Gravdal, Kathryn. Ravishing maidens. WS-0640

Graves, Pamela M. Labour women. WS-1698

Gray, Brenda Clegg. Black female domestics during the Depression in New York City, 1930-1940. WS-1999

Green, Carol Hurd, ed. American women writers: a critical reference guide from Colonial times..., v.5. WS-0096

Green, Karen. The woman of reason. WS-1085

Green, Katherine Sobba. The courtship novel, 1740-1820. WS-0375

Greene, Caroline, tr. Surviving the storm. WS-0428

Greene, Dana. Evelyn Underhill. WS-1125

Greene, Gayle, ed. Changing subjects. WS-0323

Greene, Gayle. Changing the story. WS-0328

Greene, Gayle. Doris Lessing: the poetics of change. WS-0558

Greene, Sandra E. Gender, ethnicity, and social change on the upper Slave Coast. WS-1599

Greenspan, Karen. The timetables of women's history. WS-0014

Greer, Mary K. Women of the Golden Dawn. WS-2140

Greiner, Donald J. Women without men. WS-0752

Gretlund, Jan Nordby. Eudora Welty's aesthetics of place. WS-0897

Griffin, Gabriele, ed. Outwrite. WS-0308

Griffin, Gabriele. Heavenly love? WS-0376

Griffin, Morwenna. Feminisms and the self. WS-1086

Griffiths, Trevor R., ed. British and Irish women dramatists since 1958. WS-1034

Grinstein, Louise S., ed. Women in chemistry and physics. WS-0135

Grisi, Laura. Laura Grisi. WS-0240

Grogan, Susan K. French socialism and sexual difference. WS-1734

Gromada, Thaddeus V., ed. Jadwiga of Anjou and the rise of East Central Europe. WS-1579

Gross, Rita M. Buddhism after patriarchy. WS-1126

Grossman, Barbara W. Funny woman. WS-1046

Grosz, Elizabeth, ed. Sexy bodies. WS-2305

Grosz, Elizabeth. Volatile bodies. WS-1087

Group, Thetis M. Feminism and nursing. WS-1289

Gruber, Mayer I. Women in the biblical world: a study guide. [v.1:] Women in the world of Hebrew scripture. WS-0015

Gudorf, Christine E. Body, sex, and pleasure. WS-1127

Guerrier, Edith. An independent woman. WS-1874

Guider, Margaret Eletta. Daughters of Rahab. WS-1128

Gupte, Pranay. Mother India. WS-1620

Gurin, Patricia. Women, politics, and change. WS-2050

Gustafson, Sigrid B. Female life careers. WS-2174

Gustafson, Susan E. Absent mothers and orphaned fathers. WS-0612

Guttmann, Allen. Women's sports. WS-1326

Gutwirth, Madelyn, ed. Germaine de Staël. WS-0636

Gutwirth, Madelyn. The twilight of the goddesses. WS-1735

Guy, Donna J. Sex & danger in Buenos Aires. WS-1773

Guy, Mary E., ed. Women and men of the states. WS-2120

Gygax, Franziska. Serious daring from within. WS-0898

~ H ~

Haarsager, Sandra. Bertha Knight Landes of Seattle, big-city mayor. WS-2000

Hakim, Catherine. Key issues in women's work. WS-1438

Hale, Janet Campbell. Bloodlines. WS-1875

Halecki, Oscar. Jadwiga of Anjou and the rise of East Central Europe. WS-1579

Hall, Ann C. "A kind of Alaska." WS-0753

Hall, Catherine. White, male and middle class. WS-1643

Hall, Colette T. Redefining autobiography in twentieth-century women's fiction. WS-0310

Hall, Kim F. Things of darkness. WS-0458

Hall, Kira, ed. Gender articulated. WS-0298

Hall, M. Ann. Feminism and sporting bodies. WS-1327

Hall, Marie-Beth. Crossed currents. WS-1995

Hall, Richard. Patriots in disguise. WS-1948

Hallett, Mary. Firing the heather. WS-1905

Hallissy, Margaret. Clean maids, true wives, steadfast widows. WS-0459

Hamburger, Jeffrey F. The Rothschild Canticles. WS-0210

Handler, Richard. Jane Austen and the fiction of culture. WS-0377

Hanley, Lynne. Writing war. WS-0329

Hanmer, Trudy J. Making connections. WS-2173

Hannam, June. British women's history: a bibliographical guide. WS-0062

Hansen, Carol. Woman as individual in English Renaissance drama. WS-0460

Hansen, Debra Gold. Strained sisterhood. WS-1949

Hansen, Elaine Tuttle. Chaucer and the fictions of gender. WS-0461

Hansen, Jennifer Moulton, ed. Letters of Catharine Cottam Romney, plural wife. WS-1972

Hanson, Katherine, tr.. Under observation. WS-0619

Hapke, Laura. Daughters of the Great Depression. WS-0754

Hapke, Laura. Tales of the working girl. WS-0755

Haramundanis, Katherine, ed. Cecilia Payne Gaposchkin: an autobiography and other recollections. WS-1184

Haraway, Donna J. Simians, cyborgs, and women. WS-1176

Harding, Sandra. Whose science? whose knowledge? WS-1177

Harding, Wendy. A world of difference. WS-0899

Hardy, Gayle J. American women civil rights activists. WS-0148

Hare-Mustin, Rachel T. Making a difference. WS-2142

Harlow, Barbara. Barred: women, writing, and political detention. WS-0300

Harman, Barbara Leah, ed. The New nineteenth century. WS-0306

Haroian-Guerin, Gil. The fatal hero. WS-0378

Harris, Anita M. Broken patterns. WS-2191

Harris, Betty J. The political economy of the southern African periphery. WS-1490

Harris, Janice Hubbard. Edwardian stories of divorce. WS-0559

Harris, Katherine. Long vistas. WS-1950

Harris, Maxine. Sisters of the shadow. WS-2394

Harris, Sharon M., ed. American women writers to 1800. WS-0788

Harris, Sharon M., ed. Selected writings of Judith Sargent Murray. WS-0791

Harrison, Ann Tukey, ed. The Danse macabre of women. WS-0631

Harrison, Elizabeth Jane. Female pastoral. WS-0756

Harrison, Victoria. Elizabeth Bishop's poetics of intimacy. WS-0900

Harsh, Constance D. Subversive heroines. WS-0379

Hart, Gail K. Tragedy in paradise. WS-0613

Hart, Janet. New voices in the nation. WS-1644

Hart, Lynda, ed. Acting out. WS-1030

Hart, Ursula Kingsmill. Behind the courtyard door. WS-1795

Hart, Vivien. Bound by our Constitution. WS-2056

Hartel, Lynda Jones. Sexual harassment. WS-0149

Hartfield-Méndez, Vialla. Woman and the infinite. WS-0679

Hartig, Linda. Violet Archer. WS-0127

Harvey, A.D. Sex in Georgian England. WS-1699

Harvey, Elizabeth D., ed. Women and reason. WS-1111

Harvey, Elizabeth, ed. Determined women. WS-0365

Harvey, Sally Peltier. Redefining the American dream. WS-0844

~ I ~

~ J ~

Jacobs, Janet Liebman. Victimized daughters. WS-2165

Jacobs, Jerry A., ed. Gender inequality at work. WS-2414

Jacobs, Jerry. Professional women at work. WS-2416

Jacobs, Lea. The wages of sin. WS-0978

Jacoby, Robin Miller. The British and American women's trade union leagues, 1890-1925. WS-1540

Jagoe, Catherine. Ambiguous angels. WS-0680

Jahan, Rounaq. The elusive agenda. WS-1500

James, Dean. By a woman's hand. WS-0082

James, Laurie. Men, women, and Margaret Fuller. WS-1092

Jamie, Kathleen. The Queen of Sheba. WS-0564

Jancar-Webster, Barbara. Women & revolution in Yugoslavia, 1941-1945. WS-1760

Janis, Eugenia Parry. Women photographers. WS-0254

Jankowski, Theodora A. Women in power in the early modern drama. WS-0331

Jantzen, Grace M. Power, gender and Christian mysticism. WS-1133

Jaros, Dean. Heroes without legacies. WS-1199

Jay, Elisabeth. Mrs Oliphant, 'a fiction to herself.' WS-0513

Jayakar, Pupul. Indira Gandhi: an intimate biography. WS-1624

Jeansonne, Glen. Women of the far right. WS-1825

Jeffrey, Julie Roy. Converting the West. WS-1878

Jeffreys, Sheila. Anticlimax. WS-2318

Jehenson, Myriam Yvonne. Latin-American women writers: class, race, and gender. WS-0681

Jejeebhoy, Shireen J. Women's education, autonomy, and reproductive behaviour. WS-2225

Jellison, Katherine. Entitled to power. WS-2002

Jenkins, Ruth Y. Reclaiming myths of power. WS-0514

Jenkins, Walter S. The remarkable Mrs. Beach, American composer. WS-1016

Jenness, Valerie. Making it work. WS-2319

Jennings, Anne M. The Nubians of West Aswan. WS-1419

Jennings, La Vinia Delois. Alice Childress. WS-0908

Jensen, Joan M. Promise to the land: essays on rural women. WS-1826

Jensen, Katharine Ann. Writing love. WS-0645

Jenson, Deborah, ed. "Coming to writing" and other essays. WS-0628

Jewell, Helen M. Women in medieval England. WS-1649

Joannou, Maroula. 'Ladies, please don't smash these windows.' WS-0565

Jochens, Jenny. Women in Old Norse society. WS-1580

John, Angela V. Elizabeth Robins: staging a life, 1862-1952. WS-1879

Johnson, Claudia L. Equivocal beings. WS-0332

Johnson, Elizabeth A. She who is. WS-1134

Johnson, Janis Tyler. Mothers of incest survivors. WS-2397

Johnson, Pauline. Feminism as radical humanism. WS-1344

Johnson, Penelope D. Equal in monastic profession. WS-1581

Johnson, Robert A. Lying with the heavenly woman. WS-2128

Johnston, Carolyn. Sexual power. WS-2341

Johnston, Joni E. Appearance obsession. WS-2152

Jones, Ann. Next time, she'll be dead. WS-2398

Jones, Margaret C. Heretics & hellraisers. WS-0759

Jones, Margaret E.W. The same sea as every summer. WS-0701

Jones, Michael K. The king's mother. WS-1582

Jones, Suzanne W., ed. Writing the woman artist. WS-0355

Jonza, Nancylee Novell. The underground stream. WS-0909

Jordan, Judith V. Women's growth in connection. WS-2180

Jordan, LeRoy. A bibliographical guide to African-American women writers. WS-0098

Jörgensen, Beth E. The writing of Elena Poniatowska. WS-0682

Joyce, Beverly A., comp. Drama by women to 1900. WS-0066

Judd, Ellen R. Gender and power in rural North China. WS-1420

Jurik, Nancy C. Doing justice, doing gender. WS-2110

Juster, Susan. Disorderly women. WS-1135

~ K ~

Kadel, Andrew. Matrology: a bibliography of writings WS-0140

Kadish, Doris Y. Politicizing gender. WS-1736

Kadish, Doris Y., ed. Translating slavery. WS-0651

Kadue, David D. Sexual harassment in employment law. WS-1369

Kafka, Phillipa. The great white way. WS-0760

Kagal, Ayesha, ed. Present imperfect: stories by Russian women. WS-0727

Kagan, Richard L. Lucrecia's dreams. WS-1749

Kahane, Claire. Passions of the voice. WS-0381

Kahlo, Frida. The diary of Frida Kahlo. WS-0218

Kahn, Coppélia, ed. Changing subjects. WS-0323

Kahn, Robbie Pfeufer. Bearing meaning. WS-1345

Kahne, Hilda, ed. Women's work and women's lives. WS-1465

Kaminer, Wendy. A fearful freedom. WS-2226

Kaminsky, Amy K. Reading the body politic. WS-0683

Kandiyoti, Deniz, ed. Women, Islam and the state. WS-2079

Kane, Paula M. Separatism and subculture: Boston Catholicism, 1900-1920. WS-1136

Kane, Penny. Women's health from womb to tomb. WS-1246

Kane, Thomas T. Developing new contraceptives. WS-1299

Kantha, Sachi Sri, comp. Prostitutes in medical literature. WS-0054

Kapadia, Karin. Siva and her sisters. WS-1421

Kapchan, Deborah A. Gender on the market. WS-1391

Kaplan, Deborah. Jane Austen among women. WS-0515

Kaplan, E. Ann. Motherhood and representation. WS-0382

Kaplan, Gisela. Contemporary Western European feminism. WS-1650

Kaplan, Joel H. Theatre and fashion. WS-0182

Kaplan, Lawrence J. Controlling our reproductive destiny. WS-1302

Kaplan, Marion A. The making of the Jewish middle class. WS-1741

Kaplan, Sydney Janet. Katherine Mansfield and the origins of modernist fiction. WS-0566

Kappes, Marianne. Track of the mystic. WS-0849

Karcher, Carolyn L. The first woman in the republic. WS-1880

Karim, Wazir Jahan. Women and culture. WS-1422

Karl, Frederick R. George Eliot, voice of a century. WS-0516

Karras, Ruth Mazo. Common women: prostitution and sexuality in Medieval England. WS-1651

Karsten, Margaret Foegen. Management and gender. WS-1440

Kaschak, Ellyn. Engendered lives. WS-2141

Kaschnitz, Marie Luise. Long shadows. WS-0615

Kasson, Joy S. Marble queens and captives. WS-0242

Kauffman, Christopher J. Ministry and meaning. WS-1247

Kavenik, Frances M. Handbook of American women's history. WS-0061

Kay, Rebecca. No more heroines? WS-1487

Kaye, Frances W. Isolation and masquerade. WS-0850

Kazickas, Jurate. Susan B. Anthony slept here. WS-0064

Keating, AnaLouise. Women reading, women writing. WS-0761

Keddie, Nikki R., ed. Women in Middle Eastern history. WS-1806

Kelber, Mim, ed. Women and government. WS-2064

Keller, Evelyn Fox. Conflicts in feminism. WS-1359

Keller, Evelyn Fox. Refiguring life. WS-1215

Keller, Evelyn Fox. Secrets of life, secrets of death. WS-1179

Kelley, Mary, ed. The power of her sympathy. WS-0819

Kellie, Luna. A prairie populist. WS-1955

Kelly, Catriona, ed. An Anthology of Russian women's writing, 1777-1992. WS-0714

Kelly, Catriona. A history of Russian women's writing, 1820-1992. WS-0722

Kelly, Petra K. Thinking green! WS-2057

Kelly, Rita Mae. The gendered economy. WS-1468

Kemplen, Tilda. From roots to roses. WS-1881

Kendall, Richard, ed. Dealing with Degas. WS-0205

Kendrigan, Mary Lou, ed. Gender differences. WS-2315

Kenneally, James J. The history of American Catholic women. WS-1137

Kennedy, Liam. Susan Sontag: mind as passion. WS-0910

Kenny, Maurice. Tekonwatonti/Molly Brant (1735-1795). WS-0790

Kent, Susan Kingsley. Making peace. WS-1703

Kerr, Andrea Moore. Lucy Stone. WS-1956

Kerr, Barbara. Smart girls two. WS-2175

Kertzer, David I. Sacrificed for honor. WS-1750

Kessler, Carol Farley. Charlotte Perkins Gilman: her progress toward utopia with selected writings. WS-0851

Kessler-Harris, Alice. A woman's wage. WS-1482

Kesting, Jürgen. Maria Callas. WS-1017

Kestler, Frances Roe. The Indian captivity narrative. WS-1824

Keyser, Elizabeth Lennox. Whispers in the dark. WS-0810

Kiernander, Adrian. Ariane Mnouchkine and the Théâtre du Soleil. WS-1049

King, Margaret L. Women of the Renaissance. WS-1583

King, Wilma, ed. A northern woman in the plantation South. WS-1943

Kinkley, Jeffrey C., ed. Surviving the storm. WS-0428

Kinnear, Mary. Margaret McWilliams. WS-1882

Kintz, Linda. The subject's tragedy. WS-1050

Kipnis, Aaron. Gender war, gender peace. WS-2320

Kirkby, Diane. Alice Henry: the power of pen and voice. WS-1828

Kirkham, Pat, ed. Me Jane: masculinity, movies and women. WS-0989

Kirkup, Gill. Women in engineering. WS-1225

Kirsh, Andrea. Carrie Mae Weems. WS-2003

Kitch, Sally L. This strange society of women. WS-1957

Klaus, Alisa. Every child a lion. WS-1265

Klein, Anne Carolyn. Meeting the Great Bliss Queen. WS-1138

Klein, Kathleen Gregory, ed. Great women mystery writers. WS-0071

Klein, Laura F., ed. Women and power in native North America. WS-1856

Knight, Chris. Blood relations: menstruation and the origins of culture. WS-1392

Knight, Denise D., ed. The diaries of Charlotte Perkins Gilman: v.1: 1879-87; v2: 1890-1935. WS-0841

Knight, Julia. Women and the new German cinema. WS-0980

Knoph, Marcy, ed. The Sleeper wakes. WS-0867

Knox, Claire E. Louise Bogan: a reference source.. WS-0109

Ko, Dorothy. Teachers of the inner chambers. WS-1625

Koblinsky, Marge, ed. The Health of women. WS-1243

Kobylka. The Supreme Court and legal change. WS-2099

Kochendoerfer, Violet A. One woman's World War II. WS-2004

Kochersberger, Robert C., ed. More than a muckraker. WS-0269

Kohl, Seena B. Settling the Canadian-American West, 1890-1915. WS-1900

Kolin, Philip C. Shakespeare and feminist criticism. WS-0092

Kolmerten, Carol A. Women in utopia. WS-1829

Komesaroff, Paul A., ed. Troubled bodies. WS-1257

Kon, Igor S. The sexual revolution in Russia. WS-2297

Koralewski, Mary A. Sexual coercion. WS-1375

Koritz, Amy. Gendering bodies/performing art. WS-0183

Koss, Mary P., ed. No safe haven. WS-2201

Koss-Chioino, Joan. Women as healers, women as patients. WS-1294

Kosta, Barbara. Recasting autobiography. WS-0616

Kosters, Marvin H., ed. Workers and their wages. WS-1475

Kotik, Charlotta. Louise Bourgeois: the locus of memory, works, 1982-1993. WS-0198

Kowaleski-Wallace, Beth. Refiguring the father. WS-0396

Kowaleski-Wallace, Elizabeth. Their fathers' daughters. WS-0383

Kraemer, Ross Shepard. Her share of the blessings. WS-1139

Kramarae, Cheris, ed. The Knowledge explosion. WS-1521

Kranidis, Rita S. Subversive discourse. WS-0517

Krasniewicz, Louise. Nuclear summer. WS-2379

Krause, Corinne Azen. Grandmothers, mothers, and daughters. WS-1830

Kremen, Eleanor. The Feminization of poverty. WS-2392

Krieger, Susan. Social science and the self. WS-2227

Krishnaraj, Maithreyi. Gender and the household domain. WS-2289

Kritzer, Amelia Howe, ed. Plays by early American women, 1775-1850. WS-0770

Kritzer, Amelia Howe. The plays of Caryl Churchill. WS-0568

Krive, Sarah. Women and writing in Russia and the USSR. WS-0093

Krótki, Karol J. Family and childbearing in Canada. WS-2279

Krueger, Christine L. The reader's repentance. WS-1140

Krueger, Roberta L. Women readers and the ideology of gender in old French verse romance. WS-0646

Kuehn, Thomas. Law, family, & women. WS-1584

Kumar, Radha. The history of doing. WS-1626

Kunze, Bonnelyn Young. Margaret Fell and the rise of Quakerism. WS-1704

Kunzel, Regina G. Fallen women, problem girls. WS-2266

Kupper, Susan J. Surnames for women. WS-2228

Kurzweil, Edith. Freudians and feminists. WS-2192

Kutzinski, Vera M. Sugar's secrets. WS-0684

Kuzmack, Linda Gordon. Woman's cause. WS-1542

Kwolek-Folland, Angel. Engendering business. WS-1441

~ L ~

Laas, Virginia Jeans, ed. Wartime Washington. WS-1958

Ladd-Taylor, Molly. Mother-work: women, child welfare, and the state, 1890-1930. WS-2005

Lagerquist, L. DeAne. In America the men milk the cows. WS-1831

Lalande, Roxanne Decker. Intruders in the play world. WS-0647

Lambton, Gunda. Stealing the show. WS-0243

Lamont, Rosette C., ed. Women on the verge. WS-0955

Lamphere, Louise. Sunbelt working mothers. WS-2417

Landis, Jean. The crimes women commit, the punishments they receive. WS-2405

Landrine, Hope, ed. Bringing cultural diversity to feminist psychology. WS-2138

Landry, Donna. The muses of resistance. WS-0463

Lane, Maggie. Jane Austen and food. WS-0518

Lane, Roger. William Dorsey's Philadelphia and ours. WS-1832

Lang, Gladys Engel. Etched in memory. WS-0206

Lang, Kurt. Etched in memory. WS-0206

Langbauer, Laurie. Women and romance. WS-0333

Lange, Frederick W., ed. The ceramic legacy of Anna O. Shepard. WS-1194

Langer, Cassandra. Feminist art criticism. WS-0048

Langland, Elizabeth. Out of bounds. WS-0341

Lant, Antonia. Blackout. WS-0981

Lapierre-Adamcyk, Evelyne. Family and childbearing in Canada. WS-2279

Larrabee, Mary Jeanne, ed. An ethic of care. WS-2124

Larsen, Anne R., ed. Renaissance women writers: French texts/American contexts. WS-0657

Lashgari, Deirdre, ed. Violence, silence, and anger. WS-0405

Lassner, Phyllis. Elizabeth Bowen: a study of the short fiction. WS-0569

Laughlin, Karen, ed. Theatre and feminist aesthetics. WS-1062

Laurich, Robert Anthony. AIDS and women. WS-0056

LaViolette, Alyce D. It could happen to anyone. WS-2253

Lavrin, Asunción. Women, feminism, and social change in Argentina, Chile, and Uruguay, 1890-1940. WS-1774

Lawrence, Amy. Echo and Narcissus. WS-0982

Laws, Sophie. Issues of blood. WS-2229

Lazreg, Marnia. The eloquence of silence. WS-1795a

Lazzaro-Weis, Carol. From margins to mainstream. WS-0710

Leaming, Barbara. Katharine Hepburn. WS-0983

Lease, Benjamin. Emily Dickinson's readings of men and books. WS-0811

Leckie, Shirley A. Elizabeth Bacon Custer and the making of a myth. WS-1883

LeCompte, Mary Lou. Cowgirls of the rodeo. WS-0173

Leder, Gilah C. Mathematics and gender. WS-1316

Lee, Elizabeth Blair. Wartime Washington. WS-1958

Lee, Robert G., ed. Dear Miye. WS-2030

Lee, W.R. Women's work and the family economy in historical perspective. WS-1664

Leeder, Elaine J. The gentle general. WS-1884

Leeming, E. Janice. Segmenting the women's market. WS-1442

Lehmann, Jennifer M. Durkheim and women. WS-2267

Leider, Emily Wortis. California's daughter. WS-0852

Leidholdt, Dorchen. The Sexual liberals and the attack on feminism. WS-2325

Leigh, Christian. Louise Bourgeois: the locus of memory, works, 1982-1993. WS-0198

Leighton, Angela. Victorian women poets. WS-0519

Leira, Arnlaug. Welfare states and working mothers. WS-2298

Leland, Carole. Women of influence, women of vision. WS-2374

Lemberg, Raymond, ed. Controlling eating disorders with facts, advice, and resources. WS-2148

Lemke-Santangelo, Gretchen. Abiding courage. WS-2006

Lenhart, Sharyn A. The psychodynamic treatment of women. WS-2160

Lent, John A. Women and mass communications. WS-0129

Lent, John A., comp. Women and mass communications. WS-0129

Leonard, Arthur S. Sexuality and the law. WS-0151

Leong, Frederick T.L., ed. Womanpower: managing in times of demographic turbulence. WS-1453

Lepowsky, Maria. Fruit of the motherland. WS-1423

Lerner, Gerda. The creation of feminist consciousness. WS-1652

Lerner, Jacqueline V. Employed mothers and their children. WS-2418

Leslie, Julia, ed. Roles and rituals for Hindu women. WS-1154

Leslie, Kent Anderson. Woman of color, daughter of privilege. WS-1959

Lester, Neal A. Ntozake Shange: a critical study of the plays. WS-0911

Levernier, James Arthur. The Indian captivity narrative, 1550-1900. WS-0743

Levi, Enrique Jaramillo, ed. When new flowers bloomed. WS-0704

Levi, Jan Heller, ed. A Muriel Rukeyser reader. WS-0858

Levine, Amy-Jill, ed. "Women like this." WS-0600

Levine, Laura. Men in women's clothing. WS-0464

Levine, Linda Gould, ed. Spanish women writers. WS-0095

Levine, Philippa. Feminist lives in Victorian England. WS-1705

Levine, Robert M. The life and death of Carolina Maria de Jesus. WS-1775

LeVine, Sarah. Dolor y Alegría. WS-1776

Levine, Susan. Degrees of equality. WS-1522

Levinson, Nadine A., ed. Female psychology. WS-0162

Levy, Amy. The complete novels and selected writings of Amy Levy, 1861-1889. WS-0520

Levy, Anita. Other women. WS-0334

Levy, Helen Fiddyment. Fiction of the home place. WS-0762

Levy, JoAnn. They saw the elephant. WS-1961

Lewalski, Barbara Kiefer. Writing women in Jacobean England. WS-0465

Lewenson, Sandra Beth. Taking charge. WS-1287

Lewes, Darby. Dream revisionaries. WS-0303

Lewiecki-Wilson, Cynthia. Writing against the family. WS-0570

Lewin, Ellen. Lesbian mothers. WS-2342

Lewis, Gifford. The Yeats sisters and the Cuala. WS-1676

Lewis, Hanna Ballin, ed. The education of Fanny Lewald. WS-0611

Lewis, Hanna Ballin, tr. The education of Fanny Lewald. WS-0611

Lewis, Jane. Women and social action in Victorian and Edwardian England. WS-1706

Lewis, Linda L., ed. Menstrual health in women's lives. WS-1274

Lewis, Michael, ed. Mothers, babies, and cocaine. WS-1251

Lewis, Nelly Custis. George Washington's beautiful Nelly. WS-1962

Lewis, Reina. Gendering Orientalism. WS-0184

Leyser, Henrietta. Medieval women: a social history of women in England, 450-1500. WS-1585

Leyster, Judith. Judith Leyster: a Dutch master and her world. WS-0219

Lichtenstein, Diane. Writing their nations. WS-0812

Liebow, Elliot. Tell them who I am. WS-2399

Lindemann, Barbara. Sexual harassment in employment law. WS-1369

Linden, R. Ruth. Making stories, making selves. WS-1653

Lindgren, H. Elaine. Land in her own name. WS-1963

Lindroth, Colette. Rachel Crothers: a research and production sourcebook. WS-1051

Lindroth, James. Rachel Crothers: a research and production sourcebook. WS-1051

Ling, Amy, ed. Mrs. Spring Fragrance and other writings. WS-0824

Ling, Amy. Between worlds. WS-0763

Lippitt, Jill, comp. The Women's information exchange national directory. WS-0035

Liss, Peggy K. Isabel the Queen. WS-1586

Litoff, Judy Barrett, ed. Dear boys: World War II letters from a woman back home. WS-1994

Litoff, Judy Barrett, ed. Since you went away. WS-2022

Littman, Barbara. The women's business resource guide. WS-0145

Litton, Helen, ed. Revolutionary woman: Kathleen Clarke, 1878-1972. WS-1667

Litz, A. Walton, ed. Modern American women writers. WS-0112

Livia, Anna, tr. The angel and the perverts. WS-0633

Livia, Anna. Incidents involving mirth. WS-0571

Łobodzińska, Barbara, ed. Family, women, and employment in Central-Eastern Europe. WS-2287

Lochrie, Karma. Margery Kempe and translations of the flesh. WS-0466

Lock, Margaret. Encounters with aging. WS-1424

Locke, Maryel, ed. Jean-Luc Godard's *Hail Mary*. WS-0979

Lockwood, Victoria S. Tahitian transformation. WS-1393

Loeb, Lori Anne. Consuming angels. WS-1707

Loeffelholz, Mary. Dickinson and the boundaries of feminist theory. WS-0385

Loeffelholz, Mary. Experimental lives. WS-0386

Long, Bonita C., ed. Women, work, and coping. WS-2429

Loomis, F.A., ed. As long as life. WS-1267

Looser, Devoney, ed. Jane Austen and discourses on feminism. WS-0512

Lopata, Helena Znaniecka. Circles and settings. WS-2230

Lopata, Helena Znaniecka. Current widowhood. WS-2231

López-Stafford, Gloria. A place in El Paso. WS-1834

Lorde, Audre. The marvelous arithmetics of distance. WS-0913

Los Angeles County Museum of Art. Wrapped in glory. WS-0238

Loshitzky, Yosefa. The radical faces of Godard and Bertolucci. WS-0984

Loudon, Irvine. Death in childbirth. WS-1278

Loudon, Jane (Webb). The mummy! WS-0521

Lounsbury, Richard C., ed. Louisa S. McCord: political and social essays. WS-1964

Lovenduski, Joni. Contemporary feminist politics. WS-1708

Loverde-Bagwell, Elizabeth. American feminism. WS-1813

Lowe, Sarah M. Tina Modotti: photographs. WS-0249

Lowenthal, Cynthia. Lady Mary Wortley Montagu and the eighteenth-century familiar letter. WS-0467

Lu, Tonglin. Misogyny, cultural nihilism, & oppositional politics. WS-0434

Lubin, Carol Riegelman. Social justice for women. WS-2419

Lucie-Smith, Edward. Race, sex, and gender in contemporary art. WS-0220

Luddy, Maria. Women and philanthropy in nineteenth-century Ireland. WS-1709

Luebke, Barbara F. Women's studies graduates. WS-2232

Luhan, Mabel Dodge. A history of having a great many times not continued to be friends. WS-0854

Lukacher, Maryline. Maternal fictions. WS-0648

Lunneborg, Patricia W. Women changing work. WS-2420

Lunsford, Andrea A., ed. Reclaiming rhetorica. WS-0185

Lupton, Mary Jane. Menstruation and psychoanalysis. WS-2193

Lynn, Susan. Progressive women in conservative times. WS-2009

Lyons, Nona P. Making connections. WS-2173

Lyra, F., tr. Hypatia of Alexandria. WS-1076

~ M ~

Mabee, Carleton. Sojourner Truth. WS-1885

Macdonald, Myra. Representing women: myths of femininity in the popular media. WS-0266

Mack, Beverly, ed. Hausa women in the twentieth century. WS-1389

Mack, Phyllis. Visionary women. WS-1141

Mackey, Richard A. Lasting marriages. WS-2343

Macleod, Arlene Elowe. Accommodating protest. WS-2299

MacPherson, Lillian, comp. Feminist legal literature. WS-0146

Macpherson, Pat. Reflecting on *The Bell Jar*. WS-0914

MacSween, Morag. Anorexic bodies. WS-2153

Maddux, Rachel. *Communication*, the autobiography of Rachel Maddux, and her novella, *Turnip's blood*. WS-0915

Maggio, Rosalie. The dictionary of bias-free usage. WS-0075

Magill, Frank N., ed. Great women writers. WS-0072

Magill, Frank N., ed. Masterplots II. Women's literature series. WS-0078

Magnusson, David. Female life careers. WS-2174

Maher, Vanessa, ed. The Anthropology of breast-feeding. WS-1382

Mahone, Sydné, ed. Moon marked and touched by sun. WS-0926

Mahoney, M.H. Women in espionage. WS-0152

Mahony, Rhona. Kidding ourselves: breadwinning, babies, and bargaining power. WS-2344

Mahowald, Mary Briody. Women and children in health care. WS-1248

Mairs, Nancy. Voice lessons. WS-0916

Major, Devorah. An open weave. WS-0917

Makinen, Merja. Female fetishism. WS-2125

Makward, Christiane P., ed. Plays by French and Francophone women. WS-0654

Malcolm, Janet. The Silent woman. WS-0918

Malette, Louise, ed. The Montreal massacre. WS-1908

Malhotra, Inder. Indira Gandhi: a personal and political biography. WS-1627

Malinowski, Sharon, ed. Gay & lesbian literature. WS-0070

Maman, Marie. Women in agriculture. WS-0143

Mamola, Claire Zebroski. Japanese women writers in English translation. WS-0076

Mamola, Claire Zebroski. Japanese women writers in English translation: v.2. WS-0077

Mamonove, Tatyana. Women's glasnost vs. naglost. WS-1766

Mandelker, Amy. Framing Anna Karenina. WS-0725

Mangini, Shirley. Memories of resistance. WS-1751

Manlowe, Jennifer L. Faith born of seduction. WS-2154

Mann, Coramae Richey. When women kill. WS-2400

Mann, Jill. Geoffrey Chaucer. WS-0468

Mann, Patricia S. Micro-politics. WS-1093

Manning, Carol S., ed. The female tradition in southern literature. WS-0746

Manning, Rita C. Speaking from the heart. WS-1094

Manning, Susan A. Ecstasy and the demon. WS-0964

March, John. A readers companion to the fiction of Willa Cather. WS-0111a

March, Kathleen, tr. The inhabited woman. WS-0672

Marchalonis, Shirley, ed. Critical essays on Mary Wilkins Freeman. WS-0798

Marchalonis, Shirley. College girls: a century in fiction. WS-0764

Marcus, Julie, ed. First in their field. WS-1401

Marcus, Julie. A world of difference. WS-0899

Marecek, Jeanne. Making a difference. WS-2142

Marek, Jayne E. Women editing modernism. WS-0765

Margolis, Nadia, tr. The book of the duke of true lovers. WS-0626

Mark, Rebecca. The dragon's blood. WS-0920

Marks, Elaine. Marrano as metaphor. WS-0650

Marsh, Jan. Christina Rossetti: a writer's life. WS-0522

Marsh, Margaret. The empty cradle. WS-1249

Marshall, Barbara L. Engendering modernity. WS-2380

Marshall, Kimberly. Rediscovering the Muses. WS-1027

Martín Gaite, Carmen. Love customs in eighteenth-century Spain. WS-1752

Martin, Carol. Dance marathons: performing American culture of the 1920s and 1930s. WS-0965

Martin, Emily. Flexible bodies. WS-1312

Martin, Francis. The feminist question. WS-1142

Martin, Jacky. A world of difference. WS-0899

Martin, Michèle. "Hello, Central?" WS-2421

Martin, Priscilla. Chaucer's women. WS-0469

Martin, Susan Ehrlich. Doing justice, doing gender. WS-2110

Martindale, Meredith. Lilla Cabot Perry: an American Impressionist. WS-0221

Martínez, Elena M. Lesbian voices from Latin America. WS-0686

Maso, Carole. Ava: a novel. WS-0921

Mason, Andrew. Explaining political disagreement. WS-2045

Mason, J.K. Medico-legal aspects of reproduction and parenthood. WS-2046

Mason, Michael. The making of Victorian sexual attitudes. WS-1710

Mason, Michael. The making of Victorian sexuality. WS-1711

Massardier-Kenney, Françoise. Translating slavery. WS-0651

Massiah, Joycelin, ed. Women in developing economies. WS-1510

Morris, Linda A. Women's humor in the age of gentility. WS-0814

Morris, Linda A., ed. American women humorists. WS-0730

Morris, Virginia B. Double jeopardy. WS-0526

Morrison, Mary C. Roxana's children. WS-1928

Morrison, Toni, ed. Race-ing justice, en-gendering power. WS-2367

Morrissy, Mary. Mother of pearl: a novel. WS-0575

Morrow, France. Unleashing our unknown selves. WS-1372

Morse, Mary. Women changing science. WS-1182

Mortimer, Gail L. Daughters of the swan. WS-0927

Morton, Marian J. And sin no more. WS-2268

Morton, Marian J. Emma Goldman and the American left. WS-2012

Morton, Patricia, ed. Discovering the women in slavery. WS-1936

Morton, Patricia. Disfigured images. WS-1840

Mosby, Katherine. Private altars. WS-0928

Moscucci, Ornella. The science of woman. WS-1279

Moses, Claire Goldberg. Feminism, socialism, and French romanticism. WS-1737

Mosley, Charlotte, ed. Love from Nancy. WS-0572

Moulsworth, Martha. "My name was Martha." WS-0473

Mount Holyoke College/Art Museum. Perspectives on Morisot. WS-0244

Moynihan, Ruth B. So much to be done. WS-1976

Mozans, H.J. Woman in science. WS-1200

Mueller, Roswitha. Valie Export. WS-0990

Mukherjee, Meenakshi. Jane Austen. WS-0527

Mulford, Carla, ed. Only for the eye of a friend. WS-0792

Mulhern, Chieko I., ed. Japanese women writers. WS-0074

Mulhern, Chieko Irie, ed. Heroic with grace. WS-1621

Muller, Charlotte F. Health care and gender. WS-1252

Mulqueen, Maggie. On our own terms. WS-2236

Mulroy, Elizabeth A. The new uprooted. WS-2401

Mumford, Laura Stempel. Love and ideology in the afternoon. WS-0270

Muncy, Robyn. Creating a female dominion in American reform, 1890-1935. WS-2013

Munns, Jessica. Restoration politics and drama. WS-0474

Munro, K.M., comp. Feminist legal literature. WS-0146

Munt, Sally, ed. New lesbian criticism. WS-0340

Murdock, Maureen. The hero's daughter. WS-2143

Murray, Judith Sargent. Selected writings of Judith Sargent Murray. WS-0791

Musick, Judith S. Young, poor, and pregnant. WS-2176

Myers, Gloria E. A municipal mother. WS-1889

Myers, Lois E. Letters by lamplight. WS-1970

Myers, Sylvia Harcstark. The Bluestocking circle. WS-0476

~ N ~

Naddaff, Sandra. Arabesque. WS-0419

Naffine, Ngaire. Law and the sexes. WS-2047

Nakano, Makiko. Makiko's diary: a merchant wife in 1910 Kyoto. WS-1628

Namias, June. White captives. WS-1841

Napier, Nancy K. Western women working in Japan. WS-1459

Naqvi, Tahira, tr. The crooked line. WS-0430

Nardi, Marcia. The last word. WS-0859

Narrett, David E. Inheritance and family life in Colonial New York City. WS-1920

Nash, Elizabeth. The luminous ones. WS-1052

Nash, Mary. Defying male civilization. WS-1654

Nash, Stanley D. Prostitution in Great Britain, 1485-1901. WS-0168

Nasta, Susheila, ed. Motherlands. WS-0339

Nathanson, Constance A. Dangerous passage. WS-2322

National Women's Education Centre (Japan), comp. Women in a changing society. WS-1629

Nazzari, Muriel. Disappearance of the dowry. WS-1777

Neel, Carol, tr. Handbook for William. WS-1576

Nelsen, Jane Taylor, ed. A prairie populist. WS-1955

Nelson, Albert J. Emerging influentials in state legislatures: women, Blacks, and Hispanics. WS-2112

Nelson, Barbara J., ed. Women and politics worldwide. WS-2075

Nelson, Carol. Women's market handbook. WS-1443

Nelson, Claudia, ed. The Girl's own. WS-1539

Nelson, Daniel. Farm and factory. WS-1842

Nelson, Emmanuel S., ed. Bharati Mukherjee: critical perspectives. WS-0586

Nelson, Julie A. Feminism, objectivity and economics. WS-1470

Nelson, Mariah Burton. Are we winning yet? WS-1329

Nelson, T.G.A. Children, parents, and the rise of the novel. WS-0477

Nemec Ignashev, Diane M. Women and writing in Russia and the USSR. WS-0093

Nesaule, Agate. A woman in amber. WS-1545

Neth, Mary. Preserving the family farm. WS-2014

Neumaier, Diane, ed. Reframings: new American feminist photographies. WS-0192

Neuman, Shirley, ed. Autobiography and questions of gender. WS-0283

Neumann, Erich. The fear of the feminine and other essays on feminine psychology. WS-2194

New, Melvyn, ed. The complete novels and selected writings of Amy Levy, 1861-1889. WS-0520

Newcomb, Michael D. Sexual abuse and consensual sex. WS-2329

Newland, Kathleen, ed. Gender and international relations. WS-2068

Newman, Karen. Fashioning femininity and English Renaissance drama. WS-0478

Newman, Katharine D. Never without a song. WS-1023

Newsom, Carol A. The Women's Bible commentary. WS-0141

Ngcobo, Lauretta. And they didn't die. WS-0420

Nice, Vivien E. Mothers and daughters. WS-1640

Nichols, Michael P. The lost art of listening. WS-2130

Nichols, Nina daVinci. Ariadne's lives. WS-0391

Nicholson, Colin, ed. Margaret Atwood: writing and subjectivity: new critical essays. WS-0590

Nicholson, Stuart. Billie Holiday. WS-1024

Nicol, Donald M. The Byzantine lady. WS-1588

Nicolson, Paula, ed. Gender issues in clinical psychology. WS-2163

Noggle, Anne. A dance with death. WS-1762

Noli, Jean. My life. WS-1026

Nord, Deborah Epstein. Walking the Victorian streets. WS-0528

Norman, Elizabeth M. Women at war. WS-1288

Norton, Mary Beth. Founding mothers & fathers. WS-1843

Norwood, Vera. Made from this earth. WS-1218

Novy, Marianne. Engaging with Shakespeare. WS-0392

Nunokawa, Jeff. The afterlife of property. WS-0529

Nussbaum, Felicity A. Torrid zones. WS-0479

Nye, Andrea. Philosophy & feminism. WS-1097

Nye, Andrea. Words of power. WS-1098

Nye, Naomi Shihab. Red suitcase. WS-0929

~ O ~

Oates, Stephen B. A woman of valor. WS-1890

O'Barr, Jean Fox. Feminism in action. WS-1347

O'Brien, Bernard A. Lasting marriages. WS-2343

O'Brien, Michael, ed. An Evening when alone. WS-1940

O'Connell, Joanna. Prospero's daughter. WS-0688

O'Connor, Egan, ed. Preventing breast cancer. WS-1277

O'Connor, June. The moral vision of Dorothy Day. WS-1147

O'Connor, Pat. Friendships between women. WS-2239

Odamtten, Vincent O. The art of Ama Ata Aidoo. WS-0421

Odem, Mary E. Delinquent daughters. WS-2269

O'Dowd, Michael J. The history of obstetrics and gynaecology. WS-1280

Offen, Karen, ed. Writing women's history. WS-1554

Ogunyemi, Chikwenye Okonjo. Africa wo/man palava. WS-0422

Okker, Patricia. Our sister editors. WS-0815

Okruhlik, Kathleen, ed. Women and reason. WS-1111

O'Neil, Elizabeth Murrie, ed. The last word. WS-0859

Opitz, May, ed. Showing our colors. WS-2370

Ordóñez, Elizabeth J. Voices of their own. WS-0690

Orleck, Annelise. Common sense & a little fire. WS-2015

Orlin, Lena Cowen. Private matters and public culture in post-Reformation England. WS-1716

Orr, Clarissa Campbell, ed. Women in the Victorian art world. WS-0235

Osterud, Nancy Grey. Bonds of community. WS-1971

Otten, Charlotte F., ed. English women's voices, 1540-1700. WS-1691

Owings, Alison. Frauen. WS-1742

~ P ~

Packer, Joan Garrett. Rebecca West: an annotated bibliography. WS-0094

Padula, Alfred. Sex and revolution. WS-1781

Page, Louise. Plays one. WS-1054

Paget, Karen M. Running as a woman. WS-2119

Paidar, Parvin. Women and the political process in twentieth-century Iran. WS-1800

Palmer, Carole L. Margaret Atwood: a reference guide. WS-0110

Palmer, Paulina. Contemporary lesbian writing. WS-0309

Palmieri, Patricia Ann. In Adamless Eden. WS-1524

Paludi, Michele A. Academic and workplace sexual harassment. WS-0154

Paludi, Michele A., ed. Ivory power. WS-1368

Pankhurst, Helen. Gender, development and identity. WS-1502

Pantel, Pauline Schmitt, ed. A History of women in the West. WS-1645

Papke, Mary E. Susan Glaspell. WS-0115

Paravisini-Gebert, Lizabeth, ed. Green cane and juicy flotsam. WS-0299

Paravisini-Gebert, Lizabeth. Caribbean women novelists. WS-0080

Pardes, Ilana. Countertraditions in the Bible. WS-1148

Parfitt, George. A biographical dictionary of English women writers, 1580-1720. WS-0085

Paris, Yvette. Queen of burlesque. WS-1055

Parker, Marla, ed. She does math! WS-1318

Parkin-Gounelas, Ruth. Fictions of the female self. WS-0393

Parpart, Jane L. Women, employment and the family in the international division of labour. WS-1511

Parra, Teresa de la. Iphigenia. WS-0691

Parrott, Louiselle, ed. Evaluating women's health messages. WS-1242

Parson-Nesbitt, Julie. Finders: poems. WS-0930

Parsons, John Carmi. Eleanor of Castile: queen and society in thirteenth-century England. WS-1589

Partridge-Brown, Mary. In vitro fertilization clinics. WS-0055

Paterson, John. Edwardians: London life and letters, 1901-1914. WS-0576

Patterson, Beverly Bush. The sound of the dove. WS-1025

Payne-Gaposchkin, Cecilia. Cecilia Payne-Gaposchkin: an autobiography and other recollections. WS-1184

Pearlberg, Gerry. Women, AIDS, & communities. WS-1313

Pearlman, Mickey. Tillie Olsen. WS-0931

Pearson, Anne Mackenzie. "Because it gives me peace of mind." WS-1149

Pederson, Lucille M. Breast cancer: a family survival guide. WS-1281

Pedrero, Paloma. Parting gestures. WS-0692

Pellauer, Mary D. Toward a tradition of feminist theology. WS-1150

Pendle, Karin, ed. Women and music. WS-0123

Penelope, Julia, ed. Lesbian culture. WS-0853

Penelope, Julia. Speaking freely. WS-0394

Penley, Constance, ed. Male trouble. WS-0985

Pérez, Janet. Modern and contemporary Spanish women poets. WS-0694

Perkin, J. Russell. A reception-history of George Eliot's fiction. WS-0531

Perkin, Joan. Victorian women. WS-1717

Perkins, Kathy A., ed. Contemporary plays by women of color. WS-1040

Perlman, Richard. Sex discrimination in the labour market. WS-1444

Perreault, Jeanne. Writing selves. WS-0932

Perry, Gill. Women artists and the Parisian avant-garde. WS-0191

Peteet, Julie M. Gender in crisis. WS-1801

Peters, Julie, ed. Women's rights, human rights. WS-2076

Peters, Sarah Whitaker. Becoming O'Keeffe. WS-0225

Peterson, Carla L. "Doers of the world." WS-0769

Peterson, Janice, ed. The Economic status of women under capitalism. WS-1479

Petry, Alice Hall. Understanding Anne Tyler. WS-0933

Pettis, Joyce. Toward wholeness in Paule Marshall's fiction. WS-0934

Pettman, Jan. Living in the margins. WS-1348

Phelps, Louise Wetherbee, ed. Feminine principles and women's experience in American composition and rhetoric. WS-0747

Philcox, Richard, tr. I, Tituba, black witch of Salem. WS-0630

Philipp, Elliot E. The history of obstetrics and gynaecology. WS-1280

Phillips, Anne. Democracy and difference. WS-2087

Phillips, Anne. Engendering democracy. WS-2048

Phillips, Kathy J. Virginia Woolf against empire. WS-0577

Phillips, Patricia. The scientific lady. WS-1185

Piaf, Edith. My life. WS-1026

Picchio, Antonella. Social reproduction. WS-1483

Pickle, Linda Schelbitzki. Contented among strangers. WS-1845

Pierce, Jennifer L. Gender trials. WS-1445

Pietila, Hilkka. Making women matter. WS-2070

Pike, Maureen. Sex discrimination in the labour market. WS-1444

Piland, Sherry. Women artists. WS-0050

Pinnick, Kathryn. No more heroines? WS-1487

Plum, Sydney Landon, ed. Coming through the swamp. WS-1196

Poague, Leland. Another Frank Capra. WS-0992

Pointon, Marcia. Naked authority. WS-0226

Pollack, Sandra, ed. Contemporary lesbian writers of the United States. WS-0102

Pollock, Griselda, ed. Dealing with Degas. WS-0205

Polster, Miriam F. Eve's daughters. WS-2131

Pomeroy, Sarah B., ed. Women's history and ancient history. WS-1568

Pool, Robert. Eve's rib. WS-1219

Poole, Joyce. Coming of age with elephants. WS-1220

Poppema, Suzanne T. Why I am an abortion doctor. WS-1253

Porter, Elisabeth J. Women and moral identity. WS-1099

Porter, Susan L., ed. Women of the commonwealth. WS-1858

Porterfield, Amanda. Female piety in Puritan New England. WS-1151

Posadskaya, Anastasia, ed. Women in Russia. WS-1765

Pott-Buter, Hettie A. Facts and fairy tales about female labor, family and fertility. WS-1460

Potter-MacKinnon, Janice. While the women only wept. WS-1909

Potts, Lydia. The world labour market. WS-1484

Powell, Hugh. Louise von Gall: her world and work. WS-0617

Powers, Meredith A. The heroine in Western literature. WS-0395

Prang, Margaret. A heart at leisure from itself. WS-1546

Prentice, Alison, ed. Women who taught. WS-1532

Press, Andrea L. Women watching television. WS-0272

Prewitt, Terry J. Religious violence and abortion. WS-1989

Price Herndl, Diane. Invalid women. WS-0771

Price, Alan. The end of the age of innocence. WS-0860

Probert, Belinda, ed. Pink collar blues. WS-1446

Proctor, Candice E. Women, equality, and the French Revolution. WS-1738

Prussin, Labelle. African nomadic architecture. WS-0251

Pugh, Martin. Women and the women's movement in Britain, 1914-1959. WS-1718

Putney, Martha S. When the nation was in need. WS-2016

Pycior, Helena M., ed. Creative couples in the sciences. WS-1175

Pyle, Jean Larson. The state and women in the economy. WS-1493

Pyron, Darden Asbury. Southern daughter: the life of Margaret Mitchell. WS-0861

~ Q ~

Quartly, Marian, ed. Freedom bound I: documents on women in colonial Australia. WS-1618

Quay, Joyce C. Early promise, late reward: a biography of Helen Hooven Santmyer. WS-0862

Quinlan, Susan Canty. The female voice in contemporary Brazilian narrative. WS-0695

Quinn, Susan. Marie Curie: a life. WS-1201

~ R ~

Rabine, Leslie Wahl. Feminism, socialism, and French romanticism. WS-1737

Rabinovitz, Lauren. Points of resistance. WS-0993

Rabinowitz, Nancy Sorkin. Anxiety veiled. WS-0603

Rabinowitz, Paula. Labor & desire. WS-0772

Rabinowitz, Paula. They must be represented. WS-0994

Radcliffe, Sarah A., ed. 'Viva.' WS-1768

Rado, Lisa, ed. Rereading modernism. WS-0344

Ragoné, Helena. Surrogate motherhood. WS-2349

Rainey, Buck. Sweethearts of the sage. WS-0130

Raju, Saraswati, ed. Women and work in South Asia. WS-1464

Ralston, Meredith L. "Nobody wants to hear our truth." WS-2402

Ram, Kalpana. Mukkuvar women. WS-1503

Ramsay, Raylene L. Robbe-Grillet and modernity. WS-0656

Rand, Ayn. Letters of Ayn Rand. WS-0773

Randall, Margaret. Our voices/our lives. WS-1778

Randall, Margaret. Sandino's daughters revisited. WS-1779

Randall, Vicky. Contemporary feminist politics. WS-1708

Ranft, Patricia. Women and the religious life in premodern Europe. WS-1152

Rankin, Pauline. Politics as if women mattered. WS-2063

Rao, Aruna, ed. Gender analysis in development planning. WS-1498

Rao, Aruna, ed. Women's studies international. WS-1534

Rapping, Elayne. The movie of the week. WS-0995

Ratcliffe, Krista. Anglo-American feminist challenges to the rhetorical traditions. WS-0343

Rath, Sura P., ed. Flannery O'Connor: new perspectives. WS-0890

Raub, Patricia. Yesterday's stories. WS-0774

Rauch, Alan. The mummy! WS-0521

Ravoira, LaWanda. Social bonds and teen pregnancy. WS-2403

Ray, Michael. The women's business resource guide. WS-0145

Rayman, Paula. Pathways for women in the sciences. WS-1186

Raymond, Janice G. The Sexual liberals and the attack on feminism. WS-2325

Raymond, Janice G. Women as wombs. WS-1303

Rayner-Canham, Geoffrey W. Harriet Brooks: pioneer nuclear scientist. WS-1317

Rayner-Canham, Marelene F. Harriet Brooks: pioneer nuclear scientist. WS-1317

Rayor, Diane J., tr. Sappho's lyre. WS-0604

Reagin, Nancy R. A German women's movement. WS-1743

Rebolledo, Tey Diana. Infinite divisions. WS-0906

Rebolledo, Tey Diana. Women singing in the snow. WS-0775

Reddock, Rhoda E. Women labour & politics in Trinidad & Tobago. WS-2303

Reddy, Maureen T., ed. Narrating mothers. WS-0305

Redel, Victoria. Already the world: poems. WS-0935

Redel, Victoria. Where the road bottoms out. WS-0935a

Reeder, Ellen D. Pandora: women in classical Greece. WS-1565

Rees, Alan M., ed. Consumer health USA. WS-1236

Reichardt, Mary R. A web of relationship. WS-0817

Reichardt, Mary R. The uncollected stories of Mary Wilkins Freeman. WS-0816

Reilly, Mary Ellen. Women's studies graduates. WS-2232

Reilly, Niamh. Demanding accountability. WS-2066

Reinharz, Shulamit. Feminist methods in social research. WS-2270

Remer, Pam. Feminist perspectives in therapy. WS-2172

Remley, Mary L. Women in sport. WS-0174

Renne, Elisha P. Cloth that does not die. WS-1427

Reskin, Barbara F. Job queues, gender queues. WS-1447

Resnick, Stephen. Bringing it all back home. WS-2337

Reynolds, Kimberley. Girls only? WS-0533

Reynolds, Kimberley. Victorian heroines. WS-0534

Rhoads, Steven E. Incomparable worth. WS-1471

Rhode, Deborah L. Theoretical perspectives on sexual difference. WS-2145

Ribbens, Jane. Mothers and their children. WS-2350

Rich, Doris L. Queen Bess: daredevil aviator. WS-1202

Richardson, Dorothy. Windows on modernism. WS-0579

Richlin, Amy, ed. Pornography and representation in Greece and Rome. WS-1562

Riddle, John M. Contraception and abortion from the ancient world to the Renaissance. WS-1203

Riederle, Monika H. Sexual abuse and consensual sex. WS-2329

Riessman, Catherine Kohler. Divorce talk. WS-2351

Rikoon, J. Sanford, ed. Rachel Calof's story. WS-1991

Riley, Glenda. The life and legacy of Annie Oakley. WS-1056

Riney, Bobye J. Working wives and dual-earner families. WS-1473

Ring, Jennifer. Modern political theory and contemporary feminism. WS-1101

Ringe, Sharon H. The Women's Bible commentary. WS-0141

Ringer, R. Jeffrey, ed. Queer words, queer images. WS-0273

Ritchie, Maureen. Women's studies: a guide to information sources. WS-0007

Rivadue, Barry. Mary Martin. WS-0120b

Rivero, Eliana S. Infinite divisions. WS-0906

Rivers, Caryl. Slick spins and fractured facts. WS-0274

Rizzo, Ann-Marie. The integration of women in management. WS-1448

Roazen, Paul, ed. Psychoanalysis of the sexual functions of women. WS-2183

Roazen, Paul, ed. The therapeutic process, the self, and female psychology. WS-2184

Robb, Carol S. Equal value: an ethical approach to economics and sex. WS-1153

Roberts, Diane. Faulkner and southern womanhood. WS-0776

Roberts, Diane. The myth of Aunt Jemima. WS-0777

Roberts, Helen, ed. Women's health matters. WS-1260

Roberts, Joan I. Feminism and nursing. WS-1289

Roberts, Josephine A., ed. The first part of *The Countess of Montgomery's Urania*. WS-0491

Roberts, Katherine J. Fair ladies. WS-0483

Roberts, Mary Louise. Civilization without sexes. WS-1739

Roberts, Robin. A new species. WS-0397

Roberts, Terry. Self and community in the fiction of Elizabeth Spencer. WS-0936

Robertson, Elizabeth. Early English devotional prose and the female audience. WS-0484

Robertson, Janet. The magnificent mountain women. WS-1847

Robertson, Matra. Starving in the silences. WS-2158

Robinowitz, Carolyn B. Women's progress. WS-2248

Robins, Gay. Women in ancient Egypt. WS-1563

Robinson, J. Gregg. Women in engineering. WS-1225

Robinson, Jane. Wayward women: a guide to women travellers. WS-0023

Robinson, Roger, ed. Katherine Mansfield—in from the margin. WS-0567

Robinson, Sally. Engendering the subject. WS-0398

Rocheleau, Dianne. Gender, environment, and development in Kenya. WS-1506

Rodin, Judith, ed. Women and new reproductive technologies. WS-1307

Rodowick, D.N. The difficulty of difference. WS-0996

Rodríguez, Ileana. House/garden/nation. WS-0698

Rollins, Judith. All is never said. WS-1891

Rolston, Bill, ed. Abortion in the new Europe. WS-2309

Roman, Margaret. Sarah Orne Jewett: reconstructing gender. WS-0818

Romines, Ann. The home plot. WS-0778

Romney, Catharine Cottam. Letters of Catharine Cottam Romney, plural wife. WS-1972

Ronner, Wanda. The empty cradle. WS-1249

Roof, Judith. A lure of knowledge. WS-0346

Roos, Patricia A. Job queues, gender queues. WS-1447

Rose, Barbara. Magdalena Abakanowicz. WS-0245

Rose, Ferrel V. The guises of modesty. WS-0618

Rose, Gillian. Feminism and geography. WS-1547

Rose, Hilary. Love, power and knowledge. WS-1187

Rose, Jacqueline. The haunting of Sylvia Plath. WS-0937

Rose, June. Marie Stopes and the sexual revolution. WS-1678

Rose, Kalima. Where women are leaders. WS-2061

Rose, Kenneth D. American women and the repeal of prohibition. WS-2017

Rose, Nancy E. Workfare or fair work. WS-1472

Rose, Sonya O. Limited livelihoods. WS-2271

Rosenberg, Brian. Mary Lee Settle's Beulah quintet. WS-0938

Rosenblum, Naomi. A history of women photographers. WS-0252

Rosener, Judy B. America's competitive secret. WS-1449

Rosenfeld, Michel. Affirmative action and justice. WS-2114

Rosenman, Ellen Bayuk. A room of one's own. WS-0347

Rosenthal, Joel T. Medieval women and the sources of medieval history. WS-1587

Ross, Becki L. The house that Jill built. WS-2323

Ross, Ellen. Love and toil. WS-1719

Ross, John Munder. What men want. WS-2195

Ross, Lynn C. Career advancement for women in the federal service. WS-0155

Ross, Paula P., tr. Stories of women. WS-0716

Ross, Stephen David. Plenishment in the earth. WS-1102

Rosser, Sue V. Biology & feminism. WS-1221

Rosser, Sue V. Female-friendly science. WS-1188

Rosser, Sue V. Women's health—missing from U.S. medicine. WS-1254

Rosser, Sue V., ed. Teaching the majority. WS-1529

Roth, Darlene Rebecca. Matronage: patterns in women's organizations, Atlanta, Georgia, 1890-1940. WS-2018

Rothenberg, Karen H., ed. Women and prenatal testing. WS-1308

Rothman, Barbara Katz, ed. Encyclopedia of childbearing. WS-0053

Roudinesco, Elisabeth. Théroigne de Méricourt. WS-1679

Roueche, John E. Underrepresentation and the question of diversity. WS-1519

Roueche, Suanne D. Underrepresentation and the question of diversity. WS-1519

Rowe, Margaret Moan. Doris Lessing. WS-0580

Rowland, Mary Canaga. As long as life. WS-1267

Ruane, Christine. Gender, class, and the professionalization of Russian city teachers, 1860-1914. WS-1526

Rubin, Donald L., ed. Composing social identity in written language. WS-0289

Rubin, Rose M. Working wives and dual-earner families. WS-1473

Rubinstein, Charlotte Streifer. American women sculptors. WS-0246

Rudie, Ingrid. Visible women in east coast Malay society. WS-1428

Rudy, Kathy. Beyond pro-life and pro-choice. WS-1103

Russell, Denise. Women, madness and medicine. WS-2133

Russell, Diana E.H., ed. Making violence sexy. WS-1370

Russell, Letty M. Church in the round. WS-1155

Russett, Cynthia Eagle. Sexual science: the Victorian construction of womanhood. WS-1204

Russo, Ann, ed. Third World women and the politics of feminism. WS-1377

Ruthchild, Rochelle Goldberg. Women in Russia and the Soviet Union. WS-0024

Rutherford, Susan, ed. The New woman and her sisters. WS-1053

Ryan, Barbara. Feminism and the women's movement. WS-2381

~ S ~

Sachdev, Paul. Sex, abortion and unmarried women. WS-2324

Sachs, Carolyn E. Gendered fields. WS-2241

Sadker, David. Failing at fairness. WS-1527

Sadker, Myra. Failing at fairness. WS-1527

Sadlier, Darlene, ed. One hundred years after tomorrow. WS-0689

Safa, Helen I. The myth of the male breadwinner. WS-1494

Sahgal, Manmohini Zutshi. An Indian freedom fighter recalls her life. WS-1631

St. Pierre, Mark. Madonna Swan. WS-1897

St. Pierre, Simone M. The struggle to serve. WS-1164

Sakelliou-Schultz, Liana. Feminist criticism of American women poets. WS-0116

Salisbury, Joyce E. Church fathers, independent virgins. WS-1156

Samuels, Shirley, ed. The culture of sentiment. WS-0799

Samuels, Suzanne Uttaro. Fetal rights, women's rights. WS-1450

Sánchez, Magdalena S., ed. Spanish women in the golden age. WS-1660

Sanday, Peggy Reeves. Beyond the second sex. WS-1400

Sanday, Peggy Reeves. Fraternity gang rape. WS-2404

Sandefur, Gary. Growing up with a single parent. WS-2345

Sands, Kathleen M. Escape from paradise. WS-1157

Sands, Kathleen M., ed. American Indian women. WS-0003

Sangster, Joan. Earning respect: the lives of working women in small-town Ontario, 1920-1960. WS-1910

Sapiro, Virginia. A vindication of political virtue. WS-2088

Sarab'ianov, Dmitrii V. Popova. WS-0228

Sarat, Austin, ed. Law in everyday life. WS-2044

Sartori, Eva Martin, ed. French women writers. WS-0090

Saso, Mary. Women in the Japanese workplace. WS-1461

Sault, Nicole, ed. Many mirrors. WS-2155

Saunders, James Robert. The wayward preacher in the literature of African American women. WS-0779

Savageau, Cheryl. Dirt road home. WS-0594

Sawicki, Jana. Disciplining Foucault. WS-1104

Saxton, Ruth, ed. Woolf and Lessing. WS-0585

Sayer, Karen. Women of the fields. WS-1656

Sayers, Janet. Mothers of psychoanalysis. WS-2196

Scanlon, Jennifer. Inarticulate longings. WS-2242

Scarlett, Elizabeth A. Under construction. WS-0699

Schackel, Sandra. Social housekeepers. WS-2019

Schaefer, Claudia. Textured lives. WS-0700

Schanke, Robert A. Shattered applause. WS-1057

Schaub, Diana J. Erotic liberalism. WS-0658

Schaum, Melita, ed. Wallace Stevens and the feminine. WS-0783

Scheman, Naomi. Engenderings: constructions of knowledge, authority, and privilege. WS-1105

Schiebinger, Londa. Nature's body. WS-1205

Schiesari, Juliana, ed. Refiguring woman. WS-1590

Schipper, Mineke. Source of all evil: African proverbs and sayings on women. WS-0423

Schmidt, Elizabeth. Peasants, traders, and wives. WS-1602

Schmidt, Frederick W. A still small voice. WS-1158

Schmittroth, Linda, comp. Statistical record of women worldwide. WS-0027

Schneider, Carl J. American women in the Progressive Era, 1900-1920. WS-2020

Schneider, Carl J. Into the breach. WS-2021

Schneider, Carl J. The ABC-CLIO companion to women in the workplace. WS-0144

Schneider, Dorothy. American women in the Progressive Era, 1900-1920. WS-2020

Schneider, Dorothy. Into the breach. WS-2021

Schneider, Dorothy. The ABC-CLIO companion to women in the workplace. WS-0144

Schor, Hilary M. Scheherezade in the marketplace. WS-0535

Schreiner, Olive. "My other self." WS-0424

Schriber, Mary Suzanne, ed. Telling travels. WS-0780

Schroeder, Steven. Virginia Woolf's subject and the subject of ethics. WS-0399

Schuetz, Janice. The logic of women on trial. WS-2115

Schuker, Eleanor, ed. Female psychology. WS-0162

Schultz, Margie. Irene Dunne. WS-0120c

Schultz, T. Paul, ed. Investment in women's human capital. WS-1491

Schulz, Dorothy Moses. From social worker to crimefighter. WS-2423

Schumacher, Julie. The body is water. WS-0939

Schüssler Fiorenza, Elisabeth, ed. Searching the scriptures: v.1: A feminist introduction. WS-1159

Schüssler Fiorenza, Elisabeth, ed. Searching the Scriptures: v.2: A feminist commentary. WS-1160

Schuster, Marilyn R. Marguerite Duras revisited. WS-0659

Schwartz, Marian. Popova. WS-0228

Schwartz, Marilyn. Guidelines for bias-free writing. WS-0081

Schwarzkopf, Jutta. Women in the Chartist movement. WS-1720

Schweik, Susan. A gulf so deeply cut. WS-0940

Schwichtenberg, Cathy, ed. The Madonna connection. WS-1836

Scobie, Ingrid Winther. Center stage. WS-1892

Scott, Alison MacEwen. Divisions and solidarities. WS-2304

Scott, Anne Firor, ed. Southern women and their families in the 19th century, papers and diaries.

Series A, Holdings of the Southern Historical Collection, University of North Carolina, Chapel Hill [microform]. WS-1977

Scott, Anne Firor. Natural allies. WS-1848

Scott, Bonnie Kime. Refiguring modernism: v. 1 & 2. WS-0581

Scott, Cath. Mother-headed families and why they have increased. WS-2333

Scott, Catherine V. Gender and development. WS-2243

Scott, Joan Wallach. Only paradoxes to offer. WS-1657

Scott, Kesho Yvonne. The habit of surviving. WS-2369

Scott, Michael. Maria Meneghini Callas. WS-1028

Scott, Wilbur J., ed. Gays and lesbians in the military. WS-1538

Seager, Joni. Earth follies. WS-1349

Searles, Patricia. Feminism and pornography. WS-1355

Sears, Laurie J., ed. Fantasizing the feminine in Indonesia. WS-1387

Seccombe, Wally. A millennium of family change. WS-2352

Sedgwick, Catharine Maria. The power of her sympathy. WS-0819

Seeley, Charlotte Palmer, comp. American women and the U.S. armed forces. WS-0025

Segal, Daniel. Jane Austen and the fiction of culture. WS-0377

Segrest, Mab. Memoir of a race traitor. WS-1893

Seidler, Victor J. Recreating sexual politics. WS-1374

Sekaran, Uma, ed. Womanpower: managing in times of demographic turbulence. WS-1453

Selanders, Louise C. Florence Nightingale: an environmental adaptation theory. WS-1290

Seller, Maxine Schwartz, ed. Women educators in the United States, 1820-1993. WS-0046

Sellers, Susan. Hélène Cixous: authorship, autobiography and love. WS-0660

Seminar on Feminism and Culture in Latin America. Women, culture, and politics in Latin America. WS-1790

Semmel, Bernard. George Eliot and the politics of national inheritance. WS-0536

Senelick, Laurence, ed. Gender in performance. WS-1044

Senior, Olive. Working miracles. WS-1780

Sentz, Lilli, ed. Prostitution: a guide to sources, 1960-1990. WS-0169

Sered, Susan Starr. Priestess, mother, sacred sister. WS-1161

Seremetakis, C. Nadia. The last word. WS-0859

Sevenhuijsen, Selma, ed. Equality politics and gender. WS-2083

Severa, Joan L. Dressed for the photographer. WS-1548

Seymour, Bruce. Lola Montez: a life. WS-1658

Seymour-Jones, Carole. Beatrice Webb: a life. WS-1680

Shaaban, Bouthaina. Both right and left handed. WS-1802

Shah, Nandita. The issues at stake. WS-2288

Shami, Seteney. Women in Arab society. WS-1463

Shapiro, Ann R., ed. Jewish American women writers: a bio-bibliographical and critical sourcebook. WS-0108

Shapiro, Ann-Louise. Breaking the codes. WS-1659

Shapiro, Herbert, ed. "I belong to the working class." WS-2027

Shapiro, Michael. Gender in play on the Shakespearean stage. WS-1058

Sharoni, Simona. Gender and the Israeli-Palestinian conflict. WS-2306

Sharpe, Jenny. Allegories of empire. WS-0400

Sharpe, Sue. Fathers and daughters. WS-2353

Shaw, Marion. Reflecting on Miss Marple. WS-0582

Shaw, Patrick W. Willa Cather and the art of conflict. WS-0863

Shaw, Sandra, ed. Doctor Mary in Arabia. WS-1261

Shelton, Beth Anne. Women, men and time. WS-2424

Shepherd, Linda Jean. Lifting the veil. WS-1189

Shepherd, Simon. A biographical dictionary of English women writers, 1580-1720. WS-0085

Sheppard, Alice. Cartooning for suffrage. WS-0275

Sheriff, Mary D. The exceptional woman. WS-0193

Sherr, Lynn. Failure is impossible. WS-1974

Sherr, Lynn. Susan B. Anthony slept here. WS-0064

Sherwin, Susan. No longer patient. WS-1106

Sherwood, Dolly. Harriet Hosmer, American sculptor, 1830-1908. WS-0229

Shiman, Lilian Lewis. Women and leadership in nineteenth-century England. WS-1721

Shiva, Vandana. Ecofeminism. WS-2234

Shore, Lesley Irene. Tending inner gardens. WS-2168

Shteir, Ann B. Cultivating women, cultivating science. WS-1207

Shugar, Dana R. Separatism and women's community. WS-2244

Shupe, Anson. The violent couple. WS-2354

Siann, Gerda. Gender, sex and sexuality. WS-2326

Sieg, Katrin. Exiles, eccentrics, activists. WS-1059

Sigal, Gale. Erotic dawn-songs of the Middle Ages. WS-0348

Sigel, Roberta S. Ambition & accommodation. WS-2245

Silber, Nina. The romance of reunion. WS-1975

Silver, Brenda R., ed.. Rape and representation. WS-0342

Silverthorne, Elizabeth. Sarah Orne Jewett. WS-0820

Sime, Ruth Lewin. Lise Meitner: a life in physics. WS-1319

Simmons, Diane. Jamaica Kincaid. WS-0889

Simmons, Nancy Craig, ed. The selected letters of Mary Moody Emerson. WS-1973

Simon, Joan. Susan Rothenberg. WS-0230

Simon, Rachel. Change within tradition among Jewish women in Libya. WS-1803

Simon, Rita J. The crimes women commit, the punishments they receive. WS-2405

Simon, Rita J. Women's movements in America. WS-2382

Simonds, Wendy. Abortion at work. WS-2327

Simonds, Wendy. Women and self-help culture. WS-1350

Simons, Judy. What Katy read. WS-0295

Simons, Margaret A., ed. Feminist interpretations of Simone de Beauvoir. WS-0635

Simons, Minot. Women's gymnastics: a history. v.1: 1966 to 1974. WS-1330

Simpson, Amelia. Xuxa: the mega-marketing of gender, race, and modernity. WS-0276

Singer, Elly. Child-care and the psychology of development. WS-2177

Singh, Amritjit, ed. Memory and cultural politics. WS-0767

Singh, Renuka. The womb of mind. WS-1633

Singley, Carol J. Edith Wharton: matters of mind and spirit. WS-0865

Sippy, Shana. The college woman's handbook. WS-0042

Skaggs, Merrill Maguire. After the world broke in two. WS-0866

Skandera-Trombley, Laura E. Mark Twain in the company of women. WS-0821

Sklar, Kathryn Kish. Florence Kelley and the nation's work. WS-1894

Skoller, Eleanor Honig. The in-between of writing. WS-0401

Skram, Amalie. Under observation. WS-0619

Slavin, Sarah, ed. U.S. women's interest groups. WS-0030

Slocum, Robert B. New England in fiction, 1787-1990. WS-0117

Small, Helen. Love's madness. WS-0311

Small, Judy Jo. Positive as sound. WS-0822

Small, Meredith F. Female choices. WS-1222

Smart, Patricia. Writing in the father's house. WS-0595

Smith, David A. Third world cities in global perspective. WS-1549

Smith, David C., ed. Dear boys: World War II letters from a woman back home. WS-1994

Smith, David C., ed. Since you went away. WS-2022

Smith, Dawn L., ed. The Perception of women in Spanish theater of the golden age. WS-0693

Smith, Dorothy E. Texts, facts, and femininity. WS-2272

Smith, J.C. The castration of Oedipus. WS-2135

Smith, Jessie Carney, ed. Notable Black American women. WS-0022

Smith, Lillian Eugenia. How am I to be heard? WS-0868

Smith, Lois M. Sex and revolution. WS-1781

Smith, Martha Nell. Rowing in Eden. WS-0823

Smith, Merril D. Breaking the bonds. WS-1921

Smith, Patricia, ed. Feminist jurisprudence. WS-2041

Smith, Philip H. A concordance to the novels of Virginia Woolf. WS-0091

Smith, Susan L. Sick and tired of being sick and tired. WS-1296

Smulders, Sharon. Christina Rossetti revisited. WS-0538

Smyke, Patricia. Women and health. WS-1255

Snyder, Margaret C. African women and development. WS-1505

Sobol, Richard B. Bending the law. WS-2116

Sochen, June, ed. Women's comic visions. WS-1859

Soderbergh, Peter A. Women marines. WS-2024

Soderbergh, Peter A. Women marines in the Korean War era. WS-2023

Sohoni, Neera Kuckreja, tr. Sketches from my past. WS-0437

Sokoloff, Naomi B., ed. Gender and text in modern Hebrew and Yiddish literature. WS-0297

Sokoloff, Natalie J. Black women and white women in the professions. WS-2371

Solie, Ruth A., ed. Musicology and difference. WS-1022

Solinger, Rickie. Wake up little Susie. WS-2372

Solomon, Martha M., ed. A voice of their own. WS-0543

Sonnert, Gerhard. Gender differences in science careers. WS-1190

Sonnert, Gerhard. Who succeeds in science? WS-1191

Sornberger, Judith Mickel. Open heart. WS-0943

Soto, Shirlene. Emergence of the modern Mexican woman. WS-1782

Spain, Daphne. Gendered spaces. WS-1351

Spallone, Pat. Generation games. WS-1223

Spanier, Bonnie B. Im/partial science. WS-1224

Sparr, Pamela, ed. Mortgaging women's lives. WS-1492

Spector, Janet D. What this awl means. WS-1406

Spector, Robert D. Smollett's women. WS-0486

Spence, Mary Lee, ed. The Letters of Jessie Benton Frémont. WS-1960

Spencer, Jane, ed. The rover; The feigned courtesans; The lucky chance; The emperor of the moon. WS-0443

Spender, Dale, ed. The Knowledge explosion. WS-1521

Spender, Dale. Life lines. WS-1615

Spiel, Hilde. Fanny von Arnstein. WS-1744

Spigel, Lynn. Make room for TV. WS-1849

Spitzack, Carole. Confessing excess. WS-1256

Splatt, Cynthia. Life into art. WS-0963

Sprecher, Lorrie. Sister safety pin. WS-0944

Sprengnether, Madelon. The spectral mother. WS-2197

Spring, Eileen. Law, land, & family. WS-1722

Sproxton, Judy. The women of Muriel Spark. WS-0583

Spurlock, Jeanne. Women's progress. WS-2248

Squier, Susan Merrill. Babies in bottles. WS-1305

Squire, Corinne, ed. Women and AIDS. WS-2137

Stabile, Carol A. Feminism and the technological fix. WS-1228

Stacey, Jackie. Star gazing. WS-0997

Stacey, William A. The violent couple. WS-2354

Stadum, Beverly. Poor women and their families. WS-2025

Staël, Germaine de. Delphine. WS-0662

Stafford, Pauline, comp. British women's history: a bibliographical guide. WS-0062

Staggenborg, Suzanne. The pro-choice movement. WS-2383

Staiger, Janet. Bad women: regulating sexuality in early American cinema. WS-0998

Stanley, Autumn. Mothers and daughters of invention. WS-1229

Stanley, Liz. Feminist praxis. WS-2258

Stanton, Marietta P. Florence Nightingale and her era. WS-1285

Staudt, Kathleen. Women, international development, and politics. WS-2078

Staunton, Irene, comp. Mothers of the revolution. WS-1600

Stave, Shirley A. The decline of the goddess. WS-0539

Steadman, Susan M. Dramatic re-visions. WS-0131

Stecker, Ann Page. Sisters of fortune. WS-1951

Steinberg, Naomi. Kinship and marriage in Genesis. WS-1162

Steinbock, Bonnie. Life before birth. WS-1107

Steiner, Carl. Of reason and love. WS-0620

Steinman, Michael, ed. Woman battering. WS-2409

Stephen, Lynn, ed. Hear my testimony. WS-2062

Stephen, Lynn. Zapotec women. WS-1783

Sterling, David L., ed. "I belong to the working class." WS-2027

Sterling, Dorothy. Ahead of her time. WS-1895

Sterling, Fisher. Carrie Mae Weems. WS-2003

Stern, Madeleine, ed. Louisa May Alcott unmasked. WS-0794

Stern, Steve J. The secret history of gender. WS-1784

Stetson, Erlene. Glorying in tribulation. WS-1896

Stewart, Joan Hinde. Gynographs: French novels by women of the late eighteenth century. WS-0663

Stewart, Maaja A. Domestic realities and imperial fictions. WS-0540

Stichter, Sharon. Women, employment and the family in the international division of labour. WS-1511

Stitt, Beverly A. Gender equity in education. WS-0044

Stockel, H. Henrietta. Women of the Apache nation. WS-2026

Stockman, Norman. Women's work in east and west. WS-1462

Stockton, Kathryn Bond. God between their lips. WS-0402

Stokes, Rose Pastor. "I belong to the working class." WS-2027

Stoll, Anita K., ed. The Perception of women in Spanish theater of the golden age. WS-0693

Stolte-Heiskanen, Veronica, ed. Women in science. WS-1192

Stone, James S. Emily Faithfull: Victorian champion of women's rights. WS-1681

Stone, Marjorie. Elizabeth Barrett Browning. WS-0541

Stoner, K. Lynn. From the house to the streets. WS-1785

Stott-Kendall, Pamela. Torn illusions. WS-1282

Stout, Janis P. Katherine Anne Porter: a sense of the times. WS-0869

Stout, Janis P. Strategies of reticence. WS-0403

Stowasser, Barbara Freyer. Women in the Qur'an, traditions, and interpretation. WS-1163

Stowell, Sheila. A stage of their own. WS-1060

Stowell, Sheila. Theatre and fashion. WS-0182

Strand, Dana. Colette: a study of the short fiction. WS-0664

Strange, Carolyn. Toronto's girl problem. WS-1911

Streitmatter, Janice. Toward gender equity in the classroom. WS-1528

Strobel, Margaret. European women and the second British Empire. WS-1661

Strom, Sharon Hartman. Beyond the typewriter. WS-1451

Strossen, Nadine. Defending pornography. WS-1376

Strum, Philippa. The women are marching. WS-1804

Sui Sin Far. Mrs. Spring Fragrance and other writings. WS-0824

Sullivan, Amy M. Between voice and silence. WS-2178

Sullivan, Constance. Women photographers. WS-0254

Sullivan, Norma. Masters and managers. WS-1430

Sultan, Terrie. Louise Bourgeois: the locus of memory, works, 1982-1993. WS-0198

Summers, Claude J. The Gay and lesbian literary heritage. WS-0069

Sunder Rajan, Rajeswari. Real and imagined women. WS-2307

Sussman, Elisabeth. Florine Stettheimer: Manhattan fantastica. WS-0197a

Sutherland, John. Mrs Humphry Ward. WS-0542

Sutlive, Vinson H., ed. Female and male in Borneo. WS-1388

Swain, Martha H. Ellen S. Woodward: New Deal advocate for women. WS-1898

Swaisland, Cecillie. Servants and gentlewomen to the golden land. WS-1603

Swanson, Jean. By a woman's hand. WS-0082

Swantz, Marja-Liisa. Blood, milk, and death. WS-1431

Sweatman, Margaret. Fox. WS-0596

Sweeney, Patricia E. Biographies of British women. WS-0028

Swerdlow, Amy. Women Strike for Peace: traditional motherhood and radical politics in the 1960s. WS-2028

Swetnam, Susan Hendricks. Lives of the saints in southeast Idaho. WS-1850

Swinton, Elizabeth de Sabato. The women of the pleasure quarter. WS-0231

Sword, Helen. Engendering inspiration. WS-0312

Sylvester, Christine. Feminist theory and international relations in a postmodern era. WS-2072

~ T ~

Tadesse, Mary. African women and development. WS-1505

Taeuber, Cynthia M., ed. Statistical handbook on women in America. WS-0026

Tal, Kalí. Worlds of hurt. WS-2273

Tanaka, Yukiko, ed. Unmapped territories. WS-0436

Tanner, Jo A. Dusky maidens. WS-1061

Tansman, Alan M. The writings of Kōda Aya, a Japanese literary daughter. WS-0435

Tanton, Morgan, ed. Women in management. WS-1455

Tate, Claudia. Domestic allegories of political desire. WS-0825

Tate, Thelma H. Women in agriculture. WS-0143

Tatlock, Lynne, tr. Their pavel. WS-0610

Taylor, Anne. Annie Besant: a biography. WS-1682

Taylor, Avril. Women drug users. WS-1432

Taylor, Ina. The art of Kate Greenaway. WS-0247

Taylor, Jill McLean. Between voice and silence. WS-2178

Taylor, P.A.M., ed. More than common powers of perception. WS-1931

Taylor, Sully. Western women working in Japan. WS-1459

Tebbutt, Melanie. Women's talk? WS-2274

Templin, Charlotte. Feminism and the politics of literary reputation. WS-0945

Tétreault, Mary Ann, ed. Women and revolution in Africa, Asia, and the New World. WS-2065

Thébaud, Françoise, ed. A History of women in the West: v.5: Toward a cultural identity in the twentieth century. WS-1648

Theobold, Marjorie R., ed. Women who taught. WS-1532

Thomadsen, Nancy Sweet. At the boundaries of law. WS-2084

Thomas, Ann. Lisette Model. WS-0232

Thomas, Claudia N. Alexander Pope and his eighteenth-century women readers. WS-0487

Thomas, Gillian. A position to command respect. WS-0186

Thomas, Helen, ed. Dance, gender and culture. WS-0960

Thomas, Mary Martha. The new woman in Alabama. WS-2029

Thomas, Sue. How women legislate. WS-2117

Thomas-Slayter, Barbara. Gender, environment, and development in Kenya. WS-1506

Thompson, Ruby Alice Side. Ruby: an ordinary woman. WS-1683

Thorne-Finch, Ron. Ending the silence. WS-2406

Thorpe, Margaret E. Breaking the barriers. WS-1174

Thurer, Shari L. The myths of motherhood. WS-2355

Tice, Karin E. Kuna crafts, gender, and the global economy. WS-1495

Tickner, J. Ann. Gender in international relations. WS-2073

Tierney, Helen, ed. Women's studies encyclopedia: v.3: History, philosophy, and religion. WS-0039

Tierney, Helen. Women's studies encyclopedia. WS-0038

Tilly, Louise A. Women, politics, and change. WS-2050

Tinkler, Penny. Constructing girlhood. WS-1723

Todd, Janet, ed. Counterfeit ladies. WS-0451

Tokarczyk, Michelle M., ed. Working-class women in the academy. WS-1535

Tomalin, Claire. Mrs Jordan's profession. WS-1063

Tomita, Mary Kimoto. Dear Miye. WS-2030

Tomsich, Maria G., tr. Love customs in eighteenth-century Spain. WS-1752

Tong, Benson. Unsubmissive women: Chinese prostitutes in nineteenth-century San Francisco. WS-2276

Tong, Rosemarie. Controlling our reproductive destiny. WS-1302

Toorn, Karel van der. From her cradle to her grave. WS-1165

Torgovnick, Marianna. Gone primitive. WS-1396

Torre, Adela de la, ed. Building with our hands. WS-1812

Torres, Lourdes, ed. Third World women and the politics of feminism. WS-1377

Torres-Seda, Olga, comp. Caribbean women novelists. WS-0080

Toth, Emily. Kate Chopin. WS-0826

Touchton, Judith G. Fact book on women in higher education. WS-0045

Townsend, Janet Gabriel. Women's voices from the rainforest. WS-1397

Tracy, Susan J. In the master's eye. WS-0781

Trager, James. The women's chronology. WS-0029

Traub, Valerie. Desire and anxiety. WS-0404

Treggiari, Susan. Roman marriage. WS-1564

Trela, D.J., ed. Margaret Oliphant. WS-0513a

Trenton, Patricia, ed. Independent spirits: women painters of the American West, 1890-1945. WS-0217

Trigg, Janet M. Breast cancer: a family survival guide. WS-1281

Trinh, T. Minh-Ha. Framer framed. WS-0999

Tripp, Cynthia F. Segmenting the women's market. WS-1442

Troide, Lars E., ed. The Early journals and letters of Fanny Burney: v.2: 1774-1777. WS-0446

Tseëlon, Efrat. The masque of femininity. WS-2202

Tsing, Anna Lowenhaupt. In the realm of the diamond queen. WS-1398

Tsing, Anna Lowenhaupt. Uncertain terms. WS-2328

Tsurumi, E. Patricia. Factory girls. WS-1634

Tucker, Judith E., ed. Arab women: old boundaries, new frontiers. WS-1792

Tucker, Lindsey. Textual escap(e)ades. WS-0350

Tula, María Teresa. Hear my testimony. WS-2062

Turbin, Carole. Working women of collar city. WS-1978

Turner, Barbara F., ed. Women growing older. WS-2179

Tusquets, Esther. The same sea as every summer. WS-0701

Ty, Eleanor. Unsex'd revolutionaries. WS-0488

Tyler, Pamela. Silk stockings and ballot boxes. WS-1852

Tyrrell, Ian. Woman's world/woman's empire. WS-1550

~ U ~

Udall, Sharyn R. Inside looking out. WS-0233

Underhill, Lois Beachy. The woman who ran for president. WS-1979

Underwood, Malcolm G. The king's mother. WS-1582

Unesco. Women in Arab society. WS-1463

Unger, Rhoda. Women and gender. WS-2136

Uno, Roberta, ed. Unbroken thread. WS-1064

Upton, Dell, ed. Madaline: love and survival in antebellum New Orleans. WS-1835

Urofsky, Melvin I. A conflict of rights. WS-2118

Usborne, Cornelie. The politics of the body in Weimar Germany. WS-1745

Ussher, Jane M. Women's madness. WS-2146

Ussher, Jane M., ed. Gender issues in clinical psychology. WS-2163

~ V ~

Valdivia, Angharad N., ed. Feminism, multiculturalism, and the media. WS-0261

Van Den Bergh, Nan, ed. Feminist perspectives on addictions. WS-2162

Van Dyck, José. Manufacturing babies and public consent. WS-1306

Vanacker, Sabine. Reflecting on Miss Marple. WS-0582

VanEvery, Jo. Heterosexual women changing the family. WS-2356

Varma, Maha Devi. Sketches from my past. WS-0437

Vasey, Frank B. The silicone breast implant controversy. WS-1283

Vaz, Kim Marie, ed. Black women in America. WS-1809

Veeder, Nancy W. Women's decision-making. WS-2308

Velasco, Sherry M. Demons, nausea, and resistance in the autobiography of Isabel de Jesús, 1611-1682. WS-0702

Verdelle, A.J. The good Negress. WS-0946

Verduyn, Christl. Lifelines: Marian Engel's writings. WS-0597

Vest, Hilda. Sorrow's end. WS-0947

Vicker, Jill. Politics as if women mattered. WS-2063

Vickers, Jeanne. Making women matter. WS-2070

Vickers, Jeanne. Women and war. WS-1551

Vigier, Rachel. Gestures of genius. WS-0966

Vigne, Randolph, ed. A gesture of belonging. WS-0415

Villanueva, Alma Luz. Weeping woman. WS-0948

Vinikas, Vincent. Soft soap, hard sell. WS-1352

Vircondelet, Alain. Duras. WS-0665

Vogel, Lise. Mothers on the job. WS-2425

Voget, Fred W. They call me Agnes. WS-1433

Von Mehren, Joan. Minerva and the muse. WS-0827

Von Salis, Susan J., comp. Revealing documents. WS-0031

Vonville, Helena M. Sexual harassment. WS-0149

~ W ~

Wagner-Martin, Linda. "Favored strangers." WS-0870

Wagner-Martin, Linda. Telling women's lives. WS-0313

Waid, Candace. Edith Wharton's letters from the underworld. WS-0871

Waite, Linda J. New families, no families? WS-2339

Wajcman, Judy. Feminism confronts technology. WS-1230

Wakeman, Sarah Rosetta. An uncommon soldier. WS-1980

Walbert, David F., ed. Abortion, medicine, and the law. WS-1269

Walby, Sylvia. Theorizing patriarchy. WS-1379

Waldstein, Edith, ed. In the shadow of Olympus. WS-0614

Walker, Cherryl, ed. Women and gender in southern Africa to 1945. WS-1604

Walker, Cheryl. Masks outrageous and austere. WS-0782

Walker, Nancy A. The disobedient writer. WS-0351

Walker, Nancy A., ed. Communication, the autobiography of Rachel Maddux, and her novella, Turnip's blood. WS-0915

Walker, Sue Sheridan, ed. Wife and widow in medieval England. WS-1592

Walker-Hill, Helen. Piano music by Black women composers. WS-0132

Wall, Cheryl A. Women of the Harlem Renaissance. WS-0872

Wallace, Patricia Ward. Politics of conscience. WS-1899

Wallace, Ruth A. They call her pastor. WS-1166

Waller, Gary, ed. Reading Mary Wroth. WS-0481

Waller, Gary. The Sidney family romance. WS-0489

Waller, Margaret. The male malady. WS-0666

Walls, David. The activist's almanac. WS-0156

Walsh, John Evangelist. This brief tragedy. WS-0828

Walter, John C., ed. Transforming the curriculum. WS-1530

Walters Art Gallery (Baltimore, Md.). Pandora: women in classical Greece. WS-1565

Walters, Suzanna Danuta. Lives together/worlds apart. WS-2357

Walters, Suzanna Danuta. Material girls. WS-0187

Walton, Priscilla L. Patriarchal desire and Victorian discourse. WS-0544

Walton, Priscilla L. The disruption of the feminine in Henry James. WS-0352

Ward, Carol M. Rita Mae Brown. WS-0949

Ward, Jean M., ed. Pacific Northwest women, 1815-1925. WS-1844

Ward, Margaret. Maud Gonne. WS-1684

Ward, Peter. Courtship, love, and marriage in nineteenth-century English Canada. WS-1912

Ware, Susan. Still missing. WS-1208

Ware, Vron. Beyond the pale: white women, racism and history. WS-1662

Warne, Randi R. Literature as pulpit. WS-0598

Warnock, Kitty. Land before honour. WS-1805

Warren, James Francis. *Ah ku* and *karayuki-san*. WS-1636

Warren, Joyce W. Fanny Fern: an independent woman. WS-0829

Wasby, Stephen L., ed. The constitutional logic of affirmative action. WS-2101

Watkins, Marilyn P. Rural democracy. WS-2032

Watstein, Sarah Barbara. AIDS and women. WS-0056

Watt, Jeffrey R. The making of modern marriage. WS-1552

Watterson, Barbara. Women in ancient Egypt. WS-1563

Waxman, Barbara Frey. From the hearth to the open road. WS-0406

Weatherford, Doris. American women and World War II. WS-2033

Wedell, Marsha. Elite women and the reform impulse in Memphis, 1875-1915. WS-1981

Weidner, Marsha, ed. Flowering in the shadows. WS-0207

Weigle, Marta, comp. Women of New Mexico. WS-2037

Weiner, Dora B. The citizen-patient in revolutionary and imperial Paris. WS-1268

Weisbard, Phyllis Holman, ed. The History of women and science, health, and technology. WS-0134

Weisman, Leslie Kanes. Discrimination by design. WS-0253

Weiss, Penny A. Gendered community. WS-1108

Weisser, Susan Ostrov, ed. Feminist nightmares. WS-1364

Welch, Lynne Brodie, ed. Perspectives on minority women in higher education. WS-1525

Welch, Sharon D. A feminist ethic of risk. WS-1109

Weller, Barry, ed. The tragedy of Mariam, the fair queen of Jewry. WS-0448

Wells-Barnett, Ida B. The Memphis diary of Ida B. Wells. WS-0277

Welu, James A. Judith Leyster: a Dutch master and her world. WS-0219

Wenegrat, Brant. Illness and power. WS-2147

Werlock, Abby H.P. Tillie Olsen. WS-0931

Wertheim, Margaret. Pythagoras' trousers. WS-1320

Wesley, Marilyn C. Refusal and transgression in Joyce Carol Oates' fiction. WS-0950

West, Guida. Women and social protest. WS-2385

West, Kathryn. Women writers in the United States. WS-0009

West, Michael A. Women at work. WS-2428

Weston, Ruth D. Gothic traditions and narrative techniques in the fiction of Eudora Welty. WS-0951

Wetzel, Janice Wood. The world of women. WS-2049

Wexman, Virginia Wright. Creating the couple. WS-1000

Whalen, Mollie. Counseling to end violence against women. WS-2246

Wheeler, Marjorie Spruill. New women of the New South. WS-2034

Whelehan, Imelda. Modern feminist thought. WS-1380

Whissen, Anni, tr. Long shadows. WS-0615

White, Barbara A. Edith Wharton: a study of the short fiction. WS-0873

White, Jenny B. Money makes us relatives. WS-1507

White, Sarah C. Arguing with the crocodile. WS-1508

White-Parks, Annette. Sui Sin Far/Edith Maude Eaton: a literary biography. WS-0824a

Whitehorne, John. Cleopatras. WS-1567

Whites, Lee Ann. The Civil War as a crisis in gender. WS-1982

Whitford, Margaret. Luce Irigaray. WS-1110

Whittier, Nancy. Feminist generations. WS-2384

Whitworth, Sandra. Feminism and international relations. WS-2074

Whyte, Martin King. Dating, mating, and marriage. WS-2358

Wieck, David Thoreau. Woman from Spillertown. WS-2035

Wiesner, Merry E. Women and gender in early modern Europe. WS-1591

Wignaraja, Ponna. Women, poverty and resources. WS-1509

Wikander, Ulla, ed. Protecting women. WS-2059

Wilentz, Gay. Binding cultures. WS-0314

Wilkinson, Alan G. Barbara Hepworth: a retrospective. WS-0203

Willard, Charity Cannon, ed. The writings of Christine de Pizan. WS-0627

Willard, Frances E. Writing out my heart. WS-1983

Williams, Carol Traynor. It's time for my story. WS-0278

Williams, Gerhild Scholz. Defining dominion. WS-1663

Williams, Linda B. Development, demography, and family decision-making. WS-2359

Williams, Ora. American black women in the arts and social sciences. WS-0032

Williams, Rhys H. A bridging of faiths. WS-2212

Williamsen, Amy R., ed. María de Zayas: the dynamics of discourse. WS-0685

Williamson, Margaret. Sappho's immortal daughters. WS-0605

Williamson, Marilyn L. Raising their voices. WS-0490

Willis, J.H.. Leonard and Virginia Woolf as publishers. WS-0188

Willis, Sharon, ed. Male trouble. WS-0985

Wilner, Eleanor. Otherwise. WS-0952

Wilson, Carol Shiner, ed. Re-visioning romanticism. WS-0480

Wilson, Elizabeth. The sphinx in the city. WS-2407

Wilson, Fiona. Sweaters. WS-2426

Wilson, Katherina M., ed. An Encyclopedia of Continental women writers. WS-0088

Wilson, Linda. Life after death. WS-1853

Wilson, Mary Ann. Jean Stafford: a study of the short fiction. WS-0953

Wilton, Tamsin. Antibody politic. WS-1314

Win, Everjoyce. To live a better life. WS-1593

Winchell, Donna Haisty. Alice Walker. WS-0954

Winegarten, Ruthe. Black Texas women. WS-1854

Winklepleck, Julie. Resourceful woman. WS-0005

Winkler, Mary G., ed. The good body. WS-2151

Winnan, Audur H. Wanda Gág: a catalogue raisonné of the prints. WS-0248

Winnifrith, Tom. Fallen women in the nineteenth-century novel. WS-0545

Winslow, Anne. Social justice for women. WS-2419

Winter, Kari J. Subjects of slavery, agents of change. WS-0315

Wintram, Claire. Feminist groupwork. WS-2198

Wiseman, Jacqueline P. The other half. WS-2408

Wisker, Gina, ed. Black women's writing. WS-0734

Witt, Linda. Running as a woman. WS-2119

Witz, Anne. Professions and patriarchy. WS-2427

Wolf, Diane Lauren. Factory daughters. WS-1434

Wolf, Margery. A thrice-told tale. WS-1403

Wolf, Naomi. Fire with fire. WS-2247

Wolf, Naomi. The beauty myth. WS-2159

Wolfe, Joel. Working women, working men. WS-1787

Wolfe, Margaret Ripley. Daughters of Canaan. WS-1855

Wolff, Richard. Bringing it all back home. WS-2337

Wolmark, Jenny. Aliens and others. WS-0407

Wolstenholme, Susan. Gothic (re)visions. WS-0408

Women in International Security (Project). Internships in foreign and defense policy. WS-0158

Wood, Betty. Women's work, men's work. WS-1984

Wood, Ruth Pirsig. Lolita in Peyton Place. WS-0784

Wood, Sharon. Italian women's writing, 1860-1994. WS-0711

Woodhull, Winifred. Transfigurations of the Maghreb. WS-0425

Woollacott, Angela. On her their lives depend. WS-1724

Woolum, Janet. Outstanding women athletes. WS-0175

Worell, Judith. Feminist perspectives in therapy. WS-2172

Worobec, Christine D. Peasant Russia. WS-1767

Wright, Christopher J.H. God's people in God's land. WS-1167

Wright, Elizabeth, ed. Feminism and psychoanalysis. WS-0163

Wright, Marcia. Strategies of slaves & women. WS-1605

Wrightsman, Lawrence S. Rape: the misunderstood crime. WS-1354

Wrigley, Julia. Other people's children. WS-2360

Wroth, Mary, Lady. The first part of *The Countess of Montgomery's Urania*. WS-0491

Wu, Qingyun, tr. The remote country of women. WS-0427

Wu, Qingyun. Female rule in Chinese and English literary utopias. WS-0317

Wu, Yenna. The Chinese virago. WS-0438

Wu, Yenna. The lioness roars. WS-0439

Wunderlich, Roger. Low living and high thinking at Modern Times, New York. WS-1860

Wyatt, Gail Elizabeth. Sexual abuse and consensual sex. WS-2329

Wyatt, Jean. Reconstructing desire. WS-0409

Wynne-Davies, Marion. Women and Arthurian literature. WS-0410

~ X ~

Xie, Lihong. The evolving self in the novels of Gail Godwin. WS-0956

Xuewen, Sheng. Women's work in east and west. WS-1462

~ Y ~

Yaeger, Patricia. Refiguring the father. WS-0396

Yarbro-Bejarano, Yvonne. Feminism and the honor plays of Lope de Vega. WS-0705

Yates, Norris. Gender and genre. WS-0785

Yee, Shirley J. Black women abolitionists. WS-1985

Yellin, Jean Fagan, ed. The Abolitionist sisterhood. WS-1922

~ Z ~

Title Index

Index entries refer to review numbers.

~ A ~

As long as life. WS-1267
At the boundaries of law. WS-2084
At the limits of Romanticism. WS-0321
At women's expense. WS-2097
Attack of the leading ladies. WS-0968
Australian women in Papua New Guinea. WS-1610
Autobiographical tightropes. WS-0642
Autobiographics. WS-0374
Autobiography and questions of gender. WS-0283
Ava: a novel. WS-0921

~ B ~

Babe: the life and legend of Babe Didrikson Zaharias. WS-1323
Babies in bottles. WS-1305
Bachelor Bess. WS-1862
Bad girls. WS-0194
Bad women: regulating sexuality in early American cinema. WS-0998
Barbara Hepworth: a retrospective. WS-0203
Barred: women, writing, and political detention. WS-0300
Barrett Willoughby: Alaska's forgotten lady. WS-0837
Bearing meaning. WS-1345
Bearing witness: sexual harassment and beyond—everywoman's story. WS-1371
Beatrice Webb: a life. WS-1680
The beauty myth. WS-2159
Beauty queens on the global stage. WS-1337
"Because it gives me peace of mind." WS-1149
Becoming modern. WS-0832
Becoming O'Keeffe. WS-0225
Behind the courtyard door. WS-1795
Bending the law. WS-2116
Benigna Machiavelli. WS-0840
Bertha Knight Landes of Seattle, big-city mayor. WS-2000
Berthe Morisot's images of women. WS-0215
Better red. WS-0740
Between feminism and labor. WS-1466
Between the fields and the city. WS-1758
Between two absolutes. WS-2095
Between voice and silence. WS-2178
Between worlds. WS-0763
Beulah. WS-0807
Beyond economic man. WS-1478
Beyond methodology. WS-2254
Beyond pro-life and pro-choice. WS-1103
Beyond the pale: white women, racism and history. WS-1662
Beyond the second sex. WS-1400
Beyond the typewriter. WS-1451
Bharati Mukherjee: critical perspectives. WS-0586
A bibliographical guide to African-American women writers. WS-0098
Billie Holiday. WS-1024
Binding cultures. WS-0314
The biographical dictionary of British feminists. WS-0058
A biographical dictionary of English women writers, 1580-1720. WS-0085
Biographies of British women. WS-0028
Biology & feminism. WS-1221
Birth as an American rite of passage. WS-1413
Birth control politics in the United States, 1916-1945. WS-2010
Birth, death, and motherhood in classical Greece. WS-1559
Black American women in Olympic track and field. WS-0172

Black female domestics during the Depression in New York City, 1930-1940. WS-1999
Black looks. WS-2363
Black Texas women. WS-1854
Black women abolitionists. WS-1985
Black women and white women in the professions. WS-2371
Black women as cultural readers. WS-0177
Black women in America. WS-1809
Black women in America: an historical encyclopedia. WS-0059
Black women in the new world order. WS-2223
Black women's writing. WS-0734
Blackout. WS-0981
Blood relations: menstruation and the origins of culture. WS-1392
Blood, milk, and death. WS-1431
Bloodlines. WS-1875
The Bloomsbury guide to women's literature. WS-0086
The Bluestocking circle. WS-0476
Bodies of the text. WS-0958
The body is water. WS-0939
Body, sex, and pleasure. WS-1127
Bodytalk: when women speak in Old French literature. WS-0625
Bonds of community. WS-1971
The book of medicines. WS-0903
The book of Promethea—Le livre de Promethea. WS-0629
The book of the duke of true lovers. WS-0626
Both right and left handed. WS-1802
Bound and determined. WS-0737
Bound by our Constitution. WS-2056
Breaking the barriers. WS-1174
Breaking the bonds. WS-1921
Breaking the codes. WS-1659
Breast cancer: a family survival guide. WS-1281
A breath of life. WS-1818
Breath, eyes, memory. WS-0886
A bridging of faiths. WS-2212
Bridging the gap. WS-0360
The Briles report on women in healthcare. WS-1235
Bringing cultural diversity to feminist psychology. WS-2138
Bringing it all back home. WS-2337
The British and American women's trade union leagues, 1890-1925. WS-1540
British and Irish women dramatists since 1958. WS-1034
British women's history: a bibliographical guide. WS-0062
Broken patterns. WS-2191
The bronze screen. WS-0974
Buddhism after patriarchy. WS-1126
Building with our hands. WS-1812
Burdens of history. WS-1641
By a woman's hand. WS-0082
Byron's heroines. WS-0505
The Byzantine lady. WS-1588

~ C ~

California's daughter. WS-0852
Cancer sourcebook for women. WS-1272
The captured world. WS-0498
Career advancement for women in the federal service. WS-0155
The caregiving dilemma. WS-1286
Caribbean women novelists. WS-0080
Caribbean women writers. WS-0288

Caring in crisis. WS-1291
Carnal knowing. WS-1145
Carrie Mae Weems. WS-2003
Cartooning for suffrage. WS-0275
Casting her own shadow. WS-1987
The castration of Oedipus. WS-2135
Catching babies. WS-1270
Catholic girlhood narratives. WS-0293
Cecilia Payne-Gaposchkin: an autobiography and other recollections. WS-1184
Cecilia reclaimed. WS-1004
Celia, a slave. WS-1967
Center stage. WS-1892
The ceramic legacy of Anna O. Shepard. [Book] WS-1194
Challenging times. WS-2376
Change within tradition among Jewish women in Libya. WS-1803
Changing lives of refugee Hmong women. WS-1414
Changing subjects. WS-0323
Changing the story. WS-0328
Changing the subject. WS-0471
The changing worlds of older women in Japan. WS-1617
Charles Darwin's The origin of species. WS-1195
Charlotte Brontë: a passionate life. WS-0507
Charlotte Perkins Gilman: her progress toward utopia with selected writings. WS-0851
Chaucer and the fictions of gender. WS-0461
Chaucer's women. WS-0469
A checklist of women writers, 1801-1900. WS-0083
La Chicana and the intersection of race, class, and gender. WS-2361
Child-care and the psychology of development. WS-2177
Children of horizons. WS-2317
Children, families, and HIV/AIDS. WS-1310
Children, parents, and the rise of the novel. WS-0477
The Chinese virago. WS-0438
Christina Rossetti revisited. WS-0538
Christina Rossetti: a writer's life. WS-0522
Christine Brooke-Rose and contemporary fiction. WS-0547
Church fathers, independent virgins. WS-1156
Church in the round. WS-1155
The Cilappatikāram of Iḷaṅkō ṭikaḷ WS-0433
Cinderella goes to market. WS-1757
Circles and settings. WS-2230
The citizen-patient in revolutionary and imperial Paris. WS-1268
City of eros. WS-2259
The Civil War as a crisis in gender. WS-1982
The Civil War diary of Sarah Morgan. WS-1934
Civilization without sexes. WS-1739
Clean maids, true wives, steadfast widows. WS-0459
Cleopatras. WS-1567
Climbing the hill. WS-2102
Cloth that does not die. WS-1427
Codes of conduct. WS-0181
Colette: a study of the short fiction. WS-0664
Collecting souls, gathering dust. WS-0236
College girls: a century in fiction. WS-0764
The college woman's handbook. WS-0042
Colonels and cadres. WS-1597
Colonialism and gender relations form Mary Wollstonecraft to Jamaica Kincaid. WS-0554
The color of gender. WS-2098
The comfort women. WS-1622
Coming of age with elephants. WS-1220
Coming through the swamp. WS-1196
"Coming to writing" and other essays. WS-0628

~ D ~

~ E ~

Early promise, late reward: a biography of Helen Hooven Santmyer. WS-0862

Earning respect: the lives of working women in small-town Ontario, 1920-1960. WS-1910

Earth follies. WS-1349

Earth muse. WS-1071

Eating disorders. WS-2156

Echo and Narcissus. WS-0982

Ecofeminism. WS-2234

Ecofeminism and the sacred. WS-1338

The Economic status of women under capitalism. WS-1479

Ecstasy and the demon. WS-0964

Edith Wharton and the unsatisfactory man. WS-0847

Edith Wharton, a descriptive bibliography. WS-0104

Edith Wharton: a study of the short fiction. WS-0873

Edith Wharton: matters of mind and spirit. WS-0865

Edith Wharton's letters from the underworld. WS-0871

Edith Wharton's prisoners of consciousness. WS-0838

Edith Wharton's women. WS-0843

Educating for health & prevention. WS-1262

Education and female emancipation. WS-1517

The education of Fanny Lewald. WS-0611

The education of women. WS-1523

Edwardian stories of divorce. WS-0559

Edwardians: London life and letters, 1901-1914. WS-0576

Edwina Mountbatten. WS-1677

Eighteenth-century women poets. WS-0789

Einstein's wife. WS-2338

Eleanor of Castile: queen and society in thirteenth-century England. WS-1589

Eleanor Roosevelt: v.1: 1884-1933. WS-1868

Elite women and the reform impulse in Memphis, 1875-1915. WS-1981

Elizabeth Bacon Custer and the making of a myth. WS-1883

Elizabeth Barrett Browning. WS-0541

Elizabeth Bishop. WS-0896

Elizabeth Bishop: her poetics of loss. WS-0923

Elizabeth Bishop's poetics of intimacy. WS-0900

Elizabeth Bowen. WS-0561

Elizabeth Bowen: a study of the short fiction. WS-0569

Elizabeth I: the competition for representation. WS-1694

Elizabeth Robins, 1862-1952. WS-0296

Elizabeth Robins: staging a life, 1862-1952. WS-1879

Ellen S. Woodward: New Deal advocate for women. WS-1898

The eloquence of silence. WS-1795a

The elusive agenda. WS-1500

Emergence of the modern Mexican woman. WS-1782

Emerging influentials in state legislatures: women, Blacks, and Hispanics. WS-2112

Emily Davies and the liberation of women, 1830-1921. WS-1665

Emily Dickinson: daughter of prophecy. WS-0805

Emily Dickinson: woman poet. WS-0796

Emily Dickinson's readings of men and books. WS-0811

Emily Faithfull: Victorian champion of women's rights. WS-1681

Eminent rhetoric. WS-0260

Emma Goldman and the American left. WS-2012

Emma Lazarus in her world. WS-0874

Empire and sexuality. WS-1702

Employed mothers and their children. WS-2418

The Empress Matilda. WS-1573

The Empress Theophano: Byzantium and the West at the turn of the first millennium. WS-1577

The empty cradle. WS-1249

En la Lucha = In the struggle. WS-1132

En travesti: women, gender subversion, opera. WS-1009

An enabling humility. WS-0768

Encountering Mary. WS-1168

Encounters with aging. WS-1424

Encyclopedia of childbearing. WS-0053

An Encyclopedia of Continental women writers. WS-0088

Encyclopedia of women's associations worldwide. WS-0010

The encyclopedia of women's history in America. WS-0008

The end of the age of innocence. WS-0860

Ending the silence. WS-2406

The ends of history. WS-0324

Engaging with Shakespeare. WS-0392

Engendered lives. WS-2141

Engendering business. WS-1441

Engendering democracy. WS-2048

Engendering inspiration. WS-0312

Engendering men. WS-0327

Engendering modernity. WS-2380

Engendering motherhood. WS-2346

Engendering origins. WS-1077

Engendering romance. WS-0736

Engendering the Chinese Revolution. WS-1619

Engendering the subject. WS-0398

Engenderings: constructions of knowledge, authority, and privilege. WS-1105

English women's voices, 1540-1700. WS-1691

Enlightened women. WS-2204

Enterprising women. WS-2205

Entitled to power. WS-2002

Equal in monastic profession. WS-1581

Equal value: an ethical approach to economics and sex. WS-1153

Equality politics and gender. WS-2083

Equality transformed. WS-2090

Equivocal beings. WS-0332

Erotic dawn-songs of the Middle Ages. WS-0348

Erotic liberalism. WS-0658

Escape from paradise. WS-1157

Etched in memory. WS-0206

An ethic of care. WS-2124

Eudora Welty's aesthetics of place. WS-0897

European women and the second British Empire. WS-1661

Evaluating women's health messages. WS-1242

Evelyn Underhill. WS-1125

An Evening when alone. WS-1940

Every child a lion. WS-1265

Eve's daughters. WS-2131

Eve's rib. WS-1219

The evolution of women's asylums since 1500. WS-2256

The evolving self in the novels of Gail Godwin. WS-0956

The exceptional woman. WS-0193

The exiled heart. WS-0884

Exiles, eccentrics, activists. WS-1059

Experimental lives. WS-0386

Explaining political disagreement. WS-2045

Explorations in feminist ethics. WS-1078

~ F ~

Faces in the moon. WS-0880

Faces of poverty. WS-2388

Fact book on women in higher education. WS-0045

Factory daughters. WS-1434

Factory girls. WS-1634

Facts and fairy tales about female labor, family and fertility. WS-1460

Failing at fairness. WS-1527

Failure is impossible. WS-1974

Fair ladies. WS-0483

The fairy tale revisited. WS-0959

Faith born of seduction. WS-2154

Fallen women in the nineteenth-century novel. WS-0545

Fallen women, problem girls. WS-2266

Family and childbearing in Canada. WS-2279

Family values. WS-2332

Family, women, and employment in Central-Eastern Europe. WS-2287

Family: a portrait of gay and lesbian America. WS-2330

Fanny and Anna Parnell. WS-1669

Fanny Fern: an independent woman. WS-0829

Fanny von Arnstein. WS-1744

Fantasizing the feminine in Indonesia. WS-1387

Farm and factory. WS-1842

Farm wife. WS-1941

Fashioning femininity and English Renaissance drama. WS-0478

The fatal hero. WS-0378

The fatal woman: sources of male anxiety in American film noir, 1941-1991. WS-0986

Fathers and daughters. WS-2353

Faulkner and southern womanhood. WS-0776

"Favored strangers." WS-0870

Fay Weldon's wicked fictions. WS-0553

The fear of the feminine and other essays on feminine psychology. WS-2194

A fearful freedom. WS-2226

Fearless wives and frightened shrews. WS-1572

Female and male in Borneo. WS-1388

The female bildungsroman in English. WS-0068

Female choices. WS-1222

Female detectives in American novels. WS-0103

Female fetishism. WS-2125

Female heroism in the pastoral. WS-0325

Female life careers. WS-2174

Female parts. WS-0588

Female pastoral. WS-0756

Female piety in Puritan New England. WS-1151

Female psychology. WS-0162

Female rule in Chinese and English literary utopias. WS-0317

The female tradition in southern literature. WS-0746

The female voice in contemporary Brazilian narrative. WS-0695

Female-friendly science. WS-1188

Feminine endings. WS-1020

Feminine principles and women's experience in American composition and rhetoric. WS-0747

The feminine sublime. WS-0370

Femininities, masculinities, sexualities. WS-2182

Femininity in dissent. WS-0280

Femininity to feminism. WS-0508

Feminism and disability. WS-2396

Feminism and geography. WS-1547

Feminism and international relations. WS-2074

Feminism and motherhood in Germany, 1800-1914. WS-1740

Feminism and nursing. WS-1289

Feminism and philosophy. WS-1083

Feminism and pornography. WS-1355

Feminism and psychoanalysis. WS-0163

Feminism and social change. WS-1341

Germaine de Staël revisited. WS-0624

A German women's movement. WS-1743

Gertrude Jekyll. WS-1211

Gertrude Käsebier: the photographer and her photographs. WS-0250

A gesture of belonging. WS-0415

Gestures of genius. WS-0966

Getting personal. WS-0335

The "girl problem." WS-2251

Girls only? WS-0533

The Girl's own. WS-1539

Glorying in tribulation. WS-1896

God between their lips. WS-0402

Goddesses & wise women. WS-0138

Godiva's ride. WS-0525

God's people in God's land. WS-1167

Going public: women and publishing in early modern France. WS-0639

Gone primitive. WS-1396

The good body. WS-2151

The good Negress. WS-0946

Gothic traditions and narrative techniques in the fiction of Eudora Welty. WS-0951

Gothic (re)visions. WS-0408

Grace Hartigan: a painter's world. WS-0222

Grace Paley's life stories. WS-0878

Grandmothers of the light. WS-1408

Grandmothers, mothers, and daughters. WS-1830

The great white way. WS-0760

Great women mystery writers. WS-0071

Great women writers. WS-0072

Green cane and juicy flotsam. WS-0299

Growing up with a single parent. WS-2345

Guidelines for bias-free writing. WS-0081

The guises of modesty. WS-0618

A gulf so deeply cut. WS-0940

Gynographs: French novels by women of the late eighteenth century. WS-0663

The gypsy-bachelor of Manchester. WS-0496

~ H ~

H.D.: the poetics of childbirth and creativity. WS-0848

The habit of surviving. WS-2369

Hadewijch and her sisters. WS-1146

Half a revolution. WS-0720

Handbook for William. WS-1576

Handbook of American women's history. WS-0061

Happy days, Uncle Sergio. WS-0894

Harriet Brooks: pioneer nuclear scientist. WS-1317

Harriet Hosmer, American sculptor, 1830-1908. WS-0229

Harriet Martineau in the London *Daily News*. WS-0509

Harriet Martineau, first woman sociologist. WS-2262

The Hart sisters. WS-0301

Hate crimes. WS-2395

The haunting of Sylvia Plath. WS-0937

Hausa women in the twentieth century. WS-1389

Health care and gender. WS-1252

Health issues for women of color. WS-1293

The Health of women. WS-1243

Health risks of weight loss. WS-1234

Hear my testimony. WS-2062

A heart at leisure from itself. WS-1546

Heavenly love? WS-0376

Hélène Cixous. WS-1668

Hélène Cixous: authorship, autobiography and love. WS-0660

"Hello, Central?" WS-2421

Her excellency. WS-1839

Her mentor was an albatross. WS-1198

Her share of the blessings. WS-1139

Heretics & hellraisers. WS-0759

The heritage of Islam. WS-1596

Heroes without legacies. WS-1199

Heroic with grace. WS-1621

The heroine in Western literature. WS-0395

The hero's daughter. WS-2143

Heterosexual women changing the family. WS-2356

Hidden in the home. WS-1467

High anxiety. WS-0268

History & feminism. WS-1555

The history of American Catholic women. WS-1137

History of childbirth. WS-1578

The history of doing. WS-1626

A history of having a great many times not continued to be friends. WS-0854

The history of obstetrics and gynaecology. WS-1280

A history of Russian women's writing, 1820-1992. WS-0722

The History of women and science, health, and technology. WS-0134

A History of women in the West. WS-1645

A history of women in the West: v.3: Renaissance and Enlightenment paradoxes. WS-1646

A history of women in the West: v.4: Emerging feminism from revolution to world war. WS-1647

A History of women in the West: v.5: Toward a cultural identity in the twentieth century. WS-1648

A history of women photographers. WS-0252

A history of women's contributions to world health. WS-1238

Home and work. WS-1913

The home plot. WS-0778

Home to work. WS-2411

The hour of the poor, the hour of women. WS-1772

House of mist; and, *The shrouded woman*. WS-0673

The house that Jill built. WS-2323

House/garden/nation. WS-0698

Hovering. WS-1178

How am I to be heard? WS-0868

How fascism ruled women. WS-1748

How we found America. WS-0787

How women legislate. WS-2117

Human nature: poems. WS-0877

Human reproduction, emerging technologies, and conflicting rights. WS-1298

Human rights of women. WS-2069

The Human Rights Watch global report on women's human rights. WS-2043

Hypatia of Alexandria. WS-1076

~ I ~

"I belong to the working class." WS-2027

I, Tituba, black witch of Salem. WS-0630

Identity politics and women. WS-2294

If eight hours seem too few. WS-1753

Illiberal education. WS-1515

Illinois women novelists in the nineteenth century. WS-0809

Illness and power. WS-2147

Illness, gender, and writing. WS-0549

Im/partial science. WS-1224

Images of Persephone. WS-0330

Imagination transformed. WS-0492

Imperial leather: race, gender and sexuality in the colonial contest. WS-0387

Impossible dreams. WS-1068

In a shattered mirror. WS-0712

In Adamless Eden. WS-1524

In America the men milk the cows. WS-1831

In her own write. WS-0359

In the company of men. WS-2122

In the master's eye. WS-0781

In the realm of the diamond queen. WS-1398

In the shadow of Olympus. WS-0614

In the way of women. WS-2412

In these girls, hope is a muscle. WS-1322

In vitro fertilization clinics. WS-0055

The in-between of writing. WS-0401

Inarticulate longings. WS-2242

Incidents involving mirth. WS-0571

Incomparable worth. WS-1471

Independent spirits: women painters of the American West, 1890-1945. WS-0217

An independent woman. WS-1874

An index to women's studies anthologies. WS-0006

The Indian captivity narrative. WS-1824

The Indian captivity narrative, 1550-1900. WS-0743

An Indian freedom fighter recalls her life. WS-1631

Indian women's movement. WS-1613

Indira Gandhi: a personal and political biography. WS-1627

Indira Gandhi: an intimate biography. WS-1624

Inessa Armand: revolutionary and feminist. WS-1671

Infertility and patriarchy. WS-1418

Infinite divisions. WS-0906

The information world of retired women. WS-2208

The inhabited woman. WS-0672

Inheritance and family life in Colonial New York City. WS-1920

The inner quarters. WS-1616

Inscribing the daily. WS-0302

Inside looking out. WS-0233

Inside the visible. WS-0190

Inside/out. WS-2263

The integration of women in management. WS-1448

International handbook on gender roles. WS-0166

International migration policies and the status of female migrants. WS-2295

The International who's who of women. WS-0018

Internships in foreign and defense policy. WS-0158

Interpreting ladies. WS-0457

Intimate communities. WS-0758

Into the breach. WS-2021

An introduction to feminism and theatre. WS-1031

Intruders in the play world. WS-0647

Invalid women. WS-0771

The Invention of pornography. WS-1367

Investment in women's human capital. WS-1491

Inviting women's rebellion. WS-2096

Iphigenia. WS-0691

Irene Dunne. WS-0120c

Irene Rice Pereira: her paintings and philosophy. WS-0195

Iris Murdoch: a descriptive primary and annotated secondary bibliography. WS-0089

Iron in her soul. WS-1865

Iron-jawed angels. WS-1996

Is women's philosophy possible? WS-1090

Isabel the Queen. WS-1586

Isolation and masquerade. WS-0850

The issues at stake. WS-2288

Issues in reproductive technology I. WS-1301

Issues of blood. WS-2229

It could happen to anyone. WS-2253

Italian signs, American streets. WS-0750

The making of modern marriage. WS-1552

The making of the Jewish middle class. WS-1741

The making of Victorian sexual attitudes. WS-1710

The making of Victorian sexuality. WS-1711

Making peace. WS-1703

Making policy not tea. WS-2058

Making stories, making selves. WS-1653

Making violence sexy. WS-1370

Making women matter. WS-2070

Male authors, female readers. WS-0442

Male bias in the development process. WS-1501

The male malady. WS-0666

Male trouble. WS-0985

Malina: a novel. WS-0607

La Malinche in Mexican literature from history to myth. WS-0676

The man question. WS-1365

Management and gender. WS-1440

Managing lives. WS-2199

Manufacturing babies and public consent. WS-1306

Manufacturing inequality. WS-1642

Many mirrors. WS-2155

Marble queens and captives. WS-0242

Margaret Atwood. WS-0589

Margaret Atwood: a reference guide. WS-0110

Margaret Atwood: writing and subjectivity: new critical essays. WS-0590

Margaret Fell and the rise of Quakerism. WS-1704

Margaret Fuller. WS-0803

Margaret Fuller: v.1: An American romantic life. WS-1866

Margaret Fuller's New York journalism. WS-0813

Margaret McWilliams. WS-1882

Margaret Oliphant. WS-0513a

Margaret Thatcher: a bibliography. WS-0153

Margaret Webster. WS-0121

Margery Kempe and translations of the flesh. WS-0466

Marguerite Duras. WS-0637

Marguerite Duras revisited. WS-0659

Marguerite Young, our darling. WS-0919

Maria Callas. WS-1017

María de Zayas: the dynamics of discourse. WS-0685

Maria Meneghini Callas. WS-1028

Marianne Moore: questions of authority. WS-0857

Marie Curie: a life. WS-1201

Marie Stopes and the sexual revolution. WS-1678

Marietta Holley. WS-0800

Marina Tsvetaeva: the double beat of heaven and hell. WS-0719

Marine lover of Friedrich Nietzsche. WS-1091

Mark Twain in the company of women. WS-0821

Marlene Dietrich: life and legend. WS-0967

Marrano as metaphor. WS-0650

Marriage on trial. WS-1426

Martha, the life and work of Martha Graham. WS-0961

The marvelous arithmetics of distance. WS-0913

Mary Diana Dods, a gentleman and a scholar. WS-0494

Mary Grew, abolitionist and feminist, (1813-1896). WS-1864

Mary Lee Settle's Beulah quintet. WS-0938

Mary Martin. WS-0120b

Mary McCarthy: an annotated bibliography. WS-0097

Mary Wollstonecraft and the language of sensibility. WS-0450

Masks outrageous and austere. WS-0782

The masque of femininity. WS-2202

Masquerade and gender. WS-0452

Masterplots II. Women's literature series. WS-0078

Masters and managers. WS-1430

Masters of small worlds. WS-1966

Material girls. WS-0187

Maternal fictions. WS-0648

Maternal justice. WS-2219

Mathematics and gender. WS-1316

Matrology: a bibliography of writings WS-0140

Matronage: patterns in women's organizations, Atlanta, Georgia, 1890-1940. WS-2018

A matter of black and white: the autobiography of Ada Lois Sipuel Fisher. WS-1871

A matter of choices. WS-1169

A matter of people. WS-1489

Maud Gonne. WS-1684

May you live in interesting times. WS-0895

Me Jane: masculinity, movies and women. WS-0989

Medico-legal aspects of reproduction and parenthood. WS-2046

Medieval misogyny and the invention of Western romantic love. WS-1571

Medieval women and the sources of medieval history. WS-1587

Medieval women: a social history of women in England, 450-1500. WS-1585

Meeting the Great Bliss Queen. WS-1138

Memoir of a race traitor. WS-1893

Memoir of a Victorian woman. WS-1670

Memories of migration. WS-1821

Memories of resistance. WS-1751

Memory and cultural politics. WS-0767

The Memphis diary of Ida B. Wells. WS-0277

Men in women's clothing. WS-0464

Men writing the feminine. WS-0389

Men, women, and aggression. WS-2207

Men, women, and chain saws. WS-0971

Men, women, and household work. WS-2340

Men, women, and Margaret Fuller. WS-1092

The menopause industry. WS-1273

Menstrual health in women's lives. WS-1274

Menstruation and psychoanalysis. WS-2193

Micro-politics. WS-1093

Middle East avenue. WS-2283

Millay at 100. WS-0856

A millennium of family change. WS-2352

Minerva and the muse. WS-0827

Ministry and meaning. WS-1247

Miscegenation blues. WS-0591

Misogyny, cultural nihilism, & oppositional politics. WS-0434

Mistress of Riversdale. WS-1915

Modern American women writers. WS-0112

Modern and contemporary Spanish women poets. WS-0694

Modern engendering. WS-1095

Modern feminist thought. WS-1380

Modern political theory and contemporary feminism. WS-1101

Modern witchcraft and psychoanalysis. WS-2187

Modern women writers. WS-0113

Modernizing women. WS-1797

Molly Spotted Elk: a Penobscot in Paris. WS-1886

Money makes us relatives. WS-1507

The Montreal massacre. WS-1908

Moods. WS-0795

Moon marked and touched by sun. WS-0926

Moorings & metaphors. WS-0757

The moral frameworks of public life. WS-1808

The moral vision of Dorothy Day. WS-1147

Moral voices, moral selves. WS-1089

More than a muckraker. WS-0269

More than chattel. WS-1544

More than common powers of perception. WS-1931

The morning after. WS-2067

Mortgaging women's lives. WS-1492

The most difficult revolution. WS-2413

Mother India. WS-1620

Mother of pearl: a novel. WS-0575

Mother-headed families and why they have increased. WS-2333

Mother-work: women, child welfare, and the state, 1890-1930. WS-2005

Motherguilt: how our culture blames mothers for what's wrong with society. WS-2215

Motherhood and representation. WS-0382

Motherlands. WS-0339

Mothers and daughters. WS-1640

Mothers and daughters in American short fiction. WS-0100

Mothers and daughters of invention. WS-1229

Mothers and mothering. WS-0161

Mothers and their children. WS-2350

Mother's first-born daughters. WS-1969

Mothers in law: feminist theory and the legal regulation of motherhood. WS-2235

Mothers in the English novel. WS-0388

Mothers of incest survivors. WS-2397

Mothers of invention. WS-1942

Mothers of psychoanalysis. WS-2196

Mothers of the revolution. WS-1600

Mothers on the job. WS-2425

Mothers, babies, and cocaine. WS-1251

Mouth to mouth. WS-0687

The movie of the week. WS-0995

Moving beyond boundaries: v. 1 & 2. WS-0304

Mridula Sarabhai: rebel with a cause. WS-1608

Mrs Humphry Ward. WS-0542

Mrs Jordan's profession. WS-1063

Mrs Oliphant, 'a fiction to herself.' WS-0513

Mrs. Spring Fragrance and other writings. WS-0824

Mukkuvar women. WS-1503

Mules and dragons. WS-0786

Multiple voices in feminist film criticism. WS-0991

The mummy! WS-0521

A municipal mother. WS-1889

A Muriel Rukeyser reader. WS-0858

The muses of resistance. WS-0463

Music beyond sound. WS-1002

Music, gender, and culture. WS-1021

Musicology and difference. WS-1022

My body. WS-1237

"My hideous progeny." WS-0510

My life. WS-1026

"My name was Martha." WS-0473

"My other self." WS-0424

The myth of Aunt Jemima. WS-0777

The myth of the goddess. WS-1384

The myth of the male breadwinner. WS-1494

The myths of motherhood. WS-2355

~ N ~

Nadine Gordimer: a bibliography of primary and secondary sources, 1937-1992. WS-0079

Naked authority. WS-0226

Narodniki women. WS-1761

Narrating mothers. WS-0305

Narrative and desire in Russian literature, 1822-49. WS-0713

Narratives of desire. WS-0675

Natalia Ginzberg: human relationships in a changing world. WS-0707

~ O ~

~ P ~

Private woman, public person. WS-1947

The pro-choice movement. WS-2383

Pro-choice/pro-life. WS-0164

Professional women at work. WS-2416

Professions and patriarchy. WS-2427

Profitable promises. WS-1245

Progressive women in conservative times. WS-2009

Promise to the land: essays on rural women. WS-1826

Promises broken: courtship, class, and gender in Victorian England. WS-1693

Prose by Victorian women. WS-0532

Prospero's daughter. WS-0688

Prostitutes in medical literature. WS-0054

Prostitution in Great Britain, 1485-1901. WS-0168

The prostitution of sexuality. WS-2311

Prostitution: a guide to sources, 1960-1990. WS-0169

Protecting women. WS-2059

Proud past, bright future. WS-1328

Provoking agents. WS-1100

Psychoanalysis of the sexual functions of women. WS-2183

The psychodynamic treatment of women. WS-2160

The psychology of gender. WS-2144

Psychology of women. WS-2132

Putting women on the agenda. WS-2060

Pythagoras' trousers. WS-1320

~ Q ~

Queen Bess: daredevil aviator. WS-1202

Queen Christina of Sweden and her circle. WS-1637

Queen of Bohemia: the life of Louise Bryant. WS-0258

Queen of burlesque. WS-1055

The Queen of Sheba. WS-0564

Queer words, queer images. WS-0273

Quilt groups today. WS-0051

~ R ~

Race, gender, and health. WS-1295

Race, gender, and power in America. WS-2113

Race, gender, and work. WS-1476

Race, sex, and gender in contemporary art. WS-0220

Race-ing justice, en-gendering power. WS-2367

Rachel Calof's story. WS-1991

Rachel Carson. WS-1216

Rachel Crothers: a research and production sourcebook. WS-1051

Racism in the lives of women. WS-2368

The radical faces of Godard and Bertolucci. WS-0984

Radical feminist therapy. WS-2161

Radicals of the worst sort. WS-1932

Raising their voices. WS-0490

Rape and representation. WS-0342

Rape: the misunderstood crime. WS-1354

Ravishing maidens. WS-0640

Re-visioning romanticism. WS-0480

A readers companion to the fiction of Willa Cather. WS-0111a

A readers guide to the short stories of Willa Cather. WS-0111

The reader's repentance. WS-1140

Reading Mary Wroth. WS-0481

Reading the body politic. WS-0683

Reading, writing, and rewriting the prostitute body. WS-2312

Real and imagined women. WS-2307

The real facts of life. WS-2264

The real life of Mary Ann Evans. WS-0495

Rebecca West: an annotated bibliography. WS-0094

Recasting autobiography. WS-0616

A reception-history of George Eliot's fiction. WS-0531

Reclaiming myths of power. WS-0514

Reclaiming rhetorica. WS-0185

Reclaiming the past. WS-1846

Reconstructing Babylon. WS-1227

Reconstructing desire. WS-0409

Recreating Japanese women, 1600-1945. WS-1630

Recreating sexual politics. WS-1374

Red suitcase. WS-0929

Redefining autobiography in twentieth-century women's fiction. WS-0310

Redefining the American dream. WS-0844

Rediscovering forgotten radicals. WS-0578

Re(dis)covering our foremothers. WS-0593

Rediscovering the Muses. WS-1027

Reel women. WS-0119

Reel women: the world of women who fish. WS-1325

Refiguring life. WS-1215

Refiguring modernism: v. 1 & 2. WS-0581

Refiguring the father. WS-0396

Refiguring woman. WS-1590

Reflecting on Miss Marple. WS-0582

Reflecting on *The Bell Jar*. WS-0914

Reflections of Eden. WS-1212

Reflections of ourselves. WS-0265

Reframings: new American feminist photographies. WS-0192

Refusal and transgression in Joyce Carol Oates' fiction. WS-0950

Reinterpreting the Spanish American essay. WS-0696

Religion and sexuality in American literature. WS-0338

Religious violence and abortion. WS-1989

The remarkable Mrs. Beach, American composer. WS-1016

Remarkable survivors. WS-2210

The remote country of women. WS-0427

Renaissance women writers: French texts/American contexts. WS-0657

Representing feminity. WS-0501

Representing women: myths of femininity in the popular media. WS-0266

Reproducing the womb. WS-0176

Reproduction, ethics, and the law. WS-1304

The Republican virago. WS-1674

Rereading Aphra Behn. WS-0482

Rereading modernism. WS-0344

Rereading the Spanish American essay. WS-0697

Resolving the trauma of incest. WS-2166

Resourceful woman. WS-0005

The resources of poverty. WS-1417

Restoration politics and drama. WS-0474

Restructuring patriarchy. WS-1769

The resurgence of Indian women. WS-1606

Rethinking abortion. WS-2108

Rethinking ecofeminist politics. WS-2039

Rethinking ethics in the midst of violence. WS-1070

Rethinking restructuring. WS-2240

Revealing difference. WS-0622

Revealing documents. WS-0031

Revealing reveiling. WS-1807

Revising memory. WS-0623

Revolutionary woman: Kathleen Clarke, 1878-1972. WS-1667

Revolutionizing motherhood. WS-1770

Rich and strange. WS-0364

Riding astride. WS-1816

Righteous discontent. WS-1129

The rise of public woman. WS-1837

Rita Mae Brown. WS-0949

Robbe-Grillet and modernity. WS-0656

Robbing the mother. WS-0833

Roles and rituals for Hindu women. WS-1154

Roman marriage. WS-1564

The romance of reunion. WS-1975

Romantic androgyny. WS-0380

Romantic poetry by women. WS-0073

Romantic vision. WS-0638

Romantic women writers. WS-0345

Romanticism and gender. WS-0524

A room of one's own. WS-0347

Rosa Luxemburg, women's liberation, and Marx's philosophy of revolution. WS-1074

Rosa Montero's odyssey. WS-0670

Rose Scott: vision and revision in feminism. WS-1607

The Rothschild Canticles. WS-0210

Rough magic: a biography of Sylvia Plath. WS-0876

The rover; The feigned courtesans; The lucky chance; The emperor of the moon. WS-0443

Rowing in Eden. WS-0823

Roxana's children. WS-1928

Ruby: an ordinary woman. WS-1683

Rule Britannia. WS-0503

Running as a woman. WS-2119

Rural democracy. WS-2032

Russia—women—culture. WS-1655

Russia's women. WS-1763

Ruth Hanna McCormick: a life in politics, 1880-1944. WS-1887

~ S ~

Sacrificed for honor. WS-1750

Same difference. WS-2310

The same sea as every summer. WS-0701

Samplers & samplemakers. WS-0237

Sandino's daughters revisited. WS-1779

Sappho's immortal daughters. WS-0605

Sappho's lyre. WS-0604

Sarah Orne Jewett. WS-0820

Sarah Orne Jewett: reconstructing gender. WS-0818

Sassy: the life of Sarah Vaughan. WS-1015

Sati, the blessing and the curse. WS-1632

Saturday's child. WS-1903

Scenes of seduction. WS-0652

Scheherezade in the marketplace. WS-0535

Science and sensibility. WS-1206

The science of woman. WS-1279

The scientific lady. WS-1185

Script girls. WS-0973

Searching for Christ: the spirituality of Dorothy Day. WS-1144

Searching the scriptures v.1: A feminist introduction. WS-1159

Searching the Scriptures v.2: A feminist commentary. WS-1160

Secret doctors. WS-1292

The secret history of gender. WS-1784

Secret paths: women in the new midlife. WS-2203

Secrets of life, secrets of death. WS-1179

Seductive forms. WS-0440

Segmenting the women's market. WS-1442

Seldom seen, rarely heard. WS-2134

The selected letters of Mary Moody Emerson. WS-1973

Selected writings of Judith Sargent Murray. WS-0791

Self and community in the fiction of Elizabeth Spencer. WS-0936

Theoretical perspectives on sexual difference. WS-2145

Theorizing patriarchy. WS-1379

Theory on gender/feminism on theory. WS-2275

The therapeutic process, the self, and female psychology. WS-2184

Théroigne de Méricourt. WS-1679

They call her pastor. WS-1166

They call me Agnes. WS-1433

They must be represented. WS-0994

They saw the elephant. WS-1961

Things of darkness. WS-0458

Thinking green! WS-2057

Third world cities in global perspective. WS-1549

Third World women and the politics of feminism. WS-1377

Third World women's literatures. WS-0067

This brief tragedy. WS-0828

This strange society of women. WS-1957

Thread of blood. WS-1381

Threads of solidarity. WS-1594

A thrice-told tale. WS-1403

Through a window. WS-1213

Tillie Olsen. WS-0931

Tillie Olsen: a study of the short fiction. WS-0893

The timetables of women's history. WS-0014

Tina Modotti: photographs. WS-0249

Tish Sommers, activist, and the founding of the Older Women's League. [Book] WS-1877

Tituba, reluctant witch of Salem. WS-1914

To live a better life. WS-1593

To serve my country, to serve my race. WS-2366

To the ends of the earth. WS-1193

To the scaffold. WS-1672

Toddlers and their mothers. WS-2189

Tokens of affection: the letters of a planter's daughter in the Old South. WS-1851

The tongue snatchers. WS-0641

The torchbearers. WS-1988

Torn illusions. WS-1282

Toronto's girl problem. WS-1911

Torrid zones. WS-0479

Toward a feminist epistemology. WS-1075

Toward a tradition of feminist theology. WS-1150

Toward empowerment. WS-1611

Toward gender equity in the classroom. WS-1528

Toward wholeness in Paule Marshall's fiction. WS-0934

Track of the mystic. WS-0849

Tradition and the talents of women. WS-0349

Tragedy in paradise. WS-0613

The tragedy of Mariam, the fair queen of Jewry. WS-0448

Tragic muse. WS-1036

Transcendent daughters in Jewett's Country of the pointed firs. WS-0797

Transfigurations of the Maghreb. WS-0425

The transformation of rural life. WS-1986

Transforming a rape culture. WS-1378

Transforming capitalism and patriarchy. WS-1499

Transforming rural life. WS-1968

Transforming the curriculum. WS-1530

Transforming women's work. WS-1938

Transgender warriors. WS-2216

Translated woman. WS-2281

Translating slavery. WS-0651

The trauma of moving. WS-2200

Travelers, immigrants, inmates. WS-0357

Tree of heaven. WS-0830

The trial of Madame Caillaux. WS-1726

The trial of woman. WS-0287

Trials of labour: the re-emergence of midwifery. WS-1271

Trials of the earth. WS-2031

Troubled bodies. WS-1257

Turning point. WS-1276

The twilight of the goddesses. WS-1735

Two faces of protest. WS-2052

~ U ~

U.S. women's interest groups. WS-0030

Unbecoming women. WS-0369

Unbound feet: a social history of Chinese women in San Francisco. WS-2038

Unbroken thread. WS-1064

Uncertain terms. WS-2328

The uncollected stories of Mary Wilkins Freeman. WS-0816

An uncommon soldier. WS-1980

Under construction. WS-0699

Under observation. WS-0619

The underground stream. WS-0909

Underrepresentation and the question of diversity. WS-1519

Understanding Anne Tyler. WS-0933

Understanding everyday racism. WS-2362

Underwear, the fashion history. WS-0200

Unequal burden. WS-1496

Unequal protection. [Book] WS-2103

Ungodliness. WS-0924

Ungodly women. WS-1119

United States government documents on women, 1800-1990: v.1 & 2. WS-0150

Unleashing our unknown selves. WS-1372

Unmapped territories. WS-0436

Unrelated kin. WS-2373

Unruly women. WS-1930

Unsex'd revolutionaries. WS-0488

Unstable bodies. WS-1712

Unsubmissive women: Chinese prostitutes in nineteenth-century San Francisco. WS-2276

Untamed and unabashed. WS-0286

Upstaging Big Daddy. WS-1065

The usurer's daughter. WS-0462

~ V ~

Valie Export. WS-0990

Vamps, virgins and victims. WS-1311

The veil and the male elite. WS-1796

The veiled women. WS-1614

Veils and words. WS-0417

The velvet glove. WS-2365

Vera Brittain: a life. WS-0546

The victimization and exploitation of women and children. WS-2393

Victimized daughters. WS-2165

Victoria: the young queen. WS-1666

Victorian American women, 1840-1880. WS-0019

Victorian countrywomen. WS-1700

Victorian feminists. WS-1688

The Victorian governess. WS-1701

Victorian heroines. WS-0534

Victorian women. WS-1717

Victorian women poets. WS-0519

A vindication of political virtue. WS-2088

Violence against lesbians and gay men. WS-2390

Violence, silence, and anger. WS-0405

The violent couple. WS-2354

Violet Archer. WS-0127

Virginia Woolf. WS-0573

Virginia Woolf against empire. WS-0577

Virginia Woolf and the madness of language. WS-0555

Virginia Woolf and war. WS-0584

Virginia Woolf: a literary life. WS-0574

Virginia Woolf's subject and the subject of ethics. WS-0399

Virtue and venom. WS-1543

Visible women in east coast Malay society. WS-1428

Visionary women. WS-1141

Visions & longings. WS-1124

Visions of the 'neue Frau.' WS-0234

'Viva.' WS-1768

Vocation and identity in the fiction of Muriel Spark. WS-0552

Voice for the mad. WS-1873

Voice lessons. WS-0916

The voice of Sarah. WS-1123

A voice of their own. WS-0543

Voices from the Japanese women's movement. WS-1635

Voices of their own. WS-0690

Volatile bodies. WS-1087

~ W ~

The wages of sin. WS-0978

Wake up little Susie. WS-2372

Walking the Victorian streets. WS-0528

Walking with the great apes. WS-1217

Wallace Stevens and the feminine. WS-0783

A walled garden in Moylough. WS-0922

Wanda Gág: a catalogue raisonné of the prints. WS-0248

The war against women. WS-2220

War and peace through women's eyes. WS-0101

War, women and children in ancient Rome. WS-1560

Wartime Washington. WS-1958

The way we never were. WS-2335

The wayward preacher in the literature of African American women. WS-0779

Wayward women: a guide to women travellers. WS-0023

We will rise in our might. WS-1926

We will wait: wives of French prisoners of war, 1940-1945. WS-1730

Wealth and rebellion. WS-1404

A web of relationship. WS-0817

Weeping woman. WS-0948

Welfare and the State. WS-2389

Welfare states and working mothers. WS-2298

Western women working in Japan. WS-1459

What are friends for? WS-1082

What can she know? WS-1073

What is secret. WS-0703

What Katy read. WS-0295

What makes women sick. WS-1239

What men want. WS-2195

What this awl means. WS-1406

When hens crow. WS-1953

When new flowers bloomed. WS-0704

When the canary stops singing. WS-1452

When the nation was in need. WS-2016

When women kill. WS-2400

Where no man has gone before. WS-0353

Where the girls are. WS-0259

Where the road bottoms out. WS-0935a

Women of the fields. WS-1656

Women of the Golden Dawn. WS-2140

Women of the Harlem Renaissance. WS-0872

Women of the Klan. WS-1990

Women of the Mexican countryside, 1850-1990. WS-1789

The women of the pleasure quarter. WS-0231

Women of the Renaissance. WS-1583

Women of the world. WS-0316

Women of value. WS-1486

Women on the Italian literary scene. WS-0706

Women on the verge. WS-0955

Women outdoors. WS-0171

Women philosophers. WS-0136

Women photographers. WS-0254

Women readers and the ideology of gender in old French verse romance. WS-0646

Women reading, women writing. WS-0761

Women silversmiths, 1685-1845. WS-0239

Women singing in the snow. WS-0775

Women Strike for Peace: traditional motherhood and radical politics in the 1960s. WS-2028

Women travel writers and the language of aesthetics, 1716-1818. WS-0358

Women under the Bo tree. WS-1113

Women watching television. WS-0272

Women who hurt themselves. WS-2167

Women who ruled. WS-0063

Women who taught. WS-1532

Women with alcoholic husbands. WS-2387

Women without husbands. WS-2334

Women without men. WS-0752

Women writers and fascism. WS-0180

Women writers and the great war. WS-0557

Women writers in Russian literature. WS-0728

Women writers in the United States. WS-0009

Women writers of Latin America. WS-0678

Women writing about money. WS-0290

Women writing childbirth. WS-0291

Women writing in Dutch. WS-0621

Women, AIDS, & communities. WS-1313

Women, art, and society. WS-0201

Women, crime, and custody in Victorian England. WS-1725

Women, culture, and politics in Latin America. WS-1790

Women, employment and the family in the international division of labour. WS-1511

Women, equality, and the French Revolution. WS-1738

Women, feminism, and social change in Argentina, Chile, and Uruguay, 1890-1940. WS-1774

Women, gender, and world politics. WS-2077

Women, health and medicine. WS-1250

Women, identity and private life in Britain, 1900-50. WS-1695

Women, international development, and politics. WS-2078

Women, Islam and the state. WS-2079

Women, labour & politics in Trinidad & Tobago. WS-2303

Women, madness and medicine. WS-2133

Women, media and sport. WS-1332

Women, men and time. WS-2424

Women, politics, and change. WS-2050

Women, poverty and resources. WS-1509

Women, property and Islam. WS-1799

Women, sport, and culture. WS-1333

Women, the environment and sustainable development. WS-1512

Women, the state and revolution. WS-1759

Women, the state, and welfare. WS-2121

Women, work, and coping. WS-2429

The Women's Army Corps, 1945-1978. WS-2011

The women's atlas of the United States. WS-0060

The women's awakening in Egypt. WS-1794

The Women's Bible commentary. WS-0141

The women's business resource guide. WS-0145

The women's chronology. WS-0029

Women's comic visions. WS-1859

Women's culture. WS-0223

Women's decision-making. WS-2308

The women's desk reference. WS-0011

Women's education, autonomy, and reproductive behaviour. WS-2225

Women's equality, demography and public policies. WS-2293

Women's glasnost vs. naglost. WS-1766

Women's growth in connection. [Book] WS-2180

Women's gymnastics: a history. v.1: 1966 to 1974. WS-1330

Women's health care. WS-1259

Women's health from womb to tomb. WS-1246

Women's health matters. WS-1260

Women's health—missing from U.S. medicine. WS-1254

Women's history and ancient history. WS-1568

Women's humor in the age of gentility. WS-0814

Women's information directory. WS-0034

The Women's information exchange national directory. WS-0035

Women's legal guide. WS-0036

Women's lives and the 18th-century English novel. WS-0445

Women's madness. WS-2146

Women's market handbook. WS-1443

Women's movements in America. WS-2382

Women's movements in the United States. WS-2375

The women's movements in the United States and Britain from the 1790s to the 1920s. WS-1810

Women's Orients, English women and the Middle East, 1718-1918. WS-1713

Women's paid and unpaid labor. WS-2415

Women's progress. WS-2248

Women's rights, human rights. WS-2076

Women's sports. WS-1326

Women's studies encyclopedia. WS-0038

Women's studies encyclopedia: v.3: History, philosophy, and religion. WS-0039

Women's studies graduates. WS-2232

Women's studies in the 1990s. WS-1533

Women's studies index, 1989. WS-0040

Women's studies international. WS-1534

Women's studies manuscript collections from the Schlesinger Library, Radcliffe College. Series 3. Sexuality, sex education, and reproductive rights [microform]: Pt. A & B. WS-2249

Women's studies: a guide to information sources. WS-0007

Women's suffrage in America. WS-1944

Women's talk? WS-2274

Women's two roles. WS-2422

Women's voices from the rainforest. WS-1397

Women's work and the family economy in historical perspective. WS-1664

Women's work and women's lives. WS-1465

Women's work in east and west. WS-1462

Women's work, men's work. WS-1984

Women's work: the first 20,000 years. WS-1405

Women's works in Stalin's time. WS-0721

Woolf and Lessing. WS-0585

Words of power. WS-1098

Words to the wise. WS-0065

Work engendered. WS-1458

Workers and their wages. WS-1475

Workfare or fair work. WS-1472

Working miracles. WS-1780

Working wives and dual-earner families. WS-1473

Working women don't have wives. WS-2410

Working women in Russia under the hunger tsars. WS-1754

Working women of collar city. WS-1978

Working women, working men. WS-1787

Working-class women in the academy. WS-1535

The world labour market. WS-1484

A world of difference. WS-0899

The world of women. WS-2049

Worlds of hurt. WS-2273

The World's women, 1970-1990. WS-2250

The World's women, 1995: trends and statistics. WS-0041

Wrapped in glory. WS-0238

Writing against the family. WS-0570

Writing dangerously. WS-0882

Writing in the father's house. WS-0595

Writing love. WS-0645

The writing of Elena Poniatowska. WS-0682

Writing out my heart. WS-1983

Writing selves. WS-0932

Writing the woman artist. WS-0355

Writing their nations. WS-0812

Writing war. WS-0329

Writing women and space. WS-1553

Writing women in Jacobean England. WS-0465

Writing women's history. WS-1554

Writing women's literary history. WS-0454

Writing women's worlds. WS-1399

The writings of Christine de Pizan. WS-0627

The writings of Kōda Aya, a Japanese literary daughter. WS-0435

Written by herself. WS-0749

~ X ~

Xuxa: the mega-marketing of gender, race, and modernity. WS-0276

~ Y ~

The Yeats sisters and the Cuala. WS-1676

Yesterday's stories. WS-0774

You don't have to be your mother. WS-1275

Young, poor, and pregnant. WS-2176

~ Z ~

Zapotec women. WS-1783

Zora Neale Hurston: critical perspectives past and present. WS-0875

Topical Index

Index entries refer to review numbers.

Strained sisterhood. WS-1949

Strategies of slaves & women. WS-1605

Subjects of slavery, agents of change. WS-0315

Sugar's secrets. WS-0684

~

Take my word: autobiographical innovations of ethnic American working women. WS-1402

Tara revisited. WS-1814

"The changing same." WS-0766

Threads of solidarity. WS-1594

Tituba, reluctant witch of Salem. WS-1914

To live a better life. WS-1593

To serve my country, to serve my race. WS-2366

Toward wholeness in Paule Marshall's fiction. WS-0934

Transfigurations of the Maghreb. WS-0425

Transforming capitalism and patriarchy. WS-1499

Transforming the curriculum. WS-1530

~

Unbound feet: a social history of Chinese women in San Francisco. WS-2038

Unbroken thread. WS-1064

Underrepresentation and the question of diversity. WS-1519

Understanding everyday racism. WS-2362

The veiled women. WS-1614

The velvet glove. WS-2365

~

Wake up little Susie. WS-2372

The wayward preacher in the literature of African American women. WS-0779

What makes women sick. WS-1239

When the nation was in need. WS-2016

White women, race matters. WS-2218

William Dorsey's Philadelphia and ours. WS-1832

Wings of gauze. WS-1297

Woman of color, daughter of privilege. WS-1959

Womanist and feminist aesthetics. WS-0319

Women and gender in southern Africa to 1945. WS-1604

Women & sisters. WS-1861

Women in developing economies. WS-1510

Women of color: integrating ethnic and gender identities in psychotherapy. WS-2171

Women of fire and spirit. WS-1390

Women of Phokeng. WS-1595

Women of the Harlem Renaissance. WS-0872

Women on the verge. WS-0955

Women reading, women writing. WS-0761

Working miracles. WS-1780

A world of difference. WS-0899

Writing selves. WS-0932

Written by herself. WS-0749

Zora Neale Hurston: critical perspectives past and present. WS-0875

Asian and Asian American Studies

Ah ku and *karayuki-san.* WS-1636

American women writers: a critical reference guide from Colonial times..., v.5. WS-0096

Arguing with the crocodile. WS-1508

Articulate silences. WS-0739

Australian women in Papua New Guinea. WS-1610

"Because it gives me peace of mind." WS-1149

Bharati Mukherjee: critical perspectives. WS-0586

~

Changing lives of refugee Hmong women. WS-1414

The changing worlds of older women in Japan. WS-1617

The Chinese virago. WS-0438

The Cilappatikāram of Iḷaṅkō Aṭikaḷ. WS-0433

The comfort women. WS-1622

The concubine's children. WS-1901

Conflicting stories. WS-0282

Contemporary plays by women of color. WS-1040

The crooked line. WS-0430

Culture, the status of women, and demographic behaviour. WS-2280

Dear Miye. WS-2030

The demon slayers and other stories. WS-0432

Dharma's daughters. WS-2302

The elusive agenda. WS-1500

Encounters with aging. WS-1424

Engendering the Chinese Revolution. WS-1619

Factory girls. WS-1634

Fantasizing the feminine in Indonesia. WS-1387

Female and male in Borneo. WS-1388

Female rule in Chinese and English literary utopias. WS-0317

Flowering in the shadows. WS-0207

Fruit of the motherland. WS-1423

~

Gender analysis in development planning. WS-1498

Gender and power in rural North China. WS-1420

Gender and the household domain. WS-2289

Health issues for women of color. WS-1293

A heart at leisure from itself. WS-1546

Heroic with grace. WS-1621

The history of doing. WS-1626

In the realm of the diamond queen. WS-1398

An Indian freedom fighter recalls her life. WS-1631

Indian women's movement. WS-1613

Indira Gandhi: a personal and political biography. WS-1627

Indira Gandhi: an intimate biography. WS-1624

The inner quarters. WS-1616

The issues at stake. WS-2288

The Japanese woman. WS-2296

Japanese women writers. WS-0074

Japanese women writers in English translation. WS-0076

Japanese women writers in English translation: v.2. WS-0077

Keepers of the culture. WS-2282

~

Lakshmi's legacy. WS-1612

Leaves of prayer. WS-0429

The lioness roars. WS-0439

Living in the margins. WS-1348

Makiko's diary: a merchant wife in 1910 Kyoto. WS-1628

Male bias in the development process. WS-1501

Masters and managers. WS-1430

Misogyny, cultural nihilism, & oppositional politics. WS-0434

Mother India. WS-1620

Motherlands. WS-0339

Mridula Sarabhai: rebel with a cause. WS-1608

Mrs. Spring Fragrance and other writings. WS-0824

Mukkuvar women. WS-1503

Mules and dragons. WS-0786

~

A new woman of Japan. WS-1623

Nightwork: sexuality, pleasure, and corporate masculinity in a Tokyo hostess club. WS-1409

Nikki Giovanni. WS-0891

Of woman caste. WS-1410

Outsiders in 19th-century press history. WS-0271

Planning development with women. WS-1513

The political economy of gender. WS-1488

Race, gender, and health. WS-1295

Race, gender, and work. WS-1476

Real and imagined women. WS-2307

Recreating Japanese women, 1600-1945. WS-1630

The remote country of women. WS-0427

The resurgence of Indian women. WS-1606

Roles and rituals for Hindu women. WS-1154

~

Sati, the blessing and the curse. WS-1632

Sita's daughters. WS-2301

Siva and her sisters. WS-1421

Sketches from my past. WS-0437

The sound of the wind. WS-0431

Staging place. WS-0738

Sui Sin Far/Edith Maude Eaton: a literary biography. WS-0824a

Surviving the storm. WS-0428

Teachers of the inner chambers. WS-1625

A thrice-told tale. WS-1403

Toward empowerment. WS-1611

Tree of heaven. WS-0830

Two faces of protest. WS-2052

Unbound feet: a social history of Chinese women in San Francisco. WS-2038

Unbroken thread. WS-1064

Unmapped territories. WS-0436

Unsubmissive women: Chinese prostitutes in nineteenth-century San Francisco. WS-2276

The veiled women. WS-1614

Visible women in east coast Malay society. WS-1428

Voices from the Japanese women's movement. WS-1635

~

Western women working in Japan. WS-1459

What makes women sick. WS-1239

Where women are leaders. WS-2061

Wings of gauze. WS-1297

The womb of mind. WS-1633

Women and culture. WS-1422

Women and fertility in Bangladesh. WS-2277

Women and the economic miracle. WS-1609

Women and work in South Asia. WS-1464

The women elite in India. WS-2278

Women in a changing society. WS-1629

Women in developing economies. WS-1510

Women in the Japanese workplace. WS-1461

Women of color: integrating ethnic and gender identities in psychotherapy. WS-2171

The women of the pleasure quarter. WS-0231

Classical Studies

Cultural Studies

Environmental Studies

Food and Agriculture

Lesbian Studies

Latino/a Studies

Male bias in the development process. WS-1501

La Malinche in Mexican literature from history to myth. WS-0676

María de Zayas: the dynamics of discourse. WS-0685

More than chattel. WS-1544

Mouth to mouth. WS-0687

The myth of the male breadwinner. WS-1494

One hundred years after tomorrow. WS-0689

Our voices/our lives. WS-1778

Out of the Kumbla. WS-0307

Out of the shadows. WS-2054

Outsiders in 19th-century press history. WS-0271

Painful inheritance. WS-1233

Perspectives on minority women in higher education. WS-1525

A place in El Paso. WS-1834

Planning development with women. WS-1513

Power and everyday life. WS-1771

Prospero's daughter. WS-0688

~

Race, gender, and health. WS-1295

Race, gender, and work. WS-1476

Race, sex, and gender in contemporary art. WS-0220

Reading the body politic. WS-0683

Reinterpreting the Spanish American essay. WS-0696

Rereading the Spanish American essay. WS-0697

The resources of poverty. WS-1417

Restructuring patriarchy. WS-1769

Revolutionizing motherhood. WS-1770

Sandino's daughters revisited. WS-1779

The secret history of gender. WS-1784

Senhora: profile of a woman. WS-0669

Sex & danger in Buenos Aires. WS-1773

Sex and revolution. WS-1781

Sister Jamaica. WS-1385

So far from God. WS-0883

Sojourner Truth. WS-1885

Spanish women writers. WS-0095

Staging place. WS-0738

Sugar's secrets. WS-0684

Surviving beyond fear. WS-1786

Sweaters. WS-2426

Take my word: autobiographical innovations of ethnic American working women. WS-1402

Talking back. WS-0674

El Teatro Campesino: theater in the Chicano movement. WS-1037

Textured lives. WS-0700

Thread of blood. WS-1381

Translated woman. WS-2281

'Viva.' WS-1768

~

Weeping woman. WS-0948

What is secret. WS-0703

What makes women sick. WS-1239

When new flowers bloomed. WS-0704

Wings of gauze. WS-1297

Women & alcohol in a highland Maya town. WS-1416

Women & change in the Caribbean. WS-1788

Women and survival in Mexican cities. WS-2285

Women as healers, women as patients. WS-1294

Women in developing economies. WS-1510

Women in pain. WS-1264

Women of color: integrating ethnic and gender identities in psychotherapy. WS-2171

Women of the Mexican countryside, 1850-1990. WS-1789

Women reading, women writing. WS-0761

Women singing in the snow. WS-0775

Women writers of Latin America. WS-0678

Women, culture, and politics in Latin America. WS-1790

Women, feminism, and social change in Argentina, Chile, and Uruguay, 1890-1940. WS-1774

Women, labour & politics in Trinidad & Tobago. WS-2303

Women's voices from the rainforest. WS-1397

Working miracles. WS-1780

Working women, working men. WS-1787

The writing of Elena Poniatowska. WS-0682

Xuxa: the mega-marketing of gender, race, and modernity. WS-0276

Zapotec women. WS-1783

Middle Eastern Studies

Accommodating protest. WS-2299

Arab women novelists. WS-0426

Arab women: old boundaries, new frontiers. WS-1792

Arabesque. WS-0419

Behind the courtyard door. WS-1795

Both right and left handed. WS-1802

Change within tradition among Jewish women in Libya. WS-1803

Contemporary coptic nuns. WS-1120

Feminists, Islam, and nation. WS-1793

Gender and the Israeli-Palestinian conflict. WS-2306

Gender in crisis. WS-1801

Gender on the market. WS-1391

Health issues for women of color. WS-1293

Infertility and patriarchy. WS-1418

Land before honour. WS-1805

Marriage on trial. WS-1426

Modernizing women. WS-1797

Money makes us relatives. WS-1507

The Nubians of West Aswan. WS-1419

The patriarchal paradox. WS-2051

A Persian requiem. WS-0413

Populism and feminism in Iran. WS-1798

Red suitcase. WS-0929

Revealing reveiling. WS-1807

Transfigurations of the Maghreb. WS-0425

The veil and the male elite. WS-1796

Veils and words. WS-0417

~

Women and fundamentalism. WS-2291

Women and gender in Islam. WS-1791

Women and the political process in twentieth-century Iran. WS-1800

Women and words in Saudi Arabia. WS-0412

The women are marching. WS-1804

Women in Arab society. WS-1463

Women in Middle Eastern history. WS-1806

Women, property and Islam. WS-1799

The women's awakening in Egypt. WS-1794

Writing women's worlds. WS-1399

Native American Studies

American Indian women. WS-0003

American women writers to 1800. WS-0788

American women writers: a critical reference guide from Colonial times..., v.5. WS-0096

Bloodlines. WS-1875

The book of medicines. WS-0903

Conflicting stories. WS-0282

Contemporary plays by women of color. WS-1040

Converting the West. WS-1878

Countering colonization. WS-1815

Daughters of Canaan. WS-1855

Dirt road home. WS-0594

Faces in the moon. WS-0880

From mission to metropolis. WS-1411

Grandmothers of the light. WS-1408

Health issues for women of color. WS-1293

The Indian captivity narrative, 1550-1900. WS-0743

Keepers of the culture. WS-2282

Lost Bird of Wounded Knee. WS-1819

Madonna Swan. WS-1897

Memory and cultural politics. WS-0767

Molly Spotted Elk: a Penobscot in Paris. WS-1886

Native American women: a biographical dictionary. WS-0021

Outsiders in 19th-century press history. WS-0271

Race, gender, and health. WS-1295

Race, gender, and work. WS-1476

Solar storms: a novel. WS-0904

Southern Cheyenne women's songs. WS-1012

Spirit moves. WS-1811

Tekonwatonti/Molly Brant (1735-1795). WS-0790

They call me Agnes. WS-1433

What this awl means. WS-1406

White captives. WS-1841

Wings of gauze. WS-1297

Women & alcohol in a highland Maya town. WS-1416

Women and power in native North America. WS-1856

Women of color: integrating ethnic and gender identities in psychotherapy. WS-2171

Women of the Apache nation. WS-2026

Women reading, women writing. WS-0761

Zapotec women. WS-1783

Urban Studies

Bertha Knight Landes of Seattle, big-city mayor. WS-2000

Community of suffering & struggle. WS-1435

Dream revisionaries. WS-0303

Edwardians: London life and letters, 1901-1914. WS-0576

Eighteenth-century women poets. WS-0789

Elite women and the reform impulse in Memphis, 1875-1915. WS-1981

A German women's movement. WS-1743

The life and death of Carolina Maria de Jesus. WS-1775

Love and toil. WS-1719

Makiko's diary: a merchant wife in 1910 Kyoto. WS-1628

Money makes us relatives. WS-1507

Mrs. Spring Fragrance and other writings. WS-0824

Painful inheritance. WS-1233

A place in El Paso. WS-1834

Silk stockings and ballot boxes. WS-1852

The sphinx in the city. WS-2407

Staging place. WS-0738

The struggle for community. WS-2261

Sui Sin Far/Edith Maude Eaton: a literary biography. WS-0824a

Susan Sontag: mind as passion. WS-0910

Their sisters' keepers. WS-1952

Walking the Victorian streets. WS-0528

William Dorsey's Philadelphia and ours. WS-1832